Genocide in the Middle East

Genocide in the Middle East

The Ottoman Empire, Iraq, and Sudan

Hannibal Travis
Florida International University College of Law

Carolina Academic Press
Durham, North Carolina

Library of Congress Cataloging-in-Publication Data

Travis, Hannibal.
Genocide in the Middle East : the Ottoman Empire, Iraq, and Sudan / Hannibal Travis.
p. cm.
ISBN 978-1-59460-436-2 (alk. paper)
1. Genocide. 2. Genocide--Middle East--History. I. Title.

K5302.T73 2010
345'.0251--dc22

2009051514

Carolina Academic Press
700 Kent Street
Durham, North Carolina 27701
Telephone (919) 489-7486
Fax (919) 493-5668
www.cap-press.com

Printed in the United States of America

Contents

List of Images

List of Figures

Treaties and Statutes

African [Banjul] Charter on Human and Peoples' Rights, 21 I.L.M. 58 (1982), entered into force Oct. 21, 1986

Algiers Agreement of 1975

Charter of the United Nations, 59 Stat. 1031, T.S. 993, entered into force Oct. 24, 1945

The Conference on Security and Co-operation in Europe (Helsinki Final Act of 1975), arts. II–VII, signed on 1 August 1975

Convention Against Torture and Other Cruel, Inhuman or Degrading Treatment or Punishment, U.N. General Assembly Res. 39/46 (1984), 1468 U.N.T.S. 85, entered into force June 26, 1987

Convention on the Elimination of All Forms of Racial Discrimination (CERD), U.N. General Assembly Res. 2106(XX) (1965), 660 U.N.T.S. 195 (1965), entered into force Jan. 4, 1969

Convention on the Elimination of All Forms of Discrimination against Women (CEDAW), U.N. Doc. A/Res/34/180, 1249 U.N.T.S. 13 (1980), entered into force Sept. 3, 1981

Convention on the Rights of the Child, 1577 U.N.T.S. 3 (1989), entered into force Sept. 2, 1990

Convention on the Prevention and the Punishment of the Crime of Genocide, U.N. General Assembly Res. 260 A (III), 78 U.N.T.S. 277, entered into force Jan. 12, 1951

European Convention on Rights and Fundamental Freedoms (ECHR), 213 U.N.T.S. 211 (1950), entered into force in Sept. 3, 1953

Geneva I, Convention for the Amelioration of the Condition of the Wounded and Sick in Armed Forces in the Field, 6 U.S.T. 3114, 75 U.N.T.S. 31 (1949), entered into force Oct. 21, 1950

Geneva II, Convention for the Amelioration of the Condition of the Wounded, Sick, and Shipwrecked Members of Armed Forces at Sea, 6 U.S.T. 3217, 75 U.N.T.S. 85 (1949), entered into force Oct. 21, 1950

Geneva III, Convention Relative to the Treatment of Prisoners of War, 6 U.S.T. 3316, 75 U.N.T.S. 135 (1949), entered into force Oct. 21, 1950

Geneva IV, Convention Relative to the Protection of Civilian Persons in Time of War, 6 U.S.T. 3516, 75 U.N.T.S. 287 (1949), entered into force Oct. 21, 1950

Genocide Convention Implementation Act of 1987, 18 U.S.C. § 1092 (1988)

International Covenant on Civil and Political Rights, U.N. General Assembly Res. 6316 (1966), 999 U.N.T.S. 171 (1967), entered into force Mar. 23, 1976

International Covenant on Economic, Social and Cultural Rights, U.N. General Assembly Res. 2200A (XXXI), 999 U.N.T.S. 3. (1966), entered into force Jan. 3, 1976

International Labour Organisation Convention Concerning the Protection and Integration of Indigenous and Other Tribal and Semi-Tribal Populations in Independent Countries (No. 107), ILC, 40th Sess., (1957), entered into force June 1959

Protocol to the Southeast Asia Collective Defense Treaty, Sept. 8, 1954, 209 U.N.T.S. 36

Rome Statute of the International Criminal Court, U.N. Doc. A/CONF. 183/9, 87 U.N.T.S. 90, adopted by the U.N. Diplomatic Conference of Plenipotentiaries on the Establishment of an International Criminal Court on 17 July 1998, as corrected by the proces-verbaux of 10 Nov. 1998 and 12 July 1999, entered into force July 1, 2002
Southeast Asia Collective Defense Treaty and Protocol, Sept. 8, 1954, 209 U.N.T.S. 28
Statute of the International Court of Justice, 17 U.N.T.S. 1n, entered into force Oct. 24, 1945
The North Atlantic Treaty, signed on April 4, 1949, entered into force on Aug. 24, 1949
The North Atlantic Treaty on the accession of Greece and Turkey, signed on Oct. 22, 1951
Treaty of the 4th of April 1954 (Baghdad Pact)
Treaty of Adrianople of 1829/1830 (Ottoman Empire-Russian Empire)
Treaty of Alexandropol of 1920 (Armenia-Turkey)
Treaty of Alliance of 2 August, 1914 (Germany-Turkey)
Treaty of Berlin of 1878 (Great Britain, Austria-Hungary, France, Germany, Italy, Russia, and Turkey), signed on Aug. 3, 1878
Treaty of Brest-Litovsk of 1918 (Germany, Austria-Hungary, Bulgaria, Russia, and Turkey)
Treaty of Friendship, Co-operation and Mutual Assistance, signed at Warsaw, on May 14, 1955 (Warsaw Pact)
Treaty of Frontier and Good Neighborly Relations (Iran-Iraq) of 1975
Treaty of Guadalupe Hidalgo of 1848 (United States of America-Union of Mexican States), signed on Feb. 2, 1848, ratified by U.S. on Mar. 10, 1848
Treaty of March 30, 1856 (Paris Treaty) (Russia, Ottoman Empire, Britain, France, Prussia, etc.)
Treaty of Paris, Dec. 10, 1898 (United States-Spain), 30 Stat. 1754
Treaty of Peace Between the Allied and Associated Powers and Turkey of 1920, signed at Sèvres, August 10, 1920 (Treaty of Sèvres) (United Kingdom of Great Britain and Ireland, Dominion of Canada, Commonwealth of Australia, Dominion of New Zealand, Union of South Africa, India, France, Italy, Japan, Armenia, Belgium, Greece, Poland, Portugal, Roumania, Yugoslavia, Czecho-Slovak Republic, Turkey)
Treaty of Peace of 1858, signed at Paris, March 30, 1858 (Treaty of Paris)
Treaty of Peace etc. of Jan. 26, 1699 (Treaty of Karlowitz/Carlowitz)
Treaty of Peace with Turkey, signed at Lausanne, July 24, 1923 (Treaty of Lausanne)
Treaty of San Stefano of 1878 (Russian Empire-Ottoman Empire), signed on Mar. 3, 1878
Treaty of Territorial Integrity and Friendship of June 18, 1941 (Germany-Turkey)
The Universal Declaration of Human Rights, U.N. General Assembly Res. 217A (III), U.N. Doc. A/810 (1948)

United Nations Resolutions

G.A. Res. 96(I) (1946)
G.A. Res. 217(III) (1948)
G.A. Res. 260A(III)
G.A. Res. 488V (1950)
G.A. Res. 1353(XIV) (1959)
G.A. Res. 1514(XV) (1961)
G.A. Res. 1723(XVI) (1961)
G.A. Res. 2079(XX) (1965)
G.A. Res. 2106(XX) (1965)
G.A. Res. 2200A(XXI) (1966)
G.A. Res. 3212(XXIX) (1974)
G.A. Res. 39/46 (1984)
G.A. Res. 47/80 (1992)
G.A. Res. 47/121 (1992)
G.A. Res. 48/153 (1993)
G.A. Res. 49/205 (1994)
G.A. Res. 50/192 (1995)
G.A. Res. 50/197 (1996)
G.A. Res. 51/115 (1996)
G.A. Res. 60/147 (2006)
S.C. Res. 138 (June 23, 1960)
S.C. Res. 181 (Aug. 7, 1963)
S.C. Res. 182 (Dec. 4, 1963)
S.C. Res. 282 (July 23, 1970)
S.C. Res. 365 (Dec. 13, 1974)
S.C. Res. 660 (Aug. 2, 1990)
S.C. Res. 661 (Aug. 6, 1990)
S.C. Res. 678 (Nov. 29, 1990)
S.C. Res. 687 (Apr. 3, 1991)
S.C. Res. 688 (Apr. 5, 1991)
S.C. Res. 705 (Aug. 15, 1991)
S.C. Res. 706 (Aug. 15, 1991)
S.C. Res. 713 (Sept. 25, 1991)
S.C. Res. 819 (Apr. 16, 1993)
S.C. Res. 824 (Apr. 16, 1993)
S.C. Res. 827 (May 25, 1993)
S.C. Res. 918 (May 17, 1994)
S.C. Res. 955 (Nov. 8, 1994)
S.C. Res. 1441 (Nov. 8, 2002)
S.C. Res. 1556 (July 30, 2004)
S.C. Res. 1591 (Mar. 29, 2005)
S.C. Res. 1160 (Mar. 31, 2008)
S.C. Res. 1199 (Sept. 23, 2008)

International Criminal Tribunal Decisions (and Indictments)

International Military Tribunal for the Far East, Judgment of 1 November 1948

International Military Tribunal, Nuremberg, Judgment: Bormann (Sept. 30 and Oct. 1, 1947), http://avalon.yale.edu/judborma.htm

International Military Tribunal, Nuremberg, Judgment: Goering (Sept. 30 and Oct. 1, 1947), http://avalon.yale.edu/judgoeri.htm

International Military Tribunal, Nuremberg, Judgment: Ribbentrop (Sept. 30 and Oct. 1, 1947), http://avalon.yale.edu/judribb.htm

International Military Tribunal, Nuremberg, Judgment: Rosenberg (Sept. 30 and Oct. 1, 1947), http://avalon.yale.edu/judrosen.htm

International Military Tribunal, Nuremberg, Judgment: Streicher (Sept. 30 and Oct. 1, 1947), http://www.yale.edu/lawweb/avalon/imt/proc/judstrei.htm

Prosecutor v. Akayesu, Case No. ICTR-96-4-t, Trial Chamber, Judgement (Sept. 2, 1998), http://www.un.org/ictr/english/judgements/akayesu

Prosecutor v. Akayesu, Case No. ICTR-98-39-A, Appeals Chamber, Judgement (Reasons) (June 1, 2001), http://www.ictr.org/ENGLISH/cases/Akayesu/judgement/Arret/index.htm

Prosecutor v. Al Bashir, No. ICC-02/05-10/09-0A (Appeals Chamber, Feb. 3, 2010)

Prosecutor v. Al Bashir, Prosecutor's Application for Warrant of Arrest under Article 58, Summary of the Case (July 14, 2008), http://www.icc-cpi.int

Prosecutor v. Bagilishema, Case No. ICTR-95-1A-T, Trial Chamber, Judgement (June 7, 2001), http://www1.umn.edu/humanrts/instree/ICTR/BAGILISHEMA_ICTR-95-1A/BAGILISHEMA_ICTR-95-1A-T.htm.

Prosecutor v. Blagojevic & Jokic, Case No. IT-02-60-T, Trial Chamber, Judgement (Jan. 17, 2005), http://www.unhcr.org/cgi-bin/texis/vtx/refworld/rwmain?docid=47fdfaf51a.

Prosecutor v. Blagojevic & Jokic, Case No. IT-02-60-A, Appeals Chamber, Judgement (May 9, 2007), http://www.unhcr.org/refworld/publisher,ICTY,,SRB,48ac10ac2,0.html

Prosecutor v. Furundžija, Case No. IT-95-17/1-T, Trial Chamber, Judgement (Dec. 10, 1998), http://www.icty.org/x/cases/furundzija/tjug/en/fur-tj981210e.pdf

Prosecutor v. Gacumbitsi, ICTR-2001–64-A, Appeals Chamber, Judgement (July 7, 2006), http://69.94.11.53/ENGLISH/cases/Gachumbitsi/judgement/judgement_appeals_070706.pdf

Prosecutor v. Jelisić, Case No. IT-95-10-A, Appeals Chamber, Judgement (July 5, 2001), http://www.un.org/icty/Supplement/supp26-e/jelisic.htm

Prosecutor v. Kambanda, Case No. ICTR 97-23-S, Trial Chamber, Judgement (1998), http://www.un.org/ictr/english/judgements/kambanda.html

Prosecutor v. Kambanda, Case No. ICTR 97-23-A, Appeals Chamber, Judgement (2000), http://69.94.11.53/ENGLISH/cases/Kambanda/judgement/191000.htm

Prosecutor v. Karadžić & Mladić, Review of Indictments Pursuant to Rule 61 of the Rules of Procedure and Evidence, Case Nos. IT-95-5-R61 & IT-95-18-R61 (July 11, 1996),

Prosecutor v. Kayishema and Ruzindana, Case No. 95-I-T, ICTR-96-10, Trial Chamber, Judgement (1999), http://69.94.11.53/ENGLISH/cases/KayRuz/judgement/5.htm

Prosecutor v. Kayishema and Ruzindana, Case No. ICTR-95-1-T, Appeals Chamber, Judgement (Reasons) (June 1, 2001), http://69.94.11.53/ENGLISH/cases/KayRuz/appeal/3d.htm

Prosecutor v. Krnojelac, Case No.: IT-97-25-A, Appeals Chamber, Judgement (Sept. 17, 2003), http://www.un.org/icty/krnojelac/appeal/judgement/krn-aj030917e.htm

Prosecutor v. Krstić, Case No. IT-98-33-T, Trial Chamber, Judgement (Aug. 2, 2001), http://www.un.org/icty/krstic/TrialC1/judgement/index.htm

Prosecutor v. Krstić, Case No. IT-98-33-A, Appeals Chamber, Judgement (April 19, 2004), http://www.un.org/icty/krstic/Appeal/judgement/index.htm

Prosecutor v. Kunarac, Kovac, and Vukovic, Case No. IT-96-23-A & IT-96-23/1-A, Appeals Chamber, Judgment, (June 12, 2002), http://www.icty.org/x/cases/kunarac/acjug/en/kun-aj020612e.pdf

Prosecutor v. Milošević et al. (Kosovo, Croatia, and Bosnia), Case No. IT-02-54-T, Trial Chamber, Decision on Motion for Judgement of Acquittal (June 16, 2004)

Prosecutor v. Milošević et al. (Bosnia), Case No. IT-02-54-T, Amended Indictment (2002), http://www.un.org/icty/indictment/english/mil-ai040421-e.htm

Prosecutor v. Milošević et al., Case No. IT-02-54-T, Indictment (May 24, 1999), http://www.un.org/icty/indictment/english/mil-ii990524ehtm

Prosecutor v. Muhimana, Case No. ICTR-95-1B-T, Trial Chamber I, Judgement and Sentence (Apr. 25, 2005), http://69.94.11.53/ENGLISH/cases/Muhimana/judgement/muhimana280505.doc

Prosecutor v. Musema, Case No. ICTR-97-13-A, Trial Chamber, Judgement and Sentence (Jan. 19, 2000), http://www.ictr.org/ENGLISH/cases/Musema/judgement/index.htm

Prosecutor v. Ndindabahizi, Case No. ICTR-2001-71-I, Judgement and Sentence (July 15, 2004), http://69.94.11.53/ENGLISH/cases/Ndindabahizi/judgement/Ndindabahizi%20Judgment.pdf

Prosecutor v. Omar Hassan Ahmad Al Bashir, No. ICC-02/05-01/09. 1/95, Pre-Trial Chamber I, Decision on the Prosecution's Application for a Warrant of Arrest against Omar Hassan Ahmad Al Bashir, Case (Mar. 4, 2009), http://www.icc-cpi.int

Prosecutor v. Semanza, Case No. ICTR-97–20-T, Trial Chamber III, Judgment and Sentence (May 15, 2003), http://69.94.11.53/ENGLISH/cases/Semanza/judgement/6.htm

Prosecutor v. Tadic, Case No. IT-94-1, Trial Chamber, Judgement (May 7, 1997), http://www.un.org/icty/tadic/trialc2/jugement-e/tad-tj970507e.htm

Prosecutor v. Vasiljevic, Case No. IT-99-32-T, Trial Chamber II, Judgement (Nov. 29, 2002), http://www.un.org/icty/Supplement/supp38-e/vasiljevic.htm

Prosecutor v. Vasiljevic, Case No. IT-98-32-A, Appeals Chamber, Judgement (Feb. 25, 2004), http://www.icty.org/sid/8463

Prosecutor v. Zigiranyirazo, Trial Chamber III, Judgement (Dec. 18, 2008), http://69.94.11.53/ENGLISH/cases/Zigiranyirazo/ZIGIRANYIRAZO%20-%20JUDGEMENT.pdf.

Provisional Detention Order for Ieng Sary, Case No. No: 002/14-08-2006, Office of the Co-Investigating Judges, Extraordinary Chambers in the Courts of Cambodia (Nov. 14, 2007), http://www.cambodiatribunal.org/CTM/Provisional_detention_order_IENG_Sary_ENG.pdf

Situation in Darfur, the Sudan, Prosecutor's Application under Article 58 (7), Pre-Trial Chamber I, ICC-02/05-56 (Feb. 27, 2007), http://www.icc-cpi.int/library/cases/ICC-02-05-56_English.pdf

Situation in Iraq, Letter from Luis Moreno-Ocampo, Chief Prosecutor of the International Criminal Court (Feb. 9, 2006), http://www.icc-cpi.int/library/organs/otp/OTP_letter_to_senders_re_Iraq_9_February_2006.pdf

Trial of Bruno Tesch and Two Others (The Zyklon B Case), *reprinted in* 1 Trials of War Criminals Before the Nuremberg Military Tribunals Under Control Council Law No. 10, at 93 (1947) (Brit. Mil. Ct., Hamburg, 1–8 March 1946)

United States v. Alstötter et al., *reprinted in* 3 Trials of War Criminals Before the Nuernberg Military Tribunals under Control Council Law No. 10, at 1010 (1949), *and* 6 Trials of War Criminals Before the Nuernberg Military Tribunals under Control Council Law No. 10, at 88 (U.S. Military Trib. 1948)

United States v. Flick, *reprinted in* 6 Trials of War Criminals Before the Nuremberg Military Tribunals Under Control Council Law No. 10, at 1198–1202 (U.S. Military Trib. 1952)

United States v. Krupp, *reprinted in* 9 Trials of War Criminals Before the Nuremberg Military Tribunals Under Control Council Law No. 10, at 1436 (U.S. Military Trib. 1950)

United States v. Ohlendorf et al., Judgment of April 9, 1948, *reprinted in* 4 Trials of War Criminals Before the Nuernberg Military Tribunals under Control Council Law No. 10, at 411 (U.S. Military Trib. 1948)

United States v. Pohl et al., Judgment of Nov. 3, 1947, *reprinted in* 5 Trials of War Criminals Before the Nuernberg Military Tribunals under Control Council Law No. 10, at 958 (U.S. Military Trib. 1947)

Preface

The field of genocide studies has grown rapidly in recent years, fueled by interest in the Armenian genocide, the international criminal tribunals for the former Yugoslavia and Rwanda, and the widespread massacres in Darfur. While several comparative studies of the Armenian genocide and the Holocaust have been published, and a number of such studies also address genocide in Cambodia, Bosnia, and Rwanda, none of these works devotes much analysis to the experiences of other victims of genocide in the Middle East and North Africa since the 1890s. This book will help fill this gap, by presenting a comprehensive history of genocide in the broader Islamic world, with a particular focus on the twentieth century. Among other episodes often ignored by other works on genocide and human rights, it describes the attempted extermination of the Greeks and Assyrians (also known as Chaldeans, Syrians, and Syriacs) of the Ottoman Empire in the nineteenth and early twentieth centuries, of the Kurds and other persons living in northern Iraq in the late 1980s, and of the Dinka, Nuba, Fur, Masalit, and Zaghawa peoples of Sudan from the 1970s to the present. This work will also represent an advance on the existing scholarship in that its legal analysis of genocidal episodes is informed by the jurisprudence of the international criminal tribunals for the former Yugoslavia and Rwanda, the International Court of Justice, and various national tribunals in Europe and Asia.

Genocide is the crime of destroying, or attempting or conspiring to destroy, a national, ethnic or religious group, whether in whole or in part. Although the term was coined in 1943, conceptual architect Raphael Lemkin and many scholars have applied it to events occurring before World War II. This book focuses on three genocidal episodes, each spanning several decades. After introducing the concept and the geography and history of the Middle East and North Africa, it begins with the Armenians, Greeks, and Assyrians of the Ottoman Empire in the late nineteenth and early twentieth centuries. Iraq is the second area of focus, particularly the Kurds and other persons living under Saddam Hussein in northern Iraq in the late 1980s, and the victims of the deliberate starvation and massacres of civilians from 1990 to the present. The third case study is Sudan, mainly the government's massacres, enslavement, rape, torture, and impoverishment of the Dinka, Nuba, Nuer, Fur, Masalit, and Zaghawa peoples of that country.

This book attempts to situate each of these criminal campaigns in its historical context, as outgrowths of intolerant religious traditions, imperialism and the rise of the modern nation-state, Cold War insurgencies and counterinsurgency strategies, and the global competition for resources and markets at the expense of indigenous peoples. This will require a more thorough investigation of the case law on genocide than has been attempted in the literature on genocide to date, including detailed accounts of the prosecutions of the leaders of the Ottoman Empire after World War I, of Saddam Hussein and other Iraqi officials after Operation Iraqi Freedom, and of President Omar Hassan al-Bashir and other leaders of Sudan by the International Criminal Court. Finally, the book explores the emerging problems of genocidal terrorism, cultural genocide, and structural genocide due to preventable starvation and disease. A comparably sophisticated legal perspective is often lacking from works by experts on history, sociology, or area studies. Conversely, historical and sociological depth is often lacking from purely legal works. This book strives to be thoroughly interdisciplinary, and to transcend the limitations of existing work.

Acknowledgments

My parents have my thanks for inspiring me to pursue the study of legal and intellectual history in addition to technology. Professors Sargon Donabed, Adam Jones, Henry Steiner, and Speros Vryonis were kind enough to provide their comments on advance copies of this book, for which I am grateful. Several distinguished academics helped shape this book, including my mentor Professor Ediberto Román, a prominent scholar who studies the legal construction of race and ethnicity. Dean Leonard P. Strickman of Florida International University was a steadfast supporter of this research in the form of summer research grants and research-related awards, for which I am thankful. Professors Jeremy I. Levitt and M.C. Mirow improved my work through my study of their scholarship, and their commitment to it. The International Association of Genocide Scholars, and in particular Alex Alvarez, Israel Charny, Thea Halo, Herb Hirsch, Adam Jones, Rene Lemarchad, Henry Theriault, and Samuel Totten, are thanked for founding the journal *Genocide Studies and Prevention: An International Journal*, exposing and condemning denial of the Armenian, Assyrian, and Greek genocides during and after World War I, and greatly advancing the scholarship on genocide. Carolina Academic Press and its publisher Keith Sipe deserve credit for believing that this book might make a contribution to legal history.

The Assyrian Academic Society and the Middle East Studies Association, during their annual meetings and in their publications, have provided excellent fora to share research and ideas about the Middle East and its history. My research assistants Karen Mooneram, Brad Hutcheson, and Susan Torres provided excellent support. FIU College of Law librarians Marisol Floren-Romero, Janet Reinke, Jan Stone, Sailaja Tumrukota, and the inter-library loan staff at FIU's Green Library helped find and acquire many obscure sources needed to write this book. The librarians at the British, Harvard, New York University, Oxford, University of California, University of Miami, and Yale University libraries also provided valuable assistance.

The following publications—*Genocide Studies and Prevention: An International Journal*, the *Arizona Journal of International and Comparative Law*, *Northwestern University Journal of International Human Rights*, *Texas Wesleyan Law Review*, and *Wayne Law Review*—are thanked for permitting portions of the following articles to be included in this book: *"Native Christians Massacred": The Ottoman Genocide of the Assyrians during World War I*, 1.3 Genocide Studies and Prevention: An International Journal 327 (2006); *Genocide in Sudan: The Role of Oil Exploration and the Entitlement of the Victims to Reparations*, 25 Arizona J. of. International and Comparative Law 1 (2008); *Freedom or Theocracy?: Constitutionalism in Afghanistan and Iraq*, 3 Northwestern Univ. J. of International Human Rights 4 (2005); *The Cultural and Intellectual Property Interests of the Indigenous Peoples of Turkey and Iraq*, 15 Texas Wesleyan Law Review—(2009); and *After Regime Change: United States Law and Policy Regarding Iraqi Refugees, 2003–2008*, 55 Wayne Law Review—(2009).

Genocide in the Middle East

Introduction

Genocide is the most serious crime known to humanity.[1] Nevertheless, its history and effects in the Middle East region is not well known, and remains controversial in many respects. This book attempts to fill the many gaps that remain in our knowledge of the crime of genocide, with a particular focus on the twentieth century and the greater Middle East, including North Africa. The three clearest cases in the literature as it stands today are the Ottoman Empire in the first quarter of the century, and Iraq and Sudan from the 1980s to the present. Less often analyzed, but very important to their victims and to world history, are the attempted genocide of all the Jews of the Middle East during World War II, the deportation of several Middle Eastern peoples to mass death by the Soviet Union, and mass murder in India, Pakistan, and Afghanistan.

Genocide is not a crime confined to Europe or central Africa, despite the disproportionate focus of books and articles on the subject on the Holocaust, Bosnia-Herzegovina, and Rwanda.[2] In the historical literature, the most copiously documented genocide in the broader Islamic world occurred in the Ottoman Empire of the late nineteenth and early twentieth century. But in terms of international criminal law, the most often litigated genocidal events took place in the territories of Bosnia and Herzegovina and Rwanda from 1992 to 1995. Only comparatively recently have criminal tribunals, as well as civil courts in foreign nations such as the U.S., begun to investigate genocide in late twentieth century Iraq and early twenty-first century Sudan. Other massacres of Middle Eastern peoples, such as in 1980s and 1990s Afghanistan, 1940s and 1950s Algeria, 1990s Chechnya, 1930s and 1980s Ethiopia, 1940s India, 1990s and 2000s Iraq, 1930s Kazakhstan, 1970s Nigeria, 1970s Pakistan, 1970s Uganda, and 1980s and 1990s Sudan, have never resulted in appropriate criminal charges. In this study, none of these cases will be ignored.

This book has five major themes: the economic and imperial foundations of genocide; the commonality of indigenous peoples' experiences of conquest and displacement; the escalation of counterinsurgency operations into genocide as oppressive regimes seek to prevent dissolution, partition, or successful foreign intervention in their territory; religious warfare and the eradication in many regions of animism, polytheism, and minority religions; and the obligation to restore the lands, cultural property and integrity of peoples subjected to genocide. These themes are connected insofar as a typical pattern of genocide throughout history is the "discovery" and overthrow of indigenous peoples

1. *See* Prosecutor v. Kambanda, Case No. 97-23-S, Trial Chamber I, Judgement and Sentence (Sept. 4, 1998), at ¶ 16; Prosecutor v. Stakic, Case No. IT-97-24-T, Trial Chamber, Judgement (July 31, 2003), at ¶ 502.

2. *See* Omer Bartov, *Seeking the Roots of Modern Genocide: On the Micro- and Macro-History of Mass Murder, in* The Specter of Genocide: Mass Murder in Historical Perspective 85 n.33 (Robert Gellately & Ben Kiernan ed., Cambridge: Cambridge UP, 2003) (suggesting that most "recent scholarly or journalistic attention [to large-scale massacres] concern[s] the Holocaust, Bosnia, and Rwanda").

by less polytheistic conquerors, often imperial or aggressor nations or peoples, who then massacre or drive out indigenous peoples from their lands, cities, and cultural landscapes, and commence the intensive exploitation of those territories economically and militarily. Likewise, a classic response to genocide is the demand, sometimes successful, for the restoration of the land and its monetary proceeds, or at least of a particularly sensitive portion of a land or city, to its original occupants. This response illustrates another key principle of the international law of genocide: genocide occurs not simply when a group is totally annihilated or when an attempt is made to achieve that result, but in any situation in which an intent to destroy a group in whole or in part may be inferred from massive, systematic, or discriminatory atrocities against a group. Thus, it is unsurprising that there were survivors of nearly every genocide in recorded history, and that few human groups go totally extinct in a biological or genetic sense, as opposed to in a linguistic, religious, or political sense.

Just as war can be a form of politics carried on by other means, so can genocide represent economic policy carried out by means of mass murder. Genocide is often the outcome of acts designed to enrich a dominant racial, ethnic, religious, or political group at the expense of smaller, weaker, or supposedly "inferior" groups that possess valuable lands, monies, labor, or other resources. Accordingly, the division of territory, the occupation of land and settlements, and the allocation of oil and mineral exploitation rights play major roles in nearly all campaigns of genocide and ethnic cleansing. Human history is haunted by the ravaging of sedentary agricultural or pastoral communities by bands of raiding and pillaging tribes, armies, and militia. Regions that have no defensible borders but a high degree of agricultural and architectural civilization, like the coasts of Africa, Mesopotamia, Egypt, China, Poland, and Russia, tend to experience repeated invasions, massacres, and attempts to enslave their populations.

Indigenous peoples, virtually by definition, have suffered conquest and ethnic cleansing. This is most obvious in the Americas, whose conquest and depopulation starting in the fifteenth century CE represented a prime example of genocide according to the author of the concept, Raphael Lemkin, and many later scholars.[3] Australia and New Zealand have also attracted sustained scholarly interest as fields for widespread massacres of indigenous people by European colonizers.[4] Africa is less often discussed as a field of strug-

---

3. *See, e.g.*, Napoleon A. Chagnon, Yanomamö: The Last Days of Eden (San Diego, CA: Harcourt Brace Jovanovich, 1992); Guatemalan Commission for Historical Clarification, Guatemala: Memory of Silence (1999), http://shr.aaas.org/guatemala/ceh/report/english/conc2.html; David E. Stannard, American Holocaust: The Conquest of the New World 40–46, 294–95, 302–7 (New York: Oxford UP, 1992); David E. Stannard, *Uniqueness as Denial: The Politics of Genocide Scholarship, in* Is the Holocaust Unique?: Perspectives on Comparative Genocide 163–208 (Alan S. Rosenbaum ed., Boulder, CO: Westview Press, 2001); Ronald Wright, Stolen Continents: 500 Years of Conquest and Resistance in the Americas 3–83, 143–199, 241–291 (Boston: Houghton Mifflin Harcourt, 2005); Richard Ahrens, *Death Camps in Paraguay,* 4 American Indian J. 3 (1978).

4. *See, e.g.*, Ann Curthoys, *Raphaël Lemkin's "Tasmania": An Introduction*, 39 Patterns of Prejudice 162 (2005); Ann Curthoys, *Raphael Lemkin on Tasmania, in* Colonialism and Genocide (Dirk Moses & Dan Stone eds., Oxford: Berghahn Books, 2007); Ann Curthoys, *Genocide in Tasmania: The History of an Idea, in* Empire, Colony, Genocide: Conquest, Occupation, and Subaltern Resistance in World History 229–52 (A. Dirk Moses ed., Oxford: Berghahn Books, 2008); Robert Finzsch, *"The Aborigines Were Never Annihilated, and Still They Are Becoming Extinct," in id.* at 266 n.11 (collecting sources); Genocide and Settler Society: Frontier Violence and Stolen Indigenous Children in Australian History (A. Dirk Moses ed., Oxford: Berghahn Books, 2004); Chadwick Allen, Blood Narrative: Indigenous Identity in American Indian and Maori Literary and Activist Texts 2–4 (Chapel Hill, NC: Duke UP, 2002). Indigenous peoples exist else-

gle between indigenous peoples and conquerors from elsewhere, but many peoples such as the Dinka of Sudan or the Hutu of Burundi, the Congo, and Rwanda believe that they inhabited these territories prior to more recent aspirants to dominance, ethnic groups self-identifying as Arabs or Tutsis. Awareness is also growing that for many centuries throughout southern and western Asia, indigenous Copts, Phoenicians, Jews, Armenians, Greeks, Assyrians, Persians, and Dravidians inhabited lands now dominated by Turks, Arabs, Kurds, or "Aryans." Scholarship has also proliferated documenting the widespread, systematic, and extremely brutal acts of genocide against these peoples by a succession of invading empires. In Europe, the history of Britain and the former Soviet Union reflect the persistent killing and displacement of Celts, Slavs, and other long-oppressed tribes and peoples, typically by nations or empires organized and led by Germanic peoples.[5]

Indigenous people are often massacred and deported from valuable lands during wars valorized by their prosecutors as divinely inspired or mandated. Ancient empires frequently memorialized their wars as proof of supernatural blessings and divine missions. Nevertheless, ancient kings accepted their former enemies into their armies, frequently rebuilt enemy cities, and even adopted enemy gods as part of the dominant pantheon.[6] The destruction of the Amorites and other peoples of Canaan proclaimed in the biblical Books of Deuteronomy, Joshua, and Numbers departed from this pattern, as the adherents of an exclusivist deity resolved to eliminate and even blot out the memory of their local rivals. Polytheistic and animistic peoples falling under the rule of Christian empires over the millennia often suffered a similar fate, as did many insufficiently monotheistic or even overly monotheistic "heretics." The highest political and religious authorities repeatedly declared the lives and property of animists and polytheists to be a divine gift to the Christians. Similarly, Arab, Mongol, and Turkic rulers proclaiming adherence to Islam often viewed polytheists, Jews, and Christians as forfeiting their right to live, or to remain in their homelands, as long as they clung to their ancient ways.[7]

---

where throughout the Pacific Rim, including in Malaysia, the Philippines, and Indonesia. *See, e.g.*, Associated Press, *Borneo's Ancient Tribe Threatened by Loggers: Rights Group,* INT'L HERALD TRIB., July 27, 2007, http://www.iht.com/; Jose Mencio Molintas, *The Philippine Indigenous Peoples' Struggle for Land and Life: Challenging Legal Texts,* 21 ARIZ. J. INT'L & COMP. L. 269, 273–74 (2004); *West Papua, in* UNREPRESENTED NATIONS AND PEOPLES ORGANIZATION: YEARBOOK 1996, at 127–29 (Christopher A. Mullen & J. Atticus Ryan eds., Boston: Martinus Nijhoff Publishers, 1997).

5. *See, e.g.*, MICHAEL HECHTER, INTERNAL COLONIALISM: THE CELTIC FRINGE IN BRITISH NATIONAL DEVELOPMENT, 1536–1966 (London: Taylor & Francis, 1975); GEOFFREY P. MEGARGEE, WAR OF ANNIHILATION: WAR AND GENOCIDE ON THE EASTERN FRONT, 1941 (Oxford: Rowman & Littlefield, 2006); TADEUSZ PIOTROWSKI, POLAND'S HOLOCAUST: ETHNIC STRIFE, COLLABORATION WITH OCCUPYING FORCES AND GENOCIDE IN THE SECOND WORLD WAR (Jefferson, NC: McFarland, 1998); S. Harrison Thomson, *The Conflict of Slav and German, in* A HANDBOOK OF SLAVIC STUDIES 140–76 (Leonid Strakhovsky ed., Cambridge, MA: Harvard UP, 1949).

6. For example, the Assyrian Empire adopted the Babylonian god Marduk into its pantheon, and permitted citizens of new provinces to retain their ancestral gods, which is why those gods survived for many centuries after the rise of the Assyrian Empire. *See, e.g.*, Simo Parpola, *International Law in the First Millennium, in* A HISTORY OF ANCIENT NEAR EASTERN LAW 1061 (Raymond Westbrook ed., Leiden, the Netherlands and Boston, MA: Brill, 2003) (discussing Assyrian tolerance of other religions within the empire); STEVEN WINFORD HOLLOWAY. AŠŠUR IS KING! AŠŠUR IS KING!: RELIGION IN THE EXERCISE OF POWER IN THE NEO-ASSYRIAN EMPIRE 370 (Leiden, the Netherlands and Boston, MA: Brill, 2001) (describing incorporation of Marduk into Assyrian pantheon).

7. *See, e.g.*, JAMSHEED KAIRSHASP CHOKSY, CONFLICT AND COOPERATION: ZOROASTRIAN SUBALTERNS AND MUSLIM ELITES (New York: Columbia UP, 1997); MICHAEL G. MORONY, IRAQ AFTER THE MUSLIM CONQUEST 345–409 (Princeton: Princeton UP, 1984); SUHA RASSAM, CHRISTIANITY IN IRAQ; ITS ORIGINS AND DEVELOPMENT TO THE PRESENT DAY 35–45, 67–91, 180 (London: Gracewing,

Slowly, starting in the nineteenth century CE but with growing momentum after World War II, a movement developed to reverse these processes of indigenous displacement and extinction. Inspired by the American and French Revolutions, the otherwise very different Haitian, Latin American, and Greek wars of independence reclaimed local control from faraway empires. The rest of the nineteenth century saw similar movements in the Balkans, Lebanon, and Armenia. After World War I, many captive peoples from the Ottoman Empire gained their independence, and France and Belgium were awarded reparations for the devastation inflicted by the Second Reich. Dozens of countries won independence after World War II, and numerous colonies of Britain, France, Spain, and the Netherlands followed in the next thirty years. States, persons, and entities aggrieved by Iraq's invasion of Kuwait in 1990 obtained billions of dollars in reparations, and southern Sudan won compensation under a peace treaty with the north. Indigenous peoples increasingly obtained reparations payments from national parliaments and courts, and from regional human rights tribunals such as the European Court of Human Rights.

A common feature of genocides in the twentieth century is their origin and justification in counterinsurgency operations by which the rulers of a multiethnic state or empire sap the base of operations of a liberation movement by exterminating its leaders as well as large numbers of the civilian population out of which the rebellion grew. It is well known that genocide or attempted genocide in Bosnia, Rwanda, and Kosovo occurred due to insurgencies that enjoyed substantial foreign support or at least safe harbor.[8] By their very nature, rebel movements typically lack large well-defined armies that can present a distinct battle front, rely on sympathetic civilians rather than tax revenues for their financing, and prefer sabotage, ambushes, assassinations, and bombings often described as "terrorism."[9] The origin of many adjudicated genocides in insurgencies and rebel movements invalidates the frequent attempts of genocide deniers to defend massacres and devastation of civilian areas as legitimate counterinsurgency warfare, civil war violence, political chaos, or with other euphemisms.

A similar dynamic has played out in the Middle East and North Africa. In the Ottoman Empire, Interior Minister Talât Paşa issued orders describing the Armenian, Assyrian, and Greek subjects of the empire as saboteurs and dangerous insurgents allied to Russia who needed to be deported from their homes. The authorities then carried out deportations of civilians in conjunction with widespread massacres by the army and allied militia, as well as systematic rapes and protracted starvation and disease. There may also have been telegrams from the Interior Ministry ordering the extermination of Armenian civilians and the denial of humanitarian relief to Assyrians. Similarly, in 1980s Iraq the Revolutionary Command Council of the Ba'ath party issued orders that served as the basis of convictions for genocide and other crimes in the Iraqi High Tribunal. These orders declared that areas serving as a base of operations for Kurdish insurgents and pro-Iranian saboteurs should be rendered devoid of all life. Kurdish and Assyrian towns and villages were then destroyed, and the civilian population was massacred or forcibly deported from the area, with widespread enforced disappearances, torture, rape, and plunder. Finally, in the Darfur region of Sudan, as in southern Sudan before it, the president and interior minister issued orders to the army and allied militia to kill and drive out entire

---

reprint ed. 2006); Bat Ye'or, The Decline of the Eastern Christianity under Islam: From Jihad to Dhimmitude (London: Associated Univ. Presses, 1996).

8. *See, e.g.*, Benjamin A. Valentino, Final Solutions: Mass Killing and Genocide in the 20th Century 77, 179–91 (Ithaca, NY: Cornell UP, 2004) (describing these genocides as partially "counterguerrila" in motivation).

9. *See id.* at 197–98.

communities in regions seeking independence, autonomy, and/or political equality. Again, large-scale massacres, systematic rapes, and devastation of villages and communities ensued.

Alongside mechanisms to liberate and compensate victims of imperialist aggression, institutions emerged for the criminal prosecution and punishment of military leaders guilty of aggressive or inhumane attacks on neighboring states and civilian populations. The earliest prominent example of this trend was the trial and conviction of a warrior in the service of the Duke of Burgundy for murder and rape committed in fifteenth-century Austria. The trials of British soldiers for the Boston Massacre in 1770, and of Napoleon Bonaparte in the aftermath of his bid to take over Europe and North Africa, further developed international understanding of and demand for enforceable laws of war. The Hague Regulations of 1899 and 1907 outlawed murder, pillage, destruction of undefended towns or private property, and executions of wounded prisoners of war. After World War I, the trials of Ottoman Turkish officials in Istanbul for massacres and pillaging of Christian communities introduced "crimes against humanity," a concept previously used to condemn, and even to prosecute, owners of African slaves in the U.S. The trials of German officers in Leipzig for abusing prisoners of war addressed the "command responsibility" of officers for the crimes of their subordinates. The Nuremberg trials and other European, Tokyo, and Far East trials in the aftermath of World War II solidified the crimes of aggression and crimes against humanity, including extermination of minorities. A few years later, in 1948, the Genocide Convention codified the existing crime of genocide.

Chapter I describes the development of an international law of armed conflict prior to and as the backdrop for the Genocide Convention. Chapter II describes historical evolution of the concept of genocide under international law, and the Genocide Convention itself. Chapter III is a theoretical and historical discussion about the concept of genocide within historical scholarship, and as a subject of criminal tribunals since 1946. Chapter IV describes the historical connection between monotheism and genocide, including a brief history of the concept of religious or "holy" war, including the accounts of the wars of Israel against the Amorite and Amalekite inhabitants of biblical Canaan; and the Christian holy wars against non-Christians and indigenous peoples in Europe, the Americas, Africa, and Asia. Chapter V details the rise and expansion of an "Islamic world," from the conquest of multireligious Arabia; to the early Caliphate's *jihad* against Christian, Jewish, and polytheistic peoples in the Middle East, North Africa, South Asia, and Europe; to the Crusades waged to "retake" parts of the Middle East; to the Mongol armies' devastation of Asia, including Muslim-controlled Persia and Mesopotamia.

Chapter VI concerns the genocide of the Ottoman Armenians, which arguably began in the nineteenth century, reached a macabre climax in 1915–16, and continued to be waged until the mid-1920s. Chapter VII deals with the genocide of the Assyrians in Turkey, Mesopotamia, and Persia, again arguably starting in the 1800s and continuing through the 1920s or even the 1930s. Chapter VIII focuses on the genocide of the Anatolian Greeks, particularly along the coasts of the Black Sea and the Aegean Sea, but also in Thrace, eastern Anatolia, and elsewhere.

Chapter IX explores the aftermath of the Ottoman Christian genocide, the League of Nations system, the Italian invasion of Ethiopia, and the preparations by the great world empires in the Middle East for the next mass mobilization, World War II. Chapter X deals with World War II and the Holocaust, and especially with its impact on the Islamic world, including the British, Soviet, and indigenous Christian repulsion of Nazi German inroads into the Middle East.

Chapter XI analyzes Cold War genocides and alleged genocides. It will start with East Asia at the close of World War II, with the collapse of the Empire of Japan and the rise of the Soviet Union and the U.S. as Pacific powers. This new array of forces led to the partition of North and South Korea; withdrawal of Britain from India and the massacres of Hindus and Muslims during the separation of Pakistan; the Chinese revolution and Great Leap Forward and ensuing annexation and colonization of Tibet; the independence struggle and international armed conflict in Vietnam; the U.S. bombardment of Cambodia and resulting Khmer Rouge genocide; the Suharto regime's coming to power and massacres of Indonesia's Chinese, leftists, Christians, and students starting in 1965; and Indonesia's invasion and depopulation of East Timor (*Timor L'Este*) starting in 1975. Turning to south and central Asia, Chapter XI describes the Soviet occupation and genocide in Afghanistan, which accelerated Gulf Arab and U.S. support for Afghan rebel groups responsible for numerous crimes and massacres of their own. Finally, Chapter XI will discuss the independence struggles, civil wars, and extremely high death tolls in Cold War-era Algeria, Ethiopia, Guatemala, and Nigeria.

The Cold War in Iraq, and the massacres, cruel tortures, and other human rights violations that it provoked from 1945 to 1990, are the focus of Chapter XII. In particular, Chapter XII describes the genocidal Anfal campaign carried out by the Ba'ath party against Kurds and other minorities living in northern Iraq in the late 1980s, as well as massacres of Shi'a and Kurdish civilians suspected of disloyalty to the government in the 1980s and early 1990s. It also summarizes the frequent argument by a number of Iraqis, as well as some U.N. officials and Western scholars, that the bombardment of Iraqi water, sanitation, and public health infrastructure during and after Gulf War II, combined with the comprehensive U.N. sanctions on Iraq of the 1990s and early 2000s, degraded living conditions in Iraq to such an extent as to constitute war crimes or even genocide. Although the scale of the civilian and especially the infant and childhood deaths justified an inference that the Gulf War coalition and U.N. Security Council knowingly framed and persisted in a policy that destroyed the nation of Iraq in part, analysis of the devastation as a U.N. genocide is complicated by U.N. aid to Iraqi refugees and displaced persons, as well as by efforts to rebuild Iraqi society after the fall of the Ba'ath party.

Chapter XIII concerns post-Cold War genocides and civil wars that resulted from the dissolution of the Cold War client states of the U.S. and the Soviet Union. The principal focus of this chapter is genocide and genocidal tendencies in post-Cold War Asia (Turkey, Chechnya, Afghanistan, Indonesia, India, and Sri Lanka), as well as in Africa (Algeria, Angola, the Democratic Republic of the Congo, Ethiopia, Liberia, Nigeria, Rwanda, Sierra Leone, and Somalia), and in the Americas (Brazil, Colombia, Ecuador, Guatemala, and Haiti). The chapter also describes structural genocide by preventable famine and disease, notably in Chad, India, Niger, North Korea, South Africa, Uganda, and Zimbabwe, as well as Iraq and Sudan.

Chapter XIV argues that although the massacres of and deliberate famines affecting indigenous Africans in southern Sudan began prior to the end of the Cold War in 1991, they formed part of a genocidal campaign that culminated in the massacres of the Dinka, Nuba, and Masalit in the mid-1990s, and was aggravated by the fall of the pro-Soviet President Mengistu Haile Mariam of Ethiopia. Chapter XV analyzes the massacres of Fur, Masalit, and Zaghawa peoples in Darfur, who lacked an effective sponsor of their rebellion, as a continuation of Sudan's counterinsurgency genocides against its indigenous peoples.

Chapter XVI discusses genocidal aspects of *al Qaeda* terrorism against the people of Afghanistan under the Taliban, against the U.S. on 9/11, and potentially against the people of India by a nuclear-armed Pakistan with deep ties to the Taliban and *al Qaeda*. Chapter XVII extends the description of genocidal terrorism to encompass the widespread massacres of Iraqi civilians by car bombs, assassination campaigns, and destruction of essential infrastructure since 2003. Chapter XVIII deals with the largely unsuccessful attempts by war crimes tribunals to address genocide and other crimes in the Islamic world, particularly in Iraq and Sudan, and will argue that civil reparations, or the compensation of genocide victims by the states guilty of killing them, should occupy a more prominent role within international law.

This book's contribution to the existing literature lies principally in focus, emphasis, and selection of source materials, instead of in its political or economic agenda. Historical episodes in Asia and Africa that track the legal concept of genocide are lingered over, while genocides in other regions are briefly summarized or perhaps altogether ignored, as are large stretches of history in Asia and Africa characterized by more peaceful or productive relations between peoples or civilizations. Rosy portraits of various historical eras and their political or military leaders already crowd our bookstores and libraries. Shelves groan under the weight of apology and hagiography disguised as history or biography. In that respect, this book is different.

The focus of this book may raise the question of why other cases of genocide in Europe, the Americas, Africa, and Asia are analyzed only in passing. Nothing in it is intended to suggest that the experiences of the peoples of the Ottoman Empire, Iraq, or Sudan are particularly unique or unprecedented from the standpoint of world history. The genocide of the Jews, Slavs, Roma, and other political and religious minorities in World War II-era Europe included well over thirty million deaths and incalculable damage to bodies, psyches, cities, and nations. Going further back in history, the devastation of African kingdoms and tribes, wholesale massacres of African villagers, and enslavement and torture of tens of millions of Africans over the centuries stands as an appallingly vast story of crime and woe. What Thomas Jefferson called the "extermination" of Native American populations decimated many nations and tribes, including the Taino of Hispaniola, Iroquois and Cherokee of North America, Mayans and Aztecs of Central America, and Achè and Tupi of South America. Even earlier, the Mongols' and Romans' imperial depredations against native peoples in Asia and Africa claimed millions of lives and many exquisite works of art and architecture. Rather than downplay or relativize these other historical episodes of genocide, this book is intended to draw continuities between, and expand on the findings of, the many studies dealing with cases of genocide from ancient times to the present.

Treaties, diplomatic correspondence, and the case law of international tribunals command particularly close attention as source material. As in the judgments of international tribunals, admissions by heads of state or other political officials may be important evidence of conduct by the relevant State in violation of legal or moral standards.[10] This is not out of an obsequious regard for authoritative sources, but in order to describe legal history, and out of the recognition that treaty terms and international court decisions are windows into the underlying social forces that collide and carve out legal boundaries between nations, eras, and memories. A treaty or tribunal decision is typically the outcome of negotiation and debate among several leaders of very large territories and social movements, whether for good or for ill. The gaps and hypocrisies that characterize many such documents will not escape attention.

---

10. *See Military and Paramilitary Activities in and against Nicaragua (Nicaragua v. United States of America),* Merits, Judgment, I.C.J. Reports 1986, at 41, ¶ 64.

Chapter I

Before "Genocide": The Evolution of a Law to Regulate Armed Conflict

> International law becomes meaningless when any attempt is made to apply its principles equally to barbarian nations.... For the German empire to apply international law in cases like this would not be either humanity or justice; it would be shameful weakness.
>
> —Heinrich von Treitschke, German nationalist historian and Reichstag member[1]

International law, as one scholar has noted, rests on a paradox: international law regulates and therefore limits the sovereignty and independence of states, yet it owes its existence and survival to the consent of states.[2] International law protects the integrity of states, yet prevents them from taking actions that may be deemed necessary to ensure their survival.[3]

A heightened form of this paradox makes itself known in the law of genocide. International law bans genocide. International criminal law provides penalties up to and sometimes including the death penalty for those convicted of genocide, and may assure that victims receive civil compensation for genocide even decades after the fact. At the same time, international law respects the sovereignty and territorial integrity of states that owe their existence and current contours to genocide on an unimaginable scale. The international order whose stability the law respects emerged from a history of genocidal mass killing, systematic rape and theft of children, land expropriation, and cultural devastation. This

1. *Quoted in* Alain Gresh, *The West's Selective Reading of Eastern History and Values: From Thermopylae to the Twin Towers,* Le Monde Diplomatique/Japan Focus, Jan. 2009, http://www.japanfocus.org/products/details/3004.

2. *See, e.g.,* David Kennedy, *The Sources of International Law,* 2 American Univ. J. Int'l L. & Policy 1, 23 (1987) (describing paradoxical relationship between "normative autonomy" of nation-states and "normative authority" of international law); *see also* Robert Cryer, *International Criminal Law vs State Sovereignty: Another Round?,* 16 European J. International Law 979 (2005); David J. Bederman, *The 1871 London Declaration,* Rebus Sic Stantibus *and a Primitivist View of the Law of Nations,* 82 American J. International Law 1 (1988) (similar).

3. *Compare, e.g.,* U.N. Charter art. 2, para. 4 (protecting territorial integrity of states against external interference by the threat or use of force), *with* Rome Statute of the International Criminal Court, arts. 6–8, 53rd Sess., U.N. Doc. A/CONF. 183/9, adopted by the U.N. Diplomatic Conference of Plenipotentiaries on the Establishment of an International Criminal Court on 17 July 1998, as corrected by the proces-verbaux of 10 Nov. 1998 and 12 July 1999 (prohibiting a variety of acts by states within their borders, from genocide to widespread attacks on the civilian population to large-scale commission of murder, torture, or inhuman treatment).

paradox removes much of the incentive for states not to commit genocide, by failing to take away the ill-gotten gains that flow from it. As a result, the prohibition of genocide in international law has not been adequately enforced, or has been enforced selectively and sometimes disingenuously.

A. International Law in Ancient Times

The law of war in the ancient world was more developed in the areas of treaties, particularly those containing nonaggression pacts or guarantees for prisoners of war, than in the area of the substantive protections of civilian or civilian property from attack. The ancient Assyrians, Babylonians, and Egyptians entered into nonaggression treaties with neighboring peoples such as the Moabites, Hittites, and Medes.[4] While at war, however, these and other ancient empires could be indiscriminate, killing civilians and devastating occupied cities.[5]

The Greeks and Romans behaved similarly while at war, entering into peace treaties with some vassal or rival states,[6] while utterly destroying some cities and communities that opposed them. Greek authors wrote that Troy, which Plato described as part of the Assyrian empire,[7] fell before a genocidal assault by the allied city-states of Greece,[8] although

4. *See The Vassal-Treaties of Esarhaddon, in* 2 The Ancient Near East 53–69 (James Pritchard ed., Princeton: Princeton UP, 6th ed. 1992) *The Vassal-Treaties of Esarhaddon, in* 2 The Ancient Near East 53–69 (James Pritchard ed., Princeton: Princeton UP, 6th ed. 1992) (treaty between Assyrian "king of the world" and vassal prince of Babylonia, in the era of King Esarhaddon in the seventh century BCE); *Treaty between Ashurnirari V of Assyria and Mati'ilu of Arpad, in id.* at 49–51; *Treaty of Esarhaddon with Baal of Tyre, in id.* at 52–53; *see also* Simo Parpola & Kazuko Watanabe, Neo-Assyrian Treaties and Loyalty Oaths. State Archives of Assyria xv–xvi, 18–29 (Helsinki: Helsinki University Press, 1988); Parpola, *International Law in the First Millennium,* at 1051–58; Benjamin R. Foster, *Water under the Straw: Peace in Ancient Mesopotamia, in* War and Peace in the Ancient World 68, 114 (Kurt A. Raaflaub ed., London: Blackwell Publishing, 2007); *cf.* Bruce Edward Routledge, Moab in the Iron Age 204 (Philadelphia: Univ. of Pennsylvania Press, 2004); Rainer Albertz, Israel in Exile: The History and Literature of the Sixth Century BCE, at 50 (David Green trans., Atlanta: The Society for Biblical Lit., 2002).

5. *See* François Lenormant & E. Chevallier, A Manual of the Ancient History of the East to the Commencement of the Median Wars 401 (Philadelphia: J.B. Lippicott & Co., 1871) (quoting inscription of Sennacherib); *Inscription of Seti I, "Slaying Prisoners Before Amon," in* Ancient Records of Egypt : The Nineteenth Dynasty 56–58 (James Henry Breasted ed., Chicago: The University of Chicago, 1906).

6. *See* Lawrence A. Tritle, The Peloponnesian War 10–11 (Westport, CT: Greenwood Publ'g Group, 2004); John H. McNeill, *Measures for Strengthening Mutual Guarantees of Non-aggression Among States, in* International Law and International Security: Military and Political Dimensions 295 (Paul B. Stephan III & Boris Mikhaĭlovich Klimenko eds., Armonk, NY: M.E. Sharpe, 1991).

7. *See* Plato, *The Laws, in* The Dialogues on Plato 66 (trans. Benjamin Jowett, New York: MacMillan & Co., 1892). This is consistent with Herodotus' dating of the fall of Troy to 1250 BCE, a period of expansion for the Assyrian Empire. *See* J.M. Munn-Rankin, *The Expansion of Assyrian Military Power, 1300–1200 B.C., in* 2 The Cambridge Ancient History (J. B. Bury ed., Cambridge: Cambridge UP, 1975); Carol G. Thomas & Craig Conant, Citadel to City-State: The Transformation of Greece, 1200–700 BCE, at 20 (Indianapolis: Indiana UP, 2003).

8. *See* Herodotus, The Histories, bk. 1 (G. C. Macaulay trans., New York: MacMillan & Co., 1890); Strabo, The Geography, bk. 1, at 61, 179 (Horace Leonard Jones trans., New York: G.P. Putnam's Sons, 1917); *see also* 1 Encyclopedia of Genocide and Crimes Against Humanity 37, 1191 (Dinah Shelton ed., New York: Macmillan Reference, 2005); Ben Kiernan, Blood and Soil: A World History of Genocide and Extermination from Sparta to Darfur 60 (New Haven, CT: Yale UP,

modern historians and archaeologists are split as to whether this actually occurred or was merely a legend.[9] Plato arguably initiated the discourse of war crimes in the form to which we have become accustomed. In *The Republic*, Socrates, as a mouthpiece for Plato, urges that in an ideal Greek society, the army would refrain from abusing the civilian population of a conquered enemy, enslaving its defeated military, burning its houses, or ruining its agriculture.[10] These protections were to be reserved to Greeks only in Plato's view, the threat and strangeness of foreign "barbarians" depriving them of equal treatment and subjecting them to unrestricted violence.[11] The divergence of standards governing members and non-members of the dominant group has plagued much of the thinking and writing about war crimes since Plato wrote.

East and South Asia developed codes and regulations for the conduct of war from a very early period. In the twelfth century BCE, the Zhou Dynasty of ancient China issued orders threatening punishment of troops for murders, rapes, destruction of homes, or plunder of livestock.[12] In the first millennium BCE, the "Code of Si Ma Rang Ju" reportedly prohibited the killing of children, the elderly, or peaceful adults; the burning of homes; the plunder of crops or livestock; and religious persecution.[13] It has been attributed to the Minister of War at the time.[14]

Although some aspects of the Hindu law of war predated the writings of Greek philosophers on the subject such as Plato by 1,000 years or more, the principal written document that has come down to us is the Laws of Manu from about 100 or 200 BCE.[15] The Hindu Laws of Manu urged kings to resolve quarrels by "conciliation" and "gifts" rather than war, and to honor the customs of a defeated enemy when fighting cannot be avoided.[16] The precepts of Hindu ethical war (or *dharma-yuddha*) included: refusing to kill civilians or injured, retreating, or surrendering soldiers; forswearing war for greed or national aggrandizement; and exhausting negotiations and opportunities for peaceful resolution of a dispute prior to going to war.[17] The Code of Yaj-

---

2007); Mary Boyce, *Persian Religion in the Achaemenid Age, in* 1 The Cambridge History of Judaism: The Persian Period 295 (William David Davies & Louis Finkelstein eds., Cambridge: Cambridge UP, 1984); Homer, The Siege of Troy and the Wanderings of Ulysses 179, 183–84 (Charles Henry Hanson ed., London: T. Nelson & Sons, 1894).

9. For a good overview of some of the arguments on both sides, see Joachim Latacz, Troy and Homer: Towards a Solution of an Old Mystery (Oxford: Oxford UP, 2004).

10. *See* Plato, The Republic 144–46 (G.M.A. Grube trans., 1992) (380 BCE).

11. *See id.*

12. *See* Zhu Li-Sun, *Traditional Asian Approaches [to Armed Conflicts]—The Chinese View*, 9 Australian Yearbook Int'l Law 143, 144 (1985) (symposium on Traditional Asian Approaches to the Protection of Victims of Armed Conflict and Their Relationship to Modern International Humanitarian Law).

13. *See id.* at 143–44; G. Triggs, *Commentary*, 9 Australian Yearbook Int'l Law 151, 151 (1985).

14. *See* Triggs, *Commentary*, at 151.

15. *See* Timothy L.H. McCormack, *Selective Reaction to Atrocity: War Crimes and the Development of International Criminal Law*, 60 Albany Law Review 681, 686–87 (1997).

16. *See* The Laws of Manu ¶¶ 198–203 (G. Buhler trans., 1886) (200 BCE), http://www.sacred-texts.com/hin/manu/manu07.htm. *See also* L. R. Penna, *Traditional Asian Approaches: An Indian View*, 9 Australian Yearbook Int'l Law 168, 174 (1985) (dating Laws of Manu to 100 BCE) (symposium on Traditional Asian Approaches to the Protection of Victims of Armed Conflict and Their Relationship to Modern International Humanitarian Law).

17. *See* Anantanand Rambachan, *The Co-existence of Violence and Non-violence in Hinduism*, 55 Ecumenical Rev. (April 2003), http://www.findarticles.com/p/articles/mi_m2065/is_2_55/ai_106560163.

navalka, which restated and expanded upon the Laws of Manu,[18] provided that civilians and injured or surrendering prisoners of war should not be killed, and a commentator on Yajnavalka added that women, scholars (*brahmin*), and musicians ("bards") should be spared.[19]

At the same time, the treatment of non-Hindus and conquered peoples within Hindu society could be discriminatory and debilitating. A man of the Shūdra (suffering peoples) caste, could suffer various kinds of mutilation for insulting a higher-case man,[20] as well as death, or castration and loss of all property, for adultery or fornication with a higher-caste women, a crime for which a man of the highest major caste, or Brāhma*n*a, would merely pay a fine.[21] The Laws of Manu state:

> Whatever exists in the world is the property of the Brahman [caste]; on account of the excellence of his origin the Brāhma*n*a is, indeed, entitled to it all.... The dwellings of the [lower caste families] shall be outside the village, and their wealth (shall be) dogs and donkeys. Their dress (shall be) the garments of the dead, (they shall eat) their food from broken dishes, black iron (shall be) their ornaments, and they must always wander from place to place.... [A]t night they shall not walk about in villages and in towns.[22]

Even below the Shūdra caste are the untouchables or "Dalits," the casteless, impure peoples. Through the late 1990s, Dalits lived in segregated villages or portions of villages, where they were forbidden to use the water supplies of the higher-caste Hindus. Dalit rights activism triggered mass killings, rapes, and plunder of Dalit areas.[23] A Dalit liberation movement leader characterized the caste system as a relic of Aryan conquest:

> The Aryans—your ancestors—conquered us and ... you treated us even worse than slaves and subjected us to any torture you wanted. But now we are no longer your subjects ... or serfs.... We have had enough of the ... torture of the Hindus.[24]

For some leaders in the Dalit liberation movement, the struggle against caste discrimination is that of an indigenous people against the privileges and dominance of a settler population: "having its roots in the age-old historical conflict between the ancestors of today's 'lower' castes, and the 'foreign' Aryan 'invaders', from whom the 'upper'-caste Hindus trace their descent."[25]

---

18. *See* Stephen Haley Allen, 1 The Evolution of Governments and Laws 176–77 (Princeton: Princeton UP, 2d ed. 1922).

19. *See* Penna, *An Indian View*, at 187.

20. *See* L.R. Balley, *India Needs a Cultural Revolution, in* Untouchable! Voices of the Dalit Liberation Movement 155 (Barbara R. Joshi ed., London: Zed Books, 1986) (punishments included hot iron thrust into the mouth or cutting out of tongues for insulting higher caste, amputation of hands or feet for raising them in anger against higher caste, hot oil poured into the ears for lecturing a higher case individual, cutting off of lips for spitting at a higher case individual, and removal of anus for passing gas in vicinity of a higher case individual).

21. *See* The Laws of Manu 316 (Georg Bühler ed. & trans., Oxford: Clarendon Press, 1886) (parentheses added by translator for clarity); Shridhar Venkatesh Ketkar, 1 The History of Caste in India 152 (Ithaca, NY: Taylor & Carpenter, 1909).

22. The Laws of Manu 26, 414 (parentheses added in original; brackets added).

23. *See* Smita Narula, Broken People: Caste Violence Against India's "Untouchables" (New York and Washington, DC: Human Rights Watch 1999), http://www.hrw.org/legacy/reports/1999/india/India994-04.htm.

24. Kisan Faguji Bansode in 1909, *quoted in* Gail Omvedt, Dalit Visions 35 (London: Orient Blackswan, 2006).

25. Yōgīndar Sikkand, Muslims in India Since 1947, at 103 (London: Routledge, 2004).

B. International Law in Christian Thought

Aurelius Augustinus (St. Augustine) of Hippo offered an account of the justice of war that would be highly influential on theorists who helped articulate the modern law of war, such as St. Thomas Aquinas, Francisco de Vitoria, and Hugo Grotius. Augustine argued that: "In the compelling of evildoers to righteousness the Church imitates her Lord." Pope Pelagius maintained that "heretics should be restrained by the secular arm," and Pope Urban II added that killing members of the Church who had justly been excommunicated for heresy did not constitute homicide, but justice.[26]

The early Christian church declared that Christians should not initiate violence, but should respond to swords and blows with love and forgiveness.[27] After many centuries of rule by Christian kings and emperors, rather than the likes of Nero, theologians adopted a more warlike stance, and accepted the "extermination" of heretics. Augustine, for example, cited what he characterized as endorsements of violence and compulsion in the Bible to reject the claim of the dissident Donatist Christians that religious liberty and nonviolence should be the rule.[28] Thomas Aquinas, similarly, justified on the authority of Scripture the use of compulsion and violence against unbelievers and heretics after the delivery of two warnings:

> On the part of the Church, however, there is mercy, which looks to the conversion of the wanderer; wherefore, she condemns not at once, but "after the first and second warning", as the Apostle directs (Titus 3:10). After that, if he is still stubborn, the Church, no longer hoping for his conversion, looks to the salvation of others by excommunicating him and separating him from the Church; and, furthermore, she delivers him over to the secular tribunal, thereby to be exterminated from the world by death....[29]

Aquinas recognized that faith is an act of the mind and the heart, and requires a free choice, so he wrote that "unbelievers ... who have never received the faith, such as the heathens and the Jews ... are by no means to be compelled to the faith, in order that they may believe, because to believe depends on the will...." He did not view freedom of choice as being inconsistent with the compulsion of heathen groups, whom he taught "should be

---

26. Thomas Alfred Waler, A History of the Law of Nations 209 (Cambridge: Cambridge UP, 1899) (citing St. Augustine, *Epistle No. 50, in* Contra duas Epistulas Pelagianorum ad Bonifacium Papam (420 CE)).

27. *See, e.g.*, Cyril of Alexandria, *Commentary on Luke, Homily 148, in* Ancient Christian Commentary on Scripture: New Testament III, Luke 346 (2003); Justin of Caesarea, *The First Apology, in* 1 Ante Nicene Fathers 175 (Alexander Roberts & James Donaldson eds., 1903); Irenaeus of Rome, *Against Heresies, in* Ante-Nicene Fathers 512; Clement of Alexandria, Egypt, *Instructor, in* 2 Ante-Nicene Fathers 234–35; Origin, *Against Celsus, in* 4 Ante-Nicene Fathers 558; *Tertullian, in* 3 Ante-Nicene Fathers 73; Tertullian, *De Corona, in* 3 Ante-Nicene Fathers 99–100 (Roberts & Donaldson eds., New York: Scribner & Sons, 1903).

28. *See* Aurelius Augustinus, *On the Correction of the Donatists, in* 3 The Works of Aurelius Augustine, Bishop of Hippo xiii, 497–500 (Rev. Marcus Dods ed. & Rev. J.R. Kingtrans., Edinburgh: T&T Clark, 1872) (quoting Proverbs 29:19, Proverbs 13:14, Proverbs 8:14, and Luke 14:22–23, and citing Acts 9:1–18). *See also* Aurelius Augustinus, The City of God 387, 389–90 (Rev. Marcus Dods ed., Edinburgh: T&T Clark, 1871) ("'[W]ith fire of the Lord shall all the earth be judged, and all flesh with His sword: many shall be wounded by the Lord.'") (quoting Isaiah 66:15–16); Rev. Thomas Vickers, *Rejoinder, in* The Roman Catholic Church and Free Thought 36–38 (Cincinnati: The First Congregational Church, 1868) (discussing thought of Augustinus).

29. St. Thomas Aquinas, The Summa Theologica, bk. 2, pt. 2, quest. 11, art. 3 (Benziger Bros. ed., New York: Benziger Bros., 947), http://www.newadvent.org/summa/3011.htm.

compelled to be orthodox Christians "so that they do not hinder the faith, by their blasphemies, or by their evil persuasions, or even by their open persecutions."[30] By the preemption of persecutions of Christians, Aquinas probably had in mind the campaign by Christian emperors against paganism, and by the Crusaders to halt the destructions of churches and killings of Christians that had characterized the Arab conquest and colonization of southwestern Asia and North Africa.[31]

Theology prompted religious expansion, along with forcible internal consolidation. The Italian canon lawyer Gratian argued that "wars may undoubtedly be waged with justice by command of God. The Israelites justly made war on the Amorites when they were refused [safe passage through Amorite territory]."[32] Grotius cites Augustine for the same argument, declaring that Europeans had "just reasons" for conquering the Aztecs and other Indians in the Americas because they were prevented from living among them. He noted that: "We read of a similar case in the history of Moses, which we find mentioned also in the writings of Augustine, where the Israelites justly smote with the edge of the sword the Amorites because they had denied the Israelites an innocent passage through their territory...."[33]

The historian Lorenzo Veracini argues that the "settler consciousness of the European gaze" developed "around a specific interpretative tradition of the biblical book of Exodus—where a divinely elected people takes over a promised land and disperses the original Canaanite inhabitants."[34] Machiavelli, for example, became a legend by arguing for the aggrandizement of each nation by any means necessary, including murder.[35] Machiavelli translated the example of the Roman Empire and the Bible into a modern political philosophy. He argued that European princes, in emulating ancient empires, should realize that Moses, like the early kings of Rome and Persia, justifiably took measures to make the people believe in their leader "by force." He added that when leaders overcome their rivals, "and those who envied them and their success are exterminated, they will begin to be respected, and they will [again be] powerful, secure, honoured, and happy."[36] Machiavelli regarded conquest as virtue and objections as weakness.[37]

In another work, Machiavelli proclaims that settlers typically "establish themselves in cities which they find ready to their hand in the countries of which they take possession, as did Moses...." He described the events of Moses' life as a case of an entire people leaving its former home, and finding a new country to live in, "not simply with the view to establish dominion over it, but to possess it as its own, and to expel or exterminate the former inhabitants...." He wrote:

---

30. *Id.*, quest. 10, art. 8, http://www.newadvent.org/summa/3010.htm#8.

31. *See* Matthew C. Mirow & Kathleen A. Kelley, *Law and Religion from the Theodosian and Justiniac Codes, in* Religions of Late Antiquity in Practice 263–272 (Richard Valantasis ed., 2000); Garry Wills, *What Is a Just War?*, N.Y. Rev. of Books, Nov. 18, 2004, http://www.nybooks.com/articles/article-preview?article_id=17560.

32. Waler, A History of the Law of Nations, at 208.

33. Hugo Grotius, The Freedom of the Seas; Or, the Right which Belongs to the Dutch to Take Part in the East Asian Trade 9 (Ralph van Deman Magoffin trans. & James Brown Scott ed., New York: Oxford UP, 1916).

34. Lorenzo Veracini, *Colonialism and Genocides: Notes for the Analysis of the Settler Archive, in* Empire, Colony, Genocide, at 148–49 (citing Ann Curthoys, *Expulsion, Exodus and Exile in White Australian Historical Mythology*, 61 J. of Australian Studies 2 (1999)); *see also* Curthoys, *Genocide in Tasmania: The History of an Idea,* at 229–52.

35. *See* Leo Strauss, *Niccolò Machiavelli, in* History of Political Philosophy 296–315 (Leo Strauss & Joseph Cropsey eds., Chicago: Univ. of Chicago Press, 3d ed. 1987).

36. Niccolò Machiavelli, The Prince 8, 221–223 (W. K. Marriott trans., New York: E.P. Dutton, 1908) (1515 CE), ch. 6, http://www.constitution.org/mac/prince.pdf.

37. *See* Strauss, *Niccolò Machiavelli,* at 306–310.

> When these [traveling peoples] are in large numbers, they violently invade the territories of other nations, slaughtering the inhabitants, seizing on their possessions, founding new kingdoms, and giving new names to provinces; as was done by Moses, and by those tribes who overran the Roman Empire.[38]

While they could be cited in favor of extremely harsh measures against enemy nations and heretics, biblical texts motivated some prominent jurists to articulate broad prohibitions on massacring civilians. In the sixteenth century, the Spanish jurist and theologian Francisco de Vitoria condemned Spanish tactics in the Americas as "in excess of what is allowed by human and divine law."[39] He looked directly to the Books of Exodus and Deuteronomy to argue:

> The deliberate slaughter of the innocent is never lawful in itself. This is proved, firstly, by Exodus, ch. 23: "The innocent and righteous slay thou not...." [¶] Hence it follows that even in war with the Turks it is not allowable to kill children—This is clear, because they are innocent. Aye, and the same holds with regard to the women of unbelievers. This is clear, because so far as the war is concerned, they are presumed innocent; but it does not hold in the case of any individual woman who is certainly guilty. Aye, and this same pronouncement must be made among Christians with regard to harmless agricultural folk, and also with regard to the rest of the peaceable civilian population, for all these are presumed innocent until the contrary is shown. On this principle it follows that it is not lawful to slay either foreigners or guests who are sojourning among the enemy, for they are presumed innocent, and in truth they are not enemies. The same principle applies to clerics and members of a religious order, for they in war are presumed innocent unless the contrary be shown, as when they engage in actual fighting.[40]

Vitoria argued that "neither [Indian] princes nor private persons could be despoiled of their property on the ground of their not being true owners." But he maintained the position of Aquinas and Augustine with respect to evangelization of pagan lands. Absent Spanish intervention, the Indians would remain mired in sin and "outside the pale of salvation"; for this reason, and by the natural right of travel and trade, the Spanish had the right to overcome any resistance to their presence with war, removal of kings and leaders from power, and expropriation of Indian lands and movable goods.[41]

Notions of natural rights also helped lead to more humanitarian formulations of Christian-pagan relations. Bartolomé de Las Casas argued that the Spanish conquests of the Aztecs involved the killing of so many women and children that they "should be condemned not only by the law of God but by all the laws of man...."[42] He wrote that indigenous Americans "had a right to brotherly kindness and Christian love," and in that "'right instilled in man from

---

38. Niccolò Machiavelli, Discourses on the First Decade of Titus Livius 8, 221–223 (Ninian Hill Thomson trans., London: Kegan Paul, Trench & Co., 1883) (1513 CE).

39. Francisco de Vitoria, De Indis et De ivre Belli Relectiones [On the Indians Lately Discovered] § 1, ¶ 12, at 158 (John Powley Bate trans., Ernest Nys et al eds., Washington, The Carnegie Institution, 1917) (1537–38), http://www.constitution.org/victoria/victoria_5.htm.

40. Francisco de Vitoria, *On the Law of War* [*De Indis Relectio Posterior, sive de iure belli*], *in* Political Writings 315 (Anthony Pagden, Jeremy Lawrance eds,. Cambridge: Cambridge UP, 2001).

41. Francisco de Vitoria, *Of the Indians Lately Discovered* [*De Indis*], *in* The Classics of International Law (Ernest Nys ed., New York: Oceana Publications, 1964), http://www.constitution.org/victoria/victoria_4.htm.

42. Bartolomé de las Casas, The Devastation of the Indies 58 (Herma Briffault ed. & trans., Baltimore, MD: Johns Hopkins UP, 1992) (1552).

the beginning, ... [a]ll the races of humankind are one.'"[43] He eventually "secured a royal order authorizing the establishment of villages of free Indians in the New World [governing themselves] in a civilized 'political way like Spaniards,'"[44] but his precepts were not followed in the wider empire to ensure the survival and self-determination of indigenous Americans.[45]

Hugo Grotius also conceived of a sphere of "natural right" that could be determined by examination of (1) the "principles" implicit in the "rational and social nature" of man, or (2) agreement "among all nations, or among all those that are more advanced in civilization."[46] He utilized Vitoria's reasoning to acknowledge that indigenous Americans had natural rights to life and property.[47] However, he also argued, without distinguishing between races or cultures:

> [I]f within the territory of a people there is any deserted and unproductive soil, this also ought to be granted to foreigners if they ask for it. Or it is right for foreigners even to take possession of such ground, for the reason that uncultivated land ought not to be considered as occupied except in respect to sovereignty, which remains unimpaired in favour of the original people....
>
> A noteworthy example we find in the history of Moses. When he found it necessary to pass through the territories of others, he offered ... to the Amorites, these stipulations, that he would follow the king's highway and ... that if he should have need of anything belonging to them he would pay them a fair price. When these terms were refused, for that reason he waged a just war against the Amorites.[48]

Thus, Grotius, Machiavelli, and Vitoria provided a theoretical framework for European appropriation of indigenous American lands and resources, by refusing to the Indians or to any other people the ability to deny access to travelers, traders, or even foreigners seeking wives.[49]

C. International Law in Islamic Thought

Some Islamic religious texts counsel against compelling unbelievers to practice, or usurping the divine role of guidance in matters of spirituality.[50] Among these admonitions

---

43. Brian Tierney, *The Idea of Natural Rights—Origins and Persistence*, 2 Northwestern Univ. J. of International Human Rights 2, ¶¶ 28–29 (2004). *See also* Bartolome de las Casas, Historia de las Indias (1561), *reprinted in* History of the Indies (Andree Collard ed. & trans., 1971).

44. Williams, *The American Indian in Western Legal Thought*, 66–67.

45. *See* Tierney, *The Idea of Natural Rights*, at ¶ 29.

46. 2 Hugo Grotius, De Jure Belli ac Pacis: Libri Tres 23–24, 42 (James Brown Scott ed., Francis W. Kelsey et al. trans., London: Clarendon Press, 1925) (1625). *See also* Harlan Grant Cohen, *Finding International Law: Rethinking the Doctrine of Sources,* 93 Iowa L. Rev. 65, nn. 41–43 & accompanying text (2007).

47. *See* Beate Jahn, Classical Theory in International Relations 165–67 (Cambridge: Cambridge UP, 2006).

48. 2 Grotius, De Jure Belli ac Pacis Libri Tres §§ 12, 17.

49. *Id.* §§ 12 (right to pass through foreign lands regardless of their fear at the numbers entering their territory and possibility of being taken over), 15 (right to "sojourn for a time, for the sake of health, or for any other good reason" while passing through a foreign country), 16 (right of those driven from their country to take up residence in a foreign land), 19 (right to trade at fair prices and not to be expelled from a land, once admitted), 25 (right to marry foreign women).

50. *See* Muslim and Christian Reflections on Peace: Divine and Human Dimensions 108 (John Dudley Woodberry, et al., eds., 2005); M.K. Ereksoussi, *The Koran and the Humanitarian Conventions,* 14 Int'l Rev. of the Red Cross 273–78 (May 1969).

are counted several following verses of the Qur'an that may be summed up in the phrase: "Let there be no compulsion in religion; Truth stands out clear from Error...."[51] With exceptions for retaliation and those "spreading mischief" or "causing corruption," the Qur'an states that: "if any one slew a person ... it would be as if he slew the whole people."[52]

The exception for "spreading mischief" or "causing corruption," however, threatened to undermine the rule against murder, insofar as the *Anfal* Sura of the Qur'an defines cooperation among the infidels as a source of "discord in the land and great corruption," and instructs believers to tell the infidels: "If they desist from their unbelief, what is now past shall be forgiven them; but if they return to it, they have already before them the doom of the ancients!" The "doom of the ancients" is defined in a prior Sura of the Qur'an, which states that Allah "gave to Moses the Book and the Salvation," and destroyed the Egyptian "evildoers" who slaughtered the sons of Israel.[53] Believers are called upon to punish those who "strive after corruption" with being "killed or crucified, or hav[ing] their hands and feet on alternate sides cut off, or ... be[ing] expelled out of the land."[54] The *Anfal* Sura proclaims monotheism to be the destiny of the entire world: "Fight then against the[] [infidels] till strife be at an end, and the religion be all of it God's...."[55] The so-called "Sword" verses of the Qu'ran stated:

> Then, when the sacred months are drawn away,
> slay the idolaters [or Pagans] wherever you find them,
> and take them, and confine them, and lie in wait
> for them at every place of ambush. But, if they
> repent, and perform the prayer, and pay the alms,
> then let them go their way.[56]

The endorsements of peace and discussion in Islamic religious and political texts did not prevent the dramatic expansion of the Caliphate into Christian and polytheistic lands, including conquests from the Berbers and Spanish in the west to the Hindus and Buddhists in the east. One author describes the shift in Islamic jurists' conception of international law. Starting with the expansionary objective of "winning the whole world to the new faith," a legal framework was needed for regulating the relationships between be-

---

51. Qur'an 2:256 (Abdulluh Yusuf Ali trans., Elmhurst, NY, 2001); *see also* Khurshid Ahmad, *The Challenge of global Capitalism: An Islamic Perspective, in* Making Globalization Good: The Moral Challenges of Global Capitalism 204 (John H. Dunning ed., Oxford: Oxford UP, 2003).

52. Qur'an 5:32; *see also* Encyclopedia of Love in World Religions 131 (Yudit Kornberg Greenberg ed., Santa Barbara, CA: ABC-CLIO, 2007).

53. *See* Qur'an 8:20–39, *quoted in* The Koran 484 (John Medows Rodwell ed. & trans., London: Williams and Norgate, 1861); *see also* Qur'an 2:40–53, 28:29–43 (describing doom of the ancients); George F. Nafziger & Mark W. Walton, Islam at War: A History 213 (Westport, Connecticut: Greenwood Publ'g Group, 2003).

54. Qur'an 5:33, *quoted in* The Ideas that Have Influenced Civilization, in the Original Documents
250 (Oliver Joseph Thatcher ed., 1901); *see also* Nafziger & Walton, Islam at War: A History, at 213. Another translation reserves this treatment for "those who strive with might and main for mischief throughout the land." Qur'an 5:33 (Ali trans.).

55. Qur'an 8:39–42, *quoted in* Kenneth L. Vaux, Ethics and the Gulf War: Religion, Rhetoric, and Righteousness 70–71 (New York: Perseus Books Group, 1992). Another translation refers to fighting until there is no more "tumult" or "oppression" but instead "justice" and "faith in Allah ... everywhere." Qur'an 8:39 (Ali trans.).

56. Qur'an 9:5, *quoted in* A Dictionary of Islam 243(Thomas Patrick Hughes ed., London: W. H. Allen, 1885 1885). *See also* Qur'an 9:5 (Ali trans.).

lieving and unbelieving nations. Islamic jurists articulated a legal theory under which "the rest of the world outside the domain of Islam was called collectively "*dar al-harb*" (the territory of war), and the normal relationship between it and the Muslim state was considered to be war...." After "permanent war" against such large empires as those of the Byzantines and Holy Romans proved unsustainable, the jurists "reinterpreted the duty of *jihad* as meaning defensive war against those unbelievers who threatened the domain of Islam...." A third territory, or "territory of peace," was then defined as unbelieving states that were party to treaties with the empire of Islam.[57]

Another author who engaged in an extended study of the Islamic law of nations wrote that holy war (*jihad*) was considered a more direct way to paradise than prayer and good works. The Arab empire "sought to establish Islam as the dominant reigning ideology over the entire world...." This would eliminate other religions and states from the world scene. He explains:

> [A] Qur'anic injunction ... runs as follows:
>
> "... Believe in Allah and His Apostle and carry on warfare (*jihad*) in the path of Allah with your possessions and your persons...."
>
> In several Qur'anic injunctions, the Muslims are under the obligation to "fight the polytheists wherever ye may find them"; to "fight those who are near to you of the polytheists, and let them find in you sternness"; and "when you meet those who disbelieve, strike off their heads until you have massacred them...."[58]

Given the legitimacy within Islamic international law of destroying polytheists and expanding the Arab empire by force of arms, the question arose as to how to treat conquered populations and occupied territories. Ibn Khaldun, himself possibly an assimilated Arab of North African Berber origin, justified giving conquered populations a strict choice between religious assimilation, the onerous poll tax [*jizya*], or massacres:

> The other religious groups did not have a universal mission, and the holy war was not a religious duty to them, save only for purposes of defence.... [T]hey are [not] under obligation to gain power over other nations, as is the case with Islam....
>
> That is why the Israelites after Moses and Joshua remained unconcerned with royal authority for about four hundred years. Their only concern was to establish their religion.[59]

Indigenous Christian communities bemoaned the *jizya* as so heavy it caused "extreme poverty" and "grave torment." At least in Armenia, the population tried to hide from the Arab taxation authorities, triggering revolts and the branding of residents' necks with lead seals, presumably to keep track of them.[60] The combination of the *jizya* and land taxes in Mesopotamia could reach 50 percent of the agricultural produce of a peasant's farm, and render life intolerable for entire communities. The Arab conquerors exploited the settled indigenous populations to maintain themselves as a military and administra-

---

57. Gamal M. Badr, *A Survey of Islamic International Law, in* RELIGION AND INTERNATIONAL LAW 95–96 (Mark W. Janis & Carolyn Evans eds., The Hague: Kluwer Law Int'l, 1999)

58. MAJID KHADDURI, LAW AND PEACE IN THE LAW OF ISLAM 51, 75, 105 (Clark, NJ: Lawbook Exchange, Ltd., 2006) (quoting Qur'an 5:37, 9:5, 61:10–13). Another translation says "strive ... in the Cause of Allah," rather than, as Khadduri has it, "carry on warfare." Qur'an 61:11 (Ali trans.).

59. Ibn Khaldun, *Prolegomenon* [*Muqaddimah*], *quoted in* YE'OR, THE DECLINE OF EASTERN CHRISTIANITY UNDER ISLAM, at 296.

60. *See* Nina Garsoïan, *The Arab Invasions and the Rise of the Bagratuni (640–884), in* 1 THE ARMENIAN PEOPLE FROM ANCIENT TO MODERN TIMES: FROM ANTIQUITY TO THE FOURTEENTH CENTURY 130–32 (New York: Palgrave, 1997).

tive elite. An economic decline ensued in Mesopotamia, Syria, and Egypt as Arab settlers seized land and attacked farmers.[61] The government would sell tax-farming licenses (*iqta's*) to officials, court favorites, and soldiers, who would impose taxes and remit a share to the government. This caused many indigenous peasants to have to sign over their lands to holders of tax-farming licenses. Arab tax-farmers grew increasingly powerful and eventually resembled feudal lords over a subject race.[62]

The caliphate also imposed hidden taxes in the form of legal disabilities. Christian and Jewish testimony was often inadmissible against Muslims in civil and criminal cases.[63] A Muslim could own a Christian or Jewish slave, although the reverse was not true. A Christian or Jew could not inherit property from a Muslim, and sometimes the reverse was also true, although the Caliph al-Mutawakkil allowed Muslims to inherit property from their still-Christian parents. The murder or homicide of a Christian or Jew was punished less severely than that of a Muslim, including the selective application of the law of retaliation (an eye for an eye) to non-Muslims.[64]

Other than claiming land and taxes, "the jihadists ... were advised to refrain from the shedding of blood or the [unnecessary] destruction of property...."[65] Thus, the Caliph Abu Bakr reportedly issued commands to his armies stating:

> Do not kill any women, children, elders or wounded. Do not have fruit-trees or date-trees cut down. Do not burn them. Do not destroy inhabited places. Do not have cows or sheep drowned. Do not be guilty of cowardice, but do not be inspired by hatred.[66]

Another account of these orders upon the invasion of Syria summarizes them as follows:

> Do not commit treachery, nor depart from the right-path. Do not mutilate, nor kill a child, nor aged man, nor a woman. You must not slay any of the flocks or herds or the camels, save for your sustenance. Do not destroy a palm tree, nor burn it with fire and do not cut any fruit tree. You are likely to pass by peo-

---

61. *See* IRA M. LAPIDUS, A HISTORY OF ISLAMIC SOCIETIES 37–40 (Cambridge: Cambridge UP, 2d ed. 2002).

62. *See id.* at 105–106, 125.

63. *See* PHILIP KHÛRI HITTI, HISTORY OF THE ARABS FROM THE EARLIEST TIMES TO THE PRESENT 353 (New York: Palgrave Macmillan, 10th ed. 2002) (1949); PHILIP KHÛRI HITTI, THE NEAR EAST IN HISTORY: A 5000 YEAR STORY 279 (Princeton, NJ: Van Nostrand, 1961); SPEROS VRYONIS, 1 STUDIES ON BYZANTIUM, SELJUKS, AND OTTOMANS: REPRINTED STUDIES 296 (Malibu, CA: Undena Publications, 1981); BAT YE'OR, THE DECLINE OF EASTERN CHRISTIANITY UNDER ISLAM, at 81–84. The rules restricting *dhimmi* testimony continued to have force in the early modern Ottoman Empire and modern Saudi Arabia and Pakistan. *See* ARYEH SHMUELEVITZ, THE JEWS OF THE OTTOMAN EMPIRE IN THE LATE FIFTEENTH AND THE SIXTEENTH CENTURIES 40–45 (Leiden, the Netherlands: E.J. Brill, 1984); Andrew G. Bostom, *Negating the Legacy of* Jihad *in Palestine,* 13 ISRAEL AFFAIRS 819 (2007), Pages 819–836 Cees Bouma, *Non-Muslims in Pakistan: A Question of Justice and Equality,* 9 J. OF MUSLIM MINORITY AFFAIRS 35 (1988); Jeffrey K. Walker, *The Rights of the Accused in Saudi Criminal Procedure,* LOYOLA OF LOS ANGELES INT'L AND COMPARATIVE L.J. 863 (1992–1993).

64. *See, e.g.,* Choucri Cardahi, *Conflict of Law, in* 1 LAW IN THE MIDDLE EAST 335–37 (Majid Khadduri and Herbert J. Liebesny eds., Clark, NJ: The Lawbook Exchange, Ltd., 2008) (1995). For explanations of other disabilities, see *Persecution (Muhammedan), in* 18 ENCYCLOPEDIA OF RELIGION AND ETHICS 767 (James Hastings ed., Whitefish, MT: Kessinger Publishing, 2003); *Toleration (Muhammedan), in* 23 ENCYCLOPEDIA OF RELIGION AND ETHICS 367 (James Hastings ed., Whitefish, MT: Kessinger Publishing, 2003); Gerard Troupenau, *Dhimmi, in* ENCYCLOPEDIA OF THE MIDDLE AGES 432 (André Vauchez et al. eds.

65. KHADDURI, LAW AND PEACE IN THE LAW OF ISLAM, at 102.

66. Yadh Ben Ashoor, *Islam and International Humanitarian Law,* INT'L REV. OF THE RED CROSS, Mar.–Apr. 1980, at 59–69.

> ple who have devoted their lives to monastic service; leave them to what they have devoted their lives....[67]

The same caliph reportedly issued orders against carrying out "vengeance" on polytheists, or mutilating the unbelievers.[68] A treaty or declaration by the Caliph Omar stated:

> [The caliph] grants to all, whether sick or sound, security for their lives, their possessions, their churches and their crosses, and for all that concerns their religion. Their churches shall not be changed into dwelling-places, nor destroyed, neither shall they nor their appurtenances be in any way diminished, nor their crosses [nor possessions] ... nor shall any one of them be harmed.[69]

Omar's will (or testament) contained evidence of a treaty with a conquered Christian people.[70] The treaties of Omar with the Christians of Damascus, later expanded to apply to Mesopotamia, permitted the survival of Christianity but prohibited new churches, the repair of dilapidated churches, or the refusal of lodging and three days' of food to Muslims arriving at churches.[71]

D. International Law from the Renaissance to 1914

European scholars and political advisers have long recognized that civilian massacres, as well as genocide, are prohibited by sound religious doctrine and the precepts of "natural" law. These teachings would later form the basis for historic criminal tribunals. By nature, Desiderius Erasmus argued, human beings are born soft of flesh, bereft of horns or fangs, yet possessed of the "spark of divine mind." Even so, they waged war in a fashion that made the beasts of the field seem tame, and that constituted a mockery of Christianity itself:

> [S]avage troops of men, horrible in their very visages ... ; men clad in steel..., armed with weapons ... ; [let out] a mad shout..., [and begin] a cruel butchering of each other! ... Heaps of dead bodies, fields flowing with blood....
>
> [A]fter a war, ... the unoffending common people [are] robbed of their little hard-earned property; the great [are] laden with taxes; old people [are] bereaved of their children; more cruelly killed by the murder of their offspring than by the sword; ... women far advanced in age, left destitute, and more cruelly put to death, than if they had died at once by the point of a bayonet; widowed mothers, orphan children, houses of mourning; and families, that once knew better days, reduced to extreme penury....

---

67. *See* Treaty with Damascus, *quoted in Prophet in Command, in* ENCYCLOPAEDIA OF HOLY PROPHET AND COMPANIONS 273 (Shahid Ashraf ed., New Delhi, India: Anmol Publications, 2004). *See also id.* ("I commend to your [i.e., his successors'] care the dhimmis of the Apostle of God; see that the agreement with them is kept, and that they be defended against their enemies, and that no burden be laid upon them beyond their strength.").

68. *Id.*

69. *Quoted in Toleration (Muhammadan), in* 7 ENCYCLOPÆDIA OF RELIGION AND ETHICS 367 (James Hastings, ed., New York: Charles Scribner & Sons, 1922).

70. *Quoted in id.*

71. *Quoted in* KHADDURI, LAW AND PEACE, at 182–87, 193–201. *See also id.* at 213–16 (reproducing text of Omar's treaty with Jerusalem, dated to approximately 638 CE).

> The Jews waged war with foreign nations; while the christians are, with the Turks, at peace, and with one another, at war![72]

Hugo Grotius, likewise, argued in the seventeenth century that some acts "excessively violate the law of nature or of nations in regards to any persons whatsoever."[73] Sovereigns had the right and responsibility to punish other sovereigns for such wanton violations of natural law. Rulers possessed, in the Enlightenment vision, a "general responsibility for human society."[74] Reasoning from a law of nature designed to protect and advance the interests of intelligent beings, Grotius derived a power to punish extreme anti-social and anti-human behavior.[75]

Emmerich de Vattel, writing in the eighteenth century, reasoned in a manner similar to Erasmus. Specifically, he condemned tyrannical oppression as a violation of the law of nature, triggering a right of external punishment:

> [I]f tyranny, becoming insupportable, obliges the nation to rise in their own defence,—every foreign power has a right to succour an oppressed people who implore their assistance.... [W]hen a people, from good reasons take up arms against an oppressor, it is but an act of justice and generosity to assist brave men in the defence of their liberties. Whenever, therefore, matters are carried so far as to produce a civil war, foreign powers may assist that party which appears to them to have justice on its side. He who assists an odious tyrant,—he who declares for an unjust and rebellious people,—violates his duty....
>
> As to those monsters who, under the title of sovereigns, render themselves the scourges and horror of the human race, they are savage beasts, whom every brave man may justly exterminate from the face of the earth.[76]

The laws and customs of war gave rise to criminal prosecutions of military leaders responsible for massacres of civilians or other abuses, starting even before the time of Grotius. In the fourteenth century, British jurists tried and convicted the Scottish rebel William Wallace for "violations of 'the laws and usages of war,'" specifically the conducting of an insurgency by "'sparing neither age nor sex.'"[77] In the fifteenth century, a warrior in the service of the Duke of Burgundy was tried and convicted for murder and rape committed during the occupation of Austria, in violation of the "'laws of God and man.'"[78] In the seventeenth century, the King of Sweden decreed Articles of War which, among

---

72. Desiderius Erasmus [Roterdamus], The Complaint of Peace; To Which Is Added, Antipolemus, or the Plea of Reason, Religion, and Humanity, Against War 30–37 (Boston: Charles William, 1813) (1513). He added: "As to the Heathen despots, it is true, the thirst of glory goaded them to battle; but even they conquered fierce and barbarous nations, to civilize them; ... the conquerors endeavoring to render every service in their power to the people whom they had subdued." *Id.*

73. Grotius, De Juri Belli ac Pace Libri Tres, at 504. *See also* Alex J. Bellamy, *Ethics and Intervention: The 'Humanitarian Exception' and the Problem of Abuse,* 41 Journal of Peace Res. 131, 140 (2004).

74. Grotius, De Juri Belli ac Pace Libri Tres, at §44.

75. *See, e.g.,* Michael P. Zuckert, Natural Rights and the New Republicanism 232 (Princeton: Princeton UP, 1992).

76. Emmerich de Vattel, The Law of Nations, or the Principles of the Law of Nature Applied to the Conduct and Affairs of Nations and Sovereigns §56 (Charles G. Fenwick trans., Joseph Chitty ed., Philadelphia: T. & J.W. Johnson & Co., 1883) (1758), http://www.constitution.org/vattel/vattel_02.htm.

77. McCormack, *Selective Reaction to Atrocity,* at 689–90 (citing Georg Schwarzenberger, *The Judgment of Nuremberg,* 21 Tulane L.Rev. 329, 330 (1947)).

78. McCormack, *Selective Reaction to Atrocity,* at 690.

other things, declared that any attempt to "tyrannise over" unarmed men, women, or children, particularly clergy and aged people, would be subject to "punishment at the discretion of the Judges."[79] Seventeenth-century English law similarly banned attacks on civilians or prisoners of war.[80] In the eighteenth century, British troops were put on trial for the Boston Massacre, and a treaty between Prussia and the U.S. confirmed that women and children, as well as farmers, fishermen, artisans, and scholars should be protected in wartime.[81]

In the nineteenth century, European powers punished Napoleon Bonaparte with exile and loss of property for waging unjust wars, although full trials of all of the emperor's acts was withheld for fear of incriminating the British-led coalition as well.[82] The U.S. tried and convicted British nationals for massacring women and children in violation of "the law of nations" and "the laws and usages of war,"[83] the tribunal specifically condemning their " 'savage' warfare ... whereby wives and children were brutally massacred."[84] U.S. forces in Mexico established tribunals with jurisdiction to conduct trials of " '[a]ny inhabitant of Mexico' " for "violations of the 'laws of war.' "[85]

The slave trade from Africa to the Americas is an early instance of a crime being referred to as committed against "humanity." During the Federal Convention for the preparation of a U.S. Constitution, Colonel George Mason of Virginia referred to slavery as an "infernal" practice destined to bring down the "judgement of God" upon the colonies.[86] The Treaty of Ghent between the U.S. and Great Britain in 1815 stated: "Whereas the traffic in slaves is irreconcilable with the principles of humanity and justice, and whereas both His Majesty and the U.S. are desirous of continuing their efforts to promote its entire abolition," the two countries would cooperate in said abolition of the slave trade.[87] By this treaty, one author has argued that the U.S. and Britain "agreed to work to eliminate the slave trade, indicating that they were aware of the crime against African humanity and the basic norms of human rights...."[88] Upon the emancipation of British slaves in the Caribbean in 1833, failure to prevent slavery was decreed to be "a high crime against God and the Christian Religion," and its abolition a measure to "wipe out the guilt of

79. Kenneth Ögren, *Humanitarian law in the Articles of War Decreed in 1621 by King Gustavus II Adolphus of Sweden,* 313 Int'l Rev. of the Red Cross 438–442 (1996), http://www.icrc.org/Web/Eng/siteeng0.nsf/iwpList154/BC396F38899D10BEC1256B66005A2479.

80. Will Coster, *Massacre and Codes of Conduct During the English Civil War, in* The Massacre in History 96 (Mark Levene and Penny Roberts eds., 1999); McCormack, *Selective Reaction to Atrocity,* at 692–93.

81. *See* Thomas W. Simon, The Laws of Genocide: Prescriptions for a Just World 16 (Westport, CT: Greenwood Publishing Group, 2007).

82. *See* Gary Jonathan Bass, Stay the Hand of Vengeance: The Politics of War Crimes Tribunals 37–57 (Princeton: Princeton UP, 2000); Jon Elster, Closing the Books: Transitional Justice in Historical Perspective 3–76 (Cambridge: Cambridge UP, 2004); Charles Warren, *Napoleon a Precedent; Court Trial for Arch-Criminals of War Held Unnecessary,* N.Y. Times, Nov. 7, 1943, at E10; *Napoleon and the Kaiser; Parallel Between the Cases of the Two Suggested by Trial in London Plan,* N.Y. Times, July 6, 1919, at E34.

83. McCormack, *Selective Reaction to Atrocity,* at 694.

84. McCormack, *Selective Reaction to Atrocity,* at 694 (citing Jordan J. Paust, *My Lai and Vietnam: Norms, Myths and Leader Responsibility,* 57 Military Law Review 99, 114 (1972)).

85. *Id.* at 695.

86. *Quoted in* W.E.B. [William Edward Burghardt] Du Bois, The Suppression of the African Slave Trade to the United States 135 (New York: Cosimo Inc., 2007) (1896).

87. Art. X, *Quoted in id.* at 247.

88. Ronald Walters, The Price of Racial Reconciliation 195 (Ann Arbor, MI: Univ. of Michigan Press, 2008).

Slavery from the laws of civilized nations."[89] In 1860, a resolution in the U.S. House of Representatives called the slave trade "a crime against human nature," which "the most highly civilized nations have made ... a criminal offence or piracy under their own municipal laws, [and which] ought at once ... to be declared a crime by the code of international law...."[90]

E. The Law of War Circa 1914

The protagonists to World War I had clear guidance that killing civilians was a criminal action. By 1908, the Hague Regulations had prohibited occupying powers from unnecessarily compromising public safety, individual lives, family "rights," or private property.[91] They also mandated that an occupying power "shall take all the measures in his power to restore, and ensure, as far as possible, public order and safety, while respecting, unless absolutely prevented, the laws in force in the country."[92] Thus, at Nuremberg the Nazi officials in the dock were indicted for murders and abuses against civilian populations, as a "violation of the Hague Regulations, 1907," the customary law of nations, and the penal laws of the affected nations.[93]

F. The League of Nations System

World War II occurred in a context of even more stringent regulations of the initiation and prosecution of international armed conflicts. Specifically, the Versailles Treaty that issued from the Paris Peace Conference included the Covenant of the League of Nations of 1919, which "amounted to an elimination of war, not only between members of the League, but also, by reason of certain provisions of the Covenant, in the relations of non-members as well."[94] The General Treaty for the Renouncement of War of 27 August 1928, or the Kellogg-Briand Pact, which Germany and Japan had signed, even more clearly outlawed aggressive war "for the solution of international controversies" or "as an instrument of national policy."[95] The League in 1933 condemned Japan's invasion of the

---

89. *The British West Indies, in* SUPPLEMENT NO. 1 TO THE EIGHTH REPORT FROM THE SELECT COMMITTEE ON SUGAR AND COFFEE PLANTING; PARLIAMENTARY PAPERS 44 (London: House of Commons of Great Britain, 1847–48).

90. *Quoted in* DU BOIS, THE SUPPRESSION OF THE AFRICAN SLAVE TRADE, at 281.

91. Convention (No. IV) Respecting the Laws and Customs of War on Land, and its annex: Regulations concerning the Laws and Customs of War on Land, annex art. 46, 19 October 1908, entered into force 26 January 1910, 36 Stat. 2277, TREATY SERIES 539, http://www.yale.edu/lawweb/avalon/lawofwar/hague04.htm; Convention (No. II) with Respect to the Laws and Customs of War on Land and its annex: Regulations concerning the Laws and Customs of War on Land. The Hague, entered into force 4 September 1900, [1901] UKTS No. 11.

92. *Id.*, art. 43.

93. International Military Tribunal, Indictment, Count 3, *in* 1 NUREMBERG TRIAL PROCEEDINGS (1946), http://avalon.law.yale.edu/imt/count3.asp.

94. Argument of the Chief Prosecutor of the United Kingdom, *in* 7 NUREMBERG TRIAL PROCEEDINGS (1946), http://www.yale.edu/lawweb/avalon/imt/proc/02-11-46.htm.

95. *See* International Military Tribunal, Nuremberg (IMT), Judgment: Violations of International Treaties (Sept. 30 and Oct. 1, 1946), http://avalon.law.yale.edu/subject_menus/judcont.asp; Argument of the Chief Prosecutor for the French Republic, *in* 5 NUREMBERG TRIAL PROCEEDINGS (1946),

Chinese territory of Manchuria and the establishment of a Japanese puppet state as violations of international law.[96]

The League also tried to restrain abuses like the enslavement of conquered civilian populations, a common practice from ancient times through the British, French, and Ottoman empires, and even in German-occupied Europe in World War I. Several Middle Eastern countries "abolished slavery when they entered the League of Nations in the 1920s."[97]

Finally, the League administered a system of refugee flight from zones of conflict and genocidal killing. The Covenant of the League of Nations provided for "commissions for the regulation of matters of international interest" to be instituted and directed by the League.[98] In 1926, Fridtjof Nansen founded the Office of the League's High Commissioner for Russian and Armenian refugees, which had its jurisdiction expanded in 1928 to Assyrians, Assyro-Chaldeans, and Turks.[99] The office also dealt with Greek and Bulgarian refugees.[100] The definition of a refugee during the League of Nations period focused on persons who no longer "enjoy[ed] the protection" of the government of the Soviet Union, the Turkish Republic, fascist Spain, or Nazi Germany.[101] The League of Nations granted "Nansen passports" to Russian refugees in 1922, Armenians in 1924, and Assyrians, Assyro-Chaldeans, Syrians, Kurds, and Turks in 1928.[102] The office administered a passport system for one million refugees from former Ottoman Empire, Soviet Union, and Nazi-occupied Europe. After World War II, the Nansen office evolved into the United Nations High Commissioner for Refugees.[103]

---

http://www.yale.edu/lawweb/avalon/imt/proc/01-17-46.htm; Argument of the Chief Prosecutor of the United Kingdom, *in* 7 NUREMBERG TRIAL PROCEEDINGS (1946), http://www.yale.edu/lawweb/avalon/imt/proc/02-11-46.htm.

96. *See* DOROTHY J. PERKINS, JAPAN GOES TO WAR: A CHRONOLOGY OF JAPANESE MILITARY EXPANSION FROM THE MEIJI ERA TO THE ATTACK ON PEARL HARBOR 111–15 (1997). For a discussion of the case of Ethiopia before the League, see *infra* Chapter IX.

97. *Trans-Saharan and Red Sea Slave Trade, in* AFRICANA: THE ENCYCLOPEDIA OF THE AFRICAN AND AFRICAN AMERICAN EXPERIENCE 1879 (Kwame Anthony Appiah and Henry Louis Gates eds., New York: Basic Civitas Books, 1999).

98. Covenant of the League of Nations, art. 24 (1919), *reprinted in* THE LEAGUE OF NATIONS, 179–89 (Ruth B. Henig ed., New York: Harper & Row, 1973).

99. *See* ARISTIDE R. ZOLBERG, ASTRI SUHRKE, & SERGIO AGUAYO, ESCAPE FROM VIOLENCE: CONFLICT AND THE REFUGEE CRISIS IN THE DEVELOPING WORLD 19 (Oxford: Oxford UP 1989); UNHCR, COLLECTION OF INTERNATIONAL INSTRUMENTS AND LEGAL TEXTS CONCERNING REFUGEES 36 (New York: United Nations, 2007); FRIDTJOF NANSEN, ARMENIA AND THE NEAR EAST (reprint ed., New York: Da Capo Press, 1976) (1928).

100. *See* ZOLBERG, SUHRKE, & AGUAYO, ESCAPE FROM VIOLENCE, at 19.

101. UNHCR, COLLECTION OF INTERNATIONAL INSTRUMENTS, at 36.

102. *See* SANDRA LAVENEX, SAFE THIRD COUNTRIES: EXTENDING THE EU ASYLUM AND IMMIGRATION POLICIES 5 (Budapest: Central European UP 1999).

103. *See* IRWIN ABRAMS, THE NOBEL PEACE PRIZE AND THE LAUREATES: AN ILLUSTRATED BIOGRAPHICAL HISTORY, 1901–2001, at 142 (Nantucket, MA: Science History Publications/USA, 2001).

Chapter II

From "Barbarism" to "Genocide": Outlawing Mass Murder

> Sovereignty ... cannot be conceived of as the right to kill millions of innocent people.
>
> —Raphael Lemkin, architect of the Genocide Convention[1]

A. The Crime of Genocide

Despite more stringent rules against aggressive war, the law concerning the conduct of war once initiated, or *jus in bello*, stood in need of reform in light of the difficulty prosecuting German officers guilty of atrocities in World War I. Despite the prosecutions of Napoleon, German and Ottoman officers, and other soldiers tried in military courts, the doctrine of sovereignty by military occupation had become ingrained in international law. Even a famous treatise on international law insisted that a sovereign state's "'territorial supremacy'" entitled it "to treat its own citizens at its discretion," and that no matter how bad this "treatment" got, it was of no concern to other nations.[2]

In the 1930s, a Polish lawyer named Raphael Lemkin grew increasingly concerned about mass killings and atrocities. Lemkin's interest in large-scale persecutions dated to his family's flight from pogroms and wars by and between Slavs and Germans, as well as his discovery as a teenager of the massacres of Christians in ancient Rome and of Ottoman Armenians during World War I: "At the age of fifteen, Lemkin first encountered the idea of intentional mass murder of a population when news of the Turkish slaughter of Armenians reached Poland in 1915...."[3] As he described his growing interest in and study of ethnic atrocities in his draft autobiography:

---

1. *Quoted in* Steven L. Jacobs, *Raphael Lemkin and the Armenian Genocide*, *in* LOOKING BACKWARD, MOVING FORWARD: CONFRONTING THE ARMENIAN GENOCIDE 127 (Richard G. Hovannisian, New Brunswick, NJ: Transaction Books, 2003) (quoting manuscript autobiography of Raphael Lemkin, who coined term "genocide").

2. SAMANTHA POWER, "A PROBLEM FROM HELL": AMERICA AND THE AGE OF GENOCIDE 58 (New York: Basic Books, 2001) (quoting 1 L. OPPENHEIM, INTERNATIONAL LAW 583 (7th ed., 1948)).

3. American Jewish Archives, *An Inventory to the Raphael Lemkin Papers* (2003), http://www.americanjewisharchives.org/aja/FindingAids/Lemkin.htm. *See also* RAPHAEL LEMKIN, RAPHAEL LEMKIN'S DOSSIER ON THE ARMENIAN GENOCIDE: TURKISH MASSACRES OF ARMENIANS (Michael J. Bazyler ed., Glendale, CA: Center for Armenian Remembrance, 2008); Adam LeBor, "COMPLICITY WITH EVIL": THE UNITED NATIONS IN THE AGE OF MODERN GENOCIDE 10 (New Haven, CT: Yale Univ. Press, 2006) ("Lemkin's arguments [in favor of outlawing barbarism and 1930s] were

> In 1915 the Germans occupied the city of W[arsaw] and the entire area. I used this time to read more history, to study and to watch whether national, religious, or racial groups are being destroyed. The truth came out only after the war. In Turkey, more than 1,200,000 Armenians were put to death for no other reason than they were Christians....
>
> After [the British released all Turkish war criminals from Malta]. I was shocked. A nation was killed and the guilty persons were set free. Why is a man punished when he kills another man? Why is the killing of a million a lesser crime than the killing of a single individual?....
>
> Soon contemporary examples of genocide followed, such as the slaughter of Armenians in 1915. It became clear to me that the diversity of nations, religious groups and races is essential to civilization because every one of those groups has a mission to fulfill and a contribution to make in terms of culture....[4]

Lemkin's commitment to end genocide could only have been heightened by the fact that his own brother starved to death during the family's flight to the forest during a war or anti-Jewish pogrom.[5] As a young adult, Lemkin learned, from his vantage point as a public prosecutor in Poland, of the rise of Nazism in Germany and massacres of Assyrian Christians by newly independent Iraq.[6] Lemkin had already begun "to formulate his opinions on genocide, spurred on, he noted, by the massacre of Christians in Iraq in 1933 and the rise of [Hitler]."[7]

Lemkin petitioned the Legal Council of the League of Nations in 1933 to outlaw mass killings and cultural devastation as acts of "barbarism" or "vandalism."[8] Lemkin echoed the widespread designation of the Ottoman Christian massacres as a "crime against humanity" by calling the crime of barbarism "Acts Constituting a General (Transnational) Danger Considered as Offences Against the Law of Nations."[9] He defined the crime of barbarism as acts of extermination against an ethnic, religious, or social group, including "massacres, pogroms, [and] actions undertaken to ruin the economic existence of the members of a collectivity."[10] He defined the crime of vandalism as an attack on a group in the form of the systematic destruction of their cultural heritage, whether in the form of art, literature, or scholarship.[11]

The proposed crimes of barbarism and vandalism met with silence, and his native Poland suffered the brutality of Nazi occupation and genocide, as did the Soviet Union

---

based on his studies of the massacres of the Armenians and Assyrians in the Ottoman Empire during the First World War.").

4. Raphael Lemkin, Totally Unofficial Man (1958), *quoted in* Dennis R. Papazian, *Modern Genocide: The Curse of the Nation State and Ideological Political Parties: The Armenian Case*, 7 Idea: A Journal of Social Issues (2002), http://www.ideajournal.com/articles.php?sup=12.

5. *See* Tanya Elder, *What You See Before Your Eyes: Documenting Raphael Lemkin's Life By Exploring His Archival Papers, 1900–1959*, 7, J. of Genocide Research 469, 473 (2005), http://74.125.113.132/search?q=cache:cRvWyPWy9V8J:www.inogs.com/JGRFullText/Elder.pdf.

6. *See* American Jewish Archives, *The Raphael Lemkin Papers*.

7. Elder, *What You See Before Your Eyes*, at 475.

8. *Raphael Lemkin*, Europaworld (June 22, 2001), http://www.europaworld.org/issue40/raphaellemkin22601.htm.

9. Elder, *What You See Before Your Eyes*, at 475.

10. *Quoted in Raphael Lemkin: The Original Anti-Genocide Activist (Part I)* (Oct. 04, 2008), http://genocide.change.org/blog/view/raphael_lemkin_the_original_anti-genocide_activist_part_i.

11. *See* Elder, *What You See Before Your Eyes*, at 475; American Jewish Archives, *The Raphael Lemkin Papers*.

and most of Europe.[12] With the German invasion of Poland in 1939, Lemkin, who was of Jewish descent, became a resistance fighter, and his family suffered "at first hand the very acts that he was working to prevent."[13] Lemkin himself risked death under Nazi occupation: "Wounded in the Polish resistance, Lemkin was carried through German lines to Lithuania and then fled to Stockholm."[14] While in Stockholm, he negotiated for or "purloined" Nazi legal directives from Swedish authorities.[15] By 1941, he had fled German occupation via the Soviet Union to the U.S.[16] An estimated 49 members of his family died in concentration camps, death marches, and the Warsaw Ghetto.[17] Only his brother, sister-in-law, and two nephews lived.[18]

The crime of genocide as it existed prior to, during, and after the entry into force of the Genocide Convention was never limited to instances where an entire group was exterminated. In 1943, Professor Lemkin invented the term "genocide" from the Greek words *gens* (race or tribe) and Latin *cide* (killing).[19] Professor Lemkin made clear from the outset that the crime of genocide is not restricted to instances in which groups are totally destroyed, or even to instances in which one group intended to exterminate another group in its entirety, but failed to achieve its objective for whatever reason. He wrote: "Generally speaking, genocide does not necessarily mean the immediate destruction of a nation...."[20] He counted as instances of genocide several wars "in which nations and *groups of the population* were completely or *almost completely* destroyed," clearly indicating that partial genocides were included in his definition of the term.[21] Among other instances of genocide, he accused Germany of committing the crime against "the Poles, the Slovenes and the Jews," as well as against Russians, Serbs, and Czechs as peoples, and by economic means in France, Luxembourg, and other occupied territories.[22]

Professor Lemkin believed and wrote that the history of genocide, as a campaign of massacres intended by members of a dominant national, ethnic, or religious group to destroy all or part of a subordinate or weaker group, went back to ancient times. Lemkin's writings offered many examples of ancient and medieval genocides. His examples included large-scale massacres that claimed many, but by no means all, of the affected group's members. His work *Axis Rule in Occupied Europe* highlights the massacres of the following groups:

- many residents of Carthage by the Roman Empire in 146 BCE,

---

12. *See* Elder, *What You See Before Your Eyes*, at 470–75; Samantha Power, *"New Conceptions Require New Terms, in* RAPHAEL LEMKIN, AXIS RULE IN OCCUPIED EUROPE: LAWS OF OCCUPATION, ANALYSIS OF GOVERNMENT, PROPOSALS FOR REDRESS iii (Clark, NJ: The Lawbook Exchange, 2005).

13. *Raphael Lemkin*, EUROPAWORLD.

14. LEONARD ROGOFF, HOMELANDS: SOUTHERN JEWISH IDENTITY IN DURHAM AND CHAPEL HILL, NORTH CAROLINA 167 (Tuscaloosa, Alabama and London: Univ. of Alabama Press, 2001).

15. *Id.* ("purloined"). *See also* Elder, *What You See Before Your Eyes*, at 476 ("During his stay in Sweden he *persuaded* government officials to provide him with Nazi law directives, and he accumulated a thick set of documents, which would later form the basis of [his book] *Axis Rule in Occupied Europe* as well as 'Recording on military government in Europe.'") (emphasis added).

16. *See* Elder, *What You See Before Your Eyes*, at 476. *Raphael Lemkin*, EUROPAWORLD.

17. *See* U.S. Holocaust Memorial Museum, Committee on Conscience, *History: Raphael Lemkin* (2007), http://www.ushmm.org/conscience/history/lemkin.

18. *See id.*; Raphael Lemkin, *Europaworld* (June 22, 2001), http://www.europaworld.org/issue40/raphaellemkin22601.htm; POWER, "A PROBLEM FROM HELL," at 49; U.S. Holocaust Memorial Museum, Committee on Conscience, *History: Raphael Lemkin.*

19. *See* POWER, "A PROBLEM FROM HELL," at 45–65.

20. LEMKIN, AXIS RULE, at 79–81, http://www.preventgenocide.org/lemkin/AxisRule1944-1.htm.

21. *Id.* (emphasis added).

22. *See id.*, ch. 10, http://www.preventgenocide.org/lemkin/AxisRule1944-2.htm.

- many residents of Jerusalem by the Roman Empire in 72 CE,
- various groups in "the religion wars of Islam and the Crusades,"
- the victims of the Mongol invasions of Genghis Khan and Tamerlane,
- the heretical medieval Christian sects of the Albigenses and the Waldenses, and
- the Protestant residents of Magdeburg by the Holy Roman Empire in 1631.[23]

In all of these instances, there were survivors from the destroyed cities and sects. Many survivors of the Roman siege of Carthage were enslaved rather than killed.[24] The Romans destroyed much but not all of Jerusalem, and the city was rebuilt and "flourished."[25] The Mongols' massacre of inhabitants of Beijing in 1215 CE left some survivors, and the survivors of the assault on Bukhara were not generally massacred despite systematic devastation.[26] The medieval Jews, Greeks, Armenians, Assyrians, Copts, Maronites, Turks, Kurds, Arabs, and Europeans survived in substantial numbers despite repeated religious wars between and among Muslim and Christian nations and minority communities. The Albigensian Crusade left many survivors in cities that capitulated after formerly harboring "heretics."[27] After the siege of Magdeburg in 1631, during the Thirty Years War, there were about 5,000 survivors.[28]

Later in life, Professor Lemkin planned to write and publish a book entitled *The History of Genocide*, and before he died he conducted extensive research into several major colonial and imperial genocides. As historical episodes of genocide, he identified the conquests of: the indigenous peoples of both North and South America; the Herero and other African peoples under European colonialism; the Catholics and Irish of the British Empire; the Armenians, Assyrians, Bulgarians, and Greeks of the Ottoman Empire; the Jews, Slavs, and Roma under Nazi occupation in World War II; and the dissidents and minorities of the Soviet Union.[29]

Professor Lemkin justified his expansive definition and retrospective application of the crime of genocide as a matter of theoretical and conceptual clarity in describing certain historical processes involving group-based violence. He wrote that genocide is a struggle of "biological forces" between imperial and "captive nations," carried out in particular by policies likely "to destroy or cripple the subjugated peoples in their development," so that the imperial or other dominant group would enjoy "numerical, physical and economic superiority."[30] He continued:

---

23. *Id.*, ch. 9, http://www.preventgenocide.org/lemkin/AxisRule1944-1.htm.
24. Norman Davies, Europe: A History 155 (Oxford: Oxford UP, 1998).
25. Eric H. Cline, Jerusalem Besieged: From Ancient Canaan to Modern Israel 137–38 (Ann Arbor, MI: Univ. of Michigan Press, 2004).
26. Chalk & Jonassohn, The History and Sociology of Genocide, at 101, 103.
27. *Id.* at 114–38.
28. Chris Turner & John Childs, A Dictionary of Military History and the Art of War 476 (Andre Corvisier ed., Oxford: Wiley-Blackwell, 1994).
29. *See* Dominik J. Schaller & Jurgen Zimmerer, *Raphael Lemkin: The "Founder of the United Nation's Genocide Convention" as a Historian of Mass Violence*, 7 J. of Genocide Research 447, 447–52 (2005); Michael A. McDonnell & A. Dirk Moses, *Raphael Lemkin as Historian of Genocide in the Americas*, 7 J. of Genocide Research 501, 501–29 (2005); Dominik J. Schaller, *Raphael Lemkin's View of European Colonial Rule in Africa: Between Condemnation and Admiration*, 7 J. of Genocide Research 531, 531–58 (2005); Dan Stone, *Raphael Lemkin on the Holocaust*, 7 J. of Genocide Research 539, 540 (2005); Anton Weiss-Wendt, *Hostage of Politics: Raphael Lemkin on "Soviet Genocide,"* 7 J. of Genocide Research 551, 551–59 (2005); American Jewish Archives, *The Raphael Lemkin Papers.*
30. *See* Lemkin, Axis Rule in Occupied Europe, 81.

> Generally speaking, genocide does not necessarily mean the immediate destruction of a nation, except when accomplished by mass killings of all members of a nation. It is intended rather to signify a coordinated plan of different actions aiming at the destruction of essential foundations of the life of national groups, with the aim of annihilating the groups themselves. The objectives of such a plan would be ... the destruction of the personal security, liberty, health, dignity, and even the lives of the individuals belonging to such groups....[31]

Lemkin viewed genocide as filling a gap in the laws of war, so that some but not all of the acts comprising a campaign of genocide were war crimes.[32] Thus, it is wrong to draw a stark dichotomy between wars and genocides, because killing civilians frequently occurs during wars and is itself a war crime, prohibited in Lemkin's day by the Hague Regulations.[33] War spills over into genocide when military, paramilitary, or bureaucratic forces kill a people systematically, outside of the context of legitimate military action: "Genocide in a generic sense is the mass killing of substantial numbers of human brings, when not in the course of military action against the military forces of an avowed enemy, under conditions of the essential defencelessness and helplessness of the victims."[34] To define genocide so as to exclude wars would be misleading and perverse in that the Holocaust would then be denied as a genocide because the Nazis gained control over Czech, French, Dutch, Belgian, Polish and Soviet Jews, Slavs, and Roma people precisely through war and the conquest of enemy states.[35]

Professor Lemkin did not define genocide to require the total destruction of a group, among other reasons because it may take place by means other than mass killings. An article he published after the end of World War II discussed with approval the indictment by the prosecutors for whom he worked at Nuremberg of Nazi war criminals for "crimes against humanity" including "genocide, viz., the extermination of ... particular races and classes of people and national, racial, or religious groups, particularly Jews, Poles, and Gypsies and others."[36] Even though most of the world's Jews, Poles, and Gypsies were not killed during the Holocaust,[37] genocide had been committed against them by the Nazis and was so charged in an indictment. Professor Lemkin believed that genocide may be achieved by *physically* exterminating a group such as the Jews, *culturally* by devastating their religious and spiritual heritage,[38] *politically* by destroying a group's "institutions of self-government," or *economically* by stealing the wealth of a group or depriving its members of gainful employment.[39]

---

31. *Id.* at 79.

32. *See* Lemkin, Axis Rule, at 93, *quoted in* Martin Shaw, What Is Genocide? A New Social Theory 24 (New York: Polity, 2007).

33. *See id.*

34. Israel W. Charny, *Towards a Generic Definition of Genocide, in* Genocide: Conceptual and Historical Dimensions 64–70 (George J. Andreopoulos ed., Philadelphia: Univ. of Pennsylvania Press, 1994). Barbara Harff's definition is in accord, in that it says genocide is "mass murder carried out by or with the complicity of political authorities and directed at distinct communally defined groups." Shaw, What Is Genocide?, at 46 (quoting Barbara Harff & Ted R. Gurr, Ethnic Conflict in World Politics 222 (Boulder, CO: Westview Press, 1994)).

35. *See* Shaw, What Is Genocide?, at 31–32.

36. Power, "A Problem from Hell," at 50.

37. Benjamin A. Valentino, Final Solutions: Mass Killing and Genocide in the 20th Century 177 (Ithaca, NY: Cornell UP, 2004).

38. *See* Elder, *What You See Before Your Eyes*, at 469–76.

39. Lemkin, Axis Rule in Occupied Europe, at xi.

B. Cultural Genocide

According to Lemkin, genocide occurs on a cultural or religious plane when a perpetrator group systematically attacks a victim group's "cultural institutions," as by "interfering with the activities of the Church."[40] Lemkin described the crime of genocide as a crime against "the soul of a nation," so that it had to extend beyond physical killings to include "the destruction of the cultural pattern of a group, such as the language, the traditions, the monuments, archives, libraries, churches."[41] As a prominent commentator on Lemkin's work writes:

> It may seem strange at first to see listed side by side [in Lemkin's work] the mass murder of population groups and the promotion of pornography and alcohol consumption. For some scholars, it is already unacceptable to mention the mass murder of the Jews in the same breath as that of other groups. Yet, Lemkin employed a logic that is clear in his explanation of what constitutes genocide. Genocide, according to Lemkin, does not simply mean mass murder—this remains a common misconception today; the UN Genocide Convention is quite clear on this point—but can be brought about by various means....
>
> [Lemkin] did not single out the genocide of the Jews as falling into a separate category (as some historians today distinguish "Holocaust" from "genocide").[42]

In order to dispel any confusion as to the scope of the crime of genocide, Lemkin maintained in 1945, so that "the machine gun" was the "last resort," not the only method, of the genocidist.[43]

Cultural genocide is a concept to which the definition of the crime of genocide clearly applies. Although cultural genocide not accompanied by *any* physical measures against group members is not a separate crime under the Genocide Convention, Lemkin working as a consultant to the U.N. Secretary General on the drafting of the Genocide Convention urged that it include "systematically destroying historical or religious monuments."[44] Lemkin described the coercive replacement of the culture of one group by that of another as the essence of genocide.[45] The U.N. General Assembly voted against making cultural genocide a separate crime because its members believed that "culture was already covered to a large extent by the word 'religious'" in the Genocide Convention.[46] The Genocide

---

40. *Id.* at xi–xii.

41. Lemkin, Totally Unofficial Man (Dan Eshet ed., 2007) (1958), *quoted in* Stone, *Raphael Lemkin on the Holocaust,* at 549 n.9.

42. Stone, *Raphael Lemkin on the Holocaust,* at 540, 546. *See also id.* at 546 (noting that Lemkin's "comments on the Holocaust make sense only in the light of Lemkin's detailed studies of other genocides, from examples in antiquity to the annihilation of the indigenous Tasmanians to Armenia. Indeed, these earlier genocides provided Lemkin with a conceptual framework for understanding German actions: that of colonialism."); *id.* at 548 ("The extent of the persecution of Romanies, Poles, Yugoslavs, Russians, Serbs and other nationalities by the Germans is horrifying and has rightly become a significant part of the historiography of the Second World War. Where Lemkin challenges contemporary orthodoxy is in his implication that the notion of a 'Holocaust' as a specifically Jewish tragedy makes no sense, because the genocide of the Jews was just one aspect of a broad Nazi demographic plan based on extreme racial fantasies").

43. *Id.* at 540.

44. Quigley, The Genocide Convention, at 9; LeBlanc, The United States and the Genocide Convention, 25.

45. *See* Stone, *Raphael Lemkin on the Holocaust,* at 549 n.9.

46. International Law Commission, *Offences Against the Peace and Security of Mankind,* at 69.

Convention states that the infliction of serious mental harm on a group in order to destroy its distinctiveness constitutes genocide.[47] A proposal by the U.N. Secretariat to limit mental harm to "mutilations and biological experiments" was rejected.[48] A renewed attempt to require "physical" injury was similarly rejected.[49] Another U.N. Secretariat draft limiting genocide to prevention of births within a group by sterilization or abortion also failed to obtain the support of the parties to the treaty, in favor of language covering *any* means of "preventing births within the group."[50]

The drafting history of the Genocide Convention supports the conclusion that genocide cannot be reduced to a "biological" or "racial" as opposed to a "cultural" event. The Soviet Union proposed, for obvious reasons, to link genocide to "racial hatred" rather than extermination of religious, political, or cultural groups. The United States mobilized a majority of states to oppose this amendment and to enact a broader definition of genocide that included, among other things, religious groups and mental harm. The representative of Lebanon described the Soviet amendment as a dangerous invitation to commit genocide for non-racial reasons. The representative of Pakistan emphasized that cultural and "biological" genocide are inseparable, "complementary," and "had the same motive."[51] The Soviet Union proposed another amendment limiting the "intent to destroy" a group to acts "aimed at the physical destruction" of the group, which was again rejected.[52] As a result, the words "biological" and "physical" do not appear in the text of the Genocide Convention defining genocidal intent, even though they appear several times, for example, in the opinion of the International Criminal Court declining to indict the President of Sudan for genocide.[53] Moreover, Sweden successfully lobbied to extend the protection of the Genocide Convention of "ethnical" groups, which manifests a design to reach beyond racial extermination to cultural or linguistic destruction.[54]

International criminal tribunals have regarded the destruction of sacred or cultural monuments as significant evidence of a genocidal intent to kill a group, or to cleanse an

---

47. *See* QUIGLEY, THE GENOCIDE CONVENTION, at 6–9; Stephen Gorove, *The Problem of "Mental Harm" in the Genocide Convention,* 1951 WASHINGTON UNIV. LAW Q. 174–80.

48. *Compare, e.g.,* U.N. Doc. E/447, art. II(1), U.N. Secretariat, First Draft of the Genocide Convention, May 1947, *with* Genocide Convention, art. II(b). *See also* REPUBLIC OF BOSNIA AND HERZEGOVINA, MEMORANDUM OF LAW ON JURISDICTION UNDER THE GENOCIDE CONVENTION at 21.

49. *Compare, e.g.,* U.N. Doc. E/AC.25/SR.1 to 28, Ad Hoc Committee of the Economic and Social Council (ECOSOC), April 5–May 10, 1948, *with* Genocide Convention, art. II(b). *See also* REPUBLIC OF BOSNIA AND HERZEGOVINA, MEMORANDUM OF LAW ON JURISDICTION UNDER THE GENOCIDE CONVENTION, at 21.

50. *Compare, e.g.,* U.N. Doc. E/447, art. II(2), U.N. Secretariat, First Draft of the Genocide Convention, May 1947, *with* Genocide Convention, art. II(d). *See also* REPUBLIC OF BOSNIA AND HERZEGOVINA, MEMORANDUM OF LAW ON JURISDICTION UNDER THE GENOCIDE CONVENTION, at 24.

51. *See* 3 OFFICIAL RECORDS OF THE GENERAL ASSEMBLY, ch. 6, at 13, 820–22; REPUBLIC OF BOSNIA AND HERZEGOVINA, MEMORANDUM OF LAW ON JURISDICTION UNDER THE GENOCIDE CONVENTION, at 9, 13–4.

52. *See* Prosecutor v. Omar Hassan Ahmad Al Bashir, No. ICC-02/05-01/09. 1/95, Pre-Trial Chamber I, Decision on the Prosecution's Application for a Warrant of Arrest against Omar Hassan Ahmad Al Bashir, Case (Mar. 4, 2009), ¶¶ 57, 58, 60, 110, http://www.icc-cpi.int.

53. *See* Genocide Convention, art. II. The word "physical" does appear in Article II(c), defining what kinds of destruction of groups by poor living conditions are covered, but does not appear in the other prongs of Article II.

54. *See* 3 OFFICIAL RECORDS OF THE GENERAL ASSEMBLY 98, 115; U.N. Doc. No. A/C.6/230/Corr.1 (1948); REPUBLIC OF BOSNIA AND HERZEGOVINA, MEMORANDUM OF LAW ON JURISDICTION UNDER THE GENOCIDE CONVENTION at 18–19.

area of its inhabitants.[55] The U.N. Human Rights Council's minority rights bodies define cultural genocide as "[a]ny action which has the aim or effect of depriving [indigenous peoples] of their integrity as distinct peoples, or of their cultural values or ethnic identities," or "[a]ny form of assimilation or integration by other cultures or ways of life imposed on them by legislative, administrative, or other measures."[56] Based on these authorities and the writings of many scholars of genocide whose findings are described in the following pages, foremost among them Professor Lemkin himself, cultural destruction is a genocidal event.

C. Genocide and "The Nuremberg Principles"

After World War II, the Nuremberg tribunal defined as criminal violations of existing international humanitarian law, human rights law, and laws governing armed conflict. In the "Moscow Declaration" of November 1, 1943, U.S. President Franklin Delano Roosevelt, British Prime Minister Winston Churchill, and Soviet dictator (Marshal) Josef Stalin warned that:

> [T]hose German officers and men and members of the Nazi party who have been responsible for, or have taken a consenting part in [Nazi] atrocities, massacres and executions, will be sent back to the countries in which their abominable deeds were done in order that they may be judged and punished according to the laws of these liberated countries and of the free governments which will be created therein....[57]

The Genocide Convention provides a valuable conceptual and legal tool for analyzing events that occurred prior to its drafting, including the Holocaust, because it incorporates preexisting rules of customary international law. International customary law therefore recognized genocide as a crime prior to its incorporation into the Genocide Convention of 1948. The signatories to the Genocide Convention itself recognized that genocide was already a crime by adopting language providing that they "confirm[ed]" its criminality, whether committed during war or in peacetime.[58] Genocide is, as a United Nations report described it, a recent term for "an old crime."[59]

---

55. Prosecutor v. Krstić, Case No. IT-98-33-T, Trial Chamber, Judgement (Aug. 2, 2001), at ¶580, http://www.un.org/icty/krstic/TrialC1/judgement/index.htm; Prosecutor v. Karadžić & Mladić, Review of Indictments Pursuant to Rule 61, Case Nos. IT-95-5-R61 & IT-95-18-R61 (July 11, 1996), at ¶94.

56. U.N. Human Rights Council, Resolution 2006/2, Rights of Indigenous Peoples (June 29, 2006), at ¶¶7(a), 7(d), http://www.gcc.ca/pdf/INT000000021.pdf.

57. Alan A. Ryan, *Nuremberg's Contributions to International Law*, 30 Boston College International & Comparative Law Review 55, 59 (2007) (quoting The Moscow Declaration (Nov. 1, 1943), *in* The American Road to Nuremberg: The Documentary Record 1944–1945, at 13–14 (Bradley F. Smith ed., Stanford, CA: Hoover Institution Press, 1982) [hereinafter Road to Nuremberg]).

58. Yoram Dinstein, War, Aggression and Self-Defence 108 (Cambridge: Cambridge UP, 3d ed. 2001).

59. U.N. Economic and Social Council [ECOSOC], Commission on Human Rights, Sub-Commission on Prevention of Discrimination and Protection of Minorities, Thirty-eighth session, Item 4 of the provisional agenda, revised and updated report on the question of the prevention and punishment of the crime of genocide, prepared by Special Rapporteur Ben Whitaker. U.N. Doc. No. E/CN.4/Sub.2/1985/6 (July 2, 1985), ¶24, http://www.preventgenocide.org/prevent/UNdocs/whitaker/ [hereinafter ECOSOC, Report on Genocide].

For this reason, the defendants at Nuremberg could be indicted for "genocide" as a crime against humanity in 1946, before the entry into force of the Genocide Convention.[60] The British prosecutor, who was also the attorney general of Great Britain, accused the defendants of committing "genocide" seven times during his closing argument alone.[61] This raised the question how the Nazis could be prosecuted for genocide or crimes against humanity before these crimes had been codified in international treaties providing for individual criminal responsibility. The answer of the International Court of Justice is that the "principles underlying the [Genocide] Convention are recognised by civilised nations as binding on States even without any conventional [i.e., treaty] obligation."[62] Thus, before the Nuremberg tribunals or founding of the U.N., "the pre-existing rules of international law" had established "customs by which the world has sought to mitigate the brutality of war and to protect ... passive noncombatants."[63] In addition to treaties such as the Genocide Convention, international law regards as binding such general practices and principles of law adopted by civilized nations, as illustrated by national and international judicial decisions and the teachings of international law experts.[64]

The Nuremberg judgments set down precedents on a number of important legal questions relevant to individual and collective responsibility for mass violence. Among their most important findings was their rejection of three principal defenses to genocide or other crimes against humanity: "just following orders"; *nullum crimen sine lege, nulla poena sine lege* or "no crime without a law, no penalties without a law"; and *tu quoque* or "you [did it] too."

The first defense failed because, absent duress depriving an individual of any "moral choice," superior orders are not a defense to any war crimes: "That a soldier was ordered to kill or torture in violation of the international law of war has never been recognised as a defense to such acts of brutality...." The Nuremberg tribunal dismissed reliance on one's "official position" within a state because "international duties ... transcend the national obligation[] of obedience." The second defense was rejected because, among other reasons, murder and ill-treatment of civilians was prohibited by the Hague Regulations of 1907, so that no genocide prosecution may be dismissed on retroactivity grounds after that date.[65]

The third defense was also rejected of necessity, for Allied complicity in genocides of Native Americans, Africans, residents of British India, or Soviet Koreans or Ukrainians

---

60. 1 Trial of the Major War Criminals before the International Military Tribunal for the Trial of German Major War Criminals, Nuremberg, 14 November 1945–10 October 1946, at 43–44 (1947), *quoted in* Elizabeth Borgwardt, *Re-examining Nuremberg as a New Deal Institution: Politics, Culture and the Limits of Law in Generating Human Rights Norms*, 23 Berkeley J. Int'l L. 42, 401 (2005).

61. *See* Waldemer Kaempffert, *Genocide Is the New Name for the Crime Fastened on the Nazi Leaders*, N.Y. Times, Oct. 20, 1946, at E13.

62. Reservations to the Convention on the Prevention and Punishment of the Crime of Genocide, 1951 I.C.J. 15, 21–22 (Advisory Op. of May 28, 1951).

63. 19 Trial of the Major War Criminals Before the International Military Tribunal, Nuremberg, 14 November 1945–1 October 1946: Official documents, at 465–66 (Nuremberg: Secretariat of the International Military Tribunal, 1948), http://www.loc.gov/rr/frd/Military_Law/pdf/NT_Vol-XIX.pdf.

64. Statute of the International Court of Justice, Art. 36 (2)(a–d), Art. 38 (1)(a–d), http://www.icj-cij.org/icjwww/ibasicdocuments/ibasictext/ibasicstatute.htm.

65. *See* IMT, Judgment (Sept. 30 and Oct. 1, 1946), *reprinted in* Mary Ellen O'Connell, International Law and the Use of Force: Cases and Materials 152, 155 (New York: Thomson Reuters/Foundation Press, 2009).

was no barrier to the indictment and conviction of the Nazis for extermination of Jews, Slavs, Roma people, and others. Its rhetorical force, however, may have prompted the prosecutors and the tribunal to deemphasize certain Nazi crimes that were similar to Allied practices, such as aerial bombardment of densely populated areas, and submarine warfare against civilian shipping.[66] For this reason, despite the bombardment of Shanghai and other cities by the Empire of Japan during the latter's war of aggression against China, the International Military Tribunal for the Far East focused its war crimes rulings on the treatment of prisoners of war, not civilian victims.[67]

In 1950, the U.N. General Assembly adopted the "Principles of the Nuremberg Charter and Judgment." The principles restated the definitions of crimes against the peace, war crimes, and crimes against humanity, and clarified that status as a head of state, government official, or soldier or bureaucrat following superior orders was no defense to these crimes.[68] They overlapped with the Genocide Convention to the extent that murder and deportation of civilians or occupied peoples were defined as war crimes, and murder, extermination, persecution, and other inhumane acts against civilians in connection with a war crime as crimes against humanity.

The liability of Nazi officials before an international criminal tribunal for the offense of genocide as a crime against humanity disposes of a key legal argument of defenders of genocidal policies in the Iraq or Sudan. This argument is that the failure of these states to join the International Criminal Court (ICC), or a similar consent-based tribunal, deprives the United Nations and foreign states from inquiring into, condemning, or ordering reparations for such genocidal policies. The government of Sudan argues that while genocide may be a crime, it is not a party to the Statute of the ICC and the international community therefore has no standing.[69] Similarly, Saddam Hussein's lawyer argued that neither the U.S. nor the ICC had jurisdiction over his client's crimes because they occurred before the ICC came into existence in 2002.[70] But these arguments about jurisdiction miss the point. The Nazis could be indicted for genocide, and convicted of extermination as a crime against humanity, prior to the coming into force of the Genocide Convention. This is because, as stated above, there were laws criminalizing murder and genocide prior to World War I, as of 1907 or even earlier. Therefore, if the governments of Iraq or Sudan were complicit in genocide, they deserved trial.

Nevertheless, the Nuremberg judgments were incomplete condemnations of genocide in several respects, including failing to come to grips with genocidal policies internal to greater Germany prior to the outbreak of world war. The tribunal did make progress by authoritatively declaring the charged persecutions of Jews and Slavs, "committed after the beginning of the war," to be undertaken "in connection with the aggressive war, and therefore ... crimes against humanity."[71] But it did not convict any defendants for crimes targeting the women of specific religious or ethnic groups for mass rape, sexual slavery,

---

66. *See* Robert Cryer, Hakan Friman, Darryl Robinson, & Elizabeth Wilmshurst, An Introduction to International Criminal Law and Procedure 95–96 (Cambridge: Cambridge UP, 2007).

67. *See* International Military Tribunal for the Far East, Judgment of 1 November 1948, http://www.ibiblio.net/hyperwar/PTO/IMTFE/IMTFE-5.htm.

68. G.A. Res. 488V (Dec. 12, 1950).

69. *See* Associated Press, *International Criminal Court, UN Tested by Darfur Crimes,* USA Today, Dec. 1, 2007, http://www.usatoday.com/news/world/2007-12-01-un-darfur-court_N.htm.

70. *See Saddam's Unlikely Ally,* MSNBC.com, Apr. 15, 2005, http://www.msnbc.msn.com/id/7514808.

71. *See* IMT, Judgment (Sept. 30 and Oct. 1, 1946), http://avalon.law.yale.edu/imt/judviol.asp ("The persecution of Jews [prior to 1939] is established beyond all doubt.... The Tribunal is of the opinion that revolting and horrible as many of these crimes were, it has not been satisfactorily proved

sterilization, or other gender-specific crimes; or analyze the bombardment of densely populated cities as potentially criminal.[72]

These failures have significant implications for later genocides in the Middle East and North Africa, which typically arose out of "internal" wars, often targeted women and girls for violence designed to destroy the reproductive capacity and familial ties of the group, and were carried out in part by extensive aerial bombardment of undefended villages that killed hundreds or thousands of civilians and destroyed many homes and communities. More recent war crimes tribunals have remedied some of the shortcomings on the "Nuremberg principles," however.

D. The United Nations and the International Court of Justice

The U.S. and the Soviet Union rejected the principle of a universal obligation to punish persons under their power who had committed genocide, regardless of the place of its commission or the nationality of the perpetrator. Instead, they and the other signatories left the prosecution of genocide in the hands of national courts and those international tribunals to whose jurisdiction the signatories to the Convention had consented.[73]

This means that aside from the Genocide Convention, the most important source of international law respecting genocidal campaigns is the Charter of the United Nations. The Charter has produced two principal types of international tribunals hearing genocide cases: the International Court of Justice (ICJ) and ad hoc international criminal tribunals established by the U.N. Security Council, to be discussed later. The ICJ is the "principal judicial organ" of the U.N. according to Article 92 of the Charter, which attaches the statute of the ICJ to govern the court's functioning.[74] The ICJ may be the ideal candidate to define genocide and compensate its victims, given its inclusive composition and status as the judicial branch of the U.N. system.[75] All members of the U.N. are automatically parties to the ICJ statute, and all of them have agreed to abide by decisions of the ICJ in any cases in which they are parties.[76] One might imagine that, with its diverse panel of judges experienced in international law, the ICJ would be well-equipped and eager to adjudicate violations of the Genocide Convention, whether brought by aggrieved states or leaders of ethnic or religious groups (with the support of agencies of the United Nations) as requests for advisory opinions.[77]

---

that they were done in execution of, or in connection with, any such crime [within the jurisdiction of the Tribunal].").

72. *See* McCormack, *Selective Reaction to Atrocity*, at 718–20.

73. *See* Payam Akhavan, *Enforcement of the Genocide Convention: A Challenge to Civilization*, 8 Harvard Human Rights J. 229 (1995).

74. Charter of the U.N., art. 92 (1946). *See also* Statute of the ICJ, art. 1.

75. *See* ICJ, A Guide to the History, Composition, Jurisdiction, Procedure and Decisions of the Court 17, 24 (1986), http://www.icj-cij.org/icjwww/igeneralinformation/ibleubook.pdf [hereinafter Blue Book] (describing practice of ensuring "distribution of membership of the ICJ among the principal regions of the globe," which has often allocated the 15 judgeships as follows: "Africa 3, Latin America 2, Asia 3, Western Europe and other States 5, [and] Eastern Europe 2....").

76. *See* Charter of the U.N., art. 93.

77. *See* ICJ, Blue Book, at 17, 24 ("From 1946 to 1988 the Court dealt with 58 contentious cases between States and delivered 20 Advisory Opinions."). Many U.N. agencies with the factfinding capability necessary to investigate alleged atrocities during armed conflicts, and to make credible alle-

Despite lacking a criminal chamber or jurisdiction to imprison or execute persons guilty of genocide, the ICJ has already adjudicated several disputes regarding whether states, rather than individual perpetrators, have committed genocide.[78] In resolving disputes between states over the legality of genocidal campaigns, war crimes, or other violations of international law, the ICJ applies treaties, "international custom, as evidence of a general practice accepted as law," and "general principles of law recognized by civilized nations[.]"[79] As "subsidiary means" for identifying and clarifying international law, it looks to "judicial decisions and the teaching of the most highly qualified publicists [i.e. legal scholars]."[80] The U.N. Charter also permits the U.N. General Assembly to seek advisory opinions that may guide the U.N. or its member states on questions of international law.[81]

Unfortunately, the ICJ has not been very effective in identifying or sanctioning genocide. Part of the blame rests with U.N. members themselves, rather than the ICJ, in that many states implicated in genocide have not accepted the compulsory jurisdiction of the ICJ in all matters.[82] The U.S. and Soviet Union were adamant, given their entanglement in many conflicts around the world, not to make the jurisdiction of the ICJ automatically compulsory, as most independent Latin American, African, and Middle Eastern states favored during the negotiation of the Statute of the ICJ.[83] Another factor beyond the control of the ICJ is the failure of U.N. members to establish a criminal chamber with jurisdiction over individual defendants.[84]

Even when states have agreed to submit to its jurisdiction, however, the ICJ has severely circumscribed its own ability to decide interstate disputes.[85] As a result, the ICJ has

---

gations of genocide, such as the Security Council or World Health Organization, have the power to request that the ICJ issue an advisory opinion on matters of international law. *See* NAGENDRA SINGH, THE ROLE AND RECORD OF THE INTERNATIONAL COURT OF JUSTICE: 1946–48, at 392, 394 (Norwell, MA: Kluwer Academic Publishers, 1989).

78. *See, e.g.*, Memorial of Bosn. & Herz., Application of the Convention on the Prevention and Punishment of the Crime of Genocide (Bosn. & Herz. v. Yugo.) (Apr. 15, 1994), http://www.icj-cij.org/icjwww/idocket/ibhy/ibhy_written_pleadings/ibhy_memorial_19940415.pdf; ICJ, *Croatia Institutes Proceedings Against Yugoslavia for Violations of the Genocide Convention*, PRESS RELEASE 99/38 (July 2, 1999), http://www.icj-cij.org/icjwww/ipresscom/iPress1999/ipresscom9938_19990702.htm; Armed Activities on the Territory of the Congo (Democratic Republic of the Congo v. Rwanda), Application Instituting Proceedings 7 (filed 23 June 1999), http://www.icj-cij.org/icjwww/idocket/icorw/icorwapplication/icorw_iapplication_19990623.pdf.

79. Statute of the ICJ, art. 38 (1)(a–c).

80. *Id.*, art. 38 (1)(d).

81. *See* Charter of the U.N., art. 94; Statute of the ICJ, art. 59.

82. Article 36(2) of the Statute of the ICJ provides that the "states parties to the present Statute *may* at any time declare that they recognize as compulsory ipso facto and without special agreement, in relation to any other state accepting the same obligation, the jurisdiction of the Court." (emphasis added). Sudan, for example, has excluded from the jurisdiction of the ICJ any matter that, in its discretion, it determines to be "domestic" in nature. *See* FATH EL RAHMAN ABDALLA EL SHEIKH, THE LEGAL REGIME OF FOREIGN PRIVATE INVESTMENT IN SUDAN AND SAUDI ARABIA 396 (Cambridge: Cambridge UP, 2003).

83. *See* TERRY D. GILL, LITIGATION STRATEGY AT THE INTERNATIONAL COURT 9 (Norwall, Ma: Kluwer Academic Publishers, 1989).

84. The U.N. General Assembly ordered that a study be prepared on whether to add a Criminal Chamber to the International Court of Justice for the trial of genocide and other international crimes, but one was never added. *See* McCormack, *Selective Reaction to Atrocity*, at 722.

85. *See, e.g.*, Application of the Convention on the Prevention and Punishment of the Crime of Genocide (Bosn. & Herz. v. Yugo., Preliminary Objections, 1996 ICJ REP. 595, 616 (July 11)); Application of the Convention on the Prevention and Punishment of the Crime of Genocide (Bosn. & Herz. v. Yugo. (Serb. & Mont.)), Provisional Measures, 1993 ICJ REP. 3 (Sept. 13); Reservations to the Convention on the Prevention and Punishment of the Crime of Genocide, 1951 I.C.J. 15; Arrest

only nibbled around the edges of the question of genocide, disposing of mostly procedural matters.[86] Its own jurisdictional rules, rooted in notions of consent by national sovereigns and avoidance of setting broad precedents, have blocked it from awarding effective remedies.[87] The inordinate delay, procedural maneuvering, and extensions of filing deadlines by the ICJ meant that an application filed by Bosnia and Herzegovina seeking relief from genocide in 1993 did not result in a judgment until 2007,[88] more than a decade after its preliminary ruling in the case.[89]

Even when its 2007 decision was issued, the ICJ, unlike the Yugoslav tribunal which has been quite clear on this issue in several cases, equivocated in a dangerous fashion on the application of the Genocide Convention to the ethnic cleansing of an area. The ICJ declared that

> deportation or displacement of the members of a group, even if effected by force, is not necessarily equivalent to destruction of that group, nor is such destruction an automatic consequence of the displacement. This is not to say that acts described as "ethnic cleansing" may never constitute genocide, if they are such as to be characterized as, for example, "deliberately inflicting on the group conditions of life calculated to bring about its physical destruction in whole or in part", contrary to Article II, paragraph (c), of the Convention, provided such action is carried out with the necessary specific intent (*dolus specialis*), that is to say with a view to the destruction of the group, as distinct from its removal from the region.... In other words, whether a particular operation described as "ethnic cleansing" amounts to genocide depends on the presence or absence of acts listed in Article II of the Genocide Convention, and of the intent to destroy the group as such. In fact, in the context of the Convention, the term "ethnic cleansing" has no legal significance of its own. That said, it is clear that acts of "ethnic cleansing" may occur in parallel to acts prohibited by Article II of the Convention, and

---

Warrant of 11 April 2000 (Congo v. Belgium), 2002 I.C.J. 1 (Feb. 14); Case Concerning Armed Activities on the Territory of the Congo (Democratic Republic of the Congo v. Uganda), 2005 ICJ LEXIS 1 (19 Dec. 2005), http://www.icj-cij.org/icjwww/idocket/ico/ico_judgments/ico_judgment_20051219.pdf; Application of the Convention on the Prevention and Punishment of the Crime of Genocide (Bosnia and Herzegovina v. Serbia and Montenegro), Press Release 2005/27 (Dec. 21, 2005); Application of the Convention on the Prevention and Punishment of the Crime of Genocide (Bosnia and Herzegovina v. Serbia and Montenegro), 2007 I.C.J. 140 (Feb. 26, 2007), http://www.icj-cij.org/icjwww/idocket/ibhy/ibhyjudgment/ibhy_ijudgment_20070226_frame.htm.

86. Reservations to the Convention on the Prevention and Punishment of the Crime of Genocide, 1951 I.C.J. 15; Application of the Convention on the Prevention and Punishment of the Crime of Genocide (Bosn. & Herz. v. Yugo. (Serb. & Mont.)), Provisional Measures, 1993 ICJ REP. 3 (Sept. 13); Application of the Convention on the Prevention and Punishment of the Crime of Genocide (Bosnia & Herzegovina v. Yugoslavia), Preliminary Objections, 1996 ICJ REP. 595, 616 (July 11)); Arrest Warrant of 11 April 2000 (Congo v. Belgium), 2002 I.C.J. 1 (Feb. 14); ICJ, Application of the Convention on the Prevention and Punishment of the Crime of Genocide (Bosnia and Herzegovina v. Serbia and Montenegro), Press Release 2005/27 (Dec. 21, 2005).

87. The ICJ regards its own jurisdiction as being limited to cases in which States have consented to resolution by that tribunal. *See, e.g.*, ICJ, BLUE BOOK, ch. 3 (jurisdiction is "founded upon the consent of States").

88. *See* Application of the Convention on the Prevention and Punishment of the Crime of Genocide (Bosnia and Herzegovina v. Serbia and Montenegro), Judgment (Feb. 26 2007), http://tinyurl.com/chpagq.

89. *See* Application of the Convention on the Prevention and Punishment of the Crime of Genocide (Bosnia and Herzegovina v. Yugoslavia), Preliminary Objections, 1996 ICJ REP. 595, 616 (July 11).

> may be significant as indicative of the presence of a specific intent (*dolus specialis*) inspiring those acts.[90]

The ICJ concluded, citing the *Krstić* decisions, that the massacres at Srebrenica "were acts of genocide" starting on about July 13, 1995.[91] Regarding other areas, in which a few to several dozen Bosnian Muslims were killed, raped, tortured, or deported from the area at any one time, the ICJ found no genocidal intent, without much explanation or precedential support.[92]

As a result, the vice president of the ICJ, Awn Shawkat al-Khasawneh of the Hashemite Kingdom of Jordan, argued in dissent that the majority opinion was poorly reasoned. He contended that while the majority relied on several arguments to find no genocidal intent outside Srebrenica, each of them was "inadequate for the purpose, and contradictory to the consistent jurisprudence of the international criminal tribunals."[93] He noted that both the Yugoslav and Rwanda tribunals inferred genocide from a pattern of killings or discriminatory acts, and that:

> The Appeal Chamber in *Krstić* has clearly held that the pattern of conduct known as ethnic cleansing may be relied on as evidence of the *mens rea* of genocide. Coupled with population transfers, what other inference is there to draw from the overwhelming evidence of massive killings systematically targeting the Bosnian Muslims than genocidal intent?
>
> ... It is regrettable that the Court's approach to proof of genocidal intent did not reflect more closely this relevant jurisprudence.[94]

Given the fundamental flaws in its procedures and reasoning, the ICJ has not served to date, and is not serving today in any meaningful respect, as a bulwark against genocide.

E. The Postwar Treaty System Regulating Armed Conflict

The four Geneva Conventions of 1949, which entered into force in 1950, prohibit most of the acts necessary, as part of a large-scale campaign, to commit genocide. Common Article 3 of the four conventions prohibit, during civil war or other "internal armed conflict" on the territory of a signatory, murder, summary executions, torture, cruelty, degrading or inhumane treatment, or discrimination on racial or religious grounds.[95] The fourth convention further prohibits, in international conflicts between signatories, rape

---

90. Bosnia and Herzegovina v. Serbia and Montenegro, at ¶ 190.
91. *Id.* at ¶ 297.
92. *See id.* at ¶¶ 190–376.
93. *See id.*, dissenting opinion of Awn Shawkat al-Khasawneh, at ¶ 40.
94. *Id.* at ¶¶ 41, 46.
95. *See* Convention for the Amelioration of the Condition of the Wounded and Sick in Armed Forces in the Field, art. 3, entered into force Oct. 21, 1950, 6 U.S.T. 3114, 75 U.N.T.S. 31; Convention for the Amelioration of the Condition of the Wounded, Sick, and Shipwrecked Members of Armed Forces at Sea, art. 3, entered into force Oct. 21, 1950, 6 U.S.T. 3217, 75 U.N.T.S. 85; Convention Relative to the Treatment of Prisoners of War, art. 3, entered into force Oct. 21, 1950, 6 U.S.T. 3316, 75 U.N.T.S. 135; Convention Relative to the Protection of Civilian Persons in Time of War, art. 3, entered into force Oct. 21, 1950, 6 U.S.T. 3516, 75 U.N.T.S. 287. *See also* Kadic v. Karadžić, 70 F.3d 232, 242–43 (7th Cir. 1995).

or "indecent assault" on women, inflicting willful injury or great suffering, deportation, wanton destruction of private property as well as the acts prohibited in internal armed conflicts by Common Article 3. The States parties to the conventions obligated themselves to enact sweeping legal reforms and enforcement measures, including penal sanctions for war crimes, diligent searches for and trials or extraditions of offenders, and all "measures necessary for the suppression of all acts contrary to the provisions of the present Convention other than [grave breaches of it]."[96]

On May 25, 1993, the Security Council created the International Criminal Tribunal for the Former Yugoslavia ("ICTY"), to investigate and charge violations of international law committed in the former Yugoslavia in the early 1990s, including genocide, crimes against humanity, grave breaches of the Geneva Conventions, and other violations of the laws of war.[97] The International Criminal Tribunal for Rwanda, created by the Security Council to try cases of genocide, crimes against humanity, and violations of the laws of war governing internal armed conflicts, was announced on November 8, 1994.[98]

The Yugoslav and Rwandan tribunals helped define many of the elements of the precursor crimes to genocide. They defined the elements of the crime against humanity of extermination as (1) an act or combination of acts; (2) contributing to the killing of a large number of people; (3) with intent to kill, inflict grievous bodily harm, or inflict serious injury; (4) with the reasonable knowledge that such act or omission is likely to cause death, or the intention to kill multiple persons; and (5) with an awareness that the act or omission is part of a campaign in which a large number of people are systematically killed or targeted for killing.[99]

The elements of the war crime of murder/unlawful attacks are specified as: (1) attacks; (2) deliberately directed against the civilian population as such, whether directed at particular civilian objects or at civilian areas generally; *or* (1) attacks; (2) aimed at military and civilian objectives without distinction; *or* (1) attacks; (2) directed at legitimate military objectives; (3) which cause civilian losses clearly disproportionate to the military advantage anticipated. The elements of the crime of torture are: (1) the infliction of pain or suffering, whether physical or mental; (2) by intentional act or omission; (3) that aims at obtaining information, or at punishing, intimidating, humiliating or coercing the victim or a third person; (4) under circumstances that link the act or omission to an armed conflict; and (5) reveal a nexus between at least one of the persons involved and the state, or a de facto organ of the state, or another authority-wielding entity. Finally, the elements of the crime of deportation as a crime against humanity are: (1) forcibly removing individuals from the territory; (2) in which they are lawfully present; and (3) with the intent to remove the victim (which implies that the victim can or will not return).[100]

In the 1990s, the U.S. President Bill Clinton and his administration came to accept the view that an international criminal court should have "jurisdiction over ... crimes

---

96. *See* Convention Relative to the Protection of Civilian Persons in Time of War, arts. 27, 146–47.

97. S.C. Res. 827 (May 25, 1993); ICTY Statute, Articles 2–5.

98. S.C. Res. 955 (Nov. 8, 1994); ICTR Statute, Articles 2–4.

99. Prosecutor v. Vasiljevic, Case No. IT-99-32-T, Trial Chamber II, Judgement (Nov. 29, 2002), at ¶¶ 227–29, http://www.un.org/icty/Supplement/supp38-e/vasiljevic.htm; Prosecutor v. Kayishema and Ruzindana, Case No. ICTR-95-1-T, Appeals Chamber, Judgement (June 1, 2001), http://69.94.11.53/ENGLISH/cases/KayRuz/appeal/3d.htm.

100. *See* Cryer et al., An Introduction to International Criminal Law and Procedure, at 204–58.

against humanity [in] internal situations."[101] International law defines a civil war, or a non-international armed conflict, as a state of *protracted* armed struggle between the government and rebel movements, or between various such movements within a given territory. Other than duration of the fighting, the numbers of rebels and their control over territory are relevant factors in judging the existence of an internal armed conflict.[102]

The International Criminal Court ("ICC"), created by attendees at a U.N. diplomatic conference in 1998, has jurisdiction to punish and prevent the most serious international crimes committed after July 1, 2002, including genocide, crimes against humanity, war crimes and the crime of aggression.[103] The specific crimes listed in the statute are the crime of genocide, crimes against humanity, war crimes, and the crime of aggression at such time as a provision is adopted more specifically defining aggression. Genocide for purposes of the ICC has a definition that tracks that in the Genocide Convention.[104] The preparatory documents for the ICC acknowledge that genocidal intent refers simply "to the specific intention to destroy more than a small number of individuals who are members of a group."[105] The ICC defines crimes against humanity to include:

> Murder; extermination; enslavement; deportation or forcible transfer of population; imprisonment or other severe deprivation of physical liberty in violation of fundamental rules of international law; torture; rape, sexual slavery, enforced prostitution, forced pregnancy, enforced prostitution, forced pregnancy, enforced sterilization, or any other form of sexual violence of comparable gravity; persecution against any identifiable group or collectivity on political, racial, national, ethnic, religious, gender, or other grounds that are universally recognized as impermissible under international law, in connection with any act referred to in this paragraph or any crime within the jurisdiction of the Court; enforced disappearance of persons; the crime of apartheid; other inhumane acts of a similar character intentionally causing great suffering, or serious injury to body or to mental or physical health.[106]

The Rome Statute defines a crime against humanity as a knowing, systematic or widespread attack on a civilian population by such means as murder, extermination, political or religious or ethnic persecution, enslavement, torture, rape, deportation, forced disappearance, imprisonment in violation of fundamental international norms, or other inhumane acts causing great suffering. It defines the crime against humanity of persecution as a widespread or systematic attack on a civilian population by means of intentional and severe deprivation of fundamental human rights on the grounds of religious, cultural, political, or ethnic identity of the victims, and crime against humanity of extermination as intentional infliction of conditions of life that is likely to bring about the

---

101. US Statement on the International Criminal Court, Sixth Committee, 51st Session of the UNGA, October 31, 1996, A/C.6/51/SR.28, para. 62.

102. Guenael Mettraux, *International Crimes and the* ad hoc *Tribunals*, 33–36 (Oxford University Press, 2005).

103. Rome Statute of the ICC, arts. 5(1), 11(1).

104. U.N. Doc. A/CONF. 183/9, arts. 5–6, 87 U.N.T.S. 90, entered into force July 1, 2002 [Rome Statute of the ICC].

105. Report of the Preparatory Committee on the Establishment of an International Criminal Court, UN Doc. No. A/CONF.183/2/Add.l, at 13, n. l (Apr. 14, 1998).

106. Rome Statute of the ICC, art. 7(1).

destruction of part of a population.[107] It defines the crime against humanity of extermination as "the intentional infliction of conditions of life, inter alia the deprivation of access to food and medicine, calculated to bring about the destruction of part of a population."[108] There is no numerical threshold for the crime against humanity of extermination, however, because it is committed by imposing conditions of life calculated to bring about large-scale death whether judged quantitatively or qualitatively: "Notably, Akayesu was found guilty of extermination for ordering the killing of sixteen people."[109] Extermination as a crime against humanity is committed when a widespread or systematic attack on a civilian population on political or ethnic, grounds, and even if the contribution of defendant to killings may be indirect so long as it intended to subject a number of people to conditions of life that would inevitably lead to death.[110] The Yugoslav and Rwanda tribunals have defined the elements of the crime against humanity of extermination as (1) an act or combination of acts; (2) contributing to the killing of a large number of individuals; (3) with intent to kill, inflict grievous bodily harm, or inflict serious injury; (4) with the knowledge that such act or omission is likely to cause death (or the intention to kill multiple individuals); and (5) with an awareness that the act or omission is part of an enterprise systematically targeting individuals for killing.[111]

The crime against humanity of ethnic cleansing involves a widespread or systematic attack on a civilian population committed with the intent to discriminate a specific racial, ethnic, or religious group by removing them from a particular geographic or political territory.[112] The term or phrase "ethnic cleansing" was popularized as a euphemism for genocide by the Croatian and Serbian ultranationalists of the Yugoslav civil wars, a euphemism which the U.N. General Assembly declined to use instead of genocide by calling it a "form of genocide" in the 1990s.[113] Such resolutions of the General Assembly frequently create customary international law. This is because they evidence the practice of U.N. member

---

107. Rome Statute of the ICC, art. 7. *See also* BASSIOUNI, CRIMES AGAINST HUMANITY, at 329 ("crimes against humanity" include following acts directed against any civilian population in an international or internal armed conflict: murder, torture, rape, "persecutions on political, racial and religious grounds," and "other inhumane acts").

108. Rome Statute of the ICC, art. 7(2)(b).

109. Prosecutor v. Kayishema and Ruzindana, Appeals Chamber, Judgement, at ¶¶ 89, 142–46.

110. Prosecutor v. Zigiranyirazo, Trial Chamber III, Judgement (Dec. 18, 2008), at ¶¶ 429, 470, http://69.94.11.53/ENGLISH/cases/Zigiranyirazo/ZIGIRANYIRAZO%20-%20JUDGEMENT.pdf.

111. Prosecutor v. Vasiljevic, Trial Chamber II, Judgement, at ¶¶ 227–29. *See also* Prosecutor v. Kayishema and Ruzindana, Trial Chamber II, Judgement (May 21, 1999), at ¶ 144, http://www.ictr.org/ENGLISH/cases/KayRuz/judgement/4.htm (elements of crime of extermination are: "The actor participates in the mass killing of others or in the creation of conditions of life that lead to the mass killing of others, through his act(s) or omission(s); having intended the killing, or being reckless, or grossly negligent as to whether the killing would result and; being aware that his act(s) or omission(s) forms part of a mass killing event; where, his act(s) or omission(s) forms part of a widespread or systematic attack against any civilian population on national, political, ethnic, racial or religious grounds.").

112. *See* Prosecutor v. Dusko Tadic, Case No. IT-94-1-T (May 7, 1997), at ¶¶ 253–78, 574–79, 649–59; Larry May, CRIMES AGAINST HUMANITY: A NORMATIVE ACCOUNT 116–37 (Cambridge: Cambridge UP, 2005).

113. United Nations Commission on Human Rights, Human Rights and Population Transfer: Final Report of the Special Rapporteur, para. 10 (E/CN.4/Sub.2/1997/23); ROY GUTMAN, DAVID RIEFF, & KENNETH ANDERSON, CRIMES OF WAR: WHAT THE PUBLIC SHOULD KNOW (New York: W.W. Norton, 1999); ANDREW BELL-FIALKOFF, ETHNIC CLEANSING 3 (New York: St. Martin's Press, 1996); Theodor Meron, *The Case for War Crimes Trials in Yugoslavia*, FOREIGN AFF., Summer 1993, at 122, 132.

states in compliance with the view that certain conduct does or does not comport with international law.[114]

The ICC statute defines war crimes as (1) the large-scale or planned commission; (2) of certain specified acts in violation of laws of war such as the Geneva Conventions, including murder and willful killing, intentionally attacking civilians, rape, causing excessive civilian casualties under the circumstances, bombarding undefended towns or villages in another state, using poison gases or weapons causing unnecessary suffering or indiscriminate damage in another state, torture or inhuman treatment, unlawful confinement, willfully depriving a civilian or prisoner of war of a fair and regular trial, conducting criminal trials without indispensable judicial guarantees in regularly constituted courts, unlawful deportation, colonization of occupied territory of another state, pillage, intentionally attacking religious or educational buildings, and intentionally using starvation of civilians as a method of inter-state warfare.[115]

As mentioned above, the Genocide Convention did not include a critical recommendation of its drafters, namely that either a permanent international criminal court or multiple *ad hoc* international criminal courts be established "for the trial of alleged violations of the Genocide Convention."[116] The failure to provide for an independent and impartial court has resulted in delays of many years between the global awareness of genocide, in, for example, Cambodia or Sudan, and an indictment of their leaders for genocide by a criminal tribunal.[117] This enabled countries like Sudan to fall into a legal "no man's land" for decades, a jurisdictional gap that results from the decision in 1948 not to establish a permanent international court to enforce the Genocide Convention, the refusal of countries like Sudan to cooperate with the ICC after it had been established, the U.N. Security Council's delay in demanding—on the basis of the U.N. Charter—the prosecution of Sudan and other countries for genocide by the ICC or other tribunals, and the slow progress of the ICC and other tribunals in drafting indictments.[118]

---

114. *See, e.g.*, Filartiga v. Peña-Irala, 630 F.2d 864, 882–84 (2d. Cir. 1980) (citing a General Assembly resolution, as proof of customary international law); Joseph Isanga, *Counter-Terrorism and Human Rights: The Emergence of a Rule of Customary International Law From U.N. Resolutions*, 37 Denver Journal of International Law & Policy 233, 239–51 (2009).

115. Rome Statute of the ICC, arts. 7–8.

116. McCormack, *Selective Reaction to Atrocity*, at 721.

117. *Compare, e.g.*, Amnesty International, Political Killings by Governments 38–43 (London: Amnesty International, 1983) (describing mass death from summary executions in Cambodia); Eşref Aksu The United Nations, Intra-state Peacekeeping and Normative Change 192 (Manchester: Manchester UP, 2003) (describing Amnesty and other warnings of gross human rights violations in Cambodia by March 1978); Amnesty International, *Sudan: Looming Crisis in Darfur*, AI Index: AFR 54/041/2003 (July 1, 2003), http://web.amnesty.org/library/Index/ENGAFR540412003?open&of=ENG-2AF; Amnesty International, *Sudan: Empty Promises? Human Rights Violations in Government-Controlled Areas*, AI Index: AFR 54/036/2003 (July 16, 2003). Amnesty International, *Sudan: Darfur: "Too Many People Killed for No Reason*," AI Index: AFR 54/008/2004 (Feb. 3, 2004), http://web.amnesty.org/library/Index/ENGAFR540082004?open&of=ENG-2AF (reporting complaints by Fur people of western Sudan in early 2003 that they were being subjected to genocide).

118. *See* Amnesty International, *Appeal to All Governments to End Impunity for the Worst Crimes Known to Humanity*, AI Index: IOR 70/003/2001 (Dec. 1, 2001), http://web.amnesty.org/library/Index/ENGIOR700032001?open&of=ENG-2AF ("Unless a case is referred to the Prosecutor by the UN Security Council, the Court will only have jurisdiction to investigate and prosecute a case if the crime was committed on the territory of a state that has ratified the Statute or by the national of a state that has ratified it (or accepted the Court's jurisdiction over the crime)."); Human Rights Watch, *Darfur in Flames: Atrocities in Western Sudan* 14 (Apr. 2004), http://www.hrw.org/sites/default/files/reports/sudan0404.pdf ("The Statute of the International Criminal Court established the jurisdiction of the

F. International Human Rights Law

A series of postwar international treaties underscored the Genocide and Geneva Conventions in outlawing acts of violence against civilians as a general matter. In 1948, the U.N. General Assembly adopted the Universal Declaration of Human Rights, which guarantees the human rights to life, liberty, freedom of speech and religion, freedom from torture or cruel treatment, and to own and enjoy property without arbitrary interference.[119] Article 2 states: "Everyone is entitled to all the rights and freedoms set forth in this Declaration, without distinction of any kind, such as race, colour, sex, language, religion, political or other opinion, national or social origin, property, birth or other status."[120]

In 1965, the General Assembly adopted the International Convention on the Elimination of All Forms of Racial Discrimination (the "CERD"), pursuant to which States parties agree not to implement any restriction or distinction based on race, culture, or national or ethnic origin which has the purpose or effect of impairing the exercise of human rights in the political, economic, social, or cultural areas. The CERD defines "racial discrimination" to include distinctions based on "ethnic origin" that tend to impair the full enjoyment of human rights, including in the cultural sphere. Article 2(2) of the CERD calls for "concrete measures to ensure the adequate [cultural] development and protection of certain racial groups or individuals belonging to them, for the purpose of guaranteeing them the full and equal enjoyment of human rights and fundamental freedoms."[121] Iraq, Sudan, and Turkey are parties.[122]

Since 1976, States parties to the International Covenant on Civil and Political Rights (ICCPR) have foresworn executions except for the most serious crimes and after a final judgment of a competent court, as well as arbitrary denials of life, liberty, property, freedom of speech or religion, and discrimination on the basis of race, religion, language, or social origin.[123] Article 13 prohibits mass expulsions or other non-individualized deportations of civilians.[124] The U.N. Human Rights Committee has construed Article 13 to protect potential deportees from "laws or decisions providing for collective or mass expulsions."[125]

The ICCPR confirms the right of all peoples to retain their cultural and religious heritage and way of life.[126] It prohibits discrimination or adverse distinctions based upon, among other things, race, language, religion, political or cultural opinions, national or social origin, or other status. Such group identity-based discrimination is prohibited by

---

ICC to prosecute the most serious crimes affecting the international community, including crimes against humanity. Sudan has not yet ratified the ICC Statute.").

119. *See* The Universal Declaration of Human Rights, arts. 3, 5, 7, U.N. G.A. Res. 217(III) (1948).

120. *Id.*, art. 2.

121. *See* International Convention on the Elimination of All Forms of Racial Discrimination, arts. 1–3, U.N. G.A. Res. 2106(XX) (1965), 660 U.N.T.S. 195, entered into force 4 January 1969.

122. *See* Committee on Elimination of Racial Discrimination to Meet in Geneva from 18 February to 7 March 2008 (2008), http://www.knowyourrights2008.org/index.php?nav=news&key_news=2008021510272371.

123. *See* International Covenant on Civil and Political Rights, arts. 2–10, U.N. G.A. Res. 2200A (XXI), U.N. Doc. A/6316 (1966), 993 U.N.T.S. 3, 999 U.N.T.S. 171, entered into force Mar. 23, 1976.

124. *Id.*, art. 13.

125. U.N. Doc. A/41/40, Annex VI, ¶¶ 9–10 (1986).

126. ICCPR, art. 27.

the ICCPR even during a state of emergency such as an internal armed conflict. States parties signing onto the ICCPR become obligated to ban incitement to discrimination by religious hatred. They must also guarantee, subject to laws "necessary" to protect national security, public health or safety, or morals, the freedom to worship and transmission of religious beliefs, both privately and publicly, individually or communally, as well as the freedom to speak, hear, and read about all kinds of information and ideas, regardless of borders or medium of expression used.[127] International human rights law contained in other treaties and international legal materials also guarantees indigenous peoples the right of cultural and religious self-determination.[128]

In 1984, the General Assembly adopted the Torture Convention, requiring States Parties to prevent and punish torture, defined as severe physical or mental pain or suffering intentionally inflicted on a person by or with the consent of a public official in order to discriminate against the victim or another person, punish the victim or another person, or intimidate or coerce the victim or another person.[129] The Torture Convention prohibits any act by which severe pain or suffering, whether physical or mental, is intentionally inflicted on a person for such purposes as obtaining from him or her or a third person information or a confession, punishing him or her for an act he or she or a third person has committed or is suspected of having committed, or intimidating or coercing him or her or a third person, or for any reason based on discrimination of any kind, when the infliction is by or with the acquiescence of a public official or person having official status.[130]

In 1989, the International Labour Organisation promulgated Convention (No. 169) Concerning Indigenous and Tribal Peoples in Independent Countries. "Indigenous" peoples are peoples living on land that was conquered by other peoples, states, or tribes, whose "livelihoods and very existence" were endangered "lived on their land before settlers moved in as a result of conquest, occupation, colonization, etc."[131] The indigenous peoples and nations of the world have "a historical continuity with pre-invasion and pre-colonial societies" in the lands they inhabit, and consider themselves distinct from the dominant groups of those lands.[132] ILO Convention No. 169 mandates "effective protection of [indigenous peoples'] rights of ownership and possession" over traditional lands and distinct beliefs, customs, and institutions.[133]

---

127. *See id.*, arts. 4, 18(1), 19(2), 20(2), 26.

128. *See* Maivan Clech Lâm, At the Edge of the State: Indigenous Peoples and Self-Determination 51–63, 123–35 (Ardsley, NY: Transnational Publishers, 2000).

129. *See* Convention Against Torture and Other Cruel, Inhuman or Degrading Treatment or Punishment, arts. 1–4, U.N. G.A. Res. 39/46 (1984), 1465 U.N.T.S. 85, 1468 U.N.T.S. 85, 23 I.L.M. 1027, S. Treaty Doc. No. 100–20, entered into force June 26, 1987.

130. *See id.*; *see also* 8 C.F.R. § 208.18(a)(1).

131. U.N. Economic & Social Council, Comm. on Human Rights, Sub-Comm. on the Promotion & Protection of Human Rights, Working Group on Indigenous Populations, *Report of the Working Group on Indigenous Populations on its 21st Session*, ¶ 2, U.N. Doc, E/CN.4/Sub.2/2003/22 (Aug. 11, 2003).

132. José Martínez Cobo, *Study of the Problem against Indigenous Populations, vol. 5, Conclusions, Proposals and Recommendations* ¶ 379, U.N. Doc. E/CN/4/Sub 2/1986/7 Add. 4 (March 1, 1987), *quoted in* Sarah Pritchard, *Working Group on Indigenous Populations: Mandate, Standard-setting Activities and Future Perspectives, in* Indigenous Peoples, the United Nations and Human Rights 43 (Sarah Pritchard ed., 1998).

133. ILO Convention No. 169, arts. 5(a), 7(1), 8(2), 14(2).

Similarly, the Convention on Biological Diversity (CBD) of 1993 requires the preservation of indigenous peoples' "traditional lifestyles," and the equitable distribution of the benefits arising from the utilization of their cultural heritage.[134] The CBD was the outcome of the U.N. Conference on Indigenous Peoples and the Environment, which recommended stronger legal measures to protect indigenous peoples' cultural and intellectual property from damage or destruction.[135] More than 120 heads of state signed the CBD in 1993. It protects cultural diversity within the human species,[136] because "different cultures and peoples" represent a diversity of "heritages and experiences."[137] Article 8(j) calls for "national legislation" to "respect, preserve, and maintain" indigenous practices, knowledge, and innovations; to promote the "wider application" of such practices and innovations; and to secure the "approval and involvement" of indigenous peoples in any exploitation of their practices, knowledge, and innovations.[138] Sudan and Turkey are parties to the CBD; Iraq, along with the U.S. and Ethiopia, is one of a tiny minority of the world's nations that is not.[139]

In 2007, the U.N. General Assembly, by a vote of nearly 90% of U.N. member states in favor, voted to adopt the U.N. Declaration on the Rights of Indigenous Peoples.[140] For perhaps the first time in a statement of international law, the declaration guarantees indigenous people "their cultural, intellectual, religious and spiritual property taken without their free, prior and informed consent or in violation of their laws, traditions and customs," while including in the notion of "property" archaeological and historic sites, specimens of visual art, and literary works.[141] More pointedly on the issue of cultural and intellectual property, it prohibits forced assimilation, cultural destruction, dispossession of indigenous lands or properties, forced population movements, and discriminatory propaganda.[142] Article 12 provides for redress for violations of these rights by effective mechanisms for "access [to] and/or repatriation of ceremonial objects." Article 14 provides for indigenous peoples' control over their own educational systems, which can guarantee an "education in their own culture and provided in their own language." Article 15 mandates that indigenous people be allowed to establish media outlets and access those outlets, including state-owned outlets, that are not their own.[143]

---

134. *See* CBD, art. 8(j); Darrell A. Posey, *International Agreements and Intellectual Property Right Protection for Indigenous Peoples' Intellectual Property Rights, in* Intellectual Property Rights for Indigenous Peoples: A Sourcebook 232–33 (Tom Greaves ed., 1994). Turkey is a party to the CBD; Iraq is not.

135. *See* U.N. Technical Conference on Practical Experience in the Realization of Sustainable and Environmentally Sound Self-development of Indigenous Peoples, U.N. Doc. E/CN.4/Sub.2/1992/31 (1992); Posey, *Indigenous Peoples' Intellectual Property Rights,* at 229.

136. *See* CBD, art. 2.

137. Klaus Topfer, *Foreword, in* Cultural and Spiritual Values of Biodiversity xi (U.N. Environmental Programme, 1999).

138. CBD, art. 8(j).

139. *See* Secretariat of the Convention on Biological Diversity, *Countries* (2008), http://www.cbd.int/countries/.

140. U.N. Declaration on the Rights of Indigenous Peoples, U.N. Doc. A/61/L.67 (2007), http://www.un.org/esa/socdev/unpfii/en/declaration.html.

141. *Id.*, art. 11. Other international law instruments prohibited deprivations of indigenous cultural and intellectual property, but this declaration is more expansive in referring to "religious and spiritual property," including historic sites. *Id.*

142. *Id.*, art. 8.

143. *Id.*, arts. 12, 14–15.

G. Genocide and Diplomacy: Charges and Counter-charges in the United Nations

International law often develops further reach and detail by codifying "soft law" pronouncements into more binding rules of customary international law. Between the verdicts at Nuremberg in 1946, and the first verdicts by international criminal tribunals in genocide cases in the late 1990s, the law of genocide was developed in two principal fora: diplomatic communications in the United Nations, and decisions by national criminal courts. Leaving aside the latter for the next section, diplomatic charges and counter-charges in the United Nations reveal a focus on state-implemented or -supported massacres of civilians, destruction of essential infrastructure, and deprivation of humanitarian aid during counterinsurgency operations.

The legal effect of such declarations, motions, and statements is often debated. Soft law, as a category, includes "as agreements, declarations, communication, recommendations, resolutions, guidelines, notices, and positions—the list appears to be endless."[144] Diplomatic reprisals or condemnations may be a reaction to violations of international law that falls short of the use of force or economic sanctions, yet still constitute attempts to make international law "binding."[145] Specifically in the area of genocide, the Trial Chamber of the International Tribunal for the Prosecution of Persons Responsible for Serious Violations of International Humanitarian Law Committed in the Territory of the former Yugoslavia since 1991 has cited U.N. resolutions and documents short of treaties or statements of customary international law, in support of various findings as to the crime of genocide.[146] Similarly, the Appeals Chamber of the Yugoslav tribunal characterized the Nazi massacres of Jews as genocide, even though the Nuremberg tribunal did not specifically state or decide this, so that the tribunal must have relied on "softer" materials such as indictments or diplomatic materials.[147] The Appeals Chamber also drew support from the International Law Commission's 1996 Draft Code of Crimes Against the Peace and Security of Mankind, which it described as "an authoritative instrument, parts of which may constitute evidence of customary international law," and "as 'indicative of the legal

---

144. Mono Aldestarn, *Soft Law and the State Aid Policy Area, in* SOFT LAW IN GOVERNANCE AND REGULATION: AN INTERDISCIPLINARY ANALYSIS 26 (Ulrika Mörth ed., Cheltenham, UK and Nottingham, MA: Edward Elgar Publishing, 2004). *See also* Kerstin Sahlin-Andersson, *Emergent Cross-Sectional Soft Regulations: Dynamics at Play in the Global Compact Initiative, in id.* at 145 (discussing "the large number of voluntary agreements, directives, conventions and declarations in the nature of soft law"); Henrik Frykman & Ulrika Morth, *Soft Law and Three Notions of Democracy: The Case of the EU, in id.* at 156 ("Soft law can take many forms, such as codes of conducts, declarations, communications and recommendations...").

145. Sia Spiliopoulou, *Soft Law and International Financial Institutions—Issues of Hard and Soft Law from a Lawyer's Perspective, in id.* at 77.

146. *See* Prosecutor v. Krstić, Trial Chamber, Judgement, at ¶ 589 (citing a resolution of the U.N. General Assembly in support of ruling that: "[T]he intent to eradicate a group within a limited geographical area such as the region of a country or even a municipality may be characterised as genocide.").

147. *See* Prosecutor v. Krstić, Case No. IT-98-33-A, Appeals Chamber, Judgement (Apr. 19, 2004), at ¶ 13, http://www.un.org/icty/krstic/Appeal/judgement/index.htm ("Nazi Germany may have intended only to eliminate Jews within Europe alone; that ambition probably did not extend, even at the height of its power, to an undertaking of that enterprise on a global scale.").

views of eminently qualified publicists representing the major legal systems of the world.' "[148] Finally, the Commission of Inquiry on Darfur cited an internal memorandum of the Canadian government analyzing alleged genocide in Kosovo, in support of the Commission's determination that no genocide committed by Sudan's government had been proven by 2004.[149] This reliance on a unilateral Canadian declaration gives credence to such "soft law" materials.

The list of charges and countercharges of genocide in United Nations fora, and to the press by political leaders hoping to influence public debate, is incredibly long and varied. These charges typically arose during incidents of religious persecution, civilian deaths during military occupation of foreign territory, and/or suppression of insurgencies and separatist movements.

In the late 1940s, condemnation of genocide focused on religious persecution. In 1947 and 1948, representatives in exile of the Baltic states of Lithuania, Latvia, and Estonia that had been liberated from the Nazis only to be occupied by Soviet troops petitioned the United Nations to condemn the Soviet Union for genocide in the Baltics.[150] Raphael Lemkin joined this effort, hoping to build U.S. support for the still-unratified Genocide Convention, and moved by news accounts of the Soviet destruction of churches and outlawing of Christianity.[151] Pakistan charged India with genocide against Muslims in 1948, as religious massacres raged.[152]

In the 1950s, allegations of genocide emphasized crimes by members of the U.N. Security Council. Raphael Lemkin condemned the "Russian policy of genocide," citing reports from the Catholic Church that 10,000 priests were missing in countries occupied by the Soviet Union after 1943.[153] The American Federation of Labor accused the Soviet Union of an anti-Jewish genocide in 1951.[154] The next year, a petition by African-American organizations in 1951 charged the U.S. with genocide.[155] South Korea charged North Korea and its communist allies with genocide during the North's invasion starting in 1951.[156]

---

148. *Id.* at ¶ 11 n.20 (quoting Prosecutor v. Furundžija, Case No. IT-95-17/1-T, Trial Chamber, Judgement (Dec. 10, 1998), at ¶ 227).

149. *See* Report of the International Commission of Inquiry on Darfur to the United Nations Secretary-General Pursuant to Security Council Resolution 1564 of 18 September 2004, ¶ 504 & n.186 (Jan. 25, 2005) [hereinafter ICID Report].

150. *See* Anton Weiss-Wendt, *Hostage of Politics: Raphael Lemkin on "Soviet Genocide,"* 7 J. of Genocide Res. 551, 554–58 (2005), http://www.inogs.com/JGRFullText/WeissWendt.pdf.

151. *See, e.g., Papacy Strengthened to Resist Communism*, N.Y. Times, Feb. 24, 1946, http://www.nytimes.com; *Baltic Exiles Here Renew Plea to UN*, N.Y. Times, May 13, 1949, http://www.nytimes.com; *see also Catholic Clergy Exiled By Reds, Says Lith Priest*, Chicago Tribune, Oct. 14, 1941, http://www.pqasb.pqarchiver.com/chicagotribune; *Tell of Soviet War on Baltic Protestants*, Chicago Trib., June 20, 1946; Yves du Guerny, *Reds Try to Rub Out Christmas in Baltic Lands*, Chicago Trib., Dec. 25, 1951, at 20; *see also* Sabrina P. Ramet, Catholicism and Politics in Communist Societies 53–56 (Chapel Hill, NC: Duke UP, 1990).

152. *See Million Moslems Die in India Conflict, Pakistan Tells U.N.*, Chicago Trib., Feb. 7, 1948, at 7; *Jewish Body Assails Pakistan on Genocide*, N.Y. Times, Feb. 6, 1948, http://www.nytimes.com; *Move to Curb UN on Genocide Is Hit*, N.Y. Times, Oct. 21, 1948, http://www.nytimes.com.

153. *See* Weiss-Wendt, *Raphael Lemkin on "Soviet Genocide,"* at 552.

154. *See AFL Accuses Soviet and Satellites of 'Fiendish Plan' to Wipe Out Jews*, N.Y. Times, Feb. 5, 1950, at 1.

155. *See US Accused in UN of Negro Genocide*, N.Y. Times, Dec. 18, 1951, http://www.nytimes.com.

156. *See Genocide By Reds In Korea Charged; Republic Asks UN Unit to Act*, N.Y. Times, May 4, 1951, http://www.nytimes.com.

Ethnic and racial struggles with a Cold War overcast dominated charges of genocide during the 1960s and 1970s. In 1956, fifteen Asian and African governments accused France of carrying out genocide in Algeria.[157] Malaya, which gained independence from Britain in 1957, accused the People's Republic of China of genocide in occupied Tibet in 1963.[158] The Soviet Union warned against Iraq's practice of genocide against the Kurds as early as 1963, when the Iraqi government shelled Kurdish areas in opposing a second attempt by Mullah Mustafa Barzani to set up a Soviet-backed Kurdish republic in northern Iraq, and perhaps in northern Iran as well.[159] Pakistan again accused India of genocide, this time in the region of Kashmir claimed by Pakistan.[160] The short-lived independent republic of Biafra attempted to secure U.N. intervention against genocide by Nigeria against residents of the enclave.[161] The southern Sudanese similarly charged the Soviet-armed government with genocide against the south.[162] A U.N. report in 1971 saw "elements of genocide" in the deportation of Africans into barren lands by white governments allocating rich land for whites.[163] Native American groups charged the U.S. with genocide in the late 1970s.[164]

The conflict between Israel and its Arab neighbors (the Palestinians, Egypt, Iraq, Iran, Lebanon, Syria, and the Gulf Arab states) has given rise to recurring charges of genocide since the 1950s. Israel cited a risk of genocide against Jews in Syria and Iraq as early as 1949.[165] After the Suez War, several Arab governments charged Israel with genocide in the Sinai desert.[166] Egypt accused Israel of genocide against its troops during the 1967 war.[167] The Palestinian Liberation Organization, Iraq, and Libya complained of an Israeli genocide against the Palestinians in 1974–1975.[168] In return, Israel accused Iraq in 1982 of committing genocide against the town of Dujail, in southern Iraq, by killing about 150 out of a total of 2,000 persons living in the town. "The group intended to be destroyed, according to Israel's accusation, was the population of" Dujail.[169] In 2002 and again in 2008, Turkey's prime minister accused Israel of genocide

157. *See Genocide in Algeria Charged to France*, N.Y. Times, Oct. 3, 1956, http://www.nytimes.com; *French Hit Back on Algeria Issue; Move to Present Their Case to UN*, N.Y. Times, Jan. 20, 1957, at 32. *See also Algeria to France: Recognize Your Own Genocide*, Hürriyet (Turkey), Apr. 12, 2009, http://www.hurriyet.com.tr.

158. *See Malaya Tells the UN Communist China Commits Genocide in Tibet*, N.Y. Times, Oct. 4, 1962, http://www.nytimes.com.

159. *See* Henry Tanner, *Soviet Sees Peril in Kurdish Issue; Warns Iraq, Iran, Turkey and Syria on 'Genocide,'* N.Y. Times, July 10, 1963, at 3; Dana Adams Schmidt, *Kurdish Rebel Chief Says Force Is only Way to Win Autonomy*, N.Y. Times, Sept. 11, 1962, at 1; *Iran Said to Seek Offset to Russia; Fears of Aggression*, N.Y. Times, Sept. 22, 1945, at 5.

160. *See* Drew Middleton, *Pakistani Note to UN Lays 'Genocide' to India*, N.Y. Times, Oct. 23, 1965, at 1.

161. *See Nigeria*, N.Y. Times, Oct. 4, 1968, at 12, http://www.nytimes.com; *Observers Report No Nigeria Genocide*, N.Y. Times, Dec. 7, 1968, http://www.nytimes.com.

162. *See* Michael T. Kaufman, *2 Sudanese Rebels, Charging Genocide, Seek Help at UN*, N.Y. Times, Jan. 5, 1971, at 6.

163. *See* Sam Pope Brewer, *UN Rights Team Reports On Africa; Sees 'Elements of Genocide' in White-ruled Nations*, N.Y. Times, Feb. 24, 1971, at 9.

164. *See* John Kifner, *US Indians Give Complaints to Soviet for Use in Belgrade*, N.Y. Times, June 17, 1977 at A11.

165. *See Genocide Issue Raised By Israeli Against Arabs*, N.Y. Times, Mar. 31, 1949, at 10.

166. *See* Kathleen Teltsch, *Sinai Laid Waste, Arab Nations Say*, N.Y. Times, Dec. 15, 1956, at 9.

167. *See* Thomas J. Hamilton, *Egyptian Accuses Israel*, N.Y. Times, June 16, 1967, at 10.

168. *See* Paul Hofmann, *UN Panel Accredits Israel, With Libya Protesting*, N.Y. Times, Sept 30, 1975, at 12; Paul Hofmann, *Iraq, in UN, Asks Israel's Ouster; Delegate, In Harsh Attack, Charges Mass Killings of Palestinians*, N.Y. Times, Sept. 25, 1975, at 6.

169. *See* Quigley, The Genocide Convention, at 128, 177.

in the West Bank and Gaza, based on the killing of hundreds of civilians in battles with the Palestine Liberation Organization and Hamas, while at the same time censoring American Web sites like YouTube that characterized the murder of hundreds of thousands of Ottoman Christians as a genocide.[170] This followed a similar condemnation of Israeli "genocide" by an Arab Summit that soon after welcomed President al-Bashir of Sudan, accused of genocide by the ICC prosecutor, to attend.[171] Turkey maintained good relations with Sudan while accusing Israel of crimes in Gaza, and was a "direct arms supplier" to Sudan in violation of U.N. sanctions.[172] Turkey has also accused China, Cyprus, and Serbia of genocide.[173] Since 2006, Iraq's political and religious leaders have often complained of genocide by terrorists.[174] Russia accused Georgia of genocide during its 2008 bombing over South Ossetia.[175]

---

170. *See* Associated Press, *Turkey Probes Israel on 'War Crimes' in Gaza,* JERUSALEM POST, Feb. 6, 2009, http://www.jpost.com; *Transcripts of Erdogan, Moussa, Peres (and Erdogan again ...) at Davos Economic Forum* (2009) http://palestinethinktank.com/2009/01/31/transcripts-of-erdogan-moussa-peres-and-erdogan-again-at-davos.

171. *See Arab Summit at Doha Accuses Israel of War Crimes, Genocide,* WALL STREET J., Jan. 16, 2009, http://www.wsj.com.

172. *Compare, e.g., Sudanese President Officially Welcomed By Turkish President,* BBC News, Jan. 21, 2008, http://nl.newsbank.com, *Sudan's Bashir in Visit to Turkey,* BBC NEWS, Aug. 19, 2008, http://news.bbc.co.uk/1/hi/world/europe/7569901.stm, Reuters, *Iran, Russia Supplying Arms to Sudan: Rights Group,* ASHARQ ALAWSAT, Oct. 15, 2008, http://aawsat.com/english/news.asp?section=1&id=14407, *and Sudanese Official Praises Erdoğan for Davos Walkout,* TODAY'S ZAMAN, Feb. 5, 2009, http://www.todayszaman.com/tz-web/detaylar.do?load=detay&link=166049&bolum=102, *with Turkish PM Calls for Immediate Action Against Gaza Tragedy,* XINHUA NEWS SERV., Dec. 12, 2008, http://news.xinhuanet.com/english/2008-12/29/content_10577493.htm, *and* Yigal Schleifer, *Turkey: PM Erdogan's Criticism of Israel Could Damage Ankara's Aspirations as Mid-East Peace Broker,* EURASIANET, Feb 5, 2009, http://www.eurasianet.org/departments/insightb/articles/eav020509.shtml.

173. *See, e.g., China Demands Turkish Retraction,* BBC NEWS (U.K.), July 14, 2009, http://news.bbc.co.uk/2/hi/asia-pacific/8149379.stm (Turkish Prime Minister Tayyip Erdogan accused China of genocide against Turkic Uighur Muslims in 2009); Justin Huggler, *Turkey to Take Greater Role in Cyprus,* THE INDEPENDENT (U.K.), July 21, 1999 (Turkish Prime Minister accused Greek leaders of Cyprus of genocide against Turkish population prior to Turkish invasion and occupation); *Parliament Bureau, Ecevit Defends Bank Operation,* TURKISH DAILY NEWS (FINANCIAL TIMES WIRE), Dec. 29, 1999) (Turkish Prime Minister Bulent "Ecevit also reacted against ... criticism that Turkey has remained silent over Chechnya. He said that Turkey is one of the countries that is most sensitive to the Chechen problem and that Turkey's reaction was shown by both himself and the foreign minister. He added that the government had stressed that the Russian operations against the Chechen rebels amounted to genocide...."); Republic of Turkey, *Draft Resolution of the U.N. Commission on Human Rights,* E/CN.4/1992/S-2/L.2 (Nov. 30, 1992) (charging Yugoslavia with genocide against Muslim population long before Srebrenica massacre).

174. *See, e.g., Russian President Orders Probe into Georgian "Genocide,"* BBC ARCHIVE/CHANNEL ONE TV, Moscow, Aug. 10, 2008, http://www.newsbank.com; Desmond Butler, *US Dismisses Russian Claims of Genocide by Georgia,* ASSOCIATED PRESS, Aug. 20, 2008. Georgia responded by filing suit against Russia for the ethnic cleansing in the ICJ. *See* Marlise Simons, *Georgia Files Suit Against Russia, Charging Racial Discrimination,* N.Y. TIMES, Aug. 13, 2008, http://www.nytimes.com/2008/08/14/world/europe/14hague.html.

175. *See, e.g.,* Edith M. Lederer. *Iraqi President Says Recent Attacks Have Reached Level of Genocide and Crimes against Humanity,* CANADIAN PRESS, Sept. 24, 2009; *US: Ramadi Battle Kills 100-Plus Insurgents,* CNN, May 1, 2006, http://www.cnn.com/2006/WORLD/meast/05/01/iraq.main/.

H. Genocide in Court: The Era of National Tribunals

By this process, courts utilize, as evidence of the meaning of international treaties or practices accepted as international law, the statements or reports by government officials, decisions by national courts, the treatises and articles of international lawyers, and otherwise nonbinding U.N. resolutions or declarations.[176]

Without a permanent international tribunal to punish violations of the Genocide Convention, or to impose reparations for violations, the task fell to national courts and military tribunals to define the scope and applicability of the Convention to a variety of wars and internal conflicts. Since 1948, only a handful of international tribunals have adjudicated alleged genocides, while a few national courts have struggled with the issue to varying degrees of success.[177] Signatory states continued to prosecute officials for genocide, but these prosecutions were extremely rare (likely less than one conviction for every 100,000 victims).[178]

Although criminal prosecutions for genocide are rare, those that have proceeded to a final decision have established several important precedents. One key principle is that high officials may be convicted for genocide committed largely against their own ethnic and national group, as were Pol Pot and Ieng Sary of Cambodia in 1979, Francisco Macias Nguema of Equatorial Guinea in 1979, and Nicolae and Elena Ceaucescu of Romania in 1991.[179] Another principle that emerges from the case law is that an intention to kill only a portion of a group, such as its males or those sharing a certain political ideology, may suffice for genocide, as national courts found in Bolivia, Ethiopia, Lithuania, and

176. Statute of the ICJ, art. 38(1)(b). *See* Mark Gibney and Erik Roxstrom, *The Status of State Apologies*, 23 Human Rts. Q. 911, 915 (2001); Peter Malanczuk, Akehurst's Modern Introduction to International Law 39 (London: Routledge, 1997); W. Michael Reisman, *International Lawmaking: A Process of Communication*, 75 American Soc. Int'l L. Proceedings 101 (1981).

177. *See* Payam Akhavan, *Enforcement of the Genocide Convention: A Challenge to Civilization*, 8 Harv. Hum. Rts. J. 229 (1995) ("A leading commentator on genocide, writing in 1985, observed that aside from prosecutions of Nazi war criminals, there have been only two genocide trials involving political leaders [involving Cambodia and Equatorial Guinea].").

178. *See id.* (citing Attorney General of the Government of Israel v. Adolf Eichmann, 36 Int'l .L. Rep. 5 (Isr. Sup. Ct. 1962); Federation Nationale des Deportes et Internes Resistants et Patriotes and Others v. Barbie, 78 I.L.R. 125 (Fr. Cass. crim. 1985)). *See also* United States v. Ohlendorf et al., 4 Trials of the War Criminals Before the Nuernberg Military Tribunals under Control Council Law No. 10 [LRTWC] 1 (U.S. Military Trib. 1948); Poland v. Goeth, 7 LRTWC 1 (Supr. Nat. Trib. Poland 1946); Poland v. Greiser, 13 LRTWC 70 (Supr. Nat. Trib. Poland 1948); Poland v. Hoess, 7 LRTWC 11 (Supr. Nat. Trib. Poland 1948); France v. Papon, Judgment of 18 September 1996, Chambre d' Accusation de la Cour d'Appel de Bordeaux (unpublished), *aff'd*, judgment of Jan. 23, 1997, Cass. Crim., 1997 J.C.P. II G No. 22,812; Papon v. France, Application no. 54210/00, Judgment of July 25, 2002, ¶¶ 51–73 (Eur. Ct. Human Rts.), http://preview.tinyurl.com/lfk9o8; John B. Quigley, The Genocide Convention: An International Law Analysis, ch. 6 (2006) (describing genocide cases brought in Bolivia, Brazil, Cambodia, Croatia, Equatorial Guinea, Germany, Romania, and other countries); David Stout, *Paul Touvier, 81, French War Criminal*, N.Y. Times, July 18, 1996, http://www.writing.upenn.edu/~afilreis/Holocaust/touvier-obit.htm; Leila Sadat Wexler, *The Interpretation of the Nuremberg Principles by the French Court of Cassation: From Touvier to Barbie and Back Again*, 32 Colum. J. Transnational L. 289 (1994).

179. *See* Quigley, The Genocide Convention, at 38; William Schabas, *Cambodia: Was it Really Genocide?*, 23.2 Human Rights Q. 470 (2001), http://muse.jhu.edu/journals/human_rights_quarterly/v023/23.2schabas.html.

Rwanda during the 1990s.[180] A third is that deporting the members of a group en masse constitutes a genocidal act, as courts in Israel, Latvia, and Estonia have concluded.[181] Fourth, killing members of a group to facilitate their ethnic cleansing from an area constitutes genocide, as determined by the U.N. and courts in Brazil, Croatia, and Germany.[182] Such opinions of national courts constitute a source of international law.[183]

While some nations made honest efforts to enforce the Genocide Convention, others tried to avoid its strictures. In the U.S., cold warriors, foreign policy "realists," and racist segregationists spearheaded the opposition to the Genocide Convention and an international criminal court.[184] Cold warriors and "realists" Hans Morgenthau and George F. Kennan, joined by segregationists in Congress and the American Bar Association, ultimately succeeded in deferring U.S. adherence to the Genocide Convention for four decades, until the late 1980s.[185]

---

180. *See* QUIGLEY, THE GENOCIDE CONVENTION, at 36, 41, 43; WARD N. FERDINANDUSSE, DIRECT APPLICATION OF INTERNATIONAL CRIMINAL LAW IN NATIONAL COURTS 27–28 (2006).

181. *See* QUIGLEY, THE GENOCIDE CONVENTION, at 24–26, 45; Israel (Prosecutor General) v. Eichmann, Jerusalem District Court (12 December 1961), 36 INT'L L. REPORTS 340 (1968); Lauri Mälksoo, *Soviet Genocide? Communist Mass Deportations in the Baltic States and International Law*, 14 LEIDEN J. OF INTERNATIONAL LAW 757, 774–78, 780 (2001); Registrar of the European Court of Human Rights, *Press Release, Chamber Judgment: Farbtuhs v. Latvia* (Dec. 2, 2004), http://www.echr.coe.int/Eng/Press/2004/Dec/ChamberjudgmentFarbtuhsvLatvia21204.htm ("On 27 September 1999 the Riga Regional Court found him guilty of crimes against humanity and genocide for his role in the deportation and deaths of tens of Latvian citizens during the period of Stalinist repression in 1940 and 1941, when the applicant was deputy head of police in a department under the authority of the Soviet Ministry of Foreign Affairs in Latvia following the annexation of the Republic of Latvia by the Soviet Union.... On 12 January 2000 the convictions were upheld on appeal by the Criminal Division of the Supreme Court.").

182. *See* QUIGLEY, THE GENOCIDE CONVENTION, at 196; U.N. Doc. A/RES/47/121 (Dec. 18, 1992); U.N. Doc. A/RES/48/153 (Dec. 20, 1993); U.N. Doc. A/RES/49/205 (Dec. 23, 1994); U.N. Doc. A/RES/50/192 (Dec. 22, 1995); U.N. Doc. A/RES/51/115 (Dec. 12, 1996).

183. *See, e.g.*, I.C.J. Statute, art. 38(1)(d); CRYER ET AL., AN INTRODUCTION TO INTERNATIONAL CRIMINAL LAW AND PROCEDURE, at 64 ("Domestic jurisprudence may also have an impact as a source of law for international criminal courts, as the practice of the ICTY and ICTR shows.").

184. *See* Jonathan A. Bush, *Nuremberg: The Modern Law of War and Its Limitations*, 93 COLUMBIA LAW REVIEW 2022, 2064 (1993) (reviewing TELFORD TAYLOR, THE ANATOMY OF THE NUREMBERG TRIAL: A PERSONAL MEMOIR (New York: Knopf, 1992)) ("Significant opposition in the former Allied nations was confined to foreign policy 'realists' who rejected a moralistic international 'law' and multilateral institutions that might some day be turned against the United States.").

185. *See id.* at 2064 n.146; Phillips, *The Genocide Convention: Its Effect on Our Legal System*, 35 AMERICAN BAR ASSOCIATION J. 957–960 (1949); Louis Henkin, *U.S. Ratification of Human Rights Conventions: The Ghost of Senator Bricker*, 89 AMERICAN J. INTERNATIONAL LAW 341, 348–49 (1995).

Chapter III

A Crime Against All: Legal and Theoretical Approaches to Genocide

> The aim of the Genocide Convention is to prevent the intentional destruction of entire human groups, and the part targeted must be significant enough to have an impact on the group as a whole.... Those who devise and implement genocide seek to deprive humanity of the manifold richness its nationalities, races, ethnicities and religions provide. This is a crime against all of humankind, its harm being felt not only by the group [itself], but by all of humanity.
>
> —International Criminal Tribunal for the Former Yugoslavia, Appeals Chamber[1]

This chapter describes how the crime of genocide is defined under the Genocide Convention. It discusses a "Holocaust model" of genocide elaborated by the Nuremberg tribunals, the Israeli Supreme Court, and scholars of the Holocaust and other genocides. The thesis of this chapter is that in the 1990s, the international criminal tribunals for the former Yugoslavia and for Rwanda clarified that the crime of genocide does not require the destruction or intent to destroy an entire nation or religious group, may be committed by persons also motivated by the desire to plunder minority communities or carry out counterinsurgency warfare, and may be found by inferring genocidal intent from large-scale massacres and discriminatory acts. These principles, taken together, form a Bosnia or "Srebrenica" model of genocide, and a very similar Rwanda model. Finally, this chapter details an expansive Kosovo model of genocide, in which the sporadic killings of dozens of people at a time, frightening thousands into fleeing their homes, was recognized as genocide by leading framers of the Genocide Convention.

A. The Genocide Convention

After the defeat of Nazism and Japanese imperialism in World War II, the victorious allies founded the United Nations, the General Assembly of which soon passed a resolution calling for the drafting of an international treaty against genocide.[2] The General Assembly concluded that "[m]any instances of such crimes of genocide have occurred when

1. Prosecutor v. Krstić Appeals Chamber, Judgement, at ¶¶ 8, 33.
2. Quigley, The Genocide Convention, at 5–7.

racial, religious, political or other groups have been destroyed, entirely or in part."[3] Professor Lemkin successfully lobbied the U.N. to adopt a convention creating a global duty to punish genocide, and calling for criminal prosecutions of persons guilty of it, in their own countries or before competent tribunals.[4]

Although the draft prepared under his influence served as the basis for the resulting treaty prohibiting genocide, the great powers sitting on the United Nations Security Council took care to create wiggle room for themselves to pursue their traditional policies that could be described as genocidal. The Soviet Union in particular criticized the initial draft as "much too wide" and participated on a committee which narrowed its scope, after deliberations by the four permanent members of the Security Council (the Soviet Union, the U.S., France, and China) and three smaller nations.[5] The United Kingdom was anxious to ensure that the draft not contain a provision for prosecuting heads of state such as the kings and queens in whose name Ireland, the Americas, Asia, and Africa had been colonized, often resulting in massacres of the indigenous population.[6] In the U.S., members of Congress demanded clarifying language that the Genocide Convention would not prohibit "violent expressions of prejudice which is directed against individual members of groups," and that no international courts could hear cases against the U.S.[7] The U.S. also secured an amendment of the draft decriminalizing non-violent cultural genocide through policies of linguistic or cultural assimilation.[8] Nevertheless, the Congress was only persuaded to ratify the convention in the late 1980s, four decades after signature and on condition that no enforcement by civil lawsuits brought by Native Americans or other minorities against the U.S. government could be heard, only criminal cases controlled by the president.[9]

The resulting U.N. Convention on the Prevention and Punishment of the Crime of Genocide (the Genocide Convention) reaffirmed that "genocide has inflicted great losses on humanity" not simply in World War II but "at all periods of history."[10] The signatories to the Genocide Convention came together to "confirm that genocide, whether committed in time of peace or in time of war, is a crime under international law which they undertake to prevent and to punish."[11] The Genocide Convention prohibited five categories of conduct, assuming that such conduct was committed with the intent to de-

3. G.A. Res. 96(I) (Dec. 11, 1946).

4. *See* Power, "A Problem from Hell," at 56, 529 (Lemkin participated in drafting of Genocide Convention by U.N. Secretariat and U.N. Economic and Social Council); McCormack, *Selective Reaction to Atrocity*, at 721–22.

5. Lawrence J. LeBlanc, The United States and the Genocide Convention 26–28 (Chapel Hill, NC: Duke UP, 1991).

6. *See id.* at 29.

7. *See id.* at 2, 7–10, 39, 80, 228–30.

8. *See* Matthew Lippman, *The 1948 Convention on the Prevention and Punishment of the Crime of Genocide: Forty-Five Years Later*, 8 Temple International & Comparative Law J. 1, 38–39 (1999).

9. *See* Genocide Convention Implementation Act of 1987, 18 U.S.C. § 1092 (1988) (codifying crime of genocide with proviso that such codification not "be construed as creating any substantive or procedural right enforceable by law by any party in any proceeding"). The House Report to the Act stated that this language "clarifies that the bill creates no new federal cause of action in civil proceedings." H.R. Rep. 566, 100th Cong., 2d Sess., at 8 (1988). The Truman administration, often portrayed as championing the Genocide Convention, also requested that the Senate ratify the Genocide Convention "with the understanding that article IX ... not be understood as meaning that a state can be held liable in damages for injuries inflicted by it on its own nationals." *The President's Letter of Transmittal: Report of the Secretary of State*, 21 Dep't of State Bulletin 844, 846 (1949).

10. Convention on the Prevention and the Punishment of the Crime of Genocide, adopted Dec. 9, 1948, Preamble, 78 U.N.T.S. 277, 280, U.N. G.A. Res. 260A(III), A/55/207.

11. *Id.*, Preamble, 78 U.N.T.S. at 280.

stroy all or part of a national, racial, ethnic, or religious group: (1) "[k]illing members of the group," (2) "[c]ausing serious bodily or mental harm to members of the group," (3) "[d]eliberately inflicting on the group conditions of life calculated to bring about its physical destruction in whole or in part," (4) "imposing measures designed to prevent births within the group," or (5) "forcibly transferring children of the group to the other group."[12]

The drafting history of the Genocide Convention provides more detail on the type of acts the framers of the prohibition on genocide had in mind. Killing members of the group is obvious enough. Causing "serious mental harm" short of death with the intent to destroy a group was a phrase aimed at acts such as Japan's efforts to cause opium addiction in occupied China during the 1930s, which served to destroy Chinese people and their families. The ratifying document of the U.S. referred to such serious mental harm as a permanent impairment of the mental faculties.[13] The act of inflicting conditions of life calculated to bring about the destruction of a group was summarized as follows: "Obviously, if members of a group of human beings are placed in concentration camps where the annual death rate is thirty per cent [sic] to forty per cent [sic], the intention to commit genocide is unquestionable."[14] Evidently having in mind the Nazi legal regime for the prevention of births by Jews married to non-Jews, a draft of the Genocide Convention also outlawed "obstacles to marriage" as a form of "biological genocide" along with forced sterilization and "segregation of the sexes."[15] Each of these acts seems to constitute a measure designed to prevent births by group members. Finally, the drafting committee concluded with respect to the form of genocide that results from forcibly removing children from one minority racial, religious, or ethnic group to another, that:

> The separation of children from their parents results in forcing upon the former at an impressionable and receptive age a culture and a mentality different from their parents. This process tends to bring about the disappearance of the group as a cultural unit in a relatively short time.[16]

B. Genocide: The Holocaust Model

Foremost among the dozens of additional crimes against civilians in time of war defined by the Nuremberg tribunal was genocide, called the "crime of crimes" or, with aggression, as the "supreme crime." In 1945, Professor Lemkin returned to Europe to search for his family members, eventually securing a role as legal adviser to the Chief Justice Robert Jackson, Chief U.S. Prosecutor at the International Military Tribunal for the Trial of German Major War Criminals convened at Nuremberg (IMT or "Nuremberg tri-

---

12. *Id.*, art. 10.

13. *See* QUIGLEY, THE GENOCIDE CONVENTION, at 102.

14. U.N. Econ. & Soc. Council [ECOSOC], Report of the Secretary-General on the Draft Convention on the Prevention and Punishment of the Crime of Genocide, at 25, U.N. Doc. E/447 (June 26, 1947), http://www.preventgenocide.org/law/convention/drafts

15. U.N. Econ. & Soc. Council [ECOSOC], Draft Convention on the Prevention and Punishment of the Crime of Genocide, Secretariat Draft, First Draft of the Genocide Convention, U.N. Doc. E/447 (May 1947), http://www.preventgenocide.org/law/convention/drafts/.

16. U.N. Econ. & Soc. Council [ECOSOC], Report of the Secretary-General on the Draft Convention on the Prevention and Punishment of the Crime of Genocide, at 27, U.N. Doc. E/447 (June 26, 1947).

bunal").[17] In 1945, the Nuremberg tribunal indicted high Nazi officials for a variety of "crimes against humanity" that included "deliberate and systematic genocide, viz., the extermination of racial and national groups, against the civilian populations of certain occupied territories in order to destroy particular races and classes of people and national, racial, or religious groups, particularly Jews, Poles, and Gypsies and others."[18] The text of the indictment provides a further illustration that the crime of genocide was never intended to require the complete extermination of peoples, or even necessarily an intention to achieve that result, insofar as the majority of the world's Jews, Poles, and Romani people (Gypsies) had survived the Holocaust.[19]

Within a year, a panel of American, British, French, and Soviet judges[20] condemned to death Hermann Goering and other Nazi leaders for "extermination" of the Jews as a "crime against humanity."[21] Thus, they removed any doubt that mass killings falling short of the successful destruction of an entire nation could be prosecuted as genocide or "extermination."

In 1961, an Israeli District Court convicted Adolf Eichmann for his role in the "Nazi massacre." He had been captured in Argentina in an act that that country and the Security Council questioned as illegal, even though neither entity demanded his physical return.[22] The district court focused in particular on crimes against humanity committed against the Jews, the European survivors of which group made up half of Israel's citizens.[23] The court declared that the "special character" of genocide "is indicated by criminal intention necessary in this crime, which is general and total: the extermination of members of a group as such."[24] The Supreme Court of Israel affirmed the conviction, exercising prescriptive jurisdiction to declare it was no defense to the genocide charge that Eichmann was not a citizen of Israel, had committed his crimes in furtherance of Ger-

17. *See* Power, "A Problem from Hell," at 49.

18. 1 Trial of the Major War Criminals before the International Military Tribunal for the Trial of German Major War Criminals, Nuremberg, 14 November 1945 – 10 October 1946, at 43–44 (1947), *quoted in* Elizabeth Borgwardt, *Re-examining Nuremberg as a New Deal Institution: Politics, Culture and the Limits of Law in Generating Human Rights Norms*, 23 Berkeley J. International Law 42, 401 (2005).

19. *See* Valentino, Final Solutions, at 177 (64 to 70 percent of world's Jews, and 33 to 43 percent of Jews under German occupation, survived the Holocaust); Piotrowski, Poland's Holocaust, at 305 (90 percent of ethnic Poles survived the Holocaust); Norwood, 2 Strangers and Exiles, at 289–292.

20. *See Charter of the International Military Tribunal, in* 1 Nuremberg Trial Proceedings (1947), http://avalon.law.yale.edu/imt/imtconst.asp.

21. IMT, Judgment: Goering (Sept. 30 and Oct. 1, 1947), http://avalon.yale.edu/judgoeri.htm (conviction for aggression, war crimes, slave labor, and persecution of Jews); *see also* IMT, Judgment: Bormann, *in id.*, http://avalon.yale.edu/judborma.htm (conviction for slave labor program, extermination and plunder in Russia, and extermination of Jews in "greater Germany" and occupied Europe); IMT, Judgment: Rosenberg, *in id.*, http://avalon.yale.edu/judrosen.htm (conviction for aggression, war crimes, extermination of Jews, and atrocities against Soviet and other Eastern European peoples); IMT, Judgment: Ribbentrop, *in id.*, http://avalon.yale.edu/judribb.htm (conviction for aggression, extermination of Jews, and ruthless occupation of conquered territories); IMT, Judgment: Streicher, *in id.*, http://www.yale.edu/lawweb/avalon/ imt/proc/judstrei.htm (conviction for written "incitement to murder and extermination" of Jews).

22. S.C. Res. 138 (1960). *See also* S/4349 (1960).

23. Attorney General of Israel v. Adolf Eichmann, 36 Int'l L. Rep. 5, ¶ 34 (Dist. Ct. Israel 1961).

24. *See id.* at 233. *See also* Jonathan M. Wenig, *Enforcing the Lessons of History: Israel Judges the Holocaust, in* The Law of War Crimes 103 (Timothy McCormack & Gerry J. Simpson eds., Boston: Martinus Nijhoff Publishers, 1997).

man law, or had acted before Israel (1) became a state, (2) acceded to the Genocide Convention, or (3) enacted a Nazi war crimes prosecution law in 1950.[25]

The concept that genocide unlike other crimes is "general and total" has given rise to a continuing debate concerning whether massacres other than the Nazi massacres of the Jews qualify as genocide, or perhaps constitute more ordinary, less "unique," genocides. For example, German historian Eberhard Jaeckel wrote in 1986:

> The Nazi extermination of the Jews was unique because never before had a state, under the responsible authority of its leader, decided and announced that a specific group of human beings, including the old, the women, the children, and the infants, would be killed to the very last one, and implemented this decision with all the means at its disposal.[26]

The biological assumptions and objectives of the campaign, i.e., to cleanse the world's gene pool of Jewish traits, serve as the basis of the best argument for the uniqueness of Nazi crimes against Jews. This biological threat required a more complete massacre than of Slavs or communists.[27]

The uniqueness thesis is overstated, however, when its proponents maintain that only the Jews were ever subjected to an "actualized policy, to annihilate physically every man, woman, and child belonging to a specific people."[28] The overstatement occurs because not all Jews within the power of the Nazis were physically "annihilate[d]," while other groups that fell into the hands of their oppressors were murdered to the last man, woman, or child. Nazi leaders at the highest level, including Hitler, S.S. leader Heinrich Himmler, and Reich Security officer Eichmann both publicly and privately discussed "increased emigration" or "immigration," including, by one estimate, of 537,000 Jews between 1933 and late 1941.[29] For this reason, among others, Jewish victims of genocide between 1933 and 1945 do not constitute "the largest number of victims of any mass crime," even according to uniqueness theorists.[30]

Although 1942 represents, to some authors who have consulted the Nazi official documents, a transition from a policy of "emigration" to one of "evacuation," the two periods are not so easily distinguished. More than four million Jews were internally displaced or crossed international borders as refugees from Nazi rule, a substantial number of them after 1942.[31] The Nazis actively sought out territories that would accept large numbers of

---

25. Attorney General of Israel v. Adolf Eichmann, 36 INT'L L.REP. 277, 283–98 (Sup. Ct. Israel 1962).

26. Eberhard Jaeckel, *Die Elende Praxis der Untersteller*, DIE ZEIT, Sept. 12, 1986, *quoted in* DOMINICK LACAPRA, REPRESENTING THE HOLOCAUST 49 (Ithaca, NY: Cornell UP, 1996).

27. *See* VALENTINO, FINAL SOLUTIONS, at 176–78.

28. Stephen Katz, *The Uniqueness of the Holocaust: The Historical Dimension, in* IS THE HOLOCAUST UNIQUE?, at 49.

29. Protocol of the Wannsee Conference (Secret), *in* THE HOLOCAUST AND OTHER GENOCIDES: HISTORY, REPRESENTATION, ETHICS 38–39 (Helmut Walser Smith ed., Nashville, Tennessee: Vanderbilt UP, 2002).

30. Katz, *The Uniqueness of the Holocaust*, at 49.

31. *See* FREDERICK A. NORWOOD, 2 STRANGERS AND EXILES: A HISTORY OF RELIGIOUS REFUGEES 314–16, 337–344 (Nashville and New York: Abingdon Press, 1969); ALFRED J. RIEBER, FORCED MIGRATION IN CENTRAL AND EASTERN EUROPE, 1939–1950, at 11–17 (London: Routledge, 2000); MICHAEL SHERMER & ALEX GROBMAN, DENYING HISTORY: WHO SAYS THE HOLOCAUST NEVER HAPPENED AND WHY DO THEY SAY IT? 174 (2000). For example, S.S. officials allowed about 1,200 Jews to be saved by Oskar Schindler, a German industrialist who moved them to his munitions factory in Brněnec-Bruennlitz, in Nazi-occupied Czechoslovakia. *See Former Secretary of Oskar Schindler Immigrates to Israel,* DEUTSCHE PRESSE AGENTUR, Dec. 14, 2007; *Oskar Schindler, Saved 1,200 Jews,* N.Y. TIMES, Oct. 13, 1974.

Jews, from Eastern Europe to Siberia and Palestine to Madagascar.[32] Millions of Polish Jews survived for more than a year after the conquest of Poland.[33] As late as December 1941, Himmler had been authorized by Hitler to "resettle Jews from all German-controlled territories into certain Russian areas in the northeast."[34] About 75% of French Jews fled or otherwise survived, as did about a third of German Jews despite Nazi rule from 1933 onwards.[35]

The situation of the half-Jews in Germany also undermines the exclusivity thesis. The Ministry of the Interior estimated that there were 750,000 half-Jews and one-quarter Jews in Germany in 1935. They served in the German armed forces in numbers that were substantial enough for the Interior Ministry to draft an edict in 1939 stating that these partial-Jews would be treated equally to persons of German blood, with the exception of marriage. A directive authorized by Hitler himself in 1940 allowed quarter-Jews to remain in the German armed forces. When Eichmann and certain economic planners proposed in 1941 that all half-Jews and particularly racially "Jewish" quarter-Jews be deported to slave labor or death, Hitler and Göring themselves quashed the effort. Hitler was quoted as stating that "a large number of soldiers who were quarter-Jews would be affected by the new regulations in that their fathers or mothers would now be designated Jews and that that would be very undesirable for morale." The Wannsee Conference of 1942 contemplated the sterilization, but not the murder, of half-Jews. Hitler's opposition was again cited in 1942 to halt measures aimed at half-Jews and quarter-Jews. In early 1944, a period of manpower shortages, Hitler authorized exemptions of half- and quarter-Jews from discriminatory legislation regarding education and employment.[36]

Over the past two decades, it has become more common for politicians and media corporations, perhaps under the influence of the uniqueness thesis, to refer to mass killing by massacres and deprivation of access to food, water, and housing as "ethnic cleansing." This, to paraphrase Martin Shaw, was a concept popularized by perpetrators of genocide, principally Croatians who killed and deported Serbs during World War II.[37] In 1994, a U.N. commission requested to investigate war crimes in the former Yugoslavia reported that "'ethnic cleansing'" was a "relatively new expression" referring to the making of a geographic or political area "ethnically homogenous by using force or intimidation to remove persons of given groups from the area ... carried out by means of [*inter alia*] ... forcible removal, displacement and deportation of civilian population. . . ."[38] Perhaps troubled by the growth of this euphemism, the U.N. General Assembly clarified in 1991 that ethnic cleansing "is a form of genocide."[39] "Cleansing" was, indeed, Hitler's own euphemism for genocide.[40]

---

32. *See* VALENTINO, FINAL SOLUTIONS, at 170–75, 194.

33. *See id.* at 176.

34. *Quoted in* Richard Breitman, *Additional Remarks*, 9 HOLOCAUST AND GENOCIDE STUDIES 128 (1995), *and in* Vahakn Dadrian, *Comparative Aspects of Armenian and Jewish Genocide: A Sociohistorical Perspective, in* IS THE HOLOCAUST UNIQUE? PERSPECTIVES ON COMPARATIVE GENOCIDE 146 (Alan Rosenbaum ed., Boulder, CO: Westview Press, 3d ed. 2009).

35. *See* Dadrian, *Comparative Aspects of Armenian and Jewish Genocide*, at 148.

36. *See* Jeremy Noakes, *The Development of Nazi Policy towards the German-Jewish "Mischlinge" 1933–1945, in* HOLOCAUST: CRITICAL CONCEPTS IN HISTORICAL STUDIES 239–301 (David Cesarani ed., London: Routledge, 2004).

37. SHAW, WHAT IS GENOCIDE?, at 49.

38. Final Report of United Nations Commission of Experts to the Security Council, S/1994/674 (May 27, 1994).

39. SHAW, WHAT IS GENOCIDE?, at 50, 177 (quoting G.A. Res. 47/121 (1992)).

40. M. Cherif Bassiouni, *From Versailles to Rwanda in Seventy-Five Years: The Need to Establish a Permanent International Criminal Court*, 10 HARV. HUM. RTS. J. 11, 21 (1997).

Critics of the uniqueness thesis have argued that if the Holocaust is allowed to obscure other genocides, such as that of the Native Americans or nations decimated by the slave trade, its memory will reinforce barbaric potentialities that exist within the institutions of the modern nation-state.[41] Another criticism is that no event is unique in the sense of being incapable of any comparisons with another event, and that a basic assumption of historiography is that events will be compared.[42] Similarities between Nazi crimes and other genocides include mass shootings, the use of poisons, starvation, rape and torture, slave labor, and the plunder of money, gold, and houses.[43] The percentage of Jews killed, or even of those targeted, is not necessarily higher than in other genocides, such as those of Taino, Beothuk, Herero, Armenians, or Rwandan Tutsi.[44]

Other criticisms of the uniqueness thesis are more fundamental because they go to the heart of what it means to define a crime such as genocide, and to work to prevent it. In order for the international community to have effectively prevented the extermination of Jews, an outbreak of genocide had to be declared upon the outbreak of mass persecutions, *before* the total destruction of the group. Upon the killing of multiple Jews during the *Reichskristallnacht* or "night of broken glass," when many synagogues and cultural sites of Jews were also looted and/or burned, it was time or even past time to condemn and intervene against genocide.[45] This means that genocide should be defined so that a

---

41. *See* Vincent P. Pecora, *Habermas, Enlightenment, and Anti-Semitism, in* PROBING THE LIMITS OF REPRESENTATION: NAZISM AND THE "FINAL SOLUTION" 163 (Saul Friedlander ed., Cambridge, MA: Harvard UP, 1992).

42. *See* Peter Longereich, *Holocaust, in* INTERNATIONAL HANDBOOK OF VIOLENCE RESEARCH 141 (New York: Springer, 2003).

43. *See* IRIS CHANG, THE RAPE OF NANKING: THE FORGOTTEN HOLOCAUST OF WORLD WAR II (New York: Penguin Books, 1997) (drawing comparisons between Japanese imperial massacres of Chinese civilians and the Holocaust); DADRIAN, THE HISTORY OF THE ARMENIAN GENOCIDE, at 394–418 (drawing comparisons between Armenian genocide and the Holocaust); Tigran Matosyan, *Comparative Aspects of the Armenian and Jewish Cases of Genocide, in* THE ARMENIAN GENOCIDE: CULTURAL AND ETHICAL LEGACIES 291–303 (Richard Hovannisian ed., London and New Brunswick, NJ: Transaction Publishers, 2007) (expanding upon Dadrian's findings); David E. Stannard, *Uniqueness as Denial: The Politics of Genocide Scholarship, in* IS THE HOLOCAUST UNIQUE?, at 163–208 (drawing comparisons between massacres of indigenous peoples in the Americas and the Holocaust).

44. *See* VALENTINO, FINAL SOLUTIONS, at 177–78 (between 57 and 67 percent of Jews in Nazi-occupied Europe were killed by Nazis and their allies, compared to about 75 percent of Armenians in Ottoman territory killed, and 75 percent of Rwandan Tutsi population killed); *Herero People, Genocide of, in* DICTIONARY OF GENOCIDE (Samuel Totten et al eds., Westport, CT: Greenwood Publishing Group, 2008) (more than 80 percent of Herero people of present-day Namibia killed after German contact); *Beothuk People, Genocide of, in id.* at 38 (more than 90 percent of Beothuk people of Newfoundland, present-day Canada, perished after British contact, which involved mass violence); JAMES WALLER, BECOMING EVIL: HOW ORDINARY PEOPLE COMMIT GENOCIDE AND MASS KILLING 23 (Oxford: Oxford UP, 2002) (90 percent of Taino of present-day Bahamas, Cuba, Dominican Republic, Haiti, Jamaica, Puerto Rico, and St. Croix perished after Spanish contact, which involved mass violence).

45. *See* Otto Triffterer, *Genocide, Its Particular Intent to Destroy in Whole or in Part the Group as Such*, 14 LEIDEN J. OF INTERNATIONAL LAW 399, 401–2 (2001) (arguing that as of *Kristallnacht*, Hitler regime was "committing crimes later defined in the Genocide Convention 1948 and in the corresponding Article 6 of the Rome Statute [of the ICC], with the particular intent, to destroy the European part of that [Jewish] group, as such.") (brackets added); *id.* at 402. ("[W]hat happened during the 'Reichskristallnacht' 1938, when the first Jews were killed, was completed genocide, because Hitler already at that time intended to finally 'clean' Europe of this group. It therefore would have been the time to stop Hitler committing genocide right away..., for instance, by ... starting criminal ... prosecutions....").

conspiracy to commit it can be identified and prosecuted before a group has been destroyed.[46] Success should *not* be an element of genocide.

Finally, confining genocide to the experience of Jews in the last four years of the Nazi regime is contrary to the language of the Genocide Convention. The Genocide Convention was drafted and signed a few years after the discovery of the death camps at Auschwitz and other locations, and after the prosecution of Nazi officials for the extermination of the Jews. Even so, the Convention defines genocide as certain acts committed with the intent to destroy a group in whole or in part, as a group. Complete destruction, or even that intent, is not an element. The Convention was defined around the Holocaust as an archetypal crime, not a one-time event.

C. Genocide: The Srebrenica Model

Established by the Security Council pursuant to its Chapter VII powers under the U.N. Charter, the International Tribunal for the Prosecution of Persons Responsible for Serious Violations of International Humanitarian Law Committed in the Territory of the former Yugoslavia since 1991 (the "Yugoslav tribunal") has issued important rulings defining the acts and accompanying intent of the crime of genocide.[47] The first genocide conviction arising out of the Yugoslav civil wars was handed down against Radislav Krstić in 2001, almost exactly 50 years after the Genocide Convention entered into force.[48] It addressed events in Bosnia and Herzegovina, particularly the massacre of the mostly military-aged Muslim men of Srebrenica.

The context of the Srebrenica genocide was the dissolution of Yugoslavia after the fall of the Berlin Wall in 1989 and the partition of the Soviet Union starting in 1990.[49] Yugoslavia had begun to reform its economy under International Monetary Fund (IMF) pressure in the 1980s, which led to some of the highest rates of inflation and unemployment in all of Europe.[50] The standard of living for ordinary Yugoslavs took a dive, as inflation reached 200% in 1988.[51] An IMF standby arrangement called for "shock therapy" to be imposed

46. *See id.* at 401–2.

47. *See* Akhavan, *Enforcement of the Genocide Convention.*

48. *See* Edward Wong, *Saddam Charged with Genocide of Kurds*, INT'L HERALD TRIB., Apr. 5, 2006, http://www.iht.com/articles/2006/04/05/frontpage/saddam.php?page=2.

49. *See, e.g.*, Elizabeth Shogren, *Gorbachev Denounces 3 Breakaway Leaders: President Calls Their Efforts to Dissolve the Country 'Illegal and Dangerous,'* L.A. TIMES, Dec. 10, 1991, at A1 (Baltic republics declared independence in March 1990; Russia's president Boris Yeltsin declared the republic's sovereignty in May; and other republics had declared their sovereignty by late 1990); Francis X. Clines, *Ex-Communist Wins in Ukraine; Yeltsin Recognizes Independence*, N.Y. TIMES, Dec. 3, 1991, http://query.nytimes.com/gst/fullpage.html?res=9D0CE4D81039F930A3-5751C1A967958260&sec=&spon=&pagewanted=print.

50. *See* U.S. CIA, *Yugoslavia: Statistical Profile of Yugoslavia, in* COUNTRIES OF THE WORLD (1991), http://www.highbeam.com/doc/1P1-28386917.html.

51. *See* Gayle Reaves, *Fragile Union; Ethnic, Economic Strains May Splinter Yugoslavia*, DALLAS MORNING NEWS, July 2, 1989, http://tinyurl.com/cea5k5 ("Living standards have dropped by about 50 percent since the 1970s."); *Yugoslavia's Government Resigns; Rejection of Economic Plan Brings Down Mikulic Cabinet*, L.A. TIMES. Dec. 31, 1988, at 3–1 (living standards "plummeted" due to inflation, and defense spending accounted for two-thirds of the budget); Paula Butturini, *Yugoslavs Struggle Just to Keep Pace*, CHICAGO TRIBUNE, July 11, 1988, at B3 (inflation rate hit 149%, cutting savings in more than half on annual basis); *Yugoslav Parliament OKs Moves to Ease Crisis*, L.A. TIMES, Oct. 23, 1988, at 1–6 (inflation hit 217% on annual basis).

by the government, and high inflation continued.[52] Unemployment rose to 16% in 1990 from 10% in 1981.[53]

In 1989, Franjo Tudjman helped found the Croatian Democratic Union (*Hrvatska Demokratska Zajednica*), which was backed by Croatian businessmen living abroad and by forces within the Croatian Yugoslav republic. Tudjman was a political commissar who fell from grace due to his denial of the German-Croatian Holocaust of Jews and Slavs in the territory of Yugoslavia during World War II.[54] He viewed the Croats of Yugoslavia as sharing a racial affinity with the Germans and Italians of Central Europe and the Mediterranean, rather than the "eastern peoples" like Slavs or Turks.[55] His ouster from public office in 1960s Yugoslavia came for "publicly defending the creation of the Croatian Nazi puppet state (1941–1945)...."[56]

In 1990, Alija Izetbegović created the Party of Democratic Action (*Stranka Demokratske Akcije* or SDA) for "members of the Muslim cultural-historical sphere."[57] The party called for a multiethnic and democratic Bosnia and Herzegovina, but some Serbs faced with the prospect of becoming minorities in an independent state ruled by Izetbegović were troubled by the fact that he was the author of an "Islamic Declaration," which called for an Ottoman-style empire to rule a "united Islamic Community from Morocco to Indonesia."[58] Yugoslav President Slobodan Milosevic later claimed to have perceived Izetbegovic's political agenda as follows:

> [N]on-Islamic institutions cannot co-exist with Islamic institutions.... The Islamic movement can and shall take over power as soon as its numbers rise to the extent that it cannot only topple the existing non-Islamic government but build an Islamic government. Members of the Islamic faith should learn, using the example of Pakistan, what should be done and what should not be done. Nowadays, the aspiration for all the Islamic communities and all Islam believers in the world should be brought together. This is all aimed at an Islamic Community from Morocco to Indonesia, from Europe to Africa.[59]

Izetbegović proclaimed himself President of Bosnia-Herzegovina in December 1990. The GDP of Bosnia-Herzegovina sank by nearly half through 1991, and inflation was 80% per month.[60]

---

52. *See Yugoslavia, in* World Factbook 1991, http://www.gutenberg.org/dirs/etext92/world91a.txt.

53. *See id.*; *Yugoslavia, in* World Factbook 1981, http://www.archive.org/details/worldfactbook82natiilli.

54. *See* David Bruce MacDonald, Balkan Holocausts? Serbian and Croatian Victim-centred Propaganda and the War in Yugoslavia 100–17, 167–83 (Manchester, UK: Manchester UP, 2002).

55. *Id.* at 117–18.

56. *Croatian President Tudjman Dead at 77*, United Press Int'l, Dec. 13, 1999, http://www.highbeam.com/doc/1G1-58172931.html.

57. Charter [Statutes] of the *Stranka Demokratske Akcije*, *quoted in* Tone Bringa, *The Peaceful Death of Tito and the Violent End of Yugoslavia, in* Death of the Father: An Anthropology of the End of Political Authority 176 (John Borneman ed., Oxford: Berghahn Books, 2004).

58. *Quoted in* Thomas Cushman & Stjepan Gabriel Meštrović, *Introduction, in* This Time We Knew: Western Responses to Genocide in Bosnia 28 (Thomas Cushman & Stjepan Gabriel Meštrović eds., New York: NYU Press, 1996).

59. Opening Statement of Sloboban Milošević, Case No. IT-O2-54-T, Transcript No. 040901IT, at pp. 32277–78 (Sept. 1, 2004), http://www.un.org/icty/transe54/040901IT.htm (purporting to quote the Islamic Declaration).

60. *See Bosnia-Herzegovina, in* World Factbook 1992, http://www.umsl.edu/services/govdocs/wofact92/wf930037.txt.

The government of Turkey, and Turkish militias, took a leading role in attempting to reestablish an Ottoman cultural sphere in the 1990s. As Brian Glyn Williams, a former CIA officer and Professor of Islamic History at the University of Massachusetts-Dartmouth, reported:

> In the early 1990's the Turkish people, who are far from being homogenous (millions of "Turks" are actually of Balkan or Caucasian origin—the result of the ethnic cleansing of their Ottoman-Muslim ancestors by nineteenth century Orthodox Christians), began to rediscover their former *vatans* (homelands). This happened as the Serbs, Armenians, and Russians instigated ethnic wars against the Azerbaijanis, Bosnians, Chechens, and Kosovar Albanians. Thus, as Bosnians were slaughtered by the thousands in Srebrenica by Republika Srbska paramilitaries, so Albanians were massacred in places such as Racak, Kosovo, by Milosevic's security forces, Azeris were cleansed by victorious Armenian forces in Nagorno Karabakh, and Chechens were butchered in such towns as Samaskhi by Russian Federal forces. And in Turkey, moderate secularist-nationalists throughout the country (that is, those Turks who supported the secularist Turkish constitution) began to call for the defense of these *irkdashlar* (ethnic kin).
>
> The images of toppled Ottoman minarets in Bosnia, of mass burials in Kosovo, and of fleeing refugees in the Caucasus also provided a sense of déjà vu for those "Turks" whose ancestors had fled their homes to the Turkish-Anatolian core of the sultan's state in the nineteenth century.... In the process, the ethnic, religious and historical ties that bound these former Ottoman Muslims (collectively known as *Evlad-i Fatih Han*, the descendents of Sultan Mehmet the Conqueror) to those Turks of Balkan and Caucasian ancestry were rediscovered throughout Turkey....
>
> As [veterans of the Afghan *jihad* against the Soviet Union and Afghan communists] traveled to Zenica, Bosnia, to create a volunteer *Jihad* corps to defend the outgunned Bosnians from the Serbs in 1992, the Turkish government turned a blind eye to those Turks who wished to join this "Mujahideen Brigade." Together with Iran, Turkey also sent funds to the *jihadi* volunteers who formed a shock unit—one that was feared by the Serbs for its fanatical ferocity—in the Bosnian conflict of 1992–95....
>
> In a rare convergence of opposing ideologies, the perceived threat to Turkish-Muslim kin groups in the former Ottoman lands united [Turkish political parties]....
>
> The radicalization of Turks engaged in *jihad*, including even those espousing a nationalist platform calling for the defense of kin groups in the Balkans and Caucasus, is evident on such websites and in underground Islamist circles in Turkey....
>
> [A]pproximately 1,000 Turks ... waged *Jihad* in Chechnya and Bosnia....[61]

As Izetbegović mounted a Muslim-led secession of Bosnia and Herzegovina from Yugoslavia, with Turkish and Iranian backing, the Bosnian Croats and Serbs formed their own ethnic nationalist parties. By 1991, Radovan Karadžić had helped found the Serbian Democratic Party (Srpska Demokratska Stranka or SDS), which enjoyed support from within the Yugoslav republic of Serbia.[62] Others formed a Bosnian branch of the Croatian Democratic Union.[63]

---

61. Brian Glyn Williams, *Turkey's Al-Qaeda Blowback*, 2 Terrorism Monitor, issue 8 (May 19, 2005).

62. *See id.*; Bringa, *The Violent End of Yugoslavia*, at 176.

63. *See* MacDonald, Balkan Holocausts, at 223.

On June 25, 1991, Croatia and Slovenia declared their independence from Yugoslavia; the Yugoslav government denounced this action as illegal and unconstitutional.[64] The German Chancellor Helmut Kohl stressed the "absolute right to self-determination" for Croatia, in the paraphrase of *The Washington Post*, and Germany pushed the European Union towards recognizing Slovenian and Croatian independence, as early as July 1991. Serbian observers predicted a "Fourth Reich" uniting East and West Germany, and reaching southeast through Croatia.[65] The French Foreign Ministry warned against a unilateral German recognition of Croatian independence, stating that it would be "prejudicial for Europe as a whole."[66]

In September 1991, the U.N. Security Council adopted sanctions proscribing the sale or transfer of arms to the combatants in Yugoslavia.[67] Nevertheless, German intelligence (the *Bundesnachrichtendienst*) continued to ship arms to its Croatian allies under Tudjman. A study by the U.S. Strategic Studies Institute pointed to several German and Croatian sources, including Tudjman himself, for the statement that prior to the outbreak of full-scale war, German intelligence built up an insurgency to the Yugoslav army by shipping weapons to Croatia "with the knowledge of the Foreign and Defense Ministries."[68] In early 1991, "the Bosnian Minister of the Interior personally started purchasing Kalashnikovs and ammunition in Vienna."[69]

On December 24, 1991, Germany disregarded objections from the U.N. Secretary-General and the U.S. President George H.W. Bush, and recognized Croatian and Slovenian statehood.[70] In doing so, Germany certified that Croatia met three conditions for independence set forth by the European Union: "stable borders, respect for democracy, and protection of minority rights."[71] These requirements are set forth in the U.N. Charter and the Helsinki Final Act, which demand respect for the territorial integrity and political independence of states, as well as equality before the law for national minorities, and their enjoyment of human rights.[72]

64. *See* Viktor Meier, Yugoslavia: A History of Its Demise 177–78 (Sabrina P. Ramet trans., London: Routledge, 1999).

65. Marc Fisher, *Yugoslav Violence Puts Focus on Germany; Bonn's Support for Slovenia, Croatia Draws Comparisons with Expansionist Past*, Wash. Post, July 7, 1991, http://www.highbeam.com/doc/1P2-1073601.html.

66. Stephen Kinzer, *Germans Follow Own Line on Yugoslav Republics*, N.Y. Times, Dec. 8, 1991, http://query.nytimes.com/gst/fullpage.html?res=9E0CE7DF133EF93BA35751C1A967958260.

67. *See* S.C. Res. 713, ¶ 6 (Sept. 25, 1991).

68. Stephen J. Blank, *Yugoslavia's Wars and European Security*, *in* Yugoslavia's Wars: The Problem from Hell 115 (Stephen J. Blank ed., Carlisle Barracks, PA: Strategic Studies Institute, 1995).

69. The Netherlands Institute for War Documentation, Srebrenica—A 'Safe' Area: Reconstruction, Background, Consequences and Analyses of the Fall of a Safe Area (2002), appx. 2, http://srebrenica.brightside.nl/srebrenica/toc/p6_c04_s002_b01.html.

70. The U.N. Secretary-General had been tasked by the U.N. Security Council with assisting the government of Yugoslavia with bringing an end to hostilities with the parties to the rebellion. *See* S.C. Res. 713, ¶¶ 2–3 (1991).

71. *See* Stephen Kinzer, *Slovenia and Croatia Get Bonn's Nod*, N.Y. Times, Dec. 24, 1991, http://query.nytimes.com/gst/fullpage.html?res=9D0CE4D61E3FF937A15751C1A967958260.

72. *See* U.N. Charter, art. II; The Conference on Security and Co-operation in Europe (Helsinki Final Act of 1975), arts. II–VII, signed on 1 August 1975, Austria, Belgium, Bulgaria, Canada, Cyprus, Czechoslovakia, Denmark, Finland, France, the German Democratic Republic, the Federal Republic of Germany, Greece, the Holy See, Hungary, Iceland, Ireland, Italy, Liechtenstein, Luxembourg, Malta, Monaco, the Netherlands, Norway, Poland, Portugal, Romania, San Marino, Spain, Sweden, Switzerland, Turkey, the Union of Soviet Socialist Republics, the United Kingdom, the United States of America and Yugoslavia; Final Report of the United Nations Commission of Experts Established Pursuant

Close inspection reveals that Croatia did not meet the EU's conditions in late 1991. Croatia's borders were hardly "stable," because the Security Council recognized it to be part of Yugoslavia as late as September 25, 1991,[73] and although Croatia aspired to greater autonomy in 1991, the "Serb Republic of Krajina" within Croatia proclaimed its autonomous status in late 1991 as well.[74] Regarding respect for democracy, President Tudjman was democratically elected in 1990, but when Croatian Serbs demanded a referendum similar to the one that elected autonomy-minded Croatian leaders, Tudjman refused.[75] Minority rights in Croatia were brushed aside when Tudjman ordered that Serbs be fired from the police force on the basis of their ethnicity.[76] The Croatian regime fired many Serbs from their jobs and revived "hated symbols" of the World War II Nazi puppet state that massacred more than a million Jews, Serbs, and Roma people.[77] Ethnic cleansing of Serbs and Muslims by the Croatian authorities began in early 1991, targeting the Serbs in the Krajina area and in eastern and western Slavonia for murder, torture, the destruction of Serbian villages, the burning of churches, and deportations.[78]

Throughout 1991, the Croatian military ethnically cleansed Serbs from whole areas by plundering and burning houses in Serbian villages.[79] President Tudjman rendered Croatia's borders even less stable when he sought to annex part of Bosnia and Herzegovina.[80]

---

to Security Council Resolution 780 (1992), S/1994/674/Add.2 (May 27, 1994), http://www.ess.uwe.ac.uk/comexpert/IV.htm.

73. *See* S.C. Res. 713, ¶¶ 1–3.

74. *See* Associated Press, *Serbs Renew Support of UN Peace Plan*, Chicago Trib., Jan. 17, 1992, at 8. *See also* Final Report of the United Nations Commission of Experts Established Pursuant to Security Council Resolution 780 (1992), S/1994/674/Add.2 (May 27, 1994), http://www.ess.uwe.ac.uk/comexpert/IV.htm ("Between September and November 1991, ethnic Croatian regions within BiH formed their own 'Croatian Communities'.... Mate Boban, the leader of Herzegovina's Croats, urged ... the linkage of Croat controlled areas in BiH with Croatia."); Ray Mosely, *Croatian Extremist Spoiling for Wider War*, Chicago Tribune, Oct. 7, 1991.

75. *See* Piotr Eberhardt, Ethnic Groups and Population Changes in Twentieth-century Central-Eastern Europe: History, Data, and Analysis 432 (Jan Owsinski trans., White Plains, NY: M.E. Sharpe, 2003).

76. *See* Blaine Harden, *Knin's Imaginary War Reflects Yugoslavia's Woes; Serbian Enclave in Croatia Could Be at Center of Split if Federation Comes Unglued*, Wash. Post, Sept. 16, 1990, at A20.

77. Blaine Harden, *Yugoslav Truce Pact Called Vague, Complicated, Fragile; Serbian Reluctance to Sign. Underscores Accord's Weakness*, Wash. Post, Sept. 3, 1991, http://www.highbeam.com/doc/1P2-1083010.html; *Croatian President Tudjman Dead at 77*.

78. Final Report of the United Nations Commission of Experts Established Pursuant to Security Council Resolution 780 (1992), S/1994/674/Add.2 (May 27, 1994), http://www.ess.uwe.ac.uk/comexpert/IV.htm.

79. *See Yugoslav Forces Strike Karlovac From the Air*, N.Y. Times, Dec. 30, 1991, http://query.nytimes.com/gst/fullpage.html?res=9D0CEEDE153BF933A05751C1A967958260.

80. *See id.* (leader of Croatian Democratic Union, Tudjman's party, sought to unite Croatian areas of Bosnia and Herzegovina with Croatia proper); Ray Mosely, *Croatian Extremist Spoiling for Wider War*, Chicago Tribune, Oct. 7, 1991, http://pqasb.pqarchiver.com/chicagotribune/access/24504900.xml?dids=24504900:24504900&FMT=ABS&FMTS=ABS:FT&type=current&date=Oct+07%2C+1991&author=Ray+Moseley%2C+Chicago+Tribune.&pub=Chicago+Tribune+(pre-1997+Fulltext)&desc=Croatian+extremist+spoiling+for+wider+war&pqatl=google ("Dobroslav Paraga is the head of the Croatian Party of Rights, an extremist group which is waging its own private war in Yugoslavia to create a 'Greater Croatia'...."); Carol J. Williams, *Croats Joining Bosnians in Battle Against Serbs Balkans*, L.A. Times, June 18, 1992, at A4 ("Throughout the predominantly Croatian regions of western Herzegovina, ... armored troop transports with Croatia's HV [or Croatian Democratic Union] markings rumble along the rocky, sun-scorched roads and armed irregulars who answer to a Zagreb-based nationalist warlord fill the cafes and man the roadblocks.); *id.*

Bosnia and Herzegovina declared its independence on March 1, 1992.[81] Croatia established an arms pipeline from Iran to the Bosnian insurgency against Yugoslavia.[82] By mid-1992, about "4,000 Mujahedin, supported by Iranian special operations forces," started infiltrating Bosnia from Albania, Afghanistan, Chechnya, the Gulf Arab states, North Africa, and South Asia.[83] In June 1992, Turkey convened a meeting of the Organisation of Islamic Conference in Istanbul at which the Bosnian foreign minister claimed that over 40,000 had died in fighting since the previous year, and that thousands more were threatened with starvation.[84] Turkey opened multiple arms shipments routes into Croatia and Bosnia via Cyprus and other airfields, using NATO-grade C-130 and Hercules aircraft.[85] The arms shipments to the Bosnian rebels through the Turkish pipeline occurred on a scale that was truly staggering. Turkey and Iran arranged for the shipment to Bosnian and Croatian terrorists of hundreds of thousands of hand grenades, thousands of automatic rifles, thousands of rockets and landmines, and millions of rounds of ammunition.[86]

In August 1992, Iran and other members of the Organisation of the Islamic Conference "advocated the use of force against the Serbian forces in compliance with Article 42 of the United Nations Charter, and the lifting of the [Security Council's] arms embargo against Bosnia-Herzegovina."[87] Soon thereafter, Izetbegović endorsed Iran's call "for [an] Islamic army to fight Serbs," and visited Pakistan to seek aid and support.[88] Iran and Pakistan shipped large quantities of weapons and "mujahideen" to the Bosnian Muslims though Sudan's airports.[89]

Yugoslavia attempted to restore federal control over the areas occupied by Bosnian and Croatian militias. In April 1992, as the European Community prepared to recognize the independence of Bosnia and Herzegovina, the Bosnian Serb Army began the siege of Sarajevo, where between 25,000 and 70,000 Bosnian Muslim fighters were camped. By late 1994 about 10,000 people had died in the siege, or about eight per day, along with 44 wounded per day. The U.N. Children's Fund (UNICEF) estimated that 39 percent of children in the city had seen one or more family members killed, and that 19 per cent had

("U.N. Secretary General Boutros Boutros-Ghali has ... demanded that all Croatian troops return to Croatia.").

81. *See* Final Report of the United Nations Commission of Experts, S/1994/674/Add.2.

82. John Pomfret & David B. Ottaway, *U.S. Allies Fed Pipeline of Covert Arms to Bosnia*, Wash. Post, May 12, 1996, http://www.highbeam.com/doc/1P2-784643.html (President Izetbegovic reached an accord with Iran in 1992 "to open a weapons supply route to the Muslim-led government in Sarajevo through neighboring Croatia."); *id.* (Croatia's ambassador to Iran "worked out the details of the weapons pipeline along with Omer Behmen, Bosnia's ambassador to Iran, and Hasan Cengic, ... who [later became] Bosnia's deputy minister of defense.").

83. Lt. Col. John Sray, Selling the Bosnian Myth to America: Buyer Beware (Fort Leavenworth, KS: Foreign Military Studies Office, 1995), http://leav-www.army.mil/fmso/documents/bosnia2.htm.

84. *See* Center for Post-Soviet and East European Studies, *Yugoslavia Events Chronology, Jan.–June 1992* (2008), http://www.uta.edu/cpsees/yec-192.txt.

85. *See* Netherlands Institute for War Documentation, *Final Report on "Srebrenica, a 'safe' area—Reconstruction, background, consequences and analyses of the fall of a safe area"* (2002), *quoted in* Cees Wiebes, Intelligence and the War in Bosnia, 1992–1995, at 196 (Munster: LIT Verlag, 2003).

86. *Id.* at 196–97.

87. Sir Russell Johnston, The Yugoslav Conflict—Chronology of Events from 30th May 1991–8th November 1993, A/WEU/DEF (93) 14 (Nov. 29, 1993), http://ftp.funet.fi/pub/doc/world/A-WEU/Documents/yugoslavia-conflict.

88. *Id.*, http://www.uta.edu/cpsees/yec-292.txt.

89. See Millard Burr & Robert O. Collins, Revolutionary Sudan: Hasan al-Turabi and the Islamist State, 1989–2000, at 142–43 (Leiden, the Netherlands: Brill, 2003).

witnessed a massacre. Snipers targeted children, including infants. Bosnian Serb forces possessed about 1,000 artillery pieces and other heavy weapons, and they shelled the city indiscriminately, with between 300 and 3,800 shells hitting the city each day. Bosnian Serb artillery destroyed about 35,000 dwellings and 10,000 apartments, damaged 100,000 apartments, and launched shells at almost all mosques and multiple hospitals, ambulances, government buildings, libraries, telecommunications buildings and towers, electrical infrastructure, and factories. Humanitarian aid was often blocked, contributing to malnutrition at poor country levels, although the U.N. was able to carry out an airlift of humanitarian supplies for 467 days, the longest airlift in history.[90]

On May 24, 1992, U.S. Secretary of State James Baker announced a U.S. effort to persuade the U.N. Security Council to impose similar sanctions on Yugoslavia as those that afflicted Iraq since 1990. Secretary of State Baker argued that Yugoslavia's "'cleansing' and 'ethnic purifications' in trying to force Muslims and Croats" to leave Bosnia and Herzegovina were comparable to the policies of the Nazis. Within a week, Turkey's President Turgut Ozal, offered troops for a NATO force to intervene in Bosnia and Herzegovina.[91]

In late 1992, the Security Council "strongly condemn[ed] ... the unacceptable practice of 'ethnic cleansing.'"[92] The U.N. Human Rights Committee blamed the federal government of Yugoslavia of being responsible for failing to restrain Serbian nationalist militia that sought "to displace or eliminate Muslims, Croats or other nationalities and thus constitute ethnically homogeneous areas." The Committee's Special Rapporteur and various NGOs had documented widespread attacks on populated areas including Sarajevo, Dubrovnik and Vukovar, as well as summary executions, mass arrests, forced disappearances, rape, torture, and plunder by "Serbian nationalists" in Croatia and in Bosnia and Herzegovina. Camps had been established for detainees in which "thousands of civilians, women, children and elderly people [were held] in conditions unworthy of the respect due to the human person."[93]

In December 1992, the U.N. General Assembly condemned ethnic cleansing as a "form of genocide." It reiterated this conclusion on an annual basis between 1992 and 1996.[94] The U.N. Special Rapporteur on executions without trial also referred to ethnic cleansing as a mere euphemism used by perpetrators and their apologists for genocide.[95]

In April 1993, the U.N. declared Srebrenica, along with Žepa and Gorazde, as "safe havens" or protected enclaves under the watchful eye of U.N. peacekeepers.[96] Thousands of Muslim refugees sought out Srebrenica, increasing its population to more than 50,000.[97] Prior to May, Serbian and Muslim militia fought for control of the area, until Srebrenica was nearly surrounded by Bosnian Serb militia, while the Army of Bosnia and Herzegovina controlled the enclave itself. A relatively small force of lightly armed U.N. peace-

---

90. S/1994/674, Annex VI, ¶¶ 136–200.

91. Center for Post-Soviet and East European Studies, *Yugoslavia Events Chronology, Jan.–June 1992* (2008), http://www.uta.edu/cpsees/yec-192.txt.

92. G.A. Res. 47/80 (1992).

93. U.N. Human Rights Committee, Comments on the Federal Republic of Yugoslavia, U.N. Doc. CCPR/C/79/Add.16 (1992),

94. *See* U.N. Doc. A/RES/47/121 (Dec. 18, 1992); U.N. Doc. A/RES/48/153 (Dec. 20, 1993); U.N. Doc. A/RES/49/205 (Dec. 23, 1994); U.N. Doc. A/RES/50/192 (Dec. 22, 1995); U.N. Doc. A/RES/51/115 (Dec. 12, 1996); *Bosnia and Herzegovina, in* ENCYCLOPEDIA OF GENOCIDE AND CRIMES AGAINST HUMANITY, at 1076.

95. *See* U.N. Doc. No. A/51/457 (Dec. 28, 1999), http://www.un.org/documents/ga/docs/51/plenary/a51-457.htm.

96. *See* S.C. Res. 819 (Apr. 16, 1993); S.C. Res. No. 824 (Apr. 16, 1993); Prosecutor v. Krstić, Appeals Chamber, Judgement, at ¶¶ 15–16 & n.29.

97. *See* Prosecutor v. Krstić, Appeals Chamber, Judgement, at ¶ 15 & n.26.

Image 1 Srebrenica in Its Regional Context

keepers entered the safe haven, but was prevented by the Serbian militia from freely traveling into and out of it. The 28th Division of the Army of Bosnia Herzegovina, made up of between 5,000 and 12,000 armed men, "remained in the enclave" in violation of the safe haven agreement with the U.N. According to a phrase that is sometimes bandied about with regard to the war in Iraq, the Army of Bosnia and Herzegovina used the civilians in the safe haven as a "human shield," by continuing to deploy throughout the safe haven, fire on Serbian people from within it, and arm and equip itself inside of it, including by stealing international humanitarian aid from civilians.[98]

On May 24, 1993, the Security Council expressed its "grave alarm at continuing reports of widespread and flagrant violations of international humanitarian law" in Yugoslavia, and in Bosnia and Herzegovina in particular, including "reports of mass killings, massive, organized and systematic detention and rape of women, and the continuance of the practice of 'ethnic cleansing', including for the acquisition and the holding of territory." It urged a Commission of Experts that it had convened to investigate war crimes in the former Yugoslavia to report findings back to the Council. The Council established, without prejudice to the right to obtain civil reparations for injuries, an international criminal tribunal to try and convict persons responsible for war crimes in Yugoslavia from 1991 until the end of the war.[99]

Starting in April 1994, a new wave of arms arrived in Bosnia and Herzegovina, paid for by Saudi Arabia, Iran, and Turkey. About 20 Stinger anti-aircraft missiles, dozens of

98. *See* Prosecutor v. Krstić, Trial Chamber, Judgement, at ¶¶ 6–24.
99. S.C. Res. 827 (May 25, 1993).

wire-guided anti-tank missiles of Soviet or Chinese design, and 20,000 AK-47 assault rifles, were included in the shipments. Yugoslav territory became the largest arms market anywhere.[100] By August 1994, 20 planeloads of arms arrived from Iran for Bosnian and Croatian rebels.[101] The next summer, European nations expressed alarm that the U.S. was "orchestrating arms shipments to Bosnia by allies in the Muslim world."[102] Russia, in turn, helped arm Yugoslavia.[103]

In late 1994, Croatian and Bosnian Muslim assaults on Serbian civilians intensified. The U.N. force in Yugoslavia issued a report "accus[ing] the Croat army of having wreaked 'systematic and planned destruction' in September" of majority Serb villages.[104] The report of the Commission of Experts discussed above found that by early 1994, the governments, army, and militia of Croatia and Bosnia and Herzegovina operated between 170 and 478 detention camps throughout Yugoslavia.[105] Conditions in these camps led to widespread death of Serbs:

> Bosnian Government camps are reported to have been the site of cases of grave breaches of the Geneva Conventions. These allegations include killing and torture of Croatian and Serbian prisoners....
>
> The Bosnian-Croat and Croatian Defence Council camps were in Herzegovina. The Croatian Government and Croatian Army operated camps were in the Krajina area, in eastern and western Slavonia and in other parts of Croatia. Grave breaches of the Geneva Conventions have occurred in these facilities against Serbs and Bosnian Muslims, including killing, torture and rape.... [K]illings and torture [were] inflicted on the interned population.... The largest number of violations reported are in the Krajina and eastern and western Slavonia against Serbs and in Herzegovina by Bosnian Croats and the Croatian Defence Council against Bosnian Muslims.

The Bosnian and Croatian rebels adopted such military tactics as the "indiscriminate detention of civilians," their holding as hostages and human shields, their subjection to murders (which were "not uncommon"), "death camps," beatings and torture, and organized rape. The U.N. found some 44 mass graves in Croatia, and 19 throughout Yugoslavia contained the bodies of at least some Serbs. The U.N. viewed conditions in Serb-run detention camps as even more abusive, and even more mass graves containing Muslims and Croats were found.[106]

In March 1995, Radovan Karadžić, by that time regarded by many Serbs as President of the Bosnian Serb Republic (*Republika Srpska*), issued an order called Directive 7. The di-

---

100. *See* Maud S. Beelman, *In Bosnia, Arms Embargo Looks Like a Sieve*, ASSOCIATED PRESS/THE DAILY COURIER, July 31, 1994, at A12.

101. *See Iran Uses Russian Planes to Supply Bosnian Muslim, Croatian Troops*, WASH. TIMES, Aug. 2, 1994, http://www.washingtontimes.com (between May and September 1994, "30 shipments of Iranian-financed weapons [were] flown to Muslim Bosnian and Croatian troops ... in violation of the U.N. arms embargo.").

102. William Drozdiak, *U.S. Accused of Covert Bosnia Aid*, CHICAGO TRIBUNE, July 28, 1995, at A24.

103. *See, e.g.*, BURR & COLLINS, REVOLUTIONARY SUDAN, at 142; Peter Galuszka, *Listen—Take 20 Migs and I'll Throw in Some AKs*', BUSINESSWEEK, June 13, 1994, http://www.businessweek.com/archives/1994/b337661.arc.htm.

104. Johnston, *The Yugoslav Conflict*.

105. *See* Final Report of United Nations Commission of Experts, http://www.ess.uwe.ac.uk/com expert/IV_E-V.htm.

106. S/1994/674, Annex VIII, ¶¶ 245–60.

rective called for the Bosnian Serb Army to set the stage for a cease-fire by liquidating Muslim resistance in the Srebrenica area. Through "combat operations" and limitations on the entry of international humanitarian aid, the Serb forces were to "create an unbearable situation of total insecurity with no hope of further survival or life for the inhabitants of Srebrenica." By July, Bosnian Muslim civilians in Srebrenica were dying of starvation.[107]

Prompted by a Bosnian Muslim attack on a Serb village in which several people were killed and several houses were burned, the Bosnian Serb Army launched operation Krivaja 95. The operation was intended to, by "active combat operations," restrict "the Srebrenica enclave to its urban area."[108] Depleted by the Serb blockade and lacking a clear mandate, U.N. peacekeepers retreated from Bosnian Serb Army attacks. The Army of Bosnia and Herzegovina fell back into urban Srebrenica. NATO bombed the Bosnian Serb Army's tanks and artillery, but ceased fire after threats were issued that Dutch peacekeepers held captive would be executed. Thousands of civilians fled.[109]

Reinforcements from the Army of Bosnia and Herzegovina were called for but never arrived, as the defense of Sarajevo had always been a higher priority:

> The Bosnian army (ABiH) followed a deliberate strategy of using limited military actions to tie up a relatively large part of the manpower of the Bosnian Serbian army (VRS) to prevent it from heading in full force for the main area around Sarajevo. This was also done from the Srebrenica enclave. ABiH troops had no qualms about breaking all the rules in skirmishes with the VRS. They provoked fire by the Bosnian Serbs and then sought cover with a [U.N.] unit which then ran the risk of being caught [in a crossfire].[110]

On the evening of July 11, 1995, a massed force from the Army of Bosnia and Herzegovina attempted to break out of the Srebrenica enclave to reach Tuzla. Mass murder of male refugees from the Srebrenica safe haven followed, as the Bosnian Serb Army failed to discriminate between combatants and civilians, or to set up prisoner-of-war camps, or to provide food or drink to the detainees.[111] Near the former U.N. compound at Potocari, Bosnian Serbs massacred between 20 and 100 Bosnian Muslims, raped Muslim women, and burned down Muslim houses. The remaining Muslim women, children and the elderly were placed on buses to be sent away from the enclave.[112]

A column of men from the Srebrenica safe haven, including many members of the 28th Division of the Army of Bosnia and Herzegovina, broke through to Bosnian Muslim territory, from where a force from the Army of Bosnia and Herzegovina attacked and broke through. The Muslim men captured at Srebrenica or trying to escape "were slaughtered in carefully orchestrated mass executions, commencing on 13 July 1995, in the region just north of Srebrenica." On nearby "killing fields, the men were taken off the trucks in small groups, lined up and shot." At a warehouse, nearly 1,500 Bosnian Muslim men were crowded together, when Bosnian Serb troops "started throwing grenades and shoot-

---

107. Prosecutor v. Krstić, Trial Chamber, Judgement,at ¶ 28 & n.50.

108. Prosecutor v. Blagojevic & Jokic, Case No. IT-02-60-A, Appeals Chamber, Judgement (May 9, 2007), at ¶ 36, http://www.unhcr.org/refworld/publisher,ICTY,,SRB,48ac10ac2,0.html.

109. Prosecutor v. Krstić, Trial Chamber, Judgement, at ¶¶ 30–34.

110. This was one of the findings of the Netherlands Institute for War Documentation, after an inquiry requested by the government of the Netherlands, and conducted with access to its archives. *See* Netherlands Institute for War Documentation, Summary for the Press of Final Report on "Srebrenica, a 'safe' area—Reconstruction, background, consequences and analyses of the fall of a safe area" (2002), http://192.87.107.36/en/a_index.htm.

111. *See id.*

112. *See* Prosecutor v. Krstić, Trial Chamber, Judgement, at ¶ 61.

ing directly into the midst of the men packed inside." A forensic investigation found at least 2,028 separate bodies buried in mass graves. Only one was female, and about 18% were between 13 and 24 years old. There was evidence that at least one massacre began as a reprisal for a revolt by Muslim detainees.[113]

Lists prepared by the Red Cross and other sources indicated that an estimated 7,500 people present in the Srebrenica area in July 1995 were missing and presumed dead. A participant in an intercepted Bosnian Serb Army conversation, however, stated that, "4,000–5,000 have certainly kicked the bucket." The Trial Chamber of the Yugoslav tribunal found that "plunging the Bosnian Muslim residents into a humanitarian crisis was an integral component of the long-term [Bosnian Serb Army] strategy for Srebrenica." The Trial Chamber could not, however, "rule out the possibility that a percentage of the bodies in the gravesites examined may have been of men killed in combat." Mortar shells hit the U.N. compound, although the tribunal's military expert "expressed the view that … there was no evidence that shells were fired directly at civilians" by the Bosnian Serb Army.[114]

The Yugoslav tribunal indicted Major-General Radislav Krstić, the Commander of the 5th (*Drina*) Corps of the Bosnian Serb Army, as the fourth person suspected of being responsible for the events in Srebrenica. He was the first to be convicted after a full trial of culpability for the genocide at Srebrenica. The first two persons to be indicted were Karadžić, the President of the Bosnian Serb Republic, and Ratko Mladić, the former Commander of the Main Staff of the Bosnia Serb Army. The third indictment implicated a Bosnian Serb soldier who admitted doing some of the shooting during the Srebrenica massacres. He pleaded guilty in 1997.[115]

Major-General Krstić's conviction represented the first genocide conviction of a European by an international tribunal since 1946, arguably ever.[116] The Trial Chamber of the Yugoslav tribunal acknowledged that it was "impossible to determine with precision the number of Bosnian Muslim men killed by Bosnian Serb forces" after the fall of Srebrenica, but it concluded that genocide had occurred based on strong evidence that more than 7,000 men had died or gone missing.[117] Major-General Krstić committed genocide because, although he "may not have devised the killing plan" or participated in the decision to kill Srebrenica's adult Bosnian Muslim men, he *must* have "learned of the widespread and systematic killings and became clearly involved in their perpetration." The Trial Chamber concluded that the Bosnian Serb forces acted with the genocidal intent to destroy the Bosnian Muslim group, at least in part, because their killings were not "isolated or random acts." It found genocidal intent based on the killing of a "'considerable' number" of individuals, citing a pretrial ruling in the *Karadžić* case, which stated:

---

113. *See id.* ¶¶ 37–74, 205; Prosecutor v. Krstić, Appeals Chamber, Judgement, partial dissenting op. of Judge Shahabuddeen at ¶ 25.

114. Prosecutor v. Krstić, Trial Chamber, Judgement, at ¶¶ 77–83, 120, 124.

115. *See Statement by Prosecutor—Regarding the Detention of Radislav Krstić*, M2 PRESSWIRE, Dec. 3, 1998 http://www.highbeam.com/doc/1G1-53344800.html; IWPR, *General Krstić Case: Third Srebrenica Indictment; Tribunal Update 104* (1998), http://www.iwpr.net/index.php?apc_state=hen&s=o&o=p=tri&l=EN&s=f&o=167043; Tracy Wilkinson, *Bosnian Serb Is Convicted of War Crimes*, L.A. TIMES, May 8, 1997, at A1; Associated Press, *Serb Soldier Convicted in Hague*, CHICAGO TRIB., June 1, 1996, at 13. *See also* Prosecutor v. Krstić, Trial Chamber, Judgement, at ¶ 234.

116. *A Conviction From the Bosnia Tribunal (Editorial)*, N.Y. TIMES, Nov. 30, 1996, http://query.nytimes.com/gst/fullpage.html?res=9804E7DE153CF933A05752C1A960958260.

117. Prosecutor v. Krstić, Trial Chamber, Judgement, at ¶¶ 80–84.

> [Genocidal intent may be inferred from a] certain number of facts such as the general political doctrine which gave rise to the acts ... or the repetition of destructive and discriminatory acts. The intent may also be inferred from the perpetuation of acts which violate ... the very foundation of the group ... which are committed as part of the same pattern of conduct.[118]

The key fact, according to the Trial Chamber, was that the Bosnian Serb Army extended its campaign from targeting only the military forces of the Army of Bosnia and Herzegovina, to killing *all* Bosnian Muslim men. Because the executions and massacres "systematically targeted Bosnian Muslim men of military age, regardless of whether they were civilians or soldiers," they manifested a genocidal intent.[119] Thus, massacres of military-aged men are genocidal in design.

The Trial Chamber in the *Krstić* case also equated ethnic cleansing with genocide, noting that the U.N. General Assembly had made this connection in 1992. It noted that ethnic cleansing has military advantages, but threatens genocide when implemented in a way that includes systematic killings and creating humanitarian disasters by economic blockade and starvation. The prosecutor had argued that the Rwanda tribunal regarded massacres within a single locality of a country (a "commune") as a form of genocide, and the Yugoslav tribunal agreed:

> [T]he intent to eradicate a group within a limited geographical area such as the region of a country or even a municipality may be characterised as genocide. The United Nations General Assembly characterised as an act of genocide the murder of approximately 800 Palestinians detained at Sabra and Shatila, most of whom were women, children and elderly. The Jelisic Judgement [of the Yugoslav tribunal] held that genocide could target a limited geographic zone.... In a Judgement against Novislav Djajic on 23 May 1997, the Bavarian Appeals Chamber similarly found that acts of genocide were committed in June 1992 though confined within the administrative district of Foca.[120]

The Yugoslav tribunal also concluded that a person can be criminally culpable for complicity in genocide, attempted genocide, or conspiracy to commit genocide.[121] Krstić was convicted by the Trial Chamber for causing the deaths of thousands of the military-aged Muslim men of Srebrenica, even though he did not personally kill the men, or even plan to kill them.[122]

The Appeals Chamber convicted Mr. Krstić of aiding and abetting genocide rather than committing genocide himself, concluding that a "defendant may be convicted for having aided and abetted a crime which requires specific intent even where the principal perpetrators have not been tried or identified."[123] The Appeals Chamber regarded the killing of large numbers of military-aged Bosnian Muslim men "as evidence from which to infer" that Krstić and "had the requisite intent to destroy all the Bosnian Muslims of Srebrenica," because the Trial Chamber could justifiably infer from his participation in the

118. *Id.* ¶¶586 & n.1300, 633, 682 (citing Prosecutor v. Karadžić & Mladić, Review of Indictments Pursuant to Rule 61, Case Nos. IT-95-5-R61 & IT-95-18-R61 (July 11, 1996), at ¶94).

119. Prosecutor v. Krstić, Trial Chamber, Judgement, at ¶¶546–47.

120. *Id.* ¶¶561–589.

121. *See* International Commission of Inquiry on Darfur (ICID), Report to the United Nations Secretary-General Pursuant to Security Council Resolution 1564 of 18 September 2004, ¶520 (Jan. 25, 2005) [hereinafter ICID Report].

122. Prosecutor v. Krstić, Trial Chamber, Judgement, at ¶644.

123. Prosecutor v. Krstić, Appeals Chamber, Judgement, at ¶143.

killing of Bosnian Muslim men that he "shared the genocidal intent of some members of the VRS Main Staff to destroy a substantial part of the targeted group, the Bosnian Muslims of Srebrenica."[124] Thus, it is now clear that a conspiracy to commit genocide may occur even if genocide itself does not ensue on the scale of the Holocaust, for example, but rather on the scale of "substantial" local or regional killing.[125]

Acts other than killing have served as the basis for indictments for genocide before the Yugoslav tribunal. As of early 2004, the Yugoslav tribunal had indicted 13 individuals for genocide by acts of rape, recognizing the effect of rape in disrupting local communities.[126] A U.S. federal appellate court has also held that "brutal acts of rape, forced prostitution, [and] forced impregnation" were "part of a genocidal campaign" in Bosnia and Herzegovina.[127]

Burning or otherwise destroying the homes and public spaces of a deported group is strong evidence of intent to destroy that part of the group that resides within a specific region:

> The Trial Chamber finds that the physical or biological destruction of the group is the likely outcome of a forcible transfer of the population when this transfer is conducted in such a way that the group can no longer reconstitute itself—particularly when it involves the separation of its members. In such cases the Trial Chamber finds that the forcible transfer of individuals could lead to the material destruction of the group, since the group ceases to exist as a group, or at least as the group it was....

Deportation under coercive circumstances conveys a message that an ethnic or religious group has no homes or communities to return to, and deprives families within the group of their utility to the wider group.[128] The Trial Chamber convicted a colonel in the Army of the Republika Srpska for complicity in genocide based on his role in the forcible transfer of Bosnian Muslims from Srebrenica, as an act of serious bodily or mental harm committed with the intent to destroy the Srebrenica Muslims. The Appeals Chamber found insufficient genocidal intent, but held "that the forcible transfer operation, the separations, and the mistreatment and murders in Bratunac town are relevant ... in assessing whether the principal perpetrators had genocidal intent."[129]

In a conviction for crimes against humanity by the Yugoslav tribunal, the court analogized the expropriation of non-Serbian property by the Miloševiç regime to that of Jewish property in World War II. The court explained:

> [T]he finding of the Nürnberg Tribunal characterizing certain acts of economic discrimination as persecution support the conclusion that economic measures of a personal, as opposed to an industrial type, can constitute persecutory acts. The finding in the Eichmann case also supports this conclusion. Count 6 of the indictment against Adolf Eichmann alleged persecution of Jews on na-

124. *Id.* ¶¶ 19, 21.

125. *See* William A. Schabas, The UN International Criminal Tribunals: The Former Yugoslavia, Rwanda and Sierra Leone 137, 181 (2006).

126. Katherine MacKinnon, *Defining Rape Internationally: A Comment on Akayesu*, 44 Colum. J. Transnat'l L. 940, 949 n.41 (2006).

127. Kadic v. Karadžic, 70 F.3d 232, 236–37 (2d Cir. 1995).

128. Prosecutor v. Blagojevic & Jokic, Case No. IT-02-60-T, Trial Chamber, Judgement (Jan. 17, 2005), at §§ 666, 675, http://www.unhcr.org/cgi-bin/texis/vtx/refworld/rwmain?docid=47fdfaf51a.

129. Prosecutor v. Blagojevic & Jokic, Appeals Chamber, Judgement, at ¶¶ 2, 104,123.

tional, racial, religious and political grounds and Count 7 concerned property. He was convicted of crimes against humanity (Counts 5 to 7) for his activities in the Emigration Centres, deportations and the "final solution."[130]

Finally, a conspiracy or campaign to destroy the cultural or spiritual characteristics of a group, for example by destroying their sacred monuments, was regarded by the Trial Chamber of the Yugoslav as evidence of genocidal intent. The Trial Chamber stated:

> The Trial Chamber ... points out that where there is physical or biological destruction there are often simultaneous attacks on the cultural and religious property and symbols of the targeted group as well, [these are] attacks which may legitimately be considered as evidence of an intent to physically destroy the group. In this case, the Trial Chamber will thus take into account as evidence of intent to destroy the group the deliberate destruction of mosques and houses belonging to members of the group.[131]

For these reasons, a key organizing principle of the Srebrenica model of genocide is that it requires neither the complete destruction of a group nor the intent to annihilate a group completely, but simply an intent to destroy a "considerable" or "substantial" number, or geographical subsection, of an ethnic, religious, or national group.[132] As the Yugoslav tribunal concluded in the *Milošević* case itself, genocidal intent may be inferred from evidence of "'the general context, the perpetration of other culpable acts systematically directed against the same group, the scale of atrocities committed, the systematic targeting of victims on account of their membership of a particular group, or the repetition of destructive and discriminatory acts.'"[133] It was no defense that the Bosnian Serb Army spared children or the elderly, or that many (up to 3,000) wounded and apparently healthy military-age Muslim men were let go after a truce with Bosnia.[134] The tribunal went even further, and stated: "The degree to which the group was destroyed in whole or in part is not necessary to conclude that genocide has occurred. That one of the acts enumerated in the definition was perpetrated with a specific intent suffices."[135] As the Appeals Chamber ruled in finding that declarations of hatred against Muslims by a man who had killed about 80 of them justified a finding of genocidal intent, a further "plan or policy" to kill an entire group on Holocaust levels is not necessary to be shown under the Genocide Convention.[136]

---

130. Prosecutor v. Tadic, Case No. IT-94-1, Trial Chamber, Judgement (May 7, 1997), at ¶707, http://www.un.org/icty/tadic/trialc2/jugement-e/tad-tj970507e.htm.

131. Prosecutor v. Krstić, Trial Chamber, Judgement, at ¶580.

132. Prosecutor v. Milošević (Kosovo, Croatia, and Bosnia), Case No. IT-02-54-T, Trial Chamber, Decision on Motion for Judgement of Acquittal (June 16, 2004), at ¶128. *See also* Prosecutor v. Krnojelac, Case No.: IT-97-25-A, Appeals Chamber, Judgement (Sept. 17, 2003), http://www.un.org/icty/krnojelac/appeal/judgement/krn-aj030917e.htm; Prosecutor v. Jelisić, Case No. IT-95-10-A, Appeals Chamber, Judgement, at ¶¶64–71 (July 5, 2001), http://www.un.org/icty/Supplement/supp26-e/jelisic.htm (upholding prosecution appeal of acquittal of Serb on genocide charge where evidence supported an "intent to kill the majority of Muslims in [one town]").

133. Prosecutor v. Milošević, Trial Chamber, Decision on Motion for Acquittal, at ¶120 (quoting Prosecutor v. Jelisić, Appeals Chamber, Judgement, at ¶47).

134. *See* Prosecutor v. Krstić, Trial Chamber, Judgement, at ¶593.

135. Prosecutor v. Radovan Karadzić and Ratko Mladić, Review of the Indictments Pursuant to Rule 61 of the Rules of Procedure and Evidence, Case Nos. IT-95-5-R61 and IT-95-18-R61 (July 11, 1996), at ¶92.

136. Prosecutor v. Jelisić, Case No. IT-95-10-A, Appeals Chamber, Judgement, at ¶¶64–68.

D. Genocide: The Rwanda Model

Under German and then Belgian colonial rule in the first half of the twentieth century, the majority Hutus of present-day Rwanda were oppressed and marginalized, as higher-caste neighbors called Tutsis enjoyed greater wealth and political power.[137] Rwanda gained its independence in 1962.[138] The same year, Rwanda-Urundi, which later changed its name to Burundi, claimed independence from Belgium. After a coup in 1966 by Tutsi Prime Minister Michel Micombero, Hutu insurgents attacked government targets, and the military and allied militia killed about 200,000 Hutus in Burundi.[139] In the lead-up to the Rwandan genocide, massacres of Hutu by Tutsi and vice versa in Burundi killed up to 50,000 people.[140]

In the early 1990s, Rwanda was one of the poorest countries in Africa, but was "flooded with weapons," with a grenade costing less than a six-pack of beer.[141] Meanwhile, the economy entered a tailspin as coffee, a main export between 1989 and 1993, plunged in value by half. Inflation caused Rwandans' life savings to lose most of their value, and the poverty rate doubled to 30 percent.[142] Based on the standards of developed, industrialized nations, the country was poor, with a GDP per capita of only $300 in 1990.[143] As the prices of imported finished goods soared, the IMF froze the prices of coffee as a raw material, causing young men to become impoverished and radicalized. The economic crisis was taken advantage of by tiny elites with agendas of securing power.[144]

Starting in 1990, the Rwandan Patriotic Front (RPF) invaded from bases in Uganda, with the aim of taking power in Rwanda. The RPF arrived from Uganda with large

---

137. *See* Valentino, Final Solutions, at 178; Ellen Messer, Marc J. Cohen, & Jashinta D'-Costa, Food from Peace: Breaking the Links Between Conflict and Hunger 24 (Washington, DC: International Food Policy Research Institute, 1998) ("In 1899 the German colonial authority imposed Tutsi chiefs in the north and west of the country. After World War I the Belgians defined everyone who owned more than 10 cows as Tutsi [and] kept the Tutsis in power. . . ."). Originally, a Hutu could become a Tutsi by becoming wealthy or powerful, but the introduction of ethnic identity cards in the 1930s hardened identities into caste-like categories. *See* Valentino, Final Solutions, at 178; Human Rights Watch Arms Project, *Arming Rwanda: The Arms Trade and Human Rights Abuses in the Rwandan War* 4 (Jan. 1, 1994), http://www.hrw.org/en/reports/1994/01/01/arming-rwanda.

138. *See* Human Rights Watch Arms Project, *Arming Rwanda: The Arms Trade and Human Rights Abuses in the Rwandan War* 4 (Jan. 1, 1994), http://www.hrw.org/en/reports/1994/01/01/arming-rwanda.

139. *See* U.S. Dep't of State [hereinafter USDOS], Bureau of African Affairs, *Background Note: Burundi* (2000), http://web.archive.org/web/20020606133726/http://www.state.gov/r/pa/ei/bgn/2821.htm; Valentino, Final Solutions, at 183.

140. Human Rights Watch Arms Project, *Arming Rwanda,* at 7.

141. *See id.* at 4.

142. Frances Moore Lappe, Joseph Collin, & Peter Rosset, World Hunger: 12 Myths 21–4 (New York: Grove Press, 2000).

143. *See Rwanda, in* World Factbook 1992, http://www.umsl.edu/services/govdocs/wofact92/wf930206.txt.

144. *See* Gerard Prunier, The Rwanda Crisis: History of a Genocide 364–67 (New York: Columbia UP, 1995) (emphasis omitted); Eric Toussaint, Rwanda *10 Years on: Uncovering the Financiers of the Genocide,* Red Pepper, May 6, 2004, http://www.redpepper.org.uk/May2004/x-May2004-Toussaint.html; Kenneth J. Campbell, Genocide and the Global Village: Social Theory in a Globalizing Age 71–82 (New York: Palgrave Macmillan, 2001). *See also Rwanda, in* World Factbook 1992 ("Weak [coffee] prices since 1986 have caused the economy to contract and per capita GDP to decline. A structural adjustment program with the World Bank began in October 1990.").

numbers of former Uganda troops, who massed in a sports stadium in Uganda 20 kilometers from the Rwandan border. They invaded Rwanda with thousands of Kalashnikov assault rifles, rocket-propelled grenades, large-bore mortars, cannons, landmines, and Katyusha rockets. The commander of the RPF, Paul Kagame, frequently met in Uganda with Ugandan military officers, diplomats, and members of the media. The invasion from Uganda displaced one million Rwandan civilians, whom the RPF repeatedly attacked in camps and hospitals for the displaced, and by spraying mortar fire on Rwandan towns and national parks. The RPF summarily executed hundreds of Rwandans, deported possibly thousands of people to Uganda, and stole property and cattle from Hutus. It placed Belgian landmines on roads up to 150 kilometers from the front lines, indiscriminately killing Rwandan civilians as a result. The insurgency prompted ethnically-targeted reprisals against Tutsi civilians, hundreds of whom were killed in 1993.[145]

Several massacres of Hutu civilians by RPF occurred as well. Catholic priests from various parishes "estimate[d] that up to 200 civilians were extrajudicially executed by the RPF in their areas alone."[146] Rwandan Hutu leaders evoked the Burundi massacres of Hutu in 1972.[147] More than 650,000 people fled massacres of hundreds of people in 1993. Human Rights Watch condemned the Rwandan army and the RPF for "frequent incidents of indiscriminate attacks in known civilian areas as well as direct attacks on civilians"[148]

On October 5, 1993, the Security Council authorized a peacekeeping force to be called the U.N. Assistance Mission in Rwanda (UNAMIR). The force was to grow to 2,500 troops by 1994, with a mandate of monitoring a cease-fire and demilitarized zone, protecting the capital, Kigali, and reporting on the activities of the police and gendarmerie of Rwanda.[149]

On May 17, 1994, the U.N. Security Council confirmed that entire ethnic groups were being fully or partially destroyed in Rwanda, and implemented a resolution intended to prevent the sale or supply of arms to Rwanda.[150] Nevertheless, France may have violated the embargo in May and June 1994 in an attempt to prevent the pro-British RPF from gaining power.[151] France had previously supplied advisers and technical assistance directly to Rwandan army units, as well as arms.[152] China exported double the normal amount of machetes and other farm implements to Rwanda, fully 600,000 in the two years leading up to the Rwandan genocide.[153]

---

145. Human Rights Watch Arms Project, *Arming Rwanda*, at 4, 15–16, 26–30.

146. *Id.* at 11–13.

147. *See* VALENTINO, FINAL SOLUTIONS, at 183.

148. Human Rights Watch Arms Project, *Arming Rwanda*, at 10, 12, 26; Roméo Dallaire, & Kishan Manocha, *The Major Powers and the Genocide in Rwanda, in* THE CRIMINAL LAW OF GENOCIDE: INTERNATIONAL, COMPARATIVE, AND CONTEXTUAL ASPECTS 61–64, 70–71 (Ralph Henham and Paul Behrens eds., Hampshire, England, UK: Ashgate. 2007); JACQUES SEMELIN, PURIFY AND DESTROY: THE POLITICAL USES OF MASSACRE AND GENOCIDE 179, 409 (New York: Columbia UP, 2009).

149. *See* VALENTINO, FINAL SOLUTIONS, at 35; Human Rights Watch Arms Project, *Arming Rwanda*, at 30–36.

150. *See* S.C. Res. 918 (May 17, 1994).

151. *See* Roméo Dallaire & Kishan Manocha, *The Major Powers and the Genocide in Rwanda, in* THE CRIMINAL LAW OF GENOCIDE: INTERNATIONAL, COMPARATIVE, AND CONTEXTUAL ASPECTS 61–64, 70–71 (Ralph Henham and Paul Behrens eds., Hampshire, UK: Ashgate, 2007).

152. *See* Dallaire & Manocha, *The Major Powers and the Genocide in Rwanda*, at 61–64, 70–71; Linda Melvern, *The West Did Intervene in Rwanda, on the Wrong Side*, THE GUARDIAN (U.K.), Apr. 5, 2004, http://www.guardian.co.uk/world/2004/apr/05/rwanda.comment.

153. *See* JACQUES SEMELIN, PURIFY AND DESTROY: THE POLITICAL USES OF MASSACRE AND GENOCIDE 179, 409 (New York: Columbia UP, 2009).

As part of his guilty plea in the Rwanda tribunal, Rwandan Prime Minister Jean Kambanda acknowledged leading "a widespread and systematic attack against the civilian population of Tutsi, the purpose of which was to exterminate them." The attack was carried out by mass killings of Tutsi civilians, including children, in government offices, schools, churches, and sports stadiums. As prime minister, Kambanda controlled the machinery of state, and participating in the firing of a government official of a government official who opposed the Tutsi massacres, and in the appointment of a new official "to ensure the spread of massacre[s]."

He recounted a security meeting in April 1994 between himself, the president of Rwanda, and the chief of staff of the Rwandan Armed Forces, at which measures against the RPF were planned. On May 25, 1994, Kambanda issued the Directive on Civil Defence, Directive No. 024-0273, disseminated on 8 June 1994, which encouraged and abetted pro-government militia (*Interahamwe* or "those who stand/work/fight together") massacres of Tutsi civilians. He admitted that the political party *Mouvement républicain national pour la démocratie et le développement* formed the *Interahamwe* militia through the military training of young loyalists. The Rwandan Armed Forces aided in this training, and the government distributed arms to the militia. Kambanda allowed the distribution of weapons and ammunition to militias and Hutu mobs "knowing that these weapons would be used in the perpetration of massacres of civilian Tutsi," and even visited local areas "to incite and encourage the population to commit these massacres including by congratulating the people who had committed these killings."[154] The Rwandan Armed Forces and allied militias massacred between 800,000 and more than one million Rwandans, largely ethnic Tutsi civilians, often with machetes and farm implements.[155]

The International Criminal Tribunal for Rwanda helped define the crime of genocide in the context of a complex ethnic struggle. In the first genocide conviction by an international tribunal under the Genocide Convention,[156] the International Criminal Tribunal for Rwanda concluded that genocide had taken place in Rwanda "[e]ven though the number of victims is yet to be known with accuracy." The tribunal based its conclusion on "the fact that widespread killings were perpetrated throughout Rwanda in 1994." It also cited witness accounts and second-hand reports of "heaps of bodies," the gruesome manner of killings, and the presence of "many wounded persons." The tribunal declared that given this evidence of the "undeniable scale," "systematic nature," and "atrociousness" of the murderous acts, it could say they were "committed with the intent to destroy, in whole or in part, a particular group targeted as such."[157]

Under the Rwanda model of genocide, a perpetrator need not have confessed to an intention to exterminate a group in order to have committed the crime of genocide under the Genocide Convention. Genocidal intent may be inferred, according to the tribunal, from an environment of persecution, and systematic killings of group members. The intent to exterminate the Tutsi group in certain areas of Rwanda was inferred from the

154. Prosecutor v Jean Kambanda, Case No. ICTR 97–23–S, Trial Chamber, Judgement (Sept. 4, 1998), http://www.un.org/ictr/english/judgements/kambanda.html, *aff'd by* Case No. ICTR 97-23-A, Appeals Chamber, Judgement (Oct. 19, 2000), http://69.94.11.53/ENGLISH/cases/Kambanda/judgement/191000.htm.

155. *See* Dallaire & Manocha, *The Major Powers and the Genocide in Rwanda,* at 61–64, 70–71.

156. Wong, *Saddam Charged*, at 2.

157. Prosecutor v. Jean-Paul Akayesu, Case No. ICTR-96-4-t, Trial Chamber, Judgement (Sept. 2, 1998), at § 3, http://www.un.org/ictr/english/judgements/akayesu.

"massive and/or systematic nature" of the killings.[158] The "systematic expulsion from homes" of the victim group also qualified as the "deliberate inflicting on the group conditions of life calculated to bring about its physical destruction, in whole or part" under the Genocide Convention.[159]

Like the Yugoslav tribunal, the Rwanda tribunal clarified that the crime of genocide does not require even the attempt to destroy an entire racial or religious group. In handing down the first genocide conviction under the Genocide Convention, the trial chamber stated that violent acts have destructive effects that reverberate in time: "[F]or example, the murder of a particular individual, [may lead to] the realisation of an ulterior motive, which is to destroy, in whole or in part, the group of which the individual is just one element."[160] As the report on the investigation of the genocide in Darfur summarized the Rwanda tribunal's decisions: "[T]he intent to destroy a group 'in part' requires the intention to destroy 'a considerable number of individuals' or 'a substantial part,' but not necessarily a 'very important part' of the group."[161] The intent to destroy a "substantial part" of the group may be satisfied qualitatively, by targeting a group's leaders for execution, and not simply quantitatively by large numbers of victims.[162]

The Rwanda tribunal has also confirmed that genocidal intent is perfectly consistent with economic, military, or political *motives*. The appeals chamber of the tribunal held in 2001:

> [The defendant] contends ... that certain witnesses ascribed to him a personal motive for his actions (such as the elimination of business competitors) and that "a person who commits a crime, in the quest of a personal goal, such as vengeance or lucre ... is not guilty of genocide but of an ordinary crime". The Appeals Chamber notes that criminal intent (*mens rea*) must not be confused with motive and that, in respect of genocide, personal motive does not exclude criminal responsibility providing that the acts [of killing, seriously injuring, exposing to poor living conditions, etc.] were committed "with intent to destroy, in whole or in part a national, ethnical, racial or religious group".[163]

As a result in part of the Rwanda tribunal's decisions, it is now an accepted statement of international law that mixed political or economic motives do not negate a genocidal intent to destroy a group in whole or in part.[164]

---

158. *Id.* at §6.2.

159. *Id.*, at §6.3.1.

160. *Id.* at ¶¶521–22.

161. ICID Report at ¶492 (footnotes omitted) (citing Prosecutor v. Kayishema and Ruzindana, at ¶97; Prosecutor v. Jelisić, Appeals Chamber, Judgement, at ¶82; Prosecutor v. Bagilishema, Trial Chamber, Judgement (June 7, 2001), at §64); Prosecutor v. Semanza, Case No. ICTR-97-20-I, Trial Chamber, Judgement, May 15, 2003, at §316)).

162. *See* Prosecutor v. Milošević, Decision on Motion for Judgement of Acquittal, at ¶132 (citing Prosecutor v. Krstić, Appeal Chamber, Judgement, at ¶12). *See also* Prosecutor v. Ndindabahizi, Case No. ICTR-2001-71-I, Trial Chamber, Judgement and Sentence (July 15, 2004), at ¶454, http://69.94.11.53/ENGLISH/cases/Ndindabahizi/judgement/Ndindabahizi%20Judgment.pdf ("The requisite intent may be proven by overt statements of the perpetrator or, as with any crime, by drawing inferences from circumstantial evidence of intent. The actual destruction of a substantial part of the group is not a required material element of the offence, but may assist in determining whether the accused intended to bring about that result.") (footnote omitted).

163. Prosecutor v. Kayishema & Ruzindana, Case No. ICTR-95-1-T, Appeals Chamber, Judgement (Reasons) (June 1, 2001), at ¶159, http://69.94.11.53/ENGLISH/cases/KayRuz/appeal/3d.htm (footnotes omitted).

164. *See id.*; Prosecutor v. Jelisić, Appeals Chamber, Judgement, at ¶49 (noting "'the necessity to distinguish specific intent from motive. The personal motive of the perpetrator of the crime of geno-

Like the Yugoslav tribunal, the Rwanda tribunal has concluded that genocidal intent may be inferred from massacres, rapes, destruction of property, and other crimes directed at a particular group, even without any "smoking gun" documents. The Appeals Chambers stated:

> [E]xplicit manifestations of criminal intent are, for obvious reasons, often rare in the context of criminal trials. In order to prevent perpetrators from escaping convictions simply because such manifestations are absent, the requisite intent may normally be inferred from relevant facts and circumstances.[165]

Inferential proof is necessary because genocidal intent is not amenable to direct proof, because the accused has an incentive to avoid admitting it to forestall execution or revenge-killings. This requires international tribunals to infer genocidal intent from systematic killing, planning of widespread assaults, the use of weapons that kill civilians as well as military men, the targeting of the group or their property, or racist or demagogic language used against the group"[166]

In 2005, the report for the Security Council on the crisis in Darfur, Sudan summarized the Rwanda tribunal's case law as stating that genocidal intent may be *inferred* from violent *acts*:

> A number of factors from which intent may be inferred were mentioned in *Akayesu* (§§ 523–4: "the general context of the perpetration of other culpable acts systematically directed against that same group, whether ... committed by the same offender or by others"; "the scale of atrocities committed"; the "general nature" of the atrocities committed "in a region or a country"; "the fact of deliberately and systematically targeting victims on account of their membership of a particular group, while excluding the members of other groups"; "the general political doctrine which gave rise to the acts"; "the repetition of destructive and discriminatory acts" or "the perpetration of acts which violate, or which the perpetrators themselves consider to violate the very foundation of the group—acts which are not in themselves covered by the list ... but which are committed as part of the same pattern of conduct."), in *Musema* (§ 166) as well as *Kayishema and Ruzindana* (§§ 93 and 527: "the number of group members affected"; "the physical targeting of the group or their property"; "the use of derogatory language toward members of the targeted group"; "the weapons employed and the extent of bodily injury"; "the methodical way of planning"; "the systematic manner of killing" and "the relative proportionate scale of the actual or attempted destruction of a group.").[167]

---

cide may be, for example, to obtain personal economic benefits, or political advantage or some form of power. The existence of a personal motive does not preclude the perpetrator from also having the specific intent to commit genocide.'").

165. Prosecutor v. Kayishema & Ruzindana, Appeals Chamber, Judgement, at ¶ 161.

166. Prosecutor v. Gacumbitsi, Case No. ICTR-2001-64-A, Appeals Chamber, Judgement, at 15, ¶ 40 (7 July 2006), http://69.94.11.53/ENGLISH/cases/Gachumbitsi/judgement/judgement_appeals_070706.pdf. Throughout its opinion, the Rwanda tribunal in deciding this case cited to the Yugoslav tribunal's decisions in *Krstić*, *Milosevic*, and *Jelisić*.

167. ICID Report at n.185 (citing Prosecutor v. Akayesu, Trial Chamber, Judgement, at §§ 523–4; Prosecutor v. Musema, Case No. ICTR-97-13-A, Trial Chamber, Judgement and Sentence (Jan. 19, 2000), at ¶ 166; Prosecutor v. Kayishema & Ruzindana, Case No. ICTR-95-1-A, Trial Chamber, Judgement (May 21, 1999), at ¶¶ 93, 527).

The Rwanda tribunal has repeatedly concluded that large-scale or systematic rapes of women belonging to a different group prove the genocidal intent of the perpetrators of such rapes. In particular, rape and sexual assault are most likely to be genocidal acts if they cause (1) serious bodily or mental harm, (2) women to bear children of the perpetrators' ethnic group, or (3) women of the victim group to be unable or willing to give birth to new members of their own group due to the trauma they've suffered.[168] Such rapes constitute "an integral part of the process of destruction, specifically targeting [victim group] women" because they may result "in physical and psychological destruction of [victim group] women, their families and their communities," thereby "contributing to the destruction of the [victim] group as a whole."[169] As of early 2004, the Rwanda tribunal had amended nearly all of its indictments that alleged sexual assault "to charge them as genocide."[170]

As with the Yugoslav tribunal, the decisions of the Rwanda tribunal are important for this book because they help define the genocidal intent that must accompany killings, rapes, maimings, deprivations of food, shelter, medical care, or humanitarian aid, in order for the crime of genocide to have been committed. The tribunal has helpfully clarified that genocidal intent may be inferred from a series of violent acts systematically directed against a group, large-scale atrocities, atrocities of a gruesome or vicious nature, exempting the members of other groups from systematic attacks, a racist or exclusionary political movement, or acts obviously aimed at undermining efforts of the group to survive and thrive in an area as a distinct unit.

---

168. *See* Prosecutor v. Akayesu, Trial Chamber, Judgement, at §6.3.1 (holding that acts of causing serious bodily or mental harm or preventing births within a group, can constitute genocide assuming that they are committed with the requisite intent, and that "rape can be a measure intended to prevent births when the person raped refuses subsequently to procreate, in the same way that members of a group can be led, through threats or trauma, not to procreate"); *see also* Prosecutor v. Muhimana, Case No. ICTR-95-1B-T, Trial Chamber I, Judgement and Sentence (Apr. 25, 2005), at ¶¶513, 517, http://69.94.11.53/ENGLISH/cases/Muhimana/judgement/muhimana280505.doc (finding that the accused committed genocide by, among other things, raping Tutsi women, and noting that: "During the course of some of the attacks and rapes, the Accused specifically referred to the Tutsi ethnic identity of his victims."); Prosecutor v. Semanza, Case No. ICTR-97-20-T, Trial Chamber III, Judgment and Sentence (May 15, 2003), at ¶¶476–77, http://69.94.11.53/ENGLISH/cases/Semanza/judgement/6.htm (finding that defendant's "instructions about raping and killing Tutsis, the ethnic group targeted by the widespread attack" resulted in rape of a Tutsi woman that was a crime against humanity because it "was part of the widespread attack against the civilian Tutsi population and that the assailant was so aware."); Katherine MacKinnon, *Defining Rape Internationally: A Comment on Akayesu*, 44 COLUM. J. TRANSNAT'L L. 940, 947 (2006) ("survivors of rape in the Serb-led genocide against Bosnia-Herzegovina and Croatia typically understood that they had been raped precisely to destroy their ethnic and religious communities, in acts of sexual violence against women because they were not Serbian"); Kelly Dawn Askin, *Gender Crimes Jurisprudence in the ICTR: Positive Developments*, 3 J. OF INTERNATIONAL CRIMINAL JUSTICE 1007 (2005) (noting that the Rwanda tribunal has described the rape of Tutsi women as a tactic to destroy the group both physically and mentally, especially because many women and girls were murdered after being raped or died from their injuries); Karen Engle, *Feminism and Its (Dis)Contents: Criminalizing Wartime Rape in Bosnia and Herzegovina*, 99 AMERICAN J. OF INTERNATIONAL LAW 778, 791–92 (2005) (summarizing academic commentary linking rape of Bosnian Muslim women to births of part-Serbian children to Muslim women, dissolution of families, ostracizing of victims, and occasional murder of victims within their own communities); Rosalind Dixon, *Rape as a Crime in International Law: Where to Go from Here?*, 13 EUROPEAN J. OF INTERNATIONAL LAW 697, 704 (2002) (describing rape as an element of genocide when it causes forced pregnancy or maternity of children fathered by men who are non-members of the mother's ethnic group).

169. Prosecutor v. Akayesu, Trial Chamber, Judgement, at ¶731.

170. MacKinnon, *Defining Rape Internationally*, at 949 n.41. *See also id.* at 947.

E. Genocide: The Kosovo Model

Many world leaders declared in 1999 that genocide had occurred in Kosovo, a province of Yugoslavia. These leaders included the U.S. president, British prime minister, secretary-general of the North Atlantic Treaty Organization (NATO), Turkish prime minister, and others.

In July 1996, the Kosovo Liberation Army (KLA) fought Yugoslav forces for control of the town of Orahovac, with Yugoslavia charging 11 KLA members with terrorism and the KLA alleging a massacre of 52 Kosovar Albanian civilians.[171] Western media celebrated the KLA as a "resistance" to Yugoslavia, rather than as terrorists (as they describe many other groups). By early 1997, the KLA claimed responsibility for 12 assassinations of Yugoslav officials and Albanian "collaborators." Yugoslav officials claimed that nearly 40,000 KLA supporters had been trained in Albania, Iran and Pakistan, and the KLA was funded from the Middle East.[172] In mid-1998, the KLA received a "huge infusion of weapons and fighters from Albania."[173] The KLA brought in anti-tank rockets and heavy machine guns from Germany, sniper rifles from the United States, and assault rifles from Albania, Bosnia, and Croatia. KLA supports in the United States alone provided about one thousand sniper rifles.[174]

In March 1998, the Security Council called upon all U.N. members to "prevent arming and training for terrorist activities" in Yugoslavia, and to "prevent the sale or supply to the Federal Republic of Yugoslavia, including Kosovo, ... [of] weapons and ammunition...."[175] It also called upon the KLA to cease its terrorist activity, and condemned excessive force by Yugoslavia.[176] In September, the Security Council insisted that the KLA condemn all terrorist action, announced its grave concern about indiscriminate uses of force by the Yugoslav Army, and demanded that all parties to the conflict reach a cease-fire and a political solution.[177] Already by that time the Security Council noted that 230,000 had been displaced from their homes. After hundreds of thousands of refugees had fled Kosovo, some telling stories of massacres, mass rape, and ethnic cleansing, NATO began a bombing campaign against Yugoslavia.[178]

On the fifth day of their bombing campaign against targets in Serbia and Kosovo, as part of a humanitarian intervention on behalf of the Muslim Kosovar Albanians, U.S. President Bill Clinton and U.K. Prime Minister Tony Blair announced that the "Serbs are intent on genocide and inhuman violence."[179] Turkish Prime Minister Bulent Ecevit had

---

171. *See* Associated Press, *Serbs and Albanians Trade Accusations,* New Straits Times (Malaysia), July 23, 1996, at 63.

172. *See, e.g.,* Chris Hedges, *Resistance to Serbia Turns Violent in Kosovo,* N.Y. Times, Feb. 17, 1997, http://www.nytimes.com/1997/02/17/world/resistance-to-serbia-turns-violent-in-kosovo.html.

173. *See, e.g., News Summary,* N.Y. Times, June 19, 1998, http://www.nytimes.com/1998/06/19/nyregion/news-summary-497010.html.

174. *See* Henry H. Perritt, Kosovo Liberation Army: The Inside Story of an Insurgency 118–19 (Champaign, IL: Univ. of Illinois Press, 2008).

175. S.C. Res. 1160, ¶ 8 (Mar. 31, 2008).

176. *See id.* at pmbl., ¶ 2.

177. S.C. Res. 1199, pmbl., ¶¶ 1, 6 (Sept. 23, 2008).

178. *See Serb Legal Action "Abuse of Court,"* BBC News, May 11, 1999, http://news.bbc.co.uk/2/hi/europe/341169.stm.

179. *See Day by Day Guide of the Conflict So Far,* The Times (U.K.), Apr. 3, 1999, *quoted in* Hannibal Travis.

Genocide in Sudan: The Role of Oil Exploration and the Entitlement of the Victims to Reparations, 25 Arizona J. of International and Comparative Law 1, 34 (2008).

already called Yugoslavia's counterinsurgency campaign in Kosovo an ongoing genocide.[180] Later in April 1999, U.S. Secretary of State Madeleine Albright stated that "President Milosevic has unleashed a rampage of ethnic cleansing and genocide directed at the expulsion or total submission of the Kosovo Albanian community."[181] In May, Prime Minister Blair wrote: "It is no exaggeration to say what is happening in Kosovo is racial genocide."[182] He declared: "I pledge to you now—Milosevic and his hideous racial genocide will be defeated."[183] Also in May, the German defense minister forthrightly "called the crimes in Kosovo 'genocide.'"[184] The Polish foreign minister said the Yugoslavian regime was "bent on genocide."[185] NATO Secretary-General Javier Solana alleged that President Milosevic was "spearheading a campaign to rid Kosovo of ethnic Albanians.... 'We know he wanted to exterminate the people of Albania,' he said."[186] In June, President Clinton argued, in defending the bombing campaign against Serbia, that "We should not countenance genocide or ethnic cleansing anywhere in the world if we have the power to stop it."[187] In October 1999, the U.S. Congress declared that the reports of mass executions in at least 60 villages and towns, other summary executions of men, wanton destruction of homes, forcible expulsions, and widespread rape of women and young girls provided prima facie evidence of possible genocide, that the U.S. should secure the indictment of those responsible for the commission of genocide, and that there should be no amnesty for "war crimes, crimes against humanity, or genocide committed during operations in Kosovo."[188]

The breadth of the consensus that genocide occurred in Kosovo was a bit surprising because likely fewer than 10,000 people had been confirmed dead by April or May 1999. Many of the dead might have been KLA terrorists whose activities had been specifically condemned by the U.N. Security Council, although civilians were also clearly targeted in the Yugoslav response. The prosecutor of the Yugoslav tribunal did not provide an estimate of the death toll to the members of the Security Council, including the U.S., until November, long after the U.S. had pronounced that genocide was taking place. In December, the U.S. State Department released its report concluding that "probably around 10,000 Kosovar Albanians were killed by Serbian forces," and added that the true number of killings was unknown because bodies may have been burned, some mass graves

180. *See* Paul Goble, *Yugoslavia: Analysis From Washington—In Dire Straights*, Radio Free Europe/Radio Liberty, Apr. 2, 1999; *Russia Challenges NATO, Sends Seven-Ship Fleet to Mediterranean*, Turkish Daily News, Apr. 1, 1999.

181. Madeline Albright, *Testimony before the House Appropriations Subcommittee on Foreign Operations, Washington, DC, Apr. 15, 1999 on International Affairs Budget, FY 2000*, US Dep't of State Dispatch, Apr. 1999, http://canberra.usembassy.gov/hyper/1999/WF990415/epf404.htm.

182. Tony Blair, *My Pledge to the Refugees*, BBC News, May 14, 1999, http://news.bbc.co.uk/1/hi/uk_politics/343739.stm.

183. Fred Bridgland, *A Tragic Decade for Children Worldwide*, The Sunday Herald (Scotland), Dec. 26, 1999, at 7.

184. Roger Cohen, *Crisis in the Balkans: The Indictment; Tribunal Is Said to Cite Milosevic for War Crimes*, N.Y. Times, May 27, 1999, at A1.

185. William Drozdiak, *NATO's Newcomers Are Shaken by Airstrikes; Czechs, Hungarians Express Greatest Dismay*, Wash. Post, Apr. 12, 1999, at A17.

186. Lance Gay, *U.S. Unable to Prove It's Genocide But Hints Milosevic Coming Close*, Plain Dealer (Cleveland, Ohio), Apr. 1, 1999, at 8A.

187. Interview of the President by Russian Television (Jun 20, 1999), http://clinton2.nara.gov/WH/New/Europe-9906/html/Speeches/990620b.htm.

188. National Defense Authorization Act for Fiscal Year 2000, Public L. 106–65, 106th Cong. 113 Stat. 512, 785–86.

Figure 1 Estimates of Death Tolls Due to Genocide in Bosnia, Rwanda, and Kosovo

Case	Death Toll	Refugees/IDPs	Sources
Rwanda, 1994	800,000–1 million	1–2 million	The International Criminal Tribunal for Rwanda, U.S. CIA
Bosnia, 1992–1996	8,000	2.2 million	The International Criminal Tribunal for the Former Yugoslavia
Kosovo, 1999	2,100–8,000	1 million	The International Criminal Tribunal for the Former Yugoslavia (Spokesperson)

may never be discovered, and other bodies may have been buried in a chaotic and uncountable condition.[189] Figure 1 places these estimates in context.

Russia, for its part, declared that genocide was being conducted against 200,000 Serbs and other minorities driven out of Kosovo after the victory of the Kosovar Albanian rebels with NATO air support.[190] Russia also accused NATO of genocide against Serbia due to the bombing of essential infrastructure in 1995.[191] A Russian humanitarian mission to Kosovo and Metohia concluded that 190 Orthodox Christian churches had been destroyed from 1999 to 2005.[192] The representative of Serbia and Montenegro told the U.N. General Assembly in 2005 that:

> From 10 June 1999 to the present, approximately 200,000 Serbs and Montenegrins, as well as Turks, Croats, Roma, Jews and other non-Albanians, have been expelled from Kosovo. Close to 80 per cent of the territory is now inhabited only by Albanians. Several hundred Serbs have been killed, including many children. Approximately 40,000 Serbian homes have been demolished or set on fire, as well as 150 churches and monasteries that were centuries old. The remaining Serbs and other non-Albanians live in so-called enclaves, without guarantees for their personal safety and their freedom of movement. No one in present-day Europe is so tragically unprotected.[193]

Representatives of the Roma appealed for assistance to the European Union in 2004, arguing that stating that Roma people "have again been targeted for extreme violence as part of a campaign begun in 1999 by ethnic Albanians to expel minorities from the province, to seize their property and to do them serious physical harm."[194]

The Kosovo model has several noteworthy features. First, it confirms that many of the states parties to the Genocide Convention believe that it is violated when violent and "inhuman" acts are committed against a group are "directed at the expulsion or total submission" of the group.[195] Second, it reaffirms that the crime of genocide need not have a death toll that mounts into the hundreds of thousands or millions. Several different sta-

189. *See* U.S. State Department, *Ethnic Cleansing in Kosovo: An Accounting* (Dec. 1999), http://www.state.gov/www/global/human_rights/kosovoii/homepage.html#exe (citing Yugoslav tribunal, *Prosecutor Report to the Security Council* (Nov. 10, 1999), http://www.un.org).

190. *See* ITAR-TASS News Agency, *Russian Foreign Minister Says West Tacitly Consenting to "Genocide" in Kosovo*, NEWSBANK, Nov. 30, 1999, http://nl.newsbank.com.

191. *See Raids on Serbs Prompt Russia's 'Genocide' Charge*, PITTSBURGH POST-GAZETTE, Sept. 13, 1995.

192. *See* Interfax News Agency, *190 Orthodox Churches Ruined in Kosovo Since 1999 – Russian Expert*, Interfax News Agency News bulletin, Feb. 27, 2005.

193. A/60/PV.20, at 20.

194. European Roma Rights Center, *Ethnic Cleansing of 'Gypsies' in Kosovo*, Mar. 24, 2004, http://www.errc.org/cikk.php?cikk=345.

195. Albright, *Testimony on International Affairs Budget.*

tistical studies of the Kosovo war generated an overall death toll of Kosovar Albanians of fewer than 20,000, sometimes fewer than 10,000, with a high degree of confidence.[196] Third, it illustrates the centrality of ethnic cleansing to conclusions that genocide or an attempt or conspiracy to commit genocide is taking place, triggering a global obligation to prevent and punish under the Genocide Convention. Fourth, like the Bosnia and Rwanda models, the Kosovo model emphasizes committing acts intended to and likely to kill members of a group as a result of their group membership, without requiring that all or even a large percentage of a group be destroyed. An illustration of this common feature of the three models of the crime of genocide is that the ethnic Albanian population made up a higher percentage of the total population of the Federal Republic of Yugoslavia (Serbia and Montenegro) in 2000 than in 1997.[197] Similarly, the percentage of the Rwandan population that was categorized as ethnic Tutsi was higher in 1997 than in 1992.[198] Finally, it illustrates once again that genocide often arises out of counterinsurgency warfare.

F. Sociological Models

Scholars have developed a variety of theories designed to explain the incidence of genocide in the twentieth century, and to prevent its further recurrence. One of the most popular theories is that "deep ethnic, cultural, religious or class divisions" and accompanying political and economic discrimination provoke episodes of mass killing. Although this theory has a great deal of power as an account of the Holocaust, there are several problems with it. First, it is tautological in a certain sense, because the etymology, dictionary definition, and international law of genocide focus on the killing (*cide*) of identifiable ethnic or religious groups (*genos* or tribes), so that ethnic and religious divisions will naturally play a part. Second, empirical research has failed to link mass killing to ethnic differences or conflicts. Third, anecdotal evidence suggests that groups suffering genocide did not necessarily undergo significantly worse cultural and judicial discrimination than those experiencing less severe intergroup conflict. Thus, it is not clear that the German Jews of the early 1930s were more politically, economically, or culturally marginalized than African-Americans in the era of *de jure* racial segregation, or non-Europeans in apartheid South Africa. Other victims, such as peasants in China or the Soviet Union, were culturally very similar to the architects of genocidal famines or deportations.[199]

A second family of theories emphasizes dominant group ideologies that seek to solve great national or ethnic "problems" by scapegoating and exterminating minority groups.

---

196. *See, e.g.*, American Bar Association and American Association for the Advancement of Science, Political Killings in Kosova/Kosovo, March–June 1999 (Washington, DC: American Bar Association, 2000); Paul B. Spiegel & Peter Salama, *War and Mortality in Kosovo, 1998–1999: An Epidemiological Testimony* 355 Lancet 2204 (2000); Jonathan Steele, *Figures Put on Serb Killings Too High*, The Guardian (U.K.), Aug 18, 2000, http://www.guardianunlimited.co.uk/kosovo/story/0,2763,355781,00.html.

197. *Compare Serbia and Montenegro, in* World Factbook 1997, http://www.umsl.edu/ services/govdocs/wofact97/216.htm (14% ethnic Albanian), *with Serbia and Montenegro, in* World Factbook 2000, http://www.umsl.edu/services/govdocs/wofact2000/geos/sr.html (16.5% Albanian).

198. *Compare Rwanda, in* World Factbook 1992 (only 9%), *with Rwanda, in* World Factbook 1997 (19%).

199. *See* Valentino, Final Solutions, at 9–10, 16–21, 194–232, 235, 281, 283.

Anecdotal evidence seems to confirm this theory, as several architects of genocide have experienced especially acute awareness of national crises and humiliations of their dominant group, and often suffered personally from these events to an unusual degree.[200] Other architects, however, did not particularly suffer from crisis situations. Among the prosperous and secure powers implicated in genocide are Spain in the Americas, Britain in Ireland and North America, France in Algeria and Haiti, and Japan in China.[201] Even those architects of genocide who did scapegoat minorities for genuine crises, moreover, displaced their resentment in a seemingly random fashion, as did Adolf Hitler onto Jews and Slavs from the victors over Germany in the First World War (i.e., Britain, France, and the U.S.); Josef Stalin onto Ukrainian and Asian civilians from foreign capitalists and Nazi Germany; Mao Zedong onto the Tibetan and Han Chinese people from imperial

---

200. See id. at 22–26. *See also* ROBERT MELSON, REVOLUTION AND GENOCIDE: ON THE ORIGINS OF THE ARMENIAN GENOCIDE AND THE HOLOCAUST 79–80 (Chicago: Univ. of Chicago Press, 1986) (arguing that Armenian genocide shares with other notable cases the fact that it was preceded by a "series of significant military and political disasters" that undermined existing political order and resulted in new ideology which led the state to blame an ethnic or religious minority for the disasters and "to eliminate the offending communal group from the social structure").

201. On Spain in the Americas, see ROBERT BEVAN, THE DESTRUCTION OF MEMORY: ARCHITECTURE AT WAR 20 (London: Reaktion, 2006); BARTOLOME DE LAS CASAS, THE HISTORY ON THE INDIES, *reprinted in* SUSAN CASTILLO & IVY SCHWEITZER, THE LITERATURES OF COLONIAL AMERICA (London: Wiley-Blackwell, 2001); JAMES WEST DAVIDSON, NATION OF NATIONS: A CONCISE NARRATIVE OF THE AMERICAN REPUBLIC 22 (New York, 1996); Diego de Landa, *Account on Things in Yucatan, in* CASTILLO & SCHWEITZER, THE LITERATURES OF COLONIAL AMERICA (Susan P. Castillo, Ivy Schweitzer eds., New York: Wiley-Blackwell, 2001); M. ANNETTE JAIMES, THE STATE OF NATIVE AMERICA: GENOCIDE, COLONIZATION, AND RESISTANCE 81 (Boston: South End Press, 1992); HENRY KAMEN, EMPIRE: HOW SPAIN BECAME A WORLD POWER, 1492–1763, at 117, 124–25, 136–40, 203, 285, 358 (New York, 2004); MARK LEVENE, 2 GENOCIDE IN THE AGE OF THE NATION STATE 10 (London: IB Tauris, 2005); PAN AMERICAN UNION, UNION OF AMERICAN REPUBLICS, INTERNATIONAL UNION OF AMERICAN REPUBLICS, BULLETIN OF THE PAN AMERICAN UNION 473 (1948); ANNA STUBBLEFIELD, ETHICS ALONG THE COLOR LINE 27 (Ithaca, NY: Cornell UP, 2005); THE BROKEN SPEARS: THE AZTEC ACCOUNT OF THE CONQUEST OF MEXICO 64–66, 129–131 (Miguel Leon Portilla, ed., New York: Houghton Mifflin, 1962); THE INDIGENOUS PEOPLE OF THE CARIBBEAN (Samuel M. Wilson ed., Gainesville, FL: Univ. Press of Florida, 1997); James Mooney, *American Indians*, 7 THE CATHOLIC ENCYCLOPEDIA (1910), http://www.newadvent.org/cathen/07747a.htm.

On the British in Ireland, see Thomas Jefferson, *Letter to Alexander von Humboldt* (Dec. 6, 1813), *in* THE WRITINGS OF THOMAS JEFFERSON 269 (H.A. Washington ed., New York: Derby & Jackson, 1854) (noting English "extermination" of people of Ireland); JOHN RANELAGH O'BEIRNE, A SHORT HISTORY OF IRELAND 65 (Cambridge: Cambridge UP, 1994); BREANDAN O HEITHIR, A POCKET HISTORY OF IRELAND 30 (Dublin: O'Brien Press, 1989); New Jersey Commission on Holocaust Education, *The Great Irish Famine* (1998), http://www.nde.state.ne.us/SS/irish/irish_pf.html.

On the Japanese in China, see MARIA HSIA CHANG, RETURN OF THE DRAGON: CHINA'S WOUNDED NATIONALISM 80–81 (Boulder, Colo.: Westview Press, 2001) (citing CHANG, THE RAPE OF NANKING); R.J. RUMMEL, CHINA'S BLOODY CENTURY: GENOCIDE AND MASS MURDER SINCE 1900 (New Brunswick, NJ: Transaction Publishers, 2007); NICHOLAS TARLING, A SUDDEN RAMPAGE: THE JAPANESE OCCUPATION OF SOUTHEAST ASIA (Honolulu: Univ. of Hawaii Press, 2001); Gay McDougall, Final Report Submitted by Special Rapporteur on Contemporary Forms of Slavery: Systematic Rape, Sexual Slavery and Slavery-Like Practices During Armed Conflict, ECOSOC, Commission on Human Rights, U.N. Doc. No. E/CN.4/Sub.2/1998/13 (June 22, 1998), http://www.hri.ca/forthereCord1998/documentation/commission/e-cn4-sub2-1998-13.htm; Karen Parker & Jennifer F. Chew, *Compensation for Japan's World War II War-Rape Victims*, 17 HASTINGS INT'L & COMPARATIVE LAW REV. 497 (1994); Karen Parker. *War Rape*, Report to U.N. Econ. & Soc. Council [ECOSOC], Commission on Human Rights (1995), http://www.webcom.com/hrin/parker/c95-11.html; *see also* MELSON, REVOLUTION AND GENOCIDE, at 334 n.41, 378–83, 408–411; Mike Chamberlain, *The People of East Timor, in* GENOCIDE AND HUMAN RIGHTS: A GLOBAL ANTHOLOGY 238–43 (Jack Nusan Porter ed., Washington, DC: Univ. Press of America, 1982).

Japan; and Pol Pot from the U.S. and Vietnam onto urbanized Khmer, Buddhists, Cham Muslims, and Chinese.[202]

The third family of theories emphasizes undemocratic and elitist forms of government that permit government policies to be devised and implemented in relative secrecy and without accountability before affected members of the public or an independent judiciary.[203] This theory also has some anecdotal support, as a way of explaining how genocide could have occurred in dictatorial regimes in Ottoman Turkey, Nazi Germany, the Soviet Union, Maoist China, Khmer Rouge Cambodia, and Ba'athist Iraq, as well as Pakistan, Indonesia, and Guatemala under military rule.[204] President Clinton blamed genocide and crimes against humanity that took place in the former Yugoslavia and Rwanda during his presidency on a lack of democratic institutions in those countries.[205] In the case of Rwanda, he also cited the perceived "disproportionate economic and political power" of the Tutsi group, thereby suggesting that marginalized members of the Hutu group might have been scheming to seize power and resources from the Tutsi.[206] There are numerous other examples of genocidal dictatorships, as Figure 2 illustrates.

Theories of mass killing as instances of undemocratic rule, however, fail to explain genocidal actions carried out by democracies, often with great fanfare and public support.[207] For example, Britain was one of the world's first modern democracies, with an elected parliament exercising political supremacy over royal decrees as early as the seventeenth century,[208] yet British colonists "played a major role in the destruction of several native tribes in Connecticut, the Carolinas, Florida, and Virginia...."[209] Inheriting many British institutions, a democratic U.S. continued to massacre and deport from their valuable farming and hunting lands such native tribes as the Apache, Cherokee, Chickasaw, Choctaw, Comanche, Creeks, Lakota, Nez Perce, Seminole, Shoshone, Sioux, and Yuki.[210] In the twentieth century, democratic Britain, France and the U.S. killed hundreds of thousands

---

202. *See* VALENTINO, FINAL SOLUTIONS, at 264, at 126, 262, 274; MELSON, REVOLUTION AND GENOCIDE, at 271, at 262–67, 330–32; Nicholas Eberstadt, *The Great Leap Backward,* N.Y. TIMES, Feb. 16, 1997, http://www.nytimes.com/books/97/02/16/reviews/970216.16ebersta.html (reviewing JASPER BECKER, HUNGRY GHOSTS: MAO'S SECRET FAMINE (1997)); Lewis M. Simons, *Genocide and the Science of Proof,* NAT'L GEOGRAPHIC, Jan. 2006, at 30; Daniel Sutherland, *Uncounted Millions: Mass Death in Mao's China: Repression's Higher Toll: New Evidence Shows Famine, Violence Spared Few,* WASH. POST, July 17, 1994, at A1; Robert Thurman, Statement on U.S. Policy Considerations on the 40th Anniv. of the Tibetan Uprising, U.S. House of Representatives, Cmte. on International Relations, 106th Cong., 1st Sess., Mar. 11, 1999, at 10.

203. *See* VALENTINO, FINAL SOLUTIONS, at 26–27, 262.

204. *See* CHALK & JONASSOHN, THE HISTORY AND SOCIOLOGY OF GENOCIDE, at 249–383, 394–411.

205. *See* VALENTINO, FINAL SOLUTIONS, at 236.

206. BILL CLINTON, MY LIFE 948 (New York: Random House Large Print, 2004).

207. *See* VALENTINO, FINAL SOLUTIONS, at 26–28.

208. *See* John Phillip Reid, *Another Origin of Judicial Review: The Constitutional Crisis of 1776,* 64 NYU L. Rev. 963, 972 (1989) ("English Civil War of the 1640s" established "the constitutional principle of supremacy of the law over the king"); Norman B. Smith "*Shall Make No Law Abridging ...": An Analysis of the Neglected, But Nearly Absolute, Right of Petition,* 54 U. CIN. L. REV. 1153, 1179 n.164 (1986) ("Popular sovereignty developed first by establishing the legislative supremacy of parliament in the course of the English Civil War and ensuing events, and second by gaining universal manhood suffrage through electoral reform in the Nineteenth Century.").

209. CHALK & JONASSOHN, THE HISTORY AND SOCIOLOGY OF GENOCIDE, at 180.

210. *See id.* at 195–202; GARRISON, THE LEGAL IDEOLOGY OF REMOVAL, at 2–3; VALENTINO, FINAL SOLUTIONS, at 27; LEVENE, 2 GENOCIDE IN THE AGE OF THE NATION STATE, at 57, 63, 80–82, 88, 92–93, 245; CHESTER M. OEHLER, THE GREAT SIOUX UPRISING, ch. 22 (Oxford: Oxford UP, 1997); William Bradford, *Beyond Reparations: An American Indian Theory of Justice,* 66 OHIO STATE L.J. 1, 24 (2005); Lindsay Glauner, *The Need for Accountability and Reparation: 1830–1976, The United States*

Figure 2 Genocide and Dictatorship

Country/Empire	Dictator(s)	Years of Rule*	Persecuted Ethnic and Religious Groups
Mexico	Porfirio Díaz	1884–1911	Mayan, Yaqui, other peoples
Ottoman Empire	Enver Paşa, etc.	1907–1918	Armenians, Assyrians, Greeks, Yezidis, Kurds
Republic of Turkey	Mustafa Kemal	1919–1938	Armenians, Assyrians, Greeks, Yezidis, Kurds
Italy	Benito Mussolini	1925–1943	Ethiopians, Arabs, Jews, socialists
Soviet Union	Vladimir Lenin, Josef Stalin, etc.	1917–1991	Ukrainians, Kazakhs, Christians, Germans, Koreans, Chechens, Afghans
Nazi Germany	Adolf Hitler	1933–1945	Jews, Slavs, Roma people, various Christian sects
India	Jawaharlal Nehru	1947–1952	Muslims, Dalits (untouchables)
Pakistan	Muhammad Ali Jinnah	1947–1948	Hindus
People's Republic of China	Mao Tse-Tung	1931–1976	Buddhists, Taoists, Tibetans, Christians, Turkic Muslims
Democratic Republic of Korea	Kim Il-Sung, Kim Jong-Il	1945–1994	Christians, South Koreans, Americans
Vietnam	Ho Chi Minh	1945–1969	Nationalists, Christians, landlords, capitalists, etc.
Indonesia	Suharto	1965–1998	Chinese, Christians, East Timorese
Nigeria	Yakubu Gowon	1966–1975	Igbos
Cambodia	Pol Pot	1968–1979	Vietnamese, Buddhists, Muslims, intellectual or urbanized Cambodians
Pakistan	Yahya Khan	1969–1971	Hindus, Bangladeshis, Christians
Brazil	Emílio Médici, Ernesto Geisel	1969–1979	Yanomami
Uganda	Idi Amin	1971–1979	Acholi, Lango
Ethiopia	Mengistu Haile Mariam	1974–1987	Eritreans, Tigrayans
Republic of Iraq	Saddam Hussein	1976–2003	Kurds, Assyrians, Shi'a Arabs, Yezidis, communist Sunnis, etc.
Guatemala	Efraín Ríos Montt and others	1982–1996	Mayans, Catholics
Sudan	Omar Hassan al-Bashir	1989–present	Christians, Dinka, Nuba, Masalit, Fur, Zaghawa
Federal Republic of Yugoslavia	Slobodan Milosevic	1989–2000	Bosnian Muslims, Croats, Kosovar Albanian Muslims
Rwanda	Jean Kambanda	1994	Tutsis, moderate Hutus
Islamic Emirate of Afghanistan	Muhammad Omar	1994–present	Hazaras, Tajiks, other Shi'a Afghans, communist or secular Pashtuns

*—periods listed include years of partial rule of country's territory, e.g. north or south
Source: Based in part on Helen Fein, *Accounting for Genocide After 1945: Theories and Some Findings*, 1 International J. on Group Rights 79, 87–91 (1993). Updated for 2009.

Government's Role in the Promotion, Implementation, and Execution of the Crime of Genocide Against Native Americans, 51 DePaul L. Rev. 911, 934 (2001–2002).

of civilians in Asian and African colonies such as Algeria, India, Kenya, and the Philippines.[211]

A common thread among instances of genocide (which existing theories otherwise have difficulty explaining) is the presence of an overriding economic motivation to strip vulnerable groups of their wealth, property, and lands during or after mass killing campaigns against them. Raphael Lemkin, like Thomas Jefferson, blamed greed for the riches of the New World for what both men described as the genocide (or "extermination") of Native American nations.[212] The U.S. Army dispossessed Native Americans of tens or even hundreds of millions of acres, leaving Native Americans with only 48 million acres by 1934, out of two billion acres in continental U.S.[213] The slave trade built up great fortunes for plantation owners and merchants in Europe, the Americas, and Asia,[214] while inflicting genocide upon African nations and peoples, which lost at least 1.5 million people who did not survive the passage to the Americas on slave ships, while millions more died in captivity in Africa or were subjected to slavery in the Americas.[215] The exploitation of the labor and mineral resources of African colonies claimed still more lives, up to 10 million in the Congo alone in as little as 20 years.[216] In the Ottoman Empire, the Turkish majority profited tremendously by committing geno-

---

211. *See* VALENTINO, FINAL SOLUTIONS, at 27, 83, 201–2; ALISTAIR HORNE, A SAVAGE WAR OF PEACE: ALGERIA 1954–1962 (London: Macmillan, 1978, New York reprint 2006); MOORFIELD STOREY & MARCIAL PRIMITIVO LICHAUCO, THE CONQUEST OF THE PHILIPPINES BY THE UNITED STATES, 1898–1925, at 121 (New York: G. P. Putnam's Sons, 2d ed. 1926); JULIAN CODMAN & MOORFIELD STOREY, SECRETARY ROOT'S RECORD. "MARKED SEVERITIES" IN PHILIPPINE WARFARE: AN ANALYSIS OF THE LAW AND FACTS (BiblioBazaar, LLC, 2008) (1902).

212. *See* Michael A. McDonnell and A. Dirk Moses, *Raphael Lemkin as Historian of Genocide in the Americas*, 7 J. OF GENOCIDE RESEARCH 501, 505–16 (2005). In 1813, former U.S. President Thomas Jefferson wrote that "Anglo-mercantile cupidity" drove the British Empire to "delug[e] the earth with human blood" not only in its "brutalization" and potential "extermination" of the native tribes of North America, but in its campaigns against Catholic Ireland as well. Thomas Jefferson, *Letter to Alexander von Humboldt* (Dec. 6, 1813), *in* 6 THE WRITINGS OF THOMAS JEFFERSON 269 (H.A. Washington ed., New York: Derby & Jackson, 1854). In 1830, President Andrew Jackson declared the "extinction" of the "aborigines" of United States to make room for settler prosperity and democracy to be a necessary outcome, and not regrettable. Andrew Jackson, *Annual Message to Congress, Dec. 7, 1830, in* ANNUAL MESSAGES, &C OF ANDREW JACKSON, PRESIDENT OF THE UNITED STATES 60 (Baltimore: Edward J. Coale Co., 1835).

213. Bradford, *An American Indian Theory of Justice*, at 35–40.

214. *See, e.g.*, JERRY W. MARKHAM, A FINANCIAL HISTORY OF THE UNITED STATES 37 (Armonk, NY: M.E. Sharpe, 2002) (describing how slavery was integral part of economies of British colonies in America); A.J. Williams-Myers, *Re-examining Slavery in New York*, NEW YORK ARCHIVES (2002), http://www.archives.nysed.gov/apt/archivesmag/archivesmag_past.shtml ("African labor contributed ... to the enormous wealth New York State had accumulated at the start of the Revolutionary War"); Robert Westley, *Many Billions Gone: Is It Time to Reconsider the Case for Black Reparations?*, 40 B.C. L. REV 429, 465 (1998) (citing academic estimates of value of unpaid slave labor as between hundreds of billions and several trillion dollars).

215. *See* ADAM HOCHSCHILD, BURY THE CHAINS: PROPHETS, SLAVES, AND REBELS IN THE FIGHT TO FREE AN EMPIRE'S SLAVES 32 (New York: Houghton Mifflin Harcourt, 2005); JOSEPH L. GRAVES, THE EMPEROR'S NEW CLOTHES: BIOLOGICAL THEORIES OF RACE AT THE MILLENIUM 28–30 (New Brunswick, NJ: Rutgers UP, 2001); SEYMOUR DRESCHER, THE ATLANTIC SLAVE TRADE AND THE HOLOCAUST: A COMPARATIVE ANALYSIS, IN IS THE HOLOCAUST UNIQUE?, at 98–99, 114; R.J. RUMMEL, DEATH BY GOVERNMENT 48 (New Brunswick, NJ: Transaction Publishers, 1994); Anthony Gifford, *The Legal Basis of the Claim for Slavery Reparations*, AMERICAN BAR ASS'N (2000), http://www.abanet.org/irr/hr/spring00humanrights/gifford.html.

216. John Norton Moore, *Beyond the Democratic Peace: Solving the War Puzzle*, 44 VIRGINIA J. INTERNATIONAL LAW 341, 411 (2004) ("The forgotten holocaust in the Congo from 1885 to 1908, which may have killed as many as ten million, was a giant forced labor camp for the personal enrichment of King Leopold II of Belgium.").

cide against the Armenian, Assyrian, and Greek minorities who had developed most of the businesses in the banking, manufacturing, import-export, and certain local agricultural fields, all of which Turks expropriated almost completely.[217]

There is also substantial evidence regarding an economic motivation for the Holocaust, often cited as the principal example in support of non-economic theories of genocide. The Nuremberg tribunal concluded that Hermann Göring, a "prime" Nazi leader from 1922 on, architect of the first concentration camps, and "economic dictator of the Reich" by 1936, "persecuted the Jews" in Germany and the conquered territories of the Reich out of an "interest" that "was primarily economic—how to get [Jews'] property and how to force them out of the economic life of Europe."[218] Adolf Hitler and the Nazi party imagined a

---

217. *See* David Gaunt, Massacres, Resistance, Protectors: Muslim-Christian Relations in Eastern Anatolia During World War I, at 1, 19, 22, 24–5, 27–8, 71, 92, 110, 114–15, 148, 153–54, 163, 188, 210, 213, 218, 221, 224–28, 236, 239, 245, 253–55, 258, 268, 300–5, 378, 405, 445–46 (Piscataway, NJ: Gorgias Press, 2006) (describing confiscation of Assyrian Christians' property during genocide committed against these groups by Ottoman Turkey and its Kurdish allies during and after World War I); Vahakn N. Dadrian, The History of the Armenian Genocide: Ethnic Conflict from the Balkans to Anatolia to the Caucasus 222, 232, 304 (Providence, RI: Berghahn Books, 2003) (describing Ottoman Turkish seizure of so-called "abandoned" properties during and after Armenian genocide); Vahakn N. Dadrian, Warrant for Genocide: Key Elements of Turko-Armenian Conflict 34–5, 138, 180–81 (London: Transaction Publishers, 2003) (describing seizure of Armenian properties after 1914 as well as Armenian losses during nineteenth-century massacres instigated by Ottoman Sultan Abdul Hamid); Vahakn N. Dadrian, *The Documentation of the World War I Armenian Massacres in the Proceedings of the Turkish Military Tribunal*, 23 Int'l J. of Middle East Studies 549, 565, 568, 574 (1991) (describing charges against Ottoman officials for "plunder"); Charles Issawi, The Transformation of the Economic Position of the Millets in the Nineteenth Century, in Christians and Jews in the Ottoman Empire: The Functioning of a Plural Society 262–64, 266, 269–70 (Benjamin Braude & Bernard Lewis eds., New York: Holmes & Meier Publishers, 1982) (describing importance of Greeks and Armenians to Ottoman economic life prior to genocides of World War I); Feroz Ahmad, Unionist Relations with the Greek, Armenian, and Jewish Communities of the Ottoman Empire, 1908–1914, in id. at 405–6, 427 (similar); Lt. Col. Ronald S. Stafford, The Tragedy of the Assyrians (London: Allen and Unwin, 1935), http://www.aina.org/books/tota.htm (describing how Assyrians of Mesopotamia and northern Persia lost their homes to Turkish and Kurdish attacks); Hannibal Travis, *"Native Christians Massacred": The Ottoman Genocide of the Assyrians during World War I*, 1.3 Genocide Studies and Prevention: An Int'l J. 327, 332, 335, 338 (2006) (describing how Assyrian and Chaldean villages were looted by Ottoman Turks and Kurds during World War I genocide); Dickran Kouymjian, *When Does Genocide End? The Armenian Case* (2003), http://armenianstudies.csufresno.edu/faculty/kouymjian/speechs/genocide_sonoma.htm (describing confiscation of Armenian wealth and lands); Dickran Kouymjian, *Confiscation of Armenian Property and the Destruction of Armenian Historical Monuments as a Manifestation of the Genocidal Process* (1998), http://armenianstudies.csufresno.edu/faculty/kouymjian/articles/confiscation.htm (similar); Joseph Alichoran, *Assyro-Chaldeans in the 20th Century: From Genocide to Diaspora,* 8 Journal of Assyrian Academic Studies 45, 51–6 (1994) (describing plunder of Assyrian and Chaldean property by Ottoman Turks); Basile M. Nikitine, *Une Petite Nation Victime de la Guerre*, 44 Revue des Sciences Politiques 602 (1921) (describing economic losses of Assyrian and Chaldean civilians massacred by Ottoman Turks); Eugene Griselle, Syriens et Chaldeens, Leur Martyre, Leurs Esperances (1918) (similar); *Germans Inspired Turkish Atrocities Against Asiatic Greeks*, N.Y. Times, Sept. 29, 1918 (describing economic losses to Greeks of Smyrna and elsewhere in Ottoman Empire, killed by thousands); *Turks Slaughter Greeks, Sell Women to Slavery*, L.A. Times, June 9, 1918 (similar).

218. Judgment: Goering, in Judgment of the International Military Tribunal for the Trial of German Major War Criminals (1947), http://avalon.yale.edu/judgoeri.htm. Among other economic benefits of this program to the German majority and Nazi elite, Goering implemented a one billion Deutsche Mark fine against German Jews in connection with the anti-Jewish violence on *Kristallnacht* in late 1938. *See id.*

vast German empire across Europe, Asia, and Africa in which dozens of nations would enrich their German overlords, the "master race."[219] The Nazis resolved to exterminate the Jews because the Nazis' delusional narrative of history linked an international conspiracy of Jews to the rise in the East of the Soviet Union, and to victories over Germany in the West and global South by the British Empire and international capitalism in World War I.[220] German firms eventually reaped enormous benefits from seizing Jewish businesses and utilizing up to 12 million slave laborers of mostly Jewish and Slavic origin.[221]

Acts of genocide since World War II have equally manifested economic motivations. The Cold War was a global economic struggle between rival superpowers for markets, land, natural resources, military staging points, and the hearts and minds of satellite state populations. Several allies of the NATO alliance during the Cold War committed genocide against their minority populations, with unmistakable economic and political motives accompanying their intent to prevent the survival of identifiable ethnic and religious groups. The Indonesian army's execution starting in 1965 of a genocidal campaign against up to one million communists and ethnic Chinese, the latter of which were perceived as both "enemies of God" and rich traders, blocked land reform initiatives and opened the door for army leader Suharto to steal $80 billion over the next 32 years in the absence of an effective political opposition.[222] Suharto's invasion and occupation of East Timor starting in 1975 not only claimed nearly 200,000 genocide victims,[223] but also led to the ex-

---

219. *See Introduction, in* Weber and Toennies: Comparative Sociology in Historical Perspective (Joseph B. Maier & Chaim I. Waxman eds., 1995); Franz Leopold Neumann, Behemoth: The Structure and Practice of National Socialism,1933–1944, at 136–37, 156–60 (Cass) (New York: Harper & Row, 1963) (1942); Program of the National Socialist German Workers' Party, http://www.yale.edu/lawweb/avalon/imt/document/nsdappro.htm ("We demand land and territory (colonies) for the maintenance of our people and the settlement of our surplus population."); 1 Nazi Conspiracy and Aggression, ch. VII (Office of Justice Robert H. Jackson, U.S. Chief of Counsel for the Prosecution of Nazi Criminality ed., Washington, DC: U.S. Govt. Printing Ofc., 1946) [hereinafter "Nazi Conspiracy and Aggression"], http://web.archive.org/web/20031222180432/http://www.yale.edu/lawweb/ avalon/imt/document/ nca_vol1/chap_07.htm; 1 Nazi Conspiracy and Aggression, ch. X, http://web.archive.org/ web/20031222180627/http://www.yale.edu/lawweb/avalon/imt/document/nca_vol1/chap_10.htm (describing Nazi program of enslavement and deportation of civilian populations in Germany's Eastern European empire); 1 Nazi Conspiracy and Aggression, ch. XII, http://www.yale.edu/lawweb/avalon/imt/document/nca_vol1/chap_13.htm.

220. *See* Jeffrey Herf, The Jewish Enemy: Nazi Propaganda During World War II and the Holocaust, ch. 4 (Cambridge, MA: Harvard UP, 2006); Neumann, Behemoth, at 109–11.

221. *See* Michael J. Bazyler, Holocaust Justice: The Battle for Restitution in America's Courts 59–60 (New York: NYU Press, 2003) (20,000 German companies used slave labor, 400 of them from concentration camps, so German firms reaped "enormous wartime profits" by being relieved of the obligation of having to pay for the labor of half of their workers, some paid out as dividends to investors, some "reinvested in capital equipment that paved the way for [German] postwar corporate profitability") (quoting Burt Neuborne, attorney for victims of Nazi slave labor policies); Document No. 1061-PS, *in* 3 Nazi Conspiracy and Aggression, ch. XII, http://www.yale.edu/lawweb/avalon/imt/document/1061-ps.htm (report on Warsaw Ghetto uprising stating that "considerable amounts of paper money, foreign currency, gold coins, and jewelry were seized today. The Jews still have considerable property."); Neumann, Behemoth, at 117, 119 ("Aryanization chiefly served the interests of the giant enterprises, which used the opportunity to 'round off and expand' their holdings by buying out Jewish owners.... Wherever powerful Jewish firms could not be swallowed by competing Aryan enterprises, they were taken over by banks....").

222. Chalk & Jonassohn, The History and Sociology of Genocide, at 378–83; *see also* Valentino, Final Solutions, at 27; Rachel Ehrenfeld, Funding Evil: How Terrorism Is Financed—And How to Stop It 30 (Chicago: Bonus Books, 2005).

223. *See Report Cites East Timor Suffering*, CNN (Jan. 18, 2006), http://cnn.com/2006/WORLD/asiapcf/01/18/easttimor.indonesia/index.html?eref=sitesearch; Sian Powell, *UN Verdict on East Timor*, The Australian, Jan. 19, 2006, http://www.yale.edu/gsp/east_timor/unverdict.html; Melson, *The*

pulsion of ethnic Chinese and Timorese Catholics from prime real estate, as well as "the naked plunder of East Timor's resources," including "joint Indonesian-Australian" exploitation of oil and gas reserves off the coast of East Timor.[224] Pakistani dictator Yahya Khan, by carrying out genocide against up to 3 million residents of East Pakistan, hoped to quash an independence movement against "colonial exploitation" of the East by West Pakistan, which was also a movement for public provision of basic necessities, land reform, and nationalization of businesses.[225] As the army targeted Hindus for massacres, enormous holdings in lands and economic assets passed into Muslim hands.[226] The Guatemalan military committed genocide against the indigenous Mayan people, destroying more than 600 villages and killing or "disappearing" over 200,000 people,[227] in response to a social movement and accompanying insurgency, which protested the extreme poverty faced by the 75 percent of the population with little or no land on which to grow food to support themselves.[228]

Communist regimes during the Cold War period had strong economic motivations for committing genocide. The Stalinists apparently believed that the deliberate starvation of millions of Russian and Ukrainian landlords would facilitate the collectivization of

---

Armenian Genocide, at 334 n.41; Chamberlain, *The People of East Timor*, at 238–43.

224. Geoffrey C. Gunn, East Timor and the United Nations: The Case for Intervention 27–28, 58–59 (The Lawrenceville, NJ: Red Sea Press, 1997).

225. Chalk & Jonassohn, The History and Sociology of Genocide, at 394–97. *See also Awami League Manifesto,* 4 NYU J. Int'l L. & Politics 524, 524–25, 530–33, 536–37 (1971).

226. *See* Sen. Edward Kennedy, Crisis in South Asia: A Report to the Subcommittee Investigating the Problem of Refugees and Their Settlement, Submitted to the US Senate Judiciary Committee 66 (Washington, DC, 1971), *quoted in* Jaideep Saikia, *Terror Sans Frontiers: Islamic Militancy in North East India*, ACDIS Occasional Paper (July 2003), ch. 3 n.109 & accompanying text, http://www.acdis.uiuc.edu/Research/OPs/Saikia/contents/chap_three.html; Bertil Lintner, *The Plights of Ethnic and Religious Minorities and the Rise of Islamic Extremism in Bangladesh* (Feb. 2, 2003), http://www.asiapacificms.com/papers/pdf/ethnic_and_religious_minorities_bangladesh.pdf (describing how after 1971 war, Pakistanis seized Hindu properties and "[a]ccording to the US State Department: 'Approximately 2.5 million acres of land was seized from Hindus and almost all of the 10 million Hindus in [Pakistan] were affected.'.... [B]y 1975 only 13.5% of the population was Hindu, and those who remained were no longer landowners and shopkeepers. Most were poor and low caste farmers and fishermen; the new elite that had emerged was almost exclusively Muslim.").

227. Guatemalan Commission for Historical Clarification, Guatemala: Memory of Silence (1999), http://shr.aaas.org/guatemala/ceh/report/english/conc2.html (concluding that "that the reiteration of destructive acts, directed systematically against groups of the Mayan population, within which can be mentioned the elimination of leaders and criminal acts against minors who could not possibly have been military targets, demonstrates that the only common denominator for all the victims was the fact that they belonged to a specific ethnic group and makes it evident that these acts were committed 'with intent to destroy, in whole or in part' these groups"); U.N. Econ. & Soc. Council [ECOSOC], Commission on Human Rights, The Right to Food: Report of the Special Rapporteur on the Right to Food prepared by Jean Ziegler, 62nd Sess., Item 10 of the Provisional Agenda, E/CN.4/2006/44/Add. 1, ¶ 19, http://www.righttofood.org/Guatemala%20PDF.pdf ("Over 600 villages were completely destroyed and most of their residents massacred."); Jan Perlin, The *Guatemalan Historical Clarification Commission Finds Genocide*, 6 ILSA J. Int'l & Comparative L. 389 (2000) (describing context of Commission's report); *Guatemala 'Genocide' Probe Blames State*, BBC News.com, Feb. 25, 1999, http://news.bbc.co.uk/1/hi/world/americas/286402.stm.

228. *See* Guatemalan Commission for Historical Clarification [GCHC], at http://shr.aaas.org/guatemala/ciidh/dts/socmove.html ("army high command, under pressure from, and later backed by, the economic oligarchy and sectors of the extreme right, decided to implement a counterinsurgency strategy that spared no social cost in the interest of maintaining the status quo"); *id.* (the army decided "to eliminate the potential social base of the insurgency—the indigenous peasants").

agriculture and the exponential improvement of Soviet agricultural productivity.[229] The improbable vision of Mao Zedong of a "Great Leap Forward" that would rapidly industrialize China's economy along communist lines and enable it to catch up to the U.S. in a mere 15 years resulted in the deaths of up to 30 million Chinese from starvation, disease, and stepped-up persecution of wealthier peasants.[230] Similarly, the Cambodian Khmer Rouge apparently believed that ethnic minorities such as the Cham Muslims and Vietnamese, as well as members of their own Khmer ethnic group that might oppose communism, had to be "uprooted" to facilitate a modernization and collectivization of agriculture that would boost economic output several times over.[231]

The 1980s brought a continuation of this pattern of genocide as economic policy. Scholars have accused the Soviet Union of waging a campaign of genocide in the countryside of Afghanistan, in which 1.2 to 1.5 million died as a result of the bombardment of major cities, the destruction of many villages, and the massacre of many civilians by Soviet and rebel forces.[232] During that time, the Soviet Union was importing Afghan natural gas via a pipeline into the Soviet Union, paying only about half of the world market price.[233] With ample Soviet advisers and weapons, the government of Saddam Hussein massacred close to 200,000 Kurds, Assyrians, and Yezidis during the late 1980s by poison gas attacks, bombardments, attacks on Kurdish rebel armies, and summary executions at more than 200 mass grave sites.[234] About 2,000 villages were destroyed in a campaign to consolidate Arab control of a region containing "significant oil deposits,"[235] and to neu-

229. *See Famine (Ukraine), in* 3 ENCYCLOPEDIA OF GENOCIDE AND CRIMES AGAINST HUMANITY 1056–59 (Dinah Shelton ed., Farmington Hills, MI: Thomson Gale/Macmillian Reference, 2005); WENDY J. GOLDMAN, WOMEN AT THE GATES: GENDER AND INDUSTRY IN STALIN'S RUSSIA 75 (Cambridge: Cambridge UP, 2002); David Remnick, *Academician Details Stalin's 1930s Terror,* WASH. POST, Apr. 5, 1988, at A17; *The Peasant Harries the Kremlin; His Craving for a Piece of Land Complicates Each New Plan for a Communized Countryside,* N.Y. TIMES, July 22, 1951, at Magazine-130; Walter Duranty, *'Shock Period' Set to Spur Red Output,* N.Y. TIMES, Oct. 2, 1930, at 15.

230. *See* VALENTINO, FINAL SOLUTIONS, at 75, 93, 125–33, 143 (30 million); John Komlos, *On the Biological Standard of Living in the Soviet Union,* 58.1 SLAVIC REV. 71, 77 (1999) (26 million); Nicholas Eberstadt, *The Great Leap Backward,* N.Y. TIMES, Feb. 16, 1997, http://www.nytimes.com/books/97/02/16/reviews/970216.16ebersta.html (reviewing JASPER BECKER, HUNGRY GHOSTS: MAO'S SECRET FAMINE (Toronto: Owl Books, 1997)) (30 million).

231. *See* VALENTINO, FINAL SOLUTIONS, at 134–39.

232. *See id.* at 220–233; MOHAMMAD HASSAN KAKAR, AFGHANISTAN: THE SOVIET INVASION AND THE AFGHAN RESPONSE, 1979–1982, at 213–52 (Berkeley, CA: Univ. of California Press, 1997).

233. *See* LINDA RACIOPPI, SOVIET POLICY TOWARDS SOUTH ASIA SINCE 1970, at 126 (Cambridge: Cambridge UP, 1994); Situation in Afghanistan: Hearing Before the Committee on Foreign Relations, U.S. Senate, 97th Cong., 2d Sess., at 63, 73 (Mar. 8, 1982).

234. *See* John F. Burns, *In New Hussein Trial, a Grisly Portrait of Mass Killings,* N.Y. TIMES, Dec. 4, 2006, at A15 (180,000 Kurds were killed or disappeared, according to Iraqi prosecutors who filed charges against Saddam Hussein for genocide); Travis, *The Ottoman Genocide of the Assyrians,* at 346 (during military campaigns of 1980s, Iraqi armed forces disappeared 1,000 Assyrians, destroyed 200 majority Assyrian villages, and razed two-dozen Christian religious buildings); Catherine S. Knowles, *Life and Human Dignity, The Birthright of all Human Beings: An Analysis of the Iraqi Genocide of the Kurds and Effective Enforcement of Human Rights,* 45 NAVAL LAW REV. 152, 158–59, 168 (1998) (citing MIDDLE EAST WATCH, GENOCIDE IN IRAQ 297–98, 312–317, 345 (Washington, DC: Middle East Watch, 1993)). *See also* U.N. ECOSOC, Commission on Human Rights, Report on the Situation of Human Rights in Iraq, prepared by the Special Rapporteur for Iraq, Max van der Stoel, U.N. Doc. No. E/CN.4/1992/31 (suggesting a genocidal design behind "mass murder and execution of Kurds, the destruction of Kurdish towns and villages, ... and the use of excessive force, including chemical weapons, against the Kurds in times of conflict...."), *quoted in* FERHAD IBRAHIM & GÜLISTAN GÜRBEY, THE KURDISH CONFLICT IN TURKEY: OBSTACLES AND CHANCES FOR PEACE AND DEMOCRACY 43–44 (LIT Verlag Berlin-Hamburg-Münster, 2000).

235. MIDDLE EAST WATCH, GENOCIDE IN IRAQ, at 36. *See also id.* at 4, 26.

tralize Kurdish support for Iran during Iraq's war to conquer the Iranian province of Khuzestan, which "contained the bulk of Iran's oil-industry."[236]

Victims of Africa's genocides and resource wars of the 1990s suffered from a similar dynamic, with the exploitation of mineral resources taking center stage. In Rwanda, the genocide of around a million Tutsis and moderate Hutus began during a period of plummeting food production and soaring poverty due to declining world coffee and tin prices, exacerbating a "conflict of economic needs manipulated by social elites on both sides of the ethnic divide."[237] Since 1998, the Democratic Republic of the Congo has suffered "the worst hemorrhage of human life in the present generation," as "war and preventable disease had taken a death toll of 4 million people," the equivalent of "six Rwandan genocides."[238] Congo has alleged that its neighbor Uganda invaded its territory in August 1998 and "systematically looted and exploited [its] assets and natural resources," including by assuming "outright control of the entire economic and commercial system in the [illegally] occupied areas...."[239] Congo's neighbor Rwanda invaded from the east, indiscriminately killing Hutu refugees and civilians, deliberately infecting thousands of Congolese women and children with HIV/AIDS, and exploiting eastern Congo's rich deposits of diamonds, gold, tin and other resources valued at over $150 billion.[240]

---

236. Kenneth Pollack, Arabs at War: Military Effectiveness, 1948–1991, at 183, 186–87, 228 (Omaha, Nebraska: Univ. of Nebraska Press, 2002); *see also* Oles M. Smolansky & Bettie M. Smolansky, The USSR and Iraq: The Soviet Quest for Influence 215 (Durham, NC: Duke UP, 1991) (referring to "oil-rich" Khuzestan region of Iran). *See also* Christine Spolar, *Ruthless Pursuit of Power Left His Nation a Shambles*, Chi. Tribune, Dec. 15, 2003, at 1 ("Hussein was fixated on Iran's oil fields in the southwest, a mother lode he knew could make Iraq the world's largest petroleum supplier."); Middle East Watch, Genocide in Iraq, at 49–50 (describing how in 1986 Kurdish forces reached an economic and military accord under which Iran would arm the Kurds, who attacked Iraqi oilfields near Kirkuk along with a contingent of Iranian Revolutionary Guards).

237. Prunier, The Rwanda Crisis, at 364 (emphasis omitted); *see also id.* at 367; Frances Moore Lappe, Joseph Collin, & Peter Rosset, World Hunger: 12 Myths 21–4 (New York: Grove Press, 2000); Kenneth J. Campbell, Genocide and the Global Village: Social Theory in a Globalizing Age 71–82 (New York: Palgrave Macmillan, 2001); Eric Toussaint, *Rwanda 10 Years on: Uncovering the Financiers of the Genocide*, Red Pepper, May 6, 2004, http://www.redpepper.org.uk/May2004/x-May2004-Toussaint.html.

238. *Under-Secretary-General Calls For Greater Security Council Commitment to Ending Conflicts in Democratic Republic of the Congo, Northern Uganda*, US Fed News, Sept. 16, 2006 (quoting Jan Egeland, U.N. Under-Secretary-General for Humanitarian Affairs).

239. Case Concerning Armed Activities on the Territory of the Congo (Democratic Republic of the Congo v. Uganda), 2005 ICJ LEXIS 1, ¶¶ 223, 240 (Dec. 19, 2005), http://www.icj-cij.org/icjwww/idocket/ico/ico_judgments/ico_judgment_20051219.pdf [hereinafter *Congo v. Uganda*]; Boaz Atzili, *When Good Fences Make Bad Neighbors; Fixed Borders, State Weakness, and International Conflict*, Int'l Security, Winter 2006/2007, at 139, n.117 and accompanying text; Amnesty International, *Africa Update: A Summary of Human Rights Concerns in sub-Saharan Africa*, AI Index: AFR 01/005/1998 (Oct. 1, 1998), http://web.amnesty.org/library/Index/ENGAFR010051998?open&of=ENG-2AF.

240. *See* Mariano-Florentino Cuellar, *Refugee Security and the Organizational Logic of Legal Mandates*, 37 Geo. J. Int'l L. 583, 591–96 & n29 (2006) (citing Dennis McNamara, *The Protection of Refugees and the Responsibility of States: Engagement or Abdication?*, 11 Harv. Hum. Rts. J. 355 n.1 (1998)); Armed Activities on the Territory of the Congo (Democratic Republic of the Congo v. Rwanda), Application Instituting Proceedings 7 (filed June 23, 1999), http://www.icj-cij.org/icjwww/idocket/icorw/icorwapplication/icorw_iapplication_19990623.pdf [hereinafter *Congo v. Rwanda*]; Project Censored 2004: The Top 25 Censored Stories 159 (Peter Phillips ed., 2003); Thomas R. Yager, *The Mineral Industry of Congo (Kinshasa) in 2004*, in U.S. Geological Survey Minerals Yearbook—2004, at 12.2, http://minerals.usgs.gov/minerals/pubs/country/2004/cgmyb04.pdf; Thomas R. Yager, *The Mineral Industries of Burundi, Comoros, Malawi, Mauritius, Reunion, Rwanda, and Seychelles—2001*, at 7.5 (2001), http://minerals.usgs.gov/minerals/pubs/country/2001/bycnmimpfrrwsemyb01.pdf.

G. Defining Genocide for Purposes of This Book

To sum up, it is clear that genocide does not require the killing of all members of a group, for then the crime would virtually never occur. The intent to kill all the members of a group is also nearly impossible to prove, considering that even leading Nazis could waver between permitting emigration abroad or slave labor by some Jews, and ordering total eradication at once. A systematic killing campaign targeting civilian members of a distinct group, by contrast, is a standard that can be realistically applied, and has support in the indictment of the Nuremberg tribunal, the judgments of the Yugoslav and Rwanda tribunals, and the writings of Raphael Lemkin and several other prominent jurists, historians, and sociologists who have studied the matter. Similarly, the widespread destruction of religious buildings and historic cities or villages is properly analyzed as physical genocide when it is part of a larger policy that includes killing of thousands of group members, as happened in the Ottoman Empire, Iraq, and Sudan.[241]

241. Prosecutor v. Krstić, Trial Chamber, Judgement, at ¶¶80–84, 580, 589, 633; Prosecutor v. Blagojevic & Jokic, at ¶¶666, 675.

Chapter IV

Civilizing "Idolatrous People": Religion and Genocide

> To say the Truth, I had conceived a few Scruples with Relation to the Distributive Justice of Princes.... For instance, A Crew of Pyrates are driven by a Storm they know not whither, at length a boy discovers Land from the Top-mast, they go on Shore to Rob and Plunder; they see an harmless People, are entertained with Kindness, they give the Country a new Name, they take formal Possession of it for their King, they set up a rotten Plank or a Stone for a Memorial, they murder two or three Dozen of the Natives, bring away a couple more by Force for a Sample, return Home, and get their Pardon. Here commences a new Dominion acquired with a Title by Divine Right. Ships are sent with the first Opportunity, the Natives driven out or destroyed, their Princes tortured to discover their Gold; a free Licence given to all Acts of Inhumanity and Lust, the Earth reeking with the Blood of its Inhabitants: And this execrable Crew of Butchers employed in so pious an Expedition, is a modern Colony sent to convert and civilize an idolatrous and barbarous People.
>
> —Jonathan Swift, *Gulliver's Travels* (1726)[1]

A. War and Mass Killing Before Monotheism

Long before organized religion, there was mass killing. Humanity's ancestors may have exterminated the Neanderthal population of Europe.[2] Axes may have been used in Stone Age Europe to massacre women and children of enemy tribal groups.[3]

Pagan empires, from the Assyrians and Mesopotamians to the Persians, Greeks, and Romans, could be expansionist and destructive, but rarely resolved upon extermination or complete forced assimilation. The polytheistic empires that preceded Christian Rome and the Arab Caliphate left the peoples they conquered in the possession of their original religions. Ancient Egypt and Assyria stand out as empires that waged vigorous warfare, but without destroying entire nations or religions in the process.

1. Jonathan Swift, Gulliver's Travels 292 (Michael Seidel ed., New York: Barnes & Noble Classics, 2004) (1726).

2. Ben Kiernan, Blood and Soil: A World History of Genocide and Extermination from Sparta to Darfur 1 (New Haven, CT: Yale UP, 2007).

3. *See id.*

Battles and siege warfare between ancient Egyptians and their southern neighbors could involve widespread domination of the southerners, and sometimes the converse. In ancient Egypt, circa about 3,000 BCE, a general in charge of an expedition to the south remarked:

> The soldiers ... ploughed up the land of those who live upon the sand ...; laid it waste; ... overthrew the fenced cities [there] ...; ... cut down the fig trees and vines; ... cast fire among the tribes; ... slaughtered people in myriads and myriads; ... carried away countless multitudes of living captives.[4]

This pattern apparently continued for some centuries, with repeated expeditions by the Egyptians against the southern states of the "gold-land" (Nubia, possibly derived from Egyptian *nbw* for gold). Thousands of Nubian slaves were captured in such expeditions, as many as 17,000 at a time. A vizier wrote in about 2,000 BCE that "I slaughtered Nubians on several occasions, ... I came north uprooting their harvest ... and torching their houses."[5] Yet the Egyptian colony of Nubia flourished, becoming so powerful that more than two millennia after the expedition to the south described above, Nubian pharaohs came to govern all of Egypt.[6] Nubia continued to be a rich land for another two millennia after that, eventually being targeted for Arab conquest.[7]

The dynasties of Egypt typically did not resolve to eliminate rival gods and religions, instead frequently incorporating them into the Egyptian pantheon. Thus, the names of many gods worshipped in Egypt reveal foreign influence, as with Baal, Astarte, Khen, and Resheph.[8] One author concludes that "by including foreign deities in their own pantheon the Egyptians ensured that their followers could continue to worship their own gods within Egypt without displaying disloyalty to the state gods."[9] The Assyrian and Canaanite sun-god Shamash enjoyed official recognition alongside the Egyptian sun-god Amon-Ra or Aton.[10]

Present-day Iraq, is a territory the size of California, and the site of a 5,000 year-old civilization of city-states built up along the Tigris and Euphrates rivers.[11] Prior to being known as Iraq,[12] its original inhabitants wrote that it had four "corners": Akkad in the

---

4. Inscription of Una, *quoted in* ERNEST ALFRED WALLIS BUDGE, THE LIFE AND EXPLOITS OF ALEXANDER THE GREAT vii–viii (London: C.J. Clay & Sons, 1896).

5. Dr. William J. Murnane, *Three Kingdoms and Thirty-four Dynasties, in* ANCIENT EGYPT 24–27 (David P. Silverman ed., New York: Oxford UP, 2003); Donald B. Redford, *Egypt and the World Beyond, in id.* at 40–41.

6. *See* Murnane, *Three Kingdoms and Thirty-four Dynasties, in* ANCIENT EGYPT at 36–37.

7. *See* S. Birch, *Guide to the First and Second Egyptian Rooms in the British Museum, in* A THOUSAND MILES UP THE NILE, VOLUMES 1–2, at 294 (Amelia Ann Blanford Edwards ed., Leipzig: Berhard Tauchnitz, 1878).

8. *See Nubia, in* ENCYCLOPEDIA AFRICANA, at 1447; *Nubia, in* 11 THE CATHOLIC ENCYCLOPEDIA (1911), http://www.newadvent.org/cathen/11147a.htm.

9. ANN ROSALIE DAVID, HANDBOOK TO LIFE IN ANCIENT EGYPT 127 (New York: Oxford UP, 1999).

10. *See* ADOLPHE LODS, ISRAEL, FROM ITS BEGINNINGS TO THE MIDDLE OF THE VIIITH CENTURY 127 (London: Kegan Paul, 1932).

11. *See generally* GEORGES ROUX, ANCIENT IRAQ (New York; Penguin Books, 3d ed. 1992) (1964).

12. The spelling "Iraq" may derive from the Arabic *al-Iraq*, meaning the shore of a river, in this case the Tigris and Euphrates, and the arable land along it. *See* CHARLES TRIPP, A HISTORY OF IRAQ 8 (Cambridge: Cambridge UP, 2002). The term or sound of "Iraq," however, has been traced to more ancient Mesopotamian sources, i.e. the name of the Sumerian city-state of Uruk. *See* ROUX, ANCIENT IRAQ, at 68–75; A. LEO OPPENHEIM, ANCIENT MESOPOTAMIA 164–70 (Chicago: Univ, of Chicago Press, 2d ed. 1977).

north, Sumer in the south, Elam in the east, and Amurru/Martu in the west.[13] Starting in the fourth millennium BCE, the initially non-Semitic Sumerians settled among, and mated with, the native Semitic Akkadian population; thus, the Sumerians and Akkadians developed such extensive kinship, linguistic, cultural, religious, commercial, and political ties that they are frequently considered together as one Sumero-Akkadian civilization.[14] The Sumero-Akkadians developed writing and scriptures, temples, priests, myths of paradise and the underworld, poetry, schools, libraries, currency, merchants and capital investment, codified laws, contracts, family law, large-scale agriculture, mathematics, and many other fundamentals of civilized life.[15] They founded cities like Ashur and Babylon that, centuries later, became the capitals of the Assyrian and Babylonian kingdoms and empires.[16] The Sumerians were open to foreign rulers, and eventually assimilated nearly completely into the Semitic population.[17]

Assyria and Babylonia then took up and expanded upon the Sumero-Akkadian religious and poetic literature, astrology, sciences, laws, and political concepts,[18] including

---

13. *See* Piotr Michalowski, *Sumer Dreams of Subartu: Politics and the Geographical Imagination, in* LANGUAGES AND CULTURES IN CONTACT: AT THE CROSSROADS OF CIVILIZATIONS IN THE SYRO-MESOPOTAMIAN REALM 314 (Dieter Van Taillieu, Karel van Lerberghe, & Gabriela Voet eds., 1999); Emil G. Kraeling, *The Earliest Hebrew Flood Story*, 66 J. OF BIBLICAL LIT. 279 (1947); GEORGE SMITH, THE CHALDEAN ACCOUNT OF GENESIS 26–7 (London: Low, Searle, Rivington, 1876). The Sumerians, or at least a Sumerian poem dating from about 2,000 BCE [Before the Common Era], referred to Uri in the north, Sumer in the south, Shubur in the east, and Martu in the west. *See* HENRI FRANKFORT, KINGSHIP AND THE GODS: A STUDY OF ANCIENT NEAR EASTERN RELIGION AS AN INTEGRATION OF SOCIETY AND NATURE 216 (Chicago: Univ. of Chicago Press, 2d ed. 1978); Samuel N. Kramer, *Man's Golden Age: A Sumerian Parallel to Genesis XI*, 63 J. AMERICAN ORIENTAL SOC. 191 (1943).

14. *See* JEAN BOTTÉRO, MESOPOTAMIA: WRITING, REASONING, AND THE GODS 46–47, 68 (Chicago: Univ. of Chicago Press, 2d ed. 1995).

15. *See* JEAN BOTTÉRO, ANCESTOR OF THE WEST: WRITING, REASONING, AND RELIGION IN MESOPOTAMIA, ELAM, AND GREECE 19–27 (Chicago: University of Chicago Press, 2000); ANNIE CAUBET & PATRICK POUYSSEGUR, THE ORIGINS OF CIVILIZATION: THE ANCIENT NEAR EAST 149–61 (Paris: Éditions Pierre Terrail, 1998) To indicate the scale of Sumerian agriculture, one author notes that just the temple kitchens of Uruk, in Sumeria, could prepare 80,000 liters of beer, 18,000 sheep, 3,300 geese and ducks, 2,580 lambs, 720 cows, etc. *See* BOTTERO, ANCESTOR OF THE WEST, at 27. A Sumerian student was trained to account for up to 180,000 liters of barley. *See id.* at 22. To indicate their study of history, one of the oldest literary or library catalogues ever discovered, dating from about 2,000 BCE, contains several tablets dedicated to recounting and mourning the fall of cities or regions such as Akkad, Sumer, Nippur, and Ur. *See* SAMUEL N. KRAMER, SUMERIAN MYTHOLOGY: A STUDY OF SPIRITUAL AND LITERARY ACHIEVEMENT IN THE THIRD MILLENNIUM B.C. 23 (Philadelphia: American Philosophical Society, 1944). For accounts of Sumerian innovations in the codification of laws, administration of justice, formulation of religious ideas, and creation of schools, see SAMUEL N. KRAMER, HISTORY BEGINS AT SUMER: THIRTY-NINE FIRSTS IN MAN'S RECORDED HISTORY (Philadelphia: Univ. of Pennsylvania Press, 3d ed. 1989). The first code of laws, for the city of Ur, dates to the end of the third millennium BCE. *See* BOTTÉRO, MESOPOTAMIA, at 159. The Code of Ur-Nammu provides for fines to be paid in forms of legal currency, the *mina* or *shekel* of silver. *See* J.J. Finkelstein, *The Laws of Ur-Nammu*, 22 J. OF CUNEIFORM STUD. 66 (1968). The old Assyrian laws focused mainly on promoting and regulating trade between central Assyria and the Assyrian inhabitants of ancient Anatolia. *See, e.g.*, Klaas R. Veenhof, *"In Accordance with the Words of the Stele": Evidence for Old Assyrian Legislation*, 70 CHI. KENT L. REV. 1717, 1724–35 (1995).

16. *See* C.J. Gadd, *The Cities of Babylonia, in* THE CAMBRIDGE ANCIENT HISTORY 72, 98, 122–27 (John Bagnell Bury et al. eds., 1925).

17. *See* F.R. Steele, *Sumer, in* THE INTERNATIONAL STANDARD BIBLE ENCYCLOPEDIA: Q–Z, at 652 (Geoffrey W. Bromiley ed., Grand Rapids, MI: Wm. B. Eerdmans Publishing, 1995).

18. *See* Wolfgang Saxon, *Erica Reiner Is Dead at 81: Renowned Assyrian Scholar*, N.Y. TIMES, Jan. 22, 2006, at 1–32.

some of the first kings,[19] as well as assemblies of elders (called *abba* or city father) in a form of "Primitive Democracy."[20] From about 1,800 BCE on, the four "corners" of present-day Iraq had crystallized into northern and southern halves: Assyria and Babylonia.[21]

Starting in about 1,900 BCE and again in about 1,200 BCE, Assyrians administered one of the first empires, which was actually composed by a series of regional treaty relationships.[22] Invading tribes and empires, primarily the Elamites (easterners), Hittites (northerners), and Amorites (westerners), periodically conquered and destroyed the cities of the plains of Assyria and Babylon,[23] prompting the Assyrians to colonize the lands from which these tribes arrived periodically.[24] Nomadic peoples attacked the cities of the plains in order to reap the benefits of urban productivity, organization, and achievements.[25] The Assyrians "wasted the substance of their people in futile attempts to reach natural limits" in which they would be safe from foreign raiders.[26] The chronicles of the Assyrian kings record numerous efforts to establish defensible borders at the western sea (the

19. An inscription from approximately 2,000 BCE refers to a ruler of present-day Iraq as "king of Sumer and Akkad." Bottéro, Mesopotamia, at 62.

20. Frankfort, Kingship and the Gods, at 215, 218–19. *See also* Mogens Herman Hansen, A Comparative Study of Six City-state Cultures 27–32 (Copenhagen: The Danish Royal Academy, 2002).

21. *See* Bottéro, Mesopotamia, at vii, 289–90; *The Vassal-Treaties of Esarhaddon, in* 2 The Ancient Near East 53–69 (James Pritchard ed., Princeton: Princeton UP, 6th ed. 1992) (1958) (referring, in seventh century BCE, to Assyria and Babylonia, and to the gods of Assyria and Babylon).

22. *See* Parpola, *International Law in the First Millennium,* at 1051, 1054–55 (Assyrian influence extended into Babylon, Elam, Media, Scythia, Lydia, Anatolia, and Phoenicia by written treaties: "The Assyrian Empire was a union of states consisting of a core area under direct Assyrian rule (the Assyrian heartland with its provinces) and of semi-independent (vassal and allied) states bound to it by written treaties."); *id.* at 1058 (describing terms of eight such treaties with "vassal rulers"); Gunnar Lehmann, *Phoenicians in Western Galilee: First Results, in* Studies in the Archaeology of the Iron Age in Israel and Jordan 94–96 (Amihay Mazar ed., Harrisburg, PA: Continuum Int'l Publ'g Group, 2001) (describing Assyrian treaty with Phoenician ruler Baal of Tyre that reinforced Assyrian influence over Phoenicia and Palestine); Oppenheim, Ancient Mesopotamia, at 49; Caubet & Pouyssegur, The Origins of Civilization, at 94, 114–35 (describing early second millennium BCE empire of Assur and the Assyrians under the Amorite king Shamsi-Adad, and treaties called "oaths" pursuant to which Assyrian merchants established autonomous communities in Anatolian towns); *Treaty between Ashurnirari V of Assyria and Mati'ilu of Arpad, in* 2 The Ancient Near East, at 49–51; *Treaty of Esarhaddon with Baal of Tyre, in id.* at 52–53; *The Vassal-Treaties of Esarhaddon, in id.* at 53–69.

23. The Elamites "laid [Assyria] utterly waste" early in the second millennium BCE, and sacked Babylon in the twelfth century BCE. Caubet & Pouyssegur, The Origins of Civilization, at 97. The Hittites sacked Babylon in about 1,600 BCE. *See id.* at xiii, 150. The Mitannis, a non-Semitic people possibly originating in Persia, sacked Assur in about 1,400 BCE. *See* Trevor Bryce, The Kingdom of the Hittites 149 (Oxford: Clarendon Press, 1999); Romila Thapar, Early India: From the Origins to AD 1300, at 107–8 (Berkeley and Los Angeles: Univ. of California Press, 2003) (Mitannis of fourteenth century BCE spoke an Indo-Aryan language that indicates an origin in southeastern Persia). One of the earliest inscriptions in Old Assyrian, a language dating to the dawn of the second millennium BCE and related to Old Akkadian, suggested that the temple of Adad in the city of Assur had been destroyed and had to be "rebuilt." Daniel D. Luckenbill, 1 Ancient Records of Assyria and Babylonia 14 (London: Histories & Mysteries of Man, 1989) (1927) (inscription of Irishum, viceroy of Assyria). *See also* Leonard William King, Chronicles Concerning Early Babylonian Kings 126 (London: Luzac and Co., 1907) (Irishum is estimated to have ruled Assyria prior to 2,000 BCE).

24. Oppenheim, Ancient Mesopotamia, at 36.

25. *See* Roux, Ancient Iraq, at 159; Caubet & Pouyssegur, The Origins of Civilization, at 94.

26. *See* Frankfort, Kingship and the Gods, at 218.

Sea of Amurru or the Mediterranean), the east (Persia or "Parsua"), the "upper sea" (Lake Van), and the "lower sea" (the Persian Gulf).[27]

The Assyrian Empire declared respect for and offered protection to the gods of its vassal-states, such as Babylonia.[28] Assyrian priests and emperors accepted that their gods shared the heavens with a pantheon.[29] Similarly, Cyrus II of Persia stated, in a sixth century CE inscription, that the Assyro-Babylonian gods Bel, Nebo, and Marduk blessed his rule, rather than outlawing their worship.[30] There is no record of peoples under Assyrian or Persian rule vanishing or going extinct in the way that some Canaanite peoples seemingly did. Instead, these empires were generally tolerant of other peoples, and were the most technologically advanced societies in the region. Jews, Armenians, Persians, and Arabs survived and thrived in all regions, which explains their large numbers, amounting to millions or tens of millions, down to this day. The Assyrians and Persians could,

---

27. For Assyrian attempts to establish defensible borders on the shores of seas and the foothills of mountain ranges, see, LUCKENBILL, 1 ANCIENT RECORDS OF ASSYRIA, at 201, 206, 210, 235–36, 251 (inscriptions of Assyrian king Shalmaneser III, circa 820 BCE, describe conquest of lands west to Mediterranean or "sea of the setting sun," east to Parsua, north to Anatolia, i.e. "Tarsus" and the "land of the Hittites," and south to "lower sea," i.e. Persian Gulf); R.D. Barnett, *Urartu, in* THE CAMBRIDGE ANCIENT HISTORY 331 (John Boardman ed., Cambridge: Cambridge UP, 1982) (identifying upper sea with Lake Van, present-day Armenia); L.M. Diakonoff, *Media, in* THE CAMBRIDGE HISTORY OF IRAN 66 (W.B. Fischer, Ilya Gershevitch, & Ehsan Yarshster eds., Cambridge: Cambridge UP, 1993) (describing Shalmaneser's conquest of Parsua or Persia, which became an Assyrian province); Raymond P. Dougherty, *The Sealand of Arabia*, 50 J. AMERICAN ORIENTAL SOC. 1 (1930) (identifying lower sea with Persian Gulf); 4 THE ASSYRIAN DICTIONARY: "E" 113 (Ignace J. Gelb et al. eds., Chicago: Univ. of Chicago Press, 1958) (Assyrian king Sennacherib, circa 690 BCE, "conquered everything from the Upper Sea to the Lower Sea").

Countries with no defensible borders but a large agricultural output often undergo repeated attempts to conquer and exploit their people by force. The accounts of twentieth-century China, Poland, and Russia in later chapters may illustrate this. A young United States similarly expanded westward, by such policies as the Louisiana Purchase, the Indian Removal Act, Mexican-American War, later Indian Wars, Manifest Destiny, and the Spanish-American War, in order to eliminate perceived threats from European empires and indigenous peoples. *See, e.g.*, RICHARD WILLIAM LEOPOLD, THE GROWTH OF AMERICAN FOREIGN POLICY: A HISTORY 7 (New York: Knopf, 1962).

28. *See The Vassal-Treaties of Esarhaddon, in* 2 THE ANCIENT NEAR EAST, at 53–69 (treaty, in the era of King Esarhaddon in the seventh century BCE, between Assyrian "king of the world" and vassal prince of Babylonia); *Tablet of Assurbanipal No. K 3087, in* 2 LUCKENBILL, ANCIENT RECORDS OF ASSYRIA, at 365 (describing Assyrian restoration of local gods "to their places" in conquered territories, perhaps in Arabia).

29. *See, e.g.*, Michael B. Dick & Christoper Walker, *The Induction of the Cult Image in Ancient Mesopotamia: The Mesopotamian* mis pi *Ritual*, BORN IN HEAVEN, MADE ON EARTH: THE MAKING OF THE CULT IMAGE IN THE ANCIENT NEAR EAST 66 (Michael B. Dick & Christoper Walker eds., Winona Lake, Indiana: Eisenbrauns, 1999); Jonas C. Greenfield, Al Kanfei Yonah: Collected Studies of Jonas C. Greenfield on Semitic philology 284 (Leiden, the Netherlands: Brill, 2001) (discussing incorporation of Syrian god Hadad, counterpart of Assyrian storm god Adad, into Assyrian pantheon); MORRIS JASTROW, THE RELIGION OF BABYLONIA AND ASSYRIA 232 (Boston: The Athenaeum Press, 1898) (discussing several examples of foreign gods being incorporated into the Assyrian pantheon); BARBARA N. PORTER, IMAGES, POWER, AND POLITICS: FIGURATIVE ASPECTS OF ESARHADDON'S BABYLONIAN POLICY 98 (Diane Publ'g 1993) (discussing incorporation of initially foreign gods into Assyrian pantheon); *Rimmon, in* THE NEW SCHAFF-HERZOG ENCYCLOPEDIA OF RELIGIOUS KNOWLEDGE 40 (Samuel M. Jackson et al. eds., New York: Funk & Wagnalls Co., 1911) (discussing incorporation of Aramean god Martu/Ramman into the Assyrian pantheon); LEWIS SPENCE, MYTHS & LEGENDS: BABYLONIA & ASSYRIA 225 (London: Harrap, 1916, reprint 1995) (noting that "Bel'Merodach ... was absorbed into the Assyrian pantheon," and that to "Assyrians, Babylonia was the country of Bel").

30. Inscription of Cyrus, *quoted in* 1 THE ANCIENT NEAR EAST: AN ANTHOLOGY OF TEXTS AND PICTURES 206–7 (Princeton: Princeton UP, 6th ed. 1992) (1958).

of course, destroy cities in siege warfare and carry off their inhabitants into slavery, but cities were often rebuilt, and slaves could be freed by law.[31]

The Athenians could devastate conquered regions, and enslave entire peoples. An early example of genocide was committed in the first millennium BCE by the Athenians against the island and city of Melos, in the Cyclades chain between Athens and Crete.[32] Thucydides famously records that after the Melians clung to their hopes for freedom, the Athenians warned them of destruction unless they submitted to "the greatest city in Hellas, when it makes you the moderate offer of becoming its tributary ally, ... [because] upon this one deliberation depends its prosperity or ruin." The army of the great city returned to Melos and massacred all the adult men, while enslaving the women and children, and establishing an Athenian colony.[33]

Although Western writers frequently lavish effusive praise upon Alexander "the Great" of Macedon in order to legitimize Western claims to global dominance and to paint Eastern rulers and empires as uniquely barbarous and incapable of governing,[34] Alexander proved nearly as brutal as the Athenian rulers described by Thucydides.[35] For example, Alexander's armies crucified 2,000 Phoenicians in the sack of Tyre in 332 BCE.[36] Alexander's forces "carried out crucifixions on many occasions."[37] During Alexander's sack of Thebes, in Greece, 6,000 prisoners and civilians were massacred "without mercy."[38] One author describes the fall of Thebes to Alexander:

> [T]he conquerors glutted their rage with unresisted slaughter.... [T]he Thebans suffered from the utmost excesses of hostile cruelty.... [The Hellenes] revelled in the usual license of carnage, plunder, and wanton outrages on those whose age and sex left them most defenceless.... [Alexander's council decreed] that ... the lower city should be leveled with the ground, and the territory, except that part which belonged to the temples, divided among the allies; the men, women and children, sold as slaves.... The demolished buildings of Thebes may have ... [rebuilt another city]....[39]

31. *See* Klaas R. Veenhof, *A Deed of Manumission and Adoption from the Later Old Assyrian Period, in* Zikir Šumim: Assyriological Studies Presented to F.R. Kraus 359–89 (Fritz Rudolf Kraus et al eds., 1982); Patricia Crone, Roman, Provincial and Islamic Law: The Origins of the Islamic Patronate 64–65 (Cambridge: Cambridge UP, 2002).

32. *See* Frank Chalk & Kurt Jonassohn, The History and Sociology of Genocide: Analyses and Case Studies 90–115 (New Haven: Yale UP, 1990); A.P. Bosworth, *Athens and Melos, in* 1 Encyclopedia of Genocide and Crimes Against Humanity 1191 (Dinah Shelton ed., New York: Macmillan Reference, 2005).

33. Thucydides, History of the Peloponnesian War 392–401 (Richard Crawley trans., London: J.M Dent & Sons Ltd., 1910) (431 BCE), http://books.google.com/books?id=amZkx4zjmxsC.

34. *See, e.g.*, A.T. Olmstead, History of the Persian Empire 509–19 (Chicago: Univ. of Chicago Press, paperback ed. 1959) (giving extremely sanitized account of Alexander's conquest of Babylon); Anthony Pagden, Worlds at War: The 2,500–Year Struggle Between East and West 50–68, 538 (New York: Random House, 2008) (similarly sanitized account, and praising Alexander's "magnanimity" and "constrained" behavior of his army re "defeated populations," in support of author's thesis that world is still experiencing a "'clash of civilizations'" between civilized West and barbarous East on same "battle lines drawn during the Persian Wars more than twenty-three centuries ago").

35. *See* Pagden, Worlds at War, at 50–52.

36. K.C. Hanson & Douglas E. Oakman, Palestine in the Time of Jesus: Social Structures and Social Conflicts 92 (Minneapolis, MN: Fortress Press, 2002).

37. Martin Hengel, Crucifixion in the Ancient World and the Folly of the Message of the Cross 73 (Minneapolis, MN: Fortress Press, 1977).

38. David Hume, *Of the Populousness of Ancient Nations, in* 1 Essays: Moral, Political, and Literary (422 (Thomas Hill Green & T.H. Grose eds., London: Longmans, Green, and Co., 1889) (citing Diodorus Siculus 17.14).

39. Connop Thirlwall, 2 The History of Greece 165–66 (New York: Harper & Bros., 1860).

The sack of Thebes has been described as imperial terrorism designed to awe Greece's rivals.[40] In a later sack of Thebes, this time the much older city in Egypt, the city itself was destroyed to the extent that "there was nothing left to remind the Thebans of their former prosperity."[41]

Under Alexander's generals Antigonus and Seleucus, the Babylonian people were burned with fire, as Macedonian troops "plundered town and countryside."[42] Cattle were seized and the "the wretched inhabitants were left to die of starvation and disease."[43] Alexander's tactics served as a model for the Roman Empire under Julius Caesar and Trajan, and for the French Empire under Napoleon, among others.[44]

"The first classical genocide," according to Ben Kiernan of Yale University, was the Roman destruction of Carthage, which took place in the second century BCE, in present-day Tunisia in North Africa.[45] Raphael Lemkin, the architect of the Genocide Convention, cited the destruction of Carthage along with that of Jerusalem by Rome in the first century BCE as early genocides, or "wars of extermination."[46] More than 100,000 people died in the sieges of and massacres in Carthage and Jerusalem, with possibly more than half a million displaced in each city.[47] Appian described the fall of Carthage and massacre of its civilian population:

> [The Romans cast] the dead and the living together into holes in the ground, sweeping them along like sticks and stones . . . , and man was used for filling up a ditch. . . . Horses ran over them, crushing their faces and skulls. . . . Six days and nights were consumed in this kind of turmoil, the soldiers being changed so that

---

40. *See id.* ("Thebes was destroyed ... [so] that the example of its fate might strike the rest of Greece with a wholesome awe."); CHARLES ROLLIN, THE ANCIENT HISTORY OF THE EGYPTIANS, CARTHAGINIANS, ASSYRIANS, BABYLONIANS, MEDES AND PERSIANS, MACEDONIANS AND GREEKS 317, 534 (William H. Wyckoff trans. & ed., St. Louis, Missouri: Nafis, Cornish & Co., 1848), http://books.google.com/books?id=mFQZAAAAYAAJ&pg=PA98 (noting that Thebes was destroyed and that: "The dreadful example of severity towards so powerful a city as Thebes, spread the terror of [Alexander's] arms through all Greece.")

41. *Quoted in* Dorothy J. Thompson, *The Ptolemies and Egypt, in* A COMPANION TO THE HELLENISTIC WORLD 117–18 (Andrew Erskine ed., London: Blackwell Publishing, 2003). Temples were desecrated and looted. *See id.*

42. SIDNEY SMITH, BABYLONIAN HISTORICAL TEXTS RELATING TO THE CAPTURE AND DOWNFALL OF BABYLON 144 (London: Taylor & Francis, 1975) (1924).

43. *Id.* at 154.

44. *See* PAGDEN, WORLDS AT WAR, at 61–62.

45. KIERNAN, BLOOD AND SOIL, at 49.

46. RAPHAEL LEMKIN, AXIS RULE IN OCCUPIED EUROPE: LAWS OF OCCUPATION—ANALYSIS OF GOVERNMENT—PROPOSALS FOR REDRESS, ch. 9 (Washington, D.C.: Carnegie Endowment for International Peace, 1944) http://www.preventgenocide.org/lemkin/AxisRule1944–1.htm ("As classical examples of wars of extermination in which nations and groups of the population were completely or almost completely destroyed, the following may be cited, the destruction of Carthage in 146 B.C.; the destruction of Jerusalem by Titus in 72 A.D. . . ."). Some have suggested that Lemkin distinguished Carthage and other "wars of extermination" from "genocide," but he elsewhere calls the destruction of Carthage an "example[] of the destruction of entire nations, and ethnic and religious groups," while he defines genocide as "the extermination of racial and national groups " or "the crime of destroying national, racial or religious groups." Raphael Lemkin, *Genocide*, 15 THE AMERICAN SCHOLAR 227–230 (1946).

47. *See* Ben Kiernan, *The First Genocide: Carthage 146 BC*, 203 DIOGENES 27–39 (2004) (about 150,000 "exterminated" at Carthage, which was "annihilated," according to Roman sources such as Appian, Polybius, and Plutarch, displacing the surviving population of 400,000 to 700,000, including over 25,000 women who were enslaved along with a similar number of men). *See Jerusalem, in* INTERNATIONAL STANDARD BIBLE ENCYCLOPEDIA: E–J, at 1029–30 (Geoffrey W. Bromiley ed., Grand Rapids, MI: Wm. B. Eerdmans Publ'g, 1982).

> they might not be worn out with toil, slaughter, want of sleep, and these horrid sights....
>
> Scipio ... set fire to the [buildings].... The fire spread and carried everything down, and the soldiers ... pulled [the buildings] down all together.... [O]ld men, women, and young children who had hidden in the inmost nooks of the houses, some of them wounded, some more or less burned, [were] uttering horrible cries. Still others ... were torn asunder into all kinds of horrible shapes.[48]

In Jerusalem and Carthage, cultural destruction and the devastation of cities and livelihoods accompanied massacres, tortures, and enslavement of the survivors.[49] Up to 500 refugees from Jerusalem were crucified each day during the siege, according to one source.[50] Josephus placed the total dead from the siege of Jerusalem at over one million out of a population of three million.[51] As in Carthage, many of the survivors were enslaved.[52] Similarly, the Roman sack of Corinth during the Achaean revolt, when the Macedonians were holed up in the city in the same year as the fall of Carthage, resulted in a massacre of all the men, enslavement of all the women and children, and burning and razing of all the architecture.[53]

The tearing down and burning of temples and holy places was particularly caustic to national and ethnic identity.[54] Many in ancient times, and even in modern ones, would rather die than see their native city destroyed and its sacred buildings razed to the ground. The Jewish historian Josephus wrote that "I cannot but wish that we had all died before we had seen that holy city demolished by the hands of our enemies, or the foundations of our holy temple dug up after so profane a manner."[55] The Roman historian Polybius wrote, with the fall of Carthage in mind, that "those who live in pain" after the fall of their city are still "more pitiable than those who lose their lives at the moment of their misfortunes ... —unless a man thinks nothing of dignity and honor, and ... [has] a regard only to material advantage."[56]

Nomadic raids from the northeast of the settled lands of Anatolia and Mesopotamia frequently resulted in massacres within cities, and their destruction by fire. In the fourth century CE, St. Jerome, who traveled extensively through Anatolia and spoke Aramaic,

---

48. Kiernan, Blood and Soil, at 50–51 (quoting 1 Appian of Alexandria, Roman History §8.19.128–31 (Horace White trans., New York: The MacMillan Co., 1899)).

49. *See* Kiernan, Blood and Soil, at 51–60 (describing destruction of Carthage and six other Punic [Phoenician/Tyrean] cities in North Africa); Ben Kiernan, *The First Genocide: Carthage 146 BC*, 203 Diogenes 27–39 (2004).

50. *See* Mireille Hadas-Lebel & Robyn Fréchet, Jerusalem Against Rome 90 (Leuven, Belgium: Peeters Publishers, 2005).

51. *See also* Paul N. Bartorp & Samuel Totten, *The History of Genocide: An Overview, in* Teaching about Genocide: Issues, Approaches, and Resources 24 (Samuel Totten ed., Charlotte, NC: Information Age Publ'g, 2004).

52. *See* Martin Goodman, *Judea, in* 9 The Cambridge Ancient History 664–65 (Alan K. Bowman, Peter Garnsey, Dominic Rathbone eds., Cambridge: Cambridge UP, 2d ed. 2000).

53. *See* Rollin, The Ancient History, at 57.

54. *See* Kiernan, Blood and Soil, at 612 n.36.

55. Flavius Josephus, 7 The War of the Jews: Or the History of the Destruction of Jerusalem, ch. 8 (trans. William Whiston, 1737) (75 CE), http://www.ccel.org/j/josephus/works/war-7.htm.

56. Polybius, 2 The Histories 515–40 (Evelyn S. Shuckburgh trans., London: Macmillan, 1889) (circa 200 BCE), http://www.fordham.edu/halsall/ancient/polybius-corinth146.html.

wrote that the invading Huns captured countless monasteries and committed massacres.[57] He wrote of the Huns:

> Behold the wolves, not of Arabia, but of the North, were let loose upon us last year from the far-off rocks of the Caucuses, and in a little while overran great provinces. How many monasteries were captured, how many streams were reddened with human blood! ... Not even if I had a hundred tongues and a hundred mouths, and a voice of iron could I recount the name of every catastrophe.... They filled the whole earth with slaughter and panic as they flittered hither and thither on their swift horses..., and they took pity neither upon religion, nor rank nor age nor wailing childhood. Those who had just begun to live were compelled to die and, in ignorance of their plight, would smile amid the drawn swords of the enemy.... [58]

In Syria, Cyrillonas, a Christian priest, wrote that after Attila and the Huns had come: "The East has been carried into captivity, and nobody lives in the destroyed cities.... Dead are the merchants, widowed the women...."[59] Nevertheless, Christianity and the Greek, Assyrian, and Armenian ethnicities survived in Anatolia, and even thrived long after the Huns had gone.

Between the fourth and sixth centuries CE, the Sassanian or New Persian Empire, which was generally tolerant of Judaism and Assyrian Christianity, engaged in repeated outbreaks of anti-minority persecution. Thousands died, but the Persian Empire never came close to wiping out its Jewish or Assyrian Christian subjects, and left most Jewish and Assyrian areas intact.[60] In fact, Jewish identity was consolidated in Babylon under Persian rule to the extent that Babylon could be referred to as a "land of Israel," the Babylonian Talmud could be completed there, and the Babylonian Jews could claim to have restored Torah study when it was forgotten in Israel.[61] Under the Persians, the Assyrians, or Church of the East, had bishops from Palestine to China.[62]

B. Religion and Genocide in the Ancient Near East

The Canaanites worshipped the gods that had been handed down from the Sumerians and Akkadians to the Babylonians and Assyrians, namely the father-god El or Ea, the

---

57. *See* Jerome, *Letter LX, in* SELECT LETTERS OF ST. JEROME (F. A. Wright trans., New York: G. P. Putnam's Sons, 1933), http://www.archive.org/stream/selectlettersofs00jerouoft/selectlettersofs00jerouoft_djvu.txt; *Jerome, in* THE JEWISH ENCYCLOPEDIA (1906), http://jewishencyclopedia.com/view.jsp?artid=239&letter=J&search=Jerome.

58. *Quoted in* E.A. THOMPSON, THE HUNS 31–32 (Oxford: Oxford UP, 1948). *See also* JOHN MAN, ATTILA: THE BARBARIAN KING WHO CHALLENGED ROME 113–14 (New York: Bantam Press, 2005).

59. *Quoted in* MAN, ATTILA, at 113–14.

60. *See* W.A. WIGRAM, THE ASSYRIANS AND THEIR NEIGHBOURS, ch. III (London: G. Bell & Sons, 1939); Oussani, *A Historical Essay*.

61. *See* Morris Jastrow Jr., *Babylonia, in* THE JEWISH ENCYCLOPEDIA (1901–1906), http://www.jewishencyclopedia.com/view.jsp?letter=B&artid=51.

62. *See* WILLIAM A. WIGRAM, AN INTRODUCTION TO THE HISTORY OF THE ASSYRIAN CHURCH 126–264 (Piscataway, NJ: Gorgias Press, 2004) (1910).

"Mother of the Gods" Asherah, her daughter Inanna or Ishtar, and her son Bel or Baal—literally "the Lord."[63] In Jericho, there was a temple to the Assyro-Babylonian moon god, Sin.[64] The Mesopotamian account of the creation resembles its counterpart in the Book of Genesis, for it describes a time "when heaven, on high, had not (yet) been named, [and] below, the earth had not (yet) been given a name."[65] The Assyrian scriptures of the gods used very similar terms as the term *elohim* used for "God" in Genesis, in the Assyrian case *a'lu* or *i'lu*, which referred to a "league" of "divine leadership."[66] One author argues that in translating the Book of Genesis, the "'Lord God'" (*elohim*) should be translated as "'the Hebrew tribal god among the god family.'"[67]

Despite the similarities between Judaism and ancient Assyrian and Canaanite paganism, monotheism developed in a way that ensured its implacable opposition to and intolerance of paganism. A precedent that would often be cited by military leaders and legal scholars for the subjugation of "heathen" nations and tribes in the Americas, Africa, and Oceania was the story of the conquest of Canaan by the Israelites in the books of Exodus, Deuteronomy, Joshua, and Numbers.[68] In the Book of Exodus, the "Song of Moses" declares that "all the inhabitants of Canaan shall melt away."[69] In the Book of Deuteronomy, Moses instructed his followers:

> WHEN the LORD thy God shall bring thee into the land whither thou goest to possess it, and hath cast out many nations before thee, the Hittites, and the Girgashites, and the Amorites, and the Canaanites, and the Perizzites, and the Hivites, and the Jebusites, seven nations greater and mightier than thou;

---

63. *See, e.g.*, William G. Dever, Asherah, *Consort of Yahweh?*, Bulletin of the American Schools of Oriental Research, No. 255, at 21–37 (1984); *Exodus, in* Women's Bible Commentary 38 (Carol Ann Newsom & Sharon H. Ringe, Louisville, Kentucky: Westminster John Knox Press, 1998); *id.* at 35 (discussing Baal and his female counterpart); *id.* at 109–10 (discussing relations between Baal and Asherah); *id.* at 112 (discussing Baal worship in Israel); *id.* at 208 (discussing religion of Baal and other Canaanite deities in Israel, rather than Yahweh); *id.* at 211 ("The land (people) has wantonly turned away from Yahweh to worship the Canaanite storm god Baal...."); *id.* at 238 (discussing religion of Baal); 1 Kings 16:31; 19:1–3 (KJV); Saul Olyan, Asherah and the Cult of Yahweh in Israel (Atlanta: Scholars Press, 1988); Hermann Spieckermann, Juda unter Assur in der Sargonidenzeit 212–27 (Gottingen: Vandenhoeck & Ruprecht, 1982).

64. *See, e.g.*, M.V. Seton Williams, *Palestinian Temples*, 11 Iraq 77, 78 (1949).

65. 4 The Assyrian Dictionary: "E" 96 (Chicago: Univ. of Chicago Press, 1956).

66. *Compare* 4 The Assyrian Dictionary: "E" at 374 (A Leo Oppenheim & Erica Reiner eds., Chicago: Univ. of Chicago, 1958) (Mesopotamian account of the gods used the terms "a'lu" or "i'lu" as a "confederation" or "league" of "divine leadership"), *with* James Ballantyne Hannay, Christianity: The Sources of Its Teaching and Symbolism 159 (Whitefish, MT; Kessinger Publishing, 2005) (1913) (arguing that in translating the Book of Genesis into English: "The phrase 'Lord God' [i.e. *Elohim*] ... ought to be translated ... 'the Hebrew tribal god among the god family.'... For instance, in Deuteronomy xi. 16, we have: 'Serve other Elohim (gods), and bow down to *them*.'") (emphasis in original).

67. Hannay, Christianity at 159.

68. *See* Lorenzo Veracini, *Colonialism and Genocides: Notes for the Analysis of the Settler Archive, in* Empire, Colony, Genocide, at 148–49; Ann Curthoys, *Genocide in Tasmania: The History of an Idea, in id.* at 229–52; Ann Curthoys, *Expulsion, Exodus and Exile in White Australian Historical Mythology*, 61 J. of Australian Studies 2 (1999); Niccolò Machiavelli, the Prince 8, 221–223 (W. K. Marriott trans., New York: E.P. Dutton, 1908) (1515), ch. 6, http://www.constitution.org/mac/prince.pdf; Niccolò Machiavelli, Discourses on the First Decade of Titus Livius 8, 221–223 (Ninian Hill Thomson trans., London: Kegan Paul, Trench & Co., 1883) (1513).

69. Exodus 15:3–15 (KJV).

> And when the LORD thy God shall deliver them before thee; thou shalt smite them, *and* utterly destroy them; thou shalt make no covenant with them, nor show mercy unto them....[70]

In some passages of the Books of Deuteronomy, Numbers, Joshua, and Samuel, civilians, including women and children, are not spared during the conquest of Canaan.[71] As one legal scholar describes it, the Book of Joshua is "one of the earliest texts in which a deity quite plainly promotes a destruction of the people."[72] In another account, these books tell of divinely-commanded wars "against six enumerated nations occupying cities given to the Jews," disproportionate "wars of extermination—that is, of genocide—lest the survivors teach [paganism] to the Jews."[73]

The Book of Deuteronomy allows peace treaties, and tributary relationships, but counsels harsh treatment for those refusing to submit to the Israelites: "thou shalt smite every male thereof with the edge of the sword," and "take" the women, children, and cattle "unto thyself" as war "spoil."[74] However, the Book Exodus states: "The innocent and righteous slay thou not."[75]

Archaeologists regard it as unlikely that the events detailed in the books of Exodus, Deuteronomy, etc. could have actually taken place as described, so the relevance of these stories lies more in their impact on later theologies, political ideologies, and legal theories. There is "a lack of evidence of sudden destruction at several key sites—such as Jericho and Ai, neither of which appears to have been occupied" when a "military conquest of Canaan" was supposed to have taken place. Instead, Judaism may have evolved internally from polytheism in the region, not simply in Palestine but also in Mesopotamia and elsewhere.[76] One author writes that the archaeology and the chronology of the conquest

70. Deuteronomy 6:1–2, 5–6 (KJV).

71. *See* Deuteronomy 2:34 (KJV) ("We took all his [Sihon's] cities at that time, and utterly destroyed the men, the women, and the little ones, of every city, we left none to remain...."); Deuteronomy 7:1 (KJV) ("When the Lord your God brings you into the land that you are about to enter and occupy, and he clears away many nations before you ... then you must utterly destroy them. Make no covenant with them and show them no mercy."); Deuteronomy 20:16 (KJV) ("you shall let no breathing creature live"); Numbers 25:4–6 (KJV) (describing the beheading of the worshippers of the Canaanite deity Baal-Peor); Numbers 33:50–53 (KJV) ("And the Lord spake unto Moses ... saying, speak unto the children of Israel and say unto them, when ye are passed over Jordan into the land of Canaan, then ye shall drive out all the inhabitants of the land from before you ... and ye shall dispossess the inhabitants of the land and dwell therein, for I have given you the land to possess it."); Joshua 10:40 (KJV) ("So Joshua smote all the country of the hills, of the south, and of the vale, and of the springs, and all their kings: he left none remaining but utterly destroyed all that breathed, as the Lord God of Israel commanded."); Samuel 15:3 (KJV) ("Now go and smite Amalek, and utterly destroy all that they have, and spare them not, but slay both man and woman, infant and suckling, ox and sheep, camel and ass.").

72. Leonard B. Glick, *Religion and Genocide, in* 3 The Widening Circle of Genocide: Genocide, A Critical Bibliographic Review 46 (Israel W. Charny ed., New Brunswick, NJ: Transaction Publishers, 1994), *quoted in* Kelly, *The Crime of Genocide's Evolution*, at 261 n.6.

73. David Churchman, *"Just War" in Seven Cultures* (2009), http://srrn.com/abstract_id=1311532 (citing Deut. 20: 16–18).

74. Deuteronomy 20:10–14 (KJV).

75. Exodus 23:7 (KJV).

76. Jeffery L. Sheler, *The Fight for History*, U.S. News & World Report (Special Issue), Nov. 2, 2004, http://www.usnews.com. Joshua 24:2–3 actually states, "In olden times, your forefathers—Terah, father of Abraham and father of Nahor—lived beyond the Euphrates and worshiped other gods." In the biblical account, which may have been an allegory of the settlement of a less urbanized and advanced Palestinian territory by a more advanced Mesopotamian one, God orders Abraham to

of Canaan are unconvincing and unsatisfactory.[77] Another, the chair in the archaeology of Israel at the University of Jerusalem, states that the archaeological evidence wavers between outright contradiction and lack of support for the narrative of a large-scale conquest.[78] As a theological story of miraculous victories, modern scholars doubt that the stories of the Book of Joshua represent historic facts or events.[79]

More likely to have actually taken place was the elimination of animism and paganism by force of law, under periods in which theocratic religious law was in effect. When Israelites sacrificed to other gods, Moses ordered them to be exposed to the sun until they were slain.[80] Drawing on the Book of Exodus,[81] Talmudic jurisprudence imposed the death penalty by stoning for paganism, i.e., idolatry, magic, witchcraft, necromancy, blasphemy, and instigating these offenses. The reversion of Hebrews to paganism could also be punishable as apostasy, and "prophesying in the name of heathen deities" was potentially punishable by strangulation.[82]

C. The Expansion and Defense of Christendom

Although Christianity had many parallels in pagan religions that preceded it, some its leaders did not manifest an equal tolerance for other faiths.[83] Assyro-Babylonian religion

---

move his family to Canaan, adopting a new faith in the process. *See* Shammai Engelmayer, *Ivri: Naming Ourselves*, JUDAISM, Jan. 1, 2005, at 13. Abraham was called a Hebrew, but his Mesopotamian father and brother were not, due to their polytheism. *Cf.* Mark Roth, *Theologian's Mission: Interpret Violence in the Bible*, PITTSBURGH POST-GAZETTE, March 24, 2008, at A1.

77. KATHLEEN MARY KENYON, ARCHAEOLOGY IN THE HOLY LAND 209 (London: Taylor & Francis, 1985).

78. *See* Amihai Mazar, *The Patriarchs, Exodus, and Conquest Narratives in Light of Archaeology, in* THE QUEST FOR THE HISTORICAL ISRAEL 64 (Israel Finkelstein, Amihai Mazar, Brian B. Schmidt eds., Society for Biblical Literature, 2007).

79. *See, e.g.*, Israel Finkelstein, *Digging for the Truth: Archaeology and the Bible, in id.* at 15 ("[biblical] texts are highly ideological on both the political and theological levels. They represent the point of view of one elite faction of Judahite society...."); WALTER E. RAST, THROUGH THE AGES IN PALESTINIAN ARCHAEOLOGY 112 (Harrisburg, PA: Continuum International Publishing Group, 1992) (biblical texts paint a picture of "wondrous" victory in war to confirm a gift of land from God, not a straightforward historical narrative).

80. *See* Numbers 25:4–5 (KJV); DAVID W. CHAPMAN, ANCIENT JEWISH AND CHRISTIAN PERCEPTIONS OF CRUCIFIXION 35 (Tubingen: Mohr Siebeck, 2008).

81. *See* Exodus 22:18 (KJV) ("Thou shalt not suffer a witch to live."). *See also* Deuteronomy 18:10–11 (KJV) ("There shall not be found among you [any one] that maketh his son or his daughter to pass through the fire, [or] that useth divination, [or] an observer of times, or an enchanter, or a witch. Or a charmer, or a consulter with familiar spirits, or a wizard, or a necromancer"); Leviticus 20:27 (KJV) ("A man also or woman that hath a familiar spirit, or that is a wizard, shall surely be put to death: they shall stone them with stones: their blood [shall be] upon them.")

82. *See* SAMUEL MENDELSOHN, THE CRIMINAL JURISPRUDENCE OF THE ANCIENT HEBREWS §§ 19, 26, 128–29, at 44–56, 161–62 & nn. 100, 107 (Union, NJ: Lawbook Exchange, 2001) (1891).

83. The ancient Assyrians believed in a supreme god as "the only true god," along with a divine king, his son, and a divine mother, who bore the perfect son and king of the supreme god in her womb. *See*, e.g., Simo Parpola, *Sons of God: The Ideology of Assyrian Kingship*, ARCHAEOLOGY ODYSSEY, Nov./Dec. 1999, at 16, 17 ("The impact of Mesopotamian religious thought on the evolution of other ancient religious and philosophical through ... has been far greater than anyone has yet suggested.... There was a commandment to refrain from work on every seventh day of every month (plus the 19th day."); *id.* at 20 ("In Assyrian art, depictions of kings are often ... representing the holy family of divine father, divine mother, and divine son (the king)."); *id.* ("Ashur, the supreme god of the empire, defined in Assyrian sources as ... the only true god ... was thus, by implication, the 'heavenly father'

envisaged an afterlife in paradise, particularly for those who died as stillborn infants, before "their time," or with large numbers of descendents left behind to make sacrificial offerings of food and wine.[84] Its scriptures also depicted an underworld as a "grim 'hell'" of darkness, confinement, hunger, "spiritual trials," and torment by demons.[85] Nevertheless, the underworld of the Assyro-Babylonians did not hold quite the terrors of the "lake of fire" into which the Book of Revelation predicts that worshippers of the image of "the beast" (the term used in the Book of Genesis for animals, making the worship of images of animals, a standard pagan practice, the offense in context) will be "cast alive" and "tormented day and night for the ages of the ages."[86]

Jesus Christ in the Book of Matthew is fairly clear in outlawing acts of violence or retribution that could escalate into genocide. One notable declaration by Jesus to his apostles warned that "all they that take the sword shall perish with the sword."[87] The Golden Rule, of course, calls upon Christians to treat others as they would like to be treated, which is hardly consistent with murdering them.[88] And indeed, the early Christian church taught that Christians should not make war, but should respond to acts of violence with love and forgiveness.[89]

---

of the king, while the latter was his 'son' in human form."); *id.* ("The Father-Mother-Son triad constituted by Ashur, Ishtar, and the king reminds one of the Holy Trinity of Christianity...."); *id.* at 21 ("In Assyrian imperial art, Ishtar is shown nursing a king depicted as a child...."); *id.* at 24 ("According to Assyrian royal inscriptions, kings were called and predestined to their office from the beginning of time. Their features were miraculously perfected in their mother's womb by the mother goddess, that is, the spirit of god, and their intellectual and physical abilities were ... the powers and attributes of god."); *id.* at 26 ("[When the] king had committed a sin so grave that it could be atoned for only with his death. This required enthroning a substitute king, who would take upon himself the sins of the true king and die in his stead, thus enabling spiritual rebirth."); *id.* at 27 ("[T]he Assyrian Empire itself, a true 'kingdom of heaven on earth,' did not exist just for its own sake but served a higher purpose: to provide mankind with a living example of spiritual perfection, the attainment of which would open the way to eternal life.").

84. *See* JEREMY BLACK, ANTHONY GREEN & TESSA RICKARDS, GODS, DEMONS AND SYMBOLS OF ANCIENT MESOPOTAMIA: AN ILLUSTRATED DICTIONARY 27–28, 72, 85, 180–81 (6th ed., Austin, TX: Univ. of Texas Press, 2006); Alasdair Livingstone, *The Underworld Vision of an Assyrian Prince, in* 3 STATE ARCHIVES OF ASSYRIA: COURT POETRY AND LITERARY MISCELLANEA 68 (1989); Muhammad Dandamayev, *Royal* Paradeisoi *in Babylonia*, 23 ACTA IRANICA 113 (1984); Literatur Bendt Alster, *Dilmun, Bahrein, and the Alleged Paradise in Sumerian Myth and Literature, in* NEW STUDIES IN THE ARCHAEOLOGY AND EARLY HISTORY OF BAHREIN 39–74 (Daniel T. Potts ed., 1983).

85. BLACK, GREEN & RICKARDS, GODS, DEMONS, AND SYMBOLS, at 27–28, 72, 85, 180–81; Mehmet Ali Ataç, *The "Underworld Vision" of the Ninevite Intellectual Milieu*, 66 IRAQ 67, 67 (2004). The god Nergal even played a satanic role as "lord of the Underworld." Ataç, *The "Underworld Vision,"* at 69.

86. Rev. 19:20, 20:10–15 (KJV).

87. Matthew 26:52 (KJV).

88. *See* Matthew 7:12 (KJV).

89. *See, e.g.*, Cyril of Alexandria, *Commentary on Luke, Homily 148, in* ANCIENT CHRISTIAN COMMENTARY ON SCRIPTURE: NEW TESTAMENT III, LUKE 346 (Downers Grove, IL: Inter Varsity Press, 2003); Justin of Caesarea, *The First Apology, in* 1 ANTE NICENE FATHERS 175 (Alexander Roberts & James Donaldson eds., C.L. Publ'g Co. 1903); Irenaeus of Rome, *Against Heresies, in* 2 ANTE-NICENE FATHERS THE APOSTOLIC FATHERS. JUSTIN MARTYR. IRENÆUS (Grand Rapids, MI: Eerdmans, 1963); Clement of Alexandria, *Instructor, in* 2 ANTE NICENE FATHERS: FATHERS OF THE SECOND CENTURY. HERMAS, TATIAN, ATHENAGORAS, THEOPHILUS, AND CLEMENT OF ALEXANDRIA 234–35 (Alexander Roberts et al. eds., Grand Rapids, MI: Eerdmans, 1963); Origen, *Against Celsus, in* 4 ANTE-NICENE FATHERS: TERTULLIAN, PART FOURTH. MINUCIUM FELIX. COMMODIAN . ORIGEN, PARTS FIRST AND SECOND 370–80, 558 (Alexander Roberts et al. eds., Grand Rapids, MI: Eerdmans, 1964); *Tertullian, in* 3 ANTE-NICENE FATHERS 73 (Alexander Roberts et al. eds., New York: Scribner & Sons, 1903); Tertullian, *De Corona*, in 3 ANTE-NICENE FATHERS 99–100.

The conversion of the Roman emperors to Christianity, however, augured a more militantly expansionist religious orthodoxy. The Roman Emperor Constantine accomplished the destruction of temples of Aphrodite and other pagan gods.[90] His successor the Emperor Theodosius I banned the use of pagan Greek, Egyptian, or Mesopotamian shrines, temples, or idols; removed and destroyed the statue of the Greek god Zeus from his legendary temple of Olympia in the fourth century BCE, and banned the quasi-religious Olympic games.[91] Under Theodosius I, a campaign began in Alexandria and elsewhere to eliminate the indigenous Greco-Egyptian religion. Attendance at pagan temples, and sacrifices to pagan gods, were banned. The temple of Serapis in Alexandria had its pagan idols smashed and was converted into a church. The library of Alexandria was razed, and with it the only surviving copies of many ancient works.[92] Theodosius order the Temple of Zeus in Olympia to be destroyed, and its statue of Zeus, one of the seven wonders of the ancient world, may have been removed to Constantinople.[93] The temple of Athena at Ilium [Troy] was destroyed by heirs of Constantine in their religious zeal.[94] A Roman law of 341 CE banned pagan worship and rites henceforth.[95]

The Theodosian Code discriminated against Jews in political participation, livelihoods, and the ownership of property.[96] Synagogues, like pagan temples, were frequently ordered changed into churches. By the late fourth century CE synagogues were being destroyed

---

90. *See* Averil Cameron, *The Reign of Constantine, AD 306–337*, *in* The Cambridge Ancient History: The Crisis of Empire, A.D. 193–337, at 100 (Alan K. Bowman et al. eds., Cambridge: Cambridge UP, 2005); David Hunt, *Christianizing the Roman Empire: The Evidence of the Code*, *in* The Theodosian Code 143–44 (Ithaca, NY: Cornell UP, 1993) (Roman emperors starting with Constantine banned all religions but orthodox Christianity).

91. *See* Gerard Friell & Stephen Williams, Theodosius: The Empire at Bay 120 (New Haven, CT: Yale UP, 1998) (his decree stated "No person shall approach the shrines, nor walk through the temples, nor revere the images formed of mortal hands."); *id.* at 122–23 ("Temples had been attacked or destroyed at Petraea, Areopolis, Canopus, Heliopolis, Gaza and elsewhere without any imperial disapproval...."); *id.* at 135 ("Among the mass population of the countryside the church and state had a free hand to suppress (or re-christen) the local gods, ceremonies and temples;"); John Bagnell Bury, *Alaric in Greece (Appendix 7)*, *in* 5 Edward Gibbon, The History of the Decline and Fall of the Roman Empire (John Bagnell Bury ed., New York: Fred de Fau and Co., 1906) (1776–1788), http://oll.libertyfund.org/index.php?option=com_staticxt&staticfile=show.php&title=1372.

92. *See* Christopher Haas, Alexandria in Late Antiquity: Topography and Social Conflict 160–66 (Baltimore, MD: Johns Hopkins UP, 2006). *See also* Gibbon, 5 Decline and Fall of the Roman Empire, ch. xxviii, http://oll.libertyfund.org/index.php?option=com_staticxt&staticfile=show.php&title=1372 ("The ruin of Paganism, in the age of Theodosius, is perhaps the only example of the total extirpation of any ancient and popular superstition; and may therefore deserve to be considered as a singular event in the history of the human mind.... [¶] The valuable library of Alexandria was pillaged or destroyed....").

93. *See* Hellenic Ministry of Culture, *Olympia* (2007), http://odysseus.culture.gr/h/3/eh351.jsp?obj_id=2358; *The Statue of Zeus at Olympia*, Archaeopaedia (2007), http://traumwerk.stanford.edu:3455/Archaeopaedia/244.

94. Heinrich Schliemann, Troy and Its Remains 27–28, 30 (Philip Smith ed., London: John Murray, 1875).

95. *See* David Hunt, *The Successors of Constantine*, *in* The Cambridge Ancient History: The Late Empire, A.D. 337–425, at 7 (John Bagnell Bury et al. ed., Cambridge: Cambridge UP, 1998); *see also* Bury, *Did Theodosius Visit Rome in 394?*, *in* Gibbon, 5 Decline and Fall of the Roman Empire, http://oll.libertyfund.org/index.php?option=com_staticxt&staticfile=show.php&title=1372 (Emperor Theodosius I "sent a message to the senate signifying his will that pagan worship should cease").

96. *See* Thomas M. Franck, *Is Personal Freedom A Western Value?*, 91 Am. J. Int'l L. 593, 609 & n.100 (1997). *See generally* Norman F. Cantor, The Sacred Chain: The History of the Jews 110 (New York: HarperCollins, 1994).

in the empire, and the construction of new synagogues was prohibited.[97] These policies grew even worse with time, reaching a nadir in the sixth century CE when "Justinian not only reinforced these restrictions, in 535 he commanded the wholesale destruction of synagogues in Africa."[98]

Sectarian persecution among Christians could also be severe. The Edict of Unity of 405 declared Donatism to be a heresy punishable by a fine. The Donatist Christians of Roman-occupied Africa had their property confiscated and their bishops and clergy condemned to exile.[99] In 410, the Emperor Honorius decreed death for those participating in assemblies of Donatists or other heretics.[100] Massacres and "systematic persecution" of dissident Arian and Donatist Christians, as well as polytheists, persisted from the fourth to the sixth centuries CE.[101] The Code of Justinian of 534 declared that the Manicheans were to be deported from all cities, subjected to severe penalties, deprived of all access to the courts or legal remedies for murder or other violations, and have all their churches and properties confiscated for the Church.[102]

Pagan religious traditions in England and Gaul suffered organized persecution under the new Roman Empire and medieval Catholic Church. Christian scriptures declare that animism, magic, sorcery, and paganism are punishable by death.[103] Among other things, they state: "He that sacrificeth to gods, shall be put to death, save only to the Lord."[104] The Frankish king Charles I (Charlemagne) was crowned Roman emperor by the Pope Leo III in 800 CE.[105] "In Gaul, Charlemagne and, in England, Canute conducted campaigns against all survivals of pagan worship."[106] Charlemagne condemned animism, paganism, and magic as "arts of the Devil" punishable by death.[107] Not only pagan idols but astrology and love potions were thus made illegal. Pope Gregory II similarly called for a ban on paganism and spell-casting in Bavaria.[108] Estimates are that 30,000 to 500,000 pa-

---

97. *See Jews in Italy, in* MEDIEVAL ITALY: AN ENCYCLOPEDIA 580 (Christopher Kleinhenz ed., London: Routledge, 2003).

98. DON A. HALPERIN, THE ANCIENT SYNAGOGUES OF THE IBERIAN PENINSULA 2 (Gainesville, FL: University of Florida Monographs, 1969).

99. *See* David Wright, *Donatist Church, in* ENCYCLOPEDIA OF AFRICAN HISTORY 365 (Kevin Shillington ed., Boca Raton, Florida: CRC Press, 2005); DONALD X. BURT, FRIENDSHIP AND SOCIETY: AN INTRODUCTION TO AUGUSTINE'S PRACTICAL PHILOSOPHY 209–210 (Grand Rapids, MI: Wm. B. Eerdmans Publishing, 1999).

100. *See* JAMES CRAIGIE ROBERTSON, HISTORY OF THE CHRISTIAN CHURCH 371 (London: John Murray, 1854).

101. *See* James Alexander, *Donatism, in* THE EARLY CHRISTIAN WORLD 952, 956 (Philip Francis Esler ed., London: Routledge, 2000) (describing massacres of Donatist Christians by Roman Empire in fourth century CE); Claire Sotinel, *Emperors and Popes in the Sixth Century: A Western View, in* THE CAMBRIDGE COMPANION TO THE AGE OF JUSTINIAN 277 (Michael Maas ed., Cambridge: Cambridge UP, 2005) (describing Emperor Justinian's "systematic persecution against 'Donatists, Jews, Pagans, Arians and other heretics'" in sixth century CE).

102. *Quoted in* Matthew C. Mirow & Kathleen E. Kelley, *Laws on Religion from the Theodosian and Justinianic Codes, in* RELIGIONS OF LATE ANTIQUITY IN PRACTICE, 270 (Richard Valantasis ed., Princeton: Princeton UP, 2000).

103. *See* Exodus 22:18 (KJV); Deuteronomy 18:9–14 (KJV); Leviticus 20:27 (KJV).

104. Exodus 22:20 (KJV).

105. *See* EINHARD, THE LIFE OF CHARLEMAGNE 56–57 (Ann Arbor, MI: Univ. of Michigan Press, 1960).

106. WARD RUTHERFORD, CELTIC LORE: THE HISTORY OF THE DRUIDS AND THEIR TIMELESS TRADITIONS 152–53 (San Francisco: HarperCollins, 1993).

107. JULIO CARO BAROJA, THE WORLD OF THE WITCHES 54 (London: Phoenix Press, 2001).

108. *Id.* ar 54, 56.

gans, witches, and sorcerers may have been executed in the Spanish Inquisition and other massacres, public burnings, tortures, and persecutions.[109] Pagan literature was banned by the *Index Librorum Prohibitorum* of the Catholic Church.[110]

The struggle against the Donatists and other heretics helped provide the foundation for what later became the Crusades. The Code of Justinian stated that: "We prosecute Manichaeans and Donatists with deserved severity. Thus let them have nothing in common with others of the human race...."[111] St. Augustine "developed the concept of a war based upon divine command (*bellum Deo auctore*), which was directed first of all against the (Donatist) heretics, but which subsequently served to justify war against the infidels and was incorporated into the ideology of the crusades."[112] Catholic canon law accepted this theory. In the High and Late Middle Ages, the Roman Emperor assumed the right of going to war on behalf of all Christendom, or *ius ad bellum*, which triggered a *Bellum Romanum* (Roman war). With the First Crusade in 1095 CE, Pope Urban II claimed the power to declare holy war.[113] St. Anselm described the project of the Crusades as "not a vision of peace but of tribulation and the treasures of Constantinople and Babylon which must be seized with bloodstained hands."[114] The Crusaders themselves often emphasized religious and humanitarian motives, saying for example that they wanted to preserve "the grace of the pilgrimage ... and, under the protection of God, to wipe out the defilement of the pagans and the immoderate madness through which innumerable Christians have already been oppressed, made captive, and killed with barbaric fury."[115]

The First Crusade reached Jerusalem in 1099 CE. An Arab source describes a considerable massacre of the defenders, and imprisonment of the women and children. More than 70,000, including scholars and ascetics, were said to have been slain.[116] A Frankish source is to similar effect, but emphasizes a great slaughter of armed defenders and some civilians, adding that in the temple of Solomon 10,000 were killed, and neither women

---

109. *See* Rummel, Death by Government, ch. 3. *See also* Gustav Henningsen, The Witches' Advocate: Basque Witchcraft and the Spanish Inquisition, 1609–1614 (Reno, NV: University of Nevada Press, 1980); Henry Charles Lea, A History of the Inquisition of Spain 242 (Whitefish, MT: Kessinger Publishing, 2008) (1907); Juan Antonio Lorente, A Critical History of the Inquisition of Spain, from the Period of Its Establishment to the Reign of Ferdinand II (Williamstown, MA: J. Lilburne Co., 1967) (1826); E. William Monter, Frontiers of Heresy: The Spanish Inquisition from the Basque Lands to Sicily 268 (Cambridge: Cambridge UP, 2003); Joseph Perez & Janet Lloyd, The Spanish Inquisition: A History 79–101, 179–87 (New Haven, CT: Yale UP, 2006). The papal bull of Pope Innocent X authorized and enjoined the Inquisition to imprison or punish those casting "incantations, spells, conjurations, and other accursed charms and crafts." The Bull of Innocent VII (1484 CE), http://www.malleusmaleficarum.org/?p=9.

110. *See, e.g.,* Office of the Roman and Universal Inquisition, *Index Librorum Prohibitorum* (Rome, 1559 CE), http://www.aloha.net/~mikesch/ILP-1559.htm.

111. *Quoted in* Mirow & Kelley, *Laws on Religion from the Theodosian and Justinianic Codes*, at 270.

112. Wilhelm Georg Grewe, The Epochs of International Law 108 (Michael Byers trans. & rev., Berlin and New York: Walter de Gruyter, 2000).

113. *See id.* at 108–11.

114. *Quoted in* Thomas F. Madden, The Crusades: The Essential Readings 24 (London: Blackwell Publishing, 2002).

115. *Quoted in* Jonathan Riley-Smith, The Oxford Illustrated History of the Crusades 77 (Oxford: Oxford UP, 2001).

116. *See* Ibn al-Athir, *The Franks Conquer Jerusalem, in* Arab Historians of the Crusades 10–11 (Francesco Gabrieli & E.J. Costello trans. and eds., New York: Dorset Press, 1989).

nor children were "spared."[117] Some sources reports fewer deaths in the taking of Jerusalem, as few as 3,000.[118]

Large massacres of Jews occurred on the way to Jerusalem, as well. Away from home and planning a long journey over tough terrain, the Crusaders tortured for money the Jews they found along the way.[119] In the Kingdom of Lorraine and elsewhere, they fortunes plundered from Jews, who were then massacred.[120] One author claims that: "The persecutions of the Jews, so common along the march of the Peasants, was by no means, however, confined to them, being almost as widespread as the enthusiasm for the Crusade itself."[121] A German source declares, "As [the Germans from the Rhineland] were led through the cities of the Rhine and the Main and also the Danube, they either utterly destroyed the execrable race of the Jews wherever they found them ... or forced them into the bosom of the Church."[122] Hungarians too, reacting with alarm to the marauding Germans, were classified as pagans and "persecute[d] by other Christians while yet upon the expedition ... for freeing Christians."[123]

The Spanish Inquisition, which may have burned and tortured to death nearly 9,000 "heretical" persons between 1483 and 1492, had its roots in French and Italian measures against heretics that were arguably already well established by the time of Aquinas.[124] As Professor John Witte, Jr., Director of the Center for the Study of Law and Religion at Emory University, writes, not only pagans but also Christian heretics suffered persecution during the Inquisition, and after. Heretics suffered torture and enjoyed few legal rights. Protestant Lutherans, Anglicans, and Calvinists similarly directed various civil and ecclesiastical punishments against religious dissidents, including torture and execution when such were deemed appropriate.[125]

Conflicts between pagans, Catholics, and Protestants in the British Isles and Ireland could also be devastating for the civilian population. As an Englishman self-identifying as an indigenous Saxon wrote in the seventeenth century, the Norman king William the Conqueror "turned the English out, and gave the Land unto his Norman Souldiers every man his parcel to inclose."[126] The Normans depopulated Saxon areas, claiming them for the Norman crown, and subjecting the Saxons to the death penalty for hunting many birds or animals for food. Norman jurists developed the existing Saxon feudal laws of England "into the most slavish doctrines and oppressive consequences." Most court proceedings were

117. Fulk of Chartres, *The Capture of Jerusalem, 1099*, http://www.fordham.edu/halsall/source/fulk2.html. *See also* Charles Warren Hollister, Medieval Europe: A Short History 189 (New York: McGraw-Hill, 1994).

118. *See* Benjamin Z. Kedar, *The Jerusalem Massacre of 1099 in Western Historiography of the Crusades*, 3 Crusades 15 (2004), *quoted in* Thomas S. Asbridge, The First Crusade: A New History 376 (New York: Simon and Schuster, 2005).

119. August Charles Krey, The First Crusade: The Accounts of Eye-Witnesses and Participants 261 (Princeton: Princeton UP, 1921).

120. *See id.* at 56.

121. *Id.* at 19.

122. *Id.* at 44.

123. *Id.* at 54.

124. *See* Rummel, Death by Government, at 62; Joseph Blötzer, *Inquisition, in* 8 The Catholic Encyclopedia (1910), http://www.newadvent.org/cathen/08026a.htm.

125. *See* John Witte, Jr., *"Go Ye, Therefore, and Make Disciples of all Nations": The Rights and Limits of Proselytism in the New Religious World Order, in* Religion and International Peace (Thomas Banchoff ed., Oxford: Oxford UP, 2007), http://papers.ssrn.com/sol3/papers.cfm?abstract_id=1014724.

126. Jerrard Winstanley, A New-Yeers Gift for the Parliament and Armie (1650), http://www.tlio.demon.co.uk/gift.htm.

conducted in Old Norman, rather than in Old English, "as evident a badge of slavery as ever was imposed upon a conquered people." From very few capital punishments for the first offense, the Normans created hundreds. Trials by jury were often replaced with trial by combat, introduced by the Normans for the "the decision of all civil and criminal questions of fact in the last resort."[127] Embracing a false religion, or no religion, was punishable by death in the thirteenth century. An Act of Parliament in the time of Henry IV made "heretical tenets," as found by a local diocese, punishable by burning at the stake. A statute from the time of Henry VIII made "popery," as well as Catholic mass, punishable by death, in the case of "popery" to be carried out by being "burnt with fire."[128] Another act of that time made all sorcery and witchcraft punishable by death. Invoking, consulting with, feeding, or rewarding any non-Christian "spirit" similarly led to execution.[129] Many other capital crimes were related to property or authority, e.g., stealing cattle.[130]

Norman lords frequently tortured their Saxon subjects in order to extract labor and obedience. Many Saxons had no freedom to deny their labor to the Norman lords, or to leave the manors.[131] William the Conqueror viewed the English natives as enemies, stole their lands, and made them slaves. William enjoyed to hunt, so the killing by a Saxon of a rabbit or deer could result in removal of the offender's eyes, whereas under Saxon law even murder of a human being could sometimes be resolved by the payment of a fine.[132] In the event that a Saxon refused to confess to one of the many capital crimes introduced by the Normans, he or she could be stretched upon the rack, or confined in a dungeon on his or her back with as great a weight of iron placed upon him or her as could be borne, fed only three morsels of bread on alternate days.[133] "Suspicion of theft, murder, horse-stealing, embezzlement, and other similar offenses was sufficient to consign the unfortunate accused to the tender mercies of the rack, the Scavenger's Daughter [which crushed the torso and legs together], and the manacles...."[134]

---

127. *See* WILLIAM BLACKSTONE, 4 COMMENTARIES ON THE LAWS OF ENGLAND *413–416, at 324–26 (Philadelphia: J.P. Lippicott & Co., 1867) (1769).

128. *Id.* at *43–48, 29–32.

129. *See id.* at *61–62, at 43.

130. *See id.* at *65–251, at 45–207 (describing various offenses against the King, the military, the courts, and private and public property). *See also* WILLIAM BLACKSTONE, 1 COMMENTARIES ON THE LAWS OF ENGLAND 89, 293–94 (Philadelphia: Robert Bell, 1771) (describing death penalty for stealing sheep, bulls, and other cattle).

131. *See* ROBERT BARTLETT, ENGLAND UNDER THE NORMAN AND ANGEVIN KINGS, 1075–1225, at 320–25 (Oxford: Oxford UP, 2000).

132. DAVID HUME, 1 THE HISTORY OF ENGLAND FROM THE INVASION OF JULIUS CAESAR TO THE REVOLUTION IN 1688 (William B. Todd ed., Indianapolis: Liberty Fund, 1983) (1778), http://tinyurl.com/ndqzbb.

133. *See* BLACKSTONE, 4 COMMENTARIES, at *327–28, at 265.

134. HENRY CHARLES LEA, SUPERSITITION AND FORCE: ESSAYS ON THE WAGER OF LAW—THE WAGER OF BATTLE—THE ORDEAL—TORTURE 380–81 (Philadelphia, 1866). *See also* GEOFFREY ABBOTT, TORTURES OF THE TOWER OF LONDON (London: David & Charles Press, 1986); JAMES HEATH, TORTURE AND ENGLISH LAW: AN ADMINISTRATIVE AND LEGAL HISTORY FROM THE PLANTAGENETS TO THE STUARTS (Westport, CT: Greenwood Press, 1982).

D. European Colonial Genocide in the Americas

1. Introduction

This section will explore several of the genocides described by Lemkin and other historians. It focuses on genocides against the indigenous peoples of the Americas, whose fate occupied several folders of research that Professor Lemkin compiled for his planned *History of Genocide*.[135] The next section will deal with other colonial genocides, including those in Asia.

Genocide in the early modern era through World War I (1492–1914) was principally a result of the failure of national and international law to plainly recognize the humanity and entitlement to rights of indigenous people, non-citizens, and racial and religious subordinates. At the outset of the Renaissance and early modern era, religious law had developed into a form that threatened widespread killing and demonization of native "infidels." Genocide was the result.

In the fifteenth century, encouraged by news of Spanish and Portuguese conquests in Africa and other lands in the vicinity of India, Roman popes invoked divine sanction to assign to Spain and Portugal any lands, islands, ports and seas to be found in Africa or the New World unless (in the case of the New World) they were "in the actual possession of any Christian king or prince."[136] In 1436, a papal decree awarded Portugal the right to "colonize all of Africa." In 1493, Pope Alexander IV bestowed upon Spain "the right to colonize and Christianize tribal peoples in the vicinity of Columbus's discoveries in the Western Hemisphere."[137] Spain regarded the papal bull of 1493 as granting it sovereignty over

135. *See* American Jewish Archives, *Guide to the Raphael Lemkin (1900–1959) Collection, 1763–2002* (2003), http://web.archive.org/web/20051126232228/http://www.cjh.org/academic/findingaids/AJHS/nhprc/lemkin02-03.html & http://findingaids.cjh.org/?fnm=Lemkin02-03&pnm=AJHS.

136. Pope Alexander VI, *Inter Cetera* (May 4, 1493), *in* European Treaties Bearing on the History of the United States and its Dependencies 56–63 (Francis G. Davenport ed., Washington, DC: Carnegie Institution of Washington, 1917). *See also* Pope Eugenius, Romanus Pontifex (1453), *quoted in* Robert A. Williams, Jr., The American Indian in Western Legal Thought: Discourses of Conquest 72 (New York: Oxford UP US, 1993) (affirming right of Portuguese conquest of African "provinces, islands, ports, districts, and seas"); Raymond Cross, *Sovereign Bargains, Indian Takings, and the Preservation of Indian Country in the Twenty-first Century*, 40 Ariz. L. Rev. 425, 455 n168 (1998) (Spanish jurist "Juan Gines de Sepulveda (1490–1573)..., relying on the authority of Aristotle and St. Augustine, concluded that the Indian peoples were obligated to 'accept Spanish domination because of the their idolatry and human sacrifice.'") (quoting L.C. Green & Olive P. Dickason, The Law of Nations and the New World 201–09, 204 (1989)); Mark A. Michaels, *Indigenous Ethics and Alien Laws: Native Traditions and the United States Legal System*, 66 Fordham L. Rev. 1565, 1573 (1998) ("In 1455, following the fall of Constantinople, Pope Nicholas V granted King Alfonso of Portugal the authority to 'capture, vanquish, and subdue all Saracens and pagans whatsoever, and other enemies of Christ wheresoever placed' to put them into perpetual slavery and expropriate their lands."); Robert J. Miller, *The Doctrine of Discovery in American Indian Law*, 42 Idaho L. Rev. 1, 11 (2005) ("The pope agreed and issued [a papal] bull in 1436, Romanus Pontifex, which ... was reissued several times in the fifteenth century and each time significantly extended Portugal's jurisdiction and geographical rights in Africa.").

137. Michael C. Blumm, *Retracing the Discovery Doctrine: Aboriginal Title, Tribal Sovereignty, and their Significance to Treaty-Making and Modern Natural Resources Policy in Indian Country*, 28 Vermont L. Rev. 713 (2004).

most of North, South, and Central America, excepting Portuguese sovereignty over eastern South America, present-day Brazil.[138] Elaborating on their rights under papal decrees, Spanish writers and theologians justified Spanish colonial policies in the Americas by characterizing indigenous Americans "as 'barbarous, wretched sinners, and depraved infidels....'"[139]

The scramble by the Spanish, Portuguese, British, and French for empires of rich lands, abundant gold, and heathen slaves required mass killings of indigenous Americans, as well as Africans and Asians. The trade in Native American slaves had already begun within three years of their "discovery" by Christopher Columbus, and continued for centuries. Within three years of arriving in the New World, Columbus had already shipped 500 indigenous Americans to Spain as slaves, and captured a further 1,000 for use in the colony.[140] Columbus believed that the revenues earned from the enslavement and productive use of the indigenous peoples of the Indies would be "spent in the conquest of Jerusalem."[141] Columbus resolved to sell 4,000 slaves in 1498, to raise millions in gold "in the name of the Holy Trinity."[142]

The fate of the indigenous Americans within the Spanish Empire resembled that of victims of the Third Reich or the Pol Pot regime in Cambodia. "Under the awful cruelties of their Spanish conquerors and taskmasters [the Arawak and Carib natives] were virtually exterminated within two generations of the discovery."[143] The Ciboney and Arawak/Taino peoples of the Caribbean islands, especially concentrated in pre-Columbian Haiti and the Bahamas, were basically extinct by 1535, having lost about four to five million men and women, boys and girls, to massacres, slavery, overwork, starvation, and disease.[144] Today, only 3,000 self-identifying Carib Indians are left in the eastern Caribbean, with the other Caribbean peoples having died in war, massacres, hunger, or disease, or having intermarried with the colonists.[145]

The native population of western Santo Domingo, present-day Haiti, had collapsed by the early sixteenth century CE due to slave labor in the gold mines under Columbus and his successors, and as a result of massacres, torture, disease, and deportation to remote and inhospitable parts of the island.[146] By the seventeenth century, French pirates had conquered the island, reinforced by the French government. After importing thousands of settlers and African slaves, and exporting untold agricultural bounty to France, in 1790 the population of the island stood at about 50,000 free persons, including French and mixed-race persons, and nearly 500,000 slaves.[147] In 1791, a slave rebellion broke out,

---

138. *See* Siegfried Wiessner, *Rights and Status of Indigenous Peoples: A Global Comparative and International Legal Analysis*, 12 Harv. Hum. Rts. J. 57, 58–9 (1999).

139. Jeffrey N. Gesell, *Note, Customary Indigenous Law in the Mexican Juridical System*, 26 Georgia J. of Int'l & Comparative L. 643, 646 (1997).

140. *See* Williams, *The American Indian in Western Legal Thought*, at 37 n147 ("Columbus violently suppressed an Indian revolt with 500 conquistadores. Five hundred of the 1500 Indians captured were sent back as slaves to Spain. Indian slavery was thus instituted in the New World within three years of its European 'discovery.'").

141. *Quoted in* Tzvetan Todorov, The Conquest of America: The Question of the Other 11 (Univ. of Oklahoma Press, 1999).

142. *Id.* at 47.

143. James Mooney, *American Indians, in* 7 The Catholic Encyclopedia (1910), http://www.newadvent.org/cathen/07747a.htm.

144. *See* Levene, 2 Genocide in the Age of the Nation State 10; Stubblefield, Ethics Along The Color Line, at 27. *See generally* The Indigenous People of the Caribbean.

145. U.S. Dept. of State, Bureau of Western Hemisphere Affairs, *Background Note: Dominica* (Nov. 2006), http://www.state.gov/r/pa/ei/bgn/2295.htm.

146. *See also* John Relly Beard, Toussaint L'Ouverture: A Biography and Autobiography 20–30 (Boston: James Redpath Publishers, 1863).

147. *See id.* at 26.

with planters and French settlers killed en masse, and the French settlers appealing to the English at Jamaica to save them. The rebel leader accused the French settlers, "who, next to God, should have proved our fathers," of being instead "tyrants, monsters unworthy of the fruits of our labors."[148] Haiti was the most profitable European colony in the world in the 1790s, accounting for two-thirds of the coffee and about half of the sugar produced on earth. African slaves there "were lashed and beaten to work and forced to wear tin muzzles to prevent them from eating the sugar cane. If the slaves were fractious, they were roasted over slow fires, or filled with gunpowder and blown to pieces."[149]

The early example of Haiti illustrates that counterinsurgency operations and national liberation movements heighten, rather than negate or foreclose, the likelihood of genocidal mass killings of rebels and their entire racial or ethnic group. By 1801, the rebellion under Toussaint L'Ouverture had nearly unified the island under its control.[150] In 1802, First Consul Napoleon Bonaparte led 10,000 colonial forces tasked with putting down the Haitian revolution. The French troops "were under orders to kill all blacks over the age of 12. However, younger children were also killed stabbed to death, put in sandbags and dropped into the sea." The French produced sulphur dioxide by burning volcanic sulphur, and then released the gas within the holds of ships, where about 100,000 Africans in Haiti were murdered, according to the French archives. A member of the French expeditionary force wrote that: "We invented another type of ship where victims of both sexes were piled up, one against the other, suffocated by sulphur." The ship chambers into which the gas was loaded were called "chokers" (*etouffiers*). A contemporary French historian recounted "piles of dead bodies everywhere, stacked in charnel-houses." As the Ottomans and Nazis would do decades later, the French concealed their "outrages," for example by carrying them out at nighttime. In nearby Guadeloupe, to the east of Haiti, the French General Antoine Richepanse massacred African men, women and children in the march to the capital city, as well as in nearby farms and mountainous areas.[151]

The French Code Noir of 1685 prohibited all religions other than Catholicism in the Caribbean islands within the French Empire, required slaves to be baptized as Catholics, and denied slaves all legal rights in court save protection from murder or torture.[152] General Charles Leclerc of the French expeditionary force to Haiti in 1801 ordered the killing of all Haitians excepting children under twelve years of age, as being a necessary measure to overcome resistance to the reintroduction of slavery after the French Revolution. Jean-Jacques Dessalines, a Haitian revolutionary and later Emperor of Haiti, referred to the French colonists as the "people of the executions" and as "barbarians" who "drenched [Haiti] in blood for two hundred years."[153]

After an extensive review of Napoleon's record by Claude Ribbe of France's human rights commission, French scholars could confirm "the attempted massacre," in about 1800, "of an entire population over the age of 12 by methods which included gassing them in the holds of ships...." Ribbe described Napoléon as applying the principles of

---

148. *Quoted in id.* at 51.

149. Christopher Hudson, *The French Fuhrer, Napoleon Was Responsible for Thousands of Executions,* The Daily Mail (U.K.), July 25, 2008, at 34 (review of Claude Ribbe, Le Crime de Napoléon (Paris: Editions Prive, 2008)).

150. *See* Edward Paulino, *Anti-Haitianism, Historical Memory, and the Potential for Genocidal Violence in the Dominican Republic,* 1.3 Genocide Stud. and Prevention: An Int'l J. 265, 269 (2006).

151. *See* Hudson, *The French Fuhrer.*

152. *See The Code Noir (The Black Code)* (1685), http://chnm.gmu.edu/revolution/d/335/.

153. Philippe R. Girard, *Racial War in Haiti, 1802–1804, in* Colonialism and Genocide 42 (A. Dirk Moses and Dan Stone eds., London: Routledge, 2007).

scientific investigation and enlightened reason to the "the question how to eliminate, in as short a time as possible, and with a minimum of cost and personnel, a maximum of people described as scientifically inferior."[154] With the defeat of the French in 1804, the Republic of Haiti was born, and slavery banned.[155]

2. Central America

In Central America, the Spanish killed as many as 20 million of the native inhabitants —Mayans and Aztecs, among other peoples—by 1596.[156] Spanish sources estimated the population of the Aztec capital Tenochtitlán as being between 240,000 and 1.2 million people.[157] Sixty thousand people occupied the central marketplace daily.[158] The city was effectively burned down and virtually destroyed, to be refounded as Mexico City in 1521. The fresh water supply of the city was cut off at the outset of the Spanish siege, in a form of assault against noncombatants not anticipated by Aztec culture.[159] Among other atrocities, the Aztecs described a massacre of their unarmed leaders as they celebrated a religious holiday, carried out over a span of three hours inside the main temple in the capital.[160] "I intended to attack and slay them all," recounted the Spanish leader Hernando Cortés.[161] A standard history recounts:

> The people had borne with patience all the injuries and affronts hitherto put on them by the Spaniards. They had seen their sovereign dragged as a captive from his own palace, his ministers butchered before his eyes, his treasure seized and appropriated, himself in a manner deposed from his royal supremacy. All this

---

154. Hudson, *The French Fuhrer.*

155. Paulino, *Anti-Haitianism,* at 269.

156. *See* Thomas H. Charlton et al., *The Basin of Mexico A.D. 1450–1620: Archaeological Dimensions, in* The Postclassic to Spanish-era Transition in Mesoamerica: Archaeological Perspectives 56–57 (Susan Kepecs & Rani T. Alexander eds., Albuquerque, NM: Univ. of New Mexico Press, 2005); Guillermo Cook, *Brief History of the Maya Peoples, in* Crosscurrents in Indigenous Spirituality: Interface of Maya, Catholic, and Protestant Worldviews 14 (Guillermo Cook ed., Leiden, the Netherlands and Boston: Brill, 1997); Levene, 2 Genocide in the Age of the Nation State, at 10; *see also* Davidson, Nation of Nations at 22 ("In Mesoamerica, a native population of 20 million was reduced to 2 million."); Bartolome de las Casas, *The Cruelties of the Spaniards, in* The Spanish Tradition in America 106–8 (Charles Gibson ed., Columbia, SC: Univ. of South Carolina Press, 1968); Bartolome De Las Casas, The History on the Indies, *reprinted in* Susan Castillo & Ivy Schweitzer, The Literatures of Colonial America (London: Wiley-Blackwell, 2001); Diego de Landa, *Account on Things in Yucatan, in* The Literatures of Colonial America, at 72–73; M. Annette Jaimes, The State of Native America: Genocide, Colonization, and Resistance 81 (Boston: South End Press, 1992). For numbers on the Caribbean, see Pan Am. Union, Bulletin of the Pan Am. Union, at 473 (Las Casas blamed deaths of two-thirds of the natives in Spanish Caribbean by 1530 on "war, hunger, disease, overwork and sorrow").

157. *See* William M. Denevan, The Native population of the Americas in 1492, at 148 (Madison, WI: Univ. of Wisconsin Press, 1992).

158. *See* Stannard, American Holocaust, at 5.

159. *See id.* at 77–81; Helen Miller, Latin America, The Development of Its Civilization 113 (New York: Prentice-Hall, 1960); Robert James Mullen, Architecture and Its Sculpture in Viceregal Mexico 4 (Austin, TX: Univ. of Texas Press, 1997).

160. *See* The Broken Spears: The Aztec Account of the Conquest of Mexico 64–66, 129–131 (Miguel LeonPortilla, ed., New York: Houghton Mifflin, 1962).

161. *Quoted in* Stannard, American Holocaust, at 79.

> they had seen, without a struggle to prevent it. But the profanation of their temples touched a deeper feeling....[162]

As with other genocides, during conquest of the Aztecs by the Spanish Empire, kings and other leaders were among the first to die. Some were executed for "treason" against an empire of which, a few years previously, they had been entirely unaware.[163] This decapitated the Aztecs.

The Spanish invaders killed countless natives by enslaving them in gold mines, as well as subjecting them to attacks, starvation, and disease.[164] Cortés alone claimed 3,000 slaves for his personal use. The governor of Cuba had originally conceived the invasion of the Aztec empire for purposes of enslaving the natives to mine gold and grow crops, work so hazardous that the Crown of Spain and the Catholic Church feared the extinction of their subjects.[165] As one author movingly described the Aztec plight:

> It was not a Government studious to preserve civilization and order that made the Conquest, but a band of bigoted and rapacious adventurers. The administrative system of the Aztec emperors fell into decay; the reign of order was succeeded by chaos and rapacity; cultivated was neglected, the people enslaved, the collections of science scattered, and the libraries of literature destroyed. "To the mines!" was the cry of the Spaniards. Their only thought, as Christians, was to obliterate and destroy the pagan past; their only passion, as conquerors, was to possess themselves of the precious ores. The great nobles were killed or despoiled,—the priesthood, the dignitaries of the national learning and traditions, were persecuted and massacred; and the books were gathered together, and destroyed in the flames. The Indians were hurried off to work in gangs in the mines. The great cities were depopulated, and crumbled into ruins.[166]

Between dozens and hundreds of indigenous Mexican languages died out.[167]

The Mayan culture has roots going back to 1,000 or even 10,000 BCE, but reached its peak in present-day southern Mexico in the first millennium of the Common Era. It may have served as the cultural foundation of the Aztec empire encountered by the Spanish, through intermediate influence on the Toltec civilization of central Mexico. The K'iche' tribe of Mayans briefly allied themselves with the Spanish penetrated south after the fall of Tenochtitlán, but the Spanish turned on them and burned down their capital city as well. In the "Great Maya Revolt" of 1546–47, large numbers of Mayans lost their lives in

---

162. William Hickling Prescott, History of the Conquest of Mexico 331 (John Foster Kirk ed., London: Bickers & Son, 1878).

163. *See* Kiernan, Blood and Soil, at 79–80, 89–92.

164. *See* Todorov, The Conquest of America, at 136–37.

165. *See* Richard L. Greaves & Robert Zaller, Civilizations of the West: The Human Adventure, 1660 — Present 537 (New York: HarperCollins, 1991) (in the "sixteenth century the Spaniards enslaved the island populations of the Caribbean and worked them literally to extinction in the gold mines."); Gary Jennings, Aztec Blood 98 (2002) ("The indios failed miserably as slaves, their death rate in the plantations and the mines so catastrophic that Crown and Church both feared their extinction.").

166. *See The Napoleonic Idea in Mexico,* 96 Blackwood's Edinburgh magazine, Volume 96, July 1864, at 78 http://books.google.com/books?id=gg0HAQAAIAAJ&pg=PA78.

167. *See* Gretchen Peters, *Old Words Find New Life: The Race Is On to Decode Mexico's Past,* Christian Sci. Monitor, June 11, 2002, http://www.csmonitor.com/2002/0611/p11s02-legn.html ("Ever since conquistador Hernando Cortés first set foot in Mexico in 1519, dozens if not hundreds of indigenous languages have fallen victim to Spanish.").

resistance to the Spanish, so that the Mayan population stood at only 750,000, a 93% reduction, by 1621 CE. During the inquisition into paganism of 1562, 4,500 natives were tortured, many were permanently disabled, and over 100 were murdered. The Spanish razed the Mayan religious archives and libraries, and eradicated two million sacred images. Native culture went underground, with sculptures and icons hidden within churches and polytheistic priests going into hiding.[168]

The Mayan-speaking population of Mexico and its neighboring countries subsequently rebounded, reaching six million in 1992.[169] With the cession of Arizona, California, Nevada, New Mexico, Texas, and Utah to the U.S. by the Treaty of Guadalupe-Hidalgo of 1848,[170] the indigenous peoples of northern Mexico and southeastern U.S. eventually lost their ability to travel across the border to find water, gather food, pasture cattle, and trade with other cities and tribes. The native peoples, far from being consulted, were dismissed as "savage[s]" subject to the uncontrolled jurisdiction of the U.S. in the ceded territories. Land grants under Spanish rule were to be respected, but in practice were annulled in many cases. For some indigenous groups, "the impacts on their culture and traditions were horrific." In recent years, native peoples have been arrested and deported to Mexico, had their lands degraded by law enforcement or criminal gangs, and seen road access to their lands severed.[171]

In nineteenth and early twentieth century Mexico, the indigenous Yaqui and Mayans of Mexico suffered campaigns of "extermination" similar to those waged in the U.S., with the Mayans in particular targeted for depopulation in a "race war" to prevent them from outnumbering the settler society.[172] After 1900, half a million to 3.3 million indigenous people, farmers, and government opponents suffered mass death and slavery in Mexico. Genocide scholar R.J. Rummel of the University of Hawaii described these events as follows:

> Through its system of peonage and chattel slavery, ... conscription, summary executions, and political terror, pre-revolutionary and revolutionary Mexican regimes committed murder on a massive scale, surely totaling at least hundreds

---

168. *See* Cook, *Brief History of the Maya Peoples,* at 1–18; On the consequences of the Great Maya Revolt and the Spanish Inquisition, see *Maya, in* 10 Catholic Encyclopedia 83 (Charles George Herberman ed., New York: Encyclopedia Press, 1913) ("By [1597] it was estimated that the native population of Mexico had declined by three-fourths since the discovery, through massacre, famine, disease, and oppression."); Nick Rider, Yucatan & Mayan Mexico 37–39 (3rd ed. New Holland Publishers, 2005) (Mayan population only 750,000 by 1621, down 93%).

169. *See* Ronald Wright, Stolen Continents: The Americas Through Indian Eyes since 1492, at 48 (New York: Houghton Mifflin, 1992).

170. Treaty of Peace, Friendship, Limits, and Settlement with the Republic of Mexico, Treaty of Guadalupe Hidalgo, U.S.-Mex., Feb. 2, 1848, 9 Stat. 922, 930. Texas had previously declared its intent to join the United States, but Mexico disputed this claim and did not completely recognize it until signing Article V of this treaty. *See id.*, art V.

171. Eileen Luna-Firebaugh, *'Att Hascu 'Am O 'I-oi? What Direction Should We Take?: The Desert People's Approach to the Militarization of the Border,* 19 Washington University J. Law & Policy 339, 339–50 (2005). *See also* Treaty of Guadalupe-Hidalgo, art. XI (territories "occupied by savage tribes" placed under U.S. control, with agreement being that U.S. would forcibly restrain them from reentering Mexico). On the annulment of Mexican land grants north of the Rio Grande after the cession to the U.S., see, for example, Phillip B. Gonzales, *Struggle for Survival: The Hispanic Land Grants of New Mexico, 1848–2001,* 77 Agricultural Hist. 293 (2003); Guadalupe T. Luna, *Legal Realism and the Treaty of Guadalupe Hidalgo: A Fractionalized Legal Template,* 2005 Wisconsin Law Review 519 (2005).

172. Robert L. Scheinau, Latin America's Wars: The age of the caudillo, 1791–1899, at 373 (London: Brassey's, 2003).

of thousands of Indians, peons, innocent villagers, captured soldiers, and conscripts....

The right-wing Mexican dictator Porfirio Díaz murdered his political opponents *en masse* and displaced members of 5,000 indigenous communities from their ancestral homes, leaving 95 percent of the rural population landless. More than a third of the Mexican population found itself living in virtual slavery, with death rates exceeding 50% on some plantations. Forced labor on plantations contributed to more than one million deaths in Mexico from 1900 to 1920. The conditions proved particularly well-suited to destroying native communities due to the unlimited exploitation of their bodies, with two-thirds of Yaqui people and many Mayans perishing of hunger, exposure, disease, unhygienic conditions, and overwork.[173] Using various contemporary statistics, Professor Rummel calculated that from 1900 to 1920, the Mexican government massacred, executed, or starved between 600,000 to 3,300,000 people.[174]

3. South America

The Chibcha and Inca peoples of South America suffered demographic "havoc" and cultural collapse.[175] The Spanish Empire under Francisco de Pizarro and his successors devastated the Incan Empire, perhaps the largest on earth at the time of first European contact, massacring its defenders and leaders, seizing eleven tons of its gold, and conscripting the Inca people into labor in the silver mines of Peru for minimal compensation under deplorable conditions.[176] War, deportation, enslavement, and conquest contributed to the virulence of epidemics such as smallpox, which along with violence, overwork and starvation killed seven to 13 million people living in Peru before the arrival of Pizarro.[177] "The Chibcha race was virtually exterminated by the Spanish conquerors in their thirst for gold," although many Chibcha survived into the twentieth century in Ecuador, Peru, and Bolivia.[178]

The Spanish conquered present-day Paraguay in the sixteenth century, massacring and being massacred in return, executing native leaders, and taking native women as concu-

---

173. *See* R.J. Rummel, *From the Study of War and Revolution to Genocide—Power Kills, in* PIONEERS OF GENOCIDE STUDIES 169 (Samuel Totten & Steven L. Jacobs eds., New Brunswick, NJ: Transaction Publishers, 2002); R.J. RUMMEL, SAVING LIVES, ENRICHING LIFE: FREEDOM AS A RIGHT AND A MORAL GOOD ch. 5 (Univ. of Hawaii, 2001), http://www.hawaii.edu/powerkills/WF.CHAP5.HTM; *See also* COLIN G. CLARKE, CLASS, ETHNICITY, AND COMMUNITY IN SOUTHERN MEXICO: OAXACA'S PEASANTRIES 35 (Oxford: Oxford UP, 2000).

174. *See* RUMMEL, SAVING LIVES, ENRICHING LIFE; R.J. RUMMEL, STATISTICS OF DEMOCIDE: GENOCIDE AND MASS MURDER SINCE 1900, ch. 11 (New Brunswick, NJ: Transaction Publishers, 1997).

175. *See* DIRK HOERDER, CULTURES IN CONTACT-CL: WORLD MIGRATIONS IN THE SECOND MILLENNIUM 188–191, 234–40 (Durham, NC: Duke UP, 2002). *See also* HENRY KAMEN, EMPIRE: HOW SPAIN BECAME A WORLD POWER, 1492–1763, at 117, 124–25, 136–40, 203, 285, 358 (New York: HarperCollins, 2004).

176. *See* PETER IADICOLA & ANSON D. SHUPE, VIOLENCE, INEQUALITY, AND HUMAN FREEDOM 196 (London: Rowman & Littlefield, 2003); NICHOLAS A. ROBINS, GENOCIDE AND MILLENNIALISM IN UPPER PERU: THE GREAT REBELLION OF 1780–1782, at 41–43 (Westport, CT: Greenwood Publ'g Group, 2002); STANNARD, AMERICAN HOLOCAUST, at 40–46, 294–95, 302–7; Peter F. Klarén, *Historical Setting, in* A COUNTRY STUDY: PERU, ch. 1 (Washington: Library of Congress, 1992), http://lcweb2.loc.gov/cgi-bin/query/r?frd/cstdy:@field(DOCID+pe0015).

177. *See* Klarén, *Historical Setting, in* A COUNTRY STUDY: PERU, http://lcweb2.loc.gov/cgi-bin/query/r?frd/cstdy:@field(DOCID+pe0018).

178. Mooney, *American Indians.*

bines. By the middle of that century, Portuguese slave traders utilized Tupi warriors to capture members of the sedentary agricultural peoples of Paraguay, and abduct them for sale abroad. Especially prior to Jesuit influence in Paraguay, the settler population believed that by right of conquest it could legitimately enslave native peoples. In the eighteenth century, tens of thousands were taken to the great slave-market of São Paolo.[179] The Treaty of Madrid of 1750 between Spain and Portugal called for the deportation of all Indians and missionaries from the towns and villages on the eastern bank of the Uruguay River, with the soil, villages, buildings, and churches going to Portugal. The Portuguese leader had decided to Europeanize the natives of Brazil by importing large numbers of Europeans and removing the limits placed by the Jesuits on the enslavement and exploitation of the natives.[180] The implications of this policy are apparent from a Jesuit text arguing that with the mixing of the European and Indian "races," the "latter disappears in the long term and the former prevails...." Azara is today regarded as a precursor of the Charles Darwin theory of evolution.[181] Indian slavery was abolished in 1761, but a tax-farming system led to further exploitation and depopulation.[182]

Paraguay seceded from the Spanish Empire in 1811. After indigenous rights advocates attempted to establish a multi-ethnic empire in Paraguay in the late nineteenth century, Argentina, Brazil, and Uruguay invaded, and 60% to 70% of the population was lost as the coalition rampaged through the countryside in what the descendants of the vanquished regarded as the greatest genocide in the history of the Western hemisphere.[183] Paraguay may have suffered the highest rate of casualties among a military and national population in modern history.[184]

To attract foreign investment after the war, the government of Paraguay enacted legislation in the 1880s promoting the sale of state-owned lands to farmers and cattle ranchers. Smaller holdings of part-native farmers were consolidated into larger plantations, frequently owned by Europeans, Argentineans, or Brazilians. The settlers and landowners hunted the Achè people for sport and to clear the land of persons redefined by law as

---

179. *See* THOMAS JEFFERSON PAGE, LA PLATA, THE ARGENTINE CONFEDERATION AND PARAGUAY 449–535 (New York: Harper & Bros., 1859).

180. *See* Treaty of Limits of Conquests Between the Most High and Most Potent Princes Dom Joao the Fifth, King of Portugal, and Don Fernando the Sixth, King of Spain, Signed on the Thirteenth of January, 1750, at Madrid (Spain-Portugal), art. XVI, in 3 STATEMENT SUBMITTED BY THE UNITED STATES OF BRAZIL TO THE PRESIDENT OF THE UNITED STATES OF AMERICA AS ARBITRATOR, appendix at 16 (New York: The Knickerbocker Press, 1894); KENNETH MAXWELL, POMBAL, PARADOX OF THE ENLIGHTENMENT 51–64 (Cambridge: Cambridge UP, 1995)..

181. *Quoted in* GUSTAVO VERDESIO, FORGOTTEN CONQUESTS: REREADING NEW WORLD HISTORY FROM THE MARGINS 7, 15, 26, 28, 56, 99, 107 (Philadelphia: Temple UP, 2001) (dating this text of Félix de Azara to 1847). *See also Fue el Precursor de Darwin: La Comunidad Científica Española Rinde Homenaje al Naturalista y Explorador Félix de Azara*, EL MUNDO (SPAIN), Oct. 19, 2005, http://www.elmundo.es/elmundo/2005/10/19/ciencia/1129721333.html.

182. *See* PETER JOHN BAKEWELL, A HISTORY OF LATIN AMERICA: C. 1450 TO THE PRESENT 370 (New York: Wiley, 2004); Robin M. Wright, *Destruction, Resistance, and Transformation: Southern, Coastal, and Northern Brazil (1580–1890), in* THE CAMBRIDGE HISTORY OF THE NATIVE PEOPLES OF THE AMERICAS 310 (Bruce G. Trigger et al. eds., Cambridge: Cambridge UP, 2000).

183. *See* Mark Munzel, *The Manhunts: Achè Indians in Paraguay, in* CASE STUDIES ON HUMAN RIGHTS AND FUNDAMENTAL FREEDOMS: A WORLD SURVEY 370, 375–76 (Willem Adriaan Veenhoven et al. eds., Leiden, the Netherlands: Brill, 1976). See also L.A. Demersay, *Paraguay, in* 3 CYCLOPAEDIA OF POLITICAL SCIENCE, POLITICAL ECONOMY, AND OF THE HISTORY OF THE UNITED STATES 51 (John J. Lalor ed., New York: Charles E. Merrill & Co., 1893).

184. *See* Thomas Whigham & Hendrik Kraay, *Introduction, in* I DIE WITH MY COUNTRY: PERSPECTIVES ON THE PARAGUAYAN WAR, 1864–1870, at 1 (Hendrik Kraay & Thomas Whigham eds., Omaha, NE: Univ. of Nebraska Press, 2004).

trespassers and cattle-stealers. The Achè took flight at the very sight of settlers, whom they compared to carnivorous "jaguars"; to the settlers, the Achè were sometimes known as "wild rats" or "Guayaki."[185] In a 1907 settler account, "manhunters" working with a local police chief raided an Achè village, killed multiple women and children, and burned all the bows and arrows they found, potentially leaving the Achè who fled without the means to procure food.[186]

The native peoples living in present-day Brazil also suffered catastrophic declines in their populations that coincided with massacres, expropriation of lands and wealth, and enslavement. Their decimation was inextricably linked to genocidal colonialist policies. Genocide scholar Irving Horowitz described the native population of Brazil as seemingly "'doomed to extinction,'" with peoples such as the Munduchurus, Guaranis, Kadiweus, Chavantes, and Taqpaiunas having disappeared altogether or shrunk from thousands to mere dozens of members.[187] Portuguese sugar plantations withered Indian bodies, so a "massive transatlantic slave trade" was established to import Africans for use as slaves.[188] Eighty native peoples of Brazil disappeared after contact with Portuguese-speaking settlers between 1900 and 1957.[189]

In the late twentieth century, the incursion of Portuguese-speaking settlers and mining companies deeper into heavily forested native lands was achieved by policies such as annihilation by military force, confinement into concentration camps, poisoning of food, and removal from agricultural lands.[190] As described in Chapters XI (Cold War period) and Chapter XII (post-Cold War period), the Yanomami suffered further catastrophic assaults in the 1980s and 1990s, described even by Brazilian officials and judges as a form of genocide.

Except for their architecture, the native peoples of Argentina had by 1900 "almost disappeared without leaving any record."[191] The Tehuelche, Puelche, and Araucaños of Argentina were reduced to a shadow of their former numbers, their villages looted, and their female children forcibly married off to Christians.[192] Independent Argentina killed thousands of indigenous people at a time, including over 10,000 in 1800 and over 1,500 in 1879. After coming to power in 1973, Augusto Pinochet ordered a sell-off of indigenous lands. Argentina was left with the lowest percentage of indigenous peoples in South America, at about 3%.[193]

---

185. *Quoted in* Munzel, *The Manhunts*, at 370, 375–76.

186. *Quoted in* Jonathan Kandell, *Slavery Just One Threat Facing Paraguay Tribe; Slavery Just One Hazard Facing a Stone-Age Tribe in Paraguay Deaths in Land Disputes*, N.Y. TIMES, Jan. 21, 1974, at A8.

187. IRVING LOUIS HOROWITZ, TAKING LIVES: GENOCIDE AND STATE POWER 170–71 (New Brunswick, NJ: Transaction Publishers, 4th ed. 1997); *see also* ALVAREZ, GOVERNMENTS, CITIZENS, AND GENOCIDE, at 101.

188. Adrian Hastings, *Latin America, in* A WORLD HISTORY OF CHRISTIANITY (Adrian Hastings ed., Grand Rapids, MI: Eerdmans Publishing, 2000).

189. *See* Robert K. Hitchcock & Tara M. Twedt, *Physical and Cultural Genocide of Indigenous Peoples, in* A CENTURY OF GENOCIDE: CRITICAL ESSAYS AND EYEWITNESS ACCOUNTS 352 (Samuel Totten & William S. Parsons eds., London: Taylor & Francis, 2008).

190. *Id.*

191. INTERNATIONAL BUREAU OF THE AMERICAN REPUBLICS, ARGENTINE REPUBLIC: A GEOGRAPHICAL SKETCH 107 (Washington, DC: Org. of American States, 1903).

192. *See* KURT JONASSOHN, KARIN SOLVEIG BJÖRNSON, & KARIN BJORNSON, GENOCIDE AND GROSS HUMAN RIGHTS VIOLATIONS 213 (New Brunswick, NJ: Transaction Publishers, 1998).

193. *See* Marzia Rosti, *Reparations for Indigenous Peoples in Two Selected Latin American Countries, in* REPARATIONS FOR INDIGENOUS PEOPLES: INTERNATIONAL AND COMPARATIVE PERSPECTIVES 345–47, 357 (Frederico Lenzerini ed., Oxford: Oxford UP, 2008).

In Chile, the Mapuche people declined in numbers from one million in the sixteenth century, to fewer than 290,000 according to the census of 1907. After a series of massacres in the late nineteenth century, Mapuches lost 90% of their land.[194] The Mapuche were eventually "crowded into the worst farmlands of the agriculturally rich province of Cautin...." They were so marginalized in the 1970s that urban Chileans often denied the very existence of natives in their country.[195] Their numbers later rebounded, however, reaching 600,000 in 2002. Still, fewer than five percent of the population identified as indigenous in the 2002 census.[196]

4. Canada and the United States

Genocide was also practiced in the North American colonies. In Canada, for example, a 1688 order of the governor of Canadian New France paid anyone bringing in the scalps of Indians ten beaver skins as a reward, which could be sold for food or weaponry.[197] A 1756 proclamation in Nova Scotia offered a bounty for native scalps, and was still on the books in 2000.[198] Edward Cornwallis, Governor of Halifax, issued an order to British colonial forces to "take or destroy the Savages commonly known as Mic-macks, wherever they are found." He offered, with the advice and consent of the King's Privy Council, ten guineas per scalp produced to British forces at Halifax.[199] As one author writes of such bounties:

> The punishments of the Indians for wrongdoing by the English were ... harsh and ... humiliating.... The scalp bounties of the colonies included rewards for the killing of Indian women and children, although a lesser money value was set on the scalp of a [child]....[200]

Scholars regard the hiring by the British crown, through its Governors, of mercenaries to search out and murder native Americans, including children, as part of a larger "genocide campaign."[201]

The deportation of natives from the land was also common in Canada. British treaties with native leaders purporting to guarantee British Canadian respect for indigenous peoples' land rights were disregarded. Subsequently, Canadian courts ruled that title in In-

---

194. *Compare* Memoria: Presentada al Supremo gobierno por la Comisión del Censo (Santiago, Chile: Comisión Central del Censo, 1908), http://www.memoriachilena.cl//temas/documento_detalle.asp?id=MC0007943, *with* Aldisson Anguita Mariqueo, *Chilean Economic Expansion and Mega-Development Projects in Mapuche Territories, in* In the Way of Development: Indigenous Peoples, Life Projects, and Globalization 204–5 (Mario Blaser, Harvey A. Feit, Glenn McRae eds., London: Zed Books, 2004).

195. *See* Kandell, *Slavery Just One Threat Facing Paraguay Tribe*, at A8.

196. *See* Human Rights Watch, Undue Process: Terrorism Trials, Military Courts, and the Mapuche in Southern Chile 12 (New York: Human Rights Watch, 2004).

197. John Grenier, The First Way of War: American War Making on the Frontier, 1607–1814, at 39 (Cambridge: Cambridge UP, 2005).

198. *See, e.g., Two Hundred Year-Old Scalp Law Still on Books in Nova Scotia,* Canadian Broadcasting Corp. (Jan. 4, 2000), http://www.cbc.ca/canada/story/2000/01/04/mikmaq000103.html.

199. *A Proclamation, in* Selections from the Public Documents of the Province of Nova Scotia 561 (Thomas B. Akins ed., Halifax, Nova Scotia, Canada: Charles Annand, 1869).

200. John Stewart McLennan, Louisbourg, From Its Foundation to Its Fall, 1713–1758, at 65 (London and New York: Macmillan and Co., 1918).

201. Chaim David Mazoff, Anxious Allegiances 66 (Montreal: McGill-Queen's UP, 1998) (citing Virginia Miller, *The Micmac: A Maritime Woodland Group, in* Native People: The Canadian Experience 324–52 (R. Bruce Morrison & C. Roderick Wilson eds., Toronto: McLelland & Stewart, 1986)).

dian lands was held by the Crown of Great Britain and Northern Ireland, notwithstanding the lack of native consent or compensation. "Courts viewed native people as 'uncivilized' and as belonging to an inferior race and thus agreements between native peoples and the Crown were not binding on the Crown in law...." In *Regina v. Syliboy*, the Nova Scotia County Court reiterated that a "civilized nation first discovering a country of uncivilized people or savages held such country as its own until such time as by treaty it was transferred to some other civilized nation...."[202]

The French "launched their own attempted exterminatory campaigns" against the Fox tribe of the upper Midwest and the Natchez tribe of Louisiana in the 1700s.[203] The French enslaved the Natchez to clear the forest and plant crops, but they often ran off, so the French imported African slaves instead. The French traded two Indian slaves to Hispaniola/Santo Domingo for each African slave. In 1706, the governor of the French colony of Louisiana, Jean Baptiste Lemoyne de Bienville, "adopted a scalps-for-guns policy that he said had been used effectively ... in ongoing wars against the Chitimacha and Alabama...." The policy traded firearms to Indians who brought in the scalps of Indians under British rule. Bienville even persuaded some Natchez to scalp or behead members of their own tribes.[204] A French plantation director described a plan "to destroy the Natchez Indians."[205] Based on such evidence, historians declare that the French "launched campaigns of genocidal intent against Fox, Natchez, and Chickasaw communities in the early eighteenth century."[206]

Many indigenous Canadian languages verge on extinction. About half of the indigenous languages that existed in the sixteenth century CE are not remembered or spoken, and many of the remainder are near extinction, or so endangered that their survival is unlikely.[207] Exclusion from mainstream Canadian society remains a problem as well. Indigenous people made up one-tenth of the population of Canadian prisons in the 1980s; the figure reached 20% among female inmates. Indigenous life spans were 10 years shorter than for the descendents of European settlers or other migrants to Canada, due to high rates of disease, violence, and suicide.[208]

The indigenous population in the territories that later formed the U.S. declined to 300,000 by 1880, from an original figure of up to 94 million. The free fall in indigenous North American populations was attributable to a toxic cocktail of "disease, slaughter, slavery, and aggressive war."[209] Fanning out from Plymouth Rock in New England, the Puritans regarded the natives as situated similarly to the Canaanites, inclined toward heathenism and occupying land that had not been "promised" to them by the one true deity.[210]

---

202. *See* Patrick Macklem, *First Nations Self-Government and the Borders of the Canadian Legal Imagination*, 36 REVIEW DE DROIT DE MCGILL 381, 428 (1991) (quoting Rex v. Syliboy, [1929] 1 D.L.R. 307, 50 C.C.C. 389).

203. *See* LEVENE, 2 GENOCIDE IN THE AGE OF THE NATION STATE, at 63.

204. JAMES F. BARNETT, THE NATCHEZ INDIANS: A HISTORY TO 1735, at 69, 72–73, 83 (Jackson, Miss.: Univ. of Miss. Press, 2007).

205. DANIEL H. USNER, JR., AMERICAN INDIANS IN THE LOWER MISSISSIPPI VALLEY 24 (Lincoln, Nebraska: Univ. of Nebraska Press, 1998).

206. COLIN GORDON CALLOWAY, NEW WORLDS FOR ALL: INDIANS, EUROPEANS, AND THE REMAKING OF EARLY AMERICA 98 (Baltimore, Maryland: Johns Hopkins UP, 1998).

207. *See* Akira Yamamoto, *Endangered Languages in USA and Canada,* MATTHIAS BRENZINGER, LANGUAGE DIVERSITY ENDANGERED 88 (Berlin and New York: Walter de Gruyter, 2007).

208. *Id.* at 386.

209. Bradford, *An American Indian Theory of Justice*, at 23; RUMMEL, DEATH BY GOVERNMENT, at 59, 70.

210. *See* Michael Freeman, *Puritans and Pequots: The Question of Genocide*, 68.2 NEW ENGLAND Q. 278, 284–85 (1995).

The Pequots of colonial New England almost disappeared after a massacre in 1637, leaving few descendants.[211] Settlers killed about 2,000 members of the Narragansett tribe in a massacre at about the same time.[212] The Wampanoag Indians of present-day Massachusetts and Rhode Island were "nearly exterminated" by 1700.[213] Diseases like smallpox caused untold thousands of premature deaths as a result of deportations, forced contact with Europeans and Africans, and as settler leaders' distribution of blankets exposed to smallpox germs among communities of indigenous Americans.[214]

In the eighteenth century, the Iroquois suffered a "war of extirpation" and the slaughter of many women and children, up to half of their total numbers.[215] During the U.S. Revolutionary War, Continental Army commander George Washington ordered his general, John Sullivan, to wage a punitive campaign against the Iroquois of western New York. Towns such as Genesee were completely razed, and Washington became known to Iroquois as "Town Destroyer."[216]

Upon U.S. independence, the Continental Congress decided that Indians should abandon their territory and remove themselves to British territory without compensation.[217] George Washington, as commander-in-chief of the Continental Army opposing the British Empire, called the natives "beasts of prey" like "the wolf," from which they merely "differ in shape."[218] Washington commanded campaigns that resulted in the burning of Iroquois villages and food supplies during the Revolutionary War, after which the U.S. Congress

211. *See* Jonathan Smith, Michael Johnson, Indian Tribes of the New England Frontier 13 (Oxford and New York: Osprey Publ'g, 2006).

212. *See* James Wilson, The Earth Shall Weep: A History of Native America 96 (New York: Grove Press, 1999).

213. *Wampanoag, in* Grolier Online / Scholastic.com (2007), http://content.scholastic.com/browse/article.jsp?id=5099.

214. *See* John Grenier, The First Way of War: American War Making on the Frontier, 1607–1814, at 144 (New York: w York: Cambridge UP, 2005); David Shumway Jones, Rationalizing Epidemics: Meanings and Uses of American Indian Mortality since 1600, at 94–99 (Cambridge: Harvard UP, 2004); Elizabeth A. Fenn, *Biological Warfare in Eighteenth-Century North America: Beyond Jeffrey Amherst*, 86 J. of American Hist. 1553 (2000); Noble David Cook, Born to Die: Disease and the New World Conquest, 1492–1650 (New York: Cambridge UP, 1998).

215. *See* Levene, 2 Genocide in the Age of the Nation State, at 80. *See also* Chief Red Jacket (Sagoyewatha), *Address to the Chiefs of the Iroquois Confederacy (1805), in* A History of Us: Sourcebook and Index 104–5 (Steven Mintz ed., Oxford and New York: Oxford UP, 3d ed. 2003) ("The white people, Brother, had now found our country. Tidings were carried back, and more came amongst us. Yet we did not fear them. We took them to be friends. They called us brothers. We believed them, and gave them a larger seat. At length their numbers had greatly increased. They wanted more land; they wanted our country. Our eyes were opened, and our minds became uneasy. Wars took place. Indians were hired to fight against Indians, and many of our people were destroyed. They also brought liquor amongst us. It was strong and powerful, and has slain thousands.").

216. Maureen Konkle, Writing Indian Nations: Native Intellectuals and the Politics of Historiography, 1827–1863, at 225–28 (Chapel Hill: Univ. of North Carolina Press, 2003). In the 1850s, a Tonnawanda Indian recounted the lament of an Iroquois chief:

> We have been reduced and broken by the cunning and rapacity of the white race. We are now compelled to crave as a blessing that we may be allowed to live upon our own lands, to cultivate our own fields, to drink from our own spring and to mingle our bones with those of our fathers.

Id. at 226 (quoting Nicholson Parker, *The American Red Man, in* Arthur C. Parker, The Life of General Ely S. Parker: Last Grand Sachem of the Iroquois and General Grant's Military Secretary (Buffalo: Buffalo Historical Society, 1919) (1853).

217. *See* Indian Removal Act of May 28, 1830, 4 Stat. 411.

218. *Letter from George Washington to James Duane* (Sept. 7, 1783), *in* The Writings of George Washington 312 (Worthington Chauncey Ford ed., 1891).

informed the Iroquois that the U.S. "would never cease pursuing them with war while one remained on the face of the earth."[219] President Jefferson "went as far as to state several times that the U.S. would exterminate [native] tribes that resisted American expansion." He adopted measures for acquiring native lands as rapidly as possible, and selling them to pay off U.S. sovereign debt.[220] In 1813, Jefferson characterized "the extermination of this [Native American] race in our America" as "an additional chapter in the English history of the same colored man in Asia, and of the brethren of their own color in Ireland...."[221] He blamed the English for making alliances with indigenous tribes that massacred "women and children" on the frontiers of the U.S., prompting the U.S. government to "exterminat[e]" those tribes.[222]

In 1830, President Andrew Jackson announced to the nation during an annual address that true humanitarians should welcome "the fate of the aborigines" as "the extinction of one generation to make room for another." A republic of happy Americans, then 12 million strong, with cities and prosperous farms, blessed with "civilization" and "religion," was far preferable to "a few thousand savages."[223]

The Indian Removal Act of 1830 mandated the deportation of all indigenous people to lands to the west of the Mississippi River.[224] Thus, by an Act of Congress, English-speaking settlers deported the Cherokee, Choctaw, Chickasaw, Creek, and Seminole peoples of the verdant and green present-day southeast U.S. to the arid west of the continent, with "many thousands" dying in the forced march, in a process that affected some 80,000 displaced people.[225] As usual, deportation was resisted, and often resulted in mass death on both sides, but more so on the native side.[226] As one scholar describes the process:

> [T]he United States ... expelled every major Native American nation from the Southeast. Pulled up from their ancestral roots and forced to surrender their homes, farms, and livelihoods, the Cherokees, Creeks, Choctaws, Chickasaws, and Seminoles marched and rode, often at federal [military] bayonet point, to an unfamiliar territory and an uncertain future. The physical and psychological hardships of removal were terrible; the relocation decimated the populations of the Southeastern tribes.

About half of the Cherokees,[227] four thousand members of the nation, died.[228] By 1833 the federal government had ousted the indigenous population of much of the Midwestern

---

219. Kiernan, Blood and Soil, 319, 325; *see* Stannard, American Holocaust, at 119.

220. *See* Robert Miller, *Thomas Jefferson, in* Encyclopedia United States Indian Policy and Law (Washington, DC: Congressional Quarterly Press, 2009) (citing, *inter alia*, The Writings of Thomas Jefferson, vols. 1–4, 6–8, 10, 12–13, 16–17 (Andrew A. Lipscomb & Albert Ellery Bergh, eds., 1903); Thomas Jefferson, *The Limits and Bounds of Louisiana, in* Documents Relating to the Purchase & Exploration of Louisiana (1904); 1 A Compilation of Messages and Papers of the Presidents (Washington D.C.: Bureau of National Literature, James D. Richardson ed., 1913)).

221. Jefferson, *Letter to Alexander von Humboldt,* at 269.

222. *Id.* at 23.

223. Andrew Jackson, *Second Annual Message* (Dec. 7, 1830), *in* The Addresses and Messages of the Presidents of the United States, Inaugural, Annual, and Special, from 1789 to 1846, at 746 (Edwin Williams ed., New York: E. Walker, 1847).

224. *See* William Nelson Fenton, The Great Law and the Longhouse: A Political History of the Iroquois Confederacy 604–5 (Norman, Oklahoma, Univ. of Oklahoma Press, 1998).

225. *See* Kiernan, Blood and Soil, at 310–25; Levene, 2 Genocide in the Age of the Nation State, at 57, 88, 90, 93, 245; Paul Stuart, Nations within a Nation: Historical Statistics of American Indians 71–2, 79–80 (New York: Greenwood Press, 1987).

226. *See* U.S. Army Infantry, *Indian Wars* (2008), https://www.infantry.army.mil/museum/inside_tour/deSCRIPTive_tour/08_indian_wars.htm.

U.S. from their lands. The Sauk leader Black Hawk bemoaned the fate of his people under this policy, saying that they had suffered the loss of their homes, as well as disease and death.[229]

The U.S., settled by millions of English, Germans, Dutch, Spanish, French, Irish, Poles, and other Europeans, used similar tactics to those of the British, French, and Spanish empires. Standing securely within the tradition of religious law denying human rights to infidel civilians, several prominent U.S. jurists declared that: "The territory over which [the Native Americans] wandered, and which they used for their temporary fugitive purposes, was, in respect to Christians, deemed as if it were inhabited only by brute animals."[230] As infidels and savages, Native Americans could not be dealt with as sovereign nations, as U.S. Supreme Court Justice Story wrote.[231] Colonies and states such as Virginia, and later the U.S. federal government, claimed the right to extinguish native title to land, and grant it to Europeans.[232]

The U.S. Supreme Court ratified the right of European monarchs, and the U.S. after independence, to parcel out title to indigenous lands while still in possession of the natives. Justice Marshall declared for the Court: "[T]he great nations of Europe ... asserted the ultimate dominion [over native lands] to be in themselves; and claimed and exercised, as a consequence of this ultimate dominion, a power to grant the soil, while yet in possession of the natives...."[233] The U.S. Army dispossessed Native Americans of tens or even hundreds of millions of acres, leaving Native Americans with only 48 million acres by 1934, about two percent of the two billion acres in the continental U.S.[234] Several state legislatures in the U.S. defined indigenous Americans as outlaws whose murder and mistreatment could not be restrained by state authorities.[235] The law constructed the natives as subhuman.[236]

In the late nineteenth century, the United States conquered the territory to the west of the Mississippi River, home to Apache, Cheyenne, Comanche, Shoshone, and Sioux, among other peoples. An American general declared his intention to "exterminate the Sioux." "They are to be treated as wild beasts," he added. He requested authority from President Abraham Lincoln to execute 360 Sioux rebels tried by military commission.

---

227. Tim Alan Garrison, The Legal Ideology of Removal: The Southern Judiciary and the Sovereignty of Native american Nations 1–2 (Athens, GA: Univ. of Georgia Press, 2002); *see also* Glauner, *The Crime of Genocide Against Native Americans*, at 934.

228. *See* Fergus M. Bordewich, Killing the White Man's Indian 47 (New York: Doubleday, 1996).

229. Mark Wallace, *Black Hawk's "An Autobiography": The Production and Use of an "Indian" Voice*, 18 American Indian Q. 481, 489 (1994) (quoting Black Hawk, An Autobiography 69 (1833)).

230. 1 Joseph Story, Commentaries on the Constitution of the United States 135–36 (Boston: Hilliard Gray & Co., 1833). *See also* Henry Wheaton, Elements of International Law 219 (Boston: Little, Brown and Co., 6th ed., 1855) (to "the Christian powers themselves" after 1492, "the heathen nations of the other quarters of the globe were the lawful spoil and prey of their civilized conquerors.").

231. *See* Story, Commentaries on the Constitution, at 135–36 ("As infidels, heathens, and savages, they were not allowed to possess the prerogatives belonging to absolute, sovereign, and independent nations.").

232. *Id.* at 17–20, 135–38.

233. Johnson v. M'Intosh, 21 U.S. (8 Wheat.) 543, 573–74, 588 (1823). *See also* South Dakota v. Yankton Sioux Tribe, 522 U.S. 329, 343 (1998) ("Congress possesses plenary power ... to modify or eliminate tribal rights.").

234. Bradford, *An American Indian Theory of Justice*, at 35–40.

235. *See* Rennard Strickland, *Genocide-at-Law: An Historic and Contemporary View of the Native American Experience*, 34 Kansas Law Rev. 713, 718 (1986); Bradford, *An American Indian Theory of Justice*, at n.100.

236. *See* Bradford, *An American Indian Theory of Justice*, at 19–20.

Lincoln questioned whether the paperwork was in order, and ordered that 39 out of the 360 be executed, not including those guilty only of combat against U.S. forces.[237] From an estimated 12,000 Sioux and other Indians living in Minnesota in 1850, only about 5,000 remained in 1902.[238] Governments and militias had deported 2,000 Santee Sioux and Winnebago Indians in the 1860s.[239] The Sioux arrived in semi-arid Nebraska, and lost green Minnesota.[240] Chief Sitting Bull of the Lakota Sioux bemoaned that Europeans' "love of possession is a disease" that claimed "this mother of ours, the earth, for their own and fence their neighbors away," so that tithes extracted from the poor and landless "support the rich who rule."[241]

The so-called "Indian Wars" of the nineteenth century claimed about 350,000 native lives in massacres, deportations, disease, and overwork on missions and plantations.[242] Numerous massacres occurred during the Indian Wars, which saw the indigenous population decline by up to 98%. These wars increased the size of the U.S. by more than a third, and acquired hundreds of millions of acres of land for distribution to European settlers.[243] The U.S. Infantry under Colonel (later General) Nelson Appleton Miles conquered the territories of the Apache, Cheyenne, Comanche, Kiowas, Nez Pence, and Sioux.[244] Progressively, "the Seminole, Nez Perce, Lakota, Shoshone, Comanche, Apache, and other tribes were hunted, pursued, cornered, and murdered."[245] Three thousand Apache died in the conflict with the U.S., and even more starved to death prior to 1900.[246] They had previously suffered from both American and Mexican bounty hunters collecting Apache scalps.[247] General Miles led troops in the infamous massacre at Wounded Knee.[248] Starvation tactics, the destruction of homes and shelters during the freezing winter, and the killing of horses and buffalo herds ensured the submission or deportation of the survivors of the various tribes.[249]

The Yuki people of California lost seven out of every eight of its members in just 30 years by a combination of disease, starvation, kidnapping, and mass killing.[250] The population declined from the tens of thousands to only about 300 individuals.[251] In 1851,

---

237. *See* Chester M. Oehler, The Great Sioux Uprising 207–16 (New York: Da Capo Press, 1997).

238. *Compare id.* at 11, *with* E.D. Neill, *Dakota Land and Dakota Life, in* Collections of the Minnesota Historical Society 210–15 (St. Paul, Minnesota: Minnesota Historical Society, 1902).

239. *Nebraska, in* 20 Encyclopedia Americana 31 (New York: The Encyclopedia Americana Corp., 1919).

240. *See* Lieut. David L. Kingsbury, *Sully's Expedition of the Sioux in 1864, in* 8 Collections of the Minnesota Historical Society 449 (St. Paul, Minnesota: Minnesota Historical Society, 1898).

241. *Quoted in* Wright, Stolen Continents, at 304.

242. *See* Kiernan, Blood and Soil, at 363.

243. *See* Bradford, *An American Indian Theory of Justice*, at 24, 35–40.

244. *Miles, Nelson Appleton, in* 19 Encyclopedia Americana 56 (New York: The Encyclopedia Americana Corp., 1919).

245. Bradford, *An American Indian Theory of Justice*, at 24.

246. *See id.* at n. 107; Donald E. Worcester, The Apaches: Eagles of the Southwest 167 (Tulsa, Oklahoma: Univ. of Oklahoma Press, 1979).

247. *See* Neil Goodwin, The Apache Diaries: A Father-Son Journey 80–81 (Omaha, NE: Univ. of Nebraska Press, 2002); Laurence French, Psychocultural Change and the American Indian: An Ethnohistorical Analysis 81 (New York: Garland, 1987).

248. *See Archives of the West*, PBS, http://www.pbs.org/weta/thewest/resources/archives/seven/w67i_codypine.htm.

249. *See* U.S. Army Infantry, *Indian Wars.*

250. *See* Rummel, Death by Government, at 58.

251. *See* Benjamin Madley, *Patterns of Frontier Genocide, 1803–1910: the Aboriginal Tasmanians, the Yuki of California, and the Herero of Namibia*, 6 J. of Genocide Research 167 (2004).

California's first U.S. civilian governor called the "extermination" and "extinct[ion]" of the territory's natives their inescapable "destiny." The California legislature, in 1860, proclaimed that:

> Accounts are daily coming in from the counties on the Coast Range, of sickening atrocities and wholesale slaughters of great numbers of defenseless Indians.... For an evil of this magnitude, someone is responsible. Either our government, or our citizens, or both, are to blame.

The overall native population of California plummeted by four-fifths, to only 30,000 in 1865. From only 13,000 non-Indian residents after the U.S. conquest in 1847, the non-Indian settler population exploded to more than 360,000 a mere thirteen years later.[252]

Killing was not the only method used by European settlers to wipe out the indigenous cultural pattern in the Americas. Lemkin's draft history of genocide described the enslavement of the natives of North America as a genocidal strategy of destroying their culture and subjecting them to premature death. Slavery began at least in sixteenth-century Massachusetts and Connecticut, and continued in eighteenth-century Maryland, North Carolina, South Carolina, and Virginia.[253] Lemkin quoted from a lecture by an Oxford professor of political economy, who later became Under-Secretary of State for the Colonies: "The history of European settlements in America, Africa, and Australia, presents everywhere the same general feature: a wide and sweeping destruction of native races by the uncontrolled violence of individuals and colonial authorities...."[254] The mission system in Spanish colonies up to and including California and Florida involved "virtual slavery" for thousands of Native Americans.[255] In the eighteenth century, the Spanish commissioned the Franciscan missionaries to colonize California, and they used forced indigenous labor to conduct large-scale farming and husbandry to feed Spanish troops.[256] Spanish law required those having a certain quantum of Indian blood (the *indios*) to provide labor services and pay a special indigenous tax.[257] About 30,000 natives suffered enslavement in seventeenth and eighteenth century La Florida, which "devastated" nations.[258]

Frequent rapes of indigenous women and the kidnapping of thousands of indigenous children occurred in nineteenth-century California, and no doubt in other states as well.[259] In the 1850s, enslavement of natives continued to be legally endorsed in California:

> From 1850 until 1863, California Indians could legally be taken and forced to become unpaid servants. Confronting a labor shortage, on 22 April 1850, legis-

---

252. Madley, *California's Yuki Indians.*

253. *See* John Docker, *Are Settler-Colonies Inherently Genocidal?, in* EMPIRE, COLONY, GENOCIDE, at 89, 95. There were an estimated 1,400 Native American slaves in South Carolina in 1708. *See* KENNETH GORDON DAVIES THE NORTH ATLANTIC WORLD IN THE SEVENTEENTH CENTURY 282 (Minneapolis, MN: University of Minnesota Press, 1974). Dozens of natives would be bought and sold at a time in late seventeenth century Plymouth. *See* LAUBER WHEELER, INDIAN SLAVERY IN COLONIAL TIMES WITHIN THE PRESENT LIMITS OF THE UNITED STATES 111 (New York: Columbia Univ., 1913).

254. Raphael Lemkin, *Tasmania, in* COLONIALISM AND GENOCIDE, at 97.

255. *Mission System, in* THE ENCYCLOPEDIA OF NATIVE AMERICAN ECONOMIC HISTORY 165; JANET RIEHECKY, THE SETTLING OF ST. AUGUSTINE 35 (2003).

256. *See* ROBERT H. JACKSON, FROM SAVAGES TO SUBJECTS: MISSIONS IN THE HISTORY OF THE AMERICAN SOUTHWEST ix–xiii, xvi–xvii, 5–9, 18, 26–27, 75, 79, 87 (Armonk, NY: M.E. Sharpe, Inc., 2000).

257. *See id.* at 112.

258. ALAN GALLAY, INDIAN SLAVERY IN COLONIAL AMERICA 236 (Omaha, NE: Univ. of Nebraska Press, 2010).

259. *See* BRUCE E. JOHANSEN, NATIVE PEOPLES OF NORTH AMERICA: A HISTORY 230 (New Brunswick, NJ: Rutgers UP, 2006).

> lators passed an "Act for the Government and Protection of Indians," which legalized white custody of Indian minors and Indian prisoner leasing. Under the act, children could, with consent of "friends or parents," be held and worked without pay until age fifteen (for females) or eighteen (for males). The act also empowered whites to arrest Indian adults "found loitering and strolling about," or "begging, or leading an immoral or profligate course of life." ... "Any white person" could also lease labor by visiting a jailhouse and paying "the fine and costs" for any "Indian convicted of an offense ... punishable by fine." Because few Indians had access to sufficient funds, jails became low-cost labor suppliers.[260]

Settlers enslaved approximately 10,000 Indians in California during the time when the Indian slavery legislation was in force. As the *San Francisco Alta California* documented, the theft of Indian children from their families was "quite common," so that: "Nearly all the children belonging to some of the Indian tribes in the northern part of the State, have been stolen." President Franklin Pierce refused to prevent these crimes against humanity.[261] A letter apparently in possession of President Pierce in 1856 from Major General John Wool acknowledged that the U.S. was funding the anti-Indian wars in California and Oregon, where the press was openly calling for the extermination of the indigenous population.[262]

At the close of the Indian Wars, President Theodore Roosevelt welcomed the "elimination of the Indian as a distinct problem."[263] "Such conquests," he declared, "are sure to come when a masterful people ... finds itself face to face with the weaker and wholly alien race which holds a coveted prize in its feeble grasp."[264]

After the close of the Indian Wars, U.S. tactics shifted to demographic and cultural manipulation. The prevention of births within the Native American group, codified as a form of genocide in the Genocide Convention, indisputably took place in the U.S. in the 1920s and 1930s. The U.S. government sterilized at least 70,000 Native American under circumstances that the U.S. General Accounting Office described as lacking informed consent.[265] In 1942, the U.S. Supreme Court recognized that forced sterilization violates the right to have children, and "can cause races or types which are inimical to the dominant group to wither and disappear."[266]

The outlawing of indigenous culture was intended to and no doubt succeeding in dissolving communal and ethnic ties. In the nineteenth century, the U.S. Department of the Interior took a leading role in eradicating indigenous culture and religions. In regulations issued by the department in 1883, native religious ceremonies such as the "sun-dance" and "war-dance" were crimes punishable by loss of food rations or incarceration in an interior department prison for thirty days at a time. Likewise, the religious practices of native priests or "medicine-men," and the "use any of the arts of a conjurer to prevent the Indians from abandoning their heathenish rites and customs," were crimes pun-

---

260. Madley, *California's Yuki Indians.*

261. *Id.*

262. *See* Norris A. Bleyhl, *Indian-White Relationships in Northern California 1849–1920*, at 19 (1978), http://www.csuchico.edu/lbib/spc/bleyhl/bleyhl_1978.pdf (citing Message on Indian Disturbances in California. 34th Cong., 1st Sess., Senate Executive Doc. No. 26, vol. 10, February 21, 1856).

263. *Quoted in* Kiernan, Blood and Soil, at 363.

264. *Quoted in* Stannard, American Holocaust, at 245.

265. *See* Glauner, *The Crime of Genocide Against Native Americans,* at 940.

266. Skinner v. Oklahoma, 316 U.S. 535 (1942). *See also* Kermit L. Hall, The Oxford Companion to the Supreme Court of the United States 788 (Oxford: Oxford UP, 1992).

ishable by imprisonment until such time as the practitioner could persuade the court "that he will forever abandon all [such] Indian offenses." The secretary of the interior instructed his subordinates in this regard that "medicine men" were dangerously active in "prevent[ing] the people from abandoning their heathenish rites and customs...." The secretary also directed that the natives be compelled to remain in nuclear families, noting that the taking of mistresses caused births and that "the more numerous the family the greater the number of rations allowed." After the courts were in use, the commissioner of Indian affairs noted that they were successfully abolishing heathenish customs such as the sun dance, which had existed among the natives "from time immemorial." He noted in passing that the Crow Indians were in the process of being removed from three million acres in Montana.[267]

Michael Winkelman, professor of anthropology at Arizona State University, argues that legal prohibitions and increasing social stigma wiped out polytheistic shamanism in the U.S. He summarizes the process as follows:

> The decline, and even the demise of shamanism among Native American societies was due to both internal and external factors.... The Christian mind-set of the Europeans meant that they tended to view Native American practices as forms of "devil-worship" or witchcraft. Consequently, violence was often used to eradicate these indigenous practices. In many cases, the shamanic traditions ... met with brutal repression.... The shamanic practices of most Native American groups have died out....[268]

In the U.S., as in Canada and Australia and some Central and South American countries, indigenous children were subjected to forced labor in boarding schools that reminded observers of the type of penal "hard labor" that would be illegal to impose on ethnic European children.[269] These federal boarding schools forced indigenous children to abandon their ancestral religious beliefs and to worship instead according to approved Christian rites.[270] The U.S. Congress conceded in 1978 that native children were removed from their families and communities on a "wholesale basis," with a "destructive" effect on native culture and life.[271] In that same year, the American Indian Religious Freedom Act of 1978 acknowledged that U.S. law and federal policies had banned the "possession of sacred objects necessary to the exercise of [Native Americans'] religious rites and ceremonies," and "interfered with" their sacred ceremonies.[272]

With the gradual abandonment of policies of enslavement and extermination in the Americas, native populations rebounded dramatically. According to U.S. Census figures, the population of indigenous groups in the U.S. approached two million by 1990, after

---

267. *See Progress Among Indians: Annual Report of Commissioner Price*, N.Y. Times, Oct. 28, 1884, http://www.nytimes.com; U.S. Dep't of the Interior, Office of Indian Affairs, Rules Governing the Court of Indian Offenses (Washington, D.C. 1883).

268. *See* Michael Winkelman, *Overview: North America*, *in* 2 Shamanism: An Encyclopedia of World Beliefs, Practices, and Culture 278–79 (Mariko Namba Walter et al. eds., Santa Barbara, CA: ABC-CLIO, 2004).

269. *See* Olivier La Farge, *Revolution with Reservations*, 84 The New Republic, Oct. 9, 1935, at 234; Meriam Lewis Merriam, The Problem of Indian Administration (Baltimore, MD: The Johns Hopkins Press, 1928).

270. *See* Glauner, *The Crime of Genocide Against Native Americans*, at 942–43, 952.

271. Indian Child Welfare Act of 1978, H.R. Rep. No 1386, 95th Cong., 2d Sess. 9, 11, 1978 U.S.C.C.A.N 7530.

272. Pub. L. 95–341, 92 Stat 469, Aug. 11, 1978.

being tallied at less than 240,000 in 1900.[273] The population of Haiti grew from around 500,000 in 1804 to more than 10 million in 2009.[274] Mexico's indigenous population, after possibly falling from 25 million in the Aztec empire to less than six million in the early nineteenth century, surpassed 97 million in 2008 once persons of mixed ancestry are included.[275]

E. European Colonial Genocide in Africa and the Victims of Slavery

1. Religious Justifications for Slavery

Slavery enjoyed the sanction of the Western Church for many centuries. A papal bull issued in 1455 "granted to the king of Portugal 'general and indefinite powers to search out and conquer all pagans, enslave them and appropriate their lands and goods.'" The text of the papal bull acknowledged the existence of a slave trade run by Europeans and afflicting Africans.[276] One of the main justifications for slavery was military, slavery being in this perspective a consequence of defeat in battle and as preferable to execution. Other rationalizations were scriptural. In the medieval era, the Church declared the "natural inferiority" of indigenous African and American peoples, and referred to the Old Testament story of the curse of Ham "to justify African slavery."[277] As a justification for enslaving Africans as a race, proslavery Christians in Europe and America utilized a Talmudic glass on the Genesis story that Noah's three sons Ham, Shem, and Japheth fathered three human races—African, Asian, and European—with the African race being the inferior and divinely cursed one.[278]

---

273. *See* Frederick E. Hoxie, Peter C. Mancall, & James Hart Merrell, American Nations: Encounters in Indian Country, 1850 to the Present 335 (London: Routledge, 2001).

274. *Compare* Steeve Coupeau, The history of Haiti 72 (Westwood, CT: Greenwood Publishing, 2008), *with* U.N. Dep't of Economic and Social Affairs, Population Division, *World Population Prospects* (2008), http://esa.un.org/unpp.

275. *Compare* George Lockhart Rives , 1 The United States and Mexico, 1821–1848: A History of the Relations Between the Two Countries 51 (New York: Charles Scribner's Sons, 1913) (collecting estimates prior to 1825), *and* John P. Schmal, *Indigenous Mexico: An Overview* (Mar. 29, 2008), http://www.mexconnect.com/articles/372-indigenous-mexico-an-overview ("At the time of independence—1821 to 1825—the total population of Mexico is believed to have numbered around 6,800,000. Estimates by Rosenblat tell us that 54.4% of this population was classified as indigenous."), *with* Juan González, Harvest of Empire: A History of Latinos in America 4 (New York: Penguin Group, 2001) (25 million in 1500s), CIA, World Factbook 2008, http://www.bartleby.com/151/mx.html#People (Mexican population of 108.7 million, 90% indigenous or mixed, in 2008); U.N. Dep't of Economic and Social Affairs Population Division, *Demographic Transition, Mexico, 1900–2050*, http://www.un.org/esa/population/meetings/EGMPopAge/Partida_Figures.pdf.

276. James Muldoon, *Spiritual Freedom—Physical Slavery: The Medieval Church and Slavery*, 3 Ave Maria L. Rev. 69, 80–81 (2005).

277. James H. Sweet, *The Iberian Roots of American Racist Thought*, William & Mary Q. 158 (1997). The Catholic Church has since apologized and sought forgiveness for its role in the violence against indigenous Americans. *See* Steven Paul McSloy, *"Because the Bible Tells Me So": Manifest Destiny and American Indians*, 9 St. Thomas L. Rev. 37, 46 (1996).

278. *See, e.g.*, William M. Wiecek, *The Origins of the Law of Slavery in British North America*, 17 Cardozo L. Review 1711, 1726–27 (1996).

The text of the Bible, even in the King James Version, is naturally much more complex than this pro-slavery myth would suggest. The story of Ham and Shem in Genesis does not actually refer to Africa or Africans, let alone condemn Africans to slavery as a race. Ham is associated with Canaan and the ancient king Nimrod and cities Babel and Accad (Akkad), which were in the ancient Assyrian and Babylonian empires, present-day Iraq, rather than in Africa.[279] Shem, the ancestor of the Europeans in the proslavery account, went on to father both Ashur, the god of the Assyrians, and Abraham, the ancestor of the Jewish people who lived (before moving to Canaan) in "Ur of the Chaldees," Chaldea referring in this context to Babylonia.[280] There is a linkage with the stories of Moses and Joshua in the Bible, however, in that Canaan the son of Ham gave rise to most of the seven nations whose extermination is authorized in the Book of Deuteronomy, i.e., the Canaanites, Amorites, Girgasites, Hivites, and Jebusites.[281] This may have played into the theory that anyone subject to death in an ethnic struggle may be enslaved instead, as indeed women and children were taken as "plunder" in the Book of Deuteronomy.[282] Thus, the story of Ham and Canaan served as the basis for a number of Jewish, Christian, and Muslim defenses of the enslavement of Nubians, Ethiopians, and other Africans.[283]

Another precedent for slavery and extermination as state practice was the biblical story of Joshua's conquest of Jericho. A religious law analysis of the situation in the Americas prepared at the behest of King Ferdinand of Spain found that "just as the Jews had received Israel from God, Spain had likewise received the Indies through divine favor." The author argued that King Ferdinand "might justly" kill and enslave "idolatrous Indians" by same right that Joshua killed and enslaved "all the land of Canaan by force of arms." He reasoned:

> Moses sent Joshua to require the inhabitants of Jericho, the first city in the promised land of Canaan, to abandon their city because it belonged to the people of Israel inasmuch as God had given it to them; and when the people of Jericho did not give up their land Joshua surrounded them and killed them all except one woman who had protected his spies. And afterwards Joshua conquered all the land of Canaan by force of arms, and many were killed and those who were captured were given as slaves and served the people of Israel. And all this was done by the will of God because they were idolaters.... [Therefore] the king might very justly send men to require those idolatrous Indians to hand over their land to him, for it was given him by the pope. If the Indians would not do this, he might justly wage war against them, kill them and enslave those captured in war, precisely as Joshua treated the inhabitants of the land of Canaan.[284]

Although presumably no longer bound by papal decrees and Catholic theologians, the Protestant Queen Elizabeth I of England embraced a similar doctrine permitting seizure

---

279. *See* Genesis 10:6–12 (KJV).

280. *See* Genesis 10:22, 11:10–31 (KJV). *See also* SMITH, THE CHALDEAN ACCOUNT OF GENESIS, at 19–33 (describing relationships between ancient Mesopotamian cities of Ur, Akkad, Babel, and Assur, and between Mesopotamian history and Book of Genesis).

281. *See* Genesis 10:6–18 (KJV).

282. *See* Deuteronomy 20:14 (KJV).

283. *See* Robin Blackburn, *The Old World Background to Colonial Slavery*, 54 WILLIAM AND MARY Q. 65, 91–2 (1997).

284. Robert A. Williams, Jr., *The Medieval and Renaissance Origins of the Status of the American Indian in Western Legal Thought*, 57 SOUTHERN CALIFORNIA LAW REVIEW 1, 45 n.185 (1983) (quoting L. HANKE, THE SPANISH STRUGGLE FOR JUSTICE IN THE CONQUEST OF AMERICA 31–32 (1949)).

of all lands not in actual possession of Christian sovereigns, and the consequent displacement and killing of non-Christian indigenous leaders and their communities.[285] English jurists and theologians believed that the 1493 papal grant of sovereignty over most of the Americas to the Spanish and Portuguese nevertheless permitted the English to discover and colonize lands not yet settled by other Christian powers.[286] "The English Crown's charters to [the English adventurers and colonizers] Cabot, Gilbert, and Raleigh were nearly identical to the Pope's Bulls in commissioning expeditions to 'heathen and barbarous lands.'"[287] In Massachusetts, the settlers decreed the laws of Moses as being in force all the way down to the death penalty for witchcraft.[288] At the same time, they enslaved "lawfull Captives taken in just warres."[289] The English settlers even exported Indians to the slave colonies of Bermuda and Barbados.[290]

The British Empire criminalized indigenous African religious practice by its slaves in the Caribbean.[291] European-dominated slave societies criminalized "expressions of African culture, fearing the alternative world view that functioning African religions might provide...."[292] As a "threat to white hegemony," indigenous African religions were suppressed as sources of "an alternative world view," which might "prove quite effective in helping organize rebellious opposition to enslavement...." Slave societies also banned non-Christian African religions "because they were in competition with European Christianity for the conversion of, or at least influence with, indigenous Indian populations."[293] Expressions of indigenous African religions were judged to be "witchcraft" or "voodooism" and their practitioners were executed.[294] Native dancing or "reveling" by slaves was punishable by a whipping of 39 strokes in Illinois.[295]

---

285. *See* Michael C. Blumm, *Retracing the Discovery Doctrine: Aboriginal Title, Tribal Sovereignty, and their Significance to Treaty-Making and Modern Natural Resources Policy in Indian Country*, 28 Vermont Law Review 713 (2004) (noting that Elizabeth I and her advisers utilized this interpretation of the 1493 bull to disregard prior discovery of pagan lands by Europeans who were not in actual occupancy and possession of them); Williams, *The American Indian in Western Legal Thought*, at 35 n.142.

286. *See* Blumm, *Aboriginal Title* ("English scholars[] held that the Catholic King Henry VII would not violate the 1493 papal bull, which had divided the world for the Spanish and Portuguese, if English explorers restrained themselves to only finding and claiming lands not yet discovered by any other Christian prince.").

287. McSloy, *Manifest Destiny and American Indians*, at 43 (footnote omitted). King Henry II had secured a papal grant of rights to conquer and subdue the population of Ireland to "'enlarge the boundaries of the Church, ... teach rude and ignorant peoples the truth of the Christian faith, and ... stamp out the plants of evil from the field of the Lord....'" Williams, *The American Indian in Western Legal Thought*, at 22.

288. *See* St. George Tucker, Blackstone's Commentaries: With Notes of Reference to the Constitution and Laws, of the Federal Government of the United States, and of the Commonwealth of Virginia appx. note E (Philadelphia: William Young Birch, 1803), http://www.constitution.org/tb/t1e.htm.

289. Jean-Pierre Martin, *Samuel Sewall, Witch-hunter and Abolitionist*, *in* Slavery in the Americas 198 (Wolfgang Binder ed., Wurzburg: Konigshausen & Neumann, 1998).

290. *See* Janet Riehecky, The Wampanoag: The People of the First Light 30–31 (Mankato, MN: Capstone Press, 2003).

291. *See* Robert J. Cottrol, *Outlawing Outcasts: Comparative Perspectives on the Differing Functions of the Criminal Law of Slavery in the Americas*, 18 Cardozo Law Review 717, 737–38 (1996).

292. *Id.* at 738.

293. Cottrol, *Outlawing Outcasts*, at 738.

294. *See* Harriet C. Frazier, Slavery and Crime in Missouri, 1773–1865, at 37 (Jefferson, NC: McFarland, 2001).

295. Ill. Rev. Stat. 1833, *quoted in* Taliaferro Preston Shaffner, The War in America 340 (London: Hamilton, Adams & Co., 1862).

The principle that indigenous Africans and Americans had few or no rights that Europeans were bound to respect was reinforced in Anglo-American law by *Calvin's Case*, in which Lord Coke held that "infidels" remained in a state of perpetual war with Christians and had no rights before them.[296] Building on that precedent, by 1677 the highest common-law court in England held that actions for theft of African slaves under the rubric of "trespass to chattels" were available in English courts because Africans were "infidels" worthy of being "bought and sold in America as merchandise."[297] British law continued to allow Africans to be enslaved on English soil until the mid-1700s and perhaps even later.[298] When it finally abolished slavery in its Caribbean colonies (the West Indies) by the Emancipation Act of 1834, the British Empire compensated the slaves' "owners" for the loss of their chattel "property" to the tune of about £20 million.[299] This was a prodigious sum, more than the amount of the Louisiana Purchase.[300]

2. Genocidal Effects of the Slave Trade

Although the motive of the European and American slave trade may have been to extract uncompensated labor from, rather than to exterminate, the peoples of Africa, the trade was conducted with the intent to kill and maim many innocent African civilians. Some academics estimate that 40 million or more Africans may have been loaded onto slave ships for transport to the Americas during the slave trade.[301] About four million Africans were kidnapped from Angola alone, and 3.5 million from Nigeria.[302] Millions of Africans "did not survive the voyage and their bodies were thrown overboard."[303] One estimate

---

296. Calvin's Case, 77 Eng. Rep. 377, 398 (K.B. 1608), *quoted in* PAUL VANDEVELDER, COYOTE WARRIOR: ONE MAN, THREE TRIBES, AND THE TRIAL THAT FORGED A NATION 250 (New York: Little, Brown, 2004).

297. Butts v. Penny, 83 Eng. Rep. 518 (K.B. 1677). *See also* Chamberline v. Harvey, 91 Eng. Rep. 994 (K.B. 1697); Wiecew, *The Origins of the Law of Slavery*, at 1724. The common law of England later changed course, abolishing slavery on the English homeland (as opposed to in its colonies) long before its abolition on U.S. soil. *See* Smith v. Brown & Cooper, 91 Eng. Rep. 566 (K.B. 1701) ("as soon as a negro comes into England, he becomes free"); Shanley v. Harvey, 28 Eng. Rep. 844, 844–45 (Ch. 1762) ("as soon as a man sets foot on English ground he is free: a negro may maintain an action against his master for ill usage, and may have a Habeas Corpus if restrained of his liberty"); Sen. Charles Sumner, *Barbarism of Slavery*, *in* 6 CHARLES SUMNER: HIS COMPLETE WORKS 119–238 (Boston: Lee and Shepard, 1900) (1860) (arguing that slavery was inconsistent with common law of England).

298. *See* DOUGLAS HAY & NICHOLAS ROGERS, EIGHTEENTH CENTURY ENGLISH SOCIETY 126 (New York: Oxford UP, 1997).

299. *Id.* at 126. *See also Coincidences Respecting Slavery*, 27 NEW ENGLANDER & YALE REV. 95 (1868).

300. *See* RON CHERNOW, ALEXANDER HAMILTON 671 (New York: Penguin, 2004) (Louisiana Purchase made for $15 million in 1803); *Review of Richard Henry Lee*, Life of Arthur Lee, 66 NORTH AMERICAN REV. 454, 502 (1830) (estimating more than four dollars to the British pound in early nineteenth century); *Review of Alexander Hill Everett*, British Opinions on the Protecting System, 30 NORTH AMERICAN REV. 160 (1830) (estimating more than five dollars to the British pound sterling in 1830, so that $15 million would be three million pounds sterling or less).

301. *See* Charisse Jones, *Bringing Slavery's Long Shadow to the Light*, N.Y. TIMES, Apr. 2, 1995, at 1–1. *See also* Women's Health Issues: Hearings Before the Subcommittee on Departments of Labor, Health and Human Services, Education, and Related Agencies, Committee on Appropriations, United States Senate 208 (1997) (40 million); RANDALL LEE POUWELS & PHILIP J. ADLER, WORLD CIVILIZATIONS 510 (2005) (up to 40 million); RUMMEL, DEATH BY GOVERNMENT, at 46–50 (20 million).

302. *See* PETER SCHWAB, AFRICA: CONTINENT SELF-DESTRUCTS 11 (New York: Palgrave Macmillan, 2002).

303. Jones, *Slavery's Long Shadow*, at 1–1. *See also* DEREK ROBINSON, A SHOCKING HISTORY OF BRISTOL 57 (Bristol: Abson Books, 1973) ("If we count only the slaves who died at sea, it follows that, in all, something like two million black corpses were thrown overboard by English slavers."); Michel

based on shipping records is that 11 million people were crowded into slave ships for the Atlantic crossing and about 1.5 million did not survive the journey.[304] Another estimate is that English and other slave traders killed two million, and another four million died in captivity inside Africa.[305] Much larger estimates have 14 million perishing in Africa or en route, and 15 million arriving in the Americas as slaves.[306]

Mortality rates on the ships that successfully crossed the Atlantic ranged as high as 55 percent; of course, the mortality on the many that sank was complete.[307] According to written records of the trade, slaves "'were literally piled one on top of another and the unsteady motion of the ship, combined with foul air and great heat made the place simply horrible.'"[308] The holds of the ships engaged in the trade would witness enough of a flow of blood as to resemble "'a slaughter house.'"[309]

Colonial exploitation and massacres killed millions of Africans remaining on the continent. The massacres within Africa of countless political and religious leaders, and the overthrow of many governments that resisted the slave trade, may have distorted the course of African history for all time.[310] Most famously, Adam Hochschild has estimated that up to eight million Africans living under Belgian imperial rule in present-day Democratic Republic of the Congo were massacred or died from overwork, disease, or starvation.[311] Nigeria lost 3.5 million people to the slave trade, and local slave-trading political confederacies displaced most other local rulers by 1800.[312] Four million Angolans were captured and either killed or enslaved, as "Portuguese encroachments and the imposition of European rule limited the political freedom of these Africans and diminished their pros-

---

Marriott, *Remembrance of Slave Ancestors Lost to the Sea*, N.Y. Times, June 19, 1994, at A25 ("many historians note that the numbers of enslaved Africans who died at sea were so great that sharks learned to follow the slave routes because they fed on the bodies thrown overboard").

304. *See* Adam Hochschild, Bury the Chains: Prophets, Slaves, and Rebels in the First Human Rights Crusade 32 (New York: Houghton Mifflin Harcourt, 2005). Another estimate is that 15 million Africans reached the Americas. *See* Kevin Ward, *Africa, in* A World History of Christianity 203 (Adrian Hastings ed., Grand Rapids, MI: Wm. B. Eerdmans Publishing, 2000).

305. Rummel, Death by Government, at 48. *See also* Robinson, A Shocking History of Bristol, at 57 ("If we count only the slaves who died at sea, it follows that, in all, something like two million black corpses were thrown overboard by English slavers.").

306. *See* Kevin Ward, *Africa, in* A World History of Christianity, at 203 (citing estimate that 15 million Africans reached the Americas alive); Marriott, *Remembrance of Slave Ancestors*, at A25 ("Estimates of how many blacks were lost at sea in the roughly 400 years of the slave trade in the Americas vary wildly. Some, like Mr. [Tony] Akeem, [who organized a memorial,] place the figure between 100 million and 200 million. Others say perhaps as many as 14 million people perished.").

307. Neta Crawford, Argument and Change in World Politics: Ethics, Decolonization, and Humanitarian Intervention 164 (Cambridge: Cambridge UP, 2002).

308. S. Allen Counter, *Perspective on Slavery: Acknowledging a Terrible Sacrifice*, L.A. Times, Feb. 13, 1994, at 5.

309. *Id.* (quoting contemporary observer).

310. *See, e.g.*, Alan Scholefield, The Dark Kingdoms: The Impact of White Civilization on Three Great African Monarchies (London: Heinemann, 1975) (describing disruption to African governments caused by European colonization and the slave trade).

311. *See* Adam Hochschild, King Leopold's Ghost: A Story of Greed, Terror, and Heroism in Colonial Africa (New York: Houghton Mifflin, 1998); Robert July, A History of the African People (Prospect Hts., IL: Waveland Press, 4th ed. 1992) (New York: Scribner, 1970); Samuel Dumas, Knud Otto Vedel-Petersen, & Harald Westergaard, Losses of Life Caused By War (Oxford: The Clarendon Press, 1923).

312. Paul E. Lovejoy, *Historical Setting, in* A Country Study: Nigeria (Washington, DC: Library of Congress, 1991).

perity."[313] The slave trade from West Africa to the Americas "overshadowed all other commercial activities."[314] In the Ivory Coast, the French imposed onerous taxes, and the natives lost their lands and freedoms.[315]

3. Economic Motivations for European Genocide in Africa and the Americas

The economic incentives facing European leaders and colonists with the opportunity to enslave Africans and Native Americans for work on plantations or construction were compelling. The slave trade generated great fortunes for shipping magnates and other merchants in the ports and commercial centers of London, Liverpool, Bristol, and New York, among other cities.[316] Farmers and plantation owners, and those doing business with them, also reaped enormous rewards from the trade.[317] The Royal African Company,

313. Rachel Warner, *Historical Setting, in* A COUNTRY STUDY: ANGOLA (Thomas Collelo ed., Washington, DC: Library of Congress, 1987).

314. James L. McLaughlin & David Owusu-Ansah, *Historical Setting, in* A COUNTRY STUDY: GHANA (La Verle Berry ed., Washington, DC: Library of Congress, 1994).

315. *See* Rachel Warner, *Historical Setting, in* A COUNTRY STUDY: IVORY COAST (Robert E. Handloff ed., Washington, DC: Library of Congress, 1988).

316. *See* W.E.B. DUBOIS, THE SUPPRESSION OF THE AFRICAN SLAVE TRADE TO THE UNITED STATES 48, 86, 153 (New York: Cosimo Inc., 2007) (1896) (describing how southern United States plantation slavery system produced millions of bales of cotton per year by 1840s, and produced large fortunes); A.J. Williams-Myers, *Re-examining Slavery in New York*, NEW YORK ARCHIVES (2002), http://www.archives.nysed.gov/apt/archivesmag/ archivesmag_past.shtml ("African labor contributed not only to the enormous wealth New York State had accumulated at the start of the Revolutionary War, but also to the prosperity that New York merchants and the landed aristocracy enjoyed from business, including slaving.... Some of the state's most reputable and politically influential citizens ... [and] families, possessing huge manor lands, benefited from slave labor for generations...."); Jonathan Guthrie, *Apology for Slave Trade Could Be Made to Commemorate Abolition*, FIN. TIMES (UK), Sept. 21, 2006, at 2 ("The Royal African Company, a slave-trading concern based in [London] boasted lord mayors as board members and pioneered the modern form of incorporation. Lloyd's insurers were active in covering slave-trading voyages. Liverpool, whose ships transported about 1m slaves from west Africa to the New World, apologised in 1999.... However, Bristol, whose vessels carried about 500,000 people sold into exile by west African merchants, has refused."); *The Slave Trade in New York*, CONTINENTAL MONTHLY, Jan. 1862, at 87, *quoted in* Robert Trent Vinson, *The Law As Lawbreaker: The Promotion and Encouragement of the Atlantic Slave Trade by the New York Judiciary System, 1857–1862*, 20–2 AFRO-AMERICANS IN NEW YORK LIFE AND HISTORY 35 (1996) ("The number of persons engaged in the slave trade, and the amount of capital embarked in it, exceed our powers of calculation. The city of New York has been until late the principal port of the world for this infamous commerce. Slave dealers add largely to the wealth of our commercial metropolis....") (internal quotations omitted).

317. *See* HUGH THOMAS, THE SLAVE TRADE: THE STORY OF THE ATLANTIC SLAVE TRADE, 1440–1870 (New York, Simon & Schuster, 1997) (arguing that most great companies and fortunes in the Americas were built upon slave labor, including sugar holdings in Brazil and the Caribbean and cotton and rice farms in the United States, among other enterprises); Franklin W. Wright, *Caribbean Islands: The Sugar Revolutions and Slavery, in* A COUNTRY STUDY: COMMONWEALTH OF CARIBBEAN ISLANDS (Washington, DC: Library of Congress, 1987), http://lcweb2.loc.gov/cgi-bin/query/r?frd/cstdy:@field(DOCID+cx0011) ("Between 1518 and 1870, the transatlantic slave trade supplied the greatest proportion of the Caribbean population. As sugarcane cultivation increased and spread from island to island—and to the neighboring mainland as well—more Africans were brought to replace those who died rapidly and easily under the rigorous demands of labor on the plantations, in the sugar factories, and in the mines. Acquiring and transporting Africans to the New World became a big and extremely lucrative business."). *See also* JAMES A. RAWLEY, THE TRANSATLANTIC SLAVE TRADE

one of the first modern corporations based in London, oversaw much of the slave trade, and the Church of England owned large plantations in the Caribbean.[318] The Jesuits practiced virtual slavery in South America, and built up great fortunes on plantations where captive natives performed agricultural work.[319]

4. European Colonialism in Africa in the Lead-up to World War I

In the nineteenth century CE, the worst cataclysm in Muslim North Africa occurred in Algeria. The governor-general of French Algeria, Marshal Thomas-Robert Bugeaud, led 108,000 men, or a third of the French army, into Algeria in the 1840s.[320] In this French "Second Empire" period, military doctrine moved away from the formal battles that "civilized peoples" may wage, towards destroying the food, cattle, and agricultural fields that allowed Arabs and indigenous Berbers to survive in the often harsh climate of Algeria. French troops "were allowed to pillage, burn, and rape."[321] Napoleon III denied that his intention was to "drive the whole Arab population into the desert and to inflict on it the plight of the North American Indians," but the question had obviously been raised as to whether this was the policy. A French officer wrote in 1843 that his troops left piles of dead bodies frozen to death after villages were burned. A French newspaper in Algeria welcomed the "extinction of this guilty race" of Arabs, just like the "redskins."[322] One scholar estimates that 825,000 Algerians were killed.[323]

The French seized the best agricultural land in Algeria from the Arabs and Berbers after defeating a united rebellion against French rule under Abd-al Kadir. Settlers expropriated lands from their traditional owners on a wholesale basis after 1871, and burned or tore up the Ottoman administrative records of ownership and transfers of property.[324]

The clearest evidence of genocidal orders, as opposed to genocide collateral to a policy of enslavement for export to another continent in the holds of slave ships, came from present-day Namibia. The Second Reich under Kaiser Wilhelm II killed about 75,000 Herero and Nama Africans living in Namibia.[325] In 1904, General Lothar von Trotha read out an official order on behalf of the Kaiser that the "Herero nation must leave the coun-

---

(Lincoln, NE: Univ. of Nebraska Press, 1981); IRA BERLIN, MANY THOUSANDS GONE: THE FIRST TWO CENTURIES OF SLAVERY IN NORTH AMERICA (Cambridge, MA: Harvard UP, 1998).

318. *See* Guthrie, *Apology for Slave Trade*, at 2.

319. *See* Adrian Hastings, *Latin America, in* A WORLD HISTORY OF CHRISTIANITY, at 340–48.

320. *See* JONATHAN BEECHER, VICTOR CONSIDERANT AND THE RISE AND FALL OF FRENCH ROMANTIC SOCIALISM 178–80 (Berkeley, CA: Univ. of California Press, 2001).

321. Douglas Porch, *The Development of French Colonial Warfare, in* MAKERS OF MODERN STRATEGY: FROM MACHIAVELLI TO THE NUCLEAR AGE 376–79 (Peter Paret et al. eds., Oxford: Oxford UP, 1986).

322. KIERNAN, BLOOD AND SOIL, at 370–74.

323. *See* KIERNAN, BLOOD AND SOIL, at 374.

324. *See id.* at 367; Richard I. Lawless, *History of Algeria, in* THE MIDDLE EAST AND NORTH AFRICA 2004, at 158–59 (London: Routledge, 50th ed. 2004).

325. *See* T. PACKENHAM, THE SCRAMBLE FOR AFRICA: THE WHITE MAN'S CONQUEST OF THE DARK CONTINENT FROM 1876 TO 1912 (New York: Random House, 1991); MARK COCKER, RIVERS OF BLOOD, RIVERS OF GOLD: EUROPE'S CONQUEST OF INDIGENOUS PEOPLES (New York: Grove Press, 2001); *The Story of Africa*, BBC WORLD SERVICE, http://www.bbc.co.uk/worldservice/africa/features/storyofafrica/11chapter10.shtml.

try" or be shot, whether armed or unarmed, man or woman, adult or child.[326] General Trotha wrote in a letter that the Herero should be "annihilated."[327] At the insistence of the German parliament, Trotha's extermination order was rescinded, but concentration camps and slave labor were implemented in its place.[328]

The devastation of indigenous communities in modern Africa continued well after the independence of many African states in the wake of World War II. Africa's indigenous peoples, who are marked by self-identification as such, as well as marginalization, discrimination, and danger of extinction within larger African societies, have suffered catastrophic losses during the Cold War and post-Cold War period. The peoples experiencing precipitous declines in population include the Bambuti and Twa (Pygmies) of Congo and the Great Lakes Region, the Maasai of Kenya and Tanzania, the Ogoni of Nigeria, the Himba of Namibia, and the Berbers and Tauregs of Algeria, Libya, Niger, and Mali.[329] A prominent scholar described the result:

> [O]n account of the special spiritual link that members of indigenous communities have with their own ancestral lands, lifestyle, traditions and cultural roots, their forcible removal from their lands and the consequent sudden impact with the Western society could be considered as treatment entailing both "serious ... mental harm" to the prejudice of such people and infliction "on the group [of] conditions of life calculated to bring about its physical destruction in whole or in part". These acts ... may in fact lead many indigenous persons to a physical and psychological decline that may eventually bring them to death.[330]

Like native populations in the U.S., African and African-American populations expanded rapidly after the abolition of the slave trade and the unraveling of colonialism. The population of Africa has quadrupled since 1955.[331] The African-American population of the U.S. grew from about one million in 1800 to between 34 and 37 million in 2000.[332] The Afro-Brazilian population approached 85 million in 2008, four times the total population of Brazil in 1900.[333]

---

326. *See Story of Africa*, BBC; Jan-Bart Gewald, *Imperial Germany and the Herero of Southern Africa: Genocide and the Quest for Recompense, in* GENOCIDE, WAR CRIMES, AND THE WEST: HISTORY AND COMPLICITY 61 (Adam Jones ed., London: Zed Books, 2004).

327. Gewald, *The Herero of Southern Africa*, at 62.

328. *See id.* at 62.

329. *See* Nsongurua J. Udombana, *Reparations and Africa's Indigenous Peoples, in* REPARATIONS FOR INDIGENOUS PEOPLES, at 393.

330. Frederico Lenzerini, *The Status of Indigenous Peoples in International Law, in* REPARATIONS FOR INDIGENOUS PEOPLES, at 103.

331. *See* U.N. Department of Economic and Social Affairs, Population Division, *World Population Prospects.*

332. *Compare African-American Population* (2004), http://www.infoplease.com/ipa/A0922246.htm, *with* U.S. Bureau of the Census, *The Black Population: 2000*, http://www.census.gov/prod/2001pubs/c2kbr01-5.pdf.

333. *See* CIA, WORLD FACTBOOK 2008, http://www.bartleby.com/151/br.html#People. *Compare* HERMAN G. JAMES, BRAZIL AFTER A CENTURY OF INDEPENDENCE 276 (New York: The Macmillan Company, 1925) (less than 20 million in 1900).

F. Famine and Genocide in Ireland

Under British colonization, the indigenous Irish Celts suffered from genocidal colonial policies, including a nineteenth-century famine that killed more than a million people. In 1579, Sir Thomas Smith became lieutenant general for Ireland, with a commission to subdue and expel the "barbarous" and "wild" nation of the Irish, and not to permit any sales of land within his jurisdiction to Irish or Scottish people. Queen Elizabeth granted Smith a patent to divide her earldom of Ulster among such English adventurers as might join him on the island, or aid him with men or funds.[334] Ulster had recently been cleared of Irish by the military commander of the area, who killed every Irish person who was deemed to be a traitor or an associate with traitors, and murdered "every man, woman and child" of Irish castles by the sword. After the further division of land by Smith, famine struck the Irish of Ulster, left without grain by the English. In the 1580s, the Irish population fell by nearly a third, and Irish culture was overthrown.[335]

In the wake of English colonization, the Irish lost control over most of their agricultural land and their nation's economy, leaving them vulnerable to famine. Two hundred years prior to the great famine, Oliver Cromwell consolidated English control over the Ireland by, among other measures, ordering all Irish remaining east of the Shannon River to be executed or deported as slaves to the New World. "Irish landowners found east of the river Shannon after 1 May, 1654 faced the death penalty or slavery in the West Indies and Barbados."[336] Like the French in nineteenth-century Algeria, the English employed a policy of "starving-out" the Irish resistance, using scythes, for example, to "cut down the green corn" before it could ripen for consumption.[337] English supporters of Irish colonization described the Gaelic-speaking Irish as heathen savages who "live like beastes, voide of lawe and all good order."[338] The reduction to savagery was achieved in part by "great severity" against Catholic priests and nobility in Ireland by Cromwell's forces.[339] The seventeenth-century penal laws prohibited the Irish from purchasing land or even leasing valuable land, practicing a learned profession, receiving a high-quality or pro-Catholic education, or engaging in trade or commerce in a corporate town.[340] By 1700, nearly one million acres, an area roughly the size of Delaware, had been expropriated.[341]

---

334. John Strype, The Life of the Learned Sir Thomas Smith, Kt.D.C.L., Principal Secretary of State to King Edward the Sixth, and Queen Elizabeth 131–33 (Oxford: The Clarendon Press, 1820).

335. *Quoted in* Kiernan, Blood and Soil, at 192, 197, 203.

336. New Jersey Commission on Holocaust Education, *The Great Irish Famine* (1996), http://www.nde.state.ne.us/SS/irish/irish_pf.html (quoting O'Beirne, A Short History of Ireland, at 65; *see also id.* ("In 1649 Oliver Cromwell landed at Dublin with an army of 12,000 men.... Large-scale confiscation of land followed. The owners were driven off eleven million acres of land and it was given to the Protestant colonists."); O hEithir, A Pocket History of Ireland, at 30.

337. *Ireland, in* 10 Encyclopedia Britannica 267 (New York: Henry G. Allen & Co., 9th ed. 1888).

338. *Quoted in* Wiecek, *The Origins of the Law of Slavery in North America,* at 1721 (citations omitted).

339. *Ireland, in* Encyclopedia Britannica, at 267.

340. *See* John Mitchel, Jail Journal: Or Five Years in British Prisons 10 (New York: The "Citizen," 1854); *see also* N.J. Comm'n on Holocaust Education, *The Great Irish Famine* (under the Penal laws, "Irish Catholics were forbidden to receive an education, enter a profession, vote, hold public office, practice their religion, attend Catholic worship, engage in trade or commerce, purchase

When reports of large-scale starvation of Irish civilians began to surface in nineteenth century colonial Ireland, due to potato blight and other causes, British colonial administrators continued to export huge quantities of food and enormous sums of money to Britain.[342] Wholesale evictions took place of Irish natives by British landlords, the Irish being forbidden under colonial penal laws to purchase or rent much of the valuable land. Jonathan Swift, the author of *Gulliver's Travels* and Dean of St. Patrick's Cathedral in Dublin, argued that half of Ireland's domestic product was being consumed in Britain, and that rising rents turned Irish farmers into paupers and beggars, living on little more than milk and potatoes, if that. An Irish official accused the British prime minister of having "smitten and offered up as a holocaust" a total of a "million and a half Irish people."[343] The lord lieutenant of Ireland in 1849 condemned Parliament for pursuing a cold, calculating "policy of extermination."[344]

G. European and American Conquests in Asia and Oceania

1. Australia

In Asia and Oceania, the colonies of European and American powers also suffered mass devastation. British Australia's native population fell by nearly 97 percent, and British Tasmania's native population was done away with by 1876.[345] In Australia, the Aboriginal population fell to a low of under 50,000 by the early twentieth century.[346] In 1883, the British High Commissioner in Australia wrote to the British prime minister that:

> The habit of regarding the natives as vermin, to be cleared off the face of the earth, has given the average Queenslander a tone of brutality and cruelty in dealing with "blacks" which it is very difficult to anyone who does not know it, as I do, to realise. I have heard men of culture and refinement, of the greatest humanity and kindness to their fellow whites, and who when you meet them here at home

---

land, lease [out] land, ... rent land worth more than thirty shillings a year, own a horse of greater value than five pounds, ... educate their own children or send a child abroad to receive an education").

341. *Ireland, in* Encyclopedia Britannica, at 268.

342. *See* Cecil Woodham-Smith, The Great Hunger; Ireland 1845–1849, at 380 (New York: Penguin, 1991) (1970) ("huge quantities of food were exported from Ireland to England throughout the period when the people of Ireland were dying of starvation."); N.J. Commission on Holocaust Education, *The Great Irish Famine.*

343. *Quoted in* Póirtéir, The Great Irish Famine, at 173.

344. *Quoted in* Robert Gellately & Ben Kiernan, *The Study of Mass Murder and Genocide, in* The Specter of Genocide: Mass Murder in Historical Perspective 25 (Robert Gellately & Ben Kiernan eds., Cambridge: Cambridge UP, 2003); *see also* N.J. Comm'n on Holocaust Education, *The Great Irish Famine* ("During the worst months of the famine, in the winter of 1846–47, tens of thousands of tenants fell in arrears of rent and were evicted from their homes....").

345. *See* Levene, 2 Genocide in the Age of the Nation State, at 10; A. Dirk Moses, *Genocide and Settler Society in Australian History, in* Genocide and Settler Society: Frontier Violence and Stolen Indigenous Children in Australian History 3–48 (Providence, RI: Berghahn Books, 2004); Jan Kociumbas, *Genocide and Modernity in Colonial Australia 1788–1850, in id.* at 77–102; Henry Reynolds, *Genocide in Tasmania, in id.* at 127–49; Raymond Evans, *"Plenty Shoot 'Em": The Destruction of Aboriginal Societies along the Queensland Frontier, in id.* at 150–73.

346. *See* Colin Tatz, Genocide in Australia (Canberra, Australia: Australian Institute of Aboriginal and Torres Strait Islander Studies, 1999), http://web.archive.org/web/20050808002313/http://www.aiatsis.gov.au/rsrch/rsrch_dp/genocide.htm.

> you would pronounce to be incapable of such deeds, talk, not only of the wholesale butchery (for the iniquity of that may sometimes be disguised from themselves) but of the *individual* murder of natives, exactly as they would talk of a day's sport, or having to kill some troublesome animal.[347]

A British inquiry found Aboriginals in hiding that feared capture and felt "like hunted wild beasts, having lived for years in a state of absolute terror."[348]

With the advent of the "Aboriginals Preservation and Protection" legislation, the pace of killing slowed and the population resumed a trajectory of growth. Nevertheless, living conditions frequently remained poor, and conducive to premature death or injury as in Canada and the U.S. The authorities imprisoned Aboriginals at whim for pretended crimes:

> In Queensland, protection included banishment from one part of the state to another, for periods ranging from twelve months to life [for] offences such as "disorderly conduct", "uncontrollable", "menace to young girls", and "on discharge from [urban] prison". It also involved imprisonment on the settlement or mission, for a maximum of three weeks per offense, for offences only Aborigines could commit: "being cheeky", "refusing to work", ..."committing adultery", "playing cards", "arranging to receive a male person during the night", [or] "being untidy at the recreation hall." In Western Australia there was "protective" punishment for anyone who didn't "conduct themselves in a respectable manner at all times", used "obscene language", drank alcohol, didn't keep dwellings "clean and tidy", [etc.].

A Royal Commission into aboriginal deaths in custody found high death rates in prison.[349] The Commission blamed racism against Aboriginal peoples, including "the assumption [which] was underpinned by economic interest" that "it was essential to religious enlightenment that Aboriginal religious belief be obliterated where possible."[350]

2. India

The British crown (and Lord Protector Oliver Cromwell) chartered various nobles and adventurers to India, or the East Indies as it was often called. Warren Hastings, an official in the British East India Company, became the first governor-general of India in 1773. The British justified their rule in India by the argument that "heathens" lacked capacity for intelligent self-government, Hindu Indians "'being nearly limited to mere animal functions and ... with no higher intellect than a dog, an elephant or a monkey....'"[351] During famines in India, the British pursued policies of unabated exports of foodstuffs, crippling taxation for military expenditures, and bans on charitable giving that contributed to death tolls of 12 to 30 million in the last quarter of the nineteenth century alone.[352] Only 17 famines occurred in 2,000 years of recorded Indian history, compared

347. *Quoted in id.*

348. *Id.* (quoting British High Commissioner Archibald Meston).

349. *See id.* (no longer quoting High Commissioner Meston).

350. *Quoted in* Michael Mansell, *Introducing Fairness: Aboriginal Community Sentencing Tribunals, Australian Inst. of Criminology* (2001), http://www.aic.gov.au/conferences/indigenous2/mansell.pdf.

351. Lord Moira, Governor-General of India, 1813–1823, *quoted in* J.H. Plumb, England in the Eighteenth Century 178 (London: Penguin Books, 1953), *and* N.J. Commission on Holocaust Education, *The Great Irish Famine.*

352. *See* Mike Davis, Late Victorian Holocausts: El Nino Famines and the Making of the Third World 7 (London: Verso, 2001); Amartya Sen, *Apocalypse Then*, N.Y. Times, Feb. 18, 2001, http://www.nytimes.com/books/01/02/18/reviews/010218.18senlt.html?_r=1&oref=slogin.

to 31 serious famines during 120 years of British rule.[353] One-fifth of the population of the Indian plains died in the famine of the 1780s alone. One third of the population of Bengal, up to ten million people, starved in the taxation-related famine of 1770.[354]

3. China

European colonialism in China also wrought massive death and destruction. In 1842 the Treaty of Nanking sealed Chinese defeat in the First Opium War of 1839 to 1842 with the loss of Hong Kong to Britain, the opening of five Chinese ports to British opium imports, and the payment by China of six million Chinese dollars in damages for the destruction of British opium.[355] China lost thousands, if not millions, of lives to the opium trade forced upon it for nearly 150 years by the British Empire. Three million Chinese were opium addicts by the 1830s, rising to 13.5 million by 1906. The British only agreed to give up the trade after 150 years of Chinese attempts to ban it, and two wars waged by the British Navy to compel acceptance of opium imports into China from India, where Britain decreed itself a monopoly.[356] China was shipping 20 million taels (often silver currency) overseas for imports of opium and other goods under the 1842 Treaty, compared to a government budget of 80 million taels in the 1890s.[357] A British officer wrote in 1863: "[Since 1839,] our policy has been to compel the Chinese Government, contrary to its laws and moral economy, and contrary to our professed principles of free trade, to legalize the sale of opium.... [This is] the real cause of all of our aggressions...."[358]

In the anti-opium Taiping rebellion of the mid-nineteenth century, an estimated 20 to 30 million Chinese died as the British and French joined the Chinese imperial army in retaking Nanking from the rebels.[359] The Taiping insurgents "were repeatedly attacked and

353. *See* Mike Davis, *The Origins of the Third World: Markets, States and Climate* (Dec. 2002), http://www.thecornerhouse.org.uk/pdf/briefing/27origins.pdf (citing Cornelius Walford, *On the Famines of the World, Past and Present*, 41 J. of the Statistical Soc. 433, 434 (1878)).

354. *See* Vinita Damodaran, *Famine in Bengal, in* Natural Disasters, Cultural Responses: Case Studies Toward a Global Environmental History 201–210 (Christof Mauch & Christian Pfister eds., Lanham, MD: Rowman & Littlefield, 2009); Niall Ferguson, Empire: The Rise and Demise of the British World Order and the Lessons for Global Power 39–40 (New York: Basic Books, 2004); Subrata Kumar Mitra, Power, Protest, and Participation: Local Elites and the Politics of Development in India 175 (London: Routledge, 1992).

355. *See* The Treaty of Nanking (1842), http://nanking.com/; *The First Opium War*, BBC (2006), http://www.bbc.co.uk/radio4/history/empire/episodes/episode_47.shtml; Frank Sanello, The Opium Wars: The Addiction of One Empire and the Corruption of Another 181 (Naperville, IL: Sourcebooks, 2004).

356. *See Chronology of Opium through History*, U.N. IRIN (2007), http://www.irinnews.org/web specials/opium/Chronology.asp.

357. *Compare* Jean Chesneaux et al., China from the Opium Wars to the 1911 Revolution 289 (New York: Pantheon Books, 1976), *with* Shao-Kwan Chen, The System of Taxation in China in the Tsing Dynasty, 1644–1911, at 68 (New York: Columbia UP, 1914).

358. William Henry Sykes, The Taeping Rebellion in China: Its Origins, Progress, and Present Condition ii–iii (London: Warren Hall & Co., 1863). He added: "Ningpo ... was assaulted by the British Navy, ... and the Tae-pings driven out; and they have since been repeatedly attacked and slaughtered, both in the neighborhood of Ningpo and in Shanghai.... The blame must be attributed to opium traders—to British subjects, who are receiving thousands per annum as mercenaries in the service of the Tartar Government." *Id.* at iii.

359. *See* Sanello, The Opium Wars, at 167; Paul French, Carl Crow, a Tough Old China Hand 36 (Hong Kong, People's Republic of China: Hong Kong UP, 2006) ; Rinn-Sup Shinn & Robert L. Worden, *Historical Setting, in* A Country Study: China (Robert L. Worden et al. eds., Washington,. DC: Library of Congress, 1987), http://lcweb2.loc.gov/frd/cs/cntoc.html; R.R. Palmer & Joel

slaughtered, both in the neighborhood of Ningpo and in Shanghai...." Theirs was a religious movement that strove to ban opium, alcohol, prostitution, polygamy, foot-binding, and promote land reform—many of which things Maoists actually did after Nationalists lost.[360]

In 1900, the Empress Dowager endorsed the nationalist "Boxer" rebellion, which targeted British, French, German, Japanese, and Russian subjects, along with Chinese Christians, for death or expulsion from China.[361] An international force assembled by these powers plus the U.S. and a few others occupied China, and by the Protocols of Beijing they dismantled China's military capability and system of defensive forts, and demanded exorbitant reparations.[362] Perhaps 30,000 Chinese Christians and 200,000 other Chinese died in the Boxer rebellion.[363] Vladimir Lenin observed that the imperialist powers had "utilised their vaunted civilisation solely for the purpose of deception, plunder, and violence," and had "waged wars against China in order to win the right ... to drug the people," all the while having "hypocritically carried their policy of plunder under the guise of spreading Christianity."[364]

4. The Philippines

The best estimates for the Filipino death toll in the War of Independence against the United States is about 100,000 to 200,000.[365] The U.S. Army frequently shot surrendering Filipino fighters, tortured prisoners, devastated civilian areas, and moved civilians into camps where hunger and disease commonly led to death.[366] It was one of the first uses of the term "concentration camps," probably adapted from the Spanish authorities in Cuba.[367] As one member of an artillery unit wrote in 1899, a general ordered U.S. troops to burn a town that had surrendered "and kill every native on sight" in retaliation for the killing of a U.S. soldier. A report in the *New York Evening Post* suggested that no quarter was being given and hundreds of Filipino prisoners had been killed. In one camp of 400

COLTON, A HISTORY OF THE MODERN WORLD, SINCE 1815 (New York: Knopf, 6th ed., 1994) (20 million people, equivalent to entire population of Britain, died in Taiping rebellion).

360. WILLIAM HENRY SYKES, THE TAEPING REBELLION IN CHINA: ITS ORIGINS, PROGRESS, AND PRESENT CONDITION iii (London: Warren Hall & Co., 1863). *See* ANGUS MADDISON, CHINESE ECONOMIC PERFORMANCE IN THE LONG RUN 46 (Paris: Organisation for Economic Co-operation and Development, 2007), http://books.google.com/books?id=F10vEESMZlcC&pg=PA46.

361. *See* DAVID SCOTT, CHINA AND THE INTERNATIONAL SYSTEM, 1840–1949, at 143–50 (Albany, NY: State Univ. of New York Press, 2008).

362. *See id.* at 150–51.

363. *See* R.J. RUMMEL, CHINA'S BLOODY CENTURY: GENOCIDE AND MASS MURDER SINCE 1900, tbl. 2.A (Rutgers, NJ: Transaction Publishers, 1991), http://www.hawaii.edu/powerkills/CHINA.TAB2.A.GIF (citing RICHARD O'CONNOR, THE SPIRIT SOLDIERS; A HISTORICAL NARRATIVE OF THE BOXER REBELLION 73, 339 (New York: G.P. Putnam's Sons, 1973); ROGER PELESSIER, THE AWAKENING OF CHINA: 1793–1949, at 67, 225 (Martin Kieffer ed. and trans., New York: Capricorn Books, 1967).

364. *Quoted in* SCOTT, CHINA AND THE INTERNATIONAL SYSTEM, at 155.

365. *See* John Gates, *War-Related Deaths in the Philippines*, 1898–1902, 53 PACIFIC HISTORICAL REVIEW 367 (1983) (up to 362,000 excess deaths, but 137,000 were due to a cholera epidemic, which sometimes happens without war); RUMMEL, STATISTICS OF DEMOCIDE, at 201; Arthur Westing, *War as Human Endeavor: The High-Fatality Wars of the Twentieth Century,* 19 J. OF PEACE RESEARCH 261, 262, 264 (1982).

366. *See* RUMMEL, STATISTICS OF DEMOCIDE, at 201.

367. *See* Docker, *Are Settler Colonies Inherently Genocidal?*, at 100; *The Concentration Camps*, N.Y. TIMES, May 30, 1902, at 3.

Filipino prisoners, two to four died daily.[368] Counsel for General Jacob H. Smith admitted at his court-martial in Manila "that he wanted killed everybody capable of bearing arms," including "all over ten years of age." An American governor accused the troops of "laying the country waste."[369]

368. *See* MOORFIELD STOREY & JULIAN CODMAN, SECRETARY ROOT'S RECORD. "MARKED SEVERITIES" IN PHILIPPINE WARFARE 25–26, 90 (Boston: Geo. W. Ellis Co., 1902).

369. *Court-Martial Trial of General Smith, in* 12 CURRENT HISTORY AND MODERN CULTURE: A MONTHLY ILLUSTRATED 303 (1902); *The Philippines, in id.* at 301.

Chapter V

"Pillaged Mercilessly": The Birth of the Arab and Turkish Empires

> [After the Muslim conquest, there] were raids on both Monophysite and Nestorian monasteries; monks were killed, taken prisoner or driven to take refuge elsewhere....
>
> [F]ire temples were treated as state property and confiscated at the time of the conquest. There are no indications of the survival of a public Magian cult, organization or hierarchy in early Muslim Iraq....
>
> —Michael Morony[1]

A. The Muslim Conquests of the Arabian Peninsula

In the seventh century CE, Jews, and Christians, and polytheists populated Arabia. The rise of Islam led to the deportation of two large Jewish clans from the Medina region, and the massacre of a third, the Qurayza. Fearing an attack from the Qurayza clan, the Muslim army attacked them, killing all the men and selling all the women and children into bondage.[2] In this way, "persecutions, massacres, blood and fire and exile were visited on the adherents of the Talmud."[3] In addition, the polytheistic Arabs faced the difficult choice between a complete abandonment of their ancestral culture and lifestyle, and the death penalty.[4] This was the fate of the Mandaeans or Sabīans of both Arabia and Mesopotamia. The Caliph al-Qahir Billah "declared their blood licit and refused their poll tax."[5] In 640 CE all Jews and Christians were killed in or expelled from Arabia, as a holy land.[6]

1. Michael G. Morony, *Religious Communities in Late Sasanian and Early Muslim Iraq*, 17 J. of the Econ. and Social Hist. of the Orient 119, 121 (1974).

2. W. Montgomery Watt, *Muhammad, in* 1A The Cambridge History of Islam 49 (P. M. Holt, Ann Lambton & Bernard Lewis eds., Cambridge: Cambridge UP, 9th ed, 2000).

3. 10 Babylonian Talmud (Michael L. Rodkinson ed. & trans., Boston: The Talmud Soc., 1918), http://www.sacred-texts.com/jud/t10/ht111.htm.

4. *See, e.g.*, Umar bin al-Khattab, *The People of the Countries of War, in* The Dhimmi: Jews and Christians under Islam 166 (Bat Ye'or ed., David Maisel et al. trans., Rutherford, NJ: Fairleigh Dickinson UP, 1985).

5. Ibn al-Fuwati (circa 1320 CE), *quoted in* The Dhimmi, at 192. On the origins of the Mandaeans of Arabia and Yemen in a migration from Mesopotamia, see George Cruikshank, *The Monotheism of Paganism*, 99 The Living Age 259, 265 (1873).

6. *See* Bat Ye'or, *Historical Outline, in* The Dhimmi, at 47.

B. The Arab Conquest of Mesopotamia

The Assyrian homeland lies in northern Iraq, but large communities of Assyrians have lived in southeastern Anatolia and northwestern Persia since ancient times. The ancient Assyrian capitals were Assur, Calah (Nimrud), Dur-Sharrukin (Khorsabad), and Nineveh.[7] Other important Assyrian cities included Arbela, Carcemish, Harran, Hatra, Kanesh, and Kar-Tukulti-Ninurta.[8] Assyrian towns existed in Anatolia by the first millennium BCE.[9] By the seventh century BCE, the Assyrian city of Ziyaret Tepe has risen in southeastern Anatolia.[10] The Assyrian community in Persia also dates back into distant antiquity.[11] In the early first millennium BCE, the Assyrians had consolidated their presence in Persia, Assyrian *Parsua*.[12]

The Assyrians had been a people without a state for more than two millennia, since the fall of the empire and sack of Nineveh in 600 BCE.[13] Although some authors doubt that an Assyrian people could have survived from 600 BCE to the nineteenth century, many of the factors that justify recognizing Armenians, Jews, or other groups as continuously existing since ancient times also apply to the Assyrians, namely common patterns of worship, consistent self-identification, and genetic continuity.[14] Assyria became a province of Persia and Assyrians served in the Persian army.[15] The Sassanian or new Persian Empire gave the Assyrians, like the Jews, substantial autonomy to organize their own eccle-

---

7. Sarah C. Melville, *Neo-Assyrian Royal Women and Male Identity: Status as a Social Tool*, 124 Journal of the American Oriental Soc. 37 (2004); Pauline Albenda, *Western Asiatic Women in the Iron Age: Their Image Revealed*, 46 The Biblical Archaeologist 82 (1983); Khaldun S. Husry, *The Assyrian Affair of 1933 (I)*, 5 Int'l J. of Middle East Studies 164 (1974); Gibson McGuire, *Studies in the Ancient History of Northern Iraq (Review)*, 31 Journal of Near Eastern Stud. 42 (1972).

8. *See* Oppenheim, Ancient Mesopotamia, at 134, 400–7; Marc Van de Mieroop, A History of the Ancient Near East, ca. 3000–323 BC, at 137 (New York: Wiley, 2004); Klaas R. Veenhof, *"In Accordance with the Words of the Stele": Evidence for Old Assyrian Legislation*, 70 Chi. Kent L. Rev. 1717, 1719 (1995); V.S. Tuman, *The Cerberus Slab of Hatra May Represent Important Astronomical Events*, 24 Royal Astron. Soc. Q. J. 14, 14, 17–19 (1983).

9. *See* Parpola, *International Law in the First Millennium*, at 1254–55

10. *See* Ann Donkin, *Mapping the Past: An Archaeological Case Study from Southeastern Turkey*, 69 Near Eastern Archaeology 12 (2006); Henri Frankfort, *The Last Predynastic Period in Babylonia*, *in* 1 The Cambridge Ancient History, at 87, 90, 411 (similar); Veenhof, *Old Assyrian Legislation*, at 1724–35 (similar).

11. *See* D. Barnett, *Urartu*, *in* 3 The Cambridge Ancient History 352 (John Boardman ed., 1982).

12. *See* Richard Nelson Frye, The History of Ancient Iran 67 (Munich: Verlag CH Beck, 1984); I.M. Diakonoff, *Media*, *in* The Cambridge History of Iran: The Median and Achaemenian Periods 62–65 (William Bayne Fisher et al. eds., Cambridge: Cambridge UP, 1985).

13. Christopher Johnston, *The Fall of Nineveh*, 22 J. of the American Oriental Soc. 20 (1901).

14. The Greek historian Herodotus, writing almost two hundred years later, referred to all of Mesopotamia as Assyria, even though the major Assyrian cities had been destroyed in 612 BCE. *See* John Joseph, Muslim-Christian Relations and Inter-Christian Rivalries in the Middle East: The Case of the Jacobites in an Age of Transition 150 (Albany, NY: State Univ. of New York Press, 1983); Herodotus, The Histories 431 (Harry Carter trans., New York: The Heritage Press, 1958). Another two hundred years later, under Parthian rule, many Assyrian cities were "resurrected" and, with the aid of other, mostly Semitic peoples, the former capital of Assur was rebuilt to the size it had been during the Assyrian empire. *See* George Roux, Ancient Iraq, at 419.

15. *See The Large Inscription of Darius at Behistun*, at 178; Andrew Robert Burn & David Malcolm Lewis, Persia and the Greeks: the Defence of the West, c. 546–478 B.C., at 97 (Palo Alto, CA: Stanford UP, 1984); Simo Parpola, *National and Ethnic Identity in the Neo-Assyrian Empire*

siastical and family affairs.[16] As the early Christian church was growing and evangelizing distant lands, Assyrian identity survived the destruction of Nineveh.[17] Although genetic testing of the Assyrians is just getting underway, such testing as has been done supports the idea that Assyrians very rarely intermarried with the surrounding population, at least in Persia.[18]

The Assyrians and Babylonians maintained distinct cultures under Arab, Persian, and Turko-Kurdish rule, which varied in the extent to which it actually penetrated and directly ruled their traditional homelands.[19] The ancient Assyrian capital of Nineveh was a Nestorian bishopric at the time of the Islamic conquest of Mesopotamia, and Nestorian "Syrian" Christians living under the Abbasid Caliphs are credited with translating many Greek scientific and philosophical works into Arabic.[20] The modern Assyrians of

---

and Assyrian Identity in Post-Empire Times, 14 J. OF ASSYRIAN ACAD. STUDIES 1, 16–22 (2004), http://www.jaas.org/edocs/v14n1; Smith, *The Assyrian Tree,* at 69.

16. *See* Morony, *Religious Communities in Late Sasanian and Early Muslim Iraq,* at 119–25.

17. *See Ashurbanipal and the Fall of Assyria, in* 3 THE CAMBRIDGE ANCIENT HISTORY, THE ASSYRIAN EMPIRE 130–31 (CambridgeL Cambridge UP, 1954); *Parthia, in* 3 THE CAMBRIDGE ANCIENT HISTORY, THE ROMAN REPUBLIC 597–98 (Cambridge: Cambridge UP, 2d ed., 1991); PATRICIA CRONE & MICHAEL COOK, HAGARISM: THE MAKING OF THE ISLAMIC WORLD 55–60 (Cambridge: Cambridge UP, 1980); ALBERT HOURANI, MINORITIES IN THE ARAB WORLD 99 (London: Oxford UP, 1947); A.T. OLMSTEAD, HISTORY OF THE PERSIAN EMPIRE 168 (Chicago: Univ. of Chicago Press, 1948); AUBREY VINE, THE NESTORIAN CHURCHES (London: Independent Press Ltd., 1937); *see also* GEORGE PERCY BADGER, 1 THE NESTORIANS AND THEIR RITUALS (London: Darf Publishers Ltd., 1987) (1852); GEORGE PERCY BADGER, THE CHRISTIANS OF ASSYRIA COMMONLY CALLED NESTORIANS (London: W. H. Bartlett, 1869); M. A. Dandamayev, *Assyrian Traditions during Achemenid Times, in* HELSINKI ASSYRIA 1995: PROCEEDINGS OF THE 10TH ANNIVERSARY SYMPOSIUM OF THE NEO-ASSYRIAN TEXT CORPUS PROJECT 41–48 (Simo Parpola & R. M. Whiting eds., 1997);Richard N. Frye, *A Postscript to My Article [Assyria and Syria: Synonyms],* 11 J. OF ASSYRIAN ACADEMIC STUD. 35–36 (1997); Richard N. Frye, *Assyria and Syria: Synonyms,* 51 J. OF THE NEAR EAST SOCIETY 281–285 (1992); GIBBON, 8 DECLINE AND FALL OF THE ROMAN EMPIRE, ch. 67, http://oll.libertyfund.org/Home3/HTML.php?recordID=0214.08; FLAVIUS JOSEPHUS, 13 THE ANTIQUITIES OF THE JEWS, ch. 6 (William Whiston trans., 1737), http://www.ccel.org/j/josephus/works/ant-13.htm; E.W. MacDowell, *The Ancient Nestorian Church and Its Present Influence in Kurdistan,* 2 J. OF RACE DEVELOPMENT 77 (1911); Basile M. Nikitine, *La Vie Domestique des Assyro-Chaldéens du Plateau u d'Ourmiah,* ETHNOGRAPHIE, 1925, at 356–81; Parpola, *Assyrian Identity in the Post-Empire Times,* at 16–22; Simo Parpola, *Assyrians after Assyria,* 12 J. OF ASSYRIAN ACADEMIC STUDIES (2000); HORMUZD RASSAM, ASSUR AND THE LAND OF NIMRUD 173–74 (Cincinnati; Curts & Jennings, 1897).

18. Specifically, the idea that the modern Assyrians are descended from the ancient Assyrians finds some support in a genetic study conducted by researchers from the University of Newcastle upon Tyne, England, and the University of Tehran, Iran, which found that the Assyrians of Urmia in particular, and of Tehran to a lesser extent, were genetically similar to one another and supported the oral tradition of Assyrians being a "closed" population with little "intermixture" with the Muslim Iranian population. M.T. Akbari et al., *Genetic Differentiation among Iranian Christian Communities,* 38 AM J. OF HUMAN GENETICS 84 (1986). This result is somewhat analogous to the result in a study of Armenians, Arabs, Jews, and Kurds, which found "remarkable genetic continuity" among Jews based on evidence of rare intermarriage with Palestinian Muslim Arabs descended from conquerors from the Arabian peninsula. Almut Nebel et al., *The Y Chromosome Pool of Jews as Part of the Genetic Landscape of the Middle East,* 69 AM. J. OF HUMAN GENETICS 1095 (2001), http://www.pubmedcentral.nih.gov.

19. Turkish rule in the vicinity of historical Assyria and Armenia is often referred to as Turko-Kurdish in reference to the mixed parentage of its rulers, and composition of its ruling class. *See, e.g,* Lt. Col. Ralph E. Carr, *The Kurdistan Mountain Ranges, Considered in Reference to a Russian Advance on the Tigris Valley,* 22 J. OF THE ROYAL UNITED SERVICES INST. FOR DEFENCE STUD. 156, 172–73 (1879); DE COURTOIS, THE FORGOTTEN GENOCIDE, at 237; *Glossary, in* THE CAMBRIDGE HISTORY OF EGYPT: 640–1517, at 527 (M. W. Daly et al. eds., Cambridge: Cambridge UP, 1998).

20. *See* MICHAEL G. MORONY, IRAQ AFTER THE MUSLIM CONQUEST 336, 345 (Princeton: Princeton UP, 1984); George E. Kirk, *A Short History of the Middle East, in* THE MIDDLE EAST YESTERDAY

Mesopotamia and Persia have had ancient Assyrian names such as Sargon and Sennacherib since the earliest European contact with them, and their language is "extraordinary similar" to the Aramaic language of the Assyrian empire.[21] The name "Assyria" was also consistently applied to the area around the ancient Assyrian capital of Nineveh, and the Christians of Mesopotamia reaffirmed their Assyrian identity from the earliest French and British contact.[22] Archaeologists and historians have revealed substantial linguistic and religious continuity between the ancient Assyrians and Babylonians on the one hand, and the pagan and Christian inhabitants of Iraq at the time of the Persian conquests of the region, and subsequently the Greek, Arab, Mongol, and Turko-Kurdish invasions.[23] To provide just the most powerful examples, the use of ancient Assyrian and Babylonian magic, astrology, festivals, and reverence for nature (including those archetypal sites of animistic worship, sacred springs and groves of trees) survived the transition to Persian rule and Christian beliefs.[24] Ancient Mesopotamian religious imagery such as animal sacrifice and the "medicine of life" continued as a theme of the local Assyrian Christian liturgy under Persian and Arab rule.[25]

The modern Assyrians continue to speak the language of the Assyrian Empire, which became the lingua franca of the Middle East under the Empire. The Assyrians initially communicated in Old Assyrian, which diverged in around 2,000 BCE from the language of Old Akkadian.[26] The Assyrian Empire preserved Old Assyrian for elite and sacred use, but eventually adopted Aramaic for "daily use"[27] and as an administrative language.[28] Ara-

---

AND TODAY 106 (David W. Miller & Clark D. Moore eds., New York: Bantham Pathfinder, 1970); De Lacy O'Leary, *How Greek Science Passed to the Arabs*, ch. 1 (London: Routledge & Kegan Paul Ltd., 2001), http://www.aina.org/books/hgsptta.htm. Nineveh is also referred to in Jewish sources as being inhabited by Jews in Sassanian Persian times. *See Babylonia, in* THE JEWISH ENCYCLOPEDIA.

21. J.F. COAKLEY, THE CHURCH OF THE EAST AND THE CHURCH OF ENGLAND 366 (Oxford: Clarendon Press, 1992); Brig. Gen. J.G. Browne, *The Assyrians*, 85 J. OF THE ROYAL SOC. OF ARTS 182 (1937); Leela Jacinto, *Sounds of Silence: Iraqi Assyrians Speak the Language Jesus Spoke—But For How Long?*, ABC NEWS.COM, Nov. 6, 2003, http://abcnews.go.com/International/story?id=79814&page=1. *See also* THE OXFORD HISTORY OF THE BIBLICAL WORLD 279 (Michael D. Coogan ed., New York: Oxford UP, 2001).

22. *See* COAKLEY, THE CHURCH OF THE EAST, at 65, 89, 99, 149, 366–7, 382, 411. The Church of England established a mission to the "Assyrians" by the 1870s or 1880s, long before an independent Assyrian nation became an international legal and political issue after World War I.

23. *See* Parpola, *Assyrian Identity in Post-Empire Times*, at 16–22; Joel Walker, *The Legacy of Mesopotamia in Late Antique Iraq: The Christian Martyr Shrine at Melqi (Neo-Assyrian Milqia)*, 19 ARAM: THE JOURNAL OF SYRO-MESOPOTAMIAN STUDIES 483, 491–508 (2007); Amar Annus, *The Survival of the Ancient Syrian and Mesopotamian Intellectual Traditions in the Writings of Ephrem Syrus*, 38 UGARIT-FORSCHUNGEN 1–25 (2006); *see also* MORONY, IRAQ AFTER THE MUSLIM CONQUEST at 384–400; Michael Morony, *Magic and Society in Late Sassanian Iraq, in* PRAYER, MAGIC, AND THE STARS IN THE ANCIENT AND LATE ANTIQUE WORLD 83–107 (Joel Walker et al. eds., University Park, PA: Penn State Press, 2003); *The Writings of the Fathers Down to AD 325, in* 8 ANTE-NICENE FATHERS 671–672 (Alexander Roberts & James Donaldson eds., Edinburgh: Alban Books, 1994); WIGRAM, THE ASSYRIANS AND THEIR NEIGHBORS, at 33, 186–87, 202; WILLIAM A. WIGRAM, AN INTRODUCTION TO THE HISTORY OF THE ASSYRIAN CHURCH 30–32 (New York: E.S. Gorham, 1910).

24. *See* WIGRAM, THE HISTORY OF THE ASSYRIAN CHURCH, at 30–32, 71, 83, 99, 223, 304.

25. *See id.* at 71, 223; Sebastian Brock, *Syriac Culture, 337–425*, THE CAMBRIDGE ANCIENT HISTORY: THE LATE EMPIRE, A.D. 337–425, at 713 (John Bagnell Bury et al. eds., Cambridge: Cambridge UP, 1998).

26. ANDREW DALBY, DICTIONARY OF LANGUAGES: THE DEFINITIVE REFERENCE TO MORE THAN 400 LANGUAGES 12 (New York: Columbia UP, 2004).

27. BOTTÉRO, MESOPOTAMIA, at 289.

28. *See* 3 YOCHANAN MUFFS, STUDIES IN THE ARAMAIC LEGAL PAPYRI FROM ELEPHANTINE 186, 189 (Leiden, the Netherlands: Brill, 1969) ("standard Aramaic was employed all through the Assyrian Empire ... from the borders of Egypt to the borders of India"); *see also* ROUX, ANCIENT IRAQ, at 276–77;

maic is a non-Arabic Semitic language composed of a mixture of ancient Assyrian and ancient Aramaean words and grammatical forms.[29] Along with many Aramaean words, the Assyrian Empire and its provincial officials adopted the Phoenician alphabet for use in communicating with far-flung outposts.[30] The contemporary Assyrians use Phoenician letters to write many Akkadian words.

The transition from indigenous Assyro-Babylonian religion to Christianity occurred in a relatively organic and peaceful manner, rather than by force as in the Constantinian and Theodosian Roman Empire and in the later European monarchies and their overseas colonies. The rise of Christianity within the borders of ancient Assyria, from the border with India to the border with Egypt, was likely facilitated by the extensive similarities between ancient Assyro-Babylonian religion and the sacred writings of the Jews and early Christians.[31] The Assyro-Babylonian creation story and accounts of the exploits of gods and heroes are strikingly similar to the events revealed in the Book of Genesis.[32] The Assyrians believed in a supreme god as "the only true god," along with a divine king, his son, and a divine mother, who bore the perfect son of the supreme god in her womb.[33]

Aramaic Writing, in THE BLACKWELL ENCYCLOPEDIA OF WRITING SYSTEMS 23 (Florian Coulmas ed., London: Blackwell, 1999).

29. *See* AL KANFEI YONAH: STUDIES OF JONAS C. C. GREENFIELD ON SEMITIC PHILOLOGY 113. 153–56 (Shalom M. Paul et al. eds., 2001) (discussing Old Assyrian/Akkadian influence on Aramaic); S.A. KAUFMAN, THE AKKADIAN INFLUENCE ON ARAMAIC (1974) (similar); 3 MUFFS, ARAMAIC LEGAL PAPYRI, at 186 (similar).

30. *See* MUFFS, STUDIES IN THE ARAMAIC LEGAL PAPYRI, at 189; ROUX, ANCIENT IRAQ, at 276–77; *Aramaic Writing, in* THE BLACKWELL ENCYCLOPEDIA OF WRITING SYSTEMS 23 (Florian Coulmas ed., London, 1999).

31. JAMES BRYCE, THE HOLY ROMAN EMPIRE 345 (London: Macmillian, 1864) (reprint 1912) ("[Rome] could not think of the Christian people except in the form of a body of worshippers organized under a government, and a government with an autocratic head.... But to the Eastern Christians, ... the Christian people appeared in the form of a body of worshippers professing exactly the same lifegiving dogmas.").

32. *See, e.g.*, FRANÇOIS LENORMANT, THE BEGINNINGS OF HISTORY: ACCORDING TO THE BIBLE AND TO THE TRADITIONS OF ORIENTAL PEOPLES xv (New York: Scribner's, 1893) ("The very form given it in the Bible is so closely related to that which has been lately discovered in Babylon and Chaldea, it follows so exactly the same course, that it is quite impossible for me to doubt any longer that it has the same origin. The family of Abraham carried this tradition with it in the migration which brought it from Ur of the Chaldees into Palestine ... in a written or an oral form, for beneath the expressions of the Hebrew text in more than one place there appear certain things which can be explained only as expressions peculiar to the Assyrian language, as, for instance, the [references to a ziggurat] in Genesis xi. 4...."); HOWARD H. COX, THE PENTATEUCH: HISTORY OR STORY? 27 (Lanham, MD: University Press of America, 2005) (the Assyrian library at Nineveh contained an "epic [that] includes a story of the Flood with remarkable parallels to the Genesis story. The gods decide to inundate the Earth, but one of them informs a figure comparable to Noah and counsels him to build an ark to save his family and the animals. The flood comes, three birds are sent out in sequence, and the ship comes to rest on a mountain. Sacrifices are offered."); S.A. NIGOSIAN, FROM ANCIENT WRITINGS TO SACRED TEXTS: THE OLD TESTAMENT AND APOCRYPHA 55 (Baltimore London: Johns Hopkins UP, 2004) ("The story of Moses' birth, especially the account of his being abandoned and found (Exod. 2:1–9), is borrowed from the story of Sargon [of Akkad, hero and progenitor of the Assyrians], who was abandoned by his mother and set adrift...."); *id.* (birth story of Sargon stated: "My changeling mother conceived me, in secret she bore me. She set me in a basket of rushes [reeds].... She cast me into the river ... [which] bore me up and carried me to Akki, the drawer of water.... Akki took me as his son and reared me.").

33. *See, e.g.*, Simo Parpola, *Sons of God: The Ideology of Assyrian Kingship*, ARCHAEOLOGY ODYSSEY, Nov./Dec. 1999, at 16, 17–26. *Compare also, e.g.*, 4 THE ASSYRIAN DICTIONARY: "E" 96 (Mesopotamian account of "when heaven, on high, had not (yet) been named, [and] below, the earth had not (yet) been given a name"), *id.* at 374 (Mesopotamian account of the gods used the terms a'lu or i'lu as a "confederation" or "league" of "divine leadership"), *with* HANNAY, CHRISTIANITY: THE SOURCES OF ITS

Assyro-Babylonian religion envisaged an afterlife in paradise, particularly for those who died as stillborn infants, before their time, or with large numbers of descendents who could make sacrificial offerings of food and wine.[34] Its scriptures also depicted an underworld as a "grim 'hell'" of darkness, confinement, hunger, "spiritual trials," and torment by demons.[35] The god Nergal even played a satanic role as "lord of the Underworld."[36] When missionaries today highlight analogous but much less direct similarities between Christianity and other indigenous religions, the conversion process is facilitated.[37]

Judaism spread throughout Mesopotamia and Anatolia before Christianity did,[38] and was a contributing factor in the rise of a "well-developed Christian community" in Edessa in the early first millennium CE.[39] Edessa later served as a center of Christian administration. There is evidence not only of Babylonian Jews in the third century CE, but of their actively seeking converts from among practitioners of indigenous Assyro-Babylonian religions.[40] Jews had several academies in Babylon and compiled the 2.5 million or so words of the Babylonian Talmud (*Talmud Babli*) into an edited form, using a mixture of Hebrew and Aramaic, in about 500 CE.[41] Babylonia became a second "Land of Israel," according to one rabbi.[42]

The first letter of Peter portrays the apostle preaching in "Babylon," from where he wrote that the "Church of Babylon" hailed his readers in Anatolia (including Pontus) in

---

TEACHING, at 159 (arguing that in translating the Book of Genesis into English: "The phrase 'Lord God' [i.e. Elohim] ... ought to be translated ... 'the Hebrew tribal god among the god family.'.... For instance, in Deuteronomy xi. 16, we have: 'Serve other Elohim (gods), and bow down to *them*.'") (emphasis in original).

34. *See* JEREMY BLACK, ANTHONY GREEN & TESSA RICKARDS, GODS, DEMONS AND SYMBOLS OF ANCIENT MESOPOTAMIA: AN ILLUSTRATED DICTIONARY 27–28, 72, 85, 180–81 (Austin: Univ. of Texas Press, 6th ed., 2006); Alasdair Livingstone, *The Underworld Vision of an Assyrian Prince, in* 3 STATE ARCHIVES OF ASSYRIA: COURT POETRY AND LITERARY MISCELLANEA 68 (Helsinki UP, 1989); Muhammad Dandamayev, *Royal* Paradeisoi *in Babylonia*, 23 ACTA IRANICA 113 (1984); Literatur Bendt Alster, *Dilmun, Bahrein, and the Alleged Paradise in Sumerian Myth and Literature, in* NEW STUDIES IN THE ARCHAEOLOGY AND EARLY HISTORY OF BAHREIN 39–74 (Daniel T. Potts ed., Berlin: Reimer Verlag, 1983).

35. BLACK, GREEN & RICKARDS, GODS, DEMONS, AND SYMBOLS, at 27–28, 72, 85, 180–81; Mehmet Ali Ataç, *The "Underworld Vision" of the Ninevite Intellectual Milieu*, 66 IRAQ 67, 67 (2004).

36. Ataç, *The Underworld Vision of an Assyrian Prince*, at 69.

37. *See* 4 RUTHERFORD, CELTIC LORE, at 154 (describing transformation of Celtic Druidic gods into Christian saints, and of Druidic sacred places such as springs and oak groves into sites of reverence for "Our Lady").

38. *See* Clyde Haberman, *Istanbul Journal; Where 16 Synagogues Stand Among the Minarets*, N.Y. TIMES, July 30, 1990, at A4 (dating Jewish presence in Anatolia to third century BCE); PHILLIP J. KING & LAWRENCE E. STAGER, LIFE IN BIBLICAL ISRAEL 246 (Louisville, KY: Westminster John Knox Press, 2001); K. Lawson Younger, *The Deportation of the Israelites*, 17(2) J. OF BIBLICAL LIT. 201, 201 (1998) (Jews may have been among the thousands of Samarians deported to Mesopotamia and "counted ... as Assyrians" by Sargon II in eighth century BCE); Orly Halpern, *Iraq Split on Granting Jews' Minority Status*, JERUSALEM POST, July 18, 2005, at 1 (dating Jewish presence in Mesopotamia to 500 BCE).

39. ROBERT MURRAY, SYMBOLS OF CHURCH AND KINGDOM: A STUDY IN EARLY SYRIAC TRADITION 6–7 (Harrisburg, PA: Continuum International Publishing Group, 2004).

40. *See* BERNARD JACOB BAMBERGER, PROSELYTISM IN THE TALMUDIC PERIOD 255 (New York: KTAV Pub. House, 1968); WILLIAM GORDON BRAUDE, JEWISH PROSELYTING IN THE FIRST FIVE CENTURIES OF THE COMMON ERA: THE AGE OF THE TANNAIM AND AMORAIM 19 (Providence: Brown Univ., 1940). *See also* MORONY, IRAQ AFTER THE MUSLIM CONQUEST, at 306–31.

41. *See* ALFRED J. KOLATCH, MASTERS OF THE TALMUD: THEIR LIVES AND VIEWS 40, 297 (Middle Village, NY: Jonathan David Publishers, 2003).

42. *See* MENDELSSOHN, CRIMINAL JURISPRUDENCE OF THE ANCIENT HEBREWS, at 232, 236.

the first century CE.[43] The Assyrian tradition is also that the Assyrians and Babylonians started to become Christians within the first century.[44] Assyrian (Aramaic rather than Akkadian) texts refer to bishops of Adiabene, Assyria, and Arbela as of about 100 CE, and the Christian community was so large that in 160 CE the bishop of Adiabene, the name for parts of ancient Assyria after the Persian invasions, unsuccessfully applied to the king of Adiabene for an edict of formal toleration.[45] A Greek-speaking bishop found Christians in Mesopotamia and Anatolia in about 180 CE.[46]

In the second and third centuries CE, many of the indigenous peoples of Anatolia and Mesopotamia became Christians under the influence of bishops and priests tolerated and encouraged by King Abgar IV of Urhay (Edessa).[47] Christianity was "well established and organized" in Mesopotamia by the third century CE.[48] By that century, there were more than twenty bishops in the region from Edessa and Nisibis in Anatolia east through Armenia and Mesopotamia to Persia.[49] In fact, the oldest surviving dated copy of the biblical books of Genesis, Exodus, Numbers and Deuteronomy was written in the fifth century CE in Aramaic (Greek "Syriac") by a deacon in Āmid, southeastern Anatolia, which was then a part of the Byzantine Empire,[50] but which had been an Assyrian province in an-

---

43. *See* 1 Peter 1:1, 5:13 (KJV). Some have argued that "Babylon" was a term used for Rome by Jews and Christians at the time, on account of their common polytheism, and that in context Peter must have been in Rome, which was then a much larger city than Babylon, which had suffered under Greek rule and become small and obscure. *See* Wayne A. Grudem, The First Epistle of Peter: An Introduction and Commentary 30–38 (Grand Rapids, MI: Wm. Erdmans Publ'g, 1988). On the other hand, this theory assumes that Peter meant Babylon the city as opposed to the country, which was becoming the second Israel and would develop the Babylonian Talmud. Peter at one point expressly addresses the "exiles of the Dispersion" or Jewish diaspora. The same word was often used in Hebrew and Greek, as in English, for the city and the country of Babylon. Peter also assumed the title of Patriarch of Antioch sometime in the first half of the first century CE, Antioch being a location much closer to Babylon than to Rome, which would require a perilous journey by sea. Peter had "frequent absences" from Antioch and "passed through all quarters," making a visit to Babylon and its Jewish exiles quite possible. John Mason Neale, A History of the Holy Eastern Church: The Patriarchate of Antioch 3–4 (London: Rivingtons, 1873). Antioch in Syria and Seleucia in Babylon were the two capitals of the Seleucid Empire and two of the largest cities in the region after Alexandria. Antioch was about 24 degrees of longitude away from Rome, but only about eight degrees from Babylon. *Compare* George A. Rawlinson, *Map of the Sassanian Empire* (1876), http://www.gutenberg.org/files/16167/16167-h/images/sassian_empire.jpg, *with Map of Europe*, http://www.nzhistory.net.nz/files/images/nz-europe-map2.jpg. The debate remains unresolved.

44. *See* Christine Chaillot, *The Ancient Oriental Churches, in* The Oxford History of Christian Worship 161 (2006); William Baum and Dietmar Winkler, The Church of the East: A History of the Nestorian Church 7–12 (London: Routledge, 2000); A.J. Maclean, *Syrian Christians, in* 12 Encyclopædia of Religion and Ethics 170 (James Hastings ed., Edinburgh: T. & T. Clark, 1920).

45. *See* Wigram, The History of the Assyrian Church, at 32, 89.

46. *See id.*; Maclean, *Syrian Christians*, at 170 ("It is quite probable that there were Christians in Assyria in the 2nd cent...."); Murray, Symbols of Church and Kingdom, at 5–7.

47. Gabriel Oussani, *An Historical Essay on the Assyro-Chaldean Christians, in* Naayem, Shall This Nation Die?, http://www.aina.org/books/stnd.htm. *See also* Ute Possekel, *Bardaisan of Edessa: Philosopher or Theologian?*, 10 J. of Ancient Christianity 442 (2006); Jan Willem Drijvers, The Book of the Laws of Countries: Dialogue on Fate of Bardaisan of Edessa 9–10 (Piscataway, NJ: Gorgias Press, 2007) (scholar in the court of King Abgar was a Chaldean/Babylonian astronomer, born in the Assyrian month of Tammuz).

48. Jonathan Berkey, The Formation of Islam: Religion and Society in the Near East, 600–1800, at 24 (Cambridge: Cambridge UP, 2003); William Baum and Dietmar Winkler, The Apostolic Church of the East: A History of the Nestorian Church 7–12 (New York: 2000).

49. *See* Wigram, The History of the Assyrian Church, at 27, 99, 167.

50. *Frances Spiegel,* British Library: Sacred: World Faiths Brought to Book—Exhibition Running from April–Sept. (2007), http://artgalleries.suite101.com/article.cfm/sacred. By contrast, the oldest

cient times.[51] The oldest dated Christian manuscript was written in Aramaic in Urhay in 411 CE.[52]

The Church of the East flourished under the Sassanian or New Persian Empire, despite occasional anti-Christian pogroms carried out by adherents of the state religion, Zoroastrianism. Prior to the Arab conquest of Mesopotamia, the people of the Nineveh region erected a Christian church on what was probably the site of an ancient Assyrian temple.[53] In the fifth and sixth centuries CE, the Patriarch of the Chaldeans headed the bishops of the Persian Empire.[54] Starting in the fifth century CE, the Christians of Anatolia and Mesopotamia came to be known as "Nestorians," initially only by their opponents but also among themselves, as a result of the split between the Roman Catholic Church and the Patriarch of Constantinople, Nestorius, over the metaphysical nature of Jesus Christ.[55] Nineveh became the seat of a "Nestorian" bishop.[56] The Church of the East became independent from the Roman Catholic Church in the fifth century CE, after the Patriarch of Constantinople, Nestorius, refused to assent to the concept of *theotokos*, or

---

surviving fragment of the Book of Genesis dates to about 150 BCE. *See* James C. VanderKam & Peter W. Flint, The Meaning of the Dead Sea Scrolls 105 (Harrisburg, PA: Continuum International Publishing Group, 2005) ("The oldest scroll of Genesis ... is dated to the middle of the second century BCE. This manuscript is written in the ancient Hebrew script known as paleo-Hebrew, ... with only thirty-four of the fifty chapters of Genesis represented....").

51. *See* George Smith, The Assyrian Eponym Canon 67 (1875); William Ricketts Cooper, An Archaic Dictionary 319 (London: S. Bagster and Sons, 1876); *cf.* Percy M. Sykes, A History of Persia 116 (New York: Macmillan and Co., 1930).

52. Andrew Johnson, *Found at Last: The World's Oldest Syriac Missing Page,* The Independent (U.K.), Feb. 17, 2008, http://www.platformaram.nl/forum/viewtopic.php?f=9&t=3790; Martin Bailey, *Fragments of World's Oldest Christian Manuscript Found In Egyptian Monastery,* The Art Newspaper, Feb. 18, 2008, http://www.platformaram.nl/forum/viewtopic.php?f=9&t=3790.

53. *See* H.W.F. Saggs, The Might that Was Assyria 290 (England: Sedgwick & Jackson Ltd., 1984).

54. J.P. Fletcher, Notes from Nineveh and Travels in Mesopotamia, Assyria, and Syria (Philadelphia: Carey, Lea & Blanchard, 1850), http://www.aina.org/books/nfn/nfn.htm. The terms "Chaldea" and "Chaldean" refer, respectively, to the region and the people of southern and southeastern Babylonia, and are sometimes contrasted with the more northern and northwestern Amorite tribal regions of Babylonia. Some Babylonian kings, for example Hammurabi of the eighteenth century BCE, were of Amorite tribal affiliation, while others were Chaldean, for example Nebuchadnezzar II. *See, e.g.,* Caubet & Pouyssegur, The Origin of Civilization, at 101, 135, 137; Ran Zadok, *On the Amorite Material from Mesopotamia, in* The Tablet and the Scroll: Near Eastern Studies in Honor of William H. Hallo (M.E. Cohen, D.C. Snell & D.B. Weisberg eds., 1993); *Amorite, in* The Encyclopedia Britannica (2008), http://www.britannica.com/EBchecked/topic/21276/Amorite; Emil Hirsch et al., *Chaldea, in* The Jewish Encyclopedia (1906), http://www.jewishencyclopedia.com/view.jsp?artid=336&letter=C; Ghassan Hanna, *The Assyrian-Chaldean Dilemma—One Nation, Two Names, Part I* (2000), http://www.atour.com/government/docs/20000609h.html.

55. Robin E. Waterfield, Christians in Persia: Assyrians, Armenians, Roman Catholics and Protestants 23 (London: Allen and Unwin, 1973) (setting forth a balanced view of the schism); *Nestorius and Nestorianism,* The Catholic Encyclopedia, vol. X (1911), http://www.newadvent.org/cathen/10755a.htm (setting forth the Catholic view).

56. *See* De Lacy O'Leary, How Greek Science Passed to the Arabs, ch. 1 (London: Routledge & Kegan Paul, 2001) (1957), http://www.aina.org/books/hgsptta.htm; Morony, Iraq After the Muslim Conquest, at 345; Aubrey Vine, The Nestorian Churches (London: Independent Press Ltd, 1937); Hurmuzd Rassam, Assur and the Land of Nimrud (Cincinnati; Curts & Jennings, 1897); Gibbon, 8 Decline and Fall of the Roman Empire, ch. LXVII, http://oll.libertyfund.org/Home3/HTML.php?recordID=0214.08; Parpola, *Assyrian Identity in the Post-Empire Times,* at 16–22.

the idea that Mary was the mother of God, and not merely of Jesus' human form.[57] By the sixth century CE, the "Nestorians" of the Assyrian Church had established churches and other places of worship in Persia, the Persian Gulf, Bactria (Afghanistan), India, Tibet, China, Korea, and Japan.[58]

The head of the Nestorians was known as the patriarch or *catholicos* of Babylon.[59] As Patriarch of Babylon, he regarded himself as governing "Assyria." "By mid 14th century [CE], according to the 'Book of tower', by Mari Bar Shlemun (1350) (Mari ibn Sulemon), the 'Church of the East' had only six Metropolitans left. They consisted of, Gundi Shappur, Mosul and Assyria, Nissibin, Arbil and Hazza, Basra, and Beit Garmee."[60] The taking by the Nestorian patriarchs and bishops of the title Patriarch of "Babylon" was similarly significant in that it reiterated the connection with ancient Assryo-Babylonian civilization. It recalled "the native Assyrian inhabitants of Nineveh and its surroundings ..." because "those of Babylonian blood are of the same ethnic background as that of the Assyrians. ..."[61]

By 1600 CE, some of the ethnic Assyrians of Mesopotamia and Persia had entered into communion with Rome by founding the Chaldean church.[62] The Chaldeans, or Catholic Assyrians, also identified themselves with ancient Assyria and Babylon. Indeed, the Patriarch for Babylon heads the second oldest Catholic, patriarchate, formed after "the submission of the Nestorian patriarch, John Sulaga."[63] In 1553, Pope Julius III and the Catholic

---

57. Waterfield, Christians in Persia at 23; Paul Gavrilyuk, *Theopatheia: Nestorius's Main Charge against Cyril of Alexandria*, Scottish Journal of Theology 56, no. 2 (2003): 190–207; Jonathan Eric Lewis, *Iraqi Assyrians: Barometer of Pluralism*, Middle East Q. 10 (2003): 49–58; Carl E. Braaten, *Modern Interpretations of Nestorius*, Church History 32 (1963): 251–67; *Nestorius and Nestorianism, in* 10 The Catholic Encyclopedia (1911), http://www.newadvent.org/cathen/10755a.htm.

58. *See* Henry Austen Layard, Nineveh and its Remains 82 (New York: G.P. Putnam, 1850) ("From Persia, where the Chaldean Bishoprics were early established, they spread eastwards; and Cosmas Indicopleustes, who visited Asia in the early part of the sixth century, declares that they had bishops, martyrs, and priests in India, Arabia Felix, and Socotra, amongst the Bactrians, the Huns, the Persarmenians, the Medes, and the Elamites, and that their Metropolitans even penetrated into China as early as the fifth century."); Nina Garsoian, *The Marzpanate, in* 1 The Armenian People, at 99–103 (locating Huns in Caucasus and east of Persia); Suha Rassam, Christianity in Iraq: Its Origins and Development to the Present Day 35–45, 80–81 (London: Gracewing, reprint ed. 2006) (bishops of Church of the East from Mesopotamia, Persia, and present-day Afghanistan convened a theological council in fifth century CE, and other); John M. L. Young, By Foot to China: Mission of The Church of the East, to 1400, ch. 3 (1991) (1984), http://www.aina.org/books/bftc/bftc.htm; Stephen Andrew Missick, *Mar Thoma: The Apostolic Foundation of the Assyrian Church and the Christians of St. Thomas in India*, 24 J. of Assyrian Acad. Studies 33 (2000), http://jaas.org/edocs/v14n2/missick.pdf.

59. *See* Robert Eric Frykenberg & Alaine M. Low, Christians and Missionaries in India: Cross-Cultural Communication since 1500, at 36 (Grand Rapids, MI: Wm. B. Eerdmans Publishing, 2003); Gibbon, 4 Decline and Fall of the Roman Empire, ch. 47, http://www.ccel.org/g/gibbon/decline/volume2/chap47.htm ("Twenty-five metropolitans or archbishops composed [the Nestorian] hierarchy; but several of these were dispensed, by the distance and danger of the way, from the duty of personal attendance, on the easy condition that every six years they should testify their faith and obedience to the catholic or patriarch of Babylon, a vague appellation which has been successively applied to the royal seats of Seleucia, Ctesiphon, and Bagdad.").

60. Basil Bar Shumana (twelfth century CE bishop of Syrian Church), *quoted in* J.B. Segal, Edessa: "The Blessed City" 3 n. 2 (Pisctaway, NJ: Gorgias Press, 2005).

61. Ghassan Hanna, *The Assyrian-Chaldean Dilemma—One Nation, Two Names, Part II,* Al Muntada Mag., June 9, 2000.

62. Lewis, *Iraqi Assyrians*, at 50.

63. *Patriarch and Patriarchate, in* 11 The Catholic Encyclopedia (New York: Robert Appleton Company, 1911), http://www.newadvent.org/cathen/11549a.htm.

Church proclaimed a breakaway Nestorian bishop as "patriarch of 'Mosul and Athour' [Assyria]."[64] The Catholic Church designated this patriarch as ministering to "the Assyrian Nation."[65]

The Jacobite Christians of Anatolia and Mesopotamia also made the connection between themselves and the ancient Assyrians and Babylonians/Chaldeans. They traced the name of their spiritual capital, Urhay (later called Edessa), to its founding by Nimrod, the Assyrian King of Sumer and Akkad (Babylon and Assyria) who built Urhay, because Ur meant town/city and "hay" referred to Chaldeans, or the town built for the Chaldeans (who also hailed from Ur, as in the biblical "Ur of the Chaldees," Gen. 11:31).[66] Urhay or Edessa (later Urfa or Şanlıurfa, in southeastern Turkey) "was the earliest seat of Christianity in Mesopotamia and the cradle of Syriac [i.e., modern Assyrian] literature."[67] Similarly, the town of Urmia, with centuries of Assyrian heritage, was named by combining the terms "Ur" or town/city with "mia" or sea.[68]

Several premodern invasions devastated the Assyrians' cultural heritage, architecture, and literary and artistic production. In the seventh century BCE, invading Elamites (a people later incorporated into the Persian Empire) besieged and destroyed the Assyrian cities of Assur, Calah, Dur-Sharrukin, and Nineveh.[69] In the sixth century BCE, the Persians sacked Urhay and burned down many churches and monasteries in Anatolia, particularly in the historically Assyrian Tur Abdin area.[70] During the same era, the Romans, then at war with Persia, devastated the towns and villages in the vicinity of Nisibis, an Assyrian city from the imperial period.[71] In the fifth century BCE, the Persian Empire under Xerxes sacked Babylon and deported its people.[72] In the fourth century CE, St. Jerome,

---

64. Hanna, *The Assyrian-Chaldean Dilemma.*

65. *Id.* (quoting Xavier Koodapuzha, *Faith and Communion in the Indian Church of Saint Thomas Christians, in* 2 St. Thomas Christian Encyclopaedia (Kerala, India: Oriental Institute of Religious Studies, 1973)).

66. *See* Christopher Hatch MacEvitt, The Crusades and the Christian World of the East: Rough Tolerance 50 (Philadelphia: Univ. of Pennsylvania Press, 2007); Yigal Levin, *Nimrod the Mighty, King of Kish, King of Sumer and Akkad,* 52 Vitus Testamentum 350 (2002); Amir Harrak, *The Ancient Name of Edessa,* 51 J. of Near Eastern Stud. 209, 211 (1992) ("St. Ephrem the Syrian (fourth century) wrote about the famous Nimrod 'who ruled in Erech [Uruk] which is Edessa (Urhay).' He was followed in this belief ... by Patriarch Michael the Syrian (twelfth century). Edessa is thus identified with the Sumerian city of Uruk."); the first Christian kingdom, and the cradle of Syriac literature.

67. *Syriac Literature, in* 26 Encyclopedia Britannica 211 (New York: Encyclopedia Britannica, 1911). The Book of Acts portrays the Apostle Paul and his companions preaching in Antioch, near Edessa, at a very early date. *See* Acts 13:14–52 (KJV).

68. This etymology is based on oral history from a speaker of modern Assyrian from Urmia. *See* Edward A. And Irene Kliszus, *The Assyrian Diaspora. A Research Project* §2 (1999), http://www.aina.org/books/ad.htm.

69. *See* 4 World and Its Peoples: The Middle East, Western Asia, and North Africa 461 (2006) (Assur was razed, and Nineveh attacked); Edwin Oliver James, From Cave to Cathedral: Temples and Shrines of Prehistoric, Classical, and Early Christian Times 165 (1965) (Assur, Calah, Dur-Sharrukin, and Nineveh were sacked); *cf.* Christopher Johnston, *The Fall of Nineveh,* 22 J. of the American Oriental Soc. 20 (1901).

70. *See* The Roman Eastern Frontier and the Persian Wars: Part II, AD 363–630, A Narrative Sourcebook 165 (Michael H. Dodgeon & Samuel N. Lieu eds., 1991).

71. 2 The Cambridge Medieval History 277 (John Bagnell Bury et al. eds., 1913) (Roman general devastated area around Nisibis); 1 Luckenbill, Ancient Records of Assyria, at 126, 132 (Assyrian inscription stated that king Tukulti-Urta II spent time at Nisibis [Nasibina] in ninth century BCE); 2 Luckenbill, Ancient Records of Assyria, at 417, 420 (Babylonian Chronicle recounted invasion of Assyrian Nisibis by anti-Assyrian coalition in seventh century BCE).

72. Sir Percy M. Sykes, A History of Persia 196 (2003) (1915).

who traveled extensively through Anatolia and spoke Aramaic,[73] wrote that the invading Huns captured countless monasteries and committed enormous massacres, not sparing the elderly or babies.[74]

Although the Persians and Arabs of the Christian era generally did not consciously set out to eliminate the indigenous Christians and pagans from Mesopotamia, outbreaks of persecution could be severe. "During the fourth, fifth and sixth centuries, the Assyro-Chaldean Church became so extensive and powerful that it excited the fear and the hatred of the Sassanian kings of Persia, who determined to exterminate it with a series of almost uninterrupted persecutions and unheard-of cruelties."[75] The Persian Empire "alternately protected and persecuted" Mesopotamian Christians until the rise of the Caliphate and the Arab conquest of Mesopotamia in the seventh century CE.[76]

The Byzantines were less tolerant, and laid the groundwork for the Arab conquest of Mesopotamia by devastating many of its largest cities. During a Byzantine attack on the Persians, Assyria (Athur) was conquered and pagans and Magians were deported to southeastern Anatolia as slaves, which gave rise to the name of Tur Abdin for the "Mountain of Slaves."[77] When the Byzantines under the Emperor Severus reached Babylon, Seleucia, and Ctesiphon, they sacked all three cities.[78] The Byzantines massacred most of the inhabitants of Ctesiphon.[79]

Some Assyrians initially welcomed the Arab conquests of Mesopotamia and Syria as a respite from outbursts of Eastern Roman (Byzantine) and Persian Zoroastrian persecution and oppression.[80] The Abbasids continued the religious autonomy granted by the Sassanian or New Persian Empire.[81] The Nestorian patriarch may have secured charters of protection from the Abbasid caliphs.[82] Assyrian-French scholar Joseph Yacoub, a Professor of Political Science at the Catholic University of Lyon, reproduces one of them in his book, *The Assyrian Question*. The Nestorian Patriarch was called the Patriarch "of Babylon," while the other Patriarch with jurisdiction in Anatolia and Mesopotamia was called "of Antioch," so they had clearly geographically-demarcated church names. The two patriarchs exercised separate jurisdiction over nearby churches in Baghdad and other

---

73. *See* Jerome, Select Letters (F. A. Wright trans., 1993); *Jerome, in* The Jewish Encyclopedia (1906), http://jewishencyclopedia.com/view.jsp?artid=239&letter=J&search=Jerome.

74. E.A. Thompson, The Huns 31–32 (1948). *See also* John Man, Attila: The Barbarian King Who Challenged Rome 113 (2005).

75. Oussani, *A Historical Essay*.

76. Layard, Nineveh and Its Remains, at 82.

77. Ephram I Barsoum, The History of Tur Abdin 4 (Matti Mousa trans., Piscataway, NJ: Gorgias Press, 2008).

78. *See Hatra, in* International Dictionary of Historic Places: Middle East and Africa 328 (Trudy Ring et al. eds., London: Taylor & Francis, 1996); *Seleucia (Baghdad, Iraq), in id.* at 636–38.

79. *See* T. Bioy, Late Achaemenid and Hellenistic Babylon 190 (Leuven: Peeters, 2004); *Ctesiphon, in* Dictionary of Battles and Sieges: A–E, at 274 (Tony Jaques ed. Westport, CT: Greenwood Publishing Group, 2007).

80. *See* Rassam, Christianity in Iraq, at 76, 87–88. Similar reactions have been reported in Armenia, Persia, and the Levant. *See* Waterfield, Christians in Persia, at 33; Gibbon, 5 Decline and Fall of the Roman Empire, ch. 51, http://www.ccel.org/g/gibbon/decline/volume2/chap515.htm.

81. *See* Wigram, The History of the Assyrian Church, at 89, 309–10; Wigram, The Assyrians and Their Neighbours, at 51, 77.

82. At least one author states that the charter of protection or *firman* was granted to the Assyrians by the Prophet Muhammad. *See* Isabella L. Bishop, Journeys in Persia and Kurdistan—Including a Summer in the Upper Kabun Region and a Visit to the Nestorian Rayahs 300–1 (Alcester, UK: Read Books, 2006) (1891).

places.[83] As of the tenth century CE, Church of the East bishops, under the jurisdiction of the Patriarch in Mesopotamia,[84] had been established throughout Arabia, Central Asia (east and west Turkestan), India, Tibet, and China.[85]

Within several centuries, however, many churches had been destroyed or reduced to ruins as a result of the caliphate's decrees, related discrimination and oppression, the deportation of Assyro-Chaldeans and the theft of their property, and the executions of heretics.[86] The Caliph Omar launched a persecution that claimed thousands of churches and Magian temples.[87] In the ninth century CE, the Caliph Mutawakkil decreed that many churches be demolished, and the houses of Christians expropriated.[88] Several Christian centers lost their ability to transmit their cultural heritage to later generations living in the area.[89] In the succession struggle after the death of Harun al-Rashid in 809 CE, the general Amr "massacred and pillaged mercilessly" in the Jazirah region at the intersection of present-day Syria, Turkey, and Iraq, as well as in Damascus and in central Syria on the road to Aleppo. From Mesopotamia west to Palestine, the Arab armies "brought about the ruination of Christians in every place," burning churches and villages, killing women and children in repeated massacres, and bringing about famines.[90] By 724 CE Christians could be killed on penalty of paying half the monetary fine attached to a Muslim life, and Christians were prohibited from giving evidence in court or becoming judges. The Caliph Mansur went so far as to order the Christian population to be branded.[91]

---

83. *See* Joseph Yacoub, The Assyrian Question (Chicago, IL: Alpha Graphic, 1986). *See also* Joseph Yacoub, Babylone Chrétienne: Géopolitique de l'Église de Mésopotamie (Paris: Éditions Desclée de Brouwer, 1996); Joseph Yacoub, La Question Assyro-Chaldéenne, les Puissances Européennes et la Société des Nations 1908–1938, in 4 vols. (Lyon, France: Université de Lyon II, 1984).

84. *See* Samuel Hugh Moffett, A History of Christianity in Asia: 1500 to 1900, at 295 (1998).

85. *See* Rassam, Christianity in Iraq, at 34–45, 76, 87–88 (Church of the East bishops existed in Central Asia, India, and China); Rene Grousset, Empire of the Steppes: A History of Central Asia 154–55, 300–306, 369 (1970) ("Nestorian" Church of the East bishops and priests existed in Israel/Palestine, China—including the archbishop of Beijing and churches in Chenkiang/Cinghianfu, Kanchow, Ningsia, Samarkand, Kansu/Tangut, and among the Mongols, who "referred to Nestorian priests by the Syriac terms *rabban-arkagun* and bishops as *marhasia*").

86. Rassam, Christianity in Iraq, at 88–90; Kirk, *A Short History of the Middle East*, at 101; John Stewart, The Missionary Enterprise: The Story of a Church on Fire 215, 218 (London: T&T Allen, 1928); Yohannan, The Death of a Nation, at 95–98.

87. *See* Ghiyath al-Din Khwandamir, 2 Tarikh-i Habib al-Siyar (Bombay, 1857); Mīr Khwānd (Muhammad ibn Khāvand Shāh), History of the Early Kings of Persia 137 (David Shea trans., London: Oriental Translation Fund, 1832); Edward Upham, History of the Ottoman Empire, from its Establishment, Till the Year 1828, at 46 (Edinburgh: Constable & Co., 1829). *See also* Gibbon, 9 Decline and Fall of the Roman Empire, ch. 51, http://oll.libertyfund.org/Home3/HTML.php?recordID=0214.09.

88. *See* Stewart, The Missionary Enterprise, at 218; *Decree of Caliph al-Mutawakkil* (850 CE), *in* The Dhimmi, at 185–86; Bat Ye'or, The Decline of the Eastern Christianity under Islam: From Jihad to Dhimmitude 116 (London: Associated Univ. Presses, 1996)

89. *See* Rassam, Christianity in Iraq, at 67–9, 72, 74–5, 88–90 (mentioning Hira, Seleucia-Ctesiphon, and Tikrit).

90. 3 Chronique de Michel le Syrien 22–23, 52–53 (Jean-Baptiste Chabot ed. & trans., Paris: Ernest Laroux, 1899–1905), *quoted in* Ye'or, The Decline of the Eastern Christianity under Islam, at 116.

91. *See* J.B. Segal, Edessa "The Blessed City" 196–97 (Piscataway, N.J.: Gorgias Press, 2005).

C. The Arab Conquests in Syria, Palestine, and Persia

The conquest of Syria, Palestine, and Persia will of necessity be treated more briefly in this study, the focus of which is Turkey, Iraq, and Sudan. Although some Arab tribes had settled in Syria and the Syrian-Mesopotamian border area prior to the conquest by forces from the Arabian Peninsula, it required a full-scale invasion and the death in combat of 50,000 Byzantine troops—Syrian, Greek, and Roman—to conquer Syria. The Arab armies, which had prevailed against the legendary Sassanian or New Persian Empire, killed two Byzantine governors and broke through the lines of the Byzantine army.[92] A portion of the Arab army moved on to Damascus and after a six-month siege the city fell. The Church of St. John the Baptist was turned into the Great Mosque of Damascus.[93] The Church of St, Mary, the next most important site in Damascus and second only to the Holy Sepulcher, was razed in 1260.[94]

Following the loss of Syria to the Arab forces, churches and monasteries in the region were sacked, towns and farms ruined, and "villages burned down by the nomads who were overrunning the country."[95] In Aleppo and Antioch, large numbers were massacred, and the Arab conquerors plundered and enriched themselves by seizing Byzantine property and wealth.[96] In the Arab civil wars nearly two centuries later, Syria suffered further massacres and famine conditions.[97] As in Persia, Syrian lands were counted as part of the "riches, lands, and people Allah has given us." Syrians and Mesopotamians would pay a head-tax [*jiyza*] to finance Arab rule.[98] Some of the methods used to extract taxes in the early years after the conquest are set forth in a decree by the caliph Omar announcing reforms some time after the conquest: do not beat taxpayers, torture them in other ways, burn them under the sun, or jail them to extract funds.[99] The tax, at least in Arabia, could amount to half the agricultural produce of a village.[100]

The countryside in Palestine was plundered, while cities were spared. In the defense of the Gaza region, 4,000 resisters were massacred.[101] Women and children were enslaved.[102] The expression of Jewish or Christian opposition to Islam became punishable by death.[103] A decree of the caliph Mutawakkil destroyed all the Jewish synagogues built

92. *See* Hitti, History of the Arabs, at 152; David Nicolle, Yarmuk, 636 AD 43–60 (Oxford and New York: Osprey Publishing, 1994).

93. *See* John Turnbull. *Mosques, in* Medieval Islamic Civilization 520 (Josef W. Meri ed., London: Taylor & Francis, 2006).

94. *See* David Samuel Margoliouth, Cairo, Jerusalem, and Damascus: Three Chief Cities of the Egyptian Sultans 234 (New York: Dodd, Mead and Co., 1907).

95. Ye'or, The Decline of the Eastern Christianity, at 44.

96. *See id.* at 47.

97. *See* Ye'or, The Decline of the Eastern Christianity, at 116–17.

98. Umar Ibn al-Khattab, *quoted in* Abu Yusuf *and in* Ye'or, The Decline of Eastern Christianity, at 273.

99. *See* Umar Ibn al-Khattab, *quoted in* The Dhimmi, at 168.

100. *See* Sir William Muir, Annals of the Early Caliphate: From Original Sources 224 (London: Smith, Elder & Co., 1883).

101. *See* Ye'or, The Decline of the Eastern Christianity, at 44.

102. *See id.* at 47.

103. *See* Ye'or, The Dhimmi, at 56.

in the more than two centuries after the Arab conquest of Palestine.[104] The context of the decree was incipient or revived insurgencies by Africans, Armenians, and Greeks.[105]

In Persia, the native Zoroastrian culture was targeted for intentional destruction by the Arab armies. Only two of the 21 sub-parts of the main Zoroastrian scriptures, the Avesta, survived. "Civil disturbances, religious persecutions, and the burning of many Zoroastrian scriptures and books by the conquering Muslim Arabs forced the followers of Zoroaster to either abandon their faith or go into exile." Many fled to present-day India and Pakistan.[106] Massive libraries of philosophical and religious learning were "scattered."[107] During the siege of the fortress at Ctesiphon, which held off a Roman army of 100,000 in 363 CE, "famine, sickness, and death gripped the city."[108] Multitudes of Zoroastrians were brought to Mesopotamia as slaves.[109]

D. The Arab and Turkish Conquests in Africa

In Africa, witnesses and second-hand accounts reported crimes against indigenous Africans, pagan and Christian alike, occurring on a vast scale across hundreds of miles. Arab armies conquered eastern North Africa in the seventh century CE, soon after the fall of Persian Assyria and Babylonia. The conquest of Iran, Central Asia, and Spain created one of the largest empires in history. The Byzantine Empire continued to hold out near Constantinople.[110]

The Arab forces entered Egypt a few years after conquering Syria. Entire populations were massacred along the way, until the frightened survivors agreed to feed and house the raiders. The Coptic-speaking ("Copt" being an English corruption of "Egypt") natives, as with the natives of Mesopotamia, were often "reduced to slavery or bond service." Muslims remained an elite minority for some centuries, as in Syria and Mesopotamia. Copts rebelled against oppressive taxation in the eighth and ninth centuries CE, and were massacred in response. In the ninth century, "multitude[s]" of Coptic monks had been massacred, and many nuns raped or enslaved. Coptic fortress-cities were burned and their properties were plundered.[111]

Sudan lies at the crossroads between the states of north Africa that identify themselves as Arab in ethnicity and orientation, and the majority Christian indigenous African states of sub-Saharan Africa.[112] Since the time of ancient Egypt, the territory comprising present-day Sudan has been described as the "land of the blacks" or the "black land," which

---

104. *See* Muhammad ibn Jarir al-Tabari, Ta'rikh al-Rusul wa'l Muluk [History of the Prophets and Kings] (circa 915 CE), *quoted in* Ye'or, The Dhimmi, at 186.

105. *See* Sir William Muir, The Caliphate: Its Rise, Decline and Fall, from Original Sources 522–26 (London: The Religious Tract Soc., 2d ed. 1892).

106. Solomon Alexander Nigosian, The Zoroastrian Faith: Tradition and Modern Research 47–8 (Montreal: McGill-Queen's UP, 1993).

107. Sandra Mackey, The Reckoning: Iraq and the Legacy of Saddam Hussein 46–47 (New York: W.W. Norton, 2003).

108. *See* Jamsheed Kairshasp Choksy, Conflict and Cooperation: Zoroastrian Subalterns and Muslim Elites 15 (New York: Columbia UP, 1997).

109. Morony, Iraq After the Muslim Conquest, at 305.

110. *See* Lapidus, A History of Islamic Societies, at 31–37.

111. *See* Ye'or, The Decline of the Eastern Christianity, at 59–60, 63, 78, 105.

112. *See Sudan, in* Encyclopedia Africana, at 1793.

is the meaning of the term "Sudan" in Arabic and the approximate meaning of the more ancient terms "Nubia" or "Kush." The people of Nubia converted to Coptic Christianity beginning about 500 CE. In the twelfth century CE, an Arab army reported invaded Nubia from Yemen, and enslaved 70,000 Nubians. An Egyptian army later attacked Nubian churches. When Makuria, a powerful Nubian kingdom, fell to Arab armies from Egypt, the Makuria agreed to deliver an annual tribute of 360 Nubian slaves to the Arab governor of Egypt. Despite the agreement, Arabs continued to raid Nubia periodically for slaves, cattle, gold, and various other mineral resources. By 1500 CE, Arabs had thoroughly conquered Nubia.[113]

By the early nineteenth century, armies of Arabs and Turks had reached central Sudan and were frequently raiding southern Sudan for as many as 1,800 slaves per year.[114] The Arab trade in African slaves "across the Indian Ocean to the Arabian Peninsula, the Persian Gulf, and Asia" lasted nearly 1,000 years and affected up to ten million Africans, depopulating large portions of Africa.[115] The resulting devastation of Sudan by Turkish and Arab armies was vast:

> Under the new government established in 1821, which was known as the Turkiyah or Turkish regime, soldiers lived off the land and exacted exorbitant taxes from the population.... Furthermore, slave trading increased, causing many of the inhabitants of the fertile Al Jazirah, heartland of Funj, to flee to escape the slave traders. Within a year of the [Turkish] pasha's victory, 30,000 Sudanese slaves went to Egypt for training and induction into the army. However, so many perished from disease and the unfamiliar climate that the remaining slaves could be used only in garrisons in Sudan.[116]

Both Nubia and Darfur were depopulated under Arab and Turkish rule by the slave trade to Egypt and the wider Islamic world:

> According to Islamic jurists, ... slaves could not be taken from Dar al-Islam, or, the Land of Islam, but only from the Dar al-Harb, the Land of War. It became commonly accepted that this land of war was all non-Islamic lands, where indiscriminate raiding could occur, under the assumption that these were jihads, or holy wars.... For centuries in the Middle East and North Africa, peoples defeated in battle had to send slaves as a tribute or payment to the victors.... [African] slaves were often sold to work in Arabia, the lands of the Persian Gulf, or later, Turkey and other parts of the Middle East.... [117]

The Arab invaders exported large numbers of indigenous Africans to Egypt and other regions as tribute:

> The jihad slave system included contingents of both sexes delivered annually in conformity with the treaties of submission by sovereigns who were tributaries of the caliph.... From 652 until its conquest in 1276, Nubia was forced to send an annual contingent of slaves to Cairo.... [118]

---

113. *See Nubia, in* ENCYCLOPEDIA AFRICANA, at 1447; *Nubia, in* 11 THE CATHOLIC ENCYCLOPEDIA (1911), http://www.newadvent.org/cathen/11147a.htm.

114. *See Sudan, in* ENCYCLOPEDIA AFRICANA, at 1795.

115. *Indian Ocean Slave Trade, in* ENCYCLOPEDIA AFRICANA, at 995.

116. Thomas Ofcansky, *Historical Setting, in* A COUNTRY STUDY: SUDAN (Washington, DC: Library of Congress, 1991), http://lcweb2.loc.gov/cgi-bin/query/r?frd/cstdy:@field(DOCID+sd0023).

117. *Middle East, in* ENCYCLOPEDIA AFRICANA, at 1300.

118. YE'OR, THE DECLINE OF EASTERN CHRISTIANITY, at 108.

Slavery and the large-scale depopulation of indigenous African regions of Sudan, including Nubia and Darfur, continued well into the nineteenth century:

> In the firman of 13 February 1841, the Sultan Abdul Mejid ratified the governorship of the African provinces of Darfur, Nubia, [etc.] to his vassal Muhammad Ali, and added:
>
> "The raids that the troops are accustomed to make from time to time on villages in the above-mentioned countries and as a consequence of which robust young men, taken as slaves, remain in the hands of the soldiers as payment of their wages, necessarily bring about the ruin and depopulation of these lands and are contrary to Our Holy Law...."[119]
>
> The African tribes in the provinces of Bahr al-Ghazal were obliged to deliver to the Muslim sultans of Darfur a regular tribute of slaves and ivory.... In the 1870s, Rahama Zubeir Pasha, a notorious slave trader, considered "that Blacks who had no masters and were heathens, were, in accordance with the law of the Prophet, the fair spoil of the Muslims."[120]

In the late nineteenth century, the governor of Darfur described a trade in slaves from Darfur and southern Sudan that reached genocidal proportions:

> A few years ago quantities of slaves were sent ... from Darfur and the Nuba mountains by Osman Wad Adam, and were generally sold by public auction for the benefit of ... the Khalifa's private treasury.... The transport of slaves is carried on with the same execrable and heartless cruelty which characterises their capture....
>
> [T]he slaves who had the misfortune to be sent from Darfur along the broad stretches of waterless desert which lie between that province and Omdurman. These miserable creatures were mercilessly driven forward day and night; and it would be impossible for me to describe the execrable measures adopted by these brutal slave-drivers to force their prey on to their destination. When the poor wretches could go no further, their ears were cut off as a proof to the owner that his property had died on the road....
>
> Latterly, no large caravans of slaves have arrived in Omdurman, because the majority of the slave-producing districts, such as Darfur, have become depopulated, or, in some cases, the tribes, such as the Tama, Masalit, etc., have thrown off allegiance to the Khalifa.[121]

Under Ottoman-Egyptian rule in the nineteenth century, primarily Arab slave traders seized and sold more than 400,000 Sudanese in the fifteen years after 1860 alone.[122] Eu-

---

119. *Id.* at 113.

120. *Id.* at 261. "Middle Eastern countries [only] abolished slavery when they entered the League of Nations in the 1920s." *Trans-Saharan and Red Sea Slave Trade, in* ENCYCLOPEDIA AFRICANA 1879.

121. Rudolf C. Slatin, Jihad *and Slavery in Nineteenth-Century Sudan, quoted in* YE'OR, THE DECLINE OF THE EASTERN CHRISTIANITY, at 433–35. The author of this report was an Austrian subject who lived in Sudan from 1879 to 1895, was elevated to important positions in Sudan as a colonel in the Egyptian army, and became governor of Darfur. *See id.* at 471. The Khalifa to which he refers were a series of rulers who rose to power in the "jihad state" of the so-called "Mahdi" or "guide." Ofcansky, *Historical Setting*. The state founded by the Mahdi and run by the Khalifas was "run like a military camp." *Id.*

122. *See* ROBERT WILKINSON-LATHAM, THE SUDAN CAMPAIGNS, 1881–1898, at 10–11 (1976).

ropean powers, and particularly the British, eventually secured a Turkish-Egyptian agreement to abolish the trade in indigenous African slaves.[123]

E. The Turkish and Turko-Mongol Conquests in Asia

The forbears of the Armenians may have populated the Caucasus region between Mesopotamia and Russia since 1,000 BCE,[124] but the first specific references to "Arminia" and Armenians are in Persian and Greek texts from about 500 BCE.[125] Armenia formed one of the oldest Christian countries, transitioning from paganism to Christianity under Assyrian influence starting in the 300s CE.[126] In Mesopotamia, the Urartrian predecessors of the Armenians coexisted and contended with their Assyrian and later their Persian neighbors for hundreds of years before the Arab conquest.[127] Although some Armenians no doubt remained in Ottoman Mosul and independent Iraq from the time of the Assyrian and Persian empires, many were deported to Iraq, or fled there as refugees to the country during and after World War I.[128]

Although the Armenians inhabited eastern Anatolia from a very early period, the Byzantine emperors deported (or resettled) Armenian lords and their subjects to either Assyria or Cappadocia, south of the Black Sea.[129] This weakened eastern Anatolia, leaving it indefensible from the east. In the seventh century CE, the Arab armies moved on from Syria into Armenia, "shedding rivers of blood," massacring entire urban populations, and enslaving up to 35,000 persons, including many women and children. An Armenian chronicle stated that after conquering Assyria, the Arabs entered the plains of Ararat, and besieged the Armenian city of Dvin. When the city fell the "enemy's army rushed in and butchered the inhabitants of the town by the sword."[130]

---

123. *See Sudan, in* CIA, World Factbook (1990), http://www.gutenberg.org/dirs/etext91/world12.txt; *Middle East, in* Encyclopedia Africana, at 1300.

124. *See* Adam Jones, Genocide: A Comprehensive Introduction 102 (London: Routledge, 2006).

125. Unrepresented Nations and Peoples Organization: Yearbook 1997, at 132 (J. Mullen ed., Boston: Martinus Nijhoff Publishers 1996).

126. *See* Nina Garsoian, *The Aršakuni Dynasty, in* 1 The Armenian People, at 80–83; C.L. Sulzberger, *The People God Forgot*, N.Y. Times, Nov. 29, 1970.

127. *See* George A. Bournoutiam, A Concise History of the Armenian People (From Ancient Times to the Present) 5–41, 69–77 (5th ed. 2006); James Russell, *The Formation of the Armenian Nation, in* 1 The Armenian People, at 20–35; Nina Garsoian, *The Emergence of Armenia, in* 1 The Armenian People, at 37–44.

128. *See Christians, in* Historical Dictionary of Iraq 57–58 (Edmund Ghareeb & Beth Dougherty eds., Lanham, MD: The Scarecrow Press, 2004) (noting that most Armenians fled to Mesopotamia from Anatolia as a result of Ottoman persecution); Sarah D. Shields, Mosul Before Iraq: Like Bees Making Five-sided Cells 54–55 (Albany: State Univ. of New York Press, 2000) (noting Armenian presence in 1830s Iraq). A nineteenth-century traveler to the Mosul region found Armenians living among Assyrians, Jews, and Kurds. *See* H.C. Luke, Mosul and Its Minorities 14 (Piscataway, NJ: Gorgias Press, 2004) (1925). About 12,000 Armenians resided in Baghdad alone at the outset of the 2003 war. *See* Rassam, Christianity in Iraq, at 180.

129. *See* Robert Bedrosian, *Armenia During the Seljuk and Mongol Periods, in* 1 The Armenian People, at 196, 242–43.

130. Ye'or, the Decline of Eastern Christianity, at 47, 274–75.

Arab, Turkic, and Kurdish populations settled the Greek, Assyrian, Jewish, and polytheistic (some later become Yezidi) areas of Anatolia starting in the seventh century CE. Starting in the eleventh century CE, the Seljuk Turks attacked the Eastern Roman Empire (Byzantine Empire) and set about displacing its indigenous Greek and Armenian populations with Turks.[131] Over the next three centuries Smyrna, in predominantly Greek western Anatolia, was destroyed three times: first by Seljuk Turks, then by Persians, then by the Turkic-speaking Mongols under Timur Leng.[132] The Seljuks destroyed the large commercial city of Arzen or Artze, to the east of Erzerum, wiping out a metropolis, once boasting 800 churches, to the extent that its ruins could not even be found.[133] The fire at Arzen was one of the largest in history, with 140,000 people burned alive or massacred.[134] Up to 100,000 slaves, including many women and children, were carted off from Arzen and choked the slave-markets of Asia.[135] As one author argues:

> The reign of the Byzantine emperor Constantine IX Monomachus ... proved a disastrous turning point, since it was in his time that the Seljuk Turks launched their first massive ghazwa or raid into Byzantine Armenia (1048) and the Byzantine frontier in the East was forever breached. The raid—led by Ibrahim Inal, uterine brother of the sultan Toghrul Beg—was marked by the horrific sack of Arzen or Artze, a huge commercial center near the modern Erzerum.... In all places through which he passed, Ibrahim Inal left behind a tableau of stupendous devastation. The Arab chronicler Ibn al-Athir notes that Ibrahim brought back from Byzantine territory 100,000 captives and a vast booty loaded on the backs of ten thousand camels.[136]

In the next two centuries, Turkic tribes from Central Asia began to displace the inhabitants of eastern Anatolia. The words "Turk" and "Turkic" initially referred to ethnic groups having an origin in Central Asia, especially to the northeast of Persia and in the region of the Oxus River in Central Asia.[137] "Turkia" was a sixth century CE term for Central Asia, and "Turkestan" was a related term in Arab and Persian ninth and tenth century CE sources.[138] The nomadic Turkic tribes, previously without much written civilization or traditions, converted to Islam and invaded Balkh, Persia, Mesopotamia, Armenia, and Anatolia. The tribes divided Anatolia into zones for raiding and "appropriated the soil"

---

131. Richard Clogg, A Short History of Modern Greece 2 (Cambridge: Cambridge UP, 1979); Bedrosian, *Armenia During the Seljuk and Mongol Periods,* at 241–51; The Cambridge History of Islam, 231–35 (Ann K.S. Lambton, Peter Malcolm Holt, & Bernard Lewis eds., Cambridge: Cambridge UP, 1978).

132. *See* Dobkin, Smyrna 1922, at 22.

133. Jerome Van Crowninshield Smith, Turkey and the Turks: Or Travels in Turkey 229 (Boston: F. Gleason's Publishing Hall, 1852).

134. *See Arzen, in* A Dictionary of Greek and Roman Geography 229 (William Smith ed., London: John Murray, 1873).

135. *See, e.g.,* Ludwig Beck, Die Geschichte des Eisens in Technischer und Kulturgeschichtlicher 229 (Braunschweig: Verlag von Friedrich Vieweg & Sohn, 1891); George H. Filian, Armenia and Her People: Or, The Story of Armenia by an Armenian 123 (Hartford, Connecticut: American Publ'g Co., 1896); George Finlay, 2 A History of Greece: The Byzantine Empire, pt. 1, a.d. 716–1057, at 441–44 (Henry Fanshawe Tozer ed., Oxford: The Clarendon Press, 1877).

136. Paul A. Blaum, *Diplomacy Gone to Seed: A History of Byzantine Foreign Relations, A.D. 1047–57,* Int'l J. of Kurdish Studies, Jan. 2004, http://209.85.229.132/ search?q=cache:sQyPXBPgvtUJ:findarticles.com/p/articles/mi_m0SBL/is_1-2_18/ai_n13826854/.

137. *See, e.g.,* Richard N. Frye & Aydin M. Sayili, *Turks in the Middle East before the Saljuqs,* 63 J. Am. Oriental Soc. 194, 194–207 (1943).

138. Tuner Baykara, *The Early Times of the Turks, in* 1 The Turks: Early Ages 47–48 (Hasan Celâl Güzel ed., Ankara: Yeni Türkiye, 2002).

from the inhabitants of Byzantine Anatolia.[139] A Seljuk Turkish "land rush" into Anatolia followed the defeat of the Byzantines in Armenia, near Lake Van.[140] Large armies of Seljuk Turks invaded from the east and southeast and sacked Vaspurakan, Sivas or Sebastia, and other cities; nevertheless, some anti-Byzantine Armenians joined the Turkish side.[141] An Armenian chronicle recorded the results: "Our cities were devastated, our houses and palaces burned, our royal halls were reduced to ruins."[142]

About 1,000 years ago, Turks and Kurds began invading Mesopotamia from Central Asia through Persia.[143] The progressive destruction of Assyrian culture and religion in Mesopotamia was one result. One scholar's account bears quotation at some length:

> Speaking of the events of [1083 CE], Ibn Khalikan stated that during the reign of Malik Shahi Ibn Arsilan, the Seljukid Amir Artaq Ibn Aksab of Halwan marched to [mid or] Diarbekir at the head of an army comprising both Turkomans and Kurds. The city surrendered to the attackers after a fierce assault and a long siege....
>
> [T]he Kurds were living in Persian Azerbaijan, and when they joined in the invasion of Mesopotamia, they destroyed whatever they encountered, whether plants or buildings....

---

139. GROUSSET, EMPIRE OF THE STEPPES, at 150–55; *see also* 3 THE GREAT OTTOMAN-TURKISH CIVILISATION 3–5 (Kemal Çiçek ed., Ankara: Yeni Türkiye, 2000).

140. RUDI PAUL LINDNER, NOMADS AND OTTOMANS IN MEDIEVAL ANATOLIA 10–11 (1997).

141. *See* Bedrosian, *Armenia During the Seljuk and Mongol Periods*, at 244–46.

142. G.M. MANUKIAN, ARISTAKES LASTIVERTSI, MATENAGRUTYAN BANASIRAKAN KNNUTYUN (Gurgen Musheghi Manukyan ed., Yerevan, 1977) (Armenian), *quoted in* ANTRANIG CHALABIAN, ARMENIA: EMPERORS, TZARS AND COMMISSARS 114 (Michigan, n.p, 1988).

143. *See* UNREPRESENTED NATIONS AND PEOPLES ORGANIZATION: YEARBOOK 1997, at 92 (J. Mullen ed., Boston: Martinus Nijhoff Publishers, 1998) (Turks in Iraq are "originally from central Asia" and "began settling in the northern and middle regions of Iraq over a thousand years ago"); HAKAN ÖZOĞLU, KURDISH NOTABLES AND THE OTTOMAN STATE 25 (Albany: State Univ. of New York Press, 2004) (some scholars cite linguistic evidence that shows the "Kurds are one of the original Turkic clans of Central Asia"; although other scholars attempt to connect the Kurds to the ancient Medes, there is an absence of linguistic or cultural evidence for that theory, and a gap of many centuries between last mention of Medes and first mention of Kurds); OFRA BENGIO, SADDAM'S WORD: POLITICAL DISCOURSE IN IRAQ 116 (Oxford: Oxford UP, 2002) (term "Kurdistan" was first used by Seljuk Turks for part of eastern Persia); JACK DAVID ELLER, FROM CULTURE TO ETHNICITY TO CONFLICT: AN ANTHROPOLOGICAL PERSPECTIVE ON INTERNATIONAL ETHNIC CONFLICT 154 (Ann Arbor, MI: Univ. of Michigan Press, 2d ed., 1999) (Seljuk Turks "Turkified" some Kurdish tribes that lived in Persia, while some Turkish tribes became "Kurdified").

Various groups present in ancient Anatolia and Mesopotamia in ancient times, from which contemporary Turks and Kurds sometimes claim ancestry, actually had no written language or very little written literature, unlike the Sumero-Akkadians and Assyro-Babylonians, and therefore cannot be connected by means of linguistic or religious influences to present-day Turks or Kurds, the latter of whom have very little written record of their own. These peoples include the Guti, Kassite, Kurti, Khaldi, Qurtie, Manna (Mannaeans), Mards, Medes, and Mushku. *See* GEORGE RAWLINSON, 2 THE FIVE GREAT MONARCHIES OF THE ANCIENT EASTERN WORLD 73 (2004) (1881) ("the Medes have left us no written monuments"); H.M. Burton, *The Kurds*, 31 J. OF THE ROYAL CENTRAL ASIAN SOC. 64, 67 (1943) (Kurds have very little written record of their history); MORTIMER CHAMBERS ET AL., THE WESTERN EXPERIENCE 26 (New York: McGraw-Hill, 1995) (no written documents from Medes have been found); Shahrzad Mojab, *Kurdish Women, in* ENCYCLOPEDIA OF WOMEN & ISLAMIC CULTURES: FAMILY, LAW, AND POLITICS 358 (Leiden, the Netherlands and Boston: Brill, 2003) ("first history of the Kurds" dates to late sixteenth century CE; YONA SABAR, THE FOLK LITERATURE OF THE KURDISTANI JEWS xvi (New Haven: Yale UP, 1982) ("very few" mentions in Babylonian Talmud, written centuries or millennia after time of Medes, to territory sometimes referred to today as "Kurdistan," and apparently no references at all to Kurds).

> Thus, during the Seljuk invasion, the Kurds received land for their services as an inducement to secure their support and loyalty to the Seljuks. Sinjur, the Seljuk sultan, divided the western part of the mountain district, particularly the region called Kirmanshah in Persia; gave it the name of Kurdistan; and assigned it to his nephew, Sulaiman Shah....
>
> Mosul, which was historically a major Christian centre in Mesopotamia, was repeatedly sacked. Ibn Khaldun referred to its tragic fate after the Kurdish attacks, stating that "the Kurds spoiled and spread horror everywhere." Dr. Faisal al Samir also mentioned the severe attack that the city suffered, stating that people were killed and pillaged everywhere, and the only ones who managed to escape disaster were those who accepted Islam....
>
> The famed Salah al Din, known in the West as Saladin, is a clear example, in that, ... in [1185 CE], Salah al Din first unsuccessfully attacked Mosul, then turned his army to attack Miyafarqin to the north of Diarbekir (a region largely inhabited by the followers of the Church of the East and the Jacobites), but then returned once again to Mosul and put it under siege. Many contemporary Arab historians tell us that he led wars and raids throughout northern Mesopotamia, attacking, looting, and enslaving the native inhabitants. Among his targets were the famous city of Urhai (Urfa), the capital of the ancient kingdom of the same name (Edessa), and other major centres in northern Mesopotamia.[144]

In the twelfth century, the Patriarch of Antioch, Michel the Syrian, recorded that the "Turks entered with their swords and blades drawn, drinking the blood of the old and the young, the men and the women, the priests and the deacons, the hermits and the monks, the nuns, the virgins, the infants at the breast, the betrothed men and the women to whom they were betrothed!" In Edessa in 1146 CE, the "air was poisoned with the stench of corpses; Assyria was filled with captives." In 1148 CE, an army of Turks attacked Assyria, burning houses and attempting to enslave the population. An Assyrian (Syrian) chronicle recorded: "From the year 1496 [1185–86] the devastation carried out by the Turkoman people began, and for eight years they massacred and were massacred in Armenia, Assyria, Mesopotamia, Syria and Cappadocia." Turkish forces murdered many Assyrians and even Kurds, getting "carried away by the enthusiasm of pillage and slaughter." In southeastern Anatolia, many villages were "depopulated," and 26,000 Armenian men enslaved.[145] In the thirteenth century CE, an army of Kurds entered the countryside surrounding Nineveh and Mosul, and "made a great slaughter among the Christians." Kutlu Bag, the Amir of Arbil, killed the "natives of Nineveh, ... men and women alike."[146]

---

144. Aboona, Assyrians, Kurds, and Ottomans, at 94–96 (footnotes omitted) (citing Al Rahawi Al Majhul, Tarikh al Rahawi al Majhul 39 (Albert Abouna trans. into Arabic, Baghdad: n.p., 1986)); *see also* S.H. Longrigg & F. Stokes, Iraq 63 (London: Ernest Benn, 1958); Basil Nikitine, Les Kurdes. Étude Sociologique et Historique (Paris: Editions d'Audjourd'hui, 1956); 3 Abdul Rahman Ibn Khaldun, Tarikh Dewan al EbarwaDewan al Mubtadawa al Khabar 500–501 (Beirut, n.d.); 4 Ibn Khaldun, Tarikh, at 259.

145. 3 Chronique du Michel le Syrian 261–62, 270–71, 400–402, *quoted in* Ye'or, The Decline of Eastern Christianity, at 342–44, *and in* Andrew Bostom, The Legacy of *Jihad* 610–11 (Andrew Bostom ed., Amherst, NY: Prometheus Books, 2008). *See also* 11 Archaeology 151 (1958) ("In 1146 the churches were sacked and the population enslaved by Moslem troops: this marked the end of the glories of the city of Abgar [i.e. Edessa].").

146. 1 Bar Hebraeus, The Chronography of Gregory Abul-Faraj 1225–1286 ... [A] Political History of the World 441 (E.A.T. Wallis Budge ed. & trans., Amsterdam: APA-Philo, 1976) (ca. 1286 CE), *quoted in* Ye'or, The Decline of Eastern Christianity, at 346–47.

After 1200 CE, Genghis Khan led a campaign through Asia that destroyed millions of lives and many ancient cities. In Beijing in 1219, the Mongols slaughtered thousands of people and set the city ablaze, causing it to burn for a month.[147] The ambassador to Beijing from Khwarezm described epidemics spread by the mounds of corpses, stating that "the bones of the slaughtered formed mountains, that the soil was greasy with human fat." In present-day Konye-Urgench in Turkmenistan, then called Gurganj, a contingent from Genghis Khan's army, with 100,000 Mongols in all, killed over a million people, in house-to-house fighting that burned large sections of the city and prompted the Mongols to attempt to divert the local river to drown the inhabitants. Only 100,000 artisans were spared and taken away, while the other people living in Urgench in 1221 were killed, each Mongol fighter handling a couple of dozen of them.[148]

The Mongols attacked Old Merv, a city of 700,000, thereby violating a peace pact with the city's ruler. Without encountering much resistance, the Mongols gathered the population of the city into caravans, led them outside the city, and killed all but a few hundred artisans and children. Each fighter dispatched a few hundred people, so that everyone, including the women and children, fell victims to the Mongol assault. The city itself was looted, with architecture torn down and books "burned or buried." A contemporaneous estimate had 1.3 million killed.[149]

Genghis invaded Turkestan in 1218 CE, and used Turkish and Kurdish forces acquired in Central Asia to assemble a huge Turko-Mongol army invade present-day Afghanistan, Iran, Iraq, and Azerbaijan.[150] The armies organized by Genghis Khan massacred the residents of Balkh, Bukhara, Uranj, Khorasan, Nessa, Nishapur, Sabzawar, Herat, Bamiyan, Qom, Rei, Sava, Kashan, Hamadan, Seistan, Ghazni, Soldaia, Kazvin, and Maragheh (Azerbaijan). Most or all of the houses and sacred buildings in these cities were burned down. Not only the men but the children and even the animals were cut down. Genghis was a nomad who hated and mistrusted cities and wanted them cleared as buffer zones around his empire, from Iran in the southwest to northern China and Manchuria in the northeast.[151] "He made terror a system of government and massacre a deliberate and methodical institution." He famously declared the highest form of happiness to be "'to cut my enemies to pieces, drive them before me, seize their possessions, witness the tears of those dear to them, and embrace their wives and daughters!'"[152] In the *History of the World Conqueror*, the author, a contemporary of the Mongols, estimated that the population of Asia had declined by 90% due to Genghis.[153]

The century after the death of Genghis Khan in 1227 CE saw further massacres in Mesopotamia and Persia. In the mid-1200s, Genghis' grandson Hulagu Khan organized a campaign for, as a later historian described it, "the massing of troops for Holy War and uprooting the castles of heresy." He reached Baghdad in the 1250s and massacred 100,000

147. *See* John Man, Genghis Khan: Life, Death, and Resurrection 142 (New York: St. Martin's Press, 2007).

148. *See id.* at 142, 173, 177.

149. *See id.* at 173, 177.

150. *See* Leo de Hartog, Genghis Khan: Conqueror of the World 116–56 (New York: St. Martin's, 1989); Percy M. Sykes, A History of Persia 149–62 (London: Macmillan & Co., 1915); Akbar Shah Najeebabadi, 2 History of Islam 579–80 (London: Darussalam, 2000).

151. See Hartog, Genghis Khan, at 116–56; Sykes, A History of Persia, at 149–60; Grousset, Empire of the Steppes, at 167–68, 240–41, 243–45, 249, 431.

152. Grousset, Empire of the Steppes, at 248–49.

153. *See* 'Ala-ad-Din 'Ata-Malik Juvaynī, The History of the World Conqueror (John A. Boyle trans., Cambridge, MA: Harvard UP, 1958), *quoted in* Sykes, A History of Persia, at 160.

to two million people there, seizing enormous amounts of gold and treasure, destroying libraries, and soiling and ruining mosques. Mesopotamia's irrigation system was severely damaged, leaving a legacy of dependency on imported food that would have catastrophic consequences during U.N. sanctions in the 1990s.[154] In the late 1200s, the Mongols conquered northwestern Persia and "destroyed all the churches" there, and sent out messengers "to every country and town to destroy the churches and to loot the monasteries."[155] Under Ghazan Khan, the reputed great-great-great grandson of Genghis, the Mongols in the early 1300s conducted massacres and mass enslavements in Arbil, Āmid (modern Diyarbekir), and other Assyrian cities.[156]

From 1393 to 1405 CE, Turko-Mongol invaders under Timur Leng (Tamerlane) destroyed large portions of the Assyrian (Nestorian and Jacobite Christian) population centers of Nineveh, Mosul, Arbil, Tur Adbin, Mardin, and Āmid.[157] The armies of Timur, who also claimed descent from Genghis Khan, destroyed Baghdad, Bursa, Sarai, Kara Shahr, Zranj, and Delhi, and engaged in enormous massacres, piling up human heads into pyramids, at Isfahan, Sivas, Erzerum, Smyrna, Karabakh, Seistan, and Sebzewar. All buildings in Baghdad except mosques were razed. Nearly 200,000 died in Baghdad and Isfahan alone.[158] In Armenian Van, crowds of Armenians were flung from cliffs into the depths below. Armenians, Syrians, Georgians and others were deported as slaves back to Central Asia.[159] In Georgia, 700 towns and villages were sacked, with countless churches and monasteries destroyed.[160]

The Assyrians were "almost annihilated" under Timur, a small remnant fleeing to the mountains between present-day Iraq, Iran, and Turkey, and to the plains of Mosul in Iraq and of Urmia in Iran.[161] Timur himself reportedly boasted that "I have conquered most of the world and devastated thousands of towns and countries to beautify my cities...."[162] Thus, historic Assyria, a majority Christian land before the Mongol conquests, had a majority Muslim population by the early twentieth century.[163]

The armies of Timur turned their attention to Hindustan in the last years of the fourteenth century CE. An estimated 80,000 Indians perished in the siege and sack of Delhi, with pyramids again being constructed with their severed heads.[164] Timur's memoirs, the Tuzk-e-Taimuri, recorded large-scale massacres, enslavements, and urbicide (city-killing)

---

154. *See* Juvaynī, The History of the World Conqueror, *quoted in* David Nicolle, The Mongol Warlords 104, 109–11 (London: Brockhampton Press, 1990).

155. 1 Bar Hebraeus, The Chronography, at 506–8, *quoted in* Ye'or, The Decline of Eastern Christianity, at 357–59.

156. *See* Rassam, Christianity in Iraq, at 91.

157. *See* Ye'or, The Decline of Eastern Christianity, at 235; Grousset, Empire of the Steppes, at 420–52; Rassam, Christianity in Iraq, at 91–92.

158. *See* Grousset, Empire of the Steppes, at 420–52.

159. Nicolle, The Mongol Warlords, at 159–70.

160. *See* Justin Marozzi, Tamerlane 361 (New York: Da Capo Press, 2006).

161. *See* Arthur John Maclean, *Syrian Christians, in* 12 Encyclopedia of Religion and Ethics 176 (New York: Charles Scribner & Sons, 1922). *See also Nestorian, in* Encyclopædia Britannica (Chicago: Encyclopedia Britannica Online, 2009), http://www.britannica.com/EBchecked/topic/409819/Nestorians.

162. *Quoted in* Nicolle, The Mongol Warlords, at 159–70.

163. *See* Gerald Reitlinger, *Medieval Antiquities West of Mosul,* 5 Iraq 143, 147 (1938). Some parts of historic Assyria, such as areas within the Ottoman vilayets of Mosul and Diyarbekir, may have been majority Assyrian in 1914. *See* Gaunt, Massacres, Resistance, Protectors, at 406–35 (setting forth detailed statistical tables).

164. *See Timur, in* The Columbia Encyclopedia (New York, New York: Columbia UP, 6th ed. 2001), http://www.bartleby.com/65/ti/Timur.html.

on the road to Delhi, including Tulamba and Bhatnir in Punjab, present-day Pakistan. He stated that at the city of Tulamba his "hungry Tátárs, making a general assault upon [the people] like ants and locusts, plundered an enormous number of granaries, so numerous indeed as to be incalculable. . . ." The natives rebelled, so Timur ordered his generals to carry out the "extermination of these wretches," which they did by entering the jungle base of the rebels and slaughtering "two thousand of these ill fated Indians . . . , carrying off [as] captives their women and children," and much property. When the city of Bhatnir resisted Timur's armies, they besieged the city's fort, and "[i]n a short space of time all the people in the fort were put to the sword, and in the course of one hour the heads of ten thousand infidels were cut off." He added that the houses of the people were burned to the ground, and "all the goods and effects, the treasure and the grain which for many a long year had been stored in the fort became the spoil of my soldiers."[165]

Timur's memoirs relate that he ordered the massacre of 100,000 Hindus prior to the siege of Delhi, and even more civilians found inside Delhi. Timur argued that "no other course remained but that of making them all food for the sword." He gave the command that all "infidel" prisoners should be put to death. During the sack of the city of Delhi, Timur wrote that the Turks carried out the "slaughter of many of the infidel inhabitants," the Hindu men burning their wives and children in their houses and then rushing into battle. "On that day, Thursday, and all the night of Friday, nearly 15,000 Turks were engaged in slaying, plundering, and destroying." Each Turk claimed 50 to 100 captives, including children. The spoils included diamonds, rubies, pearls, gold and silver, and valuable silks. "Excepting the quarter of the *saiyids*, the *'ulamá*, and the other Musulmáns, the whole city was sacked. . . ."[166]

Outraged at reports of the persecution of Muslims in China, and guilty for his own murder of countless Muslims, in the closing years of the fourteenth century Timur set about balancing the scales of corpses of the infidel and the faithful.[167] He amassed an army of 200,000 to invade China, which no doubt would have resulted in further massacres and urbicide, as in Delhi.[168] Timur, it is noted, "might have utterly destroyed Chinese civilization and eroded Chinese society," but he died in 1405 before his plans could come to fruition.[169] Nevertheless, the toll of Mongol conquest and devastation in China may have amounted to 30 million dead, comparing the population prior to and after the Mongol invasions and related civil wars.[170]

Other Turkic conquests could be devastating to indigenous communities and productive of mass death in sieges, plunders, and confiscatory taxation. In the twelfth century CE, the Ghuri Turks invaded India prior to Timur's assault, destroyed many temples, and established crushing taxation, sometimes with the avowed purpose of depopulating

---

165. Timur Leng, *Malfúzát-i Tímúrí, or Túzak-i Tímúrí: The Autobiography or Memoirs of Emperor Tímúr (Taimur the lame), in* THE HISTORY OF INDIA, AS TOLD BY ITS OWN HISTORIANS. THE MUHAMMADAN PERIOD 389 (Henry Miers Elliot trans., John Dowson ed; London: Trubner Co., 1867–1877), http://persian.packhum.org/persian/main?url=pf%3Ffile%3D80201013%26ct%3D97.

166. *Id.*, http://persian.packhum.org/persian/main?url=pf%3Ffile%3D80201013%26ct%3D107 & http://persian.packhum.org/persian/main?url=pf%3Ffile%3D80201013%26ct%3D110; *see also* THE AUTOBIOGRAPHY OF TIMUR 44–61 (Henry Miers Elliot trans., John Dowson ed., Lahore: Sind Sagar Academy, 1974), *quoted in* GÉRARD CHALIAND, THE ART OF WAR IN WORLD HISTORY 488–90 (Berkeley, California: Univ. of California Press, 1994).

167. *See* MAROZZI, TAMERLANE, at 348–57.

168. *See* Hok-Lam Chan, *The Ming Dynasty, 1399–1435, in* THE CAMBRIDGE HISTORY OF CHINA 256–59 (Frederick W. Mote et al. eds., Cambridge: Cambridge UP, 1988).

169. GROUSSET, EMPIRE OF THE STEPPES, at 453.

170. *See* NICOLLE, THE MONGOL WARLORDS, at 48.

the Hindus and providing a pretext to torture them with blows and imprisonment. Hundreds of thousands of Hindus were reported killed, and tens of thousands of others enslaved. Prefiguring the scalp bounties of North America under the British and French, the fourteenth century Ghuri Sultan Firoz Shah offered a bounty for hundreds of severed Hindu heads.[171]

In an event that signified the reassertion by the indigenous peoples of Asia from Mongol-Turkic rule, in 1510 the Shah of Persia, claiming descent from the pre-Arabic rulers of the Persian Empire, defeated and killed the heir of Genghis Khan outside of Merv. Sedentary indigenous peoples were to strike further blows against the nomadic Turks and Mongols. A struggle ensued between the Ottoman Turks in the West, and the emerging Shi'a theocracy in Persia in the East. The Timurid ruler Baber lost to the Persians near Bukhara, establishing a Persian-Turkic border near the present-day western border of Uzbekistan.[172]

The Persian Shah Ismail I conquered Baghdad, Mosul, Āmid, and Harput in the early sixteenth century. He also took "Kurdistan," which had been created by Turks and Mongols who depopulated the Assyrians, and replaced them with Turkic peoples and Kurds, under Genghis, Ghazan, Timur, and the "Black Sheep" Turks.[173] During the 1508 invasion of Mosul, "several Christian villages of the Mosul plain were pillaged, including Alqosh, Telkepe and Tel Isqōf." Murad Bey (Bar Yak), a Turko-Mongol official, murdered many Assyrians, prompting them to take refuge in monasteries which were then plundered.[174] An Assyrian account recorded:

> Full of anger at his failure to take Mosul, Bar Yak made his way ... to the Dāsen district.... And after pillaging and burning all the villages of the region for three days, he returned to Bet Handawaya. From there he dispatched about 500 horsemen to pillage Alqōsh. The brave men of Alqōsh attacked the Mongols, routed them, and killed some of them. Bar Yak, angered by the defeat of his troops, ordered his men to go and destroy Alqōsh. It was a Sunday. The people of Alqōsh fled to a monastery, taking with them their ... animals. The infidels surrounded the monastery on all sides: 300 of them climbed to the summit of the mountain, from where they rolled down huge stones on the monastery, while the others fired arrows from below. They plundered the monastery, forced the women, seized the cattle and other animals, and carried off as captives a boy and two young girls.[175]

An Assyrian ode from Tur Abdin in the early sixteenth century stated that an Amir (presumably Ottoman or other Turko-Mongol in ethnicity) killed the civilians within the area, raped young girls, took away the survivors as captives, killed a bishop and monks in various churches and villages, looted a monastery, and stole "great quantities of gold, silver and other possessions."[176]

In response to the Safavid victories in "Kurdistan," the Ottoman Sultan Selim I settled large numbers of Kurds from Persia in traditionally Assyrian and Armenian areas.[177] In

---

171. *See* Will Durant, 1 The Story of Civilization 458–61 (New York: Simon & Schuster, 1935); Vincent Arthur Smith & Stephen Meredyth Edwardes, The Oxford History of India: From the Earliest Times to the End of 1911, at 247 (Oxford: The Clarendon Press, 2d ed., 1923).

172. *See* Guisset, Empire of the Steppes, at 483.

173. *See* Aboona, Assyrians, Kurds, and Ottomans, at 95–101.

174. David Wilmhurst, The Ecclesiastical Organisation of the Church of the East, 1318–1913, at 21, 135, 189, 223, 240–41, 259 (Louvain-la-Neuve: Peeters, 2000).

175. *Id.* at 241.

176. *See* Barsoum, The History of Tur Abdin, at 133.

177. Aboona, Assyrians, Kurds, and Ottomans, at 103.

the early seventeenth century, the Persians under Shah Abbas massacred or deported the Armenian and Assyrian Christians from dozens of cities and surrounding areas near the Ottoman-Persian border. Entire districts were "sacked and depopulated," survivors were pillaged, women and children were kidnapped, and many were tortured before death.[178] An eighteenth century Assyrian ode reported that in 1714, the Amir Bidayn "killed thousands" of Assyrians, "slaughtered priests and church officers and spilled the blood of the believers like rivers," encouraged the plundering of churches, and destroyed many churches.[179]

The Mongols and Ottomans further devastated northern Asia in the sixteenth century. The Crimean Tatars, Ottoman vassals with Turko-Mongol lineage, reached the outskirts of Moscow in 1521, and carried away up to 800,000 persons as slaves.[180] The Tatars attacked and burned down Moscow in 1571, killing 60,000 people and enslaving 100,000 Christians.[181] The Turko-Mongol slave trade involved the trafficking of 10,000 people per year, mostly Slavs, as few as 10 percent surviving the forced march to Crimea.[182] Only 30,000 out of a population of 200,000 living in Moscow prior to the burning of the city remained in the area afterwards.[183]

---

178. *See* Ye'or, The Decline of Eastern Christianity, at 362–75.

179. *See* Barsoum, The History of Tur Abdin, at 133. The affected areas included the villages of Aine, Bati, Ba Siqle, Karboran, Medon, and Zaz. *See id.*

180. *See* Alan W. Fisher, A Precarious Balance: Conflict, Trade, and Diplomacy on the Russian-Ottoman Frontier 32 (Istanbul: The ISIS Press, 1999); Alan Fisher, *Muscovy and the Black Sea Slave Trade*, 6 Canadian American Slavic Studies 580–82 (1972); Bernard Lewis, The Muslim Discovery of Europe 28 (New York: W.W. Norton & Co., 2001); Sergeĭ M. Soloviev, History of Russia 83 (Gulf Breeze, FL: Academic International Press, 1976); Peter Turchin, War and Peace and War: the Life Cycles of Imperial Nations 33 (Upper Saddle River, NJ: Pi Press, 2006).

181. *See* W.G. Clarence-Smith, Islam and the Abolition of Slavery 8 (Oxford: Oxford UP, 2006); Richard Hellie, *Migration in Early Modern Russia, in* Coerced and Free Migration: Global Perspectives 307–8 (David Eltis ed., Palo Alto, CA Stanford UP, 2002); Fisher, *Muscovy and the Black Sea Slave Trade*, at 580–82.

182. Hellie, *Migration in Early Modern Russia,* at 307–8.

183. *See* Peter A. Kropotkin, *Moscow, in* 18 Encyclopedia Britannica 894 (New York: Encyclopedia Britannica, 1911).

Chapter VI

"A Gigantic Plundering Scheme": The Genocide of the Ottoman Armenians

> The Germans are being blamed on every hand, for if they have not directly ordered this wholesale slaughter (for it is nothing less than the extermination of the Armenian race), they at least condone it....
>
> It is a gigantic plundering scheme as well as a final blow to extinguish the race....
>
> —Jesse Jackson, U.S. Consul in Aleppo, to U.S. Ambassador Henry Morgenthau[1]

In 1893, Frank Lenz set off from New York in what he hoped would be a bicycle tour around the world. He disappeared in May of 1895, having last been seen near Tabriz, Persia. It was later discovered that he had died during widespread massacres of the local population. An American medical missionary wrote to Lenz's family that he had been killed by Kurds during the anti-Armenian massacres. The U.S. minister to Turkey demanded that five Kurds identified as responsible by the British Consul at Erzerum be prosecuted for the crime, although other accounts had Turkish soldiers shooting down the bicyclist themselves.[2] The unfortunate Mr. Lenz had entered what scholars call a "zone of genocide,"[3] in this case the area between Tabriz and Erzerum from 1894 through 1896. This chapter explores how this zone was created in the late 1890s, and dramatically expanded during the First World War, in what became known as the Armenian genocide. Illiberal politics, indigenous peoples' liberation movements, the use of undisciplined militia in warfare, organized plunder, and great power rivalries all played a part.

---

1. USDOS, Record Group 59,867.4016/148, Aug. 19, 1915, U.S. Consul in Aleppo, Syria to U.S. Ambassador to the Ottoman Empire, *reprinted in* United States Official Documents on the Armenian Genocide (Ara Sarafian ed., Watertown, MA: Armenian Review, 1993), *and in* The Treatment of Armenians in the Ottoman Empire, 1915–1916, ch. XVI (Viscount James Bryce & Arnold Toynbee eds., London: His Majesty's Stationary Office, 1916), http://net.lib.byu.edu/~rdh7/wwi/1915/bryce/a15.htm.

2. *See To Get Justice in Turkey,* Chicago Daily Tribune, Sept. 4, 1895, at 8; *Lenz Was Murdered; Authentic News of the Death of the Missing Bicyclist Received,* N.Y. Times, June 21, 1895, at 3, http://query.nytimes.com/; *Wheelman Lenz Killed by Kurds,* Chicago Daily Tribune, Apr 22, 1895, at 1; *To Find Lenz,* Boston Daily Globe, Jan 8, 1895, at 1.

3. *See, e.g.,* Mark Levene, *Creating a modern 'zone of genocide': The Impact of Nation- and State-formation on Eastern Anatolia, 1878–1923,* 12.3 Holocaust and Genocide Studies 393 (1998); Shahrazad Mojab, *Kurdish Women in the 'Zone of Genocide,'* 103 Al Raida 20 (2003), http://www.utoronto.ca/wwdl/publications/english/alraida%20article.pdf.

A. The Ottoman Christians and the Reform Era

Some Ottoman Christians were prosperous prior to World War I. At the start of the eighteenth century, a tax on non-Muslims, a small fraction of the Ottoman population, provided fully 45% of government revenue.[4] Ottoman Armenians, Assyrians, and Greeks operated banks, factories, import-export firms, and farms.[5] However, many of these populations were also subject to conditions tantamount to slavery on farms and plantations. Armenian serfs were referred to as "*zerkurri*, signifying bought with gold." As a British traveller commented:

> [Armenian serfs] are bought and sold in much the same manner as sheep and cattle by the Kurdish aghas and beys. The only difference is that they cannot be disposed of individually; they are transferred with the lands which they cultivate.[6]

The Russian Empire invaded Ottoman territory in 1737 as a result of raids on Russian population centers from the Ottoman protectorate of Crimea. The Austrian Empire joined the war and reached the walls of Belgrade, across the Ottoman-held Serbian frontier.[7] The British Empire entered the fray with 16,500 German, Italian, and Swiss mercenaries within its force.[8] The war ended with treaties ceding Belgrade and Serbia to the Ottomans, from Austria, and Moldavia and Bessarabia, from Russia, whose fleet was removed from the Black Sea.[9]

After the Ottomans massacred tens of thousands of Slavs (Bulgarians and Serbians) in their western provinces, the Russian Empire declared war in 1877. Czar Alexander II announced that peaceful negotiations to assure the human rights of the Christians of the Ottoman Empire had broken down, and that Russians would cross the Ottoman frontier to liberate the "oppressed Christian population of Turkey."[10] The Russians temporarily liberated Armenia from Ottoman rule, and allowed Armenians to join local police forces, a

---

4. Halil Incalik, *State Revenues and Expenditures: Sources of Revenue, in* An Economic and Social History 55 (Halil Incalik ed., Cambridge: Cambridge UP, 1994).

5. *See* Charles Issawi, *The Transformation of the Economic Position of the Millets in the Nineteenth Century, in* Christians and Jews in the Ottoman Empire: The Functioning of a Plural Society 262–64, 266, 269–70 (Benjamin Braude & Bernard Lewis eds., 1982) (describing Greek and Armenian businesses prior to World War I); Feroz Ahmad, *Unionist Relations with the Greek, Armenian, and Jewish Communities of the Ottoman Empire,* 1908–1914, *in id.* at 405–6, 427 (similar); Dickran Kouymjian, *When Does Genocide End? The Armenian Case* (2003), http://armenianstudies.csufresno.edu/faculty/kouymjian/speechs/genocide_sonoma.htm (describing extent of Armenian wealth and lands that would later be confiscated); Vahakn N. Dadrian, *The Documentation of the World War I Armenian Massacres in the Proceedings of the Turkish Military Tribunal,* 23 Int'l J. of Middle East Studies 549, 565, 568, 574 (1991) (describing Armenian properties plundered in World War I); *Germans Inspired Turkish Atrocities Against Asiatic Greeks,* N.Y. Times, Sept. 29, 1918 (referencing economic achievements of Greeks of Smyrna and elsewhere in Ottoman Empire prior to World War I).

6. H.F.B. Lynch, 2 Armenia: Travels and Studies 430–31 (London, 1901).

7. Vahakn N. Dadrian, The History of the Armenian Genocide: Ethnic Conflict from the Balkans to Anatolia to the Caucasus 7 (Providence, RI: Berghahn Books, 1995).

8. Christopher H. Lytton, *Blood for Hire: How the War in Iraq Has Reinvented the World's Second Oldest Profession,* 8 Or. Rev. Int'l L. 307, 308 (2006).

9. *See Turkey, in* 26 Encyclopedia Britannica, at 453 (New York: The Britannica Co., 1911); *The Dream of Russia, in* 58 The Atlantic Monthly 773 (1886).

10. Dadrian, Warrant for Genocide, at 153; R.A. Hammond, A History of the Empire and People of Turkey and the War in the East 450–470 (1878).

Image 2 The Ottoman Empire

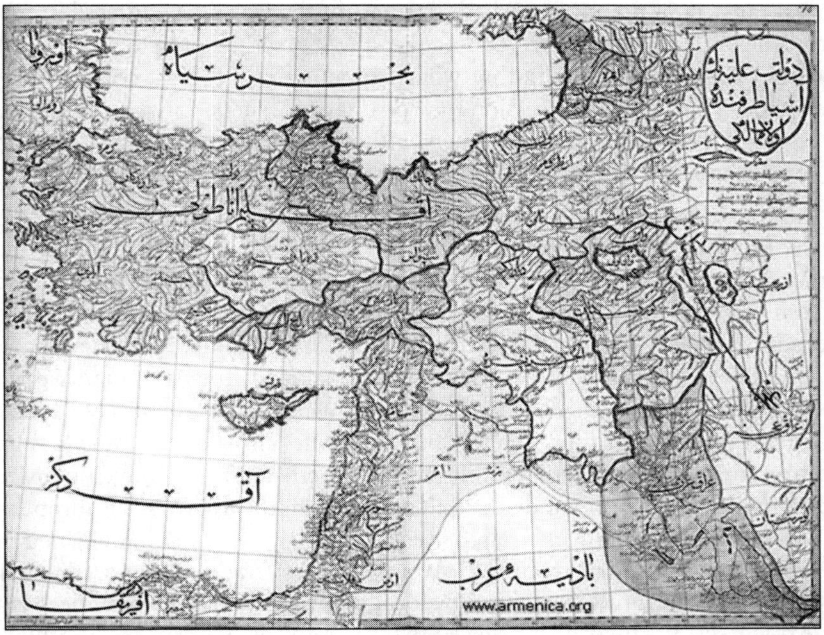

move that the Ottoman government had resisted implementing despite decades of European requests. In the overwhelmingly Christian town of Zeitoun, incorporated for the first time in the Ottoman province of Aleppo in 1860, Armenians attacked Turkish settlers, killing about seven, wounding more, and destroying settlements. Severe reprisals followed, after which the British Consul accused the Governor of Aleppo of wanton cruelty against the population of Zeitoun. Other Armenians stayed loyal. The Armenian patriarch assured the Sultan at the outset of the war of the loyalty of his people, and the Armenian General Assembly announced a mass enrollment of Armenians in the Ottomans' Civic Guard. The Sultan had ordered the enlistment of all able-bodied men between 20 and 40 years old in the Civic Guard, so it is not clear that the loyal Armenians had much choice.[11]

After the withdrawal of Russian forces from four Armenian districts situated in southeastern Anatolia, Kurds from Mesopotamia and Anatolia killed an estimated 1,400 Armenians and other Christians, carried away about 300 Armenian women and children into slavery, and plundered houses and churches. As in the Ottoman conquests of the region, and periodic wars with Persia, Kurdish militia snuffed out local resistance with indiscriminate killing and abuses against the women and children of the enemy. The British vice-consul at Mosul wrote to the British Ambassador that the Kurds "killed many an unfortunate Christian without cause or reason, and violated the women and girls...."[12]

Within the Russian Empire, the government implemented massacres and deportations of Circassians and Muslims. Circassians fled the violence, and the burning of their villages. One author writes that another precedent for total war between religious groups had been set:

---

11. *See* Şĭmşĭr, *Introduction*, *in* 1 British Documents on Ottoman Armenians, at xiv–xviii; Turkey No. 1, Nov. 28, 1877, pp. 543–548, no. 598 (1878); Dadrian, Warrant for Genocide, at 77.

12. F.O. 424/62. pp. 142–45, no. 245/1 (Vice-Consul H. Rassam to Sir A.H. Layard, British Ambassador to the Ottoman Sublime Porte, Oct. 15, 1877), *in* 1 British Documents on Ottoman Armenians, at 100.

> "This great exodus" concludes [Paul B.] Henze, "was the first of the violent mass transfers of population which this part of the world has suffered in modern times." He goes on, however, to suggest that it set the precedent for the Armenian genocide, implying that what happened was at least comparable to genocide. There was no obsession to wipe out every single Circassian, but there was a determination to get rid of them without delay, in the full knowledge that a large proportion of them were bound to perish in the process.[13]

As the war drew to a close, the Armenian Patriarch for Constantinople, Nerses II, urged the Russians to conclude a peace treaty with the Ottomans that would guarantee Armenian life and property against Kurdish and Circassian pogroms. Under Article XVI of the resulting Preliminary Treaty of San Stefano, the Ottoman Sublime Porte agreed to, "without further delay," ensure the security of Armenians against Kurdish and Circassian attacks.[14] About a month after this treaty was concluded, the Armenian patriarch requested an autonomous local government for the Armenians on the model of the Lebanon,[15] which after a massacre of more than 10,000 Maronite Christians in 1860 had been detached from the *vilayets* of Syria and Beirut, and then administered by a non-Lebanese Christian *mutasarrif* appointed by the Sultan, but with the approval of European dipomats.[16] A few months after the Patriarch's request, the Treaty of Berlin obligated the Sublime Porte to guarantee Armenian security and to "carry out, without further delay, the improvements and reforms demanded by local requirements in the provinces inhabited by the Armenians."[17] The British believed that the reforms required of the Sultan under the Treaty of Berlin included an obligation to abolish the system of tax-farming that resulted in arbitrary, duplicative, and crushing impositions on farmers and merchants, establish courts overseen by European lawyers, and create a gendarmerie in Armenia and other Asian provinces that would be "organized and commanded by Europeans."[18]

The Armenian areas of the Empire suffered from "corrupt and incapable administration," according to the British ambassador. The vice-consul for Van described the Ottoman courts as an extortionate "farce," and the Ottoman gendarmerie as the "scourge of the country."[19] The Ottoman government in 1880 consisted of the Sultan; the Sublime Porte or the court of the Sultan; the *valis* or governors-general of provinces; the *mutassarifs* or (lieutenant-)governors of districts (*sancaks*); the *kaimakams* or governors of cantons (*kazas*); the *mudirs* or administrators of village-groupings (*nahiyeh*); and the *mukhtars* or headmen of villages and town quarters.[20]

---

13. Steven D. Shenfield, *The Circassians: A Forgotten Genocide? in* THE MASSACRE IN HISTORY 157 (Mark Levene & Penny Roberts eds., New York; Oxford UP, 1999) (quoting Paul B. Henze, *Circassian Resistance to Russia, in* THE NORTH CAUCASUS BARRIER: THE RUSSIAN ADVANCE TOWARDS THE MUSLIM WORLD 111 (Marie Benningsen Broxup ed., London: 1992)).

14. Şĭmşĭr, *Introduction, in* 1 BRITISH DOCUMENTS ON OTTOMAN ARMENIANS, at xiv–xv.

15. *See id.*

16. Afaf Sabeh McGowen, *Historical Setting, in* LEBANON: A COUNTRY STUDY, ch. 1 (Washington, D.C.: Library of Congress, 3d ed. 1989).

17. Treaty of Berlin, 1878, art. LXI, *in* WHEATON, ELEMENTS OF INTERNATIONAL LAW, at 713, 728; *Introduction, in* 1 BRITISH DOCUMENTS ON OTTOMAN ARMENIANS, at xix.

18. ROLIN-JAEQUEMYNS, ARMENIA, ARMENIANS, AND THE TREATIES, at 17, 23; *Introduction, in* 2 BRITISH DOCUMENTS ON OTTOMAN ARMENIANS. at xxiii.

19. F.O. 424/63, pp. 12–27, no. 25 (Consul Wood to E.H. Stanley, the 15th Earl of Derby, British Secretary for Foreign Affairs, Nov. 27, 1877), *in* 1 BRITISH DOCUMENTS ON OTTOMAN ARMENIANS, at 125.

20. Lt. Col. Sir C. Wilson and Major Trotter, Report to F. Blackwood, the Earl of Dufferin (British Ambassador to the Ottoman Sublime Porte), Aug. 23, 1881, *in* 2 BRITISH DOCUMENTS ON OTTOMAN ARMENIANS, at 298–302; F.O. 424/63, pp. 12–27, no. 25 (Consul Wood to E.H. Stanley, the 15th Earl

The Armenian independence movement evolved from a demand for local autonomy and perhaps an Armenian governor, to a nationalist movement similar to that of the Greeks, etc. At the Congress of Berlin in 1878, the Armenian delegation requested local autonomy and an Armenian governor.[21] By late 1879, the reforms called for in the treaties of San Stefano and Berlin still had not been carried out, prompting the British ambassador to threaten the throne of the Sultan himself, and the British Navy to set sail for Ottoman waters.[22]

The oppression and poverty borne by Christian minority groups in the nineteenth century ravaged and depopulated the Christian towns and villages of the empire. The Armenian National Assembly for the Province of Van reported in 1882 that:

> Unpunished evils imposed on the population by the authorities and the wild hordes have afflicted so many, that it has arrived at the intimate conviction that the Imperial Government, far from curing her lamentable situation, is animated by an excess of zeal to depopulate Armenia of its own sons, with the intention of decreasing in this way the Christian element.[23]

The British consul reported to the special ambassador of Britain to the Ottomans that:

> In some parts nomad Kurds make raids on villages, carrying off flocks and herds and other plunder, and sometimes burning what they cannot carry away. In other parts influential Kurdish families parcel out the villages (especially Christian) in their neighbourhood among their various members, and regard them as their property. The inhabitants have to pay them black-mail ... and do for them anything they may demand....
>
> [T]he wholesale plunder by the Kurds have reduced the peasantry to the utmost straits. The rapacity of [government] officials is also always a cause of iniquity in the collection of taxation....
>
> [M]any villages have a mixed population of Turks and Armenians, and in such cases the Armenians suffer innumerable oppressions and wrongs at the hands of their Turkish neighbors. Their property, the honour of their women, and their lives are none of them safe....
>
> The hostility of the ruling race to the Christians ... renders it especially difficult for a Christian to obtain justice.[24]

Reporting in 1880 on conditions in the eastern provinces of the empire from Aleppo southeast to Baghdad, the British vice-consul for Anatolia stated that famine conditions prevailed from Erzerum in the west to Van and the Persian border. Poverty was prevalent, and the mountain villages and countryside were "suffering terribly" and in a "miserable

---

of Derby, British Secretary for Foreign Affairs, Nov. 27, 1877), *in* 1 British Documents on Ottoman Armenians, at 116–128; H. Maynard (U.S. Minister to Constantinople) to H. Fish (U.S. Secretary of State), Jan. 30, 1877, Inclosure, *in* Papers Relating to the Foreign Relations of the United States 552 (1877).

21. Taner Akçam, A Shameful Act: The Armenian Genocide and the Question of Turkish Responsibility 38 (Paul Bessemer trans., New York: Henry Holt, 2006).

22. Şĭmşĭr, *Introduction*, *in* 2 British Documents on Ottoman Armenians, at xxix.

23. F.O. 424/132, Apr. 27, 1882, p. 118, no. 88, Inclosure 1 in no. 186 (Memorandum of Armenian Patriarch of Constantinople, Nerses II, to F. Blackwood, the Earl of Dufferin, British Ambassador to the Ottoman Sublime Porte), *in* 2 British Documents on Ottoman Armenians, at 435 (my translation from original French).

24. F.O. 424/107, pp. 107–109 (Consul Trotter to G.J. Groschen, Special Ambassador to the Sublime Porte, Sept. 7, 1880), *in* 2 British Documents on Ottoman Armenians, at 651–52.

condition." The "oppressive Government" had turned entire regions with good land and climate into ruins, with hovels for homes, only ancient roads intact, desolate towns, and a declining population.[25]

The six ambassadors of the European powers that signed the Treaty of Berlin with the Ottoman Empire (i.e. Britain, France, Russia, Austria-Hungary, Germany, and Italy), echoed this account. They called the "excess of the Circassians and Kurds" a "continual source of danger to the property, honour, and life of the Armenians."[26] The ambassadors warned that the attacks created a "degree of anarchy" which, "if permitted to continue, would in all probability lead to the destruction of the Christian population of vast districts" of the empire.[27] The six ambassadors dispatched a message to the court of the Ottoman Sultan Abdul Hamid II, stating that the Ottoman Empire had violated the rights of the Ottoman Christian minorities. The ambassadors complained that Kurdish and Circassian attacks on Ottoman Christians flouted article LXI of the Treaty of Berlin, which had been intended to prevent such abuses.[28]

B. The Nineteenth Century Massacres of the Armenians under Sultan Abdul Hamid

From Erzerum in 1880, Vice-Consul William Everett wrote that the Armenians desired to "deliver their countrymen from their oppressors."[29] The movement spread to Van province by 1882, where the Young Armenian Party spoke out in favor of independence, and some Armenians received Russian arms.[30] Russian support dried up after the assassination of Czar Alexander II in 1881, however.[31] In 1883 the Ottoman authorities arrested and tried 76 members of the Armenian "Protectors of the Fatherland" party; 40 members were convicted of various crimes. This party's founders emphasized Armenian resistance to the Kurdish attacks.[32] The first Armenian party with aspirations for self-determination was the Armenakan party established in Van in late 1885.[33] Parties calling for Armenian independence soon followed, with the creation in 1887 of the Party of Hentchaks, an Armenian Marxist organization dedicated to liberating Armenia from the Empire, and the creation in 1890 of the Armenian nationalist party the *Dashnaktsutyun*.[34] Not all Ar-

---

25. Turkey No. 23, Apr. 3, 1880, pp. 183–190, No. 199/1 (Vice-Consul H. Chermside to Sir A.H. Layard, British Ambassador to the Sublime Porte), *in* 1 British Documents on Ottoman Armenians, at 701–703.

26. F.O. 424/107, pp. 191–194, no. 113/1 (1880), *in* 2 British Documents on Ottoman Armenians, at 119.

27. Turkey No. 23 (1880), pp. 279–282, no. 154/1, F.O. 424/107, pp. 191–194, no. 113/1, *in* 2 British Documents on Ottoman Armenians, at 119.

28. Bĭlâl Şĭmşĭr, *Introduction, in* 2 British Documents on Ottoman Armenians (1880–1890), at xiv (1989).

29. Lt. Col. Sir C. Wilson and Major Trotter to F. Blackwood, the Earl of Dufferin, British Ambassador to the Ottoman Sublime Porte, Aug. 23, 1881, *in* 2 British Documents on Ottoman Armenians, at 298–302.

30. Şĭmşĭr, *Introduction, in* 2 British Documents on Ottoman Armenians, at xix.

31. *Id.* at xvi.

32. *See* Christopher Walker, Armenia: Survival of a Nation 126 (2d ed. 1990).

33. Walker, Armenia, at 126.

34. Şĭmşĭr, *Introduction, in* 2 British Documents on Ottoman Armenians at xx.

menian parties opposed the Imperial government; the New Armenian Party in Van declared its "fidelity and devotion" to the Sultan.[35]

Armenian demands for sovereignty and self-rule resembled claims to aboriginal or tribal sovereignty in the Americas, Australia, New Zealand, or South Africa. Kurdish tribes and leaders behaved towards their indigenous Christian neighbors much like frontiersmen in the Americas, Australia, Tasmania, or South Africa did. Many Kurdish leaders enjoyed official authority and public offices bestowed by the Ottomans, which they utilized to "prey upon and oppress the country people," and inflict "innumerable oppressions and wrongs" upon the Armenians and Assyrians. Kurds traveled in "large bodies" of armed men, impervious to any resistance other than a "force of properly-paid and disciplined troops," which was not forthcoming from the government.[36] British reports in 1888 documented that a "large army" of Kurds attacked Assyrians in the Tiyari region on the Persian border, killing many civilians and raping many women.[37] One sign of the size and impunity of these Kurdish tribal forces is supplied by the account of a European traveler who asked the head of the Assyrians, Mar Shimun XVIII, for an escort of 12 armed men for the road to Bitlis and Erzerum, and was told that such a force would be useless against the roving Kurdish armies.[38]

Attacks by Kurds on Armenians and Assyrians continued in 1890. An Armenian church near the Russian border "was burned down maliciously by Kurds, the church property stolen," a British Consul wrote.[39] The local Ottoman governor-general blamed the Armenians. Kurds massacred five Assyrian laborers and stole their money, the governor of Erzerum admitted.[40]

In July 1895, the Ottoman authorities arrested more than 200 Armenians in Constantinople, without publicly charging them with anything.[41] On October 2, 1895, Armenian rebels wounded the former governor of Van in an assassination attempt.[42] Armenian rebels overran the garrison at Zeitoun by the first week of November, taking 420 prisoners and prompting the army to send a contingent of 25,000 men to the region.[43]

By the 1890s, the Ottoman Sultan Abdul Hamid II had created an irregular force of pro-government Kurdish horsemen called the Hamidiye.[44] The Hamidiye massacred and made refugees of the independence-minded Assyrian and Armenian peoples of the Ottoman Empire, like the contemporary Arab *Janjaweed* in Sudan have done to the indigenous Africans in Darfur.[45] The Ottomans killed tens of thousands of peace-

---

35. *Id.* at xxii.
36. *Id.* at 651, 654.
37. F.O. 424/145, p. 98, no. 97 (1888) and F.O. 424/145, p. 101, no. 102 (1888).
38. Isabella Lucy Bird, 2 Journeys in Persia and Kurdistan 320 (1891).
39. Şĭmşĭr, *Introduction, in* 2 British Documents on Ottoman Armenians at 691.
40. *Id.* at 690.
41. 4 British Documents on Ottoman Armenians, at 62.
42. Bĭlâl Şĭmşĭr, *Introduction, in* 4 British Documents on Ottoman Armenians (1895), at xiv (1990).
43. *See* 4 British Documents on Ottoman Armenians, at 438; Walker, Armenia, at 162.
44. Michael M. Gunter, *The Kurdish Question in Perspective*, World Affairs 166, 197–205 (2004), http://www.findarticles.com/p/articles/mi_m2393/is_4_166/ai_114631687/pg_2.
45. Peter Balakian, The Burning Tigris: The Armenian Genocide and America's Response 43–44, 50–51, 123 (2004). For its part, the Sudanese government sponsored a majority Arab militia called the *Janjaweed* to attack members of indigenous African tribes in Darfur associated with the Sudan Liberation Army; the militia engaged in the widespread killing and raping of civilians, looting and burning of hundreds of villages, and driving of one million people from their homes. Nsongurua J. Udombana, *When Neutrality is a Sin: The Darfur Crisis and the Crisis of Humanitarian Intervention in Sudan*, 27 Human Rights Quarterly 1149 (2005); Human Rights Watch, *Darfur Destroyed: Ethnic Cleansing By Government and Militia Forces in Western Sudan* (May 2004), http://hrw.org/reports/2004/sudan0504; Amnesty International, Sudan: *Arming the Perpetrators of*

ful, defenseless Christians in the capital, Constantinople, and in the "provincial towns of the Empire." The French vice-consul for southeastern Anatolia, told the French Ambassador to the Ottoman Empire that in Diyarbekir, "not only Armenians, but Christians of every Church, were indiscriminately slaughtered," and his own life was "in great danger."[46] He reported a campaign of terror against the Armenians and Assyrians reminiscent of *Kristallnacht* in Nazi Germany; hundreds of Christians were murdered, hundreds of Christian homes ransacked, and hundreds of Christian-owned shops looted and burned.[47] In nearby Urfa, the Edessa of Christian learning, the Sultan's genocide claimed 3,000 women and children inside the city's cathedral.[48] An historian of the Ottomans called the fire at Urfa "a human holocaust, in which nearly 3,000 persons perished."[49]

The French Ambassador, Paul Cambon,[50] wrote that Asia Minor was "'literally in flames'" with "'massacres everywhere,'" and Kurds and other Muslims "'massacring all Christians without distinction.'"[51] The Ottoman government had, "for the last few years, been pursuing its goal of gradually annihilating the Christian element" by "giving the Kurdish chieftains carte blanche to do whatever they please, to enrich themselves at the Christians' expense and to satisfy their men's whims...." The Hamidiye, the vice-consul declaimed, was "a band of official highway robbers spreading terror throughout this *vilayet* and many others." The "impunity they enjoy for the crimes they commit every day" was "ample proof" to some observers of an Ottoman policy of annihilating the Christians of the empire.[52] *Me veret*, the newspaper of the opposition Committee for Union and Progress, called the Sultan a "tyrannical" man guilty of "shameful ... massacres."[53]

On October 1, 1895, the villages of Qarabash and Sa'diye near Diyarbekir suffered massacres of the Assyrian and Armenian populations.[54] These massacres were followed by an attack on November 5, 1895, on the town of Mansuriye, near Mardin. A renewal of the attack on Mansuriye took place on November 9 and 10, along with massacres in the historic city of Nisibis, as well as the villages of Benebil and Goliye.[55] Reports of enormous massacres reached the U.S., with five to eight hundred people slain in Harput alone by mid-November 1895. Houses and religious buildings were plundered and the Ottoman Christian population was left "naked and starving."[56] In Sivas, "the massacre and pillage of Armenian villages" were widely reported in the American press.[57]

Grave Abuses in Darfur (Nov. 2004), http://web.amnesty.org/library/index/engafr541392004; USDOS, Bureau of Democracy, Human Rights, and Labor and the Bureau of Intelligence and Research, *Documenting Atrocities in Darfur* (Sept. 2004), http://www.state.gov/g/drl/rls/36028.htm.

46. Arnold Toynbee, *A Summary of Armenian History up to and Including the Year 1915, in* The Treatment of Armenians in the Ottoman Empire, 1915–1916, at 439, 623 (Viscount James Bryce, Arnold Toynbee, and Ara Sarafian eds., London: Taderon Press, 2000).

47. Gustave Meyrier, Diplomatic Dispatch #44, Dec. 18, 1895, *quoted in* Sebastien de Courtois, The Forgotten Genocide: The Eastern Christians, The Last Arameans 106 (2004).

48. Dadrian, Warrant for Genocide, at 85.

49. William Miller, The Ottoman Empire, 1801–1913, at 429 (1913).

50. M. Şükrü Hanioğlu, The Young Turks in Opposition 36, 49 (Oxford UP, 1995).

51. Paul Cambon, Correspondence.—1870–1924, vol. 1 (1878–1898)—"La Turquie d'Abdul Hamid" 395 (1940), *quoted in* de Courtois, The Forgotten Genocide, at 110.

52. Diplomatic Dispatch #2, Jan. 9, 1901, from Vice-Consul of Diyarbakir to Mr. Constans, French Ambassador to Constantinople, *quoted in* de Courtois, The Forgotten Genocide, at 138.

53. Hanioğlu, The Young Turks in Opposition, 112.

54. *See* Gaunt, Massacres, Resistance, Protectors, at 245, 250.

55. *See id.* at 208. 216, 221, 237, 265–67, 306, 314.

56. *See Massacres at Alexandretta*, Chicago Daily Tribune, Nov. 17, 1895, at 14.

57. *E.g., Sultan Openly Defies Powers*, Chicago Daily Tribune, Nov. 10, 1895, at 13.

By September 1896, up to 300,000 Ottoman Christians had perished in the massacres.[58] The British and Russians threatened military intervention unless the Ottomans reformed their pattern of persecuting their Christian subjects.[59] But the Sultan never implemented proposed reforms to protect minorities.[60] The Ottoman campaign to exterminate the Christians in the Empire had begun, as former Prime Minister William Ewart Gladstone recognized in a public speech in 1896.[61] Instead of reforms, the Ottoman government organized a massacre of over 2,000 Armenians in September 1896 in Harput province.[62]

C. The Armenian Population of the Ottoman Empire in 1914

At the Congress of Berlin in 1878, the estimate of the Armenian population of the Ottoman Empire supplied by the Armenian patriarch was three million persons.[63] This represented an increase in the Armenian population of the Empire of about one-third over the 34 years since the Ottoman survey of 1844, which was completed before pressure for Armenian autonomy prompted the government to minimize its reports of the Armenian population.[64] This also represented an increase of one-fourth in the 11 years after the Turkish "official book" of 1867.[65] By comparison, the population of the Soviet Republic

---

58. *See Armenians in Ottoman Turkey and the Armenian Genocide, in* ENCYCLOPEDIA OF GENOCIDE AND CRIMES AGAINST HUMANITY, at 71; JOHANNES LEPSIUS, ARMENIEN UND EUROPA. EINE ANKLAGESCHRIFT WIDER DIE CHRISTLICHEN GROSSMÄCHTE UND EIN AUFRUF AN DAS CHRISTLICHE DEUTSCHLAND (Berlin: Faber 1896); MORDECHAI NISAN, MINORITIES IN THE MIDDLE EAST: A HISTORY OF STRUGGLE AND SELF-EXPRESSION 165 (Jefferson, North Carolina: McFarland Press, 2002); RUDOLPH J. RUMMEL, STATISTICS OF DEMOCIDE: GENOCIDE AND MASS MURDER SINCE 1900, at 86 (Berlin: LIT Verlag, 1998); RUMMEL, DEATH BY GOVERNMENT, at 61; Benjamin Vallotin, *The Armenian Agony,* THE TRIBUNE (SWITZERLAND), *quoted in* THE ARMENIAN HERALD 324 (Boston: Armenian National Union of America, 1918); JAY WINTER, DREAMS OF PEACE AND FREEDOM: UTOPIAN MOMENTS IN THE TWENTIETH CENTURY 13(New Haven, Connecticut: Yale UP, 2008).

59. Donald Bloxham, *The Armenian Genocide of 1915–1916: Cumulative Radicalization and the Development of a Destruction Policy,* 181 PAST AND PRESENT 149, 151 (2003) [hereinafter Bloxham, *The Armenian Genocide*].

60. DADRIAN, WARRANT FOR GENOCIDE, 45, 71, 79–80, 154; DADRIAN, HISTORY OF THE ARMENIAN GENOCIDE, at 74, 85, 100, 107. Ultimately the Ottoman Christians may have enjoyed more opportunistic rhetorical expressions of support than effective military or economic aid during the periods of the worst abuses. Bloxham, *The Armenian Genocide,* at 186.

61. BALAKIAN, THE BURNING TIGRIS, at 123.

62. *See* DADRIAN, HISTORY OF THE ARMENIAN GENOCIDE, at 146.

63. *See* GUSTAVE ROLIN-JAEQUEMYNS, ARMENIA, THE ARMENIANS, AND THE TREATIES 8 (Whitefish, MT: Kessinger Publishing, 2004) (1891).

64. *See* LEVON MARASHLIAN, POLITICS AND DEMOGRAPHY: ARMENIANS, TURKS, AND KURDS IN THE OTTOMAN EMPIRE 32, 49 (Toronto: Zoryan Institute, 1991) ("the number of Armenians according to the 1844 [Ottoman] census, 2,400,000 Empire wide[,] ... is close to the [Armenian] Patriarchate's figure, 2,100,000"). The 1844 census figures are corroborated by the 1831 estimate of two million Armenians in 1833 by an official with the American Board of Commissioners for Foreign Missions. *See id.* at 36.

65. *See* HRANT PASDERMADJIAN, HISTOIRE DE L'ARMÉNIE DEPUIS LES ORIGINES JUSQU'AU TRAITÉ DE LAUSANNE 399 (Paris, 1949) ("The official book of Turkey, compiled by Sallahedin Beg in 1867, puts the Armenian population in the Ottoman Empire at 2,400,000. As soon as the Armenian question emerged, in the context of the Russian-Ottoman war of 1877–1878, the Ottoman official books showed an astonishing decrease in the number of Armenians, thanks to manipulated statistics."),

of Armenia increased by about 37% in the 20 years between the censuses of 1939 and 1959, and by about 40% in the 11 years between the censuses of 1959 and 1970.[66]

The Armenian population in 1878 included 1.3 million in the provinces of Van, Erzerum, Diyarbekir and the districts of Argana and Seghert; 670,000 in the provinces of Sivas and the district of Kayseri; 600,000 in Cilicia and other parts of Asia Minor; and 400,000 in Constantinople and Europe.[67] The British vice-consul in Van credited estimates in the 1870s of two million Armenians and up to 500,000 Assyrians (Nestorians) in the Ottoman Empire, in addition to 1.2 million Armenians in Russia and 170,000 in Persia.[68] Earlier, the British Consul for Erzerum and Diyarbekir, J.G. Taylor, who traveled throughout eastern Anatolia in 1866, estimated that 1.15 million Armenians lived in the *vilayets* of Van, Erzerum, and Bitlis alone, along with 110,000 Assyrians (or Nestorians).[69] The 1897 Population Census of the Russian Empire counted more than one million Armenians,[70] and found that about 830,000 people lived within Yerevan governorate alone, which was then the principally Armenian province of the Russian Empire.[71] The Armenian patriarch estimated around 1880 that nearly 800,000 Armenians lived in the easternmost provinces of Anatolia.[72]

Ottoman population estimates after the 1870s vary wildly, listing anywhere from 550,000 to 1.2 million Armenians.[73] Scholars regard these data as unreliable[74] because the government minimized Christian population figures relative to the Muslim population in order to resist European calls for ethnic autonomy and equal access to official posts like governorships, and because Christians evaded the census, particularly in the mountain-

---

quoted in Vahagn Avedian, The Armenian Genocide 1915 from a Neutral Small State's Perspective: Sweden, at 32 (Uppsala, Sweden: Uppsala Universiteit, 2008).

66. *See* Republic of Armenia, *National Statistical Service, A Brief Historical Review of the Censuses Conducted Previously in Armenia* (2008), http://www.armstat.am/file/doc/676.pdf; Internet Access and Training Program in Armenia, *The Number of Men and Women in Armenia (Table 3)* (2003), http://www.iatp.am/economics/migr/demog-ax.htm#3t.

67. *See* Rolin-Jaequemyns, Armenia, the Armenians, and the Treaties 8.

68. F.O. 424/106, 1879, Vice-Consul Emilius Clayton's Report on Reforms in Van, *in* 1 British Documents on Ottoman Armenians (1856–1880), at 645–46 (Bĭlâl Şĭmşĭr ed., 1980).

69. F.O. 424/107, Sept. 7, 1880, pp. 107–179, no. 104/3, Inclosure 3, Consul Trotter to G.J. Groschen, Special Ambassador to the Sublime Porte, *in* 2 British Documents on Ottoman Armenians (1880–1890), at 131, 134.

70. *See* Anna Geifman, Russia Under the Last Tsar: Opposition and Subversion, 1894–1917, at 126 (London: Blackwell Publ'g, 1999).

71. *See* Republic of Armenia, National Statistical Service, *A Brief Historical Review of the Censuses Conducted Previously in Armenia* (2008), http://www.armstat.am/file/doc/676.pdf.

72. *See* Bĭlâl Şĭmşĭr, *Introduction, in* 2 British Documents on Ottoman Armenians (1880–1890), at xiii (Bĭlâl Şĭmşĭr ed., 1989).

73. *Compare* Osmanli İmparatorluğu'nun ve Türkiye'nin Nüfusu: 1500–1927 [The Population of the Ottoman Empire and Turkey] 40–41, 46 (Cem Behar ed., Ankara, Turkey: State Institute of Statistics, 1996) (official Ottoman figures for 1885 and 1897 estimated populations of 989,000 to 1,042,000 Armenian Orthodox-Gregorian, 120,000 to 150,000 Armenian and other Catholics, and zero Assyrians-Nestorians), *with* Kemal H. Karpat, Ottoman Population 1830–1914: Demographic and Social Characteristics 192–93 (Madison, WI: Univ. of Wisconsin Press, 1985) (official Ottoman figures for 1881 and 1893 estimated populations of 500,000 to 538,000 Armenian Orthodox-Gregorian, 67,000 to 83,000 Armenian and other Catholics, and zero Assyrians-Nestorians), *and* Karpat, Ottoman Population, at 194–195 (official Ottoman figures for 1880 estimated there were 35,000 Assyrians, i.e., Nestorians, Chaldeans, Jacobite Syrians, and Syrian Catholics).

74. For a survey of sources and scholarly arguments demonstrating the incompleteness and unreliability of Ottoman census figures and estimates based upon them, see Marashlian, Politics and Demography.

ous east, fearing massacres or onerously taxation by the government.[75] After the Russian Empire asserted a renewed interest in Armenian rights, the Ottoman records "showed an astonishing decrease in the number of Armenians, thanks to manipulated statistics."[76] The Ottoman Sultan Abdul Hamid II rejected the initial conclusion of the survey that at least 900,000 Armenians resided in his Empire, and ordered his officials to reduce the count by fiat.[77]

Henry Trotter, the British Consul for Erzerum, Diyarbekir, Van, and Muş, discovered during his travels through southeastern Anatolia and northern Mesopotamia that the official population lists of the Ottoman Empire fell "considerably" short of the truth because residents wanted to avoid the Empire's military conscription and harsh taxation.[78] Although previously exempt from conscription, Christians had been warned by the Sultan, in proclamations in 1856 and 1866, that they too were liable to military conscription in the perilous cause of expanding the Ottoman Empire further into Europe, the Caucasus, the Middle East, and Africa.[79] Consul Trotter concluded that the Christian population in the rebellious Christian areas of Hakkari, Harput, and Diyarbekir, which were also some of the most distant provinces from the imperial capital, was "considerably under-estimated in the official estimate."[80] Moreover, the Ottoman census counted males only, requiring those using the data to assume that the figures counted boys as well as men, and that one may simply double the male count to get a total count.[81]

The population of the Turkish and Kurdish conquerors of Anatolia outnumbered the population of the indigenous Christians in the nineteenth century. Arab, Turkish, and Kurdish populations settled Christian, Jewish, and polytheistic areas of Anatolia starting in the seventh century. The official estimate in 1880 of the Turkish, Kurdish, and Circassian population living in the southeastern Anatolian provinces of Van, Bitlis, and Erzerum was over 800,000.[82] The Ottoman census reported the total Muslim population

---

75. *See* Bĭlâl Şĭmşĭr, *Introduction, in* 4 British Documents on Ottoman Armenians (1895), at x–xi (Bĭlâl Şĭmşĭr ed., 1990). *See also* F.O. 424/123, p. 150, no. 105/1 & Inclosure 2, *in* 2 British Documents on Ottoman Armenians, at 298–300; F.O. 424/107, Sept. 7, 1880, pp. 173–74, no. 104/1, Consul M. Trotter to G.J. Goschen, Special Ambassador to the Ottoman Sublime Porte, *in* 2 British Documents on Ottoman Armenians, at 126.

76. *See* Avedian, The Armenian Genocide, at 32 (citing Pasdermadjian, Histoire de L'Arménie, at 399).

77. *See* Dadrian, Warrant for Genocide, 173 (citing Ottoman Turkish sources including an 1895 memorandum by the Sultan to his officials dealing with the census of the Armenian population).

78. F.O. 424/107, Sept. 7, 1880, pp. 107–109, Consul Trotter to G.J. Groschen, Special Ambassador to the Sublime Porte, *in* 2 British Documents on Ottoman Armenians, at 126.

79. *See* Lisa Moses Leff, Sacred Bonds of Solidarity: The Rise of Jewish Internationalism in Nineteenth-Century France 147 (Palo Alto, CA: Stanford UP, 2006); James Carlile McCoan, 2 Our New Protectorate: Turkey in Asia: Its Geography, Races, Resources, and Government 209 (Oxford: Oxford UP, 1879). *See also* Marashlian, Politics and Demography, at 48 ("Armenian [community] leaders had an incentive to undercount Armenians" to avoid conscription).

80. F.O. 424/107, Sept. 7, 1880, pp. 107–109, Consul Trotter to G.J. Groschen, Special Ambassador to the Sublime Porte, *in* 2 British Documents on Ottoman Armenians, at 128. "[T]he extreme dispersal of Armenians in rural areas, often isolated from the Church (as well as from governmental control), made it physically impossible to count everyone, even those who had no desire to resist being counted." Marashlian, Politics and Demography, at 48.

81. *See* Karpat, Ottoman Population 1830–1914, at 192 n.8; Marashlian, Politics and Demography, at 36.

82. F.O. 424/107, Sept. 7, 1880, pp. 177–79, Consul M. Trotter to G.J. Goschen, Special Ambassador to the Ottoman Sublime Porte, *in* 2 British Documents on Ottoman Armenians, at 131.

of the Empire as 12.6 million in 1885, rising to 14 million in 1897 and 15 million in 1914.[83]

D. The Outbreak of World War I in Asia

At its seventeenth-century height, the Ottoman Empire stretched from the Black Sea and Persia in the northeast, to Algiers and North Africa in the southwest, to present-day Budapest and Central Europe in the northwest, to Nubia and Mecca in the southeast.[84] In the Treaty of Karlowitz of 1699, the empire returned Hungary, Transylvania, Slavonia, Dalmatia (Croatia), Polonia (part of Ukraine), and the Peloponnese peninsula to the Holy Roman Empire, the Kingdom of Poland, and the Republic of Venice.[85] It later lost Greece and the Balkans.

During the Greek War of Independence, Ottoman forces massacred tens of thousands of Greek civilians in western Anatolia and the island of Chios.[86] The empire killed up to 70,000 Greeks in 1822–1823 in retribution for the Greek uprising.[87] Multitudes died on the islands of Cyprus and Rhodes, as well as in the vicinity of the Anatolian cities of Smyrna and Pergamos.[88] There followed even more enormous massacres of Eastern Christians whose leaders aspired to greater autonomy, including 12,000 Maronite Catholics in Lebanon in about 1860; nearly 15,000 Bulgarians and thousands of Armenians in the 1870s; about 250,000 Armenian and thousands of Assyrian and Coptic Christians in the 1890s; and at least 30,000 more Armenians in the 1900s.[89]

The Crimean War of 1853 to 1856 had an extremely damaging impact on Ottoman Christian communities. It left them insecure and placed them on an unsustainable course. In that conflict, the British Empire committed military forces to defend the Ottoman Em-

---

83. *See* THE POPULATION OF THE OTTOMAN EMPIRE AND TURKEY, at 46.

84. *See* Halil Inalcik, *The Heyday and Decline of the Ottoman Empire, in* 1A THE CAMBRIDGE HISTORY OF ISLAM 330–37 (P.M. Holt et al., eds., Cambridge: Cambridge UP, 2006).

85. *See, e.g.*, RICHARD C. FRUCHT, EASTERN EUROPE: AN INTRODUCTION TO THE PEOPLE, LANDS, AND CULTURE 422 (Santa Barbara, CA: ABC-CLIO, 2005).

86. Bryce, *Preface, in* NAAYEM, DEATH OF A NATION, at v; DADRIAN, HISTORY OF THE ARMENIAN GENOCIDE, at 12; THEA HALO, NOT EVEN MY NAME 100 (New York, NY: Picador, 2000); M.M. Mangasarian, *Armenia's Impending Doom: Our Duty*, THE FORUM, June 1896, *in* THE ARMENIAN MASSACRES, 1894–1896: U.S. MEDIA TESTIMONY 167 (Arman Dzhonovich Kirakosian ed. Detroit: Wayne State UP, 2004); GILLES NÉRET, EUGÈNE DELACROIX, 1798–1863. THE PRINCE OF ROMANTICISM 16 (Cologne, Germany: Taschen, 2000); THOMAS ALLOM, J.C.M. BELLEW, & ROBERT WALSH, CONSTANTINOPLE AND THE SCENERY OF THE SEVEN CHURCHES OF ASIA MINOR 166 (Piscataway, NJ: Gorgias Press, 2006).

87. William Easterly, Roberta Gatti, & Sergio Kurlat, *Development, Democracy, and Mass Killings*, 11 J. OF ECONOMIC GROWTH 129, 150–56, appx. 2; RUMMEL, STATISTICS OF DEMOCIDE, ch. 10; RUMMEL, DEATH BY GOVERNMENT. at 230.

88. *Scio, in* D.K. SANDFORD, 6 THE POPULAR ENCYCLOPEDIA, at 134 (Glasgow: Blackie and Son, 1846); *Greece (Revolution), in* 3 D.K. SANDFORD, THE POPULAR ENCYCLOPEDIA, at 536–38 (Glasgow: Blackie and Son, 1841).

89. Chamberlain, *The Alexandria Massacre*, at 14–39; DADRIAN, HISTORY OF THE ARMENIAN GENOCIDE, 53–55, 106, 155, 215; Easterly, Gatti, & Kurlat, *Development, Democracy, and Mass Killings*, at 150–56; GEORGE HORTON (U.S. Consul-General in the Middle East), THE BLIGHT OF ASIA, AN ACCOUNT OF THE SYSTEMATIC EXTERMINATION OF CHRISTIAN POPULATIONS BY MOHAMMEDANS AND OF THE CUZLPABILITY OF CERTAIN GREAT POWERS; WITH THE TRUE STORY OF THE BURNING OF SNYRNA, ch. 1 (Indianapolis: Bobbs-Merrill Co., 1926); Travis, *Ottoman Genocide of the Assyrians*, at 329–330.

pire against a Russian campaign to protect the Ottoman Christians.[90] The Crimean War "was due mainly to the efforts of the Czar Nicholas to extend his protection over the Greek Christians in Turkey." On an uncharitable view, Britain and France entered the fray on the side of the Ottoman Empire because they "wished to play a great part in the world" and "resented the encroachments of Russia in the East."[91] Article IX of the treaty denied the Russian Empire of its power to intercede on behalf of the oppressed Christians of the Ottoman Empire, while referencing a *firman* of toleration by the Sultan.[92] The press remarked that Britain had "destroyed the security which Russia had extorted from the Turkish Government at San Stefano and substituted for the sterling guarantee of Russia, the worthless paper-money of Ottoman promises."[93]

In the late 1850s, the Druzes of Ottoman Lebanon, for example, "used to kill a Christian for the least thing," with the government adopting a permissive attitude towards such crimes. Reports circulated that the Christians supported French rule, and would soon kill all the Muslims. In 1860, attacks on largely defenseless Christian communities in Lebanon led to 10,000 deaths, compared to 800 Druzes. Christians were particularly targeted for praying to the cross. In Damascus, the "greatest massacre" occurred, with Turkish troops, Kurds, Druzes, and Bedouin Arabs attacking native Christians, as well as Western diplomats and an Irish missionary.[94]

In the early twentieth century, the Ottoman Empire suffered a string of setbacks that set its leaders on a much more violent and fanatical course. The massacres of Armenians and other Christians spread to Sasun in 1904, and Adana and Cilicia in 1909.[95] A coalition of Austrian, Greek, Bulgarian, and Serbian forces drove the Turkish occupiers out of their erstwhile imperial provinces in Europe, routing their armies and inflicting thousands of casualties.[96] An ultranationalist group called the Committee of Union and Progress or "Young Turks" emerged after 1905 and steadily gained control over the Ottoman government and legal system.[97] After a coup in 1913, the Young Turks seized power, forming a military dictatorship run by the triumvirate of Ismail Enver Paşa, Minister of War, Mehmet Talât Paşa, Minister of Interior Affairs, and Ahmet Cemal Paşa, Minister of the

---

90. Sneh Mahajan, British Foreign Policy, 1874–1914: The Role of India 27 (London: Routledge, 2002); Robert B Edgerton, Death Or Glory: The Legacy of the Crimean War 12–13 (Boulder, CO: Westview Press, 1999).

91. John Holland Rose, The Development of the European Nations, 1870–1914, at 161 (New York, NY: G.P. Putnam's Sons, 5th ed. 1915), http://www.gutenberg.org/files/14644/14644-h/14644-h.htm.

92. *See* Treaty of Peace, signed at Paris, March 30, 1858, *in* Pictorial History of the Russian War 1854–56, at 549–65 (George Dodd ed. 1856).

93. Westminster Gazette, Dec. 18, 1894, *quoted in* Arsen Berberian, *British Reaction Regarding the First Massacres in Turkey* (2004), http://tinyurl.com/kvjr2b. *See also* George Buchan, 2 A History of the Great War 10 (London: Nelson, 1921); Daniel S. Gregory, The Crime of Christendom, or The Eastern Question from Its Origin to the Present Time (New York: Abbey Press, 1900).

94. *See* F.O. 195/604, Nov. 8, 1858, James Finn, British Consul in Jerusalem, to the British Secretary of State for Foreign Affairs, the Earl of Malmesbury, on the plunder of christian families in Palestine; F.O. 195/604, July 21 1860, Peter Meshullam, British Commissioner in the Ottoman Empire, to Consul James Finn.

95. Bloxham, *The Armenian Genocide*, at 149.

96. Edward J. Erickson, Defeat in Detail: The Ottoman Army in the Balkans, 1912–1913, at xvii, xix, 3, 38, 94, 114, 121, 135–36, 240, 329 (Westport, CT: Praeger Publishers, 2003).

97. Stephen Hemsley Longrigg, Iraq: 1900 to 1950: A Political, Social, and Economic History, at 41–42 (Oxford: Oxford UP, 1953); Alan Palmer, The Decline and Fall of the Ottoman Empire, at 200 (New York, NY: Barnes & Noble Books, 1992)

Image 3 Enver Paşa and Talât Paşa

Navy.[98] The Young Turks imposed "Ottomanization" and began conscripting Christians into the army for the first time in many years, driving many Assyrians and other Christians to flee the empire.[99]

Before the Ottoman Empire even joined the war, its Interior Minister Talât Paşa told the American Ambassador to the Ottoman Empire, Henry Morgenthau, of a plan to "get rid of these alien peoples" like the Armenians by large-scale murders and deportations.[100] The Ottoman government organized economic boycotts and large-scale dismissals of Christian employees in cities such as Constantinople and Smyrna. The government's "passion for Turkifying the nation seemed to demand logically the extermination of all Christians," Morgenthau later wrote.[101]

The German Empire had enjoyed prodigious growth in its industrial and military capacity during the nineteenth century, and in the twentieth century it turned its attention to world conquest.[102] It occupied present-day Cameroon, Ghana, Namibia, Tanzania, and Togoland in the 1880s, and the western Samoan islands in the 1900s. The U.S. Navy believed in the early 1900s that Germany had designs on Venezuela, Colombia, Haiti, and St. Thomas.[103] Kaiser Wilhelm II's Operational Plan III of 1903 called for a 100,000-man

98. Turkey, A Country Study, ch. 1 (Helen Chapin Metz ed., Washington, DC: Library of Congress, 5th ed. 1996), http://lcweb2.loc.gov/cgi-bin/query/r?frd/cstdy:@field(DOCID+tr0019).

99. Longrigg, Iraq: 1900 to 1950, 43, 52, 58.

100. Henry I. Morgenthau, Ambassador Morgenthau's Story 35 (Garden City, NY: Doubleday, Page & Co., 1918) [hereinafter Ambassador Morgenthau's Story]; Henry Morgenthau, United States Diplomacy on the Bosphorus: The Diaries of Ambassador Morgenthau, 1913–1916 (Ara Sarafian ed., Ann Arbor, MI: Gomidas Inst., 2004).

101. Morgenthau, Ambassador Morgenthau's Story, at 35, 200.

102. Melson, Revolution and Genocide, at 105–6.

103. *See* Steven T. Ross, American War Plans, 1890–1939, at 35–38 (London: Routledge, 2002).

German invasion of the U.S. East Coast, as he condemned U.S. "greed, ... land-grabbing, ... and murder."[104]

German "*Weltpolitik*" stressed Germany's right to equalize the extent of its colonial possessions to those of France and Britain, with the jewels in their respective crowns being French Algeria and Indochina, and British Australia, Canada, Egypt, India, and South Africa. The German leadership wanted its "share" of Africa and Asia. As one author, a former professor of history in Constantinople, described prior to the outbreak of the First World War, Germany seemed destined to exercise political power in proportion to its share of the world's wealth, industrial activity, naval strength, and due to the "superiority of the German people." It was hypocritical, under this view, for "France with the greater part of northern and central Africa, and an important corner of Asia under her flag; and Great Britain with her vast territories in every portion of the globe, [to] raise the cry of 'Wolf! Wolf!'" at the rise of German imperialism.[105] Germany sought to partake in colonialism, or the "domination of people of another culture."[106]

Echoing the German poet Friedrich von Schiller, who was reported to have remarked that Britain and Russia would someday fall, and only the Lutheran faith would remain, the Kaiser proclaimed: "The German people will be the block of granite on which our Lord will be able to elevate and achieve the civilization of the world!"[107] One of the few remaining recordings of the Kaiser has him say: "Now the sword must decide.... Germany united has never been conquered.... We will advance with God on our side, as he was with our forefathers."[108]

Great Power rivalries facilitated Turkish violations against the Armenians, Assyrians, Greeks, and other Christian and non-Christian minorities, both during the waning years of the Ottoman Empire and in the independent Kemalist Turkey that followed it. Britain's alliance with Turkey during the Crimean War repelled a Russian attempt to liberate the Ottoman Christians from the subjugation and periodic slaughter to which they had been condemned by Turkish rule. By the nineteenth century, the Ottoman Empire had become the front line between the British Empire and its Prussian allies on the one hand, and the Russian Empire on the other. Britain reinforced the Ottomans with fortifications and military aid designed to frustrate Russian designs on liberating the Ottoman Greeks and Armenians. The Prussians gave the Ottomans superior arms, and advice from some of the most talented military strategists in Europe.[109]

After a German alliance with Austro-Hungarian Empire, the British, French, and Russian empires formed the Anglo-Russian Entente, or "Triple Entente." The Ottoman Empire allied itself with the German Reich in August 1914, creating the Central Powers. The Treaty of Alliance between Germany and Turkey of 2 August, 1914, between Baron von

---

104. Quoted in Channel Four, *The First World War: Global War* (transcript of television broadcast, Sept. 2003), http://www.channel4.com/history/microsites/F/firstworldwar/pdf/p03-script.pdf.

105. Herbert Adams Gibbons, The New Map of Europe (1911–1914), at 25, 30 (New York: The Century Co., 1914).

106. Philip D. Curtin, *The Black Experience of Colonialism and Imperialism, in* Slavery, Colonialism, and Racism 23 (Sidney W. Mintz ed., New York: W.W. Norton, 1974).

107. Gibbons, The New Map of Europe, at 31.

108. *Quoted in* Channel Four, *The First World War: Under the Eagle* (transcript of television broadcast, Sept. 2003), http://web.archive.org/web/20040617190942/http://www.warkclements.com/first worldwar/.

109. 2 Shaw et al., A History of the Ottoman Empire, at 45, 56.

Wangenheim and Grand Vizier Said Halim Paşa, obligated Germany to defend Ottoman territory from Russia.[110]

During its war with the Triple Entente, Germany conquered Belgium and Poland and large swaths of French and Russian territory.[111] In doing so, the Germans enslaved hundreds of thousands of civilians in Belgium, Poland, and Southwest Africa.[112] All told, German, Austrian, and Ottoman aggression against Russia claimed about 4.7 million Russian dead and wounded.[113] In Africa, between 100,000 and 200,000 Africans died in service or bondage to the British Empire, at war with Germany for supremacy on Africa's east coast.[114] The call for a broad anti-British coalition of the world's peoples failed in India, which furnished 1.7 million men to the British forces.[115] This included a third of the British force bearing the brunt of German aggression in France.[116]

A German commander, General Limon von Sanders, assumed command of the Ottoman army in September 1914, immediately leading it in the "feverish" construction of war fortifications.[117] That month, the Ottoman ambassador to the U.S. reported that an Ottoman army of 1,000,000 men had been raised, and other Ottoman officials leaked plans to invade Russia.[118] By 1916, Germany's military leaders would further tighten their control over the Ottoman, Austrian, and Bulgarian armies.[119] Approximately 30,000 German troops served as an integral part of the Ottoman army.[120]

The Ottoman Empire launched a war against the Triple Entente of Britain, France, and Russia in October 1914, by allowing German commanders to use the Ottoman fleet to bombard Russian cities and sink Russian ships.[121] An army of 400,000 Turkish troops was poised to invade Russia by that time, and Germany had prepared a $50 million loan

---

110. *See* Treaty of Alliance Between Germany and Turkey of 2 August, 1914, http://avalon.law.yale.edu/20th_century/turkgerm.asp.

111. Martin Gilbert, The First World War: A Complete History 194, 247–48, 287, 398, 425, 449, 460 (New York: Macmillan 2004); Jan-Bart Gewald, *Imperial Germany and the Herero of Southern Africa: Genocide and the Quest for Recompense, in* Genocide, War Crimes, and the West: Ending the Culture of Impunity 60–64 (Adam Jones ed., London: Zed Books, 2004).

112. Gilbert, The First World War, at 194, 247–48, 287.

113. *Id.* at 294.

114. *See* Channel Four, *Global War.* African service to the British was often secured by compulsion, which arguably constituted kidnapping and slavery under the circumstances, or even crimes against humanity in that over 100,000 Africans perished. *See* Peter James Marshall, The Cambridge Illustrated History of the British Empire 78 (Cambridge: Cambridge UP, 2001). Since 1926, factors illustrating enslavement include measures taken to prevent escape, force or threat of force, subjection to cruel treatment, and forced labour. *See* Prosecutor v. Kunarac, Kovac, and Vukovic, Case No. IT-96-23-A & IT-96-23/1-A, Appeals Chamber, Judgment (June 12, 2002), at ¶¶ 119–23, http://www.icty.org/x/cases/kunarac/acjug/en/kun-aj020612e.pdf (citing, *inter alia*, U.S. v. Oswald Pohl and Others, Judgement of 3 November 1947, *reprinted in* 5 Trials of War Criminals Before the Nuernberg Military Tribunals under Control Council No. 10, at 958, 970 (1997)).

115. *See* Channel Four, *Global War. See also* Niall Ferguson, Empire: The Rise and Demise of the British World Order and the Lessons for Global Power 255 (New York: Basic Books, 2004); Hew Strachan, The First World War: To Arms 204, 805–14 (Oxford: Oxford UP, 2003).

116. *See* Ferguson, Empire, at 255.

117. *Turks Feverishly Fortifying,* N.Y. Times, Sept. 3, 1914, at 1.

118. *Hit Russia First, Is Turks' Strategy,* N.Y. Times, Sept. 4, 1914, at 4; *Turk to Attack Two of Allies,* N.Y. Times, Sept. 3, 1914, at 1.

119. Gilbert, The First World War, at 283; Isabel V. Hull, The Entourage of Kaiser Wilhelm II, 1888–1918, at 236–37, 268–73 (Cambridge: Cambridge UP, 2004) (describing creation of German-led Supreme Command).

120. *See* Wolfgang G. Schwanitz, *The German Middle East Policy, 1871–1945, in* Germany and the Middle East, 1871–1945, at 9 (Wolfgang G. Schwanitz ed., Princeton: Markus Wiener, 2004).

121. Dobkin, Smyrna, at 40; *Fighting Between Turks and Russians,* at 1.

to finance the war.[122] About $5 million in German gold reportedly arrived in Ottoman banks the very week of the attack on Russian cities.[123] Under General von Sanders, the Ottoman 9th, 10th, and 11th Army Corps invaded Persia and the Russian Empire in an attempt to conquer the Caucasus region.[124] Russia, not unprepared for war, invaded the Ottoman Empire in retaliation.[125]

From 1914 to 1917, the German Reich under the Kaiser encouraged its Ottoman Turkish allies in World War I to declare a "holy war" against the indigenous Christian populations living in present-day Turkey, Greece, Iraq, and Iran. As Britain and France cultivated potential Greek, Arab, and Maronite allies, and as Russia cultivated Armenian and Assyrian allies, the Kaiser believed that an Ottoman holy war, or *jihad*, would improve the German Empire's situation against the Triple Entente, declaring: "Our consuls and agents in Turkey and India must inflame the whole Mohammedan World to wild uprising...."[126]

The Kaiser wanted to mobilize Muslim support for the Caliphate against the British and Russian empires. The German General Chief of Staff (Commander in Chief), Hellmuth von Moltke, the nephew of the Prussian pioneer of "total war" against the French, encouraged Enver Paşa to declare a *jihad* to incapacitate the Ottoman extremists' internal rivals, i.e. the Christians. Max von Oppenheim, a German diplomat and archaeologist, developed a detailed plan for the *jihad*, and led an Oriental News Department in the German Foreign Office to disseminate the *jihad* call widely throughout Ottoman and other Muslim lands. The German Society for the Study of Islam published a book entitled *Haqīqat al-jihād* (The Truth of *Jihad*) in early 1915, a critical point in time for the anti-Christian movement in the Ottoman Empire. The Germans also published a periodical out of Berlin entitled simply *Al-Jihād*.[127]

The German Ambassador to Constantinople, Baron Konrad von Wangenheim, actually "directed Holy War operations from his Constantinople embassy."[128] An alliance of Africans, Turks, Kurds, Persians, Afghans, and Indians united in a holy war could splinter and destroy the British Empire, he hoped.[129] The German steel magnate and industrialist August Thyssen "dearly wished to see India and its priceless raw materials torn from Britain's grasp," and advocated the seizure of lands "rich in the natural resources most needed by German industry," including Persian Azerbaijan's oil-rich areas.[130] August Thyssen's son Fritz became an early Nazi and lavish sponsor of Hitler's rise to power.[131]

---

122. *Turks Take the Offensive,* N.Y. Times, Nov. 2, 1914, at 1.

123. *Fighting Between Turks and Russians Begun Near Trebizond*, N.Y. Times, Nov. 3, 1914, at 1.

124. *See* James B. Macdonald, *The Russian Campaign in Turkey, in* 8 The New York Times Current History: The European War 1083 (1917).

125. *Russians Invade Armenia*, N.Y. Times, Nov. 4, 1914, at 11.

126. Channel Four, *Global War*; *see also* Peter Hopkirk, Like Hidden Fire: The Plot to Bring Down the British Empire 1 (New York: Kodansha America, Inc., 1994) (paraphrasing the Kaiser as stating: "Our consuls and agents in Turkey and India must inflame the whole Muslim World against [Britain,] this hateful, lying and unscrupulous nation.").

127. *See* Schwanitz, *The German Middle East Policy, 1871–1945,* at 4–9; James J. Reid, *Total War, the Annihilation Ethic, and the Armenian Genocide, 1870–1918, in* The Armenian Genocide: History, Politics, Ethics 25–32 (Richard G. Hovannisian ed., New York: Palgrave Macmillan, 1992) (describing pioneering of Prussian doctrine and practice of total war by elder General von Moltke).

128. Hopkirk, Like Hidden Fire, at 145.

129. *See id.* at 1–2, 62.

130. *Id.* at 55.

131. *See, e.g.*, Jeffrey R. Fear, Organizing Control: August Thyssen and the Construction of German Corporate Management 64 (Cambridge, MA: Harvard UP, 2005); Itamar Levin, His Majesty's Enemies: Great Britain's War Against Holocaust Victims and Survivors 162 (Natasha Dornberg & Judith Yalon-Fortus trans., Westport, CT: Greenwood Publ'g Group, 2001); Oliver

The Germans' call to pan-Islamic unity against Eastern Christians was entirely consistent with Ottoman rulers' own objectives of expanding their Empire throughout Asia and Africa using a German-trained army.[132] It was welcome to Ottoman leaders like Talât, for whom the empire cried out to be "Ottomanized" to prevent Christians from achieving political equality with European help.[133] A comprehensive study of the diplomatic traffic between the German and Ottoman Empires concluded that the Ottomans craved territorial and political supremacy in "North Africa and western Asia," especially Egypt, Libya, Persia, and southwestern Russia.[134]

The Kaiser announced to the world on November 14, 1914 that the Sheikh al-Islam, sometimes described as the highest religious authority in the Ottoman Empire, had declared holy war on behalf of the entire Islamic world against Britain, France, and Russia.[135] For some time, Germany's leadership had anxiously anticipated the Caliph's mobilization of the Islamic world against Britain and France.[136] Within two weeks after the Ottoman Empire declared war on the Entente (Great Britain, France, and Russia), the Sultan, still acting as a figurehead for the Young Turk regime, declared a *jihad* or holy war "against the enemies of Islam, who have proven their hostility by their attacks on the Caliphate."[137] The next day, a key CUP official led a march through Istanbul "meant to demonstrate the people's agreement with the Sultan's declaration of holy war against the enemies of Islam."[138] The Ottoman Minister of War, Enver Paşa, issued a proclamation to the army urging it on: "Forward, always forward! Victory, glory, and paradise are before us, death and disgrace behind."[139]

The Sheikh al-Islam, who was also a Committee of Union and Progress (CUP) appointee, endorsed the declaration of *jihad* and proclaimed it in print; violence against Christian Armenians followed quickly.[140] The declarations of *jihad* incited genocide against the Armenians.[141] The German general Limon von Sanders encouraged the Ottoman army to "throw[] these infidels [i.e., the Greeks of the Aegean region] into the sea."[142] The outbreak of religious warfare led to widespread massacres by Ottoman Turks against Christian villagers, including Armenians, Assyrians, and Greeks.[143]

THOMSON, MASS PERSUASION IN HISTORY: AN HISTORICAL ANALYSIS OF THE DEVELOPMENT OF PROPAGANDA TECHNIQUES 114 (New York: Crane, Russak & Co., 1977).

132. *See* GILBERT, THE FIRST WORLD WAR, at 389.

133. DADRIAN, THE HISTORY OF THE ARMENIAN GENOCIDE, at 378.

134. ULRICH TRUMPENER, GERMANY AND THE OTTOMAN EMPIRE, 1914–1918, at 114–15 (Princeton: Princeton UP, 1968).

135. *Kaiser Informs Son of Moslem Holy War*, N.Y. TIMES, Nov. 19, 1914, at 1.

136. *See* HOPKIRK, LIKE HIDDEN FIRE, at 54–55; TRUMPENER, GERMANY AND THE OTTOMAN EMPIRE, at 117.

137. *Proclamation of the Grand Council of Ulema*, LA TURQUIE, Nov. 16, 1914, *quoted in* DE COURTOIS, THE FORGOTTEN GENOCIDE, at 153.

138. *Yesterday's Great March*, LA TURQUIE, Nov. 15, 1914, *quoted in* DE COURTOIS, THE FORGOTTEN GENOCIDE, 152.

139. *Proclamation by Enver; Says Turks with Allah's Help Will Destroy Their Enemies*, N.Y. TIMES, Nov. 15, 1914, at 5.

140. BALAKIAN, THE BURNING TIGRIS, at 169–70.

141. *See id.*; JACK ZAKARIAN, THE ARMENIAN GENOCIDE: NEWS ACCOUNTS FROM THE AMERICAN PRESS: 1915–1922, at xiii (Richard Kloian ed., Richmond, CA: Anto Publishing, 1988).

142. TANER AKÇAM, FROM EMPIRE TO REPUBLIC: TURKISH NATIONALISM AND THE ARMENIAN GENOCIDE 146 (London: Zed Books, 2004); Travis, *Ottoman Genocide of the Assyrians*, at 342.

143. AKÇAM, FROM EMPIRE TO REPUBLIC, at 146–47; Travis, *Ottoman Genocide of the Assyrians*, at 331–32, 341–42.

E. Ottoman Sources on the Armenian Genocide: The Deportations, 1914–1917

In notes written after a meeting with Young Turk leaders, Max Erwin von Scheubner-Richter, the commander of a joint German-Turkish special guerrilla force, described plans to "destroy" the Armenians of the Ottoman Empire. He wrote:

> The first item on this agenda concerns the liquidation of the Armenians. Ittihad will dangle before the Allies a specter of an alleged revolution prepared by the Armenian Dashnak party. Moreover, local incidents of social unrest and acts of Armenian self-defense will deliberately be provoked and inflated and will be used as pretexts to effect the deportations. Once en route, however, the convoys will be attacked and exterminated by Kurdish and Turkish brigands, and in part by gendarmes, who will be instigated for that purpose by Ittihad.[144]

Within three months from the Sultan's declaration of war on the Christians, most Armenians in the Ottoman army had been "worked to death or murdered" in labor battalions or massacres.[145]

The Ottoman archives confirm in abundant detail the existence of a plan to attack and exterminate Armenian villagers and deportees. In one Ottoman document, Abbas Halim Paşa, Minister of Public Works in 1915, is described as "a member of the cabinet which ordered the deportations entailing the massacre of hundreds of thousands of Christians."[146] The motion in the Ottoman Parliament of 1918 to investigate wartime offenses against civilians made clear that these were no ordinary murders or relocations, but breaches of "the rules of law and humanity."[147] In July 1919, an Extraordinary Court-Martial convicted Talât Paşa and other defendants of massacres committed in Trabzon *vilayet* and the districts of Ankara and Yozgat.[148] On February 5, 1919, in its verdict on the Yozgat series of court-martials, an Ottoman tribunal found the defendants, including the governor of the Ottoman province that included Ankara, guilty of the "mass murder and plunder of Armenian deportees."[149] On March 3, 1919, the Ottoman Sultan described the offenses being investigated as "crimes against humanity."[150]

An Ottoman court-martial convicted several wartime ministers of "the crime of massacre," the term "genocide" having yet to be invented.[151] In late April 1919, during the

---

144. *Quoted in* DEBORAH DWORK & ROBERT JAN VAN PELT, THE HOLOCAUST: A HISTORY 38 (2002).

145. Robert Melson, *Responses to the Armenian Genocide: America, the Yishuv, Israel*, 20.1 HOLOCAUST AND GENOCIDE STUDIES 103, 107 (2006).

146. *Quoted in* GUENTER LEWY, THE ARMENIAN MASSACRES IN OTTOMAN TURKEY: A DISPUTED GENOCIDE 125 (Salt Lake City, UT: Univ. of Utah Press, 2007).

147. *Quoted in* Vahakn Dadrian, *The Historical and Legal Interconnections Between the Armenian Genocide and the Jewish Holocaust: From Impunity to Retributive Justice*, 23 YALE J. OF INT'L L. 503, 551 (1998).

148. *Quoted in Turkish Military Tribunal's Verdict, in* ENCYCLOPEDIA OF GENOCIDE 89–90 (Israel W. Charny ed., Santa Barbara, CA: ABC-CLIO, 1999).

149. Guenter Lewy, *Revisiting the Armenian Genocide*, MIDDLE EAST Q., Sept. 22, 2005, http://www.highbeam.com/doc/1G1-135763439.html.

150. *Quoted in* Dadrian, *The Historical and Legal Interconnections,* at 501.

151. *See* WILLIAM SCHABAS, "THE CRIME OF CRIMES": GENOCIDE IN INTERNATIONAL LAW 21 (Cambridge: Cambridge UP, 2000). *See also* Trabzon verdicts, No. 3616, 3617, *cited in* DADRIAN, HISTORY OF THE ARMENIAN GENOCIDE, at 308, and Dadrian, *The Historical and Legal Interconnections,*

Constantinople trials of Turkish officials for the Armenian massacres, the prosecutor declared "in opening the trial, [that] it was necessary to punish the authors of the massacres which had filled the whole world with a feeling of horror."[152] At the Constantinople trials, General Vehib Paşa, commander of the Ottoman Third Army, condemned "the murder and extermination of the Armenians and the plunder and robbery of their property." He accused a high-ranking CUP official of having "procured and engaged in the command zone of the Third Army, the butchers of human beings.... He organized gallows birds as well as gendarmes and policemen with blood on their hand and blood in their eyes."[153] The head of the Special Bureau of the Interior Ministry, and the Deputy Director of the Office for the Resettlement of Tribes and Refugees, provided evidence to the Turkish Military Tribunal that the purpose of the deportations, according to Talât Paşa, was the extermination of the Armenians.[154]

Talât Paşa told the Swedish military attaché in Constantinople, Captain Einar af Wirsén, that press reports that "we would have executed, or in other ways killed none less than 800,000 Armenians" were untrue, because "it was only 600,000."[155] Talât's successor acknowledged that a commission convened by the Ottoman government to study the subject concluded after an investigation that 800,000 Armenians had perished during the war.[156] Halil Bey, commander of the Ottoman Army Group East, boasted in his postwar memoirs that he caused about 300,000 Armenian deaths in this way, although he "didn't count." In 1918, Halil, who was the uncle of Enver Paşa, proclaimed that "I have tried to wipe out the Armenian nation to the last individual."[157] Halil is estimated today to have killed 15,000 Armenians and other Christians in concentration camps established in the Mosul area for the Anatolian deportees.[158]

The memoirs of other Ottoman officials lay the blame for the Armenian massacres squarely on the head of Talât Paşa, the Ottoman Minister of the Interior. The president of the Ottoman Chamber of Deputies wrote in his memoirs that Talât Paşa "proposed that the country be cleansed of its treacherous elements."[159] Talât's own memoirs described the so-called Special Organization (*Teşkilat-ı Mahsûsa*), which was the focus of the Constantinople trial's findings that the deported Armenians were murdered, as an agency of the Ottoman Empire.[160] The Special Organization was run by an aide to the Sultan, Cevat Bey, as well as by the director-general of security from the Interior Ministry, a representative of the War Ministry, Behaeddin Şakir of the CUP Supreme Directorate, and the Ottoman Minister of Education, Dr. Mehmed Nazim.[161] It recruited members of crimi-

---

at 508; Vahakn N. Dadrian, *The Turkish Military Tribunal's Prosecution of the Authors of the Armenian Genocide: Four Major Court-Martial Series*, 7 Holocaust and Genocide Studies 28, 33–34 (1997); *see generally* Dadrian, The History of the Armenian Genocide, at 330–41.

152. *Turks Hang Kemal Bey for Armenian Massacres*, N.Y. Times, Feb. 12, 1919, at 1.

153. *Quoted in* Lewy, *Revising the Armenian Genocide*.

154. *See id.*; Akçam, A Shameful Act, at 153–54.

155. Einar af Wirsén, Minnen Från Fred och Krig 132 (Stockholm: Bonnier, 1942), *quoted in* Avedian, The Armenian Genocide.

156. *See* Akçam, A Shameful Act, at 183; Akçam, From Empire to Republic, at 199; Kiernan, Blood and Soil, at 415.

157. *Quoted in* Vahakn Dadrian, *The Armenian Genocide: An Interpretation, in* America and the Armenian Genocide of 1915, at 65 (Jay M. Winter ed., Cambridge: Cambridge UP, 2003). *See also* Dadrian, The History of the Armenian Genocide, at 405; Kiernan, Blood and Soil, at 413.

158. *See* Bloxham, The Great Game of Genocide, at 88.

159. Akçam, A Shameful Act, at 51, 92.

160. *See id.* at 94.

161. *See* Akçam, A Shameful Act, at 94–95, 131 (Cevat Bey was on committee that ran Special Organization); Dadrian, *The Historical and Legal Interconnections*, at 526; S. Tanvir Wasti, *The Last*

nal gangs, Kurdish tribes, and Muslim refugees from the Russian Empire to serve as irregular forces under the control of the Ottoman army.[162]

An Ottoman officer stationed in the Ottoman General Headquarters accused the Special Organization of an "enormous crime" and stated: "These felons who were released from the prisons committed the greatest crimes during the Armenian horrors."[163] A leader of the Special Organization wrote in his memoirs that the reason for its existence was the Armenian persecutions, not intelligence as was claimed as a cover story.[164] Another leader testified in Constantinople that the Interior Minister ordered that the deported Armenians be massacred.[165] Prior to that, Dr. Nazim and Dr. Şakir participated in secret CUP meetings "meant to resolve the Armenian question by radical means," at which meetings the "attendees outlined the measures to be taken and the methods to be used for the liquidation of Ottoman Armenians."[166] An Ottoman military tribunal convicted Talât, Enver, Cemal, and Nazim of the crime of "massacre," and along with Şakir these defendants received death sentences from the tribunal.[167]

A Venezuelan officer who became inspector-general of the Turkish forces in Armenia described witnessing "hordes" of corpses belonging to Armenian women and children deported from Anatolia by Ottoman officials.[168] He concluded that:

> [U]pon the breaking out of the World War the massacres recommenced with such violence that, of the two and one-half million Armenians that lived in Turkey before 1914, I believe not even one-half million remain, including the three or four hundred thousand who dwelt in Constantinople and Smyrna, and who, by means of I know not what miracle, escaped the deportations and lived....
>
> There can be no doubt that the massacres and deportations took place in accordance with a carefully laid-out plan for which the responsibility lay with the retrograde party, headed by the Grand Vizier Talaat Pasha and the civil author-

---

Chroniclers of the Mabeyn, in TURKEY: IDENTITY DEMOCRACY, POLITICS 1, 4 (Sylvia Kedourie ed., London: Taylor & Francis, 1998) (Cevat Bey was successor of Tahsin Pasha); AYKUT KANSU, THE REVOLUTION OF 1908 IN TURKEY 124 (Leiden, the Netherlands and Boston, MA: Brill, 1997) (Tahsin Pasha was First Secretary to the Ottoman Sultan).

162. *See* AKÇAM, A SHAMEFUL ACT, at 94–95, 131–35 (describing formation and recruitment of Special Organization death squads); AKÇAM, FROM EMPIRE TO REPUBLIC, at 161 (Cevat Bey called Special Organization "part of the army"); G.S. GRABER, CARAVANS TO OBLIVION: THE ARMENIAN GENOCIDE, 1915, at 166–67 (New York: J. Wiley, 1996) (reproducing testimony of Cevat Bey on Special Organization); *see also* Dadrian, *The Historical and Legal Interconnections,* at 526–27 & n.106 (stating that Dr. Şakir "directed and supervised the killing operations in the interior of Turkey," and that "Special Organization Chieftain Major Yakub Cemil, who played a major role in the Armenian genocide, openly declared: 'If my fatherland's interests required that I kill my father, I would not hesitate for a moment.'").

163. *Quoted in id.* at 93.

164. *See id.* at 94–95.

165. *See* AKÇAM, A SHAMEFUL ACT, at 123, 158, 164, 399.

166. Dadrian, *The Historical and Legal Interconnections,* at 526 (citing Vahakn N. Dadrian, *The Secret Young-Turk Ittihadist Conference and the Decision for the World War I Genocide of the Armenians,* 7 HOLOCAUST & GENOCIDE STUDIES 173 (1993)).

167. See KIERNAN, BLOOD AND SOIL, at 415 (citing Vahakn Dadrian, *The Armenian Genocide in Official Turkish Records,* 22 J. OF POLITICAL AND MILITARY SOCIOLOGY 58–168 (1994)).

168. RAFAEL DE NOGALES MÉNDEZ, FOUR YEARS BENEATH THE CRESCENT 17, 136–37 (Muna Lee trans., New York: C. Scribner's Sons, 1926); *see also* GAUNT, MASSACRES, RESISTANCE, PROTECTORS, at 110.

> ities under his orders. They aimed to make an end first of the Armenians, then of the Greeks and other Christians, Ottoman subjects in the Empire.[169]

A former district-governor or *Kaimakam*[170] of Harput/Mamouret-el-Azîz also confirmed that the deportees were systematically massacred by Kurdish tribes allied to the Ottoman forces:

> There is no doubt that what is related as to the proceedings of the gendarmes and the Kurdish tribes actually took place. On receiving a caravan of Armenians the gendarmes searched them one by one, men and women, taking any money they might find, and stripping them of the better portions of their clothing. When they were satisfied that there remained no money, good clothes, or other things of value, they sold the Armenians in thousands to the Kurds, on the stipulation that none should be left alive....
>
> After purchasing the caravans, the Kurds stripped all the Armenians, men and women, of their clothes, so that they remained entirely naked. They then shot them down, every one.... [171]

He described the fate of those Armenians who initially resisted deportation from Urfa:

> As they were aware of what had happened to their kinsmen ... [the Armenians] did not give up their arms [when ordered to do so], but showed armed resistance, killing one man of the police and three gendarmes. The authorities of Urfa applied for a force from Aleppo, and by order of Jemal Pasha—the executioner of Syria—Fakhry Pasha came with cannon. He turned the Armenian quarters into a waste place, killing the men and the children, and great numbers of the women, except such as yielded themselves to share the fate of their sisters—expulsion on foot to Deir-el-Zûr, after the Pasha and his officers had selected the prettiest amongst them. Disease was raging among them; they were outraged by the Turks and Kurds; and hunger and thirst completed their extermination.[172]

As in Nazi-occupied Eastern Europe, the Armenians who had gold teeth suffered their being ripped out; those who swallowed their savings had their entrails examined for gold coins.[173]

Contemporaneous Ottoman documents other than court-martial testimony or postwar memoirs, stored in archives until recently, corroborate these accounts of a large-scale forcible deportation of Armenians from their ancestral homelands to Syria or Mesopotamia. These documents are similarly incriminating of the Ministry of the Interior. Massacres of Assyrians in Persia (described in Chapter VII) and arrests in Van prompted armed re-

---

169. De Nogales, Four Years Beneath the Crescent, at 136; Dadrian, *Documentation of the Armenian Genocide in German and Austrian Sources*, at 113.

170. For sources on the responsibilities of a *Kaimakam*, see H.F.B. Lynch, 2 Armenia, Travels and Studies 4 (New York: Longmans, Green, and Co., 1901); June Starr, Law as Metaphor: From Islamic Courts to the Palace of Justice 79 (Albany, NY: SUNY Press, 1992).

171. Fa'iz El-Ghusein, Martyred Armenia 28–29 (English trans., New York: George H. Doran Co., 1918).

172. *Id.* at 9.

173. *See* El-Ghusein, Martyred Armenia, at 28–29. For the Nazi practice, see for example the Nuremberg trial proceedings, which quote a Nazi document stating that at a prison in Minsk in 1943, "all German and Russian Jews who were turned over to us had their gold bridgework, crowns, and fillings pulled or broken out" before being "finished off." 3 Nuremberg Trial Proceedings 563, http://avalon.law.yale.edu/imt/12-14-45.asp.

sistance by the Christians of Van, whom Talât then ordered deported *en masse* in December 1914.[174] An order in May 1915 from Talât to the Fourth Army calls for reprisals against Muslims hiding Christians from persecution, specifically in the form of military commissions for such protectors of the innocent.[175] On May 27, 1915, the Ministry of the Interior issued an order to the provinces for Van, Erzerum, and Bitlis for the deportation of the Armenians.[176] Shortly after ordering an attack on the Assyrian Christians of Van by the *vali* of Mosul, Talât issued orders to the *valis* of Diyarbekir, Harput, Trebizond, and Sivas for the "deportation" of "[a]ll Armenians" to Mosul, Urfa, or Deir-el-Zor/Zûr.[177]

Reşid Bey, the *vali* of Diyarbekir, confirmed to the Ministry of Interior in September 1915 that there were no Armenians left in Diyarbekir to deport.[178] In 1916, a decree from the ministry to the provinces (and to the Ministry of War) indicated that large numbers of Armenian orphans were to be taken into Turkish or Kurdish homes, and others placed in orphanages.[179]

The Ottoman Minister of Foreign Affairs and Grand Vizier, Said Halim, made exaggerated claims to Morgenthau that were reminiscent of Adolf Hitler's claims of millions of German deaths at the hands of Jewish Bolsheviks in the lead-up to World War II. He protested to Morgenthau that "Armenian 'rebels' had killed 120,000 Turks at Van." Morgenthau found such claims to be "absurd" and attempts to demonize a "persecuted race." On other occasions, even the vizier admitted that massacres, "excesses and violations ... have been committed," which he said he "deplore[d]." He explained the position of the Sultan and the Foreign Ministry as being that there was "no justification," but "extenuating circumstances," for the massacres. He described a conflict within the Ottoman regime, as 40 troops "lost their lives defending the Armenians," while the "gendarmes committed many deplorable excesses."[180]

A foreign soldier serving as an Ottoman artillery officer wrote that the Ottoman forces purposefully sent shell after shell into Van, a historic Armenian city, thereby destroying it:

> Our ferocious onslaught and our heavy artillery fire had turned two-thirds of Van into a smouldering, fiery shambles, which was erupting at our feet like a blazing volcano, gushing out enormous puffs of smoke mingled with red tongues of flame and innumerable cascades of crimson sparks. It was a Dantesque scene....

---

174. *See* Başbakanlik Osmanlı Arşivi Dâhiliye Nezâreti, Şifre Kalemi [Prime Ministerial Ottoman Archives, Istanbul, hereinafter abbreviated as "BOA.DH.SFR"] No. 48/38 and 48/39, Dec. 18, 1914, *cited in* GAUNT, MASSACRES, RESISTANCE, PROTECTORS, at 132.

175. *See* BOA.DH.SFR 53/85, May 23, 1915, Talât to Fourth Army, *cited in* GAUNT, MASSACRES, RESISTANCE, PROTECTORS, at 67.

176. *See* BOA.DH.SFR 53/129, May 27, 1915, Ministry of Interior to several vilayets, entitled "Regulation for resettlement of Armenians relocated to other places because of war conditions and emergency political requirements." An image of this decree is viewable at http://wikipedia.7val.de/wiki/Tehcir_Law.

177. *See* BOA.DH.SFR 54787, June 21, 1915, Ministry of Interior to several vilayets, *cited in* Gaunt, *Ottoman Bystanders,* at 11.

178. *See* BOA.DH.BUM. 2Sb 68/71, Sept. 18, 1915, Reshid Bey to Ministry of Interior, *cited in* GAUNT, MASSACRES, RESISTANCE, PROTECTORS, at 69.

179. *See* BOA.DH.SFR 63/142, Apr. 30, 1916, Talât Pasha to Minister of War Enver Pasha and provinces of Adana, Erzerum, Edirne, Halep, Hudavendigar, Sivas, Diyarbekir, Mamuretulaziz, Konya, Kastamonu, Trabzon, and districts of Izmit, Canik, Eskisehir, Karahisar-I Sahib, Kayseri ve Nigde Maras, and Urfa.

180. MORGENTHAU, AMBASSADOR MORGENTHAU'S STORY, at ch. 26, http://net.lib.byu.edu/estu/wwi/comment/morgenthau/Morgen26.htm.

> I could not help shuddering every time I looked from the top of the fortress at the burning villages [in the countryside surrounding Van]....
>
> We are credited with having fired over sixteen thousand cannon shots into that city during the first two weeks of the siege.... Wherever our shells exploded buildings collapsed....[181]

Morgenthau recounted unstinting Ottoman efforts to block humanitarian aid from saving Armenians from starvation and disease. Defense Minister Enver and Foreign Minister Halim "were ever insistent on the point which they constantly raised, that no foreigners should furnish relief to the Armenians." Djemal Paşa, who had "jurisdiction over the Christians in Syria," insisted that Morgenthau "order" American consuls to stop helping the dying Armenians.[182]

The cover-up of the Armenian massacres reached the highest levels of the Ottoman regime. Talât issued secret telegrams countermanding widely publicized orders to protect the convoys of Armenian deportees from massacres and starvation.[183] As one author argues:

> Many telegrams sent by Talât are used in Turkish sources to prove that the Ottoman government did not intend to annihilate the Armenians, but merely deport them. In these telegrams [Talât] talks about orderly deportation and humane treatment of the deportees. Most of these were sent by Talât to appease the German ambassador in Istanbul.... Talât sent telegrams to the provinces merely to silence the foreign ambassadors and then immediately followed them up with a second cable cancelling the first ...[184]

Foreign Minister Halim "complained to [Morgenthau] that the American consuls were sending facts about the Armenians to America and ... insisted that [the reports] should be stopped."[185] The German consul in Adana reported that a Ministry of the Interior inspector followed up on such a telegram to see that it was not carried out, and indiscriminate deportations continued.[186]

The Patriarch of the Ottoman Armenians, Zaven Ter Eghiayan, submitted a report to German ambassador, which confirmed the accounts of Ottoman politicians and military:

> In several provinces, the male population when they were over ten years old, has been massacred, young women are abducted by Muslims and children forcibly snatched from their parents and distributed to Muslim families.

181. Rafael De Nogales, Memoirs of a Soldier of Fortune 270 (Whitefish, MT: Kessinger Publishing, 2006) (1932).

182. Morgenthau, Ambassador Morgenthau's Story, at ch. 26, http://net.lib.byu.edu/estu/wwi/comment/morgenthau/Morgen26.htm.

183. The telegrams were considered by a German court that trial Talât Pasha's assassin for murder in the 1920s. *See* Jacques Derogy, Resistance and Revenge: The Armenian Assassination of the Turkish Leaders Responsible for the 1915 Massacres and Deportations 91–106 (A.M. Berrett trans., New Brunswick, NJ: Transaction Publishers, 1990). One, for example, dated December 12, 1915, stated: "Collect and keep only those orphans who do not remember the tortures to which their parents have been subjected. Send the rest away with the caravans." *Quoted in id.* at 101. Another, dated, September 16, 1915, called for an "end" to the Armenian "existence," no matter how "criminal the measures taken may be," and without regard to age, sex, or conscience. *Quoted in* Encyclopedia of Genocide, at 96 (Israel W. Charny ed., Santa Barbara, CA: ABC-CLIO, 1999).

184. Akçam, A Shameful Act, at 169–70.

185. Morgenthau, Ambassador Morgenthau's Story, ch. 26.

186. *See* Akçam, A Shameful Act, at 170.

> In other provinces, the Armenian population has been completely destroyed [*vernichtet worden*]. The fields and the major roads are covered with dead bodies.... There is no cruelty and no destruction [*Vernichtungsmittel*], which has not occurred, even when we have believed that they were a relic of the barbaric centuries before the Christian era....
>
> The churches and monasteries are mostly in ruins, and most of them have been desecrated and by contemptuous uses tainted. The sacred cult objects have been dishonored and sold. In several provinces, the clergy were massacred. The number of priests killed is in the thousands.

The patriarch wrote that 800,000 to 1,000,000 Armenian souls had already been deported towards the Mesopotamian and Syrian deserts and "mercilessly destroyed" (*Vernichtung*).[187]

Armenian oral histories reflect that the kidnapping of women and girls from Armenian families, and their transfer to Turkish families, which fits within the core definition of genocide under the Genocide Convention, were common:

> Now there are many Armenian women among the Turks. They were taken in and remained with them and bore their children. They are all Turkicized [sic] now—gone from our blood. The children don't know their identity, only their mothers do.... After the deportations they gathered up a lot of the ... women and children. Many of them objected and did not want to leave because they had nowhere to go and no one to go to. Many of them would have left if they had had parents living. But here they were with children and a home, after all, and did not want to leave.... There are many such cases....[188]

Once removed from their families, Armenian women and children "were no longer seen as representatives of the Armenian people," and "became vulnerable to sexual abuse and victimization as a slave labor force," thus destroying the Armenian group in part.[189] For example, documents from the French archives indicate wholesale violations against girls:

> Soldiers were pushing in front of them 300 or 400 naked Armenian girls and women. These were put up for auction and the whole lot disposed of, some for two, three, and four francs. Only Mohammedans were allowed to buy. The salesman kept on exclaiming: "Rejoice oh ye faithful in the shame of the Christians."[190]

Numerous other sources document the targeting of Armenian women and girls for torture, abuse, and murder, resulting in severe disruptions of Armenian reproduction and family life. The indictment of wartime Ottoman leaders by a postwar Turkish Military Tribunal stated that during the Armenian deportations, Ottoman gendarmes committed atrocities against the convoys of deportees, including massacres, rapes, plunders, and "all sorts of tortures and shameful acts." The police chief of Trabzon testified in 1919

187. German Foreign Office, Political Archives [hereinafter DE/PA-AA], Doc. No. DE/PA-AA/R14089, 1915-A-35070, Dec. 4, 1915, report by the Ambassador in Extraordinary Mission in Constantinople, Wolff-Metternich, to the German Imperial Chancellor, Bethmann Hollweg, enclosing confidential report by Armenian Patriarch in Turkey to the German Ambassador, dated Nov. 10, 1915.

188. Derderian, *Gender-Specific Aspects of the Armenian Genocide*, at 13 (quoting oral history interview of Kevork Voskeritchian, male native of Urfa).

189. *Id.* at 14.

190. Les Grandes Puissances: L'Empire Ottoman et les Arméniens Dans Les Archives Françaises: Receuil de Documents 206 (Arthur Beylerian, ed., Paris: Université de Paris I, 1983), *quoted in* Katharine Derderian, *Common Fate, Different Experience: Gender-Specific Aspects of the Armenian Genocide*, 1915–1917, 19.1 Holocaust and Genocide Studies 1, 10–11 (2005).

that during the war he sent half a dozen Armenian girls as a "gift" from the local governor to members of the Ottoman ruling party. An Ottoman customs inspector testified that the Red Crescent building was used as a "pleasure-dome for ... the governor [who] had been satisfying his lust...."[191]

F. German Sources on the Armenian Genocide: The Deportations, 1914–1917

Numerous German sources also confirm large-scale massacres of Anatolian Armenians between 1914 and 1917. Officials of the German Empire, allied with the Ottoman Empire in World War I, corroborated the accounts of the victims, Ottoman officials, and Entente diplomats of widespread massacres, rapes, and devastation. German military officers, diplomats, and civilians actually witnessed the planning and execution of the Ottoman Christian genocide as it unfolded. The accounts of German ambassadors and other officials dealing with the Ottoman Empire are replete with such terms as "extermination,"

191. *See, e.g.,* Vahakn N. Dadrian, *The Documentation of the World War I Armenian Massacres in the Proceedings of the Turkish Military Tribunal,* 23 Int'l J. of Middle East Studies 549, 556, 559–60, 567, 574 (1991) (indictment of wartime Ottoman leaders by postwar Turkish Military Tribunal stated that during the Armenian deportations, Ottoman gendarmes committed "rape" and "all sorts of tortures and shameful acts"); *id.* at 574 (police chief of Trabzon testified in 1919 that during the war he sent half a dozen Armenian girls as a "gift" from the local governor to members of the Ottoman ruling party); *id.* (Ottoman customs inspector testified that Red Crescent building was used as a "pleasure-dome for indulging in lasciviousness where the governor had been satisfying his lust"); *id.* (Oscar Heizer, U.S. Consul for Trabzon, reported mass rapes); Annette Hoss, *The Trial of Perpetrators by the Turkish Military Tribunals: The Case of Yozgat, in* The Armenian Genocide: History, Politics, Ethics, at 217 (according to testimony before Turkish military tribunal, most Armenian women were raped during the war, often repeatedly); DE/PA-AA/R14087, K.No. 81/B. 1645, June 27, 1915, report from Consul in Aleppo, Walter Rößler, to the German Imperial Chancellor, Bethmann Hollweg ("The Turkish government has driven its Armenian subjects, the innocent ones, mark you, into the desert in thousands upon thousands, under the pretext of having to remove them from the war areas, exempting neither the sick nor pregnant women..., has driven the women to such desperation that they set out their babies and newborns by the wayside, has sold their adolescent daughters, with the result that they have thrown themselves even with their small children into the river. It has left them to the mercy of their guards and therefore to dishonour; an escort which dragged away the girls and sold them. It has driven them into the hands of the Bedouins, who have plundered and kidnapped them."); DE/PA-AA/R14090, 1916-A-02889, Enclosure 1, BN. 944, Jan. 13, 1916, report from Consul in Aleppo, Rößler, to the German Ambassador in Extraordinary Mission in Constantinople, Wolff-Metternich ("The accounts of the survivors ... of the plundering, the violation, abduction and sale of women, girls and boys by the accompanying guards and local inhabitants are made credible by the obvious condition of the survivors in Aleppo...."); *see also* U.S. National Archives, General Records of the Dep't of State, Record Group 59 (Decimal File, 1910–1929), Doc. No. 59,867.4016/74, U.S. Amb. Henry Morgenthau to U.S. Secretary of State Williams Jennings Bryan, May 25, 1915, *quoted in* Armen Hairapetian, *"Race Problems" and the Armenian Genocide: The State Department File,* 37 Armenian Rev. 41, 47 (1984) (reporting mass rapes against Armenians); U.S. National Archives, General Records of the Dep't of State, Record Group 59 (Decimal File, 1910–1929), Doc. No. 59,867.4016/72, Jesse Jackson, U.S. Consul in Aleppo, to Amb. Morgenthau, May 12, 1915, *quoted* Hairapetian, *"Race Problems" and the Armenian Genocide,* at 46 (similar); U.S. National Archives, General Records of their Dep't of State, Record Group 59 (Decimal File, 1910–1929), Doc. No. 59,867.4016/373/encl., Jesse Jackson, U.S. Consul in Aleppo, to Amb. Morgenthau, Mar. 4, 1918, *quoted* Hairapetian, *"Race Problems" and the Armenian Genocide,* at 44–45 (similar); Melson, Revolution and Genocide, at 334 n.41, 378–83, 408–411 (similar reports from various sources).

"massacre," "destruction," "slaughter," "systematic butchery," and "murder of thousands of human beings."[192] As the main ally of the Ottomans in World War I, the Germans had military officers "stationed throughout the Empire," trained and led Turkish troops, and their "military commanders and soldiers undoubtedly knew, saw, and it is alleged [indirectly] participated" in the genocide of Ottoman Christians.[193] In September 1916, Kaiser Wilhelm I, through Field-Marshal Paul von Hindenburg, actually "obtained effective command" of the Ottoman armies.[194] The Ottoman Supreme Military Command participated from near the beginning in the Armenian deportations.[195]

The Interim German Ambassador to the Ottoman Empire, Wilhelm von Radowitz, reported in October 1915 that 1.2 million Armenians had been massacred and the remainder were at extreme risk.[196] His detailed statistical survey of Armenian orphans in 1916 estimated that 1.5 million Armenians had perished.[197]

The German Ambassador, Count Paul von Wolff-Metternich, concluded in 1916 that the Ottomans were "exterminating the Armenian race" and that they refused to be deterred by either requests of their German allies or threats by their British and Russian enemies. In July 1916, he wrote that the Armenian concentration camp at Ras ul-Ain was liquidated as part of a campaign for the resolution of "the Armenian question by the destruction of the Armenian race."[198] He informed the chancellor that 30,000 Armenians had been deported from Istanbul alone, and plans were in place to remove the remaining 80,000 from their homes and communities.[199] His predecessor, Ambassador Baron Hans von Wangenheim, wrote to the imperial chancellor that:

> It has come to light that the banishment of the Armenians is not only motivated by military considerations. The Minister of the Interior, Talaat Bey, recently spoke about this without reservation to Dr. Mordtmann, who is currently

---

192. Dadrian, *Documentation of the Armenian Genocide in German and Austrian Sources,* at 100, 101, 124.

193. Yair Auron, The Banality of Indifference: Zionism and the Armenian Genocide 49 (New Brunswick, NJ: Transaction Publishers, 2003).

194. *See Eastern European Front Campaigns, in* 30 The Encyclopædia Britannica 886, 911 (New York: Encyclopedia Britannica, 12th ed. 1922); Gilbert, The First World War, at 183.

195. *See* Donald Bloxham, *Internal Colonization, Inter-Imperial Conflict and the Armenian Genocide, in* Empire, Colony, Genocide, at 337–38.

196. *See* Johannes Lepsius, Deutschland und Armenien: Sammlung diplomatischer Aktenstücke 295–96 (Potsdam: Tempelverlag, 1919) ("[W]enn man nun die Gesamtzahl der türkischen Armenier auf 2 Millionen unde die Zahl der Verschickten auf 1½ Million veranschlagt und dasselbe Verhältnis zwischen Überlebenden und Umgekmmenen wie bei den Waisen der Schwester Rohner annimmt, so gelangt man zu einer Zahl von über 1175000 von Umgekommenen und rund 325,000 Überlebenden.").

197. *See* Vahakn Dadrian, *Documentation of the Armenian Genocide in German and Austrian Sources, in* The Widening Circle of Genocide, at 121.

198. DE/PA-AA/R14092, 1916-A-18548, A53a/1916, July 10, 1916, the German Ambassador on Extraordinary Mission in Constantinople, Wolff-Metternich, to the German Imperial Chancellor, Bethmann Hollweg. *See* Vahakn Dadrian, *Documentation of Armenian Genocide in German Sources, in* Encyclopedia of Genocide 91 (Israel W. Charny ed., Santa Barbara, CA: ABC-CLIO, 1999) (Count Metternich quoted as stating that Ottomans were carrying out their "purpose to resolve the Armenian Question by the destruction of the Armenian race" and refused to be deterred); Dadrian, *Documentation of the Armenian Genocide in German and Austrian Sources*, at 121 ("Die türkische Regierung hat sich in der Durchführung ihres Programms: Erledigung der armenischen Frage durch die Vernichtung der armenischen Rasse....").

199. *See* Dadrian, *Comparative Aspects of the Armenian and Jewish Cases of Genocide: A Sociohistoric Perspective, in* Is the Holocaust Unique?, at 170; Dadrian, The History of the Armenian Genocide, at xxviii.

employed by the Imperial Embassy. He said "that the Porte is intent on taking advantage of the World War in order to make a clean sweep of internal enemies —the indigenous Christians—without being hindered in doing so by diplomatic intervention from other countries. Such an undertaking will serve the interest of the Germans, the Allies of Turkey, which thus in turn could be strengthened."

A few days later the Armenian Patriarch explained to the same official that the measures of the Porte were intended not only to make the Armenian people temporarily harmless, but to expel them from Turkey or rather to eradicate them altogether. Deportation is just as bad as massacring and it would not be surprising if the Armenians finally retaliated, even if they had no chance of succeeding, "like a tormented animal that turns against its tormentors."[200]

Another German Ambassador, Prince Ernst zu Hohenlohe-Langenburg, reported that Interior Minister Talât told him in August 1915 that the Armenian question no longer existed.[201]

The German consul in Aleppo, Walter Rößler, who personally witnessed the deportees near the end of their journey, decried the government's "ruination of hecatombs of innocent people."[202] He protested to the German embassy that many children were dying and women were being raped during the deportations. After the Germans forwarded Rößler's protests to Talât, they received the reply that the government intended "to take advantage of the World War to make a clean sweep of its internal enemies—the indigenous Christians of all confessions—without being hindered in doing so by diplomatic intervention from other countries."[203] Later in June, Rößler wrote directly to the German Imperial Chancellor Bethmann Hollweg to say that:

> In Diyarbekir, as [Swiss eyewitness] Mr. [Jakob] Künzler describes, the most gruesome things have taken place against the Armenians, and indeed as a consequence of the stance of the Vali. We have been in possession of reports concerning this since the beginning of June.... I deduce from an occasional remark made to me by the local Vali, Djelal Bey, including a reprimand from the Vali of Diyarbekir, that something terrible must have happened. The insurrection in Diyarbekir, which in the meantime has been reported, is therefore probably a result of the mistreatment of the Armenians.[204]

---

200. DE/PA-AA/R14086, DuA Dok. 081 (gk.), June 16, 1915, German Ambassador in Constantinople, Wangenheim, to the German Imperial Chancellor, Bethmann Hollweg. *See also Richard G. Hovannisian, Introduction: History, Politics, Ethics, in* The Armenian Genocide: History, Politics, Ethics, at xi–xii.

201. *See* Hilmar Kaiser, *The Baghdad Railway and the Armenian Genocide, 1915–1915: A Case Study in German Resistance and Complicity, in* Remembrance and Denial: The Case of the Armenian Genocide 102 (Richard G. Hovannisian ed., Detroit: Wayne State UP, 1992).

202. *Quoted in* Dadrian, History of the Armenian Genocide, at 205. *See also* Akçam, A Shameful Act, at 120–125.

203. DE/PA-AA/Bo. Kons./B. 169, June 6, 1915, telegram from the Consul in Aleppo, Rößler, to the German Embassy in Constantinople. Rößler wrote to the German embassy: "In all respect I again beg you to allow me to raise a protest. The larger part of the Armenian deportees are women. They would be defenceless and liable to be violated during transport and in the villages. Would it not be possible to deport only the men and leave the women and children in Aleppo? Numerous children have already fallen victim to the deportations." *Id.*

204. DE/PA-AA/R14086, 1915-A-22125, June 29, 1915, report from the Consul in Aleppo, Rößler, to the German Imperial Chancellor, Bethmann Hollweg.

In July he could confirm "systematic killing by the authorities," as Armenian bodies were "thrown into the river by soldiers."[205]

In January 1916, Rößler reported to Ambassador Wolff-Metternich that due to the massacres, rapes, killing of children, spread of typhus and dysentery, and lack of food and water, "there is not much difference between the deportation of the Armenians and their extermination."[206] He added that he had received written reports from German engineers and missionaries near Urfa and Tell-Abiad that the Armenians were suffering "the conscious and deliberate destruction [*Vernichtung*] by the Turkish government." The Armenians were banned [*Verbannt*] on a "death march" [*zu Tode zu wandern*]. Government institutions were implicated in the extermination of the Armenians. The deported Armenians were sick and exhausted, camped outdoors and subjected to attacks by dogs. The smell of corpses permeated the air.[207]

In April 1916, Rößler told the German embassy that the 14,000 "unarmed inmates of the Ras ul-Ain concentration camp" had been "butchered." He added:

> In Aleppo, in March and the first half of April, not only were the Armenians hunted down who had come from elsewhere, and were severely hunted down, but also the deportation of those Armenians who were living here began. Individual women and girls were also picked up in the streets and this condition was utilised by the organs of the government, who committed arbitrary acts. It would

---

205. Report No. 120–21, *in* Lepsius, Deutschland und Armenien, at 108ff.

206. DE/PA-AA/R14090, A53a/1916/284, report from the Consul in Aleppo, Rößler to the German Ambassador on Extraordinary Mission in Constantinople, Wolff-Metternich, Jan. 3, 1916. These reports to the German ambassador are corroborated by Dr. Martin Niepage, who was in Aleppo in 1915 after teaching at a secondary school there, and says in his memoirs that:

> When I returned to Aleppo in September 1915, ... I heard I heard with horror that a new phase of Armenian massacres had begun which were far more terrible than the earlier massacres under Abdul-Hamid, and which aimed at exterminating, root and branch, the intelligent, industrious, and progressive Armenian nation, and at transferring its property to Turkish hands.
>
> Such monstrous news left me at first incredulous. I was told that, in various quarters of Aleppo, there were lying masses of half-starved people, the survivors of so-called "deportation convoys."
>
> In order, I was told, to cover the extermination of the Armenian nation with a political cloak, military reasons were being put forward, which were said to make it necessary to drive the Armenians out of their native seats, which had been theirs for 2,500 years, and to deport them to the Arabian deserts. I was also told that individual Armenians had lent themselves to acts of espionage.
>
> After I had informed myself about the facts and had made inquiries on all sides, I came to the conclusion that all these accusations against the Armenians were, in fact, based on trifling provocations, which were taken as an excuse for slaughtering 10,000 innocents for one guilty person, for the most savage outrages against women and children, and for a campaign of starvation against the exiles which was intended to exterminate the whole nation.
>
> As a result of the censorship, it is first now that it has been possible to publish this manuscript. Its first edition was actually only revealed to members of the Parliament....

Martin Niepage, The Horrors of Aleppo, Seen by a German Eyewitness 3–4 (London: T. Fisher Unwin, 1916). *See also* Tessa Hoffman, *German Eyewitness Reports of the Genocide of the Armenians, 1915–16, in* The Crime of Silence: The Armenian Genocide 66 (London: Zed Press, 1985) (Niepage wrote to U.S. President Woodrow Wilson in 1919: "In the decrepit caravanserais, people lay apathetically among the heaps of dead and emaciated bodies, waiting for death; ... [they had] nothing to eat but grass and the few grains of corn they could find in the horses' dung...."); Avedian, The Armenian Genocide, at 70.

207. DuA Doc 226 (r. gk), No. 16/K.Nr.2, Jan. 3 1916, report by the Consul in Aleppo, Rößler, to the German Imperial Chancellor, Bethmann Hollweg.

> not have been surprising if the Armenians, whose religion and the honour of their wives had been violated by such deeds, had been driven to acts of despair.[208]

In June 1916, he confirmed that few Armenians at Ras ul-Ain concentration camp could have survived.[209] He described starvation and disease in the camps due to unhygienic conditions.[210]

The German Consul in Erzerum, Dr. Max Erwin von Scheubner-Richter, reported that the commander of the Ottoman 3rd Army "ordered the immediate and most ruthless deportation of all Armenians," and that his supporters "openly admit that the final goal of their actions against the Armenians is their total annihilation in Turkey."[211] He added: "So long as this goal is not attainable through the various massacres, one hopes that the deprivation on the long journey to Mesopotamia and the unaccustomed climate there will finish the task."[212] Dr. Scheubner-Richter estimated that 10,000 to 20,000 Armenians from the plains of Erzerum had been massacred by early August 1915.[213] In 1916 he described directly to the imperial chancellor "the atrocious sight of the slain Armenians in the devastated villages of the areas we travelled through as far as Bitlis...."[214] His account of Armenian resistance recalls the Warsaw Ghetto Uprising of 1943: the "so-called [Armenian] 'rebels' were people who had barricaded themselves for fear of being massacred and who would have gladly been prepared to give up their weapons if only they were assured of being left alive."[215]

The German Vice-Consul in Mosul, Walter Holstein, reported to the German Imperial Chancellor that newspapers published in Anatolia warned in May 1913 of imminent Armenian massacres. The conflict with the Russian Empire and a Kurdish independence movement inflamed tensions, as did the fact that: "Almost all Armenians belong to the Armenian party '*Dachnaktsutiun*', whose program is addressed to administrative decentralization in the Armenian provinces, implementation of land rights for the Armenians, the introduction of Armenian as an official language in the schools, and to freedom regarding the schools." The Ottoman government confiscated the newspapers, cowing the Armenians into silence regarding their fears.[216] Later, Holstein reported that: "Seven hundred of the Christian inhabitants of the town of Mardin (mostly Armenians) and the Ar-

---

208. DE/PA-AA/R14091, DuA Dok. 260 (gk.), K. No. 47/No. 1189, May 16, 1916, 1916-A-12911, report from the German Consul in Aleppo, Rößler, to the German Imperial Chancellor, Bethmann Hollweg.

209. DE/PA-AA/R14092, 1916-A-17939, K. No. 61 / No. 1703, June 17, 1916, report from the German Consul in Aleppo, Rößler, to the German Imperial Chancellor, Bethmann Hollweg.

210. *See* DE/PA-AA/R14089, 1915-A-35045, Nov. 8, 1915, report from the German Consul in Aleppo, Rößler, to the German Imperial Chancellor, Bethmann Hollweg.

211. DE/PA-AA/Bo. Kons./B. 170, July 28, 1915, report from the German Consul in Erzerum, Scheubner-Richter, to the German Ambassador to Constantinople, Wangenheim.

212. *Id. See also* AKÇAM, A SHAMEFUL ACT, at 121, 405.

213. *See* Report Nos. 129 & 149, *in* LEPSIUS, DEUTSCHLAND UND ARMENIEN, at 117, 138ff.

214. DE/PA-AA/R14094, 1916-A-33457, Dec. 4, 1916, report from the German Consul in Erzerum, Scheubner-Richter, to the German Imperial Chancellor, Bethmann Hollweg.

215. *Id. See also id.* ("A supposedly prepared revolution of the [Armenian revolutionary] Dashnak Party was put forward as a pretext.... Furthermore, local unrest and self-protection measures on the part of the Armenians were exaggerated and taken as an excuse to justify the evacuation of the Armenians from endangered border districts. At the instigation of the committee, the Armenians were murdered along the way by Kurd and Turkish gangs, in places also by gendarmes.").

216. DE/PA-AA/R14079, 1913-A-12315, May 22, 1913, report from the Vice-Consul in Mosul, Holstein, to the German Imperial Chancellor, Bethmann Hollweg.

menian bishop of Mardin were slaughtered like lambs."[217] On June 13, 1915, Holstein observed:

> The massacre of the Armenians in the Diyarbekir vilayet becomes more known with every day and creates increasing unrest among the population, which may easily cause uncontrollable consequences due to the foolish lack of conscience and the weakness of the local government. In the districts of Mardin and Amadia the situation has developed into a genuine persecution of Christians (*Christenverfolgung*)....
>
> We will soon have a great uproar everywhere if the Turkish central government doesn't change its program of persecuting the Christians. Armenian massacres must absolutely be prevented.[218]

On July 10, 1915, Holstein wrote that: "The vali of Diyarbekir, Reshid Bey, rages like a mad blood-hound among the Christians of his vilayet." His depredations claimed 700 Christians in Mardin, "predominantly Armenians," and he continued "his bloody work among the innocent, whose number until today reached two thousand."[219] On July 16, Holstein warned; "As long as the government does not undertake anything against the Vali of Diyarbakir, it cannot be assumed the massacres will stop." He wrote to Constantinople that 600 women and children had arrived in Mosul after the massacre of their husbands and fathers.[220] In November, he defended the Assyrians and remaining Armenians who mounted an armed resistance in the Mardin area:

> I would like to point out that it would not fit the facts, should the Christians (Syrians and, to a small extent, Armenians), who have entrenched themselves between Midiat and Mardin (near Azik) and against whom the aforementioned troops were to proceed, be addressed and treated as rebels. Rather, these are Christians who were able to flee from the massacres and who are now defending their lives instead of being slaughtered like mutton. It can be assumed that after the Turkish troops have stormed Azik, none of the Christians there will be left alive.[221]

The consul in Trabzon, Dr. Bergfeld, protested repeatedly to his superiors during the Armenian genocide. In late June 1915, he wrote to the German Embassy in Constantinople:

> About 30000 persons are affected by the deportations just in the Vilayet of Trapezunt. A mass transport of this kind for hundreds of kilometres along routes

217. *Quoted in* GERHARD FALK & CLIFFORD FALK, MURDER, AN ANALYSIS OF ITS FORMS, CONDITIONS, AND CAUSES 69 (Jefferson, NC: McFarland, 1990). *See also* AKÇAM, FROM EMPIRE TO REPUBLIC, at 179.

218. DE/PA-AA/BoKon/169, A53a/1915/3612, June 13, 1915, telegraphic report from the Vice-Consul in Mosul, Holstein, to the German Embassy in Constantinople; *see also* Tessa Hoffman, *The Ottoman Genocide against Aramaic speaking Christians and the Present Situation of Christian Minorities in the Republic of Turkey* 8 (2007), www.aga-online.org/downloads/de/news/attachments/Vortrag_Bruessel.pdf.

219. DE/PA-AA/BoKon/169, A53a/1915/4184, July 10, 1915, telegraphic report from the Vice-Consul in Mosul, Holstein, to the German Embassy in Constantinople, *quoted in* Hoffman, *The Ottoman Genocide,* at 9.

220. DE/PA-AA/BoKon/169, A53a/1915/4262, July 16, 1915, telegraphic report from the German Vice-Consul in Mosul, Holstein, to the German Embassy in Constantinople; *see also* Gabriele Yonan, *Lest We Perish: A Forgotten Holocaust, The Extermination of the Christian Assyrians in Turkey and Persia* §3, at 18–19 (1996), http://www.aina.org/books/lwpcontents.htm.

221. DE/PA-AA/BoKon/171, A53a/1915/6381, Nov. 4, 1915, telegraphic report from the German Vice-Consul in Mosul, Holstein, to the German Embassy in Constantinople, http://tinyurl.com/mnnrph.

> that are lacking in accommodation and supplies, and where 300 kilometres must count as being completely infested with typhus fever, would claim enormous numbers of victims, particularly among the women and children. This would cause damage to the moral image not only of Turkey, but also of its allies. I am absolutely no friend of the Armenians, but I consider myself to be obliged to point out to Your Excellency the dangers of this mass deportation from the standpoint of humanity and prestige. The local Vali simply refers to instructions from Constantinople.
>
> My Austrian colleague is telegraphing a similar message to his Embassy. Also, there is a danger of the deportees spreading the typhus fever. Perhaps the Sublime Porte can refrain from deporting the women and children....[222]

On July 9, 1915, Dr. Bergfeld issued one of the most damning reports of the widespread and systematic victimization of civilians that would emerge from World War I. He reported, directly to the imperial chancellor and with every motive of patriotism and personal safety to report the contrary, i.e., that the German-Ottoman operations in Anatolia were humane, that:

> On 24 June, the local leaders of the Armenian committee were arrested and exiled to the interior of the country via Samsun. The same day I heard that the deportation of all Armenians was being considered and that there was a trend towards using this occasion to instigate excesses against the local Armenians.... On 26 June, the Armenians were then told to prepare themselves for deportation into the interior of the country with only 5 days' notice. Only the sick were allowed to remain behind and accommodation was planned for them in hospitals. The sale of any of their possessions was prohibited.... Money was to be brought to the post office for gradual forwarding at later intervals.
>
> About 30000 people in the province of Trapezunt were affected by the deportation. A mass transport of this kind on routes where there is a lack of food and accommodation and which is said to be completely infested with typhus fever along the first 300 kilometres, must have claimed numerous victims among the Armenians, in particular among the women and children. This must have provoked justified criticism of such extreme measures both abroad and perhaps also in Germany. I have therefore informed the Imperial Embassy in Constantinople of the situation.... The sick and the pregnant women were also allowed to stay in their homes ... [but later], all the exceptions made so far, except for the permission for children to remain, were revoked....
>
> In fact, between Erzinghian and Diarbekir Armenians have been massacred on the mountain road, allegedly by Kurds, and larger bands of ambushers under French-speaking leaders have been seen near Erzerum and Baiburt....
>
> The Consul of Austria-Hungary has drawn the attention of his immediate authorities to the great dangers for women and children which are presented by the mass deportation. My Austrian colleague has placed his intervention with the local Vali for some children, the American Consul for the Persian Armenians under his protection, both in vain. The Italian colleague has had a nervous breakdown....[223]

222. DE/PA-AA/Embassy Constantinople/Vol. 169. DuA doc. 100, No. 5, June 27, 1915, report from the German Consul in Trabzon, Dr. Bergfeld, to the German Embassy in Constantinople.

223. DuA Doc.109, No. 35/J.No.Geh.(secr.) 316, July 9, 1915, report from the German Consul in Trabzon, Dr. Bergfeld, to the German Imperial Chancellor, Bethmann Hollweg.

After the deportation had been completed, Dr. Bergfeld documented its results for the new Imperial Chancellor, Georg Friedrich Graf von Hertling. Bergfeld sought mercy:

> Anyone who knows the Orient will agree with me that the Armenians are blessed with hardly a trait that humans find attractive. Despite this, the excesses that took place during their deportation—the mass murders of the men, numerous rapes of women and children, and theft of their possessions—cannot be condemned severely enough....
>
> [T]he differential treatment that is accorded today not only to the few Armenian men still living, but also to their women and children and their possessions, must strengthen the obvious assumption that the Turkish government was at least not unhappy about the attacks against the Armenians that led to their almost complete annihilation in East Anatolia, and still holds this opinion today. This attitude will also make our position more difficult during peace negotiations....
>
> Furthermore, the special regulation that applies to Armenians, forbidding them to move from one town to another without the permission of the Ministry of the Interior, should be revoked, at least with regard to women and children.[224]

In contrast to the more honorable actions of the German diplomatic corps, the German military insisted on massacres and deportations as part of its strategic and tactical doctrine. German military doctrine in the early twentieth century, formulated in the aftermath of the "total war" between Prussia and France in which Paris itself was set ablaze,[225] emphasized that "the violent force of the conqueror in the conquered land is completely unlimited."[226] Under this Prussian-German military doctrine: "The enemy was not merely the enemy army, but the enemy nation and the culture through which it defined itself." Thus, "Germany went to war in 1914 with a concept of the 'war of annihilation' that was based on the military doctrine developed by Alfred von Schlieffen, chief of the Prussian general staff from 1895 to 1905."[227]

The Ottoman Imperial School of Military Science brought Prussian officers, including a key veteran of the Franco-Prussian war, to Anatolia to preach the gospel of "total war." The doctrine emphasized the encirclement and annihilation of an enemy using devastating firepower in the form of artillery and rifle volleys. The Ottomans began to practice total war under Prussian influence in the late nineteenth century, to hold onto the empire's holdings in Europe, such as in Macedonia where Enver Paşa carried out total war operations. Massacres of civilians occurred with increasing regularity and staggering scale in the Ottoman Empire after the Greek War of Independence, notably in Greece and Chios in the 1820s, Armenia and Georgia in the 1850s, Armenia and Bulgaria in the 1870s, Armenia and Assyria in the 1890s, and Armenia and Macedonia in the 1910s.[228]

---

224. DE/PA-AA/R14104, 1918-A-38986, Sept. 18, 1918, report from the German Consul in Trabzon, Dr. Bergfeld, to the German Imperial Chancellor, Hertling.

225. *See* Jeremy Black, The Age of Total War, 1860–1945, at 38 (Westport, CT: Greenwood Publ'g Group, 2006).

226. Alan Kramer, Dynamic of Destruction: Culture and Mass Killing in the First World War 26 (Oxford: Oxford UP, 2007) (quoting Germany's *Handbook of International Law* circa 1915). *See also id.* (*German War Book* published by Prussian General Staff in 1902 "claimed that most attempts during the nineteenth century to codify [civilian protections during wartime] had 'completely failed'").

227. *Id.* at 31.

228. *See* James J. Reid, *Total War, the Annihilation Ethic, and the Armenian Genocide, 1870–1918, in* The Armenian Genocide: History, Politics, Ethics, at 27–38; Edward Blaquiere, The Greek Revolution, Its Origin and Progress 129, 344–45 (London: G. & W.B. Whittaker, 1824); De

German geo-strategic thought, as well as tactical military doctrine, provided a basis for ordering the mass deportation of a civilian population targeted on a racial or ethnic basis. In 1913, the German orientalist scholar Paul Rohrbach advocated the deportation of the Armenian population to Mesopotamia as a security measure for the Ottomans. Rohrbach declared that "Armenia should be evacuated of the Armenians. They should be dispersed in the direction of Mesopotamia and their places should be taken by Turks, in such a fashion that Armenia should be freed of all Russian influence and that Mesopotamia might be provided with farmers which it now lacked."[229] As the most popular German imperialist propagandist and a regular contributor to the influential *Frankfurter Allgemeine Zeitung*, Rohrbach was a supporter of German settlement activity and the Herero genocide, and served as a colonial administrator in German Namibia.[230] Rohrbach, who was a "champion of the idea of German expansionism in the Near East,"[231] argued that like the British, the Germans should develop extensive colonial holdings, and a sense of superiority in carrying "the German Idea" around the world.[232] He has therefore been identified as above any other, "the theoretician who implanted in Turkish minds the idea of the expediency of the evacuation of the Armenians from their ancestral territories in eastern Turkey and their relocation to Mesopotamia...."[233]

Friedrich Naumann, the pan-German thinker, similarly described "the violent massacre of from 80,000 to 100,000 Armenians" starting in 1895 or so as intuitively "abominable," but as rational in a long-term sense, in the way that Charlemagne's massacres of the Saxons were rational. He wrote that "the Armenian question and Armenian massacres [are] a matter of internal Turkish policy, merely an episode of the agony through which a great empire is passing, which does not propose to let itself die without making a last attempt to save itself by bloodshed." Western attempts to promote "the rights of man, or of humanity, or of civilization, or of political liberty" created a danger that the Armenians could constitute "a political force," ending the Ottoman occupation of eastern Anatolia. Sound German "[n]ational policy," or in other words, the policy of the Kaiser for a "greater, independent Germany," was a "profound moral reason why we must, as statesmen, show ourselves indifferent to the sufferings of the Christian peoples of Turkey, however painful that may be to our human feelings...."[234]

Courtois, The Forgotten Genocide, at 109–21, 132–38, 143; *see also* John Lee Comstock, History of the Greek Revolution: Compiled from Official Documents of the Greek Government 145, 161, 178, 189–90, 220–28 (New York: William Reed & Co., 1828); Charles MacFarlane, Constantinople in 1828: A Residence of Sixteen Months in the Turkish Capital and Provinces 41 (London: Saunders and Otley, 1829); The History of Modern Greece 99 (Boston: Nathan Hale, 1833).

229. Morgenthau, Ambassador Morgenthau's Story, at ch. 27, http://net.lib.byu.edu/estu/wwi/comment/morgenthau/Morgen27.htm (quoting Paris *Temps*).

230. Woodruff D. Smith, The Ideological Origins of Nazi Imperialism 160 (Oxford: Oxford UP, 1989). Rohrbach was not alone in this, defending the Armenian atrocities against British criticism by reference to Britain's own crimes, as this article from the *Frankfurter Zeitung* shows: "Reports have come from the Americans in Armenia that the Turks there were guilty of atrocities against the rebellious Armenians.... If the Turks then took harsh counter-measures, it is the fault of the rebellious Armenians themselves; the joint responsibility, however, does not lie with Germany, but rather with British, Russian and French rabble-rousers." DE/PA-AA/R14089, 1916-A-00468, Dec. 20, 1915, enclosure 1 to the report from the German Consul in Aleppo, Rößler, to the German Imperial Chancellor, Bethmann Hollweg.

231. Dadrian, The History of the Armenian Genocide, at 254.

232. Smith, The Ideological Origins, at 160–62.

233. Dadrian, The History of the Armenian Genocide, at 254.

234. Morgenthau, Ambassador Morgenthau's Story, at ch. 27, http://net.lib.byu.edu/estu/wwi/comment/morgenthau/Morgen27.htm.

The position of Rohrbach and Naimann also accords with what an Armenian told Morgenthau he heard a German theorist prescribe for Ottoman ethnic policy in a public lecture: "His main point was that throughout their history the Turks had made a great mistake in being too merciful toward the non-Turkish population." The theorist advocated action "without any sentimentality toward all the subject nationalities and races in Turkey who did not fall in with the plans of the Turks." The German naval attaché in Constantinople, Lieutenant Commander Hans Humann, similarly told Morgenthau in distinctly proto-Hitlerite terms of a racial struggle for survival:

> [B]oth Armenians and Turks cannot live together in this country. One of these races has got to go. And I don't blame the Turks for what they are doing to the Armenians. I think that they are entirely justified. The weaker nation must succumb. The Armenians desire to dismember Turkey; they are against the Turks and the Germans in this war, and they therefore have no right to exist here.[235]

Leading CUP writers and propagandists incorporated German geo-strategic theory into their program for a division of the world between Germans and Turks. The CUP leader and propagandist Yusuf Akcura wrote that Germans and Turks constituted the two legitimate "masters of the universe." The Germans, he argued, would reunite the Turks occupying Anatolia with their ethnic forbears and origins in Central Asia, in a large, powerful empire.[236] In June 1915, the CUP leader Yenibaceli Nail declared in a public speech that the modern Turks were descendents of the medieval Genghis Khan and Timur Leng, and that they would "show to the Europeans of Christian faith, to the infidel Russians, and to their friends [amongst us] the power of our sword."[237] Thus, "[t]he massacre in 1914–1916 of one and a half million Armenians was largely conditioned by the desire of the Young Turks to eliminate the Armenian obstacle which separated Ottoman Turks from the Turks of Azerbaijan, and to prepare the way for the territorial unification of the 'Oguz', or southeastern group [of Turks]."[238]

As Rößler, Holstein, Bergfeld, Scheubner-Richter protested the Armenian massacres, some German officers seemed actively to encourage and endorse the deportation and killing of the Armenians. The highest-ranking German officer on the ground in Anatolia for extended periods of time during the war gave "direct orders" for the deportation and massacre of the Armenians.[239] As the Chief of Staff at the Ottoman General Headquarters, General Major Fritz Bronsart von Schellendorf convened a meeting with ministers designated by the War Ministry to request action against Armenian saboteurs, and "severe" (*şedide*) measures against the Armenians conscripted into labor battalions.[240] General Bronsart declared that the Armenians brought their "extermination" (*Ausrottung*) upon themselves by becoming "traitors" to the empire.[241] He had been guilty of ordering

---

235. *Id.*

236. *See* DADRIAN, THE HISTORY OF THE ARMENIAN GENOCIDE, at 285.

237. *Quoted in id.* at 406.

238. SERGE A. ZENKOVSKY, PAN-TURKISM AND ISLAM IN RUSSIA 111 (Cambridge, MA: Harvard UP, 1967), *quoted in* DADRIAN, THE HISTORY OF THE ARMENIAN GENOCIDE, at 372.

239. There are "many reports indicating that General Bronsart von Schellendorf, as Chief of the Turkish General Staff, gave direct orders for the Armenians to be deported. He used the actual Turkish word *shedide* [*şedide*], meaning stern measures, which in the orders was the code name for massacre." HUBERTA VON VOSS, PORTRAITS OF HOPE: ARMENIANS IN THE CONTEMPORARY WORLD 65 (Alasdair Lean trans., Providence, RI: Berghahn Books, 2007). On the use of "*şedide*" in this sense, see for example JOHANNES LEPSIUS, ARMENIË EN EUROPA: EEN SCHRIFTELIJKE AANKLACHT 133 (Dutch trans., Amsterdam: D.A. Daamen, 1896).

240. *See* DADRIAN, HISTORY OF THE ARMENIAN GENOCIDE, at 256.

241. *Quoted in* Vahakn I. Dadrian, *Documentation of the Armenian Genocide in German and Austrian Sources, in* THE WIDENING CIRCLE OF GENOCIDE, at 86, 374.

a massacre of all the military-aged men of Andenne, Belgium in 1914.[242] His stress at that time on executing "men capable of bearing arms" illustrated his methods in war, focused on annihilating the capacity of an occupied nation to defend itself.[243]

In 1921, General Bronsart wrote an article in which he attempted to justify the deportation of Armenians, despite the many thousands of deaths.[244] He compared the Armenians to Jews who acted like "parasite[s]" and "agitators" outside their homeland, practicing usury and emigrating to "Kurdish territory" just like "Polish Jews" emigrating to Germany, provoking "the hatred, which, in a medieval form, has unleashed itself against [Armenians] as an unpleasant people, entailing their murder."[245] He compared the deportation of the Armenians to a potential imprisonment or deportation of all "Polish activists" or "violent Communists," which he thought the German people would applaud.[246] Bronsart mocked Morgenthau's defense of the murdered Armenians as a stratagem of a wily Jew.[247]

In October 1915, Dr. Ernst von Kwiatkowski, the Consul-General at Trabzon for the Austro-Hungarian Empire, which was allied with the German Empire, reported to the Austro-Hungarian Ambassador that "the first suggestion for the liquidation [*Unschädlichmachung*] of the Armenians ... came from the German camp."[248] A report from another Austro-Hungarian consul to his country's ambassador and foreign minister confirmed that "Germany wanted the enactment of the anti-Armenian measures."[249] The Ambassador, Johnn Markgraf Pallavicini, could not have been more clear about the genocidal character of this process: "[T]he Armenian massacres and deportations that have been going on now for decades ... [were] cold bloodedly designed and planned and carried out by the Government."[250] Dr. Kwiatkowski later reported a German cover-up; he informed the Austro-Hungarian Foreign Minister Stephan Baron Burian that the German

---

242. *See* Kramer, Dynamic of Destruction, at 16–17; John N. Horne & Alan Kramer, German Atrocities 1914: A History of Denial 33, 37 (New Haven, CT: Yale UP, 2001) (130 to 150 Belgian civilians died in the massacre ordered by Bronsart).

243. Kramer, Dynamic of Destruction, at 17.

244. *See* General Major Fritz Bronsart von Schellendorf, *A Witness for Talaat Pasha*, Deutsche Allgemeine Zeitung, July 24, 1921. He wrote:

> The Minster of the Interior was Talaat, and he had to make the decisions and give the directives. The Army was in its most vital stage of fighting. The Moslem inhabitants were fleeing from the terror of the Armenians. In this critical situation, the whole ministry came to the difficult decision to name the Armenians dangerous to the state, and to remove them from the border areas to a less inhabited, but fruitful area, to Northern Mesopotamia. The Minister of the Interior gave the task to the Gendarmerie, trained to deal with this assignment....
>
> [I]nto my hands came requests and demands to the Army to assist whenever possible, to provide food, shelter, doctors and medicine to the civilians under way. Unfortunately, even with all the help that was possible, thousands of Moslems as well as Armenians died....
>
> Considering that there would not have been any way to stop the Moslem population from fleeing, removing the Armenians was necessary.

Id., http://armenians-1915.blogspot.com/2005/07/78-german-officers-genocide-eyewitness.html.

245. *Quoted in* Dadrian, History of the Armenian Genocide, at 259.

246. Schellendorf, *A Witness for Talaat Pasha*.

247. *See* David Allan Mayers, Dissenting Voices in America's Rise to Power 230 (Cambridge: Cambridge UP, 2007).

248. Austrian Foreign Ministry Archives, Vienna, PA 12, Karton 463, No. 70/P. Trabzon, Oct. 22, 1915, *quoted in* Dadrian, The History of the Armenian Genocide, at 257.

249. Austrian Foreign Ministry Archives, Vienna, PA 12, Karton 209, Zl.100/P and No. 96/P. C., Nov. 10, 1915, telegram nos. 20 and 23, *quoted in* Dadrian, The History of the Armenian Genocide, at 283.

250. Dadrian, The History of the Armenian Genocide, at 426.

Consuls at Trabzon and Erzerum were being forced to "tone down" reports of massacres.[251] In 1916, he wrote that General Bronsart had warned the successor of Dr. Scheubner-Richter as Consul at Erzerum *not* to try to save the Armenians as his predecessor had.[252] Finally, in 1918 Dr. Kwiatkowski estimated that one million Armenians had already been cruelly deported and very few could possibly have survived.[253]

When Dr. Johannes Lepsius, a humanitarian missionary and fundraiser for orphanages for Armenian children whose parents had perished in the massacres of 1896, arrived in the Ottoman Empire in 1915, he asked Ambassador Morgenthau for permission to review the reports of American consuls. After reading them, Lepsius told Morgenthau about "the humiliation which he felt, as a German, that the Turks should set about to exterminate their Christian subjects, while Germany, which called itself a Christian country, was making no endeavours to prevent it." Enver Paşa suggested to Dr. Lepsius that the government "at last had an opportunity to rid themselves of the Armenians and that they proposed to use it."[254]

In 1916, Dr. Lepsius published an account of what he called the "*Todesgang*" (death march) of the Armenian people.[255] His book described a large-scale massacre starting in May 1915 of Armenians and Assyrians living in the *vilayet* of Diyarbekir. First, about 1,200 intellectual, religious, and spiritual leaders of the Armenians and Assyrians were arrested. Then, Ottoman officials loaded nearly 700 of them onto rafts purportedly for transport to Mosul. On board the rafts, their money and clothing was stripped from them. Then they were cast into the river to drown, and the gendarmes were ordered to kill any victims trying to swim ashore.[256] A German present in Erzerum described the intensification of the killing process:

> The *vali* [provincial governor] allowed the sick, families without men, and single women to stay in Erzerum [initially]. This humane procedure, for which I also interceded, was suddenly brought to an end by some influence from the [CUP]. . . . The papers already distributed to the women and the sick still remaining in the town were taken away again and they were driven onto the road—to a certain death.[257]

A Swiss deacon named Jakob Künzler provided regular eyewitness accounts from Urfa to German officials. He reported the "elimination of entire Armenian cities," the deportation of their inhabitants to be left "sick and dying on the roads" or to arrive in dire circumstances in an "uneconomic, waterless" desert region, Djebel Abdul Aziz in present-day

---

251. *Quoted in* Wolfdieter Bihl, 1 Die Kaukasus-Politik der Mittelmache 334, n.405 (Vienna, 1975), *and in* Dadrian, The History of the Armenian Genocide, at 282.

252. *See* Austrian Foreign Ministry Archives, Vienna, PA 12, Karton 380, Zl.21, folio 209, May 26, 1917, *quoted in* Dadrian, The History of the Armenian Genocide, at 257.

253. *See* Dadrian, *Documentation of the Armenian Genocide, in* The Widening Circule of Genocide, at 122.

254. *Quoted in* Morgenthau, Ambassador Morgenthau's Story, at ch. 26, http://net.lib.byu.edu/estu/wwi/comment/morgenthau/Morgen26.htm.

255. Johannes Lepsius, Bericht über die Lage des armenischen Volkes in der Türkey (Potsdam: Tempelverlag, 1916).

256. *See* Johannes Lepsius, Der Todesgang des Armenischen Volkes; Bericht über das Schicksal des Armenischen Volkes in der Türkei während des Weltkrieges 76 (Heidelberg: 1980) (new edition of Lepsius, Der Todesgang des Armenischen Volkes, (Potsdam: Tempelverlag, 1919).

257. Johannes Lepsius, Deutschland und Armenien, 1914–1918: Sammlung Diplomatischer Aktenstücke 113 (Potsdam: Der Tempelverlag, 1919), *quoted in* Derderian, *Gender-Specific Aspects of the Armenian Genocide*, at 3.

Syria. Armenians were resisting the assaults upon their people, fleeing to the mountains. He recalled that the Turkish official Nafis Bey had "said that after this war we need to eradicate [*ausrotten*] the Armenian people, or force them to emigrate," and he expressed his "fear that the time of the war will just used to decimate as far as possible, this intelligent, albeit with many flaws, [Armenian] people."[258] After the war, he published a memoir of what he had seen.[259]

G. Entente Sources on the Armenian Genocide: The Deportations, 1914–1917

Although they were bitterly opposed to the German government, British officials agreed to a remarkable extent with their German counterparts about the nature and extent of the Ottoman crimes against Armenians. The British Empire was the most vocal in condemning the Armenian massacres and the participation of German officers in the anti-Armenian persecutions. British politicians, diplomats, and military officers described horrifying massacres of Armenians.

Sir Lois Mallet, the British ambassador to the Ottoman Empire (technically to Constantinople), "left no doubt in [his] dispatches, books, articles, and interviews of the guilt of the Young Turk leaders."[260] The British ambassador to the U.S., James Bryce, wrote that the massacres were as "unprovoked," "widespread," and "terrible" as any in the history of Asia. He edited a volume calling the Ottoman massacres of Armenians "an effort to exterminate a whole nation, without distinction of age or sex, whose misfortune it was to be the subjects of a Government devoid of scruples or pity."[261] Under Bryce's leadership, the British government published an account of an American interview with a German eyewitness, stating:

> Toward the middle of April [1915] we heard rumours that there were great disturbances in Van. We have heard statements both from Turks and from Armenians, and as these reports agree in every respect, ... stat[ing] that the Ottoman Government sent orders that all Armenians were to give up their arms, which the Armenians refused to do on the ground that they required their arms in case of necessity. This caused a regular massacre. All villages inhabited by Armenians were burnt down. The Turks boasted of having now got rid of all the Armenians. I heard it from the officers myself, how they revelled in the thought that the Armenians had been got rid of.[262]

Another report from a German eyewitness republished by the British government stated:

---

258. DE/PA-AA/R14086, 1915-A-22125, June 20, 1915, German Consul in Aleppo, Rösler, to German Embassy in Constantinople.

259. Jakob Künzler, Im Lande des Blutes und der Tränen. Erlebnisse in Mesopotamien während des Weltkrieges (1914–1918) (Potsdam: Tempelverlag, 1921).

260. *Court-Martial Gives Death Sentence to Enver Pasha, Talaat Bey, and Djemal Pasha*, N.Y. Times, July 13, 1919, http://www.armeniapedia.org/index.php?title=Turkey_Condemns_Its_War_Leaders_-nyt19190713.

261. Viscount Bryce, *Preface*, *in* The Treatment of Armenians, at 19.

262. American Committee for Armenian and Syrian Relief, *Moush: Statement by a German Eye-Witness of Occurrences at Moush*, *in* The Treatment of Armenians in the Ottoman Empire, http://net.lib.byu.edu/~rdh7/wwi/1915/bryce/a04.htm#III.

> If there is no visible prospect of a change for the better, a few months more will see the end of [all the members of the Armenian nation who are in exile here in Aleppo, Syria]. They are succumbing in thousands to famine, pestilence and the inclemency of the weather.... [A]long the Euphrates, they are driven from place to place, plundered and maltreated. Many of our friends are dead.[263]

A report from a foreign resident whose name was withheld declared that a "direct attack and massacre" against Armenians was taking place because "the men and boys have been deported from their homes in great numbers and disappeared *en route*, and later on the women and children have been made to follow." All male Armenians were initially targeted, and there were "great numbers of bodies along the roadside or floating in the Euphrates River." Turkish police (gendarmes) and Kurdish militia cooperated in committing "unthinkable outrages" against Armenian women and children, including "the killing of many of the victims."[264]

Based on such testimonies, the British government concluded that a campaign of what Lemkin later called genocide had been undertaken by the Ottoman authorities.

> A detachment of gendarmerie was assigned to every convoy [of deported Armenians], to guard them on the way.... The mental misery of exile was sufficiently acute, but it was soon ousted by more material cares. A few days, or even a few hours, after the start, the carters would refuse to drive them further.... So the carts turned back, and the exiles had to go forward on foot. This was the beginning of their physical torments, for they were not travelling over soft country or graded roads, but by mule-tracks across some of the roughest country in the world. It was the hot season, the wells and springs were sometimes many hours' journey apart, and the gendarmes often amused themselves by forbidding their fainting victims to drink. It would have been an arduous march for soldiers on active service, but the members of these convoys were ... the women and children, the old and the sick. Some of the women had been delicately brought up and lived in comfort all their lives; some had to carry children in their arms too young to walk; others had been sent off with the convoy when they were far gone with child, and gave birth on the road. None of these latter survived, for they were forced to march on again after a few hours' respite; they died on the road, and the new-born babies perished with them. Many others died of hunger and thirst, sunstroke, apoplexy or sheer exhaustion.... The Government which condemned them to exile knew what the journey would mean, and the servants of the Government who conducted them did everything to aggravate their inevitable physical sufferings. Yet this was the least part of their torture; far worse were the atrocities of violence wantonly inflicted upon them by fellow human beings.
>
> From the moment they left the outskirts of the towns they were never safe from outrage.... There were ... horrible outrages when they came to the mountains, for here they were met by bands of "*chettis*" and Kurds. The "*chettis*" were brigands, recruited from the public prisons; they had been deliberately released by the authorities on a consideration which may have been tacit but which both parties clearly understood. As for the Kurds, they ... knew well what they were

---

263. *See* Fräulein O., *Aleppo* (Feb. 17, 1916), *in* THE TREATMENT OF ARMENIANS IN THE OTTOMAN EMPIRE, http://net.lib.byu.edu/~rdh7/wwi/1915/bryce/a15.htm#142.

264. American Committee for Armenian and Syrian Relief, *Aleppo: Series of Reports by a Foreign Resident*, *in* THE TREATMENT OF ARMENIANS IN THE OTTOMAN EMPIRE, http://net.lib.byu.edu/~rdh7/wwi/1915/bryce/a15.htm#142.

> allowed and what they were intended to do. When these Kurds and *chettis* waylaid the convoys, the ... first to be butchered were the old men and boys—all the males that were to be found in the convoy except the infants in arms—but the women were massacred also. It depended on the whim of the moment whether a Kurd cut a woman down or carried her away into the hills. When they were carried away their babies were left on the ground or dashed against the stones. But while the convoy dwindled, the remnant had always to march on. The cruelty of the gendarmes towards the victims grew greater as their physical sufferings grew more intense; the gendarmes seemed impatient to make a hasty end of their task. Women who lagged behind were bayoneted on the road, or pushed over precipices, or over bridges. The passage of rivers, and especially of the Euphrates, was always an occasion of wholesale murder. Women and children were driven into the water, and were shot as they struggled, if they seemed likely to reach the further bank....[265]

As in other genocides, the profit motive was ever-present. The Ottoman correspondent of the British publication *The Morning Post* wrote:

> It is probably true that never before have the Turks in the empire been so rich. An ordinary policeman in Pera is estimated to be worth anything between 10,000 and 15,000 Turkish pounds.
>
> This accumulation of wealth has been a part of the program of the committee to enrich the Turks at the expense of the Christians.... The [CUP], by means of requisitioning from the Christians, has concentrated all the trade in the hands of the Mohammedans. German officers had their share also in this plunder.[266]

French sources document the Armenian genocide in some detail. A report from a retired French consul with extensive contacts in Anatolia and Syria, described conditions in Aleppo. He declared that "in the provinces of Adana, Aleppo and Kurdistan that I have inhabited for many years," the Armenian population was suffering "persecution" and "extermination." He added that the Armenian deportees rarely "escaped death because of abuse and atrocities committed against them by the police en route...." The military was working together with civilian officials to exterminate the Armenian populations of Bitlis, Diyarbekir, Harput, Aleppo, Adana, Trabzon, Erzerum, Samsoun, Sivas, and Constantinople. Large numbers of bodies and body parts were seen floating down the Euphrates, he wrote. Entire cities had been burned down.[267]

By December 1915, a report in the French archives put the number of Armenian victims at more than 500,000, and declared that the entire Armenian population of Anatolia was under a death sentence, under German advisers' watchful eyes.[268] A French Dominican priest concluded that more than 69,000 Armenians disappeared from the vi-

---

265. Arnold Toynbee, *The Deportations of 1915—Procedure: A Summary of Armenian History Up to and Including the Year 1915, in* The Treatment of Armenians in the Ottoman Empire, http://net.lib.byu.edu/~rdh7/wwi/1915/bryce/a18.htm#hist6.

266. *Millions Slain by Turks: Moslems Made Money in the Midst of War Slaughter,* N.Y. Times, Dec. 6, 1918, http://spiderbites.nytimes.com/free_1918/articles_1918_12_00002.html.

267. Albert Guys, *Report Submitted to the Embassy of France* (July 24, 1915), *in* Les Grandes Puissances: L'Empire Ottoman et les Arméniens Dans Les Archives Françaises: Receuil de Documents 50, 56, 130, 152–53 (Arthur Beylerian, ed., Paris: Université de Paris I, 1983), http://www.imprescriptible.fr/documents/archives/francaises/561.htm (translation into English by Google).

268. *See Note by the Department on the Armenian Massacres* (Dec. 1915), *in* Les Grandes Puissances, http://www.imprescriptible.fr/documents/archives/francaises/561.htm.

layet of Diyarbekir during the massacres of 1915 to 1916.[269] This priest and scholar, who was under house arrest in Diyarbekir province through late 1916, wrote that Rashid Bey's campaigns murdered 97% of Gregorian Orthodox Armenians and 92% of Catholic Armenians. Along with Orthodox and Catholic Assyrians, the priest estimated that 144,185 persons perished, which included 82% of the Armenian and Assyrian populations. About 50,000 Christians deported from other provinces were killed in Diyarbakir province.[270] Another French Dominican priest estimated that tens of thousands of Armenian deportees of whom he was aware were massacred in 1915, and provided estimates broken down by month, day, and location.[271] Under President Jacques Chirac, France made denial of the Armenian genocide a crime in 2004, and instructed Turkey that it could not be admitted to membership in the EU unless it acknowledged the Armenian genocide.[272]

Russian diplomats and military officers were situated close to ground zero for the Armenian genocide, in and near the Ottoman border regions of Van, Erzerum, Sasoun, Zeitoun, Cilicia, etc. The Russian Empire joined with Britain and France in May 1915 to issue the following denunciation of Ottoman policy in these border regions:

> Massacres have taken place from mid April in Erzerum, Terjan, Eghine, Bitlis, Moush, Sasoun, Zeytoun and throughout Cilicia. The inhabitants in almost a hundred villages around Van have been completely murdered and the Armenian quarters in Van are under siege by Kurds. At the same time, the Ottoman government has acted mercilessly against the defenceless Armenian population in Constantinople.[273]

By the end of April, 1915, the Russian Ambassador to the U.S. submitted an official plea to the State Department to stop the Armenian massacres, and to prevent further similar crimes.[274] The Russian Consul in Urmia, Basil Nikitine, reported that 6,000 Armenians had been massacred in Van by May 15, 1915.[275] In August 1915, the minister for foreign affairs stated in the Duma that the Armenians and Greeks were "suffering terrible persecutions."[276] A resolution of the lower house of the Duma voted in 1995 to call on Turkey to acknowledge the Armenian genocide.[277]

The archives of reports by American diplomats in the Ottoman Empire during and after the First World War confirm the Ottoman, German, Russian, and British accounts of an Armenian genocide. Henry Morgenthau, the U.S. Ambassador to the Ottoman Empire stated in 1918 that the Empire "massacred fully 2,000,000 men, women, and chil-

---

269. *See* Gaunt, Massacres, Resistance, Protectors, at 433–36 (citing Jacques Rhétoré, Les Chrétiens aux Bétes: Souvenirs de la Guerre Sainte Proclamée par les Turcs Contre les Chrétiens en 1915, at 136 (Joseph Alichoran ed., Paris: Editions Cerf, 2005)).

270. *See* Gaunt, *Ottoman Bystanders*, at 15 (citing Rhétoré, Les Chrétiens aux Bétes, at 136).

271. *See id.* at 164–65, 436–40.

272. *Turkey "must admit Armenia dead,"* BBC News, Dec. 13, 2004, http://news.bbc.co.uk/2/hi/europe/4092933.stm.

273. *Quoted in* Richard G. Hovannisian, Armenia on the Road to Independence (Los Angeles, 1967), *and in* Avedian, The Armenian Genocide, at 33–34.

274. *See Appeal To Turkey to Stop Massacres,* N.Y. Times, Apr. 28, 1915, at 2.

275. *See 6,000 Armenians Killed*, N.Y. Times, May 18, 1915, http://www.cilicia.com/armo10c-nyt19150518.html; *cf.* William C. King, King's Complete History of The World War, at 169 (Springfield, MA: The History Associates, 1922); Francis Joseph Reynolds et al., The Story of the Great War: History of the European War from Official Sources 352, 421 (New York: P.F. Collier and Son, 1916).

276. *Quoted in Russian Duma. Speeches at Opening,* The Argus (Australia), Aug. 3, 1915, at 7.

277. *See* Yair Auron, The Banality of Denial: Israel and the Armenian Genocide 102 (New Brunswick, NJ: Transaction Publishers, 2004).

dren—Greeks, Assyrians, Armenians; fully 1,500,000 Armenians." He described the massacres of the Armenian men serving in the Ottoman army or associated forced labor battalions as follows:

> In almost all cases, the procedure was the same. Here and there squads of 50 or 100 men would be taken, bound together in groups of four, and then marched out to a secluded spot a short distance from the village. Suddenly the sound of rifle shots would fill the air, and the Turkish soldiers who had acted as the escort would sullenly return to camp. Those sent to bury the bodies would invariably find them stark naked.... [Sometimes] the murderers ... compell[ed the victims] to dig their graves before being shot.[278]

He described "frequent instances of rape, pillage, and murder" against "peaceful Armenian population[s]."[279] He characterized the Ottomans' treatment of Armenians as the most "beastly and diabolical cruelties" in the history of the world:

> The final and worst measure used against the Armenians was the wholesale deportation of the entire population from their homes and their exile to the desert, with all the accompanying horrors on the way. No means were provided for their transportation or nourishment. The victims ... had to walk on foot, exposed to attacks of bands of criminals especially organized for that purpose. Homes were literally uprooted; families were separated; men killed, women and girls violated daily on the way or taken to harems. Children were thrown into rivers or sold to strangers by their mothers to save them from starvation.[280]

Morgenthau described what happened in Anatolia as the "elimination of this [Armenian] race."[281] His successor, Ambassador Abram Elkus, similarly reported massacres, "deportations accompanied by studied cruelties," kidnapping of women and girls, an official "policy of extermination through starvation," and atrocities unparalleled in Turkish history.[282]

Morgenthau and Elkus had a strong basis for their statements in the reports of American consuls to the American Embassy in Constantinople. The American chargé d'affaires in Constantinople reported that in the region of Mesopotamia in which the camps for the deported Armenians were established, the "death rate from starvation and sickness was very high," with the Armenians eating dead human and animal bodies, grass, herbs, and locusts in a wretched attempt to survive.[283] An American military mission to Armenia concluded that systematic massacres took place, with young men killed en masse, women

278. Morgenthau, Ambassador Morgenthau's Story, at 303.

279. U.S. National Archives, General Records of the Dep't of State, Record Group 59 (Decimal File, 1910–1929), Doc. No. 59,867.4016/74, U.S. Amb. Henry Morgenthau to U.S. Secretary of State Williams Jennings Bryan, May 25, 1915, *quoted in* Armen Hairapetian, *"Race Problems" and the Armenian Genocide: The State Department File*, 37 Armenian Rev. 41, 47 (1984).

280. Henry Morgenthau, The Tragedy of Armenia 6–8 (1918), *quoted in* Michael J. Kelly, *Can Sovereigns Be Brought to Justice? The Crime of Genocide's Evolution and the Meaning of the Milosevic Trial*, 76 St. John's L. Rev. 257, 268–69 (2002).

281. Morgenthau, Ambassador Morgenthau's Story, at ch. 26, http://net.lib.byu.edu/estu/wwi/comment/morgenthau/Morgen26.htm.

282. U.S. National Archives, Doc. No. 59,867.4016/299, *quoted in* Dadrian, *The Documentation of the World War I Armenian Massacres in the Proceedings of the Turkish Military Tribunal*, at 567.

283. *Quoted in* Dadrian, History of the Armenian Genocide, at 243, 246. *See also* Hoffman, *German Eyewitness Reports of the Genocide of the Armenians, 1915–1916*, *in* A Crime of Silence, at 79; Hilmar Kaiser, At the Crossroads of Der Zor: Death, Survival, and Humanitarian Resistance in Aleppo, 1915–1917, at 64–66 (Princeton, NJ: Gomidas Institute, 2002) (reporting similar desperate measures by starving Armenians).

and children deported to Syrian deserts and "malarial" Mesopotamian lands, in what was described as "the most colossal crime of all ages."[284]

Leslie Davis, the American Consul in Harput, Anatolia, witnessed the condition of surviving deportees in refugee camps:

> There are very few men among them, as most of them have been killed on the road. All tell the same story of having been attacked and robbed by the Kurds. Most of them were attacked over and over again, and a great many of them, especially the men, were killed. Women and children were also killed. Many died, of course, from sickness and exhaustion on the way, and there have been deaths each day that they have been here.... Those who have reached here are only a small portion, however, of those who started. By continuing to drive these people on in this way, it will be possible to dispose of all of them in a comparatively short time.[285]

Davis visited mass grave sites and found that most victims had been killed with bayonets to maximize the efficiency of the operation in terms of number of bullets expended.[286] He reported that the Ottoman policy "seems to be to have bands of Kurds awaiting them on the road to kill the men especially and incidentally some of the others. The entire movement seems to be the most thoroughly organized and effective massacre this country has ever seen."[287]

Oscar Heizer, U.S. Consul for Trabzon, reported that female deportees were "first outraged by the officers of the gendarmerie and then turned over to the gendarmes to be disposed of," with the "best looking" girls "kept in houses for the pleasure of the members of the gang."[288] He wrote that the adult Armenians from Trabzon were deported from the city in July 1915 and killed shortly thereafter. About 3,000 Armenian orphans remained behind until Nail Bey ordered the orphanages to be closed, with some Armenian orphans were appropriated by Muslim families, some boys enslaved on farms, and the female caretakers of orphans sexually enslaved.[289] "Many of the children were loaded into boats and taken out to sea and thrown overboard."[290]

Jesse Jackson, U.S. Consul in Aleppo, Syria, compiled a 25-page report entitled "Armenian Atrocities" for the U.S. Secretary of State in 1918, Robert Lansing.[291] In the report,

---

284. Maj. Gen. James G. Harbord et al., Conditions in the Near East: Report of the American Military Mission to Armenia, 66th Cong., S. Doc. No. 266, at 7 (1920).

285. U.S. National Archives, Doc. No. 59,867.4016/122, *quoted in* Leslie A. Davis, The Slaughterhouse Province: An American Diplomat's Report on the Armenian Genocide 144–45 (Susan Blair ed., New Rochelle, NY: AD Caratzas, Orpheus Pub., 1990).

286. *See* Davis, The Slaughterhouse Province, at 83, *quoted in* Dadrian, *The Documentation of the World War I Armenian Massacres in the Proceedings of the Turkish Military Tribunal*, at 567.

287. U.S. National Archives, Doc. No. 59,867.4016/122, *quoted in* Christoper J. Walker, *World War I and the Armenian Genocide, in* 2 The Armenian People from Ancient to Modern Times: The Fifteenth Century to Modern Times, at 260 (Richard Hovannisian ed., New York: Palgrave Macmillan, 1997).

288. U.S. National Archives, Doc. No. 59,867.4016/210, U.S. Consul in Trabzon, Oscar Heizer, Aug. 13, 1915, *quoted in* Dadrian, *The Documentation of the World War I Armenian Massacres in the Proceedings of the Turkish Military Tribunal*, at 574.

289. *See* Oscar Heizer, Reports to Amb. Morgenthau in July 1915, *cited in* Ara Sarafian, *The Absorption of Armenian Women and Children into Muslim Households as a Structural Component of the Armenian Genocide, in* In God's Name: Genocide and Religion in the Twentieth Century 212 (Providence, RI: Berghahn Books, 2001).

290. Oscar Heizer, Report No. 24 to Amb. Morgenthau, *quoted in id.* at 220.

291. *See* Balakian, The Burning Tigris, at 422.

he described "massacres" of 60,000 Armenians outside of the town and district of Deir el-Zor in Mesopotamia. He blamed the governor of Deir el-Zor for "the most horrible butcheries imaginable." Ras ul-Ain was a stop on the rail line to Deir el-Zor. A few hours from Deir el-Zor, the Armenians were "set upon by bands of Turkish, Circassian, and Kurdish ex-convicts that had been liberated from prisons and taken there for that purpose," a description which matches other accounts of the formation of the Special Organization bands. The death toll in the area was at least 300,000, Jackson wrote. He documented "the unlimited suffering and death of famished women and children, the unbelievable brutality of the accompanying gendarmes towards young girls and more attractive women, [and] the carrying off by the Kurds and Turks of beautiful girls, women, and children, and countless other atrocious crimes."[292] Jackson had previously reported to Ambassador Morgenthau that during the Armenian deportations, "the accompanying gendarmes are told they may do as they wish with the women and girls."[293]

In 1919, President Woodrow Wilson referred to the Armenians as "a Christian people, helpless, at the mercy of a Turkish government which thought it the service of God to destroy them." He told a U.S. Senator that the Armenian persecutions were "outrages more terrible, I believe, than history ever before witnessed...."[294] By that time, the American Committee on Armenian and Syrian Relief estimated that four million Armenians, Assyrians, and Greeks had died.[295] Wilson announced in a public appeal in 1917 that there were 400,000 orphans and two million people facing starvation among the surviving Armenians and Syrians (presumably including Arabs in the latter category).[296] The American Red Cross had reported by then that one million deportees were starving.[297] Former President Theodore Roosevelt referred to the Armenian massacres as a "wholesale slaughter"[298] and as the "greatest crime of the war."[299]

Several other U.S. presidents and presidential candidates have since recognized the Armenian genocide. In 1978, U.S. President Jimmy Carter condemned the Ottoman Empire's "elimination" of its Armenian population. President Ronald Reagan followed suit in 1981 by acknowledging the Armenian genocide. The House of Representatives of the U.S. has passed several resolutions recognizing the genocide of the Armenians.[300] The

---

292. U.S. National Archives, Doc. No. 59,867.4016/373 & encl., Mar. 4, 1918, U.S. Consul in Aleppo, Jesse Jackson, to U.S. Secretary of State, Lansing and U.S. Ambassador to the Ottoman Empire, Morgenthau, *quoted in* Hairapetian, *"Race Problems" and the Armenian Genocide,* at 44–45. The report is available at this address: http://tinyurl.com/lqqzvf.

293. U.S. National Archives, Doc. No. 59,867.4016/72, May 12, 1915, U.S. Consul in Aleppo, Jesse Jackson, to Ambassador Morgenthau, *quoted* Hairapetian, *"Race Problems" and the Armenian Genocide,* at 46.

294. 62 Wilson Papers 259–60, *quoted in* Lloyd E. Ambrosius, *Wilsonian Diplomacy and Armenia: The Limits of Power and Ideology, in* America and the Armenian Genocide of 1915, at 135; 63 Wilson Papers 71, *quoted in* John Milton Cooper, Jr., *A Friend in Power? Woodrow Wilson and Armenia, in id.* at 118.

295. *See The Total Killed,* The Manchester Guardian (U.K.), Feb 27, 1919, at 6.

296. *See Aid Starving Refugees,* Wash. Post, Oct. 29, 1917, at 3.

297. *See Thousands in Western Asia Starving, Red Cross Relief Committee Finds,* Wash. Post, Sept. 22, 1917, at 3.

298. Theodore Roosevelt, Fear God and Take Your Own Part 379 (New York: Cosimo Books, 2005) (1915).

299. *Quoted in* Balakian, The Burning Tigris, at 293.

300. *See* Travis, *Ottoman Genocide of the Assyrians,* at 345; Days of Remembrance of Victims of the Holocaust (Proclamation 4838), 1981 Public Papers of the Presidents 375, April 22, 1981; H. Res. 316, 109th Cong., 1st Sess., June 14, 2005, http://thomas.loc.gov/cgi-bin/query/z?c109:H.RES.316; Warren Tolman & Dikran Kaligian, *It's Elementary: Turks Committed Genocide,* Boston

current U.S. President, Barack Obama, stated while running for office that he would recognize the Armenian Genocide Congress as President, and that Congress should pass an Armenian Genocide Resolution clearly describing the events as "genocide" and "race extermination."[301] At least 23 U.S. state governments have passed Armenian genocide resolutions.[302]

Even smaller nations such as Norway, Sweden, Denmark, and Switzerland had diplomats and aid officials who were situated to witness Ottoman massacres of Armenians. A Swedish military officer stationed in Persia corroborated these American accounts of Ottoman massacres of Armenians in concentration camps [*"koncentrationsläger"*].[303] Several German reports speak of *"Konzentrationslager"* or *"Konzentrationslagern,"* confirming among other things that thousands of Armenians were slaughtered in the Ras ul-Ain concentration camps.[304] The American, German, Swiss, and Swedish reports confirm the account of an Armenian genocide contained in Ottoman documents published in 1920 after a leak from Naim Bey, a conscience-stricken functionary in the Ottoman bureaucracy, which reported 70,000 civilian deaths at Ras ul-Ain[305] Other Ottoman officials confirmed

---

HERALD, Dec. 9, 2005, at 33. The declarations of the various U.S. presidents over the years are reproduced at http://www.armenian-genocide.org.

301. *See* Calvin Woodward, *Promises, Promises: Obama, Armenians and Genocide,* ASSOCIATED PRESS/FOX NEWS, Apr. 24, 2009, http://www.foxnews.com/ wires/2009Apr24/0,4670,USObamaArmenia BrokenPromise,00.html. The resolution President Obama mentioned, House Resolution 106, states that the "Armenian Genocide was conceived and carried out by the Ottoman Empire from 1915 to 1923, resulting in the deportation of nearly 2,000,000 Armenians, of whom 1,500,000 men, women, and children were killed, 500,000 survivors were expelled from their homes, and which succeeded in the elimination of the over 2,500-year presence of Armenians in their historic homeland," and that "Raphael Lemkin, who coined the term 'genocide' in 1944, and who was the earliest proponent of the United Nations Convention on the Prevention and Punishment of Genocide, invoked the Armenian case as a definitive example of genocide in the 20th century." H. Res. 106, 110th Cong., 1st Sess., introduced Jan. 30, 2007, http://www.govtrack.us/congress/billtext.xpd?bill=hr110-106. It was adopted by the House Committee on Foreign Affairs on Oct. 10, 2007. *See* U.S. Congress, *H.RES.106, All Congressional Actions* (2009), http://thomas.loc.gov.

302. *See* H. Res. 316; Fergal Keane, *Armenians Say US Failed Them,* BBC NEWS, Jan. 26, 2003, http://news.bbc.co.uk/1/hi/programmes/correspondent/2572667.stm; *US House Committee to Discuss Genocide Resolution,* TURKISH DAILY NEWS, Sept. 9, 2005, http://www.turkishdailynews.com.tr; Jason Wermers, *Massacres Genocide?; 23 States Have Legislation That Recognizes Stance of Armenians,* RICHMOND TIMES DISPATCH, Apr. 2, 2001, at B1.

303. MAJOR GUSTAV HJALMAR PRAVITZ, FRÅN PERSIEN I STILTJE OCH STORM 221 (1918), *quoted in* AVEDIAN, THE ARMENIAN GENOCIDE, at 26.

304. *See, e.g.,* DE/PA-AA/R14106, 1919-A-21605, July 19, 1919, article in Berliner Tageblatt; DE/PA-AA/R14092, 1916-A-18548, A53a / 1916, July 10, 1916, the German Ambassador on Extraordinary Mission in Constantinople, Wolff-Metternich, to the German Imperial Chancellor, Bethmann Hollweg (concentration camp at Ras ul-Ain was completely cleared of Armenians as part of a campaign for the resolution of "the Armenian question by the destruction of the Armenian race"); DE/PA-AA/R14092, 1916-A-17939 1916-A-17939, K. No. 61/No. 1703, June 17, 1916, the German Consul in Aleppo, Rößler, to the German Imperial Chancellor, Bethmann Hollweg (reporting that few Armenians at Ras ul-Ain concentration camp could have survived). *See also* Tessa Hoffman, *German Eyewitness Reports of the Genocide of the Armenians, 1915–1916, in* A CRIME OF SILENCE, at 80.

305. *See* Vahakn N. Dadrian, *The Naim-Andonian Documents on the World War I Destruction of Ottoman Armenians: The Anatomy of a Genocide,* 18 INT'L J. OF MIDDLE EAST STUDIES 311, 334 (1986); Kaiser, *The Baghdad Railway and the Armenian Genocide,* at 72–75; MERRILL D. PETERSON, "STARVING ARMENIANS": AMERICA AND THE ARMENIAN GENOCIDE, 1915–1930 AND AFTER 46–47 (Charlottesville, VA: Univ. of Virginia Press, 2004); The History of the Armenian Genocide: Hearing before the Committee on International Relations, House of Representatives. 104th Cong., 2nd Sess., Mav 15, 1996, at 53 (Washington, DC: Govt. Printing Office, 1996) ("[Armenians] were sent to specific killing sites, such as Ras-ul-Ain and Deir-el-Zor."). *See generally* ARAM ANDONIAN, THE MEMOIRS OF

massacres in Ras ul-Ain.[306] A Norwegian nurse working with the Red Cross in Anatolia reported during the summer of 1915 that:

> In March, 1915, we learnt through an Armenian doctor, who died later on of typhus, that the Turkish Government was preparing for a massacre on a grand scale.... Through the good offices of the German Consul at Erzerum, ... we were engaged by the Red Cross at Erzindjan, and worked there seven weeks....
>
> After [the Armenian deportation order], several days' grace was given to the population of Erzindjan for the sale of their property, which was naturally realised at ludicrous prices....
>
> Our Turkish cook came to us crying, and told us how the Kurds had attacked the unhappy convoy at Kamakh Boghaz, had pillaged it completely, and had killed a great number of the exiles. This must have been the 14th June....
>
> [On] the 11th June, a party of regular troops (belonging to the 86th Cavalry Brigade) were sent out to keep the Kurds in order.
>
> We heard subsequently from these soldiers how the defenceless Armenians had been massacred to the last one. The butchery had taken four hours. The women threw themselves on their knees, they had thrown their children into the Euphrates, and so on.[307]

The Swiss deacon Dr. Jakob Künzler dismissed attempts to characterize Turkish-Armenian conflict as legitimate combat, instead calling it a campaign of extermination (*ausrotten*).[308] A prominent Swedish official rejected allegations of meaningful Ottoman Armenian aggression against Turkish villages in cooperation with Russian troops, and wrote:

Naim Bey: Turkish Official Documents Relating to Deportation and Massacres of Armenians (Newton Square, PA: Armenian Historical Research Ass'n, 1965). Rößler wrote of the Naim Bey documents in 1921:

> I have received the book by Aram Andonian on the Armenian massacres that was kindly sent to me and while reading it I vividly felt myself to be back in Aleppo. In the following review I will first state some reservations and then go into the value of Naim Bey's report and the documents....
>
> Apart from these issues I must say that the contents of the book in its individual features make a credible impression and that, compared with the course of things, the documents certainly have an inner plausibility....
>
> In his preface, the author mentions the Office of Deportation (Sousdirection générale des déportés sise à Alep) as being the main organisation for deportation. He is no doubt correct. When ... I approached the Commissioner of Deportation with a request to release some Armenians who were employed by Germans, he refused this in the most brusque manner and said to me in an incredibly arrogant tone of voice which I will never forget, "You do not understand what we want. We want an Armenia without Armenians."

DE/PA-AA/NL/Rößler/Bd.1, Mar. 25, 1921, letter from former German Consul in Aleppo, Rößler, to Dr. Lepsius.

306. *See* Dadrian, *The Naim-Andonian Documents*, at 334.

307. DE/PA-AA/R14093, 1916-A-24663, Sept. 10, 1916, enclosure no. 1 to letter from the Chief of the Kaiser's Civil Cabinet, Valentini, to the German Imperial Chancellor, Bethmann Hollweg. *See also* Matthias Bjørnlund, *'A Fate Worse Than Dying': Sexual Violence during the Armenian Genocide, in* Brutality and Desire: War and Sexuality in Twentieth Century Europe 21 (Dagmar Herzog ed., New York: Palgrave, 2009); *Turkey's Historical Amnesia,* Boston Globe, Sept. 1, 2007, http://www.boston.com/news/globe/editorial_opinion/editorials/articles/2007/09/01/turkeys_historical_amnesia/.

308. *See* DE/PA-AA/R14086, 1915-A-22125, June 29, 1915, report from the Consul in Aleppo, Rößler, to the German Imperial Chancellor, Bethmann Hollweg; Künzler, Im Lande des Blutes und der Tränen, *passim*; Tessa Hoffman, *Mit einer Stimme sprechen: Gegen Völkermord, in* Ver-

> Officially, [the Ottomans] had the goal to move the entire Armenian population to the steppe regions of Northern Mesopotamia and Syria, but in reality they aimed to exterminate [*utrota*] the Armenians, whereby the pure Turkish element in Asia Minor would achieve a dominating position....
>
> The annihilation of the Armenian nation in Asia Minor must revolt all human feelings.... The way the Armenian problem was solved was hair-raising. I can still see in front of me Talaat's cynical expression, when he emphasized that the Armenian question was solved.[309]

Danish and Swiss missions corroborated German and American reports of the Armenian massacres.[310] A Danish book published in 1928 reproduced a telegram from Talât Paşa to the police in Aleppo stating that "by the order of the [CUP] the Government have determined completely to exterminate the Armenians living in Turkey."[311]

H. The Armenian Genocide in The Caucasus and Elsewhere, 1918–1925

In March 1918, the German ambassador reported to the German Foreign Office that atrocities by Armenian resisters were on the rise. He described an plan in Ottoman "leading circles of "pan-Islamism" designed to forge a wider empire of "the Mohammedans of Asia, be they Tartars, Georgians or Persians and so on, ... [in] brotherhood [with] the Turks."[312] After the Treaty of Brest-Litowsk, German officials contacted Ottoman officials to urge the peaceful treatment of the Armenians. Still, the Ottoman official telegraph services began to distribute reports that Armenian bands were committing atrocities against Turks, which the Allies viewed as "mak[ing] excuses in advance for their intended, ruthless acts against the Armenians."[313]

On May 23, 1918, a German military representative in Batum, present-day Georgia, wrote to the German ambassador that:

> As I am continuously reporting, the aim of Turkish policy is the permanent occupation of the Armenian districts and the extermination of the Armenians.... In Constantinople, the extreme anti-Armenian trend has gained the upper hand....
>
> [A]n advance has been made on Baku to drive off the Bolsheviks there and for the Turks to take up their position there. Turkish troops are on the front to the south of Achalkal, advancing against Tiflis and Erivan. Kurd and Tartar volunteers accompany the army, robbing and murdering in the Armenian towns. All of the men are taken away. In order to avoid conflicts, Armenian troops get out

---

FOLGUNG, VERTREIBUNG UND VERNICHTUNG DER CHRISTEN IM OSMANISCHEN REICH 1912–1922, at 32 (Tessa Hofmann ed., Berlin: LIT Verlag, 2006)

309. AF WIRSEN, KRIG, at 132–33, 232, 226, *quoted in* AVEDIAN, THE ARMENIAN GENOCIDE.

310. *See* FRIDTOF NANSEN, ARMENIA AND THE NEAR EAST 298–307 (New York: Da Capo Press, 1976) (1928).

311. *Id.* at 307. For other Danish sources, see sources cited in Bjørnlund, '*A Fate Worse Than Dying*,' at 42–58.

312. DE/PA-AA/R14099, DuA Dok. 376 (re.), 1918-A-11778, Mar. 16, 1918, report from the German Ambassador in Constantinople, Bernstorff, to the German Foreign Office.

313. DE/PA-AA/R14099, DuA Dok. 377 (re. gk.), 1918-A-11280, Mar. 19, 1918, notes by the German Foreign Office.

> of the way by going east. The Armenian population is fleeing to the east and must soon encounter the Tartars which will lead to massacres. Turkish policy indicates that it will avoid an ultimatum and achieve a fait accompli with regard to the possession of territory. No space will be left for the Armenian population to live on.... Through Leishman, the authorised Delegation of the Armenian National Council has requested Germany's protection against the complete annihilation of the Armenian people and that the remainder of the Armenian territory be placed under German protectorate. I have in hand an official document in this matter. If the extermination of the Armenians is to be prevented, it is necessary to put immediate and permanent pressure on Turkey.[314]

He warned on June 3 that Talât planned to expand the anti-Armenian extermination campaign [*Armenier ausrotten*] "outside Turkey." The foreign minister agreed, writing that "the Turks systematically are pursuing their plan of annihilation of the Armenians in the Caucasus."[315]

In late June 1918, Armenia declared its independence from the Ottoman Empire, and dispatched a foreign minister to the empire.[316] The Armenians fought to defend their homes in historic Armenia, but were deported and murdered wholesale.[317] On June 30, 1918, Ambassador Wolff-Metternich told Johannes Lepsius that: "The Armenians are finished.... Hellenism [the Greeks] ... will be destroyed as the Armenian element was."[318] He added that the CUP "demands the destruction of the last remnant of the Armenians." Turkification, he inferred, was a process requiring "to expel or kill all that is not Turkish, to destroy or misappropriate by violence other people's property."[319]

In July, the head of the German delegation in the Caucasus reported that "more than half a million Armenians [had] abandoned their villages in the areas occupied and threatened by the Turks," and had fled to the Yerevan area where "they are unable to obtain anything to eat, even with hard cash. For weeks, many, many thousands have been surviving only on grass."[320]

British troops withdrew from Baku, in present-day Azerbaijan, which they had entered as part of an agreement with the Bolsheviks, in August 1918. The British Prime

---

314. DE/PA-AA/R14100, DuA Dok. 395 (re.), 1918-A-21877, May 23, 1918, report from the German Ambassador in Constantinople, Bernstorff, to the German Foreign Office.

315. *Quoted in* Dadrian, *Comparative Aspects of the Armenian and Jewish Cases of Genocide*, at 166.

316. *See Armenians Assert Liberty! Government Set Up in Caucasian Region and Envoys Sent to Turks*, N.Y. Times, June 29, 1918, http://www.nytimes.com.

317. *Id.*; *see also* Ternon, *Report on the Genocide of the Armenians*, at 107–19.

318. *Quoted in* Peterson, "Starving Armenians," at 124; *see also* Derogy, Resistance and Revenge, at 95.

319. *Quoted in* Nansen, Armenia and the Near East at 319. *See also* Morgenthau, Ambassador Morgenthau's Story, at 35 (Interior Minister Talât's "passion for Turkifying the nation seemed to demand logically the extermination of all Christians"); Johannes Lepsius, Der Völkermord an den Armeniern vor Gericht: Der Prozess Talat Pascha 61 (Tessa Hofmann ed., Göttingen: Gesellschaft für bedrohte Völker, 1985) (1921) ("Count Metternich, who was German Ambassador in Constantinople in 1918, wrote in a report of 30 June: 'The Armenians are finished. The Young Turkish pack now prepares with impatience for the moment, when Greece will turn against Turkey. The Greekhood [*Griechentum*] forms the cultural element of Turkey. In that case, it will be annihilated, as was the Armenian [element].' That was the view of Count Metternich."), *quoted in* Tessa Hofmann, *Co-Victims in Genocide: The Christians during the last Decade of Ottoman Rule* 35 (2007), http://www.genocidescholars.org/blog/wp-content/uploads/2007/08/co-victims_1.pdf.

320. DE/PA-AA/R14103, DuA Dok. 405 (gk.), 1918-A-31345, July 11, 1918, report from the head of the German Delegation in the Caucasus, Kress von Kressenstein, to the German Imperial Chancellor, Hertling.

Minister judged that "it would be better for us for the Turks to hold Baku...." In September 1918, a Turkish army entered the city, where the head of the telegraph agency reported that: "In the whole town massacres of the Armenian population and robberies of all non-Muslim peoples were going on. They ... dragged out men, women and children and killed them in the street." Some 20,000 Armenians perished in Baku, perhaps even more.[321] Nevertheless, U.S. President Woodrow Wilson endorsed a "secure sovereignty" in the "Turkish portions of the present Ottoman Empire," while paying lip service to non-Turks' "security of life" in a sovereign Turkey.[322]

President Wilson dispatched emissaries to meet with Mustafa Kemal in 1919, who impressed them "as a realist." In the Republic of Armenia, they discovered that half a million refugees verged on starvation, with Yerevan packed with "wretched refugees in rags, hungry, diseased, demoralized." Wilson suffered a serious stroke and delayed half a year in submitting the plan of his emissaries for U.S. intervention to save the Armenians. The U.S. Senate voted against the plan, after which the British prime minister vetoed efforts to establish a viable Armenian republic in the traditionally Armenian areas from Erzerum to Yerevan.[323]

A Turkish army attacked the Republic of Armenia in September 1920. The previous summer, the *New York Times* had reported: "Turkish Army Moves to Destroy the Armenians; Ottomans, Aided by Tartars, Advancing on Three Sides in War of Extermination."[324] The German chief of staff to the Turkish commander of Turkish Army Groups East wrote in 1920 that: "The evacuation of Anatolia by the Russians furnished the desired opportunity to clear out also the Russian Armenians.... The annihilation campaign against the Armenians proceeded ... with inexorable ruthlessness." In five months in 1920 and 1921, about 200,000 Armenians died in eastern Anatolia and Russian Armenia.[325] The *New York Times* headline in December 1920 was: "Armenia Death. Loss Half of Population."[326] In 1922, it received a cable from the head of Near East Relief, Major Yewell, who described interference with humanitarian aid to Armenians, the confiscation of nearly all Armenian property by Turkey, "virtual slavery" of Armenian civilians including the abduction of Armenian women and holding of Armenian men in prison for ransom, and the deaths of more than 5,000 Greeks deported from Sivas.[327]

Scholars have shown that the Ottoman Empire drove waves of refugees from their homes and ancestral communities, resulting in dramatic resettlements of peoples. Nearly two million Ottoman Christians fled widespread massacres and destruction of cities and villages between the 1890s and 1920s, which rendered uninhabitable such cultural and population centers as Armenian Van, much of Baku and Yerevan, as well as the Pontus region, the Smyrna area, and the Assyrian villages in Hakkari including the Assyrian spiritual capital of Qudshanis.[328] Although claiming far fewer lives of members of other groups, Ot-

321. *Quoted in* Walker, Armenia, at 260–61.

322. *Quoted in id.* at 264.

323. *See id.* at 276–81.

324. N.Y. Times, July 31, 1919, at 1.

325. *Quoted in* Dadrian, *Comparative Aspects of the Armenian and Jewish Cases of Genocide*, at 166–67, *and in* Dadrian, *Documentation of the Armenian Genocide in German and Austrian Sources*, at 124–25.

326. *Armenia Death. Loss Half of Population. 100,000 Refugees Fleeing Through Snow in Last Stages of Want. Cut To A Little Republic,* N.Y. Times, Dec. 3, 1920, at 8.

327. *Killing by Turks Has Been Renewed*; *American Says They Plan to Exterminate the Christians in Asia Minor,* N.Y. Times, May 6, 1922, at 2.

328. *See* Rieber, Forced Migration, at 11–13; Norwood, 2 Strangers and Exiles, at 254–70; Akçam, A Shameful Act, at 106–7, 269–70; Akçam, From Empire to Republic, at 118, 146–47; Do-

toman policies targeted Muslim Shi'a and Kurds, Iraqi Jews and Yezidis, and Lebanese Maronite Christians and Druzes, prompting hundreds of thousands of members of these groups to seek to escape.[329] During and after a variety of Ottoman border conflicts and wars of independence, the Russian Empire and other Europeans at war with the Ottomans drove more than a million Muslim Turks, Bosnians, Rumelians, Circassians, etc. from lands they had settled for some centuries.[330] Circassian leaders believed that two million of their people had moved from Russia to Turkey.[331]

I. The Toll of the Armenian Genocide in Lives Taken Directly

Historians and legal scholars have combined the above accounts, and many others, to paint the following outline of the Armenian genocide. As the civilians from eastern Anatolia and Cilicia/Armenia were deported, Ottoman death squads and allied Turkish and Kurdish militia attacked them "again and again" in massacres, while survivors largely died of hunger, lack of water, or exposure to the elements.[332] One million Armenians died of these causes between 1915 and 1918, out of about two million Armenians.[333] During the first half of 1915, Ottoman Minister of War Enver Paşa ordered the mass murder of 200,000 or more Armenian men who had been drafted into or volunteered for the Ottoman armed forces.[334] On April 24, 1915, Interior Minister Talât Paşa ordered the first of thousands of Armenian religious and political leaders to be arrested throughout the Empire; hundreds of leaders imprisoned in Constantinople were later executed.[335] The "clearance"

---

minik J. Schaller & Jürgen Zimmerer, *Late Ottoman Genocides: The Dissolution of the Ottoman Empire and Young Turkish Population and Extermination Policies*, 10 J. of Genocide Res. 7, 7–10 (2008); Edwin I. James, *Turks Proclaim Banishment Edict to 1,000,000 Greeks*, N.Y. Times, Dec. 2, 1922, at 1. For sources on the destruction of Van, see Armenian Van/Vaspurakan (Richard G. Hovannisian ed., Costa Mesa, CA: Mazda Publishers, 2000); Rafael De Nogales, Memoirs of a Soldier of Fortune 270 (2006) (1932).

329. *See* Schaller & Zimmerer, *Late Ottoman Genocides*, at 11–13.

330. *See* Akçam, A Shameful Act, at 86–89, 98–99, 261, 267; Akçam, From Empire to Republic, at 93; Ryan Gingeras, Sorrowful Shores: Violence, Ethnicity, and the End of the Ottoman Empire, 1912–1923, at 125 (Oxford and New York: Oxford University Press, 2009) (Circassian leaders believed that two million Circassians from the northwestern Caucasus region became "suspicious" of the Russian Empire and "emigrated to Turkey."

331. *See* Ryan Gingeras, Sorrowful Shores: Violence, Ethnicity, and the End of the Ottoman Empire, 1912–1923, at 125 (Oxford and New York: Oxford University Press, 2009).

332. Melson, Revolution and Genocide, at 107.

333. *See id.*; Donald Bloxham, The Great Game of Genocide: Imperialism, Nationalism, and the Destruction of the Ottoman Armenians 10 (Oxford and New York: Oxford UP, 2005); Bevan, The Destruction of Memory, at 54; Dadrian, The History of the Armenian Genocide, at 62, 299, 388; Gaunt, Massacres, Resistance, Protectors, at 25, 176–77, 228–30, 250–56, 300–15; Gilbert, The First World War, at 167; Emile Hilderbrand, *Emile. Kemal Promises More Hangings of Political Antagonists in Turkey,* Los Angeles Examiner, Aug. 1, 1926, at 1; Hoffman, *German Eyewitness Reports of the Genocide of the Armenians, 1915–16, in* The Crime of Silence, at 83.

334. *See* Akçam, A Shameful Act, at 141–145; Dickran H. Boyajian, Armenia: The Case for a Forgotten Genocide 288–89, 333–34 (Westwood, NJ: Educational Book Crafters, 1972); Rummel, Death by Government, at 216–17; Howard M. Sachar, The Emergence of the Middle East: 1914–1924, at 98 (New York: Knopf, 1969).

335. Balakian, The Burning Tigris, at 211–15; Dadrian, History of the Armenian Genocide, at 221.

of Armenian cities and towns throughout the Empire occupied the rest of 1915,[336] as the army, Special Organization, and militia exterminated the Christian population of entire Ottoman provinces such as Diyarbekir.[337] The Ottoman Empire's assaults on Armenian civilians expanded into a campaign of massacres and deportations that affected the vast majority of Armenians living in eastern Anatolia and Cilicia:

> The lines of Armenian deportees were set upon again and again by Turkish and Kurdish villagers who in many cases had been incited and were led by specially designated killing squads, *Teshkilat-i Makhsusiye*, organized at the highest levels of the CUP. Those Armenians who escaped massacre were very likely to perish of hunger, dehydration, or exposure on the way.[338]

By October 1915, 1.5 million Armenians had been deported, of whom about 1.2 million were dead and the rest were in dire straits, according to a report received by the German Imperial Chancellor Theobald von Bethmann-Hollweg from his ambassador to the Ottoman Empire.[339] Between 1918 and 1923, Turkish nationalists killed 500,000 more Armenians.[340] In about five months in 1920 and 1921, about 200,000 Armenians died in eastern Anatolia and Russian Armenia.[341] As noted above, 20,000 Armenians died in Baku alone.[342] The sum of one million through 1918 and 500,000 from 1918 through 1925 leads to 1.5 million. This constituted between 50 and 75 percent of the Armenians of the former Ottoman Empire.[343] It is also similar to a German educator's estimate of two million Armenian casualties by 1918.[344]

An Armenian-American described the result, as he saw it in 1995, of the Ottoman Empire's and Turkish Republic's policies of eliminating the Armenian population:

> The most common type of church we visited [in Turkey] was the ruined variety such as in Kharpert, Husenig, Kessirig, Tallas and Germir. The Armenian districts of the former city of Kharpert cease to exist except for the eastern wall

336. DADRIAN, HISTORY OF THE ARMENIAN GENOCIDE, 219–20.

337. DE NOGALES, FOUR YEARS BENEATH THE CRESCENT, at 133–36; Dadrian, *Documentation of the Armenian Genocide in German and Austrian Sources, in* THE WIDENING CIRCLE OF GENOCIDE, at 113.

338. MELSON, REVOLUTION AND GENOCIDE, at 107.

339. *See* JOHANNES LEPSIUS, DEUTSCHLAND UND ARMENIEN: SAMMLUNG DIPLOMATISCHER AKTENSTÜCKE 295–96 (Potsdam: Tempelverlag, 1919) ("[W]enn man nun die Gesamtzahl der türkischen Armenier auf 2 Millionen unde die Zahl der Vershickten auf 1½ Million veranschlagt und dasselbe Verhältnis zwischen Überlebenden und Umgekommenen wie bei den Waisen der Schwester Rohner annimmt, so gelangt man zu einer Zahl von über 1175000 von Umgekommenen und rund 325,000 Überlebenden.").

340. *See* BLOXHAM, THE GREAT GAME OF GENOCIDE, at 10; BEVAN, THE DESTRUCTION OF MEMORY, 54; DADRIAN, THE HISTORY OF THE ARMENIAN GENOCIDE, at 62, 299, 388; GAUNT, MASSACRES, RESISTANCE, PROTECTORS, at 25, 176–77, 228–30, 250–56, 300–15; GILBERT, THE FIRST WORLD WAR, at 167; MELSON, REVOLUTION AND GENOCIDE, at 107; RUMMEL, DEATH BY GOVERNMENT, at 228–29; Hilderbrand, *Kemal Promises More Hangings*, at 1.

341. *Quoted in* Dadrian, *Comparative Aspects of the Armenian and Jewish Cases of Genocide*, at 166–67.

342. *See, e.g.*, WALKER, ARMENIA, at 260–61.

343. *See* ROBERT MELSON, REVOLUTION AND GENOCIDE: ON THE ORIGINS OF THE ARMENIAN GENOCIDE AND THE HOLOCAUST 107 (Chicago: Univ. of Chicago Press, 1992).

344. The author, the head of a school for the blind in Turkey, wrote: "The losses to the Armenian people during the period since the deportation in the summer of 1915 until today have surpassed 2 million." DE/PA-AA/R14097, DuA Dok. 356 (gk.), 1917-A-23271, July 15, 1917, report from member of the Board of Governors of the German Mission for the Blind in the Middle East to the German Foreign Office.

of Saint Garabed and Saint Hagop Churches. Even the cemeteries have disappeared.

In Urfa and Aintab, Armenian churches that survived intact over the years have been converted into mosques in recent decades....

How could the physical record of 2,500 years of Armenian civilization be so erased in only seventy years?[345]

J. The Treaty of Sèvres

After the defeat of the Ottoman Empire and the Second Reich, the postwar Treaty of Sèvres between the Allied Powers and the Ottoman Empire called for the restitution of properties of non-Turkish subjects of the empire who lost their homes due to massacres or their flight from massacres. Article 144 required the Turkish Government to repeal the law of 1915 expropriating Armenian homes and businesses (the Law on Abandoned Properties or *Emval-I-Metroukeh*), and to regard this law as "null and void, in the past as in the future."[346] The treaty also stated that:

> The Turkish Government solemnly undertakes to facilitate to the greatest possible extent the return to their homes and re-establishment in their businesses of the Turkish subjects of non-Turkish race who have been forcibly driven from their homes by fear of massacre or any other form of pressure since January 1, 1914. It recognizes that any immovable or movable property of the said Turkish subjects or of the communities to which they belong, which can be recovered, must be restored to them as soon as possible, in whatever hands it may be found....[347]

The frontiers of Armenia were to be settled by arbitration of U.S. President Wilson.[348] The Ottoman Sultan Mehmed VI agreed to this procedure and remained in power until 1922, while President Wilson's award was issued in November 1920.[349]

The Treaty of Sèvres depended heavily on the Russian Empire to allow the president of the U.S. to arbitrate the borders between Turkey and the independent Armenia recognized by the Ottoman Empire in the treaty, and to permit Azerbaijan and Georgia to enter into a treaty with Armenia establishing their mutual borders in the Caucasus.[350] The German Empire, however, had conspired with Bolshevik terrorists inside of Russia, led by Vladimir I. Lenin and Josef Stalin, who overthrew the czarist regime and occupied much of Rus-

---

345. Gregory C. Norsigian, *Chasing Ghosts in Turkey*, THE ARMENIAN REPORTER, Jan. 14, 1995, http://www.highbeam.com/doc/1P1-2297219.html.

346. *See* Treaty of Sèvres, art. 144, http://web.archive.org/web/20050218105411/ www.hri.org/docs/sevres/part4.html. *See also* 15 AMERICAN J. OF INT'L L. 210; 2 THE TREATIES OF THE PEACE, 1919–1923 (New York: Carnegie Endowment for International Peace, 1924).

347. Treaty of Sèvres, art. 142.

348. *See* GILBERT, THE FIRST WORLD WAR, at 527–28.

349. *See id.*; *see also* Treaty of Sèvres, art. 89; HAROLD ARMSTRONG, TURKEY IN TRAVAIL: THE BIRTH OF A NEW NATION 27, 113 (London: John Lane, 1925); ARNOLD J. TOYNBEE & KENNETH P. KIRKWOOD, TURKEY 151 (New York: Charles Scribners, 1927); *Sultan Mehmed VI, in* THE ENCYCLOPEDIA OF WORLD WAR I 779 (Spencer C. Tucker ed., Santa Barbara, California: ABC-CLIO, 2005).

350. *See* Treaty of Sèvres, arts. 89–92, http://web.archive.org/web/20050218105411/www.hri.org/docs/sevres/part3.html.

sia.[351] The Bolsheviks reached a peace treaty with the German, Austrian, and Ottoman empires that transferred Armenian lands to Turkey.[352] The Bolsheviks occupied Azerbaijan in spring 1920, and absorbed Russian Armenia in 1922.[353] In this war, Armenia entered a long night. Nearly 60,000 Armenians and Greeks would be deported to Kazakhstan between 1922 and 1950.[354]

K. Denial of the Armenian Genocide

The rhetorical strategies of writers who deny the occurrence of genocides are similar, whether they are writing about Native Americans, Armenians, Jews, Slavs, or other peoples. First, they argue that the crime of genocide did not exist until 1948, and that no jurisdiction exists to investigate or remedy mass killings prior to that time. Second, they ignore the most directly incriminating documents, or dismiss them as forgeries without subjecting the documents they rely on to such obstinately skeptical scrutiny. Third, they disregard the victims' own stories as being fabricated for purposes of obtaining reparations payments or furthering nationalist or secessionist political agendas, and minimize estimates of the populations of victim groups prior to the commencement of genocidal campaigns, including census results that support such estimates, in order to suppress the death toll by arithmetic gymnastics. Fourth, they equate Turkish military deaths with Ottoman Christian civilian deaths, and condemn the trials of the perpetrators of genocide as biased, and all of the testimony as lies. Fifth, they blame the victims for "terrorism" and treasonously acting in league with enemy states, and saddle the victims with responsibility for the crimes and casualties of enemy states to "even the scales," which also requires equating fallen soldiers or victims of war crimes with systematically massacred civilians. In this vein, they argue that killing civilians connected to rebels is right and lawful.

1. Legal and Factual Distortions

First, the present-day Republic of Turkey, as well as its defenders and certain scholars, concedes that killings or even massacres of Christians took place within the Ottoman Empire during World War I, but rejects the notion that these massacres fit the technical legal definition of genocide because genocide was not a crime at all in 1915 or 1916. As the Web site of the Turkish government points out, the term "genocide" was not invented

---

351. *See* Gilbert, The First World War, at 398 (describing "German financial backing for the Bolsheviks"); Simon Sebag Montefiore, Young Stalin 313 (New York: Knopf, 2007) (describing German support for Lenin's return to Russia from exile). German intelligence resolved in 1915 to fund Lenin and the other Bolsheviks, delivering tens of millions of gold marks to them. *See* Roman Brackman, The Secret File of Joseph Stalin 143 (London: Routledge, 2001); Terry Crowdy, The Enemy Within: A History of Espionage 298 (Oxford: Osprey Publishing, 2006).

352. Gilbert, The First World War, at 402.

353. *See id.* at 282–83, 339.

354. *See* Anne Applebaum, Gulag: A History 95, 301 (New York: Doubleday, 2003); P.M. Polian, Against Their Will: The History and Geography of Forced Migrations in the USSR 102, 62, 164, 169, 221, 333, 345, 358, 399 (Budapest: Central European UP, 2004); Public Radio of Armenia, *Historian Rafael Hambartsumyan Condemns Russia of Supporting the Armenian Genocide* (Apr. 21, 2006), http://www.armradio.am/news/?part=pol&id=559 ("In 1918–1948 Russia exiled thousands of Armenian intellectuals to Siberia, thus continuing the extinction of Armenians.").

until 1944, and the crime was not definitively codified into law until 1948.[355] The liability of Nazi officials before an international criminal tribunal for the offense of genocide as a crime against humanity disposes of a key legal argument of defenders of genocidal policies in the Ottoman Empire, Iraq, and Sudan. Therefore, if the Ottoman Empire committed genocide against its Christian population during World War I, this conduct was certainly criminal, as the Ottoman government later admitted. The same goes for the governments of Iraq, Sudan, or any other country.

Second, self-proclaimed "historians" who refuse to acknowledge the Armenian genocide nearly inevitably have to ignore crucial documents and sources to maintain their untenable position. They criticize the serious scholars of the Armenian genocide (among whom the overwhelming consensus is that it occurred), on the grounds that some of them cannot read Ottoman Turkish documents in the original. An increasingly broad array of scholars who acknowledge the Armenian genocide and can also read Turkish, and regularly cite to Ottoman Turkish documents, proves the irrelevance of this point. In addition to Taner Akçam and Vahakn Dadrian, the sources for many of the court-martial and postwar memoir quotations collected above, there are numerous volumes by Turkish scholars and publishers such as Fikret Adanir, Selim Deringil, Ali Ertem, Fatma Müge Göçek, Dilek Kurban, and Ragip Zarakolu.[356]

One example of a scholar who denies the existence and scope of the Turkish, British, French, German, and U.S. archival material documenting the Armenian genocide is David Cuthell, who is the Executive Director of the Institute for Turkish Studies, and a professor with both the School of Foreign Service at Georgetown University and Columbia University's School of International and Public Affairs. Professor Cuthell has admitted that his Institute has probably never sponsored any research characterizing the Armenian massacres as genocide, and parrots the Turkish government line that there is no "smoking gun" from the genocide despite the many statements of Ottoman judges and officials, the Ottoman and German archives, the records of the U.S. and the United Kingdom, the many Armenian memoirs, and voluminous other sources. The Executive Director of the

355. Republic of Turkey, Directorate General of Press and Information, *The Armenian Allegation of Genocide: Facts* (2001), http://www.byegm.gov.tr/yayinlarimiz/newspot/2001/mar_apr/n5.htm.

356. *See* Fikret Adanir, *Die Armenische Frage und der Völkermord an den Armeniern im Osmanischen Reich, in* ERLEBNIS—GEDACHTNIS—SINN: AUTHENTISCHE UND KONSTRUIERTE ERINNERUNG, ed 237–63 (Frankfurt am Main, 1996); Fatma Müge Göçek, *The Decline of the Ottoman Empire and the Emergence of Greek, Armenian, Turkish and Arab Nationalism, in* SOCIAL CONSTRUCTIONS OF NATIONALISM IN THE MIDDLE EAST 15–84 (Fatma Müge Göçek ed., Albany, NY: State Univ. of New York Press, 2001); Fatma Müge Göçek, *Through a Glass Darkly: Consequences of a Politicized Past in Contemporary Turkey,* 617 THE ANNALS OF THE AMERICAN ACADEMY OF POLITICAL AND SOCIAL SCIENCE 88–106 (2008); Dilek Kurban, *Confronting Equality: The Need for Constitutional Protection of Minorities on Turkey's Path to the European Union,* 35 COLUMBIA HUMAN RIGHTS L. REVIEW 151 (2003); *Academics' Armenia Apology to Test Taboos,* HÜRRIYET (Turkey), Apr. 11, 2009 http://www.hurriyet.com.tr/english/domestic/10566612.asp?gid=244; Vincent Lima, *Another Crack Made in "Wall of Silence" at Genocide Workshop in Chicago, IL,* ARMENIAN REPORTER, Apr. 1, 2000, http://www.highbeam.com/doc/1P1-79123234.html; Stephen Kinzer, *Turkish Region Recalls Massacre of Armenians,* N.Y. TIMES, May 10, 2000, http://www.nytimes.com/2000/05/10/world/turkish-region-recalls-massacre-of-armenians.html; Robert Tait, *Turkish Publisher Convicted Over Armenian Genocide Claims,* THE GUARDIAN (U.K.), June 19, 2008, http://www.guardian.co.uk/world/2008/jun/19/turkey.humanrights?gusrc=rss&feed=global; *Turkish and Kurdish Representatives from Germany Commemorate Armenian Genocide,* ARMENIAN TV CHANNEL 1 (YEREVAN, ARMENIA), Apr. 25, 2001, http://nl.newsbank.com; *Turkish Delegation Censures 1915 Genocide at Commemoration in Armenian Capital,* SNARK NEWS AGENCY (ARMENIA), Apr. 26, 1999, http://nl.newsbank.com; *Turkish Professors Condemn Reaction to Conference on Armenian Issue,* NTV TELEVISION (Turkey), May 25, 2005, http://nl.newsbank.com/.

Institute stated that those scholars who study the Armenian genocide "are not qualified to do the work because they can't read the archival material," to which the Turkish state manipulates access in its favor.[357] Other major denialists include the members of the Board of Directors of the Institute for Turkish Studies, including Heath W. Lowry, Ataturk Professor of Ottoman and Modern Turkish Studies, Princeton University, Jenny B. White of Boston University, and Justin McCarthy of the University of Louisville.[358]

Few of the "scholars" who are affiliated with the Institute of Turkish Studies are completely independent searchers for the truth, however, for the Institute has accepted $3 million from the Republic of Turkey, in what has been reported as a renewable annual grant. The institute allows the Turkish ambassador to the U.S. to control what scholars affiliated with the Institute can and cannot say regarding Armenians. For example, in 2006 the former Chairman of the Board of Directors of the Institute, Donald Quataert, wrote a favorable review of a book recognizing the Armenian genocide, and condemned the "self-censorship" that characterizes "Ottoman history writing." In response, the executive director of the institute told the chairman to report to the Turkish ambassador to the U.S. on his activities, during which report the ambassador informed the chairman that unless he resigned, "that funding for the institute would be withdrawn by the Turkish government and the institute would be destroyed." Another board member, Fatma Müge Göçek of the University of Michigan, called the Turkish government's intervention a violation of "academic freedom" and proof that Turkish money came to the Institute "with strings attached with respect to the research the scholars do." [359]

2. Blame Games and False Equivalencies

So-called historians who deny the Armenian genocide resort to "blame-the-victim" strategies that would not be accepted to justify any other mass murder. For example, the Turkish ultranationalist writer Sonali Sonyel, has widely published, in Turkish books and on the Internet, his theory that "the revolt of Ottoman Armenians in 1914–1915, on the instigation by the Allies (mainly by Russia, France and Britain), in order to dismember the Ottoman state," resulted in a campaign by "the British Intelligence and Information Services, some political and military advisers and Armenophile enthusiasts such as Lord Bryce, Arnold Toynbee, ... and others, ... to publicise the Turco-Armenian incidents such as 'Armenian massacres.' "[360] Bernard Lewis advanced what is known as a "provoca-

---

357. *See* Scott Jaschik, *Is Turkey Muzzling U.S. Scholars?*, INSIDE HIGHER ED, July 2, 2008, http://www.tinyurl.com/534bwg. In another recent article, Professor Cuthell called Turkey an "honest broker" of peace in the Middle East despite its support for Bosnian mujahideen, war crimes and torture in its own counterinsurgency campaign against Kurdish separatists and human rights activists, blockade of landlocked Armenia, and illegal occupation and looting of Cyprus. *See* Joel Brinkley, *Allies in Middle East Ignore Lame-Duck Bush*, S.F. CHRON., June 22, 2008, http://www.tinyurl.com/6je4ng.

358. *See* Institute for Turkish Studies, *Board of Governors* (2009), http://www.turkishstudies.org/index.php?id=3.

359. *See* Susan Kinzie, *Board Members Resign to Protest Chair's Ousting: Leader in Georgetown-Based Agency Encouraged Scholars to Research Mass Killing of Armenians*, WASH. POST, July 5, 2008, at B05.

360. Salâhi Sonyel, *War-time Disinformation and "The Blue Book"* (2005), http://armenians-1915.blogspot.com/2005/07/35-war-time-disinformation-and-blue.html. *See also* SALÂHI SONYEL, MINORITIES AND THE DESTRUCTION OF THE OTTOMAN EMPIRE (Turkish Historical Soc. Printing House, 1993); SALÂHI SONYEL, THE GREAT WAR AND THE TRAGEDY OF ANATOLIA: TURKS AND ARMENIANS IN THE MAELSTROM OF MAJOR POWERS (Turkish Historical Soc. Printing House, 2000); SALAHI RA-

tion theory" of the Armenian genocide, which blames the Armenian people for creating "the deadliest of all threats" to pan-Turkish imperialism.[361] Professor McCarthy, likewise, has called any description of Ottoman officials as "victimizers" of minority groups a "racist" form of history. He equates the deaths of "five and one half million" Muslims in various wars with the massacres of the Ottoman Christians. In so doing, he attempts to place on the same plane the Ottoman Empire's avowed campaign to make a "clean sweep" of its Christian populations in less than a decade with the military casualties of 17 Ottoman and Turkish wars which he himself describes as being waged over two *centuries* in order to "subjugate internal enemies and expand centralized control of the empire."[362] The Ottoman Empire, in these wars, had to maintain control of huge portions of three continents inhabited by dozens and dozens of peoples with histories dating back millennia, from Serbia in the northwest to Uganda in the southwest to Persia in the east.[363]

To place the Ottoman Empire's casualties in an aggressive enterprise on three continents on a similar moral footing with those of the Ottoman Armenians, Greeks, and Assyrians is very similar to placing German deaths during the Nazis' attempt to conquer Europe, half of Asia, and large parts of Africa on a par with the Holocaust.[364] The flagship publication of the Institute for Turkish Studies, Professor McCarthy's *Death and Exile: The Ethnic Cleansing of the Ottoman Muslims, 1821–1922*, closely resembles the publications and conference presentations connected to the Institute of Historical Review, which is the center of the Holocaust denial movement in the U.S.[365] For example, McCarthy equates

---

MADAN SONYEL, FALSIFICATION AND DISINFORMATION: NEGATIVE FACTORS IN TURCO-ARMENIAN RELATIONS (Center for Strategic Research, 2000).

361. *Quoted in* A. Christian van Gorder, *Armenian Christians and Turkish Muslims: Atrocity, Denial and Identity* 59 (2004), http://www.samford.edu/lillyhumanrights/papers/VanGorder_Armenian.pdf.

362. JUSTIN MCCARTHY, DEATH AND EXILE: THE ETHNIC CLEANSING OF OTTOMAN MUSLIMS, 1821–1922, at 1–6 (Princeton, NJ: Darwin Press, 1995).

363. The external and internal wars McCarthy includes in his tally of Muslim dead include those waged by the Ottomans and their allies against: the British, French, and Russian Empires, the Commonwealth of Australia, the Dominion of New Zealand, and Egyptian, Arab, and Persian forces in 1914–18; the British and French Empires, Armenia, and Greece in 1919–23; Bulgaria, Greece, Serbia, and Montenegro in 1911–13; the Russian Empire from 1806–12, 1828–29, 1832–33, 1853–56, and 1877–78; Greece in 1897; Romania in 1877–78; Egypt in 1839–40; as well as the first and second Serbian War of Independence in 1804 and 1815–17; Greek War of Independence (in which the British Empire was also involved) in 1821–30; failed Cretan War of Independence in 1866–68; Bosnian and Bulgarian Wars of Independence in 1875–76; and the Armenian and Cretan Greek independence struggles and Hamidian massacres in 1896–97. He might have added the invasion of Persia in 1821 and 1914 and of Montenegro in 1852; the siege and bombardment of Belgrade in 1862; the Ottoman-Egyptian wars against indigenous peoples in present-day Ethiopia, Sudan and Uganda in 1863–79, and various other aggressive enterprises of the Ottomans. McCarthy subsumes most of these independence-striving regions into what he calls a "vast Muslim land ... in Anatolia, the Balkans, and southern Russia," even though he admits Ottoman settlers were often a minority. *Id.* at 1.

364. Germany lost over five million soldiers and civilians during World War II, including over one million German prisoners of war who died in captivity. Some 15 million ethnic Germans or German citizens were deported after the war from communist countries, during which deportations two to 4.5 million Germans died. *See* JEFFREY K. OLICK, IN THE HOUSE OF THE HANGMAN: THE AGONIES OF GERMAN DEFEAT, 1943–1949, at 100–104 (Chicago: Univ. of Chicago Press, 2005); RUMMEL, DEATH BY GOVERNMENT, at 298, 403; RUMMEL, STATISTICS OF DEMOCIDE, at 134–45; RUDOLPH J. RUMMEL, DEMOCIDE: NAZI GENOCIDE AND MASS MURDER 13, 16 (New Brunswick, NJ: Transaction Publishers, 1992).

365. U.S. Holocaust Memorial Museum, *Combating Holocaust Denial: Holocaust Deniers and Public Misinformation, in* HOLOCAUST ENCYCLOPEDIA (2008), http://www.ushmm.org/wlc/article.php?lang=en&ModuleId=10007272.

the Ottoman Christian genocide with losses incurred in the Ottomans' bid for world dominance, just like the Institute for Historical Review equates the Holocaust with Allied war crimes against Germans,[366] and argues that the Holocaust is "atrocity propaganda against Germany," which led to the "most murderous peace plan in history," including three million German deaths.[367] While the Institute for Historical Review falsely claims that Nazi Germany did not start World War II, but was a victim of some combination of British and Soviet aggression, McCarthy baldly asserts that Russia started World War I in the East by invading Ottoman territory on November 2, 1914, whereas a casual search of diplomatic sources quoted in contemporary publications reveals that the Ottoman Empire invaded Russian and Persian territory in August 1914 and blockaded and then bombarded Russian ports on the Black Sea in October 1914.[368]

3. Myth of the Incompatibility of Genocide and Counterinsurgency

Finally, scholars connected to the Institute for Turkish Studies celebrate the killing and race-based deportation of Armenians as a legitimate counterinsurgency measure. According to Bernard Lewis, Professor Emeritus of History at Princeton University and an Honorary Fellow with the Institute for Turkish Studies, the Armenian case was a normal war because the Armenians rose in armed rebellion to the Ottomans, while all the Jews were unarmed victims of the Nazis:

> [N]owadays the word "genocide" is used very loosely even in cases where no bloodshed is involved at all and I can understand the annoyance of those who feel refused. But in this particular case, the point that was being made was that the massacre of the Armenians in the Ottoman Empire was the same as what happened to Jews in Nazi Germany and that is a downright falsehood. What happened to the Armenians was the result of a massive Armenian armed rebellion against the Turks, which began even before war broke out, and continued on a larger scale....
>
> Armenian rebels actually seized the city of Van and held it for a while intending to hand it over to the invaders. There was guerilla warfare all over Anatolia. And it is what we nowadays call the National Movement of Armenians

366. *See, e.g.*, Richard J. Evans, *David Irving, Hitler and Holocaust Denial: Electronic Edition, in* Irving v. Lipstadt: Defense Documents (2008), http://www.holocaustdenialontrial.com/trial/defense/evans/350?view=print ("Examined carefully, all the other speakers at the Institute [for Historical Review]'s conferences" indirectly deny the Holocaust "by claiming that the Western Allies were engaged in the same kind of thing, or worse.").

367. *See, e.g.*, Austin J. App, *The "Holocaust" Put in Perspective*, 1 J. of Historical Rev. [of the Institute for Historical Review] 3 (1999), http://www.ihr.org/jhr/v01/v01p-43_App.html.

368. *See Turks Paralyze Black Sea Trade; Closing of the Dardanelles a Heavy Blow to Once Busy Russian Ports*, N.Y. Times, Oct. 16, 1914, at 4; *Turkey Begins War with Russia in Black Sea*, Fairbanks Daily Times, Oct. 20, 1914, at 1; *Suspect Black Sea Battle; Russian Fleet vs. Turkish*, N.Y. Times, Oct. 21, 1914, at 2; *Russian and Turkish Ships Fight In the Black Sea, Berlin Believes*, Wash. Post, Oct. 21, 1914, at 2; *Turkey Enters War and Bombards Russian Ports*, Atlanta Const., Oct. 30, 1914, at 1. The Russian mine-layer *Pruth* sank with 250 men aboard, and 21 other Russian ships were lost. *See* Telegram from Hans Humann to Berlin (Nov. 2, 1914), *cited in* Dadrian, *The Historical and Legal Interconnections*, at 519. "According to the memoirs of party secretary Arif Cemil, attacks on Russia had already begun by the end of August [1914]." Akçam. A Shameful Act, at 123.

> Against Turkey. The Turks certainly resorted to very ferocious methods in repelling it.[369]

This argument, of course, is dependent on the idea that there was no "rebellion" or "guerilla warfare" during World War II, and no "ferocious methods" needed on the part of the Germans. It also appears to assume that Jewish components of the resistance to the Nazis in Europe never seized a town or city like Van while working in conjunction with the British or Russians.

In fact, Jewish leaders fought German imperialism and Nazism even prior to 1933. Most notably, the German Spartacists under Karl Liebknecht and Rosa Luxemburg, whose families were Jewish, mounted a purportedly Soviet-backed uprising against the German government in early 1919, occupying several cities and resulting in a large number of casualties on all sides, including 1,500 deaths in Berlin.[370] About 1,000 Spartacists and other communists perished in an attempt to create a Bavarian Soviet Socialist Republic.[371] In the aftermath of the failed communist revolution, right-wing German militias gained more than 200,000 members after 1919, and political murders in the 1920s claimed numerous Jews, including Luxemburg, Gustav Landauer, and Kurt Eisner. Munich became an unsafe place for Jews.[372] In 1934 and 1935, a number of Jews were tried and sentenced for alleged treason and underground activity, including conspiring to blow up the Nazi propaganda newspaper *Der Sturmer*.[373] Jews participated in political resistance to Nazi rule as early as 1933, with 2,500 actively en-

---

369. *See* Assembly of Turkish American Associations, *Statement of Professor Bernard Lewis, Princeton University, Distinguishing Armenian Case from Holocaust* (April 14, 2002), http://www.ataa.org/reference/pdf/lewis.pdf. For a similarly obtuse argument, see Nick Danforth, *Moving Beyond Black and White on the Armenian Genocide,* The American Prospect, Apr. 24, 2009, http://www.prospect.org/ ("The Holocaust was unique in being so irrational, unprovoked and completely one sided.... [B]efore and during World War I, there were Armenian terrorists who set off bombs in Istanbul, Armenian soldiers who fought for Russia against the Ottoman Empire, and Armenian guerrillas who massacred Muslim children.").

370. *See* Jack Fischel, The Holocaust 7 (Westport, CT: Greenwood Publishing Group, 1998) ("Rosa Luxemburg and Karl Liebknecht, both nominal Jews, were the leaders of the revolt. Right-wing propagandists made the point of connecting these two Jews with all Jews as being supportive of a Bolshevik Germany."); Saul S. Friedman, A History of the Holocaust 50 (London, Vallentine Mitchell, 2004) ("A second Berlin rising in March left 1500 dead, including Spartacist leaders Rosa Luxemburg and Karl Liebknecht....."); Associated Press, *German Troops Take Red Towns,* N.Y. Times, Apr. 4, 1920, http://www.nytimes.com (describing combat in Duisburg and capture by Reichswehr of the rebels' 2,000 rifles); Associated Press, *Loss 20 Times as Big as in First Revolt,* N.Y. Times, Jan. 10, 1919, http://www.nytimes.com (followers of Karl Liebknecht and Rosa Luxemburg engaged in "heavy fighting" in Berlin); Associated Press, *Trace Liebknecht Link with Moscow,* N.Y. Times, Jan. 16, 1919, http://www.nytimes.com (evidence of Soviet support found at Liebknecht's home); *German Reds Plan a New Uprising,* N.Y. Times, Sept. 8, 1920, http://www.nytimes.com.

371. *See* Mary Fulbrook, A Concise History of Germany 160 (Cambridge: Cambridge UP, 2004) (one thousand deaths in failed attempt to create Bavarian Soviet republic in April); Ernest Hamburger, *One Hundred Years of Emancipation*, 24 Leo Baeck Institute's Year Book 1, 38 ("The establishment of the shortlived Bavarian 'Soviet' Republic ... in April 1919 fanned the flames of antisemitism. The prominent appearance among its leaders of Jewish anarchists and Socialists had a considerable impact on the rural and urban population.").

372. *See* Frank Bajohr, *The "Folk Community" and the Persecution of the Jews: German Society under National Socialist Dictatorship, 1933–1945*, 20 Holocaust and Genocide Studies 180, 184–88 (2006).

373. *See* Helmut Eschwege, *Resistance of German Jews against the Nazi Regime*, 15 Leo Baeck Institute's Year Book 165–67 (1970).

gaged in 1933–1945. Some anti-Nazi Jews returned to Germany to fight fascism after being interned in concentration camps by the Gestapo and released on the condition that they leave Germany.[374]

There were numerous Jewish resistance groups, military units, and militias arrayed against the Germans during World War II, just as the Christians resisted Ottoman imperialism in Asia. The Soviet Orleanski Battalion had a Third Jewish Company.[375] One German death squad killed 1,100 persons its records identified as Soviet Jewish soldiers.[376] More than 50,000 Jews served as members of underground resistance movements and partisan armies in various occupied countries. "Jewish resistance units operated in France, Belgium, the Ukraine, Belorussia, Lithuania, and Poland. Jews also fought in general French, Italian, Yugoslav, Greek, and Soviet resistance organizations."[377] Up to 20,000 Jews participated in the communist Yugoslav partisan resistance to the Nazi occupation of Yugoslavia.[378] About 13,000 Jews fought the Axis occupiers of Greece and Macedonia, mainly in the Greek National Liberation Front and National People's Liberation Army.[379] More than 10,000 Jews participated in the French resistance.[380] Nearly 20,000 Palestinian Jews fought in the British forces, including as paratroopers into occupied Europe.[381] A concise summary of the research done since 1945 on Jewish resistance to the Nazis states: "In conclusion it may suffice to say German Jews were to be found on all fronts where battle was joined for the defeat of Nazism."[382]

The most dramatic example of Jewish resistance, somewhat reminiscent of the Armenian defense of Van, and smaller episodes in other Armenian towns and villages, was the Warsaw Ghetto Uprising. Jewish and Polish anti-Nazi resistance groups collaborated before the war, and two Jewish fighting organizations participated in the Warsaw Ghetto Uprising: the *Zydowska Organizacja Bojowa* (Jewish Fighting Organization), and the *Zydowski Zwiazek Wojskowy* (Jewish Military Organization).[383] During several major bat-

---

374. *See* Arnold Paucker, *German and Austrian Jews in the Fight against National-Socialist Germany,* 40 Leo Baeck Institute's Year Book 3, 10–11 (1995) (citing Konrad Kwiet, *Problems of Jewish Resistance Historiography*, 24 Leo Baeck Institute's Year Book 37–57 (1979)).

375. *See* Jewish Resistance During the Holocaust: Proceedings of the Conference on Manifestations of Jewish Resistance, Jerusalem, April 7–11, 1968, at 222 (Meir Grubsztein & Moshe M. Kohn eds., Jerusalem: Yad Vashem, 1972).

376. *See* Megargee, War of Annihilation, at 116.

377. U.S. Holocaust Memorial Museum, *Armed Jewish Resistance: Partisans* (2008), http://www.ushmm.org/wlc/article.php?lang=en&ModuleId=10005213. *See also* Reuben Ainsztein, Jewish Resistance in Nazi-occupied Eastern Europe: With a Historical Survey of the Jew as Fighter and Soldier in the Diaspora (New York: Barnes & Noble Books, 1974); Shmuel Krakowski, The War of the Doomed: Jewish Armed Resistance in Poland, 1942–1944 (New York: Holmes and Meier, 1984); Nechama Tec, Defiance: The Bielski Partisans (New York: Oxford UP, 1993).

378. *See* Paucker, *German and Austrian Jews in the Fight against National-Socialist Germany,* at 16.

379. *See* Stephen Bowman, *Freedom or Death: The Jews in the Greek Resistance* (2002), http://hcc.haifa.ac.il/Departments/greece/events/holocaust_greece/bowman.pdf; Yiannis D. Stefanidis, *Macedonia in the 1940s,* 2 Modern and Contemporary Macedonia, 64, at 7, http://www.macedonian-heritage.gr/VirtualLibrary/downloads/Stefan01.pdf.

380. *See* Paucker, *German and Austrian Jews in the Fight against National-Socialist Germany,* at 17–19; Jewish Resistance During the Holocaust, at 384.

381. *See* Mark A. Tessler, A History of the Israeli-Palestinian Conflict 249–50 (Indianapolis, IN: Indiana UP, 1994); Bowman, *The Jews in the Greek Resistance.*

382. Eschwege, *Resistance of German Jews against the Nazi Regime*, at 180.

383. *See* Moshe Arens, *The Jewish Military Organization (ZZW) in the Warsaw Ghetto*, 19.2 Holocaust and Genocide Studies 201, 201, 214 (2005).

tles, Jewish fighters "succeeded in holding off German and Ukrainian troops in continuous fighting for four days."[384]

Nearly every other genocide, with perhaps the exception of conquests and exterminations of weak and defenseless indigenous peoples living in a premodern state, featured resistance on the part of the victim group, and some sort of background ethnic or political struggle analogous to the Spartacist uprising of 1919 that propagandists for genocide could use to incite mass murder. In fascist dictatorships like Guatemala, Indonesia, Iraq, it is the threat of communist subversion or ethnic secessionism, two threats that were often linked by the Cold War. In communist societies, it is the ever-present danger of imperialism and capitalist counterrevolution, as in the Soviet Union, Maoist China and Tibet, Ethiopia, Soviet-occupied Afghanistan, and North Korea. In post-Cold War nations, it is often ethnic secessionism backed by ancient enemies blamed for past genocides or colonialism, such as the Bosnian "Turks" and Croatian "Ustaše" of the former Yugoslavia, the Rwandan Patriotic Front, or Sudanese rebels whose fight for self-determination is linked with U.S. or "Zionist" imperialism in the view of the Sudanese government.[385] Thus, after studying the Armenian genocide and the Holocaust at length, one scholar concludes that war and insurgency increase the probability of genocide by providing a motivation to adopt violent measures against groups labeled as alien, dangerous, and potentially treasonable.[386] Often, the practitioners of genocide are acutely aware of the threat that rebellious groups may pose to those in power, insofar as parties like the Nazis frequently came into power themselves through illegal means, and maintained their rule by using violence against political rivals.

After World War II and the Genocide Convention, the Armenian genocide received widespread recognition by scholars and heads of state. Raphael Lemkin described the Armenian genocide as one of history's "examples of the destruction of entire nations."[387] As noted above, several U.S. presidents from Woodrow Wilson to Barack Obama have described the Armenian massacres as genocide or as the worst crime in history, which is arguably a harsher condemnation. The United Nations (Economic and Social Council), European Parliament, and French, Russian, Canadian, Argentinean, Polish, Greek, Swiss, and Belgian parliaments have issued statements or resolutions recognizing the Armenian genocide.[388]

---

384. *Id.* at 218.

385. *See* Prosecutor v. Akayesu, Case No. ICTR-98-39-A, Appeals Chamber, Judgement (Reasons) (June 1, 2001), at ¶¶ 232–41, http://www.ictr.org/ENGLISH/cases/Akayesu/judgement/Arret/index.htm (recounting cross-examination of defendant concerning his incitement of mass killings of Tutsi by calling them rebels); *Sudan Says US Efforts on Darfur for Internal Political Agenda*, SUDAN TRIBUNE, Sept. 24, 2006 (recounting allegations that U.S. and Israel are behind the pressure on Sudan to end genocide in Darfur, and are supporting Darfurian rebel groups); *US Hypocritically Using ICC to Pressure Sudan*, TEHRAN TIMES, July 14, 2008 (blaming Darfur pressure on the "Zionist regime's plots").

386. *See* MELSON, REVOLUTION AND GENOCIDE, at 270–84.

387. Raphael Lemkin, EUROPAWORLD, http://www.europaworld.org/issue40/raphaellemkin22601.htm; Lemkin, *Genocide*, http://www.preventgenocide.org/lemkin/americanscholar1946.htm.

388. *See* Jason Wermers, *Massacres Genocide?; 23 States Have Legislation That Recognizes Stance of Armenians*, RICHMOND TIMES DISPATCH, Apr. 2, 2001, at B1; U.K. Parliament, Lords Hansard, *Armenian Massacre, 1915, ed. Her Majesty's Stationery Office, column 826, answer by Baroness Ramsay of Cartvale to question by Baroness Cox to the government* (Apr. 14, 1999), http://www.publications.parliament.uk/pa/ld199899/ldhansrd/vo990414/text/90414-09.htm; *Turkey Protests 'Genocide' Reference*, 9.10 CATHOLIC INSIGHT 23 (Dec. 2001); Warren Tolman & Dikran Kaligian, *It's Elementary: Turks Committed Genocide*, BOSTON HERALD, Dec. 9, 2005, at 33; H. Res. 316, 109th Cong., 1st Sess., June 14, 2005, http://thomas.loc.gov/cgi-bin/query/z?c109:H.RES.316:; Days

The trend towards U.S. recognition of the Armenian genocide was broken by administration of George H.W. Bush, whose extreme pro-Turkish position would be emulated at times by his successors Bill Clinton and George W. Bush. The elder Bush opposed a Senate bill to recognize the Armenian genocide, which died due to a procedural technicality, i.e., a filibuster.[389] In 1992, President Bush praised Turkey as a key ally and his "second home."[390]

Since the first President Bush adopted a denialist pose, Turkey has criminally prosecuted Turks, Armenians, and Assyrians who mention the country's history of genocide. Death, persecution, or exile has been the fate of intellectuals who grapple with Ottoman history, including Armenians like Hrant Dink, Assyrians like Yusuf Akbulut, and Turkish anti-racists like Orhan Pamuk and Taner Akçam.[391] After Hrant Dink was murdered for exercising his human right of free expression on the Armenian genocide, Turkey prosecuted his son Arat Dink for "insulting Turkishness" and sentenced him to a year in prison.[392]

Both the European Union and the U.S. have confirmed that Turkey has criminalized the very history of the Armenians, as well as the history of the Assyrians, Greeks, Jews, and other minorities such as the Yezidis who have suffered at the hands of the Ottoman or Turkish Nationalist government or army. Such policies violate principles fundamental to the European Union, including the right to maintain minority cultural and educational institutions, to access the media and public life on equal terms, and to practice minority religions in their mother tongues.[393] As part of the accession process, the Euro-

---

of Remembrance of Victims of the Holocaust (Proclamation 4838), 1981 PUBLIC PAPERS OF THE PRESIDENTS 375, April 22, 1981; Fergal Keane, *Armenians Say US Failed Them*, BBC NEWS, Jan. 26, 2003, http://news.bbc.co.uk/1/hi/programmes/correspondent/2572667.stm; *Turkey "Must Admit Armenia Dead,"* BBC NEWS, Dec. 13, 2004, http://news.bbc.co.uk/2/hi/europe/4092933.stm; *US House Committee To Discuss Genocide Resolution*, TURKISH DAILY NEWS, Sept. 9, 2005, http://www.turkishdailynews.com.tr; *Swiss Accept Armenia 'Genocide,'* BBC NEWS, Dec. 16, 2003, http://news.bbc.co.uk/2/hi/europe/3325247.stm; Armenian National Cmte. of America, *Quotes* (2004), http://www.anca.org. Some quotations are reproduced at the following Web addresses: http://www.armenian-genocide.org/Affirmation.55/current_category.4/affirmation_detail.html,

http://www.armenian-genocide.org/Affirmation.63/current_category.4/affirmation_detail, http://www.armenian-genocide.org/current_category.7/affirmation_list.html

389. *Genocide Topic Spurs Koligian to Write Bush*, FRESNO BEE, Nov, 26, 1989, http://www. NewsBank.com; *Resolution on Armenia in Doubt; Baker's Remarks to Senators Cloud Commemoration of Mass Deaths*, SACRAMENTO BEE, Jan. 24, 1989, at A7.

390. HUMAN RIGHTS WATCH, HUMAN RIGHTS WATCH WORLD REPORT 1992, at 581 (New York: Human Rights Watch, 1991).

391. *See* S. Res. 65, 110th Cong. (2007), http://www.govtrack.us/congress/billtext.xpd?bill=sr110-65; Amnesty International, *Turkey: Article 301: How the Law on "Denigrating Turkishness" Is an Insult to Free Expression* (2006), http://web.amnesty.org/library/index/engeur440032006; Nichlas Jubber, *Who Remembers the Armenians?*, CATHOLIC WORLD REPORT (2001), http://www.catholiceducation.org/ articles/persecution/pch0028.html; Michelle Pauli, *Pamuk Believed to Be in Exile in US*, THE GUARDIAN (U.K.), Feb. 14, 2007, http://books.guardian.co.uk/ news/articles/0,,2012979,00.html; Stephen Sackur, *Taner Akcam*, BBC NEWS.COM (Aug. 30, 2007), http://news.bbc.co.uk/1/hi/programmes/hardtalk/ 6970332.stm; *Turkish Priest Arrested After Genocide Claim*, CATHOLIC WORLD NEWS, Oct. 5, 2000; Savannah Waring Walker, *Turkey: Priest on Trial*, N.Y. TIMES, Dec. 22, 2000, http://www.nytimes.com.

392. *See* Amnesty International, *Turkey: Article 301*.

393. *See* Organization for Security and Cooperation in Europe (OSCE), *Document of the Copenhagen Meeting of the Conference on the Human Dimension* ¶¶31, 32.2 (1990), http://www.osce.org/item/13992.html; Framework Convention for the Protection of National Minorities ¶4(2), ¶9(1), ¶9(1), ¶9(4) (1995), http://conventions.coe.int/Treaty/EN/Treaties/Html/157.htm; OSCE High Commissioner on National Minorities, *The Oslo Recommendations Regarding the Linguistic Rights of National Minorities* (1998), http://www.osce.org/item/2930.html; OSCE Vienna Document, *Co-operation in Humanitarian and Other Fields* ¶¶32, 45, 59 (1989),

pean Parliament investigates the status of human rights and minority rights in applicant states, including, in recent years, those in Turkey. The Treaty on the European Union provides that any "European State" which respects certain principles may apply for EU membership, which shall be decided upon by decision of the Council of Europe after it receives a vote in favor of membership by the European Parliament.[394] The principles required to be respected by the applicant European State are those on which the EU is founded, including "the principles of liberty, democracy, respect for human rights and fundamental freedoms, and the rule of law...."[395] The European Council has identified "respect for and protection of minorities" as a principle with which an applicant should demonstrate compliance.[396] Candidates for EU membership must demonstrate "respect for and protection of minorities," as well as "institutions guaranteeing ... human rights" during the accession process.[397] Turkey is one of three countries currently applying for EU membership, along with Croatia and Macedonia.[398]

In 2005, the EU's rapporteur on Turkey, Camiel Eurlings, criticized the Turkish state's censorship of Armenian and other indigenous peoples' history, stating that freedom of speech is a "fundamental necessity" to join the EU.[399] Article 301 of the Turkish Penal Code (TPC) continued to outlaw attempts by historians or other intellectuals to "'denigrate Turkishness' or the government or the army."[400] In 2006, the European Parliament "stresse[d] that, although the recognition of the Armenian genocide ... is indispensable for a country on the road to membership to come to terms with and recognise its past," and called for "the Turkish authorities to facilitate the work of researchers, intellectuals and academics working on this question, ensuring them the access to the historical archives and providing them with all the relevant documents...."[401] In 2009, the European Parliament condemned Turkey for prosecutions of non-violent opinions under Article 301 and other articles of the Press Law, Penal Code, and Anti-Terror Law, and said that "frequent website bans ... and lawsuits against critical press"

---

http://www1.umn.edu/humanrts/peace/docs/madrd83e.htm; Max van der Stoel, OSCE High Commissioner on National Minorities, *The Protection of Minorities in the OSCE Region* 5–7 (2000), http://www.osce.org.

394. Treaty on European Union (Maastricht Treaty), 92/C 191/01, art. 49 (1992).

395. *Id.*, art. 6(1).

396. Copenhagen European Council of 1993, *quoted in* European Commission, *Economic Accession Criteria* (2008), http://ec.europa.eu/economy_finance/int_economic_issues/enlargement196_en.htm.

397. *See* Stoel, *The Protection of Minorities in the OSCE Region,* at 5–7.

398. European Commission, *Acceding and Candidate Countries* (2008), http://ec.europa.eu/economy_finance/int_economic_issues/non_eu_economies209_en.htm.

399. *Eurlings: Turkey Has Achieved Little Progress in Religious Freedoms,* Turkish Daily News, Oct. 22, 2005, http://www.turkishdailynews.com.tr/article.php?enewsid=26503&contact=1.

400. *See id.*; Sebnem Arsu, *Turkish Court Delays Novelist's Trial EU Observers Keep Watch on Proceedings,* Int'l Herald Trib., Dec. 16, 2005, http://www.iht.com.

401. European Parliament Resolution of 27 September 2006 on Turkey's progress towards accession, ¶ 56, A6-0269/2006, P6_TA(2006)0381, http://www.europarl.europa.eu/sides/getDoc.do?type=TA&reference=P6-TA-2006-0381&language=EN&ring=A6-2006-0269; European Union, *Press Release: European Parliament Critical of Slowdown in Turkey,* Sept. 28, 2006, http://www.scoop.co.nz/stories/WO0609/S00552.htm; *Turkey Says EU Report Smacks of Political Bias,* Turkish Daily News, Sept. 6, 2006, http://www.turkishdailynews.com.tr ("Turkey criticized a European Parliament report urging it to recognize an alleged genocide of Armenians at the hands of the late Ottoman Empire to advance its bid to join the European Union.... [T]he report slams Turkey for dragging its feet and ... it says Turkey should recognize alleged genocide of Armenians....").

were destroying "freedom of expression and freedom of the press" in Turkey.[402] U.S. reports on human rights in Turkey, as well as articles in the international press, have confirmed the validity of these concerns.[403] In 2006, the European Parliament adopted a report confirming ongoing discrimination against Christians, including the confiscation of churches and monasteries, and the prohibition on the training of Christian clergy, and stating that "no progress has been made since Parliament's last report in addressing the difficulties faced by religious minorities, ... thus falling short of EU standards and the expectations both of religious communities...."[404]

An appropriate analogy to Turkey's response to the Armenian genocide by its Ottoman forebears could only be made if, instead of acknowledging the Holocaust, making Nazism a crime, and paying billions of dollars in reparations to Holocaust survivors and the state of Israel, postwar Germany denied ever having committed genocide, prohibited giving public speeches that referenced the Holocaust, refused to pay any compensation, and actually blockaded Israel, reducing its residents to extreme poverty. Actually, to complete the analogy, the U.S. would have to, instead of ostracizing this pro-Nazi Germany, forge a strong alliance with it and send its Holocaust-denying leaders billions of dollars in weapons and military equipment. That is precisely the situation confronting the U.S. today in its relations with Turkey.

402. European Parliament Resolution of 12 March 2009 on Turkey's progress report 2008, B6-0105/2009, P6_TA-PROV(2009)0134, http://www.europarl.europa.eu/sides/getDoc.do?type=TA&reference=P6-TA-2009-0134&format=XML&language=EN.

403. *See* U.S. Dep't of State, *Country Reports on Human Rights Practices for 2007: Turkey*, http://www.state.gov/g/drl/rls/irf/2007/c23545.htm (reporting "serious restrictions on freedom of expression," including censorship of writing on ethnic or religious "minorities," Armenian history, and other "non-violent opinions"); *Cicek Signals Changes in Article 301*, TURKISH DAILY NEWS, Oct. 7, 2006, http://www.armeniapedia.org/index.php?title=Article_301 ("Despite government arguments that the new [Turkish Penal Code], which came into effect last year, constituted significant progress in terms of rights and freedoms, Article 301, which criminalizes insulting Turkishness, state institutions and Ataturk, has created an uproar with one celebrated writer after another being tried as a result."); Thomas Crampton, *Court Blocks Access to YouTube in Turkey*, INT'L HERALD TRIB., Mar, 7, 2007, http://www.iht.com ("The law—Article 301 of the Turkish penal code—has resulted in prosecutions against leading Turkish intellectuals, including the author Orhan Pamuk, a Nobel laureate, and Hrant Dink, an Armenian-Turkish journalist murdered in January."); National Public Radio, *Schism: Free Speech vs. 'Insulting Turkishness'* (Oct. 4, 2006), http://www.npr.org/templates/story/story.php?storyId=6196764 ("Armenian-Turkish newspaper editor Hrant Dink wasn't so lucky. He received a six-month suspended sentence for talking about the genocide, and faces two more trials for similar charges."); Robert Tait, *Turkish Publisher Convicted over Armenian Genocide Claims*, THE GUARDIAN (U.K.), June 19, 2008, http://www.guardian.co.uk/world/2008/jun/19/turkey.humanrights?gusrc=rss&feed=global ("The publisher of a book by a British author acknowledging the 1915 Armenian genocide has been convicted under Turkey's notorious Article 301...."); Ercan Yavuz, *Government Shelves Amendment to Article 301*, ZAMAN (TURKEY), Mar. 11, 2008, http://www.todayszaman.com/tz-web/detaylar.do?load=detaylar.do?load=detay&link=136090 ("Article 301 criminalizes denigrating the Turkish state, government and military and a vague concept it terms 'Turkishness,' in ambiguous wording making it possible to charge and convict people over the slightest criticism of official policy...," including journalists and intellectuals).

404. *See* European Parliament Resolution of 27 September 2006 on Turkey's progress towards accession, ¶ M; European Union, *Press Release: European Parliament Critical of Slowdown in Turkey*.

Chapter VII

"Native Christians Massacred": The Genocide of the Ottoman and Persian Assyrians

> The entire Christian nations of the Armenians and Assyrians are undergoing the process of extermination....
>
> The suffering Nestorians who live in the extreme eastern part of Turkey and in the western part of Persia, adjoining Turkey, have suffered as greatly, and perhaps more generally than those in Persia....
>
> A general massacre took place in ... the valley of the Tigris, close to the ruins of Nineveh.... [T]he chief settlements of this region ... [were] wiped out of existence....
>
> —Abraham Yohannan, Department of Oriental Languages, Columbia University[1]

During World War I, newspapers in London, Paris, New York, and Los Angeles regularly reported on the massacres of Assyrians living under Ottoman occupation.[2] Like the

1. Abraham Yohannan, Death of a Nation, or the Ever Persecuted Nestorians or Assyrian Christians 115, 146, 149 (New York and London: G.P. Putnam's Sons, 1916).

2. In this chapter, I will refer to the Assyrians, Nestorians, Chaldeans, and Syrian/Syriac Christians collectively as Assyrians. All of them are descended from the indigenous inhabitants of Mesopotamia, southeastern Anatolia, and northwestern Persia; Persian, Greek, and Arab rulers, as well as Chaldean Patriarchs, Syrian/Syrian priests and monks, and their Armenian neighbors, have referred to all three groups together as "Assyrians." *See, e.g.*, Hirmis Aboona, Assyrians, Kurds, and Ottomans : Intercommunal Relations on the Periphery of the Ottoman Empire 23, 30 (Amherst, NY: Cambria Press, 2008); Barsoum, The History of Tur Abdin, at 4; *Chaldean Catholic Church, in* The HarperCollins encyclopedia of Catholicism 295 (Richard P. McBrien, Harold W. Attridge eds., New York: HarperCollins, 1995); 3 Chronique de Michel le Syrien 22–23, 52–53 (Jean-Baptiste Chabot ed. & trans., Paris: Ernest Laroux, 1899–1905) (circa 840 CE), *quoted in* Ye'or, The Decline of Eastern Christianity, at 116, 342–44; Sargon Donabed, Remnants of Heroes; The Assyrian Experience 13–14, 33 (Chicago: Assyrian Acad. Soc. Press, 2003); *The Large Inscription of Darius from Behistun, in* Assyrian and Babylonian Literature: Selected Translations 178 (Robert Francis Harper ed., New York; D. Appleton & Co., 1904); Xavier Koodapuzha, Faith and Communion in the Indian Church of Saint Thomas Christians 59 (Kottayam, Kerala: Oriental Institute of Religious Studies, 1982); Agnes G. Korbani, The Political Dictionary of Modern Middle East 26 (University Press of America, 1995); Hormuzd Rassam, Ashur and the Land of Nimrod (London and New York, 1897); Sidney Smith, *Notes on the Assyrian Tree*, 4 Bulletin of the School of Oriental and African Studies 69 (1926); William A. Wigram, The Assyrians and their Neighbors 4, 162, 178, 185 (Piscataway, NJ: Gorgias Press, 2002) (1929). "Nestorian" is the Western denominational term for the indigenous Assyrians and Chaldeans of Mesopotamia, to distinguish them from Mesopotamian peoples loyal to the Catholic or Protestant churches introduced by missionaries starting in the seventeenth or eighteenth centuries CE. Assyrians, Chaldeans, and Syriac/Syrian Orthodox are religious denominations of the ethnic Assyrians of Iraq and

Armenians, the Assyrians living in Anatolia, Mesopotamia, Persia, and Azerbaijan became victims of genocidal massacres inspired by the Ottoman Sultan and carried out by the Young Turk regime of Enver Paşa. Ottoman and Turkish officials at the highest levels of government admitted to policies encouraging or carrying out massacres, deportations, and the deprivation of food and shelter. The German allies in World War I, American and British officials, legions of foreign journalists and missionaries, and of course the countless civilian victims of the war's massacres and deportations, confirmed these policies in great detail. These sources confirm that the Ottoman Turks and their Kurdish allies massacred hundreds of thousands of Assyrians in order to exterminate the Christian population, raped and enslaved hundreds and more likely thousands of Assyrian women in a systematic fashion, and deported the Assyrian population *en masse* from their ancestral lands under conditions that led to famine and widespread death.

A. The Nineteenth Century Massacres of the Ottoman Assyrians

Several Europeans visited the Assyrians in the mid-nineteenth century, describing them as the "only Christians in the East who [have] maintained their independence" from the Ottomans and other Muslim nations of Asia and North Africa.[3] They reported that the Assyrians were "very formidable" in their mountain villages, a "bold and hardy race ... [that] maintains its territory, its property, and its rights by force of arms."[4] These Assyrians were "independent of all foreign rules," and under the jurisdiction of their patriarch, Mar Shimun.[5] There were up to 200,000 independent Assyrians, mostly in the Hakkari mountains.[6] There were another 200,000 to 300,000 Assyrians subject to Ottoman, Russ-

---

Turkey, who all shared an ancestry group designation in the 2000 U.S. Census, even though Chaldean-Americans sometimes call themselves part of a distinct ethnic group from the Assyrians identified with southern Assyria, also known as Babylon or Chaldea. *See* Nicholas Kulish, *Chaldeans, Assyrians Vexed by Count*, WALL ST. J., Mar. 18, 2001, at C8, http://www.wsj.com; *U.S. Judge Rejects Assyrian Protest*, RISK MONITOR BRIEFING, Oct. 22, 2000, http://www.rferl.org/content/Article/1343271.html. Although this usage is controversial among some Chaldean Catholics, it accurately conveys the fact that Nestorian, Syrian/Syriac, and Chaldean are religious denominations whose members are descended principally from the inhabitants of ancient Assyria, who converted to Christianity starting in the first or second century A.D. *See* GEORGE M. LAMSA AND WILLIAM CHAUNCEY EMHARDT, THE OLDEST CHRISTIAN PEOPLE 20–22, 49, 78–79, 92–95 (New York, NY: Macmillan, 1926); Jackie Lyden, *Despite Turmoil, Christians Place Faith in New Iraq*, NATIONAL PUBLIC RADIO (Aug. 13, 2005), http://www.npr.org/templates/story/story.php? storyId=4799390.

3. C. JAMES RICH, NARRATIVE OF A RESIDENCE IN KOORDISTAN AND ON THE SITE OF ANCIENT NINEVEH WITH JOURNAL OF A VOYAGE DOWN THE TIGRIS TO BAGHDAD 1:277 (2d ed., London: J. Duncan, 1895), *quoted in* ABOONA, ASSYRIANS, KURDS, AND OTTOMANS, at 36–37.

4. F.O. 78/2698, July 2, 1840, James Brant, British Consul for Erzerum, to British Ambassador Palmerston, *quoted in* ABOONA, ASSYRIANS, KURDS, AND OTTOMANS, at 37.

5. HORATIO SOUTHGATE, NARRATIVE OF A VISIT TO THE SYRIAN [JACOBITE] CHURCH OF MESOPOTAMIA 158 (New York: D. Appleton, 1844), *quoted in* ABOONA, ASSYRIANS, KURDS, AND OTTOMANS, at 37.

6. *See* GAUNT, MASSACRES, RESISTANCE, PROTECTORS, at 406 (reproducing estimate of 165,000 Assyrian in Hakkari region in 1914, and 117,000 in nearby Diyarbekir province which has mountainous parts); *Massacre of the Nestorian Christians*, THE TIMES (U.K.), Sept. 6, 1843 (estimate of 190,000 people living in the Hakkari mountains, in context estimate is of Assyrians); THOMAS LAURIE, DR. GRANT AND THE MOUNTAIN NESTORIANS 279 (Edinburgh: Johnstone & Hunter, 1855) (citing initial estimate of 100,000, later revised downward, by American missionary Dr. Asahel Grant);

ian, or Persian rule.[7] This was down from tens of millions of Church of the East prior to the invasions of Genghis, Timur Leng, and the Seljuk and Ottoman Turks, which reduced the ranks of the most populous Christian church in the world by about 90%.[8]

Historians of the Assyrians record that their first massacre in modern times took place in the 1840s in northern Mesopotamia. The Ottoman Emir of Hakkari and Kurdish forces under the Ottoman governor of Djezireh, Badr Khan Bey, massacred ten thousand Assyrians, enslaving many women and children, and plundering and burning their villages.[9] As The *Times* of London reported in 1844 the Emir of a powerful Kurdish tribe joined the forces of Djezireh, Badr Khan Bey to "unexpectedly attack[]" the Tiyari tribe. The Ottomans and Kurds, "put the male inhabitants to the sword, carried off the women and children into captivity, and returned with a rich booty to Djezireh, after appointing one of

---

Aboona, Assyrians, Kurds, and Ottomans, at 13, 45–46 (citing, in addition to Dr. Grant's estimate of 100,000 Assyrians of independent tribes, estimates of 80,000 by Mrs. Bishop who traveled through Persia and Turkey, and of 100,000 by William A. Wigram who visited the region as missionary for the Anglican church).

7. *See* Gaunt, Massacres, Resistance, Protectors, at 406 (reproducing estimates of 563,000 Assyro-Chaldeans in 1914, including 165,000 in Hakkari who would frequently have been independent tribes); F.O. 424/106, 1879, Vice-Consul Emilius Clayton's Report on Reforms in Van, *in* 1 British Documents on Ottoman Armenians (1856–1880), at 645–46 (Bĭlâl Şĭmşĭr ed., 1980).

8. *See Mission to the Assyrian Church,* The Times (U.K.), June 19, 1894, http://archive.timesonline.co.uk/tol/archive/; Miran Sevasly, Armenia and Her Claims to Freedom and National Independence, S. Doc. No. 316, 65th Cong., 3d Sess., at 7 (1918) (30 million); Sydney E. Ahlstrom & David D. Hall, A Religious History of the American People 995 (New Haven, CT: Yale UP, 2d ed. 2004) (1972).

9. *See* F.O. 195/204 Mosul July 20, 1843, Rassam to Taylor; F.O. 195/228 Mosul July 29, 1843, Rassam to Canning, *quoted in* Aboona, Assyrians, Kurds, and Ottomans, at 197–98 ("Dr. Grant arrived here yesterday from Tiyari, bringing with him intelligence that the united forces of Bedr Khan Beg and the Emeer of Hakkari had plundered the Nestorian Christians in the province of Diz, killing a great number of individuals, including two (some say five) brothers of Mar Shimon the Patriarch and took captive one of his sisters."); Henry Ross, Letters From the East 33 (J. Ross ed., London: J. M. Dent & Co., 1902), *quoted in* Aboona, Assyrians, Kurds, and Ottomans, at 203 ("Bedr Khan sent to Mohammed Pasha, the Turkish Governor of the Pashalic of Mosul, and asked permission to punish the Christians. This was at once granted, for their power and reputed wealth had long aroused the jealousy and the cupidity of the Turks"). The British archaeologist and consular official wrote:

> It was near Lezan that occurred one of the most terrible incidents of the massacre;.... We soon saw evidences of the slaughter. At first a solitary skull rolling down with the rubbish; then heaps of blanched bones; further up fragments of rotten garments. As we advanced, these remains became more frequent—skeletons, almost entire, still hung to the dwarf shrubs. I was soon compelled to renounce any attempt to count them. As we approached the wall of rock, the declivity became covered with bones, mingled with the long platted tresses of the women, shreds of discoloured linen, and well-worn shoes. There were skulls of all ages, from the child unborn to the toothless old man. We could not avoid treading on the bones as we advanced, and rolling them with the loose stones into the valley below.

1 A. Henry Layard, Nineveh and Its Remains 188–89 (London, 1850), *quoted in* Aboona, Assyrians, Kurds, and Ottomans, at 209–10. In a later book, he stated that "Bedr Khan Bey, in 1843, invaded the Tiyari districts, massacred in cold blood nearly 10,000 of their inhabitants, and carried away as slaves a large number of women and children." A. Henry Layard, A Popular Account of Discoveries at Nineveh 122 n. (London: John Murray, 1851), *quoted in* Aboona, Assyrians, Kurds, and Ottomans. Other sources are in accord. *See, e.g.*, Abraham Yohannan, The Death of a Nation, at 2–3, 111–12 (forces of Bedr Khan Beymassacred nearly ten thousand Assyrians and took many women and children captive as slaves, intending to "exterminate" them all from the Hakkari mountains where they had made their home from before the coming of Islam); Lt. Col. Ronald Sempill Stafford, The Tragedy of the Assyrians, ch. 1 (London: Kegan Paul, 1935), http://www.aina.org/books/tota.htm; William Ainger Wigram, The Assyrians and Their Neighbours, ch. 8 (1929), http://www.aina.org/books/aatn.htm.

his creatures governor of the country." The Assyrians fought back, but 3,800 of them were slain, along with many of their princes (*Maliks*). The report concludes, "the rest of the women and younger children were reduced to slavery."[10]

Another report in *The Times* confirmed the genocidal character of the Kurdish massacre of the Tiyari and other independent Assyrian tribes:

> The houses of the wretched inhabitants were fired, and they themselves hunted down like wild beasts and exterminated. Neither sex nor age met with favour or mercy; the mother, brothers, and sisters of the patriarch were the objects of peculiar barbarity, the former being literally sawed in two, and the latter most shockingly mangled and mutilated.... No sooner had their country been exploited by missionaries, and the interest of learned and scientific men been awakened with respect to them, than this terrible visitation befel them, and the public is called upon to sympathize with them in their destruction, before, perhaps, it had become generally aware of their existence.[11]

Several American missionaries described the 1843 massacre of the Assyrians, hemmed in on the south by a Turkish army dispatched by the paşa of Mosul, and on the north by Kurds. They described the Tiyari and Dis tribes as being massacred, their villages destroyed.[12] The Turkish army and Kurdish forces swept through the lands of the independent Assyrian tribes in the Hakkari mountains and neighboring valleys. After the attack on Tiyari, a Turkish army joined Badr Khan Bey and the other Kurds to encircle and destroy Assyrian villages:

> The Kurdish host now followed down the western bank of the Zab, and crossed it at the venerable church of Mar Sawa. This they tried to demolish, burning what they could, and even destroying some of the massive masonry by gunpowder; but this was so difficult they soon desisted.... This beautiful place now formed the headquarters of Badir Khan Bey, as it had been a favorite resort of the Nestorians. Troops were sent out ... in every direction to destroy the surrounding villages. The war was little more now than a succession of massacres. The Kurds passed from place to place, slaying the people and burning the houses at their leisure, generally without even a shadow of resistance....
>
> Women neither young nor handsome were butchered on the spot. Those too young to travel were killed, to save their captors trouble. Infants were taken from their mothers' arms and dashed against the rocks when carrying them prevented their keeping up with the rest....
>
> If the captives are to be pitied, those who remained in the mountains fared but little better. After the slaughter, the remaining tribes sent in their submission, and were spared, for the sake of the revenue they might afford the conquerors. They were subject to unmeasured oppression. The half of their crops next season were claimed by the Kurds; and their lives were in constant danger....

---

10. *Nestorian Christians—Kurdistan*, THE TIMES (U.K.), Jan. 5, 1844, http://www.atour.com/cgi-bin/LT.cgi.

11. *Massacre of the Nestorian Christians*, THE TIMES (U.K.), Sept. 6, 1843, http://www.atour.com/cgi-bin/LT.cgi.

12. Thomas Laurie, Azariah Smith, & Mrs. Hinsdale, *Mission to the Nestorians*, *in* ANNUAL REPORT OF THE AMERICAN BOARD OF COMMISSIONERS FOR FOREIGN MISSIONS 145–47 (Boston: Crocker & Brewster, 1844).

> [In the valley of Ashitha,] the soldiers [of Zeiner Bey] swept through the valley as far as the Zab [river], sparing neither age nor sex. Out of three hundred houses in Ashitha only four were left unburned....[13]

Other reports by Western missionaries and humanitarian workers documented the imposition on the Assyrians by their neighbors of conditions of life calculated to kill them all:

> [The Kurds swept] with fire and sword swept through the country, sparing neither young nor old, male nor female, except a few whom they could carry away into a captivity worse than death....
>
> The invaders entered the district where the patriarch resided, ... [and] slew his mother, and many more of his relatives, and took others prisoners. Thence they pushed on toward Tyary, laying waste every settlement of the Nestorians, who were too feeble to make any successful resistance. A brave band did indeed dispute the progress of the fiery invaders..., but they were soon borne down by superior numbers, and only four out of the forty heroes ... escaped with their lives. The whole of Tyary, with the exception of four or five villages, was laid in ruins, the houses burned....
>
> The long winter wore away, during which the scattered remnants of the Nestorians suffered miserably from cold and famine. Many of them perished in their mountain solitudes, with none to succour, none to pity them in their wretchedness. Many of them perished in their mountain solitudes, with none to succour, none to pity them in their wretchedness....
>
> Some of the most venerated churches, which for centuries had been the sanctuaries of these people..., were now spoiled ... [and blown] to fragments with [gun]powder. The valuable library of the patriarch was burnt, and in the flames perished a collection of manuscripts, dear to the Nestorians, and venerated by all.[14]

As one Assyrian author recounted these events, citing British diplomats and American missionaries stationed in the area as witnesses, and while clarifying that the people themselves prefer to be called "Assyrian" rather than "Nestorian," the Kurds "intend[ed] to burn, kill, destroy and if possible exterminate the Christian race from the mountains...." Nearly ten thousand Assyrians were killed, and almost that many "women and children were taken captive, most of whom were sent to Jezireh to be sold as slaves...."[15]

Similar assaults on Assyrian villages and massacres of the Assyrian population occurred to the southeast of the districts of the Tiyari and Diz tribes, i.e., the Mergawar district near Persia:

---

13. Laurie et al., *Mission to the Nestorians*, at 269–76.

14. The Nestorians of Persia, A History of the Origin and Progress of that People, and of Missionary Labours Among Them, with an Account of the Nestorian Massacres by the Koords 101–3, 110 (Philadelphia: American Sunday-School Union, 1848).

15. Yohannan, The Death of a Nation, at 111. The author stated: "This name [Nestorians] ... was first used by Roman Catholics, who found it necessary to bestow upon them such a title in contradistinction to the name 'Chaldeans' which they applied only to the Assyrian proselytes to Rome.... [T]he name 'Nestorians' is disliked and disavowed by the people themselves." *Id.* at 4. He dedicated his book to the "Assyrian Christians." *Id.* at iii.

> The chief [of Rawanduz] himself had only one eye, and may have taken special pleasure in reducing others to the same condition. He was usually called Koor Bey (blind chief).... His footsteps were marked with the blood of Christians and all unbelievers, and his coffers were filled with the plunder of villages and churches, from Aderbijan [sic] to Mesopotamia, and as far north as Amadia and Jezira. The Yezidees [sic], especially, were mercilessly slain.... Many Christians still pine in the slavery to which he consigned them. When Dr. Grant came to Oroomiah [i.e., Urmia], [the chief] stripped Mergawer of everything, and put to the sword all who resisted....[16]

Some Assyrians who survived the invasions fled to the Berwer area, only to be killed there.[17]

The Yezidis of Anatolia and Mesopotamia, "mercilessly slaughtered" in the 1840s along with the Assyrians, follow a syncretic religion that combines Assyrian, Mandaean and Zoroastrian rituals like the reverence of fire, statues, towers, animal sacrifice, and religious festivals, with Jewish, Christian, and Muslim accounts of the prophets and angels.[18] Yezidis are divided as to whether or not they are ethnically Kurdish, although they are certainly religiously different.[19] According to a fifteenth-century CE manuscript, the holy shrine of the Yezidis was an Assyrian (Nestorian) monastery that was devoted to Yezidi rituals by its former steward.[20] In the nineteenth century, they suffered repeated Ottoman harem-slavery raids:

> Yearly expeditions have been made by the governors of [southern Ottoman] provinces into [Yezidi] districts; and while the men and women were slaughtered without mercy, the children of both sexes were carried off, and exposed for sale in the principal towns. These annual hunts were one of the sources of revenue of Beder Khan Bey; and it was the custom of the Pasha[s] of Baghdad and Mosul to let loose the irregular troops upon the ill fated Yezidis, as an easy method of satisfying their demands for arrears of pay. This system was still practiced to a certain extent within a very few months of my visit; and gave rise to atrocities scarcely equaled in the better known slave-trade.[21]

---

16. Laurie et al., *Mission to the Nestorians*, at 170–71.

17. *See id.* at 278.

18. *See Yezidis, in* 28 Encyclopedia Britannica 919 (11th ed., 1911) (Yezidi religion "has points of connexion with old Iranian and Assyrian beliefs and traces of Manicheaism and Nestorianism"); Harry Charles Luke, Mosul and Its Minorities 124–28, 136–37 (2004) (1925) (discussing syncreticism of Yezidi faith and their use of oil fires, statues, towers, and animal sacrifice); Austen Henry Layard, Discoveries at Nineveh (1854), http://mcadams.posc.mu.edu/txt/ah/Layard/DiscNineveh02.html (noting that Yezidis' traditions spoke of a migration north from parts of southern Iraq inhabited by Chaldeans and Mandaean Sabaeans, that their religion is a "mixture of [Mandaean] Sabaeanism, Gnosticism, Manicheanism, Christianity, and Islam, and that "it is not improbable that the sect may be a remnant of the ancient [Babylonian] Chaldees, who camouflaged their ancient beliefs to stave off "oppression"); Layard, Nineveh and Its Remains, at 95–109 (describing Yezidi religious practices).

19. *See* USDOS, *International Religious Freedom Report 2002: Iraq* (2003), http://atheism.about.com/library/irf/irf02/blirf_iraq.htm; Layard, Discoveries at Nineveh, ch.2, http://mcadams.posc.mu.edu/txt/ah/Layard/DiscNineveh02.html.

20. *See* Luke, Mosul and Its Minorities, at 130, 136.

21. Layard, Discoveries at Nineveh, http://mcadams.posc.mu.edu/txt/ah/Layard/ DiscNineveh08.html.

The Yezidis were nearly wiped out by massacres carried out by Turks and Kurds in the 1890s and 1910s.[22] Their numbers fell from a quarter of a million to about 50,000.[23] In the 1920s, a leader of the Yezidis told British and German visitors how a half-century of massacres and forced assimilation had depopulated the Yezidi community.[24] The accounts of the Yezidi massacres are important corroboration of an Ottoman policy to eliminate religious minorities.

As the assault on the Assyrian mountaineers wound down, the British consul from Samsun arrived to negotiate with Badr Khan Bey for the freeing of Assyrian children kidnapped in order to be raised as Kurds.[25] Sir Stratford Canning, the British Ambassador to the Ottoman Empire, who had an interest in Assyrian culture, was behind the initiative.[26] After "a certain number" of the children were released, *The Times* remarked that Canning had "prevent[ed] the destruction of an entire Christian population in Kurdistan...."[27]

Slavery was a common fate of Ottoman Christians in the nineteenth century. Slave markets in and around Istanbul, and the kidnapping of Armenians and other Christians for slavery, survived legally until the end of the Ottoman Empire.[28] In the empire, "enslaving Christians had been elevated to something approaching state policy" from the 1500s, if not earlier.[29] In 1840, the British ambassador to the Ottomans called slavery an "institution closely interwoven with the frame of society in this country, and

---

22. *See* LUKE, MOSUL AND ITS MINORITIES, at 128, 130, 136 (massacres of Yezidis in 1890s and 1910s reduced population by four-fifths); *see also* LAYARD, DISCOVERIES AT NINEVEH, http://mcadams.posc.mu.edu/txt/ah/Layard/DiscNineveh02.html (noting that during Ottoman period, the Bey of Rowandiz massacred Yezidis and destroyed a cherished temple); LAYARD, DISCOVERIES AT NINEVEH, http://mcadams.posc.mu.edu/txt/ah/Layard/DiscNineveh02.html (noting that Bey of Rowandiz was chief of Kurdish tribal confederation, that massacres by Ottoman Turks and Kurds reduced Yezidi population by three-fourths, and that Yezidis "took refuge in caves, where they were either suffocated by fires lighted at the mouth, or destroyed by discharges of cannon"); LAYARD, NINEVEH AND ITS REMAINS, at 93 (similar); *Devil Worshipers of Mosul, in Turkey, Are Tortured to Death by the Moslems,* WASH. POST, June 14, 1914, at 13 (similar).

23. *See* LUKE, MOSUL AND ITS MINORITIES, at 128 (massacres in 1890s and 1910s reduced Yezidi population from 250,000 to 50,000).

24. *See* JOHN S. GUEST, THE YEZIDIS: A STUDY IN SURVIVAL? 171–79 (London: Routledge, 1993).

25. *See The Nestorian Christians—Urmia,* THE TIMES (U.K.), Jan. 29, 1845, http://www.atour.com/cgi-bin/LT.cgi ("British consul ... Mr. Stevens[,] who speaks the Turkish language fluently, used his utmost efforts to obtain from Bader Khan that the Nestorian children who had been made prisoners, and were compelled to become Mahomedans, by the Kurds, should be set at liberty, and restored to their parents.").

26. *See Recent Britain and Foreign Intelligence,* THE HOBART COURIER AND GAZETTE (AUSTR.), Mar. 6, 1847, http://nla.gov.au; *The Nestorian Christians—Urmia*; *Turkey,* THE LIVING AGE, Feb. 15, 1845, at 392.

27. *The Nestorian Christians—Urmia.*

28. *See* James J. Reid, *Total War, the Annihilation Ethic, and the Armenian Genocide, 1870–1918, in* THE ARMENIAN GENOCIDE: HISTORY, POLITICS, ETHICS, at 43; Y. HAKAN ERDEM, SLAVERY IN THE OTTOMAN EMPIRE AND ITS DEMISE, 1800–1909 (London: Macmillan, 1996); EHUD R. TOLEDANO, SLAVERY AND ABOLITION IN THE OTTOMAN MIDDLE EAST (Seattle and London: Univ. of Washington Press, 1996); EHUD R. TOLEDANO, THE OTTOMAN SLAVE TRADE AND ITS SUPPRESSION, 1840–1890 (Princeton: Princeton UP, 1983); *Curb White Slavery In Constantinople; Ambassador Morgenthau's Efforts Effectively Seconded by the Sultan's Police,* N.Y. TIMES, Feb. 1915, at 4; *Slavery Problem Confronts League; Application of Abyssinia,* N.Y. TIMES, Aug. 26, 1923. The Ottoman Sultan purported to outlaw the main slave-market of Istanbul in 1846, but auctions of Armenians and other non-Turks continued to occur. *See* TOLEDANO, THE OTTOMAN SLAVE TRADE, at 108; *Mass Rape as a Crime Against Humanity, in* DICTIONARY OF GENOCIDE 272 (Samuel Totten et al. eds., Westport, CT: Greenwood Publ'g Group, 2008).

29. ROBERT C. DAVIS, CHRISTIAN SLAVES, MUSLIM MASTERS: WHITE SLAVERY IN THE MEDITERRANEAN, THE BARBARY COAST AND ITALY, 1500–1800, at 28 (New York: Palgrave Macmillan, 2003).

intimately connected with the law and with the habits, and even the religion, of all classes of the people...."[30] In the nineteenth century, Assyrian women and children were enslaved and sold, while Assyrian women would leap to their deaths from cliffs, with their children tied to their backs, in order to escape captivity, rape, and impregnation.[31] A confidential memorandum to the British Foreign Office in 1876 reported that the Turkish paşa of Mosul was "very oppressive in his conduct towards" the Assyrians, and that "by his heavy exactions ... he was fast reducing the country to the lowest state of misery and destitution." Similarly, the Assyrians of Urmia "endured great sufferings" at the hands of Persian tribes, including slavery, forced labour, and monetary exactions.[32]

In the 1890s, the Ottoman Sultan, in response to Russian expansion and an Armenian uprising, authorized Kurdish chieftains to lead irregular cavalry militia, called "*Hamidiye*" after Sultan Abdul Hamid, in the pillage of Christian villages inhabited by Assyrians.[33] According to a report by the British consul, the Ottoman leadership had granted the Kurdish horsemen "assurances that they will not be called before the tribunals for any acts of oppression committed against the Christians."[34] The Sultan had "consenting awareness" of the massacres of the Assyrians and Armenians within his empire by the Hamidiye, which is to say, an awareness of the same character used to indict heads of states and armies for war crimes and genocide.[35]

Massacres and pogroms occurred in the historically Assyrian cities and towns of Āmid (Diyarbekir), Urhay (Urfa), Benebil, Ka'biye, and Sa'diye.[36] The Assyrians and other Ottoman Christians found themselves "dispersed" to other regions and living in "deplorable conditions."[37] Their religious leaders predicted that "the Christian element will slowly disappear, either by apostasy, emigration, or massacre."[38] The Ottoman-instigated atrocities of the Kurdish Hamidiye prompted the leaders of the Eastern Christian denominations within the empire to expect the "complete disappearance of the Christian element."[39]

---

30. Viscount Ponsonby, *Slavery in Turkey*, The Times (U.K.), Dec. 27, 1840, *reprinted in* The Living Age, Feb. 8, 1845, at 352.

31. *See* Sir Edward Hertslet, Librarian and Keeper of Archives, British Foreign Office, 1857–94, *Memorandum Respecting the Persecutions of the Nestorian Christians by the Turks, Persians and Khoordish Chiefs, Dec. 2, 1876, in* 6 Minorities in the Middle East: Christian Minorities 1838–1967: Assyrian Communities in the Levant and Iraq (Volume I) 1880–1938, at 49, 356–57 (Bejtullah Destani ed., Slough, U.K.: Cambridge Archive Editions Limited, 2007).

32. *Id.* at 347, 359

33. Diplomatic Dispatch #17, Aug. 13, 1902, from Vice-consul of Diyarbakir to Mr. Constans, French Ambassador to Constantinople, *quoted in* De Courtois, The Forgotten Genocide, at 144; Diplomatic Dispatch #10, June 2, 1904, from Vice-consul of Diyarbakir to Mr. Constans, French Ambassador to Constantinople, *quoted in* de Courtois, The Forgotten Genocide, at 137; Diplomatic Dispatch #12, July 27, 1904, from Vice-consul of Diyarbakir to Mr. Constans, French Ambassador to Constantinople, *quoted in* de Courtois, The Forgotten Genocide, at 145.

34. Balakian, The Burning Tigris, at 51.

35. Bloxham, *The Armenian Genocide*, at 149.

36. *See* Gaunt, Massacres, Resistance, Protectors, at 17, 43–46, 155, 208, 230, 250–52, 264–65.

37. Diplomatic Dispatch #6, Aug. 9, 1903, from Vice-consul of Diyarbakir to Mr. Constans, French Ambassador to Constantinople, *quoted in* de Courtois, The Forgotten Genocide, at 143.

38. Diplomatic Dispatch #2, Jan. 9, 1901, from Vice-consul of Diyarbakir to Mr. Constans, French Ambassador to Constantinople, *quoted in* de Courtois, The Forgotten Genocide, at 145.

39. Diplomatic Dispatch #21 Feb. 14, 1902, from M. Constans, French Ambassador, to M. Declasse, Minister of Foreign Affairs, *quoted in* de Courtois, The Forgotten Genocide, at 145.

B. The Ottoman Genocide of the Assyrians during World War I

Starting in 1914 and with particular ferocity in 1915 and 1918, Ottoman soldiers and Kurdish and Persian militia subjected hundreds of thousands of Assyrians to a deliberate campaign of massacre, torture, abduction, deportation, impoverishment, and cultural and ethnic destruction. Established principles of international law outlawed this campaign of extermination before it was embarked upon, and ample evidence of genocidal intent has surfaced in the form of admissions by Ottoman officials. Nevertheless, the international community has been hesitant to recognize the Assyrian experience as a form of genocide. The Assyrian genocide is, however, indistinguishable in principle from the Armenian genocide, despite being smaller in size.

The Assyrian survivors of the 1915–1925 massacres in the Ottoman Empire described an attempt by Ottoman Turks and allied Kurds to destroy a distinct national, ethnic and religious group in whole or in part. As in other recognized genocides, the Ottomans and their local allies the Kurds and Persians demonstrated a pattern of deliberate and systematic targeting of Christians as such, including Assyrians, for murder, maiming, enslavement, rape, dispossession, impoverishment, and cultural and ethnic destruction including the razing of sacred and historic buildings and assassination of intellectual leaders. Nevertheless, governments and historians have not been as willing to recognize the Assyrian experience during and after World War I as a form of genocide, or even to acknowledge the existence and criminality of the Ottoman atrocities against Assyrians. The more rapid legal recognition and establishment of compensation mechanisms for the Ottoman genocide of Armenians may be attributable to the larger numbers of Armenian victims and survivors, as well as more copious evidence of an intention on the part of the Young Turks to wipe out the Armenian people.

1. The Outbreak of the Assyrian Genocide of 1914–1925

As described in the previous chapter, in 1914 the Ottoman Sultan, acting on behalf of the empire, declared a jihad or holy war "against the enemies of Islam, who have proven their hostility by their attacks on the Caliphate."[40] These declarations of *jihad* "incited wrath toward Christian minorities in the Ottoman lands," facilitated a program of genocide against the Ottoman Christians.[41] For example, a 1915 declaration of this kind stated:

---

40. *Proclamation of the Grand Council of Ulema,* La Turquie, Nov. 16, 1914, *quoted in* de Courtois, The Forgotten Genocide, at 153.

41. Jack Zakarian, The Armenian Genocide: News Accounts from the American Press: 1915–1922, at xiii (Richard Kloian ed., Richmond, CA: Anto Publishing, 1988). The author adds:

> The Ottoman Empire was the center of the Islamic world, and the Sheikh-ul-Islam was the chief religious authority for all Muslims. The Sheikh was usually appointed by the Sultan, but the CUP chose their own candidate, Mustafa Hayri Bey, who was not from the religious elite and who had served in other political offices, unlike previous Sheikhs. The Sheikh was compelled by the CUP dictators and the German government to issue a "Jihad", or a declaration of Holy War, on November 23, 1914. Ignoring the fact that Germany and Austria were Christian allies of Turkey, the Jihad appealed to all Muslims to fight a holy war against "the unbelievers".

Id.

"Kill them: God will punish them in your hand and put them to shame; and ye will overcome them. He will rejoice the hearts of believers, and take away the wrath from the hearts unbelievers."....

You have become slaves of the people of the Cross....

Your enemies are trembling under your hand. Attack them from every side. Whenever you meet them, kill them. Quicken the failing proclamation of the Unity by the fire of your rifles and cannon, and by the blows of your swords and knives....

The great God is ordering you to fight with your foes everywhere.[42]

The Ottoman armies, reinforced by Kurdish irregulars, invaded Russian-controlled northern Persia in the winter of 1914, and in early January 1915 forced a Russian evacuation of the northern Persian cities of Urmia, Tabriz, Salamas, Diliman, and Gulpashan, among others.[43] Kurdish irregulars would serve as important allies to the Ottoman military in World War I, as the *Hamidiye* contingents had done prior to the turn of the century.[44]

As the Ottoman Empire began to dissolve in the nineteenth century, Turkish officials ordered massacres of the Assyrians as another group that, along with the Armenians and Greeks, aspired to enjoy their human rights, which could only happen with independence or foreign protection. The testimony of the Assyrian victims themselves describes a genocidal campaign, led by Ottoman Turkish military but often carried out by Kurdish irregular forces, to exterminate the Assyrian population in their native lands. In the late 1890s, the Ottoman sultan gave Kurdish cavalry authority to slaughter hundreds of thousands of Armenian and many Assyrian subjects. As the Ottoman Empire entered World War I at the behest of Germany, the Assyrian Catholics of upper Mesopotamia and southeastern Anatolia joined their Armenian and Greek counterparts in suffering genocidal killings, rapes, and deportations. The statements of Ottoman leaders, both during and after the war, confirm that a campaign of anti-Assyrian massacres occurred, as do German, U.S., U.K., and other diplomatic sources, and the testimony of the victims themselves.

2. Official Confirmation of the Assyrian Genocide

Ottoman and Turkish Republic documents confirm the testimony of Assyrian and European eyewitnesses. An order in October 1914 from Interior Minister Talât to the governor (*vali*) of Van province required the deportation of the Assyrians so as to preclude their being useful to Russia after the Ottoman Empire carried out its planned attack on Russia's Black Sea ports and Caucasian provinces.[45] The order indicates the reasoning behind the Interior Ministry's cleansing of its minority communities:

> The government's lack of trust in [the Assyrians] results in their chastisement [or punishment]—their deportation and expulsion from their locations to suitable provinces such as Ankara and Konya. They are to be transferred and dispersed

42. *A "Jihad" Appeal to Moslems, in* The Armenian Genocide: News Accounts, at 19.

43. *See* Gaunt, Massacres, Resistance, Protectors, at 105–120; The Treatment of Armenians in the Ottoman Empire, at 135.

44. Gunter, *The Kurdish Question in Perspective.*

45. *See* BOA.DH.SFR 46/78, Oct. 26, 1914, Minstry of the Interior to Van vilayet, *cited in* Hilmar Kaiser, *A Deportation That* Did Not [Sic] *Occur*, Armenian Weekly, Apr. 26, 2008, at 17, 18.

> so that they henceforth will not live together in a mass, but will live exclusively among Muslim people, and in no location are they to exceed twenty dwellings..., with the proviso that the government will not undertake to provide any type of support....[46]

This was after the interior ministry had received complaints from Russia about Ottoman troops and Kurdish militia invading northwestern Persia and massacring Assyrian villages there.[47]

The October 1914 deportation order required the Assyrians to "depart from Van."[48] This "deportation" was actually the extermination of the Assyrians of Van, and the destruction of their culture. To effectuate this order, in June 1915 the interior ministry ordered the *vali* of Mosul to attack the Assyrian tribes that spanned the *vilayet* of Van and upper Mesopotamia, i.e., the tribes of Jilu, Diz, Baz, Tiyari, Tekhuma, etc. These assaults claimed many lives, destroying entire districts (i.e., the district of Tiyari) that had been laboriously rebuilt since the Kurdish assaults of the 1840s and 1890s, and causing entire groups (e.g., the Jilu tribe) to flee to Persia.[49] Djevdet Bey, the Ottoman governor of Van, organized massacres of the Assyrians living in Seert, Bitlis, and the towns surrounding Urmia, Persia.[50] Halil Bey, who also oversaw massacres in the Hakkari region, joined Djevdet Bey in the Urmia region to fight the Russians and the Assyrian resistance, and led the huge massacres in Seert and Bitlis.[51]

After the war, the leader of the new Turkish Republic recognized that massacres of at least 800,000 Ottoman citizens had occurred. After the war, Mustafa Kemal "Ataturk" declared that the Ottoman Empire's leaders were guilty of "evil deeds" and "nefarious acts of deportation and massacre."[52] A number of official Ottoman documents acknowledge that 2,000 other Christians, likely Assyrians, were included in the Armenian massacres in the Diyarbekir region, and that the homes and businesses of Christians living in Diyarbekir region were distributed to the Turkish and Kurdish population.[53] Ottoman archives establish that Ottoman officials who opposed the massacre of all Christians were executed, including the governor of Basra province and a high official in the Midyat region where many Assyrians lived, and that several governors of Ottoman provinces were fired for refusing to carry out massacres of Christians.[54] These documents are corroborated by the memoirs of the former district-governor of Harput:

---

46. BOA.DH.SFR 46/78, Oct. 26, 1914, Ministry of the Interior to Van vilayet, *quoted in* Gaunt, Massacres, Resistance, Protectors, at 446–47 (reproducing facsimile of ciphered telegram and English translation in full). *See also id.* at 128.

47. *See* BOA.DH.SFR 45/242, Oct. 12, 1914, Ministry of the Interior to Van and Mosul vilayets, *cited in* Gaunt, Massacres, Resistance, Protectors, at 99.

48. BOA.DH.SFR 46/78, Oct. 26, 1914, Ministry of the Interior to Van and Mosul vilayet, *quoted in* Gaunt, Massacres, Resistance, Protectors, at 447.

49. *See* BOA.DH.SFR 53/276, June 7, 1915, Ministry of the Interior to Mosul vilayet, *cited in* Gaunt, Massacres, Resistance, Protectors, at 142; BOA.DH.SFR 54/81, June 20, 1915, Ministry of the Interior to Mosul vilayet, *cited in* Gaunt, Massacres, Resistance, Protectors, at 143.

50. *See* Gaunt, Massacres, Resistance, Protectors, at 82–98, 106, 109, 138–40, 250–56, 313, 322.

51. *See id.* at 83, 92, 100, 107, 118, 140, 252, 273, 281–884, 312–15.

52. *Quoted in* Akcam, From Empire to Republic, at 194.

53. *See* Prime Ministry Directorate of State Archives, Osmali Belgelerinde Ermeniler (1915–1920) [Ottoman Documents on Armenians, 1915–1920] 69 (Record 71), *cited in* Taner Akçam, *Deportation and Massacres in the Cipher Telegrams of the Interior Ministry in the Prime Ministerial Archive (Başbakanlık Arşivi),* 1.3 Genocide Studies and Prevention: An International Journal 305, 310 (2006).

54. Akçam, From Empire to Republic at 171.

> When the Government at Diarbekir gave orders to the officials to kill the Armenians, a native of Baghdad was Kaimakâm of El-Beshîri, in that Vilayet, and an Albanian was Kaimakâm of Lîjeh. These two telegraphed to the Vilayet that their consciences would not permit them to do such work, and that they resigned their posts. Their resignations were accepted, but they were both secretly assassinated.... [T]he name of the Baghdad Arab was Sabat Bey El-Sueidi.... [T]hey performed a noble act for which they should be commemorated in history....[55]

Raphael de Nogales, an Ottoman officer and divisional commander in the Turkish armies, wrote of his experiences riding into one of the scenes of massacre, this one in Seert (Siirt):

> The ghastly slope was crowned by thousands of half-nude and still bleeding corpses, lying in heaps, or interlaced in death's final embrace.... Overcome by the hideous spectacle, and jumping our horses over the mountains of cadavers, which obstructed our passage, I entered Siirt with my men. There we found the police and the populace engaged in sacking the homes of the Christians. At the Seraglio I met various sub-Governors of the province, assembled in council under the presidency of the chief of the local gendarmes ... who had directed the massacre in person. From their talk I realized at once that the thing had been arranged the day before by Jevdet Bey. Meanwhile I had taken up my lodging in a handsome house belonging to Nestorians, which had been sacked like all the rest. There was nothing left in the way of furniture except a few broken chairs. Walls and floors were stained with blood.[56]

The German archives confirm the Ottoman documents and memoirs. In July 1915, the German ambassador in Constantinople described to the German imperial chancellor how the Ottoman governor of Diyarbekr, Rashid Bey, had supervised the systematic extermination (*systematischen Ausrottung*) of the Christian population of his district, without regard to ethnicity or creed (*der Rasse und der Konfession*), but including in particular Chaldean and Nestorian Assyrians (non-uniate Syrians, German *nicht unierten Syrer*).[57] He confirmed that Talât's "policy of 'Turkification' meant 'to expel or to kill everything that is not Turkish,' and to destroy or appropriate other people's property."[58] In August 1915, the ambassador wrote again to the German imperial chancellor to confirm that:

> The systematic slaughter of the Armenian people who had been deported from their homes had taken on such an extent over the past few weeks that a renewed, forcible representation on our part against this coarse action, which the government not only tolerated but apparently supported, appeared to be im-

55. El-Ghussein, Martyred Armenia, at 40.

56. De Nogales, Four Years Beneath the Crescent, at 123–25.

57. DE/PA-AA/R14094, 1916-A-33457, No. 477, July 31, 1915, telegram from the German Ambassador on Extraordinary Mission in Constantinople, Hohenlohe-Langenburg, to the German Imperial Chancellor, Bethmann Hollweg.

58. *"Kultur" in Armenia*, The Times (U.K.), Aug. 27, 1919 (review of Lepsius, Deutschland und Armenien 1914–1918), http://archive.timesonline.co.uk/tol/archive/. For other references to a "Turkification" policy, see *More Turkification?*, N.Y. Times, May 19, 1918, http://www.nytimes.com; *The Late Talaat Pasha*, The Times (U.K.), Mar. 17, 1921, http://archive.timesonline.co.uk/tol/archive; *Kemal as He Looks to the Mohammedan World*, N.Y. Times, Dec. 17, 1922, at Magazine-67; *German Aims in Turkey*, The Times (U.K.), Feb. 28, 1924, http://archive.timesonline.co.uk/tol/archive; *Iraq Recognizes Kurds.; Permits Their Language in Areas Where They Predominate,* N.Y. Times, Mar. 4, 1926, at 9, http://www.nytimes.com; *Turkey in the World War,* The Times (U.K.), Aug. 1, 1930, http://archive.timesonline.co.uk/tol/archive.

> perative, particularly as in various places the Christians of other races and confessions were also no longer being spared.[59]

The ambassador's successor reiterated the call for a public German condemnation of the massacres of Ottoman Christians in December 1915, to which the chancellor replied:

> The proposed public reprimand of an ally in the course of a war would be an act which is unprecedented in history. Our only aim is to keep Turkey on our side until the end of the war, no matter whether as a result Armenians do perish or not. If the war continues much longer, we will need the Turks even more. I cannot understand how [the ambassador] can make such a suggestion....[60]

In July 1915, the German Consul in Mosul, Walter Holstein, blamed Rashid Bey for the massacre of the exclusively Chaldean population of the village of Faysh Khabour near Jazirah.[61] He reported in July 1915 that the Assyrian (Chaldean and Syrian) and Armenian men of the towns of Seert, Mardin and Faysh khabour had been massacred, with twelve hundred of their female relatives and children arriving or about to arrive in Mosul in "indescribable" conditions, with the women and children dying of hunger "daily."[62] On July 10, he wrote that Rashid Bey "rages like a mad blood-hound among the Christians of his vilayet," and has "slaughtered them like sheep."[63] In September, Holstein reported that Turkish troops marching to Baghdad had massacred local Chaldeans along with local civilian officials and ethnic Kurds.[64] He had previously warned his superiors that:

> The massacre of the Armenians in the Diyarbekir vilayet becomes more known with every day und creates increasing unrest among the population, which may easily cause uncontrollable consequences due to the foolish lack of conscience and the weakness of the local government....
>
> In the districts of Mardin and Amadia the situation has developed into a genuine persecution of Christians. Undoubtedly this is the fault of the government: Undoubtedly Christians are outlawed here, too. To name just one of numerous incidents, the local old and respectable Khaldean patriarch—I just returned from him—had been summoned by a common policeman to a military court without giving any reasons. From the side of the government this is a childish provocation of the local Christian community.[65]

A dispatch in fall 1915 from Walter Rößler, the German Consul in Aleppo, to the German ambassador in Constantinople described a wholesale massacre of Assyrians:

---

59. DE/PA-AA/R14087, DuA Dok. 136, Aug. 12, 1915, report from the German Ambassador on Extraordinary Mission in Constantinople, Hohenlohe-Langenburg, to the German Imperial Chancellor, Bethmann Hollweg.

60. DE/PA-AA/R14089, DuA Dok. 209 (gk.). Dec. 17, 1915, note by the German Imperial Chancellor, Bethmann Hollweg.

61. DE/PA-AA/R14094, 1916-A-33457, No. 11, July 15, 1915, report from the German Vice-Consul in Mosul, Holstein, to the German Ambassador on Extraordinary Mission in Constantinople, Hohenlohe-Langenburg.

62. DE/PA-AA/R14094, 1916-A-33457, No. 14, July 21, 1915, report from the German Vice-Consul in Mosul, Holstein, to the German Ambassador on Extraordinary Mission in Constantinople, Hohenlohe-Langenburg.

63. DE/PA-AA/BoKon/169, A53a/1915/4184, No. 8, July 10, 1915, telegraphic report from the German Vice-Consul in Mosul, Holstein, to the German Embassy.

64. DE/PA-AA/BoKon/170, A53a/1915/5247, No. 39, Sept. 10, 1915, telegraphic report from the German Vice-Consul in Mosul, Holstein, to the German Embassy in Constantinople.

65. DuA Dok. 080 (re. gk.), No. 3, June 13, 1915, telegraphic report from the German Vice-Consul in Mosul, Holstein, to the German Embassy in Constantinople (translation by Tessa Hoffman with my revisions).

> Further evidence has been found that the measures [i.e., extermination and deportation] I described in my report dated 3 September—B.No. 1950—which were to be taken against the Armenians in the eastern Vilayets have now become such against the Christians. The acting Syrian (Syrian Catholic) bishop told me that a total of 300 children and older women from his denomination have arrived here from Kharput, Diarbekr, Weranscheher and Mardin. The rest of the parishioners has probably been killed or kidnapped....
>
> The Chaldeans in Söird (Vilayet Bitlis) and Djeziret ibn Omar (Vilayet Diarbekir) and all of the Christians in Djebel et Tor north of Mardin have been exterminated.[66]

According to Rößler, two-thirds of the Armenians and other Christians deported from Diyarbekir and Harput had arrived in Aleppo alive; the rest, including all the males over the age of 11, had been "either killed or abducted." A previous report from Rößler had confirmed that in the eastern provinces of the Ottoman Empire, Nestorian, Catholic, and Jacobite Assyrians had "[a]lready for a long time" been reported either "killed" (*getötet*) or "banished" (*verbannt*).[67]

Similarly, the German consul in Erzerum, Max Erwin von Scheubner-Richter, reported to the German imperial chancellor that by 1916, the Assyrians of Van ("Eastern Kurdistan"), "after brave resistance, were turned out of their domiciles by the Vali from Mosul, Haidar Bey, and annihilated in part."[68] He added that: "Their fields and homes were ravaged. The survivors fled to the Russians and are now fighting in their ranks against Turkey."[69] Figure 3 quotes from a few of the official German reports of the Assyrian genocide in 1915.

The German government officially protested the murders ongoing in the Ottoman Empire during the summer of 1915.[70] The German consul in Adana had complained to the ambassador that the measures against the Armenians were being applied to all Christians and that German and indeed all Western trade with the Ottoman Empire would be harmed as a result.[71] During and after the war, German missionary Johannes Lepsius, who had been in close contact with the German government as reflected in its ambassadors' reports,[72] "produced two publications containing unique documentary material about the political links between imperial Germany and the extermination policy of the Young Turks"; a significant portion of these accounts were devoted to the Assyrian genocide.[73]

---

66. DE/PA-AA/R14094, 1916-A-33457, No. A53a/1915/5779, Sept. 27, 1915, report from the German Consul in Aleppo, Rößler, to the German Ambassador on Extraordinary Mission in Constantinople, Hohenlohe-Langenburg.

67. DE/PA-AA/R14087. R14095, 1915-A-28019, No. 90/B. No. 1950, Sept. 3, 1915, report from the Consul in Aleppo, Rößler, to the German Imperial Chancellor, Bethmann Hollweg.

68. DE/PA-AA/R14094, 1916-A-33457, DuA Dok. 309, Dec. 4, 1916, the German Vice-Consul in Erzerum, Max von Scheubner-Richter, to German Imperial Chancellor, Bethmann Hollweg.

69. *Id.*

70. *See* Auron, The Banality of Indifference, at 50. The Germans condemned the "massive and indiscriminate expulsions ... accompanied by acts of violence such as massacres and pillages." Dadrian, *Documentation of the Armenian Genocide*, at 98.

71. DE/PA-AA/BoKon 96/Nr. 166–169, J. No. 654, July 24, 1915, the German Consul in Adana, Büge, to the German Ambassador in Constantinople, Wangenheim.

72. Dadrian, *Documentation of the Armenian Genocide*, at 100.

73. *See* Johannes Lepsius, Deutschland und Armenien 1914–1918, Sammlung diplomatischer aktenstücke [Germany and Armenia, 1914–1918: A Collection of Diplomatic Documents] (Potsdam: Tempelverlag, 1919); *see also* Johannes Lepsius, Bericht uber die Lage des armenischen Volkes in der Turkei [Report on the Situation of the Armenian People in Turkey] (Potsdam: Tempelverlag, 1916); Johannes Lepsius, Le Rapport Secret du Dr. Johannes Lepsius, President de la Deutsche Orient Mission et de la Societe Germano-Armenienne,

Figure 3 German Archival Files Documenting the Assyrian Genocide

Reporting Official	Date	Documentation of Genocidal Acts and Intent
German Ambassador	July 1915	"[T]he vali of Diyarbekir, Reshid Bey, started a systematic extermination of the Christian population of his jurisdiction, without distinction as to race or confession. Of these particularly the Catholic Armenians of Mardin and Tel-Armen and the Chaldean Christians and non-Uniate Syrians in the districts of Midyat, Jezire, and Nisibin have been victim[s]."
German Consul in Mosul	July 1915	The entire population of Faysh Khabour, made up "exclusively of Chaldean Christian population, was massacred."
German Consul in Aleppo	July 1915	"So far, about six hundred women and children (Armenian Chaldean Syrian) whose male relatives in Seert, Mardin and Feihschahbur have been massacred have arrived here; just as many will be arriving in the coming days." "The misery of these people is indescribable; every day women and children die of hunger, and their clothes rot on their bodies."
German Consul in Mosul	Sept. 1915	"Apart from the Armenians, not only the Nestorians, but also Ancient Syrians (Jacobites), Catholic Syrians (Syrians) and other Christians have also been deported in the eastern provinces. For a longer period of time it has been indicated here that such Christians were also killed. I have asked a European acquaintance of mine [about it]...." "According to him, there is a large number of non-Armenian, Christian women who arrived here without their husbands. Almost the only possible conclusion is that the men were killed."
German Consul in Aleppo	Sept. 1915	Non-elderly adults of Kharput, Diarbekr, Weranscheher and Mardin killed; children and elderly deported. "The Chaldeans in Söird (Vilayet Bitlis) and Djeziret ibn Omar (Vilayet Diarbekir) and all of the Christians in Djebel et Tor north of Mardin have been exterminated."
German Consul in Erzerum	Dec. 1916	"A large part of the Young Turkish Committee is of the opinion that the Ottoman Empire should only be built upon a purely Mohammedan, pan-Turkish foundation. Those inhabitants who are neither Mohammedan nor Turkish should be made to become so by force or, if that is not possible, annihilated.... "[1).] The first item on their programme was the execution of the Armenians. "A supposedly prepared revolution of the Dashnak Party was put forward as a pretext for those powers, who are allied with Turkey. Furthermore, local unrest and self-protection measures on the part of the Armenians were exaggerated and taken as an excuse to justify the evacuation of the Armenians from endangered border districts. At the instigation of the committee, the Armenians were murdered along the way by Kurd and Turkish gangs, in places also by gendarmes. "2.) At about the same time, the Nestorians in eastern Kurdistan, after brave resistance, were turned out of their domiciles by the Vali from Mosul, Haidar Bey, and annihilated in part. Their fields and homes were ravaged. The survivors fled to the Russians and are now fighting in their ranks against Turkey."

Sources: Lepsius, Deutschland und Armenien; Gaunt, Massacres, Resistance, Protectors, at 275–76; German Foreign Office, Political Archives (DE/PA-AA)

Other evidence of German military and diplomatic awareness and complicity in the Ottoman genocide of Armenians and other Christians is so voluminous as to fill an entire book.[74]

British, American, French, and Russian documents corroborate the German and Ottoman ones in describing the Assyrian experience in very similar terms, even though they lost millions of soldiers and civilians fighting the Ottomans and Germans during World War I. The former British Attorney-General and Lord Chancellor, the 1st Viscount Hailsham, stated in the House of Lords that in 1917 the Assyrians "found themselves face to face with attacks from Turks and Kurds and Persians, and it was only by taking shelter under the cover of the British occupation at that time that they were able to escape annihilation."[75] William Francis Hare, later the Minister of State for Colonial Affairs, declared that "the Assyrians fought on our side during the War," and "being encircled by the Turks and exceedingly short of ammunition, they lost altogether by the end of the War about two-thirds of their total number."[76]

A high British official in Mesopotamia during and after the war wrote, "[the Assyrians] had twice been betrayed by the Russians, but they still carried on, trusting now to the British. As a reward they have lost their former homes and more than one-third of their original numbers...." He noted that the Arab allies of the British had won several independent countries of their own with "infinitely less suffering and loss...."[77] Sir Percy Cox, British High Commissioner for the British Mandate of Iraq, remarked that: "In Persia, the rising of the Christians appeared as almost a slave insurrection, in which the slaves had shown themselves better men than their masters—an unforgivable offense!" After discussing the vicissitudes of Assyrian politics in the period since 1917, he concluded that the Assyrians from Urmia had "practically ceased to exist as a community."[78] A telegram to the British High Commissioner in Egypt estimated in 1919, based on Turkish documents and interviews with Christian leaders, that 58,000 Assyrians (Syrians and Chaldeans) perished in Diyarbekir vilayet during the war.[79] A list provided by the Syrian Orthodox archbishop to the British Prime Minister on behalf of "our ancient Assyrian nation" stated that the victims included 90,000 Syrian Orthodox and 90,000 Assyrian Orthodox and Chaldeans.[80]

SUR LES MASSACRES D'ARMENIE (Paris: Payot et cie., 1918); Gabriele Yonan, *Holy War Made in Germany: New Light on the Holocaust against the Christian Assyrians during World War I* (Aug. 25, 2000), http://www.nineveh.com/Holy%20War%20Made%20in%20Germany.html (paper presented at the international conference on "Assyrians After Assyria: Persecutions and Massacres of Syriac-speaking Christians," organized by the Centre for Comparative Genocide Studies at Macquarie University and the Dep't of Semitic Studies at the University of Sydney, Australia, July 2, 2000).

74. *See* VAHAKN N. DADRIAN, GERMAN RESPONSIBILITY IN THE ARMENIAN GENOCIDE: A REVIEW OF THE HISTORICAL EVIDENCE OF GERMAN COMPLICITY (Cambridge, MA: Blue Crane Books, 2d ed. 1996).

75. *Assyrians in Iraq, in* 90 THE PARLIAMENTARY DEBATES (OFFICIAL REPORT)—HOUSE OF LORDS, Nov. 28, 1933, at 145 (London: His Majesty's Stationery Office, 1934).

76. *Id.* at 142.

77. LT. COL. RS STAFFORD, THE TRAGEDY OF THE ASSYRIANS, ch. 2 (London: George Allen & Unwin, 1935, reprint 2003).

78. HIS MAJESTY'S HIGH COMMISSIONER, IRAQ: REPORT ON IRAQ ADMINISTRATION: OCTOBER, 1920–MARCH, 1922, 102–9 (London: His Majesty's Stationery Office).

79. 5 MINORITIES IN THE MIDDLE EAST: CHRISTIAN MINORITIES 1838–1967: THE TREATMENT OF ARMENIANS IN TURKEY AND THE LEVANT (VOLUME II) 1915–1958, at 252 (Slough, U.K.: Cambridge Archive Editions Limited, 2007).

80. CAB/29/30, Mar. 8, 1920, Mar Severius Barsaum, Archbishop of Syria, to British Prime Minister, Lloyd George, on the Position of Assyro-Chaldeans, *in* 6 MINORITIES IN THE MIDDLE EAST: CHRISTIAN MINORITIES 1838–1967: ASSYRIAN COMMUNITIES IN THE LEVANT AND IRAQ (VOLUME I) 1880–1938, at 80–82 (Slough, U.K.: Cambridge Archive Editions Limited, 2007).

Viscount James Bryce, the former British ambassador to the U.S., described Turkish crimes against Assyrians during World War I as follows:

> The bloodstained annals of the East contain no record of massacres more unprovoked, more widespread or more terrible than those perpetrated by the Turkish Government upon the Christians of Anatolia and Armenia in 1915. It was the sufferings of the Armenians that chiefly drew the attention of Britain and America because they were the most numerous among the ecclesiastical bodies, and the slaughter was, therefore, on a larger scale. But the minor communities, such as the Nestorian and Assyro-Chaldean churches, were equally the victims of the plan for exterminating Christianity, root and branch, although the Turks had never ventured to allege that these communities had given any ground of offense. An account of these massacres, organized and carried out with every circumstance of cruelty by Enver and Talaat, chiefs of the ruffianly gang who were then in power in Constantinople, has been given in the Blue Book, published by the British Foreign Office in 1916, and entitled "Treatment of the Armenians in the Ottoman Empire.".... [S]imilar cruelties [were] perpetrated upon members of the Assyro-Chaldean Church in which about half of them, men, women and children, perished at the hands of Turkish murderers and robbers.[81]

The Blue Book is indeed a key source of evidentiary support for the existence of the Armenian and Assyrian genocides. Viscount Bryce and Arnold Toynbee, a historian affiliated with Oxford University, compiled this book for release by the British Foreign Office under the title, *The Treatment of Armenians in the Ottoman Empire 1915–16.* The British government commissioned Viscount Bryce and Mr. Toynbee to prepare a "general narrative" of the "accounts of massacres and deportations of the Christian population of Asiatic Turkey," accounts which had increased in "number and fullness of detail." Most of these accounts were communicated to Mr. Toynbee via the U.S., then professing neutrality in World War I, from citizens of neutral countries, often American missionaries. Over three dozen of the reports in the Blue Book constituted official State Department records. Viscount Bryce, something of a "champion of the Ottoman Armenians," removed the reference to Assyrian Christians in the title of the Blue Book prior to its publication by Her Majesty's Stationer's Office.[82] The original title of this compilation of American and European eyewitness testimony and documentation of the Armenian and Assyrian genocides was *Papers and Documents on the Treatment of Armenians and Assyrian Christians by the Turks, 1915–1916, in the Ottoman Empire and North-West Persia.*[83] The deletion of the accounts of the Assyrian massacres from the French translation of the Blue Book presented to the Paris Peace Conference of 1919–20 further distorted the historical record.[84]

Viscount Bryce acknowledged, however, that the Blue Book contained evidence from both native and "neutral" witnesses of "massacres and deportations of the Armenian *and other Eastern Christians* dwelling in Asia Minor, Armenia, and the north-west corner of

81. Lord James Bryce, *Preface, in* JOSEPH NAAYEM, SHALL THIS NATION DIE?, at v (New York, NY: Chaldean Rescue, 1921), http://www.lulu.com/items/volume_2/140000/140495/2/preview/Naayem_Preview.pdf.

82. Ara Sarafian, *Introduction, in* THE TREATMENT OF ARMENIANS IN THE OTTOMAN EMPIRE, at vii, xii–xv; Viscount Bryce, *Letter to Viscount Grey of Fallodon, Secretary of State for Foreign Affairs, in* THE TREATMENT OF ARMENIANS IN THE OTTOMAN EMPIRE, at 14, 19, 28, 33–40.

83. F.O. 96/205–210, 3 Class 96, Miscellaneous, Series II, six files (London: Foreign Office Archives, 1916), *cited in* THEA HALO, NOT EVEN MY NAME 328 (New York, NY: Picador, 2000).

84. HALO, NOT EVEN MY NAME, at 328.

Persia."[85] By March 1915, it was known that 5,000 to 6,000 Assyrians had died on the plains of Urmia or in flight to Russia.[86] There were an estimated 8,500 deaths in the Assyrian villages surrounding Urmia, Persia, during five months in 1915 alone.[87] These villages included Salamas, Gulpashan, and others. The book also documented thousands of deaths of Assyrians in Armenia (Ottoman vilayet of Van), and the destruction of dozens of villages and the massacre of thousands of people in the Hakkari mountains that span from northeastern Iraq into southeastern Turkey and northwestern Persia.[88] There was a "general massacre" of Assyrians in the Bohtan district, during which the Christians of all the local villages were slain.[89]

The Blue Book documented how under Turkish occupation and "urged on and followed by Turkish officers and troops," the Kurds and other Muslims in and around Urmia "set to work robbing and looting, killing men and women and outraging the women." According to an American missionary in Persia, later American Vice-Consul for Urmia, Turkish forces directly massacred the Christian population, and failed to prevent many other massacres, leading to "the murder of over one thousand people—men, women, and children; the outraging of hundreds of women and girls of every age—from eight or nine years old to old age; the total robbing of about five-sixths of the Christian population; and the total destruction of about the same proportion of their houses." At least 4,000 perished from disease while or after being driven from their homes or lands. Kidnapping and sexual slavery were employed as methods of destroying the Christian community: "Over two hundred girls and women were carried off into captivity...."[90]

The head of the American hospital in Urmia wrote in 1916 that the Assyrian districts on the Ottoman-Persian border, including Mergawar, Tergawar, and Dasht "had been destroyed even before the war began," leaving the villages there "entirely in ruins." The Assyrian refugees from the Hakkari mountains had no food or farmland anymore.[91] Another American eyewitness whose testimony was recorded in the Blue Book stated that in the largest "Syrian" or Assyrian village in Urmia,[92] all of the men were hauled over to the cemetery to be murdered, while the "women and girls [were] treated barbarously," and sixty

85. Viscount Bryce, *Preface, in* THE TREATMENT OF ARMENIANS IN THE OTTOMAN EMPIRE, at 19 (emphasis added).

86. *See* F.N. Jessup, *Tabriz, in* THE TREATMENT OF ARMENIANS, 152–53.

87. *See* Jacob Sargis, *Urmia, in* THE TREATMENT OF ARMENIANS, at 189–91.

88. *See* Paul Shimmon, *Hakkiari, in* THE TREATMENT OF ARMENIANS, at 201; Paul Shimmon, *Urmia, Salmas, and Hakkiari, in* TREATMENT OF THE ARMENIANS, at 195–96; Paul Shimmon, *Urmia, Salmas, and Hakkiari: Fuller Statement, in* TREATMENT OF THE ARMENIANS, at 581–82. *Cf.* GERTRUDE BELL, REVIEW OF THE CIVIL ADMINISTRATION OF MESOPOTAMIA (London: Her Majesty's Stationery Office, 1920), http://www.archive.org/details/reviewofciviladm00iraqrich; GAUNT, MASSACRES, RESISTANCE, PROTECTORS, at 302.

89. E.W. McDowell, *The Nestorians of the Bohtan District, in* THE TREATMENT OF ARMENIANS, at 211.

90. William A. Shedd, *Urmia, in* THE TREATMENT OF ARMENIANS IN THE OTTOMAN EMPIRE, at 137–39. *See* Viktor Shklovsky, A SENTIMENTAL JOURNEY: MEMOIRS, 1917–1922, at 272 (Richard Sheldon trans., Normal, IL: Dalkey Archive Press, 2004); MARY LEWIS SHEDD, THE MEASURE OF A MAN: THE LIFE OF WILLIAM AMBROSE SHEDD, MISSIONARY TO PERSIA 221 (Piscataway, NJ: Gorgias Press, 2006).

91. H.P. Packard, *Plight of Assyria,* N.Y. TIMES, Sept. 18, 1916, http://www.nytimes.com.

92. It was common at the time of World War I for the British and Americans to refer interchangeably to the non-Armenian Christian population of Mesopotamia and Persia as "Nestorians (from their religion), 'Syrians' (from their language) or Chaldeans (from their race)." *Preface, in* THE TREATMENT OF ARMENIANS, at 135, 137.

men were removed from the French Mission and summarily shot.[93] An American missionary who lived with the Hakkari Assyrians for some 35 years wrote that:

> In January, 1915, an organized Turkish army entered the Urmia plain from the south. The Russians retired northward. Turks and Kurds and local Persians fell upon the subject Christians of the Urmia plain, looted and destroyed their villages and massacred the inoffensive inhabitants. Some ten thousand fled with the retreating Russians: twelve thousand took refuge with the American missionaries in the City of Urmia.[94]

Many other Assyrians in Persia suffered a similar fate under the Turks. In Salamas, a district in Persia inhabited by over 2,000 Assyrians, the Turks gathered together and massacred about 800 Christians, mostly women and older men, prior to the Turkish withdrawal from the area.[95] Some Christian men "were tied with their heads sticking through the rungs of a ladder and decapitated, others hacked to pieces or mutilated before death."[96] In Diliman, Persia, "[a]ll the males above twelve years of age ... were taken to two neighboring villages, tortured and shot."[97] As an American missionary stationed in Tabriz, Persia reported, about a fifth of the 30,000 Nestorians living in Urmia and its surrounding villages had died, and their villages had been burned for the most part, with their cultural property, their churches, reduced to ruin.[98] Another missionary who later became the American Vice-Consul for Urmia reported that Kurds murdered the Assyrian patriarch along with a hundred of his men in a "massacre" that was "followed by an attack by the Christians on Kohna Shahr, which was plundered and destroyed with large loss of life."[99]

In southeastern Anatolia, the Assyrians were caught up with the Armenians in a common genocidal campaign against Christians. In Bashkala, "many hundreds (perhaps some thousands) of Armenians and Syrians ... [were] massacred." Armenians reported that the women and children of that region had either been killed or forced into "a captivity worse than death."[100] An American missionary stationed in Mardin reported that the Kurds there "had interpreted the deportations of the Armenians as another decree against all Christians."[101] Organized "butcheries" followed in that region.[102]

By the summer of 1915 the Kurds had carried out the "proclamation of Jihad" and had "ravaged" Assyrian villages of Mesopotamia, driving the Assyrians into uninhabit-

---

93. Robert M. Labaree, *Azerbaijan, Behind the Russian Front, in* The Treatment of Armenians, at 146.

94. U.S. National Archives, General Records of the Dep't of State, Record Group 59 (Decimal File, 1910–1929), Doc. No. 59,867.4016/79, Aug. 24, 1923, E. W. McDowell, Presbyterian Church Board, Mosul, to Allen Dulles, Near East Division, U.S. Dep't of State, *quoted in* Genocides Against Assyrians 112–114 (George Davis ed., 1999).

95. William A. Shedd, *Urmia, in* The Treatment of Armenians, at 137–39.

96. F.N. Jessup, *Tabriz, in* The Treatment of Armenians, 152–53.

97. Labaree, *Azerbaijan, Behind the Russian Front, in* The Treatment of Armenians, 146.

98. *See* Jessup, *Tabriz, in* The Treatment of Armenians, at 152–53.

99. U.S. National Archives, General Records of the Dep't of State, Record Group 59 (Decimal File, 1910–1929), Doc. No. 59,891.48/126, Apr. 2, 1918, William A. Shedd, Urmia, Persia, to Robert Speer, the Board of Foreign Missions of Presbyterian Church in the U.S., *quoted in* Genocides Against Assyrians, at 18.

100. Labaree, *Azerbaijan, Behind the Russian Front, in* The Treatment of Armenians, at 147.

101. Alpheus N. Andrus, *Mardin, in* "Turkish Atrocities": Statements of American Missionaries on the Destruction of Christian Communities in Turkey, 1915–1917, at 100–101 (James L. Barton ed., Ann Arbor, MI: Gomidas Institute, 1998).

102. Armenian Colony in Egypt, *Cilicia, in* The Treatment of Armenians, at 481.

able mountains and a desperate flight to Urmia.[103] In the Hakkari mountains of northern Mesopotamia, which also extend into northern Persia and southeastern Anatolia, the Ottomans and their Kurdish allies destroyed many Christian villages and plundered the crops and goods there, condemning the Christian population to mass starvation. Forty villages in one district alone had only seventeen survivors. Assisted by Ottoman troops, Kurds entered Goele, a village of 300 Assyrian Catholic and Protestant families, and murdered the men, enslaved off the women and children, and pillaged the houses in the village. In another Assyrian village of 50 houses, Kurds attacked and killed the entire defenseless population.[104] The Governor General of the Azerbaijan province of Persia wrote to the Prime Minister of Persia in 1919 to report that Kurds in Urmia "set about massacring some Assyrians," and then "sacked the villages of the environs, massacred the peasants and occupied all the shores of [Lake Urmia]."[105]

The Russian revolution and dissolution of the czarist army destroyed Assyrian hopes of independence under the protection of their Russian allies. Instead, the Assyrian nation embarked upon a "routed, headlong, and massacre-haunted straggle" out of northern Persia and over the mountains back into British-controlled Mesopotamia.[106] The British accepted the "remnant" of the Assyrian population into refugee camps, only one-third having survived the depredations of the Turks and Kurds.[107] After the war, the Turks prevented Assyrian refugees from returning to the Hakkari mountains.[108] Rather than facilitating their return, forces loyal to Mustafa Kemal "Atatürk" murdered many of the surviving men, raped many young girls and sold others into harem slavery, and deported 8,000 Christians from Mesopotamia into the interior of Turkey.[109]

American diplomatic sources confirmed Ambassador Bryce's charge of an Ottoman policy to exterminate Christians other than the Armenians. According to Ambassador Morgenthau, widely regarded as a principal source of information on the Armenian genocide:

> The Armenians are not the only subject people in Turkey which have suffered from this policy of making Turkey exclusively the country of the Turks. The story which I have told about the Armenians I could also tell with certain modifications about the Greeks and the Syrians. Indeed the Greeks were the first victims of this nationalizing idea.[110]

Ambassador Morgenthau wrote that the Assyrians (which he called "Nestorians" and "Syrians") were subjected to the "same methods" of deportation and "wholesale massacre" as the Armenians and Greeks. He declared that the Ottoman Turks had massacred

---

103. LONGRIGG, IRAQ: 1900 TO 1950, at 97.

104. Paul Shimmon, *Hakkiari*, *in* THE TREATMENT OF ARMENIANS, at 201.

105. U.S. National Archives, General Records of the Dep't of State, Record Group 59 (Decimal File, 1910–1929), Doc. No. 59,867.4016/45, July 16, 1919, U.S. Chargé d'Affaires in Persia to U.S. Secretary of State, *quoted in* GENOCIDES AGAINST ASSYRIANS, at 34–35.

106. LONGRIGG, IRAQ: 1900 TO 1950, at 97–98.

107. *Id.*; *see also* EFRAIM KARSH AND INARI KARSH, EMPIRES OF THE SAND: THE STRUGGLE FOR MASTERY IN THE MIDDLE EAST, 1789–1923, at 160 (Cambridge, MA: Harvard UP, 2001).

108. R. S. Stafford, *Iraq and the Problem of the Assyrians*, 13 INT'L AFFAIRS 164 (1934).

109. George Seldes, *Chaldeans Outraged as Massacred by Turks*, L.A. TIMES, Oct. 25, 1925, at 1.

110. HENRY I. MORGENTHAU, AMBASSADOR MORGENTHAU'S STORY 323 (New York: New Age Publishers, 1975) (1918). Morgenthau sometimes referred to Assyrians as "Syrians," which is the Greek term for Assyrian that was often used in the West, especially when referring to those Orthodox Assyrians adhering to the Syrian Orthodox Church, as opposed to the Chaldean Assyrians of the Catholic faith. *See Preface*, *in* THE TREATMENT OF ARMENIANS, at 135, 137. As pointed out below, he later clarified that by "Syrians" he meant "Assyrians."

1.5 million Armenians and 500,000 Assyrians and Greeks, this time using the term "Assyrians" rather than the religious denominational terms "Nestorians" and "Syrians." Morgenthau therefore confirmed that sometime after April 1915, the "Turks afterward decided to apply the same methods on a larger scale" to the Assyrians and Greeks as well as the Armenians.[111] In December 1918, the *Los Angeles Times* reported that Ambassador Morgenthau told an audience in Chicago that the Turks "have massacred fully 2,000,000 men, women, and children—Greeks, Assyrians, Armenians; fully 1,500,000 Armenians."[112] Ambassador Morgenthau wrote to the White House that "in Turkey we see the evil spirit of Germany at its worst—culminating at last in the greatest crime of all ages, the horrible massacre of helpless Armenians and Syrians."[113]

A lower-ranking American diplomat, Leslie Davis, wrote to the U.S. Ambassador in 1915 that both the Assyrians and the Armenians were deported from the Harput area, in a convoy of many thousands including children, and that deportation meant a "lingering and ... dreadful death."[114] The U.S. still proclaimed neutrality in the war at that time. Davis argued that Ottoman deportees from Eastern Anatolia were destined to a dreadful death because:

> In fact, the Turks have been taking their choice of these children and girls for slaves, or worse. In fact, they have even had their doctors there to examine the more likely girls and thus secure the best ones. There are very few men among them, as most of them have been killed on the road. All tell the same story of having been attacked and robbed by the Kurds. Most of them were attacked over and over again, and a great many of them, especially the men, were killed. Women and children were also killed. Many died, of course, from sickness and exhaustion on the way, and there have been deaths each day that they have been here ... Those who have reached here are only a small portion, however, of those who started. By continuing to drive these people on in this way, it will be possible to dispose of all of them in a comparatively short time.[115]

The U.S. consul in Aleppo wrote that the "Syrians" and "Caldeans" [sic] were deported from the Mardin area.[116] An American diplomat stationed in Urmia, Persia stated that the Assyrian refugees there were "massacred" after the "Turkish consul at Urumiah forced his way into the [American Christian] mission with a number of regular Turkish troops and removed some Assyrian Christian refugees."[117] An official of the Board of Missions

---

111. MORGENTHAU, AMBASSADOR MORGENTHAU'S STORY, ch. 24, http://www.cilicia.com/morgenthau/Morgen24.htm.

112. *Morgenthau Urges Carving of Turkey,* L.A. TIMES, Dec 12, 1918, at I–1.

113. *Quoted in* LEWY, THE ARMENIAN MASSACRES IN OTTOMAN TURKEY, at 140.

114. LESLIE A. DAVIS, THE SLAUGHTERHOUSE PROVINCE: AN AMERICAN DIPLOMAT'S REPORT ON THE ARMENIAN GENOCIDE, 1915–1917, at 143–44 (New Rochelle, NY: Aristede D. Caratzas, 1989); Anahit Khosroeva, *The Assyrian Genocide in the Ottoman Empire and Adjacent Territories, in* THE ARMENIAN GENOCIDE: CULTURAL AND ETHICAL LEGACIES, at 270–73.

115. U.S. National Archives, General Records of the Dep't of State, Record Group 59 (Decimal File, 1910–1929), Doc. No. 59/867.4016/122, Aug. 10, 1915, Leslie A. Davis to Secretary of State Robert Lansing, *quoted in* Gaunt, *Ottoman Bystanders*, at 19. *See also* TREATMENT OF ARMENIANS, at 290.

116. *Quoted in* 1 UNITED STATES OFFICIAL DOCUMENTS ON THE ARMENIAN GENOCIDE 54 (Ara Sarafian, ed., Watertown, MA: Armenian Review Press, 1993).

117. *Quoted in More Violence by Turks,* L.A. TIMES, Mar. 27, 1915, at II–1. *See also Consul's Death in Persia Told. Occidental College Teacher Hears of Brother; Running Fight with Turks is Related in Letter,* L.A. TIMES, Dec. 21, 1918, at II–8.

of the Presbyterian Church of the U.S. wrote that the districts of Mergawar, Tergawar, and Dasht had been razed.[118] These districts, containing previously rich agricultural plains, were plundered by Kurds by October 1914.[119] Another American missionary reported meeting starving refugees in Persia, who reported the killing of all the men over the age of 13 by the Ottomans, the criminal abuse of the women and girls, and the looting or destruction of all their property.[120]

French accounts are similar. The French consulate in Mesopotamia reported to the French foreign minister in 1918 that nearly 8,000 Chaldeans, had been "completely exterminated" in Seert and Bitlis.[121] A French Dominican scholar present in Diyarbekir through late 1916 tallied the results. Through late 1916, he estimated that 90% of the Chaldeans in Diyarbekir were killed, as were 72% of Syrian Orthodox, 62% of Syrian Catholics, and 67% of Protestants. The loss of life approached 150,000 in Diyarbekir, "representing 82% of the combined Armenian and Assyrian population."[122] By 1919, the Dominicans stated that at least 18,000 Assyrian Chaldeans had perished, including the archbishop of Seert, the bishop of Jazirah, and dozens of priests, nuns, and monks.[123]

Finally, Russian sources provide very powerful evidence of the Assyrian genocide. A Russian diplomat in Urmia, Basil Nikitine, "published captured Ottoman documents that used the expression 'Great Jihad' for the ethnic cleansing of Christians from the Turkish Iranian border region."[124] In 1916, Nikitine wrote that the Turks "performed mass executions" of Christians from the French Mission near Urmia and in the vicinity of Gulpashan, and that over 4,500 Christians died from disease over the winter. He reported:

> Turkish authorities have imposed severe control over the territory of the Turkish Syriacs [Assyrians] and take reprisals against their leaders. Mar Shimun was called to Van and the bishop of Shamdinan, Mar Khnanisho, was arrested. But the people nevertheless demand autonomy. Now [Assyrians] from the villages of Sheitan, Bitlo, Nerdish, Segin, Hilanek, Derboder, and Diru have been deported

---

118. *See* William Walker Rockwell, The Pitiful Plight of the Assyrian Christians in Persia and Kurdistan 25–27 (New York; American Committee for Armenian and Syrian Relief, 1916).

119. *See* Gaunt, Massacres, Resistance, Protectors, at 93; Dr. William A. Shedd, *The Situation in West Persia, in* 38 The Missionary Review of the World 781 (New York: New York: Missionary Review Publishing Co., 1915); Paul Shimmon, *Urmia, Salmas, and Hakkiari, in* Treatment of Armenians, at 195; Paul Shimmon, *Urmia, Salmas, and Hakkiari: Fuller Statement, in* Treatment of Armenians, at 581–82; *cf. Humane Work by Russians in Persia Is Told*, Christian Sci. Monitor, Dec. 8, 1915, at 12; *Says Turks Aided Recent Massacres; Troops Allowed Kurds to Kill Hundreds, American Missionary Reports,* N.Y. Times, Apr. 29, 1915, at 2.

120. *See Crimes in Persia Told By Witness: Terrible Slaughter of Armenians at Hands of Turks,* Toronto World, Oct 12, 1915, at 3.

121. Joseph Tfinkdji, The Victims of the Chaldean Nation during the Massacres in Armenia: Report of a Chaldean Clergyman (Paris: Pichon, 1918), *quoted in* Gabriele Yonan, Ein vergessener Holocaust: Die Vernichtung der christlichen Assyrer in der Türkei 309–12 (Göttingen: Gesellschaft für bedrohte Völker, 1989). *See also* Father Dakras, *What Father Dakras Saw of Massacres in Turkey*, Wash. Post, Nov. 28, 1915, at M5; Khosroeva, *The Assyrian Genocide*, at 270, 273; Travis, *Ottoman Genocide of the Assyrians,* at 333.

122. Gaunt, *Ottoman Bystanders*, at 15 (citing Jacques Rhétoré, "Les Chrétiens aux Bêtes": Souvenirs de la Guerre Sainte Proclamée par les Turcs Contre les Chrétiens en 1915, at 136 (Joseph Alichoran ed., Paris: Cerf, 2005)).

123. *See* Gaunt, Massacres, Resistance, Protectors, at 164, 173–77, 208–10, 212–13, 216–27, 250–53, 323–24.

124. *Id.* at 63.

> to Persia. The Turks burned down the [Assyrian] villages and confiscated the property of the inhabitants.[125]

After the war, Nikitine wrote that three quarters of Assyrian villages were razed and thousands "exterminated" (*exterminés*) by attacks and diseases acquired in flight to safety.[126]

3. Eyewitness Accounts of the Assyrian Genocide

Paul Shimmon, who represented Mar Shimun XXI in Britain, reported that by 1915, at least 1,000 people had been massacred in and around Urmia in a few months' time, 4,000 had died of disease, 70 towns and villages had been plundered and destroyed, and the Vatican of the Assyrians, the seat of Mar Shimun and the Church of the East in Qudshanis, "was attacked by regular troops and Kurds, destroyed and plundered."[127] A nearly identical report from an American missionary in Persia stated that at least 2,000 more died in flight to Russia.[128]

The memoirs of a victim of the Ottoman Christian genocide declared that by October 1914, the Turkish government had impelled an organized army of Kurds to "expel[] several thousand Christians" from Turkish villages adjoining Persia and to "plunder and burn the Christian villages" in Persia adjoining eastern Turkey. On the road north to Russia, this missionary and another eyewitness saw thousands of Christians starving to death in the fields, children dying by the hundreds, as well as dozens of abandoned orphans.[129] In the Catholic Mission in Urmia, dozens of Christians, including an Episcopal bishop, "were bound together one night, taken to Gagain mountain and there shot down."[130] A reverend affiliated with the Church of England's mission to Assyrians reported that "[t]hose who died from the slaughter and raiding of villages numbered 6,000."[131] Another report estimated 8,500 deaths in and around Urmia in five months in 1915. In Gulpashan, Persia, dozens of men were tied together to be shot outside the village, their "wives and daughters distributed among the Turks, Kurds, and Persian Mohammedans."[132] The *Washington Post* reported an eyewitness account that in Adana, Anatolia, only 150 of 4,000 Chaldeans survived the swords and knives of the Ottomans, and that about 500 Christians had met their end in a general massacre inside a Chaldean church.[133]

---

125. AVPRI, I.F. 293, des. 571, dossier 420, list 59–61, *quoted in* GAUNT, MASSACRES, RESISTANCE, PROTECTORS, at 127–28.

126. Basile Nikitine, *Une Petite Nation Victime de la Guerre: Les Chaldéens*, 44 REVUE DES SCIENCES POLITIQUES 602, 622 (1921).

127. Paul Shimmon, *Hakkiari, in* THE TREATMENT OF ARMENIANS IN THE OTTOMAN EMPIRE, at 200–203 (describing destruction of many Assyrian villages in Hakkari mountains and neighboring Mesopotamian plains); *see also* Lady Surma, *Refugees from Hakkiari, in* THE TREATMENT OF ARMENIANS IN THE OTTOMAN EMPIRE, at 203–218; GAUNT, MASSACRES, RESISTANCE, PROTECTORS, at 135.

128. *See Crimes in Persia Told By Witness*, at 3.

129. *See* YONAN H. SHAHBAZ, THE RAGE OF ISLAM: AN ACCOUNT OF THE MASSACRE OF CHRISTIANS BY THE TURKS IN PERSIA, 170–71 (Philadelphia: Roger Williams Press, 1918).

130. Dr. Jacob Sargis, *Urmia, in* THE TREATMENT OF ARMENIANS, at 189.

131. Y.M. Nisan, *Urmia, in* THE TREATMENT OF ARMENIANS, at 187.

132. Sargis, *Urmia, in* THE TREATMENT OF ARMENIANS, at 189, 191. Gulpashan was "wholly ransacked," the men slaughtered and the attractive women kidnapped. YOHANNAN, THE DEATH OF A NATION, at 127.

133. Father Dakras, *What Father Dakras Saw of Massacres in Turkey*, WASH. POST, Nov. 28, 1915, at M5.

The slaughter of Christians described in the Blue Book was not confined to Turkey or northern Persia, but extended into Mesopotamia.[134] Mar Shimun XXI Benyamin, the spiritual leader of traditionalist Assyrians who had not joined the Catholic, Protestant, or Syrian Orthodox churches, wrote to the Russian viceroy of the Caucasus region that the Assyrians had abandoned their native lands and ancient churches because the Turks had "determined to kill all of us." He was with the Assyrians in Mesopotamia and Persia through the duration of the war and its aftermath. After suffering "massacres and aggressions" instigated by Turkish officials and carried out by Kurds,[135] Mar Shimun had declared independence from the Ottomans, giving the "best of pretexts" to the Kurds to attack them "under Turkish instigation."[136] Before declaring independence, and war upon the Ottoman Empire, he had issued a demand that the murders end:

> Mar Benjamin Shimun, Patriarch, and the Assyrian leaders communicated an ultimatum to the Government of the Sultan to stop the massacres and aggressions committed against the Assyrians of Gawar and Albaq districts by Kurdish tribesmen who were instigated by the said officials, and having received no satisfaction "due probably to Turkish pre-occupation in other theatres of war" an armed conflict was unavoidable. Mar Benyamin was, however, informed by the Turkish government that his brother, Hormizd, a student in Stamboul would be executed if the Assyrians rose and joined the Allied Powers. Mar Benyamin replied that he was prepared to sacrifice his one brother rather than sacrifice the whole nation.[137]

Mar Severius Barsaum, the representative in France of the Syrian Orthodox Patriarch, wrote that 90,000 Syrian Orthodox Assyrians had been killed and 156 churches razed.[138] An estimated 90,000 Syrian Orthodox Assyrians were "slaughtered" in upper Mesopotamia and southeastern Anatolia by massacres culminating in 1915.[139] More than 300 villages and 150 churches were damaged or destroyed.[140] Other Assyrian authors, like Malik Cambar, Yonan Shahbaz, and Abraham Yohannan, confirmed the widespread massacres of Assyrians, rapes of Assyrian women and girls, and destruction of Assyrian villages in Van, Di-

---

134. Upper Mesopotamia, or "Syrian Mesopotamia," extends into the area of ancient Nisibis and Āmid, modern-day Nusaybin and Diyarbekir in Turkey. *See* Michael H. Dodgeon & Samuel N. C. Lieu, The Roman Eastern Frontier and the Persian Wars, Part II, AD 363–630, at 5 (Boca Raton, FL: CRC Press, 2002).

135. Yusuf Malek, The British Betrayal of the Assyrians, ch. 18 (Warren Point, NJ: The Kimball Press, 1936), http://www.aina.org/books/bbota.htm. See also Paul Shimmun, *The Plight of Assyria*, N.Y. Times, Sept. 18, 1916, http://www.nytimes.com (Assyrian persecutions began prior to World War I). The massacres began with the declaration of *jihad* in 1914, and not with the Assyrian declaration of independence in 1915. *See* Lepsius, Bericht über die Lage des Armenischen Volkes in der Türkei, at 109–110, *quoted in* Yonan, Lest We Perish, at 113–14; Surma D'Bait Mar Shimun, Assyrian Church Customs and the Murder of Mar Shimun 76–89 (London, Faith Press, 1920); Otto Wendt, Report from Urmia, June 1915, *quoted in* Yonan, Lest We Perish, at 70; *see also* Yonan, Lest We Perish, at 86 (describing "a campaign of destruction against the defenseless Christian farmer population in the Turkish-Persian border areas as early as late 1914").

136. Longrigg, Iraq: 1900 to 1950, at 97.

137. Malek, The British Betrayal of the Assyrians, ch. 18.

138. *See* Gaunt, Massacres, Resistance, Protectors, at 227, 303; CAB/29/30, Mar. 8, 1920, Mar Severius Barsaum, Archbishop of Syria, to British Prime Minister, Lloyd George, on the Position of Assyro-Chaldeans, *in* 6 Minorities in the Middle East: Christian Minorities 1838–1967: Assyrian Communities in the Levant and Iraq (Volume I) 1880–1938, at 80–82 (Slough, U.K.: Cambridge Archive Editions Limited, 2007).

139. *See* Baum, The Christian Minorities of Turkey, at 102–3.

140. *See id.* at 103.

yarbekir, Bitlis, Seert, Harput, Mardin, Urfa, Jazirah, Mansurieh, the Hakkari mountains, the Urmia region, etc.[141]

Scholars estimate that 70,000 Catholic Assyrians, or Chaldeans, died between 1914 and 1918.[142] The Chaldean Patriarch, Yousef Emmanuel II Thomas, reported the loss of 5,000 of his parishioners in the diocese of Jazirah, in upper Mesopotamia near the borders between present-day Iraq, Syria, and Turkey. He further reported the loss of 4,000 Chaldeans in Seert. Another Chaldean leader reported in 1918 that the Hakkari mountains were empty of Assyrians, Turks having shelled and burned the villages there. Jacques-Eugene Manna, archbishop of the Chaldean Church, reported that more than 100 families and 150 individuals had been massacred in the province of Van, along with all the inhabitants of 20 villages in the district of Gawar.[143]

The Chaldean archbishop of Seert was slain, and his secretary reported hundreds of Chaldean victims in Seert, Ardoun, Artoun, Der-Mar-Yacoub, Dohuk, Hadidé, Ketmes, Mar-Gourye, Sadagh, Tellimachâr, and elsewhere.[144] A Chaldean vicar reported that the military governor of Van, Djevdet Bey, after encountering resistance to Ottoman expansion on the part of Russians, Armenians, and Assyrians, "entered into Seert with 8,000 soldiers which he called '*Kassab Tabouri*' (the butcher battalion) and ordered the massacre of the Christians," including all the Christians of Bitlis and the Chaldean diocese of Séert, and that the diocese of Séert had its villages "plundered, ransacked, burned and the inhabitants put to the edge of the sword." In addition to Djevdet Bey, Naayem identified the governor of Séert, Hilmi Bey, and the commander of the gendarmerie, Hamdi Bey, as well as other officials, as being responsible.[145]

The Assyro-Chaldean delegation to the Paris Peace Conference estimated that 250,000 Assyrians had been massacred or died defending their towns in Persia and in the Ottoman provinces of Diyarbekir, Van, Bitlis, Mamouret ul-Aziz, Adana, and Urfa.[146] The President of the Assyrian National Associations of America, Joel Werda, claiming to speak on behalf of Mar Shimun XXII Paulos, successor to Mar Shimun XXI Benyamin, estimated at the Paris Peace Conference that "during the so called Armenian massacre and exile, fully

141. *See* MALIK CAMBAR, VIE ET COUTUMES DES MALIKS: PRINCES DE CHALDÉE ET D'ASSYRIE (Marseille, France: Imp. Guiran, 1924); NAAYEM, SHALL THIS NATION DIE?, *passim*; Shimmun, *Hakkiari, in* THE TREATMENT OF ARMENIANS, at 200–203; Lady Surma, *Refugees from Hakkiari, in* THE TREATMENT OF ARMENIANS IN THE OTTOMAN EMPIRE, 1915–1916, at 203–218;YOHANNAN, THE DEATH OF A NATION, *passim.*

142. "The Chaldean Catholics suffered heavily from massacres during World War I (1918) when four bishops, many priests, and about seventy thousand faithful died." ANTHONY O'MAHONY, EASTERN CHRISTIANITY: STUDIES IN MODERN HISTORY, RELIGION AND POLITICS 24 (London: Melisende, 2004). *Accord* RONALD ROBERSON, THE EASTERN CHRISTIAN CHURCHES: A BRIEF SURVEY 127 (Rome: Edizioni Orientalia Christiana, 5th ed. 1995).

143. *See* GAUNT, MASSACRES, RESISTANCE, PROTECTORS, at 145–46, 227, 255, 303 (citing NAAYEM, SHALL THIS NATION DIE? [French ed.], at 48–96; YVES TERNON, MARDIN 1915: ANATOMIE PATHOLOGIQUE D'UNE DESTRUCTION, REVUE D'HISTOIRE ARMENIENNE, NUMERO SPECIAL 183 (Paris: Center for Armenian Remembrance, 2000)). *See also* NAAYEM, SHALL THIS NATION DIE?, at 123.

144. *See* NAAYEM, SHALL THIS NATION DIE?, at 123; Jean Naayem, *Les Assyro-chaldéens et les Arméniens Massacrés par les Turcs* (Feb. 18, 1918), http://www.imprescriptible.fr/documents/naayem/d03.htm (my translation from the original French).

145. Naayem, *Les Assyro-chaldéens et les Arméniens Massacrés.*

146. See GAUNT, MASSACRES, RESISTANCE, PROTECTORS, at 300; Gaunt, *Ottoman Bystanders*, at 2 ("[The losses included] Assyrians of all denominations—Nestorian, Syrian Orthodox, Chaldean, Protestants and Catholics and residents of both the Ottoman Empire and Iran. Delegations to the Paris Peace Conference estimated these losses to 250,000 amounting to half of the original population."); Khosroeva, *The Assyrian Genocide,* at 267–68.

Figure 4 Estimates of the Death Toll of the Assyrian Genocide

Deaths, estimate	Source
250,000	*Assyrian Genocide, in* 1 Dictionary of Genocide 24–26 (Samuel Totten, Paul Robert Bartrop, and Steven L. Jacobs eds., Westport, CT: Greenwood Publishing Group, 2008)
250,000	*Chaldean Victims of the Turks*, The Times (U.K.), Nov. 22, 1919, at 11
250,000	*Morgenthau Urges Carving of Turkey*, L.A. Times, Dec. 12, 1918, at I-1 (estimate for "Syrians," minus 250,000 Greeks)
250,000	*L'Asie française*, no. 115, 1919, at 190, *cited in* Khosroeva, *The Assyrian Genocide*, at 271
250,000	*The Claims of the Assyrians Before the Conference of the Preliminaries of Peace at Paris, 1919, in* The Flickering Light of Asia, or The Assyrian Nation and Church (Joel Werda ed., 1924)
70,000	The HarperCollins Encyclopedia of Catholicism 295 (Richard P. McBrien, ed., New York, 1995) (just "Chaldeans")

175,000 Assyrians perished, and were listed under the Armenian atrocities." He explained that many Assyrians in Van spoke Armenian, so that they "became identified with the Armenian people and were counted as the Armenians." He added that: "If Turkey failed to exterminate the remainder of the Assyrians, and confiscate their property, she did so because she failed in her war."[147] Figure 4 sets forth various estimates of Assyro-Chaldean deaths during and shortly after World War I:

4. Journalistic Confirmation of the Assyrian Genocide

The American press documented the genocide of Assyrians by the Turks and their Kurdish allies. These reports tended to focus on the Urmia region of northwestern Persia, the cities of Seert, Jazirah, Faysh Khabour, Diyarbekir, and Adana in Anatolia, and in villages within the mostly Armenian vilayet of Van. Early in 1915, in an article entitled "Native Christians Massacred," the Associated Press correspondent reported that in the vicinity of Urmia, "Turkish regular troops and Kurds are persecuting and massacring Assyrian Christians...." Close to 800 were confirmed dead in Urmia, and another 2,000 had perished from disease. Two hundred Assyrians had been burned to death inside a church, and the Russians had discovered more than 700 bodies of massacre victims in the village of Hafdewan outside Urmia, "mostly naked and mutilated," some with gunshot wounds, others decapitated, and still others carved to pieces.[148]

A few days earlier, the Associated Press had relayed a report from the American consul at Tabriz stating that "the Turkish consul at Urumiah forced his way into the [Amer-

147. Joel E. Werda, *The Claims of the Assyrians Before the Conference of the Preliminaries of Peace at Paris, 1919, in* The Flickering Light of Asia, or The Assyrian Nation and Church (Chicago: 1924), http://www.aina.org/books/fla/fla.htm#c31.

148. *Native Christians Massacred; Frightful Atrocities in Persia,* L.A. Times, Apr. 2, 1915, at I–1.

ican Christian] mission with a number of regular Turkish troops and removed some Assyrian Christian refugees, who were then massacred."[149] Those "who did not escape or were made slaves, perished." Thousands of Assyrians, indeed close to 30,000, fled their homes for Russian or American protection; many died en route.[150]

Other leading British and American newspapers corroborated these accounts of the Assyrian genocide. The *New York Times* reported that by October 1915, about 12,000 Persian Christians had died of massacre, hunger, or disease; thousands of girls as young as seven had been raped or forcibly converted to Islam; 120 Christian villages had been destroyed; and three-fourths of Christian villages burned to the ground.[151] Among other violence, Turks and Kurds exterminated 12,000 Nestorian and Assyrian civilians in Urmia, with huge mass graves holding up to 1,500 bodies being dug.[152] The Ottomans and their allies plundered and burned about 150 Nestorian villages. Their Persian allies seized the opportunity to kidnap and enslave women and children, and forcibly convert them to Islam. The Persian governor of Urmia had steel and lime dust baked into the bread purchased by Christian missionaries tending to Assyrian refugees, so that thousands of the refugees perished from eating contaminated food before local doctors realized what was happening.[153]

The *Washington Post* similarly reported in 1915 that "Turkish regular troops and Kurds are persecuting and massacring Assyrian Christians."[154] According to a letter from an American eyewitness, many of the thousands of Christian refugees in Urmia were "murdered in cold blood and with cruel tortures by the Kurds," with "women and children carried off" into slavery.[155] The *Post* also described how rampaging Kurds, spurred on by the Ottoman Empire's declaration of *jihad* the previous winter, exterminated the local population of Christians unable to flee because they were too old, sick, or incapacitated.[156] In Gulpashan, Kurds tore 65 Christian men out of missions to which they had fled to safety, and hanged them.[157]

In March 1918, Ottoman and Kurdish forces massacred more than two thousand Assyrians in Khoi, Persia. Nearly 800 civilians, who had lost their young men earlier in the war, met a similar fate at about the same time.[158] A few months later, the Ottomans occupied Urmia and "massacred 200 persons, mostly old men."[159] Persian gendarmes mur-

---

149. *More Violence By Turks,* L.A. Times, Mar. 8, 1915, at II–1.

150. *People Flee From Kurds,* L.A. Times, May 3, 1915, at I–2.

151. *Turkish Horrors in Persia,* N.Y. Times, Oct. 11, 1915, http://www.cilicia.com/armo10c-nyt19151011d.html.

152. *Urumiah Massacres. Death of 12,000 Nestorian Christians,* The Times (U.K.), Oct. 9, 1915, http://archive.timesonline.co.uk/tol/archive.

153. *Id.*

154. *Massacres Kept Up,* Wash. Post, Mar. 26, 1915, at 1.

155. *40 Die Daily in Mission,* Wash. Post, Apr. 11, 1915, at R4.

156. *Massacred by Kurds; Christians Unable to Flee from Urmia Put to Death,* Wash. Post, Mar. 14, 1915, at 10.

157. *Christians in Danger; Fearing New Massacre by Kurds, State Department Acts,* Wash. Post, Mar. 27, 1915, at 1.

158. *See* Martin Tamcke, *Der Genozid an den Assyrern/Nestorianern, in* Verfolgung, Vertreibung und Vernichtung der Christen im Osmanischen Reich 1912–1922, at 109 (Tessa Hofmann ed., 2d ed. Münster, 2007); Dr. Tessa Hofmann, *The Ottoman Genocide against Aramaic speaking Christians and the Present Situation of Christian Minorities in the Republic of Turkey*, at 5; Werda, The Flickering Light of Asia, at 156–58.

159. *See Persian Armenia Ravaged by Turks,* N.Y. Times, Oct., 11 1918, at 6; *Turkish Massacres,* The Times (U.K.), Oct. 11, 1918.

dered the Apostolic Delegate of the Catholic Church, along with 600 other persons at his mission in Urmia.[160]

Nearly 100,000 Assyrians fled northern Persia in 1918, with half perishing on the road to Hamadan and British lines.[161] About 14,000 who remained behind in Urmia were slain.[162] The French mission estimated 6,000 deaths among just the Chaldeans due to Turks, Kurds, and Turko-Persians.[163] When the Assyrians reached Hamadan, they died in large numbers; due to all the travails they had experienced, they died at a rate of about sixty a day. "On the way down from Urmiyah they had already suffered greatly from dysentery and even typhus."[164] More than 3,000 died in the last three months of 1918, "chiefly as a result of the dreadful sufferings undergone by them previous to their arrival at Baqubah."[165] Their hunger and exposure had long been reported.[166]

In August 1918, the U.S. Consul at Kashin, Persia reported that the Assyrian population of Urmia was fleeing to Tehran, "driven on by the Turkish invasion."[167] In Tehran, civilians were lying prostrate in the streets from hunger and exhaustion. "Children came to our rest houses with flesh hanging on bones," a telegram to the American Committee for Armenian and Syrian Relief reported, with their "voice gone, buy eyes pleading and imploring for a crust" of bread.[168] A U.S. aid mission to Persia and Turkey estimated that four million people, including 400,000 orphans, were in need of food assistance, particularly the "Armenians, Greeks, and Syrians, victims of Turkish oppression during the war."[169] President Wilson declared that these four million people were "homeless sufferers, whom the vicissitudes of war and massacre had brought to the extremest need."[170] One million persons "in advanced destitution" needed help in Persia alone.[171] This included 80,000 "starving and destitute" Assyrians made subject to an appeal by the Archbishop of Canterbury in 1918.[172]

By December 1918, the *Los Angeles Times* carried the story of a Syrian, or most likely Assyrian, merchant from Urmia who stated that his city was "completely wiped out, the

160. *See* Paul Shimmun, *Persian Debt and Credit (Letter to the Editor),* N.Y. Times, June 29, 1919, at 38.

161. *See* Baumer, The Church of the East, at 263; Alichoran, *Assyro-Chaldeans in the 20th Century*, at 63.

162. *See* Baumer, The Church of the East, at 263; David D. Newsom, *Rescue at Urmia*, Foreign Service Journal, Nov. 2005, at 58; Alichoran, *Assyro-Chaldeans in the 20th Century*, at 64 (20,000 persons died in flight to Hamadan, survivors were taken to Baquba).

163. *See* Ant Clarys, French Catholic Mission at Urmia, to Ernest Bristow, British Consul at Tabriz, Apr. 3, 1919, on losses suffered by the Christians or Urmia and Salmas during the war, *in* Middle East Minorities: Christian Minorities 1838–1967, at 146–48; Alichoran, *Assyro-Chaldeans in the 20th Century*, at 63 (3,800).

164. Stafford, Tragedy of the Assyrians, ch. III.

165. Brigadier-Gen. H. H. Austin, The Baqubah Refugee Camp: An Account of Work on Behalf of the Persecuted Assyrian Christians, ch. II (London: The Faith Press, 1920).

166. *See 25,000 Syrians Starving*, N.Y. Times, Oct. 30, 1915 ("The Foreign Office has received a dispatch from Mr. Shipley, the British Consul at Tabriz, Persia, which says that 25,000 Syrian mountaineers from the Tyari and adjacent districts have taken refuge in Salmas and that 10,000 more are expected there. All are destitute; and unless help is received many of them will inevitably perish, as Winter is close at hand.").

167. *Dr. Shedd Dies in Persia,* Wash. Post, Aug. 25, 1918, at 12.

168. *Starving Die in Persian Streets*, Wash. Post, Aug. 25, 1918, at 17.

169. *Aid Will Go to Turks' Victims*, Wash. Post, Dec. 20, 1918, at 6.

170. *Wilson Asks U.S. to Aid Refugees,* Wash. Post, Dec. 15, 1918, at 47.

171. *Starvation in East Near End*, Wash. Post, Nov. 7, 1918, at 5.

172. *See The Assyrian Massacres*, Manchester Guardian, Dec. 5, 1918, at 4.

inhabitants massacred," 200 surrounding villages ravaged, 200,000 of his people dead, and hundreds of thousands of more starving to death in exile from their agricultural lands.[173] In early 1919, representatives of the Assyrians of Mesopotamia pleaded with the U.S. that Western countries help set them on a path towards self-rule.[174] In May 1919 in Urmia, the Persian and Kurdish population invaded and destroyed the French and American missions, killing 1,000 civilians.[175] Like the Turks, the Persians tried to accuse the Assyrians of atrocities against Muslims out of all proportion of the power of the Assyrians to commit them, and with few or no specifics provided about where or when. It is possible that atrocities by Russians were multiplied by several orders of magnitude and then blamed on Assyrians, as with the Armenians.

The devastation of so many villages left their former residents starving and exposed to bitter cold and repeated outbreaks of disease. As Colonel Stafford explains:

> Assyrians and Armenians in Urmiyah fled south and the retreat soon became a panic-stricken rout.... As the territory through which they were making their painful way was largely Kurdish, the Kurdish attacks were the most numerous; the fact that any got through at all is proof that the Kurds, as usual, were anxious to loot rather than face bullets.... Not only were they the object of continual attacks by night and ambushes by day, but the struggling and starving mass were stricken by all manner of disease—typhus, dysentery, smallpox, cholera, and fevers. Many of those who did not succumb to disease dropped out and died by the wayside of sheer exhaustion. The line of the retreat was marked by an endless trail of dead: men, women, and children who had dropped in their tracks while on the march or were left dying when the camp was struck each tragic dawn. They had little food and little water, and Colonel McCarthy, who had by now come up, had described how whenever they camped for the night the site next morning was littered with dead and dying.... More than seventy thousand Assyrians started out on this dreadful retreat; fewer than fifty thousand reached Hamadan. Those who died in their tracks were perhaps fortunate; ten thousand were cut off by marauding tribesmen and have never been heard of again. Their men were no doubt massacred and their women and girls distributed round the countryside.[176]

In 1919, a German working with the Swedish mission in Urmia wrote that women and children had to cover 70 kilometers per day on foot, without shoes and laden down with supplies. "On our way, we were eight times surrounded by enemies; a few thousands were killed or made prisoners or taken away," he added. "Nursing women left their babies lying on the road and fled away." Orphans crying for help lined the roads. Nearly everyone came down with dysentery, and many fell victim to cholera.[177]

The Times of London was perhaps the first widely respected publication to document that 250,000 Assyrians and Chaldeans had died in the Assyrian genocide by late 1919,[178]

173. *Syrian Tells of Atrocities,* L.A. Times, Dec. 15, 1918, at I–1.

174. *See A Plea from Mesopotamia,* N.Y. Times, Jan. 9, 1919, at 3.

175. *See* Stephanie Cronin, The Making of Modern Iran: State and Society under Riza Shah 1921–1941, at 88 (London: Routledge, 2003).

176. Stafford, Tragedy of the Assyrians, ch. III.

177. Martin Tamcke, *World War I and the Assyrians, in* The Christian Heritage of Iraq 212–13 (Piscataway, NJ: Gorgias Press, 2009).

178. *Chaldean Victims of the Turks,* The Times (U.K.), Nov. 22, 1919, at 11.

a figure which many journalists and scholars have subsequently accepted.[179] About half of the Assyrian nation died of murder, disease, or exposure as refugees by 1920, according to the head of the Anglican Church, which had a mission to the Assyrians.[180] Famine and want were the fate of the survivors, whose homes, villages, churches and schools were wiped out.[181] In 1920, a Chaldean archbishop told a meeting convened by the Mayor of London that Chaldeans had been starving since 1918, as nearly all young Chaldeans had been killed.[182] By the next year, Assyrian boatpeople became a prominent news story around the world.[183]

In 1924, Turkish forces attacked and destroyed Assyrian homes and villages, driving 6,000 across the Mesopotamian border to Amadia.[184] The deportees had lost virtually all their savings and assets, reducing them "to absolute destitution."[185] The slaughter of the Christians of some areas, such as the Goyan district, was reportedly part of the "removal of an entire people."[186] Some of the Assyrian refugees reported that in Turkish concentration camps, no food was provided and the population was reduced to surviving on acorns. The Turkish forces massacred 40 men on a single occasion, and in driving the deportees onward shot dead those children or elderly persons who fell to the ground from hunger, exhaustion, or the cold.[187] The number massacred during the death march reached 300 children and elderly people.[188] The entire period during which Britain and Turkey contested control over the Mosul region and historic Assyria witnessed attacks and plundering of Assyrian villages, and the mass flight of refugees who, "desperate and starving," carried "blood-curdling tales of Turkish cruelties."[189]

---

179. *See, e.g.*, Bloxham, Great Game of Genocide, at 98 (estimating 250,000 Assyro-Chaldean victims of massacres, starvation, and deportations); *Assyrian Genocide, in* 1 Dictionary of Genocide 24–26 (Samuel Totten, Paul Robert Bartrop, and Steven L. Jacobs eds., Westport, CT: Greenwood Publishing Group, 2008) (similar); Jonathan Eric Lewis, *Iraqi Assyrians: Barometer of Pluralism,* 10.3 Middle East Q., (2003); http://www.meforum.org; Uwe Siemon-Netto, *Terror Fallout Hurts Iraqi Christians,* United Press International, Nov. 5, 2001; Uwe Siemon-Netto, *Attacks Defy the Prophet's Wish,* Wash. Times, Aug. 3, 2004, http://washingtontimes.com/; Gaunt, Massacres, Resistance, Protectors, at 300; Yonan, Ein vergessener Holocaust; Gabriele Yonan, "Holy War Made in Germany: New Light on the Holocaust against the Christian Assyrians during World War I," Aug. 25, 2000, http://www.nineveh.com/Holy%20War%20Made%20in%20Germany.html (paper presented at the international conference on "Assyrians After Assyria: Persecutions and Massacres of Syriac-speaking Christians," organized by the Centre for Comparative Genocide Studies at Macquarie University and the Dep't of Semitic Studies at the University of Sydney, Australia, July 2, 2000), http://www.nineveh.com/Holy%20War%20Made%20in%20Germany.html.

180. *See Assyrians' War Sufferings,* The Times (U.K.), June 15, 1920, http://archive.timesonline.co.uk/tol/archive.

181. *Chaldean Victims of the Turks,* at 11.

182. *See Starving Chaldeans,* Manchester Guardian, Jan. 14, 1920, at 7.

183. *See 1,000 Assyrians Sail for America in Small Vessels,* Wash. Post, Aug. 6, 1921, at 3; *Assyrian Christians Coming on Small Sailing Vessels,* Hartford Courant, Aug. 6, 1921; *Seize Smuggled Assyrians,* Wash. Post, July 9, 1922, at 24.

184. *See Britain's Smallest Ally: The Deeds and Needs of the Assyrians,* Manchester Guardian (U.K.), Nov. 12, 1924, at 11.

185. *Assyrian Christians,* Irish Times, Dec. 21, 1923, at 5.

186. Associated Press, *Turk Deportations Protested by Priests,* Wash. Post, Sept. 18, 1925, at 3.

187. *See* Associated Press, *Mosul Awarded to British; More Turk Killings Alleged,* Wash. Post, Dec. 16, 1925, at 1.

188. *See* George Seldes, *300 Chaldeans Die at Hands of Turks; 8,000 Go to Exile,* Wash. Post, Oct 25, 1925, at 1, 18.

189. Marguerite Harrison, Asia Reborn 177 (London: Harrap, 2007).

C. The Question of Intent: The Ottoman Plan to Exterminate the Assyrians

Assuming the Genocide Convention or some other law criminalizing genocide did apply in 1914, Turkey and its defenders argue that the Genocide Convention requires "specific intent" to destroy members of a group as such, which was lacking in the Ottoman Empire's approach to its Christian minorities such as the Armenians and Assyrians. For example, the Web site of the Turkish government states that Armenians were killed by "local Muslims," but the Ottoman armies neither ordered nor participated in this. Indeed, the Ottoman authorities ordered their subordinate officials to "protect relocated Armenians" from local Muslims.[190] The British government appears to agree with this general line of argumentation, condemning "the massacres of 1915–16 ... as a tragedy of historic proportions," but not recognizing them as "genocide" due to "the absence of unequivocal evidence to show that the Ottoman administration took a specific decision to eliminate the Armenians under their control at the time...."[191]

Absent a governmental intention to exterminate the Christians of the empire, it would be nearly impossible to explain how the massacres, rapes, deportations, and dispossessions of the Armenian, Assyrian, and Greek Christians living in the Ottoman Empire at the time of World War I could have taken place on such a vast scale.[192] How could such a remarkable degree of coordination and common purpose in slaughtering civilians, ravaging women, orphaning children, and stealing money and property have emerged without organization and direction from above? Indeed, it takes little searching to uncover abundant evidence of planning for genocide.

Interior Minister Talât, initially the most powerful member of the CUP, believed in "Turkey for the Turks," or getting rid of the ancient Christian peoples stranded in the Ottoman Empire.[193] After the 1908 coup that propelled the Young Turks to positions of power in the Ottoman government, the German ambassador to Athens reported having a conversation with the Turkish prime minister in which he learned: "The Turks have decided upon a war of extermination against their Christian subjects."[194] In 1910, the leaders of the CUP held a party conference during which they discussed how "'the complete Ottomanization of all Turkish subjects must be effected, but it was becoming clear that this could never be achieved by persuasion, and recourse must be had to force of arms.'"[195]

---

190. Republic of Turkey, Directorate General of Press and Information, *The Armenian Allegation of Genocide: Facts* (2001), http://www.byegm.gov.tr/yayinlarimiz/newspot/2001/mar_apr/n5.htm.

191. U.K. Parliament, Lords Hansard, *Armenian Massacre, 1915*.

192. "Genocide as a form of state crime has required a cooperative endeavor by individuals operating on many different levels of the state, with dramatically different orientations, objectives and motivations." David O. Friedrichs, *The Crime of the Century? The Case for the Holocaust*, 34 CRIME, LAW & SOCIAL CHANGE 29 (2000).

193. MORGENTHAU, AMBASSADOR MORGENTHAU'S STORY, at 10, 20, 34.

194. Hans Freiherr von Wangenheim, *quoted in* HALO, NOT EVEN MY NAME, at 126.

195. President of the CUP, *in The Salonika Congress; The Young Turks and their Programme*, THE TIMES (U.K.), Oct. 3, 1911, at 3, *cited in* Panayiotis Diamadis, *The Assyrians in the Christian Asia Minor Holocaust* (July 2000), http://www.nineveh.com/The%20Assyrians%20in%20the%20Christian%20Asia%20Minor%20Holocaust.html.

In 1911, a prominent Young Turk declared the "'nations that remain from the old times in our empire are akin to foreign and harmful weeds that must be uprooted.'"[196]

When the Russians advanced in the Caucasus, and the British marched north from Mesopotamia, the Ottoman "policy of [Christian] oppression broadened across the empire and increased to genocidal proportions...." Soon after the Sultan's declaration of jihad in 1914, the Ottomans, seized with "anti-Christian chauvinism," deported into other parts of Anatolia the entire Christian populations of the Gallipoli peninsula and the area around the Sea of Marmora, more than 60,000 people. "Christians ... were cast as collective targets" for reprisals encouraged by the CUP leaders for any Muslim war dead.[197]

By 1914, the Ottomans had built yet another apparatus of "ethnic war." The *Te kilat-Mahsûsa* or Special Organization, was a force of more than 30,000 men under arms, composed of Turkish law enforcement officers and criminal bands under the command of Ottoman army officers and CUP political leaders. The Special Organization eventually became "a dedicated instrument of indiscriminate mass murder."[198]

In June 1915, Interior Minister Talât told the German ambassador that the Ottomans were exploiting the crisis of the war to "thoroughly clear Turkey of her internal enemies, i.e. the Christians." Ambassador Ernst Wilhelm Hohenlohe-Langenburg reported that the Ottoman "government is resolved ... to eliminate the indigenous Christians."[199] By 1915, therefore, the CUP had created extermination squads and adopted "a crystallized policy of empire-wide killing and death-by-attrition."[200] The Ottoman government's religious figurehead, the Sheik al Islam, resigned from the Sultan's Cabinet after protesting "the extermination of the [Ottoman] Christian elements."[201]

Along with the Armenians, the Assyrians were targeted as a group of non-Turkish Christians in a way that "can only be explained by the CUP's increasingly radical ideology of ethnic [and religious] exclusivity."[202] As Peter Balakian has demonstrated, by 1915 one million people had died in "the extermination of innocent civilians in Turkey (the Armenians, but also Syrian and Assyrian Christians and large portions of the Greek population ...)."[203] Such a speedy and well-organized annihilation of the indigenous Christians of the Ottoman Empire could scarcely have taken place other than as a result of intentional planning and execution.

In any event, the intention on the part of Ottoman officials to exterminate their Armenian and Assyrian subjects need not be proven by the exclusive means of confessions or admissions. As the international criminal tribunals for the former Yugoslavia and for Rwanda have made clear, "genocidal intent [may] be inferred from the physical acts and specifically 'their massive and/or systematic nature of their atrocity.'" The tribunals have recognized that even "[i]n the absence of a confession from the accused, his intent can be inferred from ... the perpetration of other culpable acts systematically directed against that

196. *Quoted in* Bloxham, *The Armenian Genocide*, at 156–57.

197. *Id.*

198. Bloxham, *The Armenian Genocide*, 152.

199. *Quoted in* Dadrian, *Documentation of the Armenian Genocide*, 99–100.

200. Bloxham, *The Armenian Genocide,* at 152.

201. *Defense Committee Corners Supplies*, N.Y. Times, Sept. 13, 1915, http://www.umd.umich.edu/dept/armenian/facts/islam.html.

202. Bloxham, *The Armenian Genocide,* at 142.

203. Balakian, The Burning Tigris, at 286.

same group, whether these acts were committed by the same offender or by others." Additionally, mixed motives are no defense.[204]

Thus, the element of specific intent to commit genocide may be based upon the testimony of the victims and direct physical evidence, and a confession or admission of genocidal intent is not necessary. Specifically, Ottoman officials' targeting of the Assyrians for massacre, torture, or other violence on a large scale and in diverse contexts proves their specific intent to commit genocide, even without any more evidence.[205] Rapes targeting the Assyrians, and the consequent interference with births within and reproductive survival of the group, also manifested a genocidal intent.[206] The deportation of the Assyrians, and its consequent deprivation of its established means of sustenance, shelter, and dignified living, was a genocidal policy.[207] The dispossession of the Assyrians from their homes and agricultural lands, moreover, inflicted serious mental harm and tended to deprive the Assyrian people of the conditions necessary for bare life, let alone a civilized or dignified life, and therefore served to destroy the group as such.[208] In sum, the "inhuman

---

204. Prosecutor v. Akayesu, Trial Chamber, Judgement, at § 6.3.1, *quoted in* Prosecutor v. Jelisic, Case No. IT-95-10-A, Appeals Chamber, Judgement (July 5, 2001), http://www.un.org/icty/Supplement/supp26-e/jelisic.htm.

205. An inference of genocidal intent is warranted due to "the scale of atrocities committed," and "the general context in which other culpable acts were perpetrated systematically against the same group, regardless of whether such other acts were committed by the same perpetrator or even by other perpetrators." *Id.*

206. *See* Prosecutor v. Akayesu, Trial Chamber, Judgement, at ¶¶ 698–734; Karen Engle, *Feminism and Its (Dis)Contents: Criminalizing Wartime Rape in Bosnia and Herzegovina*, 99 American J. of Int'l Law 791, 791–94 (2005); Rosalind Dixon, *Rape as a Crime in International Law: Where to Go from Here?*, 13 European J. of Int'l Law 703, 703–4 (2002).

207. *See* Prosecutor v. Akayesu, Trial Chamber, Judgement, at ¶¶ 505–08 (actus reus of "deliberate inflicting on the group conditions of life calculated to bring about its physical destruction, in whole or part," includes, among other acts, "systematic expulsion from homes."); Prosecutor v. Blagovjevic and Jokic, Trial Chamber, Judgement, at ¶¶ 647–54 & n.2072 ("”In the decision on the review of the indictment against Karadzic and Mladic pursuant to Rule 61, it is stated that cruel treatment, torture, rape and deportation could constitute serious bodily or mental harm done to members of a group under a count of genocide.... The International Law Commission included 'deportation' and 'forcible transfer of members of the group, particularly when it involves the separation of family members' in this subparagraph [of the Genocide Convention].") (citing Prosecutor v. Radovan Karadzić and Ratko Mladić, Review of the Indictments pursuant to Rule 61 of the Rules of Procedure and Evidence, Case Nos. IT-95-5-R61 and IT-95-18-R61 (July 11, 1996), at ¶ 93); Prosecutor v. Krstic, Trial Chamber, Judgement, at ¶ 513 ("inhuman treatment [...] and deportation are among the acts which may cause serious bodily or mental injury"); Prosecutor v. Musema, Case No. ICTR-97-13-A, Trial Chamber, Judgement and Sentence (Jan. 19, 2000), at ¶ 157 ("The Chamber holds that the means of deliberately inflicting on the group conditions of life calculated to bring about its physical destruction, in whole or in part, include subjecting a group of people to a subsistence diet, systematic expulsion from their homes and deprivation of essential medical supplies below a minimum vital standard."); Prosecutor v. Eichmann, 36 Int'l L. Reports ¶ 199, at 238, 340 (serious bodily or mental harm may result from "enslavement, starvation, deportation and persecution," as well as detention in degrading circumstances, "deprivation of [a people's] rights as human beings, and ... inhumane suffering and torture"). At least two former Soviet republics, Latvia and Estonia, have convicted communist-era officials for genocide based on evidence that they deported members of ethnic or national groups with the intent to destroy the group in part. Lauri Mälksoo, *Soviet Genocide? Communist Mass Deportations in the Baltic States and International Law*, 14 Leiden J. of Int'l L. 774–78, 780 (2001).

208. "Genocide means any of the following acts committed with intent to destroy, in whole or in part, a national, ethnical, racial or religious group, as such: ... (c) Deliberately inflicting on the group conditions of life calculated to bring about its physical destruction in whole or in part...." Genocide Convention, art. II. The phrase "deliberate inflicting on the group conditions of life calculated to

treatment, torture, rape, sexual abuse and deportation" of the Assyrians, along with the "deliberate destruction" of their houses and places of worship, established an intention by Ottoman officials to exterminate them as a group.[209]

D. The Struggle for Recognition of the Assyrian Genocide

In contrast to the Armenian genocide, no U.S. presidents, congressional bodies, or state legislatures have recognized the Assyrian genocide; the United Nations, most European states, and some scholars of the Armenian genocide have also declined to do so.[210] New York governor George Pataki was perhaps the first prominent public official to recognize the Assyrian genocide.[211] The European Parliament followed suit by urging Turkey to recognize the Assyrian and Pontic Greek genocides along with the Armenian genocide, as a step towards coming to terms with its past.[212] Other leaders' reluctance may be due to the more extensive historical documentation of Ottoman confessions and admissions of anti-Armenian extermination policies.[213] Although a great deal of the evidence of genocidal intent deals with Christians more broadly, much of it is specific to the elimination of the Armenian people.[214]

---

bring about its physical destruction, in whole or part," includes, among other acts, "systematic expulsion from homes." Prosecutor v. Akayesu, Trial Chamber, Judgement, at ¶¶ 507–08. International tribunals infer genocidal intent from patterns of such acts which tend to "violate the very foundation of the group." Prosecutor v. Karadžić and Ratko Mladić, Trial Chamber, at ¶ 94. Thus, "attacks on the cultural and religious property and symbols of the targeted group ... may legitimately be considered as evidence of an intent to physically destroy the group." Prosecutor v. Krstić, Trial Chamber, Judgement, at ¶ 580.

209. Prosecutor v. Krstić, Trial Chamber, Judgement, at ¶ 513.

210. Afram Barryakoub, *Academic Conference on Seyfo Held in Sweden,* ZINDA MAG., Nov. 19, 2005, http://www.zindamagazine.com/html/archives/2005/11.19.05/index_sat.php.

211. *See Assyrian Genocide, in* 1 DICTIONARY OF GENOCIDE 24–26 (Samuel Totten, Paul Robert Bartrop, and Steven L. Jacobs eds., Westport, CT: Greenwood Publishing Group, 2008).

212. European Parliament Resolution of 27 September 2006 on Turkey's progress towards accession, ¶ 56, A6-0269/2006, P6_TA(2006)0381, http://www.europarl.europa.eu/sides/getDoc.do?type=TA&reference=P6-TA-2006-0381&language=EN&ring=A6-2006-0269; *EP Report Drops Genocide Clause, Calls for Investigation,* ZAMAN (TURKEY), Sept. 28, 2006, http://www.todayszaman.com/tz-web/detaylar.do?load=detay&link=36881 ("The Turkey report prepared by Dutch parliamentarian Camiel Eurlings was adopted Wednesday at a European Parliament (EP) meeting.... [The report] called for the indirect recognition of the Assyrian and Pontus Greek genocides.... Asserting that the report's references to the Pontus and Assyrian 'genocides' were not calls for genocide recognition, Eurlings stated that they were meant to encourage Turkey to face its past."); *Turkey Says EU Report Smacks of Political Bias,* TURKISH DAILY NEWS, Sept. 6, 2006, http://www.turkishdailynews.com.tr ("Turkey criticized a European Parliament report urging it to recognize an alleged genocide of Armenians at the hands of the late Ottoman Empire to advance its bid to join the European Union.... Bowing to pressure from Greek parliamentarians the document also cited alleged genocides of other communities, namely the Assyrians in southeastern Turkey and Pontus Greeks in the Black Sea region, which is the first time that a European Parliament document refers to such allegations.").

213. As a prominent scholar of the Armenian genocide stated upon being asked whether the Armenian parliament should recognize the Assyrian genocide, "we do not know much about your experience." *Quoted in* Afram Barryakoub, *Academic Conference on Seyfo Held in Sweden.*

214. Vahakn Dadrian has compiled much of the extant evidence of Ottoman admissions of genocidal intent to exterminate the Armenians in particular, although much of this evidence also supports an intention to wipe out or "cleanse" Ottoman Christians more broadly. DADRIAN, THE HISTORY OF

A requirement of a confession or other direct evidence of genocidal intent is not supported by the law, however. The evidence of Ottoman-directed massacres, rapes, deportations, and property expropriations is more than sufficient to establish a pattern of systematic and discriminatory attacks on Assyrians from which a genocidal intent may be inferred.[215] As the tribunal hearing the case of Slobodan Miloševiç held, while direct evidence of genocide is theoretically possible, genocidal intent will more typically be inferred from systematic attacks on or targeting of a group, atrocities on a large scale, or repetitive "destructive and discriminatory acts."[216]

Since 2001, the Turkish Historical Society has published two books advancing several "minimization" and "blame the victim" arguments, all of them nearly identical to arguments made by Holocaust deniers such as David Irving. First, they point out that the Ottoman Empire was at war with the British and Russian Empires, and that the Turks lost millions of men in the war. Second, they cite very low estimates of the Assyrian and Armenian populations derived from Ottoman census data. Third, they claim that the Ottoman Interior Ministry wanted the Christians to be deported to other areas, not killed. And finally, they note that the Assyrians declared war on the Ottoman Empire after the outbreak of massacres, and linked up with Russian and British forces.[217] These arguments

---

The Armenian Genocide, at 219–48; Dadrian, Warrant for Genocide, 85–105, 123–33; Vahakn Dadrian, German Responsibility in the Armenian Genocide: A Review of the Historical Evidence of German Complicity; Dadrian, *Documentation of the Armenian Genocide in German and Austrian Sources*, at 98–101; Vahakn Dadrian, *Documentation of the Armenian Genocide in Turkish Sources, in* 2 Genocide: A Critical Bibliographic Review 86–138 (Israel W. Charny ed., New York: Facts On File, 1991); Dadrian, *The Documentation of the World War I Armenian Massacres in the Proceedings of the Turkish Military Tribunal*; Vakahn Dadrian, *The Secret Young-Turk Ittihadist Conference and the Decision for the World War I Genocide of the Armenians*, 7 Holocaust and Genocide Studies 173–201 (1993); Vahakn Dadrian, *The Turkish Military Tribunal's Prosecution*, at 35, 38–9, 43, 48, 54: 51–2; Vahakn N. Dadrian, *The Naim-Andonian Documents on the World War I Destruction of Ottoman Armenians: The Anatomy of a Genocide*, 18 Int'l J. of Middle East Stud. 311 (1986).

215. The International Criminal Tribunal for Rwanda, for example, found the requisite genocidal intent in a case bearing some similarities to the massacres of Assyrians in northern Mesopotamia and Persia, noting that "explicit manifestations of criminal intent are, for obvious reasons, often rare in the context of criminal trials," and that to "prevent perpetrators from escaping convictions simply because such manifestations are absent, the requisite intent may normally be inferred from relevant facts and circumstances." Prosecutor v. Kayishema and Ruzindana, Appeals Chamber, Judgement, at ¶ 159. The Tribunal found to be adequate evidence of intent the facts that the defendant transported attackers to sites of violent conflict, "directed attackers to kill and offered payment in exchange for the severed heads of well known Tutsis or identification cards of murdered Tutsis," carried weapons, and was believed to be purchasing weapons for attackers. *Id.*, at ¶ 158.

216. Prosecutor v. Milošević, Trial Chamber, Decision on Motion for Judgement of Acquittal, at ¶ 120 (citing Prosecutor v. Jelisić, Appeals Chamber, Judgement, at ¶ 37, and Prosecutor v. Akayesu, Trial Chamber, Judgement, at ¶¶ 698–734).

217. *See, e.g.*, Salâhi Ramadan Sonyel, The Assyrians of Turkey: Victims of Major Power Policy 184–88, 195–97 (Turkish Historical Society Printing House, 2001); Israfil Kurtcephe, *Birinci Dünya Savaşinda bir Süryani Ayaklanmasi*, 1 Osmanli Tarihi Arastirma ve Uygulama Merkezi Dergisi 290 (1993). *See also* David Gaunt, *Assyrian Genocide 1915* (2008), http://www.seyfocenter.se/index.php?sid=2&aID=36 ("Recently the Turkish Historical Society established an Assyrian section. Its first publication also blames the victims and echoes the theme of Assyrian treason.") (citing Bülent Özdemir, Süryanilerin Dünü Bugünü: 1. Dünya Savaş'da Süryaniler (Ankara: Turkish Historical Society Printing House, 2008)); *Assyrian Genocide Claims 'Bogus,' Says Turkish Historian*, The New Anatolian, Dec. 27, 2006, http://www.aina.org/news/20061227125027.htm ("Bulent Ozdemir, head of the Turkish Historical Society's (TTK) Assyrian Studies Section, responded yesterday to a draft report by Dutch Christian Democrat parliamentarian Camiel Eurlings, in which

are frozen in time since the Turkish government's filings with the League of Nations in the 1920s, which made virtually identical points.[218]

The abundant evidence recited above of massacres in conjunction with or instead of deportations or expulsions puts these claims to rest. First, the fact that the Ottoman Empire was as war with Britain and Russia is totally irrelevant, for Nazi Germany was at war with these same powers at the height of the Holocaust, which was no excuse for its genocide against Jews and others. Genocide nearly inevitably occurs during a backdrop of war or insurgency, which motivates empires and nation-states to eliminate minority populations during aggressive wars or counterinsurgency operations. The examples are legion, but they include, most notably, the coincidence of the Holocaust with Nazi aggression and anti-partisan warfare, the links between the Bosnian and Kosovar Albanian insurgencies and the genocide against these peoples, the invasion of Rwanda and related war crimes by the Rwandan Patriotic Front in 1993, and rebel attacks on government installations in the lead-up to the southern Sudan and Darfur genocides.

Second, efforts to ascribe low numbers of Assyrian survivors in the Republic of Turkey after 1925 by referencing unreasonably low census figures do not hold water. In an attempt to minimize Assyrian casualties, historians linked to the Turkish Historical Society or the Institute for Turkish Studies give estimates of the Assyrian population of the Ottoman Empire of 144,000 to 250,000.[219] But the Ottoman population estimates after the 1870s are even lower, giving from zero to 35,000 Assyrians (Nestorians), or perhaps 83,000 including Catholics.[220]

As with the Armenian population, Western estimates of the Assyrian population are far higher. In 1859, Western travelers estimated that there were 400,000 non-Armenian, non-Greek Christians in Anatolia, Syria, and Mesopotamia, including Nestorians, Chaldeans, and Jacobites.[221] The British Consul estimated in 1869 that 100,000 Assyrians lived in Erzerum vilayet alone, along with 110,000 in Van.[222] Earlier, the British Consul for Erzerum and Diyarbekir, J.G. Taylor, who traveled throughout eastern Anatolia in

---

she asserted that Turkey should accept Pontic Greek and Assyrian genocide claims, in addition to those by Armenians.... [She added:] They chose a side in the war and combat occurred under the rules of war.").

218. *See Question of the Frontier Between Turkey and Iraq*, 6 League of Nations Official J. 1437–38 (1925).

219. *See* Sonyel, The Assyrians of Turkey, at 12; Justin McCarthy: Muslims and Minorities: The Population of Ottoman Anatolia and the End of the Empire 105, 110 (New York: NYU Press, 1983).

220. *Compare* Osmanli İmparatorluğu'nun ve Türkiye'nin Nüfusu: 1500–1927 [The Population of the Ottoman Empire and Turkey] 40–41, 46 (Cem Behar ed., Ankara, Turkey: State Institute of Statistics, 1996) (official Ottoman figures for 1885 and 1897 estimated populations of 989,000 to 1,042,000 Armenian Orthodox-Gregorian, 120,000 to 150,000 Armenian and other Catholics, and zero Assyrians-Nestorians), *with* Kemal H. Karpat, Ottoman Population 1830–1914: Demographic and Social Characteristics 192–93 (Madison, WI: Univ. of Wisconsin Press, 1985) (official Ottoman figures for 1881 and 1893 estimated populations of 500,000 to 538,000 Armenian Orthodox-Gregorian, 67,000 to 83,000 Armenian and other Catholics, and zero Assyrians-Nestorians), *and* Karpat, Ottoman Population, at 194–195 (official Ottoman figures for 1880 estimated there were 35,000 Assyrians, i.e. Nestorians, Chaldeans, Jacobite Syrians, and Syrian Catholics).

221. *See* Thomas Milner, The Ottoman Empire: The Sultans, the Territory, and the People 296, 312 (London: The Religious Tract Soc., 1799) (citing Abdolonyme Ubicini, Lettres sur la Turquie, ou, Tableau Statistique, Religieux, Politique, Administratif, Militaire, Commercial, etc. de l'Empire Ottoman 22 (Paris: Librarie Militaire de J. Dumaine, 2d ed. 1853)).

222. Turkey No. 16, Mar. 19, 1869, pp. 16–36 & Inclosure 1, nos. 13 & 13/1, Consul J.G. Taylor to G.W.F. Villiers, the 4th Earl of Clarendon and British Secretary of State for Foreign Affairs, *in* 1 British Documents on Ottoman Armenians (1856–1880), at 54, 63, 67.

1866, estimated that 1.15 million Armenians lived in the *vilayets* of Van, Erzerum, and Bitlis, along with 110,000 Assyrians (or Nestorians).[223] The British Vice-Consul in Van, Henry Trotter, credited estimates in 1879 of two million Armenians (as opposed to Ottoman estimates of as few as 550,000) and up to 500,000 Assyrians (Nestorians).[224] Consul Trotter, a "very highly regarded consul" for the British Empire in eastern Anatolia, estimated that 259,600 Assyrians (Nestorians and other Eastern Christians) lived in just the *vilayets* of Van, Diyarbekir, Erzerum, and Harput.[225] The Syrian Orthodox Church (*syrienne ancienne Orthodoxe en Mesopotamie et en Armenie*) probably had 150,000 to 200,000 members, as it claimed 90,000 dead in 1915–1918 alone.[226] Estimates of Assyrians in Persia reached 40,000 by 1873, and likely increased thereafter.[227]

By the late 1890s, therefore, it seems reasonable to assume an Ottoman and Persian Assyrian population of 650,000 to 750,000, given population growth of 25% in the 20 years from 1859 to 1879 and again from 1879 to 1899.[228] One must deduct several thousand from these totals due to the Hamidiye massacres described below, which still leaves well over 600,000. This is in fact the estimate adopted by leading Ottomanist Donald Bloxham.[229]

The discrepancy with the official census figures is readily explained. First, the census only counted adult males.[230] More importantly, the majority Turkish population, and in

---

223. F.O. 424/107, Sept. 7, 1880, pp. 107–179, no. 104/3, Inclosure 3, Consul Trotter to G.J. Groschen, Special Ambassador to the Sublime Porte, *in* 2 British Documents on Ottoman Armenians (1880–1890), at 131, 134.

224. F.O. 424/106, 1879, Vice-Consul Emilius Clayton's Report on Reforms in Van, *in* 1 British Documents on Ottoman Armenians (1856–1880), at 645–46 (Bĭlâl Şĭmşĭr ed., 1980).

225. *See, e.g.*, Kemal H. Karpat, The Politicization of Islam: Reconstructing Identity, State, Faith, and Community in the Late Ottoman State 210 (Oxford: Oxford UP, 2001).

226. *See* Archevéché Syrien de Syrie, *Liste des dommages que la nation ienne ancienne Orthodoxe en Mesopotamie et Armenie, a subit pendent la guerre en 1915–1918, in* De Courtois, The Forgotten Genocide, at 336. Nineteenth-century sources put the Syrian Orthodox (or "Jacobite") Church at about 200,000 members, mostly in the Tur Abdin, Mardin, Urfa, and Gawar areas. *See* De Courtois, The Forgotten Genocide, at 78 (citing Oswald H. Parry, Six Months in a Syrian Monastery vi (Piscataway, NJ: Gorgias Press, 2004) (1895)).

227. *See* Aboona, Assyrians, Kurds, and Ottomans, at 46 (citing Rufus Anderson, 2 History of the Missions of the American Board of Commission for Foreign Missions to the Oriental Churches 208 (Boston: Congregational Publishing Society, 1873); Asahel Grant, The Nestorians, or the Lost Tribes, 49, 127–128 (New York and London, 1841)). The Nestorian pastor Pera Johannes, with the Evangelical Lutheran mission institution in Persia, estimated in 1908 that there were 100,000 Assyrians in Persia. *See* Yonan, Lest We Perish, at 63–65.

228. As noted above, the Ottoman census and Armenian patriarchate's figures reflect population growth of 20% every 20 years to be reasonable. In the Soviet Union, the population of the Armenian republic nearly doubled in one 20-year period. *See* Republic of Armenia, National Statistical Service, *A Brief Historical Review of the Censuses Conducted Previously in Armenia*; IATP-Armenia, *The Number of Men and Women in Armenia (Table 3)* (2003). By way of further comparison, the population of Iraq increased by nearly 75% between the censuses of 1947 and 1965, from 4.8 to 8 million. *See Iraq: A Country Study*, http://countrystudies.us/iraq/25.htm. Turkey's population increased by nearly 40% from 1927 to 1945, and by nearly 50% from 1945 to 1965. *See* Cevat Geray, *Urbanization Im Turkey* (1965), http://dergiler.ankara.edu.tr/dergiler/42/435/8751.pdf; WHKMLA, *Turkey 1960–1971* (2007), http://www.zum.de/whkmla/region/asmin/turkey19601971.html (citing International Historical Statistics : Africa, Asia & Oceania 1750–2000 (B.R. Mitchell ed., Basingstoke: Palgrave MacMillan, 4th ed. 2003)); *Turkey: A Country Study* (Helen Chapin Metz ed., 1995), http://countrystudies.us/turkey/24.htm.

229. *See* Bloxham, Great Game of Genocide, at 98 ("In total, the victims of outright massacre, wartime privation, and a few deportation marches, reach perhaps 250,000 of a pre-war Anatolian and Persian Assyro-Chaldean population of up to 619,000 people.").

230. *See* Karpat, Ottoman Population 1830–1914, at 192 n.8; Marashlian, Politics and Demography, at 36.

particular the chauvinistic Turks of Abdul Hamid's time, had an obvious incentive to minimize minority population figures in order to deny self-government and equal rights to substantial non-Turkish Christian minorities. Assyrians and other Christians, for their part, had every reason to avoid registering for possible conscription in a war against other Christians in the British or Russian empires, not to mention in lost causes like the occupation of the Balkans, Arabia, or Africa. Moreover, the Ottoman census figures lack corroboration in either other Ottoman censuses or Western estimates, in contrast to the mutually-reinforcing figures provided by representatives of ethnic and religious minorities such as the Armenian and Assyrian churches[231] and the European travelers who conducted population surveys prior to 1914.

Third, the narrative of a humane "relocation" policy is refuted by the massacres and rapes, destruction of houses and churches, and other wanton atrocities. As numerous German, Austrian, U.S., and British diplomats pointed out at the time, the manner in which the "deportations" were carried out made them a death sentence due to hunger, disease, rape, and massacres of deportation convoys. If only relocations were planned, moreover, why did the Ottomans execute their own officials who resisted the deportation orders, for why would officials resist a mere relocation order to such a point?[232] Why was the provision of aid to Assyrian and other Christian populations banned?[233] Why were Kurds and other Muslims threatened with executions under military law for sheltering Christians, and a Kurdish chief killed for trying to save an elderly Chaldean priest?[234] Why would Mustafa Kemal condemn the CUP for "nefarious acts of deportation and massacre"?[235] And why did an Ottoman military commander describe "thousands of half-nude and still bleeding corpses" after a "massacre" of "Nestorians"?[236]

Turning to sources from outside Ottoman officialdom, why did German officials repeatedly condemn the Ottoman officials implementing the humane relocation policy, the *valis* of Diyarbekir, Erzerum, Van, and Mosul, respectively Rashid Bey, Taschin Bey, Djevdet Bey, and Haidar Bey, as well as Third Army commander General Kalil Paşa and Army Group East commander Halil Bey, as ruthless killers of civilians?[237] Why did U.S.

---

231. For example, the Armenian patriarch estimated around 1880 that nearly 87,000 Assyrians ("Syriens-Nestoriens" in French) lived in Van province alone, which nearly equals McCarthy's count for Nestorians, Chaldeans, and Jacobites in the entire Ottoman Empire. *See* Şĭmşĭr, *Introduction, in* 2 British Documents on Ottoman Armenians, at 433. In 1912, the Armenian patriarch of Istanbul estimated that there were 60,000 "Syrians" (Nestorians, Chaldeans, and Jacobites) living in Diyarbekir province, which already puts the Assyrians over McCarthy's limit without getting into Mosul, Aleppo, Harput, Bitlis, or other *vilayets. See* Mesrob K. Krikorian, Armenians in the Service of the Ottoman Empire, 1860–1908, at 20 (London: Routledge, 1978).

232. El-Ghussein, Martyred Armenia, at 40.

233. *See* BOA.DH.SFR 46/78, Oct. 26, 1914, Ministry of the Interior to Van vilayet, *quoted in* Gaunt, Massacres, Resistance, Protectors, at 446–47 (prohibiting government from providing "any type of support" to Assyrians). *Cf.* Bloxham, The Great Game of Genocide, at 88–90 (government refused to make provision for deportees).

234. *Quoted in* BOA.DH.SFR 54787, June 21, 1915, *cited in* Gaunt, *Ottoman Bystanders*, at 30. *See also* Gaunt, Massacres, Resistance, Protectors, at 253–56, 436–37; The Treatment of Armenians, at 120; *Armenians' Heroic Stand in Mountains*, N.Y. Times, Nov. 27, 1915, at 4.

235. *Quoted in* Akcam, From Empire to Republic, at 194.

236. De Nogales, Four Years Beneath the Crescent, at 123–25 (Assyrians "after brave resistance, were turned out of their domiciles by the Vali from Mosul, Haidar Bey, and annihilated in part").

237. *See* DE/PA-AA/BoKon/169, A53a/1915/3922, June 26, 1915, telegraphic report from the German Consul in Erzerum, Scheubner-Richter, to the German Embassy in Constantinople (Kalil Pasha's order to deport all Armenians was illegitimate and founded on "racial hatred" [*Rassenhaß*]); DE/PA-AA/BoKon/169, A53a/1915/4184, No. 8, July 10, 1915, telegraphic report from the German Vice-

and British leaders believe that there were millions of starving Ottoman Christians, and thousands of rape victims, even to the extent of funding their relief to the tune of $100 million,[238] if the relocations were so humane and respectful of civilian life?

Consul in Mosul, Holstein, to the German Embassy in Constantinople (Rashid Bey "rages like a mad blood-hound among the Christians of his vilayet," and has "slaughtered them like sheep"); DE/PA-AA/BoKon/169, A53a/1915/4257, July 15, 1915, telegraphic report from the German Vice-Consul in Mosul, Holstein, to the German Embassy in Constantinople (describing how entire population of Faysh Khabour in vilayet Diyarbekir, made up exclusively of Chaldean Assyrians, was massacred); DE/PA-AA/BoKon/169, A53a/1915/4262, July 16, 1915, telegraphic report from the German Vice-Consul in Mosul, Holstein, to the German Embassy in Constantinople (describing massacres under the authority of vali of Diyarbekir); DE/PA-AA/BoKon/169, A53a/1915/4352, July 21, 1915, telegraphic report from the German Vice-Consul in Mosul, Holstein, to the German Embassy in Constantinople (describing arrival of 1,200 women and children, Armenians, Assyrians, and Chaldeans, whose husbands were "massacred" in Seert, Mardin, and Faysh Khabour); DE/PA-AA/BoKon/170, A53a/1915/4429, July 28, 1915, telegraphic report from the German Vice-Consul in Mosul, Holstein, to the German Embassy in Constantinople (condemning the vali of Diyarbekir for "extreme" persecutions that prompted a Christian rebellion to "save their skins" [*welche sich ihrer Haut wehren*]); DE/PA-AA/R14094, 1916-A-33457, No. 477, July 31, 1915, telegram from the German Ambassador on Extraordinary Mission in Constantinople, Hohenlohe-Langenburg, to the German Imperial Chancellor, Bethmann Hollweg (Rashid Bey systematically exterminating Christians in his vilayet regardless of denomination); DE/PA-AA/R14087, 1915-A-25335, Aug. 11, 1915, report from the German Consul in Aleppo, Rössler, to the German Embassy in Constantinople (in the vicinity of Urfa, "two of the [CUP's] emissaries, Halil and Ahmed Bey, are running a reign of terror"); DE/PA-AA/R14087; R14095, 1915-A-28019, Sept. 3, 1915, report from the German Consul in Aleppo, Röessler, to the German Imperial Chancellor, Bethmann Hollweg ("Apart from the Armenians, not only the Nestorians, but also Ancient Syrians (Jacobites), Catholic Syrians (Syrians) and other Christians have also been deported in the eastern provinces. For a longer period of time it has been indicated here that such Christians were also killed."); ("The Chaldeans in Söird (Vilayet Bitlis) and Djeziret ibn Omar (Vilayet Diarbekir) and all of the Christians in Djebel et Tor north of Mardin have been exterminated"); DE/PA-AA/BoKon/171, DuA Dok. 190 (re.), Nov. 4, 1915, telegraphic report from the German Vice Consul in Mosul, Holstein, to the German Embassy in Constantinople ("Halil Bey arrived here yesterday with his staff.... A colonel from his staff just informed me that the Armenians in Mosul must also be massacred and it is his intention to do so. He will not be prevented from doing so, not even by me.... It is imperative that immediate and very forceful orders be sent to Halil Bey to prevent further massacres at all events."); DE/PA-AA/R14089, DuA Dok. 209 (gk.), Dec. 7, 1915, report from the German Ambassador in Extraordinary Mission in Constantinople, Wolff-Metternich, to the German Imperial Chancellor, Bethmann Hollweg ("I have seriously discussed the Armenian atrocities during the course of the past week with Enver Pasha, with Halil Bey and today with Djemal Pasha and pointed out ... that unless these atrocities are stopped," Germany and other foreign countries might withdraw their support from Turkey, while "Colonel von Kress, Djemal's Chief of Staff, tells me that the misery simply defies every description and transcends all accounts. At the same time, rumour has it that the Germans actually wanted these massacres."); DE/PA-AA/BoKon/99, 10/12/1916/2934, Jan. 1, 1916, report from the German Ambassador in Extraordinary Mission in Constantinople, Wolff-Metternich, to the German Imperial Chancellor, Bethmann Hollweg ("Turkish police, gendarmes and soldiers were involved in killing those who were resettled, partly upon the orders of their superiors and partly without any authorisation. In this respect, the Vali of Diyarbekir, Reshid Bey, the Vali of Erzurum, Tachsin Bey, the Chief of Police in Erzurum, Chulussi Bey, and a certain Machmud Kiamil Pasha are particularly heavily incriminated."); DE/PA-AA/R14094, DuA doc. 309, Dec. 4, 1916, report from the German Administrator in Erzerum, Scheubner-Richter, to the German Imperial Chancellor, Bethmann Hollweg ("the Nestorians in eastern Kurdistan, after brave resistance, were turned out of their domiciles by the Vali from Mosul, Haidar Bey, and annihilated in part"). *See also* De Nogales, Four Years Beneath the Crescent, at 123–25 (Assyrians "after brave resistance, were turned out of their domiciles by the Vali from Mosul, Haidar Bey, and annihilated in part"); Hoffman, *German Eyewitness Reports of the Genocide of the Armenians, 1915–16, in* The Crime of Silence: The Armenian Genocide, at 105 (Djevdet Bey "crossed into Persia and massacred the Assryo-Chaldeans").

238. *See* Peterson, "Starving Armenians," at 149. *See also* Balakian, The Burning Tigris, at 289, Suzanne Moranian, *The Armenian Genocide and American Missionary Relief Efforts, in* America

Finally, evidence of Assyrian resistance to genocidal assaults also prove nothing, for the Jews of Europe also engaged in armed uprisings in Poland, Lithuania, Byelorussia, Ukraine, Yugoslavia, France, and Greece, some linking up with French, Polish, Yugoslav, and Soviet Red Army forces. Of course, numerous American, British, French, Polish, and Soviet Jews also fought the Nazis in the armed forces of their respective countries. Much more difficult than uncovering evidence of resistance to genocide is trying to name a genocide that was *not* resisted, from Carthage through European colonialism to Darfur. The same governments of Turkey, the U.S., and Britain that deny the Assyrian genocide, as well as Turkish "historians" who take the same line, call the experience of Bosnian and Kosovar Muslims during the Yugoslav civil wars "genocide" even though these groups fielded large armies and linked up with international terrorist groups.[239] Recalling Chapter III, Britain, Turkey, and the U.S. accused the Serbs of "genocide" in Kosovo even though probably fewer than 20,000 Kosovars died, and the percentage of the population of the Federal Republic of Yugoslavia that was Albanian may have increased, in stark contrast to the Ottoman Empire and Turkey after 1914.[240]

Aside from such denialist chicanery and related quibbles about the sufficiency of the documentary evidence, the Assyrians may have struggled unsuccessfully to achieve recognition of their experience of genocide because fewer absolute numbers of them survived the Ottoman genocide of Christians than did the Armenians. As a smaller population, the Assyrians suffered fewer total deaths than the Armenians, failed to win statehood after World War I as the Armenians did, and did not mount similarly ambitious and effective lobbying efforts. The worldwide Armenian population stands at an estimated nine to ten million people, substantially more than the estimated four million Assyrians living around the world.[241] The three million Armenians living in and controlling the state of Armenia substantially outnumber the 550,000 Assyrians living in but largely excluded from political power in their traditional Mesopotamian homeland.[242] The estimated one million Armenians living in the U.S., concentrated in southern California, also exercise dramatically more political clout than the 350,000 marginalized Assyrians living in central California, Michigan, and Illinois.[243] As a result, more states have recognized the Armenian

---

AND THE ARMENIAN GENOCIDE OF 1915, at 197–200 (listing multi-million dollar cash and in-kind contributions of U.S. and U.K.).

239. *Compare, e.g.*, SONYEL, THE ASSYRIANS OF TURKEY, *with* SALÂHI RAMADAN SONYEL, THE MUSLIMS OF BOSNIA: GENOCIDE OF A PEOPLE 10 (The Islamic Foundation, 1994).

240. *Compare, e.g., Serbia and Montenegro, in* WORLD FACTBOOK 1997, http://www.umsl.edu/services/govdocs/wofact97/216.htm (14% ethnic Albanian), *with Serbia and Montenegro, in* WORLD FACTBOOK 2000, http://www.umsl.edu/services/govdocs/wofact2000/geos/sr.html (16.5% Albanian).

241. Summary Record of the 1530th Meeting, Committee on the Elimination of all Forms of Racial Discrimination (Aug. 14, 2002), CERD/C/SR.1530, http://www.unhchr.ch/tbs/doc.nsf/0/81d55fc0366b053cc1256c17002f1a16/%24FILE/G0243887.doc; Lyden, *Despite Turmoil, Christians Place Faith in New Iraq*; Sabrina Tavernise, *In a Muslim City in Iraq, a Christian Group Enjoys Its Lively Quarter*, N.Y. TIMES, May 23, 2003, at A2.

242. *Compare Armenia, in* WORLD FACTBOOK 2006, http://www.cia.gov/cia/publications/factbook/geos/am.html, *with* USDOS, 2008 INTERNATIONAL RELIGIOUS FREEDOM REPORT—IRAQ, http://www.state.gov/g/drl/rls/irf/2008/108483.htm (estimated 550,000 Assyrians in Iraq in 2008). *See also* UNREPRESENTED NATIONS AND PEOPLES ORGANIZATION: YEARBOOK 1997, at 44 (3.3 million Assyrians were dispersed among 30 countries outside Middle East by mid-1990s, compared to only 2.5 million in Middle East, including hundreds of thousands of refugees in Syria, Jordan, and Lebanon).

243. Michael Mainville, *Armenian Angst; Poverty, Corruption Spur Sense of Powerlessness*, WASH. TIMES, Sept. 14, 2005, at A15. "An estimated 350,000 Assyrians have migrated to the United States, many of them concentrated in the Turlock-Modesto-Ceres [California] areas and in Detroit and Chicago." California Assembly Joint Resolution No. 31—Relative to Assyrians in Iraq (Apr. 23, 2003), http://info.sen.ca.gov.

genocide than the Assyrian genocide, and the resolutions of Congress on genocide in the Ottoman Empire mention only Armenians.

E. Cultural and Political Legacies of the Assyrian Genocide

Scholars have drawn a number of analogies between the experience of the Ottoman Christians during World War I, and other acknowledged genocides such as the Holocaust of Jews, Slavs, Roma people, and leftists under Nazi occupation during World War II.[244] The Assyrians and other Ottoman Christians, like the Jews and Roma, had suffered from centuries of discrimination and official segregation; were charged with being agents of foreign powers and scapegoated for military defeats and looming threats in a rhetoric of ethnic elimination; and were physically and culturally exterminated in large numbers by massacres, rapes, expulsions, and attacks on homes and religious institutions carried out by genocidal state apparatuses and local irregular forces.[245] Just as in Nazi Germany the Holocaust reached its full expression only after the invasion of Poland and the world war with Britain and the Soviet Union, so in the Ottoman Empire the genocide of Christian populations reached its most intense phase after the outbreak of war with Britain and Russia and the Ottoman invasion of northern Persia.[246]

Although the primary blame for the genocide of the Assyrians lies with the Ottoman officials who authored and distributed the proclamation of holy war, massacred civilians and outraged women, and instigated their Kurdish and Persian allies to do the same, the West bears a heavy responsibility. After the Hamidiye massacres and during World War I, the Germans played the role of the Christian ally of the Ottomans, actually encouraging the Sultan to declare a *jihad* against the Christian allies of the British, who became enemies of the Turks.[247]

As the West, and the world in general, becomes more familiar with the history of the Armenians, Assyrians, and other victims of genocide, the prospects may improve for the future prevention of such events. This chapter has demonstrated that the Ottoman genocide of the Assyrians followed centuries of violent persecution of the Assyrians by Turkish and Kurdish rulers, that it intensified after the outbreak of international war against Western Christian nations, and that it was implemented by Ottoman troops and their local militia allies via massacre, systematic rape, deportation, the destruction of homes and villages, and cultural annihilation.

---

244. Power, "A Problem from Hell," at 47; Barry A. Fisher, *No Roads Lead to Rom: The Fate of the Romani People under the Nazis and in Post-War Restitution*, 20 Whittier L. Rev. 513 (1999).

245. For a fairly comprehensive account of this pattern in Nazi-occupied Europe, see Shirer, The Rise and Fall of the Third Reich, at 872–78, 1223–92.

246. Bloxham, *The Armenian Genocide*, at 189; William A. Schabas, *Darfur and the 'Odious Scourge': The Commission of Inquiry's Findings on Genocide*, 18 Leiden J. of Int'l Law 875 (2005).

247. *See* Frederick Jones Bliss, *The Ottoman Empire, 1801–1913 [Review]*, 19 American Hist. Rev. 356 (1914).

Chapter VIII

"A Virgin Field": The Genocide of the Anatolian Greeks

> Quietly and gradually the same treatment is being meted out to the Greeks as to the Armenians and Syrians.... Along with the Armenians most of the Greeks of the Marmora regions and Thrace have been deported on the pretext that they gave information to the enemy.
>
> —Frank Jackson, Chairman of the Relief Committee for Greeks of Asia Minor[1]

A. The Greeks and the Turks in Anatolia and Its Environs

Prior to their conquests by Turkic peoples, the ancient Greeks inhabited not only the present-day country of Greece but also many surrounding territories in Anatolia (Turkey), northern Epirus (southern Albania), Magna Graecia (southern Italy), and Krimeia (southern Ukraine). Under international law, these Greeks' were the indigenous people of these areas, living there "before [other] settlers moved in as a result of conquest, occupation, colonization, etc.," endangering their "livelihoods and very existence."[2]

The ancient Greek historian Strabo described Smyrna, present-day Izmir on the western coast of Anatolia, as "'the finest city in Asia'" with paved streets, a temple, library, and gymnasium. Smyrna was a center of learning and philosophy to rival Ephesus, and Saint Paul preached Christianity in Greek to these and other cities. In a little over three centuries, Smyrna was destroyed three times: first by Seljuk Turks, then by Persians, then by the Turkic-speaking Mongols under Tamerlane.[3] Other prominent Greek cities in western Anatolia included Nicaea, Ephesus, Pergamos, Sardis, Colophon, Philadelphia, and Chalcedon.[4]

1. Press Association, *Greek Persecution in Turkey,* The Scotsman (U.K.), Nov. 6, 1917, at 5.

2. El Hadji Guissé, *Working Paper on Globalization and the Economic, Social and Cultural Rights of Indigenous Populations,* U.N. Doc. No. E/CN.4/Sub.2/2003/22, ¶ 2 (June 15, 2003), http://www.unhchr.ch; Martinez Cobo, *Study of the Problem against Indigenous Populations, vol. 5, Conclusions, Proposals and Recommendations,* U.N. Doc. No. E/CN/4/Sub 2/1986/7 Add 4, at 379; Pritchard, *Working Group on Indigenous Populations,* at 43; Luis Rodríguez-Piñero, Indigenous Peoples, Postcolonialism, and International Law: The ILO Regime (1919–1989), at 163 (Oxford: Oxford UP, 2005).

3. Dobkin, Smyrna, at 22.

4. An Abridgement of Universal Geography: Modern and Ancient 465–68 (Adriano Balbi & Thomas Gamaliel Bradford eds., New York: Freeman Hunt & Co., 1835).

The Greeks historically referred to the Black Sea, which borders Turkey, Russia, Ukraine, and a few smaller countries, as the "Pontus Euxinus" or "hospitable sea."[5] Greeks settled its shores and navigated its expanses starting in about the eighth century BCE.[6] The principal Greek cities on the Black Sea were Trebizond (Trabzon), Samsous (Samsun), Sinope (Sinop) and Pontica Heraclea (modern Karadeniz Ereğli). Trebizond was the most legendary among these, as an ancient trading center with a road southeast to Mesopotamia and Persia, and southwest to the Aegean and Mediterranean seas. Trade with the Far East reached the Mediterranean via Trebizond by transport over land through Afghanistan, Persia, and Mesopotamia.[7] In medieval times, Trebizond remained a commercial metropolis that thrived on the import-export trade between Europe and Persia, India, and China.

Prior to becoming the capital of the Eastern Roman Empire, the port of Constantinople served as a way-station between Europe, Africa, and Asia. As a geopolitical fulcrum, the Black Sea region surrounding Constantinople has witnessed the passage of ancient and modern empires from Xerxes and Alexander to Churchill, Hitler, and Stalin.

The Ottoman Empire claimed Greece in the fourteenth century CE. Upon conquering Greek cities like Thessalonica, the Ottomans sold the Greek inhabitants into chattel slavery, converted churches into mosques, and appropriated the prime real estate for themselves.[8] The Greek commercial metropolis of Trebizond in Anatolia became a "desolat[e]" place under Turkish rule.[9] The island of Cyprus, rich in agricultural capacity and mineral resources, was poor and sparsely populated as an Ottoman possession.[10]

Poverty and desolation were the fate of many cities falling under Ottoman jurisdiction, as over-taxation, corruption, and mismanagement transformed once prosperous cities such as Baghdad into collections of hovels and dilapidated ruins.[11] The American author Mark Twain, touring the Ottoman Empire around 1900, described Ottoman Greece, Syria, and Palestine as impoverished, unproductive, desolate, and "ground down" by Ottoman taxation and corruption.[12] In 1919, Lord George Curzon, a top British official and lead negotiator at the Paris Peace Conference, summed up the result in Europe: "The presence of the Turks in Europe has been a source of unmitigated evil to everybody

---

5. Heinz Heinen, *Greeks, Iranians and Romans on the Northern Shore of the Black Sea, in* North Pontic Archaeology: Recent Discoveries and Studies 1 (Gocha R. Tsetskhladze ed., Boston: Brill, 2001).

6. *See id.* at 4.

7. Edward Gibbon, 7 A History of the Decline and Fall of the Roman Empire 17, 23, 69–70 (J.B. Bury ed., London: Metheun Publishers, 1900).

8. Phillip Mansel, *Jerusalem on the Aegean,* The Spectator, Oct. 30, 2004, at 48; Mark Mazower, Salonica: The City of Ghosts: Christians, Muslims and Jews, 1430–1950, ch. 1 (New York: Knopf, 2005).

9. *See, e.g., Desolation at Trebizond,* N.Y. Times, Apr. 22, 1883, at 6.

10. *Cyprus, in* A Dictionary of Greek and Roman Geography 86–87 (William Smith ed., London: Spottiswoodes & Shaw, 1854).

11. *See, e.g.,* George Percy Badger, The Nestorians And Their Rituals: With the Narrative of a Mission to Mesopotamia and Coordistan in 1842–44, at 79 (London: Joseph Masters, 1852); Austen Henry Layard, A Popular Account of Discoveries at Nineveh 22–23 (New York: Harper & Bros., 1852); *Bagdad and Its People,* The Argus (Australia), Dec. 11, 1915, at 8; *Baghdad (Saturday Review),* Brisbane Courier (Australia), Nov. 28, 1885, at 9; *British Found Bagdad in Ruins,* Boston Daily Globe, June 17, 1917, at 20.

12. Mark Twain, Innocents Abroad: Or, The New Pilgrim's Progress 16–17, 26, 116, 290–92, 443 (Leipzig: Bernhard Tauchnitz, 1879).

concerned. I am not aware of a single interest, Turkish or otherwise, that during nearly 500 years has benefited by that presence."[13] (Of course, he did not foresee World War II and the Holocaust, during which the Germans, Croatians, and their allies engaged in the mass murder of Jews, Slavs, and Roma people who had survived Ottoman rule in Greece and the Balkans[14]).

The Byzantine Greeks, weakened by Western European Crusaders who looted and destroyed their cities, lost their independence to Ottoman invasions.[15] During the fourteenth and fifteenth centuries CE, the Ottoman Turks, originally Central Asian nomads and raiders, conquered northwestern Anatolia and the Balkans, and occupied nearly all Greek cities and islands including the ancient Greco-Roman capital of Constantinople. The descendent of one of the Seljuk conquerors of eastern Anatolia, Utmân or Osman I, led a Turkish holy-war or *ghaza* emirate in the early fourteenth century CE. His successor Orkhan brought about the nearly complete conquest of the Christian Byzantines in Anatolia, leaving them only Constantinople and Trebizond. Very few Greeks were not under Turkish rule after the late fifteenth century, while very few Turks ever fell under Greek dominion except for brief periods.[16]

Under Orkhan, the Turks began to colonize Europe in large numbers, with "a great deal of massacre, deportation and plunder; Europe became a field for the ghazis to practice their profession of holy warfare as they had done in Asia." Orkan's successor Murâd I declared himself Sultan and established a large foothold in Europe by conquering Adrianople, Thessaloniki, Bulgaria, and Serbia.[17] In one of the last crusades, Murâd defeated an army organized out of Burgundy, which hoped to be relieved in its campaign to defend Serbia, Hungary, and Austria by the English, French, and Teutonic armies (the latter was distracted by its campaign to seize Polish and Lithuanian lands).[18]

After a period of vulnerability typified by this final crusade and the ravages of Timur in Anatolia, the Ottomans resumed their expansion under Murâd II.[19] Murâd liquidated potential challengers to his Sultanate and instituted the *devshirme* (captured) system of enslaving Christian boys and young men, mainly from Europe, to be raised as soldiers and imperial officials.[20] More than 200,000 Christians passed through the *devshirme* system over the next 250 years, leaving their communities smaller and defenseless. The Ottoman Turks also selected Christian women for their households.[21] The system removed some of the most promising Greek breadwinners and community leaders out of their cultural

---

13. Margaret MacMillan, Paris 1919: Six Months that Changed the World 373 (New York: Random House, 2003).

14. Mansel, *Jerusalem on the Aegean,* at 48

15. Charles Howland, *Greece and Her Refugees*, 4 Foreign Affairs 614, 619 (1926).

16. *See* George Holmes, Europe: Hierarchy and Revolt, 1320–1450, at 167 (London: Wiley-Blackwell, 2d ed. 2000) (1975); Arnold Toynbee, The Western Question in Greece and Turkey: A Study in the Contact of Civilizations 265–70 (New York: Houghton Mifflin, 1922).

17. *See* Holmes, Europe, Hierarchy and Revolt, 1320–1450, at 172.

18. *See* Jonathan Riley-Smith, The Oxford Illustrated History of the Crusades 276–335 (Oxford: Oxford UP, 2001); Lucien Gubbay, Sunlight and Shadow: The Jewish Experience of Islam, at 96–97.

19. *See* Holmes, Europe, Hierarchy and Revolt, 1320–1450, at 172–76.

20. *See* Gubbay, Sunlight and Shadow, at 96–97.

21. *See* Speros Vryonis, The Decline of Medieval Hellenism in Asia Minor: and the Process of Islamization from the Eleventh Through the Fifteenth Century 175, 241–43 (Berkeley: Univ. of California Press, 1971). In a sign of his abjectly hagiographic attitude towards the Ottoman Empire, Bernard Lewis describes these child-slaves as being "recruited." Bernard Lewis, Istanbul and the Civilization of the Ottoman Empire 87 (Tulsa: Univ. of Oklahoma Press, 1972).

context, sending them to serve instead under the Sultan and his elite troops, the Janissaries. Greeks viewed the process as an organized kidnapping of their children and youth.[22]

Mehmet II, son of Murâd II, led the siege of Constantinople and fusion of the European and Asian portions of the Ottoman Empire into a continuous expanse.[23] In the fifteenth century, an army of 258,000 Turks under Mehmet II slaughtered many Greek civilians during the three-day sack of Constantinople and mass rape of its women.[24] The Ottoman Sultan seized half of the city's churches for conversion into mosques, appropriated the Christians' other properties and religious endowments, and banned Christianity outside private homes and churches. The Ottoman armies moved on, ravaging the city of Trebizond and invading Europe, soon reaching Belgrade but halted there by reinforcements from neighboring lands.[25]

B. The Mass Murders of Ottoman Greeks during Their War of Independence

Ottoman Greek leaders considered their people as not simply inhabiting a distinct nation or adhering to a common religion, but even as belonging to an identifiable "race." A speaker before the Constituent Assembly of Athens declared in 1844:

> The Kingdom of Greece is not Greece. [Greece] constitutes only one part, the smallest and poorest part. A Greek is not only a man who lives within this kingdom but also one who lives in Jannina, in Salonika, in Serres, in Adrianople, in Constantinople, in Smyrna, in Trebizond, in Crete, in Samos and in any land associated with Greek history or the Greek race.... There are two main centers of Hellenism: Athens, the capital of the Greek Kingdom, [and] "The City" [Constantinople], the dream and hope of all Greeks.[26]

Although the Ottoman Empire generally categorized its subjects by religious denomination rather than ethnicity, it classified as Greek not only those adhering to the Greek Orthodox Church but also those of "Greek race and speech."[27] Many thousands of Ottoman subjects living in the Pontus Euxinus region were "Crypto-Christians," so called because they feared to acknowledge their private practice of Greek Orthodox Christianity in the officially Islamic public sphere of the Ottoman Empire.[28] Greek writers and politicians referred to "the persecutions that were practised against Ottoman subjects of Greek race."[29]

---

22. *Ottoman, in* ENCYCLOPEDIA OF MODERN GREEK LITERATURE 306 (Bruce Merry ed., Westport, CT: Greenwood Publishing Group, 2004).

23. *See* LUCIEN GUBBAY, SUNLIGHT AND SHADOW: THE JEWISH EXEPERIENCE OF ISLAM, New York: Other Press LLC, 97–98 .

24. NICOLÒ BARBARO, DIARY OF THE SIEGE OF CONSTANTINOPLE [GIORNALE DELL' ASSEDIO DI CONSTANTINOPOLI] (Melville Jones trans., New York: Exposition Press, 1969) (1453); ARCHIBALD DUNN, THE RISE AND FALL OF THE RULE OF ISLAM 122–29 (London: Tinsley, 1877); KATE FLEET, EUROPEAN AND ISLAMIC TRADE IN THE EARLY OTTOMAN SLATE: THE MERCHANTS OF GENOA AND TURKEY 122–26 (Cambridge: Cambridge UP, 1999).

25. *See* DUNN, RULE OF ISLAM, at 127.

26. Richard Clogg, *The Greek Millet in the Ottoman Empire, in* 1 CHRISTIANS AND JEWS OF THE OTTOMAN EMPIRE: THE FUNCTIONING OF A PLURAL SOCIETY 193 (Benjamin Braude and Bernard Lewis eds., New York: Holmes and Meier, 1982).

27. J.P. XENIDES, THE GREEKS IN AMERICA 67 (New York: George H. Doran Co., 1922).

28. Clogg, *The Greek Millet in the Ottoman Empire*, at 186.

29. ELEFTHERIOS VENIZELOS ET AL., THE VINDICATION OF GREEK NATIONAL POLICY 1912–1917; A REPORT OF SPEECHES DELIVERED IN THE GREEK CHAMBER, AUGUST 24–26, at 173, 184 (London: George Allen & Unwin, 1917).

A report by a British official stated that Greeks referred to themselves as a "race," whether living "in the Turkish Empire or free Greece or in any other country. . . ." After the Greek War of Independence of 1821–1830, "Greek" and "Hellene" also became national and not simply ethnic identities.[30]

From the early modern era until World War I, Britain, France, Russia, the Ottoman Empire, and other powers struggled militarily and diplomatically for control over what the ancient Greeks called the Hellespont and Bosporus, relatively narrow sea-lanes between the Black Sea and the Mediterranean (via the Sea of Marmara and the Aegean Sea). The Russian czars claimed descent from Byzantine throne by marriage.[31] In the late eighteenth century, Russia seized the historically Greek and Byzantine north shore of the Black Sea, known as the Crimea region, from its Turkic-speaking Tatar conquerors. This ended centuries of slave raids that had taken hundreds of thousands of Russians captive.[32] Britain and France, in response, joined together to defend the Ottoman Empire in order to block Russian access to the Mediterranean, and frustrate attempts to establish the Russian Empire as a protector of the Orthodox Christians of the Ottoman Empire.[33]

By forcing Russia to accept the Treaty of Paris of 1856, which ended the Crimean War with a Russian guarantee not to maintain naval defenses in the Black Sea, the Western European empires devastated the Orthodox Christian position in southwestern Asia, leaving it untenable. Article IX of the treaty prohibited the Russian Empire from intervening to save the Christians of the Ottoman Empire from persecution.[34] The security formerly guaranteed by the nearby Russian Empire had been sold for "the worthless paper-money of Ottoman promises."[35] The British bestowed 200 million pounds' worth of gold upon the Sultan to equip his army and naval fleet to Western standards, and to build roads and railways throughout his Empire.[36] The French administered the Imperial Ottoman Bank, and by 1914 had loaned or invested three billion francs in Ottoman credit, manufactures, commercial paper, and securities.[37]

In the 1820s, the movement for an independent Greece gained momentum. In response to outbursts of Greek rebellion, Ottoman forces in 1822 massacred tens of thousands of Greek civilians living in the city of Smyrna and the island of Chios, in what has been described as a genocidal attack on an entire community.[38] Up to 70,000 Greeks died

---

30. *See* SIR ANTON BERTRAM ET AL., THE ORTHODOX PATRIARCHATE OF JERUSALEM 13 (Oxford: Oxford UP, 1928).

31. *See* MICHAEL PRAWDIN & GÉRARD CHALIAND, THE MONGOL EMPIRE: ITS RISE AND LEGACY 515–16, 553 (New Brunswick, NJ: Transaction Publishers, 2005).

32. ANDREW BELL-FIALKOF, THE ROLE OF MIGRATION IN THE HISTORY OF THE EURASIAN STEPPE: SEDENTARY CIVILIZATION VS. "BARBARIAN" AND NOMAD 60 (New York: Palgrave Macmillan, 2d ed. 2000).

33. *See* NORMAN MCCORD & BILL PURDUE, BRITISH HISTORY 1815–1914, at 190, 270–71 (Oxford: Oxford UP, 2007).

34. *See* Treaty of Peace, signed at Paris, March 30, 1858, *in* PICTORIAL HISTORY OF THE RUSSIAN WAR 1854–56, at 549–65 (George Dodd ed. 1856).

35. WESTMINSTER GAZETTE, Dec. 18, 1894, *quoted in* Arsen Berberian, *British Reaction Regarding the First Massacres in Turkey* (2004), http://tinyurl.com/kvjr2b. *See also* GEORGE BUCHAN, 2 A HISTORY OF THE GREAT WAR 10 (London: Nelson, 1921); DANIEL S. GREGORY, THE CRIME OF CHRISTENDOM, OR THE EASTERN QUESTION FROM ITS ORIGIN TO THE PRESENT TIME (New York: Abbey Press, 1900).

36. DUNN, RULE OF ISLAM, at 4.

37. *See* DADRIAN, HISTORY OF THE ARMENIAN GENOCIDE, at 76–77; MARIAN KENT, THE GREAT POWERS AND THE END OF THE OTTOMAN EMPIRE 2 (London: Routledge, 1996).

38. *See* Bryce, *Preface, in* THE TREATMENT OF ARMENIANS, at 23; DADRIAN, HISTORY OF THE ARMENIAN GENOCIDE, at 12; THEA HALO, NOT EVEN MY NAME: FROM A DEATH MARCH IN TURKEY TO

in massacres in 1822–1823 as part of Turkish reprisals for the Greek War of Independence.[39] Many perished on the islands of Cyprus and Rhodes, as well as in and about the cities of Smyrna and Pergamos.[40]

C. The Genocide of the Anatolian Greeks during World War I

Despite the neutrality of the Greek state throughout most of World War I, the Greeks of Anatolia suffered genocidal persecutions and massacres. Elite opinion in Greece initially revealed a division between the attitude of Prime Minister Eleutherios (the "Liberator") Venizelos, who supported the Entente, and the Greek King Constantine, who inclined toward neutrality or even cooperation with the German Empire. Constantine argued that Britain and France simply wanted to use Greece for their own advantage and that Greece, if it joined them, faced the same destruction that had befallen Serbia and was threatening Romania, both of whose capitals fell to invading armies.[41] Venizelos, by contrast, was convinced that a German-Ottoman victory in the war would result in "the eradication of the Hellenic element in Turkey."[42] In June 1917, Britain and France issued a demand to Constantine that he abdicate the throne.[43] As a result, Venizelos gained power, founded the Greek republic in Athens, and declared war on the Ottoman Empire.[44]

The extermination of the Greek population furthered the Ottomans' plan for "Turkifying" their empire by removing "alien" races of Christians. Before the Ottoman Empire even joined the war, its Interior Minister Talât told Ambassador Morgenthau of a plan to "get rid of these alien peoples" like the Greeks by large-scale murders and deportations.[45] The Ottoman government organized economic boycotts and large-scale dismissals of

---

A New Home in America, a Young Girl's True Story 100 (2000); M. M. Mangasarian, *Armenia's Impending Doom: Our Duty, in* The Armenian Massacres, 1894–1896, at 164, 167 (Arman J. Kirakossian ed., 2004); Néret, *Delacroix: 1798–1863,* 16; Constantinople and the Scenery of the Seven Churches of Asia 166 (Thomas Allom et al. eds., 2006).

39. William Easterly, Roberta Gatti, & Sergio Kurlat, *Development, Democracy, and Mass Killings,* 11.2 J. of Econ. Growth 129, appendix 2 (June 2006), http://www.nyu.edu/fas/institute/dri/DRIWP/DRIWP10.pdf; Rummel, Death by Government, ch. 10.

40. Allan Cunningham et al., 3 The Popular Encyclopedia 536–38 (London: Blackie & Son, 1836); Allan Cunningham et al., 6 The Popular Encyclopedia 134 (London: Blackie & Son, 1846).

41. *See* Sir Martin Gilbert, The First World War: A Complete History 294 (New York: Henry Holt & Co., 2d ed. 2004); Constantine I, *Letter to Neutrals* (Jan. 14, 1917), http://www.firstworldwar.com/source/greece_constantineprotest.htm.

42. *Quoted in* Buchan, 2 A History of the Great War, at 353.

43. *Allied Ultimatum Demanding Abdication of King Constantine I* (June 11, 1917), http://www.firstworldwar.com/source/greece_jonnart1.htm. Britain and France initially landed at the Greek port of Piraeus in late 1916 in an effort to pressure King Constantine to allow them to move supplies through Greek territory, as Constantine had allowed the Germans' allies the Bulgarians to do since summer 1916. Forces loyal to Constantine, however, defeated an attempt by the Provisional Government of Prime Minister Venizelos to take Athens in late 1916, thus maintaining Greek "neutrality." *See* Gilbert, The First World War, at 278, 302–3.

44. *See* Toynbee, The Western Question, at 365.

45. *Quoted in* Henry Morgenthau, Ambassador Morgenthau's Story 35 (Whitefish, MT: Kessinger Publishing, 2004) (1919).

Christian employees in cities such as Constantinople and Smyrna.[46] In this way, Talât intended to "Turkify Smyrna" and other Greek population centers, and establish Turkey as "the land exclusively of the Turks."[47] The government's "passion for Turkifying the nation seemed to demand logically the extermination of all Christians," Morgenthau later wrote.[48]

The German general Limon von Sanders encouraged the Ottoman army to "throw[] these infidels [i.e., the Greeks of the Aegean region] into the sea."[49] The declaration of religious warfare incited widespread killings of Greeks and others.[50] In May 1914, Talât dispatched orders to the prefect of Smyrna that the "Greeks occupying the coastline of Asia Minor be compelled to evacuate their villages and install themselves in the vilayets of Erzerum and Chaldea." Talât's communiqué included orders to obtain certificates from the expelled Greeks falsely representing that they had left "their homes on their own initiative," so that the Ottomans would not face property-related "political complications ensuing from their displacement." The expulsions were far from voluntary, however. Talât added that: "If [the Greeks] should refuse to be transported to the appointed places, kindly ... induce the Greeks, through excesses of all sorts, to leave their native places of their own accord."[51]

The month after Talât's orders were issued, Prime Minister Venizelos condemned the Ottoman campaign aiming at "the elimination of populations which had been living in those places for several thousand years."[52] Thousands of refugees had already arrived in Greece from Anatolia, and thousands more were following them. An estimated 100,000 refugees were living in Greece or were on their way to Greece by June 1914.[53] Armed bands of Turks accompanied by police officers massacred 100 civilians in Phocea, a town northwest of Smyrna, prompting nearly 4,000 Greeks from the area to flee for Greece.[54] By October, the Ottomans had deported 1,500 more Greeks from the city of Ereğli west of Constantinople.[55]

The Ottoman leaders in Constantinople began reprisals in August 1914 against local Christians, drawing on public outrage about a British decision not to deliver two battleships under construction for the Ottoman navy. The Ottoman police and secret service began to press-gang all non-Muslims for forced labor as servants to Turkish soldiers.[56] Morgenthau wrote in his memoirs that both the Greeks and the Armenians were transferred into labor battalions in which untold thousands died of "cold, hunger and other deprivations."[57] During the first ten days of this policy, thousands of Greeks fled Con-

---

46. *See id.* at 35.
47. *Id.*, 93, 196, 201.
48. *Id.*, 200.
49. *Quoted in* Akçam, From Empire to Republic, at 146; Travis, *Ottoman Genocide of the Assyrians*, at 342.
50. *See* Akçam, From Empire to Republic, at 146–47; Travis, *Ottoman Genocide of the Assyrians*, at 331–32, 341–42.
51. *Quoted in* Halo, Not Even My Name, at 127.
52. *Greece Tells Turks to Stop Expulsions*, N.Y. Times, June 13, 1914, at 3.
53. *Id.*
54. *Turks Slay 100 Greeks. Massacre in a Town Near Smyrna—Police Are Accused*, N.Y. Times, June 17, 1914, at 6.
55. *Turks Expel 1,500 Greeks*, N.Y. Times, Oct. 14, 1914, at 5.
56. *Turkey Learns of the War,* N.Y. Times Current History, A Monthly Magazine, Mar. 1915, http://www.gutenberg.org/files/20521/20521-h/20521-h.htm.
57. Morgenthau, Ambassador Morgenthau's Story, at 148, 222, 287; Akçam, From Empire to Republic, at 146.

stantinople, many for the U.S.[58] Turkish officers ordered between 300,000 and 500,000 Greeks to be deported from eastern Thrace during the first few months of World War I.[59] In the process, about half of the deportees, or 250,000, were murdered or died from hunger or exposure to the elements. Greek children wandered the streets as orphans "half-naked and begging for bread"; and millions of dollars of Greek property passed into Turkish hands.[60]

Talcott Williams, director of the Pulitzer School of Journalism at Columbia University, wrote to the *New York Times* in 1915 that: "At least one-half of the Greek population has been deported from the cities and hamlets on the coast of Asia Minor from the Black Sea to the eastern end of Cilicia, or around three-fourths of the coast of this peninsula."[61] He continued: "The deportation of 700,000 Greeks ... means slavery and death to the deported."[62] In 1918, a Turkish parliamentarian estimated that more than half a million Greeks who were deported from the Black Sea, Aegean, Marmara, and other regions had been "killed and annihilated."[63]

In June 1915, the "Young Turk" leaders at the helm of the Ottoman Empire adopted a resolution directed to "[t]aking the commerce of the East out of Greek hands." The resolution also envisioned "[t]he Turkification of the Greek element by force through the establishment of mixed communities, ... [and by] compelling mixed marriages."[64]

Pursuant to this "Turkification" policy the Greek population of Anatolia suffered systematic murder, rape, and the deprivation of the essentials for life. A "violent onslaught" on the whole Greek "race" occurred, in the judgment of Ambassador Morgenthau.[65] Many "Greek men and women were ... tortured just as were their fellow Armenians," and "Greek girls, just like Armenian girls, were stolen and taken to Turkish harems." Greek homes and businesses were expropriated, in a campaign of "plundering on a wholesale scale." The Greek chargé d'affaires complained to the Ottoman Vizier about the persecution of Greek civilians, but the Vizier replied that such efforts to ameliorate Greek suffering would result in further reprisals.[66]

Further large-scale massacres of Greeks followed in 1916 and 1917, carried out by Turkish forces in Constantinople, Adrianople, and Smyrna.[67] The Austro-Hungarian consul stationed in the city of Samsun on the Black Sea wrote to the German foreign minister that the Greeks in the area were being exterminated (*ausgerottet werden*) by Turkish troops under the pretext of lawful military operations.[68] As the U.S. consul-general in Anatolia reported:

---

58. *Turkey Learns of the War.*

59. *See* Akçam, From Empire to Republic, at 147.

60. *Id.*; *Turks Slaughter Greeks, Sell Women to Slavery*, L.A Times, June 9, 1918, http://www.latimes.com.

61. Talcott Williams, *Greek Deportations. The Needs of the Latest Victims of Turkish Cruelty*, N.Y. Times, Oct. 8, 1917, at 10; Shanon Lawson, *Special Collections Department: Talcott Williams Papers 1894–1925* (Oct. 27, 2003), http://www.lib.udel.edu/ud/spec/findaids/wllms_ta.htm.

62. Williams, *Greek Deportations*, at 10.

63. *Quoted in* Akçam, From Empire to Republic, at 147–48.

64. *Germans Inspired Turkish Atrocities Against Asiatic Greeks,* N.Y. Times, Sept. 29, 1918, http://www.nytimes.com.

65. Morgenthau, Ambassador Morgenthau's Story, at 223.

66. *Id.* at 223, 245.

67. *Extermination of Greeks in Turkey,* The Times (U.K.), Aug. 23, 1917, at 5, http://www.greek-genocide.org/press/23081917.html; *Massacres of Greeks in Turkey Reported.*

68. Ernst von Kwiatkowski, *Letter to Ottokar Czernin von und zu Chudenitz Re: the Persecutions of Greeks in Bafra*, http://www.greek-genocide.org/doc_afo_potgib_1.html.

> In January 1916, the Greek deportations from the Black Sea began. These Greeks came through the city of Marsovan by thousands, walking for the most part the three days' journey through the snow and mud and slush of the winter weather. Thousands fell by the wayside from exhaustion and others came into the city of Marsovan in groups of fifty, one hundred and five hundred, always under escort of Turkish gendarmes. Next morning these poor refugees were started on the road and destruction by this treatment was even more radical than a straight massacre such as the Armenians suffered before.[69]

During World War I, "over 500,000 Greeks were deported, of whom comparatively few survived."[70] About 170,000 Christian women and children were kidnapped and enslaved by Turks and Kurds.[71] The British estimated that 100,000 Greeks died between August 1917 and 1918 alone, *before* the destruction of Smyrna.[72] Other estimates, including one cited by Greek Prime Minister Venizelos, indicate that between 240,000 and 300,000 Greeks died of starvation, disease, forced work, and exposure during the period of Greek deportation from Anatolia and Thrace.[73] A work published in 1919 by several professors of history in the U.S., including professors affiliated with Harvard, estimated fully 900,000 Greek civilian deaths.[74]

D. The Unraveling of the Postwar Armistice

While France made renewed efforts after the war to protect the indigenous Christians of the former Ottoman Empire, the British frustrated these efforts. On October 30, 1918, Turkey reached an armistice agreement with the Allies.[75] Imperial and commercial rivalries between Britain and France unraveled the post-war settlement in Turkey and opened the way for ultra-nationalists under Mustafa Kemal to cleanse most remaining Christians from the country.[76] Specifically, Britain blocked French efforts to disarm the former Ottoman armies.[77]

Although Italy had been an ally of Britain and France during the world war, it was jealous of its own "zone on influence" and therefore opposed Greece's liberation of the Smyrna area from Ottoman rule.[78] The Italian high commissioner in Constantinople had orders issued for Mustafa Kemal to "restore law and order" in northeastern Anatolia by disbanding illegal militias and securing munitions depots.[79] This was reckless at best from

69. Horton, The Blight of Asia, at 194.

70. F.O. 371/7876 (1922), at 1 (G.W. Rendel, Memorandum on Turkish Massacres and Persecutions of Minorities since the Armistice (1922)), http://www.greek-genocide.org/doc_bfo_rm_1.html.

71. *See id.* at 1–2.

72. *See* Baum, The Christian Minorities of Turkey, at 127.

73. Akçam, From Empire to Republic, at 146–47; Rummel, Death by Government, at 229; Sachar, Sachar, The Emergence of the Middle East, at 309.

74. *See* Arthur L. Frothingham et al., Handbook of War Facts and Peace Problems (NY, National Security League, 1919), http://net.lib.byu.edu/~rdh7/wwi/comment/WarFacts/wfacts7.htm#11.4.

75. Toynbee, The Western Question, at 365.

76. Auguste Gauvain, *French Policy in the Near East,* 3 Foreign Aff. 277, 277 (1924).

77. *Id.*, 279.

78. Andrew Mango, Atatürk: The Biography of the Founder of Modern Turkey 204–5 (New York: The Overlook Press, 2000).

79. Dobkin, Smyrna, at 60–61.

the Allies' perspective because during the world war, Kemal had fought with the German Empire to repel the British Commonwealth's attack on the Gallipoli peninsula, and had been promoted to colonel and awarded the Iron Cross First Class for his efforts.[80] Starting in the summer of 1919, Kemal organized a rebellion against the post-war Turkish government that had dared to prosecute criminally the perpetrators of the "annihilation" of the Armenians and the plunders of all Christians.[81] Kemal looted munitions depots left unguarded by the Allies and raised a "Nationalist" army.[82]

The Bolshevik rulers of Russia had obvious reasons to support Mustafa Kemal, and "engineered" and "furnished the money and ammunition" for Nationalist offensives against Allied positions administering the Treaty of Sevres.[83] On September 11, 1918, American troops had invaded Russia at Archangel, joining a British force at Murmansk, and a French force at Vladivostok.[84] At the outset of Turkish-Bolshevik cooperation in 1918, German armies had occupied the Baltic, Black Sea, Caspian, Crimean, Ukrainian, and White Russian regions of the Russian Empire.[85] After negotiating a peace with Germany, the new Soviet Union reportedly signed a treaty with the Nationalists in 1923 in which it pledged to invade British-controlled Mesopotamia in the event of a British intervention on the side of the Greeks against Turkey.[86]

Even France eventually tilted towards Kemal, providing his forces with arms and ammunition to attack Greek communities along the Aegean coast.[87] Frustrated by British policies favoring a Syria independent from France, and hostile to British policy towards Greece and the Balkans, the French responded by papering over Nationalist massacres of French missionaries and prisoners of war.[88] The French press grumbled about "English domination" of Turkey and praised the "loyal" Nationalists.[89] French financiers advocated a Nationalist victory from which they would "profit marvelously," presumably by liquidating the Greek and Armenian competition.[90]

The French also relied on the representations of Morgenthau, who led the negotiations, that the U.S. would assume responsibility for Armenian affairs, which it later completely abandoned to Nationalist depredations.[91] The American high commissioner for Constantinople tasked the U.S. Navy with guarding American oil and tobacco interests rather than Greek cities, and advocated "destroying all European influences" in Turkey to open up "a virgin field for American business."[92] As the highest-ranking U.S. diplomat in Turkey, he dismissed Greeks, Armenians, and "Syrians" as inferior races to the Turks, and therefore unfit for self-government.[93] The Angora Convention between France and Turkey ultimately ignored the treaty obligations of Turkey not to persecute, but instead to guarantee

---

80. Gilbert, The First World War, at 180–82.
81. Rummel, Death by Government, at 230.
82. Gauvain, *French Policy*, at 281.
83. *Killing by Turks Has Been Renewed,* at 2.
84. Gilbert, The First World War, at 398, 425, 449, 460.
85. *Id.*, 398, 425, 449, 460; Bülent Gökay, A Clash of Empires: Turkey between Russian Bolshevism and British Imperialism 1918–1923, at 18–33, 87, 120 (1997).
86. *Soviet Pledge to Help Turkey in War Signed at Lausanne, Paper Says*, N.Y. Times, Jan. 29. 1923, at 1.
87. *Who Equipped Kemal? The Soviet, One Report,* N.Y. Times, Sept. 17, 1922, at 2.
88. Gauvain, *French Policy*, at 282–83.
89. *Id.*, 284.
90. *Id.*, 283.
91. *Id.* at 284–85; Dobkin, Smyrna, at 72–83.
92. Dobkin, Smyrna, at 74, 78–9.
93. *Id.*, 73, 76, 78.

autonomy to, the Armenians, the Smyrna Greeks, and the Assyro-Chaldeans.[94] The ultimate result would be that "populations which were settled [in Anatolia] for thousands of years before the Turks made their appearance in history [were] driven out *en masse* by a treaty of peace to leave room for the Turkish invaders...."[95]

E. The Genocide of the Anatolian Greeks by the Nationalists after 1918

In July 1919, the Kemalist Nationalists redoubled their efforts to wage war on the Allies notwithstanding the armistice agreement.[96] The Nationalists pardoned violent criminals and recruited them for the gendarmerie, which proceeded to "round[] up" those Christians "still at large."[97] A British admiral reported in late 1919 that:

> Every district has its bands of brigands posing as patriots, and even in the vicinity of Constantinople robbery under arms is a daily occurrence, the principal victims being naturally the unprotected Christian villagers. Behind all these elements of disorder stands Mustapha Kemal.... The Government cannot, and will not, move a finger to help the Christians....[98]

By 1920, the Nationalists had burned alive or otherwise massacred about 12,000 Pontic Greeks throughout at least two dozen towns and villages. The Greek towns in the districts of Amissos, Paffra, and Arba had "completely disappeared." In Trabzon all Greek men who were not Russian subjects were reportedly killed. Fourteen villages surrounding Trabzon were burned down. The Turks burned down all the villages in Pontus, whose inhabitants were either killed or driven away, to die on the roads for the most part.[99]

Pursuant to the Treaty of Sèvres of August 10, 1920 between the Ottoman Empire, Greece, and other powers, the Ottomans transferred to Greece the rights of sovereignty and administration over the city of Smyrna and the surrounding territory about 100 miles inland from the coast, including the maintenance of "the military forces required for the maintenance of order and public security."[100] The treaty envisioned that the Kingdom of Greece would annex the Smyrna district by plebiscite after five years had passed.[101] The Greek army took possession Smyrna pursuant to the treaty in 1921, and achieved some victories over Turkish rebels before supplies of arms and food ran out.[102] Greek forces committed atrocities during reprisals, including murders of Turkish villagers and the looting or burning of Turkish property.[103]

---

94. Gauvain, *French Policy*, at 284, 288.
95. *Id.* at 277.
96. Toynbee, The Western Question, at 366.
97. Rendel, *Memorandum*, at 1.
98. *Id.*
99. F.O. 286/833, Mar. 6, 1921, report from Vice Admiral, Head of British Naval Mission of Athens to the British Foreign Office on the Condition of the Greeks in Pontus, at 1–3.
100. Treaty of Sèvres, arts. 65–83; *The Turkish Empire, in* 27 The Catholic Encyclopedia: An International Work of Reference on the Constitution, Doctrine, Discipline and History of the Catholic Church 744 (Edward A. Pace, et al. eds., New York: The Encyclopedia Press, Inc., 1922). http://books.google.com/books?id=e0wcodwSBckC&pg=PA346&dq.
101. Treaty of Sèvres, art. 83.
102. Gauvain, *French Policy*, at 286–89.
103. Mango, Ataturk, at 329; Toynbee, The Western Question, at 259–319.

A Nationalist attack in 1921 on Greek-administered Smyrna routed the Greek army, and Greek civilians fled with them in fear of massacres, rapes, and other reprisals by the occupying Turkish forces.[104] Widespread massacres against the Greek population of Anatolia followed. Arnold Toynbee, an officer in the Political Intelligence Department of the British Foreign Office and part of the British delegation to the Paris Peace Conference in 1919, wrote that the Angora government of Mustafa Kemal Pa a extended its "war of extermination" against the Greeks from the Smyrna area to the Pontus region.[105] In 1921, Nationalist firing squads massacred about 550 mostly Greek men deported from Samsun, in the Pontus region.[106] An American naval officer confirmed, in a document declassified in 1958, that 2,500 girls deported from the Samsun area had been assaulted "so badly ... they could hardly walk. ..."[107] An American humanitarian worker described what he saw from a vantage-point in Samsun:

> After leaving Samsoun on my return trip to Harpoot, I passed the old men of Samsoun, Greeks who were being deported. Many of these men were feeble with age, but in spite of that they were being pressed forward at a rate of thirty miles a day and there was no transport available for those who were weak or ill. There was no food allowance for them and any food they could obtain had to be procured by money or sale of small articles that they could carry with them. On this trip I passed many corpses of Greeks lying by the roadside where they had died from exposure. Many of these were the corpses of women and girls with their faces toward the sky, covered with flies.[108]

The massacres in the Pontus region began as the Turkish General Staff expected a large-scale Greek army attack against the Nationalist capital of Angora.[109] The Turkish authorities alleged after the fact that the Greek army had begun arming the Pontic Greeks to attack the Turkish army from the rear.[110] The American consul-general in the Middle East ridiculed this theory of "Turkish propagandists" that "the massacred [Greeks] were as bad as their executioners."[111]

In early 1922, Greek civilians suffered deportation from the Black Sea coast and war front into the hinterland of Anatolia.[112] The Near East Relief organization estimated that of these 30,000 refugees fleeing from their homes, about 14,000 had died. It stated: "The Turkish authorities were frank in their statements that it was the intention to have all Greeks die and all of their actions ... seem to fully bear this statement out." The Nationalists, the organization reported, drove the deportees through "severe snow storms" and "did practically everything within its power to prevent any relief to [them]." It sent the deportees towards Bitlis, "a place totally destroyed, with no industry and located far up in the mountains." Two thirds of the victims were women and children; the "main causes of

104. Gauvain, *French Policy*, at 290–91.

105. Toynbee, The Western Question, at 190.

106. Lieut. Murray, *Report from the USS Overton* [stationed off coast of Turkey] (Aug. 28, 1921) [Declassified by U.S. State Dep't May 5, 1961], http://www.greek-genocide.org/doc_usfo_sflm_1.html.

107. *Id.*

108. Stanley K. Hopkins (Near East Relief), *Report on Conditions in the Interior of Anatolia under the Turkish Nationalist Government* (Nov. 16, 1921), declassified 1961, at 2, *quoted in* Alfred de Zayas, *The Ottoman Genocide Against the Greeks and Other Christian Minorities in the Light of the Genocide Convention* 5 (2007).

109. Toynbee, The Western Question, at 275.

110. *Id.*, 275–76.

111. Horton, Blight of Asia, at 193 (rejecting ideas that massacres were "'50–50,'" because there was "very little" evidence of that).

112. Jackson, *Treatment of Christians by Turks*, 1–2.

death were starvation, exposure, typhus, and dysentery." Continuously as the deportees followed the road to Bitlis, bands of Turks and Kurds attacked and raped the women and girls.[113]

The Nationalists prohibited Near East Relief from aiding Greek deportees by giving them food, clothing, or money. Without American aid, all of the deportees would die, the organization predicted. Nevertheless, the Nationalists seized many of the facilities utilized by Near East Relief, including food storage, administrative offices, two orphanages, a nursery, a kindergarten, and a home for the disabled. The Angora government of Mustafa Kemal denied food aid to the displaced by ordering the director of Near East Relief to stop his work and leave the country.[114]

In May 1922, the Greek foreign minister detailed the massacre of more than 300,000 Anatolian Greeks in the districts of Trabzon, Amasia, Kolenia, New Cesarea, and Rodopolis.[115] The head of the Near East Relief Hospital of Harput, Anatolia, declared in June 1922 that: "the Turks are planning the extermination of this Christian minority [in Asia Minor]."[116] He stated that the Greeks "are now being indiscriminately massacred by the thousand," and their condition "is as bad as that of the Armenians."[117]

On August 31, 1922, Archbishop Chrysostomos of Smyra, also the Ecumenical Patriarch to Constantinople, wrote a letter intended for publication in the U.S. in which he stated warned of "terrible slaughters" should the Kemalist forces occupy Smyrna and other historically Greek cities. He predicted a recurrence of the Greek community's experience of "massacre and devastation" as the "continuous and inevitable" accompaniment to Turkish military operations. In the most direct terms conceivable, he cautioned: "Hundreds of thousands of Greeks will perish without the possibility of the slightest defense...." The archbishop was among those massacred during the next month in the Turkish sack of Smyrna.[118]

In September 1922, nearly 200,000 Greek and Armenian Christians died when Turkish troops burned down the Christian neighborhoods of Smyrna, and deported the remaining population to Turkish and Kurdish regions of Anatolia where they perished of attacks, hunger, disease, and exposure.[119] Defenders of the Kemalists occasionally deny responsibility for the "holocaust" at Smyrna, but this does not bear scrutiny:

> So many testimonials exist, from victims, and also from other European nationals and North Americans, that it seems impossible to deny that the Turks deliberately staged the fire.... Several witnesses reported Turks moving about with cans of fuel, soaking structures in the Greek and Armenian quarters.... [T]he Turks had controlled the city for several days, and the Turkish quarters remained intact after the two-day-long inferno.[120]

As the fires died down, Mustafa Kemal ordered "that all Greek and Armenian men between the ages of eighteen and forty-five were to be considered prisoners of war, thus

113. Mark H. Ward & F.D. Yewell, *Letter to American Consul Jesse B. Jackson (*1922), at 2–5, http://www.greek-genocide.org/doc_usfo_tocbt_3.html.

114. *Id.*, 3–16.

115. *303,238 Massacred, Greek Minister Says*, N.Y. Times, June 2, 1922, at 3.

116. *Predicts Greatest Massacre in History*, N.Y. Times, June 4, 1922, at 31.

117. *Id.* He announced this in Paris on his way to meetings with the U.S. State Dep't to seek "strong action by America and the other world powers." *Id.*

118. *Slain Archbishop Foresaw Massacre*, N.Y. Times, Sept. 24, 1922, at 35.

119. Bevan, The Destruction of Memory, at 54; Dobkin, Smyrna, at 6–7, 30, 66, 83, 201–2; Horton, The Blight of Asia, at 114–16; Prentiss, *Smyrna's Horror*, at 1–2; Rummel, Death by Government, at 233–34.

120. Matthew Stewart, *Catastrophe at Smyrna*, 54 History Today 24, –31 (2004).

paving the way for further roundups and death marches."[121] An Inter-Allied Commission of Inquiry concluded that Kemalist nationalist troops and "bands" also carried out "massacres on a large scale" against the Christian population in the region of Nicaea. In Aidin, Turkish militia "wiped out the Greek quarter," hunting down and murdering women and children "like rats," looting all valuables, and burning everything else down.[122] Turkish forces under Kemal "terrorized" the Greek population in scenes of massacre, carnage, and rapine. About 10,000 Greeks deported into the interior of Anatolia for forced labor soon perished.[123]

Near the end of 1922, the League of Nations official tasked with formulating policy on Turkey reported that "all Greeks under Turkish sovereignty [must] be got away quickly to save them from starvation or death...."[124] The *New York Times* opined in an editorial later that week that:

> The great cultured nations of Western Europe which watch calmly the annihilation of some of the oldest stocks of European culture may be calm because they think they will get a bigger share of the business with resident business men out of the way.... [T]he killing off of the races that have done the business hitherto will merely widen the field for [them].[125]

Eventually, over a million Greeks were deported from Turkey to Greece, along with almost 400,000 Turks and other Muslims who fled Greece for Turkey.[126] The Greek refugees found themselves languishing in tents, caves, huts, schools, and the like.[127] The demography of Turkey had changed forever, its Greek, Armenian, and Assyrian communities exterminated or deported *en masse*.[128]

For his leadership in the war of extermination against the Greeks and other Christian minorities, Mustafa Kemal was celebrated with the title *ghazi* or infidel-killer.[129] *Ghazi* was the Seljuk Turks' and Ottomans' term for warriors "taking revenge" on infidels and "blazing forth the way of Islam from East to West." The *ghazi* warriors raided Christian cities in Armenia and Greek Anatolia in order to loot, and to spread the faith.[130]

The definition of genocide in the Genocide Convention and the writings of Professor Lemkin capture what Talât, Enver, and Kemal achieved in World War I by massacring, raping, and plundering Greek communities, causing thousands to flee. Even those Greeks not actually killed between 1914 and 1922 had their personal security destroyed by their deportation from the country under circumstances of widespread massacres of civilians. The Ottoman and Nationalist leaders of Turkey employed numerous and devastating exclusionary policies, including mass dismissals of Christian employees, destruction of Christian businesses, destruction or expropriation of Christian churches and educational institutions, and forced Turkification.

---

121. *Id.*; Renée Hirschon, Heirs of the Greek Catastrophe: The Social Life of Asia Minor Refugees in Piraeus 8–9 (Oxford: Clarendon Press, 1989).

122. Toynbee, The Western Question, at 273–75.

123. *See* Charles Howland, *Greece and Her Refugees*, 4 Foreign Aff. 614–15 (1926).

124. Edwin I. James, *Turks Proclaim Banishment Edict to 1,000,000 Greeks*, N.Y. Times, Dec. 2, 1922, at 1.

125. *The Statesmanship of Extermination (Editorial)*, N.Y. Times, Dec. 4, 1922, at 16.

126. Howland, *Greece and Her Refugees*, at 613–16; James, *Turks Proclaim Banishment Edict*, at 1.

127. Howland, *Greece and Her Refugees*, at 622.

128. Mango, Ataturk, at 332.

129. John Gunther, Inside Europe 477 (New York: Harper Publishers, 1940); Ghazi Mustapha Kemal, A Speech Delivered by Ghazi Mustapha Kemal, President of the Turkish Republic, October 1927, at 1, 7 (Leipzig: K.F. Koehler, 1929).

130. *See* Turnbull, The Ottoman Empire 1326–1699, at 17.

Chapter IX

"Great Schemes": The Middle East from Lausanne to World War II

> The Germans were, as long as they lasted, the active allies of the Turks, and during this period nearly a million Armenians and many thousands of Greeks perished; after the Armistice and during the period which led up to the destruction of Smyrna and the accompanying massacre, the French and Italians were allies of the Turk, and furnished him moral and material support; ... the Americans gained the reputation of being pro-Turk, true friends, who would ultimately, on account of this friendship, be given the permission to put through great schemes, which would result in the development of the Ottoman Empire and, incidentally, fill certain American pocketbooks. The Turks confidently believed that commercial avarice would prevent us from interfering with their savagery, or even strongly condemning it....
>
> And in all this tangle of conflicting interests, during which the Turk continued massacring, the thoughtful observer is impressed with one thing—the clearness of [Britain's] vision.... There are copious oil wells ... not far from Basra, on the Persian Gulf, where the British landed early in the war. There are rich oil fields at Mosul.... No wonder the State Department says that it kept out of that.
>
> —George Horton, U.S. Consul-General in the Middle East[1]

A. The Consolidation of a Monocultural Turkey

The period from the mid-1920s to the late 1930s was one of forced assimilation, and continued cultural devastation for minorities and indigenous peoples. In Turkey and Iraq, as in Germany, the U.S., Mexico, much of South America, Australia, the Soviet Union, and other places, minorities remained at risk of massacres, lynchings, prohibitions of their culture and language, and loss of their ancestral lands. To replace the empty Christian cities and villages, Turkey "continued to accept Muslims speaking Turkic languages as immigrants and did not discourage the emigration of members of non-Turkic minorities."[2]

---

1. The Blight of Asia, ch. 28.
2. *Turkey: A Country Study*, http://countrystudies.us/turkey/24.htm.

The Treaty of Peace with Turkey signed at Lausanne in 1923 was criticized at the time for contemplated the expulsion of the Greek Christian expulsion from Turkey, and few mechanisms to prevent or punish crimes against Armenians, Assyrians, or Kurds during or since the war.[3] The British Foreign Secretary, George Curzon, announced his regret that the treaty contained no special protections for Armenians and Assyro-Chaldeans, because the Turks refused to hear these peoples' pleas. A column in the *New York Times* remarked that Turkish minorities had a "dark future" after being "sacrificed" in this way in favor of securing British oil interests.[4] After a campaign by prominent U.S. officials described the treaty as a disgraceful surrender to criminality and tyranny, the Senate defeated it in 1926 and 1927.[5]

In the early 1920s, Kemal Atatürk thwarted the League of Nations' investigation into a possible Assyrian homeland in northern Iraq by destroying the villages left after the Ottoman genocide before the League delegation could document their existence.[6] He was abetted in such crimes by a complicit array of world powers. As a retired U.S. Admiral, William Colby Chester, indignantly exclaimed: "The Turks were falsely maligned during World War I, [since] their policy toward the minorities had been one of utmost benevolence."[7] He explained that Armenians had simply been relocated to sunnier climes, like New Yorkers moving to Florida.[8] Privately, Admiral Mark L. Bristol revealed U.S. diplomatic concerns to center around "get[ting] Turkey away from Russia and mak[ing] her a strong bulwark in the Near East against bolshevism."[9] He hoped that American corporations would form a cartel to control the Turkish trade, rather like the British East India Company or Royal Africa Company.[10]

B. The Cultural Cleansing of Arabia

Winston Churchill, then a British colonial official with responsibilities of managing the Middle East in the British interest, acted with his deputy Sir Percy Cox to empower Ibn Saud, a Wahhabi Arab warlord, to conquer the Muslim holy cities of Mecca and Medina. Churchill and Cox paid Saud an exorbitant annual subsidy of 100,000 pounds per year.[11]

---

3. *See* Treaty of Peace with Turkey, signed at Lausanne, July 24, 1923, *in* 2 The Treaties of Peace 1919–1923; Dadrian, The History of the Armenian Genocide, 333, 341; Hans Köchler, Global Justice or Global Revenge? International Criminal Justice at the Crossroads 58 (New York: Springer, 2004); Peterson, "Starving Armenians," at 134–35; Bassiouni, *From Versailles to Rwanda*, at 17.

4. Edwin James, *Allies Abandoning Minorities' Cause*, N.Y. Times, Jan. 10, 1923, at 4.

5. *See A Minority Refuses*, Time Mag., Jan. 31, 1927, http://www.time.com/time/magazine/article/0,9171,729871,00.html; *Calls Lausanne Treaty Insult to Christianity*, Chicago Daily Tribune, May 17, 1926, at 14; *Score Turk Treaty As Disgrace to US; Ex-Ambassador Gerard and His Guests Call Lausanne Pact Indefensible*, N.Y. Times, Nov. 25, 1923, at E1.

6. *See* George Seldes, *Chaldeans Outraged as Massacred by Turks*, L.A. Times, Oct. 25, 1925, at 1.

7. *Quoted in* A. Christian van Gorder, *Armenian Christians and Turkish Muslims: Atrocity, Denial and Identity* 48 (2004), http://www.samford.edu/lillyhumanrights/papers/VanGorder_Armenian.pdf.

8. *See* Marjorie Housipian Dobkin, *What Genocide? What Holocaust? News from Turkey, 1915–1923: A Case Study, in* The Armenian Genocide in Perspective 103 (Richard G. Hovannisian ed., New Brunswick, NJ: Transaction Books, 1987).

9. *Quoted in* Donald Bloxham, *The Roots of American Genocide Denial: Near Eastern Geopolitics and the Interwar Armenian Question*, 8 J. of Genocide Research 27, 36 (2006).

10. *See id.* at 34.

11. *See* Christopher Catherwood, Churchill's Folly: How Winston Churchill Created Modern Iraq 110, 138–39 (New York: Carroll & Graf, 2005).

Ibn Saud named the resulting entity after himself, calling it Saudi Arabia.[12] The British intelligence operative and colonial officer Harry St. John Philby called Ibn Saud "the greatest Arab since the prophet Muhammad."[13]

In 1902, Ibn Saud occupied Riyadh, cutting off his rivals' heads and displaying them on spikes at the city gates. "His followers burned 1200 people to death." Ibn Saud spent British money to "expand and subsidize" the Wahhabi militia, then known as the *Ikhwan*, or "brothers." The militia's "savagery wreaked havoc across Arabia" as they massacred the population of Taif, Bureida, Al Huda, and other cities, and damaged pre-Wahhabi Muslim architecture. As many as 250 tribal and political opponents were beheaded on a single occasion. "Between 1916 and 1928 there were no fewer than 26 anti-House of Saud rebellions by the Bedouins and each of them ended with the *Ikhwan*-led forces of Ibn Saud indulging in mass killings of mostly innocent victims including women and children...." Ibn Saud founded, and the *Ikhwan* administered, the Committee for the Advancement of Virtue and the Elimination of Sin, which whipped and tortured people for singing, growing flowers, adorning themselves with gold or silk, not having long beards, wearing Western suits or dresses, or utilizing perfume or tobacco. Ibn Saud and the Committee forced many women into marriage with their allies. Ibn Saud himself told "Philby and others that he had had several hundred virgins and he was in the habit of deflowering young girls then giving them away as presents." As the leader of a nation, he "personally own[ed] hundreds of slaves," not in the 1740s or 1840s but in the 1940s.[14]

Despite the Saudi royal family's extreme form of totalitarian rule, Western money flowed into their coffers in torrents. By 1945, Saudi Arabia could produce 300,000 barrels of oil per day, an amount that rose rapidly to nine million barrels per day in the 1990s. In the 1970s the country could afford to subsidize Yaser Arafat's PLO to the tune of $100 million per year. By 1980 the U.S. had become its number one client for oil, and the country had a surplus of $100 billion. As many as 50 members of the royal family became billionaires. The king himself claimed up to $5 billion a year in oil proceeds as his personal share. Saudi Arabia's military budget averaged $18 billion per year in the late 1980s and early 1990s, an average of $1.5 million per soldier per year. This was even as its leaders spent $30 billion throughout the 1980s to prop up Saddam Hussein during his internal and external depredations.[15]

C. Independent Iraq, and a New Massacre of the Assyrians

In the twentieth century, Iraq has proven to be a difficult piece of land to hold by force, so foreign occupation armies and indigenous dictators alike have resorted to brutal and unusual methods to put down vigorous resistance from local populations. After World War I, the British Empire occupied the territory from what was then called Palestine in the

12. *See* Catherwood, Churchill's Folly, at 138–39.

13. Said K. Aburish, The Rise, Corruption and Coming Fall of the House of Saud 9 (New York: Palgrave Macmillan, 1996); *see also* Matthew Ellis, *King Me: The Political Culture of Monarchy in Interwar Egypt and Iraq*, ch. 2 (2005), http://users.ox.ac.uk/~metheses/EllisThesis.htm.

14. Aburish, The House of Saud, at 14–15, 18–19, 24–27, 32.

15. *See id.* at 26, 36, 53, 61, 134, 169, 187–88, 295.

west, to Mesopotamia in the east, as a result of its victory over the Ottoman Empire.[16] Britain took over oil exploration in Iraq from the Turkish Petroleum Co., and it was well known in the U.S. and Europe at the time that Britain's tight grip on Mesopotamia was motivated by the substantial oil deposits to be found under its soil.[17] As a full-scale rebellion broke out in Mesopotamia, the British army burned down villages and undertook "barbaric" reprisals.[18] The Royal Air Force (RAF) responded with bombings and machine-gun fire from the air, claiming thousands of Iraqi lives.[19] The British "practically wiped out" whole villages, and experimented with new weapons such as incendiary phosphorous bombs, "liquid-fire," and "man-killing shrapnel."[20] About 10,000 Mesopotamians and other Arabs died in the summer of 1920 alone.[21]

After Mesopotamian rebels killed a handful of British occupation troops in the Kurdish areas around Mosul, Churchill ordered hundreds of them to be "punished," that is killed, with poison mustard gas.[22] Churchill remarked: "I do not understand the squeamishness about the use of gas. I am strongly in favour of using poisonous gas against uncivilised tribes."[23]

By 1921, Churchill recognized "the absolute need" of "appeasing Arab sentiment" to avert being "forced by the expense of the garrisons to evacuate the territories which each country [i.e., Britain and France] gained in the war."[24] British taxpayers spent 33 million pounds fighting the Iraqi insurgents in 1921–1922 a huge fortune at the time.[25]

The Arab revolt in Mesopotamia prompted the British into consider putting an Iraqi "face" on their efforts to protect their Middle Eastern oil resources for use against other empires[26]—yesteryear's version of "Vietnamization"[27] or "as the Iraqis stand up, we will stand down."[28] Mr. Philby, by 1921 an adviser in Baghdad, lobbied for Minister of the Interior Sayyid Talib to be made king of Iraq.[29]

To put an Arab face on the occupation, in 1921 Britain appointed as Iraq's first King a non-Iraqi Ottoman general, the former Emir of Mecca who, like his father Ibn Saud, claimed descent from the prophet Muhammad.[30] The British colonial administrator ac-

---

16. *See* Catherwood, Churchill's Folly, at 62, 67.

17. *See id.* at 67–68, 75, 103–4.

18. *See* Geoff Simons, Iraq: From Sumer to Post-Saddam 212–13 (New York: Palgrave Macmillan, 3d ed. 2004).

19. *See* Catherwood, Churchill's Folly, at 89.

20. Simons, Iraq, at 214.

21. *See* Martin Walker, *The Making of Modern Iraq*, The Wilson Q. 27–2, Apr. 1, 2003, 2003 WL 13111748 (quoting legendary British officer "Lawrence of Arabia").

22. *See* Catherwood, Churchill's Folly, at 83, 85.

23. Simons, Iraq, at 181; *see also* Gary Younge, *Churchill—the Truth*, The Guardian (U.K.), Sept. 30, 2002, http://www.guardian.co.uk/comment/story/0,3604,801386,00.html.

24. Catherwood, Churchill's Folly, at 99. *See also id.* at 119–20, 129–31.

25. *See also id.* at 129–31. *See id.* at 119–20.

26. *See id.* at 119–31; Ellis, *King Me*, at nn. 91–92 & accompanying text.

27. *See More GI Withdrawals from Vietnam Expected,* San Mateo Times, June 9, 1969, at 1; *How the Troop Decision Was Made*, Time Mag., June 20, 1969, http://www.time.com/time/magazine/article/0,9171,844853,00.html.

28. "Our strategy can be summed up this way: As the Iraqis stand up, we will stand down." Associated Press, *Text of President Bush's Speech,* USA Today, June 28, 2005, http://www.usatoday.com/news/washington/2005-06-28-bush-text_x.htm.

29. *See* Ellis, *King Me*, at nn. 91–92 & accompanying text.

30. *See* Catherwood, Churchill's Folly, at 110, 138–41; Mark Lewis, *Historical Setting, in* Iraq: A Country Study, ch. 1 (Helen Chapin Metz ed., Washington, DC: Library of Congress, 1988), http://lcweb2.loc.gov/cgi-bin/query/r?frd/cstdy:@field(DOCID+iq0019).

knowledged that Faisal was viewed by Iraqis as a "puppet king, propped up by our bayonets."[31] Churchill maintained four "Imperial battalions" in Iraq, but hoped to use the RAF to save millions of pounds by using aerial bombardment and Arab troops to reduce the ranks of the British army, so costly to maintain in the field.[32] Churchill would not accept Faisal "having a free hand" given the extensive British military presence in Iraq.[33] The British held a "bogus 'referendum'" on Feisal's enthronement, claiming that 96% of Iraqis welcomed Feisal to be their king.[34]

Iraq gained its formal independence and admission to the League of Nations in 1932.[35] Its Assyrian Christian minority, from which the British had recruited many of its local troops, feared a post-colonial backlash. When the survivors of the Assyrian genocide had reached British lines in 1918, they had been disarmed, placed in refugee camps, and their appeal for an autonomous region of their own submitted to the League of Nations. Assyrian Christian leaders petitioned the League of Nations for autonomy, protection, and a guarantee of freedom to emigrate out of Iraq in the event of pogroms against them.[36] These requests were rejected out of hand, as the British in particular felt relieved of "any obligation to protect the [Assyrian] community as a whole...."[37]

Having secured oil concessions and established a network of air bases, the British proclaimed Iraq's independence to the League of Nations in 1932.[38] Sir Percy Cox, civilian governor of the British Mandate of Iraq before 1918 and again after 1920, noted that: "The Assyrians ... had been recognised as Allies by Great Britain in the War, and had been used by her in the campaign of 1919 in Kurdistan. A definite promise of settlement under a benevolent, if not a British government, had been made to them," but this promise was never fulfilled.[39] The British civil commissioner in Iraq from 1918 to 1920 later wrote that the Assyrians had "not been fairly treated; the crimes of which they have been victims are the consequence of their dispersion." Thousands of impoverished Assyrian women and children living in refugee camps had "seen their menfolk murdered in cold blood." He added:

> The Assyrian problem, as it now exists, is thus largely of our own creation and a solution has been made more difficult by our own action, or rather inaction. It was our duty to settle the Assyrians before we gave up the mandate. Our efforts were half-hearted and had no result.[40]

A British traveler though Iraq in the 1930s found it strange that the Assyrians could have survived the caliphate, the Mongols, and the Ottoman Turks, only to be in "danger

---

31. Toby Dodge, Inventing Iraq: The Failure of Nation-Building and a History Denied 26–27 (London: C. Hurst & Co. Publishers, 2003). Faisal headed one of a series of "pro-British client monarchies" in Saudi Arabia, the Transjordan, and Iraq. Catherwood, Churchill's Folly, at 141. Churchill and his deputy Sir Percy Cox had also financed Faisal's father Ibn Saud, a Wahhabi Arab warlord, in his war of conquest and extermination throughout Arabia. *See id.* at 110, 138–39; Simons, Iraq, at 253.

32. *See* Catherwood, Churchill's Folly, at 168–69.

33. *Id.* at 172.

34. Tripp, A History of Iraq, at 48.

35. *See* Tripp, A History of Iraq, at 75.

36. *See id.*

37. *Id.*

38. Bloxham, The Great Game of Genocide, at 177.

39. British Mandate in Iraq, Official Report on Iraq Administration: October, 1920–March, 1928, at 102.

40. Lt.-Col. A.T. Wilson, M.P., The Crisis in Iraq, 19th Century and After 411–422 (London: Constable and Co., 1933), *quoted in* Yusuf Malek, The British Betrayal of the Assyrians, ch. 19 (Fair Lawn, NJ: Assyrian National Federation, 1935).

of extinction as a race" under the British Mandate of Iraq.[41] A trenchant editorial in 1939 stated:

> The Assyrian nation ... was brought from its homeland by the British promises. They fought for Britain in the War and continued to act as cheap British troops in Iraq for years afterwards. They were solemnly promised a homeland; but, when their usefulness was at an end, they were told to remain amongst the people they had held down, and so antagonized, in Britain's behalf. They were given solemn guarantees that they should be safe. What happened? All the world knows. They were shot, hanged, burned, driven across the borders to stagnate in a pestiferous valley in Syria.[42]

The expected backlash against Assyrians came soon after Iraq's independence, when the leader of the Assyrians, Mar Shimun, was arrested as he pled for an autonomous region, and its army, joined by marauding Kurdish tribesmen, organized a massacre of hundreds of Assyrian civilians, looting their villages.[43] When the Assyrians continued to put up resistance, the Iraqi army and local Kurds massacred the inhabitants of 65 Assyrian villages, including up to 3,000 around Semele, Iraq, causing thousands of Assyrians to flee to Syria.[44] As a key British official in Iraq described the events:

> Suddenly and without the least warning the troops opened fire upon the defenseless Assyrians. Many fell, including women and children, and the rest ran into the houses to take cover.... A cold blooded and methodical massacre of all the men in the village followed.... This took some time. Not that there was any hurry, for the troops had the whole day ahead of them. Their opponents were helpless and there was no chance of any interference from any quarter whatsoever. Machine gunners set up their guns outside the windows of the houses in which the Assyrians had taken refuge, and having trained them on the terror-stricken wretches in the crowded rooms, fired among them until not a man was left standing in the shambles. In some other instances the blood lust of the troops took a slightly more active form and men were dragged out and shot or bludgeoned to death and their bodies thrown on a pile of dead.[45]

Many Assyrians ended up in League of Nations camps around Mosul until at least 1939.[46] The British thought that only 20,000 Assyrian non-Catholics remained in Iraq as of World War II.[47]

---

41. Archibald Hamilton, Road Through Kurdistan 135 (London: Faber & Faber, 1937).

42. *A Pledge Betrayed*, Dublin Review, July, 1939, at 32, *quoted in* David Barsum Perley, Whither Christian Missions? Reflections on the Works of a Missionary and on the Assyrian Case 98 (Paterson, NJ: Assyrian National Federation, 1946).

43. *See* Tripp, A History of Iraq, at 80.

44. Bloxham, The Great Game of Genocide, at 178. *See* USDOS, Office of Strategic Services, *Transfer of the Assyrians of Iraq* (Oct. 31, 1944), http://cgsc.cdmhost.com/cgi-bin/showfile.exe?CISOROOT=/p4013coll8&CISOPTR=646; *see also* Burchard Brentjes, The Armenians, Assyrians & Kurds: Three Nations, One Fate? 64–65 (Varanasi, India: Rishi Publ'ns, 1997); Kanan Makiya, Republic of Fear: The Politics of Modern Iraq 160–77, 183–87, 311–12 (Berkeley, CA: Univ. of California Press, 1998); International Federation for Human Rights, *Iraq: Continuous and Silent Ethnic Cleansing: Displaced Persons in Iraqi Kurdistan and Iraqi Refugees in Iran* 17 (2003), http://www.fidh.org/IMG/pdf/iq350a.pdf..

45. Ronald S. Stafford, The Tragedy of the Assyrians 159–60 (Piscataway, NJ: Gorgias Press, 2006).

46. *See Settlement of the Assyrians of Iraq*, League of Nations Official Journal 372–401 (1939).

47. *See* E 7587/7587/G, at ¶ 6, Anthony Eden, Secretary of State for Foreign Affairs, to Secretary of State for Air, Archibald Sinclair, Jan. 22, 1945, *in* 7 Minorities in the Middle East: Christian Minorities 1838–1967: Assyrian Communities in the Levant and Iraq (Volume II) 1938–1951,

Raphael Lemkin had two examples of genocide in mind prior to the Nazi seizure of power and invasion of Poland. The first was the Ottoman massacres of Armenians during the World War I. The second was the killings of Assyrians in Iraq during the 1930s.[48]

D. A Coup in Afghanistan: Setting the Mold for Later Interventions

Like many countries, Afghanistan had no written constitution prior to the twentieth century. The land was ruled either as a province of another empire, or independently by an Afghan monarch or local tribal leaders.[49] For many centuries, the legal system had its basis in a combination of Sharia law[50] and ancient customs such as the *jirga*, a council of tribal elders convened to settle important issues,[51] and *Pashtunwali*, the Pashtun code of conduct emphasizing conservative family values and the seclusion of women from public view.[52] Around the turn of the twentieth century, Afghanistan opened up to secular influences and women's rights by abolishing some forced marriages, raising the minimum marriageable age, liberalizing women's access to divorce and rights of inheritance, and prohibiting extravagant gifts to a bride's family that could be used in essence to purchase a girl from her parents.[53]

The events leading up to and following the adoption of the first Afghan constitution would be repeated many times in Afghan history: a set of policies looking towards the future and the West infuriated fundamentalists, whose opposition was violently suppressed but eventually succeeded, with foreign intervention, in deposing the regime responsible for the new policies.

---

at 568 (Bejtullah Destani ed., Slough, U.K.: Cambridge Archive Editions Limited, 2007); CP(45)11, Secretary of State for the Colonies to the Secretary of State for Foreign Affairs, Anthony Eden, June 7, 1945, on the Future of the Assyrians, *in id.* at 586.

48. *See* Elder, *What You See Before Your Eyes*, at 475; Tanya Elder, *Guide to the Raphael Lemkin (1900–1959) Collection,* (American Jewish Historical Society, Center for Jewish History ed., 2003), http://www.cjh.org/academic/findingaids/AJHS/nhprc/lemkin02-03.html; *Raphael Lemkin*, EUROPA-WORLD, June 15, 2001, http://www.europaworld.org/issue40/raphaellemkin22601.htm.

49. *See* MARTIN EWANS, AFGHANISTAN: A SHORT HISTORY OF ITS PEOPLE AND POLITICS 12, 15–17, 42–70 (New York: Harper Perennial, 2002); WILLEM VOGELSANG, THE AFGHANS 36, 114–35, 176–212, 217–227, 245–62 (London: Wiley-Blackwell, paperback ed. 2002).

50. In the modern Middle East, sharia law is generally understood to mean a loose system of uncodified laws that the supreme deity of Islam, Allah, revealed to humanity in various passages of the Islamic holy book the Qur'an, and in the sayings and deeds of the Prophet Muhammad. *See* Kristen A. Stilt, *Islamic Law and the Making and Remaking of the Iraqi Legal System*, 36 GEO. WASH. INT'L L. REV. 695, 721 (2004); SUDAN: A COUNTRY STUDY at appx. (Helen Chapin Metz ed., Washington, DC: Library of Congress, 1991), http://lcweb2.loc.gov/frd/cs/sudan/.

51. *See* AHMED RASHID, TALIBAN 83, 95 (New Haven, CT: Yale UP, 2000); United Nations High Commissioner for Refugees (UNHCR), *Update of the Situation in Afghanistan and International Protection Considerations,* 4, ¶ 3 (July 2003).

52. *See id.*; Niloufer Qasim Mahdi, *Pukhtunwali: Ostracism and Honor Among the Pathan Hill Tribes*, 7 ETHOLOGY AND SOCIOBIOLOGY 295–304 (1986).

53. *See* Mariam Nawabi, *Women's Rights in the New Constitution of Afghanistan* at 8 (2003), http://www.cic.nyu.edu; Huma Ahmed-Ghosh, *A History of Women in Afghanistan: Lessons Learnt for the Future*, 4 J. INT'L WOMEN'S STUD. 3 (May 2003), http://www.bridgew.edu/SoAS/jiws/May03/Afghanistan.pdf.

On April 9, 1923, Amanullah Khan, the Amir of Afghanistan, secured the ratification by a *Loya Jirga* of Afghanistan's first written constitution.[54] The 1923 constitution set forth a blueprint for modernizing Afghanistan and assuring greater rights for Afghan women and religious minorities within the framework of Islamic governance. It guaranteed that all Afghan subjects would have "equal rights in accordance with Sharia and the laws of the state."[55] Some Afghans interpreted this provision as entitling Afghan women to citizenship and equal rights.[56] It abolished torture, slavery, and forced labor;[57] created a legislature, although the Amir would appoint the prime minister and many of its members; and decreed that followers of religions other than Islam, such as Hinduism and Judaism, were entitled to the protection of the state. Elementary education became compulsory for all Afghan "citizens."[58]

The constitution promised greater rights to religious minorities such as the Hazaras, who as Shi'a Muslims had been labeled as infidels and massacred and enslaved in the nineteenth century for this reason. It has been estimated that nearly two-thirds of Hazaras were massacred by the former regime of Amir Abdur Rahman, with the survivors sold into slavery or deported from the country.[59] The Amir bestowed Sunni Afghans with the title of *ghazi* or infidel-killer, familiar from the life of Mustafa Kemal as discussed above, for committing massacres of Hazaras. In an example of nation-building by liquidation of minority institutions, the Hazara system of self-rule was dismantled, Hazara land was stolen, and Hazaras bought and sold in the bazaar.[60]

Taking on centuries-old customs, Amir Amnullah Khan also introduced ambitious legislative reforms improving Afghan women's rights. In 1921, he enacted a Family Code banning child marriage, marriages between close relatives, excessive dowries, and the exchange of women as "blood money" in payment of interfamilial disputes.[61] He opened girls' schools and sent women students abroad for higher education.[62] After 1923, the Amir introduced Afghanistan's first civil code,[63] which abolished polygamy and marriages to all girls under the age of 18.[64] His wife Soraya appeared unveiled in public and participated actively in politics, citing the example of women in the "early years of Islam."[65]

---

54. *Loya Jirga* (or Great Council in the Pashto language) is an institution that has served in Afghan history as a mechanism for involving the Afghan people in decisions of great historic significance by calling an assembly of tribal elders and national leaders to reach an accord. *See* G. Rauf Roashan, *Loya Jirga: One of the Last Political Tools for Bringing Peace to Afghanistan* (July 30, 2001), http://www.institute-for-afghan-studies.org/.

55. Const. of Afgh. 1923, art. 16.

56. *See* Vogelsang, The Afghans, at 279.

57. *See* Const. of Afgh. 1923, art. 10.

58. *See id.*, arts. 2, 26, 28, 68.

59. *See* Masouda Gizabi, Testimony to the Congressional Human Rights Caucus on the Post Taleban Era: Human Rights and the Role of Women in Afghanistan (Dec. 18, 2001); Mir Hekmatullah Sadat, *Afghan History: Kite Flying, Kite Running and Kite Banning*, Lemar Aftaab Afghanmagazine.com, June 2004, http://www.afghanmagazine.com/2004_06/articles/hsadat.shtml.

60. *See* Sadat, *Afghan History*.

61. *See* International Crisis Group, *Afghanistan's Flawed Constitutional Process* (June 12, 2003); *Emir (King) Amanullah, in* The Encyclopedia of World History: Ancient, Medieval, and Modern 757 (Peter N. Sterns ed., New York: Houghton Mifflin, 6th. ed. 2001).

62. *See* Mir Hekmatullah Sadat, *Modern Education in Afghanistan*, Lemar—Aftaab Afghanmagazine.com, Mar. 2004, http://www.afghanmagazine.com/2004_03/articles/education.shtml.

63. *See* Rashid, Taliban, at 83.

64. *See* Nawabi, *Women's Rights*, at 8.

65. Louis Dupree, Afghanistan 46 (Princeton: Princeton UP, 1973), *cited in* Nawabi, *Women's Rights*, at 8.

Not satisfied with the constitution's gestures towards theocracy, and disappointed with King Amanullah's record as the "protector" of Islam, Afghanistan's religious elite quickly moved to overthrow and reverse his modernizing reforms. The head of a prominent religious family, which served as "king makers" in Afghan society,[66] immediately denounced the 1923 constitution as a "communist" document.[67] A rebellion reached the outskirts of the capital Kabul, and was only repelled when the Amir mobilized his new air force to strafe and bomb the advancing insurgents,[68] and then executed the revolt's leaders.[69]

Rebels having nearly toppled his regime, the Amir called a *Loya Jirga* to amend the 1923 constitution in several important respects designed to pacify Afghanistan's religious elite. One amendment reestablished Islam as the official religion.[70] Additional concessions from the Amir included "watering down" the rights of women,[71] reintroducing torture when "in accordance with the rules of the Sharia,"[72] and allowing a Council of Islamic Scholars to "decide whether new laws were in accordance with Islamic law."[73]

After Amir Amanullah became King of Afghanistan in 1926, he announced further sweeping reforms aimed at helping Afghan women.[74] He endorsed expanding Afghan girls' access to education, proclaimed his opposition to the compulsory veiling of women, and imposed Western dress within the capital of Kabul.[75] In response, Afghan religious leaders once again led conservative Afghan tribes in rebellion. Under siege, King Amanullah abdicated the throne in early 1929.[76] Historians tend to blame the King's overhasty reforms for his downfall, especially those dealing with mandatory veiling, the seclusion of women, and forced and underage marriages.[77]

The West failed to support the King who admired its modern movements towards secular government, women's rights, and minority protection. Instead, the British Empire actively worked to overthrow him. Many Afghans and even the British press believed that the British Empire was behind Amanullah's fall from power, given the empire's poor relations with him.[78] The Soviet Union backed the anti-British King, drawing Afghanistan further into its centuries-long struggle with the British Empire, which had unsuccessfully intervened on the side of the Russian monarchy, disliked Soviet expropriations of British property, feared Soviet expansion towards British holdings in the Middle East, and fought Soviet influence in China.[79] When pro-Amanullah and anti-Amanullah armies fought

66. *See* Rashid, Taliban, at 84.

67. Ewans, Afghanistan, at 93.

68. *See id.* at 94.

69. *See id.*

70. *See id.* Jews and Hindus, moreover, would be forced to wear distinctive clothing and pay a special tax. *See* Const. of Afgh. 1923, art. 2.

71. Ewans, Afghanistan, at 94.

72. *See* Const. of Afgh. 1923, art. 24, as amended January 28, 1925.

73. Vogelsang, The Afghans, at 280.

74. *See id.* at 281.

75. *See id.*

76. *See id.* at 281–82; Craig Baxter, *Historical Setting, in* Afghanistan: A Country Study 45–46 (Richard F. Nyrop & Donald M. Seekins, eds., Washington, DC: Library of Congress, 1986).

77. *See, e.g.*, Ewans, Afghanistan, at 96–98; Edgar O'Ballance, Afghan Wars: Battles in a Hostile Land 75 (London: Brassey's, 2002).

78. *See* Ewans, Afghanistan, at 96–105.

79. *See* Associated Press, *Turns Harbin Into Military Camp; Troops Isolate Soviet Consulate—British and American Consuls Reject Japanese Plan*, N.Y. Times, Jan. 25, 1926, http://www.nytimes.com; *Britain Rejects the Soviet*, N.Y. Times, Feb. 13, 1920, http://www.nytimes.com; John Clayton, *Allies Keeping Eyes on Reds*, L.A. Times, Sep. 21, 1922, at I8; Charles Dailey, *Peking Defies Russia; War By Soviet Feared*, Chicago Daily Tribune, Apr. 7, 1927, at 1; Alfred L.P. Dennis, *Soviet's Poker Game*

over the king's future, the anti-Amanullah forces under Nadir Khan prevailed with British support.[80] The British allowed Nadir to pass through its Indian colony and raise an army with which to invade Afghanistan.[81]

King Amanullah's successors quickly overturned his reforms. But in doing so, they did not return Afghanistan to a pre-modern or pre-constitutional condition. Instead, they established an Islamic constitutional monarchy with deeply theocratic tendencies. A *Loya Jirga* in 1930 created Afghanistan's next stable government and pronounced Nadir Shah as Afghanistan's king.[82] The king promulgated the second Afghan constitution in 1931.[83] With a few minor changes, it endured as Afghanistan's governing charter for more than 30 years.[84]

E. Italy in Ethiopia and Libya: Camps, Gas, and Starvation Before 1939

Benito Mussolini witnessed, if he paid attention, Turkey's invasion of and massacres in historical Armenia, Pontus, the Smyrna region, and northern Mesopotamia, the Soviet annexation of Armenia, Georgia, and Azerbaijan, and the British invasion and occupation of Mesopotamia under a League of Nations "mandate." Mussolini admired Mustafa Kemal and has been classed with him as a dictator who restored a majority population's flagging spirits by stoking the fires of militarism, racial hatred, and expansionism.[85] Years before Germany's entry into Poland, Mussolini's fascist regime utilized tactics that are today and will long be associated with the Nazis, including widespread massacres, concentration camps, poison gas, racial discrimination, and destruction of civilian infrastructure. Scholars estimate that anywhere from 300,000 to 800,000 Ethiopians died, mostly from gunfire and starvation, but also tens of thousands in concentration camps,

---

in Asia; First Map Showing Routes of Bolshevism in Asia, N.Y. Times, July 30, 1922, at 88; United Press Int'l, *Russia Breaks With China*, Chicago Tribune, Apr. 10, 1927, at 1. *See also* Clifford Kinvig, Churchill's Crusade: The British Invasion of Russia, 1918–1920 (Harrisburg, PA: Continuum Int'l Publ'g Group, 2006).

80. *See* Douglas A. Borer, Superpowers Defeated: Vietnam and Afghanistan Compared 14 (London: Routledge, 1999); Ewans, Afghanistan, at 100; Angelo Rasanayagam, Afghanistan 18–30 (London: I.B. Tauris, 2005); *see also* Leon B. Poullada, Reform and Rebellion in Afghanistan, 1919–1929: King Amanullah's Failure to Modernize a Tribal Society 191 (Ithaca, NY: Cornell UP, 1973).

81. *See* Rasanayagam, Afghanistan, at 23–24.

82. *See* Leon B. Poullada & Leila D.J. Poullada, The Kingdom of Afghanistan and the United States: 1828–1973, at 86 (Omaha, NE: The Center for Afghanistan Studies at the Univ. of Nebraska, 1995); Ewans, Afghanistan, at 102; Afghanistan Country Study, at 49.

83. *See* Vogelsang, The Afghans, at 285.

84. *See* Ewans, Afghanistan, at 101.

85. *See, e.g.*, Denis Mack Smith, Mussolini 153 (New York: Knopf, 1982); Luigi Villari, Italian Foreign Policy under Mussolini 40 (New York: Devin-Adair Co., 1956). *See also* Paul Hollander, Political Pilgrims: Western Intellectuals in Search of the Good Society 169 (New Brunswick, NJ: Transaction Publ'ers, 1998); Francis A. Ridley, Mussolini over Africa 88 (London: Wishart Books, Ltd., 1935); Esmonde Manning Robertson, Mussolini as Empire-builder: Europe and Africa, 1932–36, at 13–20 (New York: Macmillan, 1977).

by aerial bombardment, and via summary executions and massacres.[86] In Libya more than 100,000 Arabs died resisting the Italian fascist occupation.[87]

The case of Ethiopia manifested similar failures of international order as that of Armenia, Assyria, and Pontic Greece from 1914 to 1925. Ethiopia appealed to the League of Nations for an investigation of Italian war crimes and reprisals, with an eye towards preventing the continued use of poison gas on Ethiopian nationals. The League of Nations imposed economic sanctions on Italy for invading Ethiopia without warrant under international law.[88] But it was unable to alter Italy's behavior through sanctions alone,[89] and basically "abandoned [the] Ethiopian people."[90] Ethiopian Emperor Haile Selassie telegraphed the league from exile in Jerusalem to call for an immediate "end to the most sweeping, the most unjust, and the most inhuman war of modern times by leaving the country in order to avoid the extermination of the Ethiopian people."[91] The league's sanctions on Italian exports were rendered ineffective by the decision by the U.S., Nazi Germany, and the Soviet Union to maintain or increase their levels of trade with fascist Italy.[92] Not only the U.S. but also Germany and Japan were non-members of the league, and continued to trade with Italy.[93] Italy entered World War II strong.

Nazi Germany and Imperial Japan may have been emboldened in their crimes of the late 1930s and early 1940s (prior to Pearl Harbor) by the U.S. and Soviet responses to the Ethiopian massacres.[94] The Soviet Union kept up a "lively trade" with Italy despite sanctions, at fully 83 percent of its level of prewar exports in 1935. Profit trumped human rights in the U.S. as well:

> Americans took advantage of Italy's war needs to increase trade. It was legal to do so, and many businessmen rejected the notion of a moral embargo....
>
> [E]xports from the United States [to fascist Italy] increased—above all in oil.

American oil, cars, trucks, and tractors greased the Italian path into Ethiopia.[95]

---

86. *See* George W. Baer, Test Case: Italy, Ethiopia, and the League of Nations 92–93 (Stanford, CA: Hoover Inst. Press, 1976); A.J. Barker, The Rape of Ethiopia 106–29 (New York: Ballentine, 2d ed. 1971) (1936); Angelo Del Boca, The Ethiopian War 1935–1941 (P.D. Cummins trans., Chicago: University of Chicago Press, 1969); Alberto Sbacchi, Ethiopia Under Mussolini: Fascism and the Colonial Experience (Totowa, NJ: Biblio Distribution Center, 1985); *See also* Michael B. Lentakis, Ethiopia: A View From Within 50 (2005); Nicholas Farrell, Mussolini: A New Life 275 (London: Janus Publishing Co. 2005); John W. Turner, *Mussolini's Invasion and the Italian Occupation, in* A Country Study: Ethiopia (Washington, DC: Library of Congress, 1991), http://lcweb2.loc.gov/cgi-bin/query/r?frd/cstdy:@field(DOCID+et0029).

87. *See* Robert Gerwarth, Twisted Paths: Europe 1914–1945, at 163–64 (Oxford: Oxford UP, 2007) (estimating 100,000 Arab deaths and 500,000 in flight from Libya during Italian rule in 1920s and 1930s); Waniss Otman & Erling Karlberg, The Libyan Economy: Economic Diversification and International Repositioning 14 (London: Springer, 2007) (Libyan population cut in half due to deaths and emigration by 1937).

88. *See* United States General Accounting Office, Economic Sanctions: Effectiveness as Tools of Foreign Policy 26 (Washington, DC: U.S. GAO, 1992).

89. *See* Baer, Test Case, at 183, 274.

90. *Id.* at 281 (quoting Ethiopian delegation).

91. *Id.*

92. *See id.* at 66, 170, 199–214, 290–96.

93. *See* Ciro Paoletti, A Military History of Italy 160–67 (Westport, CT: Greenwood Pub-l'g Group, 2008).

94. *See* Baer, Test Case, at 303 ("Albert Speer records the lesson Hitler learned. '... The Western governments had ... proved themselves weak and indecisive.'").

95. *Id.* at 200.

Chapter X

The Elimination of Asiatic Influence: Genocide in World War II

> The most important goal of the campaign against the Jewish-Bolshevik system is the complete crushing of the instruments of power and the eradication of the Asiatic influence in the European cultural sphere.
>
> —Field Marshal Walter von Reichenau, Sixth Army, Army Group South, 1941[1]

This chapter describes some of the links between the Ottoman Christian genocide and the Holocaust, including comparisons by Hitler and other Nazis of their policies to those of the Ottomans and Turkish Nationalists. Starting with a brief sketch of Nazi Germany's imperial ambitions, it will explore the German occupation of Eastern Europe and genocide against Jews, Slavs, and other groups, and the actions of Germany's allies and adversaries in World War II. This chapter then outlines the impact of the Holocaust on the Islamic world, and in particular the means by which the Allies prevented the planned extermination of numerous Asian and North African populations of Jews. To achieve this, it is necessary to describe Germany's hopes to dominate the Middle East, and its plan to enlist Arab, Turkish, and Persian leaders in a campaign to exterminate the Jews of southwestern Asia and North Africa. Finally, this chapter discusses the contribution of some the victims of the Ottoman Christian genocide, especially the Assyrians and Greeks, to blocking the Germans' murderous advance into southwestern Asia.

A. The Holocaust in Europe

Viewing themselves as the equals or even the cultural and intellectual betters of the British, French, and Spanish who had wrested such great empires from indigenous Americans, Africans, and Asians, the Germans developed imperial ideologies and legal theories of their own. German "geopolitics" evinced an ever-increasing emphasis on colonial space or *Raum* (eventually "living space" or *Lebensraum*). This tendency surfaced with Alexander von Humboldt's anthropological study of British and Spanish colonization of the Americas. In the twentieth century, Kaiser Wilhelm II practiced a new form of Ger-

1. *Quoted in* Megargee, War of Annihilation, at 124.

man geopolitics with his settlement of new African colonies, and mass killings of indigenous Africans.[2]

The Enlightenment was a seventeenth and eighteenth-century movement towards inter-denominational Christian toleration in Europe. The thinkers associated with it also developed rationalist and empiricist philosophy, liberal constitutionalism, and laissez-faire economic theory. In what has been termed the "dialectic of Enlightenment," the movement advocated greater personal and political liberty on the one hand, while paradoxically championing state intervention on an instrumental ends-justify-the-means basis that led to totalitarian ideologies such as communism and fascism.[3] The ideas of Fichte and Hegel gave away after the passage of more than a century to those of Hitler and Rosenberg; Pugachev's paved the way for Lenin's.

The nation-state, which Friedrich Nietzsche called the "cold monster" in a moment of deep insight, became a fetish for the Enlightenment German philosophers. The chair in philosophy at the University of Berlin, Johann Gottleib Fichte, was an expert on Machiavelli. He proclaimed in the early nineteenth century CE that the German race, of purer blood than the mixed Mediterranean races, would reorder and organize the productive forces of the world in a new progressive era.[4] From Machiavelli, he synthesized the doctrine that all humans are wicked and must be kept in check by a rigid, proto-totalitarian, system of regimentations.[5]

George Wilhelm Friedrich Hegel succeeded Fichte as chair of philosophy in Berlin. He described the State as having "the supreme right against the individual, whose supreme duty is to be a member of the State." The State represented the actuality of the "ethical mind," the march of the "world spirit" through the world to the "end of days," the fulfillment of the "Christian idea" of ordered liberty.[6] Hegel emphasized the sovereignty of States, the primacy of their drive to pursue their own interests (or "welfare," as he called it), and the impracticality of Immanuel Kant's idea of a league of nations that would peacefully arbitrate disputes among its members. War, for Hegel, was a cleansing trial improving the "ethical health of peoples corrupted by a long peace." Heroes, in Hegel's system, had the right to found new States by divine inspiration or "force and wrong," including by treating other peoples as "barbarians" if they "lag behind." He explained:

> War is not to be regarded as an absolute evil..., because philosophy ... sees in its essence, necessity. It is necessary that the finite—property and life—should be definitely established as accidental.... The transience of the finite becomes a

---

2. *See Introduction, in* WEBER AND TOENNIES: COMPARATIVE SOCIOLOGY IN HISTORICAL PERSPECTIVE (Joseph B. Maier & Chaim I. Waxman eds., New Brunswick, NJ: Transaction Publishers, 1995); Werner J. Callman, *Rudolf Hess, or an Introduction to the Emergence of German Geopolitics, in id.*, at 319–36; WOODRUFF D. SMITH, POLITICS AND THE SCIENCES OF CULTURE IN GERMANY, 1840–1920, at 12, 146, 148–9, 202–3, 209–15 (Oxford: Oxford UP, 1991).

3. *Cf.* THEODOR W. ADORNO & MAX HORKHEIMER. DIALECTIC OF ENLIGHTENMENT (Edmund Jephcott trans., Stanford: Stanford UP, 2002) (1944).

4. *See* WILLIAM L. SHIRER, THE RISE AND FALL OF THE THIRD REICH: A HISTORY OF NAZI GERMANY 143 (New York: Simon & Schuster, 1992) (1959).

5. *See* RUDOLF ROCKER, NATIONALISM AND CULTURE 188 (Ray E. Chase trans., Montreal: Black Rose Books Ltd., 1998). *See also* JOHANN GOTTLIEB FICHTE, REDEN AN DIE DEUTSCHE NATION (Berlin, 1808); JOHANN GOTTLIEB FICHTE, 2 THE POPULAR WORKS OF JOHANN GOTTLIEB FICHTE (William Smith trans., London: Trubner & Co., 1889); JOHANN GOTTLIEB FICHTE, VOLK UND STAAT: EINE AUSWAHL AUS SEINEN SCHRIFTEN (Munich, 1921).

6. *Quoted in* SHIRER, THE RISE AND FALL OF THE THIRD REICH, at 144. *See also* Pierre Hassner, *Georg W.F. Hegel, in* HISTORY OF POLITICAL PHILOSOPHY 752–58 (Leo Strauss & Joseph Cropsey eds., London and Chicago: Univ. of Chicago Press, 3d ed. 1987).

> willed passing away, and the negativity lying at the roots of the finite [is revealed]....
>
> War is the state of affairs which deals in earnest with the vanity of temporal goods and concerns.[7]

In Hegel's philosophically idealist account of war, it played the necessary part of establishing the finitude, ideality, and impermanence of particular individuals and their property.[8]

Other key contributors to the philosophical climate of twentieth century CE Europe were Karl Marx, Friedrich Nietzsche, Arthur de Gobineau, and Stewart Chamberlain. Marx's materialism regarded the world order as the outcome of a process of violent "primitive accumulation," and advocated a new form of revolution in which an enlightened vanguard would become dictators, remaking the world system in a rational mold.[9] Nietzsche valorized power and brutality over rights, justice, and humanitarianism, repeatedly praising Napoleon, Italian aristocrats, and Roman emperors over Christian "sheep," socialist "women," or English "shopkeepers."[10] De Gobineau, a former aide to Alexis de Tocqueville, became influential for his theory that a superior Aryan race, hailing from Central Asia, was destined to rule inferior black and yellow races. Finally, Chamberlain was a scion of a British military family and confidant of Kaiser Wilhelm II. He wrote that Germans—or Teutons, as he called them—were destined to follow in the steps of the Aryan (sic) prophet Jesus Christ in advancing the "true religion" of "Indo-European peoples." Chamberlain, in his old age, met Adolf Hitler, a young veteran, and encouraged him to become a world leader and do "mighty things" with his life.[11]

The Enlightenment paved the way for totalitarianism in some respects, including by reorienting the rationality of law from its content, or its substantive justice, to its form, or its duly enacted character. Judges were urged in the Enlightenment era not to legislate abstract justice, but merely to apply decrees of the legislative or executive branches. Thus, an apparently unjust decision in a particular case may be necessary to advance the long-term interests of the nation. Jean-Jacques Rousseau argued that in a republic, the laws *cannot* be unjust because they will issue from the people, and the people cannot be un-

---

7. Georg W.F. Hegel, The Philosophy of Right 107, 111–14 (T.M. Knox trans., Chicago: Encyclopedia Britannica, Inc. 1952).

8. *See also* Michael H. Mitias, Moral Foundation of the State in Hegel's Philosophy of Right 177–81 (Amsterdam: Editions Rodopi BV, 1984); Shirer, The Rise and Fall of the Third Reich, at 144.

9. *See* Karl Marx, *Manifesto of the Communist Party, in* 1 Marx/Engels Selected Works 98–137 (Frederick Engels ed. and Samuel Morre trans., Moscow: Progress Publishers, 1969), http://www.marxists.org/archive/marx/works/1848/communist-manifesto/index.htm; Karl Marx, 1 Capital, ch. 26–33 (Frederick Engels ed. and Samuel Moore & Edward Aveling trans., Moscow: Progress Publishers, 1887) (1867), http://www.marxists.org/archive/marx/works/1867-c1/index.htm; Karl Marx, *Critique of the Gotha Programme*, Die Neue Zeit, No. 18 (1890–91), *reprinted in* 3 Marx/Engels Selected Works 13–30 (Moscow: Progress Publishers, 1970), http://www.marxists.org/archive/marx/works/1875/gotha/index.htm; Vladimir I. Lenin, *Marxism and Insurrection, in* Lenin's Collected Works 22–27 (Moscow: Progress Publishers, 1972) (1917), http://www.marxists.org/archive/lenin/works/1917/sep/13.htm; Leon Trotsky, *A Necessary Discussion with Our Syndicalist Comrades* (1923), http://www.marxists.org/archive/trotsky/1931/unions/1-discussion.htm.

10. Friedrich Nietzsche, Twilight of the Idols 38 (R. J. Hollingdale trans., London: Penguin Books, 2003). *See also* Robert B. Pippin, *Overcoming Oneself: Neitzsche on Freedom, in* Nietzsche und Europa-Nietzsche in Europa 135 (Volker Gerhardt & Renate Reschke eds., Berlin: Akademie Verlag, 2007).

11. *See* Shirer, The Rise and Fall of the Third Reich, at 145–62.

just to itself.[12] To Charles de Secondat, Baron de Montesquieu, the judge possesses a "terrible power," but *should* act as "no more than the mouth that pronounces the words of the law, … incapable of moderating … its force.…"[13]

The political scientist and adviser to the Nuremberg prosecutors, Franz Neumann, wrote that such formalism dictates that the "judge's sole function is to perceive the law," so that the process of judicial review of laws using higher standards of fairness or justice is denied. This process reached its nadir with National Socialism, which "completely destroy[ed] … the independence of the judiciary and the prohibition of retroactivity" in criminal law. Acts contrary to "healthy racial feeling" became crimes under the German penal code in force in 1935. The judge became a mere "police official." In the thought of Nazi jurist Carl Schmitt, for example, the principles of National Socialism are "exclusively valid" as "general standards of conduct [applied] through the judge.…"[14] The actions of the Gestapo became unreviewable as a matter of administrative law. Judges came to accept, after some resistance, the "absolute and arbitrary power of the Gestapo over all personal liberties." Non-Aryans were purged from the Supreme Court. The civil service act rendered judges subject to being fired or transferred if they acted contrary to the policies of the leader or the interests of the national security state. Military courts and special commissions proliferated for the *Schutzstaffel* (S.S.) Nazi vanguard, *Sturmabteilung* (S.A.) brownshirts, and labor disputes. People's courts staffed by military officials or SS officials began to sentence defendants without the semblance of any trial, i.e., without choice of counsel, discovery of evidence, appeal, or public hearings. The death penalty applied to all political crimes and attempts at such crimes, and to intentionally listening to English or Russian language broadcasts. Under pure formalism, all of these materials and institutions remained legal in nature and effect; under natural law, all were null and void.[15]

Hitler's views were forged in the crucible of the First World War and the economic depression in Germany and Austria that followed it. A listener to Hitler's public speaking in 1925 noted that he "dwelt at length on patriotism and national pride and quoted approvingly the role of Kemal Ataturk of Turkey and the example of Mussolini, who had marched on Rome" a few weeks before the speech.[16] Nazism emerged in Germany at a time when extreme right-wing anti-communist ideologies were gaining traction even in "liberal" countries like Britain and the U.S. The American automobile magnate Henry Ford, a virulent anti-Semite, was looked to as a "source of funds" for the nascent Nazi movement.[17] There is evidence that Ford may have indirectly funded the rise of the Nazi party in the 1920s.[18] Even Winston Churchill praised Hitler, writing in 1938 that "if Great

---

12. *See* Jean-Jacques Rousseau, The Social Contract, or Principles of Political Right 33 (Ernest Rhys ed., New York: E.P. Dutton & Co., 1920) (1762).

13. Charles de Secondat, Baron de Montesquieu, The Sprit of Laws, bk. XI, ch. VI (Thomas Nugent trans., London: Nourse & Valliant, 4th ed. 1766).

14. Franz Leopold Neumann, Behemoth: The Structure and Practice of National Socialism 442–47 (Oxford: Oxford UP, 1942).

15. *See id.* at 447–58.

16. Martyn Housden, Hitler: Study of a Revolutionary 47 (London: Routledge, 2000).

17. Ernst Hanfstaengl, Hitler: The Missing Years 34 (John Toland trans., New York: Arcade Publ'g, 1994) ("The only American figure for whom he had time was Henry Ford, and then not so much as an industrial wonder-worker but rather as a reputed anti-Semite and a source of funds.").

18. *See* Max Wallace, The American Axis: Henry Ford, Charles Lindbergh, and the Rise of the Third Reich 64 (New York: St. Martin's Press, 2004).

Britain were defeated in war, I hoped we should find a Hitler to lead us back to our rightful position among the nations."[19]

Hitler planned a German Empire (*Reich*) enslaving the non-Germanic peoples of Europe, Asia, and Africa in colonial subjugation to their German overlords, the "master race."[20] The Nazis perceived two main obstacles to their imperial ambitions, one the Soviet Union in the East, and the other the British Empire in the West and global South; the Nazis' delusional narrative of history linked these threats through an international conspiracy of Jews.[21] After a leading figure in the regime of Kaiser Wilhelm II appointed Hitler to be Chancellor of the German Reich, a proclamation issued on behalf of the Nazis announced that they had "shattered Marxism" and thwarted the plan to "make Germany into a Soviet Jewish criminal colony."[22]

Nazi anti-Semitism had deep roots in German culture, including jealousy of their holdings in gold and currency dating back to the time of Martin Luther, and identification with 1930s socialist and anarchist revolutionaries, much like the Armenians were identified decades before.[23] The Holocaust began in 1933 with a boycott of Jewish merchants and professionals, and arrests of Jews, Communists, Social Democrats, and others for "subversive" and "Bolshevist" activities. The Nazis established concentration camps for persons in custody, including not simply Jews, Communists, and Social Democrats but also Roma people, various Christian sects, homosexuals, immigrants, and the left. In the late 1930s, mass arrests occurred of Jews, as well as seizure or destruction of Jewish properties, and segregation of Jews and non-Jews.[24] Jews were confined into ghettos and enslaved in the "'interest of War Economy.'"[25]

The Nazis declared both the Jews and the Eastern European Slavs to be sub-human (*Untermenschen*).[26] Nazi anthropologists identified "Near Asian Jewry" as the source of Europe's problems,[27] and studied the skulls of Jewish Bolshevists for racial affiliation. The University of Berlin's chair in Race Studies published influential studies on the racial origins of the Jewish and German peoples in the 1920s and 1930s, concluding among other things that Jews were a mixture of Asian, African, and European peoples and were therefore, like other "peoples of Near Eastern origin[,] ... deficient in the area of state-build-

---

19. The Times, Nov, 7, 1938, *quoted in* Walter Alfred Peter Phillips, The Tragedy of Nazi Germany 159 (London: Taylor & Francis, 1969).

20. *See* Franz Neumann, Behemoth: The Structure and Practice of National Socialism 136–37, 156–60 (New York: Oxford UP, 2d ed. 1963); 1 Nazi Conspiracy and Aggression, ch. VII, http://www.yale.edu/lawweb/avalon/imt/document/nca_vol1/chap_.htm (describing plans for empire of "'racial Germans'"); 1 Nazi Conspiracy and Aggression, ch. X., http://www.yale.edu/lawweb/avalon/imt/document/nca_vol1/chap_10.htm.

21. *See* Jeffrey Herf, The Jewish Enemy: Nazi Propaganda During World War II and the Holocaust, ch. 4 (Cambridge, MA: Harvard UP, 2006).

22. *Be On Your Guard! (Poster)* (1933), *in* Concentration Camp Dachau: 1933–1945, at 31 (Barbara Distel & Ruth Jakusch eds., Comité international de Dachau, 1978).

23. *See* Neumann, Behemoth, at 109–11.

24. *See* Concentration Camp Dachau: 1933–1945, at 31, 38–48, 58, 85, 100–4.

25. 1 Nazi Conspiracy and Aggression, ch. XII, http://www.yale.edu/lawweb/avalon/imt/document/nca_vol1/chap_12.htm.

26. *See* Megargee, War of Annihilation, at 123–28; Wiecek, *The Origins of the Law of Slavery in North America,* at 1722; Jack Achiezer Guggenheim, *Art & Atrocity: Cultural Depravity Justifies Cultural Deprivation*, 8 Fordham Intellectual Property, Media & Entmt. Law J. 699, 713 (1998) (citing Shirer, The Rise and Fall of the Third Reich, at 937).

27. *Quoted in* J. John Loughran, Developing a Pedagogy of Teacher Education 176 (London: Taylor & Francis, 2006).

ing and statecraft."[28] Hitler admired the ancient Spartans, who put "weak" children to death.[29] He was familiar with U.S. racial science and eugenics laws, which aimed to reduce births among Jews, Eastern Europeans, Native Americans, African-Americans, Asians, Hispanics, Italians, and the poor.[30]

The Holocaust was announced in dramatic form with systematic assaults on synagogues and Jewish homes and businesses in Germany. Although attacks on synagogues and their routine desecration dated back to 1933, it was in 1938 that an organized campaign emerged for the "'breakup of the synagogues,'" and the removal of Jewish symbols such as the Star of David.[31] During *Kristallnacht*, the night of the broken glass, November 9–10, 1938, the Nazis and German mobs killed between several dozen and 200 Jews, burned or destroyed more than 200 synagogues and 800 Jewish shops, and arrested 20,000 Jews.[32] The Berlin Secret State Police Headquarters was behind the organized violence, and ordered the German police to regulate it:

> a. Only such measures should be taken which do not involve danger to German life or property. (For instance synagogues are to be burned down only when there is no danger of fire to the surroundings.)
>
> b. Business and private apartments of Jews may be destroyed but not looted. The police is [sic] instructed to supervise the execution of this order and to arrest looters.[33]

On January 30, 1939, Hitler declared to the Reichstag that faced with the choice of a "Jewish victory" and "bolshevization of the earth" on the one hand, and the "annihilation of the Jewish race in Europe" on the other, he would choose the latter.[34] That same day, he told the Czechoslovakian foreign minister that: "We are going to destroy the Jews. They are not going to get away with what they did in [World War I]."[35] In June 1940, Hitler decreed that "all Jews, gypsies and communist political functionaries" should be murdered throughout the Soviet Union.[36] In July 1941, Goering ordered Reinhard Heydrich, Chief of the Reich Central Security Office, to effectuate a "total solution of the Jewish question" in the East.[37] At the Wannsee Conference in 1942, Heydrich announced to other high Nazi officials a scheme of deportation somewhat reminiscent of the Armenian, Assyrian, and Greek deportations, and the enslavement of Armenians and Greeks in labor battalions in 1915:

---

28. *See* ALAN E. STEINWEIS, STUDYING THE JEW: SCHOLARLY ANTISEMITISM IN NAZI GERMANY 20–32, 60 (Cambridge, MA: Harvard UP, 2006).

29. *See* MIKE HAWKINS, SOCIAL DARWINISM IN EUROPEAN AND AMERICAN THOUGHT, 1860–1945: NATURE AS MODEL AND NATURE AS THREAT 276 (Cambridge: Cambridge UP, 1997).

30. *See* Edwin Black, *Eugenics and the Nazis—The California Connection,* S.F. CHRON., Nov. 9, 2003, http://www.sfgate.com/cgi-bin/article.cgi?file=/chronicle/archive/2003/11/09/ING9C2QSKB1.DTL

31. Minutes of a Nazi meeting in Nuremberg in 1938, *quoted in* STEINWEIS, STUDYING THE JEW, at 20–32, 60.

32. *See* SHIRER, THE RISE AND FALL OF THE THIRD REICH, at 581–82.

33. Nuremberg Document No. 3051-PS, Nov. 10, 1938, Berlin Secret State Police Headquarters to German police chiefs, *quoted in* 1 NAZI CONSPIRACY AND AGGRESSION, ch. XII, http://avalon.law.yale.edu/imt/chap_12.asp.

34. *Quoted in* MICHAEL ZALAMPAS, ADOLF HITLER AND THE THIRD REICH IN AMERICAN MAGAZINES, 1923–1939, at 189 (Madison, WI: Univ. of Wisconsin Press, 1989).

35. *Quoted in* ERICH FROMM, THE ANATOMY OF HUMAN DESTRUCTIVENESS 444 (New York: Macmillan, 1992).

36. *Quoted in* Ian Hancock, *The Romani Holocaust, in* IS THE HOLOCAUST UNIQUE?: PERSPECTIVES ON COMPARATIVE GENOCIDE, at 83 (2001).

37. *Quoted in* CHRISTOPHER R. BROWNING, THE ORIGINS OF THE FINAL SOLUTION 315 (Omaha, NE: University of Nebraska Press, 2004).

> Under proper guidance, in the course of the final solution the Jews are to be allocated for appropriate labor in the East. Able-bodied Jews, separated according to sex, will be taken in large work columns to these areas for work on roads, in the course of which action doubtless a large portion will be eliminated by natural causes.
>
> The possible final remnant will, since it will undoubtedly consist of the most resistant portion, have to be treated accordingly, because it is the product of natural selection and would, if released, act as the seed of a new Jewish revival (see the experience of history).[38]

That elimination was the objective of Nazi officials after 1942, and likely earlier as well, is made clear by the declaration of Governor-General of Poland, Nazi jurist Hans Frank, that: "As far as the Jews are concerned, I want to tell you quite frankly that they must be done away with one way or another.... We must annihilate the Jews, wherever it is possible."[39] The German Jews fared somewhat better, with up to four-fifths being allowed to emigrate.[40]

Three to four million Jews, Roma, Slavs, and others died in Nazi extermination camps operated in Auschwitz-Birkenau, Treblinka, Belzec, Chelmno, Majdanek, Ravensbrück, Sachsenhausen, and Skarzisko Kamienno.[41] At Treblinka camp alone, as estimated 850,000 Jews were killed in gas chambers or by other means.[42] Films taken by the Allied military forces that liberated the extermination camps showed emaciated camp inmates and huge mounds of bodies being bulldozed into mass graves.[43] An assistant to Adolf Eichmann, head of the Central Office for Jewish Emigration and ultimately the S.S. official under Himmler who was in charge of transportation logistics for the "Final Solution to the Jewish Question," later testified that Eichmann admitted that "he had five million people on his conscience."[44]

Most of the estimated two million Jews who died on the Eastern front were "'shot by operational [death] squads of the Security Police during the campaign against Russia.'"[45] These Nazi security police (*Einsatzgruppen*), actually death squads, murdered whole fam-

---

38. The Wannsee Protocol of January 20, 1942, *in* "NON-GERMANS" UNDER THE THIRD REICH: THE NAZI JUDICIAL AND ADMINISTRATIVE SYSTEM IN GERMANY AND OCCUPIED EASTERN EUROPE, 1939–1945, at 559 (Diemut Majer ed., Washington, D.C.: United States Holocaust Memorial Museum, 2003).

39. *Quoted in* Arthur S. Gold and William R. Coulson, *The Nuremberg War Crimes Trials: 60 Years Later*, 20 CANADIAN BAR ASS'N RECORD 38, 43 (2006).

40. *See* Eric Solsten, *Historical Setting, in* A COUNTRY STUDY: GERMANY (Eric Solsten ed., Washington, D.C., Library of Congress, 1995), http://lcweb2.loc.gov/frd/cs/detoc.html ("[T]he Jewish population in Germany ... had numbered about 600,000 in the early 1930s.... A large number (about 4.5 million) of those killed came from Poland and the Soviet Union; about 125,000 German Jews were murdered.").

41. *See* International Military Tribunal, Judgment: Crimes Against Humanity, http://avalon.yale.edu/judwarcr.htm; RUMMEL, DEATH BY GOVERNMENT, at 117–18; DANIEL JONAH GOLDHAGEN, HITLER'S WILLING EXECUTIONERS: ORDINARY GERMANS AND THE HOLOCAUST 8, 166–67 (New York: Vintage Books, 1997); SIMON SEBAG MONTEFIORE, HISTORY'S MONSTERS 190 (New York: Metro Books, 2008); RUMMEL, DEATH BY GOVERNMENT, at 118.

42. *See Demjanjuk Appeals War-Crimes Verdict*, CHICAGO TRIBUNE, July 1, 1988, at 12.

43. *See* Gold & Coulson, *The Nuremberg War Crimes Trials*, at 43.

44. *Id.* at 43–44. *See also* Israel v. Eichmann, 36 INT'L LAW REPORTS 5, 18–53 (Israel District Court 1961), *aff'd*, 36 INT'L LAW REPORTS 277 (Isr. Sup. Ct. 1962).

45. 1 NAZI CONSPIRACY AND AGGRESSION, ch. XII, http://www.yale.edu/lawweb/avalon/imt/document/nca_vol1/chap_12.htm (quoting Affidavit of Dr. Wilhelm Hoettl, Deputy Group Leader of the Foreign Section of the Security Section, AMT VI, of the RSHA).

ilies and villages by machine-gun fire.[46] Like the Ottoman death squads and local militia, the *Einsatzgruppen* were authorized by the state and "formed for the purpose of breaking the resistance of the population of the areas lying behind the [imperial] armies in the East...."[47] The evidence at Nuremberg showed that: "In 1941, special killing units traveled with or just behind the German army as it moved eastward. Their task was to find, remove, and kill Jews in those areas, which they did largely through firing squads."[48] As with the deployment of the Ottoman Special Organization against Ottoman Christians, Goering and the Nazis hoped that by organizing gangsters and convicts into such death squads, they would murder, rape, and loot their way through the East, decimating hostile populations and enriching the War Economy.[49]

The *Einsatzgruppen* and Gestapo killed about two million Jews and many Soviet prisoners of war, commissars, and "others who were thought to be ideologically hostile to the Nazi system."[50] Large massacres of Jews or suspected Jews included 150,000 in Bessarabia area, 100,000 in Ponary area, 75,000 plus in Minsk, 70,000 in Lodz, 43,000 deported from Salonika, 33,500 in Wilna (Vilnius), 30,000 in Brest, 26,000 in Riga, 18,000 in Vinnitsa, 16,000 in Lida, 15,000 in Pinsk, 10,000 in Novogrudok, 7,000 in Borisov, 7,000 in Polotsk, 7,000 in Mogilev, 7,000 in Vilejka, 3,500 in Stolbsky, 3,000 in Zhitomir, 3,000 in Dubossary, and 420 victims per day in the territory of Einsatzgruppen B starting in late September 1941. In East Upper Silesia in Poland, they murdered Jews and destroyed shops and synagogues in order to drive Jewish families east into a "reservation." They would seize all records in Poland and elsewhere of Jews, communists, other leftists, Catholic bishops and other leaders, and Polish nationalist anti-German organizations.[51] Nazi General Otto Ohlendorf testified that the Nazi *Einsatzgruppen* death squads under his command wiped out 90,000 men, women, and children, primarily Jews and Soviet citizens.[52] For these reasons, it is now accepted that "a large percentage of Nazi victims ... perished by shooting and starvation in the manner of their Armenian predecessors."[53] Many of the Jews falling into the clutches of Einsatzgruppen and the S.S. were killed by mobile gas chambers approved by Adolf Eichmann in late 1941.[54]

Other Jews were murdered in the German bombardment of Warsaw and other Polish and Soviet cities starting in 1939 (for Soviet cities, 1941). In a 1939 appeal, President Franklin D. Roosevelt described the "ruthless bombing from the air of civilians in unfortified centres of population during the course of the hostilities," which had already

---

46. *See* RUMMEL, DEATH BY GOVERNMENT, at 115–17.

47. IMT, Judgment: Crimes Against Humanity (Sept. 30 and Oct. 1, 1946), http://avalon.law.yale.edu/subject_menus/judcont.asp.

48. Alan A. Ryan, *Nuremberg's Contributions to International Law*, 30 BOSTON COLLEGE INT'L & COMPARATIVE LAW REV. 55, 57 (2007).

49. 9 NUREMBERG TRIAL PROCEEDINGS 563, *quoted in* JOSEPH TENENBAUM, RACE AND REICH: THE STORY OF AN EPOCH 493 (New York: Twayne Publishers, 1956).

50. IMT, Judgment: Kaltenbrunner (Sept. 30 and Oct. 1, 1946), http://avalon.law.yale.edu/imt/judkalt.asp.

51. *See* MEGARGEE, WAR OF ANNIHILATION, at 13–14, 16–17, 94–98, 121–30; Avraham Barkai, *In a Ghetto without Walls, in* GERMAN-JEWISH HISTORY IN MODERN TIMES: RENEWAL AND DESTRUCTION, 1918–1945, at 368 (Columbia: Columbia UP, 1998); *Belorussia, in* THE HOLOCAUST ENCYCLOPEDIA 62–64 (Judith Tydor Baumel ed., New Haven, CT: Yale UP, 2001); *Lodz, in id.* at 403–5; *Chronology, in id.* at xxvlii–xxxiv.

52. *See* Gold & Coulson, *The Nuremberg War Crimes Trials*, at 44.

53. Robert Melson, *The Armenian Genocide as Precursor and Prototype of Twentieth-Century Genocide, in* IS THE HOLOCAUST UNIQUE?: PERSPECTIVES ON COMPARATIVE GENOCIDE 125, 135 (Alan S. Rosenbaum ed., Boulder, CO: Westview Press, 2009).

54. *See Chronology, in* THE HOLOCAUST ENCYCLOPEDIA at xxx; *Gas Chambers, in id.* at 227–33.

killed "thousands of defenseless women and children," as a "sort of inhuman barbarism" that killed people "who are not even remotely participating in the hostilities...."[55] The French ambassador to Warsaw reported to the French foreign minister that as of September 1, 1939 the Germans had already bombed "a great number of localities."[56]

It is impossible to completely distinguish the Holocaust as an "ethnic" or "racial" genocide from other "military" or "counterinsurgency" genocides, as the Nazis had significant military and counterinsurgency motives for their campaign of mass killing. Many Jews, for example, perished during Nazi operations against partisan insurgents fighting against Nazi occupation of Eastern Europe. The U.S. prosecutor Telford Taylor argued at Nuremberg that:

> [On] the Eastern Front, ... the German forces were fighting among a hostile population and had to face extensive partisan activities behind their lines. I propose to show here that the activities of the German Armed Forces against partisans and against other elements of the population became a vehicle for carrying out Nazi political and racial policies and a vehicle for the massacre of Jews and numerous segments of the Slav population which were regarded by the Nazis as undesirable. I will show that it was the policy of the German Armed Forces to behave with the utmost severity to the civilian population of the occupied territories; and that its military operations, particularly against partisans, were so conducted as to advance the Nazi policies to which I have referred.[57]

Colonel Taylor's argument had ample foundation in captured Nazi documents. In support of his argument to the Nuremberg tribunal, Taylor offered a May 1941 order from Hitler declaring that because "the collapse of Germany in 1918, the subsequent sufferings of the German people, and the fight against National Socialism which cost the blood of innumerable supporters of the movement, were caused primarily by Bolshevistic influence," any "attacks by enemy civilians on the Armed Forces, its members, and employees, are to be suppressed at once by the military, using the most extreme methods, until the assailants are destroyed."[58] This was followed in June 1941 by a directive from Berlin to all prisoner of war camps, singling out for "special handling" and "execution" each member of a list of groups, unless they had intelligence:

1. all outstanding functionaries of the State and of the Party, especially
2. professional revolutionists,
3. the functionaries of the Comintern,
4. all leading Party functionaries of the Russian Secret Police [KPdSU] and their associated organizations in the Central, district, and county Committees,
5. all the Peoples' Commissars and their Assistants,
6. all the former Polit-Commissars in the Red Army,
7. all leading personalities of the Central and Middle Offices among the State authorities,

55. President Franklin D. Roosevelt, *Appeal to Great Britain, France, Italy, Germany and Poland*, Sept. 1, 1939, *in* The French Yellow Book, No. 325, http://www.ibiblio.org/pha/fyb/part_6f.html.

56. M. Léon Nöel, French Ambassador in Warsaw, to M. Georges Bonnet, Minister for Foreign Affairs, Sept. 1, 1939, *in* The French Yellow Book, No. 331, http://www.ibiblio.org/pha/fyb/part_6f.html.

57. 4 Nuremberg Trial Proceedings 454 (Jan. 7, 1946), http://avalon.law.yale.edu/imt/01-07-46.asp.

58. Nuremberg Exhibit USA-554, *quoted in id.* at 455–56.

8. the leading economic personalities,
9. the Soviet Russian Intelligence agents,
10. all Jews,
11. all persons who are established as being instigators or fanatical communists.[59]

A few months after the invasion of the Soviet Union, a Nazi document stated that due to the fact that "Communist insurrection movements have broken out everywhere in the area occupied by Germany," the standing orders were that the "death penalty for 50–100 Communists should generally be regarded in these cases as suitable atonement for one German soldier's death."[60] Another high official declared soon after those orders were issued, that:

> The most essential aim of war against the Jewish-Bolshevistic system is a complete destruction of their means of power and the elimination of Asiatic influence from the European culture.... The soldier in the Eastern Territories is ... the avenger of bestialities which have been inflicted upon German and racially related nations.
>
> Therefore, the soldier must have full understanding for the necessity of a severe but just revenge on subhuman Jewry.
>
> The Army has to aim at another purpose, that is the annihilation of revolts in the hinterland, which as experience proves, have always been caused by Jews.[61]

Jews made up 20,000–30,000 members of the Soviet partisan resistance to Nazi occupation. Several large forests and rural areas in the Nazi eastern provinces of Poland, Ukraine, and Ostland (the Baltics) were held to varying degrees of success by Jewish and allied partisan armies.[62] In 1942, the *Reichskommissar* of Ostland (the Baltics, Belorussia, etc.) received a report that: "In all armed skirmishes with the partisans in Belorussia it has become clear ... that Jewry is the main inspiration of the partisan movement."[63]

One of the largest pitched battles of the war between Jewish and allied partisan groups, and Nazi occupation armies, occurred in Warsaw, and ended with more than 20,000 deaths. A Nazi document portrays a well-organized and well-armed resistance force in Warsaw:

> When only a few days had passed, it became apparent that the Jews no longer had any intention to resettle voluntarily, but were determined to resist evacuation with all their force and by using all the weapons at their disposal. So-called battle groups had been formed, led by Polish-Bolshevists; they were armed and paid any price asked for available arms.
>
> During the large-scale action we succeeded in catching some Jews who had already been evacuated and resettled in Lublin or Treblinka, but had broken out from there and returned to the Ghetto, equipped with arms and ammunition.
>
> During this armed resistance the women belonging to the battle groups were equipped the same as the men; some were members of the Chaluzim movement. Not infrequently, these women fired pistols with both hands. It happened time

59. Nuremberg Document No. 078-PS, *quoted in* 3 Nazi Conspiracy and Aggression, http://avalon.law.yale.edu/imt/078-ps.asp.

60. Nuremberg Exhibit USA-555, *quoted in id.* at 457–58.

61. Nuremberg Exhibit USA-556, *quoted in id.* at 458–59.

62. *Resistance in Eastern Europe, in* The Holocaust Encyclopedia, at 545–546.

63. *Quoted in Belorussia, in id.* at 64.

> and again that these [women] had pistols or hand grenades ... to use against the men of the Waffen SS, Police, or Wehrmacht.

The document notes that in addition to grenades, the resistance employed machine guns.[64]

The Nazi official in charge of the Warsaw Ghetto ordered it liquidated with the "greatest severity," which resulted in an uncompromising massacre:

> The resistance put up by the Jews and bandits could be broken only by relentlessly using all our force and energy by day and night. On 23 April 1918 the Reichsfuehrer SS issued through the higher SS and Police Fuehrer East at Cracow his order to complete the combing out of the Warsaw Ghetto with the greatest severity and relentless tenacity. I therefore decided to destroy the entire Jewish residential area by setting every block on fire, including the blocks of residential buildings near the armament works. One concern after the other was systematically evacuated and subsequently destroyed by fire....
>
> Only through the continuous and untiring work of all involved did we succeed in catching a total of 56,065 Jews whose extermination can be proved. To this should be added the number of Jews who lost their lives in explosions or fires but whose numbers could not be ascertained....
>
> Now, there are no more factories in the former Ghetto. All the goods, raw materials, and machines there have been moved and stored somewhere else. All buildings etc., have been destroyed....
>
> The remaining Jews and bandits must be deprived of any chance of survival by destroying all remaining buildings and refuges and cutting off the water supply.

The document stated that 7,000 Jews died in the ghetto massacres, 5,000 to 6,000 in explosions and fires, 7,000 in the Treblinka T-II extermination camp, and another 42,000 taken prisoner. Some of the prisoners were to harvest the bricks, metal, and other rubble of the Warsaw ghetto. Nazi troops seized about 10 million Polish *zloty* in currency and even more foreign currency.[65]

Up to 6.3 million Jews perished in the Holocaust, and 4.4 million people were displaced as refugees or IDPs.[66] Lemkin wrote that the Nazis "intended to do away with the Jews, the Gypies, the 'inferior' races like the Poles and other Slavs—with the exception of the strong, dumb workhorses." There was little difference, in his view, between an extermination camp and forced labor in a concentration camp, given the poor rations and conditions in the latter.[67]

---

64. Nuremberg Exhibit USA-275 (Document No. 1061-PS), *quoted in* 3 Nuremberg Trial Proceedings, http://avalon.law.yale.edu/imt/1061-ps.asp.

65. *Id.*

66. The International Military Tribunal concluded that six million Jews had been exterminated by the Nazis and their allies. *See* IMT, Judgment: Kaltenbrunner (Sept. 30–Oct. 1, 1946), http://avalon.yale.edu/judkalt.htm. More detailed statistical analyses have estimated that between 5.1 and 6.3 million Jews were exterminated. *See, e.g.*, D. D. Guttenplan, The Holocaust on Trial 115–116 (New York: W.W. Norton & Co., 2001); Michael Shermer & Alex Grobman, Denying History: Who Says the Holocaust Never Happened and Why Do They Say It? 174 (Berkeley, CA: Univ. of California Press, 2000); Stannard, *The Politics of Holocaust Scholarship: Uniqueness as Denial, in* Is the Holocaust Unique?, at 282 (2001). The figure for Jewish refugees from Nazi-occupied Europe comes from Shermer & Grobman, Denying History, at 174.

67. Raphael Lemkin's Thoughts on Nazi Genocide: Not Guilty?, at 154 (Steven L. Jacobs, ed., Lewiston: Edwin Mellen Press, 1992), *quoted in* Stone, *Raphael Lemkin on the Holocaust*, at 544–45.

B. The Fate of the Jews of the Former Ottoman Empire and Persia

In former domains of the Ottoman Empire, the experience of Jews varied according to the relative vitalities of the countries in which they found themselves, and the orientation of those countries towards the Nazis. Perhaps one of the worst places to be a Jew in the former Ottoman Empire during the war was Greece. Eighty to ninety percent of Jews perished in Greece and Serbia, which were unsympathetic to Nazi ambitions and adopted a pro-British line, unlike Italy and Bulgaria, which were initially pro-German, or Turkey, which supplied much of the Reich's chromite and facilitated Nazi access through the Bosphorus.[68] Approximately 60% to 80% of Jews in relatively compliant Belgium, France, and Italy survived. In Denmark nearly all survived. The militarization versus local autonomy of an area made much of the difference.[69] The areas with the stiffest local resistance typically had the highest Jewish mortality rates, with the Soviet republics, Poland, and Greece all having rates over 70%.[70]

Greece was less able to resist the Germans after its struggle with the Ottoman Empire in World War I and the Turkish Nationalists in the 1920s weakened its institutions and drained its resources.[71] Where Bulgaria was able, by petitions and telegrams, to call a halt to the deportations of Jews, saving 50,000, the Greeks were too weak to resist the Bulgarian occupation of their own country, as a result of which the Jews of Thrace, Macedonia, and Dobrudjia, 20,000 in all, were deported, the Jews of Thrace all dying on arrival at Treblinka.[72] Turkey, after reaching a treaty of friendship and cooperation with Germany in 1941, was spared an invasion, and its Jews survived.[73] Similarly, in formerly Ottoman Bulgaria a pro-German government resisted the deportation of Jews, due in part to Bulgarian Orthodox church appeals.[74] Bulgaria may have had the highest survival rate of war-affected countries other than Denmark.[75]

About 46,000 Jews from Thessaloniki were deported to Auschwitz and Birkenau by August 1943. About 5,000 Jews from Athens had been deported by summer 1944.[76] Many of the Jews of Athens survived by taking fishing boats to Turkey and traveling overland

---

68. *See* R.A.C. Parker, Struggle for Survival: The History of the Second World War 268 (Oxford: Oxford UP, 1989).

69. *See* Marnix Croes, *The Holocaust in the Netherlands and the Rate of Jewish Survival,* 20.3 Holocaust and Genocide Studies 474–499 (2006); George M. Kren, *The Holocaust as History, in* Echoes from the Holocaust: Philosophical Reflections on a Dark Time 35 (Philadelphia, PA: Temple UP, 1990).

70. *See* Ronnie S. Landau, The Nazi Holocaust 316 (London: I.B.Tauris Publishers, 1990).

71. Greece was already $15 million in debt to the United States by late 1920. See Houston Advises Larger Taxation on Smaller Incomes, N.Y. Times, Dec. 9, 1920, at 1; 10 Nations to Pay Us $180,282,628 in 1926, N.Y. Times, Nov. 16, 1925, at 31.

72. Jonathan Steinberg, All or Nothing: The Axis and the Holocaust, 1941–1943, at 94 (London: Routledge, 1991).

73. *See* Encyclopedia of World War II: A Political, Social, and Military History 1537 (Spencer C. Tucker ed., Santa Barbara, CA: ABC-CLIO, 2005) (citing Treaty of Territorial Integrity and Friendship of June 18, 1941 (Germany-Turkey)).

74. *See Bulgaria, in* Encyclopedia of the Holocaust, at 103. Bulgaria proclaimed its independence from the Ottoman Empire in 1908, but entered World War I on the side of the German, Austrian, and Ottoman empires.

75. *See* Landau, The Nazi Holocaust, at 316.

76. *See Greece, in* Jewish Virtual Library, http://www.jewishvirtuallibrary.org/jsource/Holocaust/greece1.html.

to Palestine after undergoing interrogation in Aleppo. Perhaps 3,000 escaped in this manner, and Greek Orthodox monasteries sheltered many Jewish children, returning them to their parents or the Jewish community after the war.[77] Salonika, as noted above, was particularly targeted, with the deportation of 43,000 Jews to their deaths.

The Jews of Iran, a community of more than 130,000 in 1944, faced the formidable prospect of a pro-Nazi Shah in the 1930s and 1940s.[78] Reza Shah Pahlavi, an opponent of continued British and Russian/Soviet designs on Iran, looked to Germany for economic assistance, and declared neutrality in the war. Britain invaded Iran from Iraq, and the Soviet Union invaded from the direction of Armenia and Azerbaijan. They replaced the Shah with his son, Muhammad Reza Pahlavi, who reigned until 1979.[79]

During the war, British, Soviet, and U.S. troops consumed much of Iran's food, driving up prices and contributing to a famine in the aftermath of the poor harvest of 1942. The cost of living increased from seven to ten times between 1939 and 1944. State spending on economic development projects declined by 80% as U.S. officials controlled Iran's budget.[80] Peasants lost much of their land, and were reduced to being the "property" of their landlords in many cases, with the average peasant farmer living on less than a third of a dollar a day.[81] In the postwar period, Iran suffered from the "world-wide famine" blamed on the war by former U.S. President Herbert Hoover.[82] Most foreign troops withdrew in 1946.

The Germans and Italians in World War II had a strategy of employing Arab troops under the leadership of the Grand Mufti of Jerusalem, Amin el Husseini, to fight "Anglo-Jewish domination and exploitation" with the support of Mussolini, who declared himself the "Protector of Islam."[83] Hitler and Himmler envisioned at least temporarily utilizing the

---

77. See Yitzchak Kerem, *Greek Righteous Gentiles in the Holocaust, A Renewed Look and Their Current State of Being Recognized*, Yad Vashem (2006), http://www1.yadvashem.org/education/conference 2006/Kerem,%20Yitzchak.pdf.

78. *See* Eric Hooglund, *The Society and Its Environment, in* A Country Study: Iran (Washington, DC: Library of Congress, 1987), http://www.country-data.com/cgi-bin/query/r-6443.html.

79. *See* Elena Andreeva, *Iran, in* Encyclopedia of World War II, at 742–43.

80. *See* Nikki R. Keddie, Modern Iran: Roots and Results of Revolution 106–9 (New Haven, CT: Yale UP, 2006).

81. *See id.* at 114–15.

82. *See, e.g.*, Herbert Hoover, 4 An American Epic: The Guns Cease Killing and the Saving of Life from Famine Begins, 1939–1963, at 122, 278, 293, 303 (Chicago: H. Regnery Co., 1964) ("One of my major activities was to co-ordinate the food resources of all nations in the battle against this world-wide famine in 1946."); *see also* Herbert Hoover, 3 An American Epic: The Guns Cease Killing and the Saving of Life from Famine Begins, 1939–1963, at xvii (Chicago: H. Regnery Co., 1959) (listing Iran as being recently at risk of famine); Felix Belair, Jr., *4 Calls to Country; ... Hoover Warns Millions Face Death,* N.Y. Times, Apr. 20, 1946, at 1; Waldo Drake, *Future of Billion in Asia Seems Bleak,* L.A. Times, Dec. 29, 1947, at 2; Waldo Drake, *War's End Fails to Bring 'Freedoms' to Poverty-Stricken Peoples of Asia,* L.A. Times, Aug. 10, 1947, at 5; Bees Furman, *Americans Are Asked to Cut Wheat Use 40%, Fats 20%,* N.Y. Times, Mar. 12, 1946, at 1; Bess Furman, *Truman Says Food Crisis Is 'Worse Than Is Painted'; Tells Editors of Famine Abroad...,* N.Y. Times, Apr. 19, 1946, at 1; *Hoover Asks Famine Aid,* N.Y. Times, Mar. 23, 1946, at 27; *Hoover Asks Food for 800,000,000 by Filling 'Gap' of 3,600,000 Tons; Hoover Asks Food Lest Millions Die,* N.Y. Times, May 18, 1946, at 1; *Hoover Bids U.S. Save 500,000,000 in Famine Nations,* N.Y. Times, Mar. 17, 1946, at 1; Will Lissner, *Russia Whips Up Interest in Iran,* N.Y. Times, June 14, 1948, at 3; *The Text of Mr. Hoover's Plea to Halt Famine,* N.Y. Times, Mar. 17, 1946, at 24.

83. *Quoted in* Camille Cianfarrab, *Exiled Arab Mufti Turns up in Rome,* N.Y. Times, Oct. 28, 1941, at 7. *See also* Colonial Office 733/309/75872/51, Jan. 4, 1939, Sir Harold MacMichael to Malcolm MacDonald; F.O. 371/24568, 1940, The Mufti: Proposed Visit to Ibn Saud to Discuss Palestine Question: Mr. Stokes' Visit to Bagdad; F.O. 371/Persia 1941/34-27149, British Minister to the Foreign Office, The Situation in Persia.

mufti to administer autonomous Muslim areas of the Third Reich, such as Bosnia and parts of Serbia. The Nazis recruited Albanian volunteers into the mufti-inspired 21st SS division, tasked with reprisals against Jews and Serbs. This division arrested and deported large numbers of Jews to Bergen-Belsen and other extermination camps.[84] The mufti wrote in his journals that he had received Hitler's "explicit undertaking to allow us to solve the Jewish problem ... according to the scientific methods innovated by Germany in the handling of its Jews." This was, he believed, "a free hand to eradicate every last Jew from Palestine and the Arab world."[85]

The mufti fled Iran with the British and Soviet invasion of August 1941.[86] Few Jews were massacred in wartime Iran as a result, but some 45,000 migrated to Israel between 1945 and 1978.[87] About three-fourths of the remaining 80,000 or so have left since 1979.[88]

The Jews of Iraq, a community of over 115,000 with nearly 3,000 years of history dating back to Assyrian and Babylonian times, also came under severe threat in the 1930s and 1940s.[89] The ultranationalist pro-Nazi rulers of Iraq in the 1930s dismissed hundreds of Jews from government jobs and propagandized against Jews as an "enemy" people in the public schools.[90] In the early 1940s, as the British and Nazi German empires fought for control of Iraq, Iraqi soldiers and police murdered hundreds of Iraqi Jews.[91] In the aftermath of a pro-Nazi coup, Iraqi soldiers and pro-army mobs killed or wounded 2,200 Jews and plundered hundreds of shops and houses.[92]

David Ben-Gurion and the other leaders of the Jewish community in Palestine prior to the establishment of the state of Israel developed a plan to ensure that the Iraqis were included in the one million Jews in Islamic countries that eventually migrated to Israel.[93] "'There's no need to wait until [the Iraqis] slaughter them,' Ben-Gurion said of Iraq's Jews."[94] The example of the Assyrian massacres by the Iraqi army and allied tribes in 1933 was prominent in the writings of Zionists like Ben-Gurion and Chaim Weizmann. In appeals to the U.S., Ben-Gurion criticized proposals that would leave the Jews an "Assyrian minority," in reference to the fact that the Assyrians had been "exterminated" in 1933.[95] Weizmann referred to what one author calls the "genocide of the Assyrians" in 1933 as a

---

84. *See* Raul Hilberg, The Destruction of the European Jews 751 (New Haven, CT: Yale UP, 2003) (1961).

85. *Quoted in* Jonathan Schanzer, *Hitler's 'Grossmufti von Jerusalem'*, Jerusalem Post, Sept 4, 2008, http://www.jpost.com/servlet/Satellite?cid=1220526711479&pagename=JPost%2FJPArticle%2FPrinter.

86. *See* Cianfarrab, *Exiled Arab Mufti Turns up in Rome*, at 7.

87. *See* Hooglund, *The Society and Its Environment.*

88. *See* Rafael Medoff, *The Jews in Iran, and Iran's Rank in the World (Letter to the Editor),* N.Y. Times, Mar. 23, 2009, http://www.nytimes.com.

89. *See* Orly Halpern, *Iraq Split on Granting Jews' Minority Status*, Jerusalem Post, July 18, 2005, at 1; Carole Basri, *The Jews of Iraq: A Forgotten Case of Ethnic Cleansing* (2004), at http://www.worldjewishcongress.org/policystudies/study_026.html.

90. *See* Carole Basri, *The Jewish Refugees from Arab Countries: An Examination of Legal Rights—A Case Study of the Human Rights Violations of Iraqi Jews*, 26 Fordham Int'l L.J. 656, 670 (2003).

91. *See* Joel Rayburn, *The Last Exit from Iraq*, 85 Foreign Aff. 29, 37–38 (2006).

92. *See* Basri, *The Jewish Refugees from Arab Countries* , at 671–73.

93. *See* Dalia Karpel, *"It could have been paradise here,"* Haaretz (2004), at http://www.haaretzdaily.com/hasen/pages/ShArt.jhtml?itemNo=355218.

94. Tom Segev, The Seventh Million: The Israelis and the Holocaust 122 (1991).

95. Allon Gal, David Ben-Gurion and the American Alignment for a Jewish State 20 (Bloomington, IN: Indiana UP, 1991). *See also* Auron, The Banality of Indifference, at 25.

key argument in favor of the Zionist cause.[96] "Do not submit to the fate of the Assyrians and give up Jewish Palestine," was Weizmann's call to American Jews.[97] New Zionist Organization leader Uriel Heilperin similarly argued that, alongside the Ottoman massacres of the 1860s and 1910s, "the horrors of the Assyrian slaughter in Iraq (1933)" was a stark warning of the risks of being a small minority.[98]

As Germany and Japan gained strength, Iraqi leaders pressed Iraq's historical title to Kuwait, openly criticized British colonialism in the Middle East, and eventually demanded that Britain withdraw its troops and warplanes. The mufti, working directly with Hitler and Himmler on an Arab-Nazi alliance, found a sympathetic ear in Iraqi Premier Rashid Ali al-Gaylani.[99] The mufti came forward at a critical time of struggle between pro-British and pro-German forces in Iraq, declaring holy war against Britain as the "greatest foe of Islam."[100]

Iraqi army generals, emboldened by promises of German or Italian aid, surrounded the British bases in Iraq with troops and artillery, including the Habbaniya air base.[101] The Assyrians, including many displaced from Turkey or Persia during World War I, enlisted in British units, and defended the remnant of the British forces until reinforcements could arrive. Several British officers argued that the Assyrian Levies' defense of the British Habbaniya air base in Iraq was the only thing that prevented the Nazis from cutting off the main Allied forces fighting in Europe and North Africa from British forces in India and the rest of Asia, as well as from the rump of the Soviet Union.[102] About 1,200 Assyrian Levies at Habbaniya joined 350 British army and hundreds of Kurdish Levies in repelling an Iraqi Army of 9,000 soldiers and artillery units, supported by Italian air planes and the German Reich.[103] "It is generally conceded that Assyrian Levies, numbering about eight hundred, bore the brunt of the attack by an 18,000 strong Iraqi Army" against Habbaniya, and their fierce resistance won the battle.[104] The Allied victory prevented Rashid Ali and the Germans from consolidating their power in Iraq.

Britain responded to the rise of Nazi influence in Iraq by bombing Iraqi cities and reinforcing its bases by invading the country from Jordan in the west and Basra in the south.

---

96. SHABTAI TEVETH, BEN-GURION: THE BURNING GROUND, 1886–1948, at 682 (New York: Houghton Mifflin, 1987).

97. *Quoted in* HERBERT DRUKS, THE UNCERTAIN FRIENDSHIP: THE U.S. AND ISRAEL FROM ROOSEVELT TO KENNEDY 7 (Westport, CT: Greenwood Publ'g Group, 2001).

98. JOSEPH HELLER, THE STERN GANG: IDEOLOGY, POLITICS, AND TERROR, 1940–1949, at 28 (London: Routledge, 1995).

99. *See* MAJID KHADDURI, ARAB CONTEMPORARIES: THE ROLE OF PERSONALITIES IN POLITICS 78 (Baltimore, MD: Johns Hopkins UP, 1973); IBRAHIM AL-MARASHI, IRAQ'S ARMED FORCES: AN ANALYTICAL HISTORY 59–65 (Sammy Salama trans., London: Routledge, 2008); ROBERT SATLOFF, AMONG THE RIGHTEOUS: LOST STORIES FROM THE HOLOCAUST'S LONG REACH INTO ARAB LANDS 24–25 (New York: Public Affairs, 2007).

100. *Quoted in* SAMIR AL-KHALIL, REPUBLIC OF FEAR: THE INSIDE STORY OF SADDAM'S IRAQ 179 (New York: Pantheon Books, 1989).

101. *See* Jack Kalpakian and Spencer Tucker, *Iraq, in* ENCYCLOPEDIA OF WORLD WAR II, at 744.

102. *See* APRIM, THE ASSYRIANS, at 203–4 (collecting sources).

103. See DAVID KENNETH FIELDHOUSE, KURDS, ARABS, AND BRITONS: THE MEMOIR OF WALLACE LYON IN IRAQ 1918–44, at 31 (London: I.B. Tauris, 2002); GEORGE E. KIRK, A SHORT HISTORY OF THE MIDDLE EAST: FROM THE RISE OF ISLAM TO MODERN TIMES 199 (New York: Frederick A. Praeger, 1957); P.W. PITT, ROYAL WILTS: THE HISTORY OF THE ROYAL WILTSHIRE YEOMANRY, 1920–1945, a 67 (London: Burrop, Mathieson, 1946).

104. JOSEPH B. SCHECHTMAN, POPULATION TRANSFERS IN ASIA 77 (New York: Halisby Press, 1949). *See also* FIELDHOUSE, KURDS, ARABS, AND BRITONS, at 31–32.

Iraqi resistance crumbled, and the pro-Axis government fell.[105] Former Iraqi Prime Minister Nuri al-Said, and many Arabs in North Africa who saved Jews from Nazi or Vichy persecution, shared the Assyrians' opposition to Arab Nazism.[106] After Nuri was reinstated in office, Iraq became part of the vital supply line to the Soviet Union. Iraq declared war on Germany, Italy, and Japan in early 1943, as did Iran later that year.[107]

The pro-Nazi Iraqis lost power, but the government in the 1950s expropriated $200 million worth of synagogues, schools, homes, and other properties.[108] The defeat of the pro-German Iraqi nationalists by the British and the resulting breakdown of law and order ushered in a pogrom against the Jews of Baghdad in which 200 died and many Jewish businesses were looted and destroyed.[109] In 1948, Ben-Gurion expressed fears of a complete massacre of Jews by Syria and Iraq; as one historian has written: "The Iraqi massacre of 3,000 non-Arab Christian Assyrians in Simele in August 1933 had not been forgotten."[110]

The United Nations declared an independent Israel in 1948. Iraq, Syria, Egypt, and a coalition of other Arab nations invaded Palestine to reverse the establishment and expansion of the state of Israel, but were defeated. About 750,000 Palestinian Arabs were expelled or fled from their homes, cities, and villages as a result. By 2005, their descendents amounted to three million residents, many categorized as refugees, in Jordan, and 700,000 in Syria and Lebanon.[111] In the aftermath of the 1948 Arab-Israeli war, physical and verbal attacks against Iraqi Jews, as well as racist laws and regulations and looting of Jewish properties, steadily escalated.[112] As anti-Jewish persecution in Israel's enemy states continued, U.S. President Harry Truman and the Israeli government organized the airlift to Israel of 120,000 Jews. Many of them lived in tents, cabins, or camps in Israel for up to 12 years. By 1951, the state of Israel had airlifted about 100,000 Jews out of Iraq in "Operation Ezra and Nehemiah."[113] Israeli agents even frightened some Iraqi Jews into leaving by bombing Jewish targets in Iraq.[114] The vast majority of Jews had fled Iraq by 1952.[115]

Prior to 1958, the Iraqi government expropriated $200 million worth of synagogues, schools, homes, and other properties from Iraq's Jewish residents. In the late 1950s, Iraqi President Abdul Karim Qasem abolished many discriminatory Iraqi laws and embraced a provisional constitution that declared the equality of Iraqi minorities.[116] After Qasem was deposed by the Ba'ath Party in a U.S.-backed coup in 1963, the Iraqi government once again cancelled Jews' citizenship and confiscated their properties. The Jewish population plum-

---

105. *See* Tripp, A History of Iraq, at 98, 103–6; Frederick A. Aprim, The Assyrians: From Bedr Khan to Saddam Hussein 106–16, 155–59, 190–209 (Xlibris, 2006).

106. *See* Satloff, Among the Righteous, 98–172.

107. *See* Kalpakian & Tucker *Iraq, in* Encyclopedia of World War II, at 744; Andreeva, *Iran, in id.* at 743.

108. *See* Basri, *The Jewish Refugees from Arab Countries,* at 677–78, 681, 683–85. The parliament cancelled the citizenship of tens of thousands of Jews, and then expropriated the property of all Jews who had lost their citizenship. *See id.* at 681–85.

109. *See* Tripp, A History of Iraq, at 103–6.

110. Colin Shindler, A History of Modern Israel 45 (Cambridge: Cambridge UP, 2008).

111. World Health Org., *Social Determinants of Health in Countries in Conflict: The Eastern Mediterranean* 16 (2007), http://www.who.int/entity/social_determinants/links/events/conflicts_and_sdh_emro_revison_06_2007.pdf.

112. *See* Tripp, History of Iraq, at 123–25; Simons, Iraq, 238–40.

113. *See* Basri, *The Jews of Iraq*; Ahron Bregman, Israel's Wars, 1947–1993, at 26 (2000).

114. *See* Bregman, Israel's Wars, at 26–27.

115. *See* Tripp, A History of Iraq, at 126.

116. *See The Jewish Refugees from Arab Countries,* at 685.

meted from 160,000 Jews in the 1940s, to only 1,000 by 1990, and only several dozen by 2003.[117]

C. The Holocaust against Slavs, Roma, German Leftists, Homosexuals, the Mentally Ill, and the Handicapped

1. The Slavs and Other Soviet Peoples

Professor Lemkin did not accept the argument of some contemporary scholars that only Jews died in the Holocaust, or that the term "Holocaust" should only be applied to Jews. He wrote:

> The Nazi plan of Genocide was related to many peoples, races, and religions....
>
> As a matter of fact, Hitler wanted to commit [genocide] against the Slavic peoples, in order to colonize the East, and to extend the German Empire up to the Ural [mountains]....
>
> Nazi Germany embarked upon a gigantic plan to colonize Europe, and since there are no free spaces local populations had to be removed in order to make room for Germans. Nazi Germany did not have a fleet to protect overseas colonial possessions. Moreover Germany had never had good experiences in the past with overseas colonization. It was thus much simpler to colonize the European continent....
>
> Hitler's plan covered the Poles, the Serbs, the Russians, the Frenchmen.... [118]

As noted above, Lemkin described the Nazi plan as extending to Romani and Slavs.[119]

Hitler modeled his military and political ambitions on legendary conquests and genocides throughout history. In 1931, he told a right-wing German newspaper:

> We must already be thinking of resettlement of millions of men from Germany and Europe.... Are we really going to remain a nation of have-nots forever? Why should the sources of raw material not be equitably distributed? We have the capacity to rouse and lead the masses against this situation. We intend to introduce a great resettlement policy in Germany; in 1923 little Greece could resettle a million men. Think of the biblical deportations and the massacres of the Middle Ages (Rosenberg refers to them) and remember the extermination of the

---

117. *See id.* at 659, 667, 685–86, 692; *see also* Ron Grossman, *Jewish Refugee Families Press for Equity*, Chicago Trib., Apr. 12, 2007, http://www.accessmylibrary.com/coms2/summary_0286-30297022_ITM (only 52,000 Jews remained by 1952); Julia Magnet, *The Terror Behind Iraq's Jewish Exodus*, The Daily Telegraph (U.K.), Apr. 17, 2003, http://www.telegraph.co.uk/news/1427599/The-terror-behind-Iraqs-Jewish-exodus.html (only dozens left in 2003); USDOS, *Country Reports on Human Rights Practices—Iraq 2008* (only 10 may remain in 2008).

118. Raphaël Lemkin, "The Hitler case" (unpublished ms), at 1, *quoted in* A. Dirk Moses, *Empire, Colony, Genocide: Keywords and the Philosophy of History, in* Empire, Colony, Genocide, at 20–21. *See also* Stone, *Raphael Lemkin on the Holocaust,* at 546.

119. Raphael Lemkin's Thoughts on Nazi Genocide: Not Guilty?, at 154 (Steven L. Jacobs, ed., Lewiston: Edwin Mellen Press, 1992), *quoted in* Stone, *Raphael Lemkin on the Holocaust*, at 544–45.

> Armenians. One eventually reaches the conclusion that masses of men are mere biological plasticine [i.e., clay to be molded at will].[120]

Hitler was living in Berlin in 1921, when the trial of an Armenian for the murder of Talât Paşa became an internationally famous battle of experts on the guilt of the Ottoman Empire itself.

Hitler's objectives were colonial and imperial in nature. The Nazis called in their party platform of 1933 for the conquest of new German "land and territory (colonies) for the maintenance of our people and the settlement of our surplus population."[121] Hitler proclaimed that in an imperial age, "[s]mall sovereign states no longer have a right to exist," because "[o]ne cannot keep by democratic institutions what one has acquired by force."[122]

There was little question as to where the land for German settlements could be found. In *Mein Kampf*, Hitler declared that new territory had to come "at the expense of Russia, and the new Reich would have to ... give soil to the German plow by means of the German sword, and to give daily bread to the nation.'"[123] In a speech to his military commanders poised to invade Poland in 1939, Hitler remarked: "Our strength consists of our speed and in our brutality. Genghis Khan led millions of women and children to slaughter—with premeditation and a happy heart. History sees in him solely the founder of a state."[124] Hitler explained:

> I have issued a command.... that our war aim does not consist in reaching certain lines, but in the physical destruction of the enemy. Accordingly, I have placed my death-head (SS) formations in readiness ... with orders to them to send to death mercilessly and without compassion, men, women, and children of Polish derivation and language. Only thus shall we gain the living space (*Lebensraum*) which we need. Who, after all, speaks today of the annihilation of the Armenians?
>
> Poland will be depopulated and then settled by the Germans.[125]

After the invasion of the Soviet Union in 1941, Hitler gave similar orders to Goering and Rosenberg, stating that partisan warfare "gives us the opportunity to exterminate anyone who is hostile to us.... Naturally, the vast area must be pacified as quickly as pos-

---

120. *Quoted in* Roger W. Smith, Eric Markusen & Robert Jay Lifton, *Professional Ethics and Denial of the Armenian Genocide*, 9 Holocaust and Genocide Stud.1–22 (1995). *See also* K.B. Bardakjian, Hitler and the Armenian Genocide 6, 28, 43 (London: Zoryan Institute 1985); Richard Breiting & Edouard Calie, Secret Conversations with Hitler: The Two Newly-Discovered 1931 Interviews, at 10–14, 80–81 (Richard Barry trans., New York: The John Day Co., 1971); *Modern Genocide: The Curse of the Nation-State and Ideological Political Parties,* 7 Idea: The J. of Social Issues n.10 (2002).

121. Program of the National Socialist German Workers' Party, http://www.yale.edu/lawweb/avalon/imt/document/nsdappro.htm.

122. *Quoted in* Alan Clark, Barbarossa: The Russian-German Conflict, 1941–45, at 60 (NY: Morrow, 1965).

123. *Quoted in* 1 Nazi Conspiracy and Aggression, ch. VII, http://web.archive.org/web/20031222180627/http:// www.yale.edu/lawweb/avalon/imt/document/nca_vol1/chap_7.htm.

124. Balakian, The Burning Tigris, at 164.

125. A German dissident sent the text of this speech to the head of the Associated Press bureau in Berlin in August 1939; he was later executed for conspiring to overthrow Hitler. *See* Michael Berenbaum, *The Holocaust, in* Teaching About Genocide: Issues, Approaches, and Resources 130 (Samuel Totten ed., Information Age Publ'g, 2004); Bardakjian, Hitler and the Armenian Genocide, at 20; Peter Hoffman, The History of the German Resistance, 1933–1945, at 214 (Montreal: McGill—Queen's UP, 1996).

sible; this will happen best by shooting anyone who even looks sideways at us.[126] The actual orders delivered to German soldiers were that each German loss must result in a "death sentence of from fifty to one hundred communists" as a "deterrent effect."[127] It was a fairly simple recipe for mass murder.

Nazi imperial policy therefore involved the reconquest of "the territories lost by Germany as the result of the World war of 1914–1918, and other territories in Europe asserted to be occupied by so-called 'racial Germans,'" as living space in Poland and the Soviet Union.[128] After the invasion of Poland and the Soviet Union, a high official in the Ministry for the Occupied Eastern Territories, led by Alfred Rosenberg, declared: "'In the East, Germany is carrying on a three-fold war: a war for the destruction of Bolshevism, a war for the destruction of the greater Russian Empire, and finally a war for the acquisition of colonial territory for colonizing purposes and economic exploitation.'"[129] Himmler agreed strongly with Hitler on the need for the utmost brutality. Speaking in 1945, he said:

> What happens to a Russian, to a Czech, does not interest me in the slightest.... Whether nations live in prosperity or starve to death interests me only in so far as we need them as slaves for our Kultur: otherwise, it is of no interest to me. Whether 10,000 Russian females fall down from exhaustion while digging an anti-tank ditch interests me only in so far as the anti-tank ditch for Germany is finished.[130]

The S.S. under Himmler regarded Slavs as "sub-human," "wild," and "inferior to any animal as regards intellect and soul."[131] Like Native Americans, Slavs seemed to be ill-suited to rule.

The German colonial administrations (*Reichskommissariats*) in Poland, Russia, Ukraine, the Baltic States, Belarus, the Caucasus, and satellite states in the Balkans, Hungary, Bulgaria, Greece, and Romania would provide millions of slave laborers and inestimable expanses of farmland for German settlement.[132] Poland suffered the expropriation of farmland for distribution to German settlers, and enslavement of Polish civilians by Germans in Poland or by deportation to labor inside Germany.[133] Mass killings of Slavic and Jewish civilians occurred not only in Poland but in the Soviet Union:

> The murder and ill-treatment of civilian populations reached its height in the treatment of the citizens of the Soviet Union and Poland. Some four weeks before the invasion of Russia began, special task forces of the SIPO and SD [SS intelligence], called Einsatz Groups, were formed on the orders of Himmler for the purpose of following the German armies into Russia, combating partisans and members of Resistance Groups, and exterminating the Jews and communist leaders and other sections of the population....[134]

---

126. Browning, The Origins of the Final Solution, at 309.

127. Clark, Barbarossa, at 153.

128. 1 Nazi Conspiracy and Aggression, ch. VII.

129. 1 Nazi Conspiracy and Aggression, ch. XII.

130. 1 Nazi Conspiracy and Aggression, ch. X.

131. *See* Rummel, Death by Government, at 117–18 (quoting S.S. directive).

132. *See* Institut für Zeitgeschichte, *Besetzes Europa* (1999), http://www.obersalzberg.de/cms_d/content/de_ausstellung_weltkrieg_besetztes/besetztes_5.html (map of *Reichkommissariats*, German satellite states, and occupied territories in Europe); Yitzhak Arad, The Holocaust in the Soviet Union 1–5, 96–218, 263–273, 311–97 (Omaha, Nebraska: Univ. of Nebraska Press, 2009).

133. 1 Nazi Conspiracy and Aggression, ch. X.

134. IMT, Judgment: Crimes Against Humanity (Sept. 30 and Oct. 1, 1446), http://web.archive.org/web/20010107061100/http://www.yale.edu/lawweb/avalon/imt/proc/judwarcr.htm. *See also id.* (an order issued about a month after the invasion of the Soviet Union stated: "In view of the vast size of the occupied areas in the East the forces available for establishing security in these areas will be sufficient only if all resistance is punished, not by legal prosecution of the guilty, but by the spreading

The Nazis gunned down, shelled, starved, or otherwise killed more than 10 million Soviet civilians, two to 2.5 million Polish civilians, one million Yugoslav civilians, and 14 to 18 million Soviet soldiers.[135] In all, the Nazi plan for the occupied Soviet Union anticipated 40 million deaths.[136] Nazi planning documents for occupation of Soviet Union stated that: "Many tens of millions of people in this area will become redundant and will either die or have to emigrate to Siberia."[137] At the Nuremberg trials, a Soviet prosecutor stated: "[T]his document discloses, on its face, a studied plan to murder millions of people through starvation."[138] Nazi plans came to fruition in the actual death toll of 20 to 30 million Russians and Soviet citizens who died in massacres by *Einsatzgruppen* and other Nazi units, huge tank and infantry battles, aerial and artillery bombardments of cities, siege warfare and the deliberate starvation of civilians, deportation and slave labor in grueling circumstances, and other atrocities.[139]

A few days prior to his order to "exterminate" all hostiles, Hitler had announced that Moscow and Leningrad must be "rubbed out [*ausradieren zu lassen*]."[140] His "firm decision" on Leningrad was to "level the town, make it uninhabitable and relieve us of the necessity of having to feed the population through the winter."[141] The German military drafted plans to:

> Seal off Leningrad hermetically, then weaken it by terror [i.e., aerial and artillery bombing] and growing starvation. In the spring we shall occupy the town ... remove the survivors into captivity in the interior of Russia, and level Leningrad to the ground with high explosives.

One million people starved to death as the Nazis placed the city under siege, and sent one artillery shell and sniper bullet after another into the city and its people.[142]

In its ability to support life if not in its population, Stalingrad fared even worse than Leningrad. The Germans' Army Group South made its way in July and August 1941 southeast towards the Crimea region, Stalingrad, and the Soviet-Turkish border. In October and

---

of such terror by the armed forces as is alone appropriate to eradicate every inclination to resist among the population.... Commanders must find the means of keeping order by applying suitable draconian measures.").

135. *See* Phillip S. Meilinger, Airwar: Theory and Practice 193 (London, Frank Cass, 2003); Gene Smith, The Dark Summer: An Intimate History of the Events That Led to World War II, at 286 (New York: Macmillan, 1987); Hilary Ingham & Mike Ingham, EU Expansion to the East: Prospects and Problems 58 (Cheltenham: Edward Elgar, 2002); Christopher Duffy, Red Storm on the Reich: The Soviet March on Germany, 1945, at 3 (New York: Da Capo Press, 1993) (27 million total Soviet dead, for 17 million dead Soviet soldiers, subtracting 10 million Soviet civilians); The Fourth Dimension of Warfare 14 (Michael Elliott-Bateman ed., Manchester: Manchester UP, 1970) (1.7 million Yugoslav dead); Patrizia Albanese, Mothers of the Nation: Women, Families, and Nationalism in Twentieth-Century Europe 109 (Toronto: University of Toronto Press, 2006) (1.7 million Yugoslav dead); Debórah Dwork & Robert Jan Van Pelt, Holocaust: A History 185 (2002) (11 percent of Yugoslav population and even more Poles perished during World War II).

136. *See* Judt, Postwar, at 248 (citing Alexander Dallin, German Rule in Occupied Russia, 1941–1945: A Study in Occupation Policies 278 (New York: Macmillan, 1957)).

137. 1 Nazi Conspiracy and Aggression, ch. XIII, http://web.archive.org/web/20031222180627/http://www.yale.edu/lawweb/avalon/imt/document/nca_vol1/chap_13.htm.

138. *Id.*

139. *See* Megargee, War of Annihilation, at xi, 37–41, 59–62, 89–92, 115–19, 141–42; Parker, Struggle for Survival, at 281–87.

140. Judt, Postwar, at 248.

141. *Quoted in* Clark, Barbarrosa, at 120.

142. *Id.* at 120–207.

November 1941, the Soviets suffered 750,000 dead and more than 1.2 million wounded.[143] Stalingrad was bombarded from the air and shelled from the ground into smoldering ruins.[144] More than a thousand German aircraft dropped millions of bombs that killed thousands of civilians.[145]

The Nazi occupation forces systematically exterminated Soviet prisoners. In camps and compounds alone, about two million perished, with 1.3 million listed in one German document under the heading, "Exterminations; Not accounted for; Deaths and disappearance in transit."[146] More recent estimates are of 3.3 million Soviet prisoners dead due to starvation, exposure to the cold and other elements, and torture and mistreatment. By contrast, most of the 3.5 million German, Austrian, Romanian and Hungarian occupation forces captured by the Soviets were repatriated after World War II.[147] Gas chambers equipped with Zyklon B, the cyanide gas used at Auschwitz, were tested on Soviet prisoners of war. Soviet prisoners were worked to death and fed starvation rations, some no more than three hundred calories a day.[148] They were stripped of their winter clothing and left in "'cages,' often without shelter, much less heating." As a result, hundreds of thousands of them "literally froze to death."[149] A German soldier described the pitiable condition of these Soviet prisoners of war: "Several of them burnt by flamethrowers had no longer the semblance of a human face. They were blistered shapeless bundles of flesh. A bullet had taken away the lower jaw of one man.... Each of them left behind a flow of blood which spread in an ever-increasing stream."[150] The Soviet prisoners shipped to Germany plummeted in number by 30% in five months in 1941, a loss of 150,000 or more.[151]

During the war, British Prime Minister Winston Churchill called the Nazis' "'methodical, merciless butchery' of the Russians" a "crime without a name."[152] More than 1,700 Soviet cities and 70,000 towns and villages had been partially or totally wiped out.[153] Alfred Rosenberg was convicted at Nuremberg for atrocities against Soviet and other Slavic peoples.[154] Martin Bormann was convicted of "extermination" in the Soviet Union.[155]

In Ukraine and further East, Hitler authorized the Nazi official in charge of "manpower" to demand of the Reichsminister for the Occupied Eastern Territories, Alfred Rosenberg, to deport two million civilians to Germany for the "armament industry." Hitler expected Rosenberg to lead a "ruthless commitment of all resources." An internal memorandum circulated within Rosenberg's ministry described these "ruthless" methods:

> We now experienced the grotesque picture of having to recruit millions of laborers from the Occupied Eastern Territories.... In the prevailing limitless abuse

---

143. *See* MEGARGEE, WAR OF ANNIHILATION, at 76, 110–20.

144. *See* Ralph Parker, *Stalingrad Onslaughts Crushed,* N.Y. TIMES, Nov. 5, 1942, at 8; Konstantin Simonov, *From Stalingrad's Ruins,* TIME MAG., Oct. 5, 1942, http://www.time.com/time/magazine/article/0,9171,773745,00.html.

145. *See Stalingrad Subjected to Blitz Attack; Million Tons of Bombs on City,* CANBERRA TIMES (AUSTRALIA), Sept. 8, 1942, at 1; *Stalingrad Epic,* N.Y. TIMES, Sept. 20, 1942, at E1.

146. CLARK, BARBAROSSA, at 207. *See also* SHAW, WHAT IS GENOCIDE? , at 40–42.

147. *See* JUDT, POSTWAR, at 19.

148. *See* MEGARGEE, WAR OF ANNIHILATION, at 89–90, 115.

149. CLARK, BARBAROSSA, at 206.

150. *Quoted in id.* at 147.

151. *See* MEGARGEE, WAR OF ANNIHILATION, at 118–19.

152. Elder, *What You See Before Your Eyes,* at 495 n.7.

153. *See* Harry Schwartz, *Soviet Economic Reconversion*, 1945–46, 37 AMERICAN ECON. REV. 611, 611 (1947).

154. Judgement: Rosenberg.

155. Judgement: Bormann.

> of the Slavic humanity "recruiting" methods were used which probably have their origin in the blackest periods of the slave trade. A regular manhunt was inaugurated. Without consideration of health or age the people were shipped to Germany where ... more than 100,000 had to be sent back because of serious illnesses and other incapabilities for work.

Another million people were demanded about six months after 1942 request for two million. Guerilla activity accelerated in response to the roundups and deportations.[156]

Millions of Poles were killed by the Nazis, and over 10 million were enslaved and/or displaced.[157] The Nazi plan was that the indigenous population in the East, to whatever extent it survived, would be enslaved. Hans Frank, the Nazi Governor-General of the Government-General of Poland, ordered one million Polish workers, both male and female, agricultural and industrial workers, to be deported into the German Reich in order to maximize farming and replace German workers.[158] A "Compulsory Labour Service" would achieve this by "raid" and "deportation" of Poles. The S.S. administered the seizure of Polish farms to facilitate the exile of the farmers. In a letter, a community leader complained to Governor-General Frank that:

> Everybody is exposed to the danger, to be seized anywhere and at any time by members of the police, suddenly and unexpectedly and to be brought into an assembly camp. None of his relatives knows what has happened to him, only months later ... [receiving] news of his fate by a postcard.

The Nazis imported about 4.8 million civilians and 1.9 million prisoners of war for purposes of slave labor. As for conditions inside the Reich, these may be described as calculated to bring about the deaths of large numbers of group members within the meaning of the Genocide Convention. The head of Nazi Manpower stated: "All the men must be fed, sheltered and treated in such a way as to exploit them to the highest possible extent at the lowest conceivable degree of expenditure." Poles were forbidden from having sex or bearing children. S.S. rules and regulations denied Polish workers the right to acquire food on the private market, or to obtain government aid. A work camp doctor wrote that "Polish workers' rations were insufficient to stave off hunger, particularly during hard labor." The workers' meals consisted of two meals of a watery soup, and that even these meals were frequently withheld. He described the sanitary conditions in the camps as "atrocious," with insufficient and overflowing toilets, and few opportunities or facilities for washing. Most medical cases were denied care due to inadequate supplies of medicine, bandages, and other equipment. He added:

> Tuberculosis was particularly widespread among the eastern workers. The T.B. rate among them was 4 times the normal rate.... The Tartars [i.e., Soviet Turks] and Kirghis suffered most; as soon as they were overcome by [T.B.] they collapsed like flies. The cause was bad housing, the poor quality and insufficient quantity of food, overwork, and insufficient rest....
>
> Beatings of workers were expressly allowed by [S.S.] rules and regulations.

Polish community leaders took the bold step of complaining to the Polish Governor-General about the suffering and death of Polish children at German hands. They explained that starvation and intestinal diseases afflicted children in particular, and that "there are

156. 1 NAZI CONSPIRACY AND AGGRESSION, ch. XII, http://avalon.law.yale.edu/imt/chap_12.asp.
157. *See* PIOTROWSKI, POLAND'S HOLOCAUST, at 305.
158. 1 NAZI CONSPIRACY AND AGGRESSION, ch. XII.

cases of 8-year-old delicate and undernourished children put to forced labor and perishing from such treatment."[159]

Hitler ordered his manpower chief to import "400,000–500,000 selected, healthy and strong girls from the territories of the East for Germany." The rationale was purportedly to relieve the condition of the hard-working German housewife, but slavery and abuse obviously resulted. Rosenberg also approved a plan to deport up to 50,000 children below age 14 in order to weaken enemy races. In sum, the Nazi slave labor program separated "children from their parents, and by the imposition of conditions so inhuman that countless numbers perished."[160]

2. The Romani People, Suspected Leftists, Homosexuals, and the Disabled

In English, the word "gypsy" refers to a "member of a wandering race (by themselves called Romany [Romani]), of Hindu origin, which first appeared in England about the beginning of the 16th c. and was then believed to have come from Egypt."[161] They have resided in Europe for many centuries, longer than some of their European neighbors.[162] The German religious reformer Martin Luther blamed the Gypsies for poisoning Christians' water and stealing their children. Nazi anthropologists emphasized their racial inferiority, arguing that both Gypsies and Jews were of "Oriental" or "West Asian" race.[163] Even before the Nazis, Weimar Germany passed a Romani person registration law. The Nazis banned marriages between Germans and Romani people or "Negroes" in November 1933. The Nuremberg laws, in banning German marriages to Jews or Romani, grouped them together as non-European blood.[164]

In 1939, the Nazi Office of Racial Hygiene ordered that as a racially "sick" population, the Romani people should be subject to "elimination," and that "without hesitation." In 1941, the *Einsatzkommandos*, a key instrument of the Jewish Holocaust, were instructed to "kill all Jews, Gypsies and mental patients."[165] Adolf Eichmann equated the Jewish and Romani "Questions." In December 1942, the S.S. ordered all Romani deported to Auschwitz.[166]

---

159. *Id.*

160. *Id.*

161. *Gipsy, gypsy, n., in* Oxford English Dictionary (2d ed. 1989), http://dictionary.oed.com.

162. *See* Susan Tebbutt, Sinti and Roma: Gypsies in German-speaking Society and Literature 152 (New York and Oxford: Berghahn Books, 1998); The Gypsies During the Second World War 22 (Karola Fings et al., eds., Hertfordshire: University at Hertfordshire Press, 1997). Cf. Barbara Jane Davy, Introduction to Pagan Studies 2–3, 96 (2007); Thomas S. Noonan, *European Russia, c.500–c.1050, in* 3 The New Cambridge Medieval History: c.900–c.1024, at 497–98 (Timothy Reuter, Rosamond McKitterick, & David Abulafia eds., Cambridge: Cambridge UP, 1999).

163. *See* Gilad Margalit, Germany and Its Gypsies: A Post-Auschwitz Odyssey 9, 18, 36 (Madison, WI: Univ. of Wisconsin Press, 2002).

164. Ian Hancock, *Responses to the Porrajmos: The Romani Holocaust, in* Is the Holocaust Unique?, at 89–90.

165. *Id.* at 79. *Quoted in Roma: Genocide of Roma in the Holocaust, in* Encyclopedia of Genocide, at 506.

166. *See* Hancock, *The Romani Holocaust,* at 80, 83.

About 250,000 to one million Romani people perished in the Holocaust.[167] This represented a third to half of all Romani people in Europe, and nearly 90 percent of those in Germany.[168] The rate of Romani death in Germany may have been higher than for the Jews.[169]

Nazis also systematically murdered thousands of homosexuals, leftists, handicapped or mentally ill persons, and other undesirables were also, often in death camps.[170] About 80,000 disabled or mentally ill Germans were butchered prior to 1942.[171] In the camps, "between 5,000 and 15,000 homosexual men were imprisoned in concentration camps, where many died from starvation, disease, exhaustion, beatings, and murder." In a campaign called "'extermination through work,' homosexuals and other so-called security suspects were assigned to grueling work in ceaselessly dangerous conditions."[172]

D. Victims of Japan's Holocaust in Asia

Ethnic nationalist claims reached new levels of intensity before and during World War I, not simply in Europe but in East Asia as well, including Japan.[173] Starting in the late nineteenth century, Japanese Westernizers introduced new ideas of race, Darwinian competition, and Lamarckian inheritance of acquired characteristics.[174]

Ultranationalists enshrined Emperor Hirohito in 1927 and orchestrated a "revival" of the Shinto religion, which deified the emperor and emphasized "self-sacrifice" on behalf of the nation.[175] This intensified the doctrine inherited from the Meiji Constitution that the emperor, rather than the people or the parliament, was sovereign and even divine.[176]

---

167. *See* Barry A. Fisher, *No Roads Lead to Rom: The Fate of the Romani People under the Nazis and in Post-War Restitution*, 20 Whittier Law Rev. 513 (1999). *See also* Phillip Freeman, *The Extermination of the Gypsies, in* Genocide and Human Rights, at 151–57; Dora E. Yates, *Hitler and the Gypsies, in id.* at 158–65; Jerzy Ficowski, *The Fate of Polish Gypsies, in id.* at 166–77; Gabrielle Tyrnauer, *"Mastering the Past": Germans and Gypsies, in id.* at 178–93.

168. *See* James F. Brown, Hopes and Shadows: East Europe after Communism 225 (Durham, NC: Duke UP, 1994) (Germans killed a third to half of Roma people during the Holocaust); Ian Hancock, *The Romani Holocaust, in* Is the Holocaust Unique?, at 75, 86.

169. *See* Vahakn Dadrian, *Comparative Aspects of Armenian and Jewish Genocide,* at 146 (about a third of German Jews, or about 165,000, survived the Holocaust by emigrating after Nazi takeover); *compare also* Valentino, Final Solutions, at 177 (most Jews worldwide survived the Holocaust), *with* Hancock, *The Romani Holocaust,* at 85 (only 5,000 Romani are recorded as surviving the Holocaust in Germany).

170. *See* Rieber, Forced Migration, at 11–17; Norwood, Strangers and Exiles, at 296–314. The Soviet Union also massacred thousands of Poles and Germans, and deported hundreds of thousands of Poles and others, before and during World War II. *See* Rieber, Forced Migration, at 15–20; Mikhail Koptelov, Consul General of the USSR in Pahlavi, to Stalin on the Completion of the Polish Army's Evacuation from the USSR, Cipher Telegram No. 18105, Sept. 5, 1942, *quoted in* Anna M. Cienciala, Katyn: A Crime without Punishment 304 (New Haven, CT: Yale UP, 2008).

171. *See* Shaw, What Is Genocide?, at 40.

172. U.S. Holocaust Memorial Museum, *Nazi Persecution of Homosexuals 1933–1945* (2009), http://www.ushmm.org/museum/exhibit/online/hsx/.

173. *See* Kevin M. Doak, *What Is a Nation and Who Belongs? National Narratives and the Ethnic Imagination in Twentieth-Century Japan*, 102 American History Review 283, 287 (1997).

174. *See* Tessa Morris-Suzuki, *Debating Racial Science in Wartime Japan*, 13 Osiris 354, 358 (1998).

175. *The Rise of the Militarists, in* A Country Study: Japan (1994), http://lcweb2.loc.gov/cgi-bin/query/r?frd/cstdy:@field(DOCID+jp0045).

176. *See* Donald M. Seekins, *The Political System, in* A Country Study: Japan (Washington, DC: Library of Congress, 1994), http://lcweb2.loc.gov/cgi-bin/query/r?frd/cstdy:@field(DOCID+jp0204).

Under State Shinto, even militarists outside of the royal family could be elevated to Shinto gods, by virtue of their wartime conquests.[177] The militarists ordered the invasion of China within a year or two of taking power in 1927, occupied Manchuria by 1931, and reached Shanghai by 1932.[178]

During World War II, the Empire of Japan engaged in genocidal policies of indiscriminate mass murder of occupied peoples, enslavement of civilian populations, and destruction of infrastructure necessary for supporting human life. Japan carried out "*sanko*" operations, shorthand for "Burn All, Kill All, Steal All."[179] By such means, Hirohito and the militarists mounted a vast offensive against China and various Western colonies in Asia, with the stated aim of establishing a "Greater East Asia Co-prosperity Sphere" in which the "Yamato [Japanese] race" would take a "leading" role on account of the "purity of its blood."[180]

The Japanese signed an anti-communist pact with Nazi Germany in 1936, and occupied Shanghai and the Chinese capital Nanjing in 1937.[181] President Roosevelt's State Department castigated the Empire of Japan in the late 1930s for its bombing of civilians in China, as "barbarous" violations of the "elementary principles" of ethical warfare. The U.S. Senate issued an "unqualified condemnation of the inhuman bombing of civilian populations."[182] Brigadier Guilio Douhet, an Italian air power strategist, described the rationale behind such bombing of civilian cities: "Today it is not the armies but whole nations which make war; and all civilians are belligerents and all are exposed to the hazards of war. The only salvation will be in caves, but those caves cannot hold entire cities, fleets, railways, bridges, industries, etc."[183]

The Japanese invasion claimed 10 to 20 million Chinese lives, the homes of 40 million people, 50 percent of the arable farmland, up to one-third of farm animals, 300,000 kilometers of roads, 100,000 tons of ships, and $100 billion in property damage and defense costs.[184] The Japanese army went about "indiscriminately massacring" the Chinese civil-

---

177. *See* David Pilling, *Let Sleeping Gods Lie*, Financial Times (U.K.), Feb. 19, 2005, at 14 (describing elevation of Japanese militarists and war criminals to status of Shinto gods after the war). *See also* William Chapman, *Japan's Wartime Leaders Enshrined*, Wash. Post, Apr. 21, 1979, at A3 ("The revelation of the enshrinement [of Japanese militarists] ... sparked immediate charges that it was an attempt to reverse the official split between state and religion, a small step toward the prewar nationalism that is seen by leftist critics as a growing threat.").

178. *See* Robert L. Worden, *Historical Setting, in* A Country Study: Japan, http://lcweb2.loc.gov/cgi-bin/query/r?frd/cstdy:@field(DOCID+jp0271).

179. Japanese veterans admitted to such genocidal "*sanko*" operations in a bestseller published in Japan, entitled "Burn All, Kill All, Steal All." Herbert P. Bix, Hirohito and the Making of Modern Japan 657 (New York: HarperCollins, 2000).

180. *Tojo's War Aims*, The Economist, July 19, 1975, at 102 (reviewing Japan's Greater East Asia Co-Prosperity Sphere in World War II (Joyce C. Lebra ed., Oxford: Oxford UP, 1975)). *See also The Rise of the Militarists, in* A Country Study: Japan ("The Greater East Asia Coprosperity Sphere was to integrate Asia politically and economically—under Japanese leadership—against Western domination....").

181. *See Rise of the Militarists*; *World War II, in* A Country Study: Japan, http://lcweb2.loc.gov/cgi-bin/query/r?frd/cstdy:@field(DOCID+jp0271); Chao-ying Pan, American Diplomacy Concerning Manchuria (Washington, DC: Catholic University of America, 1938); Manley Ottmer Hudson, The Verdict of the League: China and Japan in Manchuria (Boston: World Peace Foundation, 1933); Refugees from Northeast China in Consequence of Japanese Invasion, What the Japanese Have Done in Northeast China (Manchuria) Since September 18, 1931 (1932).

182. *Quoted in* Michael S. Sherry, The Rise of American Air Power: The Creation of Armageddon 58–60 (New Haven. Connecticut: Yale UP, 1989).

183. *Quoted in* Mark Levene, 1 Genocide in the Age of the Nation State: The Meaning of Genocide 57 (London: I.B. Tauris, 2005).

184. *See* Maria Hsia Chang, Return of the Dragon: China's Wounded Nationalism 80–82 (Boulder, Colo.: Westview Press, 2001).

ian population, for example in the "'Rape of Nanjing.'"[185] The occupation forces murdered at least 250,000 and possibly 350,000 civilians in Nanjing, raped 20,000 to 80,000 Chinese women, and systematically mutilated and tortured victims.[186] The Japanese general in command of some of the forces that committed these crimes was tried and convicted by a military tribunal of failing to discipline his men properly during their rampages.[187]

Chinese families had their life savings wiped out as hyperinflation increased prices by 2,000 times.[188] As a result of the occupation and its aftereffects, the Nationalist government went bankrupt and fell to the communists, while China's development was postponed by 50 years, so the average earnings of a worker were one-sixth as much in 1985 as they would have been had the invasion not occurred.[189]

By 1941 the Japanese also occupied French Indochina (Vietnam, Cambodia, and Laos), the American Philippines, the Dutch East Indies (Indonesia), British Malaya and Singapore, and previously independent Burma and Thailand.[190] About 3.5 million Filipino, Vietnamese, Korean, Cambodian, Laotian, Indonesian, Malayan, Burmese, Thais, Americans, British, Dutch, and Australians died from Japanese atrocities and slave labor campaigns carried out in these territories.[191] Of these, nearly two million were starved to death in Vietnam and one million died in the Philippines.[192] The Japanese military's system of conscripting 200,000 native females as "comfort women," i.e., sex slaves for Japanese forces, may have caused tens of millions of rapes against Chinese, Korean, Filipino, Burmese, Indonesian, and Dutch women.[193] As a result, hundreds of thousands of non-Japanese

---

185. *Sino-Japanese War, in* A Country Study: Japan, http://lcweb2.loc.gov/cgi-bin/query/r?frd/cstdy:@field(DOCID+jp0272).

186. *See* Chang, Return of the Dragon, at 80–81; *see generally* Iris Chang, The Rape of Nanking: The Forgotten Holocaust of World War II (New York: BasicBooks/HarperCollins, 1997).

187. *See* Ilias Bantekas, *The Contemporary Law of Superior Responsibility*, 93 American Journal of International Law 573, 574 n.8 (1999). Another tribunal convicted Japan's foreign minister for failing to halt these violations of the laws of war, upon being informed of their commencement and continuation. *See id.*

188. *See* Chang, Return of the Dragon, at 82.

189. *See id.* at 80–82.

190. *See War in the Pacific, in* A Country Study: Japan, http://lcweb2.loc.gov/cgi-bin/query/r?frd/cstdy:@field(DOCID+jp0273). The colonization of Korea began much earlier, being firmly established by 1910. *See* Bruce G. Cumings, *Historical Setting, in* North Korea: A Country Study (1993), http://lcweb2.loc.gov/cgi-bin/query/r?frd/cstdy:@field(DOCID+kp0020).

191. *See* Bix, Hirohito, at 690; *see also* Ann Marie Prevost, *Race and War Crimes: The 1945 War Crimes Trial of General Tomoyuki Yamashita*, 14 Human Rights Q. 303 (1992); Timothy P. Maga, Judgment at Tokyo: The Japanese War Crimes Trials 135 (Lexington: Univ. Press of Kentucky, 2001); Nicholas Tarling, A Sudden Rampage: The Japanese Occupation of Southeast Asia (London: Hurst, 2001); William Chalek, Guest of the Emperor: 1941 to 1945 in the Philippines, Surviving the War, and as a POW 189 (iUniverse, 2002); Matsuoka Hajime, *The Fukuoka Court Judgment of Chinese Forced-labor Lawsuit* (Nov. 15–17, 2002), http://members.tripod.com/~cpri/cpr2002/fukuoka.pdf.

192. *See* Bix, Hirohito, at 690.

193. Karen Parker, War Rape, Submission to United Nations Commission on Human Rights, 51st Sess., Agenda Item 11, http://www.webcom.com/hrin/parker/c95-11.html. *See also* U.N. ECOSOC, Commission on Human Rights, Sub-Commission on Prevention of Discrimination and Protection of Minorities, Final report on Contemporary Forms of Slavery: Systematic Rape, Sexual Slavery and Slavery-Like Practices During Armed Conflict prepared by Special Rapporteur Gay J. McDougall, U.N. Doc. No. E/CN.4/Sub.2/1998/13 (June 22, 1998), http://www.hri.ca/forthereCord1998/documentation/commission/e-cn4-sub2-1998-13.htm; Karen Parker & Jennifer F. Chew, *Compensation for Japan's World War II War-Rape Victims*, 17 Hastings Int'l & Comparative Law Rev. 497 (1994).

women died of disease, suicide, forced marches, or proximity to the front lines, or lost their ability to have children.[194]

E. German and Japanese Victims of the War

Scholars have also raised the question whether Allied bombardment of German and Japanese cities, and the detonation of atomic weapons on Hiroshima and Nagasaki, qualify as genocidal attempts to exterminate large portions of the German or Japanese civilian populations.[195] The bombardment of German cities such as Berlin, Hamburg, and Dresden killed about 300,000 to 600,000 persons.[196] Conventional, incendiary, and atomic bombing of Japan also claimed the lives of 330,000 to 900,000 Japanese civilians in cities such as Tokyo, Yokohama, Nagoya, Osake, Kobe, Hiroshima, and Nagasaki.[197] About 20 percent of German homes were destroyed, as were the homes of 30 percent of Japan's urban population.[198] A sense of the scale of the bombing of Japan may be gleaned from the following statistics:

- 160,800 tons of bombs percent were dropped on Japan's "home islands,"
- raids against Tokyo, Nagoya, Osake, and Kobe destroyed 31 square miles of those cities, including 15 square miles of Tokyo's "most densely populated area,"
- "some 40 percent of the built-up area of the 66 [Japanese] cities attacked was destroyed,"

---

194. *See* Parker & Chew, *Japan's World War II War-Rape Victims,* at 499 (citing Japanese estimate that 75% of sex slaves died from abuse and 145,000 Korean sex slaves alone died); Roy L. Brooks, When Sorry Isn't Enough: The Controversy Over Apologies and Reparations for Human Injustice 97 (New York: NYU Press, 1999).

195. *See* Leo Kuper, *Theoretical Issues Relating to Genocide: Uses and Abuses, in* Genocide: Conceptual and Historical Dimensions, at 33; Israel W. Charny, *Toward a Generic Definition of Genocide, in id.* at 64–94; Helen Fein, *Genocide, Terror, Life Integrity, and War Crimes, in id.* at 100; Eric Markusen and David Kopf, The Holocaust and Strategic Bombing: Genocide and Total War in the Twentieth Century (Boulder, Colo.: Westview Press, 1995); Samuel Totten, *Horizontal Nuclear Proliferation and Its Genocidal Implications, in* 3 The Widening Circle of Genocide: A Critical Bibliographic Review 290–322 (Israel Charny ed., London and New Brunswick, NJ: Transaction Publishers, 1994); Leo Kuper, Genocide: Its Political Use in the Twentieth Century 46, 207–8 (New Haven, CT: Yale UP, 1983); Israel W. Charny, How Can We Commit the Unthinkable?: Genocide, The Human Cancer (Boulder, Colo.: Westview Press, 1982).

196. *See* Eric Langenbacher, *The Allies in World War II: The Anglo-American Bombardment of German Cities, in* Genocide, War Crimes, and the West, at 118.

197. *See id.* at 129 (citing John Dower, War Without Mercy: Race and Power in the Pacific War (New York: Pantheon, 1986), and Markusen & Kopf, The Holocaust and Strategic Bombing); United States Strategic Bombing Survey, Summary Report (Pacific War) 16–17, 20 (July 1, 1946) (estimating that "[t]otal civilian casualties in Japan, as a result of 9 months of air attack, including those from the atomic bombs, were approximately 806,000" with about 330,000 fatalities). The Survey's estimate of 330,000 Japanese civilian deaths, including Hiroshima and Nagasaki, seems not to have been an underestimate at the time it was made, perhaps because the full scope of radiation-, hunger- and disease-related mortality was not yet known. *See, e.g.,* Joseph Coleman, *1945 Tokyo Firebombing Left Legacy of Terror, Pain,* Associated Press, Mar. 10, 2005, http://www.ap.org (one night of incendiary bombing of Tokyo is now thought to have killed 100,000 people); Greg Mitchell, *Poll Shows Americans, For First Time, Divided on Use of A-Bombs in 1945,* Editor & Publisher, July 24, 2005 (Hiroshima and Nagasaki bombings alone had caused an estimated 200,000 deaths by 2005).

198. *See* United States Strategic Bombing Survey, Pacific War, at 16–21 (30 percent of Japan's urban dwellers were made homeless); Langenbacher, *The Allies in World War II,* at 117, 129.

- "221,000 tons of foodstuffs ... were destroyed by air attacks," and
- fewer than 10% of bombs hit their targets, being dropped from about 30,000 feet.[199]

The British and American treatment of German and Japanese civilians and prisoners of war, during and after the war, was generally humane, and the economies of Germany and Japan enjoyed miraculous growth, seemingly disproving any intention to exterminate these groups beyond the extent necessary to break their will to fight.[200] There is less precedent regarding the applicability of the Genocide Convention to the aerial bombardment of civilians, unaccompanied by massacres and mass rapes on the ground as in the Holocaust, Srebrenica, or Rwanda. Among other indicia of continuing controversy, no international tribunal recognized by the United Nations has convicted any leaders of genocide in connection with the aerial bombardment of civilians standing alone, while the World War II, Yugoslav, and Rwandan tribunals have all convicted persons of genocide or crimes against humanity for massacres on the ground.[201]

F. Victims of Stalinist Genocide in Soviet-occupied Europe and Asia

A variety of authors have accused the Soviet Union, both before and during World War II, of being nearly as guilty of imperialism and crimes against humanity as the Nazis and militarist Japanese. Soviet empire-building and killings and/or deportations of ethnic and religious minorities surely took place on a grand scale. Millions of non-Russians, as well as hundreds of thousands or even millions of Russians suspected of disloyalty by the government, suffered starvation, summary execution, torture, and slave labor under Soviet rule.

German intelligence decided in 1915 to support and finance the rise of the Bolsheviks with 50 million gold marks.[202] The Bolsheviks, with fewer than 24,000 members earlier in the war, eventually commanded the loyalty of 60,000 Russian troops.[203] Hoping to prevent another massacre of Russians by Western Europeans such as the British, French, and Germans, due to Russian "backwardness" before the European threat, Vladimir Lenin and Josef Stalin planned to make the Soviet Union a great power.[204] This, they believed, required the defeat of the landholding farmers, referred to as kulaks and accused of feudalism.[205] As Stalin wrote in 1918:

> Either the kulaks massacre vast numbers of workers, or the workers ruthlessly suppress the revolts of the predatory kulak minority of the people against the

---

199. United States Strategic Bombing Survey, Pacific War, at 16–17, 20–21.

200. *See* Langenbacher, *The Allies in World War II,* at 117, 121–28.

201. *See* Samuel Totten, *The United Nations and Genocide*, Society, May/June 2005, at 6, 9 (discussing U.N. Security Council's establishment of two "ad-hoc international courts" to try persons indicted for genocide, etc.).

202. *See* Roman Brackman, The Secret File of Joseph Stalin 143 (London: Routledge, 2001); Robert Conquest, Stalin: The Breaker of Nations 298 (New York, Viking, 1991).

203. *See* Montefiore, Young Stalin, at 319. *Compare* Ronald Hingley, Russian Writers and Soviet Society 1917–1978, at 4 (London: Taylor & Francis, 1981).

204. *See, e.g.*, Rummel, Death by Government, at 10, 82–3.

205. *See, e.g.*, Simon Sebag Montefiore, Stalin; Court of the Red Tsar, at 45–65 (New York: Knopf, 2003).

> working class.... These leeches have sucked the blood out of the working people and grown richer.... These vampires have been gathering the landed estates into their hands; they continue to enslave the poor peasants. Ruthless war on the kulaks![206]

In power, the Bolsheviks executed millions of their ethnic and political opponents and deported millions of people from their traditional homelands, including Poles, Ukrainians, Chechens, Circassians, Armenians, Assyrians, Jews, Greeks, Central Asians, Catholics, Germans, Koreans, Mongolians, and other peoples.[207] Soviet law facilitated such crimes by concentrating power in the person of Josef Stalin and by declaring resistance to socialism to be punishable by death.[208] The Soviet Criminal Code of 1926 established a framework for widespread killing and Gulag slave labor by erecting vague and broadly interpreted bans on terror, subversion, espionage, etc.[209]

As the Soviet dictator, Stalin exhibited a cruel and cavalier disregard for human life, and a resolve to stamp out potential insurgencies and liberation movements in their infancy.[210] In the late 1920s and early 1930s, Stalin's government murdered three million peasants and landlords during the forced collectivization of Soviet agriculture.[211] In the wake of peasant uprisings in 1930 and 1931, the communists under Stalin "used the gun, the lynch mob and the Gulag camp to break the villages."[212] Between 1931 and 1933, Stalin and his officials intentionally created a famine that killed five to seven million in the Ukraine and Kazakhstan.[213] Ukrainians ate tree bark, grass, earthworms, and dead bodies to stay alive.[214] The government deported two million people to Kazakhstan or Siberia, with one million surviving in the Gulag as of 1935. Perhaps 3.5 million suffered deportation from their homes and communities by 1933, and another 3.5 million lost their homes while remaining in the same general area. The communist party issued orders starting in July 1937 to execute nearly 400,000 people. The Soviet interior ministry or NKVD targeted "Polish diversionists" for genocide, killing 100,000. Up to 15 million persons experienced deportation by 1937, and many of them perished.[215]

---

206. *Quoted in* Luciano Pellicani, Revolutionary Apocalypse: Ideological Roots of Terrorism 183 (Westport, CT: Greenwood Publishing Group, 2003).

207. Eric D. Weitz, A Century of Genocide: Utopias of Race and Nation 79–80 (Princeton, NJ: Princeton UP, 2003); Chloe Arnold, *Russia: Cobblers Face the Boot in Moscow*, Radio Free Europe/Radio Liberty (Oct. 14, 2007), http://www.rferl.org/content/article/1078944.html.

208. *See* David F. Forte, *Western Law and Communist Dictatorship*, 32 Emory Law Journal 135, 177–78 (1983) (citing Soviet Const. of 1936); 1 Alexander Solzhenitsyn, The Gulag Archipelago: 1918–1956, at 290–91, 438–39 (Thomas P. Whitney trans., New York: Harper & Row, 1991) (1973).

209. *See* Solzhenitsyn, The Gulag Archipelago, at 60–76.

210. Most sentiments are captured in an aphorism attributed to Stalin within the Soviet Union: "There is a person, there is a problem; no person, no problem." *Quoted in* Abel Gezevich Aganbegian, Perestroika 1989, at 188 (New York: Charles Scribner's Sons, 1988).

211. *See, e.g.*, Rummel, Death by Government, at 8 ("Stalin ... ordered the death of millions ... and as the ultimate dictator, was responsible for the death of still millions more killed by his henchmen."); *see also id.* at 8–10, 28, 82–3.

212. Montefiore, Stalin, at 64.

213. *See* Komlos, *On the Biological Standard of Living in the Soviet Union,* at 75, 77.

214. *See* Julia Belluz, *She Lived Through the Ukrainian Famine, and Never Forgot What Hunger Felt Like,* Globe and Mail (Canada), Oct. 5, 2009, http://www.theglobeandmail.com/deaths/she-lived-through-the-ukrainian-famine-and-never-forgot-what-hunger-felt-like/article1309349/; Askold Krushelnycky, *Ukraine: Famine—Survivors Recall the Horrors of 1933 (Part 2),* Radio Free Europe/Radio Liberty, May 8, 2003, http://www.rferl.org/content/Article/1103170.html.

215. *See* Montefiore, Stalin, at 64, 84–85, 228–29.

The Soviet leadership killed nearly five million people by deportation to and mistreatment in labor camps and inhospitable territories such as Siberia.[216] Alexander Solzhenitsyn describes an appalling catalogue of non-Russian peoples, often Muslims or Catholics, deported to Siberia or confined in the corrective-labor camp (Gulag) system starting in the late 1920s and accelerating after the German invasion in 1941. Victims included Chechens, Ingush, Balkars, Tatars, Kazakhs, Kalmyks, Cossacks, Bulgarians, Poles, Armenians, Assyrians, Greeks, Iranians, Azeris, Kurds, Turks, Mongols, Koreans, Poles, Czechs, Finns, Germans, and even Russian or other Slavic ethnic groups subjected to German occupation.[217] Once inside the Gulag system, Soviet officialdom physically and psychologically tortured civilians belonging to these peoples using merciless beatings, stress positions, sleep deprivation, starvation, unremitting hard labor, inhuman sanitary and health conditions, and threats of reprisals against loved ones.[218] Within five years of their deportation, about 25% of the members of several peoples had perished. Among the dead were 300,000 Germans, 100,000 Chechens, 40–80,000 Crimean Tatars, 40,000 Koreans, 23,000 Ingushes, and smaller numbers of other ethnic and religious minorities.[219] About 20 million persons under Soviet control died by 1955.[220]

At least two former Soviet republics, Latvia and Estonia, have convicted Communist-era officials for genocide based on evidence that they deported members of ethnic or national groups with the intent to destroy the group in part.[221] Scholars in the former Soviet republics argue that beneath Leninist or Stalinist political repression, there was an underlying policy of replacing non-Russian ethnic communities with Russian ones.[222] About a third of the Latvian population died under Nazi and Soviet occupation from 1940 to 1954.[223]

---

216. *See, e.g.*, Rummel, Death by Government, at 10, 82–3.

217. *See* Stephane Courtois et al., The Black Book of Communism: Crimes, Terror, Repression (Cambridge, MA: Harvard UP, 1999); Polian, Against Their Will, at 64, 102, 140, 184, 327–372 (documenting deportations of Armenians, Bulgarians, Crimean Tatars, Finns, Greeks, Kalmyks, Kurds, Poles, Romanians, and Turks); Solzhenitsyn, The Gulag Archipelago, at 24–6, 51, 72, 77–9, 81–5 (referring to Balkars, Chechens, Cossacks, Crimean Tatars, Czechs, Finns, Germans, Ingush, Kalmyks, Koreans, Kazakhs, and Mongols); Lynne Viola, The Unknown Gulag: The Lost World of Stalin's Special Settlements 3, 33, 49, 52, 85, 101–4, 111, 117–18, 126–27, 135, 140, 145–47, 153, 165, 188 (Oxford: Oxford UP, 2007) (describing terrible living conditions in Soviet concentration camps and settlements, including executions, starvation, disease, and exposure to the elements, and stating: "The already perilous conditions within the special settlements eased the work of the famine."); Sargis G. Osipov, *Lawlessness Is Our Destiny*, Zinda Mag., Mar. 14, 2004, http://www.zindamagazine.com/html/archives/ 2004/3.15.04/index.php (describing deportation of Assyrians of Georgia and Azerbaijan to Kazakhstan and Eastern Siberia in 1949 and 1950); Elena Ryumina, *Assyrians Ring in the Year 6750*, Moscow Times, April 1, 2000, http://www.zindamagazine.com/html/archives/2000/zn040400.htm ("In 1949, [the Assyrians] were declared a "repressed nation of the Soviet Union" (like the Chechens), and were forcibly removed by Stalin from Azerbaijan and Georgia and sent to Siberia and Kazakhstan."); *see also* Rummel, Death by Government, at 28 ("During World War II, the Soviets committed genocide against at least nine of their distinct ethnic-linguistic subnations, including ethnic Germans, ethnic Greeks, Crimean Tartars, and Balkars.").

218. *See* Solzhenitsyn, The Gulag Archipelago, at 104–17.

219. *See* Michael Rywkin, Moscow's Lost Empire 67 (Armonk, NY: M.E. Sharpe, 1994).

220. *See* Lewis M. Simons, *Genocide and the Science of Proof*, National Geographic, Jan. 2006, at 30.

221. Lauri Mälksoo, *Soviet Genocide? Communist Mass Deportations in the Baltic States and International Law*, 14 Leiden J. of Int'l L. 757, 774–78, 780 (2001).

222. *See Soviet Trials in the Baltic States*, *in* Yearbook of International Humanitarian Law —2004, at 398–99 (Cambridge: Cambridge UP, 2004).

223. *See* USDOS, *Background Note: Latvia* (May 2009), http://www.state.gov/r/pa/ei/bgn/5378.htm.

The Soviets deported an estimated 50,000 Estonians to face mass death in 1949.[224] Russians, often settlers and their progeny, made up about a third of the Latvian and Estonian population in 1989, up from about 10 percent in the 1930s.[225]

---

224. See R.J. Rummel, *Soviet Union, Genocide in, in* ENCYCLOPEDIA OF GENOCIDE, at 521.
225. *See* RYWKIN, MOSCOW'S LOST EMPIRE, at 94.

Chapter XI

"The Greatest Danger": Cold War Genocides

> Soviet leaders almost certainly believe that as Soviet nuclear capabilities increase, the unwillingness of the US and its allies to risk general war will correspondingly increase, and that the Kremlin will therefore have greater freedom of action to promote its objectives....
>
> We believe that the USSR will continue to pursue its expansionist objectives and to seek and exploit opportunities for enlarging the area of Communist control.
>
> —CIA, Memorandum on Soviet Capabilities and Probable Course of Action, 1954[1]

This chapter analyzes the problem of genocide in the Cold War era, particularly in the Middle East and broader Islamic world, from Nigeria to Indonesia. It begins with reports of genocide and mass death in Maoist China, occupied Tibet, North and South Korea, Vietnam, and Cambodia. It then turns to communist Afghanistan, Angola, and Ethiopia; British-ruled Malaya and Kenya; French-ruled Algeria; and fascist Indonesia, Nigeria, Pakistan, and Uganda. A comparison of some other often-discussed genocides during the Cold War reveals that while the death tolls did not approach those of the Holocaust, they did reach into the millions, as did the numbers of persons made refugees and internally displaced persons (IDP). Figure 5 summarizes findings concerning the scale of some Cold War massacres and atrocities by the United Nations, U.N. member states, international criminal tribunals, and truth and reconciliation commissions.

A. The Cold War: Clashes of Empires

It is often insufficiently recognized that the charter of the Nuremberg tribunal was a pact between four empires or near-empires: the British, French, Soviet, and U.S. governments.[2] Between them they dominated or indirectly controlled much of the rest of the world, including most of Europe and much of Africa, Asia, the Caribbean, and Cen-

1. Revised Conclusions, National Intelligence Estimate, Nov. 4, 1954, Box 10, White House Office, Office of the Special Assistant for National Security Affairs Research, classified Top Secret, declassified in 1981.

2. Agreement by the Government of the United Kingdom of Great Britain and Northern Ireland, the Government of the United States of America, the Provisional Government of the French Republic, and the Government of the Union of Soviet Socialist Republics for the Prosecution and Punishment of the Major War Criminals of the European Axis, 82 U.N.T.S. 280.

Figure 5 Estimates of Death Tolls in Cold War Genocides

Case	Death Toll	Refugees/IDPs	Sources
Cambodia, 1975–1979	2 million	500,000	U.N. Economic and Social Council, Commission on Human Rights
North Korea, 1945–present	1–4 million	1–2 million	THE BLACK BOOK OF COMMUNISM; U.S. Institute of Peace
Bangladesh, 1970–1971	1–3 million	7–10 million	Government of India; U.S. Consulate (Dacca, Bangladesh)
Nigeria, 1967–1970	1–2 million	1–5 million	U.S. Department of State
Afghanistan, 1979–1992	1–1.5 million	5 million	U.S. Department of State
Indonesia, 1965–1966	500,000 to 1 million	Unknown	U.S. Department of State
Algeria, 1954–1962	220,000 to 1 million	Over 1 million	France, Algeria
East Timor, 1976–2000	200,000	50,000 to 400,000	United Nations
Burundi, 1972	100,000 to 300,000	113,000	U.N. Economic and Social Council, Commission on Human Rights
Northern Iraq, 1968–1992	50,000 to 200,000	1.1 to 5 million	Iraqi High Tribunal
Guatemala, 1960–1996	200,000	1.2 million	Historical Clarification Commission of Guatemala
Brazil, 1973–?	10,000	20,000	Press reports re Yanomami Indians

tral America. Britain had significant constitutional and legislative powers in Australia, Canada, New Zealand, and South Africa, as well as mandates in Israel/Palestine, Jordan, and Tanzania; protectorates in parts of Nigeria, Gambia, Kuwait, Bahrain, Qatar, Malaysia, South Yemen, and Uganda; and colonies in Burma, India, Pakistan, and Bangladesh, the Bahamas, Jamaica, other Caribbean islands, Kenya, Sierra Leone, Sudan, Zambia, and Zimbabwe. France had colonies (formally colonial protectorates) in Algeria, Benin, Burkina Faso, Chad, Congo, Guinea, Ivory Coast, Mali, Mauritania, Niger, Senegal, Guadeloupe, Martinique, Saint Martin, Vietnam, Cambodia, and Laos, claimed a mandate in Cameroon, and maintained informal rule in Syria. The Soviet Union had troops from Manchuria and North Korea to Bulgaria and Saxony, and actively supported revolutionary movements in the Americas, China, Europe, and Iran.[3] The U.S. ruled Alaska, Hawaii, Puerto Rico, various Pacific islands, and the Philippines, stationed troops in Europe, China, Japan, other parts of Asia, and the Caribbean; had used force in several Central American and Caribbean nations, leading to thousands of deaths; and asserted the right

3. *See, e.g.*, MAZIAR BEHROOZ, REBELS WITH A CAUSE: THE FAILURE OF THE LEFT IN IRAN 22–34 (London: I.B.Tauris, 2000); JUNG CHANG & JON HALLIDAY, MAO: THE UNKNOWN STORY 19–75, 373 (London: Jonathan Cape, an imprint of Random House, 2005); FRIEDRICH ENGELBERT SCHULE, MEXICO BETWEEN HITLER AND ROOSEVELT 60–62 (Albuquerque, New Mexico: Univ. of New Mexico Press, 1999); STANLEY E. HILTON, BRAZIL AND THE SOVIET CHALLENGE, 1917–1947 (Austin, Texas: University of Texas Press, 1991).

to intervene overtly or covertly to protect its military and economic interests around the world.[4]

The rival superpowers constructed divergent understandings of Nazi terror and genocide. The Soviet view regarded them as deterministically natural consequences of cartel capitalism and its demands for abundant sources of raw materials, markets, and sources of cheap slave labor. Nazi crimes, in this conception, resembled European imperialism in the Americas, Africa, and Asia, and were linked to the global dominance of the U.S. after the war. As early as 1917, Stalin had described World War I as a campaign for the "seizure (annexation) of foreign, chiefly agrarian, territories by capitalistically developed states" in search of "new markets," shipping routes, and "raw materials and mineral wealth" to be "secure[d] ... regardless of the internal regimes in the countries they seek to annex."[5] At the outbreak of World War II, he complained of Nazi Germany's intention "to seize our lands watered by the sweat of our brows, to seize our grain and oil secured by the labour of our hands," "to restore the rule of the landlords [and] tsarism," and to "turn [Soviet citizens] into the slaves of German princes and barons."[6] In 1942, he declared German fascism to be an imperialist movement to "seize foreign countries and suck their blood in order to enrich the German bankers and plutocrats."[7] The Soviet victory, he proclaimed, was the defeat of a German movement, across the ages, to enslave persons of Slavic race and language.[8]

American historians and officials, on the other hand, viewed Nazi crimes as an outgrowth of totalitarianism and undemocratic forms of government, thereby placing fascism and communism on a more equivalent footing. According to the widely praised and credited words of George F. Kennan, chief of the U.S. mission in Moscow at the conclusion of World War II, Lenin and Stalin did not "tolerate rival political forces," and clung to a "brand of fanaticism, unmodified by any of the Anglo-Saxon traditions of compromise, [which] was too fierce and too jealous to envisage any permanent sharing of power." The Communist Party demanded that it dominate all "forms of collective human activity or association."[9] As George Orwell paraphrased the debate between West and East: "Capitalism leads to ... the scramble for markets, and war. Collectivism leads to concentration camps, leader worship, and war."[10]

---

4. *See* National Security Act of 1947, § 503(e), Public Law 253, 80th Cong., July 26. 1947, 61 Stat. 495, as amended by Public Law 216, 81st Cong., August 10, 1949, 63 Stat. 578; Ediberto Román, The Other American Colonies: An International and Constitutional Law Examination of the United States Nineteenth and Twentieth Century Island Conquests (Durham, NC: Carolina Academic Press, 2006); Douglas T. Stuart, Creating the National Security State: A History of the Law that Transformed America 230–79 (Princeton: Princeton UP, 2008); Ellen C. Collier, *Instances of Use of U.S. Forces Abroad, 1789–1993* (1993), http://www.history.navy.mil/wars/foabroad.htm.

5. *The War,* Pravda No. 10, Mar. 16, 1917, http://www.marxists.org/reference/archive/stalin/works/1917/03/16.htm. He cited German and other socialists gathered at Zimmerwald in 1915 and 1915 who characterized the war as imperialist in nature. *See id.*

6. Josef V. Stalin, *Radio Broadcast* (July 3, 1941), http://www.marxists.org/reference/archive/stalin/works/1941/07/03.htm.

7. Josef V. Stalin, *Order of the Day, No. 130* (May 1, 1942), http://www.marxists.org/reference/archive/stalin/works/1942/05/01.htm.

8. *See* Josef V. Stalin, *Stalin's Address to the People/Victory Speech* (May 9, 1945), http://www.marxists.org/reference/archive/stalin/works/1945/05/09a.htm (victory speech: "age-long struggle of the Slavonic peoples for their existence and independence").

9. George Kennan, *The Sources of Soviet Conduct,* Foreign Aff., 1947, http://www.historyguide.org/Europe/kennan.html.

10. George Orwell, *Review: The Road to Serfdom by F.A. Hayek and The Mirror of the Past by K. Zilliacus, in* III The Collected Essays, Journalism and Letters of George Orwell: As I Please,

Throughout the Cold War, which was referred to starting in the 1940s as a "Pax Americana," most of the world enjoyed peace and rising prosperity, most of the time.[11] With notable exceptions such as Hanoi and Kandahar, global cities were rarely the scene of sustained bombing or military maneuvers. Global population surged from 2.5 billion in 1950 to more than five billion in 1990. Cities like Lagos (Nigeria), Kinshasa (Kenya), and Dhaka (Bangladesh) increased in population by more than 40 times. Seoul, South Korea, New Delhi, India, Sao Pãolo, Brazil, Lima, Peru, and Mexico City, Mexico multiplied their metropolitan populations by nearly 20 times each. Beijing, Shanghai, Jakarta, Calcutta, Tehran, Istanbul, Rio de Janeiro, Buenos Aires, and Bogotá all had more than ten times as many residents in 2004 as they did in 1950.[12] In real terms, global economic output more than tripled from 1950 to 1990.[13] Both population and economic activity probably increased by greater amounts from 1945–1990 than in the prior four million years, combined.[14] From only 45% of the world's population making more than $400 per year in 1950, over 75% of humans earned that much income in 1992, at the end of the Cold War.[15]

The superpowers' divergent worldviews and friction at the intersection of their spheres of influence in Germany, the Balkans, Iran, China, and Korea erupted into Cold War in 1946. The start of the nearly 50-year struggle is often dated to British Prime Minister Winston Churchill's speech at Fulton, Missouri, an appeal to the still fairly new U.S. President Harry Truman for a common English-speaking front against Soviet totalitarianism. A key component of the plan would be support for British colonies around the world. Churchill proclaimed:

> [T]he liberties enjoyed by individual citizens throughout the British Empire are not valid in a considerable number of countries, some of which are very powerful. In these States control is enforced upon the common people by various kinds of all-embracing police governments. The power of the State is exercised without restraint, either by dictators or by compact oligarchies operating through a privileged party and a political police.[16]

Stalin responded that Churchill's speech and policies represented a revival of Nazism with an Anglo-American face. While Hitler started out with a race theory proclaiming the "German-speaking people" to be a master race, Churchill simply replaced them with the English-speaking nations without abandoning the theory of national supremacy. Stalin added:

> The German race theory led Hitler and his friends to the conclusion that the Germans, as the only superior nation, should rule over other nations. The Eng-

---

1943–1945, at 117–19 (Sonia Orwell & Ian Argus eds., New York: Harcourt, Brace, and Jovanovich, 1968).

11. *See* William Safire, Safire's Political Dictionary 525–26 (Oxford: Oxford UP, 2008). *See also* James Henry Roberts Cromwell, Pax Americana: American Democracy and World Peace (New York: A. Kroch and Son, 1941); Charles L. Mee, The Marshall Plan: The Launching of the Pax Americana (New York: Simon & Schuster, 1984).

12. *See* Mike Davis, Planet of Slums 2–4 (London: Verso, 2006).

13. *See* International Monetary Fund, World Economic Outlook 150 (International Monetary Fund, 2000).

14. *See* Lester Russell Brown, Plan B: Rescuing a Planet Under Stress and a Civilization in Trouble 6 (New York: W.W. Norton & Co., 2003).

15. *See* Peter G. Prontzos, *Collateral Damage: The Human Cost of Structural Violence, in* Genocide, War Crimes, and the West, at 305.

16. Winston Churchill, *The Sinews of Power* (Mar. 5, 1946), http://www.churchill-society-london.org.uk/Fulton.html.

> lish race theory leads Mr. Churchill and his friends to the conclusion that the English-speaking nations, as the only superior nations, should rule over the rest of the nations of the world.[17]

Soviet propaganda charged the U.S. with invading the Soviet Union after the Bolshevik revolution, and setting up concentration camps and massacring tens of thousands of Russians and other Soviet peoples in a bid to make a weakened Russia into an American colony. When that failed, the U.S. aided the rise of Hitler, and prolonged the war to sap Soviet strength.[18]

By the Warsaw Pact of 1955, the Soviet Union and its allied satellite states condemned "the participation of a remilitarized West Germany" in a North Atlantic (NATO) military alliance, as a way of "increasing the danger of a new war and creating a threat to the national security of peace-loving States."[19] Soviet theory regarded capitalist nations' alliances as respites between wars of imperialist aggression, and as untrustworthy.[20]

Despite their divergent worldviews, the Cold War superpowers adopted many of the officials, tactics, and technologies of the Nazi empire in the furtherance of their own interests. These tactics included the subversion of independent states and democratic institutions, aerial bombardment of population centers, assassination of political and religious leaders, the invasion of neighboring countries hosting rebels, prohibited zones, counterinsurgency tactics that drained the civilian "swamp" to kill the rebellious "snakes," and the use of food as a weapon of warfare. The outcome was genocidal, as the superpowers vied for global dominance across most continents while deploying "total war" tactics, frequently disregarding human and indigenous peoples' rights. When the superpowers did not themselves participate in combat, they encouraged and organized counterinsurgency warfare in a variety of post-colonial client states by providing extensive military training, armaments, financial support, and diplomatic backing.

In 1945 the Soviet Union occupied half of Europe, from the Ural Mountains to Saxony, and, in Churchill's phrase, from the Baltic to the Adriatic.[21] Meanwhile, the growth in Soviet economic output rivaled or even surpassed that of Germany in the lead-up to World War II. In the Soviet zone of Germany, raw steel output rose from just 120,000 tons in 1946 to over 2 million tons by 1953. In the Soviet Union, steel production quadrupled from 1940 to 1960, and quadrupled again by 1980.[22] Access to nutrition increased from a "very low" level of about 2,100 calories prior to 1914, to a healthy 3,400 calories by 1970.[23] Despite the loss of over 20 million people in World War II, the Soviet popula-

---

17. Josef V. Stalin, *Interview to "Pravda" Correspondent Concerning Mr. Winston Churchill's Speech at Fulton* (Mar. 1946), http://www.marxists.org/reference/archive/stalin/works/1946/03/x01.htm.

18. *See* Harry Schwartz, *Soviet Intensifies Anti-U.S. Campaign*, N.Y. Times, Apr. 10, 1951, at 11; *Soviet Historians Make U.S. Villain*, N.Y. Times, Aug. 28, 1951, at 8.

19. Treaty of Friendship, Co-operation and Mutual Assistance, signed at Warsaw, on May 14, 1955 (Warsaw Pact), Albania, Bulgaria, Czechoslovakia, East Germany, Hungary, Poland, Romania, and the Soviet Union.

20. Richard Szawlowski, The System of the International Organizations of the Communist Countries 1–2 (Leiden, the Netherlands: Brill, 1976).

21. *See* Judt, Postwar, at 118, 170, 592; George Frost Kennan & John Lukacs George F. Kennan and the Origins of Containment, 1944–1946, at 4 (Columbia, MO: U. of Missouri Press, 1997).

22. *See* Judt, Postwar, at 118, 170, 592; William J. Eaton, *Economy on Target Overall, Soviets Say*, L.A. Times, Nov. 27, 1985, at 4; Harrison E. Salisbury, *Steel Output Due to Mount in Soviet*, N.Y. Times, Jan. 15, 1951, at 3; Harry Schwartz, *High Steel Goal Is Set by Soviet*, N.Y. Times, Aug, 24, 1958, at 19; Michael Warder, ... *And Why It's Needed*, Chicago Tribune, Jan. 20, 1986, at Perspective–15.

23. *See* Robert C. Allen, *A Reassessment of the Soviet Industrial Miracle*, Comparative Economic Studies, June 2005, http://www.entrepreneur.com/tradejournals/article/print/133684229.html.

tion increased from 190 million in 1940 to 209 million in 1959, a level unmatched by the U.S. until the 1970s.[24]

By 1947, the CIA had concluded that "[t]he greatest danger to the security of the U.S. is the possibility of an economic collapse in western Europe and the consequent accession to power of Communist elements."[25] The U.S. response was a massive program of military and development aid to non-communist nations; in the five years after World War II that included the European Recovery Program (ERP) or the "Marshall Plan," West Germany received $9.5 billion, the United Kingdom $12 billion, France $9.8 billion, Italy $5 billion, Austria $2 billion, Belgium $2 billion, Greece $1.5 billion, Denmark $1.5 billion, Yugoslavia $290 million, etc.[26]

Proxy wars and "massive state-to-state military assistance" gave most local, regional, and international struggles an overlay of superpower competition.[27] The Cold War contest of superpowers led to "competing patterns of client states, and allowed geopolitical considerations to override a client's domestic [human rights] record."[28] The Soviet Union and the U.S. "fueled" most wars, either by direct participation, proxy support, or "massive state-to-state military assistance."[29] Weapons of mass destruction proliferated from the superpowers to their allies, including Britain, France, China, North Korea, India, Pakistan, and Israel.[30]

"Disappearances," a tactic used by the Nazis in occupied Europe to whisk away persons dangerous to "German security" without a trace, became popular during the Cold War among Latin American military regimes supported by the U.S., in countries like Iraq supported primarily by the Soviet Union but also by the West, and in 1990s Algeria, backed by France.[31] Millions of refugees flowed across Africa, Central America, and Asia, as their "strategic geopolitical value" was used at times to "discredit" their home countries.[32]

---

24. *See* Robert H. Donaldson & Joseph L. Nogee, The Foreign Policy of Russia 19 (Armonh, NY: M.E. Sharpe, 2003).

25. Judt, Postwar, at 97, 170.

26. *See id.* at 90, 96, 140; Sean Price, *Marshall's Plan: Pay For Peace*, N.Y. Times, Sept. 6, 2002, http://findarticles.com/p/articles/mi_m0BUE/is_1_135/ai_n18614877/pg_2; The Marshall Plan Marches On, Time Mag., Mar. 6, 1964, http://www.time.com/time/magazine/article/0,9171,938499,00.html; U.S. Embassy to Austria, Marshall Plan 60th Anniversary (2007), http://www.usembassy.at/en/embassy/speeches/060507.htm.

27. Human Rights Watch, *World Report 1998*, http://209.85.165.104/search?q=cache:khCI78UzqCQJ:www.hrw.org/worldreport/Back-02.htm.

28. Human Rights Watch, World Report 1993, http://209.85.165.104/search?q=cache:r1VRg2CJlEUJ:www.hrw.org/reports/1993/WR93/Mew.htm.

29. Human Rights Watch, World Report 1998, http://209.85.165.104/search?q=cache:khCI78UzqCQJ:www.hrw.org/worldreport/Back-02.htm.

30. *See, e.g.*, Catherine Scott-Clark and Adrian Levy, Deception: Pakistan, the United States, and the Secret Trade in Nuclear Weapons 9–55 (New York: Walker & Co., 2007); Jita Mishra, The NPT and the Developing Countries 49, 123–91 (New Delhi: Concept Publishing Co., 2008); Shuja Nawaz, Crossed Swords: Pakistan, Its Army, and the Wars Within xxiv, 100–125, 376–78 (Oxford: Oxford UP, 2008); *Nuclear Forces, in* China: A Country Study (Robert L. Worden et al., eds., Washington, D.C.: Library of Congress, 1987), http://lcweb2.loc.gov/cgi-bin/query/r?frd/cstdy:@field(DOCID+cn0400); Sharon Squassoni, *Nuclear Threat Reduction Measures for India and Pakistan*, Congressional Research Serv. Report No. RL31589 (2005), http://digital.library.unt.edu/govdocs/crs/permalink/meta-crs-6185:1.

31. *See* Human Rights Watch, World Report 1998, http://209.85.165.104/search?q=cache:SCCTXoOj1TMJ:www.hrw.org/backgrounder/usa/us1004/4.htm.

32. Human Rights Watch, World Report 2001, http://209.85.165.104/search?q=cache:p9o9ufrB-C8J:www.hrw.org/wr2k1/print/refugees.pdf.

B. The Specter of Nuclear Genocide

Scientists warned early on that the atomic bomb, and even more so the hydrogen bomb (H-bomb), had the potential to inflict millions of casualties or even to snuff out all human life. In 1955, Albert Einstein and other famous scientists issued a manifesto warning that "war with H-bombs might possibly put an end to the human race," for there "will be universal death, sudden only for a minority, but for the majority a slow torture of disease and disintegration."[33]

The advent of the intercontinental nuclear missile, and the stockpiling of such weapons by the U.S., the Soviet Union, and other powers, only increased the risk of a mass-casualty event. U.S. officials estimated in the 1970s, before the Reagan build-up, that 113 million Soviet citizens could die in a U.S. nuclear missile launch against Soviet military and industrial centers.[34] As President Reagan, who presided over a buildup of nuclear missiles in the U.S. and Europe before agreeing to arms treaties with the Soviet Union, remarked:

> By the time the 1980s rolled around, we were placing our entire faith in a weapon whose fundamental target was the civilian population.... [¶] The Pentagon said at least 150 million Americans would be lost in a nuclear war with the Soviet Union—even if we "won.".... [¶] The planet would be so poisoned the "survivors" would have no place to live. [¶] Even if a nuclear war did not mean the extermination of mankind, it would certainly mean the end of civilization as we knew it.[35]

The International Court of Justice ruled, in a widely praised advisory opinion sought by the World Health Organization in the 1990s, that the "threat or use of nuclear weapons would generally be contrary to the ... rules of humanitarian law."[36] The separate opinion of Justice Weeramantry concluded that the use of nuclear weapons would likely constitute genocide against one's adversaries, as well as against other affected peoples due to radioactive fallout.[37]

C. The Cold War in East Asia

During the Cold War, governments repeatedly committed genocide against persons in the same national and ethnic group as their leaders, but with the complication of for-

---

33. Albert Einstein et al., *Manifesto by Scientists for Abolition of War*, Albert Einstein Archives No. 33–209, released July 9, 1955, http://www.pugwash.org/about/manifesto.htm.

34. *See* Robert C. Grogin, Natural Enemies: The United States and the Soviet Union in the Cold War 296 (Lanham, MD: Lexington Books, 2000).

35. Ronald Reagan, An American Life 549–50 (New York: Simon & Schuster, 1999) (1990).

36. *See* Legality of the Threat or Use of Nuclear Weapons (Advisory Opinion), 1996 I.C.J. 226, ¶ 105(2)(E).

37. *Id.* ¶¶ 429–536 (separate opinion of Justice Weeramantry); Richard Falk, *Nuclear Weapons, International Law and the World Court: A Historic Encounter*, 91 American J. of International Law 64 (1997).

eign assistance and intervention on the one hand, and intensified persecution of minorities on the other. A case in point is Maoist China and occupied Tibet.

Stalin financed the takeover by Mao Zedong, Wang Ming, and the Chinese Communist Party of the mainland of China.[38] Mao's forces sapped the Nationalist resistance to the Japanese occupation of China.[39] The communists killed 33,000 Nationalists by 1940. With Chinese resistance weakened, the Soviet Union forged a Neutrality Pact with the Empire of Japan in the spring of 1941.[40] Mao's faction grew rich from opium dealing during the war.[41]

The Soviet occupation of Manchuria gave communist forces in China a base of operations and an abundant source of supply. Within a few years after the end of World War II, they had overwhelmed the Nationalist forces and assumed power in China.[42] The Soviet Union then demanded that Mao's government assume China's U.N. seat.[43] The Chinese communists declared a "Chinese Soviet Republic," copied the Soviet legal system, and created a Chinese version of the Soviet secret police.[44] The Chinese constitution of 1954 was "based upon the model of Stalin's constitution of 1936."[45]

Mao's sights were set on world revolution; he hoped to set up an Earth Control Committee "to make a uniform plan for the Earth." He told the Soviets that he was willing to "sacrifice 300 million Chinese" in this cause. At the outset of the famine of the late 1950s and early 1960s, he declared to the communist party congress of 1958 that: "Half the population wiped out—this happened quite a few times in Chinese history." With nearly two thousand large military-related construction projects underway in 1958, Mao told his key aides that "with all these projects, half of China may well have to die. If not half, one-third, or one-tenth—50 million—die."[46]

In fact, China's population nearly doubled (a rise of 400 million) between 1950 and 1975, rather than being cut in half.[47] But assuming that 10 percent of Chinese arrested and jailed by the communists died, executions and forced labor deaths in China may have reached 27 million after the fall of the Nationalist regime.[48] Mao and his government's officials admitted to killing up to nine million peasants and 830,000 "ene-

---

38. *See* Jung Chang & Jon Halliday, Mao: The Unknown Story 49, 62, 71, 205, 218–27, 315, 361–74 (New York: Random House/Anchor Books, 2006). By the 1920s, Stalin had "ordered" the Chinese communists to form an army composed of their supporters in the Nationalist army. *See id.* at 49. Stalin's government invited and financed a 1928 congress of Chinese communists outside Moscow in 1928, at which Mao assumed control over the Chinese Red Army. *See id.* at 62. Soviet Red Army aid to the Chinese communists commenced in early 1929. *See id.* at 64. Soviet propaganda elevated Mao to China's "leader" in the same way that Stalin was promoted as Russia's leader. *See id.* at 72. By 1938 the Soviets had financed the Chinese Red Army's expansion to thirty divisions, with the equivalent of over $40 million in today's dollars. *See id.* at 205. The Chinese Communist Party enjoyed a subsidy of $45–50 million (in today's dollars) per year from Stalin starting in 1940. *See id* at 217–18, 267–69.

39. *See id.* at 211–73.

40. *Id.* at 217. 219, 221, 231.

41. *See id.* at 270–71.

42. *See id.* at 275–303, 306–319; Arthur Waldron, *China Without Tears, in* What If? Eminent Historians Imagine What Might Have Been 381, 390–91 (New York: Putnam, 2001).

43. *See* Montefiore, Stalin, at 607.

44. Forte, *Communist Dictatorship,* at 191.

45. *Id.* at 195.

46. *See* Chang & Halliday, Mao, at 418–31.

47. *See Robert Rheinold, China's Millions Are Still Hard to Count,* N.Y. Times/The Ledger (Florida), Nov. 26, 1978, at 28; Chang & Halliday, Mao, at 418–31.

48. *See* Chang & Halliday, Mao, at 319.

mies of the people."[49] After Mao died in 1976, Chinese communist authorities condemned his former officials for fomenting "terror" in the Chinese population, and Chinese human-rights activists confirmed the existence of a Chinese Gulag system.[50] One activist, Harry Wu, estimated that more than 16 million were confined in the Chinese Gulag system by 1992, and that 50 million people had passed through it, including Catholics rounded up in purges during the 1950s in an effort to prohibit Roman Catholicism.[51]

The worst crimes in Maoist China were famine-related. Government officials told peasants in 1959 that grain production would skyrocket in a "Great Leap Forward," so peasants ate much of the grain that should have been used to plant the next crop. As production fell, government requisitions of grain increased, and exports doubled as the Soviet Union imported 50% more grain from China, and as North Korea, North Vietnam, and Albania enjoyed large grain subsidies.[52] The Soviet Union, in turn, exported a wide variety of military equipment to the People's Liberation Army, including nuclear weapons technology that Chinese leaders demanded to ensure their country's imperviousness to foreign invasions (e.g., by Japan).[53] The government prevented peasants from fleeing their districts, covered up the scale of the disaster, and rejected offers of international aid.[54] Average caloric intake per person resembled levels allotted to slave-laborers at Auschwitz.[55] Up to 38 million Chinese died in a three-year period from starvation, disease, and stepped-up persecution of wealthier peasants and "rightists."[56]

In 1950, Stalin and Mao agreed upon the need to subdue the Tibetans and bring them within the communist sphere by force. Stalin advised a version of his own Baltic and Far East strategy for China: surround the Tibetans with Han Chinese settlers.[57] The Chinese army invaded Tibet and incorporated large portions of northern and eastern Tibet into the Chinese provinces of Xinjiang, Qinghai, and Yunnan.[58] The United Nations General Assembly characterized the result of these Chinese actions as follows: the "people of Tibet have been forcibly denied" their "fundamental human rights and freedoms,"[59] China has suppressed "the distinctive cultural and religious life which they have traditionally en-

---

49. *See* Rummel, Death by Government, at 100; Daniel Sutherland, *Uncounted Millions: Mass Death in Mao's China: Repression's Higher Toll: New Evidence Shows Famine, Violence Spared Few*, Wash. Post, July 17, 1994, at A1.

50. Forte, *Communist Dictatorship*, at 205–9.

51. *See* Kerry Kennedy et al., Speak Truth to Power: Human Rights Defenders Who Are Changing Our World 241 (New York: Umbrage, 2003); Hongda Harry Wu, Laogai—the Chinese Gulag 15, 25, 231 (Ted Slingerland trans., Boulder, Colo: Westview Press, 1992).

52. *See* Nicholas Eberstadt, *The Great Leap Backward*, N.Y. Times, Feb. 2, 1997, http://www.nytimes.com/books/97/02/16/reviews/970216.16ebersta.html (reviewing Jasper Becker, Hungry Ghosts: Mao's Secret Famine (1997)).

53. *See Nuclear Forces, in* China: A Country Study, http://lcweb2.loc.gov/cgi-bin/query/r?frd/cstdy:@field(DOCID+cn0400) ("China began developing nuclear weapons in the late 1950s with substantial Soviet assistance."); Federation of American Scientists, *Institutional Trends—China Nuclear Forces* (Mar. 31, 2000), http://www.fas.org/nuke/guide/china/ agency/trends.htm.

54. *See* Eberstadt, *The Great Leap Backward*; Becker, Hungry Ghosts *passim*; Chang & Halliday, Mao, at 418–31.

55. *See* Chang & Halliday, Mao, at 429.

56. *See* Becker, Hungry Ghosts, at 274 (30 million); Chang & Halliday, Mao, at 430 (close to 38 million); *see also* Komlos, *On the Biological Standard of Living in the Soviet Union*, at 77 (26 million).

57. *See* Chang & Halliday, Mao, at 445.

58. *See* Laura S. Ziemer, *Application in Tibet of the Principles on Human Rights and the Environment*, 14 Harvard Human Rights J. 233, 235–37 (2001).

59. G.A. Res. 1353 (XIV), U.N. GAOR, 14th Sess., Supp. No. 16, at 61, U.N. Doc. A/4354 (1959).

joyed," and the Tibetan people have endured "severe hardships" and a "large-scale exodus of Tibetan refugees to the neighboring countries."[60] Mass killings ensued:

> [Tibetan history after 1949] was a long history of disasters—1.2 million people were killed, 6,000-plus monasteries were destroyed, the entire economy and the resource base of Tibet, its forests, were depleted, and in general, Tibetan religion was utterly and totally suppressed where it became criminal to have a religion in Tibet.... Mao Zedong vowed in 1950 to have 60 million Han Chinese living in Tibet by 1960....[61]

The Chinese destroyed more than 90% of the Tibetan Buddhist monasteries.[62]

Thailand characterized the killings of Tibetans as genocide in the United Nations, and India, Ireland, and the Philippines joined it with charges of systematic killings, cultural destruction, and theft of children.[63] The International Commission of Jurists issued a report in 1959 characterizing the killing and deportation of Tibetans as a violation of the Genocide Convention:

> The account of wanton killings in Tibet points to killings on a wider scale than that of religious groups. Particular attention should be paid to the evidence of indiscriminate air attacks, and of deliberate shooting of Tibetans who were in no way engaged in hostilities.... It should also be stressed that the alleged deportation of 20,000 Tibetan children [to China] is directly contrary to Article 2 (e) [of the Genocide Convention].[64]

Some scholars and advocates for the people of Tibet have raised the charge of genocide.[65] In 2001, U.S. Secretary of State Colin Powell argued that "the Chinese sending more and more Chinese in to settle Tibet ... seems to be a policy that might well destroy that society."[66] The U.N. Secretary-General documented this phenomenon in the early 1990s:

---

60. G.A. Res. 1723 (XVI), U.N. GAOR, 16th Sess., Supp. No. 17, Vol. 1 at 66, U.N. Doc. A/5100 (1961); *see also* G.A. Res. 2079 (XX), U.N. GAOR, 20th Sess., Supp. No. 14, at 3, U.N. Doc. A/6014 (1965).

61. Robert Thurman, Professor of Indo-Tibetan Studies, Columbia University, Statement on U.S. Policy Considerations on the 40th Anniv. of the Tibetan Uprising & the Dalai Lama's Flight into Exile, Hearing Before the U.S. House of Representatives, Cmte. on International Relations, 106th Cong., 1st Sess., p. 10 (Mar. 11, 1999). *Accord Tibet, in* UNREPRESENTED NATIONS AND PEOPLES ORGANIZATION YEARBOOK: YEARBOOK 1995, at 128 (Mary Kate Simmons, ed., Boston: Martinus Nijhoff Publishers, 1996).

62. *See* CHANG & HALLIDAY, MAO, at 448.

63. *See* Kathleen Teltsch, *Harsh Peking Rule in Tibet Is Charged by Asians in U.N.*, N.Y. TIMES, Dec. 15, 1965, at 13.

64. International Commission of Jurists, *Report on the Question of Tibet and the Rule of Law* (1959), http://www.tibetjustice.org/materials/govngo/govngo1.html.

65. *See, e.g.*, International Commission of Jurists, *Tibet and the Chinese People's Republic: A Report to the International Commission of Jurists* (1960), http://www.tibet.com/resolution/icj60.htm; DALAÏ LAMA XIV ET AL., THE WORLD OF TIBETAN BUDDHISM: AN OVERVIEW OF ITS PHILOSOPHY AND PRACTICE viii (Somerville, MA: Wisdom Publications, 1995); Sino-American Relations: One Year After the Massacre at Tiananmen Square: Hearing Before the Committee on Foreign Relations, Subcommittee on East Asian and Pacific Affairs 96, 150 (1997); Freedom from Religious Persecution Act of 1997: Hearing Before the Committee on International Relations 10 (1998); Maura Moynihan, *Genocide in Tibet*, WASH. POST, Jan. 25, 1998, http://www.refugeesinternational.org/content/article/detail/1112. *See also* Henry Bradsher, *Tibet Struggles to Survive*, FOREIGN AFF., June–July 1969, at 763.

66. *Senate Foreign Relations Committee Questions Secretary of State Designee Colin Powell* (CNN television broadcast, Jan. 17, 2001), *quoted in* Barry Sautman, *Is Tibet China's Colony?: The Claim of Demographic Catastrophe*, 15 COLUM. J. ASIAN L. 81, 109 (2001).

> Thousands of civilian Chinese have moved into Tibet with the active encouragement of the Government of China. In all major Tibetan cities—which are the economic, political, and cultural centers of the distinct Tibetan people—Chinese now appear to outnumber Tibetans. In some of the most fertile agricultural areas, particularly those of the eastern provinces of Kham and Amdo, Chinese settlers have established farms and pushed Tibetans into less fertile and less accessible areas.[67]

The Han Chinese outnumbered the Tibetans inside Tibet by the early 1990s.[68] U.N. reports have described the widespread torture of Tibetan resisters by Chinese occupation forces, and the displacement of indigenous Tibetans. One report stated that Tibetan detainees were "systematically tortured and ill-treated," including by stress positions, beatings, electric shocks on the genitals or inside the mouth, sleep deprivation, exposure to extreme cold, and denial of medical care while in detention.[69]

China declares that it has "no indigenous peoples' question," while hypocritically condemning the tactics it utilized in Tibet, including murder, expropriation of lands and homes, oppression, discrimination and massacres as "colonial policies." China argues that indigenous peoples may not define themselves as such without the consent of the government currently occupying them and their territory, which conveniently and completely excludes the Tibetans.[70]

D. The Partition of India and the Hindu-Muslim Massacres

In 1933, a Muslim Indian student at Cambridge University proposed to create an Islamic state on the territories of several provinces of British India, including Punjab, Northwest Frontier, Kashmir, Indus, and Baluchistan. The Muslim League of this former student, Muhammad Ali Jinnah, as well as the Congress party of Jawaharlal Nehru, abetted extremist factions within their ranks.[71] Jinnah announced after World War II that India's Muslims

---

67. U.N. Secretary-General Boutros Boutros-Ghali, Report on the Situation in Tibet, U.N. Doc. No. E/CN.4/1992/37 (1992), http://www.tibetjustice.org/materials/un/un8annex2.2.html.

68. *See* International Committee of Lawyers for Tibet, *The Relationship Between Environmental Management and Human Rights in Tibet* (July 14, 1992), http://www.tibetjustice.org/reports/env_human_rights.html ("Since its occupation of Tibet, the Chinese government has ... establish[ed] a range of incentives to attract Chinese to settle in Tibet.... The policy has been extremely successful in terms of altering the population makeup in Tibet. At this point Chinese are estimated to outnumber Tibetans in Tibet by 7.6 million compared to 6.1 million.... [I]n Lhasa, the capital of Tibet, Chinese civilians and militia are estimated to outnumber Tibetans almost two to one.") (report prepared for Fatma Zohra Ksentini, U.N. Special Rapporteur, for the Study of Human Rights and the Environment pursuant to Resolutions 1990/7 and 1990/27 of U.N. ECOSOC, Commission on Human Rights, Sub-Commission on Prevention of Discrimination and Protection of Minorities).

69. Boutros-Ghali, *Situation in Tibet*, annex II.1, http://www.tibetjustice.org/materials/un/un8annex2.1.html (quoting Amnesty International, *China—Amnesty International's Concerns in Tibet*, ¶ 17).

70. *See* Phutoli Shikhu Chingmak, *International Law and Reparations for Indigenous Peoples in Asia, in* REPARATIONS FOR INDIGENOUS PEOPLES, at 416–19.

71. *See* Adam Jones, *Review of* The Long Partition *and* Partitioned Lives, 10 J. OF GENOCIDE RES. 621, 623 (2008).

would "make any sacrifice" to create Pakistan, or "the Land of the Pure."[72] Like the Bolsheviks, his faction tapped into popular anger at corrupt officials, voracious landlords, and wartime famine conditions.[73]

After the Muslim League and Congress party rejected a proposed federation, the British declared in 1947 that a new Muslim state in the north and east of British India would be created as Pakistan.[74] The partition of British India into India and Pakistan resulted in the murders of hundreds of thousands of Muslims and Hindus by their "religious opponents."[75] Up to one million people died, as entire villages were burned alive, cut down by firing squad, or sliced apart with knives and agricultural tools. Between 80,000 and 100,000 women suffered abduction or rape. In Lahore, women were burned alive by the thousands.[76] In the Indian army's campaign in Hyderabad state, up to 200,000 Muslims were massacred, and women were raped in large numbers, as the troops also looted the state. Up to 20 million were displaced.[77]

In 1947, Abul Alaa al-Mawdudi founded the Islamic Association (*Jama'at-I Islami*), the Pakistani branch of the Egyptian Islamic revolutionary movement the Muslim Brotherhood. The association agitated for a society ruled by an elite of fundamentalist religious scholars, and succeeded in ensuring that the Pakistani Constitution of 1973 banned non-Muslim Presidents.[78] The Pakistani constitutions of 1956 and 1963 had already established an Islamic state. Fundamentalism grew in influence under Zulqifar 'Ali Bhutto and Zia ul-Haq in the 1970s and 1980s, and under Zia and his successors, the government and Islamic Association sponsored the Taliban movement in neighboring Afghanistan, as described in more detail below.[79]

In 1951, there were 10 million Hindus in Pakistan and 35 million Muslims in India.[80] Ten years later there were still 10 million Hindus in Pakistan, but nearly 50 million Muslims in India. The 1970s genocide in East Pakistan claimed most of the remaining Hindus in the country, either by death or forced displacement. By the sixtieth birthday of independent India and Pakistan, there were only two to three million Hindus "living in perpetual fear" in Pakistan, but 130 to 150 million Muslims in India, with numerous cultural and religious centers.[81]

---

72. *See Jinnah Warns of Tragedy; Moslem Fight for Pakistan*, SYDNEY MORNING HERALD, Mar. 22, 1946, at 2; Bertil Lintner, *Religious Extremism and Nationalism in Bangladesh* (Aug. 19–22, 2002), http://www.asiapacificms.com/papers/pdf/religious_extremism_bangladesh.pdf.

73. *See* LAPIDUS, HISTORY OF ISLAMIC SOCIETIES, at 637.

74. *See id.* at 639–40; Lintner, *Religious Extremism and Nationalism in Bangladesh.*

75. ERIC HOBSBAWM, THE AGE OF EXTREMES: A HISTORY OF THE WORLD, 1914–1991, at 219 (New York: Pantheon Books, 1994).

76. *See* Prabhjot Parmar, *"Moving Forward Though Still Facing Back": Partition and the South Asian Diaspora in Canada, in* PARTITIONED LIVES: NARRATIVES OF HOME, DISPLACEMENT, AND RESETTLEMENT 198 (Anjali Gera Roy & Nandi Bhatia eds., Pearson Education India, 2008); Nonica Data, *Transcending Religious Identities: Amrita Pritam and Partition, in* PARTITIONED LIVES, at 5.

77. *See* Jones, *Review*, at 621–22, 628 (citing YASMIN KHAN, THE GREAT PARTITION (New Delhi: Penguin Books India, 2007)).

78. *See* JOHN K. COOLEY, UNHOLY WARS: AFGHANISTAN, AMERICA, AND INTERNATIONAL TERRORISM, at 34–40 (London: Pluto Press, 2000).

79. *See* LAPIDUS, HISTORY OF ISLAMIC SOCIETIES, at 645–49.

80. *See* DONALD NEWTON WILBER & DONALD ATWELL, PAKISTAN, ITS PEOPLE, ITS SOCIETY, ITS CULTURE 52 (New Haven, CT: HRAF Press, 1964).

81. *Hindu Traders Threaten Strike After Kidnapping,* DAILY TIMES (PAKISTAN), July 20, 2004, http://www.dailytimes.com.pk/default.asp?page=story_20-7-2004_pg7_31. *See also* Miranda Kennedy, *Rumors of Jihad,* BOSTON GLOBE, Apr. 4, 2004, http://www.boston.com/news/globe/ideas/articles/2004/04/04/rumors_of_jihad/; LAPIDUS, HISTORY OF ISLAMIC SOCIETIES, at 643 (describing expansion of Muslim madrasas, mosques, colleges, and schools in postwar India).

E. The Cold War in Northeast and Southeast Asia

In late 1950, the U.S. faced the daunting prospect of a communist Soviet Union and China spanning the continent of Asia, building nuclear bombs, and killing millions of ethnic, religious, and political minorities within their respective territories. The CIA estimated the following in forces built up along the communist-capitalist fault lines: 250,000 Chinese communist troops in North Korea, an additional 300,000 nearby in Manchuria, 13,000 communist rebels in South Korea, 147,000 North Korean troops receiving Chinese and Soviet aid and training, and nearly 300,000 Chinese troops within striking distance of Vietnam and Cambodia.[82] Up to two million had died or were dying in India, Pakistan, and Tibet. The Kremlin had nearly established Soviet republics in Azerbaijan and Iranian "Kurdistan."[83] The CIA described long-range Soviet programs to topple pro-U.S. governments in Iran, Malaya, Burma, the Philippines, Greece, and West Germany.[84]

The Korean War began as the communists who had fought the Japanese from bases in China took over from Soviet occupation forces in 1948. Led by Kim Il-Sung, they established the Democratic People's Republic of Korea, and invaded South Korea using Soviet tanks in 1950.[85] The North Korean government caused one to two million probably avoidable deaths over the next 50 years.[86]

After the U.S. and the U.N. Security Council described the fighting in Korea as North Korean aggression against South Korea, the U.S. mobilized for war and rearmed at a furious pace. The defense budget soared to $50 billion from $15 billion the previous year. President Truman articulated the "Truman doctrine" in 1947 with the statement that "free peoples" would be saved by the U.S. from "attempted subjugation by armed minorities or by outside pressures."[87] The CIA assessed that the Soviet Union was "willing to pursue ... war-by-proxy despite a considerable risk of vastly enlarging the areas of armed conflict."[88] The U.S. instituted a program to train 100,000 foreign military personnel by 1959, from Iran, Iraq, Jordan, Lebanon, Sudan, Pakistan, Burma, Thailand, Haiti, Honduras, Peru, the Philippines, and Venezuela.[89]

The Korean War included major atrocities on the U.S. side as well. The bombing and shelling of Pyongyang and other cities by the U.S., among other things, may have claimed from one to three million North Korean civilian lives. Military losses included 200,000 North

82. *See* CIA, *Situation Summary* (Dec. 12, 1950), declassified 1978.

83. *See* Andrew D.W. Forbes, Warlords and Muslims in Chinese Central Asia 261–62 (Cambridge: Cambridge UP, 1986).

84. *See* CIA, *Review of the World Situation*, CIA 11–50, at 3 (Nov. 1950), declassified 1977.

85. *See* Bruce G. Cumings, *Historical Setting, in* A Country Study: North Korea (Washington, D.C.: Library of Congress, 1993), http://lcweb2.loc.gov/cgi-bin/query/r?frd/cstdy:@field(DOCID+kp0022), lcweb2.loc.gov/cgi-bin/query/r?frd/cstdy:@field(DOCID+kp0023), lcweb2.loc.gov/cgi-bin/query/r?frd/cstdy:@field(DOCID+kp0024).

86. *See* R.J. Rummel, *Democide in Totalitarian States, in* 3 The Widening Circle of Genocide, at 38.

87. *See* Stephen E. Ambrose, *From Korea to Vietnam: The Failure of a Policy Rooted in Fear, in* 2 Past Imperfect: Alternative Essays in American History 202–10 (Blanche Cook et al. eds., New York: Knopf, 1978).

88. CIA, *Review of the World Situation*, at 3.

89. *See* Operations Coordinating Board, *Special Report on Military Training in the U.S. of Foreign Nationals from Selected Countries* (Mar. 18, 1959), declassified 1981.

Korean troops killed or missing in action, up to 400,000 killed or missing Chinese troops, and up to 600,000 North Korean and Chinese troop deaths from disease.[90] An estimated 260,000 South Korean civilians died due to North Korean or U.S.-led coalition action, along with up to 160,000 South Korean troops.[91] Some estimates reach three million Korean civilian dead, 1.5 million dead Chinese troops, and one million Korean military killed or missing.[92]

Recent revelations, as recently as 2008, only continue to magnify the toll of Korean losses. In the late 1940s, South Korea rounded up about 30,000 suspected communists and leftists. After the North's invasion, the government of South Korea under President Syngman Rhee, in flight from the fall of the Seoul to the North in 1950, began massacring potential collaborators with the North, killing 100,000 people. Kim Dong-Chyoon, a member of South Korea's Truth and Reconciliation Commission, which arrived at the 100,000 figure by examining mass graves and interviewing witnesses, called the estimate conservative.[93]

In Vietnam, Ho Chi Minh and his allies, with experience in resisting the mighty Japanese empire, were fighting French colonialism. His League for the Independence of Vietnam, or Vietminh, opened a supply line to China in 1950.[94] By 1952, China provided the Vietminh with tens of thousands of rifles, thousands of machine guns, hundreds of artillery and field guns, and dozens of anti-aircraft guns; the Vietminh captured huge amounts of French weapons as well in 1950.[95] China and the Soviet Union recognized the Vietminh as the government of Vietnam in February 1950, while the French declared an independent state, within the French Union, led by Emperor Bao Dai in Saigon. After the Vietminh's siege of Dien Bien Phu, the French forces fighting to prop up Bao Dai lost the major battle of the Franco-Vietnamese war, with the Vietnminh killing 7,000 and capturing 11,000 French troops. This was the final blow to the U.S. policy to fund and advise the French.[96] In the meantime, the Vietminh may have suffered over 500,000 dead and wounded, and 300,000 civilians may have perished.[97]

Vietnamese human and economic losses to the French must also have been substantial. France had exported over 1.5 million tons of rice from Vietnam even before the surge of demand in World War II, and had nearly tripled taxes in Vietnam since the nineteenth century to 90 million gold francs.[98] During World War II, the Vichy regime delivered so

---

90. *See* Gordon L. Rottman, Korean War order of battle: United States, United Nations, and Communist Ground, Naval, and Air Forces, 1950–1953, at 211 (Westport, CT: Greenwood Publ'g Group, 2002).

91. *See* Sahr Conway-Lanz, Collateral Damage: Americans, Noncombatant Immunity, and Atrocity after World War II, at 96–99 (Boca Raton, FL: CRC Press, 2006).

92. *See* Rummel, Statistics of Democide, ch. 10 & tbl. 10.1, http://hawaii.edu/powerkills/SOD.TAB10.1.GIF.

93. Charles J. Hanley & Jae-soon Chang, *Massacre by U.S.-backed Regime in South Korea Comes to Light,* Associated Press, May 19, 2008, http://www.stltoday.com/stltoday/news/stories.nsf/world/story/ 72E8CF4F36FA87EB8625744E00062D7B?OpenDocument.

94. CIA, *Review of the World Situation,* at 4.

95. *See* Martin Windrow, The Last Valley: Dien Bien Phu and the French Defeat in Vietnam 154 (New York: Da Capo Press, 2004).

96. *See* William R. Keylor, The Twentieth Century World 384–87 (Oxford: Oxford UP, 2d ed. 1992).

97. *See* R.J. Rummel, *Vietnam Democide* (2001), http://www.hawaii.edu/powerkills/SOD.TAB6.1A.GIF; R.J. Rummel, Statistics of Democide, ch. 6, http://www.hawaii.edu/powerkills/SOD.CHAP6.HTM.

98. *See* Eric R. Wolf, Peasant Wars of the Twentieth Century 165–70 (Norman, Okla.: Univ. of Oklahoma Press, paperback ed. 1999).

much rice to its Japanese imperialist allies that the ensuing famine killed perhaps 500,000 Vietnamese.[99]

Negotiations between the Soviet Union, the U.S., Britain, and France on the political future of Vietnam opened in Geneva after the fall of Dien Bien Phu. The Final Declaration of the Geneva Accords, agreed to in 1954, provided for a temporary partition of Vietnam into northern and southern halves, with neither government receiving foreign military aid or joining foreign alliances, and an election to be held by mid-1956 under the oversight of the United Nations. The accords were primarily a pact between France on the one hand and the Vietminh, Soviets, and Chinese on the other; the U.S. and Ngo Dinh Diem, who had taken over as leader of South Vietnam from Bao Dai, did not sign. The U.S. allied itself with South Vietnam, Cambodia, Laos, and other countries in the region against the Soviets and Vietminh. Diem refused to authorize the government of South Vietnam to participate in the agreed-upon elections because North Vietnam did not afford basic civil or political rights to its people. Nearly 700,000 Catholics had fled communist persecution for South Vietnam, for example. By 1960, the elections and unification of Vietnam contemplated by the Geneva Accords not having taken place, a coalition of communist and non-communist opponents of Diem formed a National Liberation Front (NLF) based on independence and land reform.[100]

The Soviet Union and China armed and advised North Vietnam, as the U.S. did for the South. By late 1963 more than 16,000 U.S. military advisers were in South Vietnam, and after the Gulf of Tonkin incident and resulting resolution in Congress, 184,000 U.S. ground troops were sent in. In the late 1960s, more than 500,000 U.S. soldiers were stationed in South Vietnam, and large-scale U.S. bombing raids against North Vietnam, including the cities of Hanoi and Haiphong, were carried out from 1967 through 1972.[101]

Vietnamese deaths in the war may have included 900,000 to 1.8 million civilian and military dead, and up to 500,000 victims of executions in North Vietnam.[102] More than six million people became refugees or internally-displaced persons in Southeast Asia. The war cost the U.S. more than 50,000 lives and $350 billion in direct war costs and long-term care of injured and mentally-ill or retiring veterans.[103] Fourteen million tons of bombs fell on Southeast Asia during the Vietnam War era. U.S. herbicides such as Agent Orange ruined ten percent of the farmland in Vietnam, and bulldozers claimed 20 percent of the trees in its forests.[104] In some years, 10,000 artillery shells were fired by U.S. forces every day.[105] CIA director William Colby testified in 1971 that in the

---

99. *See* William R. Polk, Violent Politics 158 (New York: Harper Perennial, 2008).

100. *See* Keylor, The Twentieth Century World, at 387–89; Wolf, Peasant Wars, at 194; Southeast Asia Collective Defense Treaty and Protocol, Sept. 8, 1954, 209 U.N.T.S. 28; Protocol to the Southeast Asia Collective Defense Treaty, Sept. 8, 1954, 209 U.N.T.S. 36.

101. *See* Keylor, The Twentieth Century World, at 388–94.

102. *See* R.J. Rummel, *Vietnam Democide* (2001), http://www.hawaii.edu/powerkills/SOD.TAB6.1A.GIF; R.J. Rummel, Statistics of Democide, ch. 6, http://www.hawaii.edu/powerkills/SOD.CHAP6.HTM.

103. *See* Keylor, The Twentieth Century World, at 388–94. The U.S. Army had to seek out 1.5 million additional draftees or volunteers above its pre-Vietnam War strength. *See* United States Army Center of Military History, *The U.S. Army in Vietnam* (2001), http://www.history.army.mil/books/amh/AMH-28.htm.

104. *See* John Hart Ely, *The American War in Indochina, Part I: The (Troubled) Constitutionality of the War They Told Us About,* 42 Stanford L. Rev. 877, 880 (1990).

105. *See* The 10,000 Day War, Episode 11—Firepower (Canadian Broadcasting Corp., 1980).

anti-communist Phoenix program, 28,000 suspected Vietminh or NLF had been captured, and 20,000 killed. U.S. helicopter gunships also frequently attacked communist-infiltrated villages.[106] In attempting to isolate the Vietnamese population from the Vietminh and NLF, the U.S. and the South deported 67% of the rural population into "strategic hamlets," many ringed with barbed wire.[107] The under-five child mortality rate in parts of South Vietnam was estimated to be as high as 50%.[108] Half a million women turned to prostitution in the South, many no doubt being displaced from their homes.[109]

Despite the massive civilian death toll of the war in Vietnam, scholars question whether the events qualify as genocide, considering that the population of South Vietnam increased by two million during the war through late 1971, and that of North Vietnam by hundreds of thousands.[110] South Vietnam also received "$8.5 billion in economic aid from 1954 to 1974."[111] This seems to pose an obstacle to a possible inference of genocidal intent against non-communist ethnic Vietnamese, at any rate, insofar as Yugoslavia was not a provider of economic aid to the Muslims of Bosnia or Kosovo on such a scale, and Nazi Germany and imperial Japan looted and plundered minorities and occupied populations rather than providing aid. At the very least, resolving the question requires the examination of evidence on a local basis. Genocide might be an appropriate charge against those who massacred Vietnamese villagers, as occurred at My Lai, or during NLF persecutions of up to 37,000 people suspected of being pro-U.S. or at risk of becoming so, or of stealing food or similar offenses against the movement.[112]

When Indonesian nationalist Sukarno came to power, U.S. Secretary of State Allen Dulles declared him to be unfit to rule due to his susceptibility to communist ideology. The U.S. financed right-wing Indonesian insurgents and bombed Indonesia from the air even though the countries were not at war.[113] The Indonesian genocide pitted communists and nationalists who supported Sukarno and land reform against the military elite, landlords, Muslim fundamentalists, and Muslim political leaders.[114] After the insurgency died down, the U.S. cultivated ties with the Indonesian military, paving the way for the military coup that occurred in 1965, and 30 plus years of fascist rule. The Indonesian population, as guided by their military as in any well-governed state, eventually "snapped." One author declared:

> By late October, the official Antara news agency was reporting massacres in Central and East Java. Religious and racial tensions exploded, with ethnic Chinese singled out for the settling of old scores. The Muslim majority had long envied the Chinese for their wealth and questioned their patriotism.

---

106. *See* MICHAEL MACLEAR, THE TEN THOUSAND DAY WAR: VIETNAM, 1945–1975, at 255–85 (New York: Avon, 1982).

107. *See* POLK, VIOLENT POLITICS, at 177–78.

108. *See* Hugo Adam Bedau, *Genocide in Vietnam*, 53 B.U. L. REV. 586 (1973).

109. *See* T. LOUISE BROWN, WAR AND AFTERMATH IN VIETNAM 265 (London: Routledge, 1991).

110. *See* Bedau, *Genocide in Vietnam*, at 585–87.

111. *See* Walter A. McDougall, *Promised Land, Crusader State: The American Encounter with the World Since 1776*, at 193 (Boston: Houghton Mifflin Harcourt, 1997).

112. *See* THE 10,000 DAY WAR, EPISODE 10—THE VILLAGE WAR (Canadian Broadcasting Corp., 1980).

113. *See* Jim Mann, *CIA's Covert Indonesia Operation in the 1950s Acknowledged by U.S. Cold War*, L.A. TIMES, Oct. 29, 1994, at 5.

114. *See* Fein, *Revolutionary and Antirevolutionary Genocides*, at 805.

> As months of frenzy passed, the purge of anyone labeled a communist came to be considered a national obligation, not murder.
>
> Officials announced in 1975 that from 450,000 to 500,000 people were killed. Tens of thousands were injured.
>
> An estimated 600,000 suspects were detained without charge, among them some of the country's best known writers, poets, educators, journalists, film directors and intellectuals. The last detainees were released in 1979.[115]

The Chinese minority in Indonesia was particularly targeted, blamed for its association with Maoist China.[116] In East Java, for example, "the initiative for some killing came from local Muslim leaders determined to extirpate an enemy whom they saw as an infidel."[117]

The Indonesian army, led by Suharto and other fascist generals, disseminated propaganda portraying the Indonesian Communist Party as on the brink of taking power, and as sexually mutilating Indonesian military leaders. The army trained and armed the militias that actually carried out the massacres, as suggested by a death toll that has been estimated as reaching up to three million.[118] After two and a half decades of military rule, the Indonesian GDP per capita was only $500.[119]

Suharto turned next to the tiny island of East Timor, where the Portuguese were preparing to withdraw after hundreds of years of colonial rule. U.S. President Gerald Ford happened to visit Indonesia the day before the Indonesian invasion, and acquiesced actively or by silence upon being informed of the invasion plan. The indigenous Timorese paid the price:

> In their forcible takeover, the Indonesians more than decimated the native population of 700,000. Four years later, State Department officials were privately making estimates of between 100,000 and 200,000 dead. Since then, year after year, Amnesty International has chronicled torture and detentions without trial.

After the invasion, Secretary of State Henry Kissinger proclaimed that "we understand Indonesia's position." Hearings in Congress revealed that 90% of Indonesia's weaponry was imported from the U.S.[120]

In the late 1960s, Cambodia had become a key supplier of rice to the Vietnamese communists, whom the U.S. believed ran their operations in South Vietnam from a base across the border in Cambodia. Prince Norodom Sihanouk, who had nationalized Cambodia's foreign trade in 1963 only to see rice exports plummet in value by 50% by 1969, and faced an increasing risk of communist revolution, announced a deal with the Vietnamese com-

---

115. Kenneth L. Whiting, *Indonesia Still Dealing With Carnage of 25 Years Ago After Failed Coup Uprising*, L.A. TIMES, Feb. 10, 1991, at 3 (citing PETER DALE SCOTT, UNITED STATES AND THE OVERTHROW OF SUKARNO (1991)).

116. Fein, *Revolutionary and Antirevolutionary Genocides*, at 805.

117. *Indonesia, in* ENCYCLOPEDIA OF GENOCIDE AND CRIMES AGAINST HUMANITY, at 519.

118. *See id.* at 516–19.

119. *See* Whiting, *Indonesia Still Dealing With Carnage of 25 Years Ago*, at 3.

120. Alexander Cockburn, *Can 50 More Deaths Change U.S. Hypocrisy?*, L.A. TIMES, Nov. 14, 1991, at 7. In March 1977, the Indonesian Foreign Minister stated that "50,000 people or perhaps 80,000 might have been killed during the war in Timor." *Quoted in* Ben Kiernan, *The Demography of Genocide in Southeast Asia: The Death Tolls in Cambodia, 1975–79, and East Timor, 1975–80*, 35:4 CRITICAL ASIAN STUDIES 584, 594 (2003).

munists in March 1970 under which Vietnamese would intensify their control of the border areas.[121] As the North Vietnamese and South Vietnamese armies occupied large swaths of Cambodia, Cambodian troops began to massacre the Vietnamese, causing 200,000 to flee for South Vietnam.[122] The Cambodian communists surged from a few thousand troops to 75,000 members in 1970, and then doubled their strength to 150,000 in 1971.[123]

U.S. bombardment increased to approximately 100,000 tons per year between 1969 and 1972, then more than doubled to more than 250,000 tons in 1973.[124] Napalm and cluster bombs claimed civilian villagers, and three million Cambodians had been displaced from their homes by 1973 or 1974.[125] President Nixon ordered "a massive bombing campaign in Cambodia," to the extent of ordering "anything that flies on anything that moves."[126] The war and U.S. bombardment may have killed or prevented the births of 600,000 Cambodians, representing the difference between 8.5 million at normal survival rates, and 7.9 million after the war.[127]

The Khmer Rouge, fearing a bombing campaign against Cambodian cities, instead diverted its anger, and resentment of the U.S. and Vietnam for recent humiliations, onto local capitalists, intellectuals, Vietnamese, Muslims, and Chinese.[128] The Khmer Rouge liquidated the ethnic and religious minorities of Cambodia such as the Muslims and Vietnamese, as well as potentially hostile Cambodian Khmer.[129] The original Cambodian estimates were of over three million dead due to the Khmer Rouge. Between one-third and two-thirds of the Muslim population of Cambodia perished.[130] Nearly all Buddhists and Vietnamese who had not fled as refugees by 1976 were massacred. The Pol Pot regime resolved to "uproot[]" Buddhism culturally and economically, killing over 95% of Buddhist monks and welcoming the "disintegrat[ion]" of Buddhism. Half of the Chinese population may have been executed, starved, or succumbed to disease. A comparison of population estimates from 1970 or 1974–75 to estimates for 1979 reveals a loss of 1.2 to 1.7 million, of whom some 500,000 to 700,000 may have become refugees in Thailand be-

---

121. *See* Donald Kirk, *Cambodia's Economic Crisis*, 11 ASIAN SURVEY 238, 238–47 (1971).

122. *See id.* at 247–54.

123. *Compare id.* at 241, *with* Ben Kiernan, *The American Bombardment of Kampuchea, 1969–1973*, 1 VIETNAM GENERATION 4, 4–7 (1989).

124. *See* Kiernan, *The American Bombardment*, at 6.

125. *See id.* at 7–8, 12; Ben Kieman, *Cambodia's Refugees* 2, REFUGEES STUDIES CENTER (1990), http://repository.forcedmigration.org/pdf/?pid=fmo:845.

126. Michael Dobbs, *Haig Said Nixon Joked of Nuking Hill; Transcripts of Phone Talks Are Released by Archives*, WASH. POST, May 27, 2004, at A29.

127. *See* Kiernan, *The Demography of Genocide in Southeast Asia*, at 586, 588–90; SEYMOUR M. HERSH, THE PRICE OF POWER: KISSINGER IN THE NIXON WHITE HOUSE 59–68 (New York: Summit Books, 1983); WILLIAM SHAWCROSS, SIDESHOW: KISSINGER, NIXON AND THE DESTRUCTION OF CAMBODIA 19–35 (New York: Simon and Schuster, 1987). *See also* JONES, GENOCIDE, at 189–90, 193 (five million acres of rice farms were rendered unusable by the bombing campaign, which incinerated villages, left huge craters, and caused some civilians to go insane).

128. JONES, GENOCIDE, at 193. *See* VALENTINO, FINAL SOLUTIONS, at 264 at 126, 262, 274; MELSON, REVOLUTION AND GENOCIDE, at 271, 262–67, 330–32; Nicholas Eberstadt, *The Great Leap Backward*; Simons, *Genocide and the Science of Proof*, at 30; Daniel Sutherland, *Uncounted Millions: Mass Death in Mao's China: Repression's Higher Toll: New Evidence Shows Famine, Violence Spared Few*, WASH. POST, July 17, 1994, at A1.

129. *See* VALENTINO, FINAL SOLUTIONS, at 134–39.

130. *See* Ben Kiernan, *The Demography of Genocide in Southeast Asia: The Death Tolls in Cambodia, 1975–79, and East Timor, 1975–80*, 35:4 CRITICAL ASIAN STUD. 584, 586, 588–90 (2003).

tween 1970 and 1980.[131] In 1979, Pol Pot and Ieng Sary were convicted of genocide after a Vietnamese invasion, but went unpunished.[132]

The U.S. actually backed them against Vietnam for a time in the 1980s under President Reagan.[133] In the first Bush administration, Secretary of State James Baker "announced that the Khmer Rouge had to be accepted as a 'fact of life,'" and he advocated support for a four-party government composed of the current Hun Sen government, the Khmer Rouge, and the non-Communist factions, with Sihanouk as head of state.[134] The Vietnamese opposed Khmer Rouge participation in a transitional Cambodian government, while the "Baker formula" called for their participation despite their record of ethnic and religious genocide.[135] Thus, "the United States led a group of states within the United Nations in a move to deny the [post-Khmer Rouge] government its seat in the General Assembly, insisting that the Khmer Rouge was still the legitimate government!"[136]

In 2001, Cambodia enacted a law creating the Extraordinary Chambers of the Courts of Cambodia for the Prosecution of Crimes Committed During the Period of Democratic Kampuchea. The tribunal has jurisdiction over genocide, among other crimes.[137] Although the tribunal's prosecutors have so far focused their charges on crimes against humanity and war crimes rather than genocide,[138] they have access to abundant evidence around which to frame genocide charges. Among other documents discovered since the 1980s are transcripts of Khmer Rouge radio broadcasts calling on each Cambodian to kill 30 Vietnamese, so that two million Cambodian troops would kill 50 million Vietnamese. Communist party officials also declared that no Vietnamese could be left alive in Cambodia. Pol Pot warned that Buddhism was banned, and documents in the late 1970s found that up to 95% of monks had "disappeared."[139] It is expected that many potential defendants may be dead before convictions will be issued.

---

131. *See* JONES, GENOCIDE, at 199–201; KIERNAN, BLOOD AND SOIL, at 548–54; Ben Kiernan, *The Cambodian Genocide: Issues and Responses, in* GENOCIDE: CONCEPTUAL AND HISTORICAL DIMENSIONS, at 191–93, 218–19; Associated Press, *Hands Off Thailand, USSR Told*, TOLEDO BLADE (OHIO), Jan. 27, 1980, at 1; Associated Press, *Queen Aids Refugees*, FREE-LANCE STAR (VIRGINIA), Mar. 21, 1980, at 12.

132. *See* QUIGLEY, THE GENOCIDE CONVENTION, at 38; Schabas, *Cambodia: Was it Really Genocide?*, at 470–75.

133. *See* Jim Leach, *Don't Help Pol Pot. Try Him.*, N.Y. TIMES, Sept. 27, 1989, at A29.

134. HUMAN RIGHTS WATCH WORLD REPORT 1989, http://www.unhcr.org/refworld/country,,,,KHM,,467bb489c,0.html.

135. Don Oberdorfer, *US Explores Role For Khmer Rouge; 'Minimal' Formula Aims to Break Impasse*, WASH. POST, Oct. 16, 1989, at A21.

136. W. Michael Reisman, *Acting* Before *Victims Become Victims, Preventing and Arresting Mass Murder*, 40 CASE WESTERN RESERVE U. J. OF INTERNATIONAL LAW 57, 63 (2008).

137. See Law on the Establishment of Extraordinary Chambers in the Courts of Cambodia for the Prosecution of Crimes Committed During the Period of Democratic Kampuchea (Aug. 10, 2001); STEPHEN HEDER & BRIAN D. TITTEMORE, SEVEN CANDIDATES FOR PROSECUTION: ACCOUNTABILITY FOR THE CRIMES OF THE KHMER ROUGE 13–25 (Washington, DC: War Crimes Research Office, 2001).

138. *See, e.g.*, Provisional Detention Order for Ieng Sary, Case No. No: 002/14-08-2006, Office of the Co-Investigating Judges, Extraordinary Chambers in the Courts of Cambodia (Nov. 14, 2007), http://www.cambodiatribunal.org/CTM/Provisional_detention_order_IENG_Sary_ENG.pdf; Kong Sothanarithu, *Hearing for Ill Ieng Sary Postponed*, VOICE OF AMERICA, Feb. 27, 2009, http://www.voanews.com/Khmer/archive/2009-02/2009-02-27-voa3.cfm; Muon Veasna, *Nuon Chea Charged With War Crimes, Crimes Against Humanity*, VOICE OF AMERICA, Sept. 19, 2007, http://www.voanews.com/Khmer/archive/2007-09/2007-11-28-voa5.cfm.

139. *See* Phnom Penh Radio Broadcast (May 10, 1978) (DC-Cam File No. D14789), quoted in John D. Ciorciari with Youk Chhang, *Documenting the Crimes of Democratic Kampuchea, in* BRING-

F. The Cold War in Latin America and the Caribbean

As massive human rights violations occurred in Asia, a similar, although far less massive, pattern emerged in Latin America and the Caribbean. One of the most prominent cases was Guatemala, just to the south of Mexico, where Cold War leaders targeted indigenous peoples for cultural devastation, demographic collapse, and forced removal from their traditional homelands, while torturing and disappearing human rights activists, Catholics, and potential insurgents. In the wake of the U.S.-instigated *coup d'etat* in 1954, many indigenous religious and political leaders were assassinated by the Guatemalan military.

Guatemala remained a slave society in the late nineteenth century, with a system of forced Indian labor on plantations and road construction projects. The *Zapadores* system rounded up Indians to work on construction projects, unless they were already bonded to plantation labor. In the early 1950s, President Jacobo Arbenz Guzmán had moved the country towards democracy and land reform that could have helped break the grip of rural landlords on impoverished Mayan Indians and their labor. Indians were the vast majority of recipients of land under the Agrarian Reform Law of 1952, agrarian reform being a measure that the U.S. supported elsewhere as an alternative to communism, notably in Iran. Arbenz also promised a minimum wage of 80 cents per day, when some farm workers made 15 cents a day. These reforms threatened U.S. business interests in Guatemala, however, notably those of the United Fruit Company. The CIA organized an army to overthrow Arbenz, resulting in a military dictatorship that committed grotesque massacres and crimes in the following decades.[140]

In many ways, the Guatemalan genocide of the 1980s represented a continuation of the massacres and cultural genocide of the Aztecs, Mayans, and other indigenous South Americans by the Spanish and Portuguese Empires. The regime of Guatemalan President Efrain Rios Montt wiped out more than 600 mostly Mayan villages, and killed thousands of innocent women and children, much like the Sudanese government has massacred and destroyed villages of indigenous African peoples in the south of that country. Guatemala's official Commission on Historical Clarification concluded in 1999 that the government had committed genocide against the Mayans.[141] Over 200,000 people had been murdered

---

ING THE KHMER ROUGE TO JUSTICE. PROSECUTING MASS VIOLENCE BEFORE THE CAMBODIAN COURTS 265–66, 300, n.164 (Jaya Ramji & Beth Van Schaak eds., Lewiston, [N.Y.]: E. Mellen Press, 2005), http://www.dccam.org/Archives/Documenting_the_Crimes_of_DK_by_John%26Youk.pdf; Interview by Ben Kiernan with Sin Song (Aug. 12, 1980), *quoted in id.* at 265–66, 295, 300 n.165; Interview by Ben Kiernan with Heng Samrin (Dec. 2, 1991), *quoted in id.* at 264–66, 295, 300 n.165, 301 n.174; Kiernan, *The Cambodian Genocide: Issues and Responses,* at 197–202, *quoted in id.* at 265–66, 300–301 n.172; Interview by Ben Kiernan with Kun Chhay (Oct. 16, 1980), *cited in id.* at 265–66, 301 n.173; Interview by Jeremy Stone and Gregory Stanton with Mat Ly (July 1991), *cited in id.* at 265–66, 301 n.173; Interview by Jeremy Stone and Gregory Stanton with Mat Ly (July 1991), *cited in id.* at 265–66, 301 n.174; *On Grasping and Implementing the Party's Political Line of Gathering National-Democratic Front Forces,* REVOLUTIONARY YOUTH, Sept. 1975 (DC-Cam Catalogue No. D21383), *cited in id.* at 265–67, 301 n. 175, n.181.

140. *See* Jim Handy, REVOLUTION IN THE COUNTRYSIDE: RURAL CONFLICT AND AGRARIAN REFORM IN GUATEMALA, 1944–1954, at 4–39, 70 (Chapel Hill, NC: Univ. of North Carolina Press, 1994); David E. Wilkins, *Guatemalan Political History: National Indian Policy, 1532–1954*, 9 WICAZO SA REV.: A J. OF NATIVE AMERICAN STUD. 17, 18, 24, 29 (1993).

141. GUATEMALAN COMMISSION ON HISTORICAL CLARIFICATION [CHC], GUATEMALA: MEMORY OF SILENCE, http://shr.aaas.org/guatemala/ceh/report/english/conc1.html.

or "disappeared" during the government's war against the Mayans.[142] The Commission estimated that 81% of the victims were indigenous people, mostly Mayans, and that 93% of the abuses were committed by agents of the Guatemalan government including the armed forces, "death squads," and the police.[143]

Montt used foreign-supplied weapons to massacre the indigenous people of his country.[144] President Reagan proclaimed that Montt was receiving a "bum rap," and proposed to dispatch $10 million in additional U.S. aid to the regime.[145] By this time, Amnesty International had reported that the Guatemalan government was destroying entire villages, and that President Montt was running a death squad out of his own offices.[146]

The Guatemalan military and its militia allies forced Mayans to watch family members being tortured, raped, and killed.[147] Amnesty International reported in 1982 that the rape of indigenous women became "common" under Montt. Mass rapes took place in conjunction with massacres of civilians, as later occurred in Bosnia, Rwanda, and Sudan.[148] The Commission that: "The act of targeting leaders was ... directed at destroying the foundations of the Mayan communities under attack." The Mayans suffered "indiscriminate massacres" in "scorched earth" campaigns "targeting not only leaders but also all members of the community, including men, women, children, infants, and the elderly." The army "surrounded and attacked" entire indigenous communities, with women and children "often separated from the men in order to begin the macabre ritual of torture, killing, and destruction." The CIA confirmed that: "The army's well-documented belief that the indigenous-Ixil population is almost totally in favor of [the Guerilla Army of the Poor] has created a situation where you can expect that the army will give no quarter to combatants and non-combatants alike." Tortured bodies were displayed to indigenous communities and "systematic, public and gang rapes of women," occurred in order to dissolve bonds of group cohesion and dehumanize indigenous peoples.[149]

U.S. complicity was not necessary, although helpful, to other authoritarian regimes in the Americas. Another 1954 coup, this time without U.S. participation, took place in Paraguay.[150] NATO countries viewed its leader, Alfredo Stroessner, as a key bulwark against

142. *See Guatemala 'Genocide' Probe Blames State*, BBC News, Feb. 25, 1999, http://news.bbc.co.uk/1/hi/world/americas/286402.stm.

143. CHC, Guatemala: Memory of Silence, at charts, http://shr.aaas.org/guatemala/ceh/report/english/graphics/charts/page86.gif.

144. *See* Amnesty International, *Guatemala's Lethal Legacy*, AI Index No. AMR 34/001/2002 (2002), http://tinyurl.com/ksxv69; Amnesty International, *Guatemala: Fear for Safety*, AI Index No. 34/17/2001 (2001), http://preview.tinyurl.com/nd5e7x; *Guatemala Civil War 1960–1996* (2007), http://www.globalsecurity.org/military/world/war/guatemala.htm; Guatemalan Commission on Historical Clarification [CHC], Guatemala: Memory of Silence, http://shr.aaas.org/guatemala/ciidh/dts/evol.html.

145. *See* Associated Press, *Reagan Considering Trip to the Far East*, Toledo Blade (Ohio), Dec. 6, 1982, at 19.

146. *See, e.g.*, Jack Anderson, *Violence Mounts in Guatemala*, Toledo Blade (Ohio), Dec 21, 1981, at 35.

147. CHC, Guatemala, Memory of Silence, at ch. 6, http://shr.aaas.org/guatemala/ciidh/qr/english/chap6.html.

148. http://news.amnesty.org/library/Index/ENGAMR340052000?open&of=ENG-2M2.

149. *See* Jan Perlin, *The Guatemalan Historical Clarification Commission Finds Genocide*, 6 ILSA J. Int'l & Comparative Law 389, 397–411 (2000).

150. *See* Frank O. Mora & Jerry Wilson Cooney, Paraguay and the United States: Distant Allies 125–26 (Athens, GA: Univ. of Georgia Press, 2007).

communism in the Americas.[151] Stroessner was a protégé of former Paraguayan president Raimundo Rólon, and served under Rolon's defense minister, the fascist Mutsuhito Villasboa, who named his son Adolfo Hirohito in admiration for Hitler and Hirohito during their reign.[152]

After the dictator Alfredo Stroessner came to power, accusations of genocide surfaced in his country. Starting in the 1950s, Paraguayan settlers moved into homelands of the Achè people of eastern Paraguay, murdering, enslaving, and deporting the natives as they did. The price of Achè slaves eventually reached as little as $1.15 on the open market.[153] A representative of the Department of Native Affairs of the Defence Ministry reported in 1969 that "savages" in the vicinity of Itakyry were being "liquidate[d]" under orders given to rural laborers. The Vice-Director of the Department of Native Affairs confirmed in 1968 that the Achè were near "extinction" due to "repressive action" against them and the "occupation of their lands." A Paraguayan anthropologist wrote in 1972 that Achè adults were hunted like animals, and many children had been murdered or sold as slaves. In 1974, the Department of Missions of the Paraguayan Episcopal Conference condemned "genocide" of "certain indigenous groups of Paraguay." The Achè, moved into reservations, suffered famine conditions and sold their children for food on at least one occasion. The Native Affairs Department sent Protestant missionaries into the reservation, which one observer viewed as an attempt to erase the Achè culture by designating its religious practice as paganism and "dealings with the devil." A third to half of the Achè on reservations perished in the 1960s from hunger and disease. The military and missionaries forced the surviving Achè to give up their names and language.[154] Claiming that the Achè could not survive in the forests where they had lived from time immemorial, the Native Affairs Department, run by a Stroessner loyalist, refused to preserve Achè land from theft, and mocked efforts to "preserve [Achè] like guinea pigs for anthropological study."[155]

The Achè people of Paraguay eventually lost more than 85 percent of its members as Spanish-speaking peoples settled their homelands to raise cattle and extract minerals and timber.[156] The Achè, "hunted like animals," were threatened with "extinction" by the late 1970s.[157] Apologists for indigenous genocide attempt to characterize these killings as accidental, unintentional, or mere "ethnocide" unworthy of criminalization, but fail to address why the vast numbers of children affected do not meet the definition of genocide as sustained killing of nonthreatening groups.[158] Perhaps due to the influence of such scholars, Britain, Germany, and the U.S. defended Stroessner's regime and the Paraguayan military from accusations of genocide.[159] Even the Japanese Emperor Hirohito welcomed

---

151. *See Obituary: Alfredo Stroessner*, BBC NEWS, Aug. 16, 2006, http://news.bbc.co.uk/2/hi/americas/4792281.stm.

152. *See* MORA & COONEY, PARAGUAY, at 95, 128; *Paraguayan Cabinet Is Sworn in by Rolon*, N.Y. TIMES, Feb. 1, 1949, at 14.

153. *See* ALEX HINTON, ANNIHILATING DIFFERENCE: THE ANTHROPOLOGY OF GENOCIDE 62 (Berkeley, CA: Univ. of California Press, 2001).

154. *Quoted in* Mark Munzel, *The Manhunts: Achè Indians in Paraguay, in* CASE STUDIES ON HUMAN RIGHTS AND FUNDAMENTAL FREEDOMS: A WORLD SURVEY 353–54, 357, 362–365, 385 (Willem Adriaan Veenhoven et al. eds., Leiden, the Netherlands: Brill, 1976).

155. *Quoted in* Jonathan Kandell, *Slavery Just One Threat Facing Paraguay Tribe; Slavery Just One Hazard Facing a Stone-Age Tribe in Paraguay. Deaths in Land Disputes*, N.Y. TIMES, Jan. 21, 1974, at A8.

156. *See* ALEX ALVAREZ, GOVERNMENTS, CITIZENS, AND GENOCIDE: A COMPARATIVE AND INTERDISCIPLINARY APPROACH 102 (Indianapolis: Indiana UP, 2001). *See also* Richard Arens, *The Ache of Paraguay, in* GENOCIDE AND HUMAN RIGHTS, at 218–37.

157. Arens, *The Ache of Paraguay*, at 218–37.

158. *See* HINTON, ANNIHILATING DIFFERENCE, at 62–66.

159. *See* Hitchcock & Twedt, *Physical and Cultural Genocide of Indigenous Peoples*, at 355–359.

Stroessner in a state visit with full honors in 1972, thanking him profusely for his agreement to allow 80,000 Japanese to emigrate to Paraguay and grow soybeans for export to Japan.[160] After the fall of the Stroessner regime, the number of native Guarani speakers rebounded from 800,000 in 1974 to two million in 1998.[161]

In 1964, President Lyndon B. Johnson ordered U.S. officials to organize a coup against President João Goulart of Brazil. Goulart had been elected Vice President in 1956 and 1960 and became President when the elected President Jânio Quadros resigned. President Goulart enjoyed mass support among peasants and workers for planning land reform measures and increases in wages for the poor, reflected in a 1963 referendum, which the Associated Press called a "landslide victory" for Goulart. His ouster in a coup, which President Johnson welcomed in a matter of hours while Goulart was still in Brazil, initiated 25 years of military dictatorship.[162]

The largest indigenous people enjoying their traditional lifestyle in the Americas, the Yanomami people, entered a period of serious decline in the 1970s. Starting in that decade, a highway was constructed through Yanomami ancestral lands, causing them to be deported from the region in which they had developed mechanisms of surviving, and spreading disease among the remaining members of the group. About a fifth of the remaining Yanomami died in the first year of the highway's construction. Left destitute, some Yanomami women turned to prostitution, which spread disease among the tribe even further. Law 6,001 of 1973 gave the president of Brazil the authority to expropriate indigenous lands from their traditional owners, exploit resources found there for "security and national development," and deport indigenous peoples by decree.[163] A secret project initiated by President Jose Suarney in 1985 placed the northern 20% of Brazil under military rule. Human Rights Watch reported that in the late 1980s, "serious abuses against Indians, such as expulsions from their lands by landowners and gold miners, ... have been particularly severe in areas controlled by the military, where Indians have been deprived of outside help, including medical assistance, and where the ability to monitor is limited."[164] The largely forest-dwelling Yanomami suffered horribly from this:

> In the 1980s, some 40,000 illegal wildcat miners poured into the Yanomami's ancestral lands in search of gold. The tribe was decimated by illnesses ... and by a violent physical assault aimed at expelling them from their territory. Many died from the flu or a malaria epidemic that swept the region. Others were simply shot. Human rights groups labeled what followed a "genocide". According to

---

160. *See Japanese Paraguyans, in* Encyclopedia of Japanese Descendants in the Americas: An Illustrated History 235 (Rowman Altamira, 2001).

161. *Compare* Jonathan Kandell, *Slavery Just One Threat Facing Paraguay Tribe; Slavery Just One Hazard Facing a Stone-Age Tribe in Paraguay Deaths in Land Disputes*, N.Y. Times, Jan. 21, 1974, at A8, with Clare Mar-Molinero, The Politics of Language in the Spanish-speaking World 60 (London: Routledge, 2000).

162. *See* Amnesty International, Brazil: Authorized Violence in Rural Areas 2 (London: Amnesty Int'l Publications, 1988); Jorge G. Castaneda, *Promises Will Be Hard to Keep in Latin America*, L.A. Times, Dec. 25, 1989, at B7; Jonathan Kandell, *Former President of Brazil, Is Dead in Exile at 58,* N.Y. Times, Dec. 7, 1976, at 44; National Security Archive, *Brazil Marks 40th Anniversary of Military Coup* (Mar. 31, 2004), http://www.gwu.edu/~nsarchiv/NSAEBB/NSAEBB118/index.htm.

163. *See* Yanomami v. Brazil, Case 7615 (Brazil), Inter-Am. C.H.R. Res. No. 12/85, OEA/Ser.L/V/II.66, Doc. 10, rev. 1 (1985), http://www.cidh.oas.org/annualrep/84.85eng/Brazil7615.htm; Gale Goodwin Gomez, *Indigenous Rights and the Case of the Yanomami Indians in Brazil, in* Human Rights of Indigenous Peoples 190 (Cynthia Price-Cohen ed., Ardsley, NY: Transnational Publishers, 1998) (citing Commission for the Creation of the Yanomami Park, Update # 83, at 2 (Dec. 1995)).

164. Human Rights Watch, World Report 1989, http://www.unhcr.org/refworld/country,,HRW,,BRA,4562d94e2,467bb48715,0.html.

some sources, before the government expelled the miners in 1992, up to 20% of the Yanomami people died in just seven years.[165]

As the massacres of Yanomami intensified in the late 1980s and early 1990s, U.S. President George H.W. Bush tolerated these tactics of the military rulers of Brazil. He issued no public condemnation of their genocidal policies in 1989, instead praising "the consolidation of democracy and promoted his plan to create a hemispheric free-trade zone." Such a zone might have permitted, one imagines, the import into the U.S. of gold and timber from Yanomami lands. In 1991, President Bush praised Brazil's adherence to the "rule of law," and described its President as a "great" statesman. America had become "Brazil's largest trading partner, investor and creditor."[166]

Bolivia has seen a succession of military dictators and unfair elections since 1964. An indigenous majority, composed primarily of Quechua and Aymara groups, suffered constant misrule by non-indigenous dictators until the election of indigenous leader Evo Morales in 2006.[167] The Supreme Court of Justice of Bolivia convicted dictator Luis García Meza Tejada of genocide in 1993 for planning the extermination of suspected leftists.[168] A federal prosecutor charged former President Gonzalo Sanchez de Lozada with genocide in 2005 for the massacre of 67 anti-government protestors in 2003.[169] Former President de Lozada fled to the U.S., which has refused Bolivian attempts to extradite him despite a 1996 extradition treaty.[170] In 2008, a Bolivian governor was charged with genocide for the massacre of 15 to 120 Morales supporters.[171]

At the time of the election of Evo Morales, Bolivia was the poorest country in South America.[172] In the late 1990s, its infant mortality rate, at one in 15 babies perishing in the first year or two of life, vied with Haiti's for the worst in the Americas.[173] The United Nations reported that: "In Bolivia and Peru infant death rates are four to five times higher for the children of the poorest 20% of the population than the children of the richest 20%." Nearly 90% of indigenous people lived in poverty, a share that was increasing since the 1990s, and the richest 100 families owned five times as much land as

---

165. *After the Gold Rush*, The Sunday Herald (U.K.), Jan. 12, 2008.

166. *See* Human Rights Watch, World Report 1990, http://www.unhcr.org/refworld/publisher,HRW,ANNUALREPORT,BRA,467fca2f210,0.html; Human Rights Watch, World Report 1992, http://www.unhcr.org/refworld/publisher,HRW,ANNUALREPORT,BRA,467fca44c,0.html.

167. *See Push for New Bolivia Constitution,* BBC News, Aug. 6, 2006, http://news.bbc.co.uk/2/hi/americas/5251306.stm; *Historical Setting, in* Bolivia: A Country Study (Rex A. Hudson and Dennis M. Hanratty eds., Washington: Government Printing Office, 1989); USDOS, *Background Note: Bolivia* (Dec. 2008), http://www.state.gov/r/pa/ei/bgn/35751.htm.

168. *See* Quigley, The Genocide Convention, at 39–40.

169. *See* Associated Press. *Genocide Charges against Former Bolivian President,* Malaysia Star, Feb. 22, 2005, http://thestar.com.my/news/story.asp?file=/2005/2/22/latest/21583Genocidec&sec=latest; John Friedman-Rudovsky, *Bolivia Calls Ex-President to Court*, Time Mag., Feb. 6, 2007, http://www.time.com/time/world/article/0,8599,1586707,00.html?iid=digg_share.

170. *See* Pablo Bachelet, *Bolivian Ex-president to Fight Extradition,* Miami Herald, Oct. 21, 2004, http://www.accessmylibrary.com/coms2/summary_0286-7124826_ITM; Friedman-Rudovsky, *Bolivia Calls Ex-President to Court*; Steven T. Jones, *Peru Pursues Justice; When Will the US?,* S.F. Bay Guardian, Apr. 7, 2009, http://www.sfbg.com/blogs/politics/2009/04/peru_pursues_justice_when_will.html.

171. *See* Dan Keane, *Bolivia Arrests Rebel Governor in Massacre*, S.F. Chron., Sept. 17, 2008, http://www.sfgate.com/cgi-bin/article.cgi?f=/c/a/2008/09/17/MN7O12V244.DTL&hw=morales&sn=023&sc=261.

172. *See* Reuters, *Bolivia's President Decides Not to Quit*, Boston Globe, Mar. 9, 2005, http://www.boston.com/news/world/articles/2005/03/09/bolivias_president_decides_not_to_quit/.

173. *See* U.N. Development Programme et al., World Resources 2000–2001: People and Ecosystems—The Fraying Web of Life, tbl. HD.2 (Washington, DC, 2001).

two million mostly indigenous families. Meanwhile, Bolivia's GDP per capita stood at about one-half to one-fifth the levels enjoyed by its neighbors Argentina, Brazil, Peru, and Paraguay.[174]

In Peru, indigenous Aymara, Ashaninka, and Quechua peoples have struggled to preserve their lands and lifestyles from settler depredations since the time of Pisarro. As one scholar of Peruvian history writes about Peru in the mid-1960s:

> In historical terms, [the eastern slopes of the Andes in Peru] was the site of an important rebellion in colonial times that succeeded in closing the area to Spanish influence for almost three centuries.... After 1900 this frontier area was opened rapidly to sugarcane, coffee, and fruit production. Native jungle groups were displaced and pushed around. The colonizers' image of the Ashaninka as primitive but fierce savages became part of the process of dispossessing them of their lands and converting them into cheap labor. Abuses of all kinds were common, particularly sexual abuse of Ashaninka young women and trickery with money and trade goods. The guerillas [of the 1960s] told the Ashaninka that all this victimizing would stop. They distributed arms and invited the indigenous peoples to join them in running the patrones and police out of the area.

Land in Peru was owned in an extremely unequal fashion, with "the vast majority of peasants in highland Peru [having] too little land to make a living," with "grinding poverty" the result. The Movimiento Revolucionario Tupac Amaru and Sendero Luminoso cultivated, and coerced, the indigenous peoples of Peru to join their insurgencies, sometimes massacring villagers like the Vietminh and NLF in Vietnam. The Sendero Luminoso massacred 50 Ashaninka villagers in 1993, mutilating women and children in the process.[175] Under President Alan García, a "culture of violence" developed, in which "violence [was] operating at the centre of social dynamics, a society was structured with authoritarian patterns," leading "the State, in its composition and in its behavior, to express itself as an entity that developed tendencies toward privileging the use of violence, coating it with legality."[176] After Alberto Fujimori was elected in 1990 in an unfair process from which several parties were excluded, kidnapping and mass murders of leftists occurred, one of which killed 25 in Lima in 1992, leading to Fujimori's conviction in 2009.[177]

Peru's Truth and Reconciliation Commission (TRC) concluded in 2003 that 69,000 people had died in massacres and disappearances carried out by the government and the rebel groups.[178] The TRC found "that most of the victims of human rights abuses and violations" were "indigenous peoples, peasants, Quechua speakers and people living in poverty who were illiterate or had little formal education." It declared that "it is not surprising that this Peruvian rural, Andean, jungle-dwelling, Quechua and Asháninka, peasant, poor and uneducated [population] was left to bleed for years without the rest of the

---

174. U.N. Development Programme, Human Development Report 2005, at 57, 166, 217–21 (Oxford: Oxford UP, 2005).

175. *See* Enrique Mayer, *Patterns of Violence in the Andes*, 29 Latin American Res. Rev. 141, 150–69 (1994).

176. *See* Robert H. Holden, *Constructing the Limits of State Violence in Central America: Towards a New Research Agenda*, 28 J. of Latin American Studies 435, 457 (1996) (quoting special Peruvian Senate commission).

177. *See* Adriana Leon and Chris Kraul, *Former Peru President Fujimori Convicted of Mass Murder, Kidnapping*, L.A. Times, Apr. 7, 2009, http://www.latimes.com.

178. *See Peru Strife Killed 69,000*, BBC News, Aug. 28, 2003, http://news.bbc.co.uk/2/low/americas/3187587.stm.

country feeling" the tragedy of "that 'alien people within Peru,'" and that due to "racism" and subordination of indigenous peoples, "the deaths of thousands of Quechua-speakers" was ignored by public opinion in Peru.[179] Finally, it blamed the Sendero Luminoso for "proclamations" calling for "paying the blood toll" (1982), "inducing genocide" (1985) or a "revolution [that] will cost a million deaths," (1988) as well as "conceptions of racism and superiority over indigenous peoples."[180]

In El Salvador, "a number of uprisings by peasants and indigenous groups have been violently suppressed by the State and by civilian groups armed by landowners." In 1932, the army, the National Guard, local landowners and their militias massacred over 10,000 rural people. In the late 1970s, a revolutionary movement called the Frente Farabundo Martí para la Liberación Nacional (FMLN) waged a violent campaign. In response, the government institutions mobilized heavily-armed death squads that kidnapped, tortured, and killed suspected rebels or their sympathizers. The Salvadoran Commission on the Truth reported in 2003 that "human rights violations were committed in a systematic and organized manner by groups acting as death squads." As the government "turned a blind eye, gained such control that they ceased to be an isolated or marginal phenomenon and became an instrument of terror used systematically for the physical elimination of political opponents." The president of the assembly actually ran death squads out of his parliamentary offices. The army, security forces, civil defense, and other squads were blamed in 95 percent of instances, and the FLMN in five percent.[181] In one small country, an estimated 40,000 civilians perished, 750,000 became refugees, and 500,000 IDPs.[182]

In Honduras, Roberto Suazo Cordova assumed power after elections ushered in by a military regime that excluded leftist and Christian political parties from participating.[183] Political dissidents argued that the elections were window-dressing designed to mask continued rule by generals.[184] As leftists rebelled, the U.S. trained and armed "a clandestine military death squad" that became notorious for "torture, murder and disappearance in Honduras."[185] The squad, called Battalion 3-16, kidnapped and summarily executed "scores of leftist activists—students, teachers, unionists, and would-be guerillas—who were never seen again, dead or alive."[186] The commander of Battalion 3-16 became the head of

179. Amnesty International, *Peru: The Truth and Reconciliation Commission—A First Step Towards a Country Without Injustice* (Aug. 25, 2004), http://www.amnestyusa.org/document.php?id=6E22AFDD4D87E7CB80256EEB00526B10&lang=e.

180. TRC, *Final Report: General Conclusions* (Aug. 2003), http://www.cverdad.org.pe/ingles/ifinal/conclusiones.php.

181. Commission on the Truth, *From Madness to Hope: The 12–Year War in El Salvador* (2003), U.N. Doc. No. S/25500, http://www.usip.org/library/tc/doc/reports/el_salvador/tc_es_03151993_intro.html.

182. *See* Marcelo M. Suárez-Orozco, Central American Refugees and U.S. High Schools 52 (Palo Alto, CA: Stanford UP, 1989).

183. *See* Alan Riding, *Honduran Vote Moving Doctor Toward Power; Leftist Parties Excluded*, N.Y. Times, May 26, 1980, at A4; *Christian Democratic Party of Honduras, in* Political Parties of the Americas, 1980s to 1990s, at 378 (Charles D. Ameringer ed., Westport, CT: Greenwood Publ'g Group, 1992).

184. *See* Sidney Lens, *Critics Say Honduran Military Running the Show,* Chicago Sun-Times/Courier News, July 28, 1983, at 4.

185. Human Rights Watch/Americas, The Facts Speak for Themselves: the Preliminary Report of the National Commissioner for Human Rights in Honduras 270 (New York: Human Rights Watch, 1994).

186. *Id.* at iv–vi.

the Honduran armed forces after the end of the Cold War. Members of Battalion 3-16 were responsible for executing suspected leftists.[187] Mass graves were dug in the jungle for the victims.[188]

The Caribbean saw perhaps its worst crimes of the 1980s and 1990s in Haiti. In 1964, François Duvalier proclaimed himself president of Haiti for life. He had enjoyed substantial U.S. aid for his anti-communist stance, but was cut off in the 1960s.[189] He looted $10 million annually from the Haitian treasury, according to the International Commission of Jurists. Haiti's GDP per capita actually declined by one-quarter between 1950 and 1967, while other nations were tripling and quadrupling their income per capita. The country had the lowest infant survival rate, life expectancy, and caloric consumption per person in the Western Hemisphere. There were only seven medical doctors for every 100,000 patients. These figures improved somewhat under Duvalier's son and successor Jean-Claude, although the latter's regime plundered 80% of U.S. aid, misusing more funds in the 1977–78 period than the total aid received in 1975.[190] The Haitian government, after Jean-Claude Duvalier was driven into exile in France in 1986, estimated that he had misappropriated $900 million.[191]

Sustaining the Haitian elite in power and luxury amid widespread squalor and deprivation called for harsh measures. Under François Duvalier, death squads massacred civilians in the late 1960s and early 1970s.[192] The International Commission of Jurists reported in 1967 that Haitian refugees turned back at the border of the Dominican Republic were massacred by the Duvalier regime.[193] Haitian exiles alleged that death squads were gunning down people in the streets of the capital, and that the president had a torture chamber in his palace.[194] Nevertheless, the State Department welcomed normalized relations with the elder Duvalier as being in the best interests of the U.S.[195] Under the younger Duvalier, the State Department noted that human rights situation improved, but that Haitian prisons had among the highest mortality rates in the world.[196] Starting in 1975, Haiti again received U.S. military aid, including $7 million under the Reagan and Bush administrations.[197]

---

187. *See id.* at ix, 132, 228.

188. *See* Freddy Cuevas, *Honduran Officials to Search for Mass Grave Believed to Contain the Remains of American Priest*, Associated Press, Jan. 17, 2005, http://www.highbeam.com/doc/1P1-104416017.html.

189. *See Breaking the Spell*, Time Mag., May 3, 1971, http://www.time.com/time/magazine/article/0,9171,876967,00.html.

190. *See* GAO Rep. No. 04-1006; Ndiva Kofele-Kale, The International Law of Responsibility for Economic Crimes 23–24 (London: Ashgate, 2006).

191. *See* Dan Dorfman, *On the Trail of Baby Doc*, New York Mag., July 14, 1986, at 19; Keith Richburg, *Just How Much Money Did Duvalier Take Out?*, Boca Raton News, Feb. 18, 1986, at 6.

192. *See* Raymond Alcide Joseph, *Duvalier's Tenure*, N.Y. Times, June 16, 1969, at 46; *Haiti: A Cri de Coeur*, N.Y. Times, June 2, 1971, at 41; *Novelist Says Terrorist Squads Killed Haitians*, Hartford Courant, Jan. 13, 1970, at 9.

193. *See World Jurist Commission Denounces Haiti's President*, N.Y. Times, Sept. 6, 1967, at 22.

194. *See* Tad Szulc, *Beautiful, Cruel, Explosive—Haiti*, N.Y. Times, June 9, 1963, at Magazine-224; Associated Press, *Duvalier Facing A Revolt Threat*, N.Y. Times, Apr. 28, 1963, at 14; Associated Press, *Terror Mounting in Haiti*, Hartford Courant, May 4, 1963, at 19B; Reuters, *Haitian Leader "Berserk*," The Age (Australia), May 7, 1963, at 3.

195. *See* Robert Young, *US Resumes Haiti Relations*, Chicago Tribune, June 4, 1963, at A2.

196. *See* Bernard Gwertzman, *U.S Says 6 Nations Curb Human Rights; But the State Department Asks That Military Aid Be Continued*, N.Y. Times, Jan. 2, 1977, at 1.

197. *See* Adm. Gene LaRocque (Ret.), *School of the Americas: At War with Democracy?*, Center for Defense Information (1994), http://www.cdi.org/adm/transcripts/804.

On the communist side of the Cold War, the main players in the Americas were Cuba and Nicaragua. Cuba banned all political parties except the ruling communists after the 1959 revolution, and may have executed 10,000 in the early years of the revolution. Cuban prisons and psychiatric hospitals used electric shocks, cells infested with insects, attack dogs, and mock executions to punish political dissidents.[198] The director of the Havana General Psychiatric Hospital in the 1970s reportedly told a visitor that he believed that the hospital had the highest proportion of lobotomized patients in the world.[199] Starting in 1990, with the fall of East Germany and other Warsaw Pact states, Cuba "implemented what is termed 'a special period in time of peace,' a period of draconian policy measures (increased food and energy rationing and tightened internal security) designed to ensure the survival of the socialist state under hostile conditions."[200] A food shortage followed, with health problems resulting.[201] The World Food Programme believed 600,000 Cubans to be at risk of malnutrition after a drought.[202] Average caloric intake plummeted by nearly half, from 2,900 to 1,863 calories per day.[203]

In Nicaragua, a revolutionary movement like the FLMN actually took power. Nicaragua was a U.S. protectorate during World War I, as the Marines fought rebels until 1933 to ensure that debts to U.S. banks were repaid from customs revenues and other sources. César Sandino engaged in peace negotiations with the U.S., but was assassinated by the commander of a National Guard created by U.S. forces during the occupation. The Sandinista National Liberation Front, aided by the Soviet Union and Cuba, toppled the military regime in 1979.[204] The CIA organized a rebellion by forces called *contras*, who waged a proxy war from Nicaragua's mountains and jungles against the communist-backed Sandinistas.[205] On June 28, 1986, the International Court of Justice concluded that the U.S. had trained, armed, and supplied the contras in such a way as to encourage them to violate the laws of war.[206] The Nicaraguan head of state, Daniel Ortega, complained to the U.N. Security Council that thousands of rebels armed by the U.S. in Honduras with automatic weapons, grenades, and grenade-launchers had carried out bombings aboard aircraft, in airports, and on the ground.[207]

---

198. *See* Robert M. Levine & Moisés Asís, Cuban Miami 38 (New Brunswick, New Jersey: Rutgers UP, 2000); De Courtois, The Black Book of Communism at 647.

199. *Quoted in* Mona Charen, *Reflections of a 'Red Diaper Baby',* Wash. Times, May 29, 2001, http://www.cubanet.org/CNews/y01/may01/28e11.htm; *see also* Mona Charen, Useful Idiots: How Liberals Got It Wrong in the Cold War and Still Blame America First 176–77 (Washington, DC: Regnery, 2004).

200. *Cuba, in* Political Parties of the Americas, 1980s to 1990s, at 224–26.

201. *See Serious Cuban Health Problems Ahead If Food Crisis Worsens*, Miami Herald, April 25, 1993, at 5B.

202. John M. Goshko, *U.N. Group Will Ask Aid for Cubans*, Wash. Post, Sept. 1, 1998, at A08.

203. *See* Manuel Franco, M.D. et al., *Obesity Reduction and Its Possible Consequences: What Can We Learn from Cuba's Special Period?,* 178 J. Canadian Med. Ass'n, http://www.cmaj.ca/cgi/content/full/178/8/1032. Surprisingly, the death rate decreased due to accompanying drops in diabetes and heart disease, if statistics from the Cuban Health Ministry are to be believed. *See id.*

204. *See* Stephen Kinzer, Overthrow: America's Century of Regime Change from Hawaii to Iraq 98–100 (New York: Times Books, 2007); *America Courts Third World Radicals*, L.A. Times, July 5, 1979; *Communists Ready to Take Nicaragua*, Chicago Tribune, June 28, 1979; *Over The Barrel*, N.Y. Times, June 24, 1979; Saving Nicaragua from Somoza, N.Y. Times, June 24, 1979; *U.S. Fears Unrest in Latin America*, N.Y. Times, July 22, 1979.

205. Kinzer, Overthrow, at 98–100, 241–42.

206. *See Military and Paramilitary Activities in and Against Nicaragua*, at ¶¶ 194–218.

207. *See* Daniel Ortega, *Statement to the U.N. Security Council on Mar. 25, 1982, in* The Nicaragua Reader: Documents of a Revolution under Fire 8–10 (Peter Rosset & John Vandermeer eds, New York: Grove Press, 1982).

After the Sandinistas attacked the contra bases, in Honduras, the U.S.-equipped Honduran Air Force bombed Nicaragua, and 6,000 people fled their homes in the border area.[208]

The U.S. representative to the United Nations responded that it was Nicaragua that carried out the "forced, violent transfer of Miskitu Indians," and had used weapons supplied by air and sea from Cuba to arm and equip rebels in el Salvador, who were based in Nicaragua. The U.S. accused Nicaragua of a "campaign of systematic violence" against its Indians.[209] President Reagan charged the Soviet Union with supplying tanks, artillery, trucks, planes, and helicopters to Nicaragua. As the "largest army in Central America," he argued that Nicaragua threatened Guatemala, El Salvador, Honduras, and Costa Rica with arms shipments to their rebels, and the planning of attacks by 2,000 Cuban "military and security advisers" in Nicaragua.[210] The State Department claimed that Soviet military aid to Cuba and Nicaragua was 10 times U.S. aid to all of Latin America, and that the Soviets supplied 20 times as many military advisers as the U.S. did in the area. In El Salvador, the rebels were destroying the economic infrastructure: electrical lines, bridges, schools, and buses.[211]

By the end of the Cold War, in terms of GDP per capita, Bolivia, el Salvador, Guatemala, Haiti, and Nicaragua were the poorest countries in Latin America, followed closely by Cuba.[212] Haiti was the worst off, with one in four children dying before the age of five in 1960, and one in eight in 1995. Bolivia, with its high concentration of indigenous people and history of military rule, suffered nearly as badly, with one out of 10 children dying before the age of five, down from one in four in 1960. Brazil, Guatemala, Nicaragua, and Peru all had one in 17 children die before age five in 1995, down from one in four or five in 1960. Ecuador, Honduras, Colombia, and Paraguay, by comparison, had fewer than one in 25 children die before the age of five, starting from a similar base of about one in four in 1960. Costa Rica and Cuba reached levels comparable to the U.S., although Costa Rica's under-five mortality rate was still roughly double Canada's. Life expectancy reflected these children's health figures, standing at around 60 in Haiti and Bolivia, around 70 in Guatemala and the other countries discussed above, and over 75 in Costa Rica and Cuba. All of this assumes that the official statistics are to be believed, which is often in doubt outside of the most-developed countries.[213]

G. The Cold War in Africa

In May 1945, anti-French riots broke out in Algeria after French forces opened fire on Algerian veterans of World War II and other Algerians who gathered to celebrate victory

208. *See* Peter Ford, *Contras in Honduras: Two Vantage Points. Though Angry at Managua, Many Hondurans Blame Contras for Starting Troubles*, Christian Sci. Monitor, Dec. 15, 1986, http://www.csmonitor.com/1986/1215/otown.html. The United States equipped the HAF to the most sophisticated standards in Central America. The HAF received 20 B–2 fighter-bombers, 10 F-86 fighter-bombers, 5 A-37B bombers, and 24 T-28 trainer-bombers that could be used in action. Nicaragua reportedly received 20 MiGs from Cuba. *See* Lt. Col. John H. Buchanan, *Statement to the Sub-Committee on Inter-American Affairs, Committee on Foreign Affairs, U.S. House of Representatives, Sept. 21, 1982, in* The Nicaragua Reader, at 48–53.

209. *See* Jeane Kirkpatrick, *Statement to the U.N. Security Council on Mar. 25, 1982, in id.* at 14–18.

210. Ronald Reagan, *Address to Joint Session of Congress, Apr. 27, 1982, in id.* at 18–20.

211. *See* Fred Ikle, *US Policy for Central America—Can We Succeed?, in id.* at 21–23.

212. *See* Courtois, The Black Book of Communism, at 810.

213. *See* U.N. Children's Fund, The State of the World's Children 1997, at 80–81, 88–89 (Oxford: Oxford UP, 1997).

in Europe and to demand the release of Algerians detained by the French. Between 8,000 and 45,000 were killed in what the president of independent Algeria later called the "massacres of May 8, 1945." In the ensuing Algerian war of independence, 500,000 to 1.5 million people died, thousands of children were orphaned, hundreds or even thousands of Algerians were tortured, and tens of thousands were displaced. Some 900,000 to 1.4 million French and pro-French Algerians had to leave for France, which some of them had never seen.[214] In the eastern Algerian town of Philippeville, French troops were ordered to kill every Arab on sight, and about 12,000 died as a result. Nevertheless, the insurgency gained support and claimed 25,000 French lives.[215]

After a similar but much smaller massacre of Kikuyu in British-ruled Kenya in 1952, a rebellion against the British resulted in a much smaller death toll than in Algeria. The political outcome was similar, however, with independence declared in 1963. The British used concentration camps, reservations, and fortified villages to separate the indigenous population from the independence movement, as did the French in Algeria, the U.S. in its western territories and in Vietnam, and Iraq in its northern provinces in the late 1980s.[216]

South Africa joined Egypt, Ethiopia, and Liberia as four of the first African nations to join the United Nations.[217] The country, however, would be repeatedly condemned for its "racial policies" by the Security Council, and in particular for its forcible perpetuation of a policy of racial segregation or *apartheid.*[218] An estimated 19,000 South Africans, mostly indigenous Africans or European settlers opposed to apartheid, would be killed, tortured, disappeared, or lose a family member by the time the policy came to a formal end.[219] South Africa supported an armed insurgency in Mozambique and repeatedly invaded its territory in search of African National Congress rebels, reducing it to the poorest country in the world.[220] The United Nations estimated that South African attacks on and support for rebellions within Mozambique, Angola, and Namibia killed 1.4 million people and caused $60.5 billion in economic damage.[221] Four million Africans were internally displaced by 1994.[222] Despite a U.N. arms embargo, South Africa became the "West's major supplier of such metals and minerals," including of diamonds, platinum, chrome ore, and manganese ore.[223] President Reagan pursued a policy of "constructive engagement," while at the same time sanctioning Nicaragua for lesser offenses.[224]

---

214. *See* Polk, Violent Politics, at 142–43; Wolf, Peasant Wars of the Twentieth Century, at 235–47; Reuters, *Algerians Remember Massacres of 1945,* Wash. Post, May 9, 2005, at A18.

215. *See* Polk, Violent Politics, at 137, 142–43.

216. *See id.* at 111–23.

217. *See* Keylor, The Twentieth Century World, at 434.

218. *See* S.C. Res. 181 (Aug. 7, 1963); S.C. Res. 182 (Dec. 4, 1963); S.C. Res. 282 (July 23, 1970).

219. *See* Naomi Klein, The Shock Doctrine: The Rise of Disaster Capitalism 267 (New York: Macmillan, 2005).

220. *See* Keylor, The Twentieth Century World, 451; *Mozambique, in* Encyclopedia of African History, at 1044.

221. *See* Gilbert M. Khadiagala, *How Sanctions Work: Lessons from South Africa, in* How Sanctions Work 254–55 (Neta Crawford & Audie Klotz eds., New York: St. Martin's Press, 1999). This figure includes damage to Botswana, Tanzania, Zambia, and a few other States.

222. *See Health Consequences of War and Political Violence, in* Encyclopedia of Violence, Peace, & Conflict 106 (Lester R. Kurtz & Jennifer E. Turpin eds., Academic Press, 2005).

223. Michael Parks, *Economic, Strategic Reasons S. Africa Believes West Cannot Do Without It,* L.A. Times, Jan. 1, 1985, at 1.

224. *Compare* L.A. Times News Serv., *Senators Seek New Initiative on Apartheid,* Toledo Blade (Ohio), July 22, 1986, at 1, 29, *with* Associated Press, *Reagan's Nicaragua Trade Embargo Pleases Many Legislators, But Not All,* Toledo Blade (Ohio), May 2, 1985, at 1, 4.

A major Cold War genocide arguably took place in Angola, one of Africa's earlier wars with very wide participation by other newly independent African states. With roots in the Portuguese Communist Party, the Movimento Popular de Libertacao de Angola (MPLA) was founded as an anti-colonial liberation movement in 1959.[225] A rival, initially Maoist movement called the Union for the Total Independence of Angola (UNITA) was led by Jonas Savimbi starting in the 1960s, and backed by China.[226] Portugal announced Angolan independence in January 1975, and joined the MPLA and UNITA in a transitional government, which did not halt localized fighting between the movements.[227]

In the late 1960s, China supported the MPLA rebellion against the Portuguese colonial administration in that country. The Soviet Union and Cuba joined the fray, with stepped-up Soviet aid in the 1970s, and many military advisers from these countries.[228] The U.S., Zairian dictator Mobutu Sese Seko, and Ugandan dictator Idi Amin supported the National Front for the Liberation of Angola (FNLA) in early- and mid-1975.[229] By March 1975, the MPLA was emerging as the more powerful faction due to Soviet arms shipments, and by October there were up to 1,500 Cuban troops and military advisers in Angola.[230] South Africa invaded Angola in 1975 and penetrated far beyond the border, prompting the Soviet Union to authorize massive arms shipments to the MPLA, and Cuba to send thousands of troops. This led the U.S. to take the same side as apartheid South Africa for a time, embarrassingly.[231]

South Africa's invasion, and the other conflicts on Angolan soil, cost the country billions of dollars in lost trade, foregone development, and infrastructure damage. Human Rights Watch reported in 1989 that 100,000 had died amid increasing foreign intervention. The George H.W. Bush administration nevertheless upped U.S. aid to Angolan rebels to a staggering $50 million. Both sides strewed the country with land mines and shelled civilian areas, packing hospitals with children, women and men who had lost legs or otherwise been injured by land mines.[232]

In 1990, the median age at death in Angola was only five years of age.[233] By 1992, 300,000 people were dead, over a million displaced, and billions in property had been destroyed.[234] By the late 1990s, Angola had the highest under-five infant mortality rate in

---

225. *See* Rachel Warner, *Historical Setting, in* A COUNTRY STUDY: ANGOLA, at http://lcweb2.loc.gov/cgi-bin/query/r?frd/cstdy:@field(DOCID+ao0034).

226. *See id.* at http://lcweb2.loc.gov/cgi-bin/query/r?frd/cstdy:@field(DOCID+ao0040).

227. *See id.* at http://lcweb2.loc.gov/cgi-bin/query/r?frd/cstdy:@field(DOCID+ao0044).

228. *See* EDWARD GEORGE, THE CUBAN INTERVENTION IN ANGOLA, 1965–1991, at 50–55 (London: Routledge, 2006).

229. *See* Piero Gleijeses, *Havana's Policy in Africa, 1959–76: New Evidence from Cuban Archives,* COLD WAR INTERNATIONAL HISTORY PROJECT BULLETIN, 1996, at 8–9; E.I. Afanasenko, Soviet Ambassador to the People's Republic of Angola, Memorandum of Conversation with President of the Movement for the Popular Liberation of Angola Agostinho Neto, 4 July 1975, COLD WAR INTERNATIONAL HISTORY PROJECT BULLETIN, 1996, at 32–33.

230. *See* Warner, *Historical Setting, in* A COUNTRY STUDY: ANGOLA, at http://lcweb2.loc.gov/cgi-bin/query/r?frd/cstdy:@field(DOCID+ao0045).

231. *See id.* at http://lcweb2.loc.gov/cgi-bin/query/r?frd/cstdy:@field(DOCID+ao0047).

232. HUMAN RIGHTS WATCH, WORLD REPORT 1989, http://www.unhcr.org/refworld/country,,,,AGO,,467bb486c,0.html; Dennis Hevesi, *Rights Violations in Angola Cited,* N.Y. TIMES, Apr. 9, 1989, at A15, http://www.nytimes.com/.

233. *See Children and Genocide, in* ENCYCLOPEDIA OF GENOCIDE, at 139.

234. *See* Paul Taylor, *Angolan Election Margin Narrows; Savimbi Gains in Presidential Race,* WASH. POST, Oct, 5, 1992, http://www.highbeam.com/doc/1P2-1028356.html.

the world, after Niger and Sierra Leone,[235] and about 500,000 people had died in the struggle between the Angolan government and South Africa, the UNITA rebels, and their respective allies, which in the case of UNITA included former members of the apartheid-era South African Defense Force, who were hired as mercenaries after the end of apartheid.[236] Two million Angolans were displaced from their homes or communities.[237]

Nigeria was the scene of perhaps the worst Cold War genocide in Africa, outside of Sudan. As one author described the slaughter of the minority Igbos in 1971:

> [A]fter two coups, the Igbos found themselves sidelined. They decided to secede, taking the country's newfound oil fields with them into the so-called Republic of Biafra. That led to a bitter four-year war, in which millions of Biafrans died, mainly through starvation. In the end, Biafra was suppressed.[238]

An American doctor predicted in early 1970 that a million Biafrans could die "within weeks." An expert from the Atlanta Communicable Diseases Center predicted that one to 1.5 million Biafrans would die of starvation and disease by January 1970. He argued that 85% of available food was blocked from reaching Biafra, and that up to four million people would starve without full rations, which were not being provided. Only an "around-the-clock airlift" of 6,000 to 10,000 tons of food per week could stave off this disaster, which did not occur.[239]

Despite the reports he was receiving, Kissinger described the situation in Nigeria to the President has "progressing reasonably well."[240] In a later conversation with Kissinger in 1971, however, President Richard M. Nixon characterized Nigeria's policy as "shooting starving Biafrans."[241] In a high-level meeting in 1971, a State Department official called Biafra "a real blood-bath."[242] In June 1971, the National Security Council issued the official U.S. policy paper on Nigeria, which stated that Nigeria was an important back-up source of petroleum for the U.S. and Europe, had a military strength of 250,000 men, a population of 60 million, and a growing economy that promised to be a good market for U.S. exports. Therefore, the policy paper called for further U.S. training of military and police officials in Nigeria, more arms exports, increased trade, and the suppression of "anti-Nigerian voices in the United States."[243] British Prime Minister Harold Wilson and Soviet Premier Leonid Brezhnev supplied the Federal Republic of Nigeria with abundant

---

235. U.N. Development Programme, World Resources 2000–2001, at tbl HD.2.

236. *See* Juan Carlos Zarate, *The Emergence of a New Dog of War: Private International Security Companies, International Law, and the New World Disorder*, 34 Stan. J Int'l L. 75, 94 (1998).

237. *See Health Consequences of War and Political Violence, in* Encyclopedia of Violence, Peace, & Conflict 106 (Lester R. Kurtz & Jennifer E. Turpin eds., New York: Academic Press, 2005).

238. Breffni O'Rourke, *Iraq: Assessing the Strengths and Dangers of Federalism*, Radio Free Europe/Radio Liberty (Aug. 18, 2005), http://www.reliefweb.int/rw/RWB.NSF/db900SID/VBOL-6FHGPR?OpenDocument.

239. Henry A. Kissinger, Memorandum for the President re Nigerian Relief Status Report, Jan. 19, 1970, at 1–5.

240. *Id.* at 1.

241. Transcript of Telephone Conversation Between President Nixon and His Assistant for National Security Affairs, Kissinger, Mar. 30, 1971, *in* 9 Foreign Relations of the United States, 1969–1976: South Asia Crisis, 1971, at 37 (Louis J. Smith ed., Washington, DC: United States Government Printing Office, 2005).

242. Minutes of Senior Review Group Meeting, Mar. 6, 1971, *in id.* at 16.

243. CA-5632, National Security Council Interdepartmental Group for Africa, Nigeria: Policy Planning Paper, June 1971, at 2–3, attachment to USDOS to U.S. Embassy, Lagos, Nigeria, Policy Planning Paper, declassified 2005.

weaponry to blockade, massacre, and starve to death over one million majority Christian Igbo people both prior to and during the war.[244]

In January 1971, a veteran of the British army in World War II and 1950s Kenya named Idi Amin seized power in Uganda in a coup backed by Britain, Israel, and South Africa.[245] Amin's death squads targeted regime opponents and disenfranchised ethnic groups such as the largely Christian Acholi and Lango peoples.[246] Both Britain and the U.S. "applaud[ed] this new African leader" even as he slaughtered entire communities, as he had done as a lieutenant in the British-trained Ugandan Army. Entire barracks of Acholi and Lango soldiers were herded onto buses and shot as part of Amin's campaign to transform Uganda into a "Moslem state" using Arab money and by declaring a "holy war." Amin even killed his own Christian sons. An estimated 100,000 Acholi and Lango civilians died, and countless children became orphans. With 3,000 members of death squads in the State Research Bureau, if each had killed five people a year the death toll of more than eight years of Amin's rule could have claimed a million lives in executions alone, not counting untold deaths from his looting of the country, which deprived malaria sufferers of medicines, and emptied the hospitals of all supplies.[247]

Up to 400,000 of Idi Amin's other opponents in Uganda were executed or otherwise perished in his violent defense of his claim to be "President for Life." Nevertheless, he became the head of the Organization of African Unity in 1975, and Uganda occupied a seat on the U.N. Commission on Human Rights in 1977–1979.[248] Uganda invaded Tanzania, prompting the latter to declare an ongoing genocide and occupy Uganda on humanitarian grounds in late 1978.[249] Amin retired to a luxurious lifestyle in Libya and then to a Hilton hotel in Saudi Arabia. No one in the U.S. government or U.N. system bothered to call for his trial and execution.[250]

In Ethiopia, Colonel Mengistu Haile Mariam rose to power after a military coup in 1974. A severe famine had plagued the country under the Emperor Haile Selassie in 1972. The U.S. offered $100 million in military aid to the new military junta. In the late 1970s, the Eritrean People's Liberation Front (EPLF) fought to establish an independent Eritrea, in Ethiopia's pluralistic north, where there resided a higher concentration of Muslims.[251] Somalia, whose dictator Muhammad Siad Barre was backed by the U.S., invaded Ethiopia, which Somalia blamed for persecuting Somalis and supporting rebels against Somalia.[252]

244. *See* Abdul Karim Bangura, *Multifaceted Ethnic Conflicts and Conflict Resolution in Nigeria, in* PERSPECTIVES ON CONTEMPORARY ETHNIC CONFLICT: PRIMAL VIOLENCE OR THE POLITICS OF CONVICTION? 178, 183–84 (Santosh C. Saha ed., Lanham, MD: Lexington Books, 2006).

245. *See* W.D. RUBINSTEIN, GENOCIDE: A HISTORY 272–73 (Harlow: Pearson Education, 2004).

246. *See* Michael Richardson, *Untried Murderer: Amin's Rule One of Bloodiest in African History*, THE INDEPENDENT (U.K.), Mar. 28, 1980, at 13; *see also Amin, Idi, in* DICTIONARY OF GENOCIDE, at 12; *Idi Amin, in* ENCYCLOPEDIA OF GENOCIDE, at 349; *Uganda, in* ENCYCLOPEDIA OF GENOCIDE AND CRIMES AGAINST HUMANITY, at 1053–54.

247. *See* Richardson, *Untried Murderer*, at 13.

248. *See* Reisman, *Acting* Before *Victims Become Victims*, at 67–68; JOSEPH STIGLTZ, GLOBALIZATION AND ITS DISCONTENTS 40 (New York: W.W. Norton, 2003).

249. *See* John Darnton, *Rubble and the Dead Mark Invaded Region of Tanzania*, N.Y. TIMES, Nov 23, 1978, at A1; John Darnton, *Invaders Establish Control in Kampala*, N.Y. TIMES, Apr. 13, 1979, at A1.

250. *See* Richardson, *Untried Murderer*, at 13; Riccardo Orizio, *Idi Amin's Exile Dream*, N.Y. TIMES, Aug, 21, 2003, at A25, http://www.nytimes.com/2003/08/21/opinion/idi-amin-s-exile-dream.html.

251. *See* Kristin Urbach, *Famine As a Human Rights Violation: The Case of Ethiopia and the Great Famine of the 1980s*, 1 INTERDISCIPLINARY J. OF HUMAN RIGHTS L. 24–36 (2008).

252. *See Editor's Note on the Cold War Crisis: New East-Bloc Evidence on the Horn of Africa, 1977–1978*, COLD WAR INTERNATIONAL HISTORY PROJECT BULLETIN, 1996, at 38–39.

Mengistu responded by imposing famine conditions on rebel-threatened territory, "and then use[d] international aid as a weapon of war." Alex De Waal observed that "the zone of severe famine [in Ethiopia] coincided with the war zone, and the phases of the developing famine corresponded with the major military actions." Scorched-earth warfare was the norm:

> Starting with Eritrea, the measures taken by the army and the air force shattered the ecosystem as trees were cut and forests were burned for defense purposes. Pastures that were not annihilated by phosphorous and flammable chemicals were rigged with mines, trampled on by tanks, or cratered with bombs. As land became scarce, herders could no longer graze their livestock freely and many farmers were left with poor crop yields. Whatever food peasants were able to produce and whatever livestock were able to survive were usually destroyed or confiscated by government soldiers....

In the south, where Tigray separatists mounted a separate insurgency, the regime destroyed grain, "entire villages were incinerated, and markets were relentlessly bombarded." A food blockade was imposed on rebel-held villages, and potential rebels were deported to state-held or -controlled territory.[253] The Soviet Union sent one billion dollars in arms, 12,000 Cuban troops, and 1,500 military advisers to Ethiopia.[254] Despite stepped-up Soviet and Cuban aid to Mengistu, Somali-backed rebels under Meles Zenawi of the Ethiopian People's Revolutionary Democratic Front toppled Mengistu, marching into Addis Ababa in 1991.[255]

President Mengistu was tried and convicted in absentia for genocide arising out of the killing of tens of thousands of people from 1974 to 1991, in a trial overseen by Zenawi, who became president of Ethiopia in 1991.[256] U.S. sources estimated that during President Mengistu's rule, he killed 50,000 political opponents, including many students.[257] Announcing the judgment in 2006, the High Court of Ethiopia stated:

> [Those] who are present in court today ... and those who are being tried in absentia (including Mengistu) have conspired to destroy a political group and kill people with impunity. They set up a hit squad to destroy groups opposing the Mengistu regime.

Ethiopian political analyst Fisseha Tecle noted that it took "the government of Prime Minister [and former rebel leader] Zenawi 15 years to try and convict Mengistu and company."[258] Despite his conviction and sentence of life in prison, ex-President Mengistu remained at liberty as "guest" in Zimbabwe in late 2007.[259] The High Court sentenced him to death in 2008.[260]

---

253. *See* Urbach, *Famine as a Human Rights Violation*, at 24–36 (quoting ALEX DE WAAL, FAMINE CRIMES: POLITICS & THE DISASTER RELIEF INDUSTRY IN AFRICA 115 (Bloomington: Indiana UP, (1997)).

254. *See* Ermias Abebe, *The Horn, The Cold War, and Documents from the Former East-Bloc: An Ethiopian View*, COLD WAR INTERNATIONAL HISTORY PROJECT BULLETIN, 1996, at 43.

255. *See Anarchy in the Horn*, JANE'S FOREIGN REPORT, Nov. 28, 1991; *An Archive of Murders Past; Ethiopia*, THE ECONOMIST, Sept. 29, 2007, http://www.economist.com/displaystory.cfm?story_id=9867981. *See also* Associated Press, *Eritrea Marks Independence after Years under Ethiopia*, N.Y. TIMES, May 25, 1993, at A8.

256. *See An Archive of Murders Past; Ethiopia.*

257. *See* Voice of America, *Verdict Postponed in Former President Mengistu Genocide Trial*, US FED NEWS, May 23, 2006.

258. *Kenya; Zenawi's Moral Authority to Try Mengistu Questioned*, AFRICA NEWS, Jan. 20, 2007.

259. *See An Archive of Murders Past; Ethiopia.*

260. *See Court Sentences Mengistu to Death,* BBC NEWS, May 26, 2008, http://news.bbc.co.uk/2/hi/africa/7420212.stm.

H. The Cold War in the Middle East and Central Asia, and South Asia

1. The Middle East

The initial battle of the Cold War occurred in the Middle East, and specifically at the border of Iran, Iraq, and Turkey. Soviet tanks and troops occupied northern Iran and declared a Kurdish Soviet Republic. The Soviets withdrew under Western pressure, however.

Starting in the 1930s, Turks seized Kurdish lands and banned the Kurdish language and political parties. The Turkish minister of justice pronounced that: "Those who are not of pure Turkish stock can have only one right in this country, the right to be servants and slaves." In order to disperse Kurdish communities, the Turkish government deported many Kurds from villages in which they lived, either legitimately or as a result of theft from Ottoman Christians. Kurdish language classes were banned through 2003, and Kurdish books and TV until 2001.[261]

In 1955, the prime minister of Turkey ordered an intelligence agent to conduct a covert operation designed to look like a Greek terrorist's bombing of the birthplace of Mustafa Kemal in Thessaloniki. Soon after, a newspaper in Constantinople reported the news, and a shadowy new organization called for widespread retaliation against Greek civilians. As a result, Turkish mobs killed an undetermined number of Greek civilians, up to 200 Greek women were raped, 39 Greek churches burned down and dozens more badly damaged, and more than 2,000 Greek homes and dozens of Greek schools were thoroughly looted.[262] The American consul-general in Constantinople reported to the U.S. State Department that the Turkish police "cheered on the mob." A British journalist compared the Greek sections of the city to the neighborhoods in London that suffered aerial bombardment in World War II.[263]

Turkey invaded the historically Greek island of Cyprus in 1974 and had occupied more than a third of its territory ever since. Four thousand Greek Cypriots were murdered and another two thousand went missing. Cyprus documented Turkey's acts of "indiscriminate" slaughter, torture and rape, and enslavement and forced labor against ethnic Greeks of all ages and sexes.[264] The Turkish military occupation drove out Greek populations and ransacked Greek culture:

> The Turks ethnically cleansed the north of the island, village by village, as the Greeks tried to prevent Turkish Cypriots fleeing north (and so reinforcing an ethnic divide).... Thousands of Turkish peasants were brought in from mainland Turkey to the new Turkish Republic of North Cyprus to take the place of the displaced Greeks. Attacks on Greek material culture in the North

---

261. Sautman, *Is Tibet China's Colony?*, at 191.

262. *See* Doğu Ergil, *Past as Present,* TURKISH DAILY NEWS, Sept. 12, 2005, http://www.turkishdailynews.com.tr; Skenderis, *The Ethnic Greeks of Turkey*, at 565; HUMAN RIGHTS WATCH, DENYING HUMAN RIGHTS AND ETHNIC IDENTITY: THE GREEKS OF TURKEY 7–9 (New York: Human Rights Watch, 1992); Loucas Tsilas, *Greek-Turkish Relations in the Post-Cold War Era*, 20 FORDHAM INT'L L. J. 1589, 1599–1603 (1997); Vryonis, *The Turkish Pogrom*; SPEROS VRYONIS, THE MECHANISM OF CATASTROPHE: THE TURKISH POGROM OF SEPTEMBER 6–7, 1955, AND THE DESTRUCTION OF THE GREEK COMMUNITY OF ISTANBUL (New York: Greekworks.com, 2005).

263. Skenderis, *The Ethnic Greeks of Turkey*, at 566.

264. Coufoudakis, *Cyprus v. Turkey*, at 451, 455.

> were an early signal of Turkey's intention to remain in Cyprus permanently.... The destruction of Greek heritage was an insurance against ... [an] identifiably Greek ... zone.... In the months and years following [the invasion], all but a handful of northern Cyprus's 502 Greek Orthodox churches, some of Byzantine origin, were vandalized, looted, demolished or put to new uses including as mosques, stables, latrines, stores and a cinema.... The destruction was methodical....
>
> "The vandalism and desecration is [sic] so methodical and so widespread that they amount to the institutionalized obliteration of everything sacred to a Greek."[265]

The U.N. General Assembly voted unanimously in November 1974, and the U.N. Security Council agreed shortly thereafter, that Turkey must withdraw from Cyprus.[266] The European Commission on Human Rights found that Turkey's "large scale" killing of Greek Cypriot civilians violated their human right to life, and that its rapes of civilians and mistreatment of prisoners constituted torture or at least inhuman treatment.[267] Over 30 years and many U.N. resolutions and diplomatic initiatives later, Turkey remained in Cyprus.[268] Nevertheless, the U.S. has lavished $14 billion in military aid upon Turkey, NATO member and host to nuclear weapons capable of striking the Soviet Union.[269] Americans with military and economic ties to the Turkish majority have aided and abetted Turkey's human rights abuses and genocide denial. More than 100 defense contractors and other corporations joined forces to defeat a historic resolution proposed in the Senate to acknowledge the Armenian genocide. U.S. Senate Majority Leader Bob Dole admitted that the "only genocides we can talk about [in Congress] are those which do not embarrass an ally, do not threaten an American company's profit margin."[270]

By the mid-1980s, the Kurds had become the primary target of Turkey's militaristic policies, as 2,500 villages were "depopulated" by counterinsurgency operations. As Human Rights Watch documented:

> Since 1984, southeastern Turkey has been the scene of serious fighting between government security forces and the PKK (Workers' Party of Kurdistan, "Partia Karkaren Kurdistan"), a militant armed Kurdish group whose explicit claims range from complete independence to regional autonomy within Turkey. The government intensified a counterinsurgency campaign against the PKK, forcibly evacuating and burning rural villages. The majority of the more than 2,500 villages and hamlets depopulated in the region since 1984 are believed to be the result of this campaign....[271]

Kurdish culture was long banned under Turkey's language laws, among the hostile to the survival of ethnic and religious minorities of any country in the world:

> Turkey still rigidly adheres to the concept of a single-language state.... State-sponsored schools teach no language aside from Turkish and punish students who speak other languages in the classroom. Particularly in its insistence on teaching only in Turkish, the goal of the government seems to be not only to re-

---

265. Bevan, The Destruction of Memory, at 163–64.
266. U.N. G.A. Res. 3212(XXIX) (1974); S.C. Res. 365 (Dec. 13, 1974).
267. Coufoudakis, *Cyprus v. Turkey*, at 450, 464–65.
268. Athanasopulos, *Greece, Turkey and the Aegean Sea*, 30.
269. U.S. State Department, *Background Note: Turkey*.
270. *Quoted in* Marashlian, Politics and Demography, at 127.
271. Human Rights Watch, *Violations of Free Expression in Turkey* (1999), http://www.hrw.org/en/reports/1999/04/01/violations-free-expression-turkey.

strict usage of other languages to the home, but to eradicate other languages completely.[272]

Turkey also practiced the more subtle route of "genocide-by-law."[273] This is the term of Dean Rennard Strickland of the University of Oregon School of Law for techniques by which "people are made to disappear legally, through the operation of law."[274] Turkish Kurds, Armenians, Assyrians, Greeks, and Yezidis, "have faced intense pressure to assimilate," including laws that criminalize expressions of their distinctive language, culture and history.[275] In the "genocide-by-law" period, indigenous Armenian, Assyrian, and Greek names for towns and villages, as well as names changed from Assyrian or Armenian to Kurdish names after the Turko-Kurdish invasions of the past millennium, have been changed to Turkish names. Even individual minorities have been forced to use Turkish surnames, and abandon their linguistic heritage and other markers or their ethnic identity.[276] Non-Turkish names were banned, forcing descendents of families massacred or enslaved by Turks to give their children Turkish names.[277]

Turkey's Constitution of 1982 does not contemplate minorities retaining languages other than Turkish as their mother tongue, or perpetuating minority languages in school. It contemplates only Turkish as a mother tongue and prohibits the teaching of languages that are neither Turkish nor "foreign."[278] Armenian, Assyrian, and Greek language broadcasting was prohibited by law until 2002, and is still de facto prohibited.[279]

---

272. Kurdish Human Rights Project, *Human Rights Violations against Kurds in Turkey, OSCE Submissions 2007, Language and Education Rights—Working Session 1*, at 1 (2007).

273. *Cf. Race, in* KEYWORDS: A VOCABULARY OF CULTURE AND SOCIETY 295 (Raymond Williams et al. eds., 2005) (postmodern racism is justified by reference to preservation of a nation or culture, such as that of the Hindus or Turks).

274. Rennard Strickland, *Things Not Spoken: The Burial of Native American History, Law and Culture*, 13 ST. THOMAS L. REV. 11 n.19 & accompanying text (2000).

275. Minority Rights Group International, *State of the World's Minorities 2008*, at 141. The Assyrians, for example, were not recognized as official minorities in modern Turkey, and faced "systematic repression" there. *Id.*

276. *See* Law No. 2552 § (3.7) (stating that "it is not permitted to assume names from foreign races or nations"), quoted in Orom Lahdo, *The Assimilation Policy of Turkey Continues on Surnames*, EASTERNSTAR NEWS AGENCY, Feb. 11, 2008, http://groups.google.com/group/soc.culture.assyrian/browse_thread/thread/ 0b51539dc036dfd9?hl=en#; Dickran Kouymjian, *The Destruction of Armenian Historical Monuments as a Continuation of the Turkish Policy of Genocide, in* A CRIME OF SILENCE: THE ARMENIAN GENOCIDE 173–74 (London: Zed Press, 1985) (describing changing of more than 90% of Armenian place-names to Turkish ones between 1915 and 1958); *see also* GREAT BRITAIN NAVAL INTELLIGENCE DIVISION, TURKEY 10 (1942) (describing changing of Armenian and Greek place-names to Turkish ones prior to World War II); Lahdo, *The Assimilation Policy of Turkey Continues on Surnames* ("On November 24, 1934, Turkey introduced the surname act. In Turkey, this law is called 'Soyadi kanunu.' The purpose of this law was to force all groups of people, regardless of their ethnicity or religion, to assume a Turkish last name. This law is still applied today, and it is strictly forbidden for Christians or any ethnic minorities to assume "non-Turkish names." These names are by law prohibited in Turkey.").

277. *See* U.S. Dep't of State, *Country Reports on Human Rights Practices 2003: Turkey*, (Turkish law bans "names contrary to the 'national culture' or 'customs and traditions,'" but was amended in 2003 to ban "names contrary to 'moral norms' or names that 'offend the public,'" including those with "letters ... not found in Turkish" language).

278. Const. of Turkey 1982, art. 44(9).

279. *See* Human Rights Watch, *Questions and Answers: Freedom of Expression and Language Rights in Turkey* (Feb. 13, 2002), http://www.hrw.org/press/2002/08/turkeyqa041902.htm ("Individuals in Turkey face prosecution and prison terms merely for using forbidden minority languages or expressing opinions on certain taboo subjects...."); *id.* (discussing EU challenges to Turkey's prohibitions on minorities use "of their mother tongue in TV and radio broadcasting," and Turkey's refusal to amend its Broadcasting Law); U.S. Dep't of State, *Country Reports on Human Rights Practices 2003:*

Political parties seeking to preserve regional and ethnic cultures, or to seek autonomy for their members, were prohibited in Turkey, even though they are a mainstay of politics in the United Kingdom, Canada, post-2003 Iraq, and many other countries.[280] While languages other than Turkish are banned from education and the mass media, school textbooks teach Turkish children "negative stereotypes of Armenians and other minorities."[281]

Turkish laws frequently banned the very history of Anatolia's indigenous peoples. For example, "Article 301 of the Turkish penal code for 'denigrating Turkish identity,'" which "often has been used to suppress any discussion or acknowledgement of the 1915 Armenian genocide."[282] Article 216 of the penal code imposed between one to four and a half years in prison for a person who "incites groups of the population to breed enmity or hatred towards one another by, for instance, denigrating [majority] religious values."[283] The legislative history of the provision referred specifically to the Armenian genocide as an exemplar of the type of cultural and historical speech it would prohibit.[284]

Turkey also attempted to destroy the ability of its non-Kurdish ethnic and religious minorities to preserve and pass on their minority religions to future generations. The Turkish government seized many Armenian and Greek churches on the galling rationale that the local population had fallen too low, as might be expected after an extermination of a race.[285] The government then banned new construction of churches, so that it remained illegal to build a church prior to 2003, and once this discriminatory law was amended, none received authorization to open until 2006, after an evangelical church

Turkey (2004), http://www.state.gov/g/drl/rls/hrrpt/2003/27869.htm (prior to 2003, Turkish government did not "permit[] private media outlets to broadcast in Kurdish and other traditional non-Turkish languages"); Philip Shishkin, *Turkish Vote May Pull at Diversity's Divide*, WALL ST. J., July 23, 2007 ("On a recent visit to his small Sur parish, Turkey's Assyrian Metropolitan Saliba Ozmen said the use of Aramaic is also restricted."); William Dalrymple, *Ignore the Hype*, THE SPECTATOR (U.K.), Oct. 27, 2007, http://www.accessmylibrary.com/coms2/summary_0286-33610082_ITM ("[U]ntil very recently, minority languages like the Syrian Christians' Aramaic were banned from broadcasting and teaching, and almost all seminaries had been closed. But cross into Syria at Qamishli, and you find yourself in a town that is 75 per cent Christian, with icons of Christ and his mother filling almost every shop and decorating every other car window—an extraordinary display after the paranoia of Turkey.").

280. Article 58 of Turkey's Election Law "prohibits the use of languages other than Turkish in propaganda disseminated in radio or television as well as in other election propaganda." Olgun Akbulut, *The State of Political Participation of Minorities in Turkey – An Analysis under the ECHR and the ICCPR*, 12 INT'L J. OF MINORITY & GROUP RIGHTS 375, 388 (2005). Article 81 of the Turkish Law on Political Parties bans all political parties that assert that there are any minorities within Turkey based on race, national origin, language, or religion, or that propose to "promot[e] or disseminat[e] languages or cultures other than Turkish." *Id.* at 376.

281. Minority Rights Group International, *State of the World's Minorities.*

282. *Id.*

283. Organization for Security and Co-operation in Europe, *The Representative on Freedom of the Media (Miklos Haraszti), Review of the Draft Turkish Penal Code: Freedom of Media Concerns* 3 (May 2005).

284. *See id.* at 5.

285. *See* U.S. Dep't of State, *International Religious Freedom Report 2007* (2008), http://www.unhcr.org/refworld/publisher,USDOS,,TUR,46ee679269,0.html (since 1970s, Turkey "has seized control of [Armenian and Greek] properties acquired after 1936," has "expropriate[d] properties in areas where the local 'non-Muslim' population drops significantly," including "numerous" Greek and Armenian Orthodox religious centers).

made two appeals to a Turkish court for the right to open.[286] The Armenian patriarch in Constantinople complained in 1978 that: "There are bureaucratic discriminations.... We cannot build new churches or repair old ones...."[287] An Armenian-American described the result as he saw it in 1995, with "ruined" churches being the "most common type of church" in Turkey," and the "the physical record of 2,500 years of Armenian civilization" being "erased in only seventy years."[288] Turkish law states that Armenian churches and other architecture represent national wealth that can only be repaired after navigating bureaucratic and arbitrary procedures that prevent needed repairs.[289]

Since the 1980s, thousands of neo-pagan Yezidis from Turkey have fled their villages, so that their community is "dwindling."[290] Their language, religious institutions, and history were outlawed or limited in many respects, as discussed above.

Despite regular warnings concerning violations of human rights by the Turkish state, the U.S., Great Britain, and France have financed and aided oppressive Turkish rule over the Christian remnant in Asia and even in Europe (in the case of Cyprus).[291] Western powers largely ignored abuses against Christians in Turkey and even in Iraq, continuing to extend military aid and diplomatic support.[292] The U.S. remains the principal supplier of

---

286. *See Modern Turkey's First New Church Opens in Istanbul*, TORONTO STAR, Sept. 1, 2006. *See also* U.S. Dep't of State, *International Religious Freedom Report 2007* (2008), http://www.unhcr.org/refworld/publisher,USDOS,,TUR,46ee679269,0.html ("In 1974, amid political tensions over Cyprus, the High Court of Appeals ruled that the minority foundations had no right to acquire properties beyond those listed in the 1936 declarations continuing today."); U.S. Dep't of State, *International Religious Freedom Report 2002* (2003), http://www.state.gov/g/drl/rls/irf/2002 ("Non-Muslim religious foundations legally may not acquire property for any purpose....").

287. Robert Paul Jordan, *The Proud Armenians*, 153 NAT'L GEOGRAPHIC 851 (June 1978).

288. Gregory C. Norsigian, *Chasing Ghosts in Turkey*, THE ARMENIAN REPORTER, Jan. 14, 1995, http://www.highbeam.com/doc/1P1-2297219.html.

289. *See* USDOS, *International Religious Freedom Report 2005*(2006), http://www.state.gov/g/drl/rls/irf/2005/51586.htm.

290. Human Rights Watch, *Displaced and Disregarded: Turkey's Failing Village Return Program* (2002), http://www.hrw.org/reports/2002/turkey/Turkey1002.pdf.

291. *See* Suha Bolukbasi, *Behind the Turkish-Israeli Alliance: A Turkish View*, J. OF PALESTINE STUDIES 29 (1999): 22. In the 1950s and 1960s, Turkish violence and persecution against the Greek Christians, the forcible deportation of Greek citizens, and the expropriation of their property, contributed to driving an estimated 97% of Greeks in Turkey, more than 95,000 people, to flee. Steven Stavros Skenderis, *Note & Comment: The Ethnic Greeks of Turkey: The Present Situation of the Greek Minority and Turkey's Human Rights Obligations Under International Law*, 16 ST. THOMAS LAW REVIEW 551, 564–65 (2004) (citing Human Rights Watch, *Denying Human Rights and Ethnic Identity: The Greeks of Turkey* 7–9 (Mar. 1992), and Loucas Tsilas, *Greek-Turkish Relations in the Post-Cold War Era*, 20 FORDHAM INT'L L. J. 1589, 1599–1600 (1997)). Starting in 1974, Turkey invaded and began illegally occupying and colonizing northern Cyprus. Tsilas, *Greek-Turkish Relations*, at 1603–1605.

292. As for Turkey, Congress has debated whether continuing to provide aid to Turkey is to turn a blind eye to its persecution of Christians and Kurds, blockade of Armenia, and occupation of northern Cyprus. *House Tables Foreign Aid Bill*, UNITED PRESS INT'L, June 6, 1996; Eugene T. Rossides, Prepared Statement on Behalf of the American Hellenic Institute Public Affairs Committee, Inc., et al., Before the House Appropriations Committee, Subcommittee on Foreign Operations, Export Financing and Related Programs (Apr. 25, 1996). As for Iraq, the Reagan and first Bush administrations offered critical military and financial aid to Iraq after it had embarked upon campaigns of "Arabization" and ethnic cleansing in northern Iraq, in which the Assyrians and other Christians were caught up. Lewis M. Simons, *Genocide and the Science of Proof*, NATIONAL GEOGRAPHIC, Jan. 2006: 32; CRAIG UNGER, HOUSE OF BUSH, HOUSE OF SAUD: THE SECRET RELATIONSHIP BETWEEN THE WORLD'S TWO MOST POWERFUL DYNASTIES 75–82 (New York, NY: Scribner, 2004); Joost R. Hiltermann, *Halabja: America Didn't Seem to Mind Poison Gas*, INT'L HERALD TRIBUNE, Jan. 17, 2003, http://www.iht.com.

Turkish military equipment, which is used to blockade tiny landlocked Armenia and threaten military intervention against Armenia for protecting the ethnic Armenians of Azerbaijan.[293]

2. India, Pakistan, and South Asia

In the late 1960s and early 1970s, a Bangladeshi independence movement emerged, whose priorities were manifest from their first constitution with "four cornerstones," namely "secularism, ... democracy, nationalism, and socialism." Its foreign policy "emphasized friendship with India and the Soviet Union," rather than with Islamic states like Saudi Arabia.[294]

In 1971, the fundamentalist Pakistani government "systematically slaughtered" the Hindu community in rebellious East Pakistan, present-day Bangladesh. From a Hindu population of 18.5% in the 1960s, they made up only 13.5% of Bangladesh in 1974, and only 9% in 2002. The fundamentalist leader Abdul Kader Molla "became known as 'the Butcher of Mirpur,' a Dhaka suburb which in 1971 was populated mainly by non-Bengali Muslim immigrants...." Prosecuted as a war criminal by independent Bangladesh, he was welcomed into Pakistan without charge.[295]

The Pakistan government confiscated Hindu homes and businesses, even painting some with Nazi-like yellow patches marked "H" for Hindu.[296] The Hindus of Pakistan, about eight million in all, lost most of their land and other properties when they fled to India, while the poor and middle-class Hindus who remained in Pakistan and Bangladesh were intimidated into leaving by discriminatory policies. A U.S. Senate subcommittee inquiry in 1971 found that:

> Field reports to the US Government, countless eye-witnesses, journalistic accounts, reports of international agencies such as the World Bank and additional information available to the subcommittee document the reign of terror which grips East Bengal (East Pakistan). Hardest hit have been members of the Hindu community who have been robbed of their lands and shops, systematically slaughtered, and in some cases, painted with yellow patches marked "H." All of this has been officially sanctioned, ordered and implemented under the martial law from Islamabad [West Pakistan].[297]

---

293. Burak Ege Bekdil & Umit Enginsoy, *European Firms Eye Boost in Turk Business under EU*, Defense News, Oct. 24, 2005, at 26; *Turkey Rejects U.S. Aid Loan*, Wash. Post, June 7, 1996, at A28; James Morrison, *Embassy Row*, Wash. Times, Feb. 20, 1995, at A14; Martin Sieff, *Dole Targets Nations That Impede U.S. Aid*, Wash. Times, Jan. 13, 1995, at A15; *Turkey Moves Troops to Armenian Border*, N.Y. Times, Sept. 4, 1993, at 1–5.

294. Bertil Lintner, *The Plights of Ethnic and Religious Minorities and the Rise of Islamic Extremism in Bangladesh* (Feb. 2, 2003), http://www.asiapacificms.com/papers/pdf/ethnic_and_religious_minorities_bangladesh.pdf.

295. Jaideep Saikia, *Terror Sans Frontiers: Islamic Militancy in North East India*, Acdis Occasional Paper (July 2003), Chapter Three, *at* http://www.acdis.uiuc.edu/Research/OPs/Saikia/contents/chap_three.html. *See also* Lintner, *The Plight of Ethnic and Religious Minorities in Bangladesh.*

296. *See* Saikia, *Terror Sans Frontiers: Islamic Militancy in North East India*; Lintner, *The Plight of Ethnic and Religious Minorities in Bangladesh.*

297. Senator Edward Kennedy, Crisis in South Asia: A Report to the Subcommittee Investigating the Problem of Refugees and Their Settlement, Submitted to the US Senate Judiciary Committee 66 (Nov. 1, 1971), *quoted in* Jaideep Saikia, *Terror* Sans Frontiers: *Islamic Militancy in North East India*, ch. 3 (ACDIS Occasional Paper, July 2003), http://www.acdis.uiuc.edu/Research/OPs/Saikia/contents/chap_three.html.

A more recent study emphasized the role of discriminatory legislation in persuading the Hindu enemies of state to leave their communities en masse, leaving their homes free to seize:

> In 1965, a war broke out between India and Pakistan, and a law called "the Defence of Pakistan Ordinance" was promulgated to "ensure the security, the public safety, interest and the defence of the state."
>
> This was followed by an even more draconian regulation termed "the Enemy (Custody and Registration) order II of 1965." India was declared an enemy, and the law allowed "enemy" (in practice Hindu) lands to be expropriated by the state.
>
> After Bangladesh's independence, properties left behind by the Pakistanis and the erstwhile "enemy properties" were combined to a single category. Though the principal aim of the new "Vested and Non-resident Property Act" of 1974 was to take over former Pakistani-owned properties as well as properties which once belonged to the Hindus who had fled the country during the liberation war, in practice this act was widely used against the entire Hindu community.
>
> According to the US State Department: "Approximately 2.5 million acres of land was seized from Hindus and almost all of the 10 million Hindus in the country were affected."....
>
> By the end of 1971, nearly ten million people had fled to West Bengal [from Pakistani East Bengal], where they were sheltered in make-shift refugee camps. 80% of them were Hindus, 15% Muslims, and 5% Christians and Buddhists. When the war was over, and Bangladesh created, very few of the non-Muslims returned to their homes. Therefore, by 1975 only 13.5% of the population was Hindu, and those who remained were no longer landowners and shopkeepers. Most were poor and low caste farmers and fishermen; the new elite that had emerged was almost exclusively Muslim.[298]

Hundreds of remaining Hindu temples in Pakistan were razed in 1992, after the destruction of the Bari Mosque in India. The coming to power of the Muhammad Zia ul-Haq dictatorship in 1977 radicalized the population, as did his system of martial law.[299]

Pakistani religious schools (*madrassas*) also supported and participated in the genocide in Pakistan, later trained the Afghan *mujahideen* against the Soviet Union, and then schooled the Taliban movement that conquered most of the initial *mujahideen* warlords.[300] The fundamentalist Islamic party "supported Pakistan against the Bengali nationalists during the liberation war, and most of its leaders had fled to (West) Pakistan after 1971."[301] Since at least 1986, Christian and Ahmadis Pakistanis have suffered extreme levels of persecution that, if not quite genocide under a narrow understanding of the term, certainly approach ethnic cleansing as defined by the Yugoslav and Rwanda tribunals,

---

298. Bertil Lintner, *The Plights of Ethnic and Religious Minorities and the Rise of Islamic Extremism in Bangladesh* (Feb. 2, 2003), http://www.asiapacificms.com/papers/pdf/ethnic_and_religious_minorities_bangladesh.pdf.

299. *See* Peter Jacob, *The Identity Question for Christians in Pakistan, in* 1 Religious Minorities in South Asia: Selected Essays on Post-Colonial Situations 161–63 (Monirul Hussain & Lipi Ghosh eds., New Delhi: Manak Publications, 2002); S. Zulfiquar Gilani, *Ahmedis and the Problem of National Identity in Pakistan, in id.* at 139.

300. *See* Bertil Lintner, *Bangladesh: Extremist Islamist Consolidation,* 14 Faultlines: Writings on Conflict and Resolution 1 (2003), http://www.satp.org/satporgtp/publication/faultlines/volume14/Article1.htm.

301. Hobsbawm, The Age of Extremes, at 219.

with policies by the Pakistani authorities to use the blasphemy laws to "threaten, punish, or intimidate Ahmadis, Christians, and even orthodox Muslims." The State Department notes that religious minorities "have been sentenced to death, and religious extremists have killed persons accused under the provisions." One Christian writer was shot at his 1997 trial under these laws, and sentenced to death anyway in 1998. Christianity is actually an indigenous religion of Pakistan, dating to a first century CE missionary journey.[302]

3. Afghanistan and Central Asia

The King of Afghanistan was assassinated in 1933,[303] leaving his throne to his 19-year old son Zahir.[304] King Zahir Shah would preside over the slow improvement of living conditions in Afghanistan for over 40 years after his father's death in 1933.[305] As Prime Minister, the King's first cousin Muhammad Daoud Khan strove to develop Afghanistan's economy by securing vast amounts of economic and military aid from the neighboring Soviet Union.[306] The U.S. also initiated several important development projects in Afghanistan, but declined to supply military aid.[307]

In the early Cold War period Prime Minister Daoud quelled an armed uprising in Kandahar with advanced weaponry obtained from the Soviet Union.[308] In 1959, Daoud created a major cultural crisis when the wives and daughters of the Afghan royal family appeared unveiled for the first time since Amanullah's reign. Many religious leaders publicly condemned this display, but Daoud argued that Islam did not make the veiling and seclusion of women obligatory.[309] Other educated women, particularly in Kabul, then began to abandon the veil, including growing numbers of nurses, midwives, and teachers.[310] In response, the more conservative mullahs provoked riots and acid attacks on un-

---

302. *See* USDOS, *International Religious Freedom Report 1999: Pakistan* (1999), http://atheism.about.com/library/irf/irf99/blirf_pakistan99.htm.

303. He was shot to death while visiting a school in Kabul. *See* EWANS, AFGHANISTAN, at 103.

304. *See* VOGELSANG, THE AFGHANS, at 288.

305. *See id.* at 288–89; POULLADA & POULLADA, THE KINGDOM OF AFGHANISTAN, at 163–66.

306. Daoud helped broker agreements for the Soviet Union and its satellites to supply Afghanistan with advanced Soviet military training and weaponry, including tanks, helicopters, and fighter-bombers. *See* EWANS, AFGHANISTAN, at 109–10; A COUNTRY STUDY: AFGHANISTAN (Peter R. Blood ed., Washington, DC: The Library of Congress, 2001), http://countrystudies.us/afghanistan/26.htm; USDOS, *Country Fact Sheet: Afghanistan*, DEPARTMENT OF STATE DISPATCH No. 23 (June 6, 1994) ($1 billion in Soviet aid starting in 1954). Among other projects, the Soviet Union built an international airport for Kabul, roads connecting Afghanistan's three major cities with each other and with the Soviet Union, a tunnel at 11,000 feet through 1.7 miles of the towering Hindu Kush mountains that divide Kabul from the north of Afghanistan, paved streets for Kabul, and a number of grain silos. *See* EWANS, AFGHANISTAN, at 112–13.

307. The U.S. oversaw the construction of an international airport in Kandahar and developed Afghanistan's national airline Ariana; led the building of roads from Kabul to Kandahar and from Afghanistan to Iran and Pakistan, then both friendly with the United States; and provided educational assistance. *See* EWANS, AFGHANISTAN, at 114–15. President Eisenhower also visited Kabul to proclaim American friendship. *See id.*

308. *See* M. HASSAN KAKAR, AFGHANISTAN: THE SOVIET INVASION AND THE AFGHAN RESPONSE, 1979–1982, at Introduction (1995), http://ark.cdlib.org/ark:/13030/ft7b69p12h.

309. *See* EWANS, AFGHANISTAN, at 115.

310. *See* KAKAR, AFGHANISTAN, at Introduction.

veiled women,[311] until Daoud had about 50 of them jailed and charged with treason and heresy.[312] Daoud finally released the mullahs from custody, and they brought the unrest to a halt, agreeing that each Afghan family would be allowed to decide for itself whether its women would practice *purdah*.[313]

In the 1960s, Afghanistan's third constitution propelled the nation further towards democracy and respect for human rights, but like its 1923 model it would eventually fall to a combination of foreign intervention and the violent opposition of local radicals. This time, the communists and fundamentalists would divide the country between them. King Zahir Shah set out to establish a constitutional monarchy that would provide for more democratic input and thereby build public support for the regime. Despite Daoud's large victories in winning superpower development aid and ensuring greater participation for Afghan women in public life, the King successfully pressured him to resign as Prime Minister in 1963.[314] The next year, a Loya Jirga ratified a new constitution, drafted with French assistance. Afghanistan's 1964 constitution "limited the monarch's absolute power through the creation of a parliament and the clear separation of powers."[315] The King could no longer enact laws without the approval of both houses of parliament.[316] But he retained broad executive powers, including the power to declare war and command the army.[317] The lower house of the Afghan parliament and one-third of the Afghan Senate would be elected to four-year terms by direct elections, subject to the king dissolving parliament and calling new elections at any time and for any cause.[318]

The 1964 constitution loosened the requirements of previous Afghan constitutions that the state be governed in accordance with Sharia law.[319] Like the 1923 constitution, it recognized Islam as the "sacred" and official religion of Afghanistan.[320] But the 1964 constitution did not require that all Afghan laws conform to Sharia as such, stating that "there shall be no law repugnant to the basic *principles* of the sacred religion of Islam and the other values embodied in this constitution."[321] This reference to general "principles" provided the legislature with greater leeway to enact laws that presented some tension with the tenets of Islamic law taken literally.[322] The 1964 constitution no longer gave Sharia equal status with Afghanistan's "general civil and criminal laws,"[323] but made it authoritative only where no statute existed in the area.[324] Women won the right to vote in parliamentary elections,

---

311. *See* Vogelsang, The Afghans, at 293.

312. The heresy charge was leveled on the theory that King Zahir Shah ruled Afghanistan by divine right, a notion later incorporated into Afghanistan's 1964 constitution. *See* Ewans, Afghanistan, at 115; Const. of Afgh. 1964, art. 15.

313. *See* Ewans, Afghanistan, at 115.

314. *See id.* at 115–120.

315. *The Sound of the Sixties*, The Economist, Oct. 26, 2002, at 41.

316. *See* Const. of Afgh. 1964, art. 69. *Compare id.* art. 9(8), *with id.* art. 9(7), *and id.* art. 9(10).

317. *See id.* art. 9.

318. *See id.* arts. 43–44. The constitution filled the remaining one-third of the Afghan Senate by having local provincial councils each elect one of their members to serve three-year terms in that body. *See id.* art. 44.

319. *Cf.* Ewans, Afghanistan, at 120 (1964 constitution expressed "clear preference for a secular legal system").

320. *See* Const. of Afghanistan 1964, art. 2.

321. *Id.* art. 64 (emphasis added). *Compare* Const. of Afgh. 1923, art. 72.

322. *See* Cheryl Benard et al., *Democracy and Islam in the New Constitution of Afghanistan* (2003), http://www.rand.org/publications/CF/CF186/CF186.pdf.

323. Const. of Afgh. 1923, art. 21.

324. Const. of Afgh. 1964, art. 69.

be elected to parliament, serve as members of government, and even become government ministers.[325] These rights became a reality for the first time in Afghan history, as several women won seats in parliament,[326] and a woman became minister of public health.[327]

Ultimately, the 1964 constitution's most enduring legacy may be that radical elements in Afghan society misused its freedoms to prepare the way for dictatorship and the deaths of countless Afghans. Afghan communists, some of whom had been barred from Kabul University or recalled from study or work in the U.S. for expressing their radical ideas, became free to organize.[328] Although the Kabul area elected a few leftists as representatives in the first elections under the 1964 Constitution, the parliament as a whole was dominated by the rural landowners and conservative religious leaders who could afford the high costs of running for office,[329] which led many progressive young students and middle-class Afghans in Kabul to despair of democracy, and seek more radical solutions.[330]

In 1965, Muhammad Taraki and Babrak Karmal founded the People's Democratic Party of Afghanistan (PDPA), the Communist Party of Afghanistan "in all but name."[331] The PDPA attracted a growing membership among young students and intellectuals in Kabul University and the urban Afghan middle class.[332] Afghan voters elected three PDPA members to the Afghan parliament in 1965, including Karmal.[333] The principal of Kabul Teachers College, Hafizullah Amin, joined the PDPA and was elected to parliament in 1969.[334] Each of these three men—Taraki, Karmal, and Amin—would go on to assume the helm of dictatorial left-wing Afghan regimes.

Prominent Afghan fundamentalists lacked the public support necessary to be elected as such to the parliament as PDPA members were, but they organized disciplined cadres of followers during the 1960s and 1970s. The ideas of the Egyptian fundamentalist Sayyed Qutb, the "intellectual light" of the Muslim Brotherhood, "attracted particular interest" in the Kabul Sharia faculty.[335] Al-Aznar University in Egypt, which had taken the Kabul Sharia faculty under its wing,[336] was a center of the Muslim Brotherhood's fundamentalist political activity.[337] The head of the Kabul Sharia department, Professor Ghulam Muhammad Niazi, was deeply influenced by the Muslim Brotherhood's campaign for Islamic fundamentalist rule while studying at al-Aznar University.[338] The fundamentalist program of the Muslim Brotherhood and its progeny of jihadist groups is, in brief, a holy war that would replace the corrupt monarchs of Muslim countries with Islamic states that would govern all aspects of life, strictly segregating men and women and providing "humanity a complete cure for all its ills."[339]

---

325. *The Sound of the Sixties.*

326. *See* Vogelsang, The Afghans, at 296.

327. *See* Ariane Brunet & Isabelle Helal, *Seizing an Opportunity: Afghan Women and the Constitution-Making Process* (Sept. 2003), http://www.ichrdd.ca/english/commdoc/publications/women/afghanMissionReportSept2003Eng.html.

328. *See* Ewans, Afghanistan, at 122–23.

329. *See id.* at 121.

330. *See* Vogelsang, The Afghans, at 296.

331. *See* Ewans, Afghanistan, at 122–24.

332. *See id.* at 123–24.

333. *See* Vogelsang, The Afghans, at 297.

334. *See* Ewans, Afghanistan, at 123.

335. *See* Robert Irwin, *Is This the Man Who Inspired Bin Laden?*, The Guardian, Nov. 1, 2001.

336. *See id.*

337. *See id.* at 298. Most of Afghanistan's judges were trained at Al-Azhar University. *See* Barnett R. Rubin, *The Fragmentation of Afghanistan*, Foreign Affairs, 1989, at 150.

338. *See* Vogelsang, The Afghans, at 298.

339. *See* Kakar, Afghanistan, at 2.4.

From his perch as professor of Sharia law, Professor Niazi led the fundamentalist movement in Afghanistan. He established cells in Kabul and Paghman dedicated to formulating strategy, and developed contacts with sympathetic government officials.[340] Joining Niazi in his campaign for an Islamic revolution in Afghanistan were two other graduates of al-Azhar University, whose fundamentalism would determine the course of Afghan history for generations: Burhannudin Rabbani and Abdul Rasul Sayyaf.[341] Mr. Rabbani, who had translated the writings of Sayyed Qutb into the Afghan language of Dari,[342] succeeded Professor Niazi as Amir of the Islamic Association of Afghanistan in 1972.[343] Around this time, a young student leader at Kabul University named Gulbuddin Hekmatyar joined the Muslim Brotherhood[344] and shortly became famous for throwing acid in the faces of unveiled Afghan women.[345] Rabbani, Sayyaf, and Hekmatyar would each go on to lead the fundamentalist revolt against the Afghan constitutional monarchy, then the Afghan communists, and finally against the Soviet occupation of Afghanistan. Eventually, each of them would govern entire mini-states, but none of them could ever quite manage to bring all of Afghanistan under his faction's control.[346]

Despite Afghanistan's slow but steady progress in promoting democratic input and women's rights under Zahir Shah, Afghan leftists demanded immediate and sweeping change. But the socialist and communist ideology to which they turned sparked implacable opposition in Afghanistan's conservative religious leaders, setting the stage for the decades-long struggle between Soviet-backed leftist governments and Pakistani-based fundamentalist *jihadi* fighters

With extremists organizing feverishly, the Afghan economy entered a tailspin in the early 1970s. During its long reign, and despite massive foreign aid, the monarchy had done little to improve Afghanistan's standing as one of the poorest, least healthy, and worst educated countries in the world. About 50% of Afghan children died before reaching the age of five, 80% of Afghan children received no education, and "the per capita income, at $157, was one of the lowest in the world."[347] Government corruption and a three-year drought from 1969 to 1972 brought on a famine that killed between 100,000 and 500,000 Afghans.[348]

---

340. *See id.* at B, "Niazi."

341. *See id.* at B, "Rabbani," & "Sayyaf"; VOGELSANG, THE AFGHANS, at 298.

342. *See* Irwin, *Is This the Man?*

343. *See Rabbani's Afghan Comeback*, BBC NEWS ONLINE, Nov. 14, 2001, *at* http://news.bbc.co.uk/1/hi/world/south_asia/1656013.stm.

344. *See Profile of an Afghan Warlord* (Australian Broadcasting Corp. broadcast, Nov. 22, 2001), http://www.abc.net.au/worldtoday/stories/s423361.htm.

345. *See* John F. Burns, *Afghans: Now They Blame America*, N.Y. TIMES MAGAZINE, Feb. 4, 1990, at 6–22 ("As a Kabul student leader during the early 1970's, [Hekmatyar] had dispatched followers to throw vials of acid into the faces of women students who refused to wear veils."). In the Afghan context, such attacks can be a fate worse then death, due to the importance of finding a husband for financial support. *Cf.* Lisa M. Taylor, *Saving Face: Acid Attack Laws After the U.N. Convention on the Elimination of All Forms of Discrimination Against Women*, 29 GA. J. INT'L & COMP. L. 395, 400 n.25 (2001).

346. *See* VOGELSANG, THE AFGHANS, at 298.

347. Burns, *Afghans: Now They Blame America,* at 6–22. *See also* Barry Kramer, *Out of Isolation: Afghanistan Is Pushing Toward the 20th Century With Bold Spending Plan, but Tribesman Resist,* WALL ST. J., Sept. 2, 1977, at 22 ("Afghanistan is plagued by poverty, 90% illiteracy, 50% infant mortality rate and soc[ial] and econ[omic] backwardness").

348. *Compare* EWANS, AFGHANISTAN, at 126 (stating, "100,000 people—some say more—died"), *with* Burns, *Afghans,* at 6–22 (stating that 500,000 Afghans died of starvation in the winter of 1971).

The Afghan famine provided an opening for former Prime Minister Daoud, still popular with the Afghan military,[349] to overthrow the monarchy in 1973.[350] Young officers trained in the Soviet Union executed the coup.[351] Afghanistan became a republic, and Daoud its first President.[352] Half of his cabinet ministers in were communists allied with the Parcham faction of the PDPA led by Babruk Karmal, and hundreds more communists entered government ministries and provincial officialdom.[353]

The 1977 constitution granted President Daoud near-absolute powers, a common theme among Afghan regimes following the fall of the monarchy.[354] It was also a blueprint for socialism, contemplating dramatic economic and judicial reforms. Article 2, which in all previous Afghan constitutions had proclaimed Islam the sacred religion of Afghanistan, now called for "the exercise of power by the people, the majority of whom consists of farmers, workers, the enlightened people and the youth."[355] The new constitution decreed state ownership for Afghan banks, insurers, large industries, oil and other mineral resources, and communications and transport hubs.[356] Another provision called for land reform,[357] which was sorely needed even by Western standards in that five percent of the landowners then owned 45% of all arable land, with some 400 families owning about 20,000 villages.[358]

A unicameral legislature elected by all Afghans over the age of 18, half of which would be reserved for farmers and the working class, would draft legislation.[359] All laws contrary to the "basic principles" of the religion of Islam remained unconstitutional,[360] but for the first time in Afghan history, the country's constitution specifically stated that "women and men," and not simply all Afghan "subjects" or "people," were entitled to equality before the law.[361]

Daoud saw the fundamentalists as the greatest threat to a modern Afghanistan, so he arrested Niazi and 200 other fundamentalist plotters in Kabul.[362] By one account, this action began the war between leftists and fundamentalists that continued for almost 20 years, until the near-obliteration of the Afghan left and the communist movement after the dissolution of the Soviet Union and the *mujahideen* victory in 1992.[363] The fundamentalists who had fled to Pakistan from Daoud's mass arrests, including Rabbani and Hekmatyar, helped organized a holy war against Daoud's regime from their new base in Pakistan.[364] The most successful operation was an incursion from Pakistan into Afghanistan's

---

349. *See* Vogelsang, The Afghans, at 299.
350. *See* Cooley, Unholy Wars, at 11.
351. *See id.*; Blood, Afghanistan, http://countrystudies.us/afghanistan/28.htm.
352. *See* Blood, Afghanistan.
353. *See* Kakar, Afghanistan, at 3.9–3.12.
354. *See id.* at 301.
355. Afg. Const. of 1977, art. 2.
356. *See id.* art. 13; Vogelsang, The Afghans, at 301.
357. *See id.*, art. 14
358. *See* Raja Anwar, The Tragedy of Afghanistan 130 (1988).
359. *See* Const. of Afgh. 1977, art. 21.
360. *See id.* art. 64.
361. *See id.* art. 27.
362. *See* Vogelsang, The Afghans, at 300.
363. *See id.*
364. *See id.* at 300; Ewans, Afghanistan, at 155; Antonio Giostozzi, *Re-building the Afghan Army* (2003), *at* http://bglatzer.de/arg/arp/giustozzi.pdf. Pakistan trained and armed the Afghan fundamentalists such as Hekmatyar. *See* George Arney, *The Heroes with Tarnished Haloes: The Ruthless and Murderous Conflicts of Afghanistan's Other War*, The Guardian (U.K.), Jan. 5, 1988, http://www.guardian.co.uk; Ewans, Afghanistan, at 131; John Kifner, *Afghanistan, by Custom, Has Rebels Everywhere*, N.Y. Times, May 14, 1989, at E2.

Panjshir valley led by Ahmed Shah Massoud, who would become one of Rabbani's best commanders.[365] The revolution failed, however, and the fundamentalist movement splintered into factions led by Rabbani and Hekmatyar.[366]

The Soviet Union also became concerned that Daoud was being drawn into a pro-American stance with Saudi money, and began pressuring the divided Afghan communists to unite to overthrow him, which they did. When Daoud issued an order for his communist opponents to be arrested, it triggered a revolution.[367]

In April 1978, communist military officers turned Afghanistan's air force and tanks against the Daoud regime. The air force bombed the presidential palace, killing President Daoud and many members of his family. The first decree of the leaders of the revolution bestowed ultimate authority on the head of the PDPA, Nur Muhammad Taraki.[368] Another decree gave men and women equal rights, prohibited forced marriages, established a minimum marriageable age of 16 for girls, and reduced the bride price to a low fixed minimum amount to discourage the widespread sale of young Afghan girls by their parents.[369] "The Government called for women to enjoy freedom, to dress as they please, work in the civil service, armed forces and other institutions and enjoy other equal rights."[370] Taraki's regime introduced universal education for boys and girls and a campaign against illiteracy, and enacted a "far-reaching redistribution of land" from large landlords to peasants.[371]

President Taraki's government rapidly lost control of the country to anti-regime forces, which in early 1979 led several Afghan provinces in open rebellion, including Nuristan and Hazarajat.[372] The Soviet leadership believed that the CIA was fomenting fundamentalist opposition with the purpose of replacing U.S. bases lost in Iran after the 1979 revolution.[373] Iranian fundamentalists, fresh from establishing the Iranian theocracy under Ayatollah Ruhollah Khomeini, inspired a revolt in the large Afghan city of Herat close to the Iranian border,[374] drawing on outrage there against the government's efforts to promote Afghan women's literacy. An army officer named Ismail Khan organized a mutiny of the Afghan armed forces in the Herat area. In response, the government bombed the city and waged a devastating assault with tanks and helicopters, killing up to 20,000 people and razing many buildings. These events prompted Prime Minister Amin, who had gained influence over the Afghan security services, to seize power, killing his former comrade Taraki.[375]

In July 1979, President Carter signed a national security directive authorizing secret American aid to the Pakistan-based rebellion against the Afghan government.[376] Carter's national security adviser advised him at the time that this aid would likely result in a Soviet invasion, and later boasted of "drawing the Russians into the Afghan trap."[377] The Defense

---

365. *See* Ewans, Afghanistan, at 131.

366. *See* Vogelsang, The Afghans, at 300.

367. *See* Vogelsang, The Afghans, at 301–4.

368. *See* Vogelsang, The Afghans, at 304–5. His deputies were the other two leading Afghan communists, Babrak Karmal and Hafiz Allah Amin. *See id.*

369. *See* Amnesty International, *Women in Afghanistan: Pawns in Men's Power Struggles*, Nov. 1, 1999; Vogelsang, The Afghans, at 304.

370. Richard Ehrlich, *Feminism, Afghan Style*, The Advertiser (Australia), Dec. 5, 1987.

371. *See* Vogelsang, The Afghans, at 304; Ewans, Afghanistan, at 139.

372. *See* Vogelsang, The Afghans, at 306–7.

373. *See* Cooley, Unholy Wars, at 13–19.

374. *See id.* at 306.

375. Ewans, Afghanistan, at 143.

376. *See* Phillip C. Wilcox, Striking Terror: America's New War 80 (Robert B. Silvers & Barbara Epstein eds., New York: New York Review Books, 2002); Cooley, Unholy Wars, at 13, 19–22

377. Wilcox, Striking Terror, at 80; Cooley, Unholy Wars, at 13, 19–22.

Department believed at the time that "there was value in keeping the Afghan insurgency going, 'sucking the Soviets into a Vietnamese quagmire.'"[378]

On December 27, 1979, Soviet forces in and around Kabul captured the main government ministries, neutralized key Afghan army units, and fanned out to other major Afghan cities such as Herat and Kandahar.[379] Soon the Soviet occupying army reached 85,000 men.[380] Before the Red Army's defeat almost another 700,000 men would follow.[381]

The Soviets installed PDPA founder Babruk Karmal as President of Afghanistan. Karmal promulgated a new constitution in 1980 that purported to establish the rule of the Afghan people and recognize a similar list of individual rights as those recognized in previous constitutions.[382] The constitution no longer enshrined Islam as a bulwark of the government's legitimacy. All political parties other than the PDPA were outlawed.[383] With the Red Army occupying the nerve centers of Afghan society, moreover, the Soviet leadership, rather than the PDPA or the Afghan people, was the real power in Afghanistan during the 1980s.[384]

Karmal and his Soviet handlers reaffirmed and expanded the efforts of Daoud and Taraki regimes before them to promote greater equality for Afghan women. The communists "officially sanctioned a wider public role for women, whose status improved."[385] By 1985, 65% of the students at Kabul University were women, and Afghan women worked in most government agencies, social organizations, factories, the national airline, and the health care sector.[386] By the time the communists lost power, "women accounted for 70 percent of teachers, 50 percent of government workers, and 40 percent of medical doctors."[387] Women worked as police officers, members of the military, and journalists.[388] Afghan women increasingly appeared unveiled in public, as their counterparts in Soviet Central Asia had done decades previously.[389] Communist reforms in-

---

378. ROBERT GATES, FROM THE SHADOWS: THE ULTIMATE INSIDER'S STORY OF FIVE PRESIDENTS AND HOW THEY WON THE COLD WAR 145 (New York: Simon & Schuster, 1997).

379. EWANS, AFGHANISTAN, at 146–48; BLOOD, AFGHANISTAN. The Soviet Union claimed that it had been invited into Afghanistan by the besieged Taraki regime pursuant to a mutual defense treaty, but historians tend to reject these claims, citing a lack of evidence. *See, e.g.*, KAKAR, AFGHANISTAN, at Chapter 2. Although Taraki, the initial leader of the Afghan communist government, had signed a military assistance treaty with the Soviets, and pleaded with them for both "men and weapons" after the revolt in Heart, he was dead by the time of the invasion. *See id.* While it is undisputed that Taraki's rival Karmal welcomed the Soviet invasion, some historians deny that he had the authority to invite the Soviets in because he was not even living in Afghanistan at the time. *See id.*

380. *See* EWANS, AFGHANISTAN, at 146–48

381. *See* VOGELSANG, THE AFGHANS, at 321.

382. *See id.* at 309; KAKAR, AFGHANISTAN, at ch. 2.

383. *See* VOGELSANG, THE AFGHANS, at 309.

384. *See, e.g.*, KAKAR, AFGHANISTAN, at ch. 3.

385. USDOS, *Afghanistan Human Rights Practices, 1993* (Jan. 31, 1994), *at* http://64.233.167.104/search?q=cache:wGmeiZXg-jMJ:dosfan.lib.uic.edu/ERC/democracy/1993_hrp_report/93hrp_report_sasia/Afghanistan.html+%22Afghanistan+Human+Rights+Practices,+1993+%22&hl=en.

386. *See* Valentine Moghadam, *Afghan Women and Transnational Feminism*, 16 MIDDLE EAST WOMEN'S STUDIES REV. 1–6 (2001/2002), http://www.amews.org/review/reviewarticles/transnational_feminism.htm.

387. Sharon Lerner, *A Place at the Table*, VILLAGE VOICE, Dec. 11, 2001, at 39, http://www.villagevoice.com/issues/0149/lerner.php.

388. *See* Moghadam, *Afghan Women*.

389. *See* Carlotta Gall, *Afghan Women Lose their Rights*, CALGARY HERALD, Oct. 9, 1992, at A20.

truded into Afghan family life when the communists banned the purchase and sale of young girls as wives, and provoked rage by demanding that fathers allow their daughters to learn to read. The regime's family courts were "mostly presided over by female judges" and protected women's rights in marriage and divorce and to equitable child custody and support.[390]

Whatever hope existed for true equality between Afghan women and men, rich and poor, was lost in the genocidal war between Soviet and Afghan communist forces and the fundamentalist insurgents backed by the Western and wider Islamic worlds. Soon after the Soviet invasion began, the U.S. coordinated an international campaign of support for the anti-communist *jihad* that had been waged from the fundamentalists' safe haven in Pakistan for several years prior to the Soviet intervention. Pakistan agreed to set up training camps for Afghan and foreign fighters, Saudi Arabia to contribute large sums of cash, and Egypt to bequeath their stocks of Soviet-made assault rifles.[391] The *mujahideen* eventually received over $10 billion, almost $5 billion from the U.S. and $3 billion from Saudi Arabia.[392]

President Reagan and Pakistani dictator Zia ul-Haq directed billions in American military aid for the *mujahideen*, mostly to "the more extreme Sunni fundamentalist faction led by Gulbuddin Hekmatyar."[393] Hekmatyar used the money to organize a tightly disciplined faction for the day when he would "impose an authoritarian Islamic state that would sequester women and punish Moslems who don't practice their faith."[394] With great violence, his party forced Afghan women refugees in Pakistan to bury themselves in *burqas*.[395] Several Afghan women were murdered in Pakistan simply for failing to cover their hair.[396]

Saudi Arabia favored the armies of Abdul Rasul Sayyaf,[397] whose party "recruited thousands of fighters from Arab countries."[398] Like Hetmatyar, Sayyaf had little indigenous support in Afghanistan, but grew powerful because of the prolific Saudi money and foreign weaponry at its disposal.[399] In 1980, Sayyaf recruited a number of "Afghan Arabs" to

---

390. *See* Moghadam, *Afghan Women*.

391. *See* COOLEY, UNHOLY WARS, at 15–16, 59, 65–69, 100, 95, 108–110.

392. *See* RASHID, TALIBAN, at 18; SAMUEL P. HUNTINGTON, THE CLASH OF CIVILIZATIONS AND THE REMAKING OF THE WORLD ORDER at 247 (New York: Simon & Schuster, 1998).

393. HUNTINGTON, THE CLASH OF CIVILIZATIONS, at 247. The Reagan administration awarded one-third of the CIA's financial aid to the *mujahideen* and powerful anti-aircraft Stinger missiles to Hekmatyar's faction, which used this support to gain even more influence among Afghans. *See* Ahmed Rashid, *Afghan Designs; Geneva Accord on Afghanistan*, THE NATION, May 21, 1988, at 700; Richard Ehrlich, *Afghan Rebels at Each Others' Throats*, TORONTO STAR, Jan. 31, 1988, at H3.

394. Barry Shlachter, *Most-Disciplined Afghan Rebel Faction Seeks Strict Islamic State*, ASSOCIATED PRESS, Jan. 1, 1982. At the time, Hekmatyar was on "good terms" with the regime of Ayatollah Khomeini in Iran. *Id.*

395. Christina Lamb, *Westernised Women Dread Return to a Veiled Existence*, FINANCIAL TIMES (U.K.), June 23, 1989, at 6.

396. *See* Jan Goodwin & Jessica Neuwirth, *The Rifle and the Veil*, N.Y. TIMES, Oct. 19, 2001, at A19.

397. *Grand Council to Begin Historic Work: Turbaned Delegates in High-Tech Setting Chart the Future: A New Day for Afghanistan*, EDMONTON JOURNAL (CANADA), June 9, 2002, at A4. *See also* RASHID, TALIBAN, at 131 (Saudis used Sayyaf to "promote Wahhabism"); RALPH H. MAGNUS & EDEN NABY, AFGHANISTAN: MULLAH, MARX, AND MUJAHID at 97 (Boulder, Colo.: Westview Press, 1998).

398. *Grand Council to Begin Historic Work*, at A4. The Arab-Afghans had "very good relations" with both Sayyaf and Hekmatyar according to Ahmed Shah Massoud, who was later killed on the orders of the most famous one of them, bin Laden. RASHID, TALIBAN, at viii, 132–33.

399. *See* JASON BURKE, AL-QAEDA: CASTING A SHADOW OF TERROR 55 (London: I.B. Tauris, 2003).

the Afghan cause,[400] including Osama bin Laden, who was working with the CIA at the time.[401]

Both sides abandoned laws and constitutions in a common descent into wanton violations of human rights. By 1987, the communists and fundamentalists had killed more than one million Afghans by some estimates,[402] and had driven another seven million from their homes.[403] The Soviets carpet bombed major Afghan cities such as Herat and Kandahar into ruins, wiped half of Afghanistan's villages off the map, and destroyed much of the country's farmland.[404] While Afghanistan's population declined by 1.2 million by 1990, it would have had four million more inhabitants in 1990 had its population growth resembled that of the rest of Asia.[405]

The Afghan resistance continually replenished its dead with new recruits from the millions of refugees in Pakistan and Iran, and armed them with fresh infusions of American and Saudi aid.[406] The *mujahideen* gained control of up to 90% of the countryside and became "immensely wealthy" by making it the world's second largest opium producing land.[407]

Although the scale of the bombing and shelling of Afghan cities and towns posed the greatest threat to human rights, the *mujahideen*'s fundamentalist policies promised to overturn decades of progress towards including Afghan women in public life. During the 1980s, women rarely walked the streets in rebel-controlled regions of Afghanistan. "Those who leave their homes wear the chador [or *burqa*], a voluminous shroud covering the wearer from head to toe, and may only survey the world through a 4-by-4-inch rectangle of netting extending from the tip of the nose to the eyebrows." In Pakistani refugee camps run by the rebels, women were denied access to areas containing men, and prohibiting from seeing male doctors.[408] (When the Taliban continued these policies, the U.S. cited them to help justify the war.[409])

---

400. *Id.* at 55, 66, 125, 145; Vincent Cannistraro *A Strike Against Terrorism—and Ourselves?*, Boston Globe, Aug. 23, 1998, at E1 ("At 18, [bin Laden] joined Abd'al Rauf Sayyaf, an Afghan tribal leader who was trained in Saudi Arabia by the Wahabis."). Sayyaf has even been described as a "mentor" to bin Laden. Mary Anne Weaver, Pakistan: in the Shadow of Jihad and Afghanistan 191, 201, 222, 269 (New York: Farrar, Straus, and Giroux, 2002).

401. *See* Edgar O'Ballance, Afghan Wars: Battles in a Hostile Land 245 (London: Brassey's, 2002). Bin Laden built a major CIA-financed tunnel complex and arms depot for the *mujahideen* in 1986. *See* Rashid, Taliban, at 132; Michael Moran, *Bin Laden Comes Home to Roost: His CIA Ties Are Only the Beginning of a Woeful Story*, MSNBC, Aug. 23, 1998, http://www.msnbc.com/news/190144.asp?cp1=1.

402. *See, e.g.*, Russell Watson & John Barry, *Insurgencies: Two of a Kind*, Newsweek, Mar. 23, 1987, at 32; John F. Burns, *Misery Replaces Hope in a Battered Afghanistan*, N.Y. Times, Dec. 17, 1989, at 26 (1.3 million); Lamb, *Westernised Women Dread Return to a Veiled Existence*, at 6 (1.5 million).

403. *See* Watson & Barry, *Insurgencies*, at 32; *see also* Special Rapporteur on Afghanistan of the Commission on Human Rights, Supplementary Material to the Interim Report on the Situation of Human Rights in Afghanistan, *quoted in* Juliana Geran Pilon, *The Report that the U.N. Wants to Suppress: Soviet Atrocities in Afghanistan*, Heritage Foundation Reports (Jan. 12, 1987), http://www.heritage.org.

404. *See* Burns, *Afghans*, at 6–22; Watson & Barry, *Insurgencies*, at 32. *See also* Pilon, *The Report that the U.N. Wants to Suppress.*

405. The population of Asia as a whole increased by 20% in the 1980s. *See* U.N. Dept. of Economic and Social Affairs, World Population Prospects: The 2004 Revision 680 (U.N. Publications, 2005).

406. Huntington, The Clash of Civilizations, at 247.

407. *See* Ewans, Afghanistan, at 160–61; Arney, *The Heroes with Tarnished Haloes.*

408. *See Afghan Women Face Future of Backwardness*, S.F. Chron., June 1, 1989, at A22.

409. *See* The White House, Office of Mrs. Bush, *Radio Address by Laura Bush* (Nov. 17, 2001), http://www.whitehouse.gov/news/releases/2001/11/20011117.html; USDOS, Office of the Senior Co-

In 1987, the new Soviet leader Mikhail Gorbachev decided to withdraw entirely from Afghanistan.[410] The Soviets planned to leave the country to Najib Allah, the former head of the Afghan secret police, who had taken over from Karmal as the Afghan communist leader in 1986.[411] Najib Allah convened a Loya Jirga in 1987 to signal the moderation of the communist regime's policies. The 1987 constitution it passed once again enshrined Islam as the sacred religion of Afghanistan and provided that no law could be contrary to its "principles" and the other values in the constitution.[412] It guaranteed equal rights to men and women and among religious minorities in a similar manner to previous constitutions,[413] and provided for a number of individual rights to be defined in accordance with the law.[414] The ruling communist PDPA party lost its majority of seats in parliament after elections held in 1988 pursuant to the new constitution, and a member of Daoud's pre-communist government became Prime Minister.[415] Najib Allah even reserved seats in parliament for *mujahideen* leaders, and invited them to lay down their arms and participate in a mixed government, an offer that they refused.[416]

The Soviets completed their withdrawal from Afghanistan in 1989.[417] The day after the last troops had returned, Gorbachev proposed a cease-fire between the communists and fundamentalist parties to U.S. President George H.W. Bush, with the two superpowers agreeing to halt shipments of weapons until democratic elections under U.N. supervision could be held. The Bush administration and the Afghan rebels refused to negotiate, with the result that for years, the *mujahideen* supplied by the U.S. continued indiscriminate rocket attacks on Afghan towns and cities, killing up to 40 people in each blast.[418]

Nevertheless, the Afghan communist regime of Najib Allah survived, sustained by a combination of rebel infighting and billions of dollars in Soviet military aid.[419] Najib Allah convened a *Loya Jirga* in 1990, promising to achieve national reconciliation and moderate the communist face of the Afghan government. The resulting 1990 constitution proclaimed Afghanistan a multi-party state to be governed according to laws in conformity with the principles of Islam, including the right to own and inherit property pursuant to Sharia law.[420] The commanding heights of the economy remained state property, but private investment was allowed, at least in theory.[421] The National Assembly, selected by a mixture of direct elections and appointments as under previous constitutions, approved laws prior to the president's signature,[422] with a Constitutional Commission exercising limited review.[423]

---

ordinator for International Women's Issues, *Fact Sheet: Women and Girls in Afghanistan* (Oct. 30, 2001), http://www.state.gov/p/sa/rls/fs/index.cfm?docid=5795.

410. *See* EWANS, AFGHANISTAN, at 167–68

411. *See* Craig Karp, *Afghanistan: Seven Years of Soviet Occupation*, DEP'T OF STATE BULLETIN (Feb. 1987), http://www.findarticles.com/p/articles/mi_m1079/is_v87/ai_4754840/print.

412. Const. of Afgh. 1987, art. 2, http://home.no.net/dawat1/constitution_of_afghanistan_1987.htm.

413. *See id.*, art. 38.

414. *See id.*, arts. 39–60.

415. *See* VOGELSANG, THE AFGHANS, at 319.

416. *See* Reuters, *Join Afghan Parliament, Najibullah Urges Rebels*, TORONTO STAR (CANADA), May 30, 1988, at A3.

417. *See* EWANS, AFGHANISTAN, at 168–69.

418. *See* Burns, *Afghans,* at 6–22.

419. *See* EWANS, AFGHANISTAN, at 171–72; VOGELSANG, THE AFGHANS, at 322–23.

420. *See* Const. of Afgh. 1990, arts. 2, 5, 29, http://www.afghan-web.com/history/const/const1990.html.

421. *See id.*, arts. 20, 25, 27; EWANS, AFGHANISTAN, at 175.

422. *See* Const. of Afgh. 1990, arts. 75, 81.

423. *See id.*, arts. 75, 122–24.

The "Islamic revolution" triumphed in Kabul in April 1992.[424] As many had predicted, the victory of the Afghan rebels brought civil war, fundamentalist outrages, and thousands of atrocities against civilians. The Afghan civil wars of the 1990s are a topic of Chapter XIII.

---

424. *See* Felix Ermacora, *Introduction to the Ninth Report of the Special Rapporteur of the Commission on Human Rights on the Human Rights Situation in Afghanistan*, ¶ 31 at 9, U.N. Doc. A/C.3/48/SR.40 (Nov. 23, 1993), http://www.unhchr.ch/Huridocda/Huridoca.nsf/0/c3e13fa375d96e7a80256715003d714d?Opendocument.

Chapter XII

"We Razed Their Houses": The *Anfal* Campaign

> Yes, it exterminates thousands and forces them not to eat or drink and they will have to evacuate their homes without taking anything with them.
>
> —Saddam Hussein[1]

This chapter attempts to analyze the genesis and root causes of Iraq's crime of genocide against its Kurdish and Assyrian inhabitants during the 1980s. It begins with Iraq's independent and early socialist period after the death of King Faisal, turns to the coup that overthrew Prime Minister Abd al-Karim Qasem in 1963, and traces the Kurdish insurgency that followed. The context of the genocide is the Iran-Iraq war and Kurdish rebel support for the Iranian side. The modalities of the genocide were "prohibited" or free-fire zones in northern Iraq; the deportation of the civilian population of northern Iraq into inhospitable mountainous areas; the use of assault weapons, artillery, aircraft, helicopters, and tanks to gun down, bomb, or shell civilians; and the dropping of mustard and sarin gas on inhabited areas in the north.

A. The Emergence of Iraq from Imperial and Colonial Rule

A series of military coups, invasions, and insurrections followed the death of King Faisal in 1933. In all, Iraq had 58 governments in the 37-year period from 1921 to 1958.[2] Although British and British-influenced rule had improved infrastructure and education in many areas, it failed to lift most Iraqis out of poverty or overcome the legacy of Ottoman misrule. Many Iraqis remained in virtual serfdom, as "2% of the landowners owning more than two-thirds of all the useful land." Life expectancy in Iraq was a dismal 26 years, and 90% of the population could not read.[3] Iraqi women were kept almost entirely illiterate and uneducated.[4]

Starvation and famine plagued the Kurdish north and spread to Baghdad, swelling the ranks of the Iraqi Communist Party and sparking an armed Kurdish revolt led by Mul-

---

1. *Quoted in* Kim Sengupta, *Court Hears Tape of Saddam Plotting to Gas the Kurds*, The Independent (U.K.), Jan. 9, 2007, http://www.independent.co.uk/news/world/middle-east/court-hears-tape-of-saddam-plotting-to-gas-the-kurds-431364.html.
2. *See* Catherwood, Churchill's Folly, at 217.
3. *See* Simons, Iraq, at 249, 253.
4. *See* Tripp, A History of Iraq, at 154.

lah Mustafa Barzani. In an early episode among many such defeats, the British-backed Iraqi army routed Barzani's forces, which fled to the Soviet Union.[5] Barzani had already been forced to flee in 1947 after an unsuccessful attempt to declare a Kurdish republic with Soviet backing.[6]

In 1958, left-wing military officers seized power from the heirs to the Iraqi monarchy installed by the British in 1921. The new government promised to claim a greater share of Iraq's oil revenues from the British, enact land reform to benefit poor farmers, and cut the price of food. The state budget devoted to housing, education, and health care doubled.[7] The new Prime Minister, Abd al-Karim Qasem, a half-Arab, half-Kurdish progressive, tried to bridge differences between Iraqis, and welcomed Barzani back to Iraq. The 1958 constitution promulgated by the new regime promoted the Kurds to one of Iraq's two primary nationalities along with Iraqi Arabs.[8] The Agrarian Reform Law of 1958 set a limit on personal land holdings of less than 2,000 acres per person.[9] The regime's push for land reform, however, was blunted when religious fundamentalist parties, including one led by a young mullah named Muhammad Baqir al-Sadr, protested that private property is protected under Islamic Sharia law.[10] The time frame for expropriating excess holdings in land was pushed back just before the fall of the Qasem regime.[11]

B. The Revolutionary Iraq of Qasem and al-Bakr

The Iraqi wing of the Ba'ath Arab Socialist Party was founded in 1954, inspired by the Syrian Ba'ath party established in the late 1940s.[12] The party advanced a pan-Arab secular nationalism with socialist aspirations, which at the same time was hostile to "materialist communism."[13] It regarded the Arab nation as destined to replace the narrow tribal ties of the "Days of Ignorance" with a united community or nation carrying forward its eternal continuity.[14] In stark opposition to Iraqi communists, the Ba'ath party frequently made religious and spiritual declarations, typified by its slogan, "One Arab Nation with an Immortal Message."[15] It even conscripted non-Arab historical figures such as the Babylonian emperor Nebuchadnezzar and the Kurdish Sultan Salah al-Din into service as immortal Arabs.[16]

---

5. *See id.* at 111, 113, 121.

6. *See* Massoud Bārzānī, Mustafa Barzani and the Kurdish Liberation Movement, 1931–1961, at 99–137 (New York: Palgrave Macmillan, 2003).

7. *See* Simons, Iraq, at 254, 257.

8. *See* Tripp, A History of Iraq, at 150–54; Const. of Iraq 1958, art. 3.

9. Gabbay, Agrarian Reform, 109.

10. *See* Tripp, A History of Iraq, at 160–61.

11. *See* Gabbay, *Agrarian Reform*, at 117.

12. *See* George Kerevan, *Ruling Party Learned from Nazis*, The Scotsman (U.K.) (Mar. 29, 2003), at http://thescotsman.scotsman.com/international.cfm?id=371042003.

13. Simons, Iraq, at 235.

14. *Quoted in* Samira Haj, The Making of Iraq: 1900–1963, at 90 (Albany: SUNY Press, 1997).

15. The slogan apparently dates, at least in its constituent parts, to an article written in 1946 by Syrian Ba'ath party co-founder Michel Aflaq, an Arabic-speaking Greek Orthodox Christian from Damascus. The article was entitled "On the Arab Message" and refers to that message as an "eternal message." Kanan Makiya [writing as Samir al-Khalil], Republic of Fear: The Inside Story of Saddam's Iraq 183–84, 192 (New York: Pantheon Books, 1990).

16. *See* Kiernan, Blood and Soil, at 587.

Ba'ath party activists, including a young Saddam Hussein, staged a failed attempt to assassinate Prime Minister Qasem in 1959. Saddam fled to Cairo, but his fellow party activists continued to wage a campaign of urban terror in Baghdad, Mosul, and other cities, murdering communists and their families in a manner reminiscent of Hitler's Nazi brownshirts in the 1930s.[17] The CIA reportedly trained Saddam's hit squad, after cultivating contacts with him as a law student in 1960s Cairo.[18] It later attempted to assassinate Qasem with a poisoned handkerchief.[19] A witness interviewed about the CIA's assassination capability at the time, which was referred to at the time as an "executive action capability," told Congress that the capability was developed in the early Kennedy administration, and was also directed at other potentially pro-Soviet nationalists such as Sukarno of Indonesia, Patrice Lumumba of the Congo, and Fidel Castro of Cuba.[20] There was "no want of trying" to kill foreign leaders at the time, CIA director William Colby stated.[21]

On February 8, 1963, the Ba'ath Party launched a coup against Prime Minister Qasem's government. Communist demonstrators gathering in Baghdad to support Qasem were swept aside by the more heavily armed Ba'athists. The revolutionaries seized the Ministry of Defense and executed Qasem and his lieutenants the next day. The victorious Ba'ath mounted a "systematic campaign of arrests, torture and execution against Iraqi communists and other suspected leftists,"[22] murdering thousands of people in the process.[23] One historian writes:

> Concentration camps and torture centers were set up, and the [Ba'ath] National Guard roamed the streets making arrests, beating suspects, and carrying out arbitrary executions.... Later mass graves were discovered where prisoners had been buried alive. The main targets of the persecution were the leaders of the trade unions and other leftist democratic bodies, such as the Iraqi Women's League, the General Union of Students of the Iraqi Republic (the GUSIR), and the Iraqi Communist Party.

The Ba'athist coup of 1963 resulted in the assassination of Iraq's sitting leader and the executions of thousands of suspected leftists and other civilians. Almost 1,000 Iraqis lost their lives in Baghdad within a few days of the coup.[24] The Ba'ath reign of terror killed 3,000 Iraqis in 1963 alone.[25]

U.S. officials assisted the coup plotters. In February 1963, Prime Minister Qasem, who had allied himself with the Iraqi Communist Party,[26] "received a threatening note from the U.S. State Department," only to be executed in the Ba'athist coup four days later.[27] For many years, the claim of CIA support for the Ba'ath coup could not be verified, as

---

17. *See* Tripp, A History of Iraq, at 158, 162.

18. *See* Lando, Web of Deceit, at 25–27, 272–73 (citing Richard Sale, *Saddam Key in Early CIA Plot*, United Press Int'l, Apr. 10, 2003, a report based on interviews with former U.S. officials); David Morgan, *Ex-U.S. Official Says CIA Aided Baathists*, Reuters, Apr. 20, 2003.

19. *See* David Wise, *A People Betrayed Twice Before*, L.A. Times, Apr. 14, 1991, at Magazine.

20. *See* Interview with Richard Bissel, Deputy Director for Plans, CIA, President's Commission on CIA Activities, Box 32, Apr. 21, 1975, *quoted in* Ralph Edward Weber, Spymasters: Ten CIA Officers in Their Own Words 71–80 (Wilmington, DE: Scholarly Resources Inc., 1999).

21. John Jacob Nutter, The CIA's Black Ops: Covert Action, Foreign Policy, and Democracy 119 (Oxford: Oxford UP, 2000).

22. Tripp, A History of Iraq, at 170–171.

23. *See* Kerevan, *Ruling Party Learned From Nazis*; Simons, Iraq, at 259.

24. *See* Simons, Iraq, at 261, 419 (citing Le Monde (Paris), Feb. 14, 1963).

25. *See* Tripp, A History of Iraq, at 171.

26. *See* Kerevan, *Ruling Party Learned from Nazis.*

27. Simons, Iraq, at 259.

many pertinent records remained classified, and former CIA officials kept their lips sealed. But just after the fall of Saddam Hussein in 2003, press reports surfaced that the Ba'ath coup had received critical support from James H. Critchfield, a "powerful CIA insider during the Cold War" whose responsibilities included recruiting Nazi war criminals and SS officers to spy on the Soviet Union and conduct covert action against targets in communist Eastern Europe.[28] Critchfield, it is now believed, "helped arrange the 1963 coup that overthrew [Qasem] and set in motion the Baath Party's 40-year domination of Iraqi politics."[29] "We knew perhaps six months beforehand that [the coup] was going to happen," Critchfield told The Associated Press just before he died in 2003. "You have to understand the context of the time and the scope of the [communist] threat we were facing," he said. "That's what I say to people who say, 'You guys in the CIA created Saddam Hussein.'"[30] Critchfield, whose job assignment was simply "to stop Communism in Iraq,"[31] claimed credit for "what was happening" in Iraq at the time of the coup, and said the CIA "regarded it as a great victory."[32]

Critchfield's account has been corroborated by other individuals with inside information on relations between the U.S. and Iraq in the early 1960s. The secretary general of the Ba'ath-party declared at one point: "'We came to power on a CIA train.'"[33] A former official on the National Security Council confirmed that "in 1963, two years after the ill-fated U.S. attempt at overthrow in Cuba known as the Bay of Pigs, the CIA helped organize a bloody coup in Iraq that deposed the Soviet-leaning government of [Qasem]." He added that "'it was mostly American money and even American involvement on the ground'" behind the coup. The CIA had previously tried to kill Qasem using a poisoned handkerchief delivered as a gift.[34]

The lists of communists provided by the CIA reportedly included names of leftist suspects and addresses where they could be found by the Ba'ath:

---

28. Mark Fritz, *Ex-CIA Official James Critchfield Dies*, Associated Press, Apr. 23, 2003 (Critchfield justified his "recommendation in the early 1960s that the United States support the Baath Party, which staged a 1963 coup against the Iraqi government that the CIA believed was falling under Soviet influence," by reference to the CIA's recruitment of Nazi spy officer Reinhard Gehlen). *See also* Christopher Simpson, Blowback: The First Full Account of America's Recruitment of Nazis, and Its Disastrous Effect on Our Domestic and Foreign Policy 243–45 (New York: Macmillan, 1988) (CIA financed former Nazi, Gestapo, and SS members as part of a "disturbing tapestry" of "clandestine operations" and "the abandonment of war crimes prosecutions"); Evan Thomas, The Very Best Men: Four Who Dared: The Early Years of the CIA 35–36 (New York: Simon & Schuster, 1995) (describing CIA's strategy in Critchfield's day of "methodically recruiting Nazi war criminals" to build an "underground army of anticommunists"); Joseph J. Trento, The Secret History of the CIA 29 (London: Perseus Books Group, 2005) (Critchfield acknowledged an "agreement" to support an organization that employed thousands of Gestapo, Wehrmacht, and SS officers); Timothy Naftali, *Berlin to Baghdad: The Pitfalls of Hiring Enemy Intelligence*, Foreign Aff., July/Aug. 2004, http://www.foreignaffairs.org/20040701fareviewessay83412/timothy-naftali/berlin-to-baghdad-the-pitfalls-of-hiring-enemy-intelligence.html (Critchfield was "man on the ground" subsidizing Gehlen organization of Nazi war criminals, including 100 former members of the SS); *The Violent Rise and Fall of Saddam Hussein*, Chicago Tribune, Dec. 15, 2003 at 6 ("1963: With U.S. support, the Baath Party overthrows the government. [Saddam] Hussein returns to Iraq...").

29. Naftali, *Berlin to Baghdad.*

30. Fritz, *James Critchfield Dies.*

31. Said K. Aburish, Nasser: The Last Arab 182 (New York: St. Martin's Press, 2004).

32. *See* Khidhir Hamza, Saddam's Bombmaker: The Daring Escape of the Man Who Built Iraq's Secret Weapon 44 (2000); Roula Khalaf, *A Divided Country—Will Iraq Descend Into Chaos and Ethnic Hatred After Saddam's Demise?*, Financial Times (U.K.), Mar. 18, 2003, at 19.

33. Kerevan, *Ruling Party Learned from Nazis. See also* Patrick Cockburn, *Revealed: How the West Set Saddam on the Bloody Road to Power*, The Independent (U.K.), June 29, 1997.

34. David Morgan, *Ex-U.S. Official Says CIA Aided Baathists*, Reuters, April 20, 2003.

> According to Western scholars, as well as Iraqi refugees and a British human rights organization, the 1963 coup was accompanied by a bloodbath. Using lists of suspected Communists and other leftists provided by the C.I.A., the Baathists systematically murdered untold numbers of Iraq's educated elite—killings in which Saddam Hussein himself is said to have participated. No one knows the exact toll, but accounts agree that the victims included hundreds of doctors, teachers, technicians, lawyers and other professionals as well as military and political figures.[35]

A prominent historian of Iraq puts the death toll of the 1963 massacres at up to five thousand, a toll that likely rose in later years as victims died of the aftereffects of widespread torture:

> The Ba'ath National Guard, thus briefed by U.S. spies, carried out mass executions. The ICP later claimed that five thousand Party members had been killed, either resisting the fascist coup or in the subsequent terror witch-hunts from house to house. Such claims were confirmed by other sources. Many of the killings were carried out with the utmost brutality, for example, Husein Ahmed al-Rahdi, the first secretary of the ICP, was tortured for fifteen days in the Qasr al-Nihayeh dungeons, before being crushed to death.[36]

Roger Morris, who served in the National Security Council under both U.S. Presidents Lyndon Baines Johnson and Richard Nixon in the 1960s, reported that he often heard U.S. officials "speak openly about their close relations with the Iraqi Baathists."[37] He argued that the "the CIA had chosen the authoritarian and anti-communist Baath Party 'as its instrument'" in Iraq.[38]

A lack of cohesion within the Ba'ath party led to its rapid splintering and loss of power to a non-Ba'athist Arab nationalist former military officer who had been named as President after the 1963 coup. President Abdul Salam Arif ushered in more conservative rule, repealing laws deemed by Iraqi religious leaders to contravene Sharia law principles, and requiring greater public observance of Islamic rituals and requirements. Upon his death, the chief of staff of the Iraqi Army took power, and led Iraq's forces into a supporting role in the calamitous June 1967 war with Israel. Iraq's defeat resulted in a temporary rupture of diplomatic ties with the U.S., and solicitation of Soviet and French investment in exploring Iraq's oil reserves.[39]

Due to a resurgence in communist activity in southern Iraq, the Iraqi government released many Ba'athist activists from prison. They promptly became street fighters against communists demonstrating against the government's handling of the June 1967 war. Saddam Hussein, meanwhile, had been steadily rebuilding the Ba'ath party since his inexplicable release from a prison sentence imposed for his participation in a coup against President Arif himself.[40]

Saddam directed the party's efforts to recruiting Army officers for the inevitable push to reclaim power by force. The Ba'ath Party's intensified effort bore fruits, as the heads

---

35. Roger Morris, *A Tyrant 40 Years in the Making,* N.Y. Times, Mar. 14, 2003; Roger Morris, *An Enemy 40 Years in the Making,* The Daily Telegraph (Australia), Mar. 22, 2003, at 31. For another account of CIA complicity in the mass killings that followed the 1963 coup, see Simons, Iraq, at 261.

36. Simons, Iraq, at 261.

37. Morris, *A Tyrant 40 Years in the Making.*

38. *Quoted in* Richard Sale, *Saddam Key in Early CIA Plot,* United Press Int'l, Apr. 10, 2003.

39. *See* Simons, Iraq, at 171, 173, 179, 188–91.

40. *See id.* at 188–90.

of the Republican Guard and military intelligence spearheaded the Ba'athist coup that followed on July 17, 1968. Saddam Hussein's kinsman Hasan al-Bakr became President, Prime Minister, and head of the Ba'ath party. The Ba'ath then promptly purged the very military leaders who had swept the party into power, and revived its "systematic campaign of arrest, torture, and imprisonment" against the Iraqi Communist Party. After the 1968 putsch, executions of political prisoners became commonplace, with "scores of communist members and cadres ... tortured to death."[41]

The Kurdish rebellion flared up again in 1968. Oil infrastructure in Kirkuk came under assault, "causing severe economic damage." Four Iraqi divisions were mobilized and dispatched to the north, "indiscriminately" attacking civilians along with rebel positions.[42]

In 1970, the Revolutionary Command Council, under the leadership of then-Vice President Hussein, reached an accord with Kurdish rebel leader Mullah Mustafa Barzani under which the Kurds would be granted autonomy in 1974 in exchange for ending their insurgency.[43] In addition to autonomy, the accord guaranteed the Kurds certain "cultural, linguistic, and administrative rights, the appointment of a Kurd as vice president of Iraq, and the enhancement of Kurdish representation within the state's ruling institutions." The government breached the autonomy agreement, however, including by failing to carry out an envisioned census of Kurds.[44] Kurdish leaders also "accused the Government of moving more Arabs into Kirkuk to dilute the Kurdish presence there before the holding of the census."[45]

In 1974, the rebellion was rekindled, this time with more substantial support from Turkey and the Shah of Iran.[46] The government deported tens of thousands of Kurds from the country.[47] The U.S. joined Iran and Israel in giving arms and training to the Kurdish rebels. By that time, President al-Bakr had nationalized U.S. and British oil facilities, and signed a 15-year friendship and military cooperation pact with the Soviet Union.[48] The CIA supplied the Kurdish leader Mustafa Barzani with heavy weapons and intelligence.[49]

A leaked CIA memo from shortly after the expiration date for the establishment of autonomy under the 1970 accords indicates that U.S. policymakers preferred to weaken Iraq, rather than contribute to a Kurdish victory or formalized autonomous Kurdistan. The memo stated: "We would think that [Iran] would not look with favor on the establishment of a formalized autonomous government. [Iran], like ourselves, has seen benefit in a stalemate situation ... in which [Iraq] is intrinsically weakened by [the Kurds].... Neither [Iran] nor ourselves wish to see the matter resolved one way or the other."[50] According to a congressional committee, documents unearthed during an investigation of illegal and covert U.S. support for the insurgency showed that President Nixon, "Dr.

---

41. *Id.* at 188–96, 266.

42. Efraim Karsh, *Making Iraq Safe For Democracy*, 115 COMMENTARY, April 2003, at 22–28.

43. *See* Raymond H. Anderson, *Limited Local Autonomy Granted to Kurds in Iraq*, N.Y. TIMES, Mar. 12, 1974, at 5; Dana Adams, *Iraq Recognizes Kurdish Autonomy*, N.Y TIMES, Mar. 12, 1970, at 8; *A Timetable of Tyranny and Terror—Saddam Hussein's Iraq*, COURIER MAIL (AUSTRALIA), Mar. 21, 2003, at 4.

44. Karsh, *Making Iraq Safe for Democracy*, at 22–28.

45. *See Dismissal of General Takriti*, 17 KEESING'S RECORD OF WORLD EVENTS 24292 (Nov. 1, 1970).

46. *See* Christopher S. Wren, *Soviet Charges Turks Aid Kurds; Sees 'Imperialist' Forces Behind Rebels in Iraq*, N.Y. TIMES, Apr. 27, 1974, at 5.

47. *See* Karsh, *Making Iraq Safe for Democracy*.

48. *See* Eric Black, *Iraq Through the Ages*, MINNEAPOLIS STAR TRIBUNE, Feb. 9, 2003, at 10A.

49. *See* MIDDLE EAST WATCH, GENOCIDE IN IRAQ, at 34.

50. *Quoted in* David Wise, *A People Betrayed*, L.A. TIMES, Apr. 14, 1991, at M1.

Kissinger and the [Shah] hoped that our clients [i.e. the Kurds] would not prevail. They preferred instead that the insurgents simply continue a level of hostilities sufficient to sap the resources of [Iraq]."[51] A State Department cable explained this policy in more detail:

> 3. Baath regime, for all its abhorrent traits, has given Iraq over six years of stability. In addition, it is now concentrating on economic development and energetically attempting to bring about full rapprochement with Western Europe and conservative Arab states (Baghdad 857). Whatever motives lay behind this twin policy of development and rapprochement and whatever radical rhetoric used to conceal it, characteristics of baath regime if policies successful likely to be quite different from current characteristics which admittedly often resemble those of cornered rat.
>
> 4. Kurdish leadership is fighting hopeless battle. No interested party wants to see them succeed. Even the Iranians say they will not give them enough assistance to take offensive. Their sole hope again appears to be overthrow of Baghdad regime.... [52]

After $16 million in U.S. aid and "thousands of deaths," the Kurdish rebellion under Mullah Mustafa Barzani was "abruptly cut off" by Iran, which reached the Algiers Agreement with Iraq, signed by Saddam Hussein in 1975.[53] The agreement negotiated a resolution to the countries' dispute over the Shatt al-Arab, the "river of the Arabs" and Iraq's only outlet to the Persian Gulf.[54] Control over the river and islands claimed by Kuwait near its mouth on the Gulf was a dream of Iraqi leaders since at least 1938, who hoped to build a deep water port and connect it by rail or other infrastructure to the metropolis on the river's west bank, Basra.[55] Hundreds of Kurds returned to their homes under a "right of return" guaranteed to them by the Algiers Agreement, while thousands of rebels planned to fight on from Iran or the mountains.[56] About 250,000 had been displaced from their homes, many rebels were tortured and executed, and about 1,500 villages were destroyed during this phase of the anti-Kurdish campaign.[57]

C. The Iranian Revolution and the Iran-Iraq War (Gulf War I)

In 1979, the CIA faced a difficult decision. Iraq's President Hasan al-Bakr, who had done little more than sign off on Saddam's policies in the mid-1970s, began to reassert himself after Egypt reached the Camp David peace deal with Israel in the fall of 1978. Bakr and the Ba'ath party resolved to join Syria and Jordan in confronting Israel militarily, and planned to revive the Soviet-backed United Arab Republic of the late 1950s

---

51. *Id.* (quoting so-called "Pike report" of U.S. House of Representatives).

52. U.S. Microfilm No. D740373-0224, Doc. No. 1974BAGHDA00898, Dec. 23 1974, declassified June 20, 2005.

53. Wise, *A People Betrayed*, at M1 (quoting "Pike report").

54. *See id.*; Black, *Iraq Through the Ages*, at 10A; Karsh, *Making Iraq Safe for Democracy*.

55. *See* Jasper Becker, *The Gulf War: Nation Was al-Sabah Family Business,* The Guardian (U.K.), Feb. 26, 1991.

56. *See* Juan de Onis, *Iraqis Complete Seizure of Kurdish Rebel Area*, N.Y. Times, Apr. 3, 1975.

57. *See* Barry M. Lando, Web of Deceit: The History of Western Complicity in Iraq, from Churchill to Kennedy to George W. Bush 85 (New York: Other Press, 2007).

with a union of Iraq and Syria. Saddam opposed this move due to his Iraq-first orientation, and the CIA reportedly met with him in Jordan, where he had formed an alliance with the king against Bakr and the union with Syria. Saddam believed that Syria's pro-Iranian orientation, on account of its hope that an Arab-Iranian alliance could overcome Israeli military supremacy, threatened Iraq's interest in containing the Islamic Revolution before it could spread to Iraq's Shi'as and topple the Ba'ath party.[58] The CIA may have "quietly" opened an office in Baghdad from 1979 to keep tabs on things.[59]

After taking the helm of the Ba'ath party in 1979, Saddam launched a war against Iran in 1980, which claimed the lives of 300,000 Iraqis and up to 600,000 Iranians by 1985.[60] Iran's president had threatened Iraq with an invasion in response to deportations of ethnic Iranians and arrests of Shi'a leaders.[61] The Iraqi government alleged close to 200 border incursions by Iran in the months leading up the invasion. Inside Iraq, the Iranian government called for an Islamic revolution by like-minded Shi'a, who had formed a political organization called *al-Da'wa al-Islamiyyah* (the Islamic Call) that Iran supported. Bombings took place inside Iraq, and Iraq's vice president Tariq Aziz was supposedly the target of an assassination attempt a few months before the Iraqi invasion.[62] The "Da'wa leadership moved to Iran and urged its followers in Iraq to engage in acts of terror and destruction in the hope of launching a sectarian civil war (*fitna ta'ifiyya*)."[63] After the coalition invasion in 2003 and the quasi-democratic elections of 2005, a Da'wa leader became Prime Minister of Iraq.[64]

By 1982, the Secretary-General of the U.N. had urged an end to Iraqi attacks in particular on urban civilian populations.[65] In 1988, the U.N. Secretary-General condemned Iraq's use of chemical weapons on Iranian civilians near urban centers, and the Security Council concurred.[66] The Iraqi military gassed to death an estimated 60,000 Iranian soldiers and civilians.[67] Iraq dropped both mustard and nerve gas on Iranian soldiers, and reporters described "carpets of bodies," "carnage" on an unprecedented scale in recent history, "hundreds of Iranian bodies," and Iranians "cut down ... like swathes of corn

58. *See* Said K. Aburish, Saddam Hussein: The Politics of Revenge 125, 164–170 (London: Bloomsbury, 2000).

59. Con Coughlin, Saddam: King of Terror 215 (New York: Bloomsbury, 2004).

60. *See* Makiya, Republic of Fear, at 259 n.4 (citing NATO estimates summarized in N.Y. Times, Sept. 23, 1985); *see also* Robert L. Maginnis, *Outside View: The Morality of U.S. Policy*, Insight on the News, Sept. 2, 2002, http://www.insightmag.com (similar estimate of 400,000 Iraqi deaths).

61. *See* United Press International, *War Threats Traded Between Iraq, Iran*, The Bulletin (Oregon), Apr. 10, 1980, at 1. Revolutionary Iran had also accused Iraq of joining Saudi Arabia as an agent of American imperialism by failing to vote for increased oil prices and reduced levels of production within OPEC. *See* Associated Press, *Iraq-Iran Shouting Match Highlights Opec Meeting*, Kingman Daily Miner (Arizona), June 10, 1980, at 2.

62. *See* Makiya, Republic of Fear, at 107, 265.

63. Ofra Bengio, Saddam's Word: Political Discourse in Iraq 101 (New York and Oxford: Oxford UP, 1998).

64. The elections were quasi-democratic because individuals were not allowed to run for office, certain political parties were banned, and a pervasive atmosphere of violence permeated the society, often perpetrated by forces or militias linked to the dominant political parties. *See* Kristina Arvanitis, *Lessons from Iraq: Electoral Legitimacy in the Shadow of Ethnoreligious Conflict*, 20 Temple International and Comparative Law J., 529–542, 547–48 (2006); U.N. Doc. No. S/2004/710, Report of the Secretary-General Pursuant to Paragraph 30 of Resolution 1546 (2004), at ¶¶ 4–7 (describing widespread militia violence in Iraq, including against "senior officials of various political parties.").

65. *See* U.N. Doc. No. S/16609 (1984); U.N. Doc. No. S/17036 (1985).

66. *See* U.N. Doc. No. S/23273, ¶ 8 (1988); S.C. Res. 620 (Aug. 26, 1988).

67. Robert Fisk, *Death of a King, The Terrible Legacy of the Man Who Failed the World*, Independent (UK), Aug. 2, 2005, 2005 WLNR 12122214.

Image 4 Saddam Hussein Just Prior to Becoming President in 1979

under a sickle...."[68] Iraq's air force bombed Iranian cities and other civilian targets, killing 600 people in a three-day period in 1985.[69] Iran claimed to have suffered $1 trillion in damages, and the U.N. confirmed at least $100 billion.[70] Iraqi forces attacked about 100 tankers carrying Iranian oil.[71] Up to two million Iranians were driven from their homes by fighting, while two million fled the revolution.[72]

In order to commit these crimes, Saddam's government secured massive financial and military support from an array of foreign powers, including the Soviet Union, France, China, Saudi Arabia, Kuwait, and the U.S.[73] During the Iran-Iraq War, the Soviets as-

68. *Quoted in* MAKIYA, REPUBLIC OF FEAR, at 283–84 (collecting sources).

69. GARY SICK, ALL FALL DOWN: AMERICA'S TRAGIC ENCOUNTER WITH IRAN xxiii–xxiv (New York: Penguin Books, 1986).

70. *See* R.K. Ramazani, *Who Started the Iran-Iraq War? A Commentary*, 33 VIRGINIA J. OF INTERNATIONAL LAW 69, 81–82 (1992–1993).

71. *See The War*, MIDDLE EAST REPORT, Sept.–Oct. 1987, at 24.

72. *See* Associated Press, *Some Facts And Figures on Iran*, WORCESTER TELEGRAM GAZETTE, Feb. 5, 1989.

73. *See* Robert Windrem, *Rumsfeld Key Player in Iraq Policy Shift*, MSNBC, Aug. 18, 2002, *at* http://www.independent-media.tv/item.cfm?fmedia_id=228&fcategory_desc=Under%20Reported; Robert Novak, *Following Iraq's Bioweapons Trail*, CHICAGO SUN-TIMES, Sept. 26, 2002, f http://foi.missouri.edu/terrorbkgd/following.html; Associated Press, *Iraq Got Seeds for Bioweapons from U.S.*, BALTIMORE SUN, Oct. 1, 2002, http://www.baltimoresun.com/news/nationworld/bal-te.bioweapons01oct01,0,4635016.story?coll=bal%2Dhome%2Dheadlines; Human Rights Watch, *Landmines in Iraq: Questions and Answers* (Dec. 2002), http://www.hrw.org/campaigns/iraq/iraqmines1212.htm; Associated Press, *Iraq Used Many Suppliers for Nuke Program*, FOX NEWS, Dec.

signed 5,000 military advisers to Iraq and provided the Ba'ath with apparently "unlimited access to Soviet weaponry."[74] Long after the destruction of Kurdish villages and gassing of Iranians had begun, the Soviets provided Iraq with hundreds of T-52 tanks and many Tu-22 bombers, Mi-24 helicopters, and advanced artillery.[75] France exported $25 billion worth of weapons to Iraq, about 28 percent of all Iraqi arms imports, including sophisticated Mirage fighter-bombers, Super Etendard fighter-bombers, and Exocet missiles.[76] German companies helped build chemical weapons factories.[77] China became a major supplier of weapons to both sides, and was still owed $8 billion by Iraq as late as 2003 for exports of such sophisticated weaponry as Badger fighter-bombers and Silkworm missiles.[78] Kuwait loaned Iraq $15 billion to attack Iran, but made something like $100 billion in profits, much of which it invested in U.S. and British assets, from the resulting spike in oil prices as refineries and oil platforms were destroyed, and production fell.[79] For his part, King Fahd of Saudi Arabia estimated in 1991 that the kingdom had loaned Saddam Hussein $25.7 billion for the war.[80] His country likely earned even greater profits than Kuwait did from the destruction of Iranian and Iraqi assets.[81] By the end of the 1980s, all Saudi citizens enjoyed exemption from personal income taxation, a plot of land and an $80,000 interest-free loan, and free health care and higher education.[82]

The CIA station chief in Jordan regularly visited Baghdad during the Iran-Iraq war to meet with Iraqi officials, apparently funneling U.S. intelligence to Iraq for its campaign against Iranian cities.[83] The CIA is said to have conveyed sophisticated battlefield-level satellite imagery for Gulf War I.[84] As in Afghanistan, Egypt served as the conduit for hundreds of millions' worth in Soviet-made arms to reach Iraq, reportedly with the approval of the CIA.[85]

17, 2002, http://www.foxnews.com/story/0,2933,73292,00.html; Patrick E. Tyler, *Officers Say U.S. Aided Iraq in War Despite Use of Gas*, N.Y. Times, Aug. 18, 2002, http://www.commondreams.org/headlines02/0818-02.htm; Joost R. Hiltermann, *America Didn't Seem to Mind Poison Gas*, Int'l Herald Trib., Jan. 17, 2003, http://www.commondreams.org/views03/0117-01.htm; *Iraq Must First Dig Out of Massive Debt to Recover $358b Owed*, Straits Times (Singapore), Apr. 19, 2003, http://straitstimes.asia1.com.sg/iraqwar/story/0,4395,184295,00.html; Associated Press, *France Pledges Gesture on Forgiving Debt*, Fox News, Dec. 15, 2003, http://www.foxnews.com/story/0,2933,105856,00.html.

74. Simons, Iraq, at 267.

75. *See* Coughlin, Saddam, at 123.

76. Olivier Guitta, *The Chirac Doctrine (Jacques Chirac's Foreign Relations)*, Middle East Q., Sep. 22, 2005, http://www.highbeam.com/doc/1G1-135763444.html.

77. *See* Coughlin, Saddam, at 190.

78. *See* Associated Press, *China Forgives Iraqi Debt, but How Much?*, Fox News, June 22, 2007, http://www.foxnews.com/printer_friendly_wires/2007Jun22/0,4675,ChinaIraqDebt,00.html; Molly Moore, *China Sends New Weapons to Iraqis*, Wash. Post, June 27, 1987, http://www.highbeam.com/doc/1P2-1329874.html.

79. *See* Maria Halkias, *Oil Fight Was Excuse to Invade, Analysts Say; Iraq's Accusations Called 'Trumped Up,'* Dallas Morning News, Aug. 3, 1990; John Rossant et al., *Kuwait Puts Its $ 100 Billion War Chest to Work*, Business Week, Oct. 1, 1990, at 50.

80. Simons, Iraq, at 267.

81. *See* Robert Hershey, *Iraq Halts Exports of Its Oil as Result of Damage By Iran*, N.Y. Times, Sept. 27, 1980, at 1.

82. *See* Youssef Ibrahim, *Shaping a New Saudi Arabia: Oil, Peace and a Steady Hand*, N.Y. Times, Apr. 17, 1989, http://www.nytimes.com/1989/04/17/world/shaping-a-new-saudi-arabia-oil-peace-and-a-steady-hand.html?pagewanted=2 (calling these benefits "unparalleled anywhere in the world.").

83. *See* Aburish, Saddam Hussein, at 210.

84. *See* Tim Weiner, Legacy of Ashes: The History of the CIA 491 (New York: Anchor Books, 2008).

85. *See* Lando, Web of Deceit, at 60–61.

D. The *Anfal* Campaign

In 1986, Kurdish rebels within Iraq reached an economic and military accord under which Iran, then ruled by Ayatollah Ruhollah Khomeini, would arm the Kurds, who attacked Iraqi oilfields near Kirkuk along with a contingent of Iranian Revolutionary Guards. The Iraqi regime responded with massacres, horrific tortures, the destruction of villages, and chemical warfare. The orders for the Iraqi army's massacres in northern Iraq did not refer specifically to Kurds, let alone "Kurdistan," but to "prohibited" villages or "areas," within which "the armed forces must kill any person or animal present."[86] Inside the prohibited zone, the Iraqi army massacred Kurdish men by shooting them in trenches. Babies and young children were found among the bodies later exhumed from the mass graves of the *Anfal* campaign.[87] Middle East Watch described *Anfal* as involving "mass summary executions," and the forced displacement of hundreds of thousands of villagers deported from the prohibited zones to other areas without food, shelter, or spare clothing.[88] The pattern of mass executions had long-standing precedents in Iraq, from the Assyrian massacres of 1933 to the massacre of 8,000 men related to or suspected to be sympathetic with Massoud Barzani's Kurdistan Democratic Party in 1983.[89]

The head of the northern bureau of the Ba'ath Party, Ali Hassan al-Majid, a cousin of Saddam's, commanded the First and Fourth Corps of the Iraqi Army during the *Anfal* campaign. He also assumed control of Iraq's internal security infrastructure in the north, including General Security Directorate, Foreign Intelligence Agency, and Military Intelligence.[90] He ordered the armed forces to "kill any human being or animal present within [prohibited] areas."[91] About two weeks later, he reiterated his orders to the Army to "kill the largest number of persons" in the prohibited zones with "random bombardment," and execute all persons aged 15 to 70.[92]

By the start of the First *Anfal* campaign in early 1988, the Jafati valley near the Iranian border, where Kurdish *pesh merga* ("those who face death") militia from the KDP and PUK were stationed, had suffered almost daily artillery barrages, and frequent aerial bombardment. The week of al-Majid's first directive quoted above, chemical weapons—probably nerve gas but possibly mustard gas, which the army also used—were launched into the valley's towns. Large numbers of civilians were killed, and others temporarily blinded (as occurs with mustard gas). Then the First *Anfal* assault began, as the army moved in on the valley, cut down many *pesh merga*, and drove the villagers into the mountains or grasslands towards Iran.[93]

---

86. *See* Middle East Watch, Genocide in Iraq, at 49–50, 79–84.

87. *See* Lando, Web of Deceit, at 87 (citing Jonathan Randal, After Such Knowledge, What Forgiveness? 232 (New York: Farrar, Straus and Giroux, 1997)).

88. *See* Middle East Watch, Genocide in Iraq, at 4–5.

89. *See id.* at 6–7; Coughlin, Saddam, at 224.

90. *See* Middle East Watch, Genocide in Iraq, at 3–4, 51–54, 369; Aburish, Saddam Hussein, at 232–33.

91. Directive No. 28/3650, June 3, 1987, Ali Hassan al-Majid to Commanders of the First, Second, and Fifth Army Corps, General Security Directorate of the Autonomous Region, Foreign Intelligence Agency, and Military Intelligence, *quoted in* Middle East Watch, Genocide in Iraq, at 79.

92. *See* Directive No. SF/2008, June 20, 1987, Ali Hassan al-Majid to Commanders of the First, Second, and Fifth Army Corps, *quoted in* Middle East Watch, Genocide in Iraq, at 82.

93. *See* Middle East Watch, Genocide in Iraq, at 62–3, 73, 94–99.

In March, the Iraqi Army attacked Halabja, a stronghold of the PUK and pro-Iranian Islamic Movement Party, into which Iranian Revolutionary Guards and spies had infiltrated. The Iraqi Army dropped incendiaries, possibly phosphorus, from aircraft. Iraqi Army artillery fire knocked out the electricity, and when ground forces moved in they destroyed almost all the buildings as well as the electrical infrastructure. Chemical weapons fell on Halabja, and a Kurdish researcher collected 3,200 names of Kurds who died in the siege, including children. Thousands more still-unnamed victims may have died in the town, or in flight. Other, roughly similar attacks occurred in the Qara Dagh area to the south of Suleimaniya and the west of Halabja, the Tazashar area even further south, the valley of the Lesser Zab river, the area to the north and west of Dukan lake, and the area to the east of Zakho near the Turkish border.[94]

The Kurds were joined by the ethnic and religious minorities the Yezidis and the Assyrians in undergoing mass murder as "bad Arabs" and "obstinate minorities."[95] Although the Yezidi population grew dramatically after Iraq's independence from the Ottoman Empire, eventually reaching 600,000 to one million,[96] the Ba'athist regime began to misclassify the Yezidis as Arabs, denying their ethnic identity.[97] Yezidis, along with northern Iraq's other prominent religious minority, the Assyrians, were disappeared *en masse* even after the government had declared an amnesty for rebellious Kurds.[98]

There were probably more than 1.4 million Assyrians and other Christians living in Iraq in the early 1980s.[99] As the *Anfal* campaign reached the Dohuk region, where Assyrians disproportionately resided, they "were in fact dealt with by the regime even more severely than their Kurdish neighbors."[100] Iraqi forces killed many Assyrians, tortured many Assyrians, and destroyed many Assyrian churches during the *Anfal* campaign.[101] About 1,000 Assyrians "disappeared" during the Ba'athist "Arabization" and *Anfal* campaigns of the

---

94. *See id.* at 100–8, 113–281.

95. *See id.* at 312–17.

96. *See* David Nissman, *First World Congress of Yezidis Held in Germany*, Radio Free Europe/Radio Liberty (2000), http://www.globalsecurity.org/wmd/library/news/iraq/2000/5-040200.htm; *Vision of the Bridge*, Turkish Daily News, Mar. 19, 2001, http://www.turkishdailynews.com.tr/archives.php?id=22407 (estimate of one million Iraqi Yezidis in 2001).

97. *See* USDOS, *International Religious Freedom Report 2002: Iraq*.

98. *See* Middle East Watch, Genocide in Iraq, at 315–317.

99. *See* The Government of the United Kingdom, *Home Office, Iraq Country Assessment* (Oct. 2001), http://www.asylumlaw.org/docs/showDocument.cfm?documentID=844; Danish Immigration Service, *Joint British—Danish Fact Finding Mission to Damascus, Amman, and Geneva Regarding Iraqi Asylum Seekers* (June 2002), http://www.unhcr.org/cgi-bin/texis/vtx/home/opendoc.pdf?tbl=RSDCOI&id=3f4908364; Patrick McDonnell, *After Years of Relative Peace, Christians Live in Fear,* L.A. Times, Nov. 14, 2004, http://www.armeniandiaspora.com/archive/14453.html; David Nissman, *First World Congress of Yezidis Held in Germany,* Radio Free Europe/Radio Liberty, Feb. 4, 2000, http://www.rferl.org/content/Article/1343241.html (600,000 Yezidis in 1990s, after significant refugee flight); *Vision of the Bridge,* Turkish Daily News, Mar. 19, 2001, http://arama.hurriyet.com.tr/arsivnews.aspx?id=-522807 (one million Iraqi Yezidis in 1990s). The 1987 census in Iraq revealed that about 1.4 million Assyrians lived in Iraq. *See* Michael Luo et al., *Iraq's Christian Minority Flees as Extremist Threat Worsens,* N.Y. Times, Oct. 17, 2006, http://www.nytimes.com. Various estimates over the years have counted 600,000 Iraqis as Chaldean Catholics, 300,000 to 500,000 as Assyrians (Church of the East), and 140,000 as Orthodox Christians. *See Patriarch Raphael I Bidawid (Obituary),* The Times (U.K.), July 29, 2003, at 28; Uwe Siemon-Netto, *Mob Beheads Nun in Baghdad,* United Press Int'l (Aug. 27, 2002); Ray J. Mouawad, *Syria and Iraq—Repression: Disappearing Christians of the Middle East,* Middle East Q., Dec. 1, 2001, http://www.meforum.org/article/17.

100. *See* Middle East Watch, Genocide in Iraq, at 15.

101. Travis, *The Ottoman Genocide of the Assyrians*, at 346.

1970s and 1980s.[102] "Military forces destroyed many Assyrian churches during the *Anfal* Campaign, and reportedly tortured and executed many Assyrians."[103] Assyrians suffered from chemical weapons attacks in Halabja and elsewhere.[104] Between 1963 and 1987, the Iraqi government destroyed about 200 majority Assyrian villages in the provinces of Nineveh, Dohuk, and Arbil.[105] Many of these villages housed 100–200 families each.[106] The Iraqi government razed almost 25 churches, monasteries, and religious-run orphanages during this period.[107] Thus, "the army rampaged through the country's north, attacking ethnic Kurds and systematically destroying more than 100 Christian villages, razing scores of ancient monasteries and churches and deporting thousands of Christian families to Baghdad."[108]

Figures 6 and 7 set forth a sample of the documentary evidence of genocidal intent during the *Anfal* campaign and in its early 1990s aftermath. The evidence falls into several categories: (1) the killing of all individuals making up a given collective or residing in a certain region; (2) destruction and villages and foodstuffs that could support life in a given area; and (3) embargoes and interdiction of food and nutritional supplies that could replace destroyed stocks.

Human Rights Watch pointed out at the time that there were some noteworthy omissions from the U.S. condemnations of Iraqi war crimes and genocide in the late 1980s. Among other things, there was "no public expression of concern over the Iraqi government's relocation of at least 500,000 Kurds and Assyrians," in contrast to repeated condemnation of deportations in communist Nicaragua and Ethiopia. Although the U.S. ambassador remained in Baghdad, and the Iraqi Minister of State visited Washington in September 1989, U.S. officials "did not raise with Iraqi authorities the [State Department's] findings of murder, extra-legal detention, torture and disappearance of political opponents and government critics, according to State Department sources." Instead, Secretary of State Shultz "approved a recommendation that the administration oppose Congressionally mandated sanctions against Iraq." Secretary Shultz received a commitment from Tariq Aziz that Iraq would not use chemical weapons anymore, but Kurdish representa-

---

102. Tripp, A History of Iraq, at 79–81; U.N. Office for the Coordination of Humanitarian Affairs, *Iraq: Focus on Mass Graves* (Jan. 7, 2004), http://www.irinnews.org/report.asp?ReportID=38775&SelectRegion=Iraq_Crisis&SelectCountry=IRAQ; USDOS, *Iraq Human Rights Practices, 1994* (Mar. 1995), http://dosfan.lib.uic.edu/ERC/democracy/1994_hrp_report/94hrp_report_nea/Iraq.html; International Federation of Human Rights, *Iraq: Continuous and Silent Ethnic Cleansing*, Jan. 2003, at 16; Human Rights Watch, *Claims in Conflict: Reversing Ethnic Cleansing in Northern Iraq* (Aug. 2004), http://hrw.org/reports/2004/iraq0804; Siemon-Netto, *Attacks Defy the Prophet's Wish*; Ken Joseph, Jr., *Iraq's Secret Documents*, Wash. Times, July 23, 2004, http://washingtontimes.com/upi-breaking/20040723-123038-6416r.htm).

103. USDOS, *Iraq Human Rights Practices, 1994.*

104. Dr. Katrin Michael, who met with President Bush and Vice President Cheney on March 14, 2003, pointedly introduced herself as an Assyrian Chaldean and discussed her experience as a victim of the chemical weapons attack on Halabja in 1988. The White House, News and Policies (March 2003), http://www.whitehouse.gov/news/releases/2003/03/images/20030314-26_p27771-07a-515h.html; U.S. House of Representatives, Testimony of Survivor Dr. Katrin Michael (Mar. 16, 2003), http://www.house.gov/kirk/halabja_drmichael_testimony.htm.

105. International Federation of Human Rights, *Iraq: Continuous and Silent Ethnic Cleansing*, Appendices A, H.

106. *Id.*

107. *Id.*

108. *Id. See also* Middle East Watch, Genocide in Iraq, appx. D, http://www.hrw.org/reports/1993/iraqanfal/ANFAL11.htm (Iraqi forces "burned and bulldozed" specifically "Assyrian villages like Kani Balaf (in the nahya of Berwari Bala), Mezeh (Sarseng) and Gund Kosa (Al-Doski)").

Figure 6 Genocidal Orders and Statements by Iraqi Officials in 1980s and 1990s

Official	Statement	Date	Source
General Security Directorate, Erbil Governorate	1. The names of persons who are subject to a collective judgment must only be disseminated in separate memoranda. 2. Such memoranda … should be accorded the greatest secrecy.	Jan. 1987	Human Rights Watch
Minutes of meeting of Iraqi security forces	All prohibited villages will be destroyed.	Apr. 1987	Middle East Watch
Secretary General of the Northern Bureau Command [i.e., Ali Hassan al-Majid]	1. All the villages in which … traitors to Iraq are still to be found are to be regarded as out of bounds for security reasons; 2. They shall be regarded as operational zones that are strictly out of bounds to all persons and animals and in which the troops can open fire at will … ; 4. The corps commanders shall carry out random bombardments, using artillery, helicopters and aircraft, at all times of the day or night, in order to kill the largest number of persons present in … prohibited zones …; 5. [A]ll persons captured in those villages shall be detained and interrogated by the security services and those between the ages of 15 and 70 shall be executed after any useful information has been obtained from them, of which we should be duly notified.	June 1987	Middle East Watch
Ali Hassan al-Majid	[A]ll villages in which the saboteurs—the agents of Iran [i.e., the PUK], the offspring of treason [i.e., the KDP], and similar traitors to Iraq—are still to be found shall be regarded as prohibited for security reasons…. The presence of human beings and animals is completely prohibited in these areas, and shall be regarded as operational zones in which the troops can open fire at will, without any restriction, unless otherwise instructed by our headquarters.	June 1987	Human Rights Watch Archives
Baath Party People's Command in Zakho	The entry of any kind of human cargo, nutritional supplies, or mechanical instruments into the security prohibited villages under the second stage [of the operation] is strictly prohibited…. It is the duty of the members of the military forces to kill any human beings or animals found in these areas.	June 1987	N.Y. Times
Ali Hassan al-Majid	1. It is totally prohibited for any foodstuffs or persons … to reach the villages that have been prohibited…. 5. Within their jurisdiction, the armed forces must kill any human being or animal present within these areas….	June 1987	Middle East Watch

Figure 6 Genocidal Orders and Statements by Iraqi Officials in 1980s and 1990s, *continued*

Official	Statement	Date	Source
Ali Hassan al-Majid	I will kill them all [i.e., Kurds] with chemical weapons! Who is going to say anything? The international community? Fuck them! … and those who listen to them! I will not attack them with chemicals just one day, but I will continue to attack them with chemicals for fifteen days.	1988	Human Rights Watch
Military Intelligence	1. The information we received makes clear that there are villages and separate houses in the prohibited areas which were covered by the Anfal operation but have so far not been eliminated as required. 2. It was decided to speed up the destruction and elimination operation for all the villages and scattered houses as soon as possible, and to give this matter top priority within a time frame not exceeding 10 June 1988. 3. Groups of the Corps Intelligence and the Command Intelligence will check the villages that were not eliminated. 4. Please provide us with the list that includes the coordinates of the villages, marked and unmarked, which have not yet been eliminated. Please state your engineering requirements [within 48 hours] so that we can help you in the elimination of these villages.…	May 1988	Middle East Watch
Ali Hassan al-Majid	I will prohibit large areas.… I will evacuate it as far as Gweir and Mosul.… For five years I won't allow any human existence there.	Apr. 1998	Human Rights Watch
Military Intelligence	[The] result of the bombing by our planes and our artillery on the area of Halabja and Khurmal [was that], approximately 2,000 enemy forces of the Persians and agents of Iran were killed.	June 1988	Human Rights Watch Archives
Ali Hassan al-Majid	We asked [Mosul governorate] to deport every Kurd who lives there and send them to the mountains to live like goats.… We deported them from Mosul without any compensation. We razed their houses.	Aug. 1998	Human Rights Watch
Ali Hassan al-Majid	Yes, I'll certainly look after [the Kurds]. I'll do it by burying them with bulldozers. That's how I'll do it.	Jan. 1989	Human Rights Watch

Figure 6 Genocidal Orders and Statements by Iraqi Officials in 1980s and 1990s, *continued*

Official	Statement	Date	Source
General Security Directorate, Erbil Governorate	1. Strategic security operations (such as poisoning, explosions and the burning of their houses) must be conducted against the saboteurs in the Marsh areas.... 8. The principle of economic blockade must be applied to the villages and areas in which saboteurs are operating. This will be achieved in the following manner: • [through] the withdrawal of all food supply agencies; • [through] a ban on the sale of fish; • by taking the most severe measures against persons who smuggle foodstuffs to deserters, outlaws and hostile groups; • by prohibiting goods traffic from entering those villages and areas.	Jan. 1989	Human Rights Watch
Iraqi Army, Infantry Brigade 22	2. From 15:00 on 31/5, Brigade 22 and Commando Brigade 2 of the Corps will move to assert complete control over the town of Suleimaniyeh and impose a prohibition on the movement of people and vehicles.... 6. To kill any person who walks in the town of Suleimaniyeh and tries to disturb the peace and refuses to obey orders.	June 1991	Human Rights Watch

Figure 7 Statements by U.S. Officials Relating to Genocide in Iraq

Document Title	Statement	Date	Source(s)
Country Report on Human Rights Practices, Iraq	[T]he grave human rights violations when the Iraqi armed forces moved to crush a longstanding Kurdish rebellion.... The campaign was marked by the use of chemical weapons against guerrillas and civilians alike.	Feb. 1989	U.S. Department of State
Address before the United Nations General Assembly	Thousands of Iraqis have been executed on political and religious grounds and even more through a genocidal, poison-gas war waged against Iraq's own Kurdish villagers.	Oct. 1990	U.S. President George H.W. Bush
US Expands Kurdish Relief Efforts	Hundreds of thousands of Iraqi Kurds are in difficult-to-reach mountain areas in southern Turkey and along the Turkish-Iraq border.... [D]espite these efforts, hunger, malnutrition, disease, and exposure are taking their grim toll. No one can see the pictures or hear the accounts of this human suffering—men, women, and most painfully of all, innocent children—and not be deeply moved.	Apr. 1991	U.S. President George H.W. Bush
Humanitarian Assistance in Iraq	Following the swift defeat of his military forces in Kuwait last February, Saddam Hussein was confronted by sudden and massive uprisings by disaffected Shi'a in southern Iraq and Kurds in the north. Although these uprisings caught the Government of Iraq ... by surprise, Iraq's military was able to ... quell the uprisings. These events have triggered a large humanitarian emergency in Iraq and neighboring Turkey and Iran involving more than 1.8 million Iraqis.... Saddam's continuing repression of the Kurds—including artillery bombardment of urban and residential areas and deliberate eviction of people from their homes—vastly complicates the UN's efforts to provide adequate shelter in the north before the onset of winter and to "settle" returning refugees into their homes. Nevertheless, the United Nations has successfully completed arrangements to provide adequate protection against the harsh winter climate for 350,000 people for whom plans had been made last summer and autumn. But there remain serious problems for recently displaced persons in northern Iraq.... In July, we received credible reports that a number of Shi'a, who had fled their homes following the brutal put-down of their rebellion by Iraqi forces, were trapped in the vast marsh areas separating southern Iraq and Iran. What made these reports most ominous were eyewitness accounts by UN personnel that the Iraqi army had surrounded part of these marshes and appeared intent upon keeping the Shi'a pinned down in an area totally unfit for human habitation. We are very concerned with reports that indicate that there are still numbers of people, including women and children trapped in the marshes with little food, only swamp water to drink, and unable to return to their homes because of the continuing large military presence in the area.	Jan. 1992	U.S. Department of State

Figure 7 Statements by U.S. Officials Relating to Genocide in Iraq, *continued*

Document Title	Statement	Date	Source(s)
Blockade of the North	Government food rations provided to Kurds are reduced to approximately half the amount provided to other Iraqis.	Mar. 1992	U.S. Department of State
Iraq's Continued Defiance Of the United Nations	In April, the government authorized the removal of Shi'a villages living in or near the southern marshes. This operation is reminiscent of the "anfal operations" ... in the 1980s.... One of the most serious new developments is the use of fixed-wing aircraft, including jet fighters, for the first time in bombing Shi'a villages in the southern marshes. Unfortunately, we have no reason to hope for amelioration of the situation.... Instead, we have reason to believe that additional villages will be attacked, bombed, and destroyed, and civilian casualties will rise.	Aug. 1992	U.S. Permanent Representative to the United Nations
Iraqi Harassment of UN Personnel	The blockade in the North has gone on for nearly a year; Iraq has refused to provide fuel, and delivery of humanitarian assistance is virtually non-existent.	Sept. 1992	U.S. Department of State
Containing Iraqi Aggression: The U.S. Response	Three days ago, despite clear warnings from the United States and the international community, Iraqi forces attacked and seized the Kurdish-controlled city of Irbil in northern Iraq.... It appears that one Kurdish group which in the past opposed Saddam now has decided to cooperate with him. But that cannot justify unleashing the Iraqi army against the civilian population of Irbil.	Sept. 1996	U.S. President Bill Clinton
Country Reports on Human Rights Practices for 1996—Iraq	Summary executions of perceived political opponents reportedly increased, as did reports of disappearances. Both types of repression were particularly clear in the north during and after the August 31 attack on Irbil. Tens of thousands of political killings and disappearances remain unresolved from previous years.... Several other cities and villages in northern Iraq were shelled by artillery and then were entered by government troops. The Special Rapporteur stated in November that indiscriminate shelling by Iraqi forces of civilian settlements had been a recurrent practice well before these most recent clashes.... For most of the year, the Government maintained an internal embargo against Iraq's northern governorates, blocking the shipment of food, medicine, and other goods from government-controlled territory to the Kurdish-controlled areas....	Jan. 1997	U.S. Department of State

tives were barred by France from speaking at a conference on chemical weapons usage by Iran and Iraq in 1989 that could have shed light on these commitments and their validity.[109]

In 2006, the Iraqi High Tribunal concluded that during the *Anfal* campaign, starting in 1987, the death toll "reached tens of thousands of Kurdish victims between martyrs killed by raids (whether conventional or chemical weapons), or miss[ing] individuals buried in mass graves, found and anonymous...."[110] The tribunal reproduced multiple statements from witnesses to massacres of civilians by aerial and artillery bombardment, chemical weapons, shootings, torture, starvation, deprivation of water while in custody, and demolition of homes, mosques, and villages, prompting victims to flee for Iran.[111] According to Michael Newton, a U.S. adviser to the tribunal, as the tribunal collected evidence and interviewed witnesses, estimates of the toll of the *Anfal* campaign ranged from 100,000 to 200,000 deaths, 2,000 to 4,000 villages in northern Iraq destroyed, and deportation of 500,000 Kurds into "barren concrete 'collective towns.'"[112] Middle East Watch put the death toll at 50,000 to 100,000, while noting that Kurdish parties claimed that 182,000 had disappeared. Army commander al-Majid himself said the number of Kurds disappeared "could not have been more than 100,000."[113]

E. The Iraq-Kuwait Conflict (Gulf War II)

Most accounts of the Persian Gulf War preclude an objective assessment by omitting most of the historical context of the conflict.[114] The territory now known as Kuwait was governed from cities in Iraq for many of the 5,000 years prior to Western European colonization of the Middle East, including rule from the southern Iraqi city of Basra during the hundreds of years under Ottoman rule that preceded the British presence in Iraq and Kuwait.[115] Britain retained Kuwait when it handed the province of Basra over to Iraq in 1920, primarily to retain a stopping-off point on the Gulf, between Egypt and India, while precluding Germany, Iraq, and the Soviet Union from obtaining access to such a

109. *Iraq, in* Human Rights Watch World Report 1989, http://www.hrw.org/legacy/reports/1989/WR89/Iraq.htm#TopOfPage.

110. Al Anfal, Special Verdict Pertaining to Case No 1/C Second/2006, at 22–24 (Iraqi High Tribunal, Second Criminal Court, June 24, 2007), http://law.case.edu/grotian-moment-blog/anfal/opinion.asp.

111. *See id.* at 160–190, 864–70, 874–81, 887–91.

112. Michael A. Newton, *The Significance of the Anfal Campaign Indictment, in* Saddam on Trial: Understanding and Debating the Iraqi High Tribunal 220–22 (Durham, NC: Carolina Academic Press, 2006). *See also Iraq, in* Human Rights Watch World Report 1989 ("The report also pointed out that in l988 the Iraqi government intensified its destruction of Kurdish and Assyrian villages in northern Iraq and its relocation of their inhabitants....").

113. *See* Middle East Watch, Genocide in Iraq, at xiv, xviii.

114. *See. e.g.*, The Oxford Companion to United States History 589 (Paul S. Boyer ed., Oxford: Oxford UP, 2001).

115. *See, e.g.*, Walker, *The Making of Modern Iraq* ("Under the Ottomans, there had been for centuries three vilayets, or regions, in what was then called Mesopotamia. Each region was under the separate control of a governor and had little in common with the other two. The coastal province of al-Basrah included the port of Kuwait and the 'marsh Arabs,' or Ma'dan, who dwelled in the wetlands of the great delta formed by the Tigris and Euphrates Rivers."); Con Coughlin, *In Defence of the Indefensible*, The Telegraph (U.K.) (July 4, 2004) ("Iraqis generally resent the fact that the British gave Kuwait separate status during the great carve-up of the Middle East that followed the First World War,

strategic base of operations.[116] As noted above, substantial oil deposits had been discovered in Iraq even prior to World War I; Britain's policy was to control this oil, and this no doubt influenced its decision to carve out Kuwait from Iraq into a British "protectorate,"[117] which did not gain its independence until 1961.[118]

When Britain declared Kuwait independent and announced a military treaty with its new government, Iraq's then Prime Minister Qasem revived Iraq's claim to sovereignty over the small sheikhdom that largely cut off Iraq from the Gulf.[119] Qasem dispatched the Iraqi army to the border with Kuwait, but disclaimed any intention of reclaiming its territory after British warships, tanks, and troops arrived.[120] The Arab League, led by Qasem's rival Gamal Abdel-Nasser of the United Arab Republic (comprising Egypt and Syria), voted to recognize Kuwait as a sovereign state, and deployed a force of Egyptian troops to relieve the British units.[121]

Iraq invaded Kuwait on August 2, 1990. The same day, the U.N. Security Council branded the invasion a threat to international peace and security, triggering its powers under Chapter VII of the U.N. Charter.[122] On August 6, the Security Council prohibited the export of oil and gas from Iraq, denying the country the revenue to import adequate stocks of food, agricultural inputs, and medicine.[123] Seeds, fertilizers, pesticides, farm equipment, and other essential inputs for agriculture could not be imported at all, even though the initial U.N. sanctions resolution had called for the free importation of "foodstuffs" in "humanitarian circumstances." From their 1990 levels, Iraq's production of wheat, barley, and rice fell by about one-third (wheat) to 1/20th (rice). Wounds were infected further during surgery due to the lack of medical gauze, bandages, yarn, and sterile scalpels.[124]

On November 29, the Council authorized a U.S.-led coalition to restore international peace and security in the area.[125] The next day, Saudi Arabia and other Gulf Arab states announced an aid package to the Soviet Union, perhaps offered prior to the vote in order to secure it.[126] Saudi Arabia agreed to U.S. Defense Secretary Dick Cheney's proposal for military cooperation against Iraq.[127] The U.S. military deployed to Saudi Arabia on August 7 as part of "Operation Desert Shield."[128] President Bush proclaimed a "National Day

---

when previously it had come under the administration of the Ottoman vilayet, or administrative province, of Basra, the rest of which was incorporated into the new Iraq.").

116. *See* Catherwood, Churchill's Folly, at 139 (border between Iraq and Kuwait drawn "entirely in British interests").

117. Catherwood, Churchill's Folly, at 139; *see also* Lapidus, A History of Islamic Societies, at 552.

118. *See* USDOS, Bureau of Near Eastern Affairs, *Background Note: Kuwait* (2003), http://www.state.gov/r/pa/ei/bgn/5409.htm.

119. *See* Tripp, A History of Iraq, at 165.

120. *See* Simons, Iraq, at 257–58.

121. *See id.* at 166. *See also id.* at 145, 164, 166.

122. *See* S.C. Res. 660 (Aug. 2, 1990).

123. *See* S.C. Res. 661 (Aug. 6, 1990).

124. *Id.*, ¶ 3. *See The Continuing Impacts, in* Hidden Casualties Environmental, Health and Political Consequences of the Persian Gulf War 176 (Saul Bloom et al. eds., Berkeley, CA: Arms Control Research Center, 1994); International Study Team/ACRC, *Waterborne Diseases and Agricultural Consequences, in* Hidden Casualties, at 158, 160.

125. *See* S.C. Res. 678 (1990).

126. *See Arab States, Nationalism, and the Gulf War, in* Hidden Casualties, at 39.

127. *See id.* at 38.

128. *See* U.S. News & World Report, Triumph without Victory: The Hidden History of the Gulf War 86–89 (New York: Random House, 1992).

of Prayer" in support of the war against Iraq, and stated, "America, the finest, most loving nation on Earth, is at war; at war against the oldest enemy of the human spirit—evil that threatens world peace."[129]

The war began with U.S. and U.K. bombing of Iraqi positions in Kuwait, government buildings in Iraq, and oil refineries and other economic infrastructure in Iraq. Twenty-eight oil refineries in Iraq were bombed early in the war.[130] Iraq claimed in 1993 that the coalition's bombing of the oil installations incinerated 65 million liters of oil and "caused the outflow and discharge of 22,320 cubic meters of polluted waste per day to adjacent land and surface water."[131] Eighty percent of Iraq's electricity-generating capacity was destroyed.[132] The water mains broke, causing raw sewage to contaminate the drinking water. Two-thirds of Iraq's drinking water supplies tested by international researchers were positive for disease-causing germs. Iraq's baby milk formula, sugar, fertilizer, medical, and pharmaceutical factories were bombed, halting production and causing discharges of sulfuric acid and other toxins.[133]

Gulf War II claimed the lives of about 200,000 Iraqis through 1991.[134] The Defense Intelligence Agency estimated 100,000 Iraqi military deaths. Civilian deaths ranged from 20,000 to 240,000, an estimate which may have included the tens of thousands who died as a result of Iraqi government action to suppress northern Kurdish and southern Shi'a rebellions.[135]

To understand the impact of the bombing and sanctions after 1990, some context concerning Iraq's economic and health situation is necessary. Despite the disastrous wars, rebellions, and crimes against humanity under Saddam's rule, Iraq's population had increased by almost five million people from 1980 to 1990.[136] Life expectancy increased by almost 14 years on average between 1975 and 1990, as the government helped ensure that 90% of the population had access to safe drinking water and modern facilities for sanitation and health care.[137] Iraq's rate of infant mortality was one of the lowest in all of the Middle East.[138] The country's GDP doubled from 1975 to 1987, despite Gulf War I.[139] Free education, although of low quality in any politically-related subjects, debuted in 1974.[140]

Gulf War II reversed what progress in health and infrastructure there had been between 1975 and 1990, as the U.S. deliberately bombed water purification, sewage, and electricity facilities.[141] More than 4,000 cluster bombs and 10,000 anti-personnel missiles

---

129. Quoted in Jack D. Forbes, *The Gulf War: Once Again the Drama of Human Sacrifice,* 11 Wicazo Sa Review 60, 61 (1995).

130. *See The Oil Fires, in* Hidden Casualties, at 81.

131. *Quoted in Bombing Civilian Facilities, in* Hidden Casualties, at 147.

132. *See* International Study Team/ACRC, *Waterborne Diseases, in* Hidden Casualties, at 156.

133. *See id.* at 157, 162. *See also* International Study Team/ACRC, *Environmental Assessment of Bombed Sites, and Field Notes, in id.* at 167–68.

134. *See* U.S. Census Bureau, *Iraqi War Deaths, in* Hidden Casualties, at 189–93; Beth Osborne Daponte, *Interview, in* Hidden Casualties, at 182–89; *Toting the Casualties of War,* Business Week, Feb. 6, 2003, http://www.businessweek.com/bwdaily/dnflash/feb2003/nf2003026_0167_db052.htm (Beth Osborne Daponte, demographer at U.S. Commerce Department, estimated 205,000 deaths due to Gulf War II).

135. *See* U.S. Census Bureau, *Iraqi War Deaths,* at 190, 192.

136. *See Iraq,* CNN.Com (2001), *at* http://www.cnn.com/SPECIALS/2001/gulf.war/updates/iraq.

137. *See* U.N. Children's Fund, *Situation Analysis of Children and Women in Iraq—1997, at* 10 (1998), *at* http://www.childinfo.org/Other/Iraq_sa.pdf.

138. See International Study Team, *Child Mortality, in* Hidden Casualties, at 194.

139. *See id.*

140. *See* Kerim Yildix, The Kurds of Iraq: Past, Present and Future 58 (London: Pluto Press, 2006).

141. *See* George Lopez, *Not So Clean,* Bulletin of the Atomic Scientists, Sept. 1991, http://www.thebulletin.org/issues/1991/s91/s91lopez.html; Greg Barrett, *Running Dry: Sanctions Hit*

fell on Iraq and occupied Kuwait. These munitions either tear human bodies to shreds on impact, or scatter bomblets across an area as great as 60 acres per missile. Six Iraqis per day blew up each day in late 1991 due to encounters with unexploded ordinance, a British NGO estimated.[142]

F. The U.N. Sanctions

On August 6, 1990, the U.N. Security Council imposed comprehensive economic sanctions on Iraq.[143] Iraq rejected a proposed U.N. sanctions regime that contemplated the payment of 30 percent of the proceeds of its oil sales for reparations to Kuwait, Saudi Arabia, the U.S., Israel, and other countries, as well as a barely (arguably not even) proportionate share for Kurdish areas.[144] Deprived of most of its oil revenue until the late 1990s, Iraqi national income plunged to 1940s levels and the health care system virtually collapsed.[145] The sanctions, originally imposed to pressure Iraq to leave Kuwait, were continued long after the end of the Gulf War, their basis shifting to eliminating Iraq's chemical and biological weapons and nuclear weapons development program,[146] even though Iraq had destroyed its banned weapons in 1991.[147]

Even after Iraq agreed to U.N. administration of its oil revenues with deductions for reparations to Kuwait and the Gulf War coalition, the oil-for-food program allocated only $26 to $31 billion for Iraq's food, medicine, sanitation, clothing, infrastructure, and education needs over the seven years of the program from 1996 to 2003. This was $170 per person per year, or less than half what the United Nations allocated to feed and care for dogs used in de-mining operations in Iraq and elsewhere.[148] About $34 billion that could

---

Iraq's Young the Hardest, Seattle Times, Aug. 4, 2002, http://www.commondreams.org/headlines02/0804-04.htm; Thomas J. Nagy, *The Role of "Iraq Water Treatment Vulnerabilities" in Halting One Genocide and Preventing Others* (2001), http://home.gwu.edu/~nagy/iwtv-ags.htm.

142. Geoff Simons, The Scourging of Iraq: Sanctions, Law, and Natural Justice 7, 111 (New York: St. Martin's Press, 2002).

143. *See* S.C. Res. 661 (Aug. 6, 1990); S.C. Res. 687, ¶¶ 20–29 (Apr. 3, 1991); *Iraq Condemns Embargo on 9th Anniversary of Sanctions*, CNN.Com, Aug. 6, 1999, *at* http://www.cnn.com/WORLD/meast/9908/06/iraq.sanctions (citing "United Nations estimates"); U.N. Children's Fund, *Iraq Surveys Show "Humanitarian Emergency"* (Aug. 12, 1999), http://www.unicef.org/newsline/99pr29.htm.

144. *See* Coughlin, Saddam, at 286–92. The sanctions regime proposed by the U.N. Security Council contemplated the payment of 30% of the annual value of Iraq's oil and petroleum exports for reparations until December 2000, after which the percentage was reduced to 25%, and another 13% for Iraqi Kurdistan. *See* S.C. Res. 705, ¶ 2 (Aug. 15, 1991); Office of the Director of Central Intelligence, Comprehensive Report of the Special Advisor to the DCI on Iraq's WMD (2004), https://www.odci.gov/cia/reports/iraq_wmd_2004/chap2_annxD.html.

145. *See* U.N. Children's Fund, *Situation Analysis of Women and Children in Iraq*, at 16–17; World Health Organization, *Iraqi Health System Close to Collapse, Says WHO Director-General* (Feb. 27, 1997), *at* http://www.who.int/archives/inf-pr-1997/en/pr97-16.html.

146. *See Final Report: Iraq Had No WMDs*, USA Today, Oct. 6, 2004, http://www.usatoday.com/news/world/iraq/2004-10-06-wmd_x.htm.

147. *See id.*; John Mueller & Karl Mueller, *Sanctions of Mass Destruction*, Foreign Affairs, May/June 1999, http://www.foreignaffairs.org/19990501faessay979/john-mueller-karl-mueller/sanctions-of-mass-destruction.html?mode=print.

148. *See* Lando, Web of Deceit, at 209; *Oil-For-Food Program Fails to Meet Iraq's Needs: Weekly*, Xinhua News Agency, Aug. 11, 2000 ("Iraq's crude exports since 1996 have generated 28 billion US dollars, but Iraq received goods worth only 7 billion dollars"); United Nations, Office of the Iraq Pro-

have gone to feed, clothe, and care for Iraqi children went to oil-rich Kuwait, Saudi Arabia, and wealthy corporations in the U.S. and other countries.[149]

Iraqi civilians suffered from widespread starvation and disease from the combined effects of economic sanctions and bombing of essential electrical, health, telecommunications, and economic infrastructure. Male life expectancy plummeted by 14 years, from 66.5 years in 1990 to only 52.7 years in 1991. Female life expectancy fell by nearly as much, from 67.6 to 58.4 years, despite the absence of large numbers of women in the armed forces.[150] Had Iraqi life expectancy followed world trends from the late 1980s to the late 1990s, it would have stood at 67 years; instead, it was reduced to 58.8 in the late 1990s from 65 in the 1980s.[151] Infant mortality doubled by 1994–1995. Monthly deaths of children under the age of five increased by eight times from 1990 to 1991.[152] The death rate from childhood diarrhea rose nearly sixfold.[153] The total number of deaths per year rose from 120,000 in 1985–1990 to 230,000 in 1995–2000.[154] Iraq had the highest infant mortality rate in all Asia, nearly triple the rate of Indonesia or Iran.[155]

The World Food Programme reported that seventy percent of the Iraqi population had little or no access to food, with 2.4 million children under five and 600,000 pregnant

---

gram, *Oil-for-Food* (2009), http://www.un.org/depts/oip/ ("About $31 billion worth of humanitarian supplies and equipment were delivered to Iraq under the Oil-for-Food Programme between 20 March 1997 and 21 November 2003....").

149. *See* Judy Aita, *U.N. Transfers Oil-for-Food Program to CPA, Iraqi Officials* (Nov. 20, 2003), http://www.usembassy.it/viewer/article.asp?article=/file2003_11/alia/a3112004.htm; UNCC, *At a Glance* (2007), http://www.unog.ch/uncc/ataglance.htm; UNCC, *Opening of the Sixty-Second Session of the UNCC Governing Council* (Feb. 16, 2007), http://www2.unog.ch/uncc/pressrel/pr_62o.pdf; UNCC, *United Nations Compensation Commission Governing Council Has Concluded Its Sixty-First Session* (Nov. 3, 2006), http://www2.unog.ch/uncc/pressrel/pr_61c.pdf; UNCC, *Opening of the Fifty-Sixth Session of the UNCC Governing Council* (June 24, 2005), http://www2.unog.ch/uncc/pressrel/pr_56o.pdf; UNCC Governing Council, *Report and Recommendations Made by the Panel of Commissioners Concerning Part Three of the Third Instalment of "F3" Claims*, S/AC.26/2003/15, ¶419 (June 26, 2003).

150. *See* U.S. Census Bureau, *Iraqi War Deaths,* at 190, 192.

151. *See* U.N. Department of Economic and Social Affairs (U.N. DESA), World Population Prospects: The 2006 Revision 660, 672 (U.N. Publications, 2007), http://books.google.com/books?id=ghTtZ89QOt4C. Worldwide, life expectancy increased by two years on average from the late 1980s to late 1990s, so based on that Iraq's would have gone from 65 to 67.

152. *See* U.N. Food and Agriculture Org., Technical Cooperation Program, Evaluation of Food and Nutrition Situation in Iraq, tbl. 28 (Rome: U.N. Food and Agricultural Org., 1995).

153. *See* U.S. Census Bureau, *Iraqi War Deaths,* at 190, 192; International Study Team (Harvard Group), *Child Mortality, Nutrition, and Health Care, in* Hidden Casualties, at 195.

154. *See* U.N. DESA, World Population Prospects: The 2006 Revision, at 276. Iraq's crude death rate (deaths per 1,000 inhabitants) increased from seven in the late 1980s to 10 in the late 1990s. *See* U.N. Dept. of Economic and Social Affairs, World Population Prospects: The 2004 Revision 275–77, 626 (U.N. Publications, 2005). Assuming that Iraq's population stayed constant at 17.3 million (the 1990 figure), this would have resulted in an increase in the number of annual deaths from 121,000 to 173,000. However, Iraq's population increased to about 23 million in 2000 due to a high birth rate, leading to an increase in annual deaths to about 230,000. The excess deaths due to sanctions in the late 1990s could therefore be put at about 70,000 a year, or three-thousandths of 23 million.

155. *See* U.N. DESA, World Population Prospects: The 2006 Revision, ch. VII annex, tbl. A.18, http://web.archive.org/web/20070510022958/www.un.org/esa/population/publications/wpp2006/wpp2006.htm.

and nursing women at severe risk.[156] The percentage of malnourished children quadrupled, as did mortality among young children (under five) from 1990 to the mid-1990s.[157] The price of food had skyrocketed by up to 2,000 percent as parents' wages remained constant or perhaps even fell.[158] Iraq issued rations of only 1,500 calories per day to its citizens, below the 2,700 calories per day needed by adults.[159] The rate of childhood starvation exceeded the prevailing rate in Mali or the Democratic Republic of the Congo.[160] The infant mortality rate was higher than in North Korea, Sudan, or Zimbabwe.[161]

The sanctions themselves caused more deaths than all the weapons of mass destruction ever used in the course of human history.[162] The United Nations estimated that they caused 1.5 million excess deaths among Iraqis.[163] The U.N. Children's Fund estimated that they caused 500,000 excess deaths among children under the age of five by 1998.[164] A report in the British medical journal *The Lancet* offered a similar estimate, i.e., 567,000 deaths of children between August 1990 and late 1995. A Harvard study estimated that 170,000 children under five died in 1991 alone.[165] The sanctions are therefore blamed for more deaths than several adjudicated genocides, including those in Srebrenica, Rwanda, Ethiopia, Estonia, and Latvia. One month of sanctions may have caused more deaths among children under the age of five than resulted from the chemical weapons attack on Halabja. One year of them killed more civilians than the atomic bombing of Hiroshima.

Despite several attempts by scholars to identify the U.N. sanctions as a genocidal policy, the matter of intent is complicated and disputed. Two former U.N. humanitarian coordinators for Iraq condemned the sanctions regime as genocide or at least crimes against humanity as a result of their impact on infants and small children in particular.[166] The sanctions, as noted above, sharply increased infant and child mortality rates, as well as mal-

---

156. *See* SIMONS, THE SCOURGING OF IRAQ, at viii.

157. *See* U.N. FOOD AND AGRICULTURE ORG., TECHNICAL COOPERATION PROGRAM, EVALUATION OF FOOD AND NUTRITION SITUATION IN IRAQ, tbl. 28 (Rome, 1995).

158. *See* International Study Team, *Child Mortality, in* HIDDEN CASUALTIES, at 196–97.

159. *See The Continuing Impacts, in id.* at 175.

160. *See* U.N. FOOD AND AGRICULTURE ORG., TECHNICAL COOPERATION PROGRAM, EVALUATION OF FOOD AND NUTRITION SITUATION IN IRAQ.

161. *See* U.N. DESA, WORLD POPULATION PROSPECTS: THE 2006 REVISION, ch. VII annex, tbl. A.18.

162. *See* John Mueller & Karl Mueller, *Sanctions of Mass Destruction*, FOREIGN AFFAIRS, May/June 1999, http://www.foreignaffairs.org/19990501faessay979/john-mueller-karl-mueller/sanctions-of-mass-destruction.html?mode=print; Joy Gordon, *Cool War: Economic Sanctions as a Weapon of Mass Destruction*, HARPER'S MAGAZINE, Nov. 2002, http://www.harpers.org/CoolWar.html.

163. *See Iraq Condemns Embargo* (citing U.N. estimates).

164. *See* UNICEF, U*NICEF Iraq Child and Maternal Mortality Surveys* (July 23, 2000), http://web.archive.org/web/20030628153329/http://www.unicef.org.uk/index_s.asp?sct=news&filen=../news/iraq1.htm. The report stated: "During the 1980s substantial progress was made in reducing child mortality throughout Iraq. If this reduction in child mortality had through the 1990s, there would have been half a million fewer child deaths (under-five) in the country as a whole during the eight year period 1991 to 1998." *Id. See also* U.N. CHILDREN'S FUND, CHILDREN AND WOMEN IN IRAQ: A SITUATION ANALYSIS (Mar. 1993); ERIC HOSKINS, CHILDREN, WAR, AND SANCTIONS, REPORT ON THE EFFECTS OF SANCTIONS ON IRAQI WOMEN AND CHILDREN (Apr. 1993).

165. *See* SIMONS, THE SCOURGING OF IRAQ, at ix, 51. The Harvard Study was prospective, estimating the number of deaths that would occur in 1991 if sanctions were not lifted, which in fact they were not. *See id.* at 51.

166. *See* Sophia Boukhari, *Embargo against Iraq: Crime and Punishment*, THE UNESCO COURIER, July/Aug. 2000, at 57–58; Denis J. Halliday, *The Impact of UN Sanctions on the People of Iraq,* 28 J. OF PALESTINE STUD. 29 (1999); HANS VON SPONECK, A DIFFERENT KIND OF WAR: THE UN SANCTIONS REGIME IN IRAQ (New York: Berghahn Books, 2006).

nutrition rates and the prevalence of diseases that primarily affect children and persons in a weakened state. The waste of billions of dollars by the U.N. oil-for-food program's administrators, and the overpayment of reparations claimants by several billion dollars during these nutritional and disease-related crises, create a strong inference of reckless disregard for civilian life and health.[167] The overpayments to the Kuwaiti military reached $419 million, or about the same amount allocated to feed, educate, clothe, and house 2.4 million Iraqi children during some years of sanctions.[168]

Complicating the question of intent to destroy the Iraqi people, however, are the facts that the Iraqi population steadily grew under the sanctions period, as the U.N. delivered food and medicine, albeit in quantities inadequate to prevent widespread hunger and disease.[169] A destructive intent is also undermined, as in the Vietnam War, by measures on the part of the U.N. Security Council and U.N. member states to provide assistance to sectors of the Iraqi population. The U.N. launched an effort during the sanctions period to vaccinate all children under the age of five against polio, for example.[170] The U.N. built or repaired schools and universities.[171] The complicated bureaucracy of the United Nations, the voting structure of the U.N. Security Council, and the intention to deny Iraq access to chemical weapons that could be used on Iranians or Kurds further confound attempts to infer a destructive intent by any one actor. Unlike the officials of the Ottoman Empire, Nazi Germany, Yugoslavia, Rwanda, and Iraq itself, the U.N. administrators of the sanctions did not violently kill anyone or wantonly pillage and destroy private property. In sum, many persons in the U.N. bureaucracy likely helped the Iraqi people survive to whatever extent they had the funds to do so, and the U.N.'s overall intent was complex. Thus, any attempt to characterize the sanctions on Iraq as genocidal requires conceptual and legal sophistication, and perhaps the definition of a distinct crime of blockade.

G. The Kurdish and Shi'a Rebellions of 1991

In 1991, thousands of Kurds rebelled against the government that had destroyed so many villages and waged two fruitless wars with Iran and U.N. forces. The *pesh merga* militia and local supporters summarily executed hundreds of suspected Iraqi army troops

167. *See, e.g.*, Independent Inquiry Committee Into the United Nations Oil-For-Food Programme, Briefing Paper, Internal Audit Reports On The United Nations Oil-For-Food Programme 9 (Jan. 9, 2005), http://www.iicoffp.org/documents/IAD%20Briefing%20Paper.pdf; Colum Lynch, *Volcker Probe Faults U.N. Auditors on Iraq*, Wash. Post, Jan. 10, 2005, at A14 (U.N. sanctions regime "may have wasted billions"); Stephanie Nebehay, *Gulf War Victims Overpaid by $5 Billion—UN Auditors*, Reuters (Jan. 9, 2005), http://www.odiousdebts.org/odiousdebts/index.cfm?DSP=content&ContentID=12184 (waste, fraud, and overpayments may have totaled $5 billion); Nick Wadhams, *Oil-for-food Probe Finds Mismanagement*, Associated Press, July 15, 2005, http://www.usatoday.com.

168. *See, e.g.*, Judith Miller, *Report From Panel Shows Lapses In U.N.'s Oil-for-Food Program*, N.Y Times, Jan. 10, 2005), http://74.125.47.132/search?q=cache:UfdpprFvxQ8J:query.nytimes.com/gst/fullpage.html.

169. *See* Boukhari, *Embargo against Iraq*, at 57–59; U.N. Educational, Scientific, and Cultural Organization (UNESCO), *Final Report: "Oil for Food" Programme 1996–2003*, at 9 (2004), http://www.unesco.org.

170. *See* Barbara Plett, *Iraq Struggles under Sanctions*, BBC News, Apr. 2, 2000, http://news.bbc.co.uk/1/hi/world/middle_east/698462.stm.

171. *See* UNESCO, *Final Report*, at 4–5.

and other government officials. A government counterattack drove more than a million refugees into Turkey and Iran, and provoked the Security Council to condemn the repression of the civilian population, especially in "Kurdish populated areas."[172] The army received orders to kill anyone seen walking about in the largely Kurdish city of Suleimaniyah.[173]

The Shi'a religious leadership in Iraq mounted a rebellion in the southern provinces of Basra, Missan, and more than half a dozen others. Set off by deserters from the Iraqi Army, the rebellion had been quelled by March or April 1991, with U.S. forces denying the rebels access to Iraqi Army arsenals, allowing Iraqi troops to pass through U.S. lines, and relaxing its total command of the skies to permit Iraqi forces to utilize helicopter gunships to attack rebel positions.[174] Human Rights Watch alleged that the rebels "killed hundreds, if not thousands, of members of the security forces and others allegedly working for the Baath."[175]

By October 1991, "senior Arab diplomats told the London-based Arabic daily newspaper al-Hayat in October that Iraqi leaders were privately acknowledging that 250,000 people were killed during the uprisings, with most of the casualties in the south." Indiscriminate shelling by artillery and the strafing of cities by helicopter gunships likely claimed many lives.[176] The government detained and executed hundreds, and probably thousands, of young Shi'a men were in the years following 1991, and disappeared and probably killed more than 100 Shi'a clerics.[177] The Iraqi Army looted cities upon recapturing them from the rebels, impoverishing families.[178]

Altogether, Saddam's indiscriminate response to the Iranian-backed rebellions by Kurdish and Shi'a parties may have killed more than 200,000 people.[179] Mass graves were dug to contain the large numbers of Kurdish victims in Kirkuk, Suleimaniyah, and elsewhere. In 1992, the Special Rapporteur for Iraq of the U.N. Commission on Human Rights, reported that:

> [T]he mass murder and execution of Kurds, the destruction of Kurdish towns and villages, forced urbanization and internal deportation, limits on ownership of private property by Kurds in areas designated by the authorities for inhabitance by the majority population, restrictions on agricultural activities, and the use of excessive force, including chemical weapons, against the Kurds in times of conflict ... [are] policies ... [that] bear the marks of a genocide-type design.[180]

---

172. *See* Middle East Watch, Hidden Death: Land Mines and Civilian Casualties in Iraqi Kurdistan 5 (New York: Human Rights Watch, 1992) (quoting S.C. Res. 688 (Apr. 5, 1991)).

173. Joost R. Hiltermann, Bureaucracy of Repression: the Iraqi Government in Its Own Words 124–26 (New York: Middle East Watch, 1994).

174. *See* William Polk, Understanding Iraq 151–54 (New York: Harper Perennial, 2006).

175. *Iraq, in* Human Rights Watch World Report 1992, http://www.unhcr.org/refworld/country,,,,IRQ,,467fca591e,0.html.

176. *Id.*

177. *See Iraq, in* Human Rights Watch World Report 1994, http://www.unhcr.org/refworld/country,,,,IRQ,,467fca96c,0.html.

178. *Iraq, in* Human Rights Watch World Report 1992.

179. *See* Middle East Watch, Genocide in Iraq, at § 2, http://hrw.org/reports/1993/iraqanfal/ANFAL2.htm; *Neighbours from Hell*, The Economist, Dec. 12, 2002, http://www.economist.com/world/africa/displayStory.cfm?story_id=1494035; Aburish, Saddam Hussein, at 311–13; Peter W. Galbraith, *The Ghosts of 1991*, Wash. Post, Apr. 12, 2003, at A19, http://www.washingtonpost.com/ac2/wp-dyn/A10874-2003Apr11?language=printer; Kenneth Roth, *Try Saddam in an International Court,* Int'l Herald Trib., Dec. 15, 2003, http://www.iht.com/articles/121445.html.

180. Max van der Stoel, *quoted in* The United Nations and the Iraq-Kuwait Conflict, 1990–1996, at 403 (Boutros Boutros-Ghali ed., New York: United Nations Publications, 1996).

Anywhere from 200,000 to 2.5 million fled the Iraqi army's campaign to retake the northern provinces from Kurdish *pesh merga*.[181] More than one million Kurds and 100,000 other northern Iraqis fled to Iran, along with more than 700,000 Shi'a Arabs predominantly from the south and center of the country. In June 1991, NGOs estimated that the Gulf War had displaced five million people from their homes. Doctors Without Borders estimated in 1991 that 1,000 refugees from northern Iraq, mainly Kurds but also Assyrians, died every day at the height of the crisis.[182] Some reports mentioned two million refugees.[183] As of 2000, there were still 450,000 refugees outside Iraq and 700,000 IDPs within Iraq, more than from Bosnia, Croatia, and Kosovo combined.[184]

In response to the repression, the U.S., United Kingdom, and France established a safe haven covering the cities of Dohuk, Zakho, Amadiya, and Suri, and a no-fly zone extending even further south. This empowered the *pesh merga* to control much of the Arbil, Suleimaniyah, and Kirkuk governorates as well. Iraq responded by blockading food and aid, but U.N. aid helped fill some of the gap.[185] According to the U.S. State Department, the blockade covered areas inhabited by "Kurds, Assyrians, Turkoman, and other ethnic minorities," curtailed the delivery of "food, medicine, and other humanitarian supplies to that area," and after 1992 also involved electricity cuts that shut down water, sanitation, and food delivery systems.[186]

Shortly thereafter, the Security Council condemned Iraq's policies in the north as "grave human rights abuses," which included "reported restrictions on the supplies of essential commodities, in particular food and fuel, which have been imposed by the Government of Iraq on the three northern governates of Dohuk, Erbil, and Suleimaniyya."[187] The "Arabization" campaign continued through 2001, especially in the area around Kirkuk, and drove 100,000 Kurds, Turkmen, and Assyrians from their homes and villages.[188] All the while, China, Russia, and Serbia helped rearm the Iraqi military.[189] Perhaps owing to their economic interests of the members of the Security Council, all of whom were creditors of Iraq, an international effort to sanction Iraq for genocide failed to gain traction until the Ba'ath party fell in 2003.

---

181. *See* Alan Cowell, *Kurdish Refugees, by Thousands, Flee Vengeance of the Iraqi Army*, N.Y. Times, April 4, 1991, http://query.nytimes.com/gst/fullpage.html?res=9D0CE0D9133DF937A35757C0A967958260; John Kifner, *Many Kurds Leave Border For Towns They Fled in Iraq*, N.Y. Times, May 1, 1991, http://query.nytimes.com/gst/fullpage.html?res=9D0CE3D71E39F932A35756C0A967958260; *6 US Planes Begin Airlifting Relief To Kurds in Iraq*, N.Y. Times, Apr. 8, 1991, http://query.nytimes.com/gst/fullpage.html?res=9D0CE4D91F3DF93BA35757C0A967958260.

182. *See* Judith Miller, *Displaced in the Gulf War: 5 Million Refugees*, N.Y. Times, June 16, 1991, at 39.

183. *See* Alex J. Bellamy, *Ethics and Intervention: the 'Humanitarian Exception' and the Problem of Abuse in the Case of Iraq*, 41 J. of Peace Res. 131, 138 (2004).

184. *See* Leonore Loeb Adler, Robert J. Kleiner, & Uwe P. Gielen, Migration: Immigration and Emigration in International Perspective 14 (2003); Human Rights Watch, *The Silent Treatment: Fleeing Iraq, Surviving in Jordan* 20 (2006), http://www.hrw.org/reports/2006/jordan1106/jordan1106webwcover.pdf.

185. *See* Middle East Watch, Hidden Death, at 5–9.

186. USDOS, *Country Reports on Human Rights, Iraq 1995*, http://dosfan.lib.uic.edu/ERC/democracy/1995_hrp_report/95hrp_report_nea/Iraq.html.

187. *Quoted in* Repertoire of the Practice of the Security Council: Supplement 1989–1992, at 207 (New York: United Nations Publications, 1992).

188. *See* The Government of the United Kingdom, Home Office, *Iraq Country Assessment*, at ¶¶ 6.13, 6.71 (2003).

189. *See* Coughlin, Saddam, at 286–92.

After the fall of the Saddam Hussein regime, the government of Prime Minister Nouri al-Maliki opened an investigation into unlawful killings and tortures during the events of March and April 1991.[190] In December 2008, the Iraqi High Tribunal sentenced former Interior Minister al-Majid to death for crimes against humanity during the suppression of the 1991 rebellions. The court also sentenced the head of the Ba'ath Party in southern Iraq to death.[191]

Gulf War II and the 1991 rebellions had other deleterious effects on human rights as well. Due to the crisis of legitimacy they reflected, the Iraqi regime turned to violent anti-woman policies in an effort to build support for its continued rule among religious and tribal conservatives. The regime amended Iraq's Penal Code to exempt men who murder female family members in the name of family honor, after which Iraqi men murdered more than 4,000 female relatives. Under the pretext of ending prostitution, pro-government paramilitary *Fedayeen* killed more than 200 women tied to the political opposition.[192] The policies of the Kurdish parties that controlled northern Iraq after 1991 also tended to perpetuate the oppression of women. The Kurdistan region they led passed a law allowing men to kill their wives for disobedience, an offer that an estimated 550 men accepted between 1991 and 1994.[193] An Iraqi women's rights activist blamed the Kurdish nationalist parties for complicity in more than 8,000 "honor killings" of women in the 13 years after they gained control over northern Iraq.[194]

---

190. *See* Voice of Iraq, *Investigation into 1991 Incidents Reached Advanced Stage in Southern Provinces*, Aswat al-Iraq (Aug. 19, 2007), http://en.aswataliraq.info/?p=D53021.

191. *See Chemical Ali Sentenced to Death for a Second Time*, The Telegraph (U.K.), Dec. 2, 2008, http://www.telegraph.co.uk/news/worldnews/middleeast/iraq/3542055/Chemical-Ali-sentenced-to-death-for-a-second-time.html; *"Chemical Ali" Sentenced to Death, Again*, CBS News, Dec. 2, 2008, http://www.cbsnews.com.

192. *See* USDOS, *Iraqi Women Under Saddam's Regime: A Population Silenced* (Mar. 20, 2003), http://www.state.gov/ (citing U.N. Commission on Human Rights, *Report of the Special Rapporteur on Violence Against Women* ¶ 23 (Jan. 2002), http://www.unhchr.ch). *See also* U.N. Commission on Human Rights, *Report of the U.N. High Commissioner for Human Rights and Follow-up to the World Conference on Human Rights, The Present Situation of Human Rights in Iraq*, E/CN.4/2005/4 (June 9, 2004), http://www.unhchr.ch/html/hchr/docs/iraq1.doc.

193. *See* Courtney W. Howland, *The Challenge of Religious Fundamentalism to the Liberty and Equality Rights of Women: An Analysis under the United Nations Charter*, 35 Colum. J. Transnat'l L. 271, 314 (1997).

194. *See* Houzan Mahmoud, *An Empty Sort of Freedom*, The Guardian (U.K.), Mar. 8, 2004, http://www.guardian.co.uk.

Chapter XIII

Death by "Resource Curse": Post-Cold War Genocides

> In his survey of the literature on resource abundance and civil war, [Michael L.] Ross notes that oil is associated with the onset of civil war and that certain lootable natural resources such as diamonds are associated with the duration of civil wars but that an abundance of legal agricultural commodities is not associated with conflict.
>
> —Colin H. Kahl[1]

Despite the proclamation of the end of the Cold War in 1991, the former and continuing allies and client states of the U.S. and the Soviet Union attacked their own minorities and their regional rivals. In some cases, state authorities perpetuated existing policies of displacing, torturing, and killing members of indigenous minorities (and sometimes even majorities) in order to sustain policies of conquest and subjugation, as in Indonesia, Brazil, Colombia, Ecuador, and Guatemala. In others, the collapse of all or a part of the state led to widespread killing, looting, rape, conscription of child soldiers into militias, and massive spikes in rates of malnutrition and disease as a result. Major examples of this phenomenon include Afghanistan, Liberia, Sierra Leone, and Somalia. In still others, coalitions of states have joined together to fund an insurgency in another state, which then embarked upon counterinsurgency operations using genocidal strategies such as large-scale massacres, imposition of conditions on enemy populations that were calculated to cause thousands of civilian deaths, and the rape and looting of civilians perceived to be part of a disloyal ethnic or religious group. The dynamic in these cases very much resembles the illegal and criminal response of the government of Yugoslavia to the massive international campaign to finance terrorism in and bring about the partition of that country after the fall of the Soviet Union. Other examples appeared in Asia (particularly Chechnya, Sri Lanka, and Turkey), and Africa (Algeria, Angola, and the Democratic Republic of the Congo). Finally, corrupt local elites and inhumane leaders of international financial institutions allowed large sectors of some national and ethnic groups to die in structural violence involving the denial of food, health care, and clean water. Major examples of this phenomenon include Chad, Niger, North Korea, South Africa, Uganda, and Zimbabwe.

---

1. Colin H. Kahl, States, Scarcity and Strife in the Developing World 260 (Princeton, New Jersey: Princeton UP, 2006) (citing Michael L. Ross, *What Do We Know About Natural Resources and Civil War?*, 3 J. of Peace Res. 337 (2004)).

Image 5 A Political Map of North Africa and the Middle East, Circa 1995

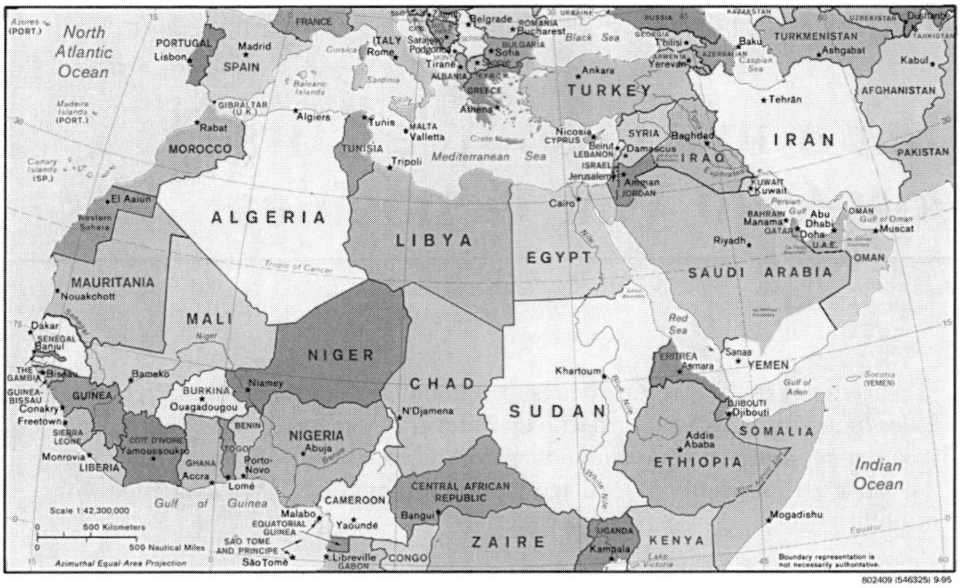

A. Counterinsurgency Massacres in Post-Cold War Asia

Several counterinsurgency campaigns during the post-Cold War period were nearly as deadly and productive of civilian displacement, as were the declared genocides in Bosnia or Kosovo. Turkey's campaign against Kurdish separatists, even after 1991, destroyed Kurdish villages, killed over many civilians, displaced thousands of people, involved widespread rape and torture of civilians, and required the forced assimilation of ethnic and religious minorities. The Turkish military has admitted that village destruction is part of its counterinsurgency strategy. Unless villagers joined anti-Kurdish independence militia groups, their homes were burned. Another motive for village destruction is thought to be preventing the growth into southeastern Turkey of the KDP- and PUK-controlled zone in northern Iraq. In 1998, the European Union called the village destructions a policy of "extreme brutality," accompanied as it is by "sexual assault and humiliation, beatings and extrajudicial executions."[2]

Turkey publicly abandoned its obligations under the Geneva Conventions and human rights law not to carry out executions except after a proper arrest, arraignment, and period of pretrial detention with bail. The European Union subsequently condemned Turkey's practice of carrying out criminal trials and sentences in violation of the laws of war and human rights law. Human Rights Watch has "noted that torture and ill-treatment in police custody are common."[3] Torture is "endemic" in Turkey, and the implements of tor-

2. *Quoted in* KERIM YILDIZ, THE KURDS IN IRAQ: THE PAST, PRESENT AND FUTURE 83 (London: Pluto Press, 2004).

3. *Quoted in* Thomas W. Smith, *The ECHR and Turkey's Human Rights Reforms, in* HUMAN RIGHTS IN TURKEY 266–69 (Zehra F. Kabasakal Arat ed., Philadelphia: Univ. of Pennsylvania Press, 2007). The Geneva Conventions, and in particular Common Article 3 of the several individual conventions, require certain indispensable judicial guarantees prior to the carrying out of prison sentences and executions. Arbitrary arrests and detention without due process violate these guarantees. *See, e.g.*, Harold

ture have been publicly displayed in front of the Turkish parliament. Education by Kurdish parents of their children in the Kurdish language remains illegal, as does the use of Kurdish letters not present in Turkish, or the exercise of freedom of speech to criticize the government or past governments.[4]

Meanwhile, Armenia loses hundreds of millions of dollars every year to a blockade on both sides by Turkey and Turkey's ally Azerbaijan. As a report prepared for the European Parliament stated, Armenia is landlocked, with both its western and eastern borders closed due to Turkish policies, and it can only import food and medicine through "expensive routes through Georgia and Iran." Thus, the entire nation's development is retarded.[5] The blockade was in breach of the Treaty of Kars in which the Soviet Union agreed to give up the Armenian Soviet Socialist Republic's claims on eastern Anatolia in exchange for the "quick[]" establishment of "railway, telegraphic, and other communications" links as well as the "free transit of persons and commodities without any hindrance." It also violated the General Agreement on Tariffs and Trade and its 1994 protocols creating the World Trade Organization.[6] Armenia's impoverished residents enjoyed a GDP per capita less than one-fourth of Israel's figure in 2004.[7] Turkey's GDP was 40 times higher than Armenia's in 2007.[8]

In the Caucasus region spanning Europe and Asia, Human Rights Watch concluded that the Russian Federation manifested a pattern of carrying out enforced disappearances in Chechnya that reached the level of a crime against humanity.[9] The Committee for the Prevention of Torture (CPT) declared that there is "continued resort to torture and other forms of ill-treatment by members of the law enforcement agencies and federal forces operating in the Chechen Republic," as well as forced disappearances in the territory of the Chechen Republic.[10] Some estimates of the death toll in Chechnya exceed 200,000. The Chechen capital of Grozny was largely shelled and bombed into rubble in the 1990s. Up to 200,000 fled as refugees in the mid-1990s, and 200,000 people were displaced within Chechnya.[11]

Hongju Koh, *The Case against Military Commissions*, 96 American J. of International Law 337 (2002).

4. *See* Zehra F. Kabasakal Arat, *Conclusion: Turkey's Prospects and Broader Implications, in* Human Rights in Turkey, at 275–82.

5. European Parliament, Directorate General for External Policies of the Union, *The Closed Armenia-Turkey Border: Economic and Social Effects, Including Those on the People; and Implications for the Overall Situation in the Region* 3 (Brussels: European Parliament, 2007), http://www.europarl. europa.eu/activities/expert/eStudies.do?languageEN. *See also*: http://www.anca.org/action_alerts/action alerts.php?aaid=14; http://www.anca.org/press_releases/press_releases.php?prid=230.

6. Treaty of Kars (Treaty of Friendship between Turkey, the Socialist Soviet Republic of Armenia, the Azerbaijan Socialist Soviet Republic, and the Socialist Soviet Republic of Georgia), adopted Oct. 23, 1921, http://groong.usc.edu/treaties/kars.html. *See also* European Parliament, Directorate General for External Policies of the Union, *The Closed Armenia-Turkey Border* at 9.

7. *Armenia, in* World Factbook 2004, https://www.cia.gov/library/publications/the-world-factbook/rankorder/2004rank.html.

8. *See* European Parliament, Directorate General for External Policies of the Union, *The Closed Armenia-Turkey Border* at 15 (statistics given are for GDP per capita at purchasing power parity).

9. "International law recognizes that a widespread or systematic pattern of enforced disappearances constitutes a crime against humanity—an act or series of acts that outrage the conscience of humankind." Disappearances become a crime against humanity when conducted on a large scale or widespread basis. Human Rights Watch, *Worse Than a War: "Disappearances" in Chechnya—A Crime Against Humanity* (2005), http://www.hrw.org/.

10. European Committee for the Prevention of Torture and Inhuman or Degrading Treatment or Punishment, *Public Statement Concerning the Chechen Republic of the Russian Federation* (July 10, 2003), http://www.cpt.coe.int/documents/rus/2003-33-inf-eng.htm.

South Asia has remained the scene of significant massacres and devastation of indigenous communities. After the assassination of Indian Prime Minister Indira Gandhi in 1984, purportedly by her Sikh bodyguards, the governing Congress party in Delhi organized large-scale massacres of Sikhs, as many as 5,000 in the vicinity of Delhi alone. About 500 were burned alive, and about 50,000 people burned out of or intimidated into leaving their homes. The Congress party rebuffed requests for an investigation and criminal prosecutions of the ringleaders.[12] Similarly, in 2002 after a massacre of over 50 Hindus aboard a train, purportedly by Muslims, a high official in the state of Gujarat organized the massacre of Muslims, killing some 2,000, displacing 150,000 from their homes and communities, and cutting down entire families.[13] The "Primitive Tribal Groups" of India confront the constant threat of eviction from their homes and villages, and their languages are at risk of extinction. Mineral extraction, industrial projects, and power stations frequently result in tribal groups losing their land.[14]

In Sri Lanka, separatist attacks in 1983 triggered widespread and systematic riots against the Tamil minority that claimed up to 3,000 lives, 100,000 refugees, many rape victims, and millions of dollars in damage to homes, shops, and factories.[15] The toll from civil war was estimated at more than 215,000 by 2008.[16] In 2009, the press reported a massacre of 20,000 trapped civilians during the final stages of the government's war against ethnic Tamils.[17] In Pakistan, churches have been burned to the grounds and Christians regularly beaten and shot by fundamentalists.[18] Terrorists suspected to be based in Pakistan killed 200 people in attacks on commuter trains and stations in Mumbai, India in 2008, and massacred 22 Hindu villagers in the Kashmir region in that same year.[19]

In Indonesia, corruption and increasing religious radicalism under the dictator Suharto led to deadly riots against the Chinese minority, and the burning or looting of several hundred churches in Jakarta and elsewhere between 1996 and 1998.[20] Suharto embezzled

---

11. *See, e.g.*, Michael Specter, *Agony of Chechen Conflict Is Felt Across Border*, N.Y. Times, Dec. 31, 1994, http://www.nytimes.com; Sabrina Tavernise, *Chechnya Is Caught in Grip of Russia's Antiterror Wrath*, N.Y. Times, Nov. 12, 2002, http://www.nytimes.com.

12. *See* Pritam Singh, Federalism, Nationalism and Development: India and the Punjab Economy 43–47 (London: Routledge, 2008).

13. *See* Mira Kamdar, Planet India: The Turbulent Rise of the Largest Democracy 234–37 (New York: Simon & Schuster, 2008); Vinay Lal, *Travails of the Nation: Some Notes on Indian Documentaries*, 19 Third Text 175, 175–78 (2005).

14. *See Primitive Tribal Groups*, *Tribal Languages*, and *Land Alienation*, *in* 2 Encyclopaedia of Scheduled Tribes in India 15–23 (P.K. Mohanty ed., New Delhi: Gyan Publishing House, 2006).

15. *See* Stanley Jeyaraja Tambiah, Sri Lanka: Ethnic Fratricide and the Dismantling of Democracy 22–24 (London: I.B.Tauris Publishers, 1986); Frances Harrison, *Twenty Years on—Riots that Led to War*, BBC News, July 23, 2003, http://news.bbc.co.uk/1/hi/world/south_asia/3090111.stm; Feizal Samath, *Sri Lanka: No Lessons Learnt from 'Black July' of 1983*, Inter Press Service, Apr. 12, 2009, http://www.ipsnews.net/news.asp?idnews=43285.

16. *See* Agence France-Presse, *Research Triples Death Toll in Wars*, The Australian, June 21, 2008, http://www.theaustralian.news.com.au/story/0,25197,23896317-31477,00.html.

17. *See* Catherine Philp, *Sri Lanka Tamil Tigers Say Struggle for Separate State Will Continue from Exile*, The Times (U.K.), June 16, 2009, http://www.timesonline.co.uk/tol/news/world/asia/article 6515025.ece.

18. *See Pakistan*, *in* Religious Freedom in the World, at 322–24 (Paul Marshall ed., London: Rowman & Littlefield Publishers, 2007).

19. *See Chronology*, *in* Conflict Between India and Pakistan 248 (Peter Lyon ed., Santa Barbara, CA: ABC-CLIO, 2008).

20. *See* Indira A. R. Lakshmanan, *In Indonesia, Another Face of Islam; Secular Ways Are Familiar in Indonesia, But The Religion Is on the Rise*, Boston Globe, Apr. 16, 1998, at A1; Willis Witter, *Churches Torched in Indonesian Unrest: Rumors Incite Riots against Christians*, Wash. Times, Nov. 23, 1998, http://www.highbeam.com/doc/1G1-56757160.html.

an estimated $15 to $35 billion from Indonesia, leaving it with a GDP per capita of less than $700 several years after he left office, a fraction of the figure for nearby Malaysia.[21] After a referendum in support of independence of East Timor in 1999, a U.N. investigation revealed a "deliberate, vicious and systematic campaign of gross violations of human rights" on the island occupied by Indonesian military and police forces. The army and police "actively assisted" local militia who were murdering civilians wholesale, burning houses, and looting homes. An estimated 70% of the buildings in East Timor were destroyed, and 60% of the population expelled from their homes and communities, with 250,000 of those fleeing East Timor altogether. The violence was planned weeks in advance and included the torture of students and the mass rape of women.[22]

B. The Continued Devastation of the Indigenous Peoples of the Americas

By the 1980s, the conditions of life experienced by indigenous peoples living in the Americas created severe risks of premature death or injury. For example, the rate among Native Americans in the U.S. of easily preventable diseases like dysentery, tuberculosis, hepatitis, influenza, pneumonia, and meningitis was 400 to 10,000 percent higher than among the rest of U.S. society. The poverty rate among Native Americans was twice as high. The suicide rate for Native American young people was 1,000 to 10,000 times higher than the rate for the general population. Poor health care and housing were often to blame. Up to 90 percent of homes on Native American reservations were classified as substandard, a euphemism for unhealthy and unsafe.[23] Native Americans lacked health insurance at the highest rate of any U.S. minority group, with the federal government spending $6,000 for each Medicare recipient, and more than $3,800 for medical care for each federal prisoner, both categories of which are mostly non-Indians, but only $2,000 per person using the Indian Health Service, despite staggering rates of Indian disease and injury.[24] The in-

21. *See* Transparency International, *Introduction to Political Corruption* 13 (Mar. 2004), http://www.transparency.org/content/download/4459/26786/file/Introduction_to_political_corruption.pdf.

22. *See* Report of the High Commissioner for Human Rights on the Human Rights Situation in East Timor, UN Doc. E/CN.4/S-4/CRP.1 (Sept. 17, 1999); *see also* Kerry B. Collison, *Indonesia: Disintegration of the Last Great Colonial Power?*, Defense & Foreign Affairs Strategic Policy, Oct. 2000, at 4, 2000 WLNR 7359792; Human Rights Watch, *Justice for East Timor* (2000), http://www.hrw.org/; Ben Saul, *Was The Conflict In East Timor 'Genocide' And Why Does It Matter?*, 2 Melbourne J. of Int'l L. 477, 484 (2001), http://www.austlii.edu.au/au/journals/MelbJIL/2001/18.html.

23. Rennard Strickland, *Genocide-at-Law: An Historic and Contemporary View of the Native American Experience*, 34 Kansas Law Rev. 713, 717 (1986).

24. These figures are from a report by two U.S. Senators who ran for President and Vice-President in 2004. See John Kerry and John Edwards, *A Plan to End the Minority Health Crisis* (2004), http://www.indianz.com/docs/kerryhealthplan.pdf. They document similar disparities in disease and injury rates. *See id.* (stating that: "Native Americans are 770 percent more likely to die from alcoholism, 650 percent more likely to die from tuberculosis, 420 percent more likely to die from diabetes, and 52 percent more likely to die from pneumonia or influenza than the rest of the United States."); Centers for Disease Control and Prevention (CDC), *Executive Summary: Atlas of Injury Mortality Among American Indian and Alaska Native Children and Youth, 1989–1998* (1999), http://www.cdc.gov/ncipc/pub-res/atlas-summary/ (Native American children and youth have highest injury death rates for suicide, car crashes, pedestrian deaths due to car traffic, and suffer from drownings, fires, and burns at rates tied with those of African-American children and youth for the highest rates); *id*, http://www.cdc.gov/ncipc/pub-res/atlas-summary/firearm.htm (firearm-related

fant mortality rate in the Pine Ridge reservation in South Dakota, for the Lakota Sioux, remains the highest on the continent of North America.[25]

Federal officials appear to have pursued policies designed to interfere with births within Native American groups. Every year in the 1970s, the Indian Health Service in the U.S. sterilized up to 3,000 Native American women under arguably coercive circumstances.[26] Up to 42% of Native American women of childbearing age in some areas may have been sterilized in this way by the 1970s and 1980s.[27] One legal scholar has argued that this "forced sterilization of Indian women in [U.S. Bureau of Indian Affairs] health clinics" was a genocidal policy.[28]

Expropriation of Native American resources served to impoverish and depopulate indigenous populations. Native Americans alleged, in a massive lawsuit filed on behalf of 300,000 class-action plaintiffs, that the U.S. government has failed to properly account for and distribute up to $100 billion in land and mineral resources and related revenues held in trust funds on the behalf of the natives. The U.S. District Court for the District of Columbia found in 2002 that the Secretary of the Interior, charged under U.S. law with administering the trust funds, "committed a fraud on the Court" in failing to properly account for the funds on behalf of 300,000 individual Native American beneficiaries.[29] The judge in the case accused Interior Department officials of racism and "cultural genocide."[30] An appellate court ordered the case be transferred to another judge because several rulings had been issued in favor of the Native Americans. The judges hearing the appeal were satisfied with testimony from the Interior Department that some progress had been made in accounting for the trust funds.[31]

One of the few instances of measures interfering with the survival of an indigenous group as a distinct entity in the U.S. receiving meaningful review by an international human rights body involves the Western Shoshone people. The Western Shoshone people were deported from 60,000 acres of their ancestral lands. The Indian Claims Commission in 1962 informed Shoshone leaders that they had no further remedy. The U.S. government planned "to store nuclear waste on Western Shoshone ancestral lands"; permit a pipeline to "drain water from aquifers beneath Western Shoshone lands"; grant approval for gold

---

death rates for Native American children and youth are double to triple rate suffered by the general population in Alaska, Arizona, and Montana).

25. *See* Shane Bauer, *Divorcing the US*, THE NEW INTERNATIONALIST, Apr. 1, 2008, http://www.newint.org/features/special/2008/04/01/lakota.

26. Bradford, *An American Indian Theory of Justice*, at 24 n110 (citing THOMAS M. SHAPIRO, POPULATION CONTROL POLITICS: WOMEN, STERILIZATION, AND REPRODUCTIVE CHOICE 91 (1985)).

27. *See id.*; Charles Rutherford, *Reproductive Freedoms and African American Women*, 4 YALE J. OF LAW AND FEMINISM 255, 273–74 (1992). *See also* Jane Lawrence *The Indian Health Service and the Sterilization of Native American Women*, 24.3 AMERICAN INDIAN Q. 400 (2000).

28. Bradford, *An American Indian Theory of Justice*, at 24.

29. Cobell v. Norton, 226 F. Supp. 2d 1, 125, 147 (D.D.C. 2002), 226 F. Supp. 2d 163 (D.D.C. 2002). *See also* UNITED STATES CONGRESS, HOUSE COMMITTEE ON APPROPRIATIONS, SUBCOMMITTEE ON THE DEPARTMENTS OF COMMERCE, JUSTICE, AND STATE, THE JUDICIARY, AND RELATED AGENCIES, DEPARTMENTS OF COMMERCE, JUSTICE, AND STATE, THE JUDICIARY, AND RELATED AGENCIES APPROPRIATIONS 441 (2004) (describing the class action as largest in history and possibly worth $100 billion); *Tribes Sue Feds, Alleging Poor Trust Fund Management*, ASSOCIATED PRESS, Jan. 11, 2007, http://www.king5.com/business/stories/NW_011107BUBtribessuitKC.2fe395ae.html.

30. Cobell v. Norton, No. 05-5269, slip op. at 29 (D.C. Cir. July 11, 2006), http://pacer.cadc.us courts.gov/docs/common/opinions/ 200607/05-5269a.pdf; Peter B. Rutledge, *A Judgment Call: A Law Professor Says Removal of Judge Lamberth From the Trust Case Was "Nothing Short of a Tragedy,"* LEGAL TIMES, Aug. 7, 2006, http://64.38.12.138/News/2006/015322.asp.

31. Cobell v. Norton, 334 F.3d 1148 (D.C. Cir. 2003).

mining and cattle grazing by "in spiritually and culturally significant areas"; condone "the sale of Western Shoshone ancestral lands [for] mining expansion plans and oil and gas leasing"; and to order or allow the "controlled burning of almost 60,000 acres of Western Shoshone ancestral lands."[32] The Inter-American Commission on Human Rights found a violation of the human right to equality as applied to the Western Shoshone people's property interests in their ancestral lands.[33]

In South America, Brazil's genocide of its Yanomami Indians, condemned by their leaders and the Brazilian authorities themselves, continued in the post-Cold War era, fueled by the prospect of lucrative gold and timber exports to the U.S. and elsewhere. A decree, formally revoked in 1991 but continually acted upon since then, "had expropriated most of the land of the Yanomami, ... and thrown it open to invasion by hordes of miners."[34] Human Rights Watch reported in 1990 that plantation owners are using some of the forested lands formerly enjoyed by the Yanomami to cut and burn cattle pasture.[35]

The Yanomami population plummeted from 20,000 in the 1970s to only 10,000 in 1991.[36] In 1993, Chief Yanomami "denounced the 'continuing genocide against the Yanomami people.'"[37] He was not alone in his concern. The federal prosecutor of Brazil accused the government of carrying out "genocidal" policies against indigenous people.[38] His office concluded that the Brazilian state had persecuted the native population "to the point of extermination."[39] Amnesty International warned of escalating violence and massacres against Yanomami people by plantation owners, clear-cutters of the forest, and gold miners.[40] A member of the Yanomami tribe explained in 1990 that: "If my people are wiped out you must destroy all photographs of us, because future generations will ... be too ashamed at such a crime against humanity."[41]

In 1996, the State Department reported that the life expectancy of indigenous Brazilians was in steep decline, down by more than five years on average since 1993. It cited estimates that 7,000 Yanomami Indians were held in forced labor on sugar and charcoal

---

32. Inter-American Commission on Human Rights, *Annual Report of the IACHR 2007*, ¶¶ 583–86, http://www.cidh.oas.org/annualrep/2007eng/Chap.3q.htm#11.140.

33. *See* Inter-American Commission on Human Rights, Report Nº 75/02, Case 11.140 (Mary and Carrie Dann v. United States), Dec. 27, 2002, ¶¶ 5–72, 127–30, 170–72, http://www.cidh.org/annualrep/2002eng/USA.11140.htm.

34. Terence Turner, *Death and Democracy in Brazil*, N.Y. Times, June 18, 1991, http://www.aaanet.org/committees/cfhr/rptyano8.htm; Human Rights Watch, *Brazil, in* World Report 1989, http://www.unhcr.org/refworld/publisher,HRW,ANNUALREPORT,BRA,467bb48715,0.html.

35. Human Rights Watch, World Report 1990, http://www.unhcr.org/refworld/publisher,HRW,ANNUALREPORT,BRA,467fca2f210,0.html.

36. *Compare The Present Situation of Indigenous People in the Amazon Region, in* Amazonia and Siberia: Legal Aspects of the Preservation of the Environment and Development in the Last Open Spaces 260 (Michael Bothe, Thomas Kurzidem, & Christian Schmidt eds., London: Martinus Nijhoff, 1993); New Gold Rush Threatens Brazil's Yanomami Indians, Reuters, Sept. 30, 2000, http://forests.org/archive/brazil/newgoldr.htm; *New Book, Article Accuses Scientists of Disrupting Yanomami Tribes*, CNN, Oct. 2, 2000, http://www.nku.edu/~humed1/darkness_in_el_dorado/documents/ 0312.htm; *Brazil Indians Call Spirits to Fight Fires*, Philadelphia Inquirer, Apr. 8, 1998, at A13.

37. *Quoted in* Valerie Taliman, *Yanomami Slaughtered For Gold*, The Circle, Sept. 1, 1993, http://www.highbeam.com/doc/1P1-2220911.html.

38. Turner, *Death and Democracy in Brazil*.

39. *Quoted in* R.M. Levine, The Brazil Reader: History, Culture, Politics 270 (1999).

40. *See* Amnesty International, *Brazil: Amnesty Calls for Protection of Indigenous Communities Following Massacre of Yanomami Indians* (Aug. 20, 1993), http://web.archive.org/web/20021216111210/http://nativenet.uthscsa.edu/archive/nl/9308/0309.html.

41. *Quoted in* Wright, Stolen Continents, at 343.

plantations, gold mines, and steel factories. Forced prostitution occurred, as did violence against slaves attempting to flee their uncompensated labor. The state governments were complicit, one governor denying that forced labor existed in his area even though inspections uncovered "some 8,000 people who were being forced to work on charcoal farms without payment and under subhuman conditions."[42] Human Rights Watch noted that plantation owners "cut and burn enormous tracts of land to turn the forest into cattle pasture, a practice . . . ," where laborers are "held against their will through threats and acts of violence, and compelled to live and work in deplorable conditions."[43]

After President Bill Clinton came to office, the State Department reported in testimony to Congress that logging and pollution in Yanomami lands was endangering their survival. An official stated:

> Logging has eroded the physical and economic base of indigenous groups. The large sums of money being made in logging on the reserves almost exclusively benefit non-indigenous investors and speculators. The roads which are developed for logging contribute to the destruction of the forest eco system and facilitate the movement of outsiders and movement in of disease to the indigenous people. . . .
>
> Messy gold mining practices have also wrought environmental damage. The use of mercury to separate the gold from other ore has resulted in extensive mercury poisoning. . . . [T]here is clearly an impact on the Yanomami's who drink from and fish in the mercury polluted rivers, thereby absorbing dangerous levels of mercury.[44]

In 1996, a Brazilian federal court concluded that genocide had been committed against the Yanomami. In 2000, Brazil's Regional Superior Court of Justice convicted gold prospectors of genocide in connection with the massacre of about 18 Yanomami people. The appellate court stated that: "The mass murder of the Yanomami, took place in a conflicting framework between the community and predatory presence of the prospectors in the region, that nurture feelings of retaliation and vengeance against an ethnic group." The court found that the acts tended to destroy the Yanomami in whole or in part because "the people against whom the crime is directed belong to an ethnic group and share the community's life."[45] In 2006, the Supreme Court of Brazil affirmed the conviction.[46]

Scholars on indigenous peoples argued that the extraction of gold, timber, rubber and oil in Brazil resulted in "regime of terror with the character of a holocaust," with the brunt of the assault being borne by "the debt-bonded indigenous population [which] was the only means to dramatically increase [the extractive industries'] short-term productiv-

---

42. USDOS, *Country Reports on Human Rights 1996: Brazil*, http://www.state.gov/www/global/human_rights/1996_hrp_report/brazil.html.

43. Human Rights Watch, World Report 1990, http://www.unhcr.org/refworld/publisher,HRW,ANNUALREPORT,BRA,467fca2f210,0.html.

44. John Shattuck, Assistant Secretary of State for Human Rights and Humanitarian Affairs, Testimony on Indigenous People and Natural Environment of Brazil to the Western Hemispheric Affairs Subcommittee, Committee on Foreign Affairs, U.S. House of Representatives, Federal News Service, May 10, 1994, http://www.lexisnexis.com.

45. *See* Quigley, The Genocide Convention, at 48–49; Lilia Toledo Diniz & Fernando Babtista, *Decision of the Superior Court of Justice—Stj Acknowledges Crime of Genocide Against the Yanomami*, Socio-Environmental Institute (2000), http://web.archive.org/web/*/http://www.socioambiental.org/website/noticias/english/rights/20000920.html.

46. *See* Survival International, *Supreme Court Upholds Genocide Ruling* (Aug. 4, 2006), http://www.survival-international.org/news/1786.

ity."[47] Brazilian production of gold, for example, nearly doubled between 1981 and 1985 alone, placing Brazil just behind South Africa and China in its capability of exporting gold to the West.[48] Brazil's exports of wood products to the U.S. quadrupled in value from 1986 to 1997. In terms of the increase in value of these exports from 1985–1997, Brazil's performance was rivaled only by that of Indonesia, China, and Mexico.[49] Exports of hardwood to the U.S. for use in hardwood flooring or carpentry, a factor in the deforestation of Yanomami lands, has increased by more than 100% (carpentry) or even more than 10 times (hardwood flooring).[50]

After the worst massacres were over in Guatemala, "extreme racism" against indigenous peoples continued to be practiced by the government, with discriminatory underinvestment of tax revenues in the regions they inhabit leading to reduced life expectancy, poverty, large-scale forced labor, and inadequate education and health care.[51] A series of recent reports by the World Bank have confirmed that Guatemala has some of the worst rates of starvation, infant mortality, preventable disease, and stunted childhood growth in all of Latin America.[52] Mayan languages were barred for long periods from public education, the courts, and public buildings.[53]

A climate for impunity with respect to killings of Mayan people prevails. A 1996 Guatemalan law prohibits prosecuting for murder any officials responsible for the worst excesses against Mayans; while it allows prosecutions for genocide and forced disappearances, Herculean efforts by Mayan activists to persuade the government to prosecute the authors of Guatemala's Mayan genocide have been rebuffed.[54] As a result, the Mayan people have had no remedy for these crimes, and must ask countries like Spain, 5,000 miles away, to bring charges against ex-President Montt and his generals.[55] On another layer of impunity, Amnesty International reported that the Guatemalan government has failed to arrest any suspects in 97% of the murders of over 2,200 women and girls since 2001.[56] Guatemala's chief of police blamed the female victims of these atrocities for getting in-

---

47. Soren Hvalkof, *Outrage in Rubber and Oil: Extractivism, Indigenous Peoples, and Justice in the Upper Amazon, in* People, Plants, and Justice: The Politics of Nature Conservation 83 (Charles Zerner ed., New York: Columbia UP, 2000).

48. *See* J.M. Lucas, *Gold, in* U.S. Bureau of Mines, Minerals Yearbook 1985: Metals and Minerals 477 (1985).

49. *See* U.S. Dep't of Agriculture (USDA), Foreign Agricultural Service (FAS), *Value of U.S. Imports of Wood Products by Country, 1985–1997* (2009), http://www.fas.usda.gov/ffpd/wood-circulars/apr98/tab114.pdf.

50. *See* USDA, FAS, *FAS Import Aggregations,* http://www.fas.usda.gov/ustrdscripts/.

51. *See* Rachel Sieder, *Recognising Indigenous Law and the Politics of State Formation in Mesoamerica,* in Multiculturalism in Latin America: Indigenous Rights, Diversity, and Democracy 200 (New York: Palgrave Macmillan, 2002).

52. Alessandra Marini, *Malnutrition and Poverty in Guatemala* (2004), http://papers.ssrn.com/sol3/papers.cfm?abstract_id=636329; Michele Gragnolati, *Health and Poverty in Guatemala* (2005), http://papers.ssrn.com/sol3/papers.cfm?abstract_id=636328; Michele Gragnolati, *Children's Growth and Poverty in Rural Guatemala* (2004), http://papers.ssrn.com/sol3/ papers.cfm?abstract_id=623945; Harry A Patrinos, *Differences in Education and Earnings Across Ethnic Groups in Guatemala* (1997), http://papers.ssrn.com/sol3/papers.cfm?abstract_id=10789.

53. *See* Perlin, *The Guatemalan Historical Clarification Commission,* at 389–91.

54. Blake v. Guatemala Case, Inter-Am. C.H.R. (ser. C) No. 36 (1998), *reprinted in* 19 Hum. Rts. L.J. 393, 405 (1998) (interpreting Article 8(1) of the American Convention on Human Rights).

55. Guatemala Genocide Case, Dec. No. 22 327/2003 (Supreme Court of Spain, Feb. 25, 2003), *reprinted in* 42 I.L.M. 686 (2003).

56. Amnesty International, *Guatemala: Killings of Women on the Rise in 2006,* AI Index Number: AMR 34/023/2006, http://web.amnesty.org/library/Index/ENGAMR340232006?open&of=ENG-GTM.

volved in "violence within the family" and "street gangs." The police have not even investigated 70% of the murders.[57]

Despite its atrocious human rights record, the U.S. supported Guatemala's bid in 2006 for a seat on the U.N. Security Council, of all places.[58] Instead of awarding it with a seat on the Security Council, the United Nations should have immediately instituted an investigation into Guatemala's climate of impunity for murder and genocide. That would have signaled the international community's intolerance to regimes tempted to commit genocide. Inviting Guatemala to occupy a seat on the Security Council sent the worst possible message to the genocidal regime in Sudan, whose crimes the Security Council was then trying to rein in.

C. The Civil Wars and Humanitarian Disasters of Post-Cold War Africa

Massacres and genocides have occurred in post-Cold War African states that rival or even surpass the genocide in Rwanda, discussed in Chapter III. The underlying conflicts are often driven by the "resource curse," or the tendency of an economy to be based on extraction of natural resources such as minerals, precious metals, or petroleum, rather than agricultural or manufactured goods.[59] In addition to the resource curse, which is best described as a statistical correlation between a certain type of economy and conflict, military or militia leaders must decide to massacre civilians or block humanitarian aid from reaching the civilian population, in order for a genocide to occur. This chapter contends that sometimes, the mismanagement of the economy and population of a country is so severe as to warrant the designation as structural genocide.

Most notably, about five million people have died in massacres and from preventable starvation and disease in the Democratic Republic of the Congo (DRC), in what the U.N. Under-Secretary-General for Humanitarian Affairs described as the equivalent of "six Rwandan genocides."[60] The DRC has alleged that "by killing, massacring, raping, throat-cutting, and crucifying, Rwanda is guilty of genocide against more than 3,500,000 Congolese, including the victims of the recent massacres in the city of Kisangani."[61] The ICJ has also found that extensive violations of laws of war and of belligerent occupation were committed during an invasion by Uganda, and ordered it to pay reparations to the DRC.[62]

Some geopolitical context for the genocide in the DRC is necessary. In the mid-1990s, the Rwandan military invaded the DRC and slaughtered tens of thousands of refugees in

57. Amnesty International, *Guatemala: No Protection, No Justice: Killings of Women (an Update)* (June 5, 2006), http://web.amnesty.org/library/Index/ENGAMR340192006?open&of=ENG-GTM.

58. Peter Heinlein, *UN Calls 'Time-Out' in Guatemala-Venezuela Battle for Security Council Seat*, Voice of America, Oct. 20, 2006, http://www.voanews.com/english/2006-10-20-voa46.cfm.

59. *See* Jeffrey Sachs & Andrew Warner, *The Curse of Natural Resources*, 45 Eur. Econ. Rev. 827, 827 (2001).

60. *Under-Secretary-General Calls For Greater Security Council Commitment to Ending Conflicts in Democratic Republic of the Congo, Northern Uganda*, US Fed News, Sept. 16, 2006; *see also* James Astill & Isabelle Chevallot, *Conflict in Congo Has Killed 4.7m, Charity Says Starvation and Disease Multiply Toll from Fighting*, The Guardian (U.K.), Apr. 8, 2003, http://www.guardian.co.uk/congo/story/0,12292,932034,00.html.

61. *Democratic Republic of the Congo v. Rwanda*, 2006 ICJ LEXIS 1, *20 (ICJ Feb. 3, 2006).

62. *Democratic Republic of the Congo v. Uganda*, 2005 ICJ LEXIS 1, at ¶¶ 203–219 (ICJ Dec. 19, 2005).

the DRC, mostly Hutus.[63] During the 1990s, a coalition made up of Rwanda, Burundi, Uganda and Tutsi rebels within the DRC controlled large amounts of territory in the DRC, where they were generally opposed by President Laurent-Desire Kabila of the DRC and the countries of Angola, Namibia, Sudan, and Zimbabwe.[64] Due to the widespread participation in it, this conflict became known as "Africa's World War."[65] In 2004, the DRC referred the case of Thomas Lubanga to the ICC, which charged him with recruiting child soldiers in eastern DRC, but apparently not with massacres, even though 60,000 have died in the eastern DRC since 1999.[66]

The government of the DRC described the following massacres and systematic rapes on its territory in a submission to the ICJ:

> By way of illustration, the [DRC] would cite the following incidents, which in no sense constitute an exhaustive list, and which are evidence of a deliberate policy operated by the Rwandan Government against the [DRC]....
>
> On 24 August 1998, more than 856 persons were massacred in Kasika, in Lwindi chieftaincy and in the territory of Mwenga, all being localities situated in the Province of Sud-Kivu.
>
> The bodies, which were found scattered over a distance of 60 kilometres between Kilungutwe and Kasika, were largely those of women and children—defenceless persons incapable of bearing arms.
>
> On the night of 31 December 1998 to 1 January 1999, 633 persons were massacred in Makobola....
>
> Two thousand Rwandan soldiers suffering from AIDS, or HIV-positive, were dispatched to the front in Orientale Province with express orders to rape Congolese women in order to spread the disease.[67]

Sudan helped form the geopolitical context for the DRC genocide. Uganda justified its invasion of the DRC on the grounds that the Congolese leader Laurent Kabila was permitting Sudan to arm and train rebels against the government of Uganda in "guerrilla bases in eastern Congo that served the [Sudanese-supported rebel group] in its raids across the Ugandan border." One expert finds the allegation of "Sudanese involvement in such activities is thus plausible, given the Sudanese leadership's policy that any enemy of Uganda was a friend of Sudan and because Uganda was assisting the rebels of southern Sudan in their fight against the Khartoum government."[68] Thousands of Ugandan children have been abducted from northern Uganda by the Lord's Resistance Army (LRA) and held in Sudan, the government of which "provides the LRA with food, weapons and

---

63. Mariano-Florentino Cuellar, *Refugee Security and the Organizational Logic of Legal Mandates*, 37 Geo. J. Int'l L. 583, 591–96 & n29 (2006) (citing Dennis McNamara, *The Protection of Refugees and the Responsibility of States: Engagement or Abdication?*, 11 Harv. Hum. Rts. J. 355 n.1 (1998)).

64. *See Congo: Elections and the Battle for Mineral Resources*, 71 Social Education, Jan.–Feb., 2007, at 24–26, http://members.ncss.org/se/7101/71010724.pdf.

65. *Id.* For further details, see Ari Nave, *Uganda, in* Encyclopedia Africana, at 1911.

66. *Lubanga Lawyers Denounce 'Unfair' ICC War Crimes Trial*, Agence France-Presse, Jan. 27, 2009.

67. Armed Activities on the Territory of the Congo (Democratic Republic of the Congo v. Rwanda), Application Instituting Proceedings 7 (filed 23 June 1999), http://www.icj-cij.org/icjwww/idocket/icorw/icorwapplication/icorw_iapplication_19990623.pdf.

68. Boaz Atzili, *When Good Fences Make Bad Neighbors; Fixed Borders, State Weakness, and International Conflict*, Int'l Security, Winter 2006/2007, at 139, n.117 and accompanying text.

relatively secure operations bases in southern Sudan."[69] Sudan's intervention in the DRC on behalf of the government has been explained as retaliation against Uganda for its support for the SPLA.[70] Thus, Uganda supported the SPLA in Sudan, which in turn supported the LRA in its fight against the government of Uganda, which invaded the DRC under the pretext of Sudan's activities in support of the LRA there.

As in most other post-Cold War conflicts, the struggle for natural resources played a prominent part. Rwanda's diamond exports soared by nearly 200 times after its invasion of the DRC, and the DRC's production of tin increased by 40 times, most exports of tin being controlled by Rwanda.[71] One expert on regional mineral economies observed: "In 2001, the United Nations Security Council issued a report that accused Rwandan Government officials, military officers, and businessmen of illegally exploiting columbium (niobium), diamond, gold, and tantalum from Congo (Kinshasa) to enrich themselves and finance their country's military presence in Congo (Kinshasa)."[72] Uganda also invaded and set about looting the resources of the DRC. The ICJ concluded in 2005 that it had "ample credible and persuasive evidence to conclude that officers and soldiers of the [Ugandan military], including the most high-ranking officers, were involved in the looting, plundering and exploitation of [the DRC's] natural resources...." The resources plundered apparently included diamonds, gold, and coffee.[73]

Congolese rebels, thus aided by Rwanda and Uganda, massacred and systematically raped many indigenous peoples of the Congo, including forest-dwelling groups such as the Batwa (Twa) and Bambuti, sometimes referred to in the media as "Pygmies." These peoples are facing extinction due to frequent violence, displacement from their forest homelands, and widespread sexual assault.[74] Their survival is at risk,[75] because their pop-

69. Amnesty International, *Africa Update: A Summary of Human Rights Concerns in sub-Saharan Africa,* AI Index: AFR 01/005/1998 (Oct. 1, 1998), http://web.amnesty.org/library/Index/ENGAFR 010051998?open&of=ENG-2AF.

70. *See* Nave, *Uganda,* at 1911.

71. *See* Project Censored 2004: The Top 25 Censored Stories 159 (Peter Phillips ed., 2003); Thomas R. Yager, *The Mineral Industry of Congo (Kinshasa) in 2004, in* U.S. Geological Survey Minerals Yearbook — 2004, at 12.2, http://minerals.usgs.gov/minerals/pubs/country/2004/ cgmyb04.pdf.

72. Thomas R. Yager, *The Mineral Industries of Burundi, Comoros, Malawi, Mauritius, Reunion, Rwanda, and Seychelles — 2001, in* U.S. Geological Survey Minerals Yearbook — 2001, at 7.5 (2001), http://minerals.usgs.gov/minerals/pubs/country/2001/bycnmimpfrrwsemyb01.pdf.

73. *Congo v. Rwanda,* 2005 ICJ LEXIS 1, at ¶¶ 240, 242.

74. *DR Congo Pygmies "Exterminated."* BBC News, July 6, 2004, http://news.bbc.co.uk/2/hi/ africa/3869489.stm; *Africa's Pygmies Facing a Terrible Future,* CTV (Canada) (Apr. 22, 2007), http://www.ctv.ca/servlet/ArticleNews/story/CTVNews/20070422/pygmies_070422/20070422?hub= TopStories; Internal Displacement Monitoring Centre, *Batwa "Pygmy" Population Has Been Displaced and Marginalized* (Aug. 12, 2003), http://www.internal-displacement.org/idmc/website/countries.- nsf/(httpEnvelopes)/ A9B47DC22230A0CC802570B8005A71E8?OpenDocument; Fergal Keane, *GPS Helps Pygmies Defend Forest,* BBC News, Jan. 30, 2008, http://news.bbc.co.uk/1/hi/world/africa/ 7218078.stm; Refugees International, *Forgotten People: The Batwa "Pygmy" of the Great Lakes Region of Africa* (Aug. 12, 2003), http://www.reliefweb.int/rw/rwb.nsf/AllDocsByUNID/a84e5cbac3ac8 c2885256d800079aaba.

75. *See Africa's Pygmies Facing a Terrible Future,* CTV (Canada), Apr. 22, 2007, http://www.ctv.ca/servlet/ArticleNews/story/CTVNews/20070422/pygmies_070422/20070422?hub= TopStories ("Africa's Pygmy people, nomadic hunters and gatherers whose mastery of the forests has been unmatched for a millennia, are facing extinction"); Internal Displacement Monitoring Centre, *Batwa "Pygmy" Population Has Been Displaced and Marginalized* (Aug. 12, 2003), http://www.internal-displacement.org/idmc/website/countries.nsf/(httpEnvelopes)/A9B47DC22230A0CC802570B8005A71E8? OpenDocument ("Civil wars, poorly planned conservation parks, lack of access to education, health-

ulation in the Great Lakes region fell by half from 2003 through 2008.[76] The leaders of the DRC's forest-dwelling peoples warn that the "survival—physical, cultural or spiritual—of thousands of Pygmies, extremely dependant on the forests, is every day sacrificed for the comfort of rich consumers of tropical timber." Timber companies are destroying the forests, killing the animals on which the forest-dwellers rely. As many as 22 million hectares are slated for exploitation by the timber industry. The World Bank initially funded the transition to large-scale industrial exploitation of timber. It later supported a moratorium on new concessions, which was flouted. A self-described Pygmy leader mourned: "The destruction of the forest is as a real tragedy for Pygmies. The forest is our supermarket, our pharmacy, our school, our temple and our cemetery."[77]

In East Africa, Somalis and Ethiopians suffered gross human rights abuses and ethnic cleansing in the post-Cold War era. In 1992, the Security Council condemned widespread violations of the law of war in Somalia, as well as the blocking of humanitarian aid.[78] An estimated 300,000 people died in the fighting and resulting famine before the United Nations intervened.[79] Tens of thousands died in the war for Eritrean independence from Ethiopia, and subsequent border wars and skirmishes, which included ethnic cleansing campaigns.[80]

In West Africa, the resource curse and various divisions in society fueled several large massacres. In Nigeria, Generals Ibrahim Badamasi Babangida and Sani Abacha implicated the state in inter-ethnic conflict and used oil revenues to perpetuate a political elite and commit gross human rights violations.[81] An independent human rights commission reported that the Nigerian military junta had viewed "the state as a conquered territory and proceeded to treat the proceeds of state as spoils of war to be shared among the members of the mil-

---

care and land, ethnic discrimination, economic hardships, and inequalities threaten to destroy Batwa cultural heritage."); Fergal Keane, *GPS Helps Pygmies Defend Forest*, BBC News, Jan. 30, 2008, http://news.bbc.co.uk/1/hi/world/africa/7218078.stm ("Now the world's hunger for tropical wood is threatening [the Batwa Pygmies'] existence."); Refugees International, *Forgotten People: The Batwa "Pygmy" of the Great Lakes Region of Africa* (Aug. 12, 2003), http://www.reliefweb.int/rw/rwb.nsf/ AllDocsByUNID/a84e5cbac3ac8c2885256d800079aaba (Batwa Pygmies are frequently subjected to violence: "Without the availability of traditional or state resources, the Batwa became the most vulnerable and the most easily exploited population during the conflicts that began in the 1990s."); John Vidal, *The Great Green Land Grab*, The Guardian (U.K.), Feb. 13, 2008, http://www.guardian.co.uk/environment/ 2008/ feb/13/conservation?gusrc=rss&feed=worldnews ("One of the worst incidents was in the 1990s, when the Bambuti Ba'twa tribe of Pygmies who used to live in" the DRC "had their lands designated a national park to protect gorillas. The Pygmies ... are now found in small groups living in squalor on the edge of the park").

76. *See* Jeff Lule, *Population of Batwa People Reduces*, New Vision, Dec. 14, 2008, http://www.newvision.co.ug/D/8/18/664591. For an explanation of the pressures on Batwa populations, see World Peasants/Indigenous Organization, *Case Study of Video Documentary "Global Warming a Concrete Experience with Pygmies Lives"* (2008), http://www.advocacynet.org/modules/fck/upload/file/ case%20study.pdf.

77. Adrien Sinafasi Makelo, *Garden Furniture for Europeans*, The New Internationalist, Apr. 1, 2008, http://www.newint.org/features/special/2008/04/01/congoart.

78. *See* S.C. Res. 794 (Dec. 3, 1992).

79. *See The Somalia Mission; UN Opposes a GI Pullout From Somalia*, N.Y. Times, Oct. 7, 1993, at A10.

80. *See Eritrea Ethiopa Claims Commission, Civilians Claims* (Eritrea v. Ethiopia), Partial Awards of Dec. 17, 2004, http://tinyurl.com/y9vlnh3. *Eritrea Reveals Human Cost of War*, BBC News, June 20, 2001, http://news.bbc.co.uk/2/hi/africa/1398446.stm; *Eritrea: 2002*, http://news.bbc.co.uk/cbbcnews; Associated Press, *Ethiopia Accuses Eritrea of Ethnic Cleansing*, Sept. 25, 1998, http://www.newsbank.com.

81. *See* Human Rights Violations Investigation Commission of Nigeria, *Summary, Conclusions and Recommendations* (May 2002), http://www.dawodu.com/oputa1.pdf.

itary, the conquering forces of occupation."[82] The military and Western oil companies burned villages belonging to ethnic minorities.[83] The Ogoni people of the Niger Delta faced the "danger of extinction" due to the poisoning of the rivers by oil corporations.[84]

The military junta embezzled $3 to $5 billion as GDP per capita hovered at around $300, and the country's under-five mortality rate in 1997 was comparable to those of war-torn DRC, Liberia, and Somalia, well as to that of extremely resource-poor Chad. The child mortality rate in 1997 was double or even triple the rate in Botswana, Namibia, South Africa, or Zimbabwe.[85]

After the 1999 election of former dictator Olusegun Obasanjo as President of Nigeria, the government's push for fundamentalist religious law provoked widespread massacres and the displacement of three million people from their homes.[86] Attacks in 2000 by Muslim Nigerians on Christians protesting the imposition of Islamic law in northern Nigeria led to 2,000 massacre victims and one thousand burned homes, churches, and mosques.[87] A controversial newspaper article about the Miss World pageant in 2002 resulted in 200 people being massacred in attacks by hundreds of rioters against over 58 Christian churches, with 1,200 people being seriously injured and 12,000 losing their homes. Corruption no doubt played a part, as the riots had their epicenter in a miserable slum in Kaduna, Nigeria.[88] Thirty churches were burned down and more than a dozen people killed in attacks on Christians in early 2006, after which over 20 Muslims perished in reprisal massacres.[89] In all, hundreds of churches may have been destroyed.[90] An estimated 10,000 died in a four-year period after Obasanjo came to power.[91] By 2007, the estimated death toll from conflicts surrounding the introduction of Sharia law stood at 60,000, many of them Christians, as all churches in some towns were razed.[92]

In 1980, Liberians of the indigenous Krahn ethnic group, led by Master Sergeant Samuel K. Doe, overturned the political order and institutional party established by the U.S. in 1847, slowing Liberia's economic growth and ushering in an era of political instability. Libya and Cote d'Ivoire supported an insurgency led by Americo-Liberians and

82. *Id.* at ¶ 114.

83. *See* Marcus Mabry, *Africa's Ailing Giant,* FOREIGN AFFAIRS, Sept./Oct. 2000, at 123 (reviewing KARL MAIER, THIS HOUSE HAS FALLEN: MIDNIGHT IN NIGERIA (New York: PublicAffairs, 2000)).

84. Nsongurua J. Udombana, *Reparations and Africa's Indigenous Peoples, in* REPARATIONS FOR INDIGENOUS PEOPLES, at 392–98.

85. *See* Transparency International, *Introduction to Political Corruption* 13 (Mar. 2004), http://www.transparency.org/content/download/4459/26786/file/Introduction_to_political_corruption.pdf.

86. *See* Agence France-Presse, *Nigeria: Churches, Mosques Among Burnt Out Buildings in Kaduna,* May 24, 2000, http://www.newsbank.com; James Astill, *The Truth Behind the Miss World Riots,* THE GUARDIAN (U.K.), Nov. 30, 2002, http://guardian.co.uk; Julia Day, *Nigerian State Issues Death Threat on Miss World Journalist,* THE GUARDIAN (U.K.), Nov. 26, 2002, http://guardian.co/uk; Princeton N. Lyman, *Nigeria Burns for Islam,* WALL STREET J., Nov. 27, 2002, at A10; *Violence Left 3 Million Bereft in Past 7 Years, Nigeria Reports,* N.Y. Times, Mar. 14, 2006, http://www.nytimes.com/.

87. *See* Agence France-Presse, *Nigeria: Churches, Mosques Among Burnt Out Buildings.*

88. *See* Astill, *The Truth Behind the Miss World Riots*; Day, *Nigerian State*; Lyman, *Nigeria Burns for Islam.*

89. *See* Dulue Mbachu, *Sectarian Mobs in Nigeria Kill 24,* BOSTON GLOBE, Feb. 21, 2006, http://www.boston.com/; Andrew Meldrum and News Agencies, *Revenge Attacks kill 20 Nigerian Muslims,* THE GUARDIAN (U.K.), Feb. 23, 2006, http://www.guardian.co.uk/world/2006/feb/23/andrew meldrum.mainsection.

90. *See* DAVID C. L. LIM, THE INFINITE LONGING FOR HOME 21–23 (New York: Rodopi, 2005).

91. *See* JACK PINKOWSKI, HOMELAND SECURITY HANDBOOK 189–90 (Boca Raton, FL: CRC Press, 2008).

92. *See Nigeria, in* RELIGIOUS FREEDOM IN THE WORLD 311 (Paul A. Marshall ed., London: Rowman & Littlefield, 2008).

called the National Patriotic Front of Liberia (NPFL), which invaded Liberia and defeated many of Doe's forces in 1989, possibly with French aid. NPFL leader Charles Taylor, in the lead-up to the fall of Doe, ordered his men to kill civilians belonging to the Krahn tribe associated with then-president Samuel Doe. At Taylor's trial before the Special Court for Sierra Leone, a NPFL death squad leader testified that he "killed so many men, women and children he had lost count."[93]

The Liberian army under President Taylor committed widespread rape and sexual violence, particularly during a rebel assault on the capital, Monrovia, which led Taylor to step down in 2003. The rebels who occupied much of western Liberia indiscriminately shelled the capital Monrovia with artillery in the lead-up to Taylor's ouster, killing hundreds of civilians. The rebels also used "forced labor, looting, rape and extrajudicial killings."[94] Ultimately a U.S.-educated politician who had funded Taylor in the past took over.[95]

In the 1990s, 250,000 died in combat, massacres, and from related hunger and disease in Liberia, and were joined by 75,000 persons in Sierra Leone. After decades of military rule in Sierra Leone, an insurgency called the Revolutionary United Front (RUF) occupied most of the country in the mid-1990s. The RUF attacked the capital Freetown in 1999, leading to a British-led intervention and the signing of a July 1999 peace accord. Meanwhile, the extraction, export, and/or sale of diamonds, timber, and rubber from Sierra Leone and Liberia made the NPFL, RUF, and Taylor tens of millions of dollars each year in the 1990s.[96] Taylor went on trial in the Hague for encouraging mass murder, mutilations, rape, and looting in Sierra Leone, and shipping arms to the RUF in return for diamonds delivered to his palace in Liberia.[97]

Many of these civil wars and insurgencies are not amenable to ready application of the Genocide Convention, given the survival of most members of the affected ethnic groups, both those with access to elite status and those identified with the insurgency. Nevertheless, they have been as productive of mass death, displaced persons, and conditions of

---

93. *See* Chris McGreal, *Charles Taylor Told Fighters to Eat Their Enemies, Court Hears,* The Guardian (U.K.), Mar. 14, 2008, http://guardian.co.uk.

94. *See* Jeremy Levitt, *Illegal Peace? An Inquiry into the Legality of Power Sharing with Warlords and Rebels in Africa,* 27 Michigan J. International Law 495, 511–17 (2006); Edward Cody, *Revenge Drives Liberian Rebels; Young Insurgents Rule by Gun in Chaotic Countryside,* Wash. Post, July 14, 1990, at A1; Human Rights Watch, *Human Rights Overview: Liberia* (2004), http://hrw.org/english/docs/2004/01/21/liberi6977.htm.

95. *See* Agence France Presse, *Sirleaf Should Be Banned from Office: Liberia Truth Commission,* July 6, 2009, http://www.channelstv.com/newsdetails.php?news_id=13329; *Bush Congratulates Liberian President-Elect* (2005), http://www.america.gov/st/washfile-english/2005/November/20051130184221HecuoR1.726931e-02.html.

96. *See* Levitt, *Illegal Peace?*, at 511–17 (citing Peace Agreement Between the Government of Sierra Leone and the Revolutionary United Front of Sierra Leone (RUF/SL), Lome, Togo, July 7, 1999, http://www.sierra-leone.org/lomeaccord.html); Jamie O'Connell, *Here Interest Meets Humanity: How to End the War and Support Reconstruction in Liberia, and the Case for Modest American Leadership,* 17 Harv. Hum. Rts. J. 207, 211–15 (2004) (citing Global Witness, The Logs of War: The Timber Trade and Armed Conflict 22–28 (2002), http://www.unglobalcompact.org/docs/issues_doc/Peace_and_Business/Logs_of_War.pdf; Ryan Lizza, *Where Angels Fear to Tread,* New Republic, July 24, 2000, at 22, 24; Report of the Panel of Experts appointed pursuant to Security Council resolution 1306 (2000), U.N. Doc. No. S/2000/1195 (2000), http://www.un.org/Docs/sc/committees/SierraLeone/SLselectedEng.htm).

97. *See* Agence France Presse, *Sirleaf Should Be Banned from Office: Liberia Truth Commission,* July 6, 2009, http://www.channelstv.com/newsdetails.php?news_id=13329; Reed Stevenson & Sophie Hares, *Liberia's Taylor to Take Stand in War Crimes Case,* Reuters, July 12, 2009, http://www.reuters.com; *World to Hear Case Against Taylor,* BBC News, Jan. 7, 2008, http://news.bbc.co.uk/1/hi/world/africa/7172443.stm.

life that impose a high risk of premature death or injury, as were the civil wars in the former Yugoslavia. Some groups, such as the Pygmies of the DRC, may be at even greater risk of complete extermination and cultural death than were the Bosnian or Albanian Muslims, or the Rwandan Tutsis.

D. "Structural" Genocide: Is It a Viable Concept?

A number of recent works, most notably by Herbert Hirsch of the International Association of Genocide Scholars, have argued for global military cooperation to suppress and punish acts of physical genocide using tools such as the U.N. Security Council, U.N. peacekeeping forces, international criminal tribunals, a proposed U.N. "rapid reaction" force, and the international law of humanitarian intervention and universal jurisdiction. Under the rubric of a "duty to protect," various U.N. reports and scholarly works persuasively make the case for military interventions to halt massacres and disruptions in the flow of humanitarian aid, and criminal prosecutions to punish and deter further such acts when they cannot be prevented.[98] Without criticizing these proposals, the remainder of this chapter will urge a similar degree of attention to the emerging crime of structural genocide, or the killing of hundreds of thousands of people by corrupt and inhumane social and economic policies, particularly in the areas of access to food and medicine.

The imposition of conditions of life that are inconsistent with healthy bodies and communities contributed to hundreds of thousands or millions of deaths in the post-Cold War era. This phenomenon in Iraq and Sudan is described at length in Chapters XIV, XV, and XVII. The denial of humanitarian aid to indigenous African populations in Sudan and the blockade of northern Iraq during the 1990s were criminal policies, and the reduction of the Iraqi people's access to food and medicine during the 1990s due to sanctions, and the related squandering of Iraq's oil resources under sanctions, warrant full-blown civil and criminal proceedings. By failing to devote their countries' resources to meeting the basic needs of their people, Iraq, Sudan, and other governments imposing or encouraging such policies may have contributed to structural genocide, in other words the intentional destruction of a people in substantial part. Under the Srebrenica model of genocide detailed in Chapter III, the fact that governments might have had corrupt or political motivations, rather than pure racial hatred, is no reason to conclude that they did not have the genocidal intent to cause widespread civilian deaths.

---

98. *See, e.g.*, HERBERT HIRSCH, ANTI-GENOCIDE: BUILDING AN AMERICAN MOVEMENT TO PREVENT GENOCIDE 115–17, 124–41, 176–77 (2002); JOHN G. HEIDENRICH, HOW TO PREVENT GENOCIDE: A GUIDE FOR POLICYMAKERS, SCHOLARS, AND THE CONCERNED CITIZEN, ch. 7, ch. 12 (2001); LEO KUPER, THE PREVENTION OF GENOCIDE (1985); Jeremy Levitt, *The Responsibility to Protect: A Beaver Without a Dam*, 25 MICH. J. OF INT'L & COMP. L. 153 (2003) (reviewing INTERNATIONAL COMMISSION ON INTERVENTION AND STATE SOVEREIGNTY, THE RESPONSIBILITY TO PROTECT (2001), and THOMAS G. WEISS & DON HUBERT, THE RESPONSIBILITY TO PROTECT: RESEARCH, BIBLIOGRAPHY, BACKGROUND (2001)); *see also* Report of the Panel on United Nations Peace Operations, A/55/305–S/2000/809 (Aug. 2000), http://www.un.org/peace/reports/peace_operations/docs/part1.htm; Aide-Memoire by France on an Agenda for Peace (Permanent Representative of France to the U.N. Secretary-General), A/50/869–S/1996/71 (Jan. 1996), http://www.un.org/documents/ga/docs/50/plenary/a50-869.htm.

It is becoming widely recognized by scholars that famines for which a state bears responsibility are justly classified as a form of genocide.[99] North Korea's government stands out as causing perhaps the gravest humanitarian disasters attributable to state policy since the end of the Cold War. In the mid- to late-1990s, the collapse of the Soviet Union, poor agricultural policies, and indifference toward the survival of large segments of the population led to two to three million famine deaths.[100] Satellite images accessible through Google Earth have revealed mass graves on nearly all the available land surrounding the city of Hamhung, which was the source of refugees to China in the late 1990s who described widespread starvation and the eating of roots and tree bark in North Korea. The same images reveal enormous palaces, yachts, manicured lakes and gardens, and private railroad systems.[101] Throughout the world in the 2000s, about 16,000 children under the age of five died from hunger and malnutrition *every day*, or about six million per year.[102]

Refusing to ensure adequate access to food, however, is not the only modality by which a government may cause hundreds of thousands of deaths. Denial of health care may inflict mass death, most notably in South Africa. During their tenure in office, President Thabo Mbeki and Health Minister Manto Tshabalala-Msimang caused 300,000 preventable deaths from the acquired immune deficiency syndrome (AIDS) by failing to provide care and medicine similar to that offered in neighboring Botswana and Namibia.[103] Throughout sub-Saharan Africa, it was estimated that in 2002, only 300,000 of nearly 30 million people with HIV were receiving proper treatment, dooming the majority of them to an early, and preventable, death.[104]

Policies that allow an avoidably high rate of infant and child mortality to persist should also be regarded as a form of structural violence or even, depending on the intent and available resources, structural genocide. If India had decreased its infant mortality rate at the

99. *See, e.g.*, JONES, GENOCIDE, at 41–2, 124–37 (describing cases in India, Ukraine, China, Cambodia, East Timor, Ethiopia, and North Korea); JASPAR BECKER, ROGUE REGIME: KIM JONG II AND THE LOOMING THREAT OF NORTH KOREA xiii, 266–273 (Oxford: Oxford UP, 2005) (arguing that the "internal devastation" in North Korea "is akin to genocide"); *Famine (Ukraine), in* 3 ENCYCLOPEDIA OF GENOCIDE AND CRIMES AGAINST HUMANITY 1056–59; VALENTINO, FINAL SOLUTIONS, at 75, 93, 125–43.

100. *See* Marcus, *Famine Crimes*, at 259–61.

101. *See* Miranda Prynne, *North Korea Uncovered: Palaces, Labour Camps and Mass Graves*, THE INDEPENDENT (U.K.), June 21, 2009, http://www.independent.co.uk/news/world/asia/north-korea-uncovered-palaces-labour-camps-and-mass-graves-1711573.html; Richard Lloyd Parry, *The Nation that Is Dying in Silence: Millions of North Koreans Have Starved to Death While Their Government Has Covered Up the Truth*, The Independent (U.K.), Aug. 23, 1998, http://www.independent.co.uk/news/the-nation-that-is-dying-in-silence-1173622.html.

102. *See* Peter G. Prontzos, *Collateral Damage: The Human Cost of Structural Violence, in* GENOCIDE, WAR CRIMES, AND THE WEST, at 299.

103. *See* Pride Chigwedere, M.D., et al., *Estimating the Lost Benefits of Antiretroviral Drug Use in South Africa*, 39 J. ACQUIR. IMMUN. DEFIC. SYN. 410, 410–11 (Dec. 2008); Harvard Sch. of Public Health, *Researchers Estimate Lives Lost Due to Delay in Antiretroviral Drug Use for HIV/AIDS in South Africa* (Oct. 20, 2008), http://www.hsph.harvard.edu/news/press-releases/2008 ... /researchers-estimate-lives-lost-delay-arv-drug-use-hivaids-south-africa.html; Clare Nullius, *South Africa's Removal of Health Minister Praised,* ASSOCIATED PRESS, Sept. 27, 2008, http://atlanticphilanthropies.org/news/news/south_africa_s_removal_of_health_minister_praised; Sarah Boseley, *Mbeki Aids Denial 'Caused 300000 Deaths'*, THE GUARDIAN (U.K.), Nov. 26, 2008, http://www.guardian.co.uk/world/2008/nov/26/aids-south-africa.

104. *See* Sarah Boseley, *Aids Epidemic 'Bringing Social Collapse'*, THE GUARDIAN (U.K.), Nov. 27, 2002, http://www.guardian.co.uk/world/2002/nov/27/aids.sarahboseley.

same pace as Vietnam, it would have saved one million infant lives every year.[105] Even in the U.S., nearly 5,000 African-American children died unnecessary deaths every year in the early 2000s due to inadequate access to health insurance and medical care.[106] American infants as a whole were twice to three times as likely not to survive their first year of life, compared with infants in Scandinavia or Japan, which more often provide free health care for infants and pregnant women.[107] The results are likely to be even worse in many countries in Asia, Africa, and the Americas, with an excess infant death toll, compared to, say, Japan or Scandinavia, that is likely in the hundreds of thousands per year. India's infant death rate, for example, was more than eight times the rate in the U.S. in 2006, and its population is also several times larger, for tens of thousands of likely infant deaths.[108]

In terms of catastrophic violations of human rights and human security, denial of health care and nutrition far outstrip the events in the former Yugoslavia or Rwanda. India's under-five infant mortality claims 1.9 million children's lives every year. When one considers that the populations of Indonesia, Brazil, Pakistan, Bangladesh, and Nigeria are between half and three-quarters that of the U.S., the risk of mass infant death is clear. It would be incomprehensible for the law of genocide to ignore such a vast scheme on the part of governments to impose conditions of life calculated to destroy their most vulnerable citizens, by corrupt or reckless policy-making.

Some countries, such as Chad and Niger, are suffering from extreme levels of malnutrition and disease that may not be explained by global conflict on the scale of an Angola or Ethiopia, or a scramble for diamonds or minerals on the scale of a Sierra Leone or DRC. These countries lag near the bottom of the U.N. Human Development Index, despite having much lower rates of HIV/AIDS infection than other countries that are improving their health care and food delivery systems, such as Botswana. A review of U.N. reports reveals that the extremely low life expectancy in these countries—45 in 2002, falling to about 44 in 2005—may be explained by very low levels of spending on clean water, health care, and women's health, with only half or a third as much spent as a percentage of GDP than in the U.S. or France. In these countries, a child has a 40% chance of dying before the age of 40, powerful evidence of structural genocide in comparison to the 9% or so rate in developing Morocco or Vietnam.[109]

Zimbabwe is perhaps the starkest case of preventable death and disease. Based on the country's mismanagement of its HIV/AIDS crisis and economic situation, life expectancy has fallen from 43 years in 2002 to only 34 years for women, and 37 for men, in 2008.[110] By contrast, the U.S. CIA, no advocate of North Korea's (it accuses the regime of "eco-

---

105. *See Child Mortality in Malawi, Vietnam and India,* BBC NEWS, Sept. 13, 2007, http://news.bbc.co.uk/nolpda/ukfs_news/hi/newsid_6992000/6992841.stm.

106. *See* Maggie Fox, *Doctors Call for Universal Health Insurance*, REUTERS, Aug. 12, 2003, http://www.defeatdiabetes.org/Articles/insurance030814.htm.

107. *See* Jeff Green, *U.S. Has Second Worst Newborn Death Rate in Modern World*, CNN, May 8, 2006, http://www.cnn.com/2006/HEALTH/parenting/05/08/mothers.index.

108. *See Infant Mortality Rate—Total (Deaths/1000 Live Births) 2006,* http://www.photius.com/rankings/population/infant_mortality_rate_total_2006_1.html (quoting CIA, WORLD FACTBOOK 2006).

109. *See* U.N. DEVELOPMENT PROGRAMME, HUMAN DEVELOPMENT REPORT 2005, at 214–43 (New York: U.N. Development Programme, 2005).

110. *Compare* U.N. DEVELOPMENT PROGRAMME, HUMAN DEVELOPMENT REPORT 2002, at 151, *with Zimbabwe in Facts and Figures,* BBC News, Mar. 25, 2008, http://news.bbc.co.uk/nolpda/ifs_news/hi/newsid_7304000/7304635.stm, *and Life Expectancy Under Mugabe Falls to Just 33*, THE DAILY MAIL (U.K.), Mar. 11, 2005, http://dailymail.co.uk.

nomic mismanagement") pegs the life expectancy in that country at over 70.[111] The Zimbabwean currency has lost more than 99.9% of its value, slum and shantytown demolitions have displaced 570,000 people, 3.4 million Zimbabweans have fled as refugees, and unemployment is 80%.[112] The blocking of humanitarian aid denied more than one million children, students, and elderly people of vital assistance, with 45% of the population estimated soon to be in need of aid.[113]

International financial institutions may bear some of the blame, or even a large part of it in certain cases, for structural violence against vulnerable children. In 1997, the U.N. Development Programme (UNDP) projected that the burden of sovereign debt in Africa was killing between five and seven million people per year due to foregone access to health care, education, sanitation, and other public goods offered by governments in East Asia, Europe, and North America. In Mozambique alone, debt took the lives of between 80,000 to 115,000 children per year due to inadequate health care and education.[114] The UNDP claimed that 21 million people's lives could have been saved between 1997 and 2000 by debt relief.[115]

Scholars have defined structural violence as "deleterious conditions that derive from economic and political structures of power, created and maintained by human actions and institutions."[116] The definition resembles one of the forms of genocide, the deliberate infliction on a group of "conditions of life calculated to bring about its physical destruction in whole or in part," with the intent to destroy the group in whole or in part.[117] If genocidal intent may be inferred in cases of the confinement of a group in concentration camps with a high death rate due to hunger and disease, this raises the question why the imposition of a high death rate due to hunger and disease outside of a camp structure is any better. As Professor Lemkin pointed out, the machine-gun may be the last resort of the architect of genocide, but it need not be the first.

---

111. *See North Korea, in* CIA, WORLD FACTBOOK 2004, http://en.wikisource.org/wiki/CIA_World_Fact_Book,_2004/Korea,_North.

112. *See Zimbabwe in Facts and Figures*; Alex Perry, *Zimbabwe Suspense: Is Mugabe Done?*, TIME MAG., Apr. 1, 2008, http://www.time.com/time/world/article/0,8599,1726790,00.html.

113. *See* Celia W. Dugger, *Zimbabwe Lifts Ban on Aid Groups, But Its Effects Linger*, N.Y. TIMES, Aug. 29, 2008, http://www.nytimes.com/2008/08/30/world/africa/30zimbabwe.html?n=Top/Reference/Times%20Topics/Subjects/P/Politics%20and%20Government.

114. *See* Robert Naiman & Neil Watkins, *A Survey of the Impacts of IMF Structural Adjustment in Africa: Growth, Social Spending, and Debt Relief*, 146 CONG. REC. H6636 (Apr. 1999).

115. *See* Canadian Center for Policy Alternatives, *Impoverishing a Continent: The World Bank and the IMF in Africa* 11–13 (July 2004), http://www.halifaxinitiative.org/updir/ImpoverishingAContinent.pdf.

116. Prontzos, *The Human Cost of Structural Violence*, at 300.

117. Genocide Convention, art. 10. *See also* Application of the Convention on the Prevention and Punishment of the Crime of Genocide (Bosnia and Herzegovina v. Serbia and Montenegro), Judgment (Feb. 26, 2007), at ¶ 190.

Chapter XIV

"Imagine": Genocide in Southern Sudan

> I lost my parents in 1985, on the day when people came to our village and burned it. My father and uncle died that day, and I lost my mother.
>
> One evening, armed men came to our village to catch certain people.... They took me and my two brothers ... to a faraway place with tents and houses made out of hay.... They made us herd sheep and small cows....
>
> —Alweel Kol, a woman from southern Sudan[1]

This chapter describes repeated campaigns of genocide and deportation against the non-Arab populations of southern Sudan. Although the depopulation of large numbers of indigenous Africans in present-day Sudan by Arab and Turkish conquerors goes back many centuries, the large-scale killing displacement of predominantly non-Arab populations has claimed more than 2.5 million lives since the seizure of power of Sudanese dictator Omar Hassan al-Bashir. The historical context of genocide in southern Sudan is the colonization, domination, and exploitation of indigenous Sudanese by Arab and Turkish invaders engaged in the large-scale export of African slaves to the Islamic world. Since the 1989 coup that brought the al-Bashir dictatorship to power, Sudanese national law has facilitated genocide against the indigenous peoples of southern Sudan in particular, and to a lesser extent in Darfur, the subject of the next chapter.

The context of genocide in southern Sudan is an economic incentive on the part of the dominant self-styled "Arab" group to exterminate indigenous non-Arab Africans and actual or perceived "infidels" in order to seize their land, enslave them, loot their villages, and exploit their scarce resources. The pace of genocide in southern Sudan has accelerated with the discovery of large amounts of oil in Sudan, which led to lucrative contracts between the regime and international oil interests including the China National Petroleum Company (CNPC), Petronas, and Talisman Energy.

A. Historical Context of Genocide in Sudan

Sudan is a closer to an empire than to a nation, at almost eight times the size of Germany and stretching across territory nearly as vast as all Western Europe.[2] As the largest country in Africa by land area, it is composed of a number of formerly independent coun-

1. *Quoted in* Out of Exile: Narratives from the Abducted and Displaced People of Sudan (Craig Walzer ed., San Francisco: McSweeney's Books, 2008).

2. *See* Safia Safwat, *Sudan*, 1 Yearbook of Islamic and Middle Eastern L. 237, 237 (1994).

tries and tribal areas that were eventually incorporated into nine federal states, some nearly as large as France.[3] Among those countries were the independent sultanates of Darfur, the home of the Fur people, and of Sinnar, where the bulk of the Dinka people lived.[4]

Peoples such as the Dinka, Nuba, Fur, Masalit, Zaghawa, etc. are the "indigenous" peoples of Sudan because they lived in the territory that became Sudan prior to conquests and colonization by Arab-speakers bearing a distinct culture and religion, that of Muslim Arabs.[5] The indigenous Africans, in Sudan or elsewhere, "are those which, having a historical continuity with pre-invasion and pre-colonial societies that developed on their territories, consider themselves distinct from other sectors of the societies now prevailing in those territories...."[6]

Sudan is composed of a number of distinct tribes; long before the recent controversies, observers recognized that many of these tribes were Arab and claimed descent from the person or the tribe of the Prophet Muhammad, while others were indigenous Africans with no Arab heritage.[7] At the time of independence in the late 1950s, only one-third of the population of Sudan was indigenous African, while the rest was estimated to be Arab and Muslim.[8] Neither Christianity nor Islam is indigenous to Africa; instead, both were imported from Asia, the former from present-day Israel and Palestine, and the latter from present-day Saudi Arabia. By 1990, war and migration had resulted in 39 percent of the Sudanese population being identified as Arab, mostly inhabiting the north, with the re-

---

3. *See id.*; Eric Hooglund, *Government and Politics, in* A COUNTRY STUDY: SUDAN (Washington, D.C.: Library of Congress, 1991), http://lcweb2.loc.gov/cgi-bin/query/r?frd/cstdy:@field(DOCID+sd0110); Tasneem Mowjee, *Humanitarian Agenda: 2015, Sudan Country Study*, TUFTS UNIV. (July 30, 2006), http://www.reliefweb.int/library/documents/2006/tufts-sdn-30jul.pdf ("Sudan is the largest country in Africa (about the size of Western Europe) and one of the most diverse. For centuries, it consisted of a number of independent countries."). The State Department has described Sudan as composed of a "collection of small, independent kingdoms and principalities from the beginning of the Christian era until 1820–21, when Egypt conquered and unified the northern portion of the country." *See* USDOS, *International Religious Freedom Report 1999—Sudan*, http://atheism.about.com/library/irf/irf99/blirf_sudan99.htm; USDOS, Bureau of African Affairs, *Background Note: Sudan* (Nov. 2006), http://www.state.gov/r/pa/ei/bgn/5424.htm.

4. *See* U.N. IRIN, *Sudan: The Escalating Crisis in Darfur*, (Dec. 31, 2003), http://www.irinnews.org/report.aspx?reportid=47856; STEPHANIE BESWICK, SUDAN'S BLOOD MEMORY: THE LEGACY OF WAR, ETHNICITY AND SLAVERY IN SOUTH SUDAN 17–20 (2004).

5. U.N. Economic & Social Council, Comm. on Human Rights, Sub-Comm. on the Promotion & Protection of Human Rights, Working Group on Indigenous Populations, *Report of the Working Group on Indigenous Populations on its 21st Session*, ¶ 2, U.N. Doc, E/CN.4/Sub.2/2003/22 (Aug. 11, 2003).

6. El Hadji Guissé, Member, U.N. Economic and Social Council, Sub-Commission on the Promotion and Protection of Human Rights, Working Group on Indigenous Populations, ¶ 2, Twenty-first session (15 June 2003), Item 4 (b) of the provisional agenda, E/CN.4/Sub.2/2003/22; Sarah Pritchard, *Working Group on Indigenous Populations: Mandate, Standard-setting Activities and Future Perspectives, in* INDIGENOUS PEOPLES, THE UNITED NATIONS AND HUMAN RIGHTS 43 (Sarah Pritchard ed., 1998) (quoting José Martínez Cobo, *Study of the Problem against Indigenous Populations, vol. 5, Conclusions, Proposals and Recommendations* ¶ 379, U.N. Doc. E/CN/4/Sub 2/1986/7 Add. 4, (March 1, 1987)). *Accord* Luis Rodríguez-Piñero, Indigenous Peoples, Postcolonialism, and International Law 163 (2005) (similar definition incorporated in International Labour Organisation Convention Concerning the Protection and Integration of Indigenous and Other Tribal and Semi-Tribal Populations in Independent Countries, art. 1 (No. 107), ILC, 40th Sess., 26 June 1957 (entry into force June 1959)).

7. *See, e.g.*, Sir Charles Wilson, *On the Native Tribes of the Egyptian Sudan, in* REPORT OF THE FIFTY-SIXTH MEETING OF THE BRITISH ASSOCIATION FOR THE ADVANCEMENT OF SCIENCE 833–34 (1887). Arab historians made no attempt to deny the fact that Sudan had been conquered and its indigenous people subjugated. *See* 2 HAROLD ALFRED MACMICHAEL, A HISTORY OF THE ARABS IN THE SUDAN 11–15 (1922).

8. *See* ABDEL SALAM SIDAHMED & ALSIR SIDAHMED, SUDAN 136 (2005).

Image 6 The Provinces of Sudan, Circa 2006

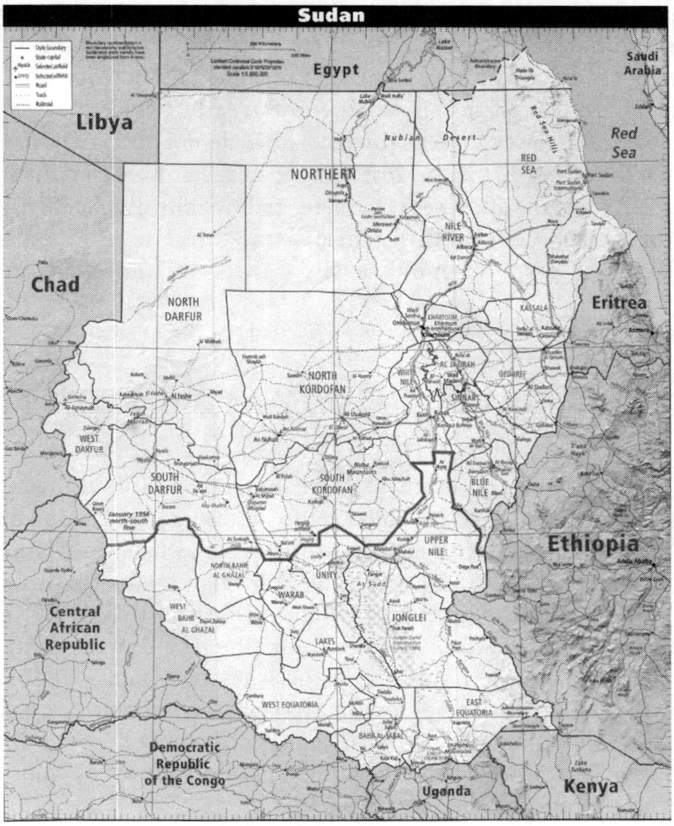

mainder being mostly indigenous Africans such as the Fur and Dinka peoples.[9] About 70 percent of the population identified as Sunni Muslim, 5 percent as Christian and 20 percent as practicing indigenous African religions.[10]

From the early 1960s until 1972, a civil war raged in the Sudan between Arab northerners and indigenous African southerners.[11] Upon independence of the Sudan from Britain in the late 1950s, the country was governed and identified as an "Arab state," with discrimination, marginalization, and "internal colonialism" the fate of the South. The southern Sudanese mounted a secessionist movement supported by Ethiopia, Uganda, Zaïre, and Israel, and charged the government with "genocide" as a million people died in the war and ensuing famine.[12]

In 1972, President Gaafar al-Nimeiry, who came to power in a Soviet-backed coup, defused the southern crisis for a time by granting autonomy to the region.[13] However, he largely abandoned more than 100,000 Darfurians, leaving them to die of famine starting

---

9. *See Sudan, in* Encyclopedia Africana, at 1798.

10. *See id.*

11. *See* Alexis Heraclides, *Janus or Sisyphus? The Southern Problem of the Sudan*, 25 J. of Modern African Studies 213, 213–15 (1987).

12. *See id.* at 213–17, 221.

13. *See* Judith Miller, *Fearful City in Southern Sudan Expects Rebel Attack*, N.Y. Times, Feb. 1, 1985, at A9; Judith Miller, *15-Year Rule Ends; Overthrow, With Nimeiry Away on Trip, Follows Increasing Unrest*, N.Y. Times, Apr. 7, 1985, at A1.

in 1984.[14] After communist and fundamentalist coup attempts, President al-Nimeiry turned rightward, declaring Arabic to be the official language of the Sudan and imposing *Sharia* or Islamic law on the country.[15] He cultivated allies in the Muslim Brotherhood, a movement whose adherents imposed fundamentalist religious law and massacred religious minorities in Afghanistan starting in the early 1990s.[16] The Muslim Brotherhood steadily gained power under Nimeiry and a democratic government of the late 1980s, and was greatly enriched by government seizures of its opponents' properties.[17] Al-Nimeiry's last years in office were characterized by southern Sudanese opposition to the imposition of Islamic law on Christian areas, and steep hikes in food and fuel prices under an austerity program recommended by the U.S. and the IMF.[18]

B. Genocide and Slavery in Southern Sudan

Sudan's constitution and governmental structure arguably lie at the root of the genocide not only in Darfur and eastern Chad but also in southern Sudan and the Nuba mountains region. Sudan's current constitution is an artifact of the Sudanese Muslim Brotherhood, which was born on the campus of Khartoum University,[19] just as the Afghan Muslim Brotherhood was born on the campus of Kabul University.[20] Hassan al-Turabi taught law at Khartoum University, and propagandized for "the Arabization of Africa and ... the rise of Islam as a form of government in [formerly] secular states." The Muslim Brotherhood became the National Islamic Front in 1985, and seized power in Sudan starting in 1989. After the revolution, Sudan's government invited any Arab or Muslim from around the world to live in Sudan, while displacing millions of non-Arabs and non-Muslims from their homes and the lands of their ancestors.[21]

After the 1989 coup, Sudan's new President Omar Hassan al-Bashir suspended the country's constitution[22] and concentrated "all effective political power [] in the hands of [the] President."[23] When President al-Bashir allowed a new constitution to be adopted in

---

14. *See* M.W. Daly, Darfur's Sorrow: A History of Destruction and Genocide 3, 227–34 (Cambridge: Cambridge UP, 2007).

15. *See* Heraclides, *The Southern Problem of the Sudan,* at 227.

16. *Id. See generally* Hannibal Travis, *Freedom or Theocracy?: Constitutionalism in Afghanistan and Iraq,* 3 Northwestern U. J. of Int'l Human Rights 4 (2005).

17. *See* U.S. Immigration and Naturalization Service (INS), *Country Reports: Sudan, Human Rights Conditions* (1993), http://www1.umn.edu/humanrts/ins/sudan93.pdf.

18. *See id.* at 227; Miller, *15-Year Rule Ends,* at A1.

19. Emily Wax, *Sudan's Unbowed, Unbroken Inner Circle,* Wash. Post Foreign Service, May 3, 2005, at A01.

20. *See* Vogelsang, The Afghans, at 292, 298; Kakar, Afghanistan.

21. *See* Emily Wax, *Sudan's Unbowed, Unbroken Inner Circle,* at A01.

22. *See Sudan, in* World Factbook 2006, https://www.cia.gov/cia/publications/factbook/print/su.html.

23. USDOS, Bureau of African Affairs, *Background Note: Sudan* (Nov. 2006), http://www.state.gov/r/pa/ei/bgn/5424.htm. *See also* S. Res. 94, 103rd Cong., 1st Sess., http://thomas.loc.gov/cgi-bin/query/z?c103:S.RES.94.IS (starting in 1989, Sudanese government "suspended the Sudan constitution, dissolved all political institutions in Sudan, and banned or dissolved all political parties, civic organizations, trade unions, professional associations, social organizations, and privately-owned mass media in Sudan").

Image 7 President Omar al-Bashir with SPLA Leader John Garang, Circa Spring 2003

1998, it included provisions imposing a duty upon every citizen to "defend the country and respond to the Jihad call."[24] This constitutional invocation is particularly significant in the African context because of the historical connection between "Jihad" and the Arab enslavement of indigenous Africans. Sudan's constitution also provides for the raising of a "volunteer Popular Defense Force from among the Sudanese people for national defense, … or to assist any regular forces."[25] Such volunteer forces—including the Popular Defense Force but also the Murahileen or Arab militias and *Mujahideen* or holy warriors—operate as pro-government forces committing genocide, crimes against humanity, war crimes, and the systematic enslavement and rape of civilians.[26]

While the constitution contains lip service to religious freedom, it makes religious law (*Sharia*) the subject of legislation, which the government has done by declaring "Islam as the state religion and … that Islam must inspire the country's laws, institutions, and policies."[27] The government banned Christian speech, bulldozed churches and other minority institutions, and fired 20,000 non-Muslims and women from federal jobs.[28] The

24. Const. of Sudan 1998, art. 35.

25. *Id.*, art. 125.

26. *See* Situation in Darfur, the Sudan, Prosecutor's Application under Article 58 (7), Pre-Trial Chamber I, ICC-02/05-56, at 4–5, 39 (Feb. 27, 2007), http://www.icc-cpi.int/library/cases/ICC-02-05-56_English.pdf. *See also* J. Millard Burr, Requiem for the Sudan: War, Drought, and Disaster Relief on the Nile 6, 11, 18–9, 29–34, 41, 72–75, 83–90 (1995). Burr describes *Murahileen* as "Arab militias, usually on horseback, used by north [of Sudan, *i.e.*, the government and its allied tribes] to attack southerners." J. Millard Burr, Quantifying Genocide in Southern Sudan and the Nuba Mountains: 1983–1998, at 8 (1998), http://web.archive.org/web/20030803023613/http://www.refugees.org/news/crisis/sudan.pdf [hereinafter Burr, Genocide].

27. USDOS, *International Religious Freedom Report 1999—Sudan*, http://atheism.about.com/library/irf/irf99/blirf_sudan99.htm.

28. *See id.*; INS, *Country Reports: Sudan* ("The imposition of Islamic law, Shari'a, on most of the Sudanese population has led to systematic legal discrimination against women and non-Muslims in northern Sudan, including over 20,000 dismissals from federal employment."); *see also* U.N. Economic and Social Council, Commission on Human Rights, Civil and Political Rights, Including the

constitution purports to guarantee an independent judiciary and parliamentary democracy; however, these provisions were undermined from 1995 to 2005 as the judiciary was "manipulated and politicized" and independent judges often dismissed.[29] Officials placed a moratorium on appointing non-Arab judges after 1989, and the judiciary since then has regarded atrocities by the government and its allied paramilitaries as minor affairs.[30] By contrast, accused civilians are very rarely represented by defense counsel and are nearly inevitably convicted in trials often lasting no longer than a few minutes. Courts regularly sentence the common people to flogging with up to 40 lashes for such offenses as violating the public dress code, unlicensed trading, or possessing alcohol.[31]

Starting in 1983, the Sudan People's Liberation Army (SPLA), led by John Garang de Mabior, a former Sudanese army colonel of Dinka ancestry, mounted a war of resistance to the Sudanese government's policies of imposing Islamic law on Christians and second-class citizenship on non-Arabs.[32] In response, the government "mobilized militias" of Arab tribesmen to "massacre[] tens of thousands of Dinka villagers [and] create[] a uniquely horrible famine in which camps of displaced people were deliberated starved to death en masse."[33] The militias massacred 20,000 Dinka people in the province of Bahr el Ghazal, enslaved 50,000 young Dinka girls, and caused the deaths, by starvation or other means, of 40,000 Dinka children fleeing to Ethiopia as refugees.[34] In 1987, Arab mobs slaughtered 1,000 to 1,500 Dinka civilians in a single incident near a railway station.[35] The government also bombed villages that had been "liberated" by the SPLA, using Soviet-designed MiG fighter-bombers.[36] By 1988, Sudan was spending three-quarters of a billion dollars a year on the war, and had lost 300,000 refugees to just one of its neighboring countries, recently famine-stricken Ethiopia.[37] War and famine in Sudan itself placed between five and six million at risk for starvation.[38]

Question of Freedom of Expression, Addendum: Visit to the Sudan, U.N. Doc. No. E/CN.4/2000/63/Add.1, ¶¶95–102, 136, 151 (Mar. 3, 2000).

29. ICID Report at ¶432.

30. *See* Elizabeth Rubin, *If Not Peace, Then Justice*, N.Y. Times, Apr. 2, 2006, at Magazine 6–42; Human Rights Watch, *Entrenching Impunity: Government Responsibility for International Crimes in Darfur*, at 55–6 (2005), http://hrw.org/reports/2005/darfur1205/darfur1205text.pdf ("The Sudanese government has failed to investigate, let alone prosecute, local, regional, and national officials who planned, coordinated, and implemented 'ethnic cleansing' or were otherwise implicated in war crimes and crimes against humanity.... Despite numerous, consistent, and credible reports documenting the existence of patterns of rape and sexual violence that may amount to war crimes or crimes against humanity, the Sudanese government consistently refuses to ... prosecut[e] the perpetrators....").

31. *See* Amnesty International, *Sudan: Empty Promises? Human Rights Violations in Government-Controlled Areas,* AI Index: AFR 54/036/2003 (July 16, 2003), http://web.amnesty.org/library/Index/ENGAFR540362003?open&of=ENG-2AF.

32. *See* Heraclides, *The Southern Problem of the Sudan*, at 228–29.

33. Alex de Waal, *Tragedy in Darfur*, 29.5 Boston Rev., Oct./Nov. 2004, http://www.bostonreview.net.

34. *See* Eric Marsden, *Charities 'Kept Quiet' on Scale of Sudan Famine*, The Times (U.K.), Sept. 4, 1988.

35. *See* Daly, Darfur's Sorrow, at 239; *Sudanese Dinkas Reported Slain By Police, Militia,* Wash. Post, Apr. 25, 1987, http://pqarchiver.proquest.com; Roger P. Winter, *In Sudan, Both Sides Use Food as a Weapon,* Wash. Post, Nov. 29, 1988, at A25.

36. *See Sudan—Air Forces,* Flight Int'l, Dec. 5, 1990; Julian Ozanne, *The Creeping Paralysis of Sudan,* Fin. Times (U.K.), May 8, 1989, at I–21.

37. *See* Editorial, *Sudan, Drowning in Troubles,* N.Y. Times, Aug. 25, 1988, at A26.

38. *See Famine Threatens Huge Areas of Africa,* St. Louis Post-Dispatch, Dec. 23, 1990, at 5B. *See also News Summary,* N.Y. Times, Dec. 19, 1990, at A2.

In 1987, the government issued a decree to kill all male children in southern Sudan.[39] Between 50,000 and 70,000 Sudanese, mostly children but including adults and children, boys and girls, fled on foot to Ethiopia, braving shootings, rapes, wild animals, disease, hunger, and extreme dehydration.[40] A southern Sudanese "Lost Boy" refugee stated in an interview:

> I will not come to Sudan. People are being shot because there is oil. They shoot small peoples like us. We don't know—they have just killed our parents. Like my father has died at that time, when I first go through Ethiopia, when we were running. We were in cattle camp. They came and shoot my father, which mean if I go now to Sudan, they can kill me again. Like my mother now, I don't know where she is with her kids. Maybe they have died. Imagine.[41]

Three out of every five of the refugees died on the 450-mile trek, as malaria, hunger, and lack of clean water took their toll.[42] The children saw each other die, buried each other, felt enormous guilt as their friends and siblings died asking them for water, food, or safety.[43] Some drank urine to survive, while older children had to bury the younger children who died.[44] An American diplomat described the children as bearing a "concentration camp stare," and comparing "poorly with pictures of Nazi concentration camp victims."[45] "An aid worker who visited one of the camps in 1987 recalled 'only naked bodies, very thin, of boys, as far as the eye could see.'"[46] Aid workers described the refugees as "skeletons" that were not even "able to stand."[47] They had walked a distance comparable to that between New York City and the Midwestern U.S.

In the late 1980s, Sudan built up the rebels of the Ethiopian Popular Revolutionary Democratic Front (EPRDF).[48] The EPRDF occupied the capital Addis Ababa in 1991. With the fall of President Mengistu, Sudan occupied SPLA territory including the Kapoeta refugee camp. About 12,000 Sudanese refugees, mostly boys below the age of 16, set off on foot to camps in Kenya.[49] Up to 100,000 Sudanese refugees in the Kakuma refugee camp in Kenya had only one U.N. protection officer to provide security, and could not

---

39. *See* Carina Chocano, *A Remarkable Odyssey from Sudan to Syracuse; 'God Grew Tired of Us' Tracks Three 'Lost Boys' on Their Journey to the United States.*, L.A. TIMES, Jan. 12, 2007, at E6.

40. *See* MARK BIXLER, THE LOST BOYS OF SUDAN: AN AMERICAN STORY OF THE REFUGEE EXPERIENCE 6 (2005); God Grew Tired of Us (National Geographic Films, 2006). *See also* Sarah O'Brien, *John Bul Dau Recounts Story of Surviving in War-torn Sudan*, THE CURRENT, Apr. 23, 2007, http://media.www.thecurrentonline.com/media/storage/paper304/news/2007/04/23/News/John-Bul.Dau.Recounts.Story.Of.Surviving.In.WarTorn.Sudan-2874587.shtml; Ellen Barry, *Strangers in a Strange Land*, BOSTON GLOBE, Jan. 7, 2001.

41. *Quoted in* GOD GREW TIRED OF US (National Geographic Films, 2006).

42. *See* BIXLER, THE LOST BOYS, at 6.

43. *See* Jane Perlez, *Trek to Misery by 12,000 Pawns in Sudan War*, N.Y. TIMES, June 10, 1992, http://www.nytimes.com/1992/06/10/world/trek-to-misery-by-12000-pawns-in-sudan-war.html; God Grew Tired of Us; Valentino Achak Deng, *Authors@Google Speech* (May 3, 2007), http://www.youtube.com/watch?v=2V7MeewG_MU.

44. *See* O'Brien, *John Bul Dau*; GOD GREW TIRED OF US.

45. BIXLER, LOST BOYS, at 6.

46. *Id.* at 57.

47. *Id.* at 6, 57.

48. *See* ALEXANDER DE WAAL, EVIL DAYS: THIRTY YEARS OF WAR AND FAMINE IN ETHIOPIA 320 (New York: Human Rights Watch, 1991); PETER WOODWARD, THE HORN OF AFRICA: POLITICS AND INTERNATIONAL RELATIONS 98 (London: I.B. Tauris, 2003).

49. *See* Jane Perlez, *Trek to Misery by 12,000 Pawns in Sudan War*, N.Y. TIMES, June 10, 1992, http://query.nytimes.com/gst/fullpage.html?res=9E0CEEDA1339F933A25755C0A964958260.

leave because Kenya "insist[ed] on confining refugees to camps"; one NGO worker described the people as lacking full "'legal rights'" and as "'not being attended to appropriately,'" some for over a decade. Human Rights Watch found that some refugee camps "are not safe and [] conditions are life threatening," and said that refugees should be allowed freedom of movement to cities.[50]

In the 1990s, the Nuba people of central Sudan began to suffer the brunt of the government's war of extermination against indigenous peoples.[51] The Nuba people comprise a substantial part of the indigenous inhabitants of Sudan; they were driven out of their traditional homelands into the mountains by "centuries of attacks."[52] Some Nuba are Christian, some Muslim, and some practice indigenous African religions. One to two million Nuba people lived in Sudan in 1989.[53]

In 1992, the Sudanese governor of South Kordofan, Lt. General al-Hussein, "declared a Holy War (Jihad) in the Nuba Mountains." There followed a campaign of "wholesale murder, abduction, rape, family separation, forced religious conversion, and the forced relocation of tens of thousands of Nuba" residents by the government and its allies, which one NGO cast as an attempt by "the Khartoum government ... to extirpate the Nuba peoples themselves."[54] As described in the journal *Foreign Affairs*:

> Declaring its purposes synonymous with the will of God, the regime [of Omar Hassan al-Bashir] has ... carr[ied] out an ambitious program to remake the country—one of Africa's most ethnically diverse—into a homogeneous, Arabized state ruled by an extremist version of Islamic law. To this end, Bashir has declared the ongoing war against southern insurgents a jihad and is pursuing a ten-year campaign of forced Islamization, pillage, rape, and murder against the people of the Nuba mountains in central Sudan, where allies of the regime covet scarce arable land....
>
> [T]he Nuba [people] ... are now threatened with cultural extinction.... [They] are facing Khartoum's onslaught alone as the international community averts its eyes, lest an acknowledgement that this is genocide entail an obligation to act.[55]

Pro-government paramilitaries destroyed crops, farmlands, and shops, triggering widespread famine. The Nuba declared that "'ethnic cleansing [was] geared towards replacing the Nuba people with the Arab tribes of Kordofan.'"[56]

---

50. Alison Parker, Hidden in Plain View: Refugees Living Without Protection in Nairobi and Kampala (New York: Human Rights Watch, 2002), http://www.hrw.org/legacy/reports/2002/kenyugan/kenyugan1002%20ap%20alter-19.htm.

51. *See* Andrew Natsios, Report on Sudan (May 31, 2002), http://fpc.state.gov/fpc/10631.htm (referring to the "indigenous Nuba people"); Mona Mohamed and Margaret Fisher, *The Nuba of Sudan, in* Endangered Peoples of Africa and the Middle East: Struggles to Survive and Thrive 115–128 (Robert Hitchcock & Alan Osborn eds., Westport, CT: Greenwood Press. 2002).

52. Millard Burr, Quantifying Genocide in Southern Sudan and the Nuba Mountains: 1983–1998, at 24, 27 (Washington, DC: U.S. Committee for Refugees, Dec. 1998), http://web.archive.org/web/20030615125913/http://refugees.org/news/crisis/sudan.pdf (footnote omitted) ("The Nuba tribes inhabited the Sudan long before the arrival of Arab tribes. However, centuries of attacks by their Arab neighbors forced the various Nuba peoples to find sanctuary in what are now called the Nuba Mountains."). *See also* Natsios, Report on Sudan (referring to the "indigenous Nuba people").

53. *See* Burr, Quantifying Genocide, at 24, 27.

54. Burr, Quantifying Genocide, at 31.

55. Gail M. Gerhart, *Africa*, 76 Foreign Aff. 147, 147–48 (May/June 1997). *See also Sudan Again Bombs Civilians in Rebel Areas*, N.Y. Times, Nov. 26, 1990; James C. McKinley, Jr., *Famine Looming, Sudan Curbs Relief to Rebel-Held Areas*, N.Y. Times, Mar. 18, 1998; Stephen Buckley and Karl Vick, *Nuba Caught Up in Sudan's Civil War,* Wash. Post, June 16, 1998.

56. Burr, Quantifying Genocide, at 29–34.

By the end of 1992, the government and its militia allies had "killed at least 500,000 civilian non-combatants since 1986," driven a third of southern Sudanese civilians from their homes,[57] and burned down "scores of villages" in the Nuba Mountains.[58] In 1993, a former logistical official with the U.S. Agency for International Development issued a report on behalf of the U.S. Committee for Refugees concluding that at least 1.3 million southern Sudanese had died since the early 1980s "as a result of war-related causes and government neglect."[59] A resolution introduced in 1993 and enjoying the support of 17 co-sponsors in the U.S. Senate accused the Sudanese government of "ethnic cleansing" against the Nuba people, killing or forcibly relocating them in the tens of thousands and placing four million people at risk.[60]

Other indigenous peoples also suffered systematic attacks. The largest of these groups is the Dinka people, with two million members in 1989, more than any other ethnic group in southern Sudan.[61] The Dinka lost hundreds of villages to government attacks between 1994 and 1998. Government trains transported Arab militias such as the *Murahileen* to the Dinka region of Bahr al-Ghazal, through which they rampaged, "looting, pillaging, and raping as they passed through."[62] The militias "burned many Dinka villages, captured hundreds of women and children as slaves, stole many thousands of heads of cattle, and caused widespread devastation."[63] Aided by Sudanese military intelligence, they "massacred tens of thousands of Dinka villagers [and] created a uniquely horrible famine in which camps of displaced people were deliberately starved to death en masse."[64] Human Rights Watch reported that the widespread famine in Bahr al-Ghazal in 1998 threatened one million people, mostly Dinka, with starvation.[65] As many as 100,000 Dinka people died in the 1998 famine alone.[66]

The government pursued a "counterinsurgency plan" against both the Dinka and Nuba peoples. These campaigns involved the depopulation of civilian areas of central and south-

57. INS, *Country Reports: Sudan*. The army, Popular Defense Force, Murahileen, and Mujahideen attacked "numerous villages" in the Nuba Mountains region, with dozens to thousands killed in many individual villages. BURR, QUANTIFYING GENOCIDE, at 31–40 (describing massacres in villages such as Ningele, Faus, Jebel Tullishi, Kuwe, Karakadi, Jebel Tabak, Nyima Hill, Kadugli, Ghulfan Range area, Lagori, Lagowa, Kamada, Ladi, Sadah, Tubira, Riwabba Jebel Heiban, Kuarten, Heiban, Otoro, Tira el Akhdar area, Kawalib, Dilling, Karkari al-Beira, Lake Abyad and Turoji area, Koya, Balol, Maryam, Shatt Tibeldi, Shatt Damam, Buram area, and many others).

58. BURR, QUANTIFYING GENOCIDE, at 28–29.

59. United States Committee for Refugees, *Press Releases: Sudan, Testimony of J. Millard Burr, Consultant, U.S. Committee for Refugees on the Crisis Against Humanity in Sudan* (May 27, 1999), http://www.reliefweb.int/rw/rwb.nsf/0/8190a73888f2c452c125677f005602fd?OpenDocument.

60. *See* S. Res. 94, 103rd Cong., 1st Sess., http://thomas.loc.gov/cgi-bin/query/z?c103:S.RES.94.IS.

61. *See* BURR, QUANTIFYING GENOCIDE, at 72.

62. *Id.* at 72, 75 (citing *By Practical Demonstration, Regime Admits the SPLA is Alive and Well, Sudan*, DEMOCRATIC-GAZETTE (UK), Jan. 1995, at 5).

63. *Id.* at 86. *See also* ICID Report at n.10 ("In March 1987, … murahilin and Arab townspeople killed 1,000 destitute Dinka displaced persons in the largely Arab town of al-Da'ien.") (citation omitted).

64. De Waal, *Tragedy in Darfur*, at 28.

65. *See* Human Rights Watch, *Famine in Sudan, 1998,* at http://www.hrw.org/reports/1999/sudan/SUDAWEB2.htm. *See also* Washington Office on Africa, *Sudan; Slavery, War and Peace in Sudan*, AFRICA NEWS, Nov. 29, 1999; Herve Creusvaux, Vincent Brown, Rosamund Lewis, Karine Coudert, & Sophie Baquet, *Research Letter: Famine in Southern Sudan*, 354 LANCET 832 (Sept. 4, 1999); Tony Freemantle, *The Hunger Weapon; Depriving Civilians of Food a Vicious Tool of Modern War*, HOUSTON CHRON., Aug. 29, 1999, at A1; *Sudan; Recurring Famine Blamed on Sudan's Devastating Conflict*, AFRICA NEWS, Apr. 9, 1999.

66. *See* ØYSTEIN H. ROLANDSEN, GUERILLA GOVERNMENT: POLITICAL CHANGES IN THE SOUTHERN SUDAN IN THE 1990S, at 128 (Uppsala, Norway: Nordiska Afrikainstitutet, 2005).

ern Sudan as a means of depriving the rebels of a base of support, and transferring wealth to ethnic Arab militias. They also served forcibly to recruit thousands of southern Sudanese children into ethnic Arab militias.[67]

Additionally, attacks by Arab militias claimed "at least two thousand members of the Masalit tribe."[68] In the 1990s, the Masalit complained that nomadic Arabs were driving them from their lands.[69] The government also targeted the Nuer people living in southern Sudan for eradication through machine-gunning, bombing, destruction of homes and villages, denial of food and medical care, and displacement into malarial marshes or forests.[70] UNICEF reported that one million Sudanese children died of malnutrition and polio in 1996–1997 alone.[71]

The U.S. Committee for Refugees estimated in 1998 that "600,000 additional people have perished in southern and central Sudan since 1993, raising the toll to an astounding 1.9 million deaths." The report condemned the Sudanese government's "effort to extirpate the Nuba tribes from the agriculturally valuable Nuba Mountain region."[72] As the Sudan Air Force bombed villages throughout southern Sudan and the Nuba Mountains hundreds of times, hundreds of victims perished, and tens of thousands of villagers fled.[73] The government transformed the Dinka tribe's homelands in southern Sudan from the country's most populous and verdant agricultural center into a "wasteland."[74]

In the mid-1990s, the Sudanese government bombed civilians from the air in violation of international humanitarian law[75] and tolerated the abduction and enslavement of ethnic and religious minorities, practices which the U.N. General Assembly in 1995 called upon the government to "cease immediately" as required by international law.[76] Hundreds of thousands of children of ethnic or religious minorities suffering abduction from their families by Sudanese armed forces for military training and religious indoctrination in secret camps.[77] Kidnapped children not sent to the camps were distributed as slaves to Arabs.[78] As the U.N. documented in 1999:

---

67. *See* Human Rights Watch, *Famine In Sudan, 1998,* http://www.hrw.org/reports/1999/sudan/index.htm/.

68. Nicholas D. Kristof, *Genocide in Slow Motion*, 53(2) N.Y. Rev. Books (2006); http://www.nybooks.com/articles/18674.

69. *Sudan: Umma Denies "Secret Deal" in Advance of NDA Meeting*, Africa News / U.N. IRIN, May 27, 1999.

70. See Figure 8 below.

71. *See* Richard Lobban, *A Concise Chronology of 1989–1999: Ten Years of the National Islamic Front,* 23 Arab Studies Q. 115, 128 (Spr. 2001).

72. U.S. Committee for Refugees, *Sudan, Testimony of J. Millard Burr. Accord* Scott Strauss, *Darfur and the Genocide Debate*, 84 Foreign Aff. 123, 125 (2005) (two million dead in conflict in southern Sudan since 1983).

73. *See* Burr, Genocide, at 14, 18.

74. U.S. Committee for Refugees, *Sudan, Testimony of J. Millard Burr.*

75. G.A. Res. 50/197, U.N. GAOR, 50th Sess., U.N. Doc. A/RES/50/107 (March 11, 1996).

76. *Id.* (citing to the International Covenants on Human Rights, the International Convention on the Elimination of All Forms of Racial Discrimination, the Convention on the Rights of the Child, the Slavery Convention, as amended, and the Supplementary Convention on the Abolition of Slavery, the Slave Trade and Institutions and Practices Similar to Slavery).

77. *See* Gáspár Biro, Situation of Human Rights in the Sudan, delivered to the U.N. Commission on Human Rights, U.N. Doc. No. E/CN.4/1994/48 (Feb. 1, 1994).

78. *See* Gáspár Biro, Report of the Special Rapporteur of the Commission on Human Rights on the Situation of Human Rights in the Sudan in Accordance with Commission Resolution 1995/77, delivered to the Commission on Human Rights, U.N. Doc. No. A/50/569 (Mar. 8, 1995). *See also* Washington Office on Africa, *Sudan; Slavery, War and Peace in Sudan*, Africa News, Nov. 29, 1999.

> Thousands, perhaps millions of southern children have been the main victims of the brutal war conducted against the civilian population by government and rebel troops alike. Children have died in droves of famine and many are still suffering from malnutrition. In Bahr-el-Ghazal an unknown number of children have been abducted during raids by Murahaleen militia.... In the Nuba Mountains, thousands of children are allegedly held in the so-called peace villages, where they are subjected to abuse.[79]

Sudan was one of only about five countries in the world to cause an outflow of at least 500,000 refugees in not only 1992–1997 but also 1997–2001.[80]

The U.S. State Department concluded in 1999 that Sudanese slavery had "a significant religious aspect since the victims are largely Christians and practitioners of traditional indigenous religions." It also stated in 2000 that slavery in Sudan had "a pronounced racial aspect, as the victims are exclusively black southerners and members of indigenous tribes of the Nuba mountains...." The "government condone[d] slavery, by allowing government troops from the North to buy, sell, and torture rebels. Estimates of those held in captivity range[d] from 14,000 to 100,000...."[81] In particular, 75,000 Dinka in Kordofan may have been enslaved. European NGOs such as Christian Solidarity International bought and freed 30,000 slaves.[82]

In 2000, the vice president of Sudan renewed the call for a holy war against the people of southern Sudan, and the government carried out this policy with extreme brutality. The air force bombed many civilian targets, creating a serious international human rights crisis.[83] The government bombed civilian areas 167 times in 2000, by one estimate. Various "human rights groups and non-governmental organizations (NGOs) working in Sudan argue that the government is destroying hospitals, schools, and feeding centers."[84] In the upper Nile region, "militias supported by military intelligence and aerial bombardment attacked with unremitting brutality. Scorched earth, massacre, pillage and rape were the norm...."[85] Armed by the government, the *murahileen* and PDF raided villages and stole children.[86] By 2001, the NGO Christian Aid reported that near "the oil fields of Sudan, civilians are being killed and raped, their villages burnt to the ground."[87] Other NGOs reported that as of 2002, more than two million people had needlessly starved to

---

79. U.N. Economic and Social Council, Commission on Human Rights, *Situation of Human Rights in Sudan*, Addendum, U.N. Doc. No. E/CN.4/1999/38/Add.1, ¶98 (May 17, 1999).

80. U.N. High Commissioner for Refugees, Statistical Yearbook 2001, maps 8–9, http://www.unhcr.org/static/statistical_yearbook/2001/maps08.pdf and http://www.unhcr.org/static/statistical_yearbook/2001/maps09.pdf.

81. USDOS, *Country Reports on Human Rights Practices—2000* (Feb. 23, 2001), http://www.state.gov/g/drl/rls/hrrpt/2000/af/822.htm.

82. *See* Richard Lobban, *Slavery in the Sudan Since 1989*, 23 Arab Studies Q. 31, 33–36 (Spr. 2001).

83. *See* Dagne, *Sudan*, at CRS-15.

84. *Id.*

85. Kristof, *Genocide in Slow Motion.*

86. John Harker, Dep't of Foreign Affairs and International Trade, Government of Canada, *Human Security in Sudan: Report of a Canadian Assessment Mission* 4–6 (2000), http://www.dfait-maeci.gc.ca/foreignp/3110186-e.pdf ("[T]he GOS provides arms, sometimes the groups of murahleen go off on their own. Tribal groups have been known to organize raids with 'representatives' from other Arab groups; returning with children, women and cattle taken in these raids, all of them have had a common celebration.").

87. Dagne, *Sudan*, at CRS-13 (citing Christian Aid. *The Scorched Earth: Oil and War in Sudan* (Mar. 2001), http://www.christian-aid.org.uk).

death, and another four million were homeless.[88] In 2002, the Congress and the president of the U.S. concluded that the actions of the Sudanese government in the south constituted genocide under the Genocide Convention.[89]

A common government program of massacres, deportation from areas capable of sustaining life, and cultural devastation led to the starvation of the Dinka and Nuba peoples:

> The government's counterinsurgency plan in Bahr El Ghazal, the central Nuba Mountains, and elsewhere is to attack civilians as a means to destroy the rebels social base, displacing, killing, or capturing civilians and stripping them of the meager assets that provide the means of survival in a harsh land. An important instrument of this policy are ethnic militias armed by the government.... [¶] The government forces abducted thousands of children and women, stole tens of thousands of cattle, burned many villages to the ground, and destroyed or pillaged food supplies....
>
> Systematic human rights abuses were the direct cause of the famine in Bahr El Ghazal. The famine agents are the government of Sudan, including the muraheleen or militia of the Baggara (Arab cattle nomads), and the rebel Sudan People's Liberation Army (SPLA).... The Bahr El Ghazal famine affected—and continues to assail—approximately one million people, a majority of them Dinka, the largest ethnic group in Sudan.[90]

Figure 8 sets forth a few of the testimonies made available by the victims of the southern Sudanese genocide over the past 10 years or so.

C. International Complicity in the Southern Sudanese Genocide

The Sudanese government's purpose in committing genocide against non-Arab groups, according to U.N. reports and victim groups, is not simply to destroy liberation movements, but to cordon off and exploit regions of the country containing significant oil deposits.[91] As the U.N. Commission on Human Rights stated, the "long-term efforts by the various Governments of Sudan to protect oil production have included a policy of forcible population displacement in order to clear oil producing areas and transportation routes of southern civilians."[92]

---

88. *Glimmer of Peace in Sudan*, Online NewsHour, PBS.org (Aug. 28, 2002), http://www.pbs.org/newshour/bb/africa/july-dec02/sudan_8-28.html.

89. *See* Sudan Peace Act, Pub. L. No. 107–245, § 2(10) (2002).

90. Human Rights Watch, *Famine in Sudan, 1998: The Human Rights Causes*, http://www.unhcr.org/home/RSDCOI/3ae6a8030.html.

91. *See* Presbyterian Church of Sudan v. Talisman Energy, Inc., 244 F. Supp. 2d 289, 300–303, 321–28 (S.D.N.Y., 2004) (recounting allegations of plaintiffs, which court assumed to be true). *See also* Second Amended Compl., ¶¶ 17–51, Presbyterian Church of Sudan v. Talisman Energy, Inc., No. 01 Civ. 9882 (AGS) (S.D.N.Y. complaint filed Aug. 15, 2003), http://www.bergermontague.com/pdfs/SecondAmendedClassActionComplaint.pdf; Human Rights Watch, *Sudan: Rebels, Religion and Oil* (Nov. 25, 2003), http://hrw.org/english/docs/2003/11/25/sudan12988.htm.

92. Second Amended Compl., ¶ 58(a), Presbyterian Church of Sudan v. Talisman Energy, Inc., No. 01 Civ. 9882 (AGS) (S.D.N.Y. complaint filed Aug. 15, 2003), http://www.bergermontague.com/pdfs/SecondAmendedClassActionComplaint.pdf.

Figure 8 Testimonies of the Victims of Genocide in Southern Sudan, 1999–2008

Victim	Date of Report	Testimony
Southern Sudanese woman from Nyongrial, in Unity State/Upper Nile region of Sudan	1999	In August and September, the GOS forces and Arab militia attacked [us]. People have been displaced from Biu, Kong, Nymrial, Pankwil, Deng Akol. The GOS used Antonovs, helicopter gunships and machine guns in the attack. They killed many people, raped women and looted our [mud huts]. We think the forces took many of our children because they disappeared and we never found their bodies. Churches were burnt in Gumriak and Nyongrial. The GOS attacked our villages because of the oil. No one is returning to those villages because the offensive is [ongoing]....
Southern Sudanese woman from Pariang, Sudanese government-controlled territory	1999	About 200 people came to Biem from Pariang. I came from Pariang.... The [government of Sudan or] GOS forces mistreated us. We were not given any services, we had to find our own food and make our own living. When the women would go to gather wood and cut grass to build shelters, the Arab militia followed us to take what we had and rape us. I tried to escape with three others from the town. The GOS shot at us. The others were killed. I was hit in the leg but managed to escape.
Southern Sudanese person from Unity State/Upper Nile region of Sudan	1999	We are going to lose our lives for oil. We know the Arabs will kill us, we are waiting for our deaths because the Arabs are chasing us, burning our villages, bombing us and killing us. Aren't we included in the human rights of the world?
Southern Sudanese person from Unity State/Upper Nile region	1999	Most of our population has died. We are blaming the world for co-operating with the Arabs to clear us from our land and take our oil. War is affecting us—because of bombs and bullets we are dying. We have been suffering since 1983 when the first shot was fired. Whenever we flee to forest, disease follows us—we have no medicine, no trained personnel, no schools for our children. The WFP is trying their best to help people but it is not enough because so many people are displaced. By the time your report is out we will be dead. The GOS will kill us because you visited us.
Southern Sudanese woman from Unity State/Upper Nile region	1999	[Our children] have been bombed and have run to the forest and we don't know where they are.... We have no food—we are eating grass and leaves—it is very hard because there is nowhere to cook it, this is all they are eating in the bush. We have to run to the forest where there are mosquitoes and people are dying because of the cold.

Figure 8 Testimonies of the Victims of Genocide in Southern Sudan, 1999–2008, *continued*

Victim	Date of Report	Testimony
Southern Sudanese woman from Unity State/Upper Nile region	1999	We are staying in a war-affected area—we have run away from bombing of our villages and our burnt our [mud huts], our people are scattered.... Since we ran away and have been displaced, we lost our cows, our tukuls have been burnt, our children have been lost, our men have been killed and there have been no births.... Since our [huts] have been burnt, our elders have died because there is no shelter, no blankets and no mosquito nets.
Southern Sudanese man from Unity State	1999	We are looking for our children. You see a few children here but most are in the forest, many have died. If they want oil they can take it peacefully. Their guns are killing us. I suggest you can stop the war. We need to stop the Arabs using their high tech weapons. We can't stop them with regular guns. Most of our people are hiding in the swamp. They have malaria and every night there is a high rate of death.
Southern Sudanese woman from Unity State	1999	The GOS and Matiep's forces looted the village and raided the livestock. They took all of our personal belongings. If any soldiers found villagers they were killed. There was no forgiveness. The Head Chief of the area and the Commissioner were killed. [Their] forces took women and girls. We don't know how many. Some they killed and some they kept.... Most of our husbands are dead.
Southern Sudanese person from Unity State	1999	The last killing was in September. 100–200 soldiers attacked and whomever they found they killed. There are not many people here. The village was burned and the church was burned in 1998.

Source: John Harker, Department of Foreign Affairs and International Trade, Government of Canada, *Human Security in Sudan: The Report of a Canadian Assessment Mission Prepared for the Minister of Foreign Affairs* (Jan. 2000), http://dsp-psd.pwgsc.gc.ca/Collection/E2-198-2000E.pdf

Figure 8 Testimonies of the Victims of Genocide in Southern Sudan, 1999–2008, *continued*

Chief Gatluak Chiek Jang, from Unity State in southern Sudan	2006	"Chief Jang is a chief of the Leek tribe. Chief Jang was displaced from Chotjara in Block 5A in July 1999, by bombers, gunships, and Government ground troops. Chief Jang went to Mankien in Block 4, but was displaced [again] .... In October 2001, he was displaced from Chotjara for a third time by bombers, gunships and Government ground troops. Chief Jang returned to Chotjara yet again, and was displaced when Chotjara was attacked in December 2002 by bombers, gunships, tanks and ... ground forces." "Chief Jang saw churches that 'had been burned by Government of Sudan forces" in villages in both Block 4 and Block 5A.'"
Chief Thomas Malual Kap, from Unity State in southern Sudan	2006	"Chief Thomas Malual Kap ... is a member of the Nuer tribe. He was displaced from Koch, located in [an oil concession in south Sudan called] Block 5A, repeatedly from 1998 to 2003. Chief Kap was first displaced from Koch in 1998, by a Government attack involving gunships, tanks and ground troops.... Chief Kap was displaced from Bieh by a Government attack during a food distribution by the World Food Program."
Chief Peter Ring Patai, from Unity State in s. Sudan	2006	"Chief Patai is the Paramount Chief of the Nuer tribe. Chief Patai ...was displaced from Nimne in Block 5A in February 2002, by an attack by bombers and gunships."
Chief Tunguar Kueigwong Rat, from Unity State in southern Sudan	2006	"Chief Tunguar Kueigwong Rat ... is the Paramount Chief of the Leek Nuer. Chief Rat was displaced from Nhialdiu in Block 5A in 2002 FN56 by an attack by Government soldiers on foot, horseback and in vehicles, including tanks, with support from bombers and gunships."
Rev. Matthew Mathian Deang, from Unity State in southern Sudan	2006	"Reverend Matthew Mathiang Deang ... was in Koch, a village several miles from Bieh, on the day of the attack. He described seeing airplanes and smoke rising from Bieh.... [He] is a member of the Southern Sudan Parliament, ... [who] was displaced by a raid on Gany, which is located in Block 5A, in September 1999 ... [when] a militia group attacked...."
Stephen Kuina, a Nuer from southern Sudan	2006	"Stephen Kuina ... is a nurse from the Nuer tribe, ... [who] was displaced from Pibor in Block 4 in 1995 by the Government and Murahaleen. Kuina moved to Mankien, ... where he was again displaced in October 1998 by fighting that included bombardment by Antonov bombers. Kuina attempted to stay in Ruathnyibol in Block 4 and built a shelter there, but was displaced by ground troops.... Upon leaving Ruathnyibol, Kuina took up residence in a displaced person's camp in Maper, ... [where] there were shortages of food and medicine.... Kuina attempted to ... build[] shelters for himself and his family ... in Block 4, but was displaced each time."
Rev. James Koung Ninrew, from Unity State in southern Sudan	2006	"Reverend Ninrew testified that he witnessed an attack that occurred in Bieh where 'people were receiving foods and helicopter gunships came and attacked people; people were killed.'" "Reverend Ninrew saw five damaged churches. Only one church showed damage from an air attack, that church, which is located in Leer in Block 5A, was 'destroyed by bombs.'"

Figure 8 Testimonies of the Victims of Genocide in Southern Sudan, 1999–2008, *continued*

Moris Bol Majok, a Dinka from southern Sudan	2006	"Moris Bol Majok is a member of the Dinka tribe.... In 2000, Sudanese Government-supported militias began attacks that drove [him] away from [his village]. [He was] subjected to attacks by Sudanese Antonovs and gunships that killed nine people.... In July 2002 ... [he] was captured and severely tortured by Sudanese security troops, causing paralysis in his hands and legs."
Puok Bol Mut, from Kordofan State in southern Sudan	2006	"Mut is a member of the Parliament of Southern Sudan. Mut was displaced from a series of villages in Block 4 between 1998 and 2002 by the "Government" and allied militias. Three of the attacks that displaced Mut, attacks on Nooriak in 1998 and 1999 and Lara in 2002, included bombers and gunships. Mut was shot in the right shoulder by a gunship during an attack at Lara in 2002."
Nyot Tot Rieth, from Unity State in southern Sudan	2006	"Nyot Tot Rieth [stated that she] lost her husband ... Joseph Thiet Makuac [who] was killed in the attack on Bieh in Block 5A and she is bringing a claim on his behalf."
Yien Nyinar Riek, from southern Sudan	2006	"Riek's people were displaced from [several villages] in 1999 after a combined air and ground attack by Sudanese forces. [After fleeing,] they suffering continued bombing by Antonovs and helicopter gunships until the end of 1999. In 2001, Government militias and soldiers attacked [other villages], burning houses and displacing [him] and his family.... [His] brother and two nephews were killed by aerial bombardment during 2000."

Source: Second Amended Complaint and Summary Judgment Ruling, *Talisman Energy v. Presb. Church of Sudan*, 453 F. Supp. 2d 633 (S.D.N.Y. 2006)

Valentino Achak Deng, a "Lost Boy" from southern Sudan	2007	"I remember leaving behind people who were weak, who could not help themselves, who were hungry, who were thirsty. They needed I remember leaving behind my people who were weak. I know what happened to them is that they died eventually.... "Some of the atrocities that I saw committed against my people were committed by the Janjaweed. The Janjaweed were known as the murahileen in southern Sudan. My village ... is one of the areas that was destroyed by the Janjaweed, the murahileen...."
Emmanuel Jal, a "Lost Boy" from southern Sudan	2008	"I saw my village in South Sudan burned to ashes, and all that we had owned we lost. I lost my mother, which cut my deeply.... When I was in a refugee camp in Ethiopia, ... hundreds starved, because we did not know how to cook. What sticks in my mind to this day is the sight of children burying the dead. Many children went crazy."
Alweel Kol, a woman from southern Sudan	2008	"I lost my parents in 1985, on the day when people came to our village and burned it. My father and uncle died that day, and I lost my mother." "One evening, armed men came to our village to catch certain people.... They took me and my two brothers ... to a faraway place with tents and houses made out of hay.... They made us herd sheep and small cows...."

Sources: Out of Exile: Narratives from the Abducted and Displaced People of Sudan (Craig Walzer ed., San Francisco: McSweeney's Books, 2008); Speech by Valentino Achak Deng at Google headquarters in 2007, http://www.youtube.com/watch?v=2V7MeewG_MU

By 1980, the U.S.-based oil company Chevron had discovered oil in Sudan.[93] Chevron planned to finance a refinery in the Upper Nile region and an oil pipeline to the Red Sea.[94] Other Western oil companies worked to develop oil projects in southern Sudan.[95] In 1984, the Chevron Oil Company of the Sudan suspended its plans to export oil from the country, due to southern Sudanese rebel attacks on its installations,[96] including an incident in which rebels seized a Chevron facility and killed three workers.[97] In 1990, Chevron sold its oil exploration rights to Arakis Energy Corporation, a Canadian company.[98] Arakis completed the oil wells that Chevron had begun to drill, and planned to complete Chevron's pipeline.[99]

In 1998, Talisman Energy, a transnational oil company traded on U.S. stock exchanges and headquartered in Canada, acquired the assets and liabilities of Arakis, including its Sudan exploration rights, for $220 million.[100] During that same year, the Sudanese government incited nomadic Arabs of Darfur and South Kordofan to attack Dinka-populated areas "to quash SPLA support in the ... region and 'secure the oil fields around Bentiu, the capital of Unity State.'"[101] As one expert described this campaign, the army achieved the "clearance of the oilfield zones" of Southern Sudan by mobilizing militias and inflicting "deliberate starvation" on civilians.[102]

In 1999, the SPLA targeted the Talisman Energy oil facilities as a source of foreign exchange for the government and allied militias to purchase weapons, and the Canadian government announced a fact-finding mission to investigate claims that Talisman's operations could be aggravating the civil war and causing human rights violations.[103] The mission discovered that there was a continuing "major displacement of civilian populations related to oil extraction," and that bomber aircraft and helicopter gunships that attacked southern Sudanese villages took off from an airstrip within the Talisman Energy oil concession.[104] In 2000, however, Canada and the U.S. refused to impose sanctions on Talisman Energy, with Canada preferring a policy of "dialogue." The U.S. imposed sanctions on the Greater Nile Petroleum Operating Co. of Sudan (GNPC), but not on its "international corporate owners," i.e., "China National Petroleum Corp. (CNPC) (40% equity interest); Petronas Carigali Overseas Shd. Bhd. of Malaysia (30%); and State Petroleum

93. *See Sudan Pushing Cotton Exports*, N.Y. Times, July 12, 1980, at 23. At that time, Sudan *imported* about $360 million in oil per year. *See id.*

94. *See Oil Project Loan to Sudan*, N.Y. Times, Aug. 20, 1981, at D10; Reuters, *Socal to Speed Up Sudan Production*, N.Y. Times, Sept. 15, 1982, at D4. Chevron reportedly spent $600 million to discover 200 million barrels of oil in Sudan, and planned to spend over $1 billion more on the pipeline. *See Socal-Sudan Deal*, N.Y. Times, Jan. 11, 1983, at D5.

95. *See* Alan Cowell, *Regional Dispute Divides the Sudan; Nimeiry Move to Subdivide the South Stirs Opposition and Fear of New Civil Strife*, N.Y. Times, Feb. 22, 1982, at A7.

96. *See State of Emergency Is Declared in Sudan*, N.Y. Times, Apr 30, 1984, at A3.

97. *See* UPI, *Sudanese Rebels Seize Chevron Oil Installation*, N.Y. Times, Feb 3, 1984, at A5.

98. *See* Dagne, *Sudan*, at CRS-10.

99. *See Sudan, in* U.S. Geological Survey, Mineral Industry Yearbook 1995, at 5, http://minerals.usgs.gov/minerals/pubs/country/1995/9248095.pdf.

100. *See* Presbyterian Church of Sudan v. Talisman Energy, Inc., 244 F. Supp. 2d 289, 299–300 (S.D.N.Y., 2004) (recounting allegations of plaintiffs, which court assumed to be true). *See also* Arakis Energy, *Talisman Agrees to Acquire Arakis* (Aug. 17, 1998), http://www.prnewswire.co.uk/cgi/news/release?id=58078.

101. Burr, Quantifying Genocide, at 83.

102. De Waal, *Tragedy in Darfur*.

103. *See* Phillip M. Mobbs, *The Mineral Industry of Sudan—1999*, http://minerals.usgs.gov/minerals/pubs/country/1999/su99.pdf.

104. *See* Second Amended Compl., Talisman Energy, at ¶ 58(b).

Corp., which was a subsidiary of Talisman Energy Inc. of Canada (25%)."[105] In March 2003, Talisman Energy sold its stake in the GNPC for $720 million to an Indian company, more than tripling its investment.[106] China succeeded where Chevron and Talisman struggled, for example by dispatching "security personnel to protect their managers and workers."[107]

Oil exports have also provided the Sudanese regime with the funding to import technologies designed to end human life on a mass scale.[108] Sudan's military and paramilitary forces utilize these technologies, ranging from military aircraft to helicopter gunships to automatic weapons, to carry out genocide against non-Arab populations. Sudan's oil exports began in 1999 and eventually earned it billions of dollars.[109] Sudan promptly doubled its military budget with the proceeds.[110] A southern Sudanese bishop described oil as a "curse" that was financing government acquisitions of assault rifles, military vehicles, and other sophisticated weapons.[111]

D. The Hope for Southern Sudanese Self-Determination

By early 2003, the Sudanese government had agreed to a peace deal with the southern Sudanese rebels.[112] The deal conceded that the southern Sudanese had a right of self-determination, and that the relationship between religion and the state had to change.[113] It

---

105. *See* Phillip M. Mobbs, *The Mineral Industry of Sudan—2000*, http://minerals.usgs.gov/minerals/pubs/country/2000/sumyb00.pdf.

106. *See* USDOS, 2003 Sudan Peace Act Report, http://www.state.gov/p/af/rls/rpt/2003/19790.htm; *Diplomatic Arm-twisting Clears Sudan Oil Deal*, The Times of India, Mar. 13, 2003, http://64.233.167.104/search?q=cache:xgC9R032-3YJ:timesofindia.indiatimes.com/articleshow/40190193.cms; Embassy of the Republic of the Sudan to India, *Canadian Firm Hopes to Sell 25% Stake in Sudan Oil Project by Month End* (2003), http://64.233.167.104/search?q=cache:EqgOarGzzR4J:www.embassysudanindia.org/news/11marongc.html.

107. Henry Lee & Dan A. Shalmon, *Searching for Oil: China's Initiatives in the Middle East*, 49 Environment 8 (2007).

108. *See* Harper, *Human Security in Sudan*; Christian Aid, *The Scorched Earth: Oil and War in Sudan* (Mar. 2001), http://sudanreport.unep.ch/sudan_website/doccatcher/data/documents/The%20scorched%20earth.pdf; Small Arms *Survey, Arms, Oil, and Darfur* (July 7, 2007), http://64.233.169.104/search?q=cache:zcVjwucTnd8J:www.smallarmssurvey.org/files/portal/spotlight/sudan/Sudan_pdf/SIB%25207%2520Arms.pdf.

109. *See* Dagne, *Sudan*, at CRS-10; USDOS, 2004 Sudan Peace Act Report (Oil Sector) ("Human Rights Watch reported in late 2003 that Sudan spent more than 60% of its 2001 oil revenues ($580.2 million) to buy weapons"); Jeffrey Gettleman, *War in Sudan? Not Where the Oil Wealth Flows*, N.Y. Times, Oct. 24, 2006, at A1 (Sudan's crude oil production of 512,000 barrels per day earned the regime billions of dollars).

110. *See* Dagne, *Sudan*, at CRS-6, CRS-10 ("[With] the new oil revenue..., the government of Sudan has been acquiring new weapons, especially helicopter gunships and fighter planes, from Russia and other countries. Critics maintain that the government of Sudan is using these newly acquired weapons to terrorize civilian populations, especially in the oil fields.").

111. *Sudan's Troubles*, Online NewsHour, PBS.org (July 25, 2001), http://www.pbs.org/newshour/bb/africa/july-dec01/sudan_7-25.html.

112. *See* Government of the Republic of Sudan and the Sudan People's Liberation Movement/Army, Landmark Sudanese Peace Agreement: Sudan Government Concludes with the SPLM/A "Machakos Protocol" and Issues a Joint Communiqué, ReliefWeb (July 20, 2002), http://www.reliefweb.int/rw/RWB.NSF/db900SID/MHII-6227SC?OpenDocument.

113. *Id.*

was claimed as a victory by U.S. officials, and was widely viewed as an outcome of U.S. pressure.[114] In 2005, the Comprehensive Peace Agreement (CPA) between the government of Sudan and the SPLA was signed. Under the CPA, South Sudan may gain its independence as early as 2011. In the three years after December 2005, nearly 300,000 southern Sudanese returned to their country from Kenya and other countries neighboring Sudan.[115]

As the CPA came into force, the remnants and aftereffects of genocide surfaced in southern Sudan's vital statistics. Life expectancy in the south was only 42 years, compared to over 56 for Sudan as a whole. About 75% of southern Sudanese were illiterate and lacked clean (or improved) water sources, compared to fewer than 40% nationwide.[116] Southern Sudan suffered from one of the highest rates of maternal mortality in the world as of mid-2009.[117] With poor roads and other infrastructure, southern Sudanese villages suffer from "catastrophically high infant mortality rates." The destruction of hospitals and feeding centers by the government means that children under the age of five "frequently die from common yet treatable diseases such as malaria, diarrhea and pneumonia...."[118]

---

114. *See, e.g.*, Jendayi E. Frazer, Assistant Secretary of State for African Affairs, *Consolidating Peace in Sudan* (June 5, 2006), http://sudan.usembassy.gov/consolidating_peace_in_sudan.html ("President Bush has made the push for peace throughout Sudan a centerpiece of his Africa agenda.... U.S. government commitment and leadership helped to resolve the North-South element of the Sudan conflict...."); Michael E. Ranneberger, Principal Deputy Assistant Secretary of State for African Affairs, *Sudan: Prospects for Peace* (Dec. 9, 2004), http://www.state.gov/p/af/rls/rm/39751.htm ("With our strong support, in large measure due to the leadership of former Special Envoy Danforth and our current Senior Representative Charles Snyder, enormous progress has been made toward a north-south accord. He laid the basis for progress through his efforts to broker a ceasefire.... The six protocols signed by the Government of Sudan and the Sudan People's Liberation Movement, taken together, constitute resolution of all the major substantive issues. The Machakos Protocol addresses the issue of religion and the state, and the right of the south to a referendum on secession."); *Sudan Leaders Try to Carve Deal*, BBC NEWS.COM, Dec. 6, 2003, http://news.bbc.co.uk/2/hi/africa/3296305.stm (describing "U.S. pressure").

115. *See* Kazuhiko Shimizu, *UNHCR Resumes Refugee Returns from Kenya to South Sudan* (Dec. 12, 2008), http://www.unhcr.org/cgi-bin/texis/vtx/newsitem?id=4942790e4.

116. *Compare* CARE, *South Sudan: Country Snapshot* (Nov. 2006), http://www.care.no/?module=files;action=file.getfile;id=2403, *with* UNDP, *Human Development Report 2005*, at 221.

117. *See* Sima Samar, Report of the Special Rapporteur on the Situation of Human Rights in the Sudan, A/HRC/11/14, ¶ 75 (June 4, 2009), http://www.un.org/apps/news/story.asp?NewsID=31031.

118. International Rescue Committee, *Saving Children's Lives*, REUTERS ALERTNET, Nov. 1, 2008, http://www.alertnet.org/thenews/fromthefield/4/122553031163.htm.

Chapter XV

Sudan Liberation: Genocide and Response in Darfur and Eastern Chad

> My village in Darfur was beautiful. It was close to mountains, valleys, and a river. There were lemon trees, guavas, and mangos. We planted okra and sugar cane. There were ... horses, camels, [and] cows.... It was a beautiful place to live.
>
> —Ahmed Ishag Yacoub, a man from Darfur[1]

Like the genocide in southern Sudan, genocide in Darfur has its foundation in a struggle between ethnic groups for land and oil deposits, and a counterinsurgency strategy of eliminating the rebellious ethnic groups by targeting their populations and villages. International apathy prevails, in part, because the allies and trading partners of the dictator Omar Hassan al-Bashir share an economic incentive to permit the clearing of oil concessions, and to profit from energy and arms deals with the government. Military and intelligence cooperation between Sudan and key permanent members of the Security Council compound the problem, and reinforce the apathetic stance of the international community. An increasingly global trade in technologies designed to end life on a mass scale also facilitates genocide in Sudan.

International actors such as the U.N. Security Council, the ICC, and other global bodies have failed to recognize and condemn genocide in Darfur and eastern Chad in a timely fashion. Although economic and geopolitical concerns lay behind the repeated refusals to mount an effective prevention and punishment of Sudan's genocidal acts, the language of international law has been used to minimize and explain away the crimes. The reasoning advanced to date rests on unjustifiable assumptions, reflected in the report of the International Commission of Inquiry on Darfur submitted to U.N. Secretary-General in early 2005, that genocide only occurs when a group is totally annihilated, or when genocide lacks any military purpose or utility. Using the definition of genocide employed by Lemkin, the Genocide Convention, and the Yugoslav and Rwanda tribunals, this chapter argues that genocide occurred in Sudan when substantial portions of identifiable groups were killed and wounded as a result of large-scale atrocities and repeated destructive and discriminatory acts.

---

1. *Quoted in* Out of Exile: Narratives from the Abducted and Displaced People of Sudan 230–31 (Craig Walzer ed., San Francisco: McSweeney's Books, 2008).

A. Genocide in Darfur and Eastern Chad

1. Phase 1: Genocide in Darfur, April 2003–July 2004

Darfur suffered throughout the 1980s and 1990s as an impoverished and insecure region of Sudan. Ten years of rule by President al-Bashir's National Islamic Front resulted in burned African villages, famine, poisoned wells, widespread torture particularly in Darfur's Shalla prison, and the imposition of the death penalty for non-Muslim worship or religious speech.[2] Like Saddam Hussein in Iraq, President al-Bashir established a Revolutionary Command Council to persecute the political opposition and confiscate its foreign currency and property holdings.[3]

Around the time of the peace deal between Sudan and the SPLA, the Sudan Liberation Army (SLA) emerged, which was modeled on the SPLA, and likewise emphasized indigenous peoples' right of self-determination within Sudan.[4] The SLA began to strike government targets, sacking an air base in April 2003.[5] SPLA leader John Garang offered "moral support" to the SLA, and was named as a possible mediator in the conflict after the CPA was reached.[6]

President al-Bashir's government retaliated by organizing local militias composed of nomadic Arab tribes into a counterinsurgency army, part of the Popular Defence Forces (PDF).[7] The racist agenda of these counterinsurgency forces soon became clear, as victims reported that their attackers repeatedly declared an intention to "exterminate" the "blacks," who were labeled "slaves."[8] The pro-government tribal militias travel on horseback; their

2. *See* Gerard Prunier, Darfur: A 21st Century Genocide vii, 69–95 (Ithaca, NY: Cornell UP, 2008); Mahgoub El-Tigani, *Solving the Crisis of Sudan: The Right of Self-determination Versus State Torture*, 23 Arab Studies Q. 41, 43–44 (Spr. 2001); Carolyn Fluehr-Lobban & Richard Lobban, *The Sudan Since 1989: National Islamic Front Rule*, 23 Arab Studies Q. 1, 1–4; Abdullahi A Gallab, *The Insecure Rendezvous Between Islam and Totalitarianism: The Failure of the Islamist State in the Sudan*, 23 Arab Studies Q. 87, 102–5; Rogaia Mustafa Abusharaf, *Migration with a Feminine Face: Breaking the Cultural Mold*, 23 Arab Studies Q. 61, 65; USDOS, *Sudan Human Rights Practices, 1995 —Sudan* ("A myriad of official and secret government security forces routinely harassed, detained, and tortured opponents or suspected opponents of the Government with impunity. Prison conditions are harsh, and the judiciary is largely subservient to the Government.").

3. *See* Lobban, *A Concise Chronology of 1989–1999*, at 115–19, 122.

4. *See* Daly, Darfur's Sorrow, at 280.

5. *See* Strauss, *Darfur and the Genocide Debate*, at 124.

6. Edmund Sanders, *Rebel Leader Turns from War to Government*, L.A. Times, July 9, 2005, http://articles.latimes.com/2005/jul/09/world/fg-garang. *See* Simon Tisdall, *Garang's Death Bodes Ill for Peace in Sudan*, The Guardian (U.K.), Aug. 2, 2005, www.guardian.co.uk/world/2005/aug/02/sudan.tisdallbriefing.

7. *See* Rubin, *If Not Peace, Then Justice?*, at 6–42. *See also* International Crisis Group, *Darfur Rising: Sudan's New Crisis*, Africa Report No. 76, at 16 (Mar. 25, 2004), http://www.crisisgroup.org/home/index.cfm?l=1&id=2550; Dianne E. Rennack, *Sudan: Economic Sanctions*, Cong. Research Serv. Rep. No. 55628, at CRS–2 (Oct. 11, 2005), http://fpc.state.gov/documents/organization/55628.pdf.

8. Eric Reeves, *Unnoticed Genocide*, Wash. Post, Feb. 25, 2004, at A25. *See also* Daly, Darfur's Sorrow, at 3–4, 246–47, 283–85, 296–305; J. Millard Burr & Robert O. Collins, Darfur: The Long Road to Disaster 286–87, 292–3 (Princeton, NJ: Markus Weiner Publishers, 2006); Alex De Waal, *Who Are the Darfurians? Arab and African Identities, Violence and External Engagement*, 104 African Aff. 181, 199 (2006); Edmund Sanders, *Battle For Darfur; Sudan War Spills Into Chad*, L.A. Times, June 6, 2006, http://articles.latimes.com/2006/jun/19/world/fg-sla19; International Commission of Inquiry on Darfur (ICID), Report to the United Nations Secretary-General Pursuant to Security Council Resolution 1564 of 18 September 2004, ¶¶ 254, 511 (Jan. 25, 2005), http://www.un.org/News/

civilian victims therefore call them "*Janjaweed*" or devils (*jinn*) on horses (*jawad*).[9] The *Janjaweed* first emerged in the late 1980s in connection with an "Arab Alliance (or Gathering)," which made a "racist" appeal for an Arab tribal "belt" across Darfur and mounted a "race war" against the Fur.[10] Its campaign of massacres against the Fur and Masalit began in the 1990s and early 2000s, with twenty-three people killed on a single day and 125 on another.[11]

Representatives of the Fur people told Amnesty International in January 2003 that "the government was not bringing the perpetrators of killings to justice and, by not doing so, was complicit in what they called 'ethnic cleansing' or even 'genocide' against their people."[12] In April 2003, the U.N. Commission on Human Rights' Sudan expert reported "sources" describing

> attacks against civilians and targeting of local tribes, to the point that some accused the Government of implementing a clear policy of ethnic cleansing aimed at eliminating African tribes from Darfur. According to information received mass executions by armed forces and aerial bombardment in areas that are densely populated have continued to take place for the past few years.[13]

By July 2003, Amnesty described a looming "humanitarian crisis" due to the killing and wounding of hundreds of people in the Darfur region of Sudan by government forces, nomads, and bandits.[14] Raids on Fur, Masalit and Zaghawa communities had claimed hundreds of lives, many grain stores, cattle and other livestock, and burned houses. Amnesty added: "Many of the Fur and other sedentary people of Darfur have said that these attacks have the intention to drive them and other sedentary peoples out of the fertile area of the Jebel Marra Mountains."[15]

Reports from an investigative team sent to Darfur in early 2004 by Physicians for Human Rights, and led by a scholar from the Harvard School of Public Health, described a repeat of the government's counterinsurgency strategy in southern and central Sudan. Specifically, the Sudanese government would bomb or "buzz" a village at about dawn,

---

dh/sudan/com_inq_darfur.pdf; Human Rights Watch, *Darfur Destroyed: Ethnic Cleansing by Government and Militia Forces in Western Sudan* (May 2004), http://hrw.org/reports/2004/sudan0504/5.htm#_Toc71531690; Human Rights Watch, *Darfur in Flames: Atrocities in Western Sudan* (Apr. 2004), http://www.hrw.org/reports/2004/sudan0404/3.htm.

9. Rubin, *If Not Peace, Then Justice?*, at 6–42. *See also* Burr & Collins, Darfur, at 286–87, 292–3. An alternative etymology would derive the term "*Janjaweed*" from the words for outlaws or guns (*Jan*) on horses, rather than for the words for a devil or evil spirit (*Jinn*) on horseback. *See* Human Rights Watch, *Darfur in Flames: Atrocities in Western Sudan 90* (Apr. 2004), http://www.hrw.org/reports/2004/ sudan0404/3.htm.

10. *See* Daly, Darfur's Sorrow, at 243–47, 262–67.

11. *See id.* at 263, 269; Amnesty International, *Sudan, Darfur: "Too Many People Killed for No Reason,"* AI Index: AFR 54/008/2004 (Feb. 3, 2004), http://web.amnesty.org/ library/index/ENGAFR540082004.

12. Amnesty International, *Sudan: Darfur: "Too Many People Killed for No Reason"*, AI Index: AFR 54/008/2004 (Feb. 3, 2004), http://web.amnesty.org/library/Index/ENGAFR540082004?open&of=ENG-2AF.

13. Mr. Gerhart Baum, Special Rapporteur of the Commission on Human Rights, Statement to United Nations Commission on Human Rights on the situation of human rights in the Sudan, (Apr. 25, 2003), http://www.ecosonline.org/back/pdf_reports/2003/speechBaum.doc.

14. Amnesty International, *Sudan: Looming Crisis in Darfur*, AI Index: AFR 54/041/2003 (July 1, 2003), http://web.amnesty.org/library/Index/ENGAFR540412003?open&of=ENG-2AF.

15. Amnesty International, *Sudan: Empty Promises? Human Rights Violations in Government-Controlled Areas*, AI Index: AFR 54/036/2003 (July 16, 2003), http://web.amnesty.org/library/Index/ENGAFR 540362003?open&of=ENG-2AF.

after which the army and *Janjaweed* militia would enter the village on vehicles or horseback, massacre the men defending the village, rape the women, steal the cattle, burn the homes, spoil the wells and irrigation works, and block humanitarian aid, making the entire area uninhabitable.[16] The report concluded:

> [T]he Sudanese government has used militia forces called Janjaweed in a sweeping campaign of attack against the non-Arab civilian population of Darfur....
>
> These features—systematic targeted assaults, massive disruption of livelihood, intensive hot pursuit, organized disruption of aid, and deliberate consignment to conditions conducive to death from exposure and disease—have prompted observers and organizations that focus on human rights to raise the issue of genocide. The people being attacked are members of identifiable ethnic and linguistic groups, targeted by an organized state authority representing other ethnic and linguistic groups.[17]

Between 2003 and early 2005, numerous admissions emerged in which Sudanese officials stated that they were attacking minority communities in Darfur on a systematic basis. These admissions are summarized in Figure 9.

By July 2004, the systematic raids had driven more than 1.3 million residents of Darfur away from their homes, and killed about 50,000 people.[18] The *Janjaweed* took inspiration from *al Qaeda* in Mesopotamia in vowing to resist any U.N. intervention to protect the Darfurians: "They say that they will fight the infidels just as the mujahideen in Iraq are doing. Iraq is their inspiration," said one Sudanese interviewed by a British newspaper.[19] The Sudanese foreign minister Mustafa Osman Ismail blamed Israel for fomenting a rebellion in the Darfur region.[20] Subsequently, a memorandum from a government office in North Darfur surfaced in which the Sudanese government ordered local "security units" to "allow the activities of the mujahedeen and the volunteers under the command of Sheikh Musa Hilal to proceed in the area[]." The commander, Musa Hilal, admitted that "all of the people in the field [in Darfur] are led by top army commanders" and "get their orders from the Western command center, and from Khartoum."[21] Hilal was promoted to an advisor to a senior government official in 2008, and was quoted in March 2009 as claiming to command 30,000 troops.[22]

---

16. Jennifer Leaning, *Diagnosing Genocide—The Case of Darfur*, 351:8 New England J. Med. 735, 735–36 (Aug. 19, 2004).

17. *Id.*

18. *See* Leaning, *Diagnosing Genocide*, at 735; Emily Wax, *Frist Calls Darfur Killing 'Genocide' Senate Leader Tours a Camp in Chad, Cites Sudan's Deadline to Stop Militia*, Wash. Post Foreign Service, Aug. 7, 2004, at A14 ("The militia, known as the *Janjaweed*, has committed atrocities across Darfur that have displaced close to 1.5 million darker-skinned African villagers and left as many as 50,000 dead, according to human rights groups and aid workers.").

19. Philip Sherwell, Janjaweed *Vow to Fight Any Intervention by 'Infidels'*, The Telegraph (U.K.), Aug. 15, 2004, http://www.telegraph.co.uk.

20. *Sudan and Arab Paranoia*, Wall St. J., Aug. 16, 2004, http://www.wsj.com.

21. *Quoted in* Human Rights Watch, *Darfur: Militia Leader Implicates Khartoum* (Mar. 2, 2005), http://www.hrw.org/fr/news/2005/03/02/darfur-militia-leader-implicates-khartoum.

22. *See* Janjaweed *Leader Is Sudan Aide*, BBC News, Jan. 20, 2008, http://news.bbc.co.uk/1/hi/world/africa/7199447.stm; Agence France-Presse, *Darfur Rebel Chief Warns Sudan Not to Harm Civilians*, ReliefWeb, Mar. 2, 2009, http://www.reliefweb.int/rw/rwb.nsf/db900sid/ASAZ-7PRHQ6?OpenDocument.

Figure 9 Evidence of Genocidal Acts and Intent in Darfur

Date	Source	Statement
2003	State Minister of the Interior Ahmed Haroun	"Haroun ... exhorted the Janjaweed and army in a speech to 'kill the Fur'...."
2003	Provincial commissioner for West Darfur	"Zaghawa, Fur and Masalit have become rebels. We will burn everything down and only leave behind the trees. They can destroy all Darfur and even if there is only one soldier left, he will fight against America. This is now jihad."
2003	President al-Bashir	"Our priority from now on is to eliminate the rebellion.... We will use the army, the police, the mujahedeen [holy warriors], the horsemen to get rid of the rebellion."
2004	President al-Bashir	"You are informed that directives have been issued ... to change the demography of Darfur and empty it of African tribes 'through burning, looting, and killing' of intellectuals and youths who may join the rebels in fighting."
2004	Sheik Musa Hilal. *Janjaweed* Commander	"What I can say about Darfur, ... is that the government came to me and to many of the other sheiks and asked for our help in fighting the S.L.A. Of course, we did so gladly.... [W]hat happened after that, if mistakes or crimes took place—well, that is the government's responsibility, not ours."
2004	Lt. Gen. Ibrahim Suleiman, former Governor of N. Darfur	"When the problems with the rebels started in Darfur, we in the government of Sudan had a number of options. We chose the wrong one. We chose the very worst one."
2004	President al-Bashir, as quoted in a *Janjaweed* communiqué	"[E]xecution of all directives from the president of the republic," including: "Change the demography of Darfur and make it void of African tribes," by "killing, burning villages and farms, terrorizing people, confiscating property from members of African tribes and forcing them from Darfur."
2004	Sudanese Brigadier General	"I talked to the Sudanese brigadier general on the ground. He told me his mission was to clear the road from Labado all the way to Khartoum, which is about 100 kilometers away. If he encountered any resistance he was going to fight back and take the villages out. Those were his orders, he told me, and they came directly from Khartoum."

Sources: Human Rights Watch, *Entrenching Impunity*, at 26; *Sudanese President Says War Against Outlaws Is Government Priority*, ASSOCIATED PRESS, Dec. 31, 2003; ALEX DE WAAL & JULIE FLINT, DARFUR: A SHORT HISTORY OF A LONG WAR 106 (London: Zed Books, 2005); Scott Anderson, *How Did Darfur Happen?*, N.Y. TIMES MAG., Oct. 17, 2004, Magazine, http://www.nytimes.com/ 2004/10/17/magazine/17 DARFUR.html?8br=&pagewanted=print&position=; Nicholas D. Kristof, *The Secret Genocide Archive*, N.Y. TIMES, Feb. 23, 2005, http://www.nytimes.com/2005/02/23/opinion/23kristof.html?_r=1&oref=login; U.S. State Department official working with the African Union Mission in Sudan (AMIS), *quoted in* Marc L. Goldberg, *Anatomy of a Genocide*, THE AMERICAN PROSPECT (Mar. 17, 2005), http://www.prospect.org/web/page.ww? section=root&name=ViewWeb&articleID=9339.

2. Phase 2: Genocide in Darfur, July 2004–December 2006

In October 2004, the World Health Organization (WHO) reported that between March and September 2004, 70,000 displaced Darfurians had died as a result of their displacement from their homes, due to causes like diarrhea, infections, and violence.[23] Up to 9,000 to 10,000 Darfurians were dying every month as a result of the violence and the poor living conditions caused by their displacement.[24] These figures did not include deaths from violence or outside WHO-accessible areas, such as refugee camps deep inside Darfur or in Chad.[25] The U.S. House of Representatives, the Committee on Conscience of the U.S. Holocaust Memorial Museum, the Congressional Black Caucus, and several African-American civil rights groups warned of genocide in Darfur.[26]

Peacekeepers entered Darfur in 2004 under the auspices of U.N. Security Council Resolution 1556[27] and a series of peacekeeping communiqués issued by the African Union Peace and Security Council (AUPSC).[28] In late 2004, the AUPSC authorized an expansion of AMIS to include more than 3,000 military personnel and civilian police.[29] Despite that, AMIS was unable to prevent multiple attacks by Sudanese government forces and *Janjaweed*.[30] Disarmament of the *Janjaweed* did not occur.[31] The African Union expanded its AMIS force to 7,000 personnel by 2006, but tens of thousands more were needed to ensure peace and security in the area.[32] Despite its inadequacies, AMIS was a limited success in that its absence might have contributed to even more widespread "mass killings of civilians and ... serious crimes."[33]

By April 2006, 2.5 million people from Darfur had been expelled from their lands and the *Janjaweed* had invaded neighboring Chad, expelling 60,000 Chadians from their homes.[34] A massacre in September 2006 by Sudanese troops and militia allies killed 72

---

23. WHO, Director-General David Nabarro, Health Action in Crises, *Sudan: Mortality Projections for Darfur* (Oct. 15, 2004), http://www.reliefweb.int/rw/rwb.nsf/AllDocsByUNID/f035e0d2e4a12d1949256f3100030846.

24. *See id.*; Warren Hoge, *U.N. Says Sudan Death Toll Reaches 70,000,* N.Y. TIMES, Oct. 16, 2004, http://www.nytimes.com/2004/10/16/international/africa/16nations.html.

25. *See Darfur's Real Death Toll*, WASH. POST, Apr. 24, 2005, atB06.

26. *See* Strauss, *Darfur and the Genocide Debate*, at 127.

27. S.C. Res. 1556 (July 30, 2004).

28. *See* Jeremy I. Levitt, *The Peace and Security Council of the African Union and the United Nations Security. Council: The Case of Darfur, Sudan, in* THE SECURITY COUNCIL AND THE USE OF FORCE 239–45 (N.M. Blokker & N.J. Schrijver eds., 2005).

29. *See id.* at 244.

30. *See id.* at 243–46; Sima Samar, *Report of the Special Rapporteur on the Situation of Human Rights in the Sudan*, A/61/469, ¶ 49 (Sept. 20, 2006), http://www.un.org/apps/news/story.asp?NewsID=20066&Cr=sudan&Cr1=.

31. *See* Samar, *Situation of Human Rights in the Sudan 2006,* at ¶ 49.

32. *See* Nicholas Leddy, *United Nations Update*, 13 HUMAN RIGHTS BRIEF 59, 60 (2006).

33. *Id. But see* Amnesty International, *Open Letter to the Chair of the Assembly of the African Union Regarding Peacekeeping in Darfur* (Nov. 22, 2006), http://web.amnesty.org/library/Index/ENGAFR220042006?open&of=ENG-2AF (stating that AMIS lacks the equipment, funding, mandate, and Sudanese compliance to prevent "major killings and displacement," which increased in 2006 despite AMIS deployment to Darfur).

34. *See* Emily Wax, *A Loss of Hope Inside Darfur Refugee Camps: Over Two Years, a Genocide Comes Into View*, WASH. POST FOREIGN SERVICE, Apr. 30, 2006, at A12.

people.[35] The death toll in Darfur had risen to about 450,000 people.[36] The Sudanese government escalated the bombing of villages using Soviet-era aircraft and helicopter gunships.[37] The *Janjaweed*, meanwhile, preyed on civilians expelled to camps for displaced persons, killing the men and raping the women, over 200 of them from a single camp in a little over a month. While doing so, one attacker chanted: "'Slave woman. Slave woman. Slave woman.'"[38] The U.N. reported that rape was being used by *Janjaweed* in Darfur and eastern Chad to "subjugate and humiliate non-Arab girls and women," with violence often tied to racial epithets and demeaning comments.[39] The U.N. Mission in Sudan confirmed that attacks on civilians "appeared to have targeted civilians from tribes of African origin in what appeared to be an attempt to drive them from the Habbania homeland and therefore completely change the ethnic balance in the area."[40]

By September 2006, the death toll in Darfur had risen to about 450,000 people, and about 2.5 million people from Darfur had been expelled from their homes and lands.[41] Several U.S. senators were told in 2004 that "even a best-case scenario will likely result in the death of more than 320,000 people between April 1, 2004 and December 31, 2004."[42] About 3,000 to 4,000 villages had been burned down or otherwise destroyed.[43] A single massacre in September 2006 by Sudanese troops and militia allies killed seventy-two people.[44] The Sudanese government escalated the bombing of villages using Soviet-era aircraft and helicopter gunships.[45] The *Janjaweed*, meanwhile, preyed on civilians expelled to camps for displaced persons, killing the men and raping the women; over 200 women from a single camp were raped by the *Janjaweed* in a little over a month.[46] These mass rapes threatened the survival of Darfur's non-Arab tribes because they caused severe phys-

---

35. *See* Craig Timberg, *In Darfur's Death Grip*, WASH. POST FOREIGN SERVICE, Sept. 6, 2006, at A01.

36. *See id.*; Jeffrey Gettleman, *Toll of Darfur Underreported, Study Declares*, N.Y. TIMES, Sept 15, 2006, http://www.nytimes.com/2006/09/15/world/africa/15darfur.html; Craig Timberg, *In Darfur, Terror From the Air*, WASH. POST FOREIGN SERVICE, Sept. 9, 2006, at A10.

37. *See* Timberg, *In Darfur, Terror from the Air*, at A10.

38. *See* Craig Timberg, *For Darfur Women, Survival Means Leaving Camp, Risking Rape*, WASH. POST FOREIGN SERVICE, Sept. 16, 2006, at A12.

39. Julia Freedson, Simar Singh and Sarah W. Spencer, *The Continuing Plight of Sudan's Children*, UN CHRONICLE, July 2007, http://www.un.org/Pubs/chronicle/2007/webArticles/072507_sudan.htm.

40. Office of the UN High Commission for Human Rights and UN Mission in Sudan, Oct. 2006, *quoted in* ERIC REEVES, A LONG DAY'S DYING: CRITICAL MOMENTS IN THE DARFUR GENOCIDE 200 (Toronto: The Key Publishing House, 2007).

41. *See* Wax, *A Loss of Hope Inside Darfur Refugee Camps*, at A12; Craig Timberg, *In Darfur, Terror From the Air*, at A20; Roger Winter, *Briefing on the Humanitarian Situation in Sudan* (July 29, 2004), http://www.usaid.gov/press/speeches/2004/sp040729.html; David Nabarro, Representative of the World Health Organization Director-General, *Sudan: Mortality Projections for Darfur* (Oct 2004), http://www.reliefweb.int/rw/rwb.nsf/AllDocsByUNID/f035e0d2e4a12d1949256f3100030846; Jeffrey Gettleman, *Toll of Darfur Underreported, Study Declares*, N.Y. TIMES, Sept. 15, 2006, at A8.

42. Comprehensive Peace in Sudan Act, section 3(13), S. 2781(RFH), 108th Cong., 2d Sess. (2004), http://www.govrecords.org/s-2781-rfh-to-express-the-sense-of-congress-regarding.html.

43. *See* Lydia Polgreen, *Shaky Peace in Darfur at Risk, As a New Confrontation Looms*, N.Y. TIMES, Aug. 13, 2006, http://query.nytimes.com/gst/fullpage.html?res=9803E3DF1E3EF932A0575BC0A9609C8B63; Lydia Polgreen, *4 Months after DPA, Darfur Heads Toward Military Confrontation*, SUDAN TRIBUNE, Sept. 1, 2006 http://www.sudantribune.com/spip.php?article17368; John Heffernan & David Tuller, *Crisis in Africa: Ending the Genocide in Darfur*, S.F. CHRON., Feb. 12, 2006, at E7.

44. *See* Craig Timberg, *In Darfur's Death Grip*, WASH. POST, Sept. 6, 2006, at A01.

45. *See* Timberg, *In Darfur, Terror from the Air*, at A10.

46. *See* Craig Timberg, *For Darfur Women, Survival Means Leaving Camp, Risking Rape*, WASH. POST FOREIGN SERVICE, Sept. 16, 2006, at A12.

ical injuries, spread the HIV virus, dissolved families, impoverished women and their children, and generally "have been among the most effective means for the government to terrorize tribal populations, break their will, and drive them away."[47] A leading Sudan expert has declared that in Darfur, "widespread rape itself is a means of [group] identity destruction or transformation."[48]

As 2006 came to a close, the top U.N. humanitarian official reported that the killing and destruction of villages in Darfur was as bad as ever.[49] The U.N. High Commissioner for Human Rights, similarly, concluded that rape was going on unabated in Darfur, unchanged from the "horrific" levels of early 2004.[50] The International Criminal Court (ICC), however, had failed to indict any Sudanese officials for genocide or the encouragement thereof, despite a legal mandate to investigate the situation and the resources to do so.[51] Even worse, the ICC reported that "direct attacks on humanitarian workers and peacekeepers, including the killing of African Union peacekeepers in 2005 and 2006" blocked the delivery of humanitarian supplies to the victims of genocide and displacement in Darfur.[52] Such attacks caused a number of aid organizations to withdraw from Darfur, "threatening the lives of millions...."[53] But as of February 2007, indictments had not been issued, although the press expected them "soon" for war crimes and crimes against humanity, but not genocide.[54] The victims in Darfur had not been compensated for the loss of their loved ones, homes, cultural treasures, or lands.[55] A non-Arab insurgent catalogued their losses: "The Arabs see black people as slaves.... There is no justice for Darfur. No schools. No healthcare. They have taken our land."[56]

The pattern of genocidal attacks spilled over into Chad in 2006 and 2007. Several hundred *Janjaweed* attacked a village in Chad 40 miles from the Sudan border, massacring up to 117 people.[57] A few months later, the situation in Chad was deteriorating:

> Hundreds of Chadians have been killed by roving groups of Arab gunmen in dozens of villages over the past 10 days, according to aid workers and human rights officials along Chad's troubled border with Sudan.
>
> At least 220 people have been killed, and dozens of wounded people have overwhelmed small, poorly equipped local hospitals, the United Nations said

---

47. Kristof, *Genocide in Slow Motion.*

48. DeWaal, *Who Are the Darfurians?*, at 199.

49. *See* Nora Boustany, *World Court Official Reports Evidence on Darfur Criminals*, WASH. POST FOREIGN SERVICE, Nov. 25, 2006, at A08.

50. *Arbour Blames Sudanese Government for Darfur Atrocities*, CBC NEWS (Canada), Nov. 29, 2006.

51. *See id.*

52. Third Report of the Prosecutor of the International Criminal Court to the UN Security Council Pursuant to UNSCR 1593 (2005) (June 14, 2006), http://www.icc-cpi.int/library/cases/OTP_Report UNSC_3-Darfur_English.pdf.

53. Third Report of the Prosecutor of the International Criminal Court to the UN Security Council Pursuant to UNSCR 1593 (2005) (Dec. 14, 2006), http://www.icc-cpi.int/library/organs/otp/OTP_ReportUNSC4-Darfur_English.pdf.

54. *See* Stephanie Nieuwoudt, *Al-Bashir Calls World's Bluff on Darfur*, IWPR, Feb. 19, 2007, http://www.iwpr.net/?p=acr&s=f&o=333337&apc_state=henpacr.

55. *See* Human Rights Watch, *Darfur Demands Sanctions, Not Words* (Dec. 13, 2006), http://hrw.org/english/docs/2006/12/12/darfur14833.htm.

56. Edmund Sanders, *Battle For Darfur; Sudan War Spills Into Chad*, L.A. TIMES, June 6, 2006.

57. See Edmund Sanders, *Sudan's Bloodshed Claws Deeper Into Its Neighbor*, L.A. TIMES, June 10, 2006.

> Tuesday. Chad's government has declared a state of emergency over the attacks and has accused Sudan, its neighbor to the east, of fomenting a crisis in Chad.[58]

U.N. envoys reported that three dozen residents of another village in Chad had been buried in mass graves after a pre-dawn attack that saw their huts burned down and food stores looted.[59] After a visit to Chad and the Central African Republic, one envoy described the devastation:

> Eastern Chad is on fire. Chadian villages are on Fire. *Janjaweed* (militias from Sudan) have reached far into Chad and joined with Arab militia in Chad to attack black African villages along the eastern border of Chad. So, what we're seeing is an identical situation with identical atrocities....[60]

As the *Janjaweed* repeatedly invaded Chad, they expelled 60,000 Chadians from their homes.[61]

3. The Involvement of the ICC and the Decision to Deny Humanitarian Aid to the People of Darfur

In late February 2007, nearly two years after the Security Council referred the Darfur case to the ICC,[62] the Office of the Prosecutor issued a "summons to appear" concerning Darfur, a document resembling an indictment.[63] The summons charged Sudan's Minister of State for the Interior and a member of the PDF with committing war crimes and crimes against humanity, but not genocide.[64] Sudan refused to surrender the suspects.[65]

In late March 2007, President al-Bashir informed Saudi Arabia and other Arab nations that he would allow the U.N. to play a role in providing logistical support to African Union peacekeepers in Darfur.[66] Throughout the rest of 2007, however, his government imposed restrictions on the U.N.'s role that the top U.N. peacekeeping official described as ensuring that the U.N. force "will not make a difference, ... will not have the capability to defend itself, and ... [will create a] risk of humiliation of the Security Council and

---

58. Lydia Polgreen, *Arab Gunmen Kill Hundreds of Villagers in Chad*, N.Y. Times, Nov. 15, 2006, at A12.

59. *See* David McKenzie, *Mia Farrow Witnesses Dire Effects of Conflict in Eastern Chad* (Feb. 22, 2007), http://www.unicef.org/infobycountry/chad_38426.html.

60. Joe DeCapua, *UNICEF Goodwill Ambassador Mia Farrow Calls for Peacekeeping Force in Chad, Darfur and CAR*, Voice of America News (Feb. 22, 2007), http://www.voanews.com/english/Africa/2007-02-22-voa57.cfm.

61. *See* Wax, *Loss of Hope Inside Darfur Refugee Camps*, at A12.

62. *See* Stephanie Nieuwoudt, *Al-Bashir Calls World's Bluff on Darfur*, IWPR, Feb. 19, 2007, http://www.iwpr.net/?p=acr&s=f&o=333337&apc_state=henpacr.

63. *See* Xan Rice, *Sudanese Minister Indicted over Darfur*, The Guardian (U.K.), Feb. 28, 2007, http://www.guardian.co.uk/sudan/story/0,,2022952,00.html.

64. *See* Situation in Darfur, the Sudan, Prosecutor's Application under Article 58 (7), Pre-Trial Chamber I, ICC-02/05-56, at 6–23, 31–33 (Feb. 27, 2007), http://www.icc-cpi.int/library/cases/ICC-02-05-56_English.pdf.

65. *See Sudan Has Failed to Cooperate With International Criminal Court, Prosecutor Says*, U.N. News Centre (Dec. 5, 2007), http://www.un.org/apps/news/ story.asp?NewsID=24933&Cr=sudan&Cr1 [hereinafter *Sudan Has Failed to Cooperate*].

66. *See* Warren Hoge, *Arabs and U.N. Chief Press Sudan's Leader to End Darfur Crisis*, N.Y. Times, Mar. 29, 2007, at A5; Challis McDonough, *Arab Leaders Discuss Regional Peace*, Voice of America News (Mar. 28, 2007), http://www.voanews.com/english/2007-03-28-voa52.cfm; Andrew Hammond & Sue Pleming, *Sudan Agrees to U.N. force But U.S. Plans New Sanctions*, Reuters/The Scotsman (U.K.), Mar. 29, 2007, http://news.scotsman.com/latest.cfm?id=493552007.

the United Nations, and tragic failure for the people of Darfur."[67] Only about a third of the planned U.N. peacekeeping force had entered Darfur by early 2008.[68] In the meantime, the Sudan Air Force carried out a massacre of civilians in a village in North Darfur, killing twenty-six, including pregnant women.[69]

The prosecutor of the ICC warned in June and December 2007 that "massive crimes continued, with rampant attacks on individuals for the purpose of destroying communities."[70] He alleged that continuing attacks on people of Darfur were not "sporadic" but represented "a calculated, organized campaign by Sudanese officials to attack individuals and further destroy the social fabric of entire communities."[71] Villages are being burned to drive out indigenous Africans, while Arabic-speaking nomads from Chad, Niger, Mali and Cameroon are resettled there.[72] The campaign tracked almost precisely the depopulation and enslavement of southern Sudanese villages in the 1980s and 1990s, with *Janjaweed* replacing *murahileen*.[73]

A report issued by a coalition of African NGOs in 2008 reported the widespread enslavement of indigenous Africans by *Janjaweed* for purposes of rape and forced agricultural labor. A woman from Darfur reported being kidnapped from a refugee camp and that she and the other captured women were "used [] like their wives in the night and during the day we worked all the time. [¶] The men they abducted with us were used to look after their livestock. We worked all day, all week with no rest." A child undergoing a similar ordeal stated: "They were treating me and the other boys very badly, they kept telling us that we are not human beings and we are here to serve them, I also worked on their farms." A Sudanese official quoted in the report said: "The army captured many children and women hiding in the bush outside burnt villages," which it then "transported by plane to Khartoum at night and divided up among soldiers as domestic workers and, in some cases, wives."[74]

In early April 2009, in the immediate aftermath of being charged with genocide by the ICC prosecutor, and with crimes against humanity by the Pre-Trial Chamber, President al-Bashir reiterated his previously-stated, but rarely followed up on, commitments to hold the perpetrators of war crimes in Darfur accountable in court, and to compensate the victims.[75] It was a moment of possibility for improvement in Darfur and eastern Chad,

---

67. Warren Hoge, *U.N. Official Criticizes Sudan for Resisting Peace Force in Darfur*, N.Y. Times, Nov. 28, 2007, at A9.

68. *See* Opheera McDoom, *Darfur Rebels Say 15 Die in Army Offensive*, Reuters (Feb. 20, 2008), http://www.washingtonpost.com/wp-dyn/content/article/2008/02/20/ AR2008022002622.html. For an account of the obstacles placed by Sudan on the deployment of this force, see U.N. Secretary-General, *Report on the Deployment of the African Union-United Nations Hybrid Operation in Darfur*, S/2007/759 (Dec. 24, 2007), http://www.un.org/Docs/sc/sgrep07.htm.

69. *See* Amnesty International, *Sudan: Arms Continuing to Fuel Serious Human Rights Violations in Darfur*, AI Index Number: AFR 54/019/2007 (2007), http://64.233.169.104/search?q=cache:UcDQOLTkvn8J:www.amnesty.org/en/alfresco_asset/8bfe199c-a2b8-11dc-8d74-6f45f39984e5/afr540192007en.pdf.

70. U.N. Security Council, *In 200,7 Security Council Faced Daunting Range of Peace, Security Challenges, Including Africa, Middle East, Nuclear Proliferation, Terrorism*, SC/9219 (Jan. 4, 2008), http://www.reliefweb.int/rw/RWB.NSF/db900SID/EGUA-7AMLKG?OpenDocument.

71. *Sudan Has Failed to Cooperate.*

72. *'Thousands made slaves' in Darfur*, BBC News (Dec. 17, 2008), http://news.bbc.co.uk/2/hi/africa/7786612.stm.

73. *See id.* ("Sudan's government has always denied the existence of slavery in the country, although Khartoum has previously admitted abductions occurred in the north-south civil war of 1983–2005, when up to 14,000 people were kidnapped.").

74. *Id.*

75. *See* U.N. System in Sudan, *Media Humanitarian Headlines, Wed., 08 April 2009*, Sudan Info. Gateway, http://www.unsudanig.org/docs/080409%20MHH%20Media%20Humanitarian%20Headlines.doc

but these hopes were quickly dashed. President al-Bashir expelled many of the NGOs that had been operating in Darfur, leaving an aid gap affecting some 3.8 million people in danger of starvation.[76]

Nevertheless, the international community continued to celebrate President al-Bashir as the leader of an increasingly wealthy country, whose GDP doubled due to the massive rise in oil prices and large-scale Chinese investment in its oil production in the wake of the Iraq war.[77] The African Union held its 2006 summit in Khartoum, Sudan, which President al-Bashir welcomed in person.[78] In the wake of the arrest warrant against him and his decision to starve out opposition to genocidal policies in Darfur by denying humanitarian aid, President al-Bashir embarked upon state visits to "friendly nations including Egypt, Eritrea, Libya, Qatar, Saudi Arabia and Ethiopia."[79] His crowning triumph seemed imminent in the fall of 2009, as U.S. President Barack Obama announced a new policy of "engagement" with and "incentives" for Sudanese regime to improve its human rights record and stay in power, in order to make sure that "Sudan remains stable to prevent it from becoming a safe haven for terrorists."[80]

B. Failures of International Law and Institutions: Silence and Denial as Genocide Spreads

1. From Indifference to an Inquiry

As of summer 2004 the government, human rights organizations, and medical community in the U.S. and elsewhere were aware that genocidal policies had been ongoing for some time in Sudan and were devastating the Darfur region of the country on a massive scale. How would the Genocide Convention be applied? A swift and sure application

(citing *Al-Bashir Vows to try Darfur War Criminals,* Khartoum Monitor, Apr. 2009; *Al-Bashir Pledges to Compensate Darfur IDPs and Refugees,* Rai Al-Sha'ab, Apr. 2009; *Vowing to Pay Collective and Individual Reparations to the Affected, Al-Bashir: Investigations Will Be Conducted on the Dead and the Killers in Darfur,* Ajras Al-Horyah, Apr. 2009; *Al-Bashir Vows to Prosecute War Criminals in Darfur,* Al-Rai Al-Aam, Apr. 2009). *See also* Cour Pénale Internationale / International Criminal Court, Warrant of Arrest for Omar Hassan Ahmad Al Bashir (Mar. 4, 2009), www.icc-cpi.int/iccdocs/doc/doc639078.pdf.

76. United Nations in Khartoum, *Sudan, Humanitarian Action in Darfur,* Weekly Bulletin 26 (July 2, 2009), http://www.unsudanig.org%2Fdocs%2FHumanitarian%2520Action%2520in%2520 Darfur%2520Bulletin%2520No.%252026.pdf.

77. Compare, e.g., CIA, World Factbook 2002: Sudan (2003), http://www.faqs.org/docs/factbook/ geos/su.html, *with* CIA, World Factbook 2008: Sudan, https://www.cia.gov/library/publications/the-world-factbook/geos/su.html.

78. See, e.g., African Union, *6th AU Summit* (2006), http://www.africa-union.org/summit/jan% 202006/home.htm.

79. See, e.g., *Timeline: The International Criminal Court and Sudan,* Reuters, Oct. 19, 2009, http://www.reuters.com/article/newsMaps/idUSTRE59I1RI20091019.

80. Scott Baldauf, *Obama Launches New 'Integrated' Approach to Sudan,* Christian Sci. Monitor, Oct. 19, 2009, http://www.csmonitor.com/2009/1019/p06s13-woaf.html. *See also* Eric Reeves, *Redefining Darfur's Agony: A Shameless Betrayal,* Sudan Tribune, Sept. 27, 2009, http://www.sudantribune.com/ spip.php?article32602; Eric Reeves, *The Phony Optimism on Darfur,* Boston Globe, Aug. 6, 2009, ttp://www.boston.com/bostonglobe/editorial_opinion/oped/articles/2009/08/06/the_phony_optimism_ on_darfur/; Bret Stephens, *Does Obama Believe In Human Rights?,* Wall St. J., Oct. 20, 2009, http://online.wsj.com/article/SB40001424052748704500604574481341183751038.html.

might prevent a further humanitarian disaster and cut short an intensifying genocide. A tardy and uncertain application, by contrast, would be a green light to al-Bashir to go forward with his declared intention to "eliminate" the rebels.[81] Victims of genocide and international aid workers looked for answers to the community of international lawyers, diplomats, and human rights experts.

Despite the growing awareness that the genocide in Sudan having claimed two million lives and displaced over 1.3 million Darfur residents and four million other Sudanese from their homes, U.N. Secretary-General Kofi Annan stated in July 2004 that "I can't at this stage call it genocide." He was not even willing to call the situation "ethnic cleansing," even though he acknowledged that "massive violations of international humanitarian law" and that "the Janjaweed militia ... are doing quite a lot of the killing...."[82] This was nearly a month after the U.N. Security Council had expressed "concern" about "reports of large-scale violations of human rights and of international humanitarian law in Darfur, including indiscriminate attacks on civilians, sexual violence, forced displacement and acts of violence, especially those with an ethnic dimension, and demand[ed] that those responsible be held accountable."[83]

In July 2004, despite recognizing "human rights and international humanitarian law violations and other atrocities" by the *Janjaweed* in Darfur, the U.N. Security Council failed to condemn them as either genocide or crimes against humanity.[84] The U.S. representative noted that the U.S. Congress had characterized these "atrocities" as "genocide," but insisted that: "it is important that we not become bogged down over words."[85] Sudan's representative admitted that Darfur was "soaked with the blood of innocent people," but pointed to the refusal of the African Union to find genocide in Darfur, and suggested that the U.S. Congress reexamine its own history of genocide and slavery. He added that Sudan had deployed 4,812 police officers to Darfur and 200 members of the *Janjaweed* had been arrested, some receiving death sentences.[86]

On September 9, 2004, U.S. Secretary of State Colin Powell testified to the U.S. Senate's Foreign Relations Committee that genocide had occurred within the meaning of the Genocide Convention and international law, and that it "may still be occurring." As evidence he cited evidence from a series of more than 1,000 interviews conducted by a State Department team and "other sources" that members of non-Arab groups had been systematically killed by "burning, shelling or bombing" by the Sudanese military and *Janjaweed* militia; subjected to a "consistent and widespread pattern of atrocities" including rapes and physical assaults; seen their "villages, foodstuffs, and other means of survival

81. *See* ICID Report, at 126–27.

82. U.N. Secretary-General Kofi Annan, *Text of Press Conference Upon Arrival at U.N. Headquarters in New York*, Federal News, June 17, 2004.

83. S/PV.4978, U.N. Security Council, Fifty-ninth year, 4978th meeting (25 May 2004), http://daccessdds.un.org/doc/UNDOC/PRO/N04/364/75/PDF/N0436475.pdf?OpenElement.

84. S.C. Res. 1556 (July 30, 2004), http://daccessdds.un.org/doc/UNDOC/GEN/N04/446/02/PDF/N0444602.pdf?OpenElement.

85. S/PV.5015, U.N. Security Council, 59th year, 5015th mtg. 4 (July 30, 2004), http://daccessdds.un.org/doc/UNDOC/PRO/N04/445/15/PDF/N0444515.pdf?OpenElement.

86. *Id.* at 14. The Peace and Security Council of the African Union had concluded earlier in July "that 'even though the crisis in Darfur is grave, with unacceptable levels of death, human suffering and destruction of homes and infrastructure, the situation cannot be defined as a genocide.'" *African Union Demands Arrest of Sudan Militia*, Detroit Free Press, July 8, 2004, at 13A.

destroyed; and blocked from receiving humanitarian aid such as food, water, and medicine to such a degree that further deaths resulted.[87]

While accurate and important in a number of respects, Secretary Powell's presentation did not fully come to grips with the legal implications of the facts as he summarized them. Powell cited Article VIII of the Genocide Convention as stating that parties "*may* call upon the competent organs of the United Nations to take such action under the Charter of the United Nations *as they consider appropriate* for the prevention and suppression of acts of genocide...."[88] He did not, however, discuss the duties of countries other than Sudan to act to stop genocide in Darfur under Article I of the convention, which provides that all parties "undertake to prevent and to punish" the crime of genocide under international law.[89]

The Security Council also instituted an arms embargo relating only to Darfur in July 2004.[90] In early 2005, the council expanded the embargo to cover the government of Sudan and the *Janjaweed* as "belligerents" in Darfur. In doing so, the council condemned the government of Sudan's air strikes in Darfur and its failure to disarm "*Janjaweed* militiamen and apprehend and bring to justice *Janjaweed* leaders and their associates who have carried out human rights and international humanitarian law violations and other atrocities." But even so, the council vacillated in the extent of its condemnation by permitting the regime to apply to a committee for permission to move weapons and military equipment into Darfur.[91] In the meantime, the death toll in Darfur far surpassed that of the wars in the former Yugoslavia.

2. A Commission of Inquiry on Darfur

In September 2004, the U.N. Security Council met to discuss Sudan's refusal to prevent violations of international humanitarian law and other atrocities in Darfur. Despite concluding that the government of Sudan had brought about a "climate of impunity in Darfur" with regards to "widespread human rights abuses and violations of international humanitarian law," the Council declined to analyze whether genocide had occurred in Sudan.[92] Instead, it requested that the Secretary-General "rapidly establish an international commission of inquiry" to determine whether "acts of genocide" had occurred and to identify their perpetrators.[93]

Secretary-General Annan arguably preordained the conclusions of the commission of inquiry called for by the Security Council. Specifically, he appointed only five commis-

87. *See* Colin L. Powell, *Written Remarks of Secretary of State to Senate Foreign Relations Committee on the Crisis in Darfur* (Sept. 9, 2004), http://www.whitehouse.gov/interactive/sudan_gen.html.

88. *Id.* (emphasis in original).

89. Genocide Convention, art. 1.

90. *See* S.C. Res. 1556 (July 30, 2004) (banning arms exports to Darfur).

91. *See* S.C. Res. 1591 (Mar. 29, 2005) (acting under Chapter VII of the UN Charter to establish an arms embargo against "all the parties to the N'djamena Ceasefire Agreement [one of which was the government of Sudan] and any other belligerents in the states of North Darfur, South Darfur and West Darfur").

92. *See* S.C. Res. 1564, ¶ 7 (Sept. 18, 2004), http://daccessdds.un.org/doc/UNDOC/GEN/N04/515/47/PDF/N0451547.pdf?OpenElement. The Council noted "the reports by the Cease Fire Commission of Government of Sudan helicopter assaults and Janjaweed attacks on Yassin, Hashaba and Gallab villages on 26 August 2004." *Id.* at ¶ 1.

93. *Id.* at ¶ 12.

Figure 10 Estimated Death Toll of Genocide in Sudan Compared to Other Genocides

Case	Death Toll	Refugees/IDPs	Sources
Southern Sudan, 1992–2001	2 million	4 million	Sudan Peace Act, Pub. L. No. 107-245, § 2(1) (2002)
Cambodia, 1975–1979	2 million	500,000	U.N. Economic and Social Council, Commission on Human Rights
Bangladesh, 1971	1–3 million	10 million	Government of India; U.S. Consulate (Dacca, Bangladesh)
Rwanda, 1994	800,000– 1 million	1+ million	The International Criminal Tribunal for Rwanda
Indonesia, 1965–1966	Up to 1 million	Unknown	FOREIGN RELATIONS OF THE U.S.
Darfur, 2003–?	200,000– 450,000	2.4 million	U.S. Secretary of State; U.N. Under-Secretary General for Humanitarian Affairs
Burundi, 1972	100,000– 300,000	113,000	U.N. Economic and Social Council, Commission on Human Rights
Bosnia, 1992–1996	8,000	2.2 million	The International Criminal Trib. for the Former Yugoslavia
Kosovo, 1999	2,100–8,000	1 million	The International Criminal Trib. for the Former Yugoslavia (Spokesperson)

sioners, and one of those was the former Minister of Information, Minister of State for Foreign Affairs, and Advisor to the President of the Arab Republic of Egypt.[94] As a member of the National Council for Human Rights of Egypt, he may even have been on the government's payroll.[95]

The government of Egypt, which a key commissioner served at the highest levels, has supported Sudan's leaders as they have waged genocide in Darfur. "Few countries have provided more diplomatic or political cover for the [al-Bashir] regime, particularly in its efforts to forestall humanitarian intervention."[96] Egypt is the most powerful member of the Arab League, and "so long as Khartoum can count on Egyptian support, it can count on support from the Arab League as a whole," whose Secretary-General is also the former foreign minister of Egypt.[97] The Arab League decided to deny the existence of genocide

94. *See* ICID REPORT, at 9 ("In October 2004 the Secretary-General appointed a five member body (Mr. Antonio Cassese, from Italy; Mr. Mohammed Fayek, from Egypt; Ms Hina Jilani, from Pakistan; Mr. Dumisa Ntsebeza, from South Africa, and Ms Theresa Striggner-Scott, from Ghana), and designated Mr. Cassese as its Chairman."); *id.* at 165 ("Mohammed Fayek ... has previously served in Egypt as Minister of Information, Minister of State for Foreign Affairs, Minister of National Guidance, and Chef de Cabinet and Advisor to the President for African and Asian Affairs.").

95. *See id* at 165 ("Mohammed Fayek ... is a member of the National Council for human rights in Egypt and the Egyptian Council for Foreign Affairs...."); National Council for Human Rights, http://www.nchr.org.eg/en/home.asp.

96. Eric Reeves, *Egypt and Darfur: Cruel Intentions*, NEW REPUBLIC ONLINE, Apr. 4, 2006, http://209.85.165.104/search?q=cache:I9lO1WHQx98J:tnr.com/doc.mhtml%3Fi%3Dw060403%26s%3Dreeves040406.

97. *Id. Accord A President's Promise*, WASH. POST, Apr. 11, 2006, at A20 ("Sudan has plenty of diplomatic cover: within the African Union, from alleged U.S. allies such as Egypt....").

in Darfur in mid-2004.[98] When the Egyptian representative received a report in 2002 from the Special Rapporteur on violations of human rights in Sudan, he complained that "discussing the question of human rights must not be a pretext to interfere with the internal affairs of a sovereign State."[99] As late as April 2006 the President of Egypt denied not only that there had been genocide but even that there had been any "massacres" at all in Sudan.[100]

On January 25, 2005, the commission of inquiry on Darfur released its report, which concluded that genocide had not occurred in Darfur. The commission, however, acknowledged that *acts* of genocide had occurred, including the "systematic killing of civilians belonging to particular tribes, [the] large-scale causing of serious bodily or mental harm to members of the population belonging to certain tribes, and [the] massive and deliberate infliction on those tribes of conditions of life bringing about their physical destruction in whole or in part (for example by systematically destroying their villages and crops, by expelling them from their homes, and by looting their cattle)." The commission was unable to persuade itself of the important element of genocidal intent because in some villages "militias and Government forces the attackers refrained from exterminating the whole population that had not fled." It also declined to find genocidal intent in light of the fact that the government forcibly expelled people from their homes but did not prevent humanitarian organizations from delivering food, water, or medicines in all instances. Ignoring the history of genocide by military operations and war-induced famine in southern and central Sudan, the commission actually concluded that the government's expulsion of ethnic Africans from their homes for "purposes of counter-insurgency warfare" meant that no genocide had taken place.[101]

The Commission of Inquiry's report suffered from many deficiencies that made it not credible as an answer to the Security Council's question regarding whether genocide had occurred in Darfur. First, it failed to apply well-established principles of international law, including the terms of the Genocide Convention, to the situation in Darfur, which it easily could have done by concluding that the Sudanese army and its *Janjaweed* allies had committed genocide by killing a considerable or significant number of individuals of specific non-Arab ethnic or tribal groups. The International Commission of Inquiry on Darfur summarized the Rwanda tribunal's conclusions: "the intent to destroy a group 'in part' requires the intention to destroy 'a considerable number of individuals' or 'a substantial part', but not necessarily a 'very important part' of the group."[102] The Commission of In-

---

98. Robert O. Collins, *Disaster in Darfur, in* Civil Wars and Revolution in the Sudan: Essays on the Sudan, Southern Sudan, and Darfur, 1962–2004, at 165 (2005).

99. U.N. Human Rights Commission, Press Release: In Third Committee, Special Rapporteurs on Myanmar, Sudan Stress Need for Human Rights-Based Approach in Building Sustainable Future, 57th General Assembly, Third Committee, 37th Mtg., http://www.unhchr.ch/huricane/huricane.nsf/view01/12872C9C3BB8C175C1256C6A002BACFD?opendocument.

100. *See President Mubarak granted Al Arabia satellite channel a TV interview which took place at the Heliopolis Presidential palace* (Apr. 8, 2006), http://www.presidency.gov.eg/html/8-April2006_press.html ("[Interviewer]: Why do not the Arab countries admit that there are mass killings in Darfur; all international reports say there are hundreds of killed people or more? [¶] President: We would admit that there are mass killings in Darfur if a commission went there and said so.... [¶] [Interviewer]: The Secretary General of the Arab League said there are mass killings, but not genocide, because the latter has another international definition. There is always a feeling that the Arabs do not admit inhumane matters and human rights. [¶] President: I want to say something. I say that there are victims and losses but I can't say there are massacres or genocides.").

101. ICID Report at ¶ 507, 513, 515, 518. *See also id.* at pp. 3–4, 37, 54.

102. ICID Report at ¶ 492 (footnotes omitted) (citing Prosecutor v. Kayishema and Ruzindana, Trial Chamber, Judgement, at ¶ 97; Prosecutor v. Jelisić, Appeals Chamber, Judgement, at ¶ 82; Prosecutor v. Bagilishema, Trial Chamber, Judgement, at § 64); Prosecutor v. Semanza, Trial Chamber, Judgement, at § 316.

quiry's determination as to whether genocide had been committed would have carried more weight had it applied these principles to documents and eyewitness testimony unearthed by other investigators of the conflict in Sudan, most notably the communiqué cited by Julie Flint and Alex de Waal describing orders from President al-Bashir to the leader of the *Janjaweed* "to change the demography of Darfur and empty it of African tribes 'through burning, looting, and killing' of intellectuals and youths who may join the rebels in fighting."[103]

As noted above, the commission made many factual conclusions that directly track the Genocide Convention's definition of the crime of genocide. The commission found a "pattern of indiscriminate attacks on civilians in villages and communities" throughout Darfur beginning in 2001 and 2002 and escalating in 2003 and 2004.[104] The commission stated:

> There are consistent accounts of a recurrent pattern of attacks on villages and settlements, sometimes involving aerial attacks by helicopter gunships or fixed-wing aircraft (Antonov and MIG), including bombing and strafing with automatic weapons. However, a majority of the attacks reported are ground assaults by the military, the *Janjaweed*, or a combination of the two. Hundreds of incidents have been reported involving the killing of civilians, massacres, summary executions, rape and other forms of sexual violence, torture, abduction, looting of property and livestock, as well as deliberate destruction and torching of villages. These incidents have resulted in the massive displacement of large parts of the civilian population within Darfur as well as to neighbouring Chad.[105]

This pattern of attacks on indigenous Africans completely destroyed at least 600 villages and hamlets and partially destroyed 100 more.[106] Perceived racial and ethnic differences clearly motivated this pattern of attacks:

> In a majority of cases, victims of the attacks belonged to African tribes, in particular the Fur, Masaalit and Zaghawa tribes. When asked why they believed they were attacked, some witnesses stated 'because they want our land and cattle' or 'they want to eliminate us from the area'. Other witnesses referred to statements made by their aggressors during some of the attacks, such as 'you are Tora Bora, the SLA are your families', 'the Fur are slaves, we will kill them', 'we are here to eradicate blacks (nuba)', 'we will drive you into poverty', 'this is not your land' or 'you are not from here'....
>
> In many cases militias attacking "African" villages tend to use derogatory epithets, such as "slaves", "blacks", Nuba", or "Zurga" that might imply a perception of the victims as members of a distinct group.[107]

---

103. Reeves, *Egypt and Darfur* (quoting Julie Flint & Alex de Waal, Darfur: A Short History of a Long War 106 (2005)). *See also* Richard Just, *Sudan and the Colonial Impulse: An Imperialist Indifference*, New Republic, May 9, 2006, http://www.tnr.com/doc.mhtml?i=20060515&s=just051506&c=2; The International Citizens' Tribunal for Sudan, Case No. ICTS-1, ¶ 15, http://www.judgmentongenocide.com/images/darfur_indictment.pdf.

104. ICID Report at ¶¶ 184, 238.

105. *Id.* at ¶ 186.

106. *See id.* at ¶ n.117.

107. *Id.* ¶¶ 254, 511.

As the Nuba people were victims of slave raids by northern Arabs for hundreds of years, the term "Nuba" is "used by the *Janjaweed* and others as a derogatory reference to ethnic Africans."[108] The term "Zurga" also apparently means "blacks" among the *Janjaweed*.[109]

The commission also made important findings that bear directly on the question of genocidal intent. The massacres in Darfur are directed from President al-Bashir down, according to the commission. The *Janjaweed*, the commission noted, was a term often used by victims unaware that their attackers were Sudanese government military.[110] To the victims, "*Janjaweed*" is "a derogatory term that ... clearly refers to 'militias of Arab tribes on horseback or on camelback.'"[111] But *Janjaweed* were typically either part of the Popular Defense Forces receive "uniforms, weapons, ammunition and payments" from them.[112] The Popular Defense Forces, in turn, receive their orders from army officers.[113] President al-Bashir declared in 2003 that: "Our priority from now on is to eliminate the rebellion.... We will use the army, the police, the *mujahedeen*, the horsemen to get rid of the rebellion."[114] Since then, observers have noted that the al-Bashir regime waged "a campaign of genocide against the 'infidels' of Darfur."[115]

The *Janjaweed* and Sudanese intelligence services subjected members of indigenous African peoples "to severe torture"; specific techniques included dragging by the neck behind horses, gouging out of eyes, and whipping, all while "abusive and insulting terms were used against the detainees, often calling them 'slaves.'" Torture was an integral "part of the systematic and widespread attacks directed at the civilian population conducted by the *Janjaweed* and Government forces." It was also inflicted upon abducted women to prevent their escape. "Extreme mental torture was inflicted on many mothers who saw their children burn alive after they were snatched from their arms by the *Janjaweed* and thrown into the fire."[116]

The government and *Janjaweed* targeted children of African tribes for murder, in violation of the Convention on the Rights of the Child and with the effect of transferring many children from non-Arab African tribes to Arab tribes, which is a form of genocide under the Genocide Convention.[117] Hundreds of children were burned alive or confined in unsanitary internment camps until they passed away from deprivation.[118] In a single

---

108. Human Rights Watch, *Darfur Destroyed: Ethnic Cleansing by Government and Militia Forces in Western Sudan* (May 2004), http://www.hrw.org/reports/2004/sudan0504/5.htm.

109. *See* Human Rights Watch, *Darfur in Flames: Atrocities in Western Sudan* (Apr. 2004), http://www.hrw.org/reports/2004/sudan0404/3.htm ("Darfur's sedentary agriculturalists are generally composed of non-Arab or African ethnic groups known as "Zurga" or blacks, and include groups such as the Fur, Masaalit, Tama, Tunjur, Bergid, and Berti....").

110. *See* ICID Report at ¶ 104.

111. *Id.* at ¶ 511.

112. *Id.* at ¶ 109. *See also* Philip Sherwell, Janjaweed *Vow to Fight Any Intervention by 'Infidels'*, The Daily Telegraph (U.K.), Aug. 15, 2004, http://www.telegraph.co.uk/ ("Across Darfur, Janjaweed have been put into the uniforms of the paramilitary Public Defence Force (PDF) and police in recent weeks as the Arab-dominated authorities attempt to disguise the role of the militia that they created but are now struggling to control.").

113. *See* ICID Report at ¶ 112.

114. *Id.* at ¶ 119 (quoting *Sudanese President Says War Against Outlaws Is Government Priority*, Associated Press, Dec. 31, 2003).

115. Niall Ferguson. *Here's a Challenge: Link the Al-Qaeda Bombs to Poverty and Global Warming*, The Daily Telegraph (UK), July 10, 2005, http://www.telegraph.co.uk/.

116. ICID Report ¶¶ 342, 364–73.

117. *See id.* ¶¶ 221, 341–45, 356, 365, 402, 490.

118. *See id.* ¶¶ 365, 373. "The Commission received many reports of random and/or targeted killing of children, sometimes in horrific circumstances such as by burning or mutilation." *Id.* at ¶ 278.

massacre in 2004, the Sudanese military and the *Janjaweed* murdered 250 civilians, including a "large number of children" torn from their mothers' protective embrace.[119]

Second, under the Srebrenica and Rwanda models of genocide, the intent to destroy a "substantial part" of the group may be satisfied qualitatively, by targeting a group's leaders for execution, and not simply quantitatively by large numbers of victims.[120] The Commission of Inquiry acknowledged this as well, citing an influential U.N. report on the Genocide Convention, which concluded that genocide includes acts directed at "a significant section of a group such as its leadership."[121] The commission could have applied this principle to infer genocide from evidence such as attacks on Kailek, a village in Darfur populated by members of the Fur tribe, where "[l]ocal community leaders" "were called out and shot in front of everyone or alternatively taken away and shot."[122] Similarly, the Sudanese "armed forces in complicity with *Janjaweed*" targeted the elders in the village of Adwa during an attack with a Soviet-era bomber, two helicopter gunships, assault rifles, rocket-propelled grenades, and high-caliber machine guns mounted on vehicles.[123] The pattern was repeated elsewhere:

> *Janjaweed* and Government forces surrounded the town of Deleig, and then went from house to house looking for specific individuals. Many men were arrested and ... transported in a truck, allegedly to [another] area. The truck would come back empty and leave again with a new group of men. Most of those taken away were executed. According to highly reliable eyewitnesses, over 120 men were killed (reportedly mainly intellectuals and leaders).[124]

Third, as a result in part of the Rwanda tribunal's decisions, it is now an accepted statement of international law that mixed political or economic motives do not negate a genocidal intent to destroy a group in whole or in part.[125] This should have disposed of the commission's argument that genocide could not be inferred from the actions of the

119. *Id.* at ¶ 272.

120. *See* Prosecutor v. Milosevic, Trial Chamber, Decision on Motion for Judgement of Acquittal, at ¶ 132 (citing Prosecutor v. Krstić, Appeals Chamber, Judgement, at ¶ 12). *See also* Prosecutor v. Ndindabahizi, Case No. 01-71-T, Trial Chamber, Judgement and Sentence (July 15, 2004), at ¶ 454 ("The requisite intent may be proven by overt statements of the perpetrator or, as with any crime, by drawing inferences from circumstantial evidence of intent. The actual destruction of a substantial part of the group is not a required material element of the offence, but may assist in determining whether the accused intended to bring about that result.") (footnote omitted); Prosecutor v. Jelisić, Appeals Chamber, Judgement, at ¶¶ 64–71 (declaring that a suspect should not be acquitted of genocide charges based on "randomness" of letting some persons under his power survive, where his intent is to kill all the members of one religious group within a particular geographic area such as a town).

121. ICID Report at n.175 (citing Report on Genocide, U.N. Doc. No. E/CN.4/Sub.2/1985/6, at § 29).

122. *Id.* at ¶ 274.

123. *Id.* at ¶ 253.

124. *Id.* at ¶ 275.

125. *See* Prosecutor v. Kayishema & Ruzindana, Trial Chamber, Judgement, at ¶ 161 ("Ruzindana contends further that certain witnesses ascribed to him a personal motive for his actions (such as the elimination of business competitors) and that 'a person who commits a crime, in the quest of a personal goal, such as vengeance or lucre ... is not guilty of genocide but of an ordinary crime'. The Appeals Chamber notes that criminal intent (mens rea) must not be confused with motive and that, in respect of genocide, personal motive does not exclude criminal responsibility providing that the acts proscribed in Article 2(2)(a) through to (e) were committed 'with intent to destroy, in whole or in part a national, ethnical, racial or religious group'.") (footnotes omitted); Prosecutor v. Jelisić, Appeals Chamber, Judgement, at ¶ 49 (noting "'the necessity to distinguish specific intent from motive. The personal motive of the perpetrator of the crime of genocide may be, for example, to obtain personal

Sudanese government because it had mixed motives of ethnic destruction and counter-insurgency warfare.[126] It should also have led the commission to reject the notion that the *Janjaweed* did not manifest a "special intent to kill a member of a group to destroy the group as such" simply because they sometimes steal camels or cattle while shooting or brutally beating their owners, and thereby obtain an economic benefit as well as inflicting an ethnic harm.[127]

Fourth, many of the facts and circumstances which the Rwanda tribunal used to infer genocidal intent on the part of the responsible government[128] are present in Darfur, including:

- "the perpetration of other culpable acts systematically directed against that same group, whether ... committed by the same offender or by others";
- "the large] scale of atrocities committed";
- "the fact of deliberately and systematically targeting victims on account of their membership of a particular group, while excluding the members of other groups";
- "the general political doctrine which gave rise to the acts";
- "the repetition of destructive and discriminatory acts";
- "the perpetration of acts which violate, or which the perpetrators themselves consider to violate the very foundation of the group—acts which are not in themselves covered by the list.... but which are committed as part of the same pattern of conduct"[129]
- "the [large] number of group members affected";[130]
- "the physical targeting of the group or their property";
- "the use of derogatory language toward members of the targeted group";
- "the weapons employed and the extent of bodily injury";
- "the methodical way of planning";
- "the systematic manner of killing"; and
- "the relative proportionate scale of the actual or attempted destruction of a group."[131]

All of these factors from which genocidal intent may be inferred are present in the case of Darfur, including large numbers of affected group members (400,000 dead and 2 million displaced people), widespread bodily injury, the repetition of acts violating the economic and familial foundation of the affected groups, systematic and deliberate targeting

---

economic benefits, or political advantage or some form of power. The existence of a personal motive does not preclude the perpetrator from also having the specific intent to commit genocide.'").

126. ICID Report at ¶ 518.

127. *Id.* at ¶ 517. *See also* Reeves, *Egypt and Darfur* ("Most egregiously, the [Commission of Inquiry] badly confused 'intent' and 'motive' in assessing the issue of 'genocidal intent,' even as international jurisprudence has consistently found genocide to be a crime of intent, with motives that may vary considerably.").

128. Prosecutor v. Kayishema & Ruzindana, Case No. ICTR-95-1-T, Appeals Chamber, Judgement (Reasons) (June 1, 2001), at ¶ 159, http://69.94.11.53/ENGLISH/cases/KayRuz/appeal/3d.htm#_ftnref221.

129. ICID Report, at n.185 (quoting Prosecutor v. Akayesu, Trial Chamber, Judgement, at ¶¶ 523–4).

130. *Id.* (citing Prosecutor v. Musema, Case No. ICTR-96-13-A, Trial Chamber, Judgement and Sentence (Jan. 27, 2000), at ¶ 166; Prosecutor v. Kayishema and Ruzindana, at ¶¶ 93, 527).

131. *Id.* (no longer citing Musema).

of non-Arabs accompanied by the exclusion of Arabs from liability to attack, routine use of language perceived to be derogatory such as "slave" or "black," involvement of the same offenders (i.e. the army, *Janjaweed*, and Popular Defense Force), utilization of weapons designed to inflict mass death such as machine guns and helicopter gunships, an exclusionary and fundamentalist political ideology at the root of the conflict, and methodical planning and execution (including timing surprise attacks at dawn, destroying food supplies, and depriving peoples of shelter).[132]

Fifth, the large-scale or systematic rapes of women belonging to the Fur, Masalit, and Zaghawa tribes living in Darfur fall squarely within the rulings of the Rwanda tribunal that such rapes demonstrate the genocidal intent of their organizers and perpetrators.[133] In particular, rape and sexual assault have destroyed substantial portions of non-Arab ethnic groups in Darfur because they have caused serious bodily or mental harm to members of these groups, prevented the births of children having both parents from within the group, caused births of other children who may be associated with the perpetrators' ethnic group, and inflicted trauma on women and entire families that disrupts the normal process of genetic and cultural reproduction.[134] Just as in Rwanda, for families and communities in Darfur systematic rape has accelerated the process of group destruction on the physical, psychological, and cultural level.[135]

---

132. *See generally id.* ¶¶ 184–402, 507–11. *See especially id.* at ¶ 516 (noting that "in a number of instances villages with a mixed composition (African and Arab tribes) have not been attacked. This for instance holds true for the village of Abaata (north-east of Zelingei, in Western Darfur), consisting of Zaghawa and members of Arab tribes.").

133. *Id.* at ¶ 513.

134. *See* Akayesu, Trial Chamber, Judgement, § 6.3.1 (holding that acts of causing serious bodily or mental harm or preventing births within a group, can constitute genocide assuming that they are committed with the requisite intent, and that "rape can be a measure intended to prevent births when the person raped refuses subsequently to procreate, in the same way that members of a group can be led, through threats or trauma, not to procreate"); see also Prosecutor v. Muhimana, Case No. ICTR-95-1B-T, Trial Chamber I, Judgment and Sentence (Apr. 25, 2005), at ¶¶ 513, 517, http://69.94.11.53/ENGLISH/cases/Muhimana/judgement/muhimana280505.doc (finding that the accused committed genocide by, among other things, raping Tutsi women, and noting that: "During the course of some of the attacks and rapes, the Accused specifically referred to the Tutsi ethnic identity of his victims."); Prosecutor v. Semanza, Case No. ICTR-97-20-T, Trial Chamber III, Judgment and Sentence (May 15, 2003), ¶¶ 476–77, http://69.94.11.53/ENGLISH/cases/Semanza/judgement/6.htm (finding that defendant's "instructions about raping and killing Tutsis, the ethnic group targeted by the widespread attack" resulted in rape of a Tutsi woman that was a crime against humanity because it "was part of the widespread attack against the civilian Tutsi population and that the assailant was so aware."); Katherine MacKinnon, *Defining Rape Internationally: A Comment on Akayesu*, 44 Colum. J. Transnat'l L. 940, 947 (2006) ("survivors of rape in the Serb-led genocide against Bosnia-Herzegovina and Croatia typically understood that they had been raped precisely to destroy their ethnic and religious communities, in acts of sexual violence against women because they were not Serbian"); Kelly Dawn Askin, *Gender Crimes Jurisprudence in the ICTR: Positive Developments*, 3 J. of Int'l Crim. Just. 1007 (2005) (noting that the Rwanda tribunal has described the rape of Tutsi women as a tactic to destroy the group both physically and mentally, especially because many women and girls were murdered after being raped or died from their injuries); Karen Engle, *Feminism and Its (Dis)Contents: Criminalizing Wartime Rape in Bosnia and Herzegovina*, 99 American Journal of International Law 778, 791–92 (2005) (summarizing academic commentary linking rape of Bosnian Muslim women to births of part-Serbian children to Muslim women, dissolution of families, ostracizing of victims, and occasional murder of victims within their own communities); Rosalind Dixon, *Rape as a Crime in International Law: Where to Go from Here?*, 13 European J. of Int'l L. 697, 704 (2002) (describing rape as an element of genocide when it causes forced pregnancy or maternity of children fathered by men who are non-members of the mother's ethnic group).

135. *Cf.* Prosecutor v. Akayesu, Trial Chamber, Judgement, at ¶ 731.

The Commission of Inquiry discovered a pattern of rapes by Sudanese soldiers and *Janjaweed* militia throughout Darfur, that "the rape of individual victims was often multiple, carried out by more than one man, and accompanied by other severe forms of violence, including beating and whipping. In some cases, women were reportedly raped in public, and in some incidents, the women were further berated and called 'slaves' or 'Tora Bora.'"[136] The commission confirmed that Popular Defense Forces led several "attacks on villages in which civilians were killed and rapes were committed."[137] Leaders of victims' groups reported that "extensive rape has been committed by the Government and the *Janjaweed*, including an alleged mass rape of 120 women in July 2003 in Tawilah," and "the Government and the *Janjaweed* have repeatedly abducted women and children," while the fact that "no Arab woman had been raped and no Arab village had been destroyed was evidence that the Government was specifically targeting African tribes." Mass rapes and abductions by the army of *Janjaweed* of young girls and older women of the Fur tribe occurred continuously from 2003 to 2004.[138]

The testimony of the victims in Darfur that the Commission of Inquiry could have obtained from other sources also demonstrates the use of mass rape as a genocidal tactic. Victims report that the circumstances in which they were raped demonstrated an intention to attack their entire ethnic group, rather than abuse them personally. For example, one leader of a victim group told U.N. monitors: "I believe this is an elimination of the black race.... The government is arming some tribes, just Arabs, they go and kill, take the belongings and rape the women."[139] Several women reported to Human Rights Watch that the rapists who attacked them used "vitriolic racial and ethnic slurs" such as "dirty black Nuba" or "slaves."[140] Other women "have reported that their attackers have used racial epithets and declared that they wanted to make more Arab babies."[141]

The systematic rape of Darfur's women also leads to death and/or dire poverty that may increase female mortality rates. Children of *Janjaweed* or other Arab attackers may have lighter skin than the indigenous inhabitants of Darfur and therefore brand their mothers as victims of rape, whose chances of marriage may be reduced, which compounds the poverty and isolation of female refugees from destroyed villages.[142] Amnesty International found that rape was spreading HIV/AIDS, destroying family ties in Darfur, driving non-Arab women into destitution, and creating vulnerability of women to further violence and human rights abuses. Civilians from Darfur find it difficult to access food and water because of *Janjaweed* patrolling for rape.[143] Moreover, rape can damage the reproductive systems of women belonging to non-Arab groups, and children born to rape survivors may be "ostracised by their community" as "a child of the 'enemy', a '*Janjawid*

136. ICID Report at ¶ 333.

137. *Id.* at ¶ 104.

138. *See id.* ¶¶ 221, 243, 253, 333–355.

139. Mindy Belz, *Brotherly Hate*, World Mag., Jan. 24, 2004, http://web.archive.org/web/20040414112434/http://www.worldmag.com/world/issue/01-24-04/international_1.asp.

140. Human Rights Watch, *Sexual Violence and its Consequences among Displaced Persons in Darfur and Chad: A Briefing Paper* (Apr. 12, 2005), http://www.hrw.org/backgrounder/africa/darfur0505.

141. *See* Lydia Polgreen, *Darfur's Babies of Rape Are on Trial from Birth*, N.Y. Times, Feb. 11, 2005, http://www.peacewomen.org/news/Sudan/Feb05/babiesofrape.html.

142. *Id.*

143. *See* Amnesty International, *Stop Violence Against Women: Sudan—Mass Rape, Abduction and Murder*, AI Index: AFR 54/125/2004 (Oct. 12, 2004), http://web.amnesty.org/library/Index/ENGAFR541252004?open&of=ENG-2AF.

child' and women can feel forced to abandon the child."[144] Under Sudanese law, being victimized by rape can even cause women to be indicted for *Zina* crimes (e.g., adultery and fornication), for which the maximum penalty is death by stoning.[145]

Finally, the Commission of Inquiry on Darfur raised the question, without expending the effort to answer it, whether Sudanese political and military officials were criminally culpable for complicity in genocide, attempted genocide, or conspiracy to commit genocide.[146] As indicated above, there is ample evidence from which to conclude that Sudanese officials have given orders to, supplied weapons to, supported, transported, and failed to investigate or punish groups such as the *Janjaweed* and PDF. Failing to analyze such actions as triggering secondary liability for genocide compounded the mistakes that characterized the commission's grossly inadequate analysis of the question of intent. Specifically, the commission cited the Yugoslav tribunal for the idea that genocidal intent is a "stringent requirement[ ]" that must be "unequivocally established," without adopting the tribunal's justification in the same case for convicting an individual who lacked such a personal genocidal intent for "complicity in genocide."[147] In the cited case, *Prosecutor v. Krstić*, the Trial Chamber of the Yugoslav tribunal convicted a general in the Bosnian Serb army for killing thousands of the military-aged Bosnian Muslim men of Srebrenica, even though he did not personally kill or plan to kill the men.[148] The Appeals Chamber convicted Mr. Krstić of aiding and abetting genocide, concluding that a "defendant may be convicted for having aided and abetted a crime which requires specific intent even where the principal perpetrators have not been tried or identified."[149] Having failed to conduct a similar analysis, the Commission of Inquiry's report (and ICC's opinion) remain unpersuasive.

The Sudanese government, immediately "seized on" the commission's conclusions "to try to defuse pressure for sanctions and prosecutions against perpetrators of war crimes." The international press reported that the commission's failure to recognize the genocide in Darfur was "significant because genocide creates a special obligation on governments to act. Under the 1948 Genocide Convention, … all countries 'undertake to prevent and to punish' genocide."[150]

Perhaps feeling the great weight of the Genocide Convention being lifted from its shoulders, the U.S. government did "little" to stop the genocide in Darfur over the next year.[151]

---

144. Amnesty International, *Sudan: Surviving Rape in Darfur*, AI Index: AFR 54/097/2004 (Aug. 9, 2004), http://web.amnesty.org/library/Index/ENGAFR540972004?open&of=ENG-2AF.

145. Amnesty International, *Sudan: Continuing Human Rights Violations*, AI Index: AFR 54/038/2005 (Apr. 13, 2005), http://web.amnesty.org/library/Index/ENGAFR540382005?open&of=ENG-SDN (describing cases where survivors of rape in Darfur "were subsequently charged with Zina (unlawful sexual intercourse …)"); Amnesty International, *Sudan: Death Sentence / Unfair Trial*, AI Index: AFR 54/020/2004 (Feb. 19, 2004), http://web.amnesty.org/library/Index/ENGAFR540202004?open&of=ENG-310 ("The Sudanese Penal Code, which is partly based on interpretation of Islamic Law, allows for penalties such as … deaths by hanging or stoning.… Article 146 of the Penal Code … states that 'whoever commits zina shall be punished with execution by stoning if [the offender] is married or flogging a hundred times if [the offender] is not married.' Zina is defined in the Sudanese Penal Code as sexual intercourse without lawful relationship.").

146. *See* ICID Report at ¶ 520.

147. *Id.* at ¶ 503.

148. Prosecutor v. Krstić, Trial Chamber, Judgement, at ¶ 644.

149. Prosecutor v. Krstić, Appeals Chamber, Judgement, at ¶ 143.

150. *70,000 Dead and 1.6m Homeless, But the UN Says It's Not Genocide*, The Times (U.K.), Feb. 1, 2005, at 29.

151. *See* John Prendergast & Don Cheadle, *Our Friend, an Architect of the Genocide in Darfur*, L.A. Times, Feb. 14, 2006.

A panel established by the U.N. Security Council to consider sanctions against Sudanese leaders failed to adopt sanctions against President al-Bashir, as China, Russia and the Gulf Arab state of Qatar opposed efforts to impose sanctions on any members of Sudan's government.[152] The Bush administration, for its part, "sought to block the inclusion of Sudan's intelligence chief and other government officials from a list of people U.N. sanctions would target...."[153] Other nations provided an even more muted response, few so much as echoing the U.S. finding of genocide.[154]

C. The Darfur Peace Agreement and the Continuing Massacres

1. The Darfur Peace Agreement

Over the past few years, the victims of genocide in Darfur have seen their prospects for compensation improve, albeit only very marginally. On May 5, 2006, two years of diplomacy by the African Union, the U.S., the European Union, and the Arab League culminated in the Darfur Peace Agreement (DPA).[155] Abdel Wahid al-Nur, the leader of the "main part" of the Sudan Liberation Army, including most of its Fur members, and the movement's founder, refused to sign the agreement, characterizing its $30 million compensation fund for genocide victims as paltry, the provisions for disarmament of the *Janjaweed* as toothless, and the continued exclusion of Darfurians from legislative and executive power as intolerable. Minni Minawi, a leader of a mostly Zaghawan faction of the Sudan Liberation Movement, did sign the DPA.[156]

Predictably, the implementation of the DPA has been lacking. The African Union took on the responsibility of overseeing the implementation, but established no plan for disarming the *Janjaweed* and monitoring the decommissioning process. Six months after the signing of the agreement, no disarmament had occurred, the *Janjaweed* were receiving even more weapons than before,[157] and the government of Sudan had breached its promise under the DPA to provide $500 million in reconstruction aid to the Darfur region.[158]

---

152. Colum Lynch, *Sanctions Against Sudanese Officials Sought Over Darfur*, WASH. POST, Feb. 23, 2006, at A20.

153. *A President's Promise*, at A20.

154. *See* Jendayi E. Frazer, Assistant Secretary, USDOS, Testimony before U.S. House Committee on International Relations on Prospects for Peace in Darfur, CQ CONGRESSIONAL TESTIMONY, May 18, 2006 ("The U.S. government has demonstrated bold leadership on Darfur in a number of ways, including the official determination of genocide in September 2004. The United States remains the only nation to make such a determination....").

155. USDOS, *Darfur Peace Agreement* (2006), http://www.state.gov/r/pa/prs/ps/2006/65972.htm.

156. Alex de Waal: *'I Will Not Sign': Alex de Waal Writes About the Darfur Peace Negotiations*, Nov. 30, 2006, LONDON REV. OF BOOKS, http://www.lrb.co.uk/v28/n23/waal01_.html.

157. *See id.*; *see also* Amnesty International, *Sudan: Arms Continuing to Fuel Serious Human Rights Violations in Darfur*; *Sudan Has Failed to Cooperate*; Sudan Presidential Aide Briefs UN, *AU Envoys on Progress of Darfur Peace Process*, BBC MONITORING MIDDLE EAST—POLITICAL, Feb. 13, 2007.

158. *See Backgrounder: Darfur's Peace Proces*, N.Y. TIMES, June 18, 2007, http://www.nytimes.com/glogin?URI=http://www.nytimes.com/cfr/world/slot3_20070618.html&OQ=_rQ3D1&OP=d15a620Q2FeqHPeQ5B_Q27mp__IjeQ27apeq_pQ7BQ5BemQ7B_IQ7DQ22jQ3CQ3CEQ3CM3s)TIQ24Q7B; *Sudan*

Leaders of the Fur people, as well as U.N. and U.S. officials, have questioned the existence and adequacy of the compensation under the DPA.[159] At least one student of the situation in Darfur has noted that, even if $30 million in compensation were paid, that amount divided among the four million people who have suffered from the government's policies would amount to less than $8 per person.[160] He notes that Darfurians living in displaced persons camps felt "tremendous anger" at being asked to accept such a pittance for all that they had suffered.[161] In any event, the compensation is unlikely to be paid. Most of the victims are scattered among refugee and IDP camps and have little capacity to file whatever forms will be required, and the Sudanese government has a long history of establishing tribunals for prosecuting crimes or compensating victims, but allowing very few actual cases to proceed.[162]

2. Denial of Humanitarian Aid in Retaliation for ICC Arrest Warrants

In March 2009, the ICC Pre-Trial Chamber I released an arrest warrant for President al-Bashir for crimes against humanity and war crimes, but not for genocide. In response to the ICC's release of its watered-down arrest warrant, the regime expelled international aid workers, revoked the licenses of many humanitarian aid agencies, and launched a new campaign of torture and enforced disappearances against aid workers and human rights activists. As the U.N. Special Rapporteur on Sudan, Sima Samar, reported:

> 61. The March 2009 expulsions of international NGOs, and revocation of three national NGO licenses has the potential to undermine the rights to health and adequate standard of living for more than one million conflict-affected civilians in Darfur. Reports were immediately received in Zam Zam IDP camp, North Darfur, of water shortages, delays in food distribution and lack of adequate medical services. In Kerenek, West Darfur, medical services, particularly reproductive health, were seriously affected and, as of May 2009, only one doctor was available to treat more than 35,000 beneficiaries. Difficulties in delivery of humanitarian assistance were also reported in Kalma IDP camp, South Darfur, and

---

Not Making Payments to Darfur Fund, SUDAN TRIBUNE, Feb. 18, 2008, http://www.sudantribune.com/spip.php?article26034.

159. *See Nigerian President Warns of "Near Genocide" in Darfur*, BBC MONITORING AFRICA—POLITICAL, Oct. 12, 2006; *Brookings-Bern Project on Internal Displacement Discussion; Subject: International Policy Toward Darfur (remarks of Jean-Marie Guehenno, Undersecretary-General, United Nations, Peacekeeping Operations)*, FEDERAL NEWS SERVICE, Nov. 20, 2006; *Dr. Al-Khalifa Holds UN Responsible for Delay*, SUNA NEWS AGENCY, Nov. 26, 2006; Andrew Natsios, *Special State Department Briefing by the President's Special Envoy on Sudan*, FEDERAL NEWS SERVICE, Nov. 20, 2006 (victims say $30 million is insufficient to rebuild damaged farms and cattle stocks).

160. *VOA News: Peace Eludes Darfur*, US FED NEWS, Nov. 29, 2006.

161. *Id.*

162. *See* Sima Samar, Report of the Special Rapporteur on the Human Rights Situation in the Sudan, U.N. Doc. No. E/CN.4/2006/111, ¶¶ 44–49, 79 (Jan. 11, 2006), http://unbisnet.un.org:8080/ipac20/ipac.jsp?session=1L05392IK7144.21469&profile=bib&uri=full=3100001~!794425~!9&ri=1&aspect=alpha&menu=search&source=~!horizon.

> in Kass, West Darfur, where gaps were reported in the sectors of water and sanitation, and health services.
>
> 62. The impact is also being felt in the area of protection of civilians. The national NGOs whose licenses were revoked were involved in important human rights and humanitarian work in Darfur. The Amel Centre was the major national NGO in North and South Darfur providing legal aid and psychosocial support to victims of human rights violations, with a special focus on torture and rape victims.[163]

The denial of food and medical care to persons living in concentration camps because their homes have been destroyed or they have been forced to flee falls squarely within the conduct element of genocide under the Genocide Convention of "[d]eliberately inflicting on the group conditions of life calculated to bring about its physical destruction in whole or in part...." It also constitutes the crime against humanity of extermination under the Rome Statute of the ICC due to the nexus with systematic attacks on civilians.[164] The crime against humanity of extermination includes "the deprivation of access to food and medicine, calculated to bring about the destruction of part of a population."[165]

D. International Complicity in the Darfur Genocide

For the campaign in Darfur, Sudan's oil revenues secured "expensive bombers, helicopters, and arms supplies" to bomb civilians and equip militias in violation of human rights.[166] The Commission of Inquiry on Darfur noted that the Sudanese air force bombarded villages in Darfur using "Mi-8 helicopters, Mi-24 helicopters and Antonov aircraft...."[167] Figure 11 charts the rise of Sudan's oil exports and its military spending during the genocides against the south and Darfur.

Although oil is not considered to be as important a factor behind the violence in Darfur as it is in the violence surrounding the GNPC oilfield, Darfur is also expected to contain significant oil deposits, which Chinese and British interests have paid millions to explore.[168] After the arrival of Chinese corporations in Sudan, the country switched from

---

163. Samar, *Situation of Human Rights in the Sudan 2009*, at ¶¶61–62, 90.

164. See *Genocide Convention, art. II(c); Prosecutor v. Musema, Trial Chamber, Judgement and Sentence*, at ¶157 ("The Chamber holds that the means of deliberately inflicting on the group conditions of life calculated to bring about its physical destruction, in whole or in part, include subjecting a group of people to a subsistence diet, systematic expulsion from their homes and deprivation of essential medical supplies below a minimum vital standard.").

165. Rome Statute of the ICC, art. 7(2)(b). *See also* Prosecutor v. Kayishema and Ruzindana, Appeals Chamber, Judgement, at ¶¶89, 142–46; Prosecutor v. Zigiranyirazo, Trial Chamber III, Judgement, at ¶¶429–31, 470.

166. Amnesty International, *Sudan: Arming the Perpetrators of Grave Abuses in Darfur* (Nov. 16, 2004), http://web.amnesty.org/library/index/engafr541392004. *See also* Ronan Farrow & Mia Farrow, *The 'Genocide Olympics,'* Wall St. J., Mar. 28, 2007, http://maloof.wordpress.com/2007/04/01/the-genocide-olympics-by-ronan-and-mia-farrow.

167. ICID Report at ¶234; Human Rights Watch, *Sudan: Government Offensive Threatens Darfur Civilians* (Apr. 26, 2006), http://hrw.org/english/docs/2006/04/26/sudan13276.htm; Human Rights Watch, World Report 2006 (2007), http://hrw.org/englishwr2k7/docs/2007/01/11/sudan14715.htm.

168. *See* Chandra Lekha Sriram, *Forum: China, Human Rights and the Sudan*, Jurist, http://jurist.law.pitt.edu/forumy/2007/01/china-human-rights-and-sudan.php; David Leigh & Adrian

Figure 11 Sudan's Oil Exports and Military Spending, 1999–2006

Year	Oil Revenue	Military Spending	Source
1999	$0.61 billion	$242 million	Human Rights Watch
2000	$0.55 billion	$250.9 million	Human Rights Watch
2001	$0.57 billion	$345 million	Human Rights Watch
2002	$1 billion	$312.7 million	Human Rights Watch *The New York Times*
2003	$2 billion	Unknown	*The Times (U.K.)*
2004	$3 billion	Unknown	*Toronto Star*
2005	$4+ billion	$733 million	Oil—ECOS Military—U.S. CIA
2006	$6.3 billion	$733 million	Oil—Foreign Affairs Military—U.S. CIA

being an oil importer to being an exporter of $2 billion in oil annually.[169] Chinese corporations have invested about $10 billion in Sudan's energy industry.[170] Indeed, in 2005, Sudan received more Chinese "investment" than any other African country.[171] About 20% of Sudan's imports originate in China; Sudan's other major trading partners are Saudi Arabia and Japan.[172]

In exchange for its investments and political and military alliance with Sudan, China is securing increasing control over Sudan's oil industry. For example, China bought seventy percent of Sudan's exports in 2006.[173] The CNPC, which is owned by the Chinese government, controls ninety-five percent of Block 6, a particularly large oil concession that

---

Gatton, *Briton Named as Buyer of Darfur Oil Rights*, THE GUARDIAN (U.K.), June 10, 2005, http://www.guardian.co.uk/sudan/story/0,14658,1503470,00.html.

169. *See* European Coalition on Oil in Sudan, *Fact Sheet II.*

170. *See Khartoum Character*, INVESTOR'S BUSINESS DAILY, April 17, 2007; Samuel Hoff, *Genocide in Sudan Must Be Halted Immediately*, THE NEWS JOURNAL (DELAWARE), Apr. 25, 2006, at 7A.

171. *See* Laura Macinnis, *Sudan Top Target for Chinese Investment in Africa*, REUTERS, Mar. 27, 2007, http://africa.reuters.com/wire/news/usnL27206739.html. China's economic ties with Sudan extend beyond Sudanese exports of oil to China. About 20% of Sudan's imports originate in China; Sudan's other major trading partners are Saudi Arabia and Japan. *See* CIA, *Sudan.* Among other China-Sudan trade, China is building the "largest hydro-electric project" in all of Africa in association with Sudan, a project valued at approximately $2 billion and capable of doubling Sudan's electricity supply. Agence France-Presse, *UN Warns Sudan to End Darfur Atrocities,* ABC NEWS ONLINE (AUSTRALIAN BROADCASTING CORPORATION), July 31, 2004, http://www.abc.net.au/; *see also Power of Displacing People*, FIN. TIMES, Mar. 14, 2007, http://archive.gulfnews.com/articles/07/03/14/10110878.html. Saudi Arabia has also exported arms to Sudan in potential violation of U.N. arms embargos. *See* Victor T. Le Vine & Ruth Iyob, *Region Requires Forceful Response*, ST. LOUIS POST-DISPATCH, Oct. 8, 2006, at B6. Like China, it has been a prominent player in the failure by the U.N. Human Rights Council to condemn the genocide in Darfur. *See* Pablo Bachelet, *Group Critical of Rights Panel*, MIAMI HERALD, Jan. 12, 2007; *China, Russia Seek to Block UN report on Darfur*, REUTERS, Mar. 19, 2007, http://www.savedarfur.org/newsroom/ clips/china_russia_seek_to_block_un_report_on_darfur/.

172. CIA, *Sudan.*

173. *See* Small Arms Survey, *Arms, Oil, and Darfur* 7 (2007), http://64.233.169.104/search?q=cache:zcVjwucTnd8J:www.smallarmssurvey.org/files/portal/spotlight/sudan/Sudan_pdf/SIB%25207%2520Arms.pdf.

Image 8 Oil Concessions in Sudan, Circa Fall 2001

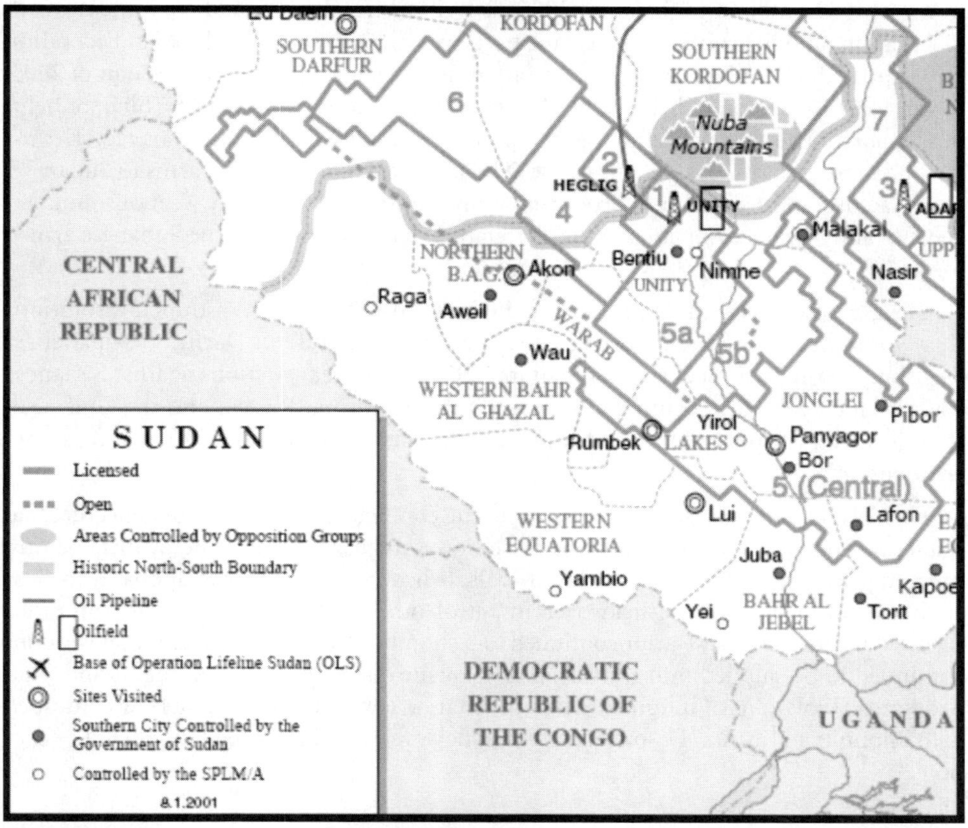

Source: U.S. Agency for International Development

includes territory within the Darfur region[174] and could be worth billions of dollars over time.[175]

Additionally, along with Saudi Arabia, China has exported arms to Sudan in violation of U.N. arms embargos.[176] During the genocide in southern Sudan, indigenous African rebels captured government bases, and found "large numbers of relatively new Chinese arms and ammunition," including tanks, howitzers (artillery), anti-personnel mines, machine guns, and ammunition.[177] Chinese engineers reportedly helped Sudan build factories for tanks, military vehicles, rocket-propelled grenades, and heavy weapons.[178] In defiance of U.N. sanctions implemented in 2005 to prohibit arms sales to the govern-

174. *See* Human Rights Watch, *Sudan, Oil, and Human Rights*, at http://www.hrw.org/reports/2003/sudan1103/sudanprint.pdf; The European Coalition on Oil in Sudan (ECOS), *Oil Development in Northern Upper Nile, Sudan* (2006).

175. *See* U.S. Dep't of Energy, Energy Information Administration, *Sudan* (2007), http://www.eia.doe.gov/emeu/cabs/Sudan/Oil.html.

176. *See* Sriram, *China, Human Rights, and Sudan*; Victor T. Le Vine & Ruth Iyob, *Region Requires Forceful Response*, St. Louis Post-Dispatch, Oct. 8, 2006, at B6. Saudi Arabia has also been a prominent player in the failure by the U.N. Human Rights Council to condemn the genocide in Darfur. *See* Pablo Bachelet, *Group Critical of Rights Panel*, Miami Herald, Jan. 12, 2007.

177. Small Arms Survey, *Arms, Oil, and Darfur*, at 5.

178. *See id.* A report issued after 2006 by a U.N. Panel of Experts documented that the ammunition being used in the Darfur was manufactured either in Sudan or in China. *See id.*

ment of Sudan as well as the SLA,[179] Chinese corporations exported arms and ammunition worth $24 million to Sudan in 2005, as well as aircraft parts and equipment worth $57 million, and helicopter and airplane parts worth $2 million. The Russian Federation also exported $21 million worth of aircraft and associated equipment to Sudan in 2005, as well as $13.7 million of helicopters. Amnesty International condemned China for helping Sudan violate the arms embargo.[180] China even built whole "munitions factories for the Sudanese government, in part to avoid being accused of exporting arms to Sudan."[181] Arms factories near Khartoum produced "ammunition, light infantry weapons, military vehicles and Sudanese versions of the T-55 tank, seen in Darfur, for the Sudanese armed forces."[182]

The Chinese government has repeatedly blocked U.N. Security Council resolutions that would have condemned or intervened against genocide in Darfur.[183] A panel established by the U.N. Security Council in 2005 to consider sanctions against Sudanese leaders failed even to recommend any sanctions, as China, Russia, and the Gulf Arab state of Qatar "opposed efforts to impose sanctions on members of Khartoum's government."[184]

The U.N. arms embargo on the parties to the conflict in Darfur was so ineffectual that it did not stop China from arming Sudanese troops to guard Chinese energy installations, or from providing Sudan with "tanks, aircraft, helicopters and other weapons ... to clear civilians and rebels from oil-fields rich in petroleum."[185] The U.N. sanctions committee reported in late 2007 that Darfur continued to be bombed by the government, that weapons continued to be shipped into Darfur on an airplane disguised as a U.N. flight, and "that widespread violations of international humanitarian law and human rights law continued with impunity in Darfur." Despite its findings, however, the U.N. failed to tighten the sanctions.[186]

---

179. *See* S.C. Res. 1556 (July 30, 2004) (banning arms exports to Darfur); S.C. Res. 1591 (Mar. 29, 2005) (condemning the Government of Sudan's air strikes in Darfur and its failure to disarm "*Janjaweed* militiamen and apprehend and bring to justice *Janjaweed* leaders and their associates who have carried out human rights and international humanitarian law violations and other atrocities," and acting under Chapter VII of the UN Charter to establish an arms embargo against "all the parties to the N'djamena Ceasefire Agreement and any other belligerents in the states of North Darfur, South Darfur and West Darfur," which includes the Government of Sudan unless it seeks prior approval from a sanctions committee to move arms or materiel into Darfur).

180. Amnesty International, *Sudan: Arms Continuing to Fuel Serious Human Rights Violations in Darfur*.

181. Lee & Shalmon, *China's Initiatives in the Middle East*.

182. Amnesty International, *Sudan: Arms Continuing to Fuel Serious Human Rights Violations in Darfur*.

183. *See* Agence France Presse, *China Offers Aid for 'Peaceful Resolution' of Darfur Conflict*, SUDAN.NET, Feb. 2, 2007, http://209.85.165.104/search?q=cache:oyxFbYv_dQoJ:www.sudan.net/news/posted/14064.html.

184. Colum Lynch, *Sanctions Against Sudanese Officials Sought Over Darfur*, WASH. POST, Feb. 23, 2006, at A20.

185. *Blood for Oil*, INVESTOR'S BUS. DAILY, May 2, 2005, http://www.investors.com/editorial/editorialcontent.asp?secid=1501&status=article&id=156744&secure=2799.

186. Security Council Committee Established Pursuant to Resolution 1591, Annual Report, S/2007/779, ¶¶ 13–27 (Dec. 31, 2007), http://daccess-ods.un.org/access.nsf/Get?OpenAgent&DS=S/2007/779&Lang=E&Area=UNDOC.

E. Conclusion

Genocide has occurred in Sudan, most notably in southern Sudan, the Nuba Mountains, and Darfur. Misled by an unreasonably narrow construction placed upon the Genocide Convention by a commission that it established to investigate the atrocities in Darfur, the U.N. Security Council and ICC have failed to act vigorously to put an end to genocide in these regions of Sudan. Applying the Genocide Convention in light of the precedents established by national and international tribunals that have construed it reveals that genocide has occurred in Sudan.

Chapter XVI

Denying the "Other": *al Qaeda*, the Taliban, and Genocidal Terrorism

Al-Qaeda combined ethnoreligious violence with territorial expansionist ambitions that resemble those of other genocidal movements.

—Ben Kiernan[1]

A. The Rise of *al Qaeda* and the Taliban

The rise of *al Qaeda* cannot be understood without reference to the Arab fighters recruited to fight the Soviet Union in Afghanistan and Pakistan during the Cold War, who formed a terrorist organization and the military backbone of the Taliban movement.[2] Abdul Rasul Sayyaf was a Wahhabi fundamentalist sent to Afghanistan in the 1980s by Saudi Arabia to promote its ideology in the context of a Cold War struggle against atheistic communism.[3] By 1980, he had become an Afghan *mujahideen* leader and a mentor to a number of "Afghan Arabs,"[4] including Osama bin Laden, who was working with the CIA at the time building arms depots and tunnel complexes.[5] The CIA supported Pakistani efforts to "recruit radical Muslims from around the world" to fight in Afghanistan.[6] More than 35,000 radicals from Muslim countries, mostly Arabs, signed up to fight in the "holy war,"[7] and 65,000 had "direct contact" with the war.[8] More than 12,000 Arabs and others

1. Blood and Soil, at 598.
2. *See* Ken Silverstein, *Two Panelists Detail Allies' Al Qaeda Ties*, L.A. Times, June 21, 2004, at A12.
3. *See* Rashid, Taliban, at 83, 131.
4. *See* Vincent Cannistraro *A Strike Against Terrorism—and Ourselves?*, Boston Globe, Aug. 23, 1998, at E1 ("At 18, [bin Laden] joined Abd'al Rauf Sayyaf, an Afghan tribal leader who was trained in Saudi Arabia by the Wahabis."). Sayyaf has even been described as a "mentor" to bin Laden. Mary Anne Weaver, Pakistan: in the Shadow of Jihad and Afghanistan 191, 201, 222, 269 (New York: Farrar, Straus & Giroux, 2002).
5. *See* O'Ballance, Afghan Wars, at 245; Rashid, Taliban, at 132; Michael Moran, *Bin Laden Comes Home to Roost: His CIA Ties Are Only the Beginning of a Woeful Story*, MSNBC, Aug. 23, 1998, http://www.msnbc.com.
6. Rashid, Taliban, at 129.
7. *See id.* at 13. *See also* Huntington, The Clash of Civilizations, at 247 (putting number at 25,000).
8. Rashid, Taliban, at 130.

received training in "bomb-making, sabotage and urban guerrilla warfare" in camps the CIA helped build.[9]

As many had predicted, the victory of the Arab and Afghan anti-communist rebels brought civil war, fundamentalist outrages, and thousands of atrocities against civilians. The "Islamic revolution" triumphed in Kabul in April 1992.[10] The military defense of communist Kabul unraveled due to the collapse of the Soviet Union in 1991 and the defection of Afghan communist military commander Rashid Dostum to the rebels in March of 1992.[11] But after the communist regime fell, the war continued. With no communists left to fight, the *mujahideen* leaders were left to wage a bitter struggle for power among themselves, as Najib Allah had predicted in 1990.[12]

The principal parties to the initial bout of post-Cold War conflict in Afghanistan were the *Hizb-i-Islami* of Gulbuddin Hekmatyar, his ally General Dostum, and the *Jamiaat-i-Islami* of Ahmed Shah Massoud and Rabbani. Hekmatyar was a KGB asset who infiltrated the Muslim Brotherhood in Afghanistan prior to the Soviet invasion, and sabotaged Massoud's insurgent forces during the Soviet-Afghan war. Nevertheless, he eventually received, along with Sayyaf, most of the U.S. and Pakistani aid to the Afghan fighters.[13]

Joined by General Dostum's tanks, Hekmatyar's forces finished the job of destroying Afghanistan's housing stock and architectural heritage by rocketing the Afghan capital Kabul into ruins.[14] The warring factions killed about 50,000 Kabulis[15] and committed many atrocities against civilians.[16] Almost 20,000 Afghans were killed or injured during the fighting in 1993 alone.[17] The *mujahideen* perpetrated frequent massacres and "indiscriminate killing," as well as "rape, torture and looting."[18] In 1994, the United Nations reported that Kabul, spared the type of bombing to which Kandahar had been subjected by the Soviets, had become "the most destroyed city in Afghanistan."[19]

The victorious fundamentalist armies subjected Afghan women to some of the worst treatment in Afghan history.[20] The State Department reported that the *mujahideen* were responsible for "innumerable cases of rape."[21] Human Rights Watch described 1992–1995 as the worst period in Afghan history, replete with "mass rapes" and the indiscriminate

---

9. Jason Burke, *Frankenstein the CIA Created*, The Guardian (U.K.), Jan. 17, 1999, http://www.guardian.co.uk/world/1999/jan/17/yemen.islam.

10. *See* Felix Ermacora, Introduction to the Ninth Report of the Special Rapporteur of the Commission on Human Rights on the Human Rights Situation in Afghanistan, ¶ 31 at 9, U.N. Doc. No. A/C.3/48/SR.40 (Nov. 23, 1993), http://www.unhchr.ch/Huridocda/Huridoca.nsf/0/c3e13fa375d96e7a80256715003d714d?Opendocument.

11. *See* Vogelsang, The Afghans, at 323–24.

12. *See* John F. Burns, *Afghan's Chief Vows to Stay in Office*, N.Y. Times, May 4, 1990, at A3.

13. This is according to a U.S. congressional report on terrorism from 1990 that was leaked to the Pakistani media in 1992. *See* Imran Akbar, *'Gulbuddin Hekmatyar had links with KGB,'* The News Int'l (Pakistan), Oct. 8, 1992.

14. *See* Ewans, Afghanistan, at 180.

15. *See* Michael Griffin, *A Gruesome Record*, The Guardian (U.K.), Nov. 16, 2001.

16. O'Ballance, Afghan Wars, at 241.

17. *See* USDOS, *Afghanistan Human Rights Practices, 1993* (Jan. 31, 1994), http://dosfan.lib.uic.edu/ERC/democracy/1993_hrp_report/93hrp_report_sasia/Afghanistan.html.

18. Felix Ermacora, *Final Report on the Situation of Human Rights in Afghanistan*, ¶ 37 at 10, U.N. Doc. E/CN.4/1995/64, http://www1.umn.edu/humanrts/commission/country51/64.htm.

19. Ermacora, *The Situation of Human Rights in Afghanistan*.

20. *See 10,000 Killed in 8 Months in Kabul*, The Frontier Post (Pakistan) Nov. 28, 1993.

21. USDOS, *Afghanistan Human Rights Practices, 1994* (Feb. 1995), http://dosfan.lib.uic.edu/ERC/democracy/1994_hrp_report/94hrp_report_sasia/Afghanistan.html.

slaughter of civilians.[22] *Mujahideen* fighters kidnapped many Afghan women for purposes of sexual slavery, as a "method of intimidating vanquished populations and of rewarding soldiers."[23] "Thousands of women and girls were systematically raped by armed thugs, and many committed suicide to avoid being sexually assaulted by them."[24]

While the soldiers of the victorious rebel armies ran amok, discipline was reserved for Afghan women. In 1994, the Supreme Court of the Islamic state of Afghanistan issued a series of rulings requiring a woman to "wear a full-body veil"[25] and stating that she "must not leave her house without her husband's permission," and "must not look at strangers."[26] Other courts issued rulings ordering that women be stoned to death for adultery or other crimes.[27]

The "valiant and courageous Afghan freedom fighters" (Reagan's phrase[28]) also persecuted religious minorities viciously.[29] On February 11, 1993, the military forces of President Rabbani and his ally Abdul Rasul Sayyaf occupied a Kabul suburb populated largely with minority Shi'a Hazaras. Their armies killed "'up to 1,000 civilians', beheading old men, women, children and even their dogs...."[30]

Prior to the Taliban revolution, Afghanistan under *mujahideen* rule became infamous for training and harboring international terrorists. Ramzi Yousef, who masterminded the 1993 World Trade Center bombing, had fought under the command of Abdul Rasul Sayyaf, the junior partner in Rabbani's *mujahideen* government.[31] The U.S. government issued a report in the 1990s in which it cited Saudi-backed *mujahideen* commander Sayyaf for "continuing to harbor and train potential terrorists." Sayyaf's faction maintained close contact throughout the 1990s with Osama bin Laden, and welcomed him back to Afghanistan in 1996.[32]

---

22. Charles M. Sennott, *A Dark Side to the Northern Alliance: Afghanistan's Anti-Taliban Militias Share History of Human Rights Abuse*, BOSTON GLOBE Oct. 6, 2001, at A1. Mariam Rawi, *Rule of the Rapists*, THE GUARDIAN (U.K.), Feb. 12, 2004, http://www.guardian.co.uk/comment/story/0,3604,1146134,00.html.

23. *See* Amnesty International, *Women in Afghanistan: A Human Rights Catastrophe* (Nov. 3, 1995), http://www.amnesty.org/ailib/intcam/afgan/afg5.htm.

24. Rawi, *Rule of the Rapists.*

25. Syed Saleem Shahzad, *Empty Words of War*, ASIA TIMES (Hong Kong), Nov. 27, 2001, http://www.atimes.com/c-asia/CK27Ag02.html. *See also* Sonali Kolhatkar, *Commentary: The Impact of U.S. Intervention on Afghan Women's Rights*, 17 BERKELEY WOMEN'S L.J. 12, 16 (2002) ("The Mujahadeen [] instituted laws banning alcohol and requiring that women be veiled. Both of these new crimes were punishable by floggings, amputations, and public executions."); USDOS, *Afghanistan Human Rights Practices, 1994* (Rabbani government imposed a mandatory "strict, conservative Islamic dress code"); *Killing for a Cause*, CALGARY HERALD (CANADA), Aug. 21, 1992, at A4 (Rabbani government "forced women to wear veils").

26. USDOS, *Afghanistan Human Rights Practices, 1994.*

27. *See id.*

28. Ronald Reagan, *Proclamation 5034—Afghanistan Day, 1983* (Mar. 21, 1983), http://www.reagan.utexas.edu/resource/speeches/1983/32183d.htm.

29. USDOS, *Country Fact Sheet: Afghanistan*, DEP'T OF STATE DISPATCH NO. 23 (June 6, 1994).

30. Griffin, *A Gruesome Record*; CHRISTINA LAMB, THE SEWING CIRCLES OF HERAT 20 (London: HarperCollins, 2002). *See also Grand Council to Begin Historic Work*, at A4; *Loya Jirga Defuses Battle of Good and Evil*, DEUTSCHE PRESSE-AGENTUR, June 12, 2002 ("Backed by hundreds of Arab recruits," Sayyaf "spearheaded a vicious campaign against the country's Shia Hazara minority.").

31. *See Empowered Through Violence: The Reinventing of Islamic Extremism, in* THE AGE OF TERROR: AMERICA AND THE WORLD AFTER SEPTEMBER 11, at 39 (Strobe Talbott et al. eds., New York: Basic Books, 2001). *See also* LAMB, THE SEWING CIRCLES OF HEART, at 21.

32. *See* BURKE, AL QAEDA, at 20–21, 66, 125, 145. *See also* LAMB, THE SEWING CIRCLES OF HEART, at 21.

Almost three years after the fall of the communist government, the *mujahideen* had failed to establish an effective central government or national judicial system.[33] Instead of establishing law and order, their forces were killing, raping, and looting at will, and had "blocked food and medical supplies desperately needed by [the Afghan] people."[34] An estimated 100,000 Afghans died in Kabul alone prior to the Taliban takeover in 1996.[35] All told, about 400,000 Afghan civilians died in the civil wars and humanitarian disasters of the 1990s.[36]

In early 1994, according to their own legend, a group of former *mujahideen* fighters and Islamic students, or Taliban, joined together to fight the "Muslims who had gone wrong," and started by freeing young boys and girls from local warlords who had kidnapped them for rape.[37] As the future President of Afghanistan, Hamid Karzai, testified before Congress, the "Taliban emerged when Afghans were desperately looking for a savior," and their "emergence was supported by the majority of the Afghan people" who hoped that they would "end the bloodshed" and bring "peace and stability."[38] The Taliban selected Muhammad Omar as their leader, a village mullah from a backward area of southern Afghanistan who had fought in the American-backed *jihad* against the post-Soviet Afghan government of Najib Allah.[39]

The U.S. and its allies in Pakistan and Saudi Arabia initially supported the Taliban movement.[40] The U.S. State Department praised the Taliban to Congress and argued publicly as late as 1996 that there was "nothing objectionable" about their fundamentalist policies.[41]

The generous international military, financial, and diplomatic aid to the Taliban transformed a ragtag gang of fighters into a sophisticated army with tanks, artillery, bombers, and an intelligence capability. U.S. allies Saudi Arabia and Pakistan also provided direct support to the *al Qaeda* brigades fighting alongside the Taliban and planning foreign terrorist attacks, including financial, intelligence, and military assistance.[42] The Taliban owed much of their military sophistication and the speed of their victory to skilled professionals in Pakistani intelligence, who trained the Taliban and provided them with thousands of Pakistani troops, 12,000 assault rifles and ammunition, and fuel and maintenance for tanks, artillery, and aircraft.[43]

With fresh infusions of foreign financing and manpower for each new offensive, the Taliban defeated every major *mujahideen* commander. The Taliban captured Kandahar in 1994 largely by bribing local commanders with over $1.5 million probably provided by

---

33. *See* USDOS, *Afghanistan Human Rights Practices, 1994*; EWANS, AFGHANISTAN, at 179.

34. USDOS, *Afghanistan Human Rights Practices, 1994. See also* Dan Chapman, *Many Afghans Haunted by Northern Alliance's Past*, THE ATLANTA JOURNAL-CONSTITUTION, Nov. 12, 2001, at 8A.

35. *See* EWANS, AFGHANISTAN, at 186.

36. *See* Scott Baldauf, *Life Under Taliban Cuts Two Ways*, CHRISTIAN SCI. MONITOR, Sept. 20, 2001, at 1.

37. RASHID, TALIBAN, at 25. *See also id.* at 115.

38. Hamid Karzai, *The Taliban: Engagement or Confrontation?*, Statement to Hearing Before the Committee on Foreign Relations United States Senate, 106th Cong., 2d Sess., S. Hrg. 106–868 (July 20, 2000).

39. *See* RASHID, TALIBAN, at 23.

40. *See id.* at 46, 158–59, 166, 176–177. *See also* Howard Schneider, *Saudi Missteps Helped Bin Laden Gain Power*, WASH. POST FOREIGN SERVICE, Oct. 15, 2001, at A01.

41. MAGNUS & NABY, AFGHANISTAN, at 184; *see* RASHID, TALIBAN, at 158–59, 166.

42. *See* Josh Meyer, *2 Allies Aided Bin Laden, Say Panel Members*, L.A. TIMES, June 20, 2004.

43. *See* EWANS, AFGHANISTAN, at 183; RASHID, TALIBAN, at 27–28, 39.

Saudi Arabia via Pakistan.[44] They doled out more cash to buy control of Uruzgan and Zabul provinces,[45] and occupied Herat with tens of thousands of Pakistani recruits and "arms, ammunition, and vehicles provided by Pakistan and Saudi Arabia."[46] In 1996, Saudi and Pakistani intelligence orchestrated the triumph of the Taliban revolution by helping ensure the fall of Kabul and Jalalabad.[47] As many as 8,000 more residents of Kabul died in the fighting and the ensuing Taliban atrocities.[48] In response, many of the *mujahideen* leaders whose factions had opened the way for the Taliban revolution by abusing the Afghan population for years formed the Northern Alliance.[49] But angered by the looting and routine violence against civilians that had characterized *mujahideen* rule, some Kabul residents initially welcomed the Taliban, even after thousands of Kabulis died in the battle for the city.[50]

The Taliban persecuted the Shi'a Muslims, who then made up as much as 20% of the Afghan population, even more brutally than had the *mujahideen* under Rabbani and Sayyaf.[51] A mutiny in Mazar-i-Sharif opened the door to Taliban occupation of that city; although 3,000 Taliban died in an uprising that followed, the Taliban retook the city in 1998, backed by Pakistani intelligence officers and even Pakistani troops.[52] The Taliban slaughtered up to 8,000 civilians in a frenzy of killing and rape directly mostly at the Shi'a Hazara.[53] The Hazara holdout of Bamiyan was the last major city to fall, with more mass murders of Shi'a the result, including of hospital patients roused from their beds.[54] The post-Taliban governor of Bamiyan has estimated that 20,000 Hazaras and other Shi'a died in this way.[55] Iran mobilized its army to intervene against the massacres and systematic rape of Shi'a civilians, but backed down under pressure from the U.N. Security Council.[56] The genocidal killing continued into 2001, as Pakistan delivered military aid to the Taliban in violation of U.N. sanctions.[57]

Saudi Arabia and some Pakistanis seized on the Taliban as a vehicle for promoting fundamentalist ideals.[58] Saudi Arabia, the primary backer of the Taliban along with Pakistan, served as the model for the Taliban state. Taliban leader Mullah Omar used to say, "Whatever Saudi Arabia wants me to do, I will do."[59] Saudi Arabia in the 1990s remained a fundamentalist monarchy, whose constitution demands allegiance to its founding king and

---

44. *See* Ewans, Afghanistan, at 184. The Pakistani Interior Minister even called the Taliban "our boys" and boasted that he was responsible for their victory in Kandahar. *See* Rashid, Taliban, at 27–29.

45. *See* Vogelsang, The Afghans, at 327; Rashid, Taliban, at 33.

46. Rashid, Taliban, at 39.

47. *See id.* at 48.

48. *See* O'ballance, Afghan Wars, at 243.

49. *See id.* at 52–53.

50. *See* Rashid, Taliban, at 51.

51. *See* UNHCR, *Update of the Situation in Afghanistan* ¶ 6, at 5.

52. *See* Rashid, Taliban, at 74–6.

53. *See id.* at 58–60, 72–74; O'ballance, Afghan Wars, at 244. The Pakistanis allocated a budget of $5 million for this operation, and the Saudis contributed as well. *See* Rashid, Taliban, at 72, 138.

54. *See id.* at 76; Gizabi, *Human Rights and the Role of Women in Afghanistan.*

55. *See* David Filipov, *Reconstruction: Hazaras Hold Key Role After Taliban Destruction*, Boston Globe, Feb. 14, 2002, http://www.afgha.com/?af=article&sid=12366.

56. *See* Rashid, Taliban, at 76.

57. *See id.* at ix–x.

58. *See* Rashid, Taliban, at 197–206, 211.

59. Steve Coll, Ghost Wars: The Secret History of the CIA, Afghanistan, and bin Laden, from the Soviet invasion to September 11, 2001, at 295 (New York, NY: The Penguin Press, 2004).

his "children's children" in the name of religion.[60] Its government tortures members of religious minorities and its religious police administer beatings to women who reveal their faces, hair, or bodies in public.[61] The Saudi government helped create the Taliban, encouraged them to give refuge to bin Laden, and tutored them in theocracy.[62] The Saudi Ministry for the Propagation of Virtue and the Prevention of Vice trained a similar Taliban agency in enforcing Saudi-style laws, including the near-total covering of women.[63]

The Taliban aimed to install a government and legal system that would revive a life like pious Muslims had lived "1,400 years ago."[64] The attorney general of the Taliban declared: "The Constitution is the Sharia so we don't need a constitution." The Taliban believed that the principal purpose of the anti-Soviet *jihad* had been the establishment of Sharia law, and indeed that is how the *mujahideen* leaders who had been fighting for Sharia from bases in Pakistan even prior to the communist coup in 1978 explained their war at the time.[65]

The resulting system of Taliban law systematically destroyed any manifestation of culture or religion that did not reflect Wahhabi orthodoxy. It featured severe criminal sanctions, enforced with great capriciousness and corruption, against any activities viewed as deviant, sinful, or otherwise harmful. The Taliban's prohibitions addressed activities prohibited by religious tradition as harmful to the person (drugs and alcohol, gambling, and usury); sexuality and Western fashions (music and dancing, British or American hairstyles, the shaving of men's beards, women's high-heeled shoes, and fashion magazines); "idolatry" (photographs, paintings, statues, and sorcery); and other relatively harmless activities that might lead to gambling or distract from prayer (television, sports, kite-flying and the keeping of birds as pets).[66] Proving the old adage that the law often falls behind advances in technology, however, the Taliban did not prohibit use of the Internet until July 2001, half a decade after banning kite-flying.[67]

The mode of enforcement of the Taliban's prohibitions proved as uncompromising as the bans themselves. Torture by various methods was routine and vicious under the Taliban. Violations of the Taliban dress code and inappropriate male-female contact were

---

60. *See* Const. of Saudi Arabia, art. 1, 5–8, http://www.the-saudi.net.

61. *See* Harvey Morris, *Saudi Arabia 'Torturing Christians'; Expatriates and Shia Minority Victimised in State-Sanctioned Persecution, Says Amnesty International*, INDEPENDENT (U.K.), Sept. 14, 1993, at 10; Mark Lattimer, *Letter: Plight of Saudi Women*, INDEPENDENT (U.K.), Oct. 24, 2000, at 2 ("Women in Saudi Arabia cannot move freely, appear in public without a hijab or gain equal access to education or employment. The al-Mutawa'een (religious police) aggressively target women, frequently beating them in the streets for perceived infractions of moral codes relating to dress or behaviour."); Robert Fisk, *Saudi Torture of Women Rampant, Says Amnesty*, INDEPENDENT (U.K.), Sept. 27, 2000, at 14 ("Amnesty International has turned its humanitarian searchlight on Saudi Arabia's justice 'system'—the quotation marks are essential—demanding to know why the kingdom's judiciary and regal authorities should subject women to arbitrary detention, arrest, flogging and execution."). In 2002, 15 Saudi girls burned to death in a fire in their dormitory after the religious police refused to allow them to leave the building without being completely covered. *See Palpitations at the Kingdom's Heart*, THE ECONOMIST, Aug. 22, 2002, http://www.economist.com/world/africa/displayStory.cfm?story_id=1291310.

62. *See* COLL, GHOST WARS, at 341–42.

63. *See id.* at 297, 613.

64. RASHID, TALIBAN, at 43.

65. *See id.* at 51, 85, 106–7.

66. *See id.* at 29, 105, 115, 218–19; LAMB, THE SEWING CIRCLES OF HERAT, at 283.

67. *See* RASHID, TALIBAN, at xii, 219.

cause for being beaten black and blue with clubs or rifle butts.[68] Implementing Taliban law required stoning adulterers and amputating the hands of criminals, medieval punishments which had been abandoned by most Muslim countries.[69]

While Afghan men suffered conscription into the Taliban army,[70] bitter fighting in the north of the country,[71] imprisonment or murder for their religious or political affiliation,[72] and denial of virtually any access to entertainment or unrelated members of the opposite sex, they enjoyed some ability to go to school, find a job, and travel. The Taliban kept Afghan women, by contrast, largely shuttered indoors.[73] Upon taking power in Kandahar in 1994, the Taliban forbade the education of girls and the employment of most women outside of their homes.[74] After becoming the rulers of most of Afghanistan in 1996, the Taliban's religious police decreed that women must wear all-covering *burqas*, which many Afghan women could not even afford (as they cost about two months' wages), effectively sentencing them to house arrest.[75] The Taliban ordered women to stay in their homes as much as possible, ended the rudimentary female education and employment that the *mujahideen* had allowed to continue.[76]

The Taliban allowed Afghan women to see only female doctors, while banning women from practicing medicine.[77] The result was one of the highest maternal mortality rates anywhere in the world.[78] By 2001, average life expectancy was only 40 years, 70% of Afghans were malnourished, and more infants died in childhood and more mothers died in childbirth than in almost any other country ever recorded in human history.[79] Mean-

---

68. *See, e.g.*, *id.* at 15–18.

69. *See* RASHID, TALIBAN, at 93; EWANS, AFGHANISTAN, at 184, 187.

70. *See* Pamela Constable, *Far From Prosperity: The Taliban Is Gone, But Drought and Corruption Have Hit Hard*, WASHINGTON POST Feb. 17, 2004, at C1. *See also* LAMB, SEWING CIRCLES OF HERAT, at 10–11.

71. Thousands of Taliban conscripts and troops died in battles for one northern city, Mazar-i-Sharif, many being roasted in metal containers in the desert into which they were packed. *See* RASHID, TALIBAN, at 59, 63.

72. *See* Physicians' Committee for Human Rights, *The Taliban's War on Women—A Health and Human Rights Crisis in Afghanistan*, "Overview" (1999), *at* http://www.phrusa.org/research/health_effects/exec.html ("Thousands of men have been taken prisoner, arbitrarily detained, tortured, and many killed and disappeared.").

73. *See* RASHID, TALIBAN, at 106, 110, 218.

74. *See id.* at 29; LAMB, THE SEWING CIRCLES OF HERAT, at 81.

75. *See* Anastasia Telesetsky, *Recent Developments: In the Shadows and Behind the Veil: Women in Afghanistan Under Taliban Rule*, 13 BERKELEY WOMEN'S L.J. 293, 296 (1998).

76. *See* LAMB, THE SEWING CIRCLES OF HERAT, at 30–31, 162. Even before the Taliban took power, more than 90% of girls and 60% of boys in Afghanistan were illiterate. *See* RASHID, TALIBAN, at 107.

77. *See* RASHID, TALIBAN, at 217–18; Robert Scheer, *Bush's Faustian Deal With the Taliban*, L.A. TIMES, May 22, 2001, http://www.robertscheer.com/1_natcolumn/01_columns/052201.htm.

78. *See* Physicians' Committee for Human Rights, *The Taliban's War on Women.*

79. *See* World Bank, *Afghanistan: Facts and Figures at a Glance* (Apr. 2002), *at* http://lnweb18.worldbank.org/SAR/sa.nsf/Attachments/dat/$File/AfgData.pdf; *Afghanistan: Government Set to Tackle Maternal Mortality*, U.N. IRIN, May 1, 2003, *at* http://www.irinnews.org/report.asp?ReportID=33189&SelectRegion=Central_Asia&SelectCountry=AFGHANISTAN.report.asp?ReportID=33819&SelectRegion=Central_Asia&SelectCountry=AFGHANISTAN; Amnesty International, *Afghanistan: Constitution Fails Women* (Nov. 26, 2003), *at* http://web.amnesty.org/library/Index/ENGASA110272003?open&of=ENG-AFG; *Plight of "Forgotten Women" Needing Health Care in Rural Areas*, U.N. IRIN (May 14, 2004), *at* http://www.irinnews.org/report.asp?ReportID=39783&SelectRegion= Central_Asia&SelectCountry=AFGHANISTAN; Physicians for Human Rights, *Women's Health and Human Rights in Afghanistan* (2001), *at* http://www.phrusa.org/campaigns/afghanistan/Afghan_report_toc.html.

while, between the 1980s and the 2000s, up to 200,000 Afghan civilians were killed or maimed by land mines, many of which were laid by the Soviet Union. About $400 million was spent after 1989 on clearance.[80]

B. September 11 and Terrorism as Genocide

Prior to the 2001 attack on the World Trade Center and targets in Washington, DC, the White House Presidential Daily Brief had documented a serious risk of hijackings of U.S. aircraft by forces loyal to Osama bin Laden.[81] Warnings of an impending attack had poured in from all corners of the globe, from the CIA, Federal Bureau of Investigation, and multiple foreign governments.[82] The Federal Aviation Administration was told "that associates with Usama Bin Ladin in the 1990s were interested in hijackings and the use of an aircraft as a weapon."[83] In an act of mass murder, the hijacking of two aircraft on the morning of September 11, and their crashing into the towers of the World Trade Center killed nearly 2,000 civilians, mostly above the floors into which the planes hit.[84] Many of those who did not die directly were either horribly burned, or had their lungs scarred by smoke and chemicals.[85]

The definition of terrorism, at least in some legal systems, overlaps to a significant degree with the definition of genocide promulgated by national and international criminal tribunals. At the time of the 9/11 attacks, U.S. law defined terrorism to include violent and illegal activity that is intended to intimidate or coerce a civilian population or government.[86] As noted in Chapters II and III, ethnic cleansing is equated with genocide by the U.N. General Assembly and international criminal tribunals created by the U.N. Security Council, and includes the mass intimidation of a group, by threat or use of vio-

80. *See* Abdul Rauf Liwal, *Loan or War Reparations: Kabul, Moscow Lock Horns*, Pajhwok Afghan News, Aug. 23, 2004.

81. *See* The National Commission on Terrorist Attacks Upon the United States, The 9/11 Commission Report: Final report of the National Commission on Terrorist Attacks Upon the United States (New York: W.W. Norton, 2004).

82. *See* Coll, Ghost Wars, at 131–32, 134–37, 144–56, 228–31, 238–39, 294–95, 297, 327, 341, 385, 439, 555; Steve Fainaru & James Grimaldi, *FBI Knew Terrorists Were Using Flight Schools,* Wash. Post, Sept. 22, 2001, http://www.washingtonpost.com; Phillip Shenon, *FBI Ignored Attack Warning: Flight Instructor Told Agency of Terror Suspect's Plan*, S.F. Chron., Dec. 22, 2001, http://www.sfgate.com; U.S. Senate, Select Committee on Intelligence, Joint Inquiry into Intelligence Community Activities Before and After the Terrorist Attacks of September 11, 2001 (Washington, D.C. 2004), http://www.gpoaccess.gov.

83. Staff of the National Commission on Terrorist Attacks Upon the United States, *Staff Statement No. 3: The Aviation Security System and the 9/11 Attacks* (Jan. 27, 2004), http://www.9-11commission.gov/.

84. *See* The National Commission on Terrorist Attacks Upon the United States, The 9/11 Commission Report, at 250–300 (2004).

85. *See* Chayes, *Ground Zero Workers Rally to Demand Reparations for Medical Care,* N.Y. Sun, Sept. 7, 2006, http://www.nysun.com/; Chen, *Ground Zero: The Most Dangerous Workplace,* The New Standard, Jan. 24, 2005, http://newstandardnews.net/.

86. *See* 18 U.S.C. § 3077 (West 2000).

lence, to flee its homeland.[87] In New York, 72,000 people were displaced from their homes and communities by terrorism on 9/11.[88]

Even under the assumption that genocide requires a massacre of thousands of people, rather than their displacement by force or intimidation, the 9/11 terrorists committed genocide. Although a death toll of 3,000 is smaller than that of the Srebrenica massacre, it represents a larger toll than some local massacres in Rwanda, such as that leading to the conviction of Jean-Paul Akayesu in 1998.[89] Moreover, it was only the heroic efforts of firemen, police officers, and other victims that saved many of the 16,400 to 18,800 civilians occupying the World Trade Center from being crushed or immolated. The attackers' approach threatened to kill 50,000 or even 100,000 people in the World Trade Center and hundreds of thousands more buried by the buildings' collapse, or incinerated by the spreading urban blaze.[90] Many survivors and persons in the area were seriously injured by inhaling particles of lead, mercury, arsenic, asbestos, concrete, glass, and dioxin.[91]

Osama bin Laden, the terrorist leader confirmed as being behind the attacks by a video released in December 2001,[92] also clearly had a genocidal intent to kill all members of a national group. On the video, he remarked that Muslims were obligated to kill non-believers until the ultimate victory of fundamentalist Islam.[93] His declaration of war on Americans called upon his allies to "kill the Americans and their allies—civilians and military," and "to kill the Americans ... wherever and whenever" they are found. Also in

87. *Compare* Final Report of United Nations Commission of Experts to the Security Council, S/1994/674, at 33 (May 27, 1994), at III.B (ethnic cleansing includes not simply the extermination of an ethnic group, but also "rendering an area ethnically homogenous by using force or intimidation to remove persons of given groups from the area...."), *with* U.N. Doc. A/RES/47/121 (Dec. 18, 1992) (ethnic cleansing is a "form of genocide"); U.N. Doc. A/RES/48/153 (Dec. 20, 1993); U.N. Doc. A/RES/49/205 (Dec. 23, 1994); U.N. Doc. A/RES/50/192 (Dec. 22, 1995); U.N. Doc. A/RES/51/115 (Dec. 12, 1996); *Bosnia and Herzegovina, in* ENCYCLOPEDIA OF GENOCIDE AND CRIMES AGAINST HUMANITY, at 1076; SHAW, WHAT IS GENOCIDE?, at 50, 177 (citing G.A. Res. 47/121 (1992). For application of the concept to Iraq, see, for example, Nina Shea, *Iraq's Future as a Tolerant, Democratic Nation Is at Stake*, NATIONAL REV. (Oct. 14, 2004), http://www.nationalreview.com/comment/shea200410140830.asp.

88. *See, e.g.*, Angelina Cappiello, *FEMA Furor As Deadline Approaches*, NEW YORK POST, June 24, 2002, at 9.

89. *See* James D. Fry, *Terrorism As a Crime Against Humanity and Genocide: The Backdoor to Universal Jurisdiction,* 7 UCLA J. OF INTERNATIONAL LAW AND FOREIGN AFFAIRS 169, 193 (2002) (noting that "Akayesu was convicted of genocide for his responsibility in the killing of '[a]t least 2,000 Tutsis ... in Taba between April 7 and the end of June, 1994, while he was still in power.' ").

90. *See, e.g.*, THE NATIONAL COMMISSION ON TERRORISTS ATTACKS UPON THE UNITED STATES, THE 9/11 COMMISSION REPORT: FINAL REPORT OF THE NATIONAL COMMISSION ON TERRORIST ATTACKS UPON THE UNITED STATES 310–16 (New York: W.W. Norton, 2004).

91. *See, e.g.*, THE NATIONAL COMMISSION ON TERRORISTS ATTACKS UPON THE UNITED STATES, THE 9/11 COMMISSION REPORT: FINAL REPORT OF THE NATIONAL COMMISSION ON TERRORIST ATTACKS UPON THE UNITED STATES 316 (New York: W.W. Norton, 2004); E. Barry, *Lost in the Dust of 9/11,* L.A. TIMES, Oct. 14, 2006, http://www.latimes.com; M. Chayes, *Ground Zero Workers Rally to Demand Reparations for Medical Care,* NEW YORK SUN, Sept. 7, 2006, http://www.nysun.com.

92. *See* Ben Fenton, *New Video Clues to bin Laden Hijack Link,* THE DAILY TELEGRAPH (U.K.), Dec. 22, 2001, http://www.telegraph.co.uk/news/worldnews/asia/afghanistan/1366082/New-video-clues-to-bin-Laden-hijack-link.html; Rupert Cornwell, *Al-Qa'ida Video Has Names of Two More Hijackers,* THE INDEPENDENT (U.K.), Dec. 22, 2001, http://www.independent.co.uk/news/world/americas/alqaida/video-has-names-of-two-more-hijackers-620914.html.

93. *See* Fenton, *New Video Clues to bin Laden Hijack Link.*

1998, he stated clearly that he did not "differentiate between those dressed in military uniforms and civilians."[94]

Genocidal intent against Americans and pro-American groups extended beyond the core leadership of *al Qaeda* and its terrorist front line. The video released by the U.S. confirming bin Laden's responsibility for 9/11 contained an account by the terrorist leader "of the enthusiastic reception in Saudi clerical circles to the successful attack." A prominent cleric appeared with bin Laden on the video itself, and apparently had entered Afghanistan with the aid of Saudi officials.[95] In 2003, Senator Bob Graham, the co-chairman of a congressional committee investigating the 9/11 attacks, told an American cable network that 28 censored pages of a classified intelligence report showed that "high officials of a foreign government 'made substantial contributions to the support and well-being of two of these terrorists and facilitated their ability to plan, practice and then execute the tragedy of Sept. 11.'"[96] He remarked that declassifying "the currently censored pages" would "allow the American people to make their own judgment about who are our true friends and allies in the war on terrorism."[97]

From 2003 to 2006, evidence of Saudi government complicity in 9/11 continued to leak out of the tight net of Bush administration denials. New York Senator Charles Schumer noted that an individual suspected of being a Saudi intelligence agent, Omar Bayoumi, had a colloquy in 2000 with a Saudi diplomatic official in Los Angeles, California, and just hours later met directly with the 9/11 hijackers. Senator Schumer characterized Bayoumi as a "key figure" in the 9/11 investigation because he "'had access to seemingly unlimited funding from Saudi Arabia' and helped out two of the hijackers who flew the plane into the Pentagon ... when the three were living in San Diego."[98] A Saudi-funded charity in Brooklyn "was effectively ... a U.S. outpost for Al Qaeda," and a Saudi-backed lobbying group in the U.S. defended *al Qaeda* as a "resistance movement."[99] An official Saudi investigation found that the kingdom's educational curriculum "encourages violence" and indoctrinates "pupils into believing that in order to safeguard their own religion, they must violently repress and even physically eliminate the 'other.'"[100] The Saudi minister of the interior blamed the Jews for 9/11.[101]

Nevertheless, the matter of Saudi responsibility for terrorism in Afghanistan and the U.S. was put to rest with the wars in Afghanistan and Iraq. After September 11, 2001, the mass media widely disseminated claims that Iraq, rather than Saudi Arabia, was the source of the 9/11 terrorists' financing and had huge stockpiles of nuclear, biological, and chem-

---

94. *See, e.g.*, Fry, *Terrorism As a Crime Against Humanity And Genocide,* at 191–92 (citing *ABC News Interview with Osama bin Laden, Interviewed by John Miller* (ABC television broadcast, May 28, 1998), *available at* http://abcnews.go.com/sections/world/dailynews/terror_980609.html; *Fatwa by Osama Bin Laden, World Islamic Front Statement, Jihad Against Jews and Crusaders* (Feb. 23, 1998), at http://www.fas.org/irp/world/para/docs/980223-fatwa.htm; *Al-Jazeera Interview with Osama bin Laden* (Al-Jazeera television broadcast, 1998), *available at* http://groups.yahoo.com/group/EDITOR_RMNEWS).

95. *See* Rupert Cornwell, *Al-Qa'ida Video Has Names of Two More Hijackers,* The Independent (U.K.), Dec. 22, 2001, http://www.independent.co.uk/news/world/americas/alqaida—video-has-names-of-two-more-hijackers-620914.html.

96. Associated Press, *White House Says Part of 9/11 Report on Saudis Will Stay Secret,* N.Y. Times, July 29, 2003.

97. *Id.*

98. Eric Herman & James Gordon Meek, *Pol: Reveal 9-11 File; Censored Pages Implicate Allies, He Says,* N.Y. Daily News, July 28, 2003.

99. Unger, House of Bush, House of Saud, at 204–205.

100. Nina Shea, *This Is a Saudi Textbook.,* Wash. Post, May 21, 2006, at B01.

101. Unger, House of Bush, House of Saud, at 263.

ical weapons.[102] Beginning in late September 2001, television and radio networks were saturated with coverage of intelligence reports, disseminated by the White House, that World Trade Center hijacker Muhammad Atta had received his orders from Iraqi intelligence officers in Prague, reports which were later shown to be baseless.[103] Television and radio corporations constantly repeated and elaborated upon the discredited theory that Iraq was responsible for the 9/11 attacks, thereby beating the drums of war.[104] Both on television and in print, scholars and former U.S. officials affiliated with the American Enterprise Institute (AEI) blamed Saudi Arabia for financing *al Qaeda* and the Taliban but advocated an attack on Iraq as a remedy.[105] AEI is led and funded by oil and oil-trading corporate executives like Lee Raymond of ExxonMobil, which was excluded from exploiting Iraqi oil by French, Russian, and Chinese oil majors,[106] and billionaire Bruce Kovner of oil trading hedge fund Caxton Associates.[107] All of the U.S. television networks

---

102. For more objective accounts of the financing of the attacks, see Burnett v. Al Baraka Inv. & Dev. Corp., 274 F. Supp. 2d 86 (D.D.C. 2003). *See also Counterterror Initiatives in the Terror Finance Program: Hearing Before the S. Comm. on Banking, Housing and Urban Affairs*, 108th Cong. 100 (2003) ("Saudi Arabia is present at every stage of Al-Qaida financing, but primarily as the major source of funding. This is an indication that Osama Bin Laden has been able to leverage his family position in the Kingdom to gain access to major sources of funding.").

103. *See* FAIR (Fairness & Accuracy in reporting), Action Alert: Fox News Spins 9/11 Commission Report, (June 24, 2004),http://www.fair.org/index.php?page=1577; Media Matters for America, *CNN's Blitzer Spun Cheney's Atta/Prague claims*, Research, Dec. 15, 2005, http://mediamatters.org/research/200512150009; DanK Is Back, *Timeline: Cheney's Claims on Saddam and Al-Qaeda*, DailyKos, June 3, 2009, http://www.dailykos.com/story/2009/6/3/738412/-Timeline:-Cheneys-Claims-on-Saddam-and-Al-Qaeda; Staff of S. Armed Services Comm., 108th Cong., Report of an Inquiry into the Alternative Analysis of the Issue of an Iraq-Al Qaeda Relationship 38–43 (Washington, DC, 2004) (Senator Carl Levin), *available at* http://levin.senate.gov/newsroom/supporting/2004/102104inquiryreport.pdf at 38–43; Roger Trilling, *Fighting Words: The Administration Builds up its Pretext for Attacking Iraq*, The Village Voice, Apr. 30, 2002, *available at* http://www.villagevoice.com/2002-04-30/news/fighting-words/1.

104. *See* Orville Schell, *Preface*, Michael Massing, Now They Tell Us: The American Press and Iraq, at v–vi (New York: New York Review of Books, 2004) ("The upper tier [of U.S. mass media], populated by the major broadcast outlets, newspapers, and magazines, allowed a much more limited bandwidth of opinion (often deferring to the Bush administration's vision of the world, especially on questions of war and peace) until the US occupation began to unravel in the spring of 2004."). Most notably, all television and many radio networks not only carried but constantly replayed claims that Iraq was not only responsible for 9/11, but planned far worse attacks with nuclear and biological weapons that could kill millions of Americans. *See* Lando, Web of Deceit, at 221–237; Tim Weiner, Legacy of Ashes: The History of the CIA 567–68 (New York: Anchor Books, 2008); Bob Woodward, Plan of Attack 17, 168–294, 379 (New York: Simon & Schuster, 2004).

105. *See, e.g.*, Michael A. Ledeen, *Iraq: A Wide War*, N.Y. Post, Feb. 21, 2003, http://web.archive.org/web/20030418093331/www.aei.org/news/newsID.16025/news_detail.asp ("We have waited too long [for war with Iraq].... [W]e want to see a free Iraq, governed by Iraqis, as quickly as possible. That is because we also want to see a free Iran and a free Syria, along with a free and moderate Saudi Arabia...."); Michael A. Ledeen, *What W. Should Say*, N.Y. Post, Oct. 7, 2002, http://web.archive.org/web/20030419092953/www.aei.org/news/newsID.15540/news_detail.asp ("When Iraq has been liberated, we will move on to the others [i.e. the other state sponsors of terrorism]–just as the president said from the beginning."); Richard Perle, *State Sponsors of Terrorism Should Be Wiped Out*, The Daily Telegraph (U.K.), Sept. 18, 2001, http://web.archive.org/web/20030831151217/www.aei.org/news/newsID.13180/ news_detail.asp (similarly arguing for prioritization of Iraq over Saudi Arabia, which merely "tolerates" terrorism).

106. *See, e.g.*, Tom Hundley, *Oil Fuels Resistance to Attacking Iraq*, Chi. Trib., Sept. 30, 2002, at 1–3. *See also* BBC News, *Iraq Halts Russian and Chinese Oil Deals*, May 26, 2003, http://news.bbc.co.uk/2/hi/business/2937702.stm; David Ivanovich, *Oil Pits U.S. Against Other Powers*, Hous. Chron., Apr. 8, 2003, at B1.

107. American Enterprise Institute (AEI), *Board of Trustees*, http://web.archive.org/web/20030430184155/www.aei.org/about/msgkey.2002121511002562,pageID.73/default.asp (last visited

described Iraq as poised to use weapons of mass destruction such as atomic bombs, or to deliver them to bin Laden.[108] Clinging to President Bush's version of events, the media ignored Saudi sponsorship of terrorist groups such as *al Qaeda*, Hamas, and the Muslim World League.[109]

Saudi Arabia earned an impressive return on its investment in *al Qaeda*, with budget surpluses (due to the oil price spike after 9/11) exceeding $150 billion in both 2007 and 2008.[110] Its GDP doubled between 2001 and 2008. Saudi government expenditures exploded from $54 billion in 2002 to $118 billion in 2007.[111] In 2002, CIA field officer Robert Baer summarized the attitude in Washington towards the pervasive Saudi funding of terrorism around the world:

> Washington fiddles and pretends Riyadh won't burn, watching passively as wealthy Saudis channel hundreds of millions of dollars to radical groups in hopes of buying protection.... Ex-presidents, former prime ministers, onetime senators and members of Congress and Cabinet members walk around with their hands out....[112]

Arms and oil exploration deals help explain the "softness" of U.S. policy on Saudi Arabia, as does the flow of $1.4 billion in Saudi investments to organizations linked to the

---

Oct. 3, 2009) (identifying Bruce Kovner of oil-trading hedge fund Caxton Associates, LLC, as Chairman of AEI Board of Trustees, and Lee Raymond, Chairman and CEO of Exxon Mobil Corporation, as Vice-Chairman of the board). *Cf. also* Christopher DeMuth, American Enterprise Institute, *Note for AEI Scholars, Fellows, and Staff*, ARTICLES & COMMENTARY, Feb. 2, 2007,http://www.aei.org/article/25586 (noting that "ExxonMobil's annual AEI support is generous and valued"); John J. Miller, *The Man Who Saved AEI*, NATIONAL REV., Jan. 26, 2009, at 34, 36 (quoting *The Guardian's* identification of ExxonMobil as "a major source of funds for AEI," but disputing it); Ian Sample, *Scientists Offered Cash to Dispute Climate Study*, THE GUARDIAN (U.K.), Feb. 2, 2007, http://www.aei.org/docLib/20070209_Guardiancontroversy.pdf ("The AEI has received more than $1.6m from ExxonMobil ... Lee Raymond, a former head of ExxonMobil, is the vice-chairman of AEI's board of trustees."); Andy Serwer, *The $11 Billion Man Hedge Fund Guru Bruce Kovner Earns Giant Returns*, CNN MONEY, Sept. 29, 2003, http://money.cnn.com/magazines/fortune/fortune_archive/2003/09/29/349918/index.htm; *The Forbes 400*, FORBES, Oct. 11, 1999, at 352 (showing Bruce Kovner as being worth nearly $1 billion).

108. These claims are described in Chapter XVII below.

109. *See* DORE GOLD, HATRED'S KINGDOM: HOW SAUDI ARABIA SUPPORTS THE NEW GLOBAL TERRORISM 2, 8 (Washington DC: Regnery, 2003) ("Commentators in the Islamic and Arab worlds have ... examined the Saudi role in the September 11 attacks, but unlike their American counterparts, they have ... investigated the root causes of terrorism, zeroing in on the main creed or version of Islam practiced in Saudi Arabia, known as Wahhabism."); *id.* at 8, 197 (arguing that Saudi extremism has "eluded the conceptual radar screen of most analysts" in the United States because Saudi Arabia's support for an Arab-Israeli peace agreement shifted the country into the peacemaking camp). *See also* RACHEL EHRENFELD, FUNDING EVIL: HOW TERRORISM IS FINANCED—AND HOW TO STOP IT 33–46 (Chicago: Bonus Books, Inc., 2005).

110. Will McSheehy, *Saudi Arabia Plans Its First Sovereign Wealth Fund (Update2)*, BLOOMBERG.COM, Jan. 23, 2008, http://www.bloomberg.com/apps/news?pid=20601014&sid=aOvveqIXjVuU&refer=funds.

111. *Compare* CIA, WORLD FACTBOOK 2002: SAUDI ARABIA, http://www.umsl.edu/services/govdocs/wofact2002/geos/sa.html (expenditures of $54 billion and GDP of $241 billion), *with* CIA, WORLD FACTBOOK 2008: SAUDI ARABIA, http://www.umsl.edu/services/govdocs/wofact2008/geos/sa.html (expenditures of $118.3 billion and GDP of $546 billion). *See also* Caryle Murphy, *G-20 Nation Profile: Saudi Arabia*, PITTSBURGH POST-GAZETTE, Sept. 16, 2009, http://www.post-gazette.com/pg/09259/998308-482.stm, *with* CIA, WORLD FACTBOOK 2001: SAUDI ARABIA, http://www.umsl.edu/services/govdocs/wofact2001/index.html

112. ROBERT BAER, SEE NO EVIL: THE TRUE STORY OF A GROUND SOLDIER IN THE CIA'S WAR ON TERRORISM 166 (Three Rivers Press, 2003).

family of President George W. Bush. The lawyer who helped President Bush win the 2000 election in the Supreme Court advised the Saudis on a $25 billion natural gas project during the Afghan war.[113]

The composition of *al Qaeda* fighters captured by the U.S. in Afghanistan also bears out Senator Graham's and former CIA agent Baer's analysis of Saudi control of the movement. By 2002, over 100 Saudis were held at the U.S. detention facility at Guantanamo Bay for suspected terrorists and pro-Taliban fighters, out of only about 150 detainees in the entire facility, and the official response of Saudi Arabia was not to apologize, but to ask for them to be let go.[114] Despite the overwhelming Saudi leadership and financing of *al Qaeda* from bin Laden on down, in 2002 the U.S. government did not require Saudis or Kuwaitis to be fingerprinted, even though it did require all qualifying persons from Middle Eastern countries, whether or not they were themselves Arabs or Wahhabis, to be fingerprinted, including all Iraqis, Syrians, Lebanese, Sudanese, Libyans, Algerians, Tunisians, and Moroccans.[115] The U.S. "registration and monitoring" regime also exempted Turks, even though a number of Turks had been captured in *al Qaeda* hideouts and battles in Afghanistan.[116] In 2003, the registration and monitoring system was expanded to include Saudis and Kuwaitis, but Turks were never included, even though North Korea, with little or no *al Qaeda* activity, was a suspect country.[117]

The top CIA counterterrorism official in Saudi Arabia confirmed that there was "zero cooperation" from the Saudis in investigating 9/11, and tens of millions of dollars in Saudi financing for *al Qaeda*.[118] Despite the clear Saudi link to *al Qaeda*, Afghanistan rather than Saudi Arabia was selected as the scene of the initial U.S. response to the 9/11 attacks. The Bush administration demanded that the Taliban cease harboring bin Laden and the *al Qaeda* terrorist organization, and threatened war and the destruction of their government if they refused. But the Taliban declined to hand over bin Laden, the former *mujahideen* leader suspected of masterminding or inspiring the 9/11 attacks. Bin Laden had contributed about $100 million to the Taliban by that time.[119] A Taliban spokesman, however, indicated that the regime would hand bin Laden over for trial, provided that the U.S. provided evidence of his responsibility for the 9/11 attacks, which the U.S. had provided only to its "key allies."[120] This did not occur.

On October 7, 2001, the U.S. began bombing *al Qaeda* terrorist targets and Afghan military, electricity, and communications facilities.[121] Special forces units on the ground pro-

---

113. *See* Unger, House of Bush, House of Saud, at 261–62, 271–73.

114. Sulaiman Al-Hattlan, *Terrorism War Magnifies U.S.-Saudi Differences*, USA Today, Feb. 17, 2002, http://www.usatoday.com/news/opinion/2002/02/18/ncguest1.htm; Bruce Shapiro, *POWs in Legal Limbo*, The Nation, Feb. 7, 2002, http://www.thenation.com/doc/20020225/shapiro.

115. Registration of Certain Nonimmigrants from Designated Countries, 67 Fed. Reg. 77136 (2002); Registration and Monitoring of Certain Nonimmigrants; Notice of Ports-of-Entry for Departure of Aliens Who Are Subject to Special Registration, 67 Fed. Reg. 61352 (2002).

116. Ilnur Cevik, *Al Qaeda Turks in US Custody*, Turkish Daily News, Jan. 17, 2002, http://www.turkishdailynews.com.tr/archives.php?id=26705.

117. Asian-American Legal Defense and Education Fund, *Special Registration Report* (2004), http://www.aaldef.org/images/01-04_registration.pdf.

118. *Quoted in* Unger, House of Bush, House of Saud, at 260.

119. *See* Schneider, *Saudi Missteps Helped Bin Laden*, at A01.

120. *Taliban Repeats Call for Negotiations*, CNN.Com, Oct. 2, 2001, http://www.cnn.com/2001/WORLD/asiapcf/central/10/02/ret.afghan.taliban.

121. Stephen Biddle, *Afghanistan and the Future of Warfare: Implications for Army and Defense Policy* 8, U.S. Army War College Strategic Studies Institute (Nov. 2002), *at* http://www.au.af.mil/au/awc/awcgate/ssi/afghan.pdf.

vided the targeting coordinates for U.S. aerial bombing, which destroyed the Taliban tanks and troops that had held off the Northern Alliance opposition for years.[122] Hundreds of Taliban conscripts and hardcore troops died in the fighting, including many prisoners of war summarily executed by Northern Alliance gunfire or suffocation in sealed truck containers.[123] Thousands of Afghan civilians died in the U.S. bombing raids and the ground operations that mopped up after them.[124] Whole families were cut down, sometimes as a result of apparently indiscriminate bombing based on inaccurate or misleading information.[125]

Driving the Taliban before them, the luminaries of the anti-Soviet *jihad* retook their former positions in Herat,[126] Bamiyan,[127] and Kandahar,[128] the prize of Kabul going to the forces of former President Rabbani, now led by Ahmed Shah Massoud's successor Muhammad Fahim.[129] Former *mujahideen* deputy foreign minister Hamid Karzai, leader of the largest Pashtun tribe, entered Afghanistan after September 11 to raise a Pashtun rebellion against the Taliban, joining Gul Agha Shirzai in taking Kandahar.[130]

The occupation of Kabul by the Northern Alliance created a political crisis for the U.S. and the U.N., which had urged their forces to hold back from taking the city until a broad-based government could be formed. Under pressure from the U.S. and other nations, Northern Alliance commanders and other Afghan military factions agreed to participate in U.N.-sponsored talks held in Bonn, Germany. Almost two dozen Afghan delegates, mostly drawn from the Northern Alliance and the circle around former King Zahir Shah, signed an accord called for the creation of an Interim Authority to rule Afghanistan until

---

122. *Id.* at 8–11, 18, 26–28; *see also* Michael Gordon, *"New" U.S. War: Commandos, Airstrikes and Allies on the Ground*, New York Times, Dec. 29, 2001, at A1; Thom Shanker, *Conduct of War is Redefined by Success of Special Forces*, New York Times, Jan. 21, 2002, at A1.

123. *See* Yvonne Abraham, *UN Backs Reports of Mass Execution*, Boston Globe, Nov. 14, 2001, at A33; Carlotta Gall, *A Nation Challenged: Prisoners*, N.Y. Times, Dec. 11, 2001, at A1; Nicholas Watt, Richard Norton-Taylor, & Luke Harding, *Allies Justify Mass Killing of Taliban Prisoners in Fort*, Guardian (U.K.), Nov. 29, 2001, http://www.globalpolicy.org/wtc/analysis/1129justify.htm; Holly J. Burkhalter, *POW Atrocities: An Ugly Lesson*, L.A. Times, Oct. 14, 2002, http://www.commondreams.org/views02/1014-04.htm; Human Rights Watch, World Report 2003, http://www.hrw.org/wr2k3/asia1.html.

124. *See* Barry Bearak, *Uncertain Toll in the Fog of War: Civilian Deaths in Afghanistan*, N.Y. Times, Feb. 10, 2002, http://www.globalpolicy.org/wtc/analysis/2002/0211fog.htm.

125. *See, e.g.*, Barry Bearak, *A Nation Challenged: The Victims*, N.Y. Times, Dec. 16, 2001, at 3B; Susan B. Glasser, *Afghans Live and Die With US Mistakes; Villagers Tell of Over 100 Casualties*, Wash. Post, Feb. 20, 2002, at A1; Human Rights Watch, *Afghanistan: U.S. Military Should Investigate Civilian Deaths* (Dec. 13, 2003), http://www.hrw.org/press/2003/12/afghanistan121303.htm. Reporting by the New York Times in Afghanistan revealed that the deaths of "as many as four hundred civilians" resulted from American forces relying "on mistaken, incomplete, inaccurate and intentionally misleading information provided by locale Afghans harboring vendettas." Matthew Lippman, *Aerial Attacks on Civilians and the Humanitarian Law of War: Technology and Terror from World War I to Afghanistan*, 33 Cal. W. Int'l L.J. 1, 59 (2002) (citing Dexter Filkins, *Flaws in U.S. Air War Left Hundreds of Civilians Dead*, N.Y. Times, July 21, 2002, at A1).

126. *See* Barry Bearak, *Unreconstructed*, N.Y. Times, June 1, 2003, http://www.nytimes.com.

127. *See* Ahmed Rashid, *Hamid Karzai Moves from Lightweight to Heavyweight in Afghan Politics*, Eurasia Insight, Dec. 10, 2001, http://www.eurasianet.org/departments/insight/articles/eav121001.shtml.

128. *See* Robert Fisk, *Warlord of the Year: Gul Agha Shirzai*, The Independent (U.K.), Aug. 9, 2002.

129. *See* Gordon, *"New" U.S. War*, at A1; Shanker, *Conduct of War*, at A1.

130. *See Ally of Afghan Leader Shot Dead*, BBC News Online, Apr. 5, 2003, http://news.bbc.co.uk/1/hi/world/south_asia/2919815.stm; Biddle, *Afghanistan and the Future of Warfare*, at 11.

a Transitional Authority government could be selected in a *Loya Jirga* six months later, and a "fully representative government" freely elected two years after that.[131] Although loyalists to the former King Zahir Shah initially voted that he return to power, the U.S. and U.N. secured the delegates' agreement to appoint Pashtun anti-Taliban leader Hamid Karzai as Chairman of the Afghan Interim Authority.[132]

More than 1,000 elected and 700 selected delegates to the June 2002 Emergency Loya Jirga established the Islamic Transitional Authority of Afghanistan and elected Hamid Karzai as its President.[133] Despite the support of a majority of delegates at one point, the former King of Afghanistan Mohammad Zahir Shah withdrew his name from consideration for the presidency, prompting Human Rights Watch to accuse the U.S. of "'brazen' interference in the loya jirga, [which was] promoted as the birth of Afghani democracy."[134] Some delegates also objected that *mujahideen* commanders who had killed innocent Afghan civilians were wielding too much control over the Afghan political process. "We were told that this loya jirga would not include all the people who had blood on their hands," said one delegate to applause.[135]

The Karzai government began as "an island in a sea of uncompromising warlords," who fielded large militias outside the framework of the Afghan National Army and exercised totalitarian theocratic powers.[136] Most rural areas and even major cities were not under the firm control of the central government, especially at night.[137] According to a member of the Afghanistan Independent Human Rights Commission, "trials do not take place in accordance with law. In provinces, warlords are the law, the judge, the government."[138] Bin Laden's mentor Sayyaf controlled much of Kabul province after the Taliban fell.[139] Two years after the rout of the Taliban, the governor of Kabul province and many of the city's police and intelligence officials were loyal to him, and his troops patrolled Kabul.[140] International peacekeepers in Kabul "publicly accused" those troops of responsibility for

---

131. *See* UN Doc. S/2001/1154, Dec. 5, 2001 (relaying the "Agreement on Provisional Arrangements in Afghanistan Pending the Re-establishment of Permanent Government Institutions" signed in Bonn).

132. *See id.* § III(A)(2); Kolhatkar, *The Impact of U.S. Intervention on Afghan Women's Rights*, at 21–22; Norimitsu Onishi, *A Nation Challenged: War in South*, N.Y. Times, Dec. 15, 2001, at A1; David Rohde, *A Nation Challenged: The Politics*, N.Y. Times, Dec. 16, 2001, at B3. The shape of the new administration came together when three former lieutenants to Northern Alliance military leader Ahmed Shah Massoud indicated their willingness to serve under Karzai rather than their titular leader, former President Rabbani, and were rewarded with positions heading the key government ministries of Defense, Foreign Affairs, and Interior. *See* Ahmed Rashid, *Hamid Karzai Moves from Lightweight to Heavyweight*; *Profile: Younis Qanooni*, BBC News, Dec. 6, 2001, ttp://news.bbc.co.uk/1/hi/world/south_asia/1695218.stm.

133. *See The Sound of the Sixties* ("Conservative elements led by Abdul Rasul Sayyaf, a warlord who destroyed much of western Kabul in the early 1990s (though he still teaches religion at Kabul University), insisted that the provisional administration be designated as 'Islamic'.").

134. *Afghans Claim U.S. Is Manipulating Loya Jirga*, Holland Online Sentinel, June 20, 2002, http://www.hollandsentinel.com; Chris Otton, *US Pressure May Undermine Karzai and Long-Term Ambitions: Analysts*, Agence France-Presse, June 20, 2002.

135. *Warlords Demand Say in Future of Afghanistan*, Toronto Star, June 14, 2002, at B4.

136. Rashid, *Hamid Karzai Moves from Lightweight to Heavyweight.*

137. *See* Michael Moran, *The Other Unfinished War*, MSNBC, June 24, 2003, http://www.msnbc.msn.com/id/3340310.

138. *See* Farangis Najibullah, *Afghanistan: Little Progress Seen in Reform of Judicial System*, Radio Free Europe, Mar. 10, 2003, http://www.rferl.org/features/2003/03/11032003204729.asp.

139. *See* John Sifton, *We're Losing The War in Afghanistan, Too*, Salon.com, Aug. 21, 2003, http://www.salon.com/news/feature/2003/08/21/afghanwar/index_np.html.

140. *Id.*

"a series of murders, abductions and extortion incidents in that sector of the city, aided by a cadre of loyalists in the police department."[141] Following mainstream Saudi ideology,[142] those forces "continue[d] to enforce strict Islamic social codes including restrictions on women's education and dress." Sayyaf's men tortured villagers and old people for such crimes as listening to music. He viewed any attempt to question his authority as a form of blasphemy, and had two newspaper editors arrested on blasphemy charges and sentenced to death for criticizing his tactics.[143]

In the north, a campaign of ethnic cleansing against Pashtuns raged in early 2002. Soldiers and armed militia in northern Afghanistan rounded up and shot dozens of Pashtun men at a time, raping many Pashtun women and young girls, a crime that can lead to the murder of its victim by members of her own family in conservative rural Afghanistan.[144] The militia of former communist officer General Dostum raped whole families of women, including girls as young as 10.[145] A U.N. official called the abuses against ethnic Pashtuns "systematic and wide scale."[146] Thousands of Pashtuns fled their homes, some living in caves to keep warm.[147]

Until 2004, a warlord ruled Herat, a historically more liberal city near the Iranian border that is widely viewed as a litmus test for human rights after the Taliban.[148] The security forces of Governor Ismail Khan borrowed a page from neighboring Iran, which Khan called "the best model of an Islamic country in the world."[149] Women complained that his regime resembled that of the Taliban, as their mode of dress was confined to two options: *burqas* or full-body veils (known as *chadoris*) that expose only the face.[150] Although President Karzai promoted Khan from governor to the Ministry of Mines in September of 2004, as a warlord he continued to field a militia, and thousands of petty warlords with similar ideologies continued to hold power in their respective fiefdoms.[151]

Under the Afghan Constitution of 2004, the Supreme Court had the power to "review compliance with the Constitution of laws, legislative decrees, international treaties, and international conventions, and interpret them, in accordance with the law."[152] The

---

141. *Loya Jirga Defuses Battle of Good and Evil*, Deutsche Presse-Agentur, June 12, 2002.

142. Saudi Arabia's "most senior Islamic cleric" has publicly warned: "'Allowing women to mix with men is the root of every evil and catastrophe.'" Robin Gedye, *Unveiled Women Are Root of All Evil, Says Saudi Cleric*, Daily Telegraph (U.K.), Jan. 22, 2004.

143. Sifton, *We're Losing*.

144. *See* Human Rights Watch, *Afghanistan: Paying for the Taliban's Crimes: Abuses Against Ethnic Pashtuns in Northern Afghanistan* (Apr. 2002), http://www.hrw.org/reports/2002/afghan2. *See also* Anna Badkhen, *Afghan Women Still Shrouded in Oppression*, S.F. Chron., Oct. 14, 2002, http://www.sfgate.com ("Soldiers loyal to the powerful northern warlord Abdul Rashid Dostum are alleged to have repeatedly raped women and girls in northern Afghanistan.").

145. *See* Anna Badkhen, *Reports of Rape, Looting by Afghan Militiamen*, S.F. Chron., Feb. 15, 2002, at A1.

146. Dexter Filkins & Barry Bearak, *A Tribe Is Prey to Vengeance After Taliban's Fall in North*, N.Y. Times, Mar. 7, 2002.

147. *See* Human Rights Watch, *Afghanistan: Paying for the Taliban's Crimes*.

148. David Brunnstrom, *Desperate Afghan Women Opt for Fiery Suicides*, Reuters, Apr. 16, 2004.

149. *See* Hersh, *The Other War*.

150. Human Rights Watch, *All Our Hopes Are Crushed: Violence and Repression in Western Afghanistan* (2002), http://hrw.org/reports/2002/afghan3/herat1002-07.htm#P1061_165296.

151. *See* Gary Thomas, *Afghan President Must Still Negotiate Political Minefield*, Voice of America, Oct. 25, 2004, http://ibb7.ibb.gov/newswire/3f7b65d5.html.

152. Const. of Afgh. 2004, art. 121.

constitution granted the Supreme Court, which the Chief Justice has packed with many sympathetic judges who lack training in Afghanistan's civil and secular laws, the power to reject human rights law or treaties as "un-Islamic."[153] The constitution barred only those actually "convicted" of crimes against humanity from becoming president, a minister, or member of the national assembly or Supreme Court.[154] The ineffectiveness of this provision resulted from the fact that despite "the enormous scale of war crimes, crimes against humanity and other serious human rights violations committed in Afghanistan, ... no one has yet been tried by a competent court for crimes committed during the long years of conflict in the country."[155] Rather than convening trials, in late 2003 coalition forces decided not to prosecute the Taliban's foreign minister for crimes against Hazaras, Americans killed on 9/11, Afghan women, or other groups. After the Karzai government took office, "many former Taliban officials [were] sitting in the same government positions they held when Mullah Mohammad Omar was still in charge."[156] Amnesty International declared the constitution's denial of power to war criminals "meaningless."[157]

In several other respects, implementation of the rights guaranteed in the constitution remained a distant dream. Shortly after the new constitution was adopted, U.N. Secretary General Kofi Annan's special envoy to Afghanistan warned that "there is no rule of law in this country yet."[158] The Afghan Independent Human Rights Commission (AIHRC) received complaints of hundreds of murders in 2003, most blamed on government officials and militia commanders.[159] The AIHRC has found that "innocent people are put in jail for a very long time and for no reason."[160] There was no sign of these practices having been put to an end by the adoption of the new constitution, which called for liberty and due process.[161]

C. *Al Qaeda's* New Base: Pakistan

About 5,000 *al Qaeda* fighters moved into Pakistan in early 2002 and "set up new bases of operations in western Pakistan and in the city of Karachi."[162] Shortly before the invasion of Iraq in March 2003, a prominent Pakistani politician declared "*jihad* against Amer-

153. Thier, *Attacking Democracy*.
154. *See id.*; Const. of Afgh. 2004, art. 62, 72, 85, 118.
155. *Quoted in* James Ingalls, *The New Afghan Constitution: A Step Backwards for Democracy*, Foreign Policy in Focus, Mar. 2004, http://www.fpif.org/pdf/papers/SR2004afghanconst.pdf.
156. Ilene R. Prusher, *Ex-Taliban Officials Change Headdress, Resume Duties*, Christian Science Monitor, Jan. 14, 2002, http://www.csmonitor.com/.
157. *Id.*
158. *Afghans Endorse New Constitution*, BBC News Online, Jan. 4, 2004, http://news.bbc.co.uk/1/hi/world/south_asia/3366455.stm.
159. *See* Carlotta Gall, *News Analysis: Afghan Constitution Offers Slim Hope in a Land Where Warlords Rule*, Int'l Herald Trib., Jan. 15, 2004, http://www.nytimes.com.
160. *Id.*
161. *See* Kathy Gannon, *Afghanistan Unbound*, 83 Foreign Aff. 35 (2004) ("The warlords have stolen people's homes, arbitrarily arrested their enemies, and tortured them in private jails"); *see also* Carlotta Gall, *Afghan Parliamentary Elections May Be Delayed Again*, N.Y. Times, July 9, 2004, at A10.
162. Kronstadt, *Pakistan-U.S. Relations*, at CRS-16.
163. Kronstadt, *Pakistan-U.S. Anti-Terrorism Cooperation*, at CRS-18.

ica that has stationed its forces in Pakistan to do away with our sovereignty."[163] The leader of his party warned in January 2003 that Pakistani groups would "break America into pieces like Russia" and "erase America from the world."[164] Afghan expert Barnett Rubin described Pakistan's policy:

> The Pakistani military will not consent to a stable Afghanistan under U.S. hegemony because it fears that the United States will reduce military aid to Pakistan the moment it no longer needs Pakistan to address terrorism or instability in Afghanistan. The Pakistani military cannot agree to a definition of Pakistani national security that is not based on the Indian threat, because that threat, in addition to being founded on the reality of Indian capabilities, provides the rationale for the military's domination of Pakistan's state, society and economy.[165]

Taliban expert and Pakistani journalist Ahmed Rashid observed in 2007 that Pakistan has provided four principal types of state sponsorship to *al Qaeda* and the Taliban. These are the following: (1) Pakistani intelligence services are permitting Taliban leader Mullah Omar to reside in Quetta, Pakistan; (2) the Pakistani military has tolerated the presence of the Taliban and allied Pakistani militia groups, and has failed to capture bin Laden and Ayman al Zawahiri, who likely reside somewhere in Pakistan; (3) Pakistani militia groups are providing safe houses, transport, and communications facilities to *al Qaeda*, as well as "manpower" and "cannon fodder" for the Taliban movement; and (4) the fundamentalist-led provincial Pakistani governments of Baluchistan and the North-West Frontier Province are permitting the Taliban to import weapons and ammunition from the Gulf Arab states as part of the imports allotted to these provinces. He identified three motivations to adopt this set of policies: (1) frustrating Indian and American influence in Afghanistan; (2) providing a foundation to take over Afghanistan after a U.S.-led coalition is defeated by the Taliban; and (3) courting fundamentalist political parties.[166]

In 2006, the AIHRC reported that 650 civilians were killed in terrorist bombings or U.S. and NATO strikes against terrorist bases.[167] A similar number were killed in just the first five months of 2008 alone, a number that increased by another 25 percent in the same period in 2009. The U.N. Secretary-General reported that "most civilian casualties stem from the activities of the Taliban and terrorist groups, deliberately targeting civilians."[168] Amid growing cross-border attacks on aid workers, Afghanistan remained one of the poorest and most desperate countries in the world in late 2008. The Taliban and perhaps some local criminals attacked 26 World Food Programme trucks bearing aid, and "[d]ozens of local and foreign aid workers" were "killed and abducted in 2008." Up to 10 million people lacked access to adequate food, nearly 40% of the population. According to the Ministry of Health, about "1.6 million children under five and 625,000 child-bearing-age

---

164. *Id.* at CRS-20 (quoting *US Trying to Destroy Muslims: Saeed*, DAWN (PAKISTAN), Jan. 9, 2003).

165. Barnett R. Rubin, *Afghan Dilemmas: Defining Commitments*, THE AMERICAN INTEREST, May/June 2008, http://www.the-american-interest.com/ai2/article-bd.cfm?Id=423&MId=19.

166. *Ahmed Rashid on the Taliban in Kunduz*, SPIEGEL ONLINE (GERMANY), May 29, 2007, http://www.spiegel.de/international/world/0,1518,485299-2,00.html.

167. *See* U.N. IRIN, *Afghanistan: Civilians the Main Victims of Conflicts*, REUTERS ALERTNET, Apr. 14, 2007, http://www.alertnet.org/thenews/newsdesk/IRIN/b5e9a58ad6c13090f76a5f18344953f2.htm.

168. *See* U.N. Secretary-General Ban Ki-Moon, Report on the Situation in Afghanistan and Its Implications for International Peace and Security, A/63/892, S/2009/323 (June 23, 2009), ¶¶ 48–49.

women" risked death in the winter of 2008/2009 due to starvation or malnutrition-related disease.[169] The Russian Federation drew attention in 2009 to a bombing incident in which U.S.-led forces in Afghanistan killed up to 150 civilians.[170]

The year 2009 drew to a close with a bitter controversy over whether Pakistan was knowingly providing safe haven to *al Qaeda*. U.S. Secretary of State Hillary Clinton argued that it was "hard to believe" that the Pakistani government did not know where bin Laden and other *al Qaeda* leaders lived in Pakistan. Her remarks came just as she announced nearly $10 billion in military and humanitarian aid to Pakistan, including $100 million for law enforcement.[171]

D. The Greatest Danger Revisited: The Threat of Nuclear War in South Asia

The arms race in India and Pakistan, several decades after the partition, posed an even greater danger of war crimes and genocide by nuclear weapons. In the 1990s, the CIA concluded that "the arms race between India and Pakistan poses perhaps the most probable prospect for future use of weapons of mass destruction, including nuclear weapons."[172]

The Cold War accelerated this prospect, with both the U.S. and the Soviet Union expanding the nuclear weapons programs of South Asia with critical nuclear and ballistic weapons assistance. In the 1960s, the U.S. built India a nuclear power plant near Bombay, and supplied enriched uranium to India until 1978. In 1974, India tested a nuclear weapon. In response, the U.S. Congress passed the Nuclear Non-Proliferation Act of 1978.[173] In late 1980s and until 1993, the Soviet Union supplied India with rocket engines that the U.S. suspected could be used to build ballistic missiles for the delivery of nuclear weapons. In 1979, the U.S. had evidence of a Pakistani nuclear weapons program, prompting President Carter to suspend aid to Pakistan pursuant to Section 101 of the Arms Export Control Act. Carter then waived the requirement to suspend military aid in order to

---

169. U.N. IRIN, *Afghanistan: Food Insecurity May Cause Deaths This Winter—Government* (Nov. 27. 2008), http://www.irinnews.org/report.aspx?ReportId=81692. *See also* U.N. IRIN, *Afghanistan: Nazia, "I work as health worker despite threats to my life"* (Dec. 01, 2008), http:// www.reliefweb.int/rw/rwb.nsf/db900SID/PANA-7LWETY?OpenDocument.

170. *See* U.N. Security Council, *Despite Progress, Civilians Continue to Bear Brunt of Conflict, Says Under-Secretary-General in Briefing to Security Council*, SC/9692, 6151st Meeting (AM & PM) (June 26, 2009), http://www.reliefweb.int/rw/rwb.nsf/db900SID/MUMA-7TE4GA?OpenDocument ("[T]he deaths of 150 civilians in May as a result of strikes by international forces in Afghanistan should be investigated carefully. It was the responsibility of all parties, including foreign forces, to protect civilians.").

171. *See* Andrew Quinn, *Clinton Puzzled at Pakistan Failure to Find al Qaeda*, REUTERS, Oct. 29, 2009, http://www.reuters.com; Lalit Jha, *Clinton Announces More Humanitarian Aid to Pak*, PRESS TRUST OF INDIA, Oct. 29, 2009, http://www.ptinews.com.

172. *See* Richard P. Cronin, *Pakistan Aid Cutoff: U.S. Nonproliferation and Foreign Policy Considerations*, CONG. RES. SERV. REPORT No. 90149 (1996), http://www.fas.org/spp/starwars/crs/90-149.htm.

173. *See id.*

174. Sharon Squassoni, *Nuclear Threat Reduction Measures for India and Pakistan*, CONG. RES. SERV. Rep. No. RL31589, at CRS-13–CRS-14 (2005), http://digital.library.unt.edu/govdocs/crs/permalink/meta-crs-6185:1.

support Afghan guerillas based in Pakistan.[174] In 1981, President Reagan resumed economic and military aid, in the form of a 6-year, $3.2 billion package.[175] A $4 billion aid package followed in 1986.[176]

Shortly after the Soviet pullout of combat troops from Afghanistan, President George H.W. Bush admitted that Pakistan may have possessed one or more nuclear weapons.[177] Nevertheless, President Bush, and later President Clinton, allowed commercial sales of weapons and spare parts, including parts for F-16 fighter-bombers and Cobra attack helicopters. In 1996, the U.S. Congress passed a law allowing aid for "antinarcotics and antiterrorism cooperation," and training of Pakistani military officers in the International Military Education and Training (IMET) program.[178] Pakistan continued to refuse to sign the Comprehensive Nuclear Test Ban Treaty of 1996, and stated that it would "never accept unilaterally any obligations which tend to compromise its nuclear program."[179]

India and Pakistan were believed by 1996 to have built or bought ballistic missiles capable of carrying nuclear warheads. The U.S. believed its satellite technology contributed to the build-up of the Pakistani missile arsenal through the intermediary of China, which imported ballistic technology from the U.S. and sent it to Pakistan.[180] Article I of the Nuclear Non-Proliferation Treaty (NPT), which entered into force in 1970, required the U.S. not to act "in any way to assist, encourage or induce any non-nuclear weapon state to manufacture or otherwise acquire nuclear weapons or other nuclear explosive devices, or control over such weapons or explosive devices."[181] Since 2001, however, Pakistani officials have claimed that the country has reached "deals for the purchase of major U.S. weapons platforms," including F-16 fighter-bombers.[182] By the mid-2000s, the U.S. believed Pakistan to be "the most crucial node of the nexus of terrorism and WMD proliferation," with a "relationship to the Taliban and Al Qaeda" and a "doctrinal preference (for first use of nuclear weapons)" in the event of war with India.[183]

In 2002, conventional terrorism threatened to spiral out of control into nuclear war and the deaths of tens of millions from radiation and infrastructure damage in India and Pakistan. Lashkar-e-Taiba, a terrorist group devoted to the liberation of Kashmir from Indian rule, and armed and backed by Pakistani state, attacked the Indian parliament with guns and grenades, killing nine and nearly reaching the office of India's foreign minister. India

---

175. *See* Cronin, *Pakistan Aid Cutoff.*

176. *See* K. Alan Kronstadt, Pakistan-U.S. Relations, Cong. Res. Serv. Rep. No. IB94041, at CRS-2 (2003), http://digital.library.unt.edu/govdocs/crs/permalink/meta-crs-4859:1.

177. *See* Squassoni, *Nuclear Threat Reduction Measures*, at CRS-14; Cronin, *Pakistan Aid Cutoff.*

178. *See* Cronin, *Pakistan Aid Cutoff.*

179. *Id.* (quoting REUTERS, Aug. 8, 1996).

180. *See id.* (U.S. overturned its 1993 "ban on the sale of satellites, satellite technology, and other advanced technology to China and Pakistan as a result of evidence that China has provided M-11 components to Pakistan" after China agreed "not to sell medium-range missiles," but continued to sell missiles that the U.S. had previously declared to be "medium range," the M-11 ballistic missiles, of which model Pakistan bought 30 from China); Kronstadt, *Pakistan-U.S. Relations* ("In 1993, the United States determined that China had transferred to Pakistan prohibited missile technology and imposed trade sanctions on one Pakistani and 11 Chinese entities (government ministries and aerospace companies) for 2 years. The U.S. intelligence community reportedly has evidence of PRC provision of complete M-11 ballistic missiles to Pakistan.").

181. NPT, art. 1.

182. K. Alan Kronstadt, *Pakistan-U.S. Anti-Terrorism Cooperation*, CONG. RES. SERV. REP. No. RL31624, at CRS-15 (2003), http://digital.library.unt.edu/govdocs/crs/permalink/meta-crs-4937:1.

183. Squassoni, *Nuclear Threat Reduction*, at CRS-1.

sent an army of 500,000 troops to the border and readied its nuclear-capable missile installations. U.S. officials believed that war was imminent, and Pakistan's dictator Pervez Musharraf warned that he would use "all countermeasures" and "all [Pakistan's] might" against the larger Indian military.[184]

---

184. *Fears of India-Pakistan Nuclear War Raged in 2002*, National Public Radio, Dec. 18, 2008, http://www.npr.org/templates/story/story.php?storyId=98443922.

Chapter XVII

"Mass Extermination" in Iraq: At What Stage Genocide?

> The daily pattern of murder in Iraq is spinning out of control; the death toll is becoming unbearable. Iraqi cleric Grand Ayatollah Ali al-Sistani ruled that the indiscriminate slaughtering of politicians and religious dignitaries, children and the elderly has assumed the dimensions of "mass extermination," and that Iraq is headed in the direction of what he called "genocide."
>
> —Georg Mascolo and Bernhard Zand[1]

A. The Evolving Policy of Regime Change in Iraq

In 1991, President George H.W. Bush authorized the CIA to depose Saddam Hussein, but its Iraqi military contacts balked or were preempted inside Iraq. The next year, however, the CIA convened a meeting in Vienna of a coalition of Iraqi rebel groups who would take power after the 2003 war between Iraq and a U.S.-led coalition.[2] In the 1990s, a civil war between two of the opposition groups organized by the CIA into an anti-Saddam coalition, the Kurdish Democratic Party (KDP) of Massoud Barzani and the Patriotic Union of Kurdistan (PUK) of Jalal Talabani. The fighting killed many Kurds and Assyrians and displaced tens or even hundreds of thousands of villagers.[3] After a Kurdish rebellion and U.S., U.K., and French intervention in 1991, the Saddam Hussein regime had ceded control over many areas of northern Iraq inhabited by Kurds to the KDP and PUK.[4] A parliament was elected for the Kurdistan safe haven, with ethnic minority representation. Alleging that the PUK received Iranian aid in expanding its territory, however, the KDP invited the Iraqi army to retake the northern city of Arbil from PUK forces in 1995, which resulted in the "indiscriminate shelling" by Iraqi artillery of Arbil and other areas of northern Iraq.[5] Kurdish politician Mahmoud Othman blamed the KDP's and PUK's "lining their pockets and wanting to achieve supremacy at the expense of each other."[6]

---

1. *Crumbling Iraq: Is the Country Heading for Civil War?*, Spiegel Online (Germany), July 22, 2005, http://www.spiegel.de/international/spiegel/0,1518,366834,00.html.
2. *See* Coughlin, Saddam, at 286–92.
3. *See* The Government of the United Kingdom, Home Office, *Iraq Country Assessment* (Apr. 2002); Alastair Bruton, *Christian Sects in Kurdish Lands Dwindle*, N.Y. Times, May 24, 1993, http://www.nytimes.com/1993/05/24/opinion/l-christian-sects-in-kurdish-lands-dwindle-021793.html.
4. U.S. Dep't of State, *Iraq: Country Reports on Human Rights Practices—2002.*
5. *Iraqi Authority to Return to Kurdistan Under Draft Accord*, Agence France-Presse, Sept. 26, 1996.
6. Aburish, Saddam Hussein, at 312–13, 358.

Image 9 Autonomous Kurdish Militia-Controlled Northern Iraq, Circa Spring 2003

Source: U.S. Central Intelligence Agency

Gross violations of human rights continued inside Iraq. Torture was very common and inflicted with extreme brutality. Children could be tortured in front of their mothers, and spouses in front of one another; torture victims could be mutilated and killed.[7] Iraq experienced a Shi'a Muslim insurgency in its southern provinces. In 1997, the State Department described "large scale burning operations in the south."[8] Iraq pointed to the economic sanctions as justification to impose amputation and branding as legal punishments for "rampant crime."[9] In the early 1990s, the Iraqi government engaged in a disproportionate response to rebellious activity emanating from the southern marshes, ordering the "burning and demolition of houses" as well as "poisoning" and "explosives" against residents suspected of "collaborating" with rebels.[10] It cleansed all towns within three

7. *See* Deborah Cobbett, *Women in Iraq, in* SADDAM'S IRAQ: REVOLUTION OR REACTION? 128–29 (London: Zed Books, 2d ed. 1990).

8. *Quoted in* GRAHAM-BROWN, SANCTIONING SADDAM, at 136.

9. Human Rights Watch, *Iraq and Iraqi Kurdistan, in* HUMAN RIGHTS WATCH WORLD REPORT 1995, *quoted in* SARAH GRAHAM-BROWN, SANCTIONING SADDAM: THE POLITICS OF INTERVENTION 125 (London: I.B. Tauris, 1999).

10. Ibrahim al-Marashi, *Dismantling the "Republic of Fear" Was a Just Cause*, 9 NEXUS 63, 66 (2004).

kilometers of the marshes of their populations, killed hundreds of residents of the marshes, and dumped toxic material into the marshes, which the Babylonians and Mandaeans used for millennia in their religious rituals of washings and baptisms.[11] Thousands of Shi'a Arabs, Kurds, Yezidis, Mandaeans, and Assyrians left their homes and villages in Iraq between 1979 and 2002,[12] so that by 2002, more Assyrians lived outside Iraq than in their homeland.[13]

The Iraq Liberation Act of 1998 declared regime change to be the policy of the U.S., based on Iraq's acts of aggression, war crimes, and poor human rights record. The Act authorized $97 million for the training and arming of Iraqi rebel groups. President Bill Clinton designated as eligible aid recipients the Supreme Council for Islamic Revolution in Iraq (SCIRI), a Shi'a religious movement founded in Iran in the 1980s, along with the KDP, PUK, and the Movement for a Constitutional Monarchy.[14] The head of the U.N. weapons inspectors in Iraq was told after the Act was passed that a bombing campaign against Iraq was in the works, and "[w]e have to have a crisis by this date...." Using intelligence acquired during the inspections process, the campaign targeted army and intelligence facilities, accelerating the subsequent fall of the regime.[15]

B. Operation "Iraqi Freedom" (Gulf War III)

The Bush administration decided in 2001 to invade Iraq and depose Saddam Hussein.[16] Bush administration Treasury Secretary Paul O'Neill described efforts shortly after the inauguration of George W. Bush as President to invade Iraq, calling the plans a form of "unilateral" pre-emption that he found to be a "really huge leap" from the norm. Secret memoranda were prepared in early 2001 with such titles as "'Plan for Post-Saddam Iraq'" and "'Foreign Suitors for Iraqi Oilfield Contracts.'" The latter document described Iraq's oilfields and multi-national claimants to the exploration rights in detail.[17]

In another development related to the planned war in Iraq, the U.S. withdrew from the treaty establishing the ICC. On May 7, 2002, the State Department under Secretary Powell "notified United Nations Secretary General Kofi Annan that the administration will not seek ratification of the treaty creating the tribunal, and considers itself free of any obligation to comply with its terms." It explained that the U.S. would "seek agreements

---

11. Melinda L. Kimble, *Humanitarian Situation in Iraq*, 3–1 Dep't of State Dispatch 223, 224 (1992).

12. *See* Jonathan Eric Lewis, *Iraqi Assyrians: Barometer of Pluralism*, Middle East Q., Summer 2003.

13. Unrepresented Nations and Peoples Organization: Yearbook 1997, at 44 (3.3 million Assyrians lived in 30 countries outside Middle East by mid-1990s, compared to only 2.5 million in Middle East); California Assembly Joint Resolution No. 31—Relative to Assyrians in Iraq (Apr. 24, 2003), http://info.sen.ca.gov/pub/03–04/statute/ch_0051-0100/ch_73_st_2003_ajr_31 (350,000 Assyrians live in California, Michigan, and Illinois).

14. *See* Public Law 105–338 (1998); Lando, Web of Deceit, at 206; Volker Franke, Terrorism and Peacekeeping: New Security Challenges 159–70 (Westport, CT: Greenwood Pub'g Group, 2005).

15. Lando, Web of Deceit, at 206–8.

16. *See Bush Sought 'Way' to Invade Iraq?*, CBS News, Jan. 11, 2004, http://www.cbsnews.com.

17. *See id.*; *Bush's Plans to Invade Iraq Began Days after Inauguration*, CBS News, Jan. 10, 2004, http://www.derechos.org/nizkor/iraq/doc/bush3.html.

around the globe barring U.S. citizens from being extradited to the court."[18] This position isolated the U.S., which had joined only China, Israel, Iraq, Libya, Qatar and Yemen in voting "no" when the ICC Statute was approved by 120 countries in 1998.[19]

Secretary of Defense Donald Rumsfeld announced on May 8, 2002 the President's decision to formally notify the United Nations that President George W. Bush had decided that the U.S. would reverse its signature on the ICC treaty and instead remain a non-party. He added that the ICC's entry into force on July 1, 2002 without U.S. ratification meant that "our men and women in uniform—as well as current and future U.S. officials—could be at risk of prosecution...."[20]

In July 2002, after widespread criticism by foreign governments and human rights NGOs of the U.S. withdrawal from the ICC, the U.S. proposed a deal to immunize its officials. As early as the very day of the announcement, the Russian Foreign Ministry criticized the decision: "'Quite a few people in the world believe that the United States is making a mistake by openly opposing the court,' the [Russian] Foreign Ministry said in a statement...."[21]

The public relations campaign to "sell" the invasion of Iraq was launched in August 2002. Ten days after reports of a new 10-year economic cooperation deal between Iraq and Russia, valued in the press at more than $40 billion, U.S. Vice President Dick Cheney warned that Iraq would have nuclear weapons soon and "no doubt" would use them on the U.S.[22] In September, President Bush and Vice President Cheney appeared on radio and television to disseminate their claims that Iraq had nuclear weapons and was seeking more, which had been disproven by the CIA and State Department in 2001.[23] President Bush, Secretary of State Powell, and other U.S. officials expressed outrage at Iraq's poor human

18. Peter Slevin, *U.S. Renounces Its Support of New Tribunal for War Crimes,* WASH. POST, May 7, 2002, http://www.highbeam.com/doc/1P2-345416.html. *See also* Harry Dunphy, *U.S. Declares It Is No Longer Bound by Treaty Creating Permanent War Crimes Tribunal,* AP WORLDSTREAM, May 6, 2002, http://www.highbeam.com/doc/1P1-52769025.html.

19. Nicole Winfield, *UN Hails US Decision to Sign War Crimes Court Treaty,* THE INDEPENDENT (U.K.), Jan. 1, 2001, http://www.independent.co.uk/news/world/americas/un-hails-us-decision-to-sign-war-crimes-court-treaty-704867.html.

20. U.S. Dep't of Defense, *Secretary Rumsfeld Statement on the ICC Treaty,* May 8, 2002, http://www.accessmylibrary.com/coms2/summary_0286-25322868_ITM.

21. *Russian Foreign Ministry Criticizes U.S. Decision to Not Be Involved in Permanent War Crimes Tribunal,* AP WORLDSTREAM, May 7, 2002, http://www.highbeam.com/doc/1P1-52839478.html.

22. *Compare* Elisabeth Bumiller & James Dao, *Eyes on Iraq; Cheney Says Peril of a Nuclear Iraq Justifies Attack,* N.Y. TIMES, Aug. 27, 2002, http://www.nytimes.com/2002/08/27/world/eyes-on-iraq-cheney-says-peril-of-a-nuclear-iraq-justifies-attack.html?pagewanted=all ("Vice President Dick Cheney today presented the administration's most forceful and comprehensive rationale yet for attacking Iraq, warning that Saddam Hussein would 'fairly soon' have nuclear weapons.... 'There is no doubt that Saddam Hussein now has weapons of mass destruction,' Mr. Cheney said. 'There is no doubt that he is amassing them to use against our friends, against our allies and against us.'"), *with* Peter Baker, *Russia, Iraq Plan Deal to Bolster Ties,* WASH. POST, Aug. 17, 2002, at A01 ("Russia and Iraq plan to sign a new five-year economic cooperation agreement worth $40 billion, reinforcing Moscow's close ties to Baghdad even as the United States weighs a military attack to drive Iraqi President Saddam Hussein from power, Iraqi and Russian officials said today.").

23. *See Senate Intelligence Committee Report Confirms Bush Administration Spun the Truth to take America to War,* U.S. Senate (June 5, 2008), http://democrats.senate.gov/journal/entry.cfm?id=298788. *Cf.* David Sirota & Christy Harvey, *They Knew,* IN THESE TIMES, Aug. 3, 2004, http://www.inthesetimes.com/article/899/they_knew (stating that in 2001, CIA found no "direct evidence that Iraq has used the period since [1998] to reconstitute its weapons of mass destruction programs," and State Department concluded that Iraq had "not developed any significant capability with respect to weapons of mass destruction").

rights record, repeatedly citing its use of chemical weapons against the Kurds and Iranians.[24] In October, President Bush claimed on all three networks that Iraq "possesses and produces chemical and biological weapons," and "is seeking nuclear weapons."[25]

In March 2003, the claims relating to Iraq's weapons escalated into the claim that Iraq was already a nuclear power that would imminently attack the U.S. In March 2003, Vice President Dick Cheney appeared on NBC, in remarks rebroadcast by other networks, to claim that Iraq "has, in fact, reconstituted nuclear weapons." In late March, Secretary of Defense Donald Rumsfeld even claimed he knew where the nuclear weapons were.[26] U.S. officials repeatedly made questionable claims about the threat that Iraq's unconventional weapons and ties to *al Qaeda* posed to international peace and security, particularly concerning the risk of a "mushroom cloud" caused by a nuclear weapon detonated in a U.S. city.[27]

U.S. Senate reports confirm that while the American public and United Nations were told that "[a]ll intelligence experts agree that Iraq is seeking nuclear weapons," internal U.S. intelligence reports, which were not released until after the war began, called these claims "weak" and "unsubstantiated." Many of the relevant documents remain classified as secret, particularly those containing evidence that Iraq possessed no weapons of mass destruction and was not in violation of pertinent U.N. Security Council resolutions.[28] Foreign intelligence provided to the U.S., but not disclosed to the public by the president or his representatives, stated that Iraq had no nuclear program remaining by 1999.[29] A Senate report concluded that the public claims were not supported by actual intelligence information.[30] Despite the stated concern about nuclear weapons, the U.S. rejected Iraq's offers to allow U.S. military wide access to suspected weapons sites, and to hold free elections.[31] Recently declassified information shows that as Iraq was becoming the focus, the U.S. terminated a program to kill the actual leaders of *al Qaeda* that *had* carried out 9/11 and *were* seeking weapons of mass destruction.[32]

---

24. *See President Bush's Address to the United Nations*, CNN, Sept. 12, 2002, http://www.cnn.com/2002/US/09/12/bush.transcript.

25. David Wise, *If Bush Is Lying, He's Not the First*, WASH. POST, June 15, 2003, at B1.

26. *See id.*; Dana Milbank, *Bush Remarks Confirm Shift in Justification for War*, WASH. POST, June 1, 2003, at A18.

27. *See, e.g.*, Nicholas Kristof, *The Man with No Ear*, N.Y. TIMES, June 27, 2003, http://www.nytimes.com/2003/06/27/opinion/27KRIS.html; Wolf Blitzer, *Did the Bush Administration Exaggerate the Threat from Iraq?*, CNN.COM, July 8, 2003, http://www.cnn.com/2003/ALLPOLITICS/07/08/wbr.iraq.claims.

28. U.S. Senate, Select Committee on Intelligence, Report on the United States Intelligence Community's Prewar Intelligence Assessments on Iraq, S. Rep. No 108-301, 108th Cong., 2d Sess. (Dec. 12, 2006), at 230–42, 290–91, http://www.gpoaccess.gov/serialset/creports.

29. *See id.* at 122.

30. *See id.* at 129.

31. *See* James Risen, *Iraq Said to Have Tried to Reach Last-Minute Deal to Avert War*, N.Y. TIMES, Nov. 5, 2003, http://www.commondreams.org/headlines03/1106-02.htm; Michael Isikoff & Mark Hosenball, *Lost Opportunity?*, NEWSWEEK (Web Exclusive), Nov. 5, 2003, http://www.msnbc.com/news/989704.asp; Julian Borger, Brian Whitaker & Vikram Dodd, *Saddam's Desperate Offers to Stave Off War*, THE GUARDIAN (U.K.), Nov. 7, 2003, http://www.guardian.co.uk/Iraq/Story/0,2763,1079769,00.html.

32. *See* Siobhan Gorman, *CIA Had Secret Al Qaeda Plan*, WALL ST. J., July 13, 2009, http://online.wsj.com/article/SB124736381913627661.html (one plan, "later scrapped, authorized officers on the ground to 'kill on sight' certain *al Qaeda* targets," including "the most senior leaders in *al Qaeda*"); Carrie Johnson, *Reckoning with Bush Anti-Terror Policies*, CBS NEWS, July 13, 2009, http://www.cbsnews.com/stories/2009/07/13/politics/washingtonpost/main5154942.shtml; Mark Mazzetti & Scott Shane, *C.I.A. Had Plan to Assassinate Qaeda Leaders*, N.Y. TIMES, July 13, 2009, http://www.nytimes.com/2009/07/14/us/14intel.html?_r=2&hp. *See also Al Qaeda Documents, Man-*

The majority of the permanent members of the Security Council did not believe that a breach of the 1991 cease-fire conditions had occurred that triggered an authority vested in the U.S. and Britain to enforce the 1990 U.N. resolutions. They rejected U.S. claims that there had been a material breach of the 1991 cease-fire, because there was insufficient evidence of banned weapons in Iraq, and U.S. and British claims that there were such weapons had been revealed to be based on doctored or unreliable intelligence reports.[33] Their joint memorandum stated that there was "no evidence" that Iraq had violated pertinent U.N. resolutions, weapons inspections were proceeding "without hindrance," and war should have been a "last resort."[34] In addition, the Security Council was "seized of the matter" of Iraq's compliance, which is an international law phrase meaning that any enforcement action against Iraq had to be decided by entire Security Council, subject to a Russian, Chinese, or French veto.[35] Finally, the supposed beneficiary of the "collective self-defense" effort in Iraq pursuant to U.N. Security Council resolutions 678 and 687, its southern neighbor Kuwait, was actually opposed to the invasion.[36] Saudi Arabia, another neighbor, declared that a war "could 'shake peace, security and stability in the region and the world.'" Jordan agreed, calling the proposed war a "tremendous mistake."[37]

The U.S., U.K., Italy, Spain, Poland, Romania, and other coalition partners argued that their invasion of Iraq was justified under Article 51 of the U.N. Charter, which permits self-defense in the event of an "armed attack." The U.S. and some members of the coalition contended that U.N. Security Council resolutions 678, 687, and 1441 required the disarmament of Iraq's chemical and biological weapons and nuclear weapons programs after the Persian Gulf War, and that resolution 1441 in particular warned of "serious consequences" for a failure to comply.[38] France, Russia, and China, the other permanent

uals Found in Kabul, CNN, Nov. 17, 2001, http://www.cnn.com; David Rohde, *In 2 Abandoned Kabul Houses, Some Hints of Al Qaeda Presence,* N.Y. Times, Nov. 17, 2001, http://www.nytimes.com/2001/11/17/world/nation-challenged-kabul-2-abandoned-kabul-houses-some-hints-al-qaeda-presence.html; *Al Qaeda Documents Outline Serious Weapons Program,* CNN, Jan. 25, 2002, http://www.cnn.com.

33. *See* Bob Drogin & John Goetz, *How US Fell Under the Spell of 'Curveball',* L.A. Times, Feb. 5, 2003, http://www.latimes.com/news/nationworld/columnone/la-na-curveball20nov20,0,5692836.story?page=1.

34. *Text of Memorandum Submitted by France, Russia, Germany,* CNN, Feb. 24, 2003, http://www.cnn.com/2003/US/02/24/sprj.irq.memo/index.html.

35. *See* Jeff Sallott, *Attack Illegal, Experts Say,* Globe and Mail (Canada), Mar. 20, 2003, http://www.theglobeandmail.com/servlet/story/RTGAM.20030320.ulaww0320/BNStory/International.

36. *Kuwait Protests Over Iraq Statement,* BBC News, Feb. 18, 2003, http://news.bbc.co.uk/2/hi/middle_east/2776819.stm.

37. *Quoted in Scorecard: For or Against Military Action in Iraq,* N.Y. Times, Aug. 27, 2002, at A8.

38. *See* S.C. Res. 678 (Nov. 29, 1990); S.C. Res. 687 (Apr. 8, 1991); S.C. Res. 1441 (Nov. 8, 2002); U.S. Dep't of Justice, Office of Legal Counsel, Memorandum for Alberto R. Gonzales. Counsel to the President, Re: Authority of the President Under Domestic and International Law to Use Military Force Against Iraq (Oct. 23, 2002); U.S. Dep't of Justice, Office of Legal Counsel, Memorandum for Alberto R. Gonzales, Counsel to the President, Re: Effect of a Recent United Nations Security Council Resolution on the Authority of the President Under International Law to Use Military Force Against Iraq, http://judiciary.senate.gov/resources/documents/upload/010509OLCDoc-UNSecurityCouncil-Resolution.pdf; *Powell Says Kay Report Confirms Iraq Defied U.N. Res. 1441* (2003), http://www.america.gov/st/washfile-english/2003/October/20031007091342nosnhojb0.5803186.html; William Howard Taft IV & T. Buchwald, *Preemption, Iraq, and International Law,* 97 American J. of Int'l L. 557, 563 (2003); William Howard Taft IV, *State: Taft on President's Auth. to Use Force in Iraq* (Mar. 20, 2003), http://www.iraqwatch.org/government/US/State/state-taft-032003.htm; Lord Goldsmith, Attorney General of the United Kingdom of Great Britain and Northern Ireland, *The Legal Basis for the Use of Force Against Iraq* (Mar. 17, 2003), http://usiraq.procon.org/viewbackgroundresource.asp?resourceID=960.

members of the Security Council, maintained that resolutions 687 and 1441 did not authorize a U.N. war against Iraq.[39]

Before the 2003 invasion of Iraq by a coalition of democratic nations, the governments that spearheaded the coalition received numerous warnings of large-scale refugee flight. U.N. projections were for 500,000 Iraqi casualties and possibly millions of refugees and IDPs. Amnesty International warned of "large-scale refugee movements," with "many thousands [] expected to leave their homes in search of safety," the majority of whom would probably be women and children.[40] The United Nations predicted 900,000 refugees and 1.1 million IDPs in the event of a war against the U.S. and U.K.[41] A U.N. official told the *Washington Post* in late 2002 that a "few million" could flee the country, and that six million might be displaced from Baghdad due to the cut-off of water and electricity.[42]

In fact, the invasion claimed the lives of up to 60,000 Iraqi soldiers, according to estimates by the American generals who oversaw its prosecution.[43] Up to 135,000 Iraqi soldiers and militia were injured in the first eight months of the war. About 10,000 Iraqi civilians died from violence in 2003, as the Baghdad morgue reported an increase in corpses received of about 500 per month. More than 1,500 cluster bombs were dropped from airplanes on Iraq in the first year of the war, killing dozens of civilians and leaving behind hundreds of "explosive projectiles designed to separate and spread when released." When they blow up, these cluster bombs scatter "fragments of munitions [that] penetrate the body, maiming or provoking lethal internal bleeding." About 1,000 Iraqi children were killed or injured by previously unexploded bombs in the first three months after the war. Up to 20 children per day were killed or injured by unexploded bombs in one Iraqi city alone. Forty percent of Baghdad's neighborhoods and forty percent of the population of Basra lost their access to drinking water, forcing them to forego food and medicine to buy water, or to drink from contaminated and polluted rivers.[44]

The infrastructure needed to sustain life in Iraq's hostile and dry climate suffered pervasive deterioration. The Ministry of Health was burned in the invasion, and terrorism and looting devastated the hospitals and aid agencies. The remains of the water and sanitation systems collapsed, accelerating epidemics of waterborne disease like diarrhea. War

---

39. *See* Associated Press, *Russia, France and China Issue Joint Interpretation of Security Council Resolution,* Augusta Chronicle, Jan. 25, 2003, http://chronicle.augusta.com/stories/012503/ira_council2.shtml.

40. *See* Amnesty International, *Iraq: Refugees and Displaced Persons—Protection First,* AI Index No. MDE14/038/2003 (2003), http://www.amnesty.org/en/library/asset/MDE14/038/2003/en/ea2fbb2d-d713-11dd-b0cc-1f0860013475/mde140382003en.html; Irwin Arieff, *U.N. Sees 500,000 Iraqi Casualties at Start of War,* Reuters, Jan. 7, 2003, http://www.commondreams.org/headlines03/0107-09.htm; Australian Broadcasting Corp., *UN Report Predicts 500000 Iraqi Dead* (Sept. 2003), http://www.abc.net.au/7.30/stories/s760655.htm; Canadian Broadcasting Corp., *Fears Iraq War Could Set Off Humanitarian Crisis* (Jan 13, 2003), http://www.cbc.ca/world/story/2003/01/13/iraqhumanitarian030113.html.

41. *See* United Nations, *Likely Humanitarian Scenarios* ¶ 11 (Dec. 10, 2002), http://www.casi.org.uk/info/undocs/war021210.pdf. *See also* Rhoda Margesson & Johanna Bockman, *Potential Humanitarian Issues in Post-war Iraq: An Overview for Congress,* Cong. Research Serv. No. RL31814.

42. *See* Rajiv Chandrasekaran & Peter Slevin, *This Time Around, War Would Hit Iraq Harder,* Wash. Post, Oct. 29, 2002, at A12; United Nations, *Likely Humanitarian Scenarios* ¶ 11.

43. *See* Bob Woodward, Plan of Attack 408 (New York: Simon & Schuster, 2004) (citing estimates of U.S. generals).

44. Medact, Continuing Collateral Damage: The Health and Environmental Costs of War on Iraq 2003, at 2–5 (London: Medact, 2003) (citing U.N. Children's Fund, *Humanitarian Briefing, Baghdad* (July 17, 2003), http://www.un.org/apps/news/infocusnewsiraq1.asp?sID=11).

and looting destroyed Iraq's hospitals and water infrastructure along with most public buildings.[45]

Many deaths resulted from policy decisions by the U.S. and the U.K. that inadvertently imposed conditions of life on the Iraqi people that were not conducive to survival. Children suffered from starvation, euphemistically referred to as "acute malnutrition," at nearly double the rate in 2002. Food rations on which more than 20 million Iraqis depended were drastically cut back. Many more Iraqis lacked access to safe drinking water, and cholera spread rapidly.[46] In the first half of 2004, the median per capita household income in Iraq was $144. The median per capita household income for all of 2003 was only $255.[47]

The CPA held $8.5 billion in cash from seized Iraqi assets and the proceeds of oil sales at the end of 2003, mostly in the Federal Reserve Bank of New York.[48] These billions had not been spent on the welfare of the Iraqi people, despite the widespread high rates of acute malnutrition, infectious disease, illiteracy, and unemployment, not to mention the looting of the country during and after regime change. About $8.8 billion from the Development Fund for Iraq, representing proceeds of Iraqi oil sales and frozen Iraqi assets, went missing under the CPA. Political operatives with no accounting experience were placed in charge of a multi-billion dollar oil economy, as a book by the *Washington Post*'s Baghdad correspondent documented.[49]

C. Genocide in Occupied Iraq?

1. The Warning Signs

Six months after the invasion of Iraq, a model for early warning of genocidal violence developed for the U.S. government described Iraq as at high risk of genocide. Iraq had

---

45. *See* Jeffrey Gettleman, *Chaos and War Leave Iraq's Hospitals in Ruins*, N.Y. Times, Feb. 14, 2004; *see also* Robert Fisk, *For the People On the Streets, This Is Not Liberation but a New Colonial Oppression*, The Independent (U.K.), Apr. 17, 2003; U.N. Children's Fund, *At a Glance: Iraq* (2004), http://www.unicef.org/infobycountry/iraq.html.

46. *See* Hussein al-Yasiri, *Anger Over Food Ration Hitches*, IWPR, Sept. 27, 2005, http://www.iwpr.net; *Children 'Starving' in New Iraq*, BBC News, Mar. 30, 2005, http://www.bbc.co.uk; Patrick Cockburn, *Cholera Spreads in Iraq As Health Services Collapse*, The Independent (U.K.), Aug. 31, 2007, http://www.independent.co.uk; Jonathan Fowler, *Expert: Malnutrition Affects Iraq Kids*, Associated Press, Mar. 30, 2005, http://www.ap.org; "*Iraq: Child Malnutrition*," Parliamentary Debates, Lords, vol. 682, HL5858 (June 5, 2006), answer by Lord Triesman, Under-Secretary of State, Foreign and Commonwealth Office, to question by the Earl of Sandwich to the Government, http://www.publications.parliament.uk/pa/ld200405/ldhansrd/pdvn/lds06/text/60605w05.htm#60605w05_sbhd3; Reuters, *Hunger, Disease Spread In Iraq—Oxfam Report*, Alertnet, July 30, 2007, http://www.alertnet.org/thenews/newsdesk/L3048136.htm; Daud Salman, *Food Rations Cut Hurting Poor*, IWPR, Mar. 29, 2006, http://www.iwpr.net; UNICEF, *Food Insecurity in Iraq Persists: Children Suffer*, May 11, 2006, http://www.unicef.org; U.N. IRIN, *Iraq: Food Prices Rise After Reduction of Monthly Rations*, U.N. IRIN, Apr. 2, 2006, http://www.un.org.

47. *See* U.N. Consolidated Appeals Process, *Humanitarian Appeal for Iraq 2008* (Feb. 12, 2008), http://ochaonline.un.org/humanitarianappeal/webpage.asp?Page=1656.

48. *See* International Advisory Monitoring Board for Iraq, *Development Fund for Iraq—Statement of Cash Receipts and Payments for the period from 22 May 2003 to 31 December 2003 (with Independent Auditors' Report)* (July 15, 2004), http://www.iamb.info/auditrep/r052203a.pdf.

49. Rajiv Chandrasekaran, *Back on Capitol Hill, Bremer Is Facing a Cooler Reception*, Wash. Post, Feb. 6, 2007, at A09.

many of the warning signs of previous genocides, such as those in Turkey, German-occupied Europe, Yugoslavia, and Rwanda, including demonization of minority groups, unfair scapegoating of minorities for the problems of the majority population, and refugee flight.[50] The war itself was a contributory factor to the risk of genocide, as such policies typically follow abrupt political change or "national upheaval," which escalate existing group conflicts into intense violence.[51] The Office of the Special Adviser of the U.N. Secretary-General on the Prevention of Genocide has argued that some of the triggering events for genocide include changes of regime outside of constitutionally-mandated procedures, upcoming elections, disqualifications of political parties from electoral eligibility, military deployments against civilians, and armed combat.[52]

The extent of political change was difficult to overstate, with fundamentalist Shi'a political parties that had been based in Iran during Gulf War I, and that were part of a long-term strategy of the Iranian theocracy to take over Iraq in the eyes of U.S. analysts, replacing a regime that had executed Shi'a religious leaders and banned many public displays of Shi'ism.[53] The new Iraqi constitution of 2005 condemned the previous regime for "sectarian oppression ... by the autocratic clique," declared Islam to be the "official religion of the State" and "source of legislation, "and established "experts in Islamic jurisprudence" on the Federal Supreme Court to review all Iraqi laws for compliance with "the established provisions of Islam."[54] The President of Iraq since 2005, Jalal Talabani, was the head of an Iranian-backed Kurdish group that actually fought on the side of Ayatollah Khomeini during the 1980s.[55]

Other so-called "accelerators" for genocide were present in post-2003 Iraq, including executions of group leaders, torture, mass political demonstrations, refugee flight, forcible resettlements and deprivations of property rights, human rights violations, formation of militias, and acquisition of arms from foreign sources.[56] Shi'a death squads based in the Ministry of Interior and elsewhere assassinated numerous Ba'athists and former Ba'athists using personnel records obtained by government officials or by private persons from looted government buildings.[57] The government announced efforts in 2003 to execute

---

50. *Iraq, Afghanistan, 11 Other States At Risk of Genocide: Expert,* Agence France-Presse, Jan. 28, 2004, http://www.keepmedia.com/pubs/AFP/2004/01/27/361322.

51. *See* Alvarez, Governments, Citizens, and Genocide, at 133.

52. *See* Office of the Special Adviser of the Secretary-General on the Prevention of Genocide, *Analysis Framework* (2009), http://www.un.org/preventgenocide/adviser/pdf/OSAPG%20Analysis FrameworkExternalVersion.pdf.

53. *See* Mark Hosenball et al., *Iran: Running the New Iraq*, Newsweek, Feb. 21, 2005, http://www.accessmylibrary.com.

54. Const. of Iraq 2005, preamble, arts. 2, 89.

55. *See* Edgar O'Ballance, The Gulf War– 133 (London: Brassey's, 1988); *Timeline: Iraq After Saddam*, BBC News, http://news.bbc.co.uk/2/hi/middle_ east/4192189.stm.

56. *See* John L. Davies, Barbara Harff, and Anne Speca, *Dynamic Data for Early Conflict Warning, in* Preventive measures: Building Risk Assessment and Early Crisis Warning Systems 79–88 (John Davies & Ted Robert Gurr eds., London: Rowman & Littlefield, 1996); Barbara Harff, *Early Warning of Humanitarian Crises: Sequential Models and the Role of Accelerators, in id.* at 70–78; Barbara Harff, *Could Humanitarian Crises Have Been Anticipated in Burundi, Rwanda, and Zaire? A Comparative Study of Anticipatory Indicators, in* Journeys Through Conflict: Narratives and Lessons 81–101 (London: Rowman & Littlefield, 2001); Barbara Harff, *The Etiology of Genocides, in* Genocide and the Modern Age: Etiology and Case Studies of Mass Death 41–59 (Isidor Walliman & Michael N. Dobkowski, eds., New York: Greenwood Press, 1987).

57. *See* Ali A. Allawi, The Occupation of Iraq: Winning the War, Losing the Peace 241, 396, 378–459, 491 (New Haven, CT: Yale UP, 2007).

Saddam Hussein and some of his key lieutenants for genocide, war crimes, and crimes against humanity.[58] Mass political demonstrations occurred on a routine basis in Baghdad, Fallujah, Mosul, and elsewhere.[59] Demonstrations in favor of theocratic Shi'a rule, and demanding elections that were widely expected to propel an alliance of Shi'a political parties to power, were frequently covered on television and in print media.[60]

Terrorist organizations and militia groups that were formed in or expanded into Iraq after the 2003 invasion include *al Qaeda* in Mesopotamia, Islamic State of Iraq, 1920 Revolution Brigades, Islamic Front of Iraqi Resistance, Mujahideen Army, *Jaysh al-Madhi* (the Mahdi Army), Badr Brigades, and Kurdish *pesh merga*.[61] The constitution of 2005 was seen as validating the continued existence of pro-government militia by allowing regional "security forces and guards" as an exception to the general ban on "militia outside the ... armed forces."[62] The coalition left about 200,000 tons of weapons unsecured, which militias eagerly snapped up. The *pesh merga* even obtained tanks and artillery seized from the regime.[63]

Amnesty International estimated that one million additional small arms (mainly automatic rifles and machine guns) were imported into Iraq after 2003 from China, Russia, the United Kingdom, and the U.S. These added to an existing stockpile of 15 million machine guns in Iraq. Amnesty International reported that the "easy availability of small arms and lack of accountability has contributed to sectarian killings by armed groups, as well as torture and other ill-treatment and sectarian extra-judicial executions by Iraqi government forces," and that many weapons were falling "into the hands of militias working as death squads or insurgents."[64] By 2009 Iraq had imported $5 billion in American weapons, supplies, and training.[65] Hundreds of thousands of small arms went missing and were believed to have armed *al Qaeda* in Iraq.[66]

---

58. *See* CPA Order No. 48, Delegation of Authority to Iraqi Special Tribunal, CPA/ORD/10 DEC 2003/48; Statute of the Iraqi Special Tribunal (Dec. 10, 2003), http://www.cpa-iraq.org; Const. of Iraq 2005, art. 48; Iraqi High Tribunal Rules of Procedure and Evidence, Law/Resolution No. 10, Official Gazette of Iraq, No. 4006, Oct. 18, 2005, in Saddam on Trial, at 220–22; Michael A. Newton, *The Significance of the Anfal Campaign Indictment, in* Saddam on Trial, at 220–22; *Timeline of the Dujail Trial, in* Saddam on Trial, at 76–82; Jim Krane, *Politics Afoot in a Bid to Rush Saddam Trial, Ousted Tribunal Director Says,* Wash. Post, Aug. 12, 2004, at A19.

59. *See* Larry Jay Diamond, Squandered Victory: The American Occupation and the Bungled Effort to Bring Democracy to Iraq 231 (New York: Times Books, 2006); Allawi, The Occupation of Iraq, at 138, 158, 212–30, 245, 268, 273, 325, 391; *Iraq: US Military Confirms Killing Iraqis in Mosul During Protest,* RadioFreeEurope/RadioLiberty, Apr. 16, 2003, http://www.rferl.org/content/Article/1102951.html; *Iraq: Security Forces Open Fire At Two Separate Protests,* RadioFreeEurope/RadioLiberty, Oct. 1, 2003, http://www.rferl.org/content/Article/1104509.html.

60. *See* Allawi, The Occupation of Iraq, at 138, 168, 212–30, 278.

61. *See* Loretta Napoleoni, Insurgent Iraq: Al Zarqawi and the New Generation 137–45, 191, 253 (New York: Seven Stories Press, 2005); James L. Jones, *The Report of the Independent Commission on the Security Forces of Iraq* 25–31 (2007), http://media.csis.org/isf.pdf.

62. Const. of Iraq 2005, art. 117. *See also* Mats Berdal, Transforming Armed Groups After Conflict: War-to-Peace Transitions 99 (London: Taylor & Francis, 2009).

63. *See* Allawi, The Occupation of Iraq, at 140.

64. Amnesty International, *Blood at the Crossroads: Making the Case for a Global Arms Trade Treaty,* AI Index No. ACT 30/011/2008 (2008), http://www.amnesty.org/en/library/asset/ACT30/011/2008/en/64decb12-6ea3-11dd-8e5e-43ea85d15a69/act300112008eng.html.

65. *See* Michael Evans, *After the Surge, the $5bn Splurge as Iraq Draws Up Wishlist for Rebuilding Its Forces,* The Times (U.K.), Feb. 17, 2009, 2009 WLNR 3063207.

66. *See* Richard Norton-Taylor, *Amnesty Warns US and UK Are Failing to Monitor Flood of Arms into Iraq,* The Guardian (U.K.), Sept. 17, 2008, http://www.guardian.co.uk/world/2008/sep/17/armstrade.humanrights.

Militia violence, sectarian strife, wartime strife, joblessness, poverty, and starvation drove 1.6 million people outside the country in the two and a half years after May 2003. Up to 700,000 had fled to Jordan, 600,000 to Syria, 100,000 to Saudi Arabia and Kuwait, and 436,000 elsewhere. An additional 1.6 million were displaced inside Iraq by December 2006.[67]

The risk of genocide against Shi'a Arabs, Kurds, and Assyrian Christians, as groups with representatives in the pro-war Iraqi National Congress, may have been heightened by detention and interrogation policies that humiliated many Sunni Arab and Ba'athist prisoners and their families, and gave rise to a bitter, organized response. An Iraqi general and several other detainees died in custody of such causes as "massive blow to the head," or being suffocated with an electrical cord while being wrapped in a sleeping bag.[68] The Red Cross reported mistreatment of prisoners by military intelligence at Camp Cropper and at Abu Ghraib prison, the Ministry of Defense and Presidential Palace in Baghdad, the Iraqi secret police headquarters in Basra, Habbaniya Camp in Ramadi governorate, a school being used as a prison in Tikrit, and a detention center at a base near the Syrian border. Prisoners reported, and the Red Cross viewed wounds consistent with, beatings with pistols and rifles, punches and kicks, stomping of faces into the ground, handcuffs so tight that nerve damage resulted, threats of imminent executions or reprisals against family members, nudity in completely dark cells, and deprivation of food, water, and sleep. The Red Cross described three incidents in mid-2003 in which prisoners at Camp Cropper outside Baghdad International Airport were fired upon after protesting or attempting to flee the conditions of their detention.[69] Red Cross medical officials observed symptoms of mental illness including acute anxiety and suicidal tendencies, which "appeared to have been caused by the methods and duration of interrogation."[70]

The initially secret report on these camps was delivered to MNF commander Lt. Gen. Ricardo Sanchez, who had his legal adviser prepare a response. The U.S. denied the Red Cross the ability to visit unannounced the areas where the worst abuses occurred.[71] In August 2003, Amnesty International described torture and "ill-treatment" of Iraqi prisoners of war by coalition forces, including "prolonged sleep deprivation, prolonged restraint in painful positions—sometimes combined with exposure to loud music, prolonged hooding and exposure to bright lights."[72] At Camp Cropper, 3,000 Iraqi prisoners lived eighty to a tent, with thin mats to sleep on, and only shovels and trenches for latrines.[73]

---

67. *See* U.N. Secretary-General, Report Pursuant to Paragraph 30 of Resolution 1546 (2004), S/2006/945, para. 36 (Dec. 5, 2006), http://daccessdds.un.org/doc/UNDOC/GEN/N06/634/80/PDF/N0663480.pdf?OpenElement.

68. *See* Human Rights First, *Command's Responsibility: Detainee Deaths in U.S. Custody in Iraq and Afghanistan* (Feb. 22, 2006), http://www.humanrightsfirst.org/us_law/etn/dic/exec-sum.asp; Hina Shamsi, *Command's Responsibility: Detainee Deaths in U.S. Custody in Iraq and Afghanistan* (Feb. 22, 2006), http://www.humanrightsfirst.org/us_law/etn/dic/statement-shamsi.asp.

69. *See* The International Committee of the Red Cross (ICRC), *Report on the Treatment by Coalition Forces of Prisoners of War and Other Protected Persons by the Geneva Conventions in Iraq During Arrest, Internment and Interrogation* 18–19 (Feb. 2004), http://msnbcmedia.msn.com/i/msnbc/Sections/News/International%20News/Mideast%20and%20N.%20Africa/Iraq%20conflict/Red%20Cross%20report.pdf.

70. *Id.* at 7, 12–13.

71. Greg Jaffe & David S. Cloud, *American Officials in Iraq Knew Last Fall of Prison Abuse*, WALL STREET J., May 19, 2004, http://www.derechos.org/nizkor/iraq/doc/torture18.html.

72. Amnesty International, *Iraq: Continuing Failure to Uphold Human Rights* (June 23, 2003), http://www.amnesty.ca/resource_centre/reports/view.php?load=arcview&article=689.

73. *See id.*; Olga Craig, *Dirty, Hunched and Hungry: Tariq Aziz Digs His Own Latrine*, THE TELEGRAPH (U.K.), July 19, 2003, http://www.telegraph.co.uk.

Numerous Iraqis told Amnesty International that large sums of money were taken from them upon their arrest in their homes.[74] Human Rights Watch, declassified U.S. military documents, and the international press reported the subjection of Iraqi detainees to beatings, stress positions, electric shock treatment, denial of food and water, exposure to extreme heat or cold, threats of more severe violence, and confinement for prolonged periods in small boxes in which it is impossible to sit or stand.[75]

The Iraqi government appointed by the coalition enshrined religion as the basis of the new Iraq. After the end of "major combat operations," the CPA established an Iraqi Governing Council (IGC) to manage the country. The U.S. handed 60% of the seats on the Iraqi Governing Council to Shi'a Muslims with long-standing ties to Ayatollah Khomeini. These council members subsequently used their power to attempt to promulgate fundamentalist laws for the country, repealing more secular laws guaranteeing women's equality with men in certain matters that had been enforced by the previous regime.[76] Religious party cadres replaced secular officials, as the CPA fired hundreds of thousands of Iraqi government workers, including tens of thousands of teachers.[77]

Iraq's economic statistics also reflected an atmosphere of national upheaval. The war "resulted in the shutdown of much of the central economic administrative structure," and Iraq's GDP shrank by a fifth.[78] The unemployment rate for Iraqis doubled to about

---

74. *See* Amnesty International, *Iraq: Continuing Failure.*

75. *See* American Civil Liberties Union (ACLU), *ACLU and HRF Ask Circuit Court to Reconsider Rumsfeld Torture Case* (Apr. 25, 2008), http://72.3.233.245/safefree/torture/feed.xml; ACLU, *ACLU Obtains Defense Department Documents about Prisoner Deaths and Interrogations* (May 14, 2008), http://72.3.233.245/safefree/torture/feed.xml; ACLU, *Army Documents Show Senior Official Reportedly Pushed Limits on Detainee Interrogations* (May 2, 2006), http://72.3.233.245/safefree/torture/feed.xml; ACLU, *Defense Department Releases Documents Relating to Detainee Abuse in U.S. Custody Overseas* (July 2, 2009), http://www.aclu.org/safefree/torture/40123prs20090702.html?s_src=RSS; ACLU, *Defense Department to Release Prisoner Abuse Photos by May 28 in Response to ACLU Lawsuit* (Apr. 23, 2009), http://72.3.233.245/safefree/torture/feed.xml; ACLU, *Documents Obtained by ACLU Provide Further Evidence That Abuse of Iraqi Prisoners Was Systemic* (Nov. 19, 2008), http://72.3.233.245/safefree/torture/feed.xml; Human Rights Watch, *Leadership Failure: Firsthand Accounts of Torture of Iraqi Detainees by the U.S. Army's 82nd Airborne Division* 9–12 (Sept. 2005), http://www.hrw.org; Human Rights Watch, *No Blood, No Foul: Soldiers' Accounts of Detainee Abuse in Iraq* 6–14 (July 2006), http://www.hrw.org; Human Rights Watch, *The New Iraq? Torture and Ill-treatment of Detainees in Iraqi Custody* 2–4 (Jan. 2005), http://www.hrw.org; Lt. Gen. Ricardo Sanchez, *CJTF-7 [Combined Joint Task Force-7] Interrogation and Counter-Resistance Policy* (Sept. 14, 2003), http:// 72.3.233.245/safefree/general/17561lgl20050329.html; U.S. Dep't of Defense, *Memo Dated June 15, 2003*, http://www.aclu.org/projects/foiasearch/pdf/DOD046342.pdf; U.S. Marine Corps, *USMC Alleged Detainee Abuse Cases Since 11 Sep 01*, http://www.aclu.org; *see also* Janis Karpinski, One Woman's Army: The Commanding General of Abu Ghraib Tells Her Story– (New York: Miramax Books, 2006); Naomi Klein, The Shock Doctrine: The Rise of Disaster Capitalism 367–72 (London: Penguin Books, 2007); John F. Burns, *Torture Alleged at Ministry Site Outside Baghdad*, N.Y. Times, Nov. 16, 2005, http://www.nytimes.com.

76. *See* Pamela Constable, *Women in Iraq Decry Decision to Curb Rights: Council Backs Islamic Law on Families*, Wash. Post, Jan. 16, 2004, http://www.washingtonpost.com.

77. *See* International Crisis Group, *Iraq's Muqtada Al-Sadr: Spoiler or Stabiliser?*, Int'l Crisis Group, Middle East Report No. 55, at 14–16 (July 11, 2006), http://www.ciaonet.org/pbei/icg/icg007/icg007.pdf; Aaron Mate, *Pillage Is Forbidden: Why the Privatisation of Iraq Is Illegal*, The Guardian (U.K.), Nov. 7, 2003, http://www.guardian.co.uk; Sami Moubayed, *Maliki on a Path to Self-destruction*, Asia Times Online, Nov. 15, 2006, http://www.atimes.com/atimes/Middle_East/HK15Ak02.html; Richard Sale, *Iraqi CPA Fires 28,000*, Wash. Times, Nov. 22, 2003, http://www.washtimes.com.

78. *See* CIA, World Factbook 2004, http://www.umsl.edu/services/govdocs/wofact2004/geos/iz.html.

70 percent,[79] which compares unfavorably to the former Yugoslavia's unemployment rate of 16% in 1990, at the outbreak of civil war and genocide in Bosnia.[80] Iraq suffered severe financial and monetary losses, with more than $11.35 billion in lost revenue and infrastructure damage due to terrorist attacks through mid-2005.[81] This figure compared to about $400 billion in U.S. direct outlays by late 2006, not counting the cost of deaths and injuries among Iraqis or Americans.[82]

Hundreds of thousands of people became homeless by 2004,[83] and nearly five million in all were made refugees or IDPs by 2007.[84] Electricity production fell after the war, and families and hospitals complained of prolonged blackouts, or rather intermittently available electricity, that destroyed lives, human health, and the quality of life. More than 3,000 schools were bombed, looted, or otherwise destroyed in the war and ensuing chaos.[85]

The CPA promulgated an interim Iraqi constitution that governed Iraq for more than a year and a half, from March 2004 until about the end of 2005.[86] The public statements of the Iraqi fundamentalist leaders who implemented the interim constitution, referred to as a Law of Administration for the State of Iraq for the Transitional Period, or "TAL," indicated that theocratic rule was their objective. Iraq's interim prime minister virtually declared allegiance to the Shi'a Ayatollah Ali Hussein al-Sistani, describing him as standing at the "forefront" of all of the country's other religious authorities during the handover of sovereignty from the CPA in June 2004.[87] The alliance of Ayatollah al-Sistani and the Supreme Council for the Islamic Revolution in Iraq (SCIRI) resembled the movement of Ayatollah Khomeini of Iran in that it demanded that fundamentalist religious law be used to deny equal rights to women and religious minorities.[88] SCIRI and al-Sistani received large donations from the spiritual capital of Iran and used them to main-

---

79. *See* CPA, *Administrator's Weekly Report, Essential Services* (Sept. 27, 2003), http://www.iraqcoalition.org.

80. *See id.*; *Yugoslavia, in* WORLD FACTBOOK 1981, http://www.archive.org/details/worldfactbook82natiilli.

81. *See* Jim Crane, *Iraq's Oil Production Declines This Year,* ASSOCIATED PRESS/N.C. TIMES, Dec. 12, 2009, http://www.nctimes.com/articles/2005/12/09/business/news/16_31_3912_8_05.txt.

82. *See* David M. Herszenhorn, *Estimates of Iraq War Cost Were Not Close to Ballpark,* N.Y. TIMES, Mar. 19, 2008, http://www.nytimes.com/2008/03/19/washington/19cost.html?pagewanted=print; Mark Mazzetti & Joel Havemann, *Iraq War Is Costing $100000 Per Minute*, L.A. TIMES/SEATTLE TIMES, Feb. 3, 2006, http://seattletimes.nwsource.com/html/politics/2002780385_spending03.html.

83. *See* Dexter Filkins, *Kurds Advancing to Reclaim Land in Northern Iraq*, N.Y. TIMES, June 20, 2004, http://www.nytimes.com; *Iraq: New Housing Project for Displaced People*, U.N. IRIN, June 8, 2004, http://www.irinnews.org/report.asp?ReportID=41465&SelectRegion=Iraq_Crisis&SelectCountry=IRAQ (50,000 people displaced due to fighting in Fallujah alone).

84. *See* Walter Pincus, *U.S. Can't Keep Up On Visas for Iraqis Refugees in Danger After Helping Coalition,* WASH. POST, July 25, 2008, http://www.washingtonpost.com; Doug Smith & Ned Parker, *2.3 Million Iraqis Reported Displaced,* L.A. TIMES, Nov. 6, 2007, http://www.latimes.com.

85. *See Iraq Reconstruction: Education*, BBC NEWS.COM, Apr. 7, 2004, http://news.bbc.co.uk/1/hi/world/middle_east/3605821.stm.

86. Rajiv Chandrasekaran, *Iraq Fails to Meet Bush Deadline,* THE AGE (AUSTRALIA), Mar. 1, 2004, http://www.theage.com.au. *See also* Rajiv Chandrasekaran, *Iraqis Divided Over Charter: Shi'ites Walk Out Amid A Dispute*, WASH. POST, Feb. 28. 2004, http://www.washingtonpost.com.

87. *Transcript: Political Authority Handover Ceremony*, WASH. POST, June 28, 2004, http://www.washingtonpost.com.

88. *See* Steven R. Weisman, *Bush Plan Will Limit Sovereignty for Iraqis,* N.Y. TIMES, Apr. 23, 2004, http://www.nytimes.com; Terence P. Jeffrey, *Is Sistani Iraq's Khomeini?*, HUMAN EVENTS, May 26, 2004, http://www.humanevents.com; Andrew Hammond, *Iraqi Shiites Oppose Power Transfer Plan: 'Real Problems' Ahead: Ayatollah Makes Rare Public Statement on U.S. Timetable,* NATIONAL POST (CANADA), Nov. 27, 2003, http://www.nationalpost.com.

tain private armies, along with a website detailing the characteristics of the planned fundamentalist state.[89] Although Ayatollah Sistani promised to be less active in politics than Ayatollah Khomeini believed that clerics should be, the latter also made reassuring statements to the West about democracy, religious freedom, and women's rights, behaving quite differently once securely in power.[90] The Iraqi Ayatollahs have been even less moderate in tone than Khomeini, in some respects;[91] they openly "'use[d] religion in order to assume power,'" in the words of the former head of the IGC, while Khomeini reassured Iranians and the West that his was an anti-imperialist and nationalist movement.[92]

In the January 2005 election, a coalition of Iraqi Shi'a fundamentalist parties claimed about half of all votes, and promptly declared that religious law would be implemented.[93] The coalition controlled more than 130 seats in the 275-member Iraqi National Assembly charged with drafting a permanent constitution.[94] Its architect and inspiration, Ayatollah Sistani, pledged that the coalition would make Islam the sole source of legislation in the permanent constitution, and prohibit any law that was contrary to his version of Islam.[95]

The close ties of leading Iraqi politicians to the Iranian theocracy did not bode well for the multi-national forces' declared objective of securing "Iraqi freedom." With opposition to the Iranian government's most conservative religious policies reportedly widespread,[96] some elements in the country's leadership resorted to torturing and executing thousands to maintain power.[97] As Iraq followed the lead of its larger neighbor, a similar drama played out, as it has in many other theocracies known to history. When the drafting of a permanent constitution was underway, with SCIRI in the lead, a pollster in Baghdad warned: "When religious men start governing Iraq, we will land in a dangerous situation. These people think they have the right solution because they have been authorised by God."[98] Iraqi author Ghassan Attiyah noted at the time: "Civil war and the partitioning of Iraq may now be difficult to avoid.[99]

---

89. *See* Graham E. Fuller, *Islamist Politics in Iraq after Saddam Hussein* (Aug. 2003), http://www.usip.org; Borzou Daragahi, *Al-Sistani Mixes Tradition with Modern Outlook*, WASH. TIMES, Mar. 9, 2004, http://www.washtimes.com.

90. *See* Daragahi, *Al-Sistani*; Jeffrey, *Is Sistani Iraq's Khomeini?*

91. *See* Jeffrey, *Is Sistani Iraq's Khomeini?*

92. *Quoted in* Edward Wong, *Iraq's Path Hinges on the Words of Enigmatic Cleric*, N.Y. TIMES, Jan. 25, 2004, http://query.nytimes.com/gst/abstract.html?res=F30913FD3D5C0C768EDDA80894DC404482.

93. David Enders, *Iraqi Vote Gives Shia Parties a Mandate for Islamic Law*, THE INDEPENDENT (U.K.), Feb. 14, 2005, at 2.

94. *See id.*; Daniszewski, *Ancient Faith Is a Reminder of Iraq's Diversity*, at A1.

95. *See* Michael Jansen, *Shia Clerics Insist on the Adoption of Islamic Law*, IRISH TIMES, Feb. 7, 2005, at 11.

96. *See, e.g.*, *Ruling Cleric Warns Iran 'On the Brink of Explosion,'* WORLDTRIBUNE.COM, June 3, 2002, http://216.26.163.62/2002/me_iran_06_03.html; *Poll on US Ties Rocks Iran*, BBC NEWS, Oct. 2, 2002, http://news.bbc.co.uk/2/hi/middle_east/2294509.stm.

97. For example, the theocratic regime in Iran executed thousands of political opponents, razed villages belonging to religious and ethnic minorities such as the Kurds, and practiced widespread torture. *See, e.g.*, USDOS, *Country Reports on Human Rights Practices for 2000: Iran* (Feb. 23, 2001), http://www.state.gov/g/drl/rls/hrrpt/2000/nea/786.htm; Amnesty International, *Iran: Executions of Prisoners Continue Unabated* (1992), http://www.amnestyusa.org/countries/iran/document.do?id=7D4EA7D35E816F03802569A600602B9A ("Between July 1988 and January 1989 alone Amnesty International recorded more than 2,500 political prisoners who were executed....").

98. ICG interview with pollster Munqeth Dagher, manager of the Independent Institute for Administration and Civil Society Studies, Baghdad, Aug. 30 2005, *quoted in* ICG, *Unmaking Iraq*.

99. *Quoted in* ICG, *Unmaking Iraq*.

Image 10 Ethno-Religious Composition of Iraq, Circa 2003

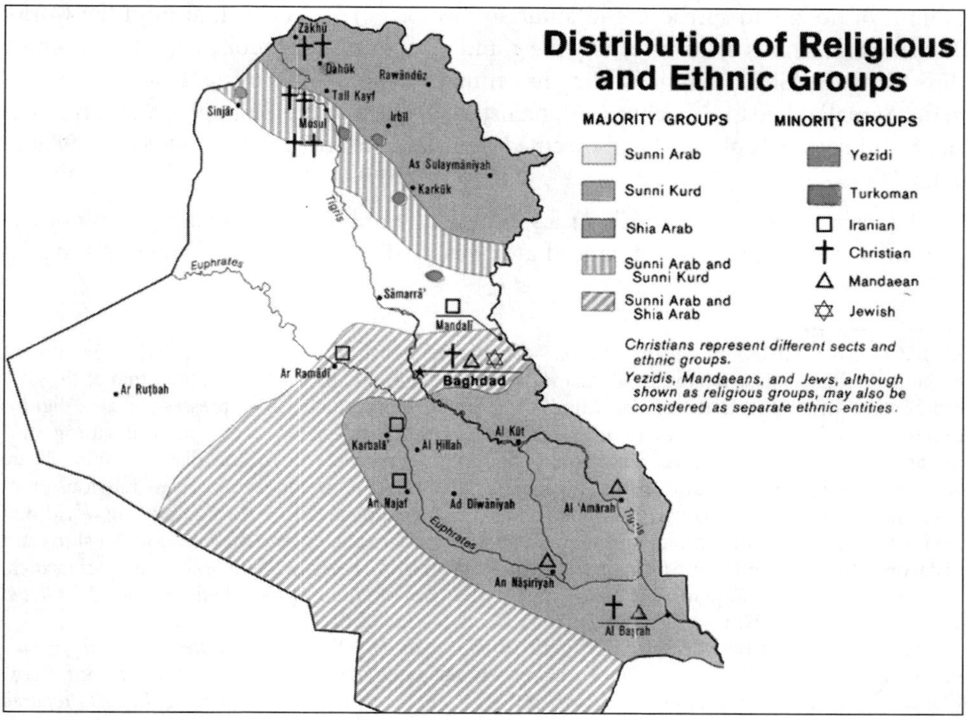

Source: CIA

2. Massacres of Iraqi Civilians by Car Bombs and Death Squads

The civil war began as Sunni Arabs in the royal families, major banks, and security services of Saudi Arabia and the Persian Gulf states financed terrorist groups like *al Qaeda* and the Islamic State of Iraq. These groups exploded huge car bombs and artillery shells in attempts to kill as many Shi'a, Kurdish, Assyrian, Yezidi, and pro-government Sunni civilians as possible, most notably in Baghdad and Mosul from 2003 to the present, Najaf in 2003, Arbil in 2004, Hilla in 2005, and Jebel Sinjar in 2007.[100] To the extent that responsibility may be assigned for the genocide in post-2003 Iraq, the Gulf Arab states have played the most unequivocally negative and destructive part. The Chairman of the Senate Foreign Relations Committee after the Democrats' 2006 takeover of Congress, Joseph Biden, recognized that the jihadists in Iraq are primarily foreigners.[101] Saudi clerics, probably the most influential globally, endorse the tactic, impliedly by voicing support for jihadist operations and on occasion expressly as well.[102]

Saudi leaders view Iraq as in essence a global terrorist factory to train fighters for and publicize the Wahhabi movement, which is the official religion of Saudi Arabia.[103] The

100. David M. Malone, The International Struggle Over Iraq: Politics in the UN Security Council 1980–2005, at 334–36 (Oxford: Oxford UP, 2006).

101. Senator Joseph Biden, *For Success in Iraq, Change Course,* Wash. Post, Sept. 14, 2005, http://www.washingtonpost.com.

102. *Saudi Clerics Still Encouraging Jihad*, MSNBC.com, Mar. 31, 2005, http://www.msnbc.com.

Saudi Muslim World League and the International Islamic Relief Organization have spent billions of dollars to spread the totalitarian ideology of Wahhabism around the world. These organizations are overseen by the grand mufti of Saudi Arabia, a figure appointed directly by the king.[104] Saudi funding has enflamed conflict in Bosnia, Israel, Egypt, Algeria, Somalia, Sudan, Chechnya, Afghanistan, Tajikistan, the Philippines, and Indonesia. Saudi nationals planned and executed most large terrorist events between 1998 and 2005.[105]

The terrorist war against Shi'a Arabs, pro-U.S. Sunni Kurds, and religious minorities in Iraq is at its base a Saudi-financed and -inspired religious war.[106] The bombings of

---

103. *See* U.S. CIRF, *Annual Report 2005—Saudi Arabia*, http://www.unhcr.org ("The government of Saudi Arabia persists in banning all forms of public religious expression other than that of the government's own interpretation of one school of Sunni Islam and forcefully represses private religious practice. Members of the Shi'a and other non-Sunni communities, as well as non-conforming Sunnis, are subject to government restrictions on public religious practices and official discrimination. There is a continuing pattern of punishment and abuse of non-Muslim foreigners for private religious practice. The government also continues to be involved in financing activities throughout the world that support extreme religious intolerance, hatred, and, in some cases, violence toward non-Muslims and disfavored Muslims."); Gaer, *Statement to Panel III of a Hearing on the Plight of Religious Minorities.*

104. *See* David E. Kaplan, *The Saudi Connection: How Billions in Oil Money Spawned a Global Terror Network*, U.S. NEWS & WORLD REPORT, Dec. 15, 2003, http://www.usnews.com.

105. *See id.*; Jean-Charles Brisard, *Written Testimony to the U.S. Senate, Committee on Banking, Housing, and Urban Affairs* (Oct. 22, 2003), http://www.senate.gov/~banking/_files/brisard.pdf; Jean-Charles Brisard, *Terrorism Financing: Roots and Trends of Saudi Terrorism Financing: Report Prepared for the President of the Security Council* (Dec. 19, 2002), http://www.nationalreview.com/document/document-un122002.pdf; *see also* Josh Meyer, *U.S. Faults Saudi Efforts on Terrorism*, L.A. TIMES, Jan. 15 2006, http://www.latimes.com ("Although Saudi Arabia has cracked down on militants within its borders, the kingdom has not met its promises to help prevent the spread of terrorism or curb the flow of money from Saudis to terrorist cells around the world, U.S. intelligence, diplomatic and other officials say."); Josh Meyer, *Two Allies Aided Bin Laden, 9/11 Panel Members Say*, L.A. TIMES, June 20, 2004, http://www.latimes.com ("Pakistan and Saudi Arabia helped set the stage for the Sept. 11 attacks by cutting financial deals with the Taliban and Osama bin Laden that allowed his Al Qaeda terrorist network to flourish, according to several senior members of the Sept. 11 commission."); Josh Meyer., *U.S. and Saudis Block Assets of Charity Group*, L.A. TIMES, June 3, 2004, http://www.latimes.com ("U.S. and Saudi officials moved to block some assets of a major Saudi charity with links to the Riyadh government, saying the group and its former leader had financed Al Qaeda and other terrorists in at least five countries in recent years."); Josh Meyer, *Report Links Saudi Government to 9/11 Hijackers, Sources Say*, L.A. TIMES, Aug. 2, 2003, http://www.latimes.com; A.B. Prados & C.M. Blanchard, *Saudi Arabia: Terrorist Financing Issues*, CONG. RESEARCH SERV. REPORT RL 32499 (Dec. 8, 2004), http://www.fas.org/irp/crs/RL32499.pdf; Craig Unger, *Saving the Saudis*, VANITY FAIR, Oct. 2003, http://www.wesjones.com/saudi1.htm; Carol J. Williams, Rich Connell & Robert J. Lopez, *Saudi Prisoner Release Gives U.S. Pause*, L.A. TIMES, Oct. 25, 2006, http://www.latimes.com ("U.S. officials, apparently caught off guard by the Saudi government's recent release of more than two dozen former Guantanamo Bay prisoners, are voicing fears that the men will join the camp of violent extremist groups. [¶] The Saudis released the 29 men from jail ..."); *see generally* COLL, GHOST WARS, at 131–32, 134–37, 144–56, 228–31, 238–39, 294–95, 297, 327, 341, 385, 439, 555; UNGER, HOUSE OF BUSH, HOUSE OF SAUD, at 111–12; David Armstrong, *Charity Cases: Why Has the Bush Administration Failed to Stop Saudi Funding of Terrorism?*, HARPER'S MAG., Mar. 2004, http://www.harpers.org/archive/2004/03/0079958; *Bin Laden Expert Steps Forward*, 60 MINUTES, Nov. 14, 2004, http://www.cbsnews.com/stories/2004/11/12/60minutes/main655407.shtml; Declan McCullagh, *Al-Qaida Proving Elusive on the Net*, CNET News.com, Oct. 14, 2005, http://news.com.com.

106. *See* Gaer and Chaput, *Protecting Iraq's Religious Minorities*, at A21; Gaer, *Statement on the International Religious Freedom Report*; Nina Shea, Director, Center For Religious Freedom, Freedom House, Testimony on Panel III of a Hearing by the U.S. House of Representatives, I Committee on International Relations, on the International Religious Freedom Report, FEDERAL NEWS, Dec. 21, 2006, http://www.fednews.com; Rep. Christopher Smith, Statement on Panel III of a Hearing by the

churches and Shi'a institutions in Iraq in multiple simultaneous explosions have occurred in a style associated with *al Qaeda* since the Africa bombings and 9/11, and blamed by Iraq's national security adviser on the Saudi-funded group that became "al Qaeda in Mesopotamia."[107] By 2006, more than 600 car bombs have blown up thousands of Shi'a Iraqis in their homes, mosques, police stations, and markets, as well destroyed a dozen Christian churches and killed hundreds of Kurds. "Eleven car bombs exploded in Baghdad and Kirkuk on New Year's Day 2006" alone. Dozens of car bombs have targeted civilians in Baghdad, e.g. in "Sadr City."[108]

The Associated Press and U.S. military officials have reported that most of the suicide bombers and most of the terrorists' money in Iraq is brought in from Saudi Arabia and other Gulf Arab states.[109] "One US defense official estimated that as of July 2005, Iraqis had directly carried out less than 10% of more than 500 suicide bombings."[110] Saudi individuals reportedly "are giving millions of dollars to Sunni insurgents in Iraq" and "several truck drivers interviewed by the Associated Press described carrying boxes of cash from Saudi Arabia into Iraq, money they said was headed for insurgents."[111] The Iraq Study Group report in 2006 found that "funding for the Sunni insurgency comes from private individuals within Saudi Arabia and other Gulf states."[112] The commander of the MNF maintained in 2005 that "insurgent activity among Iraqis was being driven by money, not ideology, and foreign jihadists were using their financial resources to get Iraqis to attack other Iraqis."[113]

By 2007, thousands had been killed in terrorist bombing campaigns. The State Department noted that bombings that targeted "densely populated Shi'a areas were common...."[114] Huge massacres based on sectarian or religious identity included those listed in Figure 12.

In excess of 400,000 more Iraqis died between 2003 and 2006 than the death rate prior to the hostilities would have indicated would die. This was the conclusion of a peer-reviewed scientific study authored by faculty from Johns Hopkins and MIT in the British medical journal *The Lancet*. According to this study, three-fourths of the violent deaths in Iraq in 2006 were due to terrorists, militia, insurgents, and unknown attackers. This

---

U.S. House of Representatives, Committee on International Relations, on the International Religious Freedom Report, Dec. 21, 2006; Testimony of Stephen Liston, Director of the State Department's Office of Religious Freedom, Before Panel III of a Hearing of the U.S. House of Representatives, Committee on International Relations, on the International Religious Freedom Report, FEDERAL NEWS, Dec. 21, 2006.

107. *See* Agence France-Presse, *Iraqi Leaders Call for Unity After Church Bombings*, Aug. 2, 2004, http://www.findarticles.com; Kim Sengupta, *Exodus of Iraqi Christians in Full Flood as Targeted Killings Grow*, THE INDEPENDENT (U.K.), Oct. 21, 2004, http://www.findarticles.com.

108. Mike Davis, *The Poor Man's Air Force*, HARPER'S MAG., Oct. 2006, at 19.

109. The commander of multi-national forces in Iraq stated in 2005 that foreigners are most often responsible for the hundreds of suicide car bombs that struck Iraq since the handover of the government ministries to Iraqis. General Abizaid similarly concluded that al Qaeda "brings foreign fighters in from Saudi Arabia and from North Africa," countries where Saudis have financially backed armed extremist groups for decades. *See* Patrick Quinn & Katherine Shrader, *Foreigners Blamed For Iraq Suicide Attacks,* ASSOCIATED PRESS, July 1, 2005, http://www.ap.org.

110. Anthony H. Cordesman, *The Role of Outsiders: Foreign Volunteers and Iraq's Neighbors in the Insurgency*, at 3 (June 23, 2006), http://www.csis.org/media/csis/pubs/060622_outsiders.pdf.

111. *Saudis Reportedly Funding Iraqi Sunni Insurgents,* USA TODAY, Dec. 8, 2006, http://www.usatoday.com/news/world/iraq/2006-12-08-saudis-sunnis_x.htm.

112. IRAQ STUDY GROUP, FINAL REPORT 29 (Washington, DC: Gov. Printing Office, 2006).

113. Cordesman, *The Role of Outsiders*, at 2.

114. USDOS, *Country Reports on Human Rights Practices: Iraq*, WESTLAW (Mar. 2007), http://web2.westlaw.com (search for "2007 WL 1040174").

Image 11 U.S. Central Command Assessment of Situation in Iraq, mid-2006

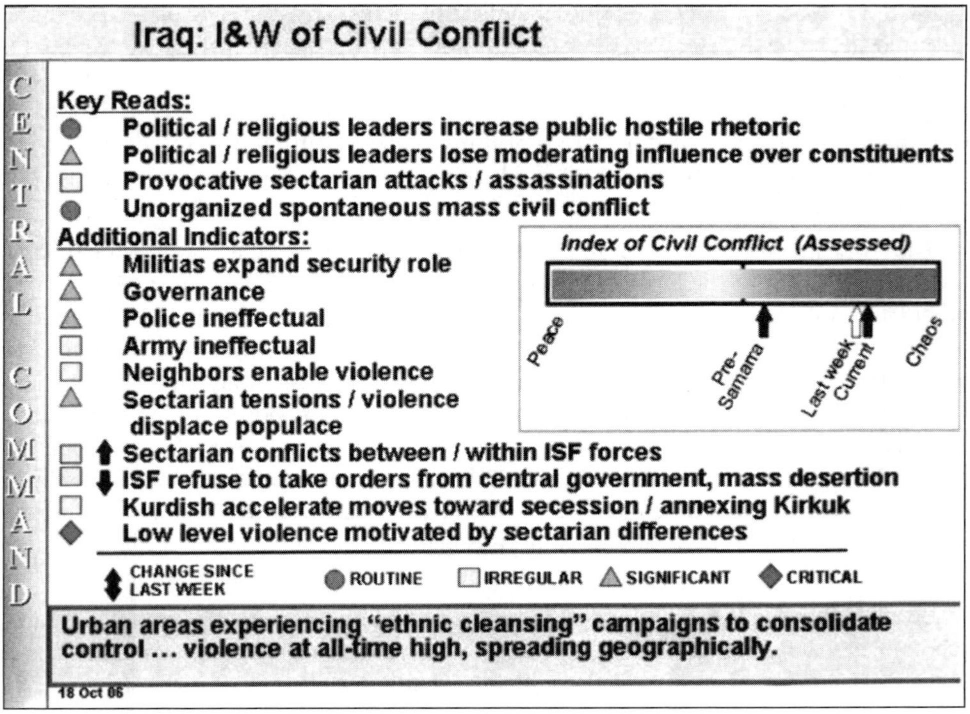

is the same methodology used to estimate the number of deaths in Kosovo, the Congo, and Darfur.[115] A poll of 1,500 Iraqi adults completed in 2007 corroborated *The Lancet* study's conclusions by suggesting a death toll of between 733,158 to 1,446,063 due to violence from March 2003 through mid-August 2007.[116]

The death rate more than doubled after the war, according to a survey of Iraqis in September 2004 which revealed that about 100,000 Iraqi civilians had died who probably would have survived had the war never taken place. This was the conclusion of a team of researchers led by the Johns Hopkins Bloomberg School of Public Health, who randomly surveyed almost 1,000 Iraqi households in September 2004.[117]

The rates of disease, malnutrition, and infant mortality in Iraq soared.[118] By 2007, a quarter of Iraqi children under the age of five exhibited stunted growth, and ten percent suffered from wasting, a condition in which muscle tissue is lost due to famine-like hunger.[119] Iraq's mortality rate for children under five was then as high as it was in 1960

115. *See* Gilbert Burnham et al., *Mortality after the 2003 Invasion of Iraq: A Cross-sectional Cluster Sample Survey*, The Lancet, Oct. 11, 2006, at 1–8; Spiegel & Salama, *War and Mortality in Kosovo, 1998–1999*, at 2204.

116. *See* Opinion Research Business (ORB), *More than 1,000,000 Iraqis Murdered*, ORB (Sept. 2007), http://www.opinion.co.uk/Newsroom_details.aspx?NewsId=78.

117. Elisabeth Rosenthal, *Iraqi Civilian Toll Since the Invasion Is Estimated at 100,000*, Int'l Herald Trib., Oct. 29, 2004, http://www.iht.com.

118. *See* European Commission, *Iraq: Commission Sets Priorities for Aid in 2004* (Mar. 4, 2004), http://europa.eu.int/comm/external_relations/iraq/news/ip04_303.htm; Maureen Fan, *Iraq: Infant Mortality Rises with Chaos*, Miami Herald, Nov. 23, 2003, http://www.miami.com/mld/miamiherald/news/world/7329400.htm.

119. *See* UNAMI, *Humanitarian Crisis in Iraq: Facts and Figures* 1 (Nov. 13, 2007), http://www.uniraq.org/aboutus/HR.asp.

Figure 12 Mass-Casualty Bombings in Iraq, 2003–2008, by Location

Date of Bombing	Death Toll as Reported	Targets and Circumstances
Aug. 31, 2005	1,000	Shi'a pilgrims trampled on or who fell off Al-Aaimmah bridge while trying to outrun a suspected suicide bomber
Aug. 14, 2007	400–520	Yezidi villages in the Sinjar area of northwestern Iraq
Nov. 23, 2006	200	Shi'a neighborhood in Baghdad
Nov. 24, 2006	200	Baghdad market
July 7, 2007	160	Amerli market
Oct. 25, 2009	155	Baghdad, Justice Ministry and provincial council offices
Mar. 27, 2007	150	Tal Afar market
Apr. 18, 2007	140	Shi'a neighborhood in Baghdad
Feb. 3, 2007	132	Shi'a neighborhood in Baghdad
Mar. 6, 2007	115	Shi'a pilgrims in Hilla
Aug. 19, 2009	100+	Baghdad, Finance Ministry and Foreign Ministry buildings
Feb. 1, 2004	100+	Kurdish political offices in Arbil
Feb. 3, 2007	100+	Baghdad market
Sept. 14, 2007	100+	Baghdad market
Feb. 1, 2008	98–100	Baghdad markets
Aug. 29, 2003	90	Outside Shi'a Imam Ali mosque in Najaf
June 20, 2009	81+	Outside Shi'a mosque near Kirkuk
Feb. 1, 2007	73	Hilla market
June 6, 2006	72	Mahmudiya market
Jan. 16, 2007	70	Mustansiriyah University in Baghdad
Apr. 24, 2009	70	Shi'a pilgrims in Baghdad

Sources: *See Large Bombings Claim Ever More Lives*, IRAQ BODY COUNT (Oct. 4, 2007), http://www.iraqbodycount.org/analysis/numbers/biggest-bombs; *see also* Damien Cave, *Cheated of Future, Iraqi Graduates Want to Flee*, N.Y. TIMES, June 5, 2007, http://www.nytimes.com; *Death Toll from Bombing in Iraq Reaches 73*, IRISH INDEPENDENT, June 21, 2009, http://www.independent.ie; Steven R. Hurst, *At Least 132 Killed in Iraq Bombing*, DENVER POST, Feb. 4, 2007; Emad Matti, *Bombings in Iraq Raise Fears of Resurging Ethnic Violence*, SEATTLE TIMES, July 10, 2009, http://seattletimes.nwsource.com; Patrick J. McDonnell & Tracy Wilkinson, *Blast Kills Scores at Iraq Mosque; Toll Tops 90 in Shiite Stronghold*, L.A. TIMES, Aug. 30, 2003, at A1; Richard A. Oppel Jr., *After The War: Bombing's Aftermath; U.S. Troops Delay Exit From Najaf*, N.Y. TIMES, Sept. 1, 2003, http://www.nytimes.com; Patrick Quinn, *Iraqi Military Hopes Security Will Last*, WASH. POST, Feb 18, 2008, at http://www.washingtonpost.com; Marc Santora, *Iraq Steps Up Criticism of Syria Over Bombings*, N.Y. TIMES, Aug. 25, 2009, http://www.nytimes.com/2009/08/26/world/middleeast/26iraq.html; Graham Usher, *Blood and Ashes in Arbil*, AL-AHRAM WEEKLY, Feb. 18, 2004, http://weekly.ahram.org.eg/2004/677/re2.htm; Timothy Williams, *Bombings in Iraq, Deadliest Since 2007, Raise Security Issue*, N.Y. TIMES, Oct. 26, 2009, http://www.nytimes.com/2009/10/26/world/middleeast/26iraq.html; Edward Wong, *Militants Attack Sunnis' Mosques in 2 Iraqi Cities*, N.Y. TIMES, Nov. 25, 2006, http://www.nytimes.com. Note: bombings resulting in fewer than 70 deaths have been omitted.

or 1970, before improvements in the health care system cut the rate by two-thirds before 1990.[120] Infant mortality doubled in some hospitals, for example in Yarmuk Hospital.[121] About $10 billion the Iraqi government had budgeted in 2006 went unspent, as children went without food and health care.[122] Due to shortages, the price of food nearly doubled in 2006, and the price of gasoline went up more than 10 times.[123] Although wages for government officials and public sector workers improved markedly, the inflation rate soared to over 30% in 2004 and 2005.[124]

The health care sector, which should have been a prime candidate for employing Iraqis and rebuilding the economy in a post-conflict society, was in shambles.[125] Iraqi mothers were dying in pregnancy or childbirth at two to three times the rate in 1989, as about half of women gave birth at home with no medical attention.[126] Thousands of Iraqis died every year, according to an investigative report by the *Los Angeles Times*, because hospitals lacked the equipment or medicines needed to treat heart attacks and cancers.[127] One report said:

> At Baghdad's Central Teaching Hospital for Children, gallons of raw sewage wash across the floors. The drinking water is contaminated. According to doctors, 80 percent of patients leave with infections they did not have when they arrived. Doctors say they have been beaten up in the emergency room....
>
> "The word 'big' is not enough to express the disaster we are facing," said Ahmed A. Muhammad, the hospital's assistant manager....
>
> "It's definitely worse now than before the war," said Eman Asim, the Ministry of Health official who oversees the country's 185 public hospitals. "Even at the height of sanctions, when things were miserable, it wasn't as bad as this...."[128]

Equipment or medicines widely used in other countries to treat heart attacks and cancers were unavailable.[129]

---

120. UNICEF, State of the World's Children 2007, at 139, *see also* http://depts.washington.edu/pspgh/lecsem/pdfs/presentations/Iraq.pdf, and http://earthtrends.wri.org/pdf_library/data_tables/pop4_2003.pdf.

121. *See* Gettleman, *Iraq's Hospitals in Ruins*.

122. *See* UNICEF, State of the World's Children 2007, at 139 (2006), http://www.unicef.org/publications/files/The_State_of_the_Worlds_Children_2007_e.pdf, U.N. Development Programme, *Iraq Living Conditions Survey* (2005), http://www.iq.undp.org/ILCS/PDF/Analytical%20Report%20-%20English.pdf; Louise Roug, *Iraq's Health Care a Shambles*, L.A. Times, Nov. 15, 2006, http://www.latimes.com; *Iraq: Food Prices Rise After Reduction of Monthly Rations*, U.N. IRIN, Apr. 2, 2006, http://www.un.org; Daud Salman, *Food Rations Cut Hurting Poor*, IWPR, Mar. 29, 2006 http://www.iwpr.net;*More Children Dying in Basra Since Iraq Invasion, Says Aid Worker*, Deutsche Presse Agentur, Mar. 21, 2006, http://www.dpa.com. *See also* al-Yasiri, *Anger Over Food Ration Hitches;* BBC, *Children Starving*; Fowler, *Expert*; Salman, *Food Rations Cut*; UNICEF, *Food Insecurity in Iraq;* U.N. IRIN, *Iraq: Food Prices.*

123. Damien Cave, *Weary Iraqis Face New Foe: Rising Prices*, N.Y. Times, Aug. 26, 2006, at A1, A5.

124. *See id.*

125. U.N. Development Programme, *Iraq Living Conditions Survey* (2005), http://www.iq.undp.org/ILCS/PDF/Analytical%20Report%20-%20English.pdf.

126. *See* Annia Ciezadlo, *In Iraq, Giving Birth is Complicated by War,* Christian Science Monitor, June 30, 2005, http://www.csmonitor.com; UNICEF, *Promoting Women's Rights Is Essential to Iraq's Recovery* (Dec. 11, 2006), http://www.unicef.org.

127. Louise Roug, *Iraq's Health Care a Shambles*, L.A. Times, Nov. 15, 2006, http://www.latimes.com. *See also* Deutsche Presse Agentur, *More Children Dying in Basra Since Iraq Invasion.*

128. Jeffrey Gettleman, *Chaos and War Leave Iraq's Hospitals in Ruins*, N.Y. Times, Feb. 14, 2004, http://www.nytimes.com.

129. Louise Roug, *Decrepit Health Care Adds to Toll in Iraq,* L.A. Times, Nov. 15, 2006, http://www.iraq-war.ru/article/108687; *see also* Deutsche Presse Agentur, *More Children Dying in Basra Since Iraq Invasion.*

Iraqi women and children suffered horribly as a result of the war. A third of violent deaths among females occurred among little girls under 15 years old.[130] A breakdown of law and order after the fall of Iraq's government resulted in the rapes of hundreds of Iraqi women.[131] Violent deaths of men, women and children tripled.[132] Young girls were sold into slavery.[133] Many women were too afraid even to leave their homes, let alone participate actively in developing a secular government that respects the equal rights of its citizens.[134]

Most of the victims of massacres in Iraq by gunfire, and perhaps also by suicide bomb or air strike, have been men, but Iraqi women and girls have suffered violence and impoverishment as well. At the time of the war, Iraq's population was about 42% under the age of 15, which likely made most of Iraq's people children or teenagers, and most of them young Iraqi girls. About one in three Iraqi women and girls have been widowed or orphaned by war. The average income of such female-headed households in 2009 was only $125, far below the cost of living. The Red Cross noted that since 2003, Iraqi women and girls "have increasingly been caught in the crossfire, killed or wounded in mass explosions and displaced from their homes."[135]

In December 2006, a report prepared for the U.N. Security Council called Iraq arguably the worst humanitarian and human rights crisis in the world, with 5,000 Iraqis dying violent deaths every month.[136] Civilian deaths in Iraq from direct violence alone were more than 30,000 in 2006 according to U.N. figures.[137] These figures are likely understated if they are drawn from Ministry of Health death certificates, which only captured about a third of all deaths even before the outbreak of war and collapse of many essential services.[138] When Iraqis are interviewed about the causes of the high death rate, as they perceive it given the deaths or maimings of their family members, they blame terrorism, gunfire, and U.S. air strikes. Among Iraqis interviewed about the deaths of family members, they reported about the victims that "48% died from a gunshot wound,

---

130. *See* Burnham, *Mortality after the 2003 Invasion of Iraq*, at 4–6.

131. *See* Agence France-Presse, *More than 400 Iraqi Women Kidnapped, Raped in Post-War Chaos: Watchdog*, ReliefWeb (Aug. 24, 2003), http://www.reliefweb.int/w/rwb.nsf/480fa8736b88bbc3c12564f6004c8ad5/c21efb4c4e3dda7e49256d8d0010bacb.

132. *See* Gettleman, *Chaos and War Leave Iraq's Hospitals in Ruins*.

133. *See* Houzan Mahmoud, *An Empty Sort of Freedom*, The Guardian (U.K.), Mar. 8, 2004, http://www.guardian.co.uk/; Debra McNutt, *Is the Iraq Occupation Enabling Prostitution?*, Common Dreams (July 11, 2007), http://www.commondreams.org/archive/2007/07/11/2453; Kavita N. Ramdas, *Women's Rights Another Victim of the Iraq Catastrophe*, Baltimore Sun, Dec. 22, 2006, http://www.commondreams.org/views06/1222-27.htm; Ruth Rosen, *The Hidden War on Women in Iraq*, Common Dreams (July 13, 2006), http://www.commondreams.org/views06/0713-33.htm.

134. *See* Lauren Sadler, *Veiled and Worried in Baghdad*, N.Y. Times, Sept. 16, 2003, http://www.nytimes.com.

135. International Committee of the Red Cross, *Iraq: Women in War*, ICRC Field Newsletter (Mar. 5, 2009).

136. Press Release, U.N. Security Council, Iraq Stands on Brink of Civil War, 'Violence Seems Out of Control', Special Representative Tells Security Council, SC/8895, 5583rd Meeting, Dec. 11, 2006, http://www.un.org; *Report of the Secretary-General*, S/2006/945, at ¶¶ 38–40.

137. *See* Sudarsan Raghavan, *Iraq Agency Tally Shows Death Spike; More Than 17,000 Police, Civilians, Slain in Last Six Months*, S.F. Chron., Jan. 8, 2007, http://www.sfgate.com/cgi-bin/article.cgi?f=/c/a/2007/01/08/MNG4PNEMKE1.DTL&feed=rss.news; Reuters, *Civilian Toll In December Put at 1,930*, Wash. Post, Jan. 2, 2007, at A12.

138. *See* Gilbert Burnham et al., *The Human Cost of the War in Iraq: A Mortality Study, 2002–2006*, at appx. C (pp. 16–17) (Oct. 2006), http://www.humansecuritygateway.info/showRecord.php?RecordId=17000.

20% from the impact of a car bomb, 9% from aerial bombardment, 6% as a result of an accident and 6% from another blast/ordnance."[139]

Unlike Iraq's religious minorities, the Kurds and Shi'a Arabs were not helpless before Saudis and insurgents, and responded in force to the numerous massacres against them. With the influx of foreign suicide bombers in 2004, more than 100,000 Arabs were displaced from their homes in the Kurdish *pesh merga*-controlled areas.[140] Iraq soon crossed the threshold into a sectarian civil war with the overlay of regional and international conflict. The epidemic of mass-casualty suicide bombings drove the growth of the Shi'a defense force the Mahdi Army from 600 members in 2003 to more than 6,000 in 2004.[141] Iran stepped up its influence and intervention in Iraq as a result of these massacres of Shi'a, as it did in Afghanistan when the Saudi-funded Taliban massacred the Shi'a there.[142]

Although it is commonly argued in mitigation of the many massacres of Sunni Arab men by Shi'a militias and Iraqi security forces that they were committed in response to the bombing of the Shi'a shrine in Samarra in February 2006, this claim does not bear scrutiny.[143] The massacres of hundreds of Sunni Arab men began in 2005 at the latest, after multiple mass-casualty suicide and/or car bombs against Shi'a Arab, Kurdish, and multi-national soldiers and civilians in 2003 and 2004.[144] Shi'a militia mobilized to re-

---

139. ORB, *More than 1,000,000 Iraqis Murdered.*

140. *See* Dexter Filkins, *Kurds Advancing to Reclaim Land in Northern Iraq*, N.Y. Times, June 20, 2004, http://www.nytimes.com.

141. *Cf.* Peter W. Galbraith, *The Mess*, N.Y. Rev. Books, Mar. 9, 2006, http://209.85.165.104/search?q=cache:kFX7i-sy1MkJ:www.nybooks.com/articles/18771.

142. *See, e.g.*, ICG, *Iraq's Civil War, the Sadrists and the Surge* 15 (Feb. 7, 2008), http://www.crisisgroup.org (Shi'a militia enjoyed "refuge and military training in Iran. Until the time Muqtada [al-Sadr] decreed a halt to Mahdi Army activities, Sadrist militants went so far as to boast of Iranian help, including courses on street combat and the transfer of sophisticated explosive devices. . . .") (footnotes omitted).

143. *See* USDOS, *Country Reports on Human Rights Practices: Iraq 2007*; USDOS, *Country Reports on Human Rights Practices: Iraq 2006.*

144. *See, e.g.*, Mohammed Al-Dulaimy, *Discovery of Secret Jail 'Like a Dream'*, Kansas City Star, Nov. 17, 2005, http://www.newsbank.com (describing "US troops' discovery of 173 mostly Sunni Arab men beaten and malnourished in a secret Interior Ministry jail. . . ."); Associated Press, *Bodies of 10 Executed Men Found in Baghdad*, RadioFreeEurope/RadioLiberty, http://www.rferl.org/content/article/1059925.html ("Members of the country's Sunni Muslim minority accuse Iraqi security forces of mistreating or killing Sunni Arab men."); Leila Fadel, *Abuse of Prisoners in Iraq Widespread, Officials Say*, Knight-Ridder News Serv., May 21, 2004, http://www.commondreams.org/headlines05/1129-03.htm ("Deputy Human Rights Minister Aida Ussayran and Gen. Muntadhar Muhi al-Samaraee, a former head of special forces at the Ministry of the Interior, made the allegations two weeks after 169 men who apparently had been tortured were discovered in a south-central Baghdad building run by the Interior Ministry."); *id.* ("While he was at the ministry, al-Samaraee said, Sunni men were beaten, tortured and killed, then thrown on the side of the road or into rivers. . . ."); Dexter Filkins et al., *Sunnis Accuse Iraqi Military of Executions*, N.Y. Times, Nov. 29, 2005, http://www.nytimes.com ("Some Sunni men have been found dead in ditches and fields, with bullet holes in their temples, acid burns on their skin, and holes in their bodies apparently made by electric drills."); Alex Rodriguez, *Sectarian Violence Poses Threat to Iraq's Future*, Chicago Trib., Oct. 3, 2005, http://www.accessmylibrary.com/coms2/summary_0286-31659703_ITM ("More than 70 young Sunni Arab men were whisked away. The fate of 36 of them became known ... in a dry riverbed 110 miles southeast of Baghdad."); Kirk Semple, *Iraq Bomber Kills 27, Most of Them Children*, Int'l Herald Tribune, July 14, 2005, http://www.iht.com ("On Sunday, at least 10 Sunni Arab men and youths suffocated after a unit of the police commando, a predominantly Shiite group, seized them from a hospital. . . ."); *U.S. Plans More Advisers After Claims of Iraq Abuse*, N.Y. Times, Dec. 30, 2005, at A1 ("Human rights groups in Baghdad say the [Iraqi] commando units may be guilty of murdering or torturing thousands of Sunni Arab men of military age.").

spond to the many massacres against Shi'a with sectarian cleansing campaigns against Sunni Arabs,[145] with the result that thousands of bodies of tortured and mutilated Sunnis turned up in Baghdad, in mass killings blamed by the U.S. and U.N. on death squads linked to the Ministry of the Interior, which has been infiltrated by the Mahdi Army.[146] It is true that reports of much larger massacres surfaced in 2007 and 2008. The U.S. State Department, for example, described "large-scale death squad[s]" and "common" executions of "military-age Sunni males."[147] In the Hurriya area, south of Baghdad, a formerly large population of Sunnis was displaced as "militias and death squads in the neighborhood killed or drove out thousands of Sunnis."[148] In one two-month period in late 2006, nearly 5,000 residents of Baghdad were massacred, often Sunnis killed by Shi'a groups linked to the government, with ample evidence of targeting of victims by religious sect.[149]

---

145. *See* ICG, *Iraq's Civil War*, at 2, 15.

146. *See* USDOS, *Country Reports on Human Rights Practices: Iraq 2007*; USDOS, *Country Reports on Human Rights Practices: Iraq 2006*; UNHCR, *Guidelines Relating to the Eligibility of Iraqi Asylum-Seekers,* at 8 ("There are growing indications that state persecution (including arbitrary arrest and unlawful detention, torture and ill-treatment as well as extra-judicial executions) is taking place in Iraq, in particular by Shiite-dominated police commandos working under the authority of the Ministry of Interior who have been accused of deliberately targeting Sunnis considered to be supporting the insurgency. The Iraqi authorities have admitted such incidents, but are currently not able to stop them"); Kim Gamel, *McCain Visits Baghdad Market, Proclaims US-Iraqi Security Crackdown Is Working,* San Diego Union Trib., Apr. 1, 2007, http://www.signonsandiego.com/news/world/iraq/20070401-1222-iraq.html ("[On] Sunday, 20 bullet-riddled bodies were found, most in Baghdad, apparent victims of so-called sectarian death squads that are believed to be run by Shiite militias. The number was low compared to the average of 50 bodies per day that were turning up before the security crackdown."); U.N. Assistance Mission for Iraq (UNAMI), *Human Rights Report: 1 September–31 October 2006*, at 1, http://www.uniraq.org/aboutus/HR.asp ("Sectarian attacks seem to be the main source of violence in the country, fuelled by action of the insurgents and militias, as well as various criminal groups. HRO received information about a large number of indiscriminate and targeted killings. During the reporting period, 3, 253 unidentified bodies were found in Baghdad."); UNAMI, *Human Rights Report: 1 January–31 March 2007*, at 1–2, 7–8, http://www.uniraq.org/aboutus/HR.asp (fifty bodies being dumped in Baghdad every day in January 2007).

147. *See* USDOS, *Country Reports on Human Rights Practices: Iraq 2007* ("[P]redominantly Shi'a militias with some ties to the Iraqi Security Forces (ISF), targeted Sunnis in large-scale death squad and kidnapping activities. While the law provides for civilian authorities' control over the security forces, there were many instances in which elements of the security forces acted independently."); USDOS, *Country Reports on Human Rights Practices: Iraq 2006* ("Executions of military-age Sunni males became common....").

148. Richard A. Oppel Jr. & Ali Hamid, *At Least 51 Are Killed In Blast At Baghdad Market*, N.Y. Times, June 18, 2008, http://www.nytimes.com.

149. *See* UNAMI, *Human Rights Report: 1 November–31 December 2006*, at 1–2, 7–8, http://www.uniraq.org/aboutus/HR.asp (stating that "6,376 civilians were violently killed in November and December 2006, with no less than 4,731 in Baghdad, most of them as a result of gunshot wounds."); Bob Woodward, The War Within: A Secret White House History, 2006–2008, at 256 (London: Pocket Books, 2009) (U.S. Secretary of State Condoleeza Rice told aides to Iraqi Prime Minister Nouri al-Maliki that: "Look, we've got reports—people going into villages, killing all the men and sending the women into exile."); Ahmad Ali & Oliver Poole, *Sunnis Learn Shia Customs to Bluff Baghdad Death Squads,* The Telegraph (U.K.), Oct. 10, 2006, http://www.telegraph.co.uk/news/worldnews/1530994/Sunnis-learn-Shia-customs-to-bluff-Baghdad-death-squads.html ("Since Saturday at least 74 bodies have been found around the capital—often, Sunnis claim, killed with the complicity of the predominantly Shia police force in the city."); Oliver Poole, *Death Squads Leave 65 More Bodies for Iraq Morgue*, The Telegraph (U.K.), Sept. 14, 2006, http://www.telegraph.co.uk/news/worldnews/1528867/Death-squads-leave-65-more-bodies-for-Iraq-morgue.html ("Sixty-five bodies have been discovered in and around Baghdad, Iraqi police said yesterday. One victim was beheaded and most of the rest were tortured before being shot in the head." Findings are described as "daily occurrence."); *see also* UNAMI, *Human Rights Report: 1 January–30 June 2008,* at 11, http://www.uniraq.org/aboutus/HR.asp ("Large numbers of unidentified bodies were found in Diyala,

3. Evidence of Genocidal Intent Due to Targeting by Religion or Sect

The religious and sectarian nature of the massacres in Iraq led to numerous condemnations of the genocidal campaigns being waged by terrorists and militias. In 2005, President Talabani declared that "radical Islamists have declared a policy of genocide against the Shiites, whom they consider infidels, and against the Kurds."[150] He complained that terrorists were "waging a genocidal war on our people."[151] He repeated his charge in 2007, explaining that *al Qaeda* in Iraq under Abu Musab al-Zarqawi had engaged in a campaign of "genocide against the Iraqi people."[152] The head of Iraq's largest political movement, the Supreme Council for Islamic Revolution in Iraq, concurred, as did Iraq's vice president and leader of the Iraqi Islamic Party.[153] Similarly, arguably Iraq's most influential religious figure, Ayatollah al-Sistani, declared in July 2005 that the suicide bombings

---

Nineveh, Anbar and Diwaniyah and mainly in Baghdad. Many of these bodies bore signs of torture, some were blindfolded and others were decapitated."); UNAMI, *Humanitarian Briefing on the Crisis in Iraq* 1 (May 2, 2007), http://www.uniraq.org/aboutus/HR.asp ("The violence is primarily taking its toll on innocent civilians, who account for the majority of casualties and fatalities at a sheer scale of which is unparalleled in any other emergency occurring in the world today"); *id.* ("In other words, 94 Iraqi civilians died violently every day throughout 2006 with a similar number wounded.... The ongoing violence has resulted in a basic survival crisis"); UNHCR, *UNHCR's Eligibility Guidelines for Assessing the International Protection Needs of Iraqi Asylum-Seekers* 39–40 (Aug. 2007), http://www.unhcr.org.au/pdfs/iraqeligiblityaug07.pdf ("Most high-profile attacks causing large numbers of civilian casualties are attributed to Al-Qa'eda in Iraq and Ansar Al-Sunna...."); *id.* at 50 ("A series of car bombs and mortar attacks in Sadr City, home to more than two million Shi'ites, on 23 November 2006 caused the death of over 200 persons and injured many more."); *id.* at 51 ("Both Sunni and Shi'ite armed groups are held responsible for running death squads that conduct kidnappings and execution-style killings in Baghdad and other parts of the country. Bodies are routinely found dumped in the streets, rivers and mass graves."); U.N. Secretary-General, Report Pursuant to Paragraph 6 of Resolution 1770 (2007), S/2007/608, ¶ 36 ("[B]oth Sunni and Shiite armed groups have carried out systematic and widespread attacks against civilians through suicide bombings, abductions and extrajudicial executions, making no distinction between civilians and combatants.") ; U.S. House of Representatives, House Committee on Government Reform: Subcommittee on National Security, Emerging Threats and International Relations, Hearing on Iraq's Progress Toward Democracy, Congressional Quarterly, (statement of Rep. Kucinich) ("Hundreds of Iraqi bodies are showing up with signs of torture and execution, with published reports linking this to the Ministry of Interior."); Ashraf Al-Khalidi & Victor Tanner, *Sectarian Violence: Radical Groups Drive Internal Displacement in Iraq* 15 (Oct. 2006), http://www.brookings.edu/fp/projects/idp/20061018_DisplacementinIraq_Khalidi-Tanner.pdf.

150. *Quoted in Talabani Knows Whereabouts of Saddam Supporters,* INTERFAX NEWS AGENCY (RUSSIA), Sept. 11, 2005, http://www.aina.org/news/20050911115231.htm; *see also* Robert F. Worth, *A Day After the Stampede, Iraqis Bury Their Dead as Some Bodies Lie Nameless,* N.Y. TIMES, Sept. 2, 2005, http://www.nytimes.com; Nikolay Kudryashov, *Russia's Policies Reflect an Unfriendly Outlook on the Situation,* KOMMERSANT (RUSSIA), Sept. 12, 2005, http://www.kommersant.com/page.asp?id=607703.

151. *Quoted in Iraqi President-elect Pledges to Work for Democratic Rule, Security,* AL-SHARQIYAH (IRAQ)/BBC ARCHIVE, Apr. 6, 2005, http://www.newsbank.com.

152. *Quoted in* Robert Reid, *Talabani Hopeful After Meeting Insurgents,* WASH. POST, May 1, 2006, http://www.washingtonpost.com/wp-dyn/content/article/2006/04/30/AR2006043000127.html. *See also US: Ramadi Battle Kills 100-Plus Insurgents,* CNN, May 1, 2006, http://www.cnn.com/2006/WORLD/meast/05/01/iraq.main.

153. *Quoted in* Atul Aneja, *Undeclared Civil War Has Broken Out, Says Iraqi Minister,* THE HINDU (INDIA), Apr. 9, 2006, http://www.hindu.com/2006/04/09/stories/2006040904151600.htm. *See also*

and shootings of Iraqi civilians had crossed the threshold into a "genocidal war."[154] And the leader of the largest Sunni Arab political movement, the Iraqi Accordance Front, warned of genocide against Sunnis in Baghdad by militias supplied and directed from Iran, which lost thousands of people to Gulf War I.[155]

Iraq's minority populations faced a larger risk relative to their populations, although far fewer deaths and injuries in absolute terms. Despite deep theological differences, their leaders were united in warning of genocide against Iraqi religious minorities. A Christian bishop in Dohuk, in northern Iraq, agreed with Iraq's president that genocide was forcing hundreds of thousands of Christians to flee for their lives.[156] Another prominent Christian, a director of antiquities at Iraq's national museum, stated that due to violence and persecution: "There will be no Assyrians in Iraq. This is an awful thing, a country where the original people from that country are driven away."[157] The leaders of Iraq's Mandaeans, adherents to John the Baptist and neo-pagan Mesopotamian religious practices, grew

---

Simon Jeffery, *25,000 Civilians Killed Since Iraq Invasion, Says Report,* The Guardian (U.K.), July 19, 2005, http://www.guardian.co.uk/world/2005/jul/19/iraq.simonjeffery.

154. *Quoted in* Golnaz Esfandiari, *Iraq: Murders Hurt Efforts to Enlist Sunnis in Politics,* RadioFreeEurope/RadioLiberty, July 20, 2005, http://www.rferl.org/content/article/1060052.html.

155. *See Coalition Troops Kill, Capture Iranian-Linked Militants in Baghdad,* Voice of America (Aug. 13, 2007), http://www.voanews.com/english/archive/2007-08/2007-08-13-voa6.cfm?CFID=259730757&CFTOKEN=75510701&jsessionid=663076d83c5b3662440231442e732f281f62.

156. *See* Jack Fairweather, *Christians Flee Genocide as Fear Sweeps Iraq,* The Telegraph (U.K.), Aug, 1, 2005, http://groups.yahoo.com/group/OrthodoxNews/message/2342. *See also* CBS, *Vicar: Dire Times For Iraq's Christians; Tells 60 Minutes Most of Iraq's Christians Have Fled or Been Killed* (June 28, 2008), http://www.cbsnews.com/stories/2007/11/29/60minutes/main3553612.shtml; *Iraq, in* Religious Freedom in the World, at 213–14 (non-Muslim minorities of Iraq are "a disproportionate percentage of the 2 million refugees … and the 2 million more who are displaced within Iraq"); Habib Malik, *Christians of the Middle East, in id.* at 25 ("As the prospects of a secular democracy that upholds the principles of equality and freedom grow dim, Iraq's Christians fail to see a place for themselves in Iraq."); *Fleeing Christians Face New Hardships in Turkey,* Compass Direct News (Nov. 14, 2008), http://www.genocidewatch.org/iraq.html; Erica Goode and Suadad Al-Salhy, *Violence in Mosul Forces Iraqi Christians to Flee,* N.Y. Times, Oct. 11, 2008, http://www.nytimes.com; *Iraq's Christian Population Cut by Half,* The New American, Sept. 4, 2006, http://www.accessmylibrary.com; Michael Youash, *Iraq's Minority Crisis and U.S. National Security: Protecting Minority Rights in Iraq,* 24 American University International L. Review 341, 369 (2008) ("With over one in three Assyrian Christians already cleansed from Iraq, it is not enough to approach reconstruction and development as a means to prevent further minority flight.With over one in three Assyrian Christians already cleansed from Iraq, it is not enough to approach reconstruction and development as a means to prevent further minority flight.").

157. *Quoted in* Angus Crawford, *Iraq's Mandaeans 'Face Extinction',* BBC News, Mar. 5, 2007, http://news.bbc.co.uk/2/hi/middle_east/6412453.stm; *see also* John Clugston, Letter Concerning the Mandaean Genocide in Iraq (June 12, 2008), Genocide Watch, http://www.genocidewatch.org/iraq.html; Genocide Watch, *Mandaeans of Iraq* (June 4, 2007), http://www.genocidewatch.org/images/Iraq4Jun07GenocideWatchIraqMandaeans.pdf ("Mandaeans also suffer the confiscation of their property, their houses being taken from them in Baghdad, Basra, and Baquba. Mandaeans flee their homes in response to threatening letters, and their property is immediately taken. The police often refuse to intervene."); Mandaean Human Rights Group, *Sabian Mandaeans in Iraq Face Annihilation* 10 (Jan. 2007), http:// mandaeanunion.org ("The Sabian Mandaeans in Iraq are looking for protection from the hate crimes that they are facing. They are looking for the USA and the international community to save their lives, their children, their future and prevent the genocide that is happening to them."); Mandaean Human Rights Group, *Mandaean Human Rights Annual Report* 7 (Mar. 2008), http://mandaeanunion.org ("Mandaeans are being targeted and killed primarily for their beliefs and secondly for their position in the community as professionals and jewellers."); Luma al-Shumary, *Ancient Sect Targeted,* Inst. of War and Peace Reporting (IWPR), Iraq Crisis Rep. No. 45, Jan. 22, 2004,

even more concerned as their numbers plummeted to the low thousands, from the tens of thousands before the most recent war. One of only five remaining Mandaean bishops warned that without assistance from the international community, "our ancient religion will die off."[158] The Yezidis of Iraq, although more numerous than the dwindling Mandaeans, likewise declared that they faced being wiped out or driven away by Arab bombings and shootings.[159]

In 2006, Secretary-General Kofi Annan's advisor on the prevention of genocide argued that "the targeting of minorities based solely on religion in Iraq, the extent of the violence there, the lack of central control, and the fact that Iraq has already experienced genocide, 'constitute warning signs that we take very seriously.'" Prominent Harvard scholar Samantha Power, currently an adviser on genocide to the White House, agreed, because "with Shi'ite and Sunni sub-groups already identifying and killing victims solely on the basis of their religious identity, 'genocidal intent' is already present in Iraq."[160] Two prosecutors of the Cambodian war crimes tribunal argued that more than 18,000 Iraqi Christians may have been killed, and that "the targeting of religious leaders and buildings accompanied by statements advocating the destruction of Iraqi Christians supports an inference of the requisite genocidal intent."[161] With far more murders than in Bosnia or Kosovo, and perhaps even more than in Rwanda, the situation in Iraq involves, at a minimum, war crimes, crimes against humanity, and conspiracy to commit genocide.[162] Acts of "murder, sexual assault, intimidation, harassment, and the destruction of sacred and cultural buildings," are war crimes, and, when they make up part of a policy or pattern of attacking civilians or a civilian population, they are a crime against humanity.[163] They are also predicate acts to the crime of genocide, when

---

http://www.iwpr.net/?p=icr&s=f&o=168543&apc_state=heniicr2004 ("Baghdad's tightly knit Mandaean community has suffered ten murders and more than 13 kidnappings in just three months").

158. *Quoted in* Wendy Griffith, *Iraqi Christians May Face Extinction* (Jan. 17, 2007), http://www.cwnews.com.

159. *See* Michael Howard, *'They won't stop until we are all wiped out.',* THE GUARDIAN (U.K.), Aug. 18, 2007, http://www.guardian.co.uk/world/2007/aug/18/iraq.topstories3.

160. Massimo Calabresi, *Is Iraq Headed for Genocide?,* TIME MAG., Nov. 29, 2006, http://www.time.com/time/world/article/0,8599,1564270,00.html.

161. *See* Robert Petit, Stuart Ford, & Neha Jain, *Exploring Critical Issues in Religious Genocide: Case Studies of Violence in Tibet, Iraq, and Gujarat,* 40 CASE WESTERN RESERVE U. J. OF INTERNATIONAL LAW 163, 196, 199 (2008).

162. *See* ORB, *More than 1,000,000 Iraqis Murdered* ("[A] new poll reveals that more than 1,000,000 Iraqi citizens have been murdered since the invasion took place in 2003.... As well as a murder rate that now exceeds the Rwanda genocide from 1994 (800,000 murdered), ... more than one million been injured."); Samantha Power, *How to Stop Genocide in Iraq,* L.A. TIMES, Mar. 5, 2007, http://www.latimes.com (arguing that "wholesale ethnic cleansing" in Iraq led 3.8 million Iraqis to flee their communities, including 50,000 each month).

163. M. CHERIF BASSIOUNI, CRIMES AGAINST HUMANITY IN INTERNATIONAL CRIMINAL LAW 329 (Dordrecht and Boston: Kluwer Law Int'l, 1999) ("crimes against humanity" include following acts directed against any civilian population in an international or internal armed conflict: murder, torture, rape, "persecutions on political, racial and religious grounds," and "other inhumane acts"); United Nations Commission on Human Rights, *Human Rights and Population Transfer: Final Report of the Special Rapporteur,* E/CN.4/Sub.2/1997/23, ¶ 10; ROY GUTMAN, DAVID RIEFF, & KENNETH ANDERSON, CRIMES OF WAR: WHAT THE PUBLIC SHOULD KNOW (1999); ANDREW BELL-FIALKOFF, ETHNIC CLEANSING 3 (1996); Theodor Meron, *The Case for War Crimes Trials in Yugoslavia,* 72 FOREIGN AFF. 132 (1993).

164. *See* Genocide Convention, art. II ("Genocide means any of the following acts committed with intent to destroy, in whole or in part, a national, ethnical, racial or religious group, as such: ... (a) Killing members of the group ... [or] (c) Deliberately inflicting on the group conditions of life calculated to bring about its physical destruction in whole or in part...."); *id.*, art. III (equating con-

genocidal intent is present.[164] As noted in Chapter III, "attacks on the cultural and religious property and symbols of the targeted group" constitutes "evidence of an intent to physically destroy the group."[165]

A targeted campaign of violence against Assyrian Christians and destruction of Christian cultural and religious symbols has raged in Iraq since 2003. The Assyrians and Chaldeans are an indigenous population that speaks a non-Arabic language handed down from the time of the Assyrian and Babylonian empires, with 1.4 million surviving into the 1980s.[166] Thousands were killed or fled during the Iran-Iraq war and Anfal genocide campaign,[167] while up to a third left Iraq over the 1990s,[168] as U.N. sanctions and the bombardment of the country in the Persian Gulf War cut the GDP of the country by two-thirds and led to over a million preventable deaths from diarrhea, malnutrition, and other causes associated with extreme poverty.[169] This left about a million Chaldean Catholics and Assyrian Church of the East members of the Assyrian ethnic group in Iraq before the war.[170]

Human rights reports issued in the years immediately preceding the 2003 war by the United Nations and the governments of the U.S. and United Kingdom cited isolated killings and

---

spiracy to commit genocide, public incitement to commit, and complicity in or an attempt to commit genocide with the substantive crime itself); *see also* Akayesu, Trial Chamber, Judgement, at ¶¶ 507–08 (actus reus of "deliberate inflicting on the group conditions of life calculated to bring about its physical destruction, in whole or part," includes, among other acts, "systematic expulsion from homes.").

165. Prosecutor v. Krstić, Trial Chamber, Judgement, at ¶ 580.

166. Christopher H. Smith, Chairman of the House International Relations Committee, Statement on the Plight of Religious Minorities: Can Religious Pluralism Survive?, U.S. House of Representatives (June 30, 2006), http://www.internationalrelations.house.gov/109/smith063006.pdf. This number likely included Armenians and Protestants as well as Assyrians and Chaldeans. *See* Petit, Ford & Jain, *Religious Genocide*, at 182.

167. UN Office for the Coordination of Humanitarian Affairs, *Iraq: Focus on Mass Graves* (Jan. 7, 2004), http://www.irinnews.org/report.asp?ReportID=38775&SelectRegion=Iraq_Crisis&SelectCountry=IRAQ; USDOS, *Country Reports on Human Rights—Iraq*, 1994 (Feb. 1995), http://dosfan.lib.uic.edu/ERC/democracy/1994_hrp_report/94hrp_report_nea/Iraq.html; International Federation of Human Rights, *Iraq: Continuous and Silent Ethnic Cleansing* 16 (Jan. 2003), http://www.fidh.org/IMG/pdf/iq350a.pdf; Human Rights Watch, *Reversing Ethnic Cleansing in Northern Iraq* 16 (Aug. 2004), http://hrw.org/reports/2004/iraq0804; Ken Joseph, Jr., *Iraq's Secret Documents*, WASH. TIMES, July 23, 2004, http://washingtontimes.com/upi-breaking/20040723-123038-6416r.htm.

168. NATALIE HENRICH & JOSEPH HENRICH, WHY HUMANS COOPERATE: A CULTURAL AND EVOLUTIONARY EXPLORATION 81 (Oxford UP, 2007) (noting that 100,000 Assyrian Chaldeans live in the metropolitan Detroit area, and others in California, Illinois, and the East Coast); California Assembly Joint Resolution No. 31—Relative to Assyrians in Iraq (Apr. 24, 2003), http://info.sen.ca.gov/pub/03–04/statute/ch_0051-0100/ch_73_st_2003_ajr_31; *Patriarch Raphael I Bidawid*, THE TIMES (U.K.), July 29, 2003, at 28; David Rieff, *Were Sanctions Right?*, N.Y. TIMES, July 28, 2003, http://www.nytimes.com; Caryle Murphy & Naseer Nouri, *Iraqi Catholics Mourn John Paul*, WASH. POST, Apr. 8, 2005, at A18; John Thavis, *Modern-Day Exodus: Flight of Catholics from Iraq Troubles Vatican*, CATHOLIC NEWS SERVICE, Feb. 28, 2003, http://www.findarticles.com; Danish Immigration Service, *Joint British–Danish Fact Finding Mission to Damascus, Amman, and Geneva Regarding Iraqi Asylum Seekers* (June 2002), http://www.unhcr.org/cgi-bin/texis/vtx/home/opendoc.pdf?tbl=RSDCOI&id=3f4908364; U.K. Home Office, *Country Assessment: Iraq* (Oct. 2001), http://www.asylumlaw.org/docs/showDocument.cfm?documentID=844.

169. *See* Economist Intelligence Unit, *Country Profile Iraq 1996* (June 1, 1996), http://www.eiu.com; State Senator John Nimrod, Statement on a Pathway to Human Rights for Northern Iraq to the U.N. Commission on Human Rights, Sub-Commission on Prevention of Discrimination and Protection of Minorities, under item 6 (Aug. 8, 1996); World Health Org., *The Health Conditions of the Population in Iraq Since the Gulf Crisis*, WHO/EHA/96.1 (Mar. 1996), http://www.who.int; Alberto Ascherio et al., *Effect of the Gulf War on Infant and Child Mortality in Iraq*, 327 NEW ENGLAND J. OF MEDICINE 931 (1992).

170. *See* USDOS, *Annual Report on International Religious Freedom for 2006—Iraq* (Sept. 2006).

widespread ethnic and religious discrimination against Assyrians.[171] By comparison, similar reports issued since 2004 have acknowledged "systematic attacks" against Assyrians.[172] Among other incidents, more than 100 Assyrians were murdered in late 2003 and early 2004,[173] including eleven people killed during bombings of Assyrian churches and seven people riding on a bus who were massacred in one day in October 2004;[174] and most Assyrian families formerly living in Basra fled fundamentalist rule.[175] A campaign of kidnappings terrorized Iraqi Christians, at a rate of two or three per week in Baghdad alone.[176]

In the first 16 months after the fall of the old regime, five churches, four of which were Assyrian, were bombed in Iraq.[177] As the State Department described these bombings:

> There were numerous incidents of violence against the Christian community this year, ranging from individual killings to intimidation.... The number of Christians leaving the country rose after bombings of 14 churches in Baghdad and Mosul from August through December [2004]. The bombings left 43 dead and 340 injured, as well as damaging the churches.[178]

Priests and archbishops were regularly kidnapped and murdered,[179] as Christian leaders were targeted.[180] By 2009, more than 40 churches had been bombed, and an archbishop killed.[181]

---

171. *See* USDOS, *Iraq: Country Reports on Human Rights Practices—2002* (Mar, 31, 2003), http://www.state.gov/g/drl/rls/hrrpt/2002/18277.htm; The Government of the United Kingdom, Home Office, *Iraq Country Assessment,* at ¶¶6.124–6.132 (Oct. 2004), http://www.ind.homeoffice.gov.uk/.

172. The Government of the United Kingdom, Home Office, *Iraq Country Assessment,* at ¶6.51.

173. *See* Kenneth Chan, *Christians Wish to Stay, Build Future in Iraq,* Christian Post, Oct. 21, 2004, http://www.christianpost.com. For similar figures, see *Christians in Iraq Caught in the Crossfire,* Associated Press, Nov. 11, 2004, http://www.ap.com.

174. The Government of the United Kingdom, Home Office, *Iraq Country Assessment,* ¶6.54 (Oct. 2004); *Seven Christians Shot Dead in Iraq 'To Arouse Religious Sedition'—Paper,* BBC Monitoring Serv., Oct. 4, 2004.

175. U.K. Home Office, *Iraq Country Assessment,* at ¶6.51; William Booth, *For Basra's Liquor Dealers, The Shots Turn Deadly,* Wash. Post, June 1, 2003, at D01.

176. *See* Jonathan Steele, *Kidnappers Find a Profitable Way to Drive out Educated Families in Baghdad,* The Guardian (U.K.), June 17, 2004, http://www.guardian.co.uk/Iraq/Story/0,2763,1240571,00.html.

177. *See* Petit, Ford, & Jain, *Religious Genocide,* at 189 ("In 2003, there was a rocket attack on a convent in Mosul, explosions in two Christian schools in Baghdad and Mosul, and an explosion in a church in Baghdad on Christmas eve."); *id.* ("[O]n December 7, 2004, a series of attacks on Armenian and Chaldean churches in Mosul caused substantial damage to property."); *id.* ("Since the U.S.-led invasion of Iraq in 2003, more than twenty-five churches in Iraq are reported to have been bombed."); *id.* at 185 ("[F]ive churches were bombed in what looked like a series of coordinated attacks in Baghdad and Mosul on August 1, 2004."); id. at 186 ("There were a series of attacks on six Christian churches in Baghdad on October 16, 2004...."); id. ("On January 29, 2006, car bombs targeted [churches in Baghdad and Kirkuk] killing at lease three people...."); Jamal-Daoud v. Gonzales, 403 F.3d 918, 925–27 (7th Cir. 2005); Sengupta, *Exodus of Iraqi Christians.*

178. USDOS, *Country Reports on Human Rights: Iraq 2004* (2005), http://www.state.gov/g/drl/rsl/hrrpt/2004/41722.htm.

179. *See* U.S. Commission for International Religious Freedom, Annual Report 9 (Washington, DC: 2008) ("ChaldoAssyrian Christians, Mandaeans, and Yazidis, who are heavily targeted in Iraq and disproportionately represented among the refugee populations in neighboring countries."); Petit, Ford & Jain, *Religious Genocide,* at 186 (leader of Iraq's Syrian Catholics, a Syrian Orthodox priest, and two Catholic nuns were killed); Youash, *Iraq's Minority Crisis,* at 348 ("The bombings and attacks on over forty churches, the regular kidnapping of priests, and gruesome murdering of priests, set in motion total panic and flight by this vulnerable minority.").

180. *See* USDOS, *Country Reports on Human Rights Practices: Iraq 2007* (2008), http://www.state.gov/g/drl/rls/hrrpt/2007/100596.htm; USDOS, *Country Reports on Human Rights Practices: Iraq 2006,* Westlaw.com (Mar. 2007), http://www.state.gov.

181. *See Christians Besieged in Iraq,* BBC News, Mar. 13, 2008, http://news.bbc.co.uk/1/hi/world/middle_east/7295145.stm; Ben Gilbert, *Christians Celebrate a Wary Christmas in Baghdad,* S.F. Chron.,

The international press and U.S. and U.K. governments have reported that hundreds of Christians have been targeted and killed based on such signifiers of "Christian" identity as doing the janitorial or translation work for multi-national forces or civilian contractors, operating convenience stores that sell alcohol, being women appearing in public with their faces or legs uncovered, for wearing fashionable Western haircuts or clothes, or listening to or selling Western music. Assyrian and other Christian children have been beheaded and in one case literally crucified. The leader of the Chaldean church in Turkey has stated that the current situation is worse than ever, with news reaching Istanbul every day of five or six more Chaldeans having been killed in Iraq. Women have suffered disfiguring acid attacks and frequent kidnapping in a climate of fundamentalist resurgence and a breakdown of government institutions.[182] Christian women and girls became "virtual prisoners in their homes," with religious services at a halt and 30 Christian women kidnapped in a month.[183]

Under international law, Christians in Iraq could be suffering from an attempt or conspiracy to commit genocide. "The context of the violence against the Iraqi Christians, along with the targeting of religious leaders and buildings accompanied by statements advocating the destruction of Iraqi Christians supports an inference of the requisite genocidal intent."[184] Many Assyrians have been targeted for killing or infliction of severe bodily or mental harm, and Iraq's Christian population has been cut by as much as half since

---

Dec. 24, 2005, http://www.sfgate.com; Paul Isaac, *Iraq's Assyrian Christians: More of the Same Old*, INT'L HERALD TRIB., Feb. 17, 2009, http://www.iht.com; *Leaders Condemn Iraq Church Bombs*, BBC NEWS, Aug. 2, 2004, http://news.bbc.co.uk/1/hi/world/middle_east/3527032.stm; Liz Sly, *Churches in Iraq Targeted in Bombings; 4 Killed*, L.A. TIMES, July 13, 2009, http://www.latimes.com/news/ nationworld/world/la-fg-iraq-bombings13-2009jul13,0,2315778.story; Wisam al-Qasi, *The Churches Are under Threat in Iraq*, THE INDEPENDENT (SOUTH AFRICA), Dec. 24, 2003, http://www.iol.co.za/ index.php?sf=2813&click_id=2813&art_id=qw1072357381117B262&set_id=6.

182. *See* Lawrence F. Kaplan, *Crossing Over: The Plight of Iraqi Christians*, THE NEW REPUBLIC, Apr. 3, 2006, at 14–18; Assyrian Academic Society, *Submission to the U.N. Commission on Human Rights, Sub-Commission on the Promotion and Protection of Human Rights, Working Group on Minorities* (June 2005), http://www.ohchr.org/english/issues/minorities/docs/11/Assyrian_3a.doc; Anna Badkhen & Danielle Hass, *Women Losing Freedoms in Chaos of Postwar Iraq*, S.F. CHRON., May 24, 2003, at A1; Felice D. Gaer and Charles J. Chaput, *Protecting Iraq's Religious Minorities*, WASH. TIMES, Dec. 22, 2006, at A21; Felice Gaer, Chair, U.S. Commission on International Religious Freedom [CIRF], Statement to Panel III of a Hearing by the U.S. House of Representatives, Committee on International Relations, on the Plight of Religious Minorities, Dec. 21, 2006, http://www.uscirf.gov; Mariam Georgis, Assyrian Aid Society of Canada, *Edited Evidence to the Canadian House of Commons, Standing Committee on Citizenship and Immigration* (Apr. 7, 2008), http://www2.parl.gc.ca; Hoffman, *U.S. Iraqi Christian Community Debates How to Help Relatives*; Human Rights Without Frontiers Int'l, *The ChaldoAssyrian Community in Iraq* (Nov. 2003), http://www.hrwf.net/reports/ext/Iraq_MissionReport_ Nov03.pdf;Isaac, *Iraq's Assyrian Christians*; Yanar Muhammed, Organization of Women's Freedom in Iraq, *Edited Evidence to the Canadian House of Commons, Standing Committee on Citizenship and Immigration* (Apr. 7, 2008), http://www2.parl.gc.ca; Sengupta, *Exodus of Iraq's Christians*; *Syrian Sanctuary for Iraq's Displaced Christians*, THE HERALD (GLASGOW, SCOTLAND), Sept. 4, 2006, http://www.theherald.co.uk; U.S. CIRF, *Annual Report of the United States Comm'n on Int'l Religious Freedom* 13 (2005), http://www.uscirf.gov/countries/publications/currentreport/2005annualRpt.pdf; Loretta Waldman, *A Voice for an Iraqi Minority*, HARTFORD COURANT, Nov. 25, 2006, at B3; Michael Youash, *Testimony to U.S. Commission on International Religious Freedom, Hearing on Threats to Iraq's Communities of Antiquity* (July 27, 2007), http://www.zindamagazine.com/ html/archives/2007/ 08.01.07/pix/USCIRF_Yoash.pdf.

183. *See* Teresa Watanabe, *War Splits Iraqi Emigres*, L.A. TIMES, Nov. 19, 2006, http://articles.latimes.com/2006/nov/19/local/me-iraqi19.

184. Petit, Ford, & Jain, *Religious Genocide*, at 199; Preti Taneja, *Assimilation, Exodus, Eradication: Iraq's Minority Communities Since 2003*, at 5, MINORITY RIGHTS GROUP INT'L, (2007), http://www.minorityrights.org/?lid=2805.

2003, from over a million down to 600,000.[185] At less than five percent of Iraq's population, Chaldeans, Assyrians and other Christians constituted 30 to 40 percent of the refugees fleeing to Syria, Jordan, Europe, the U.S. and Australia, according to the U.N. High Commissioner for Refugees.[186] Iraqi refugees interviewed in Syria by UNHCR reported being personally threatened with death by aerial bombing, shelling, or rockets, while nearly 90% saw a person be shot at.[187] One-sixth had personally been tortured, so that compared to other refugee populations, Iraqis are one of the most violence-affected populations in the history of the United Nations.[188]

Based on experience in Gulf War II, the U.S. State Department, United Nations and the press warned before the multi-national forces invaded Iraq in 2003 that the conflict could inflame existing religious tensions, causing widespread refugee flight.[189] More than 45,000 Assyrian Christians who survived Saddam fled Iraq by fall 2004.[190] About 300,000 to 400,000 Christians fled their homes in Iraq between 2003 and 2005, many languishing as refugees in Syria, Jordan, Turkey, and Iran.[191] A Chaldean painter from Baghdad who fled to Syria after his gallery and house were firebombed told the media that: "Many of the refugees were maimed by their attackers."[192] Intimidation on such a scale consti-

185. *See* Chairman Christopher H. Smith, Statement on The Plight of Religious Minorities: Can Religious Pluralism Survive?, to the Subcommittee on Africa, Global Human Rights and International Operations, International Relations Committee, U.S. House of Representatives (June 30, 2006), http://www.internationalrelations.house.gov/109/smith063006.pdf. *See also Leaders Condemn Iraq Church Bombs.*

186. *See* Kenneth H. Bacon, *A Role for Syria*, Wash. Post, Dec. 06, 2006, at A25; Allison Hoffman, U.S. *Iraqi Christians Seek Help*, Associated Press, Dec. 15, 2006, http://abcnews.go.com/US/wireStory?id=2728272; Petit, Ford, & Jain, *Religious Genocide,* at 195. *See also Pontiff Appeals for Aid for Iraqi Refugees in Syria*, Zenit, Dec. 17, 2006, http://www.zenit.org; *Syrian Sanctuary for Iraq's Displaced Christians*, The Herald (Glasgow, Scotland), Sept. 4, 2006, http://www.theherald.co.uk ("Traumatised by the killing, kidnapping and gangsterism that constitutes life in Iraq since [the war], 350,000 Iraqi Christians now live as near-penniless refugees, principally in Damascus, Syria, where they have been given safe status.").

187. *See* UNHCR, *Iraq* (2008), *Trauma Survey in Syria Highlights Suffering of Iraqi Refugees* (Jan. 22, 2008), http://www.unhcr.org/cgi-bin/texis/vtx/iraq?page=news&id=479616762.

188. *See* U.N. News Service, *1 in 5 Iraqi Refugees in Syria Suffered Torture or Violence Back Home,* Jan. 22, 2008, http://www.un.org/apps/news/story.asp?NewsID=25366&Cr=iraq&Cr1=syria.

189. *See* U.N., *Likely Humanitarian Scenarios*; USDOS, *Memo to Under Secretary of State Paula Dobriansky* (Feb. 7, 2003), http://www.gwu.edu/~nsarchiv/NSAEBB/NSAEBB163/iraq-state-03.pdf (Defense Department's "reluctance to take on 'policing' roles," and "failure to address short-term public security and humanitarian assistance concerns could result in serious human rights abuses...."); *see also* Robert Collier, *Wartime Iraq Aid Calamity Feared: Relief Agencies Predict Humanitarian Disaster,* S.F. Chron., Jan. 5, 2003, http://www.sfgate.com/cgi-bin/article.cgi?file=/chronicle/archive/2003/01/05/MN198063.DTL; Sadako Ogata, *This Time, Take Care of the Refugees,* Int'l Herald Trib., Feb. 21, 2003, http://www.highbeam.com.

190. *See* Sabrina Tavernise, *For Now, Merchants Cast Lot with a New Iraq*, N.Y. Times, Sept. 12, 2004, http://www.nytimes.com/2004/09/12/international/middleeast/12store.html?ex=1113364800&en=848f5b04b6bf7b18&ei=5070&hp; Sengupta, *Exodus of Iraqi Christians.*

191. Fairweather, *Christians Flee Genocide as Fear Sweeps Iraq*; Eshoo, *Statement in Support of the Eshoo Amendment*; Jack Fairweather, Archbishop Is Kidnapped by Iraq Insurgents, The Telegraph (U.K.), Jan. 21, 2005, http://www.telegraph.co.uk/news/worldnews/middleeast/ iraq/1481471/Archbishop-is-kidnapped-by-Iraq-insurgents.html; *Leaders Condemn Iraq Church Bombs;* Patrick McDonnell, *After Years of Relative Peace, Christians Live in Fear,* L.A. Times, Nov. 14, 2004, at A16; *see also* Rep. Anna Eshoo, Statement in Support of the Eshoo Amendment to H.R. 2601, the Foreign Relations Authorization Act for FY 2006 and 2007 (July 20, 2005), http://www-eshoo.house.gov/news/iraq072005.aspx; Lobe, *Iraqi Christians Need Protection, Too*; Shea, *Iraq's Future*; Siemon-Netto, *Attacks Defy the Prophet's Wish.*

192. Refugees International, *Iraq Is the Fastest-Growing Refugee Crisis in the World* (Dec. 6, 2006), http://www.aina.org/news/20061207013439.htm.

tutes ethnic cleansing, which the United Nations has often equated with genocide.[193] Human rights groups charged genocide in Mosul:

> Over a thousand Christian families have fled Mosul for outlying villages and villages in the Kurdistan region in search of safety, a spokesman for the Ministry of Endowment and Religious Affairs said.... "The Christian families left in Mosul are very few indeed," said Mariwan Nakshabandee, spokesman for the Ministry of Endowment and Religious Affairs, which oversees Christian communities in Mosul....
>
> The Hammurabi Association for Human Rights released a statement demanding international attention to the assassinations of Christians likening it to "genocide."[194]

When about 900,000 Kosovars fled as refugees and 1,000 were killed in 1998 and 1999, the U.S. State Department, NATO, and various European governments declared genocide to be underway, as detailed in Chapter III. By comparison, between one hundred and one thousand times as many people have died in Iraq, and they were largely targeted by religion or sect. While the largest receiving country for Kosovars, Albania, admitted 440,000 refugees, Syria admitted 750,000 Iraqi refugees[195] and Jordan admitted up to a million refugees by late 2006.[196] By late 2006, 1.6 million Iraqis had fled the country, while another 1.6 million were internally displaced within Iraq.[197] About a million more Iraqis fled in 2007, at an astonishing rate of 100,000 a month.[198] The proportionally worst-affected groups in Iraq in terms of refugee flight are religious minorities not linked to the insurgency. Even if not genocide, this campaign of ethno-sectarian "murder, sexual as-

---

193. *Compare* Final Report of United Nations Commission of Experts to the Security Council, S/1994/674, at 33 (May 27, 1994), at III.B (ethnic cleansing includes not simply the extermination of an ethnic group, but also "rendering an area ethnically homogenous by using force or intimidation to remove persons of given groups from the area...."), *with* U.N. Doc. A/RES/47/121 (Dec. 18, 1992) (ethnic cleansing is a "form of genocide"); U.N. Doc. A/RES/48/153 (Dec. 20, 1993); U.N. Doc. A/RES/49/205 (Dec. 23, 1994); U.N. Doc. A/RES/50/192 (Dec. 22, 1995); U.N. Doc. A/RES/51/115 (Dec. 12, 1996); *Bosnia and Herzegovina, in* Encyclopedia of Genocide and Crimes Against Humanity–, at 1076; Shaw, What Is Genocide?, at 50, 177 (citing G.A. Res. 47/121 (1992). For application of the concept to Iraq, see, for example, Nina Shea, *Iraq's Future as a Tolerant, Democratic Nation Is at Stake*, National Rev. (Oct. 14, 2004), http://www.nationalreview.com/comment/shea200410140830.asp.

194. Leila Fadel, *Thousands of Christians Flee Killings in Mosul,* McClatchy Newspapers, http://www.mcclatchydc.com/255/story/53808.html.

195. *See* Human Rights Watch, Under Orders: War Crimes in Kosovo 134 (New York: Human Rights Watch, 2001).

196. *See* Bacon, *A Role for Syria*, at A25 (Syria took in 750,000 Iraqi refugees from April 2003 through November 2006); *A Torch Still Burns*, Seattle Post-Intelligencer, Mar. 16, 2007, http://www.highbeam.com/doc/1G1-108474902.html (Syria took in one million Iraqi refugees by March 2007); Albert Aji, *Iraqi Refugees Trying to Adjust to Syria*, Wash. Post, Oct. 22, 2006, http://www.washingtonpost.com/wp-dyn/content/article/2006/10/22/AR2006102200467_pf.html (500,000 Iraqis in Syria by 2006); *American Morning (Transcript)*, CNN.com (June 20, 2006), http://edition.cnn.com/TRANSCRIPTS/0606/20/ltm.05.html (one million Iraqi refugees in Jordan by late June 2006); Associated Press, *Iraq Refugees Flee for Jordan, Syria*, San Fran. Chronicle (June 14, 2006), http://www.sfgate.com/cgi-bin/article.cgi?f=/n/a/2006/06/14/national/w160253D47.DTL&type=politics (650,000 Iraqis fled for Jordan and Syria in 18 months between Jan. 2005 and June 2006, making 888,000 refugees in all); Kelley Beaucar Vlahos, *U.S. Cautions Against Iraq Refugee Number Claims*, Fox News.com (May 17, 2006), http://www.foxnews.com/story/0,2933,195761,00.html.

197. U.N. Secretary-General, Report Pursuant to Paragraph 30 of Resolution 1546, at ¶ 36.

198. About "100,000 per month have left Iraq" in late 2006. *U.N.: Iraqi Civilian Death Toll Reaches New Monthly High,* CNN, Nov. 22, 2006.

sault, intimidation, harassment, and the destruction of sacred and cultural buildings" amounts to the crimes against humanity of persecution or extermination.[199]

In 2004 and 2005, Assyrian leaders proposed that a just proportion of Iraqi reconstruction spending authorized by the U.S. and the international community be specifically earmarked to security and the rebuilding of Assyrian villages.[200] Without a large militia to police their neighborhoods, the Assyrians were often defenseless and needed their own governors and police, like those possessed by the Native Americans in the U.S. The U.S. Commission on International Religious Freedom told Congress in June 2006 that Iraqi Christians "have been forced to fend for themselves in a continuing climate of impunity, and they remain particularly vulnerable given their lack of any tribal or militia structure to provide for their security." The Commission noted that Iraq's "non-Muslim religious minorities suffer a disproportionate burden of violent attacks and other human rights abuses," including "religiously motivated attacks on ... non-Muslim women." Assyrian women have suffered from "the unlawful imposition of Islamic laws and principles by grassroots vigilante groups, as well as by the operation of illegal courts that seek to impose an extremist version of Islamic law on all Iraqis, regardless of their beliefs."[201] Mass flight from Basra northwards became necessary because armed militia terrorized women and religious minorities in the streets.[202]

The U.S., Britain, and France have largely ignored the persecutions of Christians in Iraq, as well as in Egypt and Saudi Arabia, while rushing to save Muslim minorities in Bosnia and Kosovo from far less systematic destruction. Throughout the 1980s, 1990s, and 2000s, the West rejected the idea of solidarity with the Christians of the Middle East, failing to prevent their ethnic cleansing while prioritizing diplomacy based on oil interests and the Arab-Israeli conflict.[203] Even from 2003 to 2006, American troops in Iraq did not intervene against repeated instances of the persecution of Assyrians, perhaps not wanting to provoke retaliation.[204]

In an effort to stem the bloodshed, President Bush appointed a new secretary of defense, Robert Gates, in 2006, who promptly stated that the U.S. was not prevailing in Iraq on its declared objectives or bringing democracy, stability, and prosperity. This was surprising because terrorists and insurgents were clearly losing more fighters on the battlefield than the multi-national forces. Despite the disparity in human and economic losses, Iraqi insurgents and militias were said to be prevailing to a certain extent due to political perceptions. Specifically, foreign terrorist leaders and Iraqi warlords were achieving many of their political objectives, while multi-national forces and its allies in the Iraqi government seemingly were not. Assuming that the objective of the multi-national forces was, as stated in a series of U.N. Security Council resolutions, a

199. *See* Rome Statute of the ICC, art. 7; Prosecutor v. Kayishema and Ruzindana, Appeals Chamber, Judgement, at ¶¶ 89, 142–46; Prosecutor v. Zigiranyirazo, Trial Chamber III, Judgement, at ¶¶ 429, 470; Prosecutor v. Vasiljevic, Trial Chamber II, Judgement, at ¶¶ 227–29.

200. U.S. CIRF, *Annual Report 2005*, at 18. The Assyrian American National Federation proposed 5% of such funds as a just proportion. Jim Lobe, *Plight of Christians Provokes Calls for Special Protection*, Inter Press Service, Oct. 20, 2004, http://64.233.179.104/search?q=cache:g58M2R8E4TMJ:ipsnews.org/new_nota.asp%3Fidnews%3D25948.

201. Nina Shea, Vice Chair, U.S. CIRF, Testimony on The Plight of Religious Minorities: Can Religious Pluralism Survive?, to the Subcommittee on Africa, Global Human Rights, and International Operations, International Relations Committee, U.S. House of Representatives, June 30, 2006, http://www.internationalrelations.house.gov/109/she063006.pdf.

202. *See* Mohammed, *Edited Evidence to the Canadian House of Commons.*

203. Walid Phares, *Are Christian Enclaves the Solution?*, 8 Middle East Q. 69 (2001).

204. Fairweather, *Christians Flee Genocide.*

stable, secure, democratic, unified, and prosperous Iraq that was not a base for terrorism, this had not been created. By contrast, Iraqi terrorist leaders and warlords achieved many of their political objectives. *Al Qaeda* in Iraq achieved its goal of punishing the Christians and Shi'a for working with Westerners, causing hundreds of thousands of deaths and billions of dollars in economic damage to Iraq. Shi'a militia such as the Badr Brigades and Mahdi Army then consolidated their control over the Iraqi government and security forces, as well as key neighborhoods in Baghdad, and entire southern provinces.

By 2008, Sunni terrorists and insurgents, whose violence was driven in part by fears that the Kurdish north and Shi'a south would dominate Sunnis politically and impoverish the Sunni center and west by refusing to share oil revenues, had secured a degree of de facto independence from the national army and Shi'a-dominated police force. This occurred under the rubric of the "Awakening" program whereby Sunni militias are paid by the U.S. Meanwhile, the leaders of the Kurdish *pesh merga* militia, which also rejected control by the national army, established an increasingly independent mini-state with its own oil deals (that other Iraqis would not accept) with Western oil companies.[205] The president of Iraq underlined the extent of Kurdish *pesh merga* domination of Iraqi territory in 2008 when he refused to allow the Iraqi army to take over military duties in Kirkuk from the *pesh merga*. President Talabani vowed that a law calling for Iraqi army control over Kirkuk would "never" be passed.[206] Until late 2008, there were up to 30,000 *pesh merga* fighters loyal to the KDP and PUK who had not been incorporated into the Iraqi military, and who policed the borders of Kurdistan region and the disputed areas such as Kirkuk with the rest of Iraq and Iraq's neighbors. As of this writing, the Iraqi army and Kurdish *pesh merga* still struggle for territory and control in northern Iraq.[207]

D. The Systematic Expulsion of Iraq's Non-Christian Minority Communities

In 2003, nearly three quarters of a million non-Christian religious minorities lived in Iraq. These included an estimated 100,000 Mandaeans and 600,000 Yezidis.[208] Leaders of

205. "The Kurdistan government never implemented the TAL provisions calling for a single national military force or those giving Baghdad control over Kurdistan's oil and border crossings. Resentment of the TAL led the Kurds to organize a referendum in Kurdistan simultaneous with the January elections, in which 98 percent of Iraq's Kurds expressed a preference for independence." Galbraith, *The Mess*.

206. *See* Amit R. Paley, *Iraqi President Vows Veto of Election Bill*, WASH. POST, July 24, 2008, at A16.

207. *See, e.g.*, International Crisis Group, *Iraq and the Kurds: Trouble Along The Trigger Line*, Middle East Report No. 88 (July 8, 2009), http://www.crisisgroup.org/home/index.cfm?id=6207&l=1; Saif Hameed and Ned Parker, *27 Killed in Two Bombings in Iraq*, LA TIMES, Mar. 24, 2009, http://www.latimes.com/news/nationworld/world/la-fg-iraq24-2009mar24,0,4027684.story; *Iraqi Forces Revamp Hit by Oil Prices: Pentagon*, AGENCE FRANCE-PRESSE, Mar. 31, 2009; *Iraqi Kurdish Press Highlights*, BBC WORLD PRESS MONITORING SERVICE, Apr. 29, 2008, http://nl.newsbank.com; The Economist Intelligence Unit Ltd., *Iraq: Country Profile 2007*, http://www.eiu.com.

208. *See* USDOS, *Annual Report on International Religious Freedom for 2006—Iraq* (Sept. 2006) (figures for Yezidis and Baha'i); Michael J. Frank, *Justice for Iraq, Justice for All*, 57 OKLA. L. REV. 303, 310–12 (2004) (figure for Mandeans).

these other religious minorities are united with Iraq's president in declaring that Iraq is experiencing genocide.[209] Up to 90 percent of Mandaean families have fled Iraq.[210]

The Mandaean language, Mandaic, has been traced to ancient Babylonian sources.[211] Both the Mandaean and Yezidi faiths are syncretic, which is to say that they are composed of elements of ancient Assyro-Babylonian paganism, Judaism, Christianity, and, in the case of the Yezidis, Islam.[212] The Yezidis therefore revere the sun and fire, and perpetuate ancient Assyro-Babylonian beliefs.[213]

The ancient Mesopotamian religions continued to be practiced after the Persian and Arab conquests, with temples of pagan gods still standing in the sixth and early seventh centuries CE.[214] Gnostics continued the Assyro-Babylonian faith in enlightenment from a monstrous material world, which requires rituals such as baptism, magic, and "sacred meals" to "purify the soul." In Babylonia, local pagans adapted Gnostic ideas and became known as "Sābians" by Arab historians; they tended to cluster near swamps, used ritual ablutions and washings to purify their bodies and foodstuffs, and continued ancient Assyrians conceptions of the gods, their connection to the Sun and moon, and astrology.[215]

---

209. *See* Crawford, *Iraq's Mandaeans 'Face Extinction'*; Associated Press, *Mandaeans a Casualty of Iraq War* JOPLIN GLOBE (MISSOURI), Apr. 27, 2009, http://www.joplinglobe.com/weekend/local_story_040145621.html?keyword=topstory; Australian Broadcasting Corp., *Mandaeans Persecuted in Iraq*, THE RELIGION REPORT, June 7, 2006, http://www.abc.net.au/rn/talks/8.30/relrpt/stories/s1657535.htm; Patrick Jackson, *Crushing Iraq's Human Mosaic*, BBC NEWS, July 13, 2007, http://www.bbc.co.uk; Justin Vallejo, *A Baptism of Final Sadness*, THE DAILY TELEGRAPH (AUSTRALIA), Feb. 25, 2008, http://www.news.com.au/dailytelegraph/story/ 0,22049,23268209-5006009,00.html; Carol J. Williams, *Death Toll in Bombing of Sect Rises*, L.A. TIMES, Aug. 16, 2007, at A6.

210. *See* Youash, *Iraq's Minority Crisis*, at 344.

211. *See* EDMONDO LUPIERE, THE MANDAEANS: THE LAST GNOSTICS 53–54 (Charles Hindley trans., Cambridge, U.K.: William Eerdmans Publishing Co. 2002); Jonas C.C. Greenfield, *Standard Literary Aramaic, in* AL KANFEI YONAH: STUDIES OF JONAS C. C. GREENFIELD ON SEMITIC PHILOLOGY 113, 153–56 (Shalom M. Paul et al. eds., 2001); Greenfield, *The Babylonian Forerunner of a Mandaic Formula, in id.* at 509–11; Greenfield, *Aramaic and Its Dialects, in id.* at 369–75.

212. *See* JOHN S. GUEST, THE YEZIDIS: A STUDY IN SURVIVAL 55, 202–04 (New York: KPI Ltd., 2007); LUPIERE, THE MANDAEANS, at 130–31, 138–39, 176, 203–212, 252–53; W. Francis Ainsworth, *The Assyrian Origin of the Izedis or Yezidis—The So-Called "Devil Worshippers,"* 1 TRANSACTIONS OF THE ETHNOLOGICAL SOCIETY 11 (1861); Francesca Rochberg, *The Babylonian Origins of the Mandaean Book of the Zodiac*, 11–12 ARAM 237, 240–46 (1999–2000); Michael Tarelko, *A Magical Scroll from the Drower Collection*, 11–12 ARAM 249, 251 (1999–2000); *The Yezidis, A Strage Survival, in* 58 The Church Quarterly Review 119, 123–18 (1904); E.M. Yamauchi, *Mandaic Incantations*, 11–12 ARAM 253, 256*58 (1999–2000);Michael J. Frank, *Justice for Iraq, Justice for All*, 57 OKLA. L. REV. 303, 310–12 nn. 44–46 (2004) (citing John Daniszewski, *Ancient Faith is a Reminder of Iraq's Diversity*, L.A. TIMES, Mar. 10, 2003, at A5; Megan K. Stack, *Gnostic Sect in Iraq Lobbies to Protect Its Way of Life*, L.A. TIMES, Feb. 29, 2004, at A12; Susan Taylor Martin, *In Iraq, Ancient Sect Quietly Lives on Faith*, ST. PETERSBURG TIMES, Apr. 26, 2004, at 1A).

213. *See* OSWALD HUTTON PARRY, SIX MONTHS IN A SYRIAN MONASTERY 359 (Piscataway, N.J.: Gorgias Press LLC, 2d ed. 2004).

214. MORONY, IRAQ AFTER THE MUSLIM CONQUEST, at 384–85.

215. *Id.* at 401, 409; E.S. DROWER, THE MANDAEANS OF IRAQ AND IRAN: THEIR CULTS, CUSTOMS, MAGIC LEGENDS, AND FOLKLORE xviii–xxiii, 26, 40, 46, 56, 75–80, 84, 96–98, 117, 121, 229, 271, 275, 305, 318, 342–44, 399, 408, 417 (Piscataway, NJ: Gorgias Press, 2002) (1962) (describing Mandaean scriptures referring to Assyro-Babylonian gods Shamash the sun-god, Sin the moon-god, Ishtar or Dilbat the goddess identified with Venus, Bel the god identified with Jupiter, Nirgal the god identified with Mars, and Tammuz the mate of Ishtar who descends into the underworld); E.S. Drower, *The Mandaean New Year Festival*, 36 MAN 185, 187–188 (1936) (describing similarities between New Year's festival of modern Mandaeans and ancient Assyro-Babylonians, including story of descent of a god into the netherworld). The basic principle of Mandaeanism is reverence for and baptism in the holy "living water" or the fresh water of rivers, which the ancient Sumerians, Assyrians, and Babylonians also revered as holy water under the name *apzu* or *apsu* to distinguish it

In the same part of the country, perhaps a little to the north, the Mandaeans proliferated in the seventh century CE, also living near swamps and practicing ritual ablutions, and retaining the ancient Assyrian gods, magical invocations, and amulets.[216] After the introduction of Christianity in Iraq, many pagan priests reportedly adopted the new faith and transformed their temples, and others, into churches or monasteries. Christian bishops, for example in sixth-century CE Iraq, tried to ban pagan religious traditions such as astrology, divination, and spell-casting. Persians, and later Arabs, persecuted paganism as a form of sorcery punishable by death, as did the Greeks and Romans, and later the French and English, in the West.[217]

The Mandaeans today regard themselves as living on the brink of cultural extinction. Their population inside Iraq has plummeted by 90% since 2003, from 100,000 to fewer than 6,000.[218] Persecution since 2003 by former Ba'athists and foreign terrorists has caused most Mandaeans to flee Iraq:

> Today, it is estimated that only 5,000 Mandaeans [down from 100,000] remain in Iraq, mostly in Baghdad, and in the area around Basra. Since the US-led invasion of Iraq in 2003, Mandaeans have been the specific targets of violence....
>
> The community has suffered the looting and destruction of their homes and businesses....
>
> Layla al Roomi, a Mandaean who is based in the UK and is now lobbying for the Iraqi community, said, "In the last months, there have been further killings of Mandaeans in Iraq. Families are being separated, homes are being taken. It is worse than it has been so far. Despite the Bush administration saying that there is more security in Iraq, minorities are continuing to suffer." In fact, she said, "beneath the noses of the British and US troops in southern Iraq, including Basra, there has been a total cleansing of Mandaeans and Christians."....
>
> The Mandaean culture and language [are] at risk of being totally eradicated from Iraq.[219]

The Mandaean religion is in crisis because most have had to flee the rivers and marshes in Iraq that are central to their religious practice. Although Mandaeans do not have as many churches or shrines to destroy as the Assyrians do, their ability to practice their traditional religious rites has been impaired by displacement of their homes and communities, and therefore from proximity to the rivers where they are regularly baptized in rituals of "spiritual cleansing" administered by Mandaean priests.[220] In the early 1990s, the Iraqi govern-

---

from salt water, which they called Tiamat and identified with pollution and destruction because it is not fit to drink. *See* Drower, The Mandaeans of Iraq and Iran, at 95, 100–10, 117–25, 142–43, 229–36, 256; Jeremy A. Black & Anthony Green, Gods, Demons, and Symbols of Ancient Mesopotamia: An Illustrated Dictionary 26–27, 117 (Austin, Texas: Univ. of Texas Press, 1992).

216. *See* Morony, Iraq After the Muslim Conquest, at 15. They also adapted elements of Persian Magianism and Jewish faith in specific angels. *See id.*

217. *See id.* at 394–97, 410–416.

218. USDOS, *Country Reports on Human Rights, Iraq 2008*. *Compare* Nathaniel Deutsch, *Save the Gnostics*, N.Y. Times, Oct. 6, 2007, http://www.nytimes.com/2007/10/06/opinion/06deutsch.html?pagewanted=all.

219. Minority Rights Group, *State of the World's Minorities 2008*, at 141 (2008) http://www.minorityrights.org/?lid=6138.

220. *Id.*

ment attacked rebel groups active in the southern marshes, ordering the "burning and demolition of houses" as well as "poisoning" and "explosives" against residents suspected of "collaborating" with rebels.[221] It cleansed all towns within three kilometers of the marshes of their population, killed hundreds of residents of the marshes, and dumped toxic material into the marshes, which the Babylonians and Mandaeans used for millennia in their religious rituals of washings and baptisms.[222] Their language, Mandaic Aramaic,[223] in which their scriptures are written, is also listed on the U.N. Economic, Social, and Cultural Organization's (UNESCO's) *Atlas of the World's Languages in Danger of Disappearing.*[224]

The Yezidis, whose beliefs combine indigenous Assyro-Babylonian and Zoroastrian religion with Jewish, Christian, and Muslim doctrines, are also a threatened people.[225] Leaders of the Yezidis agree with those of the Mandaeans and Assyrians in declaring that an attempted genocide against them has been underway.[226] The Yezidis may have lost 100,000 members or more to violence and refugee flight.[227] About 500 Yezidis in two villages died due to four truck bombs targeting them in 2007; many others fled Iraq or ceased to practice their religious ceremonies out of fear of persecution.[228] When a much smaller massacre of Kosovar Albanians occurred in the town of Racak in 1999, the U.S., U.K., NATO, Germany, and Turkey declared soon thereafter that a genocide of Albanians on Kosovo was underway.[229]

---

221. Ibrahim al-Marashi, *Dismantling the "Republic of Fear" Was a Just Cause*, 9 Nexus 63, 66 (2004).

222. Melinda L. Kimble, *Humanitarian Situation in Iraq*, 3–1 Dep't of State Dispatch 223, 224 (1992).

223. *See* Deutsch, *Save the Gnostics*.

224. *See* Minority Rights Group, *State of the World's Minorities 2008*, at 141 (2008), http://www.minorityrights.org/?lid=6138.

225. *See Yezidis, in* 28 Encyclopedia Britannica 919 (11th ed., 1911) (Yezidi religion "has points of connexion with old Iranian and Assyrian beliefs and traces of Manicheaism and Nestorianism"); Harry Charles Luke, Mosul and Its Minorities 124–28, 136–37 (2004) (1925) (discussing syncreticism of Yezidi faith and their use of fire temples, statues, towers, and animal sacrifice); Austen Henry Layard, Discoveries at Nineveh (1854), http://mcadams.posc.mu.edu/txt/ah/Layard/Disc Nineveh02.html (noting that Yezidis' traditions spoke of a migration north from parts of southern Iraq inhabited by Chaldeans and Mandaean Sabaeans, that their religion is a "mixture of [Mandaean] Sabaeanism, Gnosticism, Manicheanism, Christianity, and Islam, and that "it is not improbable that the sect may be a remnant of the ancient [Babylonian] Chaldees, who camouflaged their ancient beliefs to stave off "oppression"); Layard, Nineveh and Its Remains, at 95–109 (describing Yezidi religious practice).

226. *See, e.g.*, Michael Howard, *'They won't stop until we are all wiped out.'*, The Guardian (U.K.), Aug. 18, 2007, http://www.guardian.co.uk/world/2007/aug/18/iraq.topstories3.

227. *Compare* David Nissman, *First World Congress of Yezidis Held in Germany*, Radio Free Europe/Radio Liberty (2000), http://www.globalsecurity.org/wmd/library/news/iraq/2000/5-040200.htm (estimate of 600,000 Yezidis in Iraq in 2000), *with* USDOS, *International Religious Freedom Report, Iraq 2008* (estimate of as few as 500,000 in 2008). By way of comparison, if the Yezidi population had grown at the same rate as the 90% of Iraq that is Muslim, i.e. by 20% since 2000, it would have gained 120,000 members. *Compare Iraq, in* World Factbook 2000, http://www.photius.com/wfb2000/countries/iraq/iraq_people.html (2000 population of 22.6 million), *with Iraq, in* World Factbook 2008, http://www.photius.com/wfb2000/countries/iraq/iraq_people.html (population of 27.5 million in 2008, a 20% jump).

228. Minority Rights Group, *State of the World's Minorities 2008*.

229. *See, e.g.*, U.S. Dep't of State, *Daily Press Briefing*, M2 Presswire (Mar. 30, 1999) (describing January 1999 incident in which "44 innocent civilians were murdered at Racak" as one of the " indicators that genocide is unfolding in Kosovo"); U.S. Secretary of State Madeleine Albright, *Address to the Brookings Institution* (Apr. 1999), http://www.pbs.org/newshour/bb/europe/jan-june99/albright_4-6.html (designating Serbian "acts of barbarism such as the massacre at Racak earlier this year" as "ethnic cleansing, war crimes, crimes against humanity and the other indicators of genocide that we see").

E. Conclusion

If the Srebrenica model of genocide is to have any meaning, it should apply to the ethnic and sectarian massacres in Iraq. Just as Bosnian Serb militia, with alleged Serbian military support, massacred military-aged Bosnian Muslim men, so Sunni Arab militia, with support and financing from Saudi Arabia, massacred Shi'a Arab, Kurdish, and religious minority communities. In response, Iraqi Shi'a Arab security forces and allied militia, with alleged Iraqi and Iranian government participation and support, massacred military-aged Sunni Arab men, by the hundreds or thousands. The U.N. should open investigations of these events as genocide. Otherwise, the implication that Iraqi lives are cheap and that the country remains a law-free zone will be reinforced, and the destruction of indigenous and minority communities will continue.

Chapter XVIII

"An Effective Remedy": Prosecutions or Reparations?

[I]ndeed it is a vain thing to imagine a right without a remedy....

—Chief Justice John Holt, in *Ashby v. White and others,* 92 Eng. Rep. 126 (1703)[1]

A. International Military Tribunals

1. Post-World War I Tribunals

The trials of German officers in Leipzig for war crimes against British prisoners and civilians in occupied Belgium articulated the "command responsibility" of officers for the crimes of their subordinates. Post-war trials charged about 900 Germans with war crimes, although few were convicted.[2] Among those who were convicted, Karl Heynen of the German military was found guilty of pistol-whipping, punching and kicking British prisoners of war.[3]

On May 24, 1915, Britain and France joined Russia in condemning the widespread crimes in eastern Anatolia after mid-April 1915. They stated: "In regard to this new crime against humanity and civilisation, the allied governments declare openly to the Sublime Porte that they will hold each member of the Turkish government personally responsible, as well as those who have participated in these massacres."[4] After World War I, Britain, France, and Russia decided upon "individual war crimes prosecutions" against "leading members of the ... Young Turks" alleged "to be responsible for the massacre of hundreds of thousands of Armenians perpetrated under the guise of wartime deportations."[5]

With international customary law on their side, Britain, France, and Russia, the Entente powers, issued a joint declaration in May 1915 by which the Entente announced

1. *Quoted in* Shelton, Remedies in International Human Rights Law, at 63.

2. *See* John C. Watkins, Jr. & John Paul Weber, War Crimes and War Crime Trials: From Leipzig to the ICC and Beyond: Cases, Materials, and Comments, ch. 1 (2004); Michele Norris & Walter Cronkite, *Listening in on the Nuremberg Trials,* National Public Radio—All Things Considered, Feb. 20, 2006.

3. *See The British Cases,* 16 American J. of Int'l Law 633 (1922). *German War Trials: Judgment in the Case of Karl Heynen,* 16 American J. of Int'l Law 674, 676, 679–81 (1922).

4. *Quoted in* Richard G. Hovannisian, Armenia on the Road to Independence (Los Angeles, 1967), *and in* Avedian, The Armenian Genocide, at 33–34.

5. M. Cherif Bassiouni, *World War I: 'The War to End All Wars' and the Birth of a Handicapped International Criminal Justice System,* 30 Denver J. of Int'l L. & Policy 244, 244 (2002).

publicly "that they [would] hold personally responsible all members of the Ottoman government and those of their agents who are implicated in these massacres."[6] The declaration recognized the Ottoman authorities' prosecution of the war as criminal and constituted "a public and joint commitment to prosecute after the war those responsible for the crimes perpetrated."[7]

After losing the war, Turkey commenced its own prosecutions of those responsible. An interim Ottoman government tried and convicted Ministers Enver, Talât, and Cemal of widespread massacres, war crimes, and atrocities, and sentenced them to death in absentia.[8] The court-martial concluded that "all the testimony and documents show that ... bands of brigands were formed for the sole purpose of massacring and destroying the caravans of the (Armenian) deportees. It is fully proven that these massacres were taking place on the immediate orders and full knowledge of Talat, Enver, and Cemal."[9] As the *New York Times* reported (July 13, 1919), the triumvirate were "condemned to death" by the court-martial "for joining in the war and for the Armenian, Greek, and Syrian atrocities and deportations."[10] A Turkish tribunal found that the orders for the Armenian massacres in particular had issued directly from Istanbul.[11] The founder of modern Turkey, Mustafa Kemal "Atatürk," later captured the sentiments in Turkey that led to the trials of those Young Turks responsible for the Ottoman genocide of the Christian population: "These left-overs from the former Young Turk Party, who should have been made to account for the lives of millions of our Christian subjects who were ruthlessly driven en masse, from their homes and massacred, have ... hitherto lived on plunder, robbery and bribery...."[12]

In 1920, the Treaty of Sèvres recognized that the "terrorist regime" of the Young Turks had victimized "subjects of non-Turkish race" with massacres, disappearances, forcible conversions to Islam, and unjust and illegal expropriations of homes and businesses.[13] The treaty denied the legitimacy of Turkish claims to lands inhabited by Christians by excluding Mesopotamia, Syria, and Greece from the boundaries of the post-imperial Turkish state, and purported to guarantee those non-Turks and Christians remaining subjects of Turkey equal rights and religious freedom.[14] Along with the Charter of the League of Nations and the Treaty of Versailles, the delegates to the Paris Peace Conference, most notably the president of the United States of America, the prime minister of Great Britain, and the premier of France, intended the Treaty of Sèvres to frame a more peaceful postwar world.

---

6. Declaration by the Governments of France, Great Britain and Russia (May 29, 1915), *in* U.N. War Crimes Commission, History of the United Nations War Crimes Commission, at 35.

7. Vahakn N. Dadrian, *The Armenian Genocide and the Legal and Political Issues in the Failure to Prevent or to Punish the Crime,* 29 U. of West Los Angeles L. Rev. 57 (1998).

8. John Shamsey, *Comment: 80 Years Too Late: The International Criminal Court and the 20th Century's First Genocide,* 11 J. of Transn. L. & Policy 336, 340–41 (2002).

9. *Id.*, 348 (quoting Vartkes Yeghiayan, The Armenian Genocide and the Trials of the Young Turks xxvi (La Verne, CA: American Armenian Int'l College Press, 1990)).

10. *Turkey Condemns Its War Leaders: Court-Martial Gives Death Sentence to Enver Pasha, Tallat Bey, and Djemal Pasha,* N.Y. Times, July 13, 1919, http://www.cilicia.com/armo10c-nyt19190713.html.

11. Vahakn N. Dadrian, *The Turkish Military Tribunal's Prosecution of the Authors of the Armenian Genocide: Four Major Court-Martial Series,* 7 Holocaust and Genocide Studies 34 (Spr. 1997).

12. Emile Hildebrand, *Kemal Promises More Hangings of Political Antagonists in Turkey,* L.A. Examiner, Aug. 1, 1926, *quoted in* Dennis R. Papazian, *Misplaced Credulity: Contemporary Turkish Attempts to Refute the Armenian Genocide,* 45 Armenian Rev. 177–178 (1992).

13. Treaty of Peace Between the Allied Powers and Turkey (Treaty of Sèvres), Aug. 10, 1920, arts. 142, 144, *reprinted in* 15 American J. of Int'l Law 179, 210 (Supplement: Official Documents, 1921).

14. *Id.*, arts. 27, 140–41, 145, 147–50, *in* 15 American J. of Int'l L. at 182–84, 208–9, 211–12.

The Treaty of Sèvres, which the Ottoman government signed in 1920, required Turkey to hand over to Allied custody those of its nationals who were "responsible for the massacres," and to recognize whatever tribunal the Allied powers designated to try the perpetrators as criminals under international law.[15] Like article 6 of the Crimea protocol of 1945 between the World War II allies, article 230 of the 1920 Treaty of Sèvres, stated:

> The Turkish Government undertakes to hand over to the Allied Powers the persons whose surrender may be required by the latter as being responsible for the massacres committed during the continuance of the state of war on territory which formed part of the Turkish Empire on 1st August 1914. The Allied Powers reserve to themselves the right to designate the Tribunal which shall try the persons so accused and the Turkish Government undertakes to recognize such Tribunal....[16]

Article 230 is regarded by the United Nations as "a precedent for Articles 6 (c) and 5 (c) of the Nuremberg and Tokyo Charters, and offers an example of one of the categories of 'crimes against humanity' as understood by these enactments."[17] In that it called for the prosecution in international tribunals of massacres of a sovereign's own subjects pursuant the laws of that very sovereign, it is a primary precedent for international justice and universal jurisdiction.

The Treaty of Sèvres resembled the post-World War II settlement in other respects as well. First, like the Tehran and Crimea conferences during World War II, the Sèvres treaty contained an agreement to strip the aggressor empire of lands used as launching pads for world conquest, primarily the Baltic states and Poland in the case of World War II, Armenia, Assyria (Kurdistan), and Mesopotamia in the case of World War I.[18] Second, the

---

15. *Id.*, art. 230, *in* 15 AMERICAN J. OF INT'L L. at 235.

16. Treaty of Sèvres, 15 AMERICAN J. OF INT'L L. at 235. Compare Protocol of Proceedings of Crimea Conference of 1945 (United States-United Kingdom-Soviet Union), art. 6 ("The conference agreed that the question of the major war criminals should be the subject of inquiry by the three Foreign Secretaries for report in due course after the close of the conference.").

17. UNITED NATIONS, WAR CRIMES COMMISSION, HISTORY OF THE UNITED NATIONS WAR CRIMES COMMISSION AND THE DEVELOPMENT OF THE LAWS OF WAR 45 (London: Her Majesty's Stationery Office, 1948).

18. *Compare* Treaty of Sèvres, art. 62 ("A Commission sitting at Constantinople and composed of three members appointed by the British, French and Italian Governments respectively shall draft within six months from the coming into force of the present Treaty a scheme of local autonomy for the predominantly Kurdish areas lying east of the Euphrates, south of the southern boundary of Armenia as it may be hereafter determined, and north of the frontier of Turkey with Syria and Mesopotamia," and for "full safeguards for the protection of the Assyro-Chaldeans and other racial or religious minorities within these areas,...."), *id.*, art. 88 ("Turkey, in accordance with the action already taken by the Allied Powers, hereby recognises Armenia as a free and independent State."), id., art. 89 ("Turkey and Armenia ... agree to submit to the arbitration of the President of the United States of America the question of the frontier to be fixed between Turkey and Armenia in the vilayets of Erzerum, Trebizond, Van and Bitlis, and to accept his decision thereupon, as well as any stipulations he may prescribe as to access for Armenia to the sea, and as to the demilitarisation of any portion of Turkish territory adjacent to the said frontier."), and *id.*, art. 94 ("The High Contracting Parties agree that Syria and Mesopotamia shall ... be provisionally recognised as independent States subject to the rendering of administrative advice and assistance by a Mandatory until such time as they are able to stand alone."), *with* Protocol of Proceedings of Crimea Conference of 1945 (United States-United Kingdom-Soviet Union), art. 7 (moving the eastern frontier of Poland further west, and Poland's western frontier must move into pre-war German territory), SIMON SEBAG MONTEFIORE, STALIN: THE COURT OF THE NEW TSAR 476 (New York: Knopf, 2003) (in 1944, British Prime Minister Churchill agreed in Moscow meeting that Soviet Union would have spheres of influence in Bulgaria, Hungary, and Romania, while Britain would predominate in Greece), id. at 482 (in 1945, allies apparently agreed at conference in Crimea that "Russia would take eastern slices of Poland in exchange for ... German territory in the west."), *and* GEOFF SWAIN, BETWEEN STALIN AND HITLER:

Treaty of Sèvres, like the Crimea agreement, involved the creation of spheres of influence whereby the allies would manage the capital and major power centers of the failed world empire in order to prevent another global conflagration.[19] Third, both the Sèvres and Crimea agreements called for reparations to be paid for the losses to the allied nations.[20]

Sèvres was more comprehensive than the Crimea agreement in that it called for individual reparations. The treaty provided for the repeal of the law of 1915 expropriating Armenian homes and businesses (the Law on Abandoned Properties or *Emval-I-Metroukeh*). It also stated that:

> The Turkish Government solemnly undertakes to facilitate to the greatest possible extent the return to their homes and re-establishment in their businesses of the Turkish subjects of non-Turkish race who have been forcibly driven from their homes by fear of massacre or any other form of pressure since January 1, 1914. It recognizes that any immovable or movable property of the said Turkish subjects or of the communities to which they belong, which can be recovered, must be restored to them as soon as possible, in whatever hands it may be found....[21]

Before long, however, the British had abandoned their prosecutions of the Young Turks and surrendered many suspects held in their custody to the new government of Atatürk, in exchange for the repatriation of British prisoners of war.[22] Atatürk had promised to prosecute these leaders in Turkish courts.[23] Raphael Lemkin describes his reaction in his draft autobiography:

Class War and Race War on the Dvina, 1940–46, at 134–35 (London: Routledge, 2004) (at Tehran conference, President Roosevelt agreed with Stalin that Baltic states would remain in Soviet sphere of influence after the war).

19. *Compare* Treaty of Sèvres, art. 197 ("The Inter-Allied Commissions of Control and Organisation may establish their organisations at Constantinople, and will be entitled, as often as they think desirable, to proceed to any point whatever in Turkish territory, or to send sub-commissions, or to authorise one or more of their members to go, to any such point"), *id.*, art. 198 ("The Turkish Government must furnish to the Inter-Allied Commissions of Control and Organisation all such information and documents as the latter may deem necessary for the accomplishment of their mission, and must supply at its own expense all labour and material which the said Commissions may require in order to ensure the complete execution of the military, naval or air clauses."), *id.*, art. 200(I) ("As the Military Inter-Allied Commission of Control it will be its special duty: ... (b) To receive from the Turkish Government the notifications relating to the location of the stocks and depots of munitions, the armament of the fortified works, fortresses and forts, the situation of the works or factories for the production of arms, munitions and war material and their operations."), and *id.*, art. 231 ("Turkey recognises that by joining in the war of aggression which Germany and Austria-Hungary waged against the Allied Powers she has caused to the latter losses and sacrifices of all kinds for which she ought to make complete reparation."), *with* Protocol of Proceedings of Crimea Conference of 1945, art. 3 ("'The United Kingdom, the United States of America and the Union of Soviet Socialist Republics shall possess supreme authority with respect to Germany. In the exercise of such authority they will take such steps, including the complete dismemberment of Germany as they deem requisite for future peace and security.'"), and *id.*, art. 4 (providing that zones in Germany should be occupied by American, British, and French forces).

20. *Compare* Treaty of Sèvres, art. 231 ("Turkey recognises that by joining in the war of aggression which Germany and Austria-Hungary waged against the Allied Powers she has caused to the latter losses and sacrifices of all kinds for which she ought to make complete reparation."), *with* Protocol of Proceedings of Crimea Conference of 1945, art. 5 ("'Germany must pay in kind for the losses caused by her to the Allied nations in the course of the war. Reparations are to be received in the first instance by those countries which have borne the main burden of the war, have suffered the heaviest losses and have organized victory over the enemy.").

21. *See* Treaty of Sèvres, art. 144, *in* 15 American J. of Int'l Law at 210.

22. Shamsey, *80 Years Too Late*, at 271–72.

23. Dadrian, *The Turkish Military Tribunal's Prosecution*, at 51–2.

> After the end of the war, some 150 Turkish war criminals were arrested and interned by the British Government on the Island of Malta. The Armenians sent a delegation to the peace conference in Versailles. They were demanding justice. Then one day, the delegation read in the newspapers that all Turkish war criminals were released. I was shocked. A nation was killed and the guilty persons were set free.[24]

In 1923, the Kemalist government declared a general amnesty for all those convicted of war crimes by courts-martial.[25]

As Atatürk threatened Mesopotamian oil reserves, Britain, France, and the U.S. decided to conclude the Treaty of Lausanne in 1923, with its "moral horror[s]" of the Orthodox Christian expulsion from Turkey, no protections for Armenians, Assyrians, or Kurds, and a secret annex providing amnesty to Turkish war criminals.[26] The former U.S. Ambassador to Germany called the treaty a "disgrace."[27] Ambassador Morgenthau called it a "purposeless and humiliating surrender to a red handed, faithless military despotism."[28] The Democratic Party defeated the treaty in the U.S. Senate on the ground that it did not protect the Christian minorities of Turkey, in contrast to the Treaty of Sèvres.[29]

Despite the success of the Kemalist revolution and the concessions wrought from the oil-thirsty Entente at Lausanne, the Ottoman government had formally acknowledged the criminal character of the massacres of Christian civilians that took place during the war. This disposes of the two principal defenses of the conduct of the Turks from the charge of genocide: that the charge that the Ottomans attempted to wipe out the Christians of the empire is merely Western propaganda, and that any alleged attempt to exterminate minority racial and religious groups did not constitute a criminal act under international law as it stood during World War I.

2. Post-World War II Tribunals

As in the aftermath of World War I, the British vacillated on the subject of Nazi war crimes trials. British leaders initially opposed holding trials, the lord chancellor worrying that trials "might be drawn out almost indefinitely, in which all sorts of things might be raised and discussed—whether legal or historical—leading to controversy and debate in the world at large...."[30] British officials were particularly anxious to avoid testimony exploring how British banks had facilitated the economic and fiscal dimensions of the Nazis'

---

24. Raphael Lemkin, Totally Unofficial Man (1958), *quoted in* Papazian, *The Armenian Case*.

25. Dadrian, The History of the Armenian Genocide, at 332–35, 340–41.

26. *See* Dadrian, The History of the Armenian Genocide, 333, 341; Köchler, Global Justice or Global Revenge?, at 58; Peterson, "Starving Armenians," at 134–35; Bassiouni, *From Versailles to Rwanda*, at 17 (Lausanne treaty had "unpublicized annex granting Turkish officials amnesty").

27. *See Score Turk Treaty As Disgrace to US; Ex-Ambassador Gerard and His Guests Call Lausanne Pact Indefensible*, N.Y. Times, Nov. 25, 1923, at E1.

28. *Calls Lausanne Treaty Insult to Christianity*, Chicago Daily Tribune, May 17, 1926, at 14.

29. *See A Minority Refuses*, Time Mag., Jan. 31, 1927, http://www.time.com/time/magazine/article/0,9171,729871,00.html.

30. Alan A. Ryan, *Nuremberg's Contributions to International Law*, 30 Boston College Int'l & Comp. L. Rev. 55, 59 (2007) (quoting Memorandum to Judge Rosenman From Lord Simon (Lord Chancellor) (April 6, 1945), *in* The American Road to Nuremberg: The Documentary Record 1944–1945, at 151–52 (Bradley F. Smith ed., Stanford, CA: Hoover Institution Press, 1982) [hereinafter Road to Nuremberg].

rise to power and embarkation on a path of world conquest.[31] British imperial rule in the Americas, India, Malaya, Kenya, Nigeria, Sudan, Iraq, Palestine, etc. also did not always emerge favorably when viewed through the lens of the laws and customs of war.

Some American officials were more enthusiastic about punishing Nazis. In 1944, Secretary of the Treasury Henry Morgenthau, Jr. argued that "the arch-criminals of this war whose obvious guilt has generally been recognized" must "be put to death forthwith by firing squads."[32] U.S. Supreme Court Justice Robert Jackson reported that Treasury Department officials wanted to hand over 500,000 Germans to the Soviet Union as reparations, "regardless of personal guilt."[33] U.S. Secretary of War Henry Stimson responded that "rudimentary" due process rights should be granted the suspects, including "dignified" punishments and trial on specific charges supported by witness testimonies before "an international tribunal."[34] Stimson supported trials not only to "punish the individual criminals, but also to expose and condemn the criminal purpose behind each individual outrage."[35] Stimson favored trials of Nazi officials for a criminal scheme that included "mass murders, imprisonments, expulsions and deportations of populations; the starvation, torture and inhuman treatment of civilians; the wholesale looting of public and private property on a scale unparalleled in history; and, after initiation of 'total' war, its prosecution with utter ruthless disregard for the laws and customs of war."[36]

After President Roosevelt's death on April 12, 1945, President Truman decided to hold trials and to name Justice Jackson as "Chief of Counsel for the Prosecution of Axis Criminality."[37] Jackson soon after concluded that the Nazi "atrocities and persecutions on racial and religious grounds" had been criminal violations of the Hague Regulations of 1907.[38] Jackson wrote that international treaties and trials designed specifically to punish Axis crimes would "themselves become sources of a newer and strengthened International Law."[39]

Endorsed by 17 nations formerly occupied by the Germans,[40] the Nuremberg trials took place on a vast scale, with 5,000 convicted, about 800 sentenced to death, and 486 actually executed.[41] The Germans continued to deny the gravity of their crimes, protest-

31. *See id.* at 71.

32. *Id.* (quoting Henry Morgenthau Jr., Punishment of Certain War Crimes and Treatment of Special Groups (Sept. 5, 1944), *in* ROAD TO NUREMBERG, at 28).

33. Henry T. King, Jr., *"The Role of Justice in Building Peace": Robert H. Jackson and the Triumph of Justice at Nuremberg*, 35 CASE W. RES. J. INT'L L. 263, 264 (2003).

34. Ryan, *Nuremberg's Contributions to International Law*, at 60 (quoting Communication from Secretary of War (Stimson) to the President (Sept. 9, 1944), *in* ROAD TO NUREMBERG, at 30–31).

35. *Id.* at 61 (quoting Draft Memorandum for the President from the Secretaries of State, War and Navy, Subject: Trial and Punishment of European War Criminals (Nov. 11, 1944), *in* ROAD TO NUREMBERG, at 44).

36. *Id.* at 62 (quoting Memorandum for the President, Subject: Trial and Punishment of Nazi War Criminal (Jan. 22, 1945), *in* ROAD TO NUREMBERG, at 118).

37. *Id.* at 66.

38. *Id.* at 68.

39. *Id.* at 69 (quoting Robert H. Jackson, *Atrocities and War Crimes: Report from Robert H. Jackson to the President*, 12 DEP'T OF STATE BULL. 1071, 1076 (1945)).

40. *See* IMT, *Opening Arguments* (Nov. 21, 1945), 2 I.M.T. 99 (1947); Agreement for the Prosecution and Punishment of the Major War Criminals of the European Axis, Aug. 8, 1945, 59 Stat. 1544, 82 U.N.T.S. 280, 280 n.1.

41. TONY JUDT, POSTWAR: A HISTORY OF EUROPE SINCE 1945, at 53 (New York: Penguin Press, 2005).

ing in "vociferous" fashion to the last execution in 1951.[42] The Allies tried between 10,000 and 100,000 Nazis or Nazi collaborators by 1950, not counting many thousands subjected to Soviet extrajudicial procedures for the execution or torture of suspected Nazi agents.[43] Up to 70,000 Nazis, Italian fascists, and fascist collaborators were summarily executed after the war.[44]

A plan to try Emperor Hirohito for massive crimes against populations occupied by the Japanese, and against Western POWs, was considered and rejected by General Douglas MacArthur, who stated:

> If he is to be tried ... his indictment will unquestionably cause a tremendous convulsion among the Japanese people, the repercussions of which cannot be over-estimated.... It is not inconceivable that all government agencies will break down, the civilized practices will largely cease, and a condition of underground chaos and disorder amounting to guerilla warfare [will] result.... It is quite possible that a minimum of a million troops would be required which would have to be maintained for an indefinite number of years.[45]

The International Military Tribunal for the Far East sentenced seven Japanese leaders to be executed for aggression, war crimes, and crimes against humanity, including wartime leader Hideki Tojo.[46] The tribunal convicted 18 other Japanese military and civilian officials, while deciding not to indict more than 200 other suspected war criminals.[47] Another military tribunal convicted the commanding general of the Imperial Japanese Army in the Philippines of a "plan ... to massacre and exterminate a large part of the civilian population of [the Philippines]," as a result of which 25,000 civilians died.[48] Ultimately more Japanese than Germans were tried for various crimes, around 5,500 in all.[49] More than 900 defendants were executed and more than 2,500 sentenced to life in prison.[50] Few or none of them actually served a life sentence after General MacArthur instituted parole in the 1950s, a move to which the Soviet Union vigorously objected as an unlawful amnesty for war criminals in violation of treaties.[51]

---

42. *See id.*

43. *Compare* Jonathan A. Bush, *Nuremberg: The Modern Law of War and Its Limitations*, 93 COLUM. L. REV. 2022, 2037 (1993) (reviewing TELFORD TAYLOR, THE ANATOMY OF THE NUREMBERG TRIAL: A PERSONAL MEMOIR (1992)) (citing figure of 10,000), *with* MARK A. DRUMBL, ATROCITY, PUNISHMENT, AND INTERNATIONAL LAW 110, 254–57 (Cambridge: Cambridge UP, 2007) (citing estimates of 10,000 Soviet trials, 65,000 French collaborator trials, and further British, Dutch, German, U.S., and other trials, along with amnesty laws, especially in France).

44. *See* DRUMBL, ATROCITY, at 110.

45. *Quoted in* KYOKO INOUE, MACARTHUR'S JAPANESE CONSTITUTION 163–64 (Chicago: Univ. of Chicago Press, 1991).

46. *See Text of the Tribunal's Verdict on Tojo*, THE NEW YORK TIMES, Nov. 13, 1948; U.S. Public Broadcasting System, *The Tokyo War Crimes Trials: 1946–1948* (2008), http://www.pbs.org/wgbh/amex/macarthur/peopleevents/pandeAMEX101.html.

47. *See International Military Tribunal: Far East, in* ENCYCLOPEDIA OF WORLD WAR II, at 739–40.

48. Bix, Hirohito, at 128 (quoting In the Matter of Yamashita, 327 U.S. 1 (1946)).

49. *See* NAZI WAR CRIMES & JAPANESE IMPERIAL GOVERNMENT RECORDS INTERAGENCY WORKING GROUP, FINAL REPORT TO THE UNITED STATES CONGRESS 7 (2007), http://www.loc.gov/rr/frd/Military_Law/pdf/NaziWarCrimes_Japanese-Records.pdf.

50. *See id.*; U.S. Public Broadcasting System, *The Tokyo War Crimes Trials: 1946–1948.*

51. *See* Walter H. Waggoner, *Russians Protest Japanese Paroles; Note Here Assails MacArthur on His New System to Free Some War Criminals MacArthur's Powers Affirmed*, N.Y TIMES, May 13, 1950; *Deaths: Teichi Suzuki*, WASH. POST, July 17, 1989; *War Crimes: The Nurnberg and Tokyo Trials, in* ENCYCLOPEDIA BRITANNICA ONLINE EDITION (2008), http://www.britannica.com/EBchecked/topic/635621/war-crime.

B. U.N.-Sponsored International Criminal *Tribunals*

The substantive findings of these tribunals were the focus of much of the discussion of the crime of genocide in Chapters II and III. Considering that those chapters dealt with the definition of genocide and other international crimes, however, the scope of criminal liability and evidentiary principles recognized by those tribunals warrant brief discussion here.

Both tribunals exercise jurisdiction over genocide, crimes against humanity, and war crimes. A suspect's acts should be closely related to the conflict in order to be triable as a violation of the laws and customs of war.[52] A superior military officer or rebel leader may be culpable for his or her subordinates' actions.[53] Failure to take objectively reasonable efforts to prevent the commission of foreseeable international crimes by subordinates may result in criminal liability.[54] Contributing to or facilitating an international crime may make persons who did not directly commit it or originate the criminal policy also responsible for it.[55] Inciting or instigating a crime results in criminal liability if it causes a crime to be committed.[56] Intent may be inferred from the passive presence and acquiescence of a responsible official at the site of a crime.[57] A joint criminal enterprise may exist due to a tacit agreement or understanding to commit or facilitate criminal acts.[58] An investigation or acquittal by a biased national court is no defense before an international criminal tribunal of the U.N.[59]

C. The ICC

The genocides in northern Iraq and southern Sudan had climaxed in the late 1980s and early 1990s, respectively, prior to the adoption of the Rome Statute of the ICC in 1998. The Rome Statute entered into force in mid-2002.[60] By it, the ICC acquired the jurisdiction to punish and prevent *some* of the most serious international crimes committed after July 1, 2002, including genocide, crimes against humanity, war crimes and the crime of aggression.[61] The ICC's principle of complementary means that member na-

---

52. *See, e.g.*, Prosecutor v. Akayesu, Trial Judgment, ¶¶ 640–42.

53. *See* Prosecutor v. Aleksovski, Case No. IT-95-14/1-T (Trial Judgment) (June 25, 1999), ¶¶ 76; Liesbeth Zegveld, *Accountability of Non-State Actors in International Law, in* Relevance of International Humanitarian Law to Non-State Actors 153, 155 (College of Europe Collegium, 2003).

54. Guénael Mettraux, International Crimes and the ad hoc Tribunals, at 297, 306 (Oxford: Oxford UP, 2005).

55. Prosecutor v. Kayishema and Ruzindana, Case No. ICTR-95-1-A (Appeal Judgment) (June 1, 2001), ¶ 185; Prosecutor v. Furundzija, Case No. IT-95-17/1-A (Trial Judgment) (Nov. 10, 2000), ¶¶ 273–75.

56. Prosecutor v. Bagilishema, Case No. ICTR-95-1A-T (Trial Judgment) (June 7, 2001), ¶ 30.

57. *See* Maria Allison & Leslie Wilson, *News from the International Criminal Tribunals*, 10 No. 3 Human Rights Brief 36 (2005).

58. *Prosecutor v. Kvocka*, Case No. IT-98-30/1-T (Trial Judgment), November 2, 2001, at ¶¶ 326–27, 407–08; Mettraux, International Crimes and the ad hoc Tribunals, at 288–89.

59. ICTY Statute, art. 10(2); ICTR Statute, art. 9(2).

60. Rome Statute of the ICC, U.N. Doc. A/CONF. 183/9, 87 U.N.T.S. 90, F. 183/9.

61. *Id.*, arts. 5(1), 11(1).

tions may divest the ICC of jurisdiction by genuinely prosecuting crimes otherwise within the ICC's subject matter jurisdiction.[62]

The ICC took its first action in 2004, and has made little progress in preventing or punishing genocide, thereby leaving the Genocide Convention relatively toothless. The ICC's substantive findings in Pre-Trial Chamber I that genocide had not occurred in the Darfur region of Sudan from 2003 to 2009 were discussed at some length in Chapter XV. The court's lack of effectiveness in prosecuting international crimes, however, merits further discussion in order to understand whether U.N.-backed criminal tribunals hold out a reasonable prospect of genocide prevention.

In March 2009, six years into the Darfur war, and four years after the Security Council referral of the Sudan case to the ICC, the court issued an arrest warrant against President al-Bashir. Five counts covered crimes against humanity, leaving two counts focused on war crimes.[63] Given the speed with which Talât Paşa, Hermann Göring, and Jean-Paul Akayesu were convicted of war crimes, and given all the advances in using books, newspapers, magazines, radio, television, and the Internet to disseminate evidence of such crimes, it is baffling why the case should have taken so long to launch. Refugees languishing in camps for years could hardly have been satisfied with the delay and uncertainty that characterized the ICC's action. Civilians fearing their governments' unlimited power over them in the absence of international justice were unlikely to be reassured by a four- to six-year delay in sanctioning mass murder and torture.

The decision, which is under appeal, falls into the same pattern as other rulings by tribunals inexperienced with and reluctant to implement the Genocide Convention, such as the ICJ or the Commission of Inquiry. Specifically, it selectively quoted from the history of the Genocide Convention to erect a standard for genocide that has never been and will never be met by any set of facts, refuses to draw the types of inferences from patterns of mass killings and systematic rapes that have become a staple of Yugoslav and Rwanda tribunal judgments, and arguably mischaracterized the relevant evidence to cabin it into categories with which the ICC is more comfortable and that may be more judicially manageable, such as murder, torture, rape, and extermination.[64]

First, in describing the elements of the crime of genocide, ICC Pre-Trial Chamber I was extremely selective in the drafting materials and historical precedents it analyzed. Like many persons unfamiliar with the complex drafting history of the Genocide Convention, the Pre-Trial Chamber relied on Lemkin's *Axis Rule in Occupied Europe* solely for the proposition that genocide is the murder of a *people* as opposed to a series of *individuals*.[65] This is lazy thinking and opinion drafting. A careful reading of *Axis Rule in Occupied Europe* reveals that Lemkin clearly stated that "genocide does *not* necessarily mean the immediate destruction of a nation," but "is intended rather to signify a coordinated plan of different actions aiming at the destruction of essential foundations of the life of

62. *Id.*, arts. 17–19.

63. *See Arrest Warrant Draws Sudan Scorn*, BBC News, Mar. 5, 2009, http://news.bbc.co.uk/2/hi/africa/7924982.stm. *See also* Amnesty International, *Sudan: Historic ICC Referral Welcome But Dismay at US Efforts to Undermine Court* (Apr. 1, 2005), http://www.amnesty.org.uk/news_details.asp?NewsID=16031.

64. *See* Prosecutor v. Omar Hassan Ahmad Al Bashir, Case No. ICC-02/05-01/09. 1/95, ICC Pre-Trial Chamber I, Decision on the Prosecution's Application for a Warrant of Arrest against Omar Hassan Ahmad Al Bashir (Mar. 4, 2009), at ¶¶ 90–109, http://www.icc-cpi.int/iccdocs/doc/doc639096.pdf.

65. *See id.* ¶ 114 & n.134.

national groups," such as "the destruction of the personal security, liberty, health, dignity, and even the lives of the individuals belonging to such groups...."[66] The Pre-Trial Chamber found precisely such a pattern of actions to destroy life, dignity, and health in upholding multiple charges of war crimes and crimes against humanity.

Second, the Pre-Trial Chamber selectively quoted from the drafting history of the Genocide Convention. Specifically, it declared that "a proposal made during the drafting of the 1948 Genocide Convention to include in the definition 'measures intended to oblige members of a group to abandon their homes in order to escape the threat of subsequent ill-treatment' was not accepted."[67] This proposal was of course overbroad in that it might include threatening homeowners in a particular area that they face eviction and criminal prosecution if they do not abandon their homes to make way for a new highway or railroad. But its rejection did not imply that driving a people into an arid desert, where they may frequently die of starvation, thirst, or exposure to the elements, cannot be evidence of genocide. Even in rejecting the proposed "abandon their homes" clause of the Genocide Convention, the Soviet representative noted that genocide may indeed force members of a group to flee for self-protection, as in World War II.[68]

To address the problem of genocide by deprivation of access to the food, water, shelter, and protection provided in a group's ancestral homeland or original location, Saudi Arabia proposed criminalizing genocide by the "intentional deprivation of elementary necessities for the preservation of health or existence."[69] The U.N. Secretariat agreed, reworking the language of the proposed provision to outlaw sending a certain group "to a wretched existence maintained ... by public charity," which fits very closely the lived experience of Darfur refugees in eastern Chad.[70] The U.S., China, and the Soviet Union endorsed these proposals, rephrasing them as the infliction or subjection of a group to conditions of life that will cause deaths within or the total or partial destruction of the group.[71] France believed the provision to be applicable to Jews confined in ghettos, but not yet concentration camps, when starvation and illness made extinction inevitable without outside intervention.[72] Given this drafting record, the Yugoslav and Rwandan tribunals have held that the Genocide Convention reaches "systematic expulsion from homes," and Professor Lemkin would definitely have agreed.[73] He wrote that genocide may be achieved by physically exterminating a group, culturally by devastating a group's heritage,[74] politically by destroying its "institutions of self-government," *or* economically by stealing its wealth and depriving its members of gainful employment.[75] Thus, Lemkin described many groups who survived and were used for various purposes by their oppressors as being subjected to genocide, including the Native American slaves and inmates of

66. LEMKIN, AXIS RULE IN OCCUPIED EUROPE, at 79 (emphasis added).

67. Prosecutor v. Al Bashir, at ¶ 144 (citing Bosnia v. Serbia 2007, at ¶ 190, and U.N. Doc. A/C6/234).

68. *See* John Quigley, *State Responsibility for Ethnic Cleansing*, 32 U.C. DAVIS L. REV. 341, 351 (1999).

69. U.N. Doc. A/C.6/86, *quoted in* SCHABAS, "THE CRIME OF CRIMES," at 165.

70. U.N. Doc. E/447, *quoted in* SCHABAS, "THE CRIME OF CRIMES," at 165.

71. *See* U.N. Doc. A/C.25/7 and A/C.25/9, *quoted in* SCHABAS, "THE CRIME OF CRIMES," at 165–66.

72. *See* U.N. Doc. A/C.25/SR.4, at 14–16, *quoted in* SCHABAS, "THE CRIME OF CRIMES," at 166.

73. *See, e.g.*, Prosecutor v. Akayesu, Trial Chamber, Judgement, at ¶¶ 507–08; Prosecutor v. Blagovjevic and Jokic, Trial Chamber, Judgement, at ¶¶ 647–54, Prosecutor v. Karadzi and Mladić, Review of the Indictments pursuant to Rule 61 of the Rules of Procedure and Evidence, at ¶ 93; Prosecutor v. Musema, Trial Chamber, Judgement and Sentence, at ¶ 157.

74. *See* Elder, *What You See Before Your Eyes*, at 469–76.

75. LEMKIN, AXIS RULE IN OCCUPIED EUROPE, at xi.

Catholic missions of the Americas, the Irish of the British Empire, the Bulgarians of the Ottoman Empire, the Slavs and French of the Third Reich, and various minorities of the Soviet Union.[76]

Third, after selectively quoting from the jurisprudence of the ICJ and the Yugoslav and Rwanda tribunals,[77] the Pre-Trial Chamber found itself unable to draw inferences of genocidal intent from mass killings and systematic rapes. Such inferences are vital to making the Genocide Convention an effective preventive and punitive treaty, rather than a hollow shell applicable only to the obtuse defendant who fails to rationalize and explain his genocidal intent.

Confessions without torture or abusive interrogation are rare, and rationalizations abound. "Only the accused himself has first-hand knowledge of his own mental state, and he is unlikely to testify to his own genocidal intent."[78] Therefore, the Yugoslav and Rwanda tribunals infer genocidal intent from repeated or systematic attacks targeting a group or its members, such as atrocities on a large scale, or widespread or massively discriminatory campaigns.[79] The Pre-Trial Chamber selectively quoted from some of these cases in an attempt to magnify and distort the requirement of genocidal intent beyond all utility or comprehensibility, while failing to note that the very same tribunals have prevented the Genocide Convention from becoming a nullity by making clear that failing to confess to genocide is not a sufficient defense standing alone.

Finally, the Pre-Trial Chamber arguably warped the law, and the evidence provided by the prosecutor, in an attempt to avoid issuing an arrest warrant for genocide. In paragraphs 124, 167, and 181, it characterized the threat to the existence of the Fur, Masalit, and Zaghawa groups as being "latent or hypothetical" because the government may simply have been "implementing political arrangements aimed at limiting their power in their homeland." Thus, the regime's "hindrance of humanitarian assistance, as well as cutting off supplies of food and other essential goods," may not prove an intent to destroy one of these groups in whole or in part. In doing so, the Pre-Trial Chamber completely ignored a great deal of evidence that these tactics not only may but already have claimed thousands of lives. It selectively quoted one U.N. document characterizing the U.N. aid operation for Darfur as the largest in the world, while failing to quote others declaring that 70,000 to 450,000 members of the Fur, Masalit, and Zaghawa were dead.[80] The Pre-Trial Chamber was completely silent on perhaps the most important allegation of the prosecutor's application for an arrest warrant, i.e. that 35,000 people or more than four times the

76. *See* LEMKIN, AXIS RULE IN OCCUPIED EUROPE, at ch. 10; Schaller & Zimmerer, *Raphael Lemkin: The "Founder of the United Nation's Genocide Convention" as a Historian of Mass Violence,* at 447–52 (2005); McDonnell & Moses, *Raphael Lemkin as Historian of Genocide in the Americas,* at 501–29; Stone, *Raphael Lemkin on the Holocaust,* at 540–45; Weiss-Wendt, *Raphael Lemkin on "Soviet Genocide,"* at 551–59; American Jewish Archives, *The Raphael Lemkin Papers.*

77. *See* Prosecutor v. Al Bashir, at ¶¶ 39 & n. 62, 135 & nn. 148–150, 139 n. 154 (citing Prosecutor v Jelisic, Appeals Chamber, Judgment, at ¶¶ 45–46, and Prosecutor v Akayesu, Trial Chamber, Judgment, at ¶¶ 510–516).

78. Prosecutor v. Gacumbitsi, Appeals Chamber, Judgement, at ¶ 40.

79. *Id.* at ¶¶ 38, 40; *see also* Prosecutor v. Jelisić, Appeals Chamber, Judgement, at ¶ 47 (genocidal intent may be inferred from "the perpetration of other culpable acts systematically directed against the same group, the scale of atrocities committed, the systematic targeting of victims on account of their membership of a particular group, or the repetition of destructive and discriminatory acts"); *id.* at ¶ 37; Prosecutor v. Milošević, Trial Chamber, Decision on Motion for Judgement of Acquittal, at ¶ 120; Prosecutor v. Akayesu, Trial Chamber, Judgement, at ¶¶ 698–734.

80. *See* Prosecutor v. Al Bashir, at ¶ 186 & n. 212 (citing John Holmes, ICC-02/05-161-Conf-AnxF, ¶ 135).

toll at Srebrenica were directly killed.[81] One U.N. official cited by the Pre-Trial Chamber to show how large the aid effort is actually confirmed 300,000 Darfurian deaths.[82]

The Pre-Trial Chamber cited evidence that children were killed on only a few occasions, and never provided any estimates, despite citing U.N. and NGO reports that have such figures. Moreover, while the Pre-Trial Chamber held that there are reasonable grounds to believe that acts of torture, deportation, and rape took place in Darfur in the context of a widespread and systematic attack on the Fur, Masalit and Zaghawa peoples, it declined to find genocidal intent with respect to these peoples.[83] The charges as described by the ICC spokesperson leave little doubt as to President al-Bashir's intent, in that they involve "being criminally responsible ... for intentionally directing attacks against an important part of the civilian population of Darfur, Sudan, murdering, exterminating, raping, torturing and forcibly transferring large numbers of civilians, and pillaging their property."[84] As outlined in Chapter III and in this chapter, these are precisely the sorts of crimes that led to genocide charges against Nazi Germans, Bosnian Serbs, and Rwandan Hutus, creating an appearance of indifference by the ICC towards similar crimes by self-styled Arabs in Sudan against the Fur, Masalit, and Zaghawa peoples. There were refugees and deportees in all of these prior conflicts that led to genocide charges, which refutes the ICC's conclusion that mass murder along with mass deportation is not genocide.[85]

The ICC may have been intimidated against issuing the kind of blunt condemnation of genocide that the World War II Allies issued against the Nazis, or that the Security Council issued against Rwanda, or that the General Assembly and international criminal tribunals issued against both Rwanda and Yugoslavia. After the ICC issued initial arrest warrants against *Janjaweed* leaders in 2007, the al-Bashir regime responded by integrating *Janjaweed* into the army, providing them with heavy weapons, ordering the army to attack indigenous African villages, resettling Arab tribes in formerly African villages, and waging war against neighboring Chad.[86] Retaliation against eyewitnesses, journalists, and human rights activists in Darfur became common, and threatened to increase if al-Bashir was indicted for genocide.[87]

---

81. *See* Prosecutor v. Al Bashir, Prosecutor's Application for Warrant of Arrest under Article 58, Summary of the Case, at 5 (July 14, 2008), http://www.icc-cpi.int.

82. *See* Associated Press, *Prosecutor Says Wanted Sudanese Minister Is Involved in Attacks on Darfur Camps,* INT'L HERALD TRIB., Apr. 25, 2008, http://www.iht.com (citing John Holmes, cited by Pre-Trial Chamber in n.212).

83. *See* Prosecutor v. Al Bashir, at ¶¶ 100–108.

84. Matt Brown, *ICC Issues Arrest Warrant for Bashir,* THE NATIONAL (CANADA), Mar. 5, 2009, http://www.thenational.ae/apps/pbcs.dll/article?AID=/20090305/FOREIGN/501677707/1001.

85. *Compare* Prosecutor v. Al Bashir, at ¶ 192 (finding "reasonable grounds to believe" that government of Sudan "subjected thousands of civilians belonging primarily to the Fur, Masalit and Zaghawa groups to acts of murder, as well as to acts of Extermination," and "subjected hundreds of thousands of civilians belonging primarily to the said groups to acts of forcible transfer"), *with id.* at ¶ 202 (concluding that there is no "direct evidence of the [government's] genocidal intent").

86. *See* International Crisis Group, *Darfur's New Security Reality,* Africa Report No. 134, 7–10, 17–18 (Nov. 2007), http://www.crisisgroup.org/home/index.cfm?id=5180&CFID=21423281&CFTOKEN=92724554.

87. *See* Amnesty International, *Statement on the Group of Experts Report on the Situation of Human Rights in Darfur* (Dec. 11, 2007), http://www.amnesty.org/en/library/asset/IOR41/028/2007/en/586328d4-afbf-11dc-b001-5f9481a8353e/ior410282007eng.html (noting that the "Group of Experts on the situation of human rights in Darfur ... assessed that contrary to recommendations, human rights defenders are still subject to arbitrary arrest, physical abuse and harassment.... Amnesty International receives reports of those who complain of human rights violations being arrested rather than the perpetrators, and of rape victims in Darfur who are sent away by the police without a hearing."); Amnesty International, *Written Statement on the Review of the Mandate of the Special Rapporteur on*

In July 2009, the ICC prosecutor announced that he had filed an appeal of the refusal by the Pre-Trial Chamber to issue an arrest warrant for genocide against President al-Bashir.[88] His appeal seemed to have promise in light of the opinion of a partially-dissenting judge on the Pre-Trial Chamber, who criticized the majority opinion for failing to account for evidence that the Sudanese government targeted all of the Fur, Masalit, and Zaghawa for killing, rapes, and destruction of homes and villages, rather than targeting only those tied to the insurgency or actively waging war. On Feb. 3, 2010, the ICC Appeals Chamber ordered the Pre-Trial Chamber to reconsider whether there are reasonable grounds to believe that genocide occurred in Darfur.[89]

The partial dissent initiated the first serious judicial inquiry into genocidal intent in Darfur by refusing to ignore the ample evidence of intent by President al-Bashir and his Darfur chief Ahmad Haroun [or Harun], Deputy Minister for Internal Affairs from April 2003 to 2005:

> In April 2003, Omar Al Bashir ... is said to have stated in front of Northern Darfur State officials and members of the Sudanese Armed Forces officials that he "did not want any villages or prisoners, only scorched earth."....
>
> At a public meeting in Al Geneina in July 2003, where Ahmad Harun is said to have called on the people to go to their sons and ask them to lay down their firearms, he is also said to have stated that "the President had handed over to him the Darfur security file and given him all the power and authority to kill or forgive in Darfur for the sake of peace and security", and that "for the sake of Darfur, they were ready to kill 3/4 of the people in Darfur so that a 1/4 could live"; and....
>
> At a public meeting in Mukjar on 7 August 2003, Ahmad Harun is said to have stated that there was a rebellion against the State in Darfur, and that, since the children of the Fur had become rebels, all the Fur and what they had, had become booty for the Mujahidin....
>
> [Also in] August 2003, Ahmad Harun is said to have stated in Camp2 that "The Fur are making headache to us.... God willing, we will kill them and make them homeless ... and Darfur land will be suitable for people better than them"; ... and (iii) at an unknown time and location, Ahmad Harun is said to have told local leaders that "You the emirs ... uh.... Clean Darfur; wipe out the blacks and this

---

the Situation of Human Rights Situation in the Sudan (Dec. 10–11, 2007), http://www.amnesty.org/en/library/asset/IOR41/028/2007/en/586328d4-afbf-11dc-b001-5f9481a8353e/ior410282007eng.html ("At least 10 journalists have been detained since June for writing articles critical of government policies or because they were investigating sensitive subjects."); Lisa Bryant, *Reports Finds Human Rights Defenders Face Increasing Suppression,* Voice of America (June 19, 2008), http://www.voanews.com/english/archive/2008-06/2008-06-19-voa30.cfm?CFID=312151428&CFTOKEN=86513581&jsessionid=88301fc71a37641ccda365721a601f74e696 ("[In] Central African Republic and Chad, where those investigating human rights abuses during conflict are increasingly under threat."); Eric Reeves, "Chaos by Design": Khartoum's Patterns of Violence in Darfur, 2008 (Sept. 13, 2008), http://www.sudanreeves.org/Article224.html ("In camps and towns, civilians—especially those thought to be too visible in their support for the rebels or the International Criminal Court in its investigation of atrocity crimes in Darfur—are subject to continuing arrest, torture, arbitrary detention, and extrajudicial execution. Darfuris who are heard or seen to be giving revealing accounts of conditions in Darfur are also beaten, raped, arrested, or even killed.").

88. Reuters, *Sudan: Prosecutor Appeals for Genocide Charge against President,* N.Y. Times, July 7, 2009, http://www.nytimes.com/2009/07/08/world/africa/08briefs-Sudan.html?ref=global-home.

89. *See* Prosecutor v. Al Bashir, No. ICC-02/05-10/09-0A (Appeals Chamber, Feb. 3, 2010).

> land will be to you and your friends from Niger, from Mahamid tribe will come and ... and live with you on this land and we are capable to change even the name of this land"....

Victim testimony quoted in this opinion confirms that the attackers of African villagers yelled "Nuba nuba" or "black" as they killed civilians and burned homes. The partial dissent also pointed out that 700 villages were destroyed in only a year and a half, and confirmed a legal principle that the majority opinion failed to acknowledge, i.e. that the Yugoslav tribunal regards ethnic cleansing as genocide so long as the "group can no longer reconstitute itself" as it was due to "the separation of its members." These criticisms begin the process of rectifying the majority opinion's flaws in terms of reasoning, source materials, and selective quotations.[90]

The aftermath of the ICC's arrest warrants against President al-Bashir showed that even when the ICC does have jurisdiction, political and security ties between heads of state charged by it and other powerful states may make its actions meaningless. The African Union issued a resolution calling for noncompliance within Africa with the ICC's attempt to try President al-Bashir for war crimes and crimes against humanity.[91] President al-Bashir has traveled freely to Saudi Arabia, Egypt, Libya, and Ethiopia since March 2009, in open and collective defiance of international law.[92] South Africa, despite ratifying the ICC treaty in parliament, has publicly called for the arrest warrant to be ignored.[93] Former South African President Thabo Mbeki, implicated in the deaths of hundreds of thousands due to an internationally condemned do-little policy on HIV/AIDS, was appointed by the African Union to try to save President al-Bashir from the ICC's charges.[94] After the ICC arrest warrant was released, Egypt declared its outrage, and took the matter to the Arab League.[95] Led by Saudi Arabia, its largest financial contributor, the Arab League declared its "solidarity with Sudan and our rejection of the ICC decision against President Omar al-Bashir." At the same time, the League called for an international prosecution of war crimes in Gaza in 2008 and 2009, where Palestinian deaths from Israeli fire likely numbered fewer than 1,500.[96] China, with hopes of importing up to three million

---

90. Prosecutor v. Al Bashir, Separate and Partly Dissenting Opinion of Tudge Anita Usacka at ¶¶ 22, 25 n.42, 52, 170, 173 & n. 195 (footnotes omitted) (citing, inter alia, Prosecutor v Blagojevic, Trial Judgment, at ¶ 666).

91. *S. Africa under Pressure over Sudanese President Warrant*, Sudan Tribune (July 16, 2009), http://www.sudantribune.com/spip.php?article31827; Moabi Phia & Phumza Macanda, *Botswana Condemns AU Resolution on Sudan's Bashir*, Reuters, July 7, 2009, http://www.reuters.com/article/idUSL750994.

92. *See* Ghazanfar Ali Khan, *Delegation to Show Arab Solidarity with Bashir*, Arab News, Aug. 3, 2009, http://www.arabnews.com/?page=1&section=0&article=125117&d=3&m=8&y=2009&pix=kingdom.jpg&category=Kingdom.

93. *See South Africa: State Seeks Legal Advice on Indicting Al-Bashir*, BuaNews (Tshwane), July 23, 2009, http://allafrica.com/stories/200907230616.html ("South Africa's position is that while it respects the ICC's efforts to end impunity for war crimes in Darfur, the court has not made enough effort to engage the AU to co-ordinate efforts to end the fighting in that country.").

94. *See Bashir Warrant: Mbeki Chosen to Intercede*, The Independent (South Africa), Mar. 5, 2009, http://www.iol.co.za/index.php?sf=1&set_id=1&click_id=68&art_id=nw20090305075531160C704046; Carli Lourens, *South Africa's Mbeki Opposes al-Bashir Indictment*, Bloomberg, July 29, 2008, http://www.bloomberg.com/apps/news?pid=20601116&sid=aQfJQlPURgxs&refer=africa.

95. *See Arrest Warrant Draws Sudan Scorn.*

96. *See In Defense of Genocide: An Arab Summit Embraces the Butcher of Darfur*, Wash. Post, Apr. 1, 2009, at A20.

barrels per day of Sudanese oil someday, and facing its own genocide charges in Tibet and East Turkestan, and from neo-Taoists, condemned "[o]utside interference in Sudan," despite failing to veto the Security Council's ICC referral.[97] The U.S., even after the ICC's arrest warrant was issued, called for Sudan to continue to enjoy the "stable" rule of al-Bashir, and held out the prospect of freer trade with his regime.[98]

D. National Courts in Iraq and Sudan, Including the Iraqi High Tribunal

At a preliminary hearing on July 1, 2004, Saddam Hussein was informed that he faced six criminal counts relating to "intended killings" during his reign: (1) "intended killing by using chemical weapons in Halabjah," (2) "intended killing of a great number of Iraqis in 1983," (3) "intended killing of a number of members of political parties without trials," (4) "intended killing of many of the Iraqi religious people," (5) "intended killing of many Iraqis in Anfal (ph) without any evidence against it," and (6) acting as "as president of the republic and the commander in chief of the army ... [that] went to [i.e., invaded] Kuwait."[99] Press reports added a seventh charge that did not appear in the publicly released transcript of the hearing: directing widespread executions of Kurdish and Shi'a rebels and civilians after Gulf War II.[100]

The Iraqi High Tribunal made important strides in clarifying that genocide may occur in the context of counterinsurgency warfare, when it is characterized by disproportionate violence, massive civilian deaths among minorities or distinct ethnic groups, use of weapons incapable of distinguishing between rebels and civilians, and large scale displacement of civilians leading to hunger, disease, and exposure to the elements. In September 2007, the Appellate Chamber of the Iraqi High Tribunal affirmed the death sentences of 'Ali Hassan al-Majid and the other defendants in the Anfal trial. According to the English translation released in October 2008, al-Majid argued that the relocation of civilians from the Iran-Iraq border regions inhabited by Kurds was necessitated by the military conflict and the presence of Iranian forces in the area, that he did not control the Iraqi forces guilty of murders or other inhumane acts, and that if he had desired to eliminate the Kurdish population he could have much more easily started with the Kurds in Baghdad, Mosul, Kirkuk, Arbil, and other large cities. The Appellate Chamber disagreed, finding him to have contributed significantly to acts targeting the civilian population.

---

97. *See* Antoaneta Bezlova, *China/Sudan: Move to Get Al-Bashir Off Genocide Charges*, Inter Press Service, July 31, 2009, http://www.ipsnews.net/news.asp?idnews=43392.

98. *See* Eric Reeves, *Redefining Darfur's Agony: A Shameless Betrayal*, Sudan Tribune, Sept. 27, 2009, http://www.sudantribune.com/spip.php?article32602; Eric Reeves, *The Phony Optimism on Darfur*, Boston Globe, Aug. 6, 2009, http://www.boston.com/bostonglobe/editorial_opinion/oped/articles/2009/08/06/the_phony_optimism_on_darfur/; Bret Stephens, *Does Obama Believe in Human Rights?*, Wall St. J., Oct. 20, 2009, http://online.wsj.com/article/SB40001424052748704500604574481341183751038.html.

99. *Transcript: Saddam Hussein Court Hearing*, Washingtonpost.com (July 1, 2004), http://www.washingtonpost.com/ac2/wp-dyn/A20462-2004Jul1?language=printer.

100. *See Charges Facing Saddam Hussein*, BBC News.com (July 1, 2004), http://news.bbc.co.uk/2/hi/middle_east/3320293.stm.

The tribunal reasoned that thousands of Kurds were killed, and 3,000 villages were destroyed. It also focused on orders by defendant al-Majid to declare areas inhabited by civilians "prohibited zones" where any person could be killed, and to use chemical weapons in these areas.[101] As in many other genocide cases, intent to destroy a group was inferred a campaign targeting it.

The Iraqi Special/High Tribunal was not perfect, however. First, the CPA trial process was explicitly one-sided, limiting the tribunal's jurisdiction to "Iraqi nationals or residents of Iraq accused of genocide, crimes against humanity, war crimes or violations of certain Iraqi laws," and to crimes committed in violation of international or Iraqi law prior to May 1, 2003.[102] Although, of course, the focus of transitional justice in Iraq needed to be on the aggression and crimes against humanity committed by Saddam Hussein and his henchmen, the rule of law could only be served by investigating the role of the international community, where appropriate. In particular, the circumstances under which the Ba'ath party and Saddam Hussein took power and eliminated their initial enemies deserved careful scrutiny. The possibility that members of the U.N. Security Council, especially the U.S. and the Soviet Union, encouraged Saddam Hussein to take and exercise power, invade Iran, and import the military equipment he needed to prosecute the war, should not have been ignored. Likewise, allegations of disproportionate force and disregard of the rights of the civilian population of Iraq, during and after both the 1991 and 2003 wars, have received too much support from U.S. and U.N. sources to be dismissed without more thorough inquiries. The factual record and international legal context permitted a reasonable charge to be leveled of numerous war crimes and crimes against humanity, first of all by the leadership of the Ba'ath party, and secondly by its allies (and adversaries) on the United Nations Security Council. The existing legal structure seemed poised to prosecute only a handful of these crimes, ignoring others that would arguably have been easier to prove with government documents and former officials' statements, such as aggression, torture, and genocide.

Second, the statute was framed so as to exclude crimes committed by the Iraqi military or police after May 1, 2003, aggravating the perception of bias and victor's justice.[103] With their impunity assured, Iraq's Internal Affairs Unit went about killing suspected former regime officials without trials, and Baghdad police killed 12 persons in its custody without due process.[104] Death squads discovered lists of former regime officials, and systematically executed them without trials, including teachers, professors, and doctors.[105] Police torture and abuse of detainees became common, including by electric shock treat-

---

101. *See* Al Anfal, Special Verdict Pertaining to Case No 1/C Second/2006, at 22–24 (Iraqi High Tribunal, Appellate Chamber, Sept. 4, 2007), at 11–14, 26, http://law.case.edu/grotian-moment-blog/anfal/cassation.asp.

102. CPA/ORD/9Dec2003/48, Coalition Provisional Authority Order Number 48 & The Statute of the Iraqi Special Tribunal.

103. *See* Robert Cryer, Håkan Friman, Darryl Robinson, & Elizabeth Wilmshurst, An Introduction to International Criminal Law and Procedure 160–61 (Cambridge: Cambridge UP, 2007).

104. *See* USDOS, *Country Reports on Human Rights Practices: Iraq 2004.*

105. *See* Allawi, The Occupation of Iraq, at 135–46; Gilbert Burnham et al., The Human Cost of the War in Iraq: A Mortality Study, 2002–2006, at 20–24 (2006); Economist Intelligence Unit, *Iraq: Country Profile 2007*, http:// www.eiu.com; Imad Harb, *Higher Education and the Future of Iraq*, U.S. Institute of Peace (2008), http://www.usip.org/pubs/specialreports/sr195.pdf.

ment.[106] The CPA amended the Iraqi Penal Code to declare that no one could be charged with torture or murder arising out of tasks performed for the CPA.[107] The CPA also shielded U.S. contractors from charges for theft or fraud, or bribery in Iraq, so that $250 million was misappropriated by Halliburton alone.[108] More than $8.8 billion may have been misspent.[109]

Third, the fairness of the proceedings was subject to serious doubt. The procedures and opinions issued by the Iraqi High Tribunal were deficient in both form and substance. Hearings were often boisterous, and judges and lawyers would often be threatened, removed, or replaced. The tribunal's decisions failed to analyze or follow applicable precedents of international criminal tribunals.[110] The documentation of crimes and analysis of the context and modalities of crimes charged was frequently shoddy. The U.S. High Commissioner for Human Rights, Louise Arbour, was moved to argue to the Iraqi High Tribunal that its proceedings failed to meet international standards of due process and fairness.[111] Her brief to the tribunal argued that the fairness of the trial was undermined by media interviews by senior public officials confirming the defendants' guilt prior to their convictions, the inability of the defendants to examine certain witnesses or impeach the reliability of documents, the murder of several defense counsel, the removal of judges from cases on political grounds, and the prohibition on all Iraqi judges living in Iraq at the time of the invasion hearing cases.[112]

Finally, and most damningly, even assuming that the restriction of the Iraqi Special Tribunal's jurisdiction to nationals or residents of Iraq during a certain period was justified, the trials themselves did not focus on the most serious crimes. Saddam Hussein was executed for the murders and torture of more than 100 residents of a Shi'a town, while the genocide of 50,000 to 200,000 by him went untried. The genocide charges against him for the Anfal campaign were dropped after his death.[113]

---

106. *See* USDOS, *Country Reports on Human Rights Practices: Iraq 2004.*

107. *See* CPA, Order 7 [Penal Code], § 3, http://web.archive.org/web/20040810044933/www.cpa-iraq.org/regulations/.

108. *See* Farah Stockman, *US Firms Suspected of Bilking Iraq Funds; Millions Missing from Program for Rebuilding,* Boston Globe, Apr. 16, 2006, http://www.boston.com/news/world/articles/2006/04/16/ us_firms_suspected_of_bilking_iraq_funds.

109. *See* Ed Harriman, *So, Mr Bremer, Where Did All the Money Go?,* The Guardian (U.K.), July 7, 2005, http://www.guardian.co.uk/world/2005/jul/07/iraq.features11.

110. *See, e.g.,* Human Rights Watch, Judging Dujail (2007), http://www.hrw.org/en/node/11112/section/6; Al Anfal judgment, Iraqi High Tribunal, Second Court of Felonies, Case No. 1/C Second/2006 (June 24, 2007), at PDF p. 25 (without citing any precedents, convicting defendant Ali Hassan al-Majid "for, within the period before Al Anfal, on 1987 June, as well as within Al Anfal campaigns in 1988, the aforementioned convict issued orders to military troops and security, intelligence and military intelligence systems, as well as bygone Ba'th Party organizations to murder Kurds in northern Iraq, causing physical and mental damages by using all types of war weapons like aircrafts and artilleries, oppressing them and imposing harsh living conditions shortage of food, medicine and fuel supplies, killing their livestock and burning their agronomic crops) aiming to partially or completely eradicate them.").

111. *UN Appeals against Iraq Execution*, BBC News, Feb. 9, 2007, http://news.bbc.co.uk/2/hi/middle_east/6344969.stm.

112. *See* Brief Amicus Curiae of the U.N. High Commissioner for Human Rights, Louise Arbour, In re Sentencing of Taha Yassin Ramadan, at ¶¶ 14–25 (Feb. 2007), http://law.case.edu/saddamtrial/entry.asp?entry_id=229.

113. *See* Human Rights Watch, *Q & A: The Anfal Trial* (2007), http://www.hrw.org/en/news/2007/06/22/q-anfal-trial ("Unlike the recently-concluded Dujail trial, which concerned horrific killings in one village, the crimes of the Anfal were massive in scale.").

E. Awarding Reparations in the ICJ or ICC

The slow pace and limited scope of ICC prosecutions reflects a more fundamental flaw with international criminal tribunals as mechanisms for the deterrence of genocide. Empirical research into the effect of the death penalty in the U.S. has shown that only large-scale executions will deter murder, and that small numbers of executions merely brutalize the population by fomenting an atmosphere of revenge-killing, thereby increasing rather than decreasing the murder rate in U.S. states that execute small numbers of offenders.[114] In addition, not only the severity of the sentence but the likelihood of suffering it is an important factor that emerges from empirical studies of deterrence.[115] A severe sanction for genocide is anything but certain, as dictators like al-Bashir and Saddam Hussein may survive for decades.

Legal scholars have questioned whether international criminal tribunals are sufficient or even helpful, standing alone, as deterrents to genocide. Among other problems with criminal deterrence, leaders often positively embrace their own and their subordinates' sacrifices for the benefit of the nation; military command structures complicate individual cost-benefit calculations; the sheer numbers of soldiers and instigators of massacres create such a mob-like mentality that punishing all perpetrators is impossible; state-sanctioned hatred and mass violence resist rational analysis and deliberation; and criminal trials may themselves valorize perpetrators of genocide as national or ethnic martyrs.[116] Under these theories, the failure of the international community to deter governments from engaging in genocide has not been due to weak international criminal procedures. If criminal sanctions could deter government officials from implementing genocide as a solution to their nations' political and economic problems, the trial and sentencing of several heads of state and high officials over the past century should already have achieved this goal.[117]

---

114. *See* Joanna M. Shepherd, *Deterrence Versus Brutalization: Capital Punishment's Differing Impacts Among States*, 104 MICH. L. REV. 203, 206–7, 247–48 (2005).

115. *See* GENNARO F. VITO ET AL., CRIMINOLOGY: THEORY, RESEARCH, AND POLICY 53–76 (Sudbury, Massachusetts: Jones & Bartlett Publishers, 2006).

116. For a sense of the literature over the past decade questioning the deterrent effect of penal sentences handed down by international criminal tribunals, in roughly chronological order, *see* Theodor Meron, *From Nuremberg to the Hague*, 149 MIL. L. REV. 107, 110 (1995); Jose E. Alvarez, *Rush to Closure: Lessons of the Tadic Judgment*, 96 MICH. L. REV. 2031, 2080 (1998); Mark A. Drumbl, *Punishment, Postgenocide: From Guilt to Shame to Crisis in Rwanda*, 75 N.Y.U. L. REV. 1221, 1254, 1321 (2000); Payam Akhavan, *Beyond Impunity: Can International Criminal Justice Prevent Future Atrocities?*, 95 AM. J. INT'L L. 8, 10 (2001); Diane Marie Amann, *Assessing International Criminal Adjudication of Human Rights Atrocities*, 2000–2003 THIRD WORLD LEGAL STUD. 169, 173–74; Laurel E. Fletcher and Harvey M. Weinstein, *Violence and Social Repair: Rethinking the Contribution of Justice to Reconciliation*, 24 HUM. RTS. Q. 573, 579–80, 592 (2002); Allison Danner & Jenny Martinez, *Guilty Associations: Joint Criminal Enterprise, Command Responsibility, and the Development of International Criminal Law*, 93 CAL. L. REV. 75, 147–48 (2005); Mark Drumbl, *Collective Violence and Individual Punishment: The Criminality of Mass Atrocity*, 99 NW. U. L. REV. 539, 589–91 (2005); Jenia Iontcheva, *Nationalizing International Criminal Law*, 41 STAN. J. INT'L L. 1, 25 (2005); Mark Osiel, *The Banality of Good: Aligning Incentives Against Mass Atrocity*, 105 COLUM. L. REV. 1751, 1770 (2005).

117. *See* Prosecutor v Jean Kambanda, Trial Chamber, Judgement, *aff'd by* Appeals Chamber, Judgement; Prosecutor v. Milosevic, Case No. IT-02-54-T, Amended Indictment (Bosnia) (2002), http://www.un.org/icty/indictment/english/mil-ai040421-e.htm; Judgment: Goering, http://avalon.yale.edu/judgoeri.htm; Judgement: Bormann, http://avalon.yale.edu/judborma.htm; Judgement: Rosenberg, http://avalon.yale.edu/judrosen.htm; Judgement: Ribbentrop, http://avalon.yale.edu/judribb.htm; Judgement: Streicher, http://avalon.yale.edu/judstrei.htm; Kirk Semple, *Iraqi Court Sentences Saddam to Death*, INT'L HERALD TRIB., Nov. 5, 2006, http://www.iht.com/articles/2006/11/05/news/saddam.php; *Saddam's YouTube Execution*, RED HERRING,

The persistence of genocide despite successful criminal convictions and private justice against architects of genocide from Talât Paşa to Saddam Hussein indicates that the international community may need to pay more attention to collective, rather than individual, responsibility for genocide, and to economic, rather than criminal, disincentives to genocide.

An underlying current in the history of genocide and mass killing is the powerful economic incentive that more powerful groups possess to exterminate and appropriate the wealth of weaker groups. This raises the question whether to effectively prevent genocide, international law should remove this incentive by ordering restitution of ill-gotten gains. Most national governments and courts outside the U.S. have been extremely slow to award reparations to victims for genocide, and when such awards have been made, they rarely made victim communities whole. This may explain why governments and peoples engage in genocide with such regularity, lacking an economic disincentive not to do so.

Victims of Japan's occupation, mass murder, and enslavement of Asian populations during World War II have received very little in reparations payments, compared to what they have lost.[118] Few of the victims of other mass killings, including those in Indonesia, Pakistan, Cambodia, Guatemala, Iraq, Bosnia, Rwanda, and the Congo, have received substantial compensation for their losses.[119] The main exception to this rule is Germany,

---

Dec. 30, 2006, http://www.redherring.com/Article.aspx?a=20519; International Criminal Tribunal for the Former Yugoslavia, Press Release, Slobodan Milosevic Found Dead in His Cell at the Detention Unit (2006), http://www.un.org/icty/pressreal/2006/p1050-e.htm; MIKI Y. ISHIKIDA, TOWARD PEACE: WAR RESPONSIBILITY, POSTWAR COMPENSATION, AND PEACE MOVEMENTS AND EDUCATION IN JAPAN 15–16 (2005); Vahakn N. Dadrian, *The Documentation of the World War I Armenian Massacres in the Proceedings of the Turkish Military Tribunal*, 23 INTERNATIONAL J. OF MIDDLE EAST STUDIES 549, 556, 561–62, 575 (1991); Gerard Chaliand, *Prologue, in* JACQUES DEROGY, RESISTANCE AND REVENGE: THE ARMENIAN ASSASSINATION OF THE TURKISH LEADERS RESPONSIBLE FOR THE 1915 MASSACRES AND DEPORTATIONS (New Brunswick, NJ: Transaction Publishers, 1990), http://www.macalester.edu/courses/intl345/docs/derogy.pdf.

118. *See* Michael J. Bazyler, *The Holocaust Restitution Movement in Comparative Perspective*, 20 BERKELEY J. INT'L L. 11, 32 (2002). Japan never paid reparations to China, the principal victim of its colonial and genocidal policies during World War II. *See* Kitaoka Shinichi, *Answering China's Japan Bashers* (Part 2 of 3), JAPAN NOW, Vol. 1, No. 2 (2005), http://www.us.emb-japan.go.jp/jicc/EJN_no2.htm (Japan never paid reparations to China); MARIA HSIA CHANG, RETURN OF THE DRAGON, CHINA'S WOUNDED NATIONALISM 80–83 (Boulder, Colo.: Westview Press, 2001) (China lost 10 to 20 million people and $100 billion to Japan's attacks). *But cf.* Melinda Liu & Christian Caryl, *Asia: Furies Unleashed*, NEWSWEEK INTERNATIONAL, April 25, 2005, http://www.msnbc.msn.com/id/7529463/site/newsweek/ (Japan distributed $34 billion in development aid to China through 2005). Japan did pay reparations to Burma, Indonesia, the Philippines, Vietnam, and South Korea, but only in the amount of about $1.3 billion not counting loans, or about $300 for each of the at least four million people it killed in these countries, assuming that neither purely economic losses nor any of the estimated 125 million rapes committed by Japanese troops were compensated. *See* Larry A. Niksch, *Japan's World War II Reparations: A Fact Sheet*, CONGRESSIONAL RESEARCH SERV. (Mar. 7, 1991), http://tinyurl.com/yd3nrnm (noting that Japan paid about $1.3 billion in reparations to Burma, Indonesia, the Philippines, and South Korea, and "minor" amounts to Vietnam, Cambodia, and Laos); MIKIO SUMIYA, A HISTORY OF JAPANESE TRADE AND INDUSTRIAL POLICY 237 (Oxford: Oxford UP, 2001) (Japan paid only $39 million in reparations to Vietnam); BIX, HIROHITO, at 657, 690 (stating that Japan claimed 2 million victims in Vietnam and 1 million in the Philippines).

119. *See, e.g.*, JOSEPH NEVINS, A NOT-SO-DISTANT HORROR: MASS VIOLENCE IN EAST TIMOR 178 (Ithaca, NY: Cornell UP, 2005) (East Timor); LOUISE KRABBE BOSERUP, HUMAN RIGHTS IN DEVELOPMENT YEARBOOK 2001, REPARATIONS: REDRESSING PAST WRONGS 64 (The Hague, Netherlands: Kluwer Law Int'l, 2003) (East Pakistan/Bangladesh); VICTOR D. MONTEJO, MAYA INTELLECTUAL RENAISSANCE: IDENTITY REPRESENTATION, AND LEADERSHIP 196–97 (Austin, TX: Univ. of Texas Press, 2005) (Guatemala); Case Concerning the Application of the Convention on the Prevention and Punishment of the Crime of Genocide (Bosnia and Herzegovina v. Serbia and Montenegro), Judgment

which finally, by 1998, paid out $60 billion in reparations to Holocaust victims; however, even Germany paid "very little" in individual compensation in the first decade after 1945.[120] It was only starting in the late 1990s, after fifty years of little to no redress, that many victims of Nazi genocide and slave labor received compensation in U.S. courts.[121] This was not "swift" punishment.

Despite the relative infrequency until recent years of cases seeking civil compensation for genocide, international law is fairly clear, when it is properly and impartially construed, that such compensation must be paid.[122] Thus, the ICC is directed by its Statute to "establish principles relating to reparations to, or in respect of, victims, including restitution, compensation and rehabilitation."[123] Similarly, the ICJ has "observe[d] that it is well established in general international law that a State which bears responsibility for an internationally wrongful act is under an obligation to make full reparation for the injury caused by that act."[124] Such reparations must compensate for all "damage caused to all natural or legal persons concerned"[125] and, "as far as possible, wipe out all the consequences of the illegal act and reestablish the situation which would ... have existed if that act had not been committed."[126]

The ICC should become a tribunal that victims of genocide and crimes against humanity can appeal to rebuild their lives, just as Holocaust victims appealed to U.S. courts

---

459–470 (I.C.J. 26 Feb. 2007), http://www.icj-cij.org/docket/index.php?p1=3&PHPSESSID=f63dc11009628f59386d98e083651b4e&case=122&code=ybh&p3=4 (Bosnia); Drumbl, *Punishment, Postgenocide*, at 1271 n.232 (Rwanda). The compensation process for dispossession of Kurdish properties has begun in Iraq, but the amounts awarded have been criticized as inadequate and too slow in coming. *See* Internal Displacement Monitoring Centre, *Iraq: Sectarian violence, Military Operations Spark New Displacement, As Humanitarian Access Deteriorates* (May 23. 2006), http://www.icmc.net/pdf/idmc_report_iraq.pdf.

120. Paul R. Dubinsky, *Justice for the Collective: The Limits of the Human Rights Class Action*, 102 Mich. L. Rev. 1152, 1189 (2004).

121. *See id.* at 1157, 1164; Bazyler, *The Holocaust Restitution Movement*, at 12, 15–25, 36–37 ($8 billion in payouts). The amount paid out by Germany and German corporations rose to $100 billion by 2006. *See* Bassiouni, *World War I*, at 219–20.

122. *See, e.g., Congo v. Uganda*, Annex ¶ 15 ("In accordance with its domestic laws and international legal obligations, a State shall provide reparation to victims for acts or omissions which can be attributed to the State and constitute gross violations of international human rights law or serious violations of international humanitarian law."); U.N. Commission on Human Rights, Basic Principles and Guidelines on the Right to a Remedy and Reparation for Victims of Gross Violations of International Human Rights Law and Serious Violations of International Humanitarian Law, U.N. Doc. E/CN.4/2005/L.48 (Apr. 13, 2005), http://www.icj.org/IMG/pdf/UNRemedyReparation.pdf ("Any human rights violation gives rise to a right to reparation on the part of the victim or his or her beneficiaries, implying a duty on the part of the State to make reparation and the possibility for the victim to seek redress from the perpetrators.... The right to reparation shall cover all injuries suffered by the victim; it shall include individual measures concerning the right to restitution, compensation and rehabilitation....").

123. Report of the Preparatory Committee on the Establishment of an International Criminal Court, UN Doc. No. A/CONF.183/2/Add.l, art. 75(1) (Apr. 14, 1998).

124. *Congo v. Uganda*, ¶¶ 259, 345, 2005 ICJ LEXIS 1, *202, 254 (citing, *inter alia*, Avena and Other Mexican Nationals (Mexico v. United States of America), Judgment, I.C.J. Reports 2004, ¶ 119 at 59).

125. *See* Legal Consequences of the Construction of a Wall in the Occupied Palestinian Territory, Advisory Opinion of 9 July 2004, at ¶ 152, General List No. 131, 2004 ICJ LEXIS 20, *147.

126. *Id.* (citing Factory at Chorzow, Merits, Judgment No. 13, 1928, P.C.I.J., Series A, No. 17, p. 47.).

to establish compensation funds.[127] The ICC, however, does not recognize the vicarious criminal liability of corporations appearing before it.[128] This is perverse, in that corporations are frequently among the greatest beneficiaries of international crimes, and civil litigation in the aftermath of crimes against humanity and genocide frequently involves corporations.[129] International law, at least since the trials of German industrialists in the aftermath of World War II, has arguably acknowledged the criminal responsibility of individuals for the facilitation of international crimes by private corporations.[130] Corporate executives may therefore be prosecuted for aiding and abetting international crimes, so the immunity of their employers is puzzling and difficult to justify. One might argue that corporations are not living beings in a corporeal sense, but that does not prevent them from incurring many legal benefits and liabilities.[131]

The ICJ provides a forum for U.N. members and states parties to the Statute of the International Court of Justice to seek declarations of illegal uses of force and reparations for violations of the law of armed conflict.[132] In an important case, that court stated:

> [R]eparation must, as far as possible, wipe out all the consequences of the illegal act and reestablish the situation which would, in all probability, have ex-

---

127. *See* G.A. Res. 60/147 (Dec. 16, 2005/Mar. 21, 2006), Basic Principles and Guidelines on the Right to a Remedy and Reparations for Gross Violation of International Human Rights Law and Serious Violations of International Humanitarian Law, http://www2.ohchr.org/english/law/remedy.htm; Redress, *Reparations for Victims of Genocide, Crimes Against Humanity and War Crimes: Systems in Place and Systems in the Making* (Mar. 2, 2007), http://redress.org/conferences/CNRC%2520Background%2520Paper%25201-2%2520March%252007.pdf.

128. Rome Statute, art. 25(1).

129. Diane F. Orentlicher, *The Future of Universal Jurisdiction, in* UNIVERSAL JURISDICTION: NATIONAL COURTS AND THE PROSECUTION OF SERIOUS CRIMES UNDER INTERNATIONAL LAW, 214, 226–27 (Stephen Macedo ed., Philadelphia: Univ. of Pennsylvania Press, 2004).

130. *See, e.g.*, United States v. Krupp, *reprinted in* 9 TRIALS OF WAR CRIMINALS BEFORE THE NUREMBERG MILITARY TRIBUNALS UNDER CONTROL COUNCIL LAW NO. 10, at 1436 (U.S. Military Trib. 1950); United States v. Flick, *reprinted in* 6 TRIALS OF WAR CRIMINALS BEFORE THE NUREMBERG MILITARY TRIBUNALS UNDER CONTROL COUNCIL LAW NO. 10, at 1198–1202 (U.S. Military Trib. 1952); Doe I v. Unocal, 395 F.3d 932, 947–53 & nn.21–22 (9th Cir. 2002), *vacated en banc*, 395 F.3d 978 (9th Cir. 2003) (citing, among other authorities in support of corporate civil responsibility for war crimes, "cases before Nuremberg Military Tribunals involving the role of German industrialists in the Nazi forced labor program during the Second World War."); Doug Cassel, *Corporate Aiding and Abetting of Human Rights Violations: Confusion in the Courts*, 6 NORTHWESTERN J. OF INTERNATIONAL HUMAN RIGHTS ¶¶ 1, 8–9 (2008) ("Corporate executives have long been held criminally liable for committing violations of human rights norms that do not require state action (Part A).... As human beings, corporate executives are no less subject to international criminal law than are other individuals. This message was laid down plainly at the principal Nuremberg trial....") (citing Trial of Bruno Tesch and Two Others (The Zyklon B Case), 1 TRIALS OF WAR CRIMINALS BEFORE THE NUREMBERG MILITARY TRIBUNALS UNDER CONTROL COUNCIL LAW NO. 10, at 93 (1947) (Brit. Mil. Ct., Hamburg, 1–8 March 1946)); *id.* at ¶ 9–10 ("In subsequent trials before British, French and American military courts, assorted German industrialists were convicted of such war crimes as plundering private property and using slave labor.... In other words, international criminal responsibility of corporate executives as accomplices has long been recognized."); Jordan Paust, *Human Rights Responsibilities of Private Corporations*, 35 VAND. J. TRANSNATIONAL LAW 801 (2002).

131. These principles received recognition in the French penal code. *See* Code Pénal (France), arts. 121–2, 213–3.

132. ICJ, Rules of Court (1978), http://www.icj-cij.org/icjwww/ibasicdocuments/ibasictext/ibasicrulesofcourt_20050929.htm; ICJ, States Members of the United Nations (2006), http://www.icj-cij.org/icjwww/ibasicdocuments/ibasictext/ibasicUNmembers.html; Islamic Republic of Iran v. United States of America: Order of 10 March 1998, http://www.icj-cij.org/icjwww/idocket/iop/ioporders/iop_iorder_980310.HTM.

> isted if that act had not been committed. Restitution in kind, or, if this is not possible, payment of a sum corresponding to the value which a restitution in kind would bear; the award, if need be, of damages for loss sustained which would not be covered by restitution in kind or payment in place of it—such are the principles which should serve to determine the amount of compensation due for an act contrary to international law.[133]

More recently, the ICJ has reaffirmed that a state "has an obligation to compensate, in accordance with the applicable rules of international law, all natural or legal persons having suffered any form of material damage as a result" of an international crime.[134]

ICJ cases recognizing the duty to pay compensation for international crimes or torts include *United States of America v. Iran*, *Nicaragua v. United States of America*, and *Bosnia and Herzegovina v. Yugoslavia*.[135] In perhaps the most significant case in this line of authority, the ICJ in 2005 ordered Uganda to pay compensation because its military invaded the Democratic Republic of the Congo and

> committed acts of killing, torture and other forms of inhumane treatment of the Congolese civilian population, destroyed villages and civilian buildings, failed to distinguish between civilian and military targets..., incited ethnic conflict and failed to take measures to put an end to such conflict; as well as by its failure ... to take measures to respect and ensure respect for human rights and international humanitarian law ... [in breach of] its obligations under international human rights law....[136]

Under general principles of international law, genocide and ethnic cleansing give rise to legally enforceable claims for reparation and restoration of property and the value of lives lost.[137] "[I]t is a principle of international law that the breach of an engagement involves an obligation to make reparation in an adequate form."[138] International human rights instruments also require that individuals be made whole for violations of their rights by their governments. For example, the International Covenant on Civil and Political Rights states that any person whose rights are violated "shall have an effective remedy...."[139] Turkey, Iraq, and Sudan are parties.[140] Similarly, the African Charter on Human and People's

---

133. Case Concerning the Factory at Chorzów (Federal Republic of Germany v. Poland), Merits, Judgment No. 13, 1928, P.C.I.J., Series A, No. 17, p. 47.

134. Legal Consequences of the Construction of a Wall in the Occupied Palestinian Territory, Advisory Opinion (ICJ July 9, 2004), 43 ILM 1009 (2004).

135. ICJ, *Basis of the Court's Jurisdiction* (2006), http://www.icj-cij.org/icjwww/ibasicdocuments/ibasictext/ibasic_basisjurisdiction.html (citing these cases). For treatises and articles discussing these cases and many others, see, for example, Dinah Shelton, Remedies in International Human Rights Law (2d ed. 2005); *Public International Law; International Human Rights*, 41 Int'l Law. 643 (2007) (citing *Congo v. Uganda*, at ¶345(1)); Christian Tomuschat, *Reparation in Cases of Genocide*, 6 J. of International Criminal Justice 905 (2007).

136. *Congo v. Uganda*, 2005 ICJ LEXIS 1, at ¶¶254–55.

137. For discussion of further decisions by the International Court of Justice and other tribunals bearing on the obligation to make restitution for violations of international law, see Malcolm N. Shaw, International Law 95, 241–42, 694–97, 714–19, 995 (Cambridge: Cambridge UP, 2003).

138. Case Concerning the Factory at Chorzów (Federal Republic of Germany v. Poland), 1927, P.C.I.J., Series A, No. 9, p. 21.

139. International Covenant on Civil and Political Rights, Art. 2(3), Dec. 16, 1966, 999 U.N.T.S. 171, 174.

140. *See* Amnesty International, *Sudan: 1.2 Million Internally Displaced People at Risk in Darfur* (July 1, 2004), http://web.amnesty.org/library/Index/ENGAFR540782004?open&of=ENG-2AF; Dickran Kouymjian, *The Destruction of Armenian Historical Monuments as a Continuation of the Turkish Policy of Genocide, in* A Crime Of Silence, at 176; Mohammed Mattar, Unresolved Questions *in the Bill of Rights of the New Iraqi Constitution: How Will the Clash Between "Human Rights" and "Islamic*

Rights[141] states that peoples despoiled of their wealth and natural resources "shall have the right to the lawful recovery of [their] property as well as to an adequate compensation."[142] Sudan has ratified this code of human rights.[143]

The requirement of an "effective remedy" for violations of law entails a thorough investigation, punishment of the guilty, and the payment of compensation.[144] The purpose of this requirement is "to protect the victims and to provide for the reparation of damages."[145] This means, in cases involving the death of a victim by genocide or other criminal behavior, the payment to his or her survivors of an amount equivalent to the victim's "lost earnings, funeral expenses, and non-pecuniary damages for torture or unlawful detention." Where property is taken from its owners unlawfully, as in genocide, it should be restored without undue delay.[146]

F. Awarding Reparations in the U.N. Security Council

In 1991, the U.N. Security Council, acting under Chapter VII of the U.N. Charter, established a compensation fund in U.N. Security Council Resolution 687, as part of the council's efforts to restore "international peace and security" after Iraq's war with Kuwait.[147] Resolution 687 created a U.N. Compensation Commission (UNCC), and a follow-up resolution required Iraq to pay compensation to persons affected by the war with Kuwait, up to a limit of "30 per cent of the annual value of the exports of petroleum and petroleum products from Iraq."[148] The UNCC, operating as a subsidiary of the U.N. Security Council, paid out more than $21.8 billion in reparations to Kuwaiti, Saudi, Jordanian, Palestinian, Israeli, and American corporations and citizens.[149] The UNCC apparently intends to distribute $30

Law" be Reconciled in Future Legislative Enactments and Judicial Interpretations?, 30 FORDHAM INTERNATIONAL LAW J. 126, 128, 137–38 (2006).

141. African (Banjul) Charter on Human and Peoples' Rights, Art. 21 (June 27, 1981), 21 I.L.M. 58 (1982), http://www1.umn.edu/humanrts/instree/z1afchar.htm.

142. *Id.*, art. 21 (June 27, 1981), 21 I.L.M. 58 (1982), http://www1.umn.edu/humanrts/instree/z1afchar.htm.

143. *See* Amnesty International, *Sudan, Darfur: "Too Many People Killed."*

144. *See, e.g.*, Mentes v. Turkey, 37 I.L.M. 858, 882 (Eur. Ct. Hum. Rts. Nov. 28, 1997); Klint A. Cowan, *International Responsibility for Human Rights Violations by American Indian Tribes*, 9 YALE HUMAN RIGHTS & DEVELOPMENT LAW J. 1, 27–8 (2006).

145. Velasquez Rodriguez v. Honduras, Judgment, Inter-Am. Ct. Human Rights (ser. C) No. 4, at ¶ 134 (July 29, 1988), http://www.javier-leon-diaz.com/enforced_disappearances/Velasquez%20Rodriguez.pdf.

146. DINAH SHELTON, REMEDIES IN INTERNATIONAL HUMAN RIGHTS LAW 303, 305 (Oxford: Oxford UP, 2d ed. 2005).

147. *See* S.C. Res. 687 (1991).

148. S.C. Res. 705 ¶ 2 (Aug. 15, 1991); S.C. Res. 706 ¶¶ 2–4 (Aug. 15, 1991); PABLO DE GREIFF, THE HANDBOOK OF REPARATIONS 364 (Oxford: Oxford UP USA, 2006). The percentage was reduced to 25 percent in December 2000. *See* OFFICE OF THE DIR. OF CENTRAL INTELLIGENCE, COMPREHENSIVE REPORT OF THE SPECIAL ADVISOR TO THE DCI ON IRAQ'S WMD, annex D (2004), https://www.odci.gov/cia/reports/iraq_wmd_2004/chap2_annxD.html.

149. *See* UNCC, *At a Glance* (2007), http://www.unog.ch/uncc/ataglance.htm; UNCC, *Opening of the Sixty-Second Session of the UNCC Governing Council* (Feb. 16, 2007), http://www2.unog.ch/uncc/pressrel/pr_62o.pdf; UNCC, *United Nations Compensation Commission Governing Council Has*

billion more, for more than $50 billion in total compensation paid out of the Iraqi people's oil resources.[150]

While the UNCC provides a provocative model for awarding reparations for genocide pursuant to the U.N. Charter, it is subject to criticism for several related reasons. First, while many Kuwaitis died in Gulf War II, they were not found to be victims of genocide. Estimates place the number of victims somewhere between a few hundred and 10,000, a ratio of one Kuwaiti victim for every fifty to 1,000 Darfurian victims.[151] Second, the UNCC administered a fund payable out of revenues that otherwise would have fed, clothed, and provided medical care to victims of genocide inside Iraq. For example, the Kuwait Petroleum Corporation received twice as much as the $10 billion in Iraqi oil revenues that was allocated between 1996 and 2000 for the nutrition and other survival needs of the entire population of Iraq.[152] The vast majority of UNCC awards represented lost revenues or profits that might have been earned by corporations, among them a $15.9 billion award to the Kuwait Petroleum Corporation, rather than payments to the survivors of war victims or to persons who lost their homes or limbs.[153] Victims of genocide in Iraq who might have benefited from these funds included the Kurdish and Assyrian survivors of the 1980s Anfal campaign. Third, the UNCC was part of a sanctions regime that reduced civilian rations for food and other essentials below subsistence levels, thereby contributing to a 160 percent increase in child mortality in Iraq,[154] and to huge declines in life expectancy, nutrition, health care, and access to education.[155] In contrast, a properly-executed compensation mechanism for genocide victims—whether it be in northern Iraq, southern Sudan, Darfur, or elsewhere—could actually improve rations and medical care, and therefore reduce mortality. Fourth,

---

Concluded Its Sixty-First Session (Nov. 3, 2006), http://www2.unog.ch/uncc/pressrel/pr_61c.pdf; UNCC, *Opening of the Fifty-Sixth Session of the UNCC Governing Council* (June 24, 2005), http://www2.unog.ch/uncc/pressrel/pr_56o.pdf.

150. UNCC, *Opening of the Sixty-Second Session.*

151. *See* Human Rights Watch, *Iraq and Occupied Kuwait, in* HUMAN RIGHTS WATCH WORLD REPORT 1990, http://www.hrw.org/reports/1990/WR90/MIDEAST.BOU-03.htm#P200_49710 (citing estimates of 600 victims in first three months of Iraqi occupation of Kuwait); Judith Miller, *Standoff in the Gulf; Atrocities by Iraqis in Kuwait: Numbers Are Hard to Verify*, N.Y. TIMES, Dec. 16, 1990, at 1–1 (citing Kuwaiti estimates of up to 7,000 victims).

152. *See* Alain Gresh, *A Debt of Dishonour; Oil for Food: The True Story*, LE MONDE DIPLOMATIQUE, Oct. 2000, http://www.globalpolicy.org/security/sanction/iraq1/oilforfood/00gresh.htm. *See also* Denis J. Halliday, *The Impact of UN Sanctions on the People of Iraq*, 28 J. OF PALESTINE STUDIES 29, 31 (1999) (only $2.6 billion available to import food in Iraq each year during sanctions period).

153. *See* Gresh, *A Debt of Dishonor*; UNCC Governing Council, *Report and Recommendations Made by the Panel of Commissioners Concerning Part Three of the Third Instalment of "F3" Claims*, S/AC.26/2003/15, ¶ 419 (June 26, 2003) ($16 billion awarded for lost profits).

154. *See* H.C. Graf Sponeck, *Sanctions and Humanitarian Exemptions: A Practitioner's Commentary*, 13 EUR. J. INT'L L. 81, 82 (2002). *See also* Halliday, *The Impact of UN Sanctions*, at 30 (former U.N. assistant secretary-general and humanitarian coordinator for Oil-for-Food Program in Iraq wrote that sanctions caused deaths of 5,000 to 7,000 Iraqi children per month in the 1990s).

155. *See* U.N. Children's Fund, *Iraq* (2008), http://www.unicef.org/infobycountry/iraq_statistics.html (life expectancy in Iraq declined from 63 years in 1990 to 60 years in 2005); Sponeck, *Sanctions and Humanitarian Exemptions*, at 81–83; Halliday, *The Impact of UN Sanctions*, at 30; Eric Herring, *Between Iraq and a Hard Place: A Critique of The British Government's Case for UN Economic Sanctions*, 28 REV. OF INT'L STUD. 39, 51–52 (2002) (mortality rate in north of Iraq where most Kurds live rose in first five years of U.N. sanctions); Abbas Alnasrawi, *Iraq: Economic Sanctions and Consequences, 1990–2000*, 22 THIRD WORLD Q. 205, 209–214 (2001) (describing U.N. sanctions on Iraq as contributing to soaring infant and child mortality rates, deaths of up to 1.5 million people, including more than 500,000 children, and deterioration in access to food, health care, electricity, and education); Mel Lehman, *Death by Sanctions: Iraqi Churches Persevere Despite U.N. Embargo*, 44 CHRISTIANITY TODAY, Oct. 2 2000, at 29 (describing adverse impact of U.N. sanctions on Iraqi Chaldeans and other Christians).

the people of Kuwait remained wealthy by regional standards despite the war with Iraq, and therefore were in much less need of compensation than the destitute civilians of Iraq or Sudan.[156] Finally, the UNCC wasted billions of dollars that could have fed Iraqis or compensated Kuwaitis, and spent an astronomical $482 million on administrative costs.[157]

After episodes of genocide by dictatorial regimes such as Iraq or Sudan, the U.N. Security Council should establish mechanisms for compensating the victims, while incorporating the lessons of the UNCC. Such mechanisms should focus on compensating victims of genocide for lost family members, health, and homes. The process should not favor large claims for lost corporate profits or business assets as the UNCC did.[158] It should also keep administrative costs under control so that reparations are not transformed into a slush fund for bureaucrats and international consultants. And governments made parties to such proceedings should be given detailed notice of, and an opportunity to respond to, claims against it, so that waste, fraud, and overpayments do not deplete the fund's resources.[159]

The Security Council had an opportunity in 1992, and again in 2002 and 2003, when it found the situation in Iraq to threaten international peace and security, to establish such a compensation fund for victims of genocide in Iraq. Another such opportunity arose in 2004, when the Security Council found a threat to international peace and security in Sudan and imposed an arms embargo, to establish a mechanism for awarding reparations to the survivors, and deterring further violations of international law. In the Anfal and Darfur genocides, the governments of Iraq and Sudan had committed much more serious crimes than Iraq did in connection with Kuwait, with a far higher toll of dead and displaced persons in northern Iraq, southern Sudan, and the Darfur region. A compensation fund for genocide victims in Iraq and Sudan would therefore have been more justifiable than the UNCC turned out to be. Such a fund could have achieved two objectives on which the international community has lavished enormous resources, including tens of billions of dollars and tens of thousands of peacekeeping troops: ensuring the survival of the groups subjected to genocide, and deterring the government and allied militia from continuing to exterminate members of minority ethnic and religious groups with the intention of stealing their land, water and mineral resources, homes, and cattle.

---

156. *See Kuwait, in* World Factbook 1992, http://es.rice.edu/projects/Poli378/CIA_Factbook/kuwait.html (Kuwait had per capita GDP of $11,100 in 1992); *Kuwait, in* World Factbook 2006, http://www.cia.gov/cia/publications/factbook/print/ku.html (Kuwait had per capita GDP of nearly $23,000 in 2005).

157. *See* Colum Lynch, *Volcker Probe Faults U.N. Auditors on Iraq*, Wash. Post, Jan. 10, 2005, at A14 (UNCC "may have wasted billions"); Stephanie Nebehay, *Gulf War Victims Overpaid by $5 Billion—UN Auditors*, Reuters (Jan. 9, 2005), http://www.odiousdebts.org/odiousdebts/index.cfm?DSP=content&ContentID=12184 (waste, fraud, and overpayments may have totaled $5 billion); Nick Wadhams, *Oil-for-food Probe Finds Mismanagement*, Associated Press, July 15, 2005, *http://www.usatoday.com/news/world/2005-07-16-food-probe_x.htm*; Independent Inquiry Committee Into the United Nations Oil-For-Food Programme, Briefing Paper, Internal Audit Reports on the United Nations Oil-For-Food Programme 9 (Jan. 9, 2005), http://www.iic-offp.org/documents/IAD%20Briefing%20Paper.pdf (commission may have made "[m]any very large potential overpayments").

158. *See* Shelton, Remedies, at 406, 408, 410–12 (UNCC set forth maximum compensation rates of: $5 million for initial awards to corporations for their lost profits, lost property, and increased expenses, compared to the following much lower amounts for individuals: $15,000 for the death of a spouse, child, or parent; $15,000 for dismemberment or permanent disfigurement; $5,000 for torture or sexual assault; or $2,500 for economic losses).

159. Iraq's government was denied the ability to examine the claims and investigate their veracity, even though it was forced to pay for the administration for the UNCC. *See* Gresh, *A Debt of Dishonour*.

People from Darfur frequently lack homes to sleep in or water to drink, and sometimes eat tree bark in a desperate bid to stay alive.[160] It was a sound assumption that voluntary agreements between the Sudanese government and representatives of the Dinka, Nuba, Masalit, Fur, Zaghawa, and other indigenous African peoples would fail to achieve adequate compensation to these peoples subjected to genocide. The international community, therefore, needed to take the lead in assuring that the government fulfills its legal obligation to pay reparations. The Holocaust litigation in the U.S. has already demonstrated the possibility that legal institutions could compensate victims and contribute to the survival of destitute survivors of genocide, notably elderly Holocaust survivors living in the former Soviet Union.[161] Reparations payments, unlike criminal prosecutions, "provide at least the possibility that victims may be compensated for lost property, for injuries suffered, or for emotional distress caused."[162]

From a deterrence perspective, the chief prosecutor of the international criminal tribunals for the former Yugoslavia and Rwanda called on the U.N. Security Council to "to break this cycle of violence" in Darfur by assessing reparations.[163] He argued that forming a "trust fund" out of a portion of Sudan's oil revenues to compensate the victims, provide humanitarian relief, and rebuild destroyed villages would provide a "strong incentive for Khartoum to admit a UN-authorized protection force and to cooperate with the International Criminal Court."[164] Without strong action by the international community to penalize the Sudanese government, it "has no incentive to stop its current campaign of atrocities."[165] Thus, both Human Rights Watch and Amnesty International have called for a compensation fund for Darfur's victims to be financed by oil revenues.[166] Therefore, the international community had a stronger basis to pierce Sudan's sovereignty and assess reparations. Insofar as both war crimes and genocide are *jus cogens* and *erga omnes* violations, there was no reason to distinguish on legal or jurisdictional grounds between Iraq's invasion of Kuwait and Sudan's genocide against non-Arabs in southern Sudan and Darfur. Thus, there is no merit to the contention of at least one prominent scholar that it would impermissibly invade Sudan's sovereignty to utilize its oil exports to pay reparations to the victims of genocide in southern Sudan and Darfur.[167] Iraq only lost its sovereignty and became subject to UNCC reparations

---

160. *See 700,000 Lack Access To Clean Water in Darfur*, UNICEF UK NEWS (May 25, 2004), http://www.unicef.org.uk/press/news_detail.asp?news_id=288; Charlotte Sector, *Aid Worker Fears 'Disaster of Biblical Proportions' in Darfur*, ABC NEWS (Mar. 31, 2006), http://abcnews.go.com/International/story?id=1786781&page=2.

161. *See* Dubinsky, *Justice for the Collective*, at 1179.

162. John F. Murphy, *Civil Liability for the Commission of International Crimes as an Alternative to Criminal Prosecution*, 12 HARV. HUM. RTS. J. 1, 48 (1999).

163. Richard Goldstone, *An 'Oil-for-Food' Program for Darfur*, INT'L HERALD TRIB., June 12, 2007, http://www.iht.com/articles/2007/06/12/opinion/edgold.php.

164. *Id.*

165. Nick Grono & John Prendergast, *To Halt Sudan's Atrocities, Follow the Money*, INT'L HERALD TRIB., Aug. 22, 2006, http://www.iht.com/articles/2006/08/21/opinion/edgrono.php.

166. *See* Human Rights Watch, *UN: Create Darfur Recovery Fund for Sudanese Oil Revenues* (Mar. 16, 2007), http://www.hrw.org/english/docs/2007/03/19/sudan15517.html; Human Rights Watch, *Sudan; Darfur Demands Sanctions, Not Words*, AFRICA NEWS, Dec. 12, 2006; Amnesty International, *Darfur: "Too Many People Killed."*

167. *See* Christian Tomuschat, *Darfur: Compensation for the Victims*, J. OF INTERNATIONAL CRIMINAL JUSTICE 579, 589 (2005) ("In the case of Iraq, ... [t]he Security Council was able to control the export shipments of oil. Revenues from those shipments were available for distribution by the UNCC. In the case of Sudan, no such monies are available. Sudan is a sovereign state which has ... [not] been deprived of its right to make sovereign determinations on its foreign trade.").

once the international community decided to impose reparations for alleged international crimes.

The sanctions framework for Iraq, including the UNCC, represented the first time that the U.N. determined the "financial liability" of a member state, and decided that a member state owed payment for such liability.[168] Such an assertion of judicial power would be morally unacceptable and potentially discriminatory if the Security Council did not take "comparable actions" in other cases, or failed to establish "clear rules of general applicability."[169] Thus, the Security Council still has an opportunity to assess reparations for genocide and crimes against humanity, not only in Iraq and Sudan, but also in Burma, Congo, and other warzones.

G. Awarding Reparations for Genocide in National Courts Exercising Universal Jurisdiction

Private litigation in national courts, for example but not necessarily in the U.S., has great promise to deter genocidal attacks and other mass killings by compensating victims' families for the value of their loved ones' lives. The U.S. federal courts have distinguished themselves by serving as a forum of last resort for victims seeking compensation for the Holocaust, the Yugoslav civil wars, and other mass killings.[170] Since 1789, U.S. law has provided a cause of action for a "violation of the law of nations," in what is often called the Alien Tort Claims Act ("ATCA"), 28 U.S.C. § 1350.[171] A leading case in this area stated that an individual may be found liable for genocide or war crimes based on acts of murder, rape, or torture intended to destroy religious or ethnic groups in part, regardless of whether an individual acted on behalf of a state.[172] Similarly, the Torture Victim Protection Act of 1991 ("TVPA")[173] recognizes that torture or extrajudicial killing gives rise to a private right of action for violation of U.S. law.[174] In addition, victims of discriminatory seizures of their property abroad have common-law claims for conversion under U.S. law.[175]

---

168. Jose E. Alvarez, *The Once and Future Security Council*, 18 WASHINGTON Q. 3 (1995).

169. *Id.*

170. *See* Bazyler, *The Holocaust Restitution Movement*, at 15–25; Dubinsky, *Justice for the Collective*, at 1157, 1164; Michael J. Bazyler & Adrienne Scholz, *Holocaust Restitution Litigation in the United States and Other Claims for Historical Wrongs—An Update*, ACLU INTERNATIONAL CIVIL LIBERTIES REPORT (2003), http://www.sdshh.com/ICLR/ICLR_2003/6_bazyler.pdf; Christine Haughney & Bill Miller, *Karadzic Told to Pay Victims $745 Million*, WASH. POST, Friday, Aug. 11, 2000, at A13.

171. 28 U.S.C. § 1350 (1948); *see* Hilao v. Estate of Marcos, 25 F.3d 1467, 1475 (9th Cir. 1994). *Accord* Presbyterian Church of Sudan v. Talisman Energy, 244 F. Supp. 2d 289, 320 (S.D.N.Y. 2003) ("ATCA provides a cause of action in tort for breaches of international law").

172. Kadic v. Karadzic, 70 F.3d 232, 240, 242 (2d Cir. 1995) (defendant could be found liable for genocide, murder, and torture against part of Bosnian Muslim population).

173. 28 U.S.C. § 1350 (2000).

174. *See* Enahoro v. Abubakar, 408 F.3d 877 (7th Cir. 2005) (TVPA provides cause of action for properly pleaded claims of torture or extrajudicial killing), *cert. denied by* Abub v. Enahoro, 2006 U.S. LEXIS 1210 (2006); Wiwa v. Royal Dutch Petroleum Company, 226 F.3d 88, 105 (2d Cir. 2000) (similar).

175. *See* Bigio v. Coca-Cola Co., 448 F.3d 176, 177 (2d Cir. 2006); Bigio v. Coca-Cola Co., 239 F.3d 440, 452 (2d Cir. 2000).

Initially, U.S. courts dismissed claims by Holocaust survivors on the grounds that international law only gave rise to claims between states and was not enforceable (or "self-executing") in the absence of implementing legislation by Congress.[176] This erroneous interpretation of section 1350 was corrected within a few years, however.[177]

In the 1980s, U.S. federal courts confirmed that under the principle of universal jurisdiction, any nation may prosecute the perpetrators of universally-condemned crimes according to its own laws and procedures.[178] Since then, the U.S. courts have exercised universal jurisdiction in a nearly unbroken line of cases involving offenses properly alleged to have been committed elsewhere in violation of international law.[179] For example,

176. *See* Dreyfus v. Von Finck, 534 F.2d 24 (2d Cir. 1976). *See also* Bernstein v. N. V. Nederlandsche-Amerikaansche Stoomvaart-Maatschappij, 173 F.2d 71 (2d Cir. 1949); Bernstein v. Van Heyghen Freres Societe Anonyme, 163 F.2d 246 (2d Cir. 1947).

177. *See* Filartiga v. Pena-Irala, 630 F.2d 876 (2d Cir. 1980); Harold Hongju Koh, *Transnational Public Law Litigation*, 100 YALE L.J. 2347, 2366 (1991).

178. *See Filartiga*, 630 F.2d 876; Demjanjuk v. Petrovsky, 776 F.2d 571, 582 (6th Cir. 1982) (United States recognizes the universality principle, i.e. that "some crimes are so universally condemned that the perpetrators are the enemies of all people," and "any nation which has custody of the perpetrators may punish them according to its law applicable to such offenses."), *judgment vacated on other grounds*, 10 F.3d 338 (6th Cir. 1994).

179. *See, e.g.*, Sosa v. Alvarez-Machain, 542 U.S. 692, 732–33 & n.20 (2004) (U.S. courts have jurisdiction over "private claims under federal common law for violations of any international law norm [that has sufficiently] definite content and acceptance among civilized nations," such as prohibition on genocide); Sarei v. Rio Tinto, PLC, 487 F.3d 1193, 1200–10 (9th Cir. 2007) (ATCA provided cause of action for racial discrimination and other violations of international law), *vacated upon grant of reh'g en banc by* 499 F.3d 923 (9th Cir. 2007); Aldana v. Del Monte Fresh Produce, N.A., Inc., 416 F.3d 1242, 1247–53 (11th Cir. 2006) (ATCA provides a cause of action for allegations of torture and crimes against humanity that are properly pleaded in the complaint), *cert. denied*, 127 S. Ct. 596 (2006); Alperin v. Vatican Bank, 410 F.3d 532, 544–58 (9th Cir. 2005); Alvarez-Machain v. United States, 331 F.3d 604, 615 n.7 (9th Cir. 2003) (resolution of claims for torts committed in violation of international law "'has been constitutionally committed ... [to] the Judiciary") (quoting *Kadic*, 70 F.3d at 249), *rev'd on other grounds*, *Sosa*, 542 U.S. 692 ; John Doe I v. Unocal Corp., 395 F.3d 932, 958–60 (9th Cir. 2002) (ATCA provides cause of action for "torture, murder, and slavery [which] are jus cogens violations and, thus, violations of the law of nations"); Abebe-Jiri v. Negewo, 1993 U.S. Dist. LEXIS 21158, No. 90-CV-2010, 1993 WL 814304, at *4 (N.D. Ga. Aug.20, 1993), *aff'd*, Abebe-Jira v. Negewo, 72 F.3d 844 (11th Cir. 1996) (ATCA provides cause of action for torture or "cruel, inhuman and degrading treatment or punishment," at least as defined by Eighth Amendment to U.S. Constitution); *Kadic*, 70 F.3d at 249 (ATCA provides a cause of action for genocide); In re Estate of Ferdinand Marcos, Human Rights Litig., 25 F.3d 1467, 1475–76 (9th Cir. 1994) (ATCA "creates a cause of action for violations of specific, universal and obligatory international human rights standards which confer fundamental rights upon all people vis-a-vis their own governments."); Telesat Roe v. Bridgestone Corp., 492 F. Supp. 2d 988, 1010–24 (S.D. Ind. 2007) (ATCA provides a cause of action for forced labor); Burnett v. Al Baraka Inv. & Dev. Corp. (In re Terrorist Attacks), 349 F. Supp. 2d 765, 826 (S.D.N.Y. 2005) (ATCA provides cause of action against foreign defendants for conspiracy to support, and aiding of abetting of, terrorist aircraft hijackings); Doe I v. Liu Qi, 349 F. Supp. 2d 1258 (N.D. Cal. 2004) (ATCA provides cause of action for "cruel, inhuman, or degrading" treatment); Tachiona v. Mugabe, 234 F. Supp. 2d 401, 437 (S.D.N.Y. 2002) (ATCA provides cause of action for torture or "cruel, inhuman, or degrading treatment"); Cabello Barrueto v. Fernandez Larios, 205 F. Supp. 2d 1325, 1331–33, 1359 (S.D. Fla. 2002) (ATCA provides cause of action for extrajudicial killing, torture, and "cruel, inhuman and degrading treatment"); Wiwa v. Royal Dutch Petroleum Co., No. 96 Civ. 8386 (KMW), 2002 WL 319887, at *8 (S.D.N.Y. Feb. 28, 2002) (similar); Doe v. Karadzic, No. 93 Civ. 0878 (PKL), 2001 U.S. Dist. LEXIS 12928, *2 (S.D.N.Y. 2001) (ATCA provides cause of action for genocide, war crimes, crimes against humanity, and other human rights abuses); Doe v. Islamic Salvation Front, 993 F. Supp. 3, 8 (D.D.C. 1998) (ATCA provides cause of action for murder, mutilation, torture, cruel or inhumane treatment, kidnapping, summary executions, and other violations of Common Article 3 of the Geneva Conventions); Xuncax v. Gramajo, 886 F. Supp. 162, 186–89 (D. Mass. 1995) (ATCA provides cause of action for torture, summary executions, disappearances, and arbitrary detention);

the U.S. Supreme Court, in the celebrated case of *Sosa v. Alvarez-Machain,*[180] held that the ATCA provides a civil action for damages under U.S. law for serious violations of international law such as genocide, torture, piracy, and slavery. The U.S. Supreme Court held in 2004 that there is a private cause of action for genocide under the ATCA as long as the prohibition against genocide is an international law norm with specific content and wide acceptance among civilized nations.[181] There can be little doubt that the Genocide Convention satisfies these criteria.[182] In another famous case, the Supreme Court held that the original owner of paintings by Gustav Klimt had civil action in U.S. against Austrian museum that gained possession of them in violation of international law due to expropriations by Nazis and Austrian government.[183] Thus, civil compensation for genocide is available to aliens in the U.S. under the ATCA.

The U.S. Court of Appeals for the Second Circuit held, in *Kadic v. Karadži*, that victims of a campaign of genocide, torture, and other violations of international law overseen by Bosnian-Serb leader Radovan Karadzic were entitled to monetary reparations in U.S. courts.[184] In more recent cases, the Second Circuit upheld awards of billions of dollars in reparations to Jewish, Polish, Roma, and other Holocaust victims.[185] In numerous other cases, U.S. courts have applied ATCA and the Torture Victims Protection Act to deter human rights violations by government officials and armed groups who sponsor terrorism, engage in ethnic cleansing, or torture political or religious minorities.[186]

Paul v. Avril, 812 F. Supp. 207 (S.D. Fla. 1993), *later proceeding at* 901 F. Supp. 330 (S.D. Fla. 1994) (ATCA provides cause of action for torture or cruel/inhuman treatment); Lafontant v. Aristide, 844 F. Supp. 128, 138–39 (E.D.N.Y. 1994) (ATCA provides cause of action for torture); Forti v. Suarez-Mason, 672 F. Supp. 1531 (N.D. Cal. 1987) (similar).

180. 542 U.S. 692, 732 (2004).

181. *See, e.g., Sosa,* 542 U.S. at 732 & n.20; *see also id.* at 748–49 (Scalia, J., dissenting) (majority opinion endorsed private right of action for genocide).

182. *See, e.g., Kadic,* 70 F.3d at 238, 242 (ban on genocide is "well-established" and "universally recognized"); Presbyterian Church of Sudan v. Talisman Energy, Inc., No. 01 Civ. 9882(DLC), 2005 WL 2082846, *2 & n.5 (S.D.N.Y. Aug. 30, 2005) (similar).

183. *See* Republic of Austria v. Altmann, 541 U.S. 677 (2004).

184. 70 F.3d 232 (2d Cir. 1995).

185. *See* In re Holocaust Victim Assets Litig., 225 F.3d 191 (2d Cir. 2000) (approving $1.25 billion settlement of claims by Jewish, Polish, Roma, and other Holocaust victims against Swiss banks); D'Amato v. Deutsche Bank, 236 F.3d 78, 2001 (2d Cir. 2001) (approving $40 million settlement of claims by Holocaust victims and their heirs and Austrian and German banks charged with violations of international law in dealings with Nazis); *U.S. Involvement in Claims by Victims of the German Holocaust or Their Heirs,* 93 AMERICAN J. INT'L L. 879 (1999) (describing these and other cases brought by Holocaust victims for reparations under U.S. law).

186. *See* Boim v. Quranic Literacy Inst., 291 F.3d 1000, 1021 (7th Cir. 2002) ("The only way to imperil the flow of money and discourage the financing of terrorist acts is to impose liability on those who knowingly and intentionally supply the funds to the persons who commit the violent acts."); Estate of Jenco v. Islamic Republic of Iran, 154 F. Supp. 2d 27, 39 (D.D.C. 2001) (after punitive damages award in case involving Hizbollah and U.S. nationals, "no reported hostage incidents" occurred); Alejandre v. Republic of Cuba, 996 F. Supp. 1239, 1251 (S.D. Fla. 1997) ("By granting large exemplary awards, courts have both expressed their condemnation of human rights abuses and attempted to deter other international actors from engaging in similar practices. Most of these cases have been brought pursuant to the authority of the Alien Tort Claims Act ... and the ... [Torture Victims Protection Act]."); *see also, e.g.,* Hilao v. Estate of Marcos, 393 F.3d 987 (9th Cir. 2004) (torture and political persecution); Abebe-Jira v. Negewo, 72 F.3d 844 (11th Cir. 1996) (similar); In re Estate of Ferdinand Marcos Human Rights Litig., 25 F.3d 1467 (9th Cir. 1994) (similar); Doe I v. Unocal Corp., 395 F.3d 932 (9th Cir. 2002) (torture and forced labor); Rein v. Socialist People's Libyan Arab Jamahiriya, 162 F.3d 748 (2d Cir. 1998) (terrorism); Kadic v. Karadzic, 70 F.3d 232 (2d Cir. 1995) (ethnic cleansing and torture); Burnett v. Al Baraka Inv. & Dev. Corp., 274 F. Supp. 2d 86 (D.D.C. 2003) (terrorism); Presbyterian Church of Sudan v. Talisman Energy, Inc., 244 F. Supp. 2d 289 (S.D.N.Y. 2003)

A common criticism of such decisions is that they constitute intrusions by the U.S. into the internal affairs of sovereign nations whose actions are entitled to deference and respect. But under the doctrine of universal jurisdiction, a nation with the capacity to do so may sanction violations of the law of nations and crimes against humanity, even if the underlying events occurred outside the sanctioning state.[187] International comity does not require U.S. courts to sit idle while genocidal regimes adjudicate their own responsibility for massacring religious minorities who have little to no hope of receiving justice in their courts.[188]

The U.S. and other nations have a strong interest in "affording alleged victims of atrocities a method to vindicate their rights."[189] Defenses such as sovereign immunity and the act of state doctrine should not stand in the way of this kind of deterrence, particularly where a foreign state is engaged in commercial activity that has a direct effect on the U.S. and has violated *jus cogens* norms of international law.[190] Genocide and crimes against humanity are almost by definition assaults on the international legal order, and are there-

---

(persecution of religious minorities); Estate of Jenco v. Islamic Republic of Iran, 154 F. Supp. 2d 27, 29–39 (D.D.C. 2001) (terrorism); Doe v. Karadzic, 192 F.R.D. 133 (S.D.N.Y. 2000) (ethnic cleansing); Eisenfeld v. Islamic Republic of Iran, No. Civ. 98-1945 RCL, 2000 WL 1918779, at 2 (D.D.C. July 11, 2000) (terrorism); Flatow v. Islamic Republic of Iran, 999 F. Supp. 1, 7–13, 18, 28 (D.D.C. 1998) (terrorism); Doe v. Islamic Salvation Front (FIS), 993 F. Supp. 3, 7 (D.D.C. 1998) (torture and politico-religious persecution); In re Estate of Ferdinand E. Marcos Human Rights Litig., 910 F. Supp. 1460, 1462 (D. Haw. 1995) (torture and political persecution); Xuncax v. Gramajo, 886 F. Supp. 162, 169 (D. Mass. 1995) (torture and political persecution); Paul v. Avril, 901 F. Supp. 330, 331 (S.D. Fla. 1994) (torture); Lafontant v. Aristide, 844 F. Supp. 128, 129–130 (E.D.N.Y. 1994) (torture and murder); Debra M. Strauss, *Enlisting the U.S. Courts in a New Front: Dismantling the International Business Holdings of Terrorist Groups Through Federal Statutory and Common-Law Suits*, 38 Vand. J. Transnat'l L. 679 (2005); Elizabeth Amon, *Coming to America*, Nat'l L.J., Oct. 23, 2000, at A1; Harold Hongju Koh, *Transnational Public Law Litigation*, 100 Yale L.J. 2347 (1991). In addition, the Antiterrorism Act of 1991 may provide a remedy to U.S. nationals. *See* 18 U.S.C. § 2333 (1992); Estates of Ungar ex rel. Strachman v. Palestinian Auth., 304 F. Supp. 2d 232, 238–39 (D.R.I. 2004) ("On April 14, 1990, Senator Charles E. Grassley (R. Iowa) introduced ... a bill providing a new, federal, civil cause of action for acts of international terrorism...."); *id.* (noting that the Act "gave victims of terrorism the remedies of traditional American tort law, including treble damages and attorney's fees.... During the floor debates, Senator Grassley spoke of holding terrorists accountable 'where it hurts them most: at their lifeline, their funds.'") (citing 136 Cong. Rec. S14279-01 (1990), 137 Cong. Rec. S4511-04 (1991)).

187. *See Sosa*, 542 U.S. at 762 (Breyer, J., concurring in the judgment) ("Today international law will sometimes similarly reflect not only substantive agreement as to certain universally condemned behavior but also procedural agreement that universal jurisdiction exists to prosecute a subset of that behavior."); Restatement (Third) of Foreign Relations Law of the United States § 404 (American Law Institute, 1987) (courts may exercise universal jurisdiction over "offenses recognized by the community of nations as of universal concern, such as piracy, slave trade, attacks on or hijacking of aircraft, genocide, war crimes, and perhaps certain acts of terrorism"); *see also* Demjanjuk v. Petroks, 776 F.2d 571, 582–83 (6th Cir. 1985).

188. *See Talisman Energy*, 244 F. Supp. 2d at 335–343.

189. *Id.* at 340.

190. *See* 28 U.S.C. § 1605(a); H.R. Rep. No. 94-1487, 94th Cong., 2nd Sess. 1976, 1976 U.S.C.C.A.N. 6604, 6618; *Rio Tinto*, 487 F.3d at 1209–10 ("Acts of racial discrimination are violations of jus cogens norms," to which deference to sovereign authority does not apply because "'[i]nternational law does not recognize an act that violates jus cogens as a sovereign act'"); *see also Unocal*, 395 F.3d at 958–60; *Kadic*, 70 F.3d at 250; Siderman de Blake v. Republic of Argentina, 965 F.2d 699, 710 (9th Cir. 1992); U.S. v. Alstötter et al. ("The Justice Case"), 3 Trials of War Criminals Before Nuremberg Military Tribunals under Control Council Law No. 10, at 983 (1946–1949) ("As the prime illustration of a crime against humanity under [Control Council] Law 10, which by reason of its magnitude and international repercussions has been recognized as a violation of common international law, we cite 'genocide'....").

Figure 13 Reported Net Income of Corporations Dealing with Sudan

MNC	Sudan Energy Consortia and Their Estimated 2007 Output	2006 Net Income	Sources
China National Petroleum Corp.	Greater Nile Petroleum Operating Co. (GNPOC) (40%), 92 million barrels; Petrodar Operating Co. (PDOC) (41%), 59 million barrels; CNPCIS, 21.9 million barrels	$13.5 billion	Petroleum Intelligence Weekly (PIW), Dec. 3, 2007, & Oct. 1, 2007
Petronas	GNPOC (30%), 92 million barrels; PDOC (41%), 59 million barrels; White Nile Production Operating Co. 1 (WNPOC) (68.9%), 9.7 million barrels	$14.4 billion	PIW, Dec.10, 2007, Dec. 3, 2007, & Oct. 1, 2007
ONGC Videsh	WNPOC 1 (24.1%), 9.7 million barrels	$3.5 billion	PIW, Dec. 3, 2007
Talisman Energy	GNPOC (25%), 92 million barrels [Talisman Energy helped develop but this consortium]	$1.9 billion	Google Finance

fore *jus cogens* and *erga omnes* norms from which there can be no valid derogation, claim of sovereign right, or jurisdictional limits.[191] Genocide is a uniquely grievous crime which warrants strong civil remedies, including the imposition of exemplary damages "as a warning or deterrence to others," and "to make an example of a defendant's conduct" to prevent its recurrence.[192]

In the 1990s, victims of genocide in southern Sudan attempted to utilize the ATCA as a "judicial forum for redressing violations of customary international law that often accompany religious persecution," and deterring further violations of international law in Sudan.[193] They sued Talisman Energy and the other oil companies doing business in Sudan for bestowing extensive financial and logistical assistance to the Sudanese government despite actual knowledge of ongoing genocide and crimes against humanity. The reported revenues and profits of corporations that have purchased oil or oil concessions from the government of Sudan are enormous, and are reported in Figure 13.

Talisman Energy, the CNPC, and other corporations knowingly providing funds or shipping arms to the governments or allied militias that commit genocide in violation of U.N. sanctions, should be held liable for aiding and abetting under long-standing legal principles.[194] Nevertheless, when a case brought by survivors of genocide and crimes against humanity in Darfur reached the U.S. Court of Appeals for the Second Circuit, the court allowed Talisman Energy to hide behind its investment in the GNPOC, and held that because it had not directly participated in any attack on a victim, and demon-

191. *See United States v. Alstötter*, at 983; Institute of International Law/Institut de Droit International, *Resolution: Obligations* Erga Omnes *in International Law*, art. 1 (2005), http://www.idi-iil.org ("For purposes of the present articles, an obligation erga omnes is: (a) an obligation under general international law that a State owes in any given case to the international community, ... so that a breach of that obligation enables all States to take action....").

192. Hilao v. Estate of Marcos, 103 F.3d 767, 771–72, 781 n.7 (9th Cir. 1996); *Filartiga*, 577 F. Supp. at 864–67 (awarding punitive damages under ATCA to effectuate international law).

193. Brief for the Presbyterian Church of Sudan as Stated Clerk of the General Assembly of the Presbyterian Church (U.S.A.) as Amici Curiae in Support of Respondent, Sosa v. Alvarez-Machain, 542 U.S. 692 (2004) (No. 03-485), http://www.nosafehaven.org/_legal/atca_pro_SudanPresbyterian.pdf.

194. *See, e.g.*, Restatement (Second) of Torts § 876 (American Law Institute, 1977).

strated no clear intent to kill any group, it could not be liable for genocide or crimes against humanity. The court conceded that the plaintiffs had evidence that Talisman Energy had funded the weapons and provided the motivation for the government to massacre the inhabitants of oil-rich areas.[195] But it found no evidence of an "improper purpose" or "purpose of facilitating attacks on civilians," even though there was evidence that attacks on the plaintiffs were launched from GNPOC airfields, and Talisman entered Sudan with the express understanding that because its "assistance would greatly advance oil exploration, it would tip the military balance in favor of the Government." Specifically, its improvements of roads leading to and airfields within the concession area enabled the Government to better supply troops and initiate offensive attacks on civilians.[196]

The result in *Talisman Energy* declares open season for multinational corporations to knowingly conspire to support attacks on civilians by their local allies. It will likely compound the existing climate of impunity for crimes against civilians in connection with the exploitation of oil, minerals, timber, and agricultural lands. The appellate court affirmed the trial court's ruling that whether or not there was genocide in southern Sudan, there was "no evidence ... that Talisman Energy intended to further it."[197] The language of the court's opinion would absolve of any culpability corporations exploiting Nazi-occupied oilfields in Russia, or oilfields in Iraq cleared by genocidal village destructions, or forests in Brazil where natives were massacred:

> Resource extraction in particular is by nature land-intensive: land is needed for exploration and engineering, equipment, rigs or mines, offices and dormitories in remote areas, transportation infrastructure, and so on. Under the best circumstances, these facilities might require relocation from a development area. But GNPOC was not operating in the best of circumstances. Sudan's oil was located in an area heavily contested in a civil war, in a region of the country that had suffered through four decades of violence before Talisman arrived. The oil facilities came under frequent rebel attack and oil workers were killed during the relevant time. Safe operation of the oil facilities therefore required tightened security; and displacing civilians from an "area within the security ring road" was not in itself unlawful.

The court dismissed at least five types of evidence: (1) findings by the U.S. Congress that genocide in southern Sudan was facilitated by oil revenues, (2) expert testimony that Talisman Energy believed that the government used oil revenues to buy weapons to wage the genocide, (3) written documents by GNPOC personnel recording the government's use of GNPOC airfields to bomb southern Sudanese populations, and (4) a report from the head of security for the firm from which Talisman Energy purchased the oil concession that Talisman Energy's assistance to the government "would tip the military balance in favor of the [g]overnment."[198]

The court's characterization of the Sudanese regime's policy in the south as "displacement" is, of course, a euphemism for mass murder, ethnic cleansing, and deprivation of food and water. As detailed in Figure 8 of Chapter XIV, the plaintiffs in the case testified that many people were killed, many women were raped, homes and churches were looted and burned, and many of the survivors suffered hunger and disease after fleeing aircraft

195. *See* The Presbyterian Church of Sudan et al. v. Talisman Energy, Inc., No. 07-0016-cv, slip op. at 10–24, 45–56 (2d Cir. Oct. 3, 2009).

196. *Id.* at 9–11, 24–25, 39–40.

197. *Id.* at 21–23.

198. *Id.* at 9–11, 50–59.

and helicopters.[199] The court's open defense of these events as legitimate economic activity stands as an invitation for other U.S. and multi-national corporations to profit from genocide and war crimes.

H. Voluntary Reparations Payments by Governments Pursuant to Peace Accords

Governments complicit in gross human rights violations have occasionally, due to international pressure or a change of regime, agreed voluntarily to pay reparations to victims of genocide. Germany famously agreed in 1952 to pay its first installment of $3.5 billion Deutsche marks to Israel and Jewish diaspora organizations.[200] The pact was announced the day after the U.S. voiced its support for bargaining with the European Coal and Steel Community, including Germany, as a single entity.[201] The question of World War II reparations was legally linked to Germany's future in coal and steel, which the new deal resolved.[202]

Truth and reconciliation commissions in Argentina, Brazil, and Chile have issued select reparations to families of the "disappeared," typically the equivalent of more than $150,000 per family. Bolivia, El Salvador, and Peru have done little in this regard, and Honduras and Guatemala have only paid reparations to successful litigations in the Inter-American Court of Human Rights, a small proportion of all victims during the Cold War.[203] Compensation was paid to indigenous groups displaced by natural gas pipeline in Bolivia, and to victims of extrajudicial killings, deportations, and oil spills in Ogoniland, Nigeria.[204] Indigenous groups suffering from cancers and the loss of their habitat in Ecuador now hope to win billions of dollars in compensation in Ecuadorian courts for pollution and displacement by Chevron.[205]

As noted above, the Darfur Peace Agreement of 2006 envisioned $30 million in compensation for the Fur people and other groups victimized by massacres, forced displace-

---

199. *See also* Second Amended Complaint and Summary Judgment Ruling, Talisman Energy v. Presb. Church of Sudan, 453 F. Supp. 2d 633 (S.D.N.Y. 2006); Presbyterian Church of Sudan v. Talisman Energy, 244 F. Supp. 2d 289 (S.D.N.Y. 2003).

200. *See* David S. Wyman & Charles H. Rosenzveig, The World Reacts to the Holocaust 409 (Baltimore, MD: Johns Hopkins UP, 1996).

201. *Compare US and Britain Give Strong Support to European Coal-Steel Community,* Christian Sci. Monitor, Sept. 9, 1952, *with Israeli Bonn Pact to Be Signed Today*, N.Y. Times, Sept. 10, 1952, http://www.nytimes.com.

202. *See Contest for Control of the Saar Imperils Europe's Plans,* L.A. Times, Apr. 6, 1952, http://www.latimes.com; *Saar Returning to German Fold,* N.Y. Times, Dec. 26, 1956, http://www.nytimes.com.

203. *See* John C. Torpey, Politics and the Past: On Repairing Historical Injustices 77 (London: Rowman & Littlefield, 2003); *Massacre Survivors to Get Compensation*, L.A. Times, Dec. 10, 2004, at A17.

204. *See Bolivian Protestors Take Over Gas Pipe Station,* Oil Daily, Aug. 22, 2006; Thomas Perreault, *Natural Gas, Indigenous Mobilization and the Bolivian State* (2008), http://se1.isn.ch/serviceengine/FileContent?serviceID=47&fileid=18A220B6-0503-D922-C69E-0F1951AAE18A&lng=en.

205. *See* John Vidal, *Shell Settlement with Ogoni people Stops Short of Full Justice*, The Guardian (U.K.) (June 9, 2009), http://www.guardian.co.uk. *See also* Chevron, *Chevron — Ecuador*, http://www.chevron.com/ecuador/; ChevronToxico, *The Campaign for Justice in Ecuador, A Rainforest Chernobyl*, http://chevrontoxico.com.

ment, and village burnings in Sudan.[206] Given that more than 300,000 had died, a million people had been displaced, and four million had lost family or community members due to the government's policies, this added up to less than $30 per person, and less than $100 per death.[207] Such an amount can hardly be characterized as compensation in the same sense as Germany, Brazil, or Chile paid out.

In Iraq, the CPA established an Iraq Property Claims Commission to hear real property restitution claims arising out of the Anfal campaign, Arabization deportation schemes, and other war crimes and crimes against humanity in 1980s and 1990s Iraq.[208] With tens of thousands of civilian victims of the regime, millions of refugees, thousands of destroyed villages, and hundreds of square kilometers of territory laced with land mines, the potential losses are vast.[209] Displaced persons filed about 17,000 claims in the first two months of the commission's opening for claims, more than 130,000 claims had been filed by early 2006, and more than 20,000 have been decided.[210] The CPA released $180 million for the program in its last days, and the Iraqi parliament allocated $500 million for the commission in 2006 and 2007.[211] Although the commission is certainly an advance over Iraqi law prior to 2003, it may be inadequate to resolve many claims equitably due to potential delays and inadequate staffing, budgetary limitations, and inapplicability of the scheme to displacement occurring after April 9, 2003.[212]

---

206. *See Nigerian President Warns of "Near Genocide" in Darfur*, BBC MONITORING AFRICA—POLITICAL, Oct. 12, 2006; *Brookings-Bern Project on Internal Displacement Discussion; Subject: International Policy Toward Darfur (remarks of Jean-Marie Guehenno, Undersecretary-General, United Nations, Peacekeeping Operations)*, FEDERAL NEWS SERVICE, Nov. 20, 2006; *Dr. Al-Khalifa Holds UN Responsible for Delay*, SUNA NEWS AGENCY, Nov. 26, 2006; Andrew Natsios, *Special State Department Briefing by the President's Special Envoy on Sudan*, FEDERAL NEWS SERVICE, Nov. 20, 2006 (victims say $30 million is insufficient to rebuild damaged farms and cattle stocks).

207. *VOA News: Peace Eludes Darfur*, US FED NEWS, Nov. 29, 2006.

208. *See* CPA Reg. No. 12, June 23, 2004, http://www.iraqcoalition.org; U.N. IRIN, *Iraq: Property Commission Gives Displaced People Hope*, RELIEFWEB, May 25, 2004, http://www.reliefweb.int/rw/rwb.nsf/AllDocsByUNID/bb9ee486020ba3d985256e9f006905ee. The commission was renamed the Commission for the Resolution of Real Property Disputes in January 2006. *See* Statute No. 2 of the year 2006 (Iraq), http://www.ipcciraq.org/en/law.php.

209. *See* Al Anfal, Special Verdict in Case No 1/C Second/2006, at 22–24; MIDDLE EAST WATCH, GENOCIDE IN IRAQ, at 4, 26–36; Kurdistan Regional Government, *U.N. Mine Clearance Projects in Kurdish Region* (Feb. 18, 2000), http://web.archive.org/web/20001202085400/http://www.krg.org/; U.N. IRIN, *Iraq: Property Commission.*

210. *See* International Organization for Migration, *IPCC Completes Second Year, Iraq Newsletter —Jan and Feb 2006* (Mar. 2006), http://www.reliefweb.int/rw/rwb.nsf/db900sid/YAOI-6VT535?OpenDocument.

211. *See* Andrew Cockburn, *Spending Iraq's Money*, CINCINNATI POST, June 23, 2004, http://www.highbeam.com/doc/1G1-118540631.html; Bay Fang, *Iraq's Human Chess Pieces: Kurds Are Moved in and Arabs Are Forced Out in a Gambit to Control Oil-Rich Kirkuk*, U.S. NEWS & WORLD REPORT, July 25, 2004, http://www.usnews.com/usnews/news/articles/040802/2kurds_3.htm; *After Several Months' Cessation [sic], the Commission for Resolution of Real Property Disputes (CRRPD) Releases Compensation Funds for Victims,* AlMashriq (Iraq), Jan. 2008, http://www.iirl.org/newsbriefs/a-1-16-01-14-08.htm.

212. *See* Brookings Institution, *The Looming Crisis: Displacement and Security in Iraq* 26 (Aug. 2008), http://www.brookings.edu ("According to [International Organization for Migration]'s Peter van der Auweraert, it will take 30 years just to address the appeals that have already been ruled on by the Judicial Committee"); Statute No. 2 of the year 2006 (Iraq) ("The provisions of this Statute are applicable to the claims for properties that fall within the jurisdiction of the Statute during the period from 17 July 1968 to 9 April 2003. . . .").

I. Compensation from Complicit Corporations for Aiding Genocidal Campaigns

Recent precedents from the U.S. federal courts provide strong support for a right to compensation for victims of violations of international law against multi-national corporations that aided or abetted the government committing the violations. This right to compensation flows from the obligation to pay civil damages for genocide under the Alien Tort Claims Act (ATCA).[213] In *Khulumani v. Barclay Nat'l Bank Ltd.*, victims of crimes against humanity and human rights violations in apartheid-era South Africa sued Shell Oil Co., Exxon Mobil, and other multi-national corporations under the ATCA and the Torture Victims Protection Act (TVPA). The plaintiffs alleged in particular that "[w]ithout oil, the police and military could not have functioned and the economy of South Africa would have come to a standstill." The Court of Appeals for the Second Circuit, a court based in New York that is one level below the U.S. Supreme Court, ruled that corporations who "aid and abet" violations of customary international law can be sued for damages under the ATCA. The court also stated that the corporations could have been sued under the TVPA if they could be linked "to state aid or the conduct of state officials." Both of the judges in the court's majority cited the Zyklon B case arising out of the Holocaust for the idea that knowingly supplying the means to commit mass murder renders the supplier equally guilty of the crime. One of the judges also cited a decision of the international criminal tribunal for the former Yugoslavia to the effect that individuals could be liable for violations of international law based on their "knowledge that [their] acts assist the commission of the specific crime of the principal."[214]

Genocide victims have repeatedly attempted to obtain reparations from corporations complicit in genocide by governments to whom they provide support. Liability for aiding and abetting genocide may extend to all instances in which a corporation acts "in concert with" a government carrying out a campaign of genocide or crimes against humanity.[215] A corporation so acts in concert with a government when it provides practical assistance with knowledge that the assistance will facilitate perpetration of a crime.[216] The

---

213. *See, e.g.*, *Kadic*, 70 F.3d at 238.

214. *Khulumani*, Nos. 05-2141-cv, 05-2326-cv, 2007 U.S. App. LEXIS 24370, *62 (internal quotations omitted) (quoting Prosecutor v. Vasiljevic, Case No. IT-98-32-A, Appeals Chamber, Judgement (Feb. 25, 2004), at ¶ 102 (ii)). *See also* Presbyterian Church of Sudan v. Talisman Energy, 454 F. Supp. 2d 633 (S.D.N.Y. 2006) (knowledge satisfies the mental element of the crime of aiding or abetting genocide, war crimes, or crimes against humanity).

215. *Kadic*, 70 F.3d at 245; John Doe I v. Unocal Corp., 395 F.3d 932, 949–56 (9th Cir. 2002).

216. *See Unocal*, 395 F.3d at 950–51. Whether Talisman Energy provided such assistance is a question of fact winding its way through the federal courts, as will similar facts raised by analogous cases in the future. *See* Presbyterian Church of Sudan v. Talisman Energy, Inc., 454 F. Supp. 2d 633 (S.D.N.Y. 2006) (granting summary judgment to defendant), *on appeal*, No. 07-0016 (2d Cir.). The district court found that Talisman's knowledge that its royalties and other payments would finance weapons purchases by Sudan did not amount to aiding and abetting its crimes, but only because the court imposed a requirement of "an intent to assist in those attacks by the payment of royalties." *Id.* at 676. Such a requirement is not supported by aiding and abetting cases decided under the ATCA and by international criminal tribunals, which impose liability based on knowledge as well as intent. *See, e.g.*, *Khulumani*, 504 F.3d at 274–76 (Katzmann, J., concurring); *id.* at 290–91 (Hall, J., concurring); *Unocal I*, 395 F.3d at 949–56.

international law ban on genocide also extends by its terms to conspiracy to commit genocide and complicity in genocide.[217] Complicity in genocide may therefore trigger civil liability in the U.S. and elsewhere.

217. *See, e.g.*, Genocide Convention, art. III.

Conclusion

Professor Lemkin planned an expansive historical analysis of the problem of genocide, which was "designed to prove that genocide is not an exceptional phenomenon, but that it occurs in intergroup relations with a certain regularity like homicide takes place between individuals."[1] Under his approach, genocide is not restricted to fascist dictatorships or outbursts of ethnic extremism, as is sometimes suggested in the literature. Instead, it has occurred in various types of societies, including ancient empires, medieval theocracies, European monarchies, communist societies, and democracies with far-flung colonies and dependencies. It constitutes a latent risk of religious intolerance, ethnic and racial divisions, economic growth, technological development, political stratification, and military theorization. The risk could be reduced by tolerant policies such as religious freedom, the promotion of diversity in education, democratic governance, self-determination of peoples, economic and social equality, but perhaps may never eradicated from the human species, much like homicide will likely remain with us.

The aspiration of the international law of genocide is to minimize the incidence of genocide, and ameliorate the immediate and long-term effect of the crime, by defining its elements and providing remedies to his victims in the form of civil and criminal proceedings. Like any branch of law, the treaties and customary international law on genocide will be repeatedly flouted, particularly in their first few centuries of existence, and may confront periods in which social norms and new technologies such as nuclear weapons make it extremely difficult to enforce. Furthermore, the concept of genocide itself may one day be done away with as outmoded and archaic, to be replaced by alternative approaches such as a right to be different,[2] the resurrection of the dead by new technologies, or a mass migration to virtual reality homes.[3]

---

1. Raphael Lemkin, *quoted in* John Docker, *Are Settler Colonies Inherently Genocidal?: Re-reading Lemkin, in* Empire, Colony, Genocide, at 87.

2. *See, e.g.*, Lawrence Rosen, *The Right to Be Different: Indigenous Peoples and the Quest for a Unified Theory,* 107 Yale Law J. 227 (1997) (book review). *Cf.* David L. Richards, *Civilizational Geography of Government Respect, in* Human Rights and Diversity 33–35 (David P. Forsythe eds., Omaha, NE: Univ. of Nebraska Press, 2003) (grouping together rights not to be tortured, disappeared, killed without trial, or imprisoned for one's political beliefs as "physical integrity rights" for purposes of empirical research across cultures).

3. *See, e.g.,* John Beckmann, The Virtual Dimension: Architecture, Representation, and Crash Culture 69, 72–75 (Princeton, NJ: Princeton Architectural Press, 1998) (describing science fiction stories in which people achieve immortality by "using virtual bodies inside virtual spaces"); Tim Guest, Second Lives: A Journey Through Virtual Worlds 273 (New York: Random House, 2008) (describing theory of psychologist and guru Timothy Leary that human minds could be uploaded to the Internet for purposes of achieving immortality); Sandra Hughes, *Scientists Clone Long-Dead Animal,* CBS News, Apr. 8, 2003, http://www.cbsnews.com/stories/2003/04/08/tech/main548333.shtml; Margaret Munro, *Resurrection of Mammoths Possible: Researchers,* Canwest News Service, Nov. 19, 2008, http://www2.canada.com/saskatoonstarphoenix/news/story.html?id=183889f6-c536-469d-8211-88224efad7c5.

Remaining for the moment within the limitations of existing technologies, and the framework of existing law, a synthesis of the findings of this study is in order. The conclusions of this study must remain provisional, restricted as it is to the published scholarship and unclassified or declassified documents reviewed by the author. Nevertheless, some common patterns of genocidal campaigns emerge from this study. Exclusionary and expansionist ideologies of powerful nations and empires rationalize and organize the destruction or forcible assimilation of smaller peoples conquered by great empires such as those of the Greeks, Romans, Spanish, Portuguese, English, French, Germans, Russians, Arabs, Turks, Mongols, Japanese, and Chinese. Myths of racial and ethnic superiority justify the exploitation of indigenous peoples. The conquest of the capital city of an indigenous people, and the resulting destruction of a people's spiritual center and main temples, renders a people vulnerable to elimination as a distinct polity. Counterinsurgency operations often include the burning of villages, massacring of civilians, and the deportation of entire peoples from their ancestral lands.

While international law has frequently privileged the prosperity and security of a few powerful states, most notably the members of the U.N. Security Council, this study has shown that small minorities and indigenous peoples have suffered some of the worst crimes since 1945. The law has paradoxically focused its protections on peoples whose sheer numbers and organization make their destruction impossible, from Americans and the French to the Russians and Chinese, while the world has witnessed massive epidemics of linguistic extinctions, the devastation of countless ancient structures and sacred or historic artifacts, widespread ethnic and sectarian violence against minorities, and the flight of millions of people away from the persecution of their cultures and religions in their ancestral lands and communities.[4]

---

4. *See, e.g.*, DANIEL NETTLE & SUZANNE ROMAINE, VANISHING VOICES: THE EXTINCTION OF THE WORLD'S LANGUAGES 1–10, 39–80, 133–50 (Oxford: Oxford UP, 2000); W. Wayt Gibbs, *Saving Dying Languages*, SCI. AM., July 2002, at 62. *See also* ADAM JONES, GENOCIDE: A COMPREHENSIVE INTRODUCTION 67–255 (2006) (describing deaths of millions of Armenians, Jews, Cambodians, Rwandan Tutsis, and other peoples due to twentieth century genocides); Meline Karakashian & Gevorg Poghosyan, *Armenian Migration and Diaspora: A Way of Life, in* MIGRATION: IMMIGRATION AND EMIGRATION IN INTERNATIONAL PERSPECTIVE 228 (Leonore Loeb Adler et al. eds., Westport, CT: Greenwood Press, 2003) (stating that present-day Turkey, Azerbaijan, Armenia, and Georgia contain the ruins of many Armenian cities that once contained thousands of churches and seminaries); Kouymjian, *The Destruction of Armenian Historical Monuments as a Continuation of the Turkish Policy of Genocide*, at 173–85 (over 1,000 Armenian churches and monasteries were totally destroyed by Ottoman and Turkish forces from 1915 to 1923, and nearly 700 additional Armenian monuments were severely damaged); Iwanowa v. Ford Motor Co., 67 F. Supp. 2d 424, 432–33, 490 (D.N.J. 1999) (describing enslavement of 7.5 million foreign citizens by the Nazis); HISTORIC CITIES AND SACRED SITES: CULTURAL ROOTS FOR URBAN FUTURES 246 (Ismail Serageldin et al. eds., 2001) (describing research finding that 2,000 to 3,000 Jewish synagogues in Germany were destroyed by 1945); Gertrude Samuels, *On the World's Conscience*, N.Y. TIMES, Jan. 16, 1955, at SM13 (there were 15 million refugees from persecution by 1955); BEVAN, THE DESTRUCTION OF MEMORY, at 52–54, 163–64 (describing devastation of Greek communities in Turkey and Turkish-occupied Cyrpus); Press Release, U.S. Committee for Refugees, *Sudan, Testimony of J. Millard Burr, Consultant, U.S. Committee for Refugees on The Crisis Against Humanity in Sudan* (May 27, 1999), http://www.reliefweb.int/rw/rwb.nsf/0/8190a73-888f2c452c125677f005602fd?OpenDocument (estimating death toll from war, famine, and government neglect in Southern Sudan as two million since 1980); *Editorial, Sudan, Drowning in Troubles*, N.Y. Times, Aug. 25, 1988, at A26 (describing flight of 300,000 refugees from Sudan to Ethiopia in 1980s); Al Anfal, Special Verdict Pertaining to Case No 1/C Second/2006, at 22–24 (Iraqi High Tribunal, Second Criminal Court, June 24, 2007), http://law.case.edu/grotian-moment-blog/anfal/opinion.asp (verdict of Iraqi High Tribunal finding that Anfal campaign, starting in 1987, inflicted a death "toll [that] reached tens of thousands"); LORI DAMROSCH, ENFORCING RESTRAINT: COLLECTIVE INTERVENTION IN INTERNAL CONFLICTS 81 (New York: Council on Foreign Relations Press, 1993) (de-

The findings of this study are consistent with Professor Lemkin's conceptual model of genocide. This book has attempted to update Professor Lemkin's historical research for 2009. Specifically, postwar scholarship has amply documented, in the form of documentary evidence, oral histories, and statistical estimates, Professor Lemkin's view that genocide occurred in the Ottoman Empire; in the British, French, Spanish, and Portuguese empires in the Americas and Africa; in the Nazi empire including in the Soviet Union; and in the Soviet Union.

After the eradication of all or most independence-minded members of an indigenous minority group, particularly its military and spiritual elite, the stage is set for genocide-by-law. Prohibitions on the language and religion of the indigenous people under the administration of a foreign empire or alien state further frustrate their attempts at cultural survival. Imperialist and ultranationalist laws often interfere with efforts to maintain indigenous or minority schools, religious institutions, and the propagation of minority cultural patterns. Indigenous peoples and minorities frequently experience biological interventions into the processes by which they would otherwise conceive, bear, and nurture the next generation. Deprivation of equal access to food, clean water, sanitation, safe housing, and health care is a common method of reducing the numbers of an indigenous or minority group, and of waging demographic warfare.

This book has attempted to chart a new course for genocide scholarship by emphasizing struggles between indigenous peoples and foreign empires, economic incentives on behalf of the latter to commit genocide, and the role that international law could play in deterring such conduct in awarding economic reparations as compensation and a deterrent. That focus represents a departure from most legal scholarship on genocide and its pre-

---

scribing Iraqi government's attacks on Kurdish civilians and villages, which led to the regime having "rounded up and murdered as many as 100,000 Kurdish men, women, and children, placing many in mass graves to be shot by soldiers and buried by bulldozers."); John Kifner, Many *Kurds Leave Border for Towns They Fled in Iraq,* N.Y. TIMES, May 1, 1991, http://www.nytimes.com (describing flight of 200,000 to 2.5 million Kurds and other persons in northern Iraq from army's onslaught on northern villages in 1991); Judith Miller, *Displaced in the Gulf War: 5 Million Refugees,* N.Y. TIMES, June 16, 1991, at 39 (estimating total refugees displaced from Iraq or its neighboring countries due to Gulf War II at 5 million); Alan Cowell, *Kurdish Refugees, by Thousands, Flee Vengeance of the Iraqi Army,* N.Y. TIMES, April 4, 1991, http://www.nytimes.com (similar); *6 US Planes Begin Airlifting Relief To Kurds in Iraq,* N.Y. TIMES, Apr. 8, 1991; *1997 in Review—Protection,* REFUGEES MAG., Mar. 1998, http://www.unhcr.org/publ/PUBL/3b681f657.html ("The year 1997 was undoubtedly an 'annus horribilis'... in the world of refugee protection ... [with] an increasing number of displaced peoples ... [and] the largest loss of refugee life in recent history."); ANTIQUITIES UNDER SIEGE: CULTURAL HERITAGE PROTECTION AFTER THE IRAQ WAR (Lawrence Rothfield ed., 2008) (describing destruction of Assyrian and other Mesopotamian heritage); FERNANDO BAEZ, A UNIVERSAL HISTORY OF THE DESTRUCTION OF BOOKS: FROM ANCIENT SUMER TO MODERN-DAY IRAQ (Alfred MacAdam trans., Atlas 2008) (2004) (describing destruction of Assyrian and other Mesopotamian manuscripts and books); JAMES RAVEN, LOST LIBRARIES: THE DESTRUCTION OF GREAT BOOK COLLECTIONS SINCE ANTIQUITY (2004); REBECCA KNUTH, LIBRICIDE: THE REGIME-SPONSORED DESTRUCTION OF BOOKS AND LIBRARIES IN THE TWENTIETH CENTURY (2003); Hisham Mohammed Ali, *Christians Abandon Iraqi City,* MCCLATCHY-TRIB. INFO. SERVICES, Nov. 28, 2008, available at http://www.ankawa.com/english/?p=2078#more-2078 (an estimated 2,000 families, representing half of Iraqi city of Mosul's remaining Christian population, fled their homes and the city itself in 2008); U.N. High Comm'r for Refugees [UNHCR], The Continuing Needs of Iraq's Displaced, THE IRAQ SITUATION (2008), http://www.unhcr.org/cgi-bin/texis/vtx/iraq?page=intro (4.7 million Iraqis were displaced from their homes by 2008 due to "spiraling violence," and are in "dire need of humanitarian care"); UNHCR, STATISTICAL YEARBOOK 2006, at 7 (2007), http://www.unhcr.org/statistics/STATISTICS/478cda572.html (there were 9.9 million refugees worldwide by 2006, along with 12.8 million internally displaced persons, and 5.8 million "stateless persons").

vention, which stresses that genocide is the outcome of intolerant political movements, and prioritizes international criminal tribunals as means of deterring genocide by threatening terms of imprisonment.

Genocide in the Ottoman Empire, Iraq, Sudan and elsewhere cannot be fully understood without reference to economic motivations on the part of dominant groups to expropriate foreign or minority populations' lands, natural resources, properties, and uncompensated labor. Economic motivations become especially powerful when oil companies hold out the prospect of generous revenues to a regime willing to kill or displace any ethnic or religious group that resists the government's efforts to exploit the national wealth in a discriminatory fashion. Accordingly, the redistribution of stolen resources and wealth to the victim groups, in the form of reparations or oil revenue-sharing, is increasingly taken center stage in genocide prevention. This is likely in accord with the wishes and needs of the survivors of genocide victims, who will benefit more from assistance with maintaining their lives and rebuilding their homes than from elaborate and expensive criminal proceedings before distant tribunals. Even if the effect of such measures in deterring genocide proves to be incomplete, their adoption will help ensure that victims of widespread massacres and deportations have some means to survive.

Index